Sherwood Anderson

Sherwood Anderson

A WRITER IN AMERICA

VOLUME I

Walter B. Rideout

Introduction by Charles E. Modlin

The University of Wisconsin Press

The University of Wisconsin Press
1930 Monroe Street
Madison, Wisconsin 53711

www.wisc.edu/wisconsinpress/

3 Henrietta Street
London WC2E 8LU, England

Copyright © 2006
The Board of Regents of the University of Wisconsin System
All rights reserved

5   4   3   2   1

Printed in the United States of America

Library of Congress Cataloging-in-Publication Data
Rideout, Walter B. (Walter Bates)
Sherwood Anderson : a writer in America / Walter B. Rideout ; introduction by Charles E. Modlin.
p. cm.
Includes bibliographical references and index.
ISBN 0-299-21530-X (cloth : alk. paper)
1. Anderson, Sherwood, 1876–1941. 2. Authors, American—20th century—Biography. I. Title.
PS3501.N4Z773   2005
813'.52—dc22   2005011164

This book was published with the support of the Brittingham Fund and the Anonymous Fund for the
Humanities of the University of Wisconsin–Madison.

To Jean

Contents

Acknowledgments

PROFESSOR RIDEOUT had virtually finished his book before illness left him unable to complete the final touches, including a list of acknowledgments. It is impossible now to compile a complete one or to include the genial words of appreciation that he would certainly have written. But we have listed here the names, so far as we can determine them, of major informants, librarians, colleagues and friends, Anderson family members, and the University of Wisconsin Press staff who have contributed to the making of this biography. We apologize for the impersonality of the lists and for omissions:

Informants: Marc and Lucile Antony, Dorothy Bartlett, William Bird, Charles Bockler, George A. Bottger, Mrs. Lorenz Carstensen, Ralph Church, John Cournos, Mrs. John Craun, George M. Day, H. Kellogg Day, William R. Dennes, Burt L. Dickinson, Mrs. Jack Dillman, Margaret E. Edwards, Wharton Esherick, Ernestine Evans, Richard Faben, Richard Faxon, James K. Feibleman, Julius Friend, Mr. and Mrs. Clarence G. Fuller, Lewis Galantiere, Albert Goldstein, Mildred Becker Fuller, Charles H. Funk, Glenn and Laura Gosling, Mrs. W. K. Graham, B. W. Huebsch, Herman Hurd, Thaddeus Hurd, Maria Jolas, Nellie Lewis, Dorothy Jones, Mr. and Mrs. W. Powell Jones, Mrs. Joel Harris Lawrence, Mrs. Alfred Newman, Anne Poor, Felix Russman, Adaline Katz Samuel, Alma Schiff, William Spratling, Mrs. James Stark, Joe Stephenson, Mrs. James Thomas, Margaret Bartlett Thornton, Raymond J. Toner, Harriet Walker Welling, Elizabeth Whaley, William L. White, Mrs. Frank Wilford, William Wright.

Librarians: Diana Haskell and Amy Wood Nyholm at the Newberry Library.

Andersonian colleagues: David D. Anderson, Hilbert H. Campbell, Charles E. Modlin, William A. Sutton, Welford D. Taylor, Kim Townsend, Ray Lewis White, Kenny Williams.

His colleagues and friends at the University of Wisconsin and elsewhere:

Jon S. Reilly, Phillip Harth, Sargent Bush, Susan Stanford Friedman, Thomas Schaub, Marton M. Sealtz Jr., Ron Wallace, and Phillip Certain.

Relatives of Anderson: Cornelia Anderson, Tennessee Mitchell Anderson, Eleanor Copenhaver Anderson, Elizabeth Prall Anderson, John Anderson, Marion (Mimi) Anderson, Mary Chryst Anderson.

Those at the University of Wisconsin Press who have made it possible for this book to be published: Raphael Kadushin, Sheila Moermond, Sheila Leary, Mary Sutherland, and Adam Mehring.

The one person to whom he would have expressed his deepest indebtedness is his dear wife, Jean Rideout, to whom this book is dedicated.

Introduction
Charles E. Modlin

ALTER RIDEOUT'S *Sherwood Anderson: A Writer in America* is a seminal work that reintroduces us to an important American writer. All writers go in and out of fashion, but the best writers always weather the passing literary mode, and Anderson is due for the kind of rousing rediscovery that Rideout's book should help launch. In fact, no other existing Anderson biography is as thoroughly researched, as founded on primary sources and interviews with a range of Anderson friends and family members, or as complete in its vision of the man and the writer.

This biography is the result of exhaustive research begun in 1959. The results are impressive, not only adding a wealth of details to what was previously known but also uncovering much new information about events and people in Anderson's life. For example, Rideout reveals that Anderson suffered a breakdown in 1907 that prefigures his famous one in 1912. He also finds in Bertha Baynes, a young woman in Anderson's boyhood home of Clyde, Ohio, the prototype of Helen White and traces his companionship with Adaline Katz during his time in New Orleans that influenced his 1923 novel *Many Marriages*. With such a comprehensive perspective on Anderson the man, this book presents his many remarkable attributes more clearly than ever before. On the other hand, Rideout makes no attempt to overstate Anderson's virtues or to overlook his weaknesses and inconsistencies as they are occasionally displayed.

Rideout also provides perceptive analyses of many of Anderson's works, pointing out previously overlooked subtleties of structure, symbolism, and characterization. He also astutely places Anderson's life and writings in such broader movements of his times as the transition of American society from rural to industrial; the shaping of a midwestern literary tradition; and the political trends of socialism, communism, and Roosevelt's New Deal.

Of great assistance to Rideout in tracing these matters were the findings of other scholars whose publications led the renaissance of Anderson studies in the last four decades of the twentieth century. As the extensive documentation of this book acknowledges, they contributed mightily to its content. But time has taken its toll, and the production of Anderson studies has lagged in recent years. Nonetheless, signs of new interest are evident this year in a reprint of *A Story Teller's Story*, a critical study by Robert Dunne, and a collection of Anderson's poetry.

∽

Anderson's life is an absorbing story in its own right, but in many ways it also provides the best possible background for an appreciation of his literary accomplishments, especially his fiction. As Anderson himself acknowledged, his fiction is often autobiographical and his memoirs are fictionalized. Professor Rideout ably sorts out the subtleties resulting from such crossovers. He shows on the one hand how Anderson's life does frequently enrich his fiction and, on the other, how the autobiographical works, even when they are embroidered by Anderson's fancy, still reveal an imaginative truth of their own.

The signature event in Sherwood Anderson's life was his dramatic departure from his Elyria, Ohio, business in 1912 and embarkation upon a career as an author. As Rideout explains, the circumstances at the time were not as simple as Anderson would have us believe in *A Story Teller's Story*, yet this important event, even as altered in Anderson's imagination, well demonstrates the cyclical course of his life. "I'm trying again . . . a man has to begin over and over . . . ," he wrote to Roger Sergel a year before his death, and indeed his life consisted of many stops and starts, which not only reveal an important part of his psychological makeup but also provide convenient demarcations of the major phases of his life.

Anderson's early years growing up in Clyde, Ohio, were a strong formative influence on him, and he drew freely from them in many of his writings. In fact his interest in the resonance of youthful experience became a major theme in his fiction. It is rendered masterfully in such short stories as "The Man Who Became a Woman" and "Death in the Woods," in which the narrators come to terms with events in their youth, though for quite different purposes. In "The Man Who Became a Woman," the narrator tells his story as a "kind of confession" that he hopes will put to rest his memories of nightmarish experiences from boyhood. The narrator of "Death in the Woods" combines his memories of an event in his childhood with adult experience and insights to piece together the full story. As he explains: "The whole thing, the story of the old woman's death, was to me as I grew older like music heard from far off. The notes had to be picked up slowly one at a time."

One of the most telling uses of Anderson's boyhood in both his fiction and autobiographies is his manner of depicting the influence of his mother and father, Emma and Irwin Anderson. Looking back upon his mother's death, which occurred in 1895 when he was eighteen, he identifies her as the main source of his artistic bent. In the dedication to her in *Winesburg, Ohio,* which remarkably anticipates his approach to the characters in the book, he credits her with having awakened in him "the hunger to see beneath the surface of lives. . . ." As he remembers her in his autobiographical works, she also becomes the victim of her husband's irresponsible conduct, having to take in laundry because of his inability to hold a job. In *Winesburg* George Willard's parents are similarly contrasted, with his mother representing the source of his capacity to dream, while his father, who is ineffectual as a provider, lectures George to "Keep your eyes on your money. Be awake." At the end of the book, when George Willard, much like Anderson himself, leaves town, he intends to follow his mother's dream of finding artistic fulfillment in his writing. But he is also aware, as he counts the money in his pocketbook, of his father's admonition to mind his finances. In 1932 when Anderson was planning a dramatic version of *Winesburg,* he identified this conflict between the mother and father as "the central theme of the play." Such opposing demands of artistic and material success would recur to the end in Anderson's life and works.

⌇

Anderson's business career, in a sense, actually began in Clyde, when he worked at such a variety of jobs that he acquired the nickname "Jobby." But it was in Chicago, following a period of manual labor, a stint in the army during the Spanish-American War, and a year at the Wittenberg Academy in Springfield, Ohio, that he began to write copy for an advertising agency. In 1904 he married Cornelia Lane, and they subsequently had three children. In the meantime he became the head of a mail-order firm in Cleveland and then another in Elyria, Ohio. Following his walking away from the Elyria business, his marriage also collapsed, and in 1913 he moved back to Chicago to resume his advertising job. He later came to despise such work, mainly because he felt that it interfered with his own writing and was a debased use of the language, manipulating words for financial profit.

Despite this apparent conflict between his business and writing careers, the fact is that Anderson did some of his finest writing, including

Winesburg, Ohio, the book generally considered to be his masterpiece, while working as an ad man. In some ways the job even provided unexpected opportunities to pursue his writing. He claimed for example to have written one of his finest short stories, "I'm a Fool," while appearing to be working on an advertisement. In *A Story Teller's Story* he recalls an occasion during a dull meeting about plows when he transformed one of the speakers into a character in a story that played out in his imagination while the meeting dragged on. In addition he enjoyed the stimulating contact with coworkers such as George Daugherty, who was gifted as an oral storyteller but unable to write up his stories and thus provided Anderson with material for his writing. The job also afforded him occasional opportunities to escape Chicago and to develop friendships with favorite clients, notably W. A. Steele and Dave Bohon in Owensboro and Harrodsburg, Kentucky, respectively, the latter even figuring in Anderson's story "I Want to Know Why." The same mix of good and bad impressions may be seen in his reactions a few years later to his lecture tours. He often complained about them, but he also enjoyed the stimulation of traveling to new places, speaking to particularly receptive audiences, and meeting interesting people.

Anderson's career as a full-time writer could be said to have begun in 1922 when he left Chicago on a train, leaving behind his advertising work and his second wife, Tennessee Mitchell. On his way to New York, he stopped off in Elyria, where he revisited his old factory, found his name missing from the door of his old office, and realized anew that he was now a writer. By the time he and his third wife, Elizabeth Prall, settled in New Orleans, he had published *Many Marriages* and *Horses and Men,* and virtually completed *A Story Teller's Story.* He was a renowned author when he became a mentor of sorts for the young William Faulkner, not only helping him to publish his first novel, *Soldier's Pay,* but, more importantly, as Faulkner explained, encouraging him to write about the world he knew best, the "little patch up there in Mississippi" that he was to draw upon in shaping the fictional world of Yoknapatawpha County.

Another change followed in 1925. After a vacation in southwestern Virginia that summer, Anderson became so fond of the people and the countryside there that he bought farm property. The following year, using the royalties from his best-selling novel *Dark Laughter,* he built a fine country house near the village of Troutdale that he called Ripshin. Within a year he had tired of being the gentleman farmer and, being anxious to take on a new role for himself, he moved to Marion, about twenty-two miles from Ripshin, to become publisher and editor of the two local newspapers. Although the work amounted to a retreat from the literary world and a return to business, he enjoyed it for awhile, especially as it afforded frequent opportunities to talk with the citizenry of that area. He wrote a large number of editorials, features, and news stories for the papers, some of which were collected in *Hello Towns!* By the end of 1928, however, he was ready for a change. Turning over the papers to his son Robert and, separating from Elizabeth Prall, he struck out in yet another new direction.

⌇

In early January 1929, Anderson began a friendship and correspondence with Eleanor Copenhaver, a Marion native who frequently returned home from her job as an industrial secretary for the YWCA in New York. Much of her work involved travel throughout the South promoting better working and housing conditions for women. Anderson not only fell in love with her but also became interested, through her influence, in factory conditions in the South. Anderson's interest in the emerging world of American industry had previously been reflected in the agrarian-industrial conflict in *Winesburg, Ohio, Poor White,* and many of his short stories, including "The Egg" and "Ohio Pagan." Now, however, his concern with industrialism became much more politically focused. Within a few months of their meeting, he began a long courtship of Eleanor that included following her movements throughout the South and using the occasions to tour mills and factories and to become involved in the labor movement. The literary results of these experiences were *Perhaps Women, Beyond Desire,* and numerous essays.

After Anderson and Eleanor Copenhaver were married in 1933, he enjoyed his only thoroughly successful marriage, his interest in radical politics waned, and his writing career took new directions. He was once again beginning a new cycle—his final one. He continued to write some fine short stories, many of which he collected in *Death in the Woods,* and also became interested in the theater. His most notable play was an adaptation of *Winesburg,* which for various reasons, especially his difficulties in attempting to collaborate with New York playwright Arthur Barton, never succeeded. At about the same time, he became attracted to the Roosevelt administration and agreed to travel around the country, meeting people and assessing their recovery from the Depression in a series of articles for *Today,* a pro-New Deal magazine. In 1935 some of these were included in his book *Puzzled America.* A year later he published his last novel, *Kit Brandon,* about rum-running during the Prohibition era.

Given the cyclical pattern of Anderson's life, it is appropriate that his last published book was *Home Town,* a pleasant paean to small-town life that in a way brought him back full-circle to his own origins. Still, he remained the restless traveler to the end. He and Eleanor were on their way to South America to visit friends in Valparaiso and to settle into the life of a small town in Chile when he died on March 8, 1941.

One can only speculate on how the South American trip would have worked out for Anderson during the planned six-month visit. Being so fond of visiting new places and meeting people, he would undoubtedly have enjoyed the South American friends he had already made and the literary figures they would have put him in touch with. However, his dream of becoming close to the ordinary people there might have been difficult because of the language barrier. Despite his diligent efforts to learn Spanish, he probably would have had the same problems communicating with non-English-speaking people that had previously frustrated him in France and Mexico. In any case it seems likely that his restlessness and longing to return to his home in Virginia would have been strong by the time for his return trip.

After Anderson's death, Eleanor resumed her work with the YWCA, which included an assignment in post–World War II Italy. She also preserved Ripshin much as her husband had left it. Over the years until her own death in 1985, she was the faithful steward of Anderson's literary estate. In 1947 she gave most of the manuscripts and correspondence that were still in her possession to the Newberry Library in Chicago, stimulating a major outpouring of critical and editorial work on Anderson that culminates in this eagerly awaited biography.

~

Sherwood Anderson's life and writings as expressions of his Americanism have long been of interest to Walter Rideout. He and Howard Mumford Jones gave as one basis for their selection of letters for *Letters of Sherwood Anderson* "the place (or lack of place) of the writer in America"; similarly the full title of the present biography is *Sherwood Anderson: A Writer in America*. In both books the theme is only suggestive, but the distinctly American patterns of Anderson's life, both as aspiring businessman and writer, are evident. As he leaves the small midwestern town of his youth to make his mark in the big world, he is squarely in the tradition of the American Dream made famous in Benjamin Franklin's autobiography, the life of Abraham Lincoln, and the novels of Horatio Alger. When Anderson picks up stakes and starts anew, he is also the characteristic American nomad, as he acknowledges in *A Story Teller's Story:* "Like all real American men of our day I wander constantly from place to place striving to put down roots into the American soil and not quite doing it." But he greatly enjoyed his many opportunities to discover and write about the places and people in all regions of the country.

Ultimately his pursuit of success, both material and artistic, became disappointing. In later years he lamented his diminished capacity to produce publishable work and the low income from work that was published. At the same time, he battled with various financial distractions such as his arrangement with publisher Horace Liveright in 1925 by which he would receive an advance of $100 a week for five years, the troublesome patronage of Mary Emmett, and his embarrassment at having to live on Eleanor's YWCA income. But eventually, as his literary reputation declined, he came to a fairly serene acceptance of his fate and adopted a kind of anti-American Dream—maintaining the importance of "thinking small" and shunning the corruptive search for success. Instead, the process, not the achievement, became the important thing. He wrote to Roger Sergel in 1927, soon after buying the Marion newspapers, that "work accomplished means so little. It is in the past. What we all want is the glorious and living present."

On the other hand, his interest in discovering America and its people never subsided. His many chances to travel, whether as businessman, writer, or tourist, helped to sustain his wandering ways. No pattern for living could be easier for Anderson because one of his remarkable gifts was his ability to be equally at home working on his farm, attending dinners with the literati in New York, visiting a men's club at a church in South Dakota, conversing with a brakeman on a train in California or coal miners in West Virginia; he made new friends wherever he traveled. He could never be an expatriate like his sometime friend Ernest Hemingway and insisted many times throughout his life that his writing was inextricably connected with his identity as an American. He was, he explained in a letter to Van Wyck Brooks on July 30, 1923, "because of the accident of my position as a man of letters, . . . a kind of composite essence of it all." In 1937 Thomas Wolfe wrote to him that "I think of you with Whitman and with Twain—that is, with men who have seen America with a poet's vision." Anderson could have wished for no finer compliment.

Sherwood Anderson

1

A Mid-American Beginning

1.

In his later years Sherwood Anderson enjoyed inventing fictitious fathers for himself and usually provided them with a Southern birth and indefinite parentage. His real father, however, Irwin McClain Anderson, was an Ohio man, a midwesterner, probably of Scotch-Irish ancestry. Irwin's father, Sherwood Anderson's grandfather, was James Anderson, who had been born in Cumberland County in south-central Pennsylvania on March 1, 1796, of parents who were themselves both from that county. In 1807, when James was eleven, his parents, Robert and Elizabeth Dickey Anderson, joined the great Scotch-Irish and German migration from Pennsylvania homesteads into southern Ohio; in the fall of 1808 they took up three hundred acres of land a mile north of West Union, the newly settled seat of Adams County, some sixty-five miles southeast of Cincinnati, close to the Ohio River. On this farm James Anderson lived until, in 1866, he moved to the nearby town of Sardinia, Ohio, where he died on May 11, 1886, at the age of ninety.[1]

During his half century of adult life in West Union, this paternal grandfather of Sherwood Anderson was a pillar of his society. A vigorous, efficient man, James farmed, hauled loads of iron and supplies for local blast furnaces, and had "a prominent place in the militia because his talents deserved it," being elected and commissioned major and then lieutenant-colonel of the First Cavalry Regiment, First Brigade, Eighth Division of the Ohio Militia. On June 2, 1831, James Anderson married Mary Baird of West Union, who bore him four sons and two daughters before her death on May 7, 1840. On November 7, 1844, he married Isabella Bryan Huggins, a thirty-eight-year-old widow with two sons of her own. James and his second wife, a woman with "the same happy and genial disposition as her husband," added yet two more sons and a daughter to a large, harmonious family. The oldest of this third and last set of children was

3

Irwin McClain, who was born August 7, 1845, and was to become the father of Sherwood Anderson.[2]

Considering Grandfather James's personal qualities, one would like to believe in a genetic chain of artistic inheritance, for this Ohio patriarch possessed the family skill of storytelling. His memory was so unusual that, as a friend and admirer subsequently wrote, he "could remember every incident of his life and everything which had ever been told him," and he "was fond of telling humorous stories." This gift for oral narrative was one expression of a firmly integrated personality, some elements of which were to reappear but in strikingly different combinations in his son Irwin and his grandson Sherwood. James Anderson enjoyed life with a direct immediacy, was "always brimful and running over with good humor," and, untroubled by trouble, "persisted in looking at the bright and cheerful side of things" with an unruffled hopefulness that another grandson was to denounce decades later as "the weakness of our clan." Yet while James had "the keenest sense of humor of any man of his time in the county," he was nevertheless "a most earnest and conscientious man." He was an antislavery Whig and then Republican, and an elder for thirty years in the Associate Reform Presbyterian Church. An honest man, he did not worry over money but "lived comfortable and easy." In sum, his friend's account concludes enthusiastically, "His life was a more valuable lesson than that taught by the Greek Philosophers, for he was up to their ideas and was a Christian beside."[3]

If James Anderson kept in intuitive balance the claims of this world and the next, his son Irwin was more concerned with the here than the hereafter. Nothing is known of the early years of Sherwood Anderson's father except that he grew up on the family farm, one child among the eleven reared by amiable parents "without a jar," and that he was educated during the 1850s in the "old stone schoolhouse" in West Union. The record becomes much more detailed with his Civil War service, which began just before his eighteenth birthday and subsequent to his father's own brief tour of active duty in 1862 as captain of a company of the irregulars known as the "Squirrel Hunters," which James Anderson led to nearby Aberdeen when a Confederate raid across the Ohio threatened. Military service, in fact, formed part of the lives of grandfather, father, and son; but it was only Irwin of the middle generation who saw any violent action. In his fanciful autobiography, *A Story Teller's Story*, Sherwood Anderson gave the impression that his father had been only a guardhouse soldier who in later years invented tales of how he and General Grant licked the Confederacy. The Civil War was indeed one of the climaxes in Irwin's life, the GAR subsequently became a focus for his social energies, and the evidence is overwhelming that he would rather talk, often about his war experiences, than work. But if in later years he became the garrulous old soldier of the American small town, he very definitely had had something to be garrulous about. For several reasons, Irwin Anderson's military career must be described in some detail here. A man whose obvious faults were to dismay and infuriate his children deserves at least his due. Furthermore, it seems likely that Sherwood Anderson's long interest in the Civil War originated in part from hearing his father's tales, whether believed or not. Most important of all, it is essential to have now the facts of Irwin's war experience in order later to understand fully the emotional conflict that was to develop between father and son.[4]

Irwin's first service appears to have been more arduous than exciting. When in the summer of 1863 a call went throughout Adams County for volunteers to make up Company G of the 129th Ohio Volunteer Infantry, a "six-month" regiment, he enlisted at West Union on July 20 as a private. On August 10, 1863, three days after Irwin turned eighteen, the regiment was mustered in at Camp Taylor near Cleveland, Ohio, proceeded to Cumberland Gap, and participated in Burnside's December campaign against Longstreet in eastern Tennessee. Nelson Evans, Irwin's boyhood friend and first lieutenant of Company G, recalled that the company "did some hard marching, much starving, and was under fire several times"; but the only fighting was a few skirmishes, and the company had no casualties. The worst enemy was the unusually bitter winter. During December the men quickly became ragged, were "nearly all without shoes," and had few and poor rations. After guarding Cumberland Gap during January, the regiment began its return north to Cleveland, where Irwin was mustered out with his company on March 8, 1864, and sent home to West Union.[5]

Irwin's next tour of duty, this time as a trooper in the Seventh Ohio Volunteer Cavalry, gave him a full taste of war. Back in the fall of 1862, the Seventh, the three-year "River Regiment," had been recruited from the counties in the southwestern part of the state along the Ohio River, Adams County contributing Company F, and had been mustered into service under Colonel Israel Garrard, a Cincinnatian, of whom the regiment's chronicler would later write that "it is an utter impossibility to hold the Colonel back when a fight is in progress." For a year and a half the Seventh had already fought frequently in eastern Kentucky and Tennessee, having been engaged, like Irwin's 129th Infantry, in Burnside's operations against Longstreet in late 1863; in July of 1864 this seasoned outfit had ridden down Sherman's extended supply line to Atlanta in time to participate in his siege of the city. On August 25, as the Confederate defense before Atlanta was crumbling, Irwin Anderson once more left off farming and enlisted as a private in the Seventh at Ironton, Ohio. By September 3, the day after Sherman's troops occupied Atlanta, the new recruit arrived in Columbus, Ohio, with a detachment of one-year volunteers assigned to Garrard's regiment.[6]

Just turned nineteen, Irwin was of average height—five feet seven inches, according to the Seventh's muster roll—and he must have been a handsome young man with his dark hair, dark complexion, and black eyes. He may have enlisted in the cavalry this time for any number of reasons, of course. Perhaps he was influenced by his father's lieutenant-colonelcy in the cavalry of the state militia, and there may well have been a persuasive recruiting drive in Adams County for replacements for Company F of the Seventh. Considering Irwin's personality as revealed in later life, however, one suspects also a temperamental attraction to this branch of the service. The Union cavalry, which in the first two years of the War was far inferior to the Confederate, had by now been reorganized, was repudiating the contemptuous commonplace of the early War years that "no one ever sees a dead cavalryman," and after Sheridan's victories in the Shenandoah Valley was taking on a glamour like that of the Air Force during World War II. Part of that glamour came from the extra long period of special training that the cavalryman needed in order to master not only his weapons but his horse and mounted maneuvers as well. Despite the fact that the muster rolls of Company F of the Seventh list Irwin as present from September 1864 through June 1865, such extended training probably kept him from active service with the regiment until after it had completed its foraging expeditions in October around captured Atlanta. There the regiment turned over its best horses to the cavalry that was to march with Sherman to the sea, and were shipped north in early November to Louisville, Kentucky, for refitting and assignment to the newly organized Cavalry Corps of the Military Division of the Mississippi under the command of James Harrison Wilson, a West Pointer and one of the meteoric bright young men of the War, who became a brevet major-general when barely twenty-seven.[7]

Probably Irwin Anderson received his training at the huge cavalry depot at Edgefield, just across the Cumberland River from Nashville, Tennessee; but he certainly was with the six hundred other men of the Seventh Ohio when in late November of 1864 the regiment was at the front again south of Franklin, Tennessee, helping to cover the withdrawal of the Federal infantry north toward Nashville before the advance of General John Hood and his cavalry commander, Nathan Bedford Forrest. Even so, Irwin was yet to be involved in his first real engagement; for the Seventh was held in reserve at the bloody Battle of Franklin, and by December 2 the whole Federal army under General George Thomas's command was safely back in Nashville.

For the next two weeks Thomas's cavalry commander, James Wilson, was pulling together his new Corps. Wilson was an extremely able and self-confident young man with revolutionary ideas on the use of cavalry. Most Union generals had regarded cavalry as of secondary importance, to be employed in small units for reconnoitering, escort work, and, at most, harassment of enemy infantry in a battle. Wilson had impressed Grant and Sherman with both his organizational and tactical skill, and was now entering on his great opportunity to test his theory that cavalry should be massed in whole corps by themselves, with the addition of small, mobile artillery units, and should use their horses for swift movement while doing most of their fighting dismounted. What he was directly anticipating was, in fact, the mobile warfare of World War II.

Wilson's theory had its first brilliant success at the Battle of Nashville on December 15–16, 1864, when the three divisions of his Cavalry Corps greatly helped to collapse Hood's left wing and turned the Confederate retreat from Nashville almost into a rout. Irwin Anderson and the rest of the Seventh Ohio were in the midst of Wilson's massive assault and would certainly have shared in the exultant feeling of invincibility that now swept the Cavalry Corps. Early on December 17, Irwin's outfit and other regiments pressed south against the retreating enemy and by itself entered the suburbs of Franklin so far in advance of the rest of their division that for an hour it was pinned down by the combined fire of a Confederate battery and a Federal one, the latter under the impression that any unit that far ahead must be Rebel. Withdrawing temporarily, the Seventh then charged through the town of Franklin and, in the words of the divisional commander, "would have pressed the pursuit farther had I not sent them word to stop." Through the rain and cold of approaching winter, along muddy roads and across a land foraged naked, the Cavalry Corps triumphantly pursued Hood's disintegrating army at a pace so demanding that hundreds of horses went lame and had to be killed. At 5 AM on Christmas Day of 1864, the single brigade containing the Seventh Ohio and two other cavalry regiments began their advance ten miles north of Pulaski, Tennessee. The brigade routed the Confederate rearguard at Pulaski, drove it seven miles south of the town, went into action again at the head of a narrow gorge called Devil's Gap, and briefly retreated only when counterattacked by eight brigades of enemy infantry. By the last day of 1864, this same Union brigade had helped push the final Confederate remnants back across the Tennessee River at the point in northwest Alabama where Hood had earlier collected his army for the disastrous Nashville campaign.

The taste of victory was in the air as Wilson established comfortable winter quarters near Florence, Alabama. For over two months he reorganized his Corps into the largest cavalry concentration yet assembled in the United States and turned it into a tough, skilled, striking force. He was particular about providing his troopers with the most effective modern weapons. Each man was issued the newly adopted shorter and lighter cavalry saber, which was considerably more wieldy than the old dragoon saber; but more important, each man received a Spencer carbine, a stubby, accurate gun only recently in mass production. Wilson enthusiastically advocated the Spencer because it was a breech-loading, seven-shot repeater that could be fired fourteen times a minute and hence enormously increased the firepower of his troops. The young general was also particular about extensive training. Daily the men drilled and practiced with their new weapons, and discipline of all sorts was rigorously enforced. One surmises that young Irwin Anderson would not have liked the drill and discipline any better than the next man; yet generally, as the historian of another regiment recalled, despite "the harsh weather and the rigid requirements of duty . . . the men were contented and happy." Because of their victory over Hood, their new and superior weapons, and their confidence that their general's theories would be further vindicated in practice, the men "were now sure of the success of their cause," and the whole Corps was in "high spirits."[8]

As soon as the heavy rains of late winter had subsided in mid-March, Wilson began moving his three picked divisions to the south bank of the Tennessee River; and on March 22 at dawn 12,500 troopers swung into the saddle and headed south on the great scythe-shaped sweep through the western Confederacy to be recorded officially as Wilson's Raid. Fanned out at first on three different routes in order to puzzle General Forrest, whose rebel cavalry was poised to repel raid or invasion, the three divisions cut swiftly down through the rugged, sparsely settled forestland of northern Alabama, converged into one great column just northwest of Elyton, the site of present-day Birmingham, and began destroying the collieries and iron mills of north central Alabama that were still supplying the Confederate war effort. The column then moved swiftly south to Montevallo, where on March 31, with the division containing Irwin's regiment in the advance, Wilson's men hit rebel troops under Forrest's direct command and drove them "in confusion," as Wilson later wrote, down the road toward Selma. On April 1, the Corps, in whom victory had established, as their young major general declared, a "spirit of great cheerfulness and confidence," again clashed victoriously with Forrest's troops at Ebenezer Church in an action so fierce that in "one company, C of the Seventh Ohio, every man was killed, wounded or had bullets through his clothes." Forrest fell back on Selma, Wilson in such close pursuit that in less than twenty-four hours his men were looking down from a low plateau onto that heavily fortified city, "beautiful in the soft light of a spring afternoon." Wilson ordered an immediate attack, and by full dark on that April 2 dismounted Union troopers had penetrated the outer fortifications, and the Seventh Ohio had participated in a massive mounted charge that helped carry the inner works. Irwin's regiment by itself was ordered to follow the fleeing enemy eastward and was so "active and unremitting" in pursuit "despite the darkness and almost impassable roads" that the Seventh captured four artillery pieces and 125 prisoners.[9]

Selma was the last major ordnance center left in the Confederacy, and Wilson's engineers did a systematic job of destroying its great machine shops and gun foundries. Then the Corps force-marched day and night due east to Montgomery, where four years earlier the Confederate States of America had been formed. Montgomery surrendered without a shot, and on April 12, Wilson's troopers rode through the city. It was "a beautiful day," one of them afterwards recalled, as perhaps Irwin Anderson did thirty years later; "the streets were lined with dooryards filled with bloom, and all the people came out to see." General Wilson, too, remembered the triumphal march.

With perfect order in column of platoons, every man in his place, division and brigade flags unfurled, guidons flying, sabers and spurs jingling, bands playing patriotic airs, and the bugles now and then sounding the calls, the war-begrimed Union troopers, batteries, ambulance, and wagons passed proudly through the city. Not a man left the ranks, not a loud word was uttered, and not an incident happened to hurt the feelings of the people. It was an example of discipline, order, and power lasting nearly all day and constituting a far more impressive spectacle than a bloody battle would have been.

Four days later the Corps reached Columbus, Georgia, then a city of twelve thousand people. Not yet informed of Lee's surrender at Appomattox a week before, Wilson threw his men into a night attack on that fortified city, which culminated in a charge by three hundred dismounted troopers across the one remaining bridge over the Chattahoochee River, a charge that opened the city to capture along with its entire garrison of twelve hundred soldiers.[10]

Columbus was the last real battle of the Civil War. By April 20, Wilson was at Macon, where he and his troops received word of the armistice. The rest of Irwin Anderson's service in the Cavalry Corps is quickly told. After Jefferson Davis was captured on May 10 near Irwinsville, Georgia, by men under Wilson's command, the Seventh Ohio was part of his train guard from Atlanta to Augusta. On May 22 the regiment began a march to Chattanooga, and on the twenty-ninth it was ordered to Nashville. Here it went into the cavalry camp at Edgefield, where in the first two weeks of the preceding December Wilson with methodical speed had been pulling together his original Cavalry Corps for the Battle of Nashville. After turning in his horse and all equipment except for his saber, saber belt, and belt plate, which he undoubtedly delighted in being allowed to keep, Irwin Anderson was mustered out with the rest of the Seventh Regiment on July 1, 1865, still a private after ten months in the cavalry, and sent back to Camp Dennison, near Cincinnati, where he was paid $151.15 for serving his country and discharged.[11]

So at age nineteen Irwin Anderson became a veteran of what E. E. Cummings was to call, speaking of World War I, "the experience of his generation." Well over a hundred and fifty years later it is of course impossible, in the absence of dependable evidence, to know specifically how Irwin Anderson was affected by the experience. How, for example, did he feel when, if the regimental historian is telling the horrifying truth in his plain account, the Seventh Ohio rode toward Andersonville Prison "for the purpose of releasing our prisoners held there"?

When within four miles of the place, they were met by a flag of truce, evidently to gain time. This was not recognized by the Seventh, who charged the place, but only in time to see the train moving out with the mass of skeletons caused by starvation. Some eighty-four men, which beggared all description, were left in the prison pen.

It cannot be know what psychic wounds, if any, Irwin may have sustained; it cannot even be established for certain that he ever received a physical wound. The records of the Adjutant General's office in the War Department "furnish no evidence of disability" for Irwin during either his infantry or his cavalry service; yet his oldest son-to-be would later recall that his "father was not a rugged man and for many years after the Civil War had a running sore on his leg from a bullet wound." But whether he fought well or badly, whether he fought for adventure, from fear of weakness or of censure, or for love of slaughter, he could truly say, however exaggerated his recollections, "I am the man, I suffer'd, I was there." Wilson's Raid, "one of the most important and fruitful expeditions of the war," as Nicolay and Hay wrote in their *Life of Lincoln*, had been as dramatic as it had been successful, indeed had been so successful in part because both enlisted men and officers felt exultantly the drama of what they did. Irwin may well have used his memories and his tales of them to carry him through the undramatic failures of his later years; but, as will be seen, the fanciful reconstructions of his tales by his storytelling son reveal more about Sherwood Anderson than about his father.[12]

Having learned the arts of war, Irwin turned to the arts of peace. Around September 5, 1865, Irwin began a year's study as one of forty-four "Gentlemen" (boys and young men), who, because their sisters were enrolled there, were registered as day scholars at the Xenia Female College, Xenia, Ohio. Irwin's fifteen-year-old sister Martha was enrolled in the "First Year" college level, and he himself probably thought it wise to invest his army pay in some education beyond the West Union public school. Xenia Female College had been founded under Presbyterian auspices as a girls' academy in 1850, when Xenia itself was a town of three thousand inhabitants, but by Irwin's time it had been taken over by the Cincinnati

Conference of the Methodist Episcopal Church, had become coeducational despite its name, and in 1865–66 enrolled 247 students at levels from high school through what would now be considered junior college. The pleasant but modest campus consisted of two three-story brick buildings—one a classroom building, the other a dormitory for women students from outside the town—set on broad, tree-shaded grounds at the top of a hill on East Church Street.[13]

Although the institution was under Methodist control, the religious and ethical emphasis was so marked as to have pleased even a lifelong Associate Reform Presbyterian like Irwin's father. All students were required to attend "Devotional Exercises every morning and evening" in the school's chapel, two additional meetings "during the week, for Prayer and Religious Conversation," and regular "Public Worship on the Sabbath, at such Church as their Parents may designate"; and the explicit aim of the Trustees was "to make the Institution a CHRISTIAN HOME, where comfort, health, morals and mind, will receive appropriate attention." The mind was attended to by a faculty of two men and six women under the presidency of William Smith, MA, who had at least the local reputation of a stern and excellent teacher. Irwin the ex-cavalryman might have taken the first year of the Scientific Course in the Collegiate Department, which emphasized algebra, grammar, general history, and one-quarter courses in physiology, botany, and physical geography; or he might have entered the Classical Course, which, besides algebra and grammar, concentrated on Latin and French. The college's interest in the inculcation of good reading habits and "a correct literary taste" for all students was taken care of by two closely supervised literary societies that met both privately and publicly for "recitations, essays, stories interspersed with piano and vocal music."[14]

No record exists of Irwin's activities at Xenia Female College or of its effect on him. Since subsequently in his early married years he at least once taught Sunday school, he presumably profited from the organization of "each College-Class . . . into a Bible-Class" so that the students could study "the Scriptures systematically" and be prepared "to teach successfully in Sabbath-School"; and considering his later involvement in declamation and dramatic performances, he might have been much interested in the meetings of whichever literary society he belonged to. The opportunities for social life in Xenia appear to have been rather restricted. Whereas Martha Anderson would have been required to live in the boardinghouse with all the other out-of-town girls under the watchful eyes of the teachers, Irwin would have had to live with a family in a private home "under right influences." It is possible that a Stella Anderson of Xenia, who was registered that year in the Preparatory Department of the College, was a relative and that he lived with her family. It is also possible that at this time he really did become acquainted with Whitelaw Reid, the distinguished Xenia-born journalist and diplomat, whose friendship he later claimed to have, though during at least most of the months Irwin would have been in school, Reid was traveling in the South observing the effects of the Civil War, including the destruction carried out in Selma by General Wilson's Cavalry Corps. And it is just barely possible that Sherwood Anderson was right when he later asserted that his father had once run a livery stable in Xenia. If so, Irwin was presumably earning his way through his one year at the college.[15]

In the Xenia of the 1860s, when most of the published local news consisted of notices of marriages, deaths, and church socials, the commencement exercises of the Female College, held on the evening of June 20, 1866, were an event. Very probably Irwin Anderson was involved in the college's public examinations held from the nineteenth through the twenty-first, but he was not one to have missed the exercises. The weather was warm, the First Methodist Episcopal Church was crowded, the spectators talked too loudly, and the evening was excessively prolonged by the reading by eight young ladies of eight essays, "which evidenced high talent and fine culture," according to the newspaper report, but not "the highest talent," that of "condensation." The next evening, "after one of the grandest thunderstorms of the season," Irwin might have heard more essays, recitations, and music at the Alumni Association exercises. These ceremonies would have ended his last year of formal education; yet it should be kept in mind that even this much academic training beyond public school, whatever the professional quality of the college, was unusual in the 1860s for the average young American.[16]

Irwin's movements over the next few years are obscure. Military service may well have stimulated, or reinforced, in the young cavalry veteran the restlessness that was to mark his future life. At any rate the account of him by his friend Nelson Evans states that after the Xenia year, "He then located in Mexico, Missouri, and was in the west and southwest from 1866 to 1870," a statement partially confirmed by Irwin's own cryptic declaration that during these years he was "traveling." He returned to Ohio in 1870 and in that year or the next settled in Morning Sun, a tiny community of 170 people in Preble County about thirty-five miles north of Cincinnati. At some earlier time, though possibly in 1870 also, he had learned the trade of harnessmaking, as his younger brother, Benjamin Dickey, did; and the evidence suggests that the loan of $150 that his father made Irwin on September 17, 1870, was designed to set the son up in business. Certainly he was living in or near Morning Sun by November 14, 1871; for, as William Sutton discovered, on this day Irwin became a member of the Hopewell (United Presbyterian) Church, the plain "Scotch architecture" building of which stood about a mile west of Morning Sun village. Established as a harnessmaker, the occupation Sherwood was to use in *Poor White* as the symbol of craftsmanship, and received into a locally popular church, Irwin lacked only one requirement to be a perfect example of the rising young American. Then one day a slender, dark-haired, dark-eyed girl named Emma Smith, who lived on a farm just south of Morning Sun, entered in her diary a reference to a carriage ride "during which something broke on the carriage and was fixed by Irv Anderson." Irwin was about to complete the accepted configuration of early success by taking a wife.[17]

2.

Of his mother, whom he loved deeply, Sherwood Anderson was to write more accurately than of his father, whom he did not. Nevertheless, about her side of the family not much is known and even less can be documented. His mother's mother, Margaret Austry, was originally from Germany. She was the daughter of one Henry Austry and was born, probably near Berlin, on September 10, 1830. When she was still a young child, her parents brought her to the United States. On December 22, 1851, at age twenty-one, she was definitely in Butler County, Ohio, some miles north of Cincinnati, for on that day she was married by a justice of the peace to William H. Smith, possibly an Englishman and a teacher, who probably lived near the town of Oxford. By this husband Margaret had two daughters. The first of these, Emma Jane, who was to become the mother of Sherwood Anderson, was born on October 1, 1852, near Oxford. Whatever William Smith may have been like, faithfulness was not one of his strong points; in March of 1854, shortly before the birth of Emma's sister, Mary Ann, he deserted his wife "without any just cause" and permanently disappeared, leaving his family without support except for that provided by Margaret's "own industry and the support of her parents." Some three years later, on July 8, 1857, Margaret Smith petitioned the Court of Common Pleas of Butler County for a divorce, custody of the children, "reasonable alimony," and restoration "to her maiden name Margaret Ostray [*sic*]." On December 4, 1857, the divorce was granted. Margaret was given "exclusive custody" of the children, and the sum of $300 was named as alimony to be paid by her husband who had abandoned her, though this would have been a legal gesture only since, according to the petition, she had "no means of knowing or finding out where he lives."[18]

The divorce decree released Margaret to marry again, and shortly thereafter, on March 29, 1858, she did marry a Louis Myers, who seems to have been a farmer or farm laborer of German extraction, to have been about two years older than she, and to have lived either in or near Oxford. But though a year later Margaret bore yet another daughter, also named

Margaret, this second marriage was hardly more fortunate than the first; for it appears that Louis Myers was killed in 1860 "by a bolt of lightning while standing under a tree," and that a son, born to Margaret that same year, died in the year following. Such a series of catastrophes may well explain why "Grandmother Myers," as she was to be known in Sherwood Anderson's family, did not marry again and why she later would be remembered as an extremely difficult person, "neurotic, suspicious, volatile" and filled with "an unrestrained anger."[19]

After he became a writer, Sherwood Anderson gave a picture of this grandmother in *A Story Teller's Story*. Characteristically, the picture is in considerable part an invention, perhaps of the "unforgettable" kind of grandmother he would like to have had. So he describes her as "the dark evil old woman with the broad hips and the great breasts of a peasant and with the glowing hate shining out of one eye," who "had shuffled off four husbands," who beat up a tramp, then got drunk with him, and "went singing off together with him down the road." Anderson the storyteller refers ambiguously to the supposed episode of the tramp as "the tale" he may sometime tell, a reference that allows him to fictionalize while seeming to claim to tell the truth; yet Anderson the person apparently did believe that his own piercingly dark eyes proved an Italian heritage through this grandmother. In actuality, Margaret Austry Smith Myers was German rather than Italian, prudish rather than passionate, Presbyterian rather than pagan; she was, in fact, "a very respectable old lady who went to church each Sunday wearing a rustling silk dress and lace mitts."[20]

Both the reality and the invention were far in the future, of course. For young Margaret Myers, left with three children from two marriages to support, life was difficult. It may be that after the death of her second husband in 1860 she had to place at least six-year-old Mary Ann, her second daughter by William Smith, with the first of a series of families willing to care for her; but it is not know how long Emma Jane, about eight years old at the time of her stepfather's death, remained with her mother. She certainly continued to live in or near Oxford, with or close to her mother, for some years; for despite the fact that Margaret Myers was a convinced Presbyterian, Emma Smith was "received" into the Oxford Methodist Church "on probation" in February, 1865, her address given as "Hamilton Road." On August 27, 1865, when she was almost thirteen, she was "Baptized and received into full membership" in that church. At some time thereafter, however, Emma was taken into the home of James I. Faris, a farmer, who lived some six or seven miles north of Oxford near the village of Morning Sun and who was, significantly for the girl's future, a member like Irwin Anderson of the Hopewell United Presbyterian Church.[21]

In later years Sherwood Anderson wrote that his mother had been a "bound girl," a term he may have found attractive because it connoted the oppression by others of one he loved and wished to commemorate; yet even if Emma was, in the strict sense of the term, "articled to service" in the Faris home, she seems to have been treated very much as one of the family. A daughter of the Farises recalled for William Sutton that her mother was fond of Emma and had characterized her as "fine in every way, . . . kind and a good housekeeper." While living on the Faris farm, Emma continued her education at the high school level, probably at the Morning Sun Academy, a private school emphasizing the classics, which occupied a "commodious brick" house in the village. Nor was her life joyless in other ways. Her student diary was "well-filled with attendances" at the social pleasures then available to young ladies—"prayer meetings, parties, croquet games, sleigh and buggy rides." It was, of course, on one such latter ride that "something broke on the carriage and was fixed by Irv Anderson."[22]

Exactly when Emma Smith and Irwin Anderson met is not known and is inconsequential anyway. Small towns are, after all, small, and their young people tend to know or know of every available person of the opposite sex. Very probably Emma attended the Hopewell Church with the Farises, there being no Methodist congregation in Morning Sun, and in town life of that day prayer meetings had social as well as religious functions. Emma Smith was strikingly good-looking with her dark hair and eyes, quietly charming in disposition, hardworking in domestic duties, and, whatever her legal relationship to the Farises, had quite sufficient social status as part of their family group. As for Irwin Anderson, besides being darkly handsome, he had about him the romantic aura of the ex-cavalryman and traveler, his gift for storytelling, more than the usual amount of education, and in addition must have seemed dependable because he knew a craft and ran his own harnessmaking business. In short, on February 26, 1873, Irwin Anderson, age twenty-seven, and Emma Smith, age twenty, were granted a marriage license by the probate judge of Preble County; and on March 11 they were united in marriage by the Reverend Joseph MacHatton, pastor for a dozen years of Hopewell Church, at a ceremony in the Faris home.[23]

Presumably it was through the influence first of the Farises and then of her new husband that Emma Smith Anderson decided to leave Methodism for Presbyterianism, for on August 21, 1873, she was received into the Hopewell Church. Religion was to be a comfort in the difficult years yet to come. The only other known event of the Andersons' early married life in Morning Sun was the birth of their first child, a son, Karl James, on January 13, 1874. Morning Sun, despite its shining name, appears to have been too small a town for the family's needs or ambitions, and around June of 1874 the Andersons began the first of a series of moves by going on to the larger town of Camden some half dozen miles to the northeast.[24]

Camden, Ohio, the town where Sherwood Anderson would be born and spend the first year of his life, had a population, according to the 1870 census, of 650. Although its large flour milling firm, busy during the Civil War, had failed disastrously just before the arrival of the Andersons, thus demonstrating "how swiftly financial ruin could sweep away and destroy" the benefits accruing "from heavy mechanical industries," the town remained the trading center of "fine farming country" and boasted of its prosperous, moral, and civic-minded citizens. Not only did it have a location with "all of the elements of practical and material advantage," including a station on the Cincinnati and Chicago Railway, but its setting was beautiful as well. Although Anderson was taken from Camden too early for him actually to remember the community, the pastoral memory of it he invented in *Tar: A Midwest Childhood* as "a little white town in a valley with high hills on each side" was true in certain respects. A "gem in appropriate setting," as a contemporary county history floridly exclaimed, Camden did lie in a valley, along the west bank of a small river, and from the hills on either side one could look down on streets lined by maples and locusts that half concealed, not the "poor little houses" that the autobiographical Tar Moorehead fancied, but neat, thrifty-looking residences.[25]

Irwin Anderson set up his harness shop in a rented two-story wooden building at Number 25 on the west side of Camden's Main Street, a few doors north of Central Street. He engaged a sixteen-year-old cobbler named James Gift to make the halters, which he disliked doing himself, and prospered so sufficiently that about June, 1875, he was one of ten businessmen in Camden to purchase advertising space in B. F. Morgan's *Directory of Preble County*. Unlike the town's other harnessmaker, he was characteristically quite willing to call attention to himself as a "Manufacturer and Dealer in Harness, Saddles, Bridles, Collars, Whips, &c" with "A large Stock always on hand, of Best Materials, and at lowest Cash prices" and "Fine Harness a Specialty." Young Jim Gift, the helper, seems to have had considerable insight into "M" Anderson, as Irwin was nicknamed, for years later Gift remembered him as "a kind employer whose chief fault was to tell glowing tales of his own experiences." Yet another townsman, Charles E. Morlatt, who subsequently became a banker, recognized the mixture of qualities in his friend Irwin. In his old age Morlatt recalled that Anderson "worked hard to support his family," but also told a story "of 'M' Anderson's drinking and standing on the street corners, swinging a silver watch on a heavy silver chain while he told of thrilling experiences he had had in the Civil War."[26]

When and where Irwin may actually have purchased that watch and chain, (which Tar Moorehead also recollected), they were a sign of the Andersons' solid standing in the community as "an average family." Irwin had an assured place in certain of Camden's social institutions. It is clear that he had some talent for music; he played in the Camden Cornet Band, and Jim Gift recalled that during "his spare moments he sat in the rear of the store and practiced on the alto horn," and he may have sung in the choir of the Presbyterian Church to which presumably his and his wife's memberships were transferred from Hopewell. Apparently more attracted to church society than to dogma, this "likeable fellow who made friends easily" taught a Sunday school class in the Methodist church for young adults such as Charles Morlatt and once convivially gave his "scholars a treat in the way of an oyster supper at his home."[27]

The class could not have been a large one even in so upright a community as Camden thought itself to be, for home to the steadily growing Anderson family was four small rooms in the north half of a modest one-story, two-family frame house at what is now 142 South Lafayette Street. Here in one of the two bedrooms the second Anderson child, a girl named Stella, was born on April 13, 1875. Jim Gift could recall Mrs. Anderson from about that time as "a small, neat, pretty woman who occasionally pushed a baby carriage to her husband's shop, while a small boy [Karl] toddled along beside her." It was also in this little house that the third child and second son, Sherwood Berton Anderson, was born on September 13, 1876. Years later older brother Karl, not quite three at the new baby's birth, recorded for Sherwood his own first memory as being connected with his brother's early infancy: "my mother, with you in her arms, had led me through a wooden gate and I had seen a railroad engine, with a swollen smoke stack cutting its way through a meadow." Considering the degree to which Sherwood Anderson's life, thought, and writings were to be bound up with the transformation of American society from rural-agrarian to urban-industrial, Karl's mental image fortuitously linking baby brother, natural scene, and train has a startling appropriateness.[28]

The Andersons stayed in Camden for perhaps a little more than three years, leaving town just before Sherwood's first birthday, so that he was correct in asserting in *Tar* that when he left he went in his mother's arms. The reason for moving is not known. In general the family appears to have been better off financially in the Camden period than it was to be for years afterward. Certainly the townspeople and the well-to-do farmers around Camden needed harnesses for their horses, for in 1880 there were three harnessmakers in town rather than the two, including Irwin, in 1875. Possibly, however, the departure was somehow linked to financial troubles on the part of Irwin's brother, Benjamin Dickey Anderson, who seems to have been at this time, though no one knows for how long, a harnessmaker in the village of Fairhaven nearby to both Morning Sun and Camden, and who was probably the Anderson of oral tradition who "skipped out of. . . . Fairhaven owing a bill for leather." Whatever the reason, the local newspaper, the Camden *Herald,* noted in its "Personal" column for the issue of September 1, 1877, that "I. M. Anderson will leave here in a few days for Independence, Ohio, where he will engage in business." Once again the Andersons were taking up their migration generally northward through Ohio.[29]

3.

The Independence to which the Andersons moved from Camden in 1877 was not the town of that name today, but rather present-day Butler in Richland County some fifteen miles southeast of Mansfield in north-central Ohio. Butler was laid out in 1848 under the name of Independence, incorporated as a village in the same year the Andersons moved there, and acquired its present name subsequent to the family's departure. In 1860 it had had a population of six hundred, but by 1880, perhaps because of the hard times of the seventies, the population had dropped to about four hundred. The town was situated "at the great bend of the B & O railroad, where a number of railroad accidents" had occurred, and Irwin may have heard about it through reports of "the terrible collision in September, 1872, during the first state fair at Mansfield." Nothing is known of the Anderson's short stay in Independence except that a fourth child, a son named Irwin M., was born there on June 18, 1878. Presumably Irwin, the father, found that it was not profitable after all to "engage in business" in that town; for sometime in 1879, probably in late winter or early spring, the family moved again, to a county just to the west of Richland.[30]

This time the Andersons tried their fortune in Caledonia, a village some ten miles northeast of the small city of Marion and on the main road to Mansfield. Caledonia, where they lived for about five years, was roughly the size of Camden, but unlike the town of Sherwood's birth it was situated on flat ground and had exceptionally wide streets laid out as with a ruler off a broad, bare, public square. From a townsman named C. S. Geddis, Irwin rented a shop building on the south side of East Marion Street, where he set up business as a "saddler," and a house for his family on the west side of South High Street. Here Sherwood Anderson lived from about age two and a half to seven and a half, and here in this house and town and immediately surrounding countryside his first "faint memories" began.[31]

Although he wrote at some length about Caledonia in *Tar,* the condensed recollections of the town in his *Memoirs* appear to be, in this as in other matters, somewhat more reliable. In neither account does he mention a first year of school that he must have taken in the two-story brick schoolhouse that the community had proudly erected on spacious grounds opposite the Methodist Church in 1874, only a year after Caledonia had been incorporated as a village; in fact, Anderson was to have singularly little to say about his schooling and his regular teachers in any of his autobiographical writings despite the fact that he became at least an average student. From Caledonia, briefer but probably more interesting matters stayed in his mind. He would remember nibbling grass in childish imitation of sheep and being stung on the mouth by a bee, seeing a spring flood, presumably of Whetstone Creek, being taken to his father's harness shop to watch the mysterious and exciting activity there, and accidentally viewing with his sister the birth of a litter of pigs, a sight that, he later asserted, stirred him with an obscure awareness of the endless procession of animal life. That he may really have had such experiences is supported by the fact that his memory of a great night fire is firmly grounded in an actual event. On "July 23, 1883, at 2:30 in the morning, there broke out the most destructive fire that ever occurred in Caledonia," a fire that "ceased not its insatiate fury until it had destroyed seventeen buildings" and fire engines had been brought by railroad flat car from Marion on the west and Galion on the east.[32]

In the *Memoirs* Anderson recalled that the family house must not have been in the path of the fire, but so much destruction would seriously have impaired village prosperity, and this in turn may well have finally convinced his father that Caledonia held no future for him. Actually, such a future had almost certainly been foreclosed already. At least during the first part of this five-year period in Caledonia, Irwin seems to have managed to make out well enough. According to people who knew him, he "worked hard, was smart," and "was always punctual in paying his rent" on house and shop. As in Camden, the family appears to have fitted into the community. Emma Anderson was a close friend of the wife of one of the town's three druggists who had a corner store on the square, and their children played together. As in Camden also, Irwin was known as "a great story teller"; and since, as his landlord later asserted, he played an instrument in what was known grandiloquently as the Caledonia Aeolian Band, the Anderson family tradition could have been correct as reported in *Sherwood Anderson's Memoirs,* that he "once played together in the same cornet band" with Dr. George Tryon Harding's fourteen-year-old son, Warren Gamaliel. Irwin must have been right in his element with that village brass band, whose name, painted on the side of the bass drum, came from Aeolus, Greek god of the winds. Young Warren Harding, who played the B-flat cornet, had collected money from the town merchants to buy the resplendent uniforms with real brass buttons and a tassel on the cap. Summer, "when picnics were abloom in the land," was the time when the band was busiest; and Saturday nights in the little town were especially merry because then the band assembled under torchlight by the town pump near the center of the wide square and played to the assembled crowd of town and farm folk regular concerts of waltzes, quicksteps, and patriotic marches.[33]

Those happy days did not last. The evidence indicates that toward the end of the Caledonia stay, probably in late 1882 or early 1883, Irwin's business failed. In the late spring of 1883 he was recorded as boarding, apparently without his family, in Mansfield some thirty miles away, at which time he may have worked as a journeyman harnessmaker in another man's shop or have had a job in the factory of the Aultman & Taylor Company, which boasted of being "among the largest producers of threshing machinery in the world." Perhaps he moved his family briefly to Mansfield in late 1883, but more likely he left them in Caledonia while he worked temporarily by himself in the city to support them, to help pay off his debts, to save up money for a permanent move from a Caledonia badly hurt by the great fire. His financial difficulties would certainly have been intensified at the time by the birth on May 21, 1883, of a fifth child, a son named Ray Maynard.[34]

The precise causes of Irwin's financial failure are not known, and his son stated in the *Memoirs* that he was himself "to hear many explanations." One cause advanced by the father in that painful fourth chapter of *Tar,* in which he comes home to his family drunk and self-pitying, was that some of the people who bought harnesses from him did not pay. Interviews with Caledonia people suggest a second possible cause. At some time during the five-year stay in Caledonia, Irwin began to get his reputation as a man who spent too much of his time in the town's several saloons, a reputation he had not had earlier in Camden. Perhaps, of course, Irwin turned to heavy drinking after his business failure as a means of coping with it psychologically; nevertheless, he did spend so much of what income he had on liquor that, according to a longtime friend of Stella, "neighbors would help out with gifts occasionally." Sherwood Anderson appears to have remembered correctly when he told Mary Helen Dinsmoor in 1939 that at the time the Andersons left Caledonia, his father "was paying less attention to his business, and partaking of the bottle more frequently."[35]

The father must indeed have felt his failure to be "a bitter dose" to take. The curve of his career had been generally upward in the approved American manner—military service, a taste of college education, travel, an independent craft-business, marriage to a beautiful and loyal wife, a growing family, status in the community. Then came the bad luck and bad choices, which deflected that movement downward and away from the happy ending of the success story. Even more important for the subject of this book was the complex effect of the father's failure on the inner, as well as the outer, life of his second son. Though other forces and causes were of course involved, that failure helped to turn an impressionable Sherwood away from his father and toward his mother, to make him as a young man define success in material terms, to cause him to set business success as his goal in his early adult years. Yet each of these effects merged with its opposite. Although never reconciled to his father, Anderson would come to an uneasy recognition of his own resemblance to this fellow "word-man," an unconscious artist lost in the little towns of Ohio, would feel compelled years afterwards to reject conventional success himself, and would in some of his best writings find a justification for failure. Only, one suspects, because he experienced as a child the family strains and insecurities resulting from his father's business defeat could the mature Anderson succeed in writing that sadly funny tale of unsuccess, "The Egg." Paradoxically, the truism is true: the writer always has the childhood he must have in order to become the writer he will be.

Irwin's stay in Mansfield could not have lasted long, for when the family took up their northward migration again in March 1884, it was from Caledonia that they departed. Leaving defeated hopes behind, they at last headed for Clyde, Ohio, the town near Sandusky and Lake Erie where Sherwood Anderson grew up and which he always thought of as his home town. In later years Karl Anderson vividly recalled the morning when the family closed the door to their Caledonia house for the last time and made their "laden way to the depot, Sherwood with a struggling pup in his arms that only a few days before a neighbor had given him." When the dog leaped from the boy's arms and fled back under the foundation of the house, Sherwood was led wailing to the railroad station by a mother gently assuring him "that the little animal would find a home" and a father emptily promising "that each of his children in the golden future was to have a better bred dog of their own." As the train whistle sounded far down the track, the mother discovered that Sherwood was missing from the family group. Karl ran back to the house again, found his brother vainly searching for the dog under the house, dragged him out through the red clay dirt by the legs, and led him back to the station, where their impassive mother did her best with a handkerchief to clean her boys' clothes and faces. As the train carried the family away from the village, Sherwood stood at the coach window sniffling at the irrevocable loss of his puppy.[36]

Karl remembered other events of that day's journey, which sharply characterize members of the Anderson family. By the time they had to change trains at a junction in the afternoon, Irwin, who "was fond of fraternizing," had gotten to know everyone in the coach car; and while Emma waited with the children at the junction depot, he had restlessly and gregariously "wandered away to inspect the village." Karl, sent to locate him, was distracted by a nearby sawmill and returned to find that his distressed mother had in turn sent Sherwood to fetch the father back, the northbound train shortly being due, but the younger brother had not carried out the mission either. Once again Karl set off toward the village, and, in a remembered scene that is an epiphany of the two personalities, found father and son "sitting on the bench outside the general store in conversation with the storekeeper and another man."

What I particularly recall was Sherwood's serious contemplation, a look of inquiry as he sat beside the storekeeper, as if he was searching the manner and character of the people, and the resistance to my insistence that he return with me in response to Mother's anxiety that we prepare for the oncoming train; that, and my father shaking hands with his genial companions, as if saying good-bye to a long-established friendship.

The Andersons arrived in Clyde after dark that evening and put up for the night in a little hotel near the station, the mother quiet, the children apprehensive in their new surroundings, only the father talkative, as always, with the waitress in the musty dining room. Karl and Sherwood "slept on a lumpy cotton mattress in a large bed at the other end of the hall from Mother and Father"—and at this point the adult Karl's recollection takes on the pathos of a *Winesburg* tale.

I remember a feeling of isolation as though I were trapped, and Sherwood was whimpering. Just at daybreak I was awakened by Sherwood crying at the window. I went over to join him, and he was whimpering over the loss of his dog. From the windows we looked over the desolate rooftops soaked with the driving rain. You could just see the town's main street in the cold rain, and Clyde was presenting to its newest citizens a dreary aspect.

Then the boys heard their mother, the dependable one, coming down the hall, and Sherwood "sniffed back the sobs." She entered the room, Karl remembered, "with a white bowl and pitcher to wash us and inspect behind our ears" in order to prepare her sons properly for "the beginning of a new life" in a new town.

2

Clyde, Ohio

1.

In later years after he had become a successful painter, Karl Anderson remembered Clyde joylessly as "a community without much beauty," a "farmers' town, without growth," through which "Main Street ran its dusty way like an arrow from field to field." Sherwood, on the other hand, remembered it as "a fair and a sweet town." The latter's pastoral recollection was to be touched with both elegy and anger, but one quite misunderstands Sherwood Anderson, both the man and the writer, if one labels him part of the Revolt from the Village. "There wasn't anything to this revolting," he told a young novelist only a few months before his death. "I liked Clyde. I saw it the way it was and I put it down the way it was. I didn't run away from Clyde. The time came, and I went."[1]

Despite his dismal introduction to the town as a child, Clyde became for the mature Sherwood Anderson what Hannibal became for Mark Twain, a writer whom he admired with reservations and with reservations resembled. Like Twain, he returned again and again, as he says in the *Memoirs,* to the "impressions gathered . . . in the first twenty years of his life, impressions of people, and events experienced during these formative years when the imagination is most alive," impressions that were "source materials for him all his life." For each writer, also, the particular experience in his community was of central importance in shaping his fundamental attitudes toward and assumptions about the meaning of experience in general, though only slowly and intuitively did each bring these attitudes and assumptions into conscious understanding. Then, too, just as Hannibal for all its dark side furnished Twain's nostalgic imagination with a kind of Golden Age against which to measure post–Civil War America, so Clyde furnished Anderson's equally nostalgic imagination with one luminous moment before the troubled twentieth century, when, as he wrote in *Poor White,* that lyric in novel form, each town in the great

Mississippi Valley "came to have a character of its own," when a "kind of invisible roof beneath which everyone lived spread itself over each town." Clyde for all its dark side provided Anderson the man and writer with a standard, less of isolation, rebellion, and hatred than of community, acceptance, and love.[2]

When Irwin and Emma Anderson and their five children came north by train that March day in 1884, Clyde was a town of about twenty-four hundred inhabitants. Situated only a few miles beyond the limits of the old Western Reserve, it lay in a region of low hills and broad flat fields in Green Creek Township, Sandusky County, seventeen miles southwest of the small city of Sandusky, which was itself roughly halfway between Cleveland on the east and Toledo on the west. Originally the town had grown up in the 1830s around Hamer's Tavern and William McPherson's blacksmith shop at the point where a wagon track north to Sandusky crossed the Maumee and Western Reserve Pike—the Trunion Pike as Anderson was to call it in *Winesburg, Ohio*—which slanted northwest from Bellevue, just inside the Western Reserve, across the then undrained Black Swamp to a point on the Maumee River just south of Toledo. The little settlement of Hamer's Corners, known among the teamsters on the Pike as "Bang All" because of the brawls ignited there by cheap tavern whiskey, developed only slowly. Then in 1852 the tracks of the north-south Indiana, Bloomington, and Western Railroad (later part of the "Big Four" system) were laid at a seventy-degree angle across the east-west line of the Lake Shore and Michigan Southern (later part of the New York Central) just south of Hamer's Corners; and the town, now named Clyde after the Clyde in New York State, grew up rapidly around this junction point. Passengers, like the Andersons, came north on the I, B & W (the "I Better Walk" of local humor) and, if they were going east or west, waited at Clyde for a Lake Shore train to Cleveland or Toledo. The wooden Gothic railroad station, functionally designed in an L-shape to face both lines of tracks, became literally the center of the town and as much a focus for the practical and imaginative life of its inhabitants as for those of Winesburg, the fictional community that Sherwood Anderson was to superimpose on the real Clyde. To accommodate such transients as traveling salesmen, two railroad hotels, the Nichols House and the Empire House Hotel, were built on either side of the station, the latter almost certainly becoming the original for the New Willard House of the Winesburg tales. Often the saloon and the dining room of the Empire House, which together took up most of the first floor of this two-story brick building, painted white, would be thronged with people waiting to change trains.[3]

From the windows on the upper floor of the Empire House one could look down, like Karl and Sherwood Anderson that rainy first morning in Clyde, into a broad Main Street, dusty in the summer, snow-packed in the winter. Main Street did indeed run straight as an arrow due north and south through the town, but Sherwood was more accurate than Karl about the attractiveness of Clyde. The angles at which the Maumee Pike and the railroad tracks crossed Main broke up the rigid grid system of so many midwestern towns; and the residence streets, which branched off somewhat unevenly from Main, were lined with neat frame houses and an occasional brick one set back from the street on green lawns, the "sidewalk of every avenue hidden from the burning sun," according to a contemporary description, "by the foliage of thrifty maples and elms." At the northeast corner of town, beyond where the Anderson family first lived, was the cemetery with its bronze statue commemorating the grave of Clyde's most famous native son, Major-General James B. McPherson, son of William the blacksmith, who at thirty-five had led the Army of Tennessee under Sherman in the Atlanta campaign until he was killed in front of the city shortly before it fell. Since nobody now knows why Irwin Anderson chose to settle in Clyde out of all the other communities in Ohio, one can only suspect that he may have been influenced by some newspaper account of the dedication ceremonies that had attracted fifteen thousand people to Clyde as recently as July 22, 1881, on which occasion General Rutherford B. Hayes was "president of the day" and Sherman himself unveiled the statue and eulogized his dead lieutenant.[4]

Diagonally across the town from the cemetery, on the southwest corner of Clyde was Raccoon Creek with its Waterworks Pond—another feature of Winesburg—and farther out its Mammy Culver swimming hole, where the village boys swam naked in the summer. On a hill sloping upward from the pond and creek was the fairgrounds with its half-mile oval racetrack and small wooden grandstand, where the Clyde Fair, one of the important annual events of the community, was held each September from 1870 until the last one in 1891. From this hill—where, in *Winesburg,* George Willard walks with Helen White one night after the town fair— one looked out on the fertile countryside that surrounded Clyde with apple and cherry orchards and great fields of cabbages and strawberries, the marketing of which gave work for the town's young people and in good years a modest prosperity for its tradesmen. One could look due north over the town, too, and see Main Street slope steadily downward between its houses and then storefronts toward the Pike. Down this slope in winter were held daily horse-and-sleigh races. It especially rejoiced the boys, and such older townspeople as were not concerned over the chance of accidents, when one-eyed George Crosby, a livery stable owner, warwhooped at his trotter Florida Monarch to bring her in fast on the home stretch by the railroad station.

Until their furniture arrived, the Andersons lived in a pleasant brick farmhouse on the edge of the village, where Karl "was paid twenty-five

cents a day to rake a half-acre lawn and orchard, and Sherwood was tag-
ging and trying to help, gathering leaves from one spot to drop them in another spot." The first of the Anderson houses to stay clearly in Sherwood's
mind was the one that Irwin next rented. Since torn down, this was the
"little brick house" at what is now 147 Duane Street in the northeast quarter of town between the station and the cemetery. Both Karl and Sherwood
would remember the huge-trunked maple tree right at the edge of the
wooden sidewalk in front. There was a cherry tree in the yard, and once
Sherwood ate so much of the fruit that he made himself sick. Though the
house was very small, the street was not a poor one. It had two churches,
and across from the Andersons, who lived on the north side of the street,
was the large yellow frame house of Charles Shuter, a German saloon
keeper, whose saloon was to be mentioned casually by name in several of
Anderson's fictions. Beside the Andersons lived Mrs. Mary Whaley, who
became fond of Emma Anderson and used to go over when she could to
help her because Emma was "so sickly and hardworking." Earl, the
youngest Anderson boy, was born in this house, on June 18, 1885, and
Mrs. Whaley helped out at the time. With six children now to manage,
Mrs. Anderson could use assistance, particularly since, in Mrs. Whaley's
opinion, Irwin was "an accommodating neighbor" but a poor provider.[5]

Mrs. Whaley was right. Some three blocks away from the Anderson
house over on the west side of Main street was the shop of J. M. Ervin,
"Manufacturer of Fine Buggy and Carriage Harness, Farm and Team Harness, Saddles, Bridles, Etc." In this one-story, gray-stone-fronted building
next to Terry's Opera House, Irwin, no longer the proprietor of his own
business, for awhile held a job as one of half a dozen hired harnessmakers. Just when or why he left this trade is not certain. According to Karl,
his father left off working indoors on the advice of a doctor because of the
running sore on his leg from a Civil War bullet wound. Sherwood himself
was to suggest in the *Memoirs* that his father might have been laid off during an economic depression—and Clyde in the mid- and late eighties was
indeed economically stagnant—or that he might have been fired for irresponsibility or for drinking. One can in addition suppose a good deal of
friction between "the boss" and a man of independent nature like Irwin
who had up until recently been his own master and who in addition disliked routine work. Sherwood was certainly correct in recalling that his father "soon lost his place." In the *Directory of Clyde and Vicinity, January
1, 1887*, Irwin is already listed as a "House and Sign Painter," an occupation he may have tried as far back as Camden days. For the rest of his active life, house and sign painting, and to a lesser extent paperhanging, was
to be his trade.[6]

Leaving a job where he was an employee for a trade where he was
again on his own probably was good for Irwin's ego, but it did not im-

prove his capacity for taking care of his wife and children. Sherwood was to recall a frightening "winter of hardship," almost certainly that of 1884–85, the family's first winter in Clyde, when his mother began to take in washing, as she was to do for years, in order to help support the family. Though they were still young, the older children helped as they could; but even when in 1887 Karl at age thirteen began a four-year apprenticeship in the same harness shop where his father had worked, he could have brought to the family only a little steady money in return for the long hours he put in "before and after school, winter and summer" as he discontentedly "served and washed smelly old harness." There is no doubt that at least during the 1880s the Andersons were, as Karl later said, "always poor, and sometimes incredibly so," though they may have had brief periods of relative affluence when Irwin was paid for a paint job.[7]

These early years of poverty in Clyde left psychological scars on both Karl and Sherwood. In later life they, like Theodore Dreiser, always dreaded the coming of winter because of its former associations with privation, and as a writer Sherwood was to show a special skill at catching sympathetically the quality of poor people's lives. More immediately important, the fact of the Andersons' poverty became entangled in the constellation of emotional relationships that gradually developed within the family, acquired extraordinary intensity, and had deep, lasting effects on both sons.

This constellation originated in the unlike temperaments of the parents. Sherwood's admiring portraits of his mother in *A Story Teller's Story, Tar,* and the *Memoirs* probably show some idealization by a loving son and a writer who always insisted on the supremacy of fancy over fact; yet unanimously those who knew Emma Anderson in Clyde have recalled her as being, despite her circumscribed position, a person out of the ordinary. The reports confirm what was known of her in Morning Sun, Camden, and Caledonia. Still striking in her dark beauty despite childbearing and hard work, she was intelligent and thoughtful, composed in manner but not withdrawn, quietly perceptive about people, loyal to her husband, and profoundly though undemonstratively devoted to her children, for whom she worked self-sacrificingly to see that they were fed and clothed. "She took in washing," one lady remembered her own upper-class mother saying of Mrs. Anderson, "but she kept her dignity." It was Emma Anderson who held the family together.[8]

That Irwin Anderson remained quite different from his wife is also well attested to by those who knew him in Clyde as in the preceding small towns where the family had lived. Still slim, trim, and alert-looking now in his forties, Irwin was known in Clyde as a potentially capable person who simply disliked to work when it did not interest him, but who "could always do something better than anyone else," as long as doing did not involve more than giving advice. It was an accepted fact in the town that he provided very inadequately, or rather very irregularly, for his family; and he seems to have treated his home rather as the bird does the bough, alighting, flying away, and briefly returning, a style of life encouraged by his paint jobs outside Clyde. Years after Irwin's death Judge Silas S. Richards, one of Clyde's leading citizens, described him to William Sutton:

> He did any kind of painting work and went out through the country soliciting work. He did good work when he worked but was fond of taking numerous vacations on impulse. He had the ability to do a good job and did do it. But he was as apt to quit in the middle of a job as at the end. He was not shiftless but a ne'er-do-well. He was not, and did not care to be, employed steadily. He destroyed the possibility of continuous employment by drinking.

Though hardly the town drunkard, Irwin did bring his habit with him to Clyde from Caledonia and improved on it to the extent of drinking, as various other Clyde people have said, "quite a bit" or "hard." In liquor or out he continued to be a great talker. A boaster, particularly about his own skills and his share in the defeat of the Confederacy, he also was known as a storyteller; and though he told tales when for his family's welfare he should have been working, the tales were good. He could, and would, stand on the street all afternoon telling stories that kept people amused and interested. The gift for oral narrative was part of his jovial, outgoing manner and of a very real personal charm that people still recalled him as possessing. It may have been part, too, of what one faintly glimpses through the memories of Clyde people as a kind of pathos. "He had set up an ideal for himself," a close friend of Sherwood said much later, "but he didn't know how to live up to that ideal." Possibly Irwin told stories, now, not only out of blind creative impulse as always but also out of his need to come to terms with that financial failure in Caledonia and with his current hard times in Clyde, perhaps even out of some sense of failure toward his family, some need for self-justification to them, yet a sense and a need not strongly or consistently enough felt to turn him into a more conventional citizen and father.[9]

No one now knows for sure how Emma Anderson really felt about her husband, how much his charm, his imagination, his disregard for the humdrum social role offset the worry and unceasing hard work his irresponsibility forced upon her. She was not one to complain to the neighbors. As Karl and Sherwood grew older, however, they began to blame their father for not shielding the family and especially their mother from the deprivations, anxieties, and humiliations of poverty. With an intensity that was Oedipal in strength whether or not it was in origin, they began to side with their mother and to detest their father, who could get rid of his troubles by dramatizing them, for turning their mother, who could not get rid of hers, into a drudge. (Years later in an interview Karl would suddenly declare apropos of nothing: "I suppose Sherwood hated our father as much as I did.") The older the boys became and the more they themselves had to work to provide where Irwin would not, the more they saw him in relation to the town as well as to the family. They were humiliated that their father could be referred to in public with raillery. "Major Anderson," commented the *Clyde Enterprise*, the local weekly newspaper, using Irwin's nickname as it never did with more highly regarded folk, "is displaying his artistic taste with the brush at Fremont this week upon Pickett's new green house." The sons were hurt and exasperated to see the discrepancy between their father's public boasting about his abilities and his failure to back up words with deeds, a failure that they felt reflected on the whole family. Largely from this antagonism toward their father for being the main cause, as they saw it, of the family's difficulties came the intense ambition of both boys to escape out of poverty and become financially successful, a characteristic that several Clyde people have recalled as marking all the Anderson children. It was the conflict between this intimately, powerfully motivated drive for a Horatio Alger success and other even stronger drives that would bring Sherwood into a major personal crisis in his mid-thirties and that would be obscurely involved in yet further crises after he had chosen the way of art over business.[10]

Actually there is documentary evidence that Karl and Sherwood's intense dislike for their father made them at that time subjectively distort the town's real attitude toward the man. As background for this evidence it is necessary to know that by the end of 1886, after having moved briefly from 147 Duane Street to another rented house on Vine Street in the northwest corner of town, the Andersons had settled for a year or so in their third residence, a small frame house at 214 Race Street in a slightly elevated area on the extreme west side of Clyde called then, as now, "Piety Hill." Like Duane Street, Piety Hill was not a "poor section" of town, but a mixed income one; in fact, several well-to-do families lived there. It was while the Andersons were in this house that Irwin, on March 15, 1887, suffered a painful accident that was serious enough to prevent his working for some time and that, as a result, may have had something to do with Karl's going into the harness shop in this year to help support the family. The story of the accident in the *Clyde Enterprise* contains several implications.

Major Anderson, of Race Street, is an old soldier. He can testify to the music there is in a bullet. He can tell you what pleasures and privations there are in camp life. His experience in being taken prisoner, and escaping in the darkness is interesting. He now has another chapter, where he was the prisoner, but failed to escape. Such was his experience last Tuesday evening, when he returned home and found his loving family prisoners in the hands of about forty of the Piety Hillyers. A strong guard stationed on the outside cut off his escape, and he willingly gave himself up to an evening of enjoyment with his friends. A pretty set of cane seated chairs was left, a gift from his friends. It was enjoyed by all, barring one accident which befell Mr. Anderson. He was crossing the street from Neighbor Tuttle's with a teakettle of hot water, when he stepped into an open ditch, spilling the hot water and scalding his right arm severely. This ditch was opened some time ago, to repair a string of tile, and has been left open some twenty rods or more, to the great danger of life and limb . . .[11]

Subsequently Sherwood Anderson was to use this incident as an important element in a highly autobiographical short story, "The Sad Horn Blowers," though, significantly, he twisted events in the tale to make the accident result from the father's rattle-brained excitability while organizing a surprise party for another Piety Hill neighbor. Of more immediate relevance are the indications of Irwin's true position in Clyde. The opening sentences confirm Irwin's gift for telling vivid, tallish tales of the war; yet though the tone at first is amused and Irwin is addressed by his nickname, the account reveals that, so soon after the family had moved to Piety Hill, this small section of town held some forty people who were sufficiently Irwin's friends to arrange a surprise party, possibly in honor of his and his wife's fourteenth wedding anniversary on March 11, and to make a substantial gift. One notes also the shift from "Major" to the formal "Mr.," the entire seriousness with which the accident, considered newsworthy, is described, and the rebuke for a public carelessness that had endangered all persons in the area. Taken with the testimonies of Clyde people, the account indicates that Irwin was not really regarded by the town as the incompetent, irresponsible buffoon he appears in some of Sherwood's fictions. Rather he was regarded as a "character," one who though not admired, because he drank and neglected his family, was definitely liked because, just as much as his wife though in a completely different way, he was a person out of the ordinary. Subsequent events were to impose this objective reality on Sherwood; and some of his fictions, it will be seen, were attempts, sometimes drastic ones, to control the true facts for more than aesthetic ends.

From both unusual parents Sherwood Anderson took influences that helped to make him the kind of writer he became. As the dedication of *Winesburg, Ohio* and the comments in *A Story Teller's Story* show, he was lovingly impressed both by his mother's "keen observations on the life about her" and by "the strength of her silences." As for his father, his dislike of the man shows as savagely in his last published book as in his first, despite a conscious effort in the *Memoirs*—the fictionlike "Discovery of a Father"—to persuade the reader otherwise. Yet quite as significant as his refection of his father was his inability to expunge that parent from memory. In *A Story Teller's Story*, published midway in his writing career, he was to try to come to terms with the remembered image of Irwin, who had died only a few years before, by portraying him as the unconscious artist, the artist *manqué* in a community that could not understand one for whom imagination took precedence over reality. Though the portrait is part of Anderson's strategy in this book to define his own place as conscious artist within American society, it does represent an attempt at an accommodation of the writer's subjective reality of hatred to the objective reality of his father's gift for storytelling and of Clyde's willingness to include the man under its invisible roof. Even in this relatively genial memoir, however, the relation between negative rejection and positive creation is intricate and ambivalent. Anderson's memories of his family in Clyde were to be a recurrent, insistent source for his later writing; the tensions built into these memories helped give the best of this writing its singular quality of surface calm and inner pressure.

All this working out of parent-child relation into ultimate effects was, of course, far in the future for Sherwood, whose physically limited childhood world of the Caledonia days now gradually expanded to include the larger world of school, friends, and the town itself. The Clyde school records indicate that Karl (aged ten) and Stella (aged nine) were both enrolled in "C Grammar," or the sixth grade, on September 1, 1884, and that Sherwood (just turned eight) was enrolled in "C Primary," or the second grade, on October 1. Possibly an illness such as that described in the fourth chapter of *Tar* accounted for the lapse of a month before the enrollment of Sherwood, who seems not to have begun school at all until he was about seven years old. In the fall of 1885, Sherwood entered the third grade, which he attended regularly. Apparently he demonstrated ability there since in the following fall he skipped the fourth grade and entered the fifth; but he attended school so little during the last of this year's three terms that in the fall of 1887 at the age of eleven he was once more enrolled in the fifth grade. Thereafter he continued in the regular course, despite considerable absence, through the eighth grade, from which he graduated in the late spring of 1891 at the age of fourteen. The indications of his scholastic ability are meager, but the few marks that have survived for his fifth grade work are all good, while those for the seventh, probably because of what Kintner calls "a staggering record of tardiness," are uneven. In that year he made good or average marks in arithmetic, geography, and reading, but in spelling he was below average, a rating which surprises no one who has looked at some of his letters written later in life.[12]

Perhaps Sherwood's scholastic record would have been more distinguished if he had not been absent so frequently either because of sickness or because of the various jobs he was beginning to hold to improve the

CLYDE, OHIO

family's finances. His marks do, however, support Karl's recollection that "Sherwood took no honors, but he was an effortless student," and he did finish grade school and go on briefly to high school. In 1891–92 he was a freshman during the seven months from September through March, and during January and February of 1893 he was a sophomore, though he missed fifteen days out of the two months. Kintner summarizes his high school scholastic record:

> In his freshman year we find him very good in algebra, average in physical geography, physiology, and grammar, and very weak in Latin and music. In his sophomore year he excelled in rhetoric ("He was a good arguer . . .") and made average grades in physics and geographical review. He received no grade in bookkeeping, algebra, and arithmetic. Yet the fact that he elected these subjects shows his interest in the business world.

Kintner also records a memory by Jennie Baker, a classmate whom Anderson liked, of a school incident, which indicates that he was not a docile student despite his fairly high record in "deportment."

> It must have been during his freshman year, for he was fifteen or thereabout when the incident occurred. A high school teacher went to the back of the classroom to reprimand a girl roughly. The classmate who relates the story [Jennie Baker] was seated too far forward to see exactly what happened, but Sherwood was not, and evidently he found the teacher brutal. For he jumped up angrily and exclaimed, "Don't you hit her again!"
> "He was mad!" explains the former classmate.[13]

Although Anderson had only nine months of high school, he received a good education by the standards of his time. The superintendent of schools during all his Clyde schooling was F. M. Ginn, a patriarchally bearded man, called "Professor" to his face and "Faker" to his back. A person of exceptional competence, though much given to paddling the pupils, he had begun his twenty-five years of service in 1870, the year that a new school building, a "large and well-arranged three-story brick structure," was opened on South Main Street on the hill beside the fairgrounds. Ginn had at once set up regular courses of study from the grades through the high school, the purpose being "to prepare pupils for any of the ordinary callings of business; in other words, to provide a good English education." Furthermore, Ginn was to take a special concern with furthering the education of Karl and Sherwood and presumably that of Stella, the most scholarly of the Anderson children. The notion that Sherwood's formal education was as inadequate as it was limited by present-day standards does not fit the facts.[14]

For Sherwood to acquire friends was in part a matter of the family's

32

settling more permanently in one section of town. Some time after March 1887, the Andersons moved to Spring Avenue (not to be confused with Spring Street), then a one-block street just west of and parallel to South Main Street, while in the fall of 1888 the children are listed in school records as living again on Vine Street, the west end of which lies in the Piety Hill area. By at least the end of April, 1889, the family was definitely back on Spring Avenue, living in the two-story frame house still standing at No. 129, which Anderson was to recall accurately in the *Memoirs* as "Our small yellow house at the foot of its street by the cattail swamp" and which in the Twainian manner he was to transport, building and grounds, to western Virginia for the setting of "Daughters," a story he wrote as late as 1935. For the first time the family had a little living space. Both Karl and Stella had small bedrooms of their own, and no longer did all meals have to be eaten at the kitchen table, for there was "a dining-room across the way from a commodious setting-room or parlor." The Andersons settled down in this house, which was to be their Clyde home at least until mid-1895 and perhaps later. Here a second daughter, Fern, the last of the children of Irwin and Emma, was born on January 21, 1890. It was here also in a spring that bubbled up into a sunken barrel in one corner of the front yard under a great beech tree that the five-year-old son of M. B. Wyatt, a drayman who lived on the other side of the street, was drowned on April 27, 1889. William Sutton has carefully compared the account of the incident in the *Clyde Enterprise* with Anderson's in the *Memoirs*, pointing out that Anderson depicts his mother, who actually discovered the child's body, as stoically competent whereas according to the newspaper she "was so frightened that she simply pulled [the drowned boy] out of the water, laid him on the grass, and fled to the house, instead of trying to resuscitate him." Quite rightly Sutton sees this as an instance of Anderson's tendency in later years to idealize his mother.[15]

Sherwood's life in the Spring Avenue house was pleasanter than this incident would suggest, however. Only a few houses away on Cherry Street where Spring Avenue ran into it lived Thaddeus Hurd, a heavily bearded, kindly man, who owned a grocery store on Main Street and had a family consisting of a wife, several daughters, and a son. The son, Herman, a small, lively boy with a quick sense of humor, had been born January 10, 1877, and was a year behind Sherwood in school. The two boys became close friends; in fact, Sherwood "practically lived" at the Hurd house from morning until night and was treated as one of the family. They would do Herman's chores together and then sit down to breakfast or dinner at the Hurd's well-filled table, where Sherwood, who loved to eat and was never sure of a full meal at his own home, ate enormously. Once he and Herman had an egg-eating contest, and Sherwood won, eight eggs to Herman's six. Occasionally Mr. Hurd would drive Sherwood out to his farm three miles south of Clyde and give him a basket of apples or potatoes to take home. Years later Herman would recall that his father, though a strict as well as hospitable man, never objected in any way to the friendship; and the fact of this long, close comradeship between the son of a "ne'er-do-well" and the son of one of Clyde's most respected citizens may have had something to do with Anderson's subsequent belief in the "invisible roof" that spread over the inhabitants of each midwest town as though they were "members of a great family" in that magical moment in American history when "mankind seemed about to take time to try to understand itself."[16]

Sometimes just for companionship Herman went along with Sherwood while the latter delivered the *Cleveland Plain-Dealer* and the *Toledo Blade* on the evening paper route that he developed when about twelve years old. Herman rarely was given pocket money, but because of his job Sherwood, the poorer boy, often had some change. While waiting for the trains to come in from the east and west with the day's papers, the boys would go to the bakery and restaurant across from the station run by Mrs. Baker, whose daughter Mary Janette, or "Jennie," later became Herman's wife. Here Sherwood would order one dish of ice cream and two spoons so that both boys could eat it. Then they would pick up the papers at the station and deliver them, helping themselves to the free lunch at the several saloons along the route. "Body" Adare's place, they agreed in their growing sophistication, had the best free lunch of all. As they walked, Sherwood would read the lead article on the front page and refer to it in the sales talk he had planned to get rid of the few papers left over after the delivery. His only competitor as town newsboy was Clifton Paden, son of a Clyde mayor and a boy about Karl's age, but Sherwood's willingness to invade the saloons with the Saturday editions and his gleeful ability to talk farmers who had come to town into buying them apparently put him ahead of Clifton. Although probably much metamorphosed in detail, the opening chapter of *Windy McPherson's Son* may record that early business rivalry.[17]

As Sherwood grew older, selling papers was not the only work he tried. He took many other jobs, so many that he was nicknamed "Jobby." Memories of his tasks frequently occur in his writings. Certainly at some time Sherwood briefly and Karl and Young Irwin for a longer period helped their father in his trade as house painter, and Anderson's description in the opening pages of *A Story Teller's Story* of the three sons helping their father letter a sign on a fence has at least a core of actuality beneath the casual denigration of his own and his father's ability. In sequence Karl, Sherwood, and young Irwin also worked for Dr. Cyrus L. Harnden, a big, active, compulsively neat man in his forties, who lived on George Street very close to the Hurd house. As it had been Karl's, so it became part of

Sherwood's job to pick up in a basket every leaf on the doctor's lawn and to sweep the walk against the doctor's exacting inspection; in fact, Anderson seems to be reporting his duties and accompanying pleasure accurately in the opening paragraphs of "Unused: A Tale of Life in Ohio."

He, the doctor, was an extraordinarily large and immaculately clean man, by whom I was at that time employed. I swept out his office, mowed the lawn before his residence, took care of the two horses in his stable and did odd jobs about the yard and kitchen—such as bringing in firewood, putting water in a tub in the sun behind a grape arbor for the doctor's bath and even sometimes, during his bath, scrubbing for him those parts of his broad back he himself could not reach. The Doctor had a passion in life with which he early infected me. He loved fishing and as he knew all of the good places in the river, several miles west of town, and in Sandusky Bay, some nineteen or twenty miles to the north, we often went off for long delightful days together.

Presumably also Anderson told the truth when he wrote later that as a boy he had driven cows to and from pasture at "twenty-five cents per week per cow," and had worked at times in the fields around Clyde, cutting corn, picking strawberries, and planting cabbages, in the last two learning the backbreaking labor on "stoop-crops" that he was to describe so well in *Poor White*. Karl was to recall that when the cabbage was harvested, "Sherwood and Irwin would don rubber boots and stamp for hours the cabbage in huge vats to start the process of making sauerkraut," a local product manufactured, canned, and so widely distributed that among the surrounding towns it won for Clyde the nickname of "Sauerkrautville," a term which may explain why Hugh McVey in *Poor White* settles in the "Pickleville" area near the Clyde-like town of Bidwell. For awhile Sherwood was delivery boy for Thaddeus Hurd's grocery and drove the Hurd's old black mare Topsy all over town. At "the age of sixteen or thereabouts" he worked for a while as clerk in George Richards's dry-goods store, a position in which he was "so clever in getting rid of job lots of goods left from the regular selling that they were always turned over to him, his fellow employees dubbing him 'Job Lots.'"[18]

The number and variety of jobs are indicative of the strength of Sherwood's continued reaction in his adolescence against his father's casualness about work. His later claim in the *Memoirs* to have held several jobs at once and to have subcontracted others to other boys is probably a satirical exaggeration of his early drive toward financial success; actually he held one job at a time but changed jobs frequently, to some extent for variety, but primarily in order to find work that paid more money. It was both a pleasure and a necessity to bring money back to a home that was never to be really comfortable economically, and to have some for his own increasing wants. Already he seems to have recognized the love of clothes, the "natural liking" for fine fabrics, that he was to indulge in himself in later years. As a small, poorly clad boy he had stood by Waterworks Pond one winter day and held the overcoat of "Hal" Ginn, son of the school superintendent, while Hal, who was back from college to visit his parents, skated. Sherwood was always to remember caressing the fabric of the expensive coat and associating money and elegance with its rich texture. Now in his teens Sherwood could afford to have only one suit at a time, bought by one-dollar installments over so long a period that sometimes the suit wore out and he had to start buying another on time before the first was fully paid for.[19]

In addition to these several motivations that drove him from job to job in search for better pay, Sherwood was discovering, as in his newsboy and clerk jobs, that he had a flair for words that could persuade other people to part with their money. Already he was unconsciously moving toward his years as an advertising writer; yet, paradoxically, even deeper currents in these and subsequent jobs he held in Clyde were drawing him toward the use of words more creatively and toward his special talent as a storyteller. Delivering groceries for Thaddeus Hurd, for example, gave him a wide acquaintance with the people and geography of his community; and his job as a newsboy, by taking him along alley, shortcut, and crosslot, made him aware of "a lot of things going on," as he was to write in *Tar*, behind the main streets and the fronts of houses, brought him literally "beneath the surface of lives," thus reinforcing his mother's gift for penetrating comment. "How much of the native novelist's competency is derived from conscious 'observation'?" Mark Twain asked in a *North American Review* article excerpted in the *Clyde Enterprise* in 1895, and he continued: "The amount is so slight that it counts for next to nothing in the equipment. Almost the whole capital of the novelist is the slow accumulation of unconscious observation—absorption."[20]

The passive as well as the active was indeed a pole of "Jobby" Anderson's unsimple temperament when he was a boy growing up in Clyde. Looking back in the *Memoirs,* he recalled that he had been "half the young hustler and half the dreamer who wanted to sit forever looking at people, listening, wondering about people." When he asked a grown man who had been a boyhood companion what the man's recollection of him had been, the man

remembered me only as a lazy fellow, sitting on the curb on the main street or before the little frame hotel at evening, listening to the tales told by traveling men. Or I sat with my back against a barn wall listening to men talking within a barn or to women gossiping in the kitchen of a nearby house.

And the companion recalled:

"I would come out of the house. I wanted you to go play ball with me or to go with me to bring home the cows.

"I remember your sitting there, your eyes glassy, and that I walked over and stood before you. I shouted but you did not hear. I had to lean over and hit you before I could get you attention.

"With a book in your hand you were ten times worse."

"But," I protested, "I was called Jobby."

"You were both a hustler and bone lazy," he said. "I do, now that you speak of it, remember periods of intense activity, when you worked feverishly at any job you could get."

Although this particular conversation may have been a self-portrait invented by Anderson, Herman Hurd, who in fact may have been this "boyhood companion," could confirm the portrait's essential truth long after the artist's death. Usually a steadily good-humored person, Sherwood was occasionally moody; much more often he was simply "dreamy." Not infrequently, while Herman and Sherwood would be walking with a group of boys who were talking among themselves, Herman would become aware that his friend was "dreaming to himself as he walked along with them." Despite the nickname "Jobby," which suggests energetic efficiency, Sherwood "was always a little late to everything. We always had to wait for him." Once the two friends had gone with a group of youths to Linwood Park, a resort on Lake Erie, where they all rented a boat and stayed on the water so long that they had to hurry ashore to catch the homeward train. The other boys leaped from the beached boat and began sprinting, leaving behind Herman and Sherwood, who was, typically, the last out of the boat. Suddenly startled out of some daydream, Sherwood excitedly held up his shoes and called to the running boys, "Hey, isn't anyone going to help with all this stuff?"—the "stuff" being only the shoes.[21]

For Anderson, the boy and young man, as well as for the middle-aged writer, there plainly existed with equal intensity both the world of reality and the world of imagination. His above-average mark in the seventh grade for reading supports his own recollections and those of Karl and of boyhood friends that he was reading widely, constantly, and with an absolute concentration "that was a source of amusement to his friends; they had to shake him to get his attention when he was reading." Not until 1903, by which time Sherwood had left Clyde, did Andrew Carnegie help provide a public library for the town, and the Andersons were too poor to own many books of their own. Subsequently Karl, who like Stella was also a reader, could recall in the Anderson house only *The Pilgrim's Progress* and Tennyson's *Complete Poems;* but Sherwood, according to Herman

Hurd read "all" the books in the small school library and borrowed books from various people, particularly from Superintendent Ginn, who enriched both of the Anderson boys' educations by granting them free access to his extensive personal library.[22]

Giving himself "utterly to the printed page," Sherwood read as indiscriminately as he did widely—from dime novels, sentimental fiction, and such adventure tales as *Robinson Crusoe* and *The Swiss Family Robinson* to many of the classic eighteenth- and nineteenth-century novels and romances. The names listed in *A Story Teller's Story* seem reasonably representative: "Laura Jean Libbey, Walter Scott, Harriet Beecher Stowe, Henry Fielding, Shakespeare, Jules Verne, Balzac, the Bible, Stephen Crane . . . Cooper, Stevenson, our own Mark Twain and Howells and later Whitman." Though he read the poetry of Longfellow and Whittier—he later found the New England writers too "frigid" for his mature taste—he was chiefly devoted to fiction but also liked history, biography, and autobiography. Whether or not his father really did sell the books in the slack time of another "hard winter," Sherwood fairly early read two reminiscences of the Civil War, Grant's *Memoirs* and *Corporal Si Klegg and His "Pard,"* both of which fed his permanent fascination with the great national conflict as well as with the lives of others. Considering his subsequent vision of himself as social prophet in his first published volumes, one can also believe Anderson's statement in the *Memoirs* that "the town photographer . . . loaned me Bellamy's *Looking Backward* which sent me off into youthful dreams of a new and beautiful social system in which I might some day live." The apocalyptic strain in Sherwood Anderson's mind and art was to run deeply and variously.[23]

Books, any books, fed his dreams or gave him a "background" on which to "construct new dreams," as he asserts in *A Story Teller's Story,* and often the life of books fed into his real life as boy and adolescent. The opening pages of that fanciful autobiography finely describe Sherwood and his younger brother Irwin enacting La Longue Carabine and Uncas out of *The Last of the Mohicans,* while an early reading of adventure yarns and of *Huckleberry Finn* appear to be connected with the digging by Sherwood, Herman Hurd, and other boys of a "pirate's cave" in what was then a high gravel bank behind the Spring Avenue house and the organizing of a pirate crew. "It was Sherwood's idea that each boy must sign his name with his own blood, on a large rock, before he could become a real pirate." In retrospect, however, Herman Hurd could recall only one indication that his friend might later become a writer. This was his ability to tell stories. In the summer the two boys would lie out on the strip of grass between sidewalk and street, and Sherwood would "tell stories by the hour," usually "hair-raising" ones, often adventure tales or stories from what he had read. Only infrequently were his stories about people in the town, however, and he never intimated any interest in becoming a writer himself.[24]

Sherwood's intermittent tendency toward dreaminess, his frequent, absolute absorption in reading, his love of storytelling were signs, if unrecognized ones, of an ultimate commitment to the life of the imagination. No more than his concentration on jobs, money, clothes, however, were they indications that he then viewed himself or that he should now be viewed as the sensitive, half-self-conscious artist, hurt by his environment, alienated from it spiritually, and forced into fighting it with silence, exile, and cunning. Clyde permeated Anderson's psyche almost as much as Dublin did Joyce's, but unlike that greater writer Anderson did not have to reject his community totally in order totally to re-create it. In his middle teens he was to grow even closer to Clyde than he had been in his boyhood.

By about 1891, when Sherwood was in his fourteenth year, things were becoming slightly easier economically for the Anderson family. As she was to do for the remaining few years of her life, Emma Anderson still took in washing, while Irwin would occasionally come home from a painting job and with the air of the lordly provider drop a load of food on the kitchen table. The older boys were now earning money with some regularity, and Stella, age sixteen in the spring of 1891, was completing her final year of high school and was soon to start earning a schoolteacher's pay. In other ways, too, the family was assuring itself a place, however qualified, in the town.

As in any American community, the educational system was part of the complex of social patterns into which the Anderson children could fit. It had, of course, proved too hard for Karl to continue formal education while apprenticed as a harnessmaker, and he had dropped out of high school after less than a year. Sherwood likewise abandoned high school at the end of February, 1893, after a total of only nine months attendance, presumably because of the need to help support the family. Even so Superintendent Ginn thought highly enough of both Anderson boys to invite them to his home one evening and advise them to continue their education beyond high school; in fact, Ginn especially encouraged Sherwood to go on to college and offered to assist him in getting a scholarship. Because Sherwood did not feel that he should be so obligated to the man and because he was too young then to want further education, he did not accept the offer. That it was made, however, indicates Sherwood's intellectual promise; and in a day when boys did not regularly finish high school, both Karl and Sherwood probably had an average amount of schooling.[25]

Stella, on the other hand, was a girl and in addition an exceptionally fine student. With only twenty-seven days of absence out of the whole four years of high school, "she was extremely good in Latin, music, geology, and English literature," and finished high school with an average of 92.1. On May 29, 1891, Stella took part in her Senior Class Day, and a few days later the Reverend George B. Wilson of the Presbyterian Church preached on 1 Corinthians 12:31 to her graduating class. (In the fall of this year a new Presbyterian church with "cathedral glass windows" would be built on Forest Street close beside a private home, thus preparing the setting for Anderson's *Winesburg* tale, "The Strength of God.") Then on the hot evening of June 11, Sherwood and the rest of the family presumably crowded into Terry's Opera House to view the commencement exercises for Stella's class, which consisted of nine girls. Members of the class, whose motto was "Ever Onward," gave orations, the last being that of Stella, the class valedictorian, a dark-haired, dark-eyed Anderson beauty of sixteen, the youngest girl in the graduating group. After Stella's address, titled "Creation's Crowning Jewel," all the young graduates received "floral trophies." Clearly at least one of the Andersons had "arrived" by Clyde standards.[26]

Before Mrs. Anderson's death four years later, when it was necessary for the daughter to take over the running of the family, Stella had a brief teaching career. During the fall term of 1892–93, she was assigned to the nearby village of York Station, but beginning on January 9, 1893, she finished the second and third terms of the school year teaching the fifth grade in Clyde itself. She taught the same grade again for the whole of 1893–94, but her failure to apply for 1894–95, which was specifically noted by the *Enterprise,* suggests that Emma Anderson was failing in health and that Stella's help in the Anderson household was more necessary than the salary she received from teaching. That Stella was worthy of what the townspeople would have considered an honor even for a class valedictorian, to be hired by Superintendent Ginn to teach in her own school, is borne out by the recollections of Herman Hurd's younger sister, Blanche, who had Stella as teacher in the fifth grade and who remembered her particularly because she was not at all sharp-tongued but "quiet and nice" as well as capable and pretty. Following a classic American pattern, Stella had briefly risen from blue-collar to white-collar class, and her rise subtly altered the way the town as a whole would regard the Andersons.[27]

In yet another way both Stella and her mother had for some time been influencing the town's regard for the family. This was their connection with the Presbyterian Church. As early as 1886 the *Clyde Enterprise* noted that Stella had recited at Children's Day and Christmas exercises in the Presbyterian Sunday school, and a month after her high school graduation she was one of a group of Clyde boys and girls who attended a state convention in Toledo of some one thousand delegates of the Presbyterian Young People's Christian Endeavor Society. Then on the Sunday of March 6, 1892, both she and Mrs. Anderson joined the Presbyterian Church.

Quite understandably, Stella seems to have been the more active in church affairs. On a Sunday evening at the church in November of 1894, she presented a "highly commended" original article titled "Search the Scriptures," and in the following January she was selected to help with the "Good Citizenship" night program during "Presbyterian Week."[28]

The only other members of the family to join the church were the two youngest children, Ray on February 11, 1893, and Earl on April 12, 1896; there is no record of church membership for the older male Andersons—Mr. Anderson, Karl, Sherwood, or young Irwin. George Richards, who employed Sherwood as dry-goods clerk and was at one time superintendent of the Presbyterian Sunday school, later recalled that despite the family's "meager earnings" Mrs. Anderson, "the real backbone of the family," managed to keep "her six children neatly dressed and always at church and Sunday school." Under the firm pressure of his mother Sherwood probably attended church and Sunday school at least in his boyhood, but Herman Hurd, who regularly went to the Methodist Sunday school, could not in later years recall that his friend ever showed any interest in religion; and indeed Sherwood was to show little interest in formal religion throughout the rest of his life, though he often read in the King James Version for its tales and its prose rhythms. Religion was meaningful to his mother and sister, however. In her later years after leaving Clyde, Stella became increasingly devout and occasionally wrote religious verse. Her mother was less demonstrative about her Presbyterianism, but she held to it strongly. Judge Silas Richards, who regularly attended the same church, was later to assert that she "was an active member of the church and performed her duties in it. Mrs. Anderson was a devout Christian if there ever was one." Religion very probably helped to console her for a life that, whatever her husband's personal charm, contained all too much economic privation, hard work, and family cares. A more specific grief may have had something to do with her joining the church when she did. This was the death three months earlier of Fern, the last born of the Anderson children. The *Clyde Enterprise* records the painful event.

A two-year-old daughter of Mr. and Mrs. I. M. Anderson died yesterday [December 9, 1891] of congestion of the brain. The little one had been ill for a week, but the parents thought nothing serious was the matter and failed to call a physician until two hours before the child died, when too late to save its life. The funeral will be held at the house on Friday at two o'clock. Burial at Clyde.

These flat factual details suggest that Emma Anderson's decision at last to unite formally with the church she had long been attending may have resulted not only from the grief of loss but also from sense of guilt at a tragic parental misjudgment.[29]

The effect of Fern's death on fifteen-year-old Sherwood is even more conjectural, for with one exception the very few references he was to make to this younger sister in his writings, including his surviving correspondence, are brief and vague. The exception is, of course, the three-page account in the semiautobiographical *Tar: A Midwest Childhood,* written years later in the mid-twenties, an account in most ways vague too because it is literally remote from reality. Yet if the few facts obtainable about this younger sister's death are juxtaposed to the recasting of them in *Tar,* an unexpected, though tentative, insight may be obtained into the question of why Anderson became a writer and of what writing meant for him.

Having stated that if your "lovely" mother "dies when you are young, what you do all your life afterwards is to use her as material for dreams," Anderson describes young Tar Moorehead's brief, self-absorbed relation to his infant sister in order to prepare for the assertion, dubious as autobiography, that a daydream of Fern as she might have become in young womanhood keeps recurring to Tar the middle-aged man. Immediately striking in the account is the fact that Fern's actual name is used, for the first names of all the other "Moorehead" (Anderson) family members have been changed. Momentarily it would seem to be the real little sister whom he is directly recalling and writing about, and indeed the assertion that "Little Fern Moorehead died when she was three weeks old" is consonant with such a later reference as the one in the *Memoirs* that she "had lived but a few weeks"; yet the records prove that Fern was nearly two years old when she died. Tar is said never to have seen the baby during the three weeks of her life because he is sick in bed; yet the real fact is that, as his school records show, Sherwood attended school fourteen and a half days in December 1891 and was absent five and a half days, though to be sure he may have been absent and ill at the time of Fern's death on a Wednesday and her funeral two days later. Because of Tar's illness his older sister "Margaret" (that is, Stella) has to stay home with him and hence both miss the funeral, by implication held elsewhere; yet according to the *Enterprise* the funeral was actually to be held in the home, hence Stella would have been present, as Sherwood himself may have been. In short, on several points the account in *Tar* is at such sharp variance with what truly happened that it must be taken as deliberate fictionalization rather than as mere misremembering.[30]

Now, clearly the creative imaginative works by transforming and synthesizing the artist's experience, and Anderson had fairly enough warned the reader in his foreword to *Tar* that he was not telling the truth. One must look, then, not for authentic details—though Fern was the last Anderson child and did die very young—but for possible authentic patterns or motifs. Two elements in the *Tar* account are at least suggestive. The first is the statement that by missing the funeral Tar missed "the kind of time when Dick [the father of the Moorehead family] would be at his worst and Dick at his worst would be pretty bad." By its very gratuitousness the comment underlines the real Anderson's real and continuing hostility to his father, whose behavior may or may not have been appropriate to the actual funeral of his child but is here flatly supposed to have been bad. The second element is an equally gratuitous assertion about another kind of death for a child: "If a child in the family dies and you knew the child alive you always think of him as he was when he died. A child dies in spasms. It is terrible to think about." Then the author adds the elliptical one-sentence paragraph: "But if you have never seen the child." Anderson had known Fern alive for nearly two years, and since she died abruptly of "congestion of the brain," it is possible that she did die "in spasms," which is indeed terrible to think about and may well require some psychological defense to deal with, such as imposing a fictional memory on the real one.

If the relation of reality and rendered reality in this episode in *Tar* provides something more than speculation but something less than certainty, it does show Anderson reversing, negating, withdrawing from distressing actualities. It may tentatively be asserted at this point, then, that for him an important function of writing would be to control reality, especially unpleasant reality, not just in the usual sense of giving it aesthetic shape, but actually of dominating experience and the memory of experience, making them tolerable, through words. Hence words themselves and the patterning of them might well come to assume for him, as in fact they did, the mysterious, potent aura of magic, by which what *is* is metamorphosed into what one desires. Art for Sherwood Anderson, it may be suggested, would often become a psychically essential device for coping with reality. Conversely such psychological maneuvering could and often did produce a remarkable kind of art.

At this point it is necessary, as Anderson the storyteller would say, to speak a bit of Karl Anderson, for what may appear at first to be a digression will turn out, as in Sherwood's tales, to have significance for the main narrative. Karl had begun sketching as a young boy, and in slack time during his four years of apprenticeship as harnessmaker from 1887 to 1891 he even made drawings on the walls of J. M. Ervin's shop. Unlike his younger brother he very sharply felt the constrictions of Clyde as "a community without much beauty," but the notion of becoming an artist did not occur to him until one summer afternoon in the late 1880s when he earned a little money by holding Hal Ginn's white pointer dog in position while "a young local artist, a farm boy named [John B.] Tichenor who had returned from a six months art education in Toledo, painted the dog's portrait" and while "the young Ginn, like a D'Medici [*sic*], sat behind the artist and directed how the portrait should be done." By the end of the afternoon Karl had decided to become a painter. Tichenor, who worked and lived in Terry's Opera House next to the harness shop, "solicited orders for crayon portraits, and sometimes did landscapes in oil," which Karl later recalled as technically untutored but "of great imagination and poetic charm." In return for Karl's cleaning of his studio on Sundays, Tichenor taught Karl "how to be a crayon portraitist." One of Karl's first portraits was of Superintendent Ginn and was hung in the entrance foyer of the Vine Street elementary school building in Clyde, formerly the town high school.[31]

For Karl, art was the key to a prison cell. He detested harnessmaking, he hated the father whose irresponsibility had forced him into the trade, he feared poverty, loathed it for its physical ugliness, and desired both artistic and financial success, a combination of strong early motivations that kept him at oil portraits later in life as a means of maintaining a standard of living even when he would have preferred to pour all of his fine sense of color into other kinds of painting. On October 19, 1891, he broke for freedom by responding to an "Artist Wanted" ad in a Cleveland newspaper. The *Clyde Enterprise* considered Karl's departure important enough to note that he had gone to Cleveland, "having secured a position in an art store in that city." He reached Cleveland only to find that someone else had already been hired, and instead he found a job retouching photographs. In the evenings he attended classes at the Art School with Hal Ginn, who was studying law during the day, and thus began a long friendship with a young man who was to achieve wealth. After a year in Cleveland he went to Chicago so eager to continue his study of art that he attended life classes at the Art Institute evenings, weekends, and even parts of some days while supporting himself, and sending money home, by full-time work in an engraving house. Here he remained until September of 1897, when he went to New York to try to make his way as an illustrator.[32]

Whatever the hardships and frustrations Karl may have endured in these early years away from home, his brief reappearances in Clyde were always news in the *Clyde Enterprise,* and the entries, though few, support the assertion of Clyde friends that the Anderson children and their mother had a strong family feeling. He returned from Cleveland to attend Fern's funeral and again, in April, 1892—one month after Mrs. Anderson and Stella had joined the Presbyterian Church—"to spend Easter with his parents." In August, 1894, the *Enterprise* announced that "Carl Anderson, who has been in Chicago attending the art school, is home for a few weeks vacation." Even more significant for its suggestion of the changing status of the Anderson family in Clyde is the accompanying item: "Miss Stella Anderson pleasantly entertained about thirty of her friends on Tuesday evening [August 7] in honor of her brother Carl. . . ."[33]

Karl's departure from Clyde and his intense commitment to art was an important influence in the life of his brother Sherwood. The most important long-range effect was to help persuade him to a similar commitment. When Sherwood left Clyde just a few years later, he had no fixed ambition except to be successful in something, anything; nevertheless, he and the rest of the family watched Karl's career proudly, and he was not simply joking when, long after he had become a writer, he told Karl, "Your going off to study art, . . . that set a bad example for me." More immediate was the effect of Karl's career on the position of the Andersons remaining in Clyde. Not only was Stella a capable teacher, and a beautiful woman in addition, but the oldest son had demonstrated that he was an artist while still in town and that he was now on his way to success in Chicago. Artists might be only artists, to be sure, as teachers only teachers; still success was also success, especially when it occurred to people far down on the social scale and thus reaffirmed America as the land of opportunity. "All our old town soon began to be proud of him," Sherwood later wrote of Karl, at a time when he felt the town would be proud of his own career as well.[34]

As Sherwood grew into his middle teens in the early 1890s, the forces that were to shatter the invisible roof that bent over him and Clyde were only beginning to gather strength; and in these first years of the decade his resentment against his father and his memories of early poverty were outweighed by the somewhat improved financial situation of the family, the local fame of Karl and Stella, his own jobs, and his friendships. All these drew him closely into the life of the town, that life which was to become his deepest imaginative source as a writer. With varying degrees of intimacy he now "knew everyone in town" from the well-to-do to the bums, and everyone, including the well-to-do and the bums, liked him. Although, as Herman Hurd was to recall, Sherwood was awkward and unskilled at games and could hardly catch a ball, he did not suffer exclusion as did, say, the young Sinclair Lewis. When in early May of 1894 a group of boys, including Herman, organized a baseball team known as the Clyde Stars, they insisted that Sherwood be in on things and made him the manager. Among the Hurd family papers there is a snapshot of the Stars taken in June or July when Sherwood was seventeen. Thin and dark-eyed, he stares out as solemnly as the other youths from his sitting position in the front row, wearing a dark suit, vest, and bowler hat, not in uniform but very much one of the group.[35]

The Stars began a fairly successful season, but for some now unremembered reason the team broke up in midsummer. In May of the following year, 1895, a new team was formed, called Taylor's Greys in honor of "Z. [Zachary] Taylor, the dry-goods king, who has donated handsome suits for the club at a cost of nearly $75." The Greys were an excellent team of older youths, and only two of the Stars were taken on, one of them being Herman Hurd at shortstop. Harry Surbeck became manager, and a backstop and grandstand were erected in Ames's Field on the east edge of town to show the community's loyal backing. The one extended reference to Sherwood Anderson in the entire extant files of the *Clyde Enterprise* up to 1898 links him with the Greys. The episode described is like a tiny window opening onto Anderson's life in those days—and onto town ballgames in any day. Under the page three head, "Clyde 9, Oakharbor O," the *Enterprise* for June 18, 1895, reported:

The Clyde Baseball Club went to Oakharbor last Sunday to play with the club at that place, and they now wish they had stayed at home and attended Sunday school. Not that they didn't have good luck playing, but the Oakharbor Swamp Angels threw up the game at the end of the eighth inning and skipped out with the gate receipts. At that time the score stood Clyde 10, Oakharbor 4, but umpire Sherwood Anderson refused to credit the Angels with a run unless they finished the game. This they refused to do, and he gave the game to Clyde by a score of 9 to 0. The Clyde boys were about $27 out of pocket on the trip, and expected to make some money from their share of the gate receipts, as a large crowd was present.[36]

Anderson as trusted baseball umpire may not at first seem to fit with Anderson as author of *Winesburg, Ohio;* yet the two were one and, whether in reality or in imagination, that one was firmly imbedded in the matrix of his community. In the opening pages of the *Memoirs,* Anderson describes a beery evening celebration held by a victorious town baseball team at the edge of the hickory woods that bordered Ames's Field, and emphasized his pleasure at being included with this group of young men who drank beer, possessed willing girls on the grassy slopes of the cemetery, and even, much to the annoyance of the town's churchly element, played baseball on Sunday. Anderson's fancy has played over the recollection, changing the names, but not the characteristics, of the team members and fabricating a place for himself on the team as right fielder; yet what objective facts there are confirm the psychological essence of the scene, the "happiness, the warm feeling I now have for these others out here with me at the edge of the wood." For Anderson, the profoundest meaning of Clyde, as of *Winesburg,* is, to repeat, not alienation but communion.

As for his own sexual adventures with willing girls, he describes in the 1969 *Memoirs* three incidents, to be commented on in more detail in chapter 32 of this biography, covering the time he wrote of them. In all three the girl was not only willing but actually initiated the adventure. The first seems to have been primarily a mutual examination of bodies; the second was an opportunity for sexual intercourse, which had, as he would write, a "ridiculous ending"; the third, when he might have been fourteen, was allegedly an affair of some duration ending in his panic lest the girl might become pregnant. There is ample evidence, however, that in the more conventionally acceptable boy-girl relationships he was fortunate and happy. Being, according to Herman Hurd, handsome, witty, clever and a good talker, he was popular with girls. As they grew older, the two young men used to go riding in a surrey with their dates, Herman with Jennie Baker, his future wife, and Sherwood "each time with a different girl." He may have had a passing interest in Jennie, and once when he had some extra money, he bought a bicycle and let her use it until a much upset Herman made him take it back. In later years Herman Hurd was to assert that his friend never had had a great affair of the heart while in Clyde and that the Helen White of *Winesburg* was only a "dream-girl"; still Herman may have forgotten a beautiful young Clyde girl named Bertha Baynes, who, if anyone, is likely to have been the prototype of George Willard's attractive companion in "Sophistication."

About the year 1895 Anderson began going fairly steadily with Bertha, who is certainly the "young girl" described in the *Memoirs* at the beginning of the section titled "The Capture of Caratura." As is typical of Anderson's method in this final review of his life, the *Memoirs* account is grounded in actuality. Bertha Baynes was indeed in her middle teens at the time, she was, much more than Helen White to George Willard, "far above him in the social scale," and though Clarence Whittaker, the man she married instead of Sherwood when she was seventeen, was not exactly "a clerk in a jewelry store," he was a watchmaker with a "bench" in a jewelry store, which would seem to be coming fairly close to fact, not just for Sherwood Anderson but for many men in their sixties recalling a sweetheart of forty years earlier. As for the "revenge" Anderson purports to have taken out on her, here his fancy may have embroidered on the facts, as indeed is the other part of the basic technique in the *Memoirs,* where fact and invention are commingled. In actuality Sherwood and Clarence were close friends, Anderson visited the couple fairly often after their marriage, and the Whittaker son customarily referred to his father's friend as "Uncle Jobby." At least for a time, however, Bertha was much charmed by Sherwood's company, and it is significant that he was accepted by the "crowd" of young people with whom she was associated and that he shared in their good times. Helen Baynes, Bertha's older sister by five years, was considerably less charmed by her sister's beau. Although he was at the Baynes house "a good deal," Helen never paid much attention to him or was much impressed by him, "for he always looked . . . as though he needed a bath, and his hair always looked as though it needed combing." Even Bertha realized that, as she subsequently confided to a niece, her admirer was far from neat in appearance and habits. He "would come to see her on Sunday morning," the niece later reported, "and if she was eating breakfast he'd just come right in, make himself at home in the living room reading the Sunday paper. Which invariably he would have scattered all over the place." But that Anderson had other more attractive qualities is shown in a description written by Bertha herself many years later, a description of the person and the times so clear and accurate that it must be quoted at length.

> I first knew Sherwood Anderson when we moved to Clyde. . . . Stella (the sister) taught school and kept house for her father and brothers—The father was a house painter—liked his liquor and was often under the influence—of it—Sherwood was about 20 years old—5 ft 7 or 8 inches tall slender—dark hair and eyes . . . would have been good looking had his face not have had so many pimples on it—
>
> He had a wonderful personality, a great gift of *Gab*—and would talk about the great things he was going to do—*some day*—Sher—was well liked in town and could always find some kind of work to do—he never worked any one place for long, was not interested in doing menial work—for this reason he was thot lazy—would never amount to much—In order to help out at home—he preferred having many odd jobs—like mowing lawns—working in a livery stable (he loved horses) part time work in stores and in a factory—having had so many different jobs—he was called *Jobby Anderson* which did not seem to bother him in the least—for he was a dreamer, liked to talk and dream of what he would do *some day*—Sher and I were in the same group of young people—In those days there were no movies—radio's nor T.V. in our town—so we made our own good times by going to different homes—some one would play a piano—we would dance, sing—pop corn—etc—It became a habit for him to *walk* home with me. We had dancing school every Friday nite where we all went—Sher loved to dance and so did I—we danced most every dance together—and afterwards would *walk* me home—This of course was during the winter month—we also had sleigh rides, parties—during the summer we would go on picknicks—[37]

This sympathetic but unsentimental portrait of the artist as a young man, pimples and all, agrees with the clear and detailed recollections of his friend Herman Hurd. These happy memories by the two persons in Clyde probably closest to Anderson outside his own family prove yet again that, with qualifications subsequently to be explored, Anderson during the last years of his youth in his hometown lived a rapport with his community that was as strong as it was subtle and complex. He knew that he too was included under the invisible roof, and he carried the warm knowledge of inclusion with him throughout adulthood as one measure of what constituted the good life. But if Anderson is not to be thought of as a rebel against the village, neither is he to be regarded even in these last Clyde years as the uncomplicated provincial. Bertha Baynes's word portrait of the townsman at twenty hardly seems to accord with the brooding image of the mature writer caught by Alfred Stieglitz's camera eye in 1923; yet again both men are one, or rather the older is implicit in the younger. Most of the time the young man seemed "normal" enough to his friends in

Clyde, who were amused and touched, as was Bertha, rather than disturbed by his unpredictable combination of dreaminess and activity, his
ability to become absorbed either in a book or his own talk. Underneath
his amiable, usually relaxed good-humored manner, however, a natural
manner emphasized as it was by the drawl that he had as a boy and kept
all his life, it was possible on rare occasions for emotional pressures to
build up, unnoticed by his friends and perhaps not even by himself, until
they broke out in some abrupt, impulsive act. Years afterward Herman
Hurd was to recall one of his friend's infrequent bursts of temper. In spring
it was the Clyde custom for every boy to get a new straw hat. One spring
Sunday afternoon Sherwood, Herman, and several other boys were hanging around a barn, fooling the time away. They began an aimless scuffling,
shoving each other about and trying to knock each other's new straw hat
off. When someone knocked but did not dislodge Sherwood's hat, he suddenly snatched off the hat himself, threw it on the barn floor, and jumped
up and down on it.[38]

It is easy, of course, to read too much significance into a minor incident; yet Herman Hurd was to advance this anecdote as having a serious,
explicit bearing on, as he put it, the later Anderson's "inability to stay with
any woman long," and similar anecdotes about sudden drastic acts are
fairly numerous about Sherwood at various stages of his life. In 1920, for
example, while he was living for a few months at Fairhope, Alabama, on
Mobile Bay, and finishing *Poor White*, he began experimenting with watercolors as a means of expressing his sense of the many-hued physical
world about him. In the company of a witty, uninhibited, Philadelphia
artist named Wharton Esherick he would occasionally go off for a day of
sketching. On one of these rambles Esherick had just introduced him to
the strong, deep palette color of cobalt blue, and Anderson began using it
heavily in a watercolor of the exposed, intertwined roots of a blown-down
pine tree. The result was, Esherick recognized, a very good little sketch despite or because of Anderson's quite typical refusal to accept instruction in
technique. On the way home Sherwood swaggered along in front of the
artist, obviously much pleased with himself, swinging the watercolor and
occasionally looking at it. Amused, Esherick called out, "Sherwood, that's
a pretty good picture, but next time why don't you use some cobalt blue?"
Immediately Anderson flashed into anger, tore the sketch in half, and
threw the pieces away. Whether it was a jumped-on hat or a ripped picture
or another shockingly abrupt word or act, the central elements of the situation would almost always be the same: a sudden resentment against a
fancied hostility from another and an equally sudden aggressive move
against that other, but an aggression expressed symbolically through self-
destructive behavior. As subsequent crises in his personal life were to indicate, this emotional pattern could unite with and reinforce more permanent

feelings of hostility against another person and result in catastrophically impulsive acts as a way out of some frustrating situation. After some thirty more years of living, the Anderson of the Stieglitz photograph with its deep, haunting eyes had come to recognize the forces of his emotional nature, and those of others, as the younger Anderson was only beginning to do in the mid-1890s.[39]

2.

The year 1895 was perhaps Sherwood Anderson's most critical one in Clyde, for its events brought experiences and emotional strains that were to echo in his life and to affect both substance and attitude in his writing. The consequences of the first of these events were to emerge far away from Clyde, but the event itself reveals him to be clearly fixed in the social context of the town. On March 28, 1895, he enlisted for a term of five years in Company I of the Sixteenth Regiment of Infantry in the Ohio National Guard, giving his occupation at the time of enlistment as "painter," an indication that he was at least temporarily helping his father in his trade.[40]

Company I, which had been organized in Clyde in 1878, was known as the McPherson Guard in honor of the town's famous general. For several years William E. Gillett, who was also township clerk and secretary of the waterworks, had been captain; and at the time Sherwood enlisted, some fifty-five men were in Gillett's command. From now on Anderson's Monday evenings were occupied with meetings and drills that began at 7:30 in the regiment's armory in the Kline Block on Main Street. The entire company also marched in Clyde's annual Memorial Day parade, participated in certain other occasions in the town's ceremonial life, and attended a week's encampment of National Guard regiments each summer. In that first year of Sherwood's service the men of Company I took part in the Clyde Memorial Day parade on May 30 and in a parade at Sandusky on June 12 in honor of the G. A R. encampment, while on June 13 they were officially inspected at Clyde. Equipped with new uniforms from the state, they went into regimental camp from July 25 through July 30 at Bryan, Ohio, where Anderson for the first time could have sensed the orderliness of large military units that helped inspire his novel *Marching Men*. In addition to such regular duties, Company I was subject at all times to the Governor's call to protect public order and private property anywhere in the state during disasters, strikes, or other emergencies. The McPherson Guard had been called out several times in 1894, that hungry, explosive year of Coxey's Army and Debs's Pullman Strike. In both June and July, Company I had been sent to the coalfields of southeastern Ohio to suppress lawlessness among striking miners, and on July 20 it had escorted through Clyde one Count Joseph Bylakowski and his "army" of

260 tramps on the march to Washington under the slogan, "Bread or blood." Yet the McPherson Guard could have other, more humanitarian functions. In January of 1895 Captain Gillett reported that "Co. I is having remarkable success in soliciting provisions for the starving miners, and that the prospects are the boys will be able to fill a [freight] car."[41]

One can only guess why Anderson joined the McPherson Guard. He may have been influenced to do so, of course, more by its efforts for the mine workers than for the mine owners; yet this is unlikely. Although he seems to have read *Looking Backward* feelingly and was considered by several friends to be "idealistic," the indications are that in his Clyde years he was not the critic of American society that he was to become. In fact, it is mildly ironic to note that in a strongly Republican town Irwin Anderson and his son were firm working-class Republicans, and Thaddeus Hurd and his son were equally firm business-group Democrats. One good reason for joining the Guard would have been the financial one. Only the captain received regular stipend, but the men were paid at such time as they were called out for duty. Another motivation may have been Sherwood's reading of Civil War writings, and there were literally dozens of men alive in Clyde who had fought for the Union, some of whom probably had told him tales of their military adventures. In addition, one former member of Company I told William Sutton that joining the Guard "was a boost socially," since the "better class of fellows generally" did join. Any such boost must have been a relative one, however, because Herman Hurd, in sociological terms a member of the town's power elite, later asserted flatly that the young men of Clyde's "better families" did not go into the Guard. What is involved here, it needs to be noticed, is not a question of possible class snobbery in a small town, but of the town's real social stratifications and mechanisms. To recognize these is to understand more exactly the complex relation of Sherwood Anderson to his community.[42]

During all the time that the Andersons were in Clyde, the center of social activity for the men was the lodges, such fraternal groups as the Elks, the Odd Fellows, the Masons. "Everyone who was anyone belonged to a lodge" when he reached the "joining age" at adulthood. Understandably, Irwin Anderson belonged to no lodge, though by the 1890s he had become active in the local post of the G. A. R., to which he belonged by right of his war service. Sherwood's enlistment in Company I did not automatically put him into the group of advantageously placed young men who could expect invitation into a lodge; it did confer some kind of status on him, however, and it did enmesh him even more thoroughly in the town's social fabric, including its values. Herman Hurd was later even certain that, had Sherwood stayed on in Clyde, Herman could have arranged his invitation into the Masonic Lodge, the prestige organization of the town. Sherwood of course did not stay on, but the significant point is his curious ambiguous position in Clyde as a young man. On the one hand, he was liked as a person generally, his mother and older sister and brother were all for varying reasons admired, and he had good friends among the "better" young townspeople as represented by Herman Hurd and Bertha Baynes; on the other hand, he had no settled occupation at the present, he had no definite prospect of one for the future, and he was "Major" Anderson's son. Midway in the nineties, then, he was, sociologically speaking, simultaneously among the favored and not among them, a marginal situation that typically produces—F. Scott Fitzgerald is an extreme instance—both psychological strain and a heightened awareness of social pressures and their symbolic indicators that the ordinary person does not perceive. For Sherwood the dreamy hustler this marginality meant an intensification of the conflict represented as going on in George Willard in the opening stories of *Winesburg,* that between "dream" and "success." Anderson was to try to solve it for some years by dreaming of success. Yet he awoke from this dream of money and social advancement, whereupon the sensitivity induced in him earlier partly by his ambiguous social situation in Clyde was fully released to augment that best gift obtained from his mother—the capacity to hear the words that people are really saying under the words that they pronounce.[43]

The scarcity of references to Sherwood in the *Clyde Enterprise* in the critical year 1895, as in other years, up to that of the Spanish-American War, is an indication of how ordinary and "unnewsworthy" he was then considered to be. Just as revealing, however, are the many appearances of his father's name in that year, most of them concerning events that would find their way into *Windy McPherson's Son* and that must now be discussed at length because of the astonishing and significant way in which Sherwood was to distort reality in this first published of his novels.

In the early and mid-1890s Irwin Anderson was himself improving the town's regard for the family by his activity in two areas. Although Karl was to claim that his father played a horn as badly as he told stories, the dislike of the oldest son for his father seems to have colored his memory. A former acquaintance of Irwin's told William Sutton that Mr. Anderson had played cornet in the Clyde band, and after Irwin's death George Richards, who had been superintendent of the Presbyterian Sunday school, recalled that he had had "a talent for music, playing the cornet sometimes in the church choir. . . ." Irwin's considerable instrumental ability, attested to beyond doubt by persons who knew him in Camden, Caledonia, and Clyde, was to enter Sherwood's first fictional portrait of him revealingly.[44]

In a second area Irwin was demonstrating an unexpected devotion to duty. This was in the affairs of the local Eaton Post No. 55 of the G. A. R., which had about a hundred members and which met regularly in Grand

Army Hall on the second and fourth Tuesdays of each month. As early as 1890 Irwin had served a year's term as Officer of the Guard, but beginning in 1894 he regularly held lesser positions in the local organization, though he was never elected to the office of commander, the ultimate honor and sign of trust. On January 9, as the new Officer of the Day for that year, he inducted into their positions the other officials of the post with, according to the *Enterprise,* "dignity and promptness." Irwin must have continued to perform his duties well. In December, 1894, he was reelected Officer of the Day and also "Delegate to Departmental Encampment," he served in 1896 and 1897 as Adjutant, and in 1898 he was to be one of two delegates at the G. A. R. state encampment at Mount Vernon, Ohio. His finest hours, however, came in his son's crucial year, 1895. On the gala evening of January 8, 1895, he was inducted into office as Officer of the Day, headed the "foraging squad" that brought in the refreshments, and gave evidence of his histrionic abilities by participating in a program of readings and recitations. Next, and much more importantly, he was made head of the post's Committee on Arrangements for the Memorial Day parade; and in item after item the *Enterprise* records, as it was not to do for the activities of any other such committee before or after 1895, the energy poured into preparations by this "ne'er-do-well," who thirty years before had ridden on Wilson's Raid and for whom the War of the Great Rebellion was still red in memory.[45]

The newspaper record, which must be recounted in detail because of its relevance to Irwin's son and the son's fiction, begins with the front-page appearance on April 30 of an item unprecedented in the career of the *Enterprise,* the full report, as adopted by Eaton Post of its Committee on Arrangements, recommending with flourishes of organizational language that are presumably Irwin's such actions as that "Comrade W. H. Jackson be selected as grand marshall of the day" and "That all military and civic societies be and they are hereby invited to attend in a body and take part in the parade and the Memorial services at McPherson cemetery in the afternoon of May 30th." The same issue notes on an inside page that "The new Clyde Cornet band has generously tendered its services to Eaton post for Memorial day." On May 17, the front page of the *Enterprise* carried, again unprecedentedly, a signed statement by the committee, two-thirds of a column long, giving, in a detail that indicates hours of "staff-work," the coming program of exercises and an elaborate order of march for the parade. The McPherson Guard, to take a pertinent example, would march second in line after the Cornet Band, while Eaton Post would come eighth and last; but at the entrance to McPherson Cemetery the marching order of the Guard and the Post was to be reversed, the Post following the Band into the cemetery and the Guard entering last. In addition to his hard-working Committee on Arrangements, Irwin headed the Resolutions Committee, which introduced at a special meeting of the post after pre-Memorial Day services in the Methodist Episcopal Church a resolution of thanks to the pastor "for his excellent memorial sermon" and to the choir "for their beautiful and appropriate music." The labors of Irwin and his committees were so diligent and so effective that on May 31 the *Enterprise,* in a first-page story titled "Honoring the Brave," once more unprecedentedly concluded its account of the previous day's ceremonies with a special statement of praise: "Take it all in all, the celebration of Memorial day in Clyde was a grand success, and the committee on arrangements in charge of the affair are to be congratulated upon the success of the event and the smoothness with which the entire day's program was carried out."[46]

Probably the most memorable sequence in *Windy McPherson's Son* begins with a crowded town meeting in "Caxton," Iowa, called for the public planning of an elaborate Fourth of July celebration. Young Sam McPherson, privileged as the town's newsboy to mix with the men, watches "with burning cheeks" as his father, Windy, drunk, garrulous, and avid as always for public attention, grandly contributes seventeen dollars to the celebration fund, while at home Sam's mother is washing the clothes of a shoe merchant who at the meeting has just contributed only five dollars. Then, on Windy's insistence that he had been a regimental bugler in the Civil War, the crowd agrees that he is to open the festivities on the Fourth by riding into town at dawn on a white horse and blowing reveille in front of the town hall. At first humiliated by what he assumes to be just another of his father's War stories, Sam is subsequently persuaded otherwise at home when Windy histrionically tells a tale of how, as bugler, he awakened his comrades to action in a surprise night attack. Sam even uses his own carefully saved money to send to Chicago for a bugle to go with Windy's newly purchased uniform. At dawn on the Fourth, Main Street is packed with people, and the three McPhersons—mother, Sam, and Kate the daughter—watch as Windy, "sitting very straight in the saddle and looking wonderfully striking in the new blue uniform," rides between the rows of silent people with "the air of a conqueror come to receive the homage of the town." In front of the town hall he rises in the saddle, looks haughtily at the crowd, puts the bugle to his lips—and blows only "a thin piercing shriek followed by a squawk." At once the people realize that "It was only another of Windy McPherson's pretensions" that he can blow a bugle, and "A great shout of laughter rolled down the street. Men and women sat on the curbstones and laughed until they were tired. Then, looking at the figure upon the motionless horse, they laughed again." Sam and his mother, standing "in a doorway leading into a shoe-store" are "white and speechless with humiliation" and do not dare look at each other. "In the flood of shame sweeping over them they stared straight before them with hard, stony eyes."

It is inescapable that in writing this sequence, and others in the first part of *Windy McPherson's Son*, Anderson was employing his "fancy," his imagination, in a way similar to his treatment of Fern's death in *Tar*, not simply to rearrange reality but actually to reverse it, here to transform fact into a fiction that was simultaneously a savage attack on his own father and a desperate defense of his rejection of the man, desperate since in the subsequent action of the novel Sam, a projection of the author, drives to the top of money success in reaction to his father's failures only to find that success to be a failure also. Clearly the Fourth of July celebration, which Clyde never had, is based on the Memorial Day one it always did, though it is a nice fictional touch for Sam to gain independence from his father on the national holiday reserved for rejoicing at a declaration of freedom rather than that for honoring the dead. Clearly also Windy McPherson's grotesque failure is the reverse image of Major Anderson's notable success, Windy's inability to blow the bugle inverts Irwin's real musical talent, and the jeering laughter of the crowds of townspeople both at the meeting and the dawn fiasco is equal but opposite to the public commendation by the newspaper, in this instance speaking as the collective voice of Clyde. Even Windy's ease in the saddle, which truly reflects Irwin's cavalry training, leads to his being set above the crowd, not to assert authority, but to stand out as the target of derision. Only the humiliation of the son is the same, but here the distortion is in terms of cause. In the novel Sam McPherson goes willingly with his mother and sister to observe only as spectator what turns out to be his father's ridiculous downfall; on May 30, 1895, Sherwood Anderson was required to participate in what turned out to be his father's glorious triumph. Only two months after his enlistment in the McPherson Guard, the son had to march as his father had directed, had to approach the cemetery gate and, halted, see the G. A. R. veterans enter the cemetery just behind the Cornet Band, he and the rest of Company I, who had never proved their manhood by firing a shot at an enemy, bringing up the rear.

Other masking and manipulation of reality occurs in *Windy McPherson's Son*. In addition to the fact that the last name of Sam McPherson, like that of "Sher" Anderson, is a three-syllable patronymic, it was the name of the Clyde cemetery where the Memorial Day ceremonies were held and of a general buried there beneath a larger-than-life bronze statue of himself, a soldier who was a true hero of the War, not a false one. Then, too, with a shock of surprise one comes across an item in the issue of the *Enterprise* for the just previous March 15 that may be only an extraordinary coincidence but in the present context is provocative. "Windy Kintz in Trouble" reads the headline over a brief note: "William, better known as 'Windy' Kintz, was arrested Monday and charged with stealing a watch about thirteen months ago." Assuming from Sherwood's wide acquaintance in Clyde that he at least knew of Windy, of the garrulity implied by the nickname, and of the arrest on a charge of stealing, how appropriate it would be for him in writing this sequence in his novel to give the father a nickname that linked him, in the author's memory, with another talker who only a few weeks before Memorial Day had been publicly charged as a petty criminal.[47]

But if this is to spin out too finely the speculation on names, the files of the *Enterprise* do make clear a specific reason for Anderson's ferocity in his fictional portrait of his father in *Windy McPherson's Son*. One more real event of this May of 1895 required imaginative containment and control. In the novel, son, daughter, and mother hurry "hand in hand toward Main Street" at "dawn on the great day"; in actuality Emma Anderson did not witness her husband's Memorial Day triumph. She had died just under three weeks before.

Once again the newspaper tells the facts. On page one of the issue for April 30, 1895, appears the initial report of Irwin Anderson's Committee on Arrangements. On page three, however, two personal items allow one to see a little "beneath the surface of lives": "Mrs. I. M. Anderson is lying very ill at her home on Spring avenue, and is not expected to recover"; and "Carl Anderson has arrived home from Chicago, being called here by the fatal illness of his mother." On May 7, a Tuesday, the *Enterprise* notes that, "Mrs. I. M. Anderson is lying unconscious to day, and her death is a matter of a few hours at best." The following Friday, May 10, the mother had appeared to have passed the crisis, for the paper states, "Mrs. I. M. Anderson, who was several times reported to be dead within the past few days, is considerably better to-day." But Emma Anderson died that afternoon.[48]

In the crowded four-page issues of the *Enterprise* of those days extended obituaries were usually printed only for the oldest inhabitants and prominent citizens. It indicates the high regard in Clyde for Emma Anderson, therefore, that she should be honored with a three-paragraph notice of her death.

Emma J., wife of I. M. Anderson, who had been lying very ill for several weeks, died at her home on Spring street on Friday afternoon, aged forty-two years, eight months and two days. The funeral was held at the house on Sunday at three o'clock, conducted by Rev. George E. Wilson; the burial was in McPherson cemetery.

The second paragraph gives, mostly accurately, such dates in her life as those of birth and marriage, dates that a husband would be most likely in a family to know, and describes her as "A faithful, consistent christian." After accurately listing her survivors—"two sisters . . . a mother, husband, five sons and a daughter"—the obituary ends with a brief statement of more than merely formal praise: "Mrs. Anderson was a most estimable lady, and leaves very many friends who sympathize with the family in their sad affliction."[49]

Sherwood Anderson's mother died, then, twenty days before Memorial Day, and when he and the rest of Company I marched into McPherson Cemetery at the end of the parade his father had so successfully organized, her grave there was still fresh. It is impossible to know whether the way Irwin took his wife's death had anything to do with another scene in *Windy McPherson's Son* in which Sam nearly strangles his drunken father in the kitchen of the McPherson home while the mother is dying in the little parlor; but perhaps even the most dignified grief on Irwin's part would not have satisfied Sherwood, who, together with Karl and Stella, had had to watch the mother, worn out from over-work, lie for "several weeks" in a final illness reported in the death record as consumption. It is clear, however, that for days before and after his wife's death Irwin was heavily occupied with the meticulous planning for the Memorial Day celebration, and being Irwin, he would have had to talk about the plans even more than work on them. The special hatred behind Windy McPherson's catastrophe would appear to come from Sherwood's witnessing how his own father in a time of death was very much in the midst of life, in a time when he should have been private and silent was public and full of words, in a time when he should have acknowledged guilt for having failed to provide properly for his family was accorded a civic triumph instead.[50]

That his mother's death was a profound shock to Sherwood Anderson is implied by the kind of inaccuracies which appear in all of his accounts of the event, fictional or nonfictional. In *A Story Teller's Story*, for example, he might have been deliberately changing the fact for effect when he writes that his mother was "to die, outworn and done for at thirty," though she actually died at forty-two, but in a letter of 1938 seriously designed to give information he could state: "I should say that my father died about twenty years ago, my mother when I was a boy of eight or ten." Irwin did die in 1919, but Emma Anderson's death occurred when Sherwood was eighteen. Perhaps the consistent chronological mistake reveals a psychological truth; his remembrance of his mother's dying may always have been associated with a strong sense of being abandoned such as a boy rather than a young man would feel. Coupled with this would always be the rage against his father, whose irresponsibility toward the family he would blame for making his mother really die "from poverty." So even in the posthumously published *Memoirs* he could insinuate that Irwin, who was actually there in Clyde busying himself with Memorial Day preparations, may have been away out of town having an adulterous affair while his wife lay dying, but that at any rate he, Sherwood, was "quite without any memory of [Irwin's] presence in our house when mother was suddenly struck down." In his last published book as in his first, as far as his father was concerned, Sherwood's chief design seems to have been to do away with him by one imaginative means or another. Once again the evidence suggests that, at least in part, Anderson would find in the craft of writing a way to deal with past, but not forgotten, emotional crises, to cope with difficult, long-standing psychic pressures, a way to use "little tricky words" to reshape unpleasant reality into what he wished his readers to think and himself to remember. One important function of art for him would be to provide the imaginative manipulation, sometimes even reversal, of personal experiences that he required, not only for aesthetic satisfaction, but for psychological relief, perhaps at times even for survival.[51]

3.

The shock of his beloved mother's death was especially great for Sherwood at this particular time, since, despite Stella's self-sacrificing attempts to act as mother for four boys, the disintegration of the Anderson family that now began echoed also his dimly growing sense that his town's invisible roof was weakening under the impact of a new force. This new force was industrialism, which of course meant additional ways for "Jobby" Anderson to make money, but which had other less attractive effects that he was to understand clearly only later. Ultimately, in *Poor White*, he was to see the story of his hometown under industrialism as referring to the development of his entire modern America, and conversely, the imagined disintegration of Bidwell in that novel was felt so deeply by its author because it referred to the real disintegration of the intimate world of his youth. Despite Bertha's and his affection for each other, Anderson's last months in Clyde were far from untroubled ones.

When he had come to Clyde in 1884, the town despite the railroad and telegraph was essentially as preindustrial as the fictional Winesburg. When he left it some dozen years later, the new age had touched the town, physically and emotionally, in irrevocable ways. The first real indication that "the time of the factories was at hand" even in Clyde was the attempt by the town's leading citizens, as satirically described in Book 1 of *A Story Teller's Story*, to get in on northern Ohio's natural gas boom of the middle 1880s; and eleven-year-old Sherwood caught his "first glimpse of the Industrial Age" when with other town boys he saw the Clyde gas well, after months of dry boring, unsuccessfully "shot" with nitroglycerine on April 14, 1887. The failure to strike gas meant to Anderson the writer that Clyde "could not become another fragrant Akron or Youngstown," yet it probably meant to Sherwood as "Jobby" what it did to the *Enterprise*, that for several years thereafter the town became "too dead to skin." In

58

1891 the last of the annual Clyde fairs failed and a short-lived piano factory shut down, but the "hustlers," as the *Enterprise* called the active businessmen, were at work. The Clyde Kraut Company, where Sherwood and
young Irwin once labored, prospered so rapidly that by 1892 the owners
were constructing a new building from which the cans of sauerkraut and
sauerkraut juice, marked with the "Silver Fleece" brand, were shipped out
to various parts of the world. Then in 1893, the year that Sherwood finished his last few months of high school education, the Mechanical Age
began to come in a rush.[52]

First were the "modern conveniences." A sewer was laid that summer
along the Maumee Pike, and then, as Anderson was to put it accurately in
Poor White, "Main Street was torn up for the purpose of laying a brick
pavement and digging a new sewer." Just as in the novel, Italian workmen
were brought in by the contractor to do the hard labor, and the "native"
American *Enterprise* commented with a superior air on the Saturday night
drunks and the tight clannishness of the "dagos." The man who used to
go about every evening with his short ladder and torch to light each of the
gasoline streetlamps of Clyde, and of Winesburg, made his last rounds on
the evening of September 6—the electric light plant had been installed,
new arc lights went on the next night, and, as the *Enterprise* boasted,
"Clyde is now the best lighted town in northern Ohio." In March of 1894,
"Jobby" Anderson himself joined progress by working as a water boy for
the "foreign workmen" who were now putting in the sewer on Buckeye
Street, and on April 6, as the *Enterprise* shows, he was paid $13.30 for his
labor. The following year, the critical year 1895, he was to serve the Industrial Age even more directly as a laborer in Clyde's local manifestation
of the Age, the new Elmore bicycle factory.[53]

At this time, however, there seems to have occurred an interlude in Anderson's life that was to be of an importance almost equal to industrialism
as a means of ordering both his thinking and his fiction. Even as a boy he
had loved harness racehorses, the trotters and pacers, with an intensity
like that described in "I Want to Know Why" and *Tar,* and had often hung
around the track up on the Clyde fairgrounds to watch them being
trained. It was apparently during the winter of 1894–95 that he held yet
another of his jobs, this one as groom in Harvey & Yetter's livery stable,
beside the Nichols House and opposite the railroad station, where, according to the *Memoirs,* a crude joke played on him by other laborers may
have made him conclude that even the slow, old livery horses were "infinitely finer and better than many . . . men." Apparently also it was in the
summer and early fall of 1895, after the death of his mother in May and
his first National Guard encampment at the end of July, that he followed
the county fair and race circuit of northern Ohio as a "swipe," or groom,
with "Tom Whitehead's string of trotting and pacing horses." Whether or

not he dreamed, as he says in the *Memoirs,* of becoming a famous harness-race driver like Ed Geers or Budd Doble, he did work with racehorses, probably at this time, and the racetrack stories he would later write have a grounding in actuality.[54]

Thomas (Tom) C. Whitehead, for example, who appears briefly as Tom Whitehead in *Tar* and as Harry Whitehead in "I'm a Fool" and "An Ohio Pagan," was very much a real person. A big man with an equally husky wife, who could drive a horse as well as he, Whitehead had taken over his father's prosperous farm a few miles northeast of Clyde and for years had been breeding, training, and selling horses. In 1891 he moved into Clyde, built a large brick house on Main Street, purchased an adjoining building where wooden brackets had once been manufactured, and turned the factory into a stable for the trotters and pacers he was training for harness racing. The narrator of "I'm a Fool" cares for a trotter named Doctor Fritz, and Dr. Fritz was the name of a four-year-old trotting horse that Whitehead owned and had sold after it set a record in 1893. In the summers of 1894–95 Whitehead's best horse was a pacer named Solarion—the pacer in "I'm a Fool" is named Bucephalus—who in 1895 frequently took prize money at such places as Toledo, Cleveland, and Sandusky. Another character in "I'm a Fool" and "The Man Who Became a Woman" is Burt, the black groom. A black groom in Clyde named Bert Ellison worked at the Harvey & Yetter livery stable and at racetracks. It would be absurd, of course, to suggest that Anderson's racetrack stories are dependable autobiography; quite the contrary, they are for the most part imaginative constructions. Nevertheless, the existence in a group of stories of autobiographical elements—some of the persons, the actual work of the swipes, the response to the atmosphere of the county fair races—indicates, as does his dependence on the Clyde setting in *Winesburg, Ohio* and *Poor White,* how much Anderson needed a thinly disguised reality as a backdrop for the play of his "fancy."[55]

Besides its usefulness for future fictional material, the job of "swiping" for Tom Whitehead served other important functions. To Sherwood the young man it gave his first sustained opportunity to satisfy his love for wandering about, a combination of restlessness, curiosity, and preference for the unhurried, clock-free life that Herman Hurd, who preferred to stay home, recalled as a marked characteristic of his friend from their earliest times together. Along the county fair circuit, too, he became acquainted with a new sort, the unconventional, raffish people who, as the narrator-protagonist of "The Man Who Became a Woman" says "hang about a race track, the touts, swipes, drivers, niggers and gamblers," a "gaudy undependable lot" whom he learned to admire and be easy with for their nonconforming independence, their ability to tell flamboyant lies, their "not saving money or thinking about morals" like the more conventional

Clyde, Ohio

small-towners. To Anderson the writer his life as a swipe would also furnish a major symbol or symbol-cluster centered on horses and their racing, a symbol of grace, courage, cleanness, and fidelity to oppose what he
saw as the ugliness, noise, dirt, and spiritual corruption of industrialism,
a symbol of the life-encouraging to set against that which, because of its
inhuman rigidity, denied vitality and destroyed it.[56]

Once back from the lazy, horsey wandering, which seems to have provided him in real life the kind of idyllic, prelapsarian interlude celebrated
at the beginning of "I'm a Fool," Anderson fell fully into the knowledge
of industrialism. The Elmore Manufacturing Company was a small
enough enterprise, but it was a big one for Clyde. Well-to-do townspeople
had brought in first an organ factory and then a piano-making company
to the long brick building on Amanda Street next to the Lake Shore and
Michigan tracks in the northwest corner of town, and had in some cases
paid double what they had invested when these businesses successively
failed. Then in June of 1894 two leading citizens, one of them the George
S. Richards who had employed Sherwood in his dry-goods store, persuaded Harmon V. Becker and his two sons, James and Burton, who had
turned a prosperous cooperage into an equally prosperous bicycle works
in the nearby town of Elmore, to move their firm to the empty factory on
Amanda Street. The *Enterprise* immediately announced a building boom
in anticipation of an increased town population; and at the same time that
it was reporting the calling out of the McPherson Guard against Count Bylakowski's "army" and striking coal miners, the paper kept the townspeople excited by bulletins on the moving of "the Elmore's" machinery to
town and the arrival of the Becker families and of the first employees. Actual operations in the new factory began in about September, and by mid-
January of 1895 the *Enterprise,* which with the new year had changed
from weekly to semiweekly in order to keep up with Clyde's new prosperity, could announce "a 10,000 edition of a handsome illustrated catalogue
showing the various styles of '95 Elmore Cycles" and a force of sixty men
at work. In February the *Enterprise* happily reported that "The busiest
place in Clyde nowadays is the Elmore Cycle factory, where seventy men
are hustling from early morn till late at night," and quoted James Becker
as saying that "The force at the factory will have to be increased to one
hundred men, and that it will be necessary to turn out thirty wheels per
day from now until the season closes in order to supply the orders now on
hand." The first manufacturing season was so prosperous, in fact, that in
the May when Emma Anderson died the Elmore purchased land for an
"extensive addition" to the factory in preparation for manufacturing ten
thousand bicycles in the yet busier season to begin, after the summer lull,
in September of 1895. By February, 1986, the Elmore was running until
10 PM daily with a force of 150 men, and soon the *Enterprise* could boast

of the beneficial effect on the town of the high wages earned. "There are men working there by day who make $100 per month and over," and unskilled laborers were making from $1.25 to $2.50 a day at piece work.[57]

Sherwood Anderson made the piece-work wage. Probably he began to work at the bicycle factory in October of 1895, shortly after returning from his wanderings with Tom Whitehead's racehorses and before, presumably, he was called with the rest of Company I to nearby Tiffin from October 27 to 29 to establish order in that town during and after a lynch mob riot. At any rate, a Clyde directory for November 1, 1895, lists him as an employee of the Elmore Manufacturing Company and as "boarding" along with Stella and "Irving" at the home of his father, a "painter," on Spring Avenue. His job was in the "enamel shed" in a little twenty-by-forty brick building connected by an elevated runway to the rear of the main factory. Here, as he was to write in the *Memoirs*, during twelve-hour work days in the winter months of 1895–96 he helped dip the bicycle frames into tanks of stinking black enamel, brush them as they dried, and then hang them in ovens for the enamel to bake hard. The work was not heavy, but the hours were long, and the enamel fumes stung the eyes and nose. As nearly as Herman Hurd could remember, Sherwood never told him whether he liked the job or not but simply regarded it as just another way to earn money. The testimony of Burton Becker's daughter, Mildred, later Mrs. Clarence G. Fuller, is extremely illuminating, however. She knew that her father, who with his brother James really ran the factory, distinctly remembered Sherwood Anderson on two counts. First, instead of tending to business on the job, Sherwood would often sit and look dreamily out the window; hence Burton Becker was relieved when Sherwood eventually left the factory, probably quitting rather than waiting to be fired. Second, when some ten years later Anderson went into business for himself in Elyria, Ohio, he wrote to Mr. Becker urging him to "go into business with him." Mrs. Fuller recalled how her father laughed over the letter, thinking the proposition enormously funny considering his feelings about Sherwood's capacity for work.[58]

If Anderson's first real confrontation with industrialism was to lose him a possible business partner, it ultimately gave him something much more important, though the immediate experience could have been an emotionally crippling one. For twelve hours a day in uncomfortable surroundings he performed repetitive acts requiring a minimum of skill. The dreaminess that even a tolerant employer noted, it becomes clear, was his means of escaping, or at least alleviating, the impact of what Karl Marx was first fully to define as "alienation," that feeling of powerlessness, meaninglessness, isolation, and self-estrangement in relation to their labor which in varying degrees affects many industrial workers. Dominated by the machine system, compelled to labor repetitively on only one small part in the whole manufacturing process, divorced both from the goals of production and from social collectivity, the alienated worker becomes separated even from himself, for his work provides him only with money and satisfies little or not at all the human need for self-expression. Since he is deprived of any sense of an organic wholeness in his experience, such a worker feels himself a fragment and "a thing," merely an object for use by others. In 1895 Anderson was a young man with a limited education and of a nature never given to systematic thought, and he certainly had not read Marx. He did not conceptualize alienation; he lived it in his tired body and bored, unhappy mind. The Elmore Manufacturing Company provided him with an experience that had complex and contradictory results. On the one hand, it reinforced his desire for financial success and his growing realization that he preferred to obtain such success, indeed could only obtain it, from using his brain rather than his physical strength. On the other, it fed those deeper and more slowly moving currents in his personality that would ultimately drive him out of business into art, that would emphasize the primacy of the imagined over the real, and that would give him his extraordinary intuitive insight into natures alienated by the machine or by life itself.[59]

It is relevant to examine here, not the somewhat unreliable evidence of the *Memoirs,* but that contained in a short piece of experimental prose that Anderson was to publish years later in 1922 in the first issue of the little magazine *Manuscripts.* Called "A Testament," this piece points toward the fiction of *Dark Laughter* and the autobiography of the *Memoirs* as well as to the prose poems of *A New Testament*, and is Anderson's only other extended comment on his Clyde factory experience. "A Testament" falls into three almost equal parts, the last being somewhat longer than the first two. The piece opens with a speaker, "I," introducing himself through interior monologue as an old man whose parents are dead, a "dreamer" who has "a lowly place" in a bicycle factory in a town of "thirty-five hundred people." He has a twisted foot as the result of an early accident while "painting roofs"—this may be in 1922 a veiled reference either to Anderson's assistance of his housepainter father in Clyde or to his emotionally damaging venture as paint seller in Elyria, Ohio from 1907 to 1913—and he does not "see very well" because his eyes are sore. Mingled with the associative detail that "flies about" in the lonely speaker's mind is considerable straightforward exposition:

I work in a bicycle factory. The man who works in the same room with me is named Biffer Smith. He is a short man with a round belly and big black mustache. The place I work in is called an enamelling shed. The enamelling shed is separated from the rest of the factory because in the enamelling of bicycles liquids are used that are likely at any time to catch fire and explode.

The exposition is followed by a transition paragraph into the second section. In this part the speaker dreams that he is "one of a flock of blackbirds" who in the spring morning have eaten their fill in a new cornfield of the blades, seed kernels, and "Young, fragrant, succulent roots" of the corn. Driven out of a wood, they fly over the town through the "sweet" air.

When I was a blackbird, flying in the May morning I flew with the other birds along a street, just skimming above the tops of maple trees. We went along a winding dirt road. Smoke rolled out at the chimney of the factory. The houses along the street were dirty. I live in an ugly house now. At the factory faces peered out at windows. The faces at the windows looked like the faces of people in a prison. We did not care. We flew high and free. It was a May morning and the young corn was just coming up in the fields.

This juxtaposition of natural freedom and squalid, man-made captivity ends section two. Section three begins with more exposition of the enameling process with its stinging vapor that hurts eyes and throat. Biffer Smith, however, is not hurt by the vapor from "the black shiny liquid," and his singing of the workman's song of release, "Saturday night and supper on the table," is directly associated with flocks of blackbirds that "fly high up overhead, going away to the fields." There follows an ugly sketch of a lime-hauler's wife, a woman of "bad reputation," who "lives in a small dirty frame house along a railroad track back of our bicycle factory" and who receives other men while her husband is away working. The final paragraph excludes all reference to Biffer Smith or flying birds and brings together vividly the images of ugliness, corruption, hurt, and failure:

My hands tremble. Bicycle frames are held by hooks to be dipped into tanks. They slip off the hooks and fall to the bottom of the tanks. I put in my arms and fish them out. My arms are brown. They used to be white but they are now brown. I cannot wash them white. Whenever a man goes into the house of the lime hauler to visit the lime hauler's wife I drop frames into the dipping tanks. My eyes are sore all the time. I cannot hold my hands steady over the tanks. In the evening when I come here to sit I cannot see the paths that run through the fields by the side of the railroad tracks.

Allowing for the passage of years and Anderson's intervening development as artist, "A Testament" nevertheless appears to constitute an emotionally true memory of the months in the Clyde factory. Whether or not this is what Sherwood may actually have been dreaming about when Burton Becker saw him looking out of the enameling shed's windows along the Lake Shore tracks, the arrangement and content of the three sections is revealing. Two sections emphasizing lack of control, purposelessness, isolation, and self-estrangement enclose, entrap as it were, a middle one in which a fantasied escape into freedom, community, and wholeness is symbolized by flocks of birds and the rebirth of nature. "A Testament," drawing on the facts of the bicycle factory as well as on fantasy, daydream, and symbolism, externalizes acutely and hauntingly the subjective state of alienation.[60]

Not unexpectedly, Biffer Smith turns out to have been based on an actual person. The foreman of the enameling shed was a man named B. M. Rice, who had been brought by the Beckers to Clyde from the earlier factory in Elmore. Anderson was to describe him at length in the *Memoirs* (1969, pp. 123–28), where he asserts that Rice "gave me the notion for the figure of Sponge Martin," the old craftsman in *Dark Laughter,* though much of Sponge's background was "all imagination." According to the *Memoirs* Rice had been an independent craftsman, an expert carriage-maker devoted to fine artisanship, who accepted his detested piece work in the bicycle factory out of a boyhood friendship with one of the Beckers and a need for money; and these details sound less like imaginative invention than the accompanying description of Rice's supposed habit of getting drunk at Body Adare's on Saturday nights and then frantically running away from the saloon in a bizarre effort to work off his own sense of alienation, a description where one suspects the creation of another Winesburg grotesque. Yet embellished as the portraits of the man may be, Rice did in fact have at least the one extraordinary and highly individualized skill that Anderson ascribes to him. When the enameled bicycle frames came hard and gleaming from the baking ovens, it was Rice's job to sweep the gold decorating stripes onto them with a special thin, pointed camel's hair brush; and just as Sherwood recalled, each stripe went on absolutely evenly at a single freehand stroke. In addition, then, to a profoundly disturbing experience of alienation Anderson gained from his first encounter with industrialism one answer to its tendency to turn human being into thing. Rice, who as Biffer Smith is not hurt by the enamel fumes and whose singing is linked with the freely flying birds, became a real-life prototype for those skilled craftsman figures recurrent in Anderson's writings that represent in a wholly human way, just as horses were to do symbolically, that which is morally and aesthetically superior to the die-stamped outer conformity and the inner disorientation of a machine civilization.[61]

It is not known how many months Sherwood worked at the Elmore, but considering his own feelings about the job, Burton Becker's observation of him as a workman, and Herman Hurd's recollection that, characteristically, his friend did not work for very long at the factory, it is extremely unlikely that he would have been among the skeleton force of twenty-five men kept on after June 8, 1896, when the company shut down six weeks earlier than usual because of the sudden slack business in bicycles all over the country resulting from overproduction and hard times. The Elmore did reopen late in the following November, but the Beckers were then shrewdly following national patterns by switching over to the manufacture of the Elmore automobile. Meanwhile Anderson's problem was to find other work in Clyde. As on the previous Memorial Day, he presumably marched with the McPherson Guard on May 30 in a parade that, this year, could not have been organized by Irwin Anderson, since no prior fanfare appeared in the *Enterprise* and the procession was markedly delayed in forming; and from the twentieth through the twenty-fifth of July, 1896, he was with his company at Camp Moses, Cleveland, for the National Guard's annual encampment. In June, Irwin, as busy Adjutant of the Eaton Post, arranged with Governor Bushnell for the return to Clyde of the Seventy-second Regiment's Civil War flag, and in September Earl, the youngest Anderson child, was seriously ill for several days. None of these distractions solved the problem of work, however, and very likely it was in the fall of 1896 that Sherwood decided to combine the search for a job with "the impulse to be on the move, a hunger to see more of the world," as he was to put it in a section of the *Memoirs* (1969, p. 129).[62]

It is not clear how long was this ensuing period when, as Anderson later recalled for a questioner, he "drifted for a time from town to town" and "worked in an iron foundry at Erie, Pennsylvania," but it seems to have been some months in the depression fall and winter of 1896–97. The details of this period are only a little less conjectural than those concerning many other young men on the road in those hard times. Certain of Anderson's subsequent writings do provide some hints, however. Since the first part of his short story "The Sad Horn Blowers" draws heavily on actual Clyde materials, distorted and telescoped in time as they are, one assumes the likelihood that the last part contains personal history in some form as well. For what the "facts" are worth, the tale states that Will Appleton and his brother had been helping their father as house painter until the father's careless self-scalding puts all three out of work one August. Will "managed to find employment during September on the farms." (Will is clearly a figure representing Sherwood himself, and for once the author is carefully specific about the time sequence.) Then, feeling momentarily "a kind of dislike of his native town, Bidwell"—a fictional community populated by people with Clyde names—because he can find no work there, Will decides to go to Erie "to get a job in a factory or on the docks," deciding on Erie because it "wasn't as big as Cleveland or Buffalo or Toledo or Chicago, or any one of a lot of other cities to which he might have gone, looking for work." One night "Early in October" he says good-bye to his older sister, Kate, hops a freight train to Cleveland, crosses the city on a street car, and catches another freight as far as Ashtabula, where he decides to enter Erie in more style and takes a passenger train. The remainder of the story describes how Will overcomes homesickness and achieves some sense of maturity while rooming in a working-class boardinghouse in Erie and working at a factory where, in a classic image of alienation, he stands all day at a machine drilling holes in boxlike truck after boxlike truck of "little, short, meaningless pieces of iron."[63]

Perhaps Anderson did perform such depersonalizing labor and then went to another job, more familiar but equally stultifying, as described in Book 2 of *A Story Teller's Story* with a sure, low-keyed sense for a reality symbolic of human waste.

It was a bicycle factory where I was employed as an assembler. With some ten or twelve other men I worked at a bench in a long room facing a row of windows. We assembled the parts that were brought to us by boys from other departments of the factory and put the bicycles together. There was such and such a screw to go into such and such a screw hole, such and such a nut to go on such and such a bolt. As always in the modern factory nothing ever varied and within a week any intelligent quick-handed man could have done the work with his eyes closed. One turned certain screws, tightened certain bolts, whirled a wheel, fastened on certain foot pedals and passed the work on to the next man. Outside the window I faced there was a railroad track lined on one side by factory walls and the other by what had started to be a stone quarry. The stone of this quarry had not, I presume, turned out to be satisfactory and the hole was being filled with rubbish carted from various parts of the city and all day carts arrived, dumped their loads—making each time a little cloud of dust—and over the dump wandered certain individuals, men and women who were looking among the rubbish for bits of treasure, bottles I fancy and bits of cloth and iron that could later be sold to junk men.

In recollecting this job from his factory years Anderson comments on how here, as in other such jobs, his fellow workers continually boasted of their sexual conquests in order to compensate in words for their actual work-induced impotence. (This was a phenomenon he was to be certain he observed also among male workers in southern textile mills in the early thirties.) Claiming that he was subject to sick headaches, he would escape the vile talk, he writes, by going to a window and opening it, "closing my eyes and trying to create in fancy a world in which men lived under bright skies, drank wine, loved women and with their hands created something of lasting value and beauty"—whereupon these same foul-mouthed men would become solicitous about his health and bring him home remedies for his supposed illness. Whatever the fabrication possibly involved in describing these episodes years later, the factory experience would be immensely valuable to him as a writer. It introduced him to a mode of existence characteristic of millions of Americans and helped prepare in him the consciously Whitmanesque feeling he later had of containing a multitude of American lives and hence being representative of his country's development; it strengthened his curiosity about the secret fantasy life of his fellows; and it stimulated his contradictory desire to escape from factory routine by substituting his own fantasy life for actuality or, conversely, by dreaming, even scheming, of how to work his way up from blue-collar shop to white-collar office. So when he moved on to yet another job in Erie, "rolling kegs of nails out of a great sheet-iron warehouse and onto a long platform, from where they were to be carted by trucks, down a short street, out to a wharf and aboard a ship," the author figure of *A Story Teller's Story* temporarily comes to terms with his conflicting needs by, paradoxically, rejecting the colorful, ordered world of his fancy, which covers ugly external reality with the "unreality inside himself," and elects instead to "become a man of action, in the mood of the American of my day." Yet if his sketch "In a Box Car" can be believed, he continued for some time in the blind drift of the unskilled worker, at one point witnessing a murder while riding in a freight car in winter "during a period of hard times" when he was "beating his way from one town to another" in the Midwest looking unsuccessfully for work and dreaming "of someday getting up in the world."[64]

Just when he definitely decided to go to Chicago is uncertain, though it would seem to have been in the spring or early summer of 1897 that he returned to Clyde before leaving for the big city. Why he went to Chicago is clearer than exactly when he went. For one thing Karl had already been there for several years and could at least help him get settled, and in fact when Sherwood did go, he lived all the time in the same house where his brother roomed. Furthermore, from the beginning of the 1890s onward there had been an especially large migration to Chicago by Clyde people, who added the attachments of friendship to the magnetic pull that the metropolis always exerted on Midwest towns. The house where Karl and Sherwood would room together was that of the Padens, a Clyde family who, until the father died in 1889, had lived next door to the Hurds. Young Clifton Paden (who later changed his name to John Emerson, became a movie producer, and married Anita Loos) had been in school with Sherwood and, though a newsboy rival in Clyde, would become a close friend during Sherwood's first residence in Chicago. Then, too, just as going to Chicago would be an exciting adventure for a restless wanderer, there was correspondingly little to hold Sherwood in Clyde with his mother dead now some two years, his sister in charge of the younger boys, his father as boastful as ever and even more officious, and any possibility of marrying Bertha Baynes contingent at least on Sherwood's finding permanent work. Although hard years had followed the closing of the 1893

Exposition, Chicago provided job opportunities immeasurably beyond what Clyde offered.[65]

This last reason was probably the strongest one for going to Chicago. Despite the picture Anderson was to give of the semiautobiographical Sam McPherson as one whom all the town elders encouraged, in actuality only Superintendent Ginn is known to have tried to help him, though doubtless there were plenty, as he himself was to write again and again, who advised him that money made the mare go. Bright, resourceful, and likeable though he was, young Sherwood Anderson was also known in Clyde as a dreamer and had repeatedly demonstrated an unwillingness to stay with any job long. He had long since turned down the chance of a college education, and he had no training for a trade except for that of his father's as painter, which he did not wish to follow. Karl had a talent as an artist, the town and Sherwood knew, and Stella had one as a teacher except that her mother's death had forced her into the role of homemaker; Sherwood, as far as anyone, including himself, could see, had no talent for anything specific, though this did not lessen his ambition for an as-yet-unspecified success. Not having the advantage of hindsight, the townspeople could regard Sherwood, for all their fondness of him, only as a young man with no future beyond that of hundreds and millions of other unskilled workers, a son of Emma Anderson but Irwin Anderson's son as well, hence a drifter and a talker with too much of his father in him to come to any solid good. Did he think Anderson would ever be famous when he left Clyde, Herman Hurd was asked years later. No, he replied, his only feeling when Sherwood left was that he had lost his best friend.[66]

Conceivably Anderson might have stayed in Clyde, found an occupation, married Bertha or some other local girl, and been invited into the Masons, "arriving" in the town's estimation with the help of Herman Hurd. Yet if such had been his future, the deep contrary impulses that family, town, and factory had fostered would most likely have continued to dispute within him, caught as he was between action and dream, reality and fancy, surface and inwardness, between the desire to wander and the love of community, between, on the one hand, his urgent hunger for success, the glimpsed sensuousness of money and power, and the redress of old humiliation over poverty, and, on the other, his obscure, dense, inarticulate, probably even as yet unformulated resistance to the use of people for material ends. Such a future could well have turned an unfocused young man into a middle-aged grotesque, estranged from the very experience that was to feed his imagination as a writer. Only by leaving Clyde could Anderson in more senses than one possess it as Winesburg.

Though the time is not established beyond question, Anderson very likely left Clyde for Chicago in the early summer or late spring of 1897. In the *Memoirs* he describes a farewell scene with an unnamed Clyde girl, certainly Bertha Baynes, on a summer evening "before definitely leaving for Chicago," and summer as the season of his departure is supported by the vague recollection of Herman Hurd. Yet in Anderson's one other extended comment about his leaving, in "City Plowman," a piece he wrote nearly forty years later in praise of Alfred Stieglitz, he speaks of going to Chicago "for the first time" in the spring when, he remembered, "the dogwood was blooming." Out of neglect, or by error, or perhaps even from a feeling that it didn't matter much anyway, the *Enterprise* unfortunately failed to note the date of his leaving and thus settle the question, an omission that would seem, whatever the cause, to be a comment on Sherwood's social marginality in his hometown. But between recollections either or neither of which may be factually accurate and where temporal difference is perhaps only a matter of a few weeks at most, it mattered little. A dramatic farewell to Bertha the night before his departure or the next day on the platform of the scrollsaw-Gothic railroad station, the usual undemonstrative farewell to his sister and brothers, perhaps even to his father now that the son was going away, these would in any case have been in character for Sherwood. Like many other young Clyde men before and after him he would have stood on the station platform, heard the four blasts of the Chicago-bound train in the distance, seen it grow larger down the track lined by the backs of houses and stores of his town. As the steam engine came grinding and hissing to a stop, he would have stepped up into the nearest coach car, seated himself, waved to any family and friends on the platform, and felt the train begin to pull him away from Clyde, though still leaving Clyde within him as a background on which to paint the dreams of his manhood.[67]

3

Young Man from the Provinces

1.

The Chicago to which Sherwood Anderson came, probably in the depression spring or summer of 1897, added sensory and emotional details to the picture of industrialism that had been sketched for him by his factory life in Clyde, Ohio, and Erie, Pennsylvania. For him as for any small town man the city was a fascinating, at first unnerving experience, one reflected perhaps in the sensations of the country boy Hugh McVey in *Poor White,* who spends two hours between trains in the "huge commercial city at the foot of Lake Michigan" and is frightened by the rushing, disordered crowds, the noise, the dirt, the ugliness, the "pall of black smoke [that] covered the sky." According to the *Memoirs* Sherwood always remembered his first impression of "the tall buildings, the crowds, so strange and terrible." He stuck close to his older brother, who had met him at the train. The immensity of the city made him feel small; the streets ran out of nowhere into nothing.[1]

Fortunately, Karl had spent several years in Chicago already. On first arriving in the fall of 1892 he had lived for perhaps two years in a variety of boarding houses. Meanwhile a Clyde man, Harkness Lay, a carpenter and contractor, had come to Chicago with his son Frank at about the same time because of the brief building boom that preceded the Exposition; and the following spring, his wife and his daughter Bessie joined them there. Meeting Mr. Lay one time, Karl mentioned that he was tired of boarding houses and would like to live with Clyde people. Mr. Lay invited him to move in with his family in their house on the far West Side near Garfield Park; so Karl lived with the Lays from 1894 to 1896 as the family moved through a succession of houses. Finally by early 1897, Karl decided that he was having to travel too far from his work, and he took up residence many blocks closer to the Loop at 708 (now 2045) Washington Boulevard, just west of what is now Damen Avenue. This was the home of another Clyde family, the Padens, who had moved to the city in mid-1893. Since Mrs. Paden and Mrs. Lay were sisters, the two families were close. Both families had been prominent in Clyde, Karl was accepted by all as a close friend, and Sherwood himself had of course known Clifton Paden well in Clyde. It was to the Paden home that Karl brought Sherwood after meeting him at the train on his arrival in Chicago.[2]

Half a century later Karl was to recall, not his younger brother's awe of the city, which Sherwood may have concealed or even exaggerated in retrospect to dramatize the rawness of his youth, but rather "his good-natured assurance" that at once "captured the hearts" of the Padens.

He told everyone on the day of his arrival that he would first get a job as a grocery clerk, and then progress upwards in a short space of time.

The following evening, Sherwood appeared at dinner with the exalted announcement that he, that day, had landed ten grocery jobs. "I'm to go to work at one of them tomorrow morning," he told us. "I haven't made up my mind at which one. I'll flip a coin. See which fellow is to have my services."

As it turned out, Sherwood did not take any of the ten positions. A girl who happened to be visiting at the house that night was so impressed by his self-confidence that she took him to her father, the owner of a large cold-storage plant. Sherwood spent the next two years wheeling meat in and out of frigid vaults.

Whether the account is accurate in all its details or not, from the time Sherwood arrived in Chicago until he left in the spring of 1898 he worked in a cold-storage warehouse "just across the river in Chicago's North Side." The few bits of evidence now available indicate that the warehouse was probably that of the Western Union Cold Storage Company, which then actually occupied a half-dozen warehouse buildings grouped on the southeast corner of North State Street and Michigan (now Hubbard) Street, made a specialty of "the cold storage of eggs, fruit, cheese, and butter," and by 1900 was said to contain the "Largest cold storage and freezing houses in the world." Anderson's job was the laborious, unskilled one of piling barrels of apples and crates of eggs in great cold rooms for ten hours a day at a wage, he recalled in the *Memoirs,* of two dollars a day. Unlike Beaut MacGregor, the hero of Anderson's novel *Marching Men,* who piles barrels of apples in a warehouse similar to the Western's, he at first found the work exhausting and would come back to the Paden home "so dog-tired at night that he was just all to pieces."[3]

Despising the work, he found some consolation in his friendship with Clifton Paden, perhaps a year older that he, who had briefly considered becoming an Episcopal minister, had taught school, and had worked in a

printing office in Tiffin, Ohio, before coming in 1893 to Chicago and a
steady job as a clerk in Marshall Field's wholesale house. Charming, generous, unpredictable, Clifton maintained a loyal, lifelong friendship with
Anderson; but from boyhood he had had a compulsive fear of poverty, and
his ruthless desire to get money made Sherwood at the time even more dissatisfied with his own lack of future. Closest to Clifton, he nevertheless
was good friends with the other young people in the Paden and Lay families and their associates who, according to Bessie Lay's later recollections,
"all thought he had charm and qualities that made him interesting." Both
Karl and Sherwood, she recalled, joined eagerly in the "idealistic" talk
about the state of the world and what to do about it that these young
Clyde people much went in for. The group of friends were all interested in
the arts as well; Karl was of course attending painting classes at the Art Institute, Clifton Paden had been an amateur actor and musician, and Bessie
Lay was studying music, having already had a year at the Heidelberg College conservatory in Tiffin.[4]

Though Sherwood was accepted into this group and spent much of his
leisure time with them, he could not help comparing his situation unfavorably with theirs. Coming from comfortable homes in Clyde and much
given to reminiscences about that town where their families had been
prominent, most of these young people had jobs superior to his in status
and pay and could look forward to more specific futures. Detesting his
own wearying unskilled labor that looked forward to nothing, he desperately longed to find something bigger and better to do whatever it might
be, and, according to Jeanette Paden, he "talked about his dissatisfaction
and unhappiness all the time."[5]

One way out of the trap could be education. Clifton Paden became a
student some time in 1897, and perhaps following his and Karl's example,
Sherwood himself decided to go to night school at the Lewis Institute, a
private academic and technical school, the main building of which, in
massive sandstone and brick, had just been completed in 1896 at the
southeast corner of West Madison and South Robey (now Damen) Street,
hardly more than a block from the Paden home. On October 25, 1897,
Anderson began taking advanced arithmetic and possibly advanced penmanship for a term that ran for five months, with a two weeks recess
at Christmas time (December 17, 1897, through January 2, 1898), and
ended March 25, 1898. For five dollars tuition he received class instruction every Monday and Thursday evenings from 7:30 to 9:30, approximately an hour for each subject, and could also attend special lectures on
Friday nights. Possibly he attended a weekly series of six lectures on Roman culture, "The Debt of the Nineteenth Century to Rome," and since
he subsequently went through a "Browning period" during his early advertising years in Chicago, he may very well have attended the series of six

lectures given by Associate Professor Edwin H. Lewis of the institute's regular academic staff on "Browning and Tennyson as Thinkers." Lectures on the treatment of "Human Emotions," "Human Conduct," and "Human Destiny" by each of these Victorian poets might have attracted the interest of an idealistic young man who lived with a group of other young people concerned with ideas and the arts, a young man, moreover, very eager to get on. If he was not too tired after work to read on the alternate nights of the week, his tuition ticket gave him free access to the shelves of the six-thousand-volume library of the institute between 7 to 10 PM.[6]

In the *Memoirs* Anderson recalled that by going to night school he hoped to move upward from unskilled labor to white-collar clerk and that he "tried to study book-keeping and accounting but it was no go." Fatigued by his work in the cold warehouse, he at once fell asleep in class and was sent home by the teacher. But in this passage Anderson's memory was tricking him or he was tricking his reader, or very likely, given his literary method, he was trying to get at the essence of his Chicago situation, the feeling of frustration and entrapment that then possessed him. The class report of John C. South, his instructor in advanced arithmetic shows that, contrary to the *Memoirs* account, he stayed awake most of the time and studied very successfully. During the entire five-months term from October to March, Sherwood was absent only twice, and of the thirty-two students in the class he ranked second highest in "Final Estimate," just one point below the top man. The course was a practical one in "commercial arithmetic" and corresponded to the regular academic division course in accounting: "A study of common and decimal fractions, addition, percentage, discounts, commission, insurance, exchange, bills, settlements, averaging accounts, and profit and loss. Special work in mental calculations." The textbook used was O. W. Powers's *The New Business Arithmetic;* the "ground covered was from page 150 to page 275, omitting Compound Interest, Taxes and Duties"; and the instructor, an excellent one judging by his written comments, taught so as to "fix the principles of each subject in mind and enable the pupil to do independent work." By October of 1897 Sherwood must have toughened to his hard work and presumably was alert enough at night and on weekends to exploit his educational opportunities if he wished. These need not have been solely commercial; the institute's library was available, and in fact it may have been at this time that he was introduced to the poetry of Walt Whitman, first, he was to claim, in a volume bowdlerized by mutilation on the part of the book's owner, but then in one which included all the verses in which "Old Walt had . . . expressed . . . his healthy animalism."[7]

Meanwhile, Karl Anderson had already left the Paden home in September of 1897 for a New York venture. After quickly finding a job on a newspaper doing illustrations, "a method of expression in which he was ill at ease and never happy," Karl was subsequently fired and then, apparently in the spring of 1898, went to Springfield, Ohio, to become the "resident artist" on the *Woman's Home Companion*. His brother's being off "living an artist's life" in New York supplied Sherwood with yet another reminder of his own present lack of success. Friendship with the Lays and Padens, the night-school work with its uncertain promise of access to a white-collar job, a brief engagement to a girl about whom nothing is known except her name, Mabel Harper, and, according to the *Memoirs,* an affair with a plain, love-starved woman who lived in a tiny apartment far out on the city's West Side, a setting he was to reproduce in his tale, "The Man's Story"—none of these could assuage his sense that his young life was already at a dead end. Like many other young men before and after him, he took refuge from his personal problems in an historical event.[8]

2.

Considering his own and his friends' interest in current events, it is likely that Anderson had followed the newspaper accounts of the Cuban Insurrection, and he could hardly have avoided the excited reports about the sinking of the battleship *Maine* in Havana harbor on the night of February 15, 1898. In later years Anderson was mostly to belittle the small part he played in the Spanish-American War, and there is no way of knowing for certain how much at that time the idealistic young man may actually have sympathized with the Cubans in their struggle for freedom from Spanish rule or favored armed intervention by the United States in that struggle. One suspects that his motives were not so cynically self-regarding as he subsequently described them, but he did recognize the possibility of war with Spain as a chance to escape from the rut of unskilled labor, to see new places and people, even, perhaps, to be a hero. Very shortly after the sinking of the *Maine* he had written Captain Gillett of Clyde's Company I: "If by any chance this war scare amounts to anything, and the company is called, please telegraph me 708 Washington Boulevard and I will be with you." The note was printed in the *Enterprise* for March 3, 1898, to illustrate Clyde's readiness for combat. Sherwood's own qualified readiness appeared in his comment in a letter to Karl, who was still in New York: "I prefer yellow fever in Cuba to living in cold storage in Chicago."[9]

During March and into April, the war crisis developed, the Hearst and certain other newspapers finding patriotism profitable and feeding the honest desire of many Americans to come to Cuba's rescue. While Company I drilled intensively in Clyde, Anderson completed his successful term at the Lewis Institute on March 25 and apparently made arrangements for his younger brother Irwin to come to Chicago, take over his room at the Padens', and find a job. Perhaps he stayed in Chicago until just after April 22, when President McKinley ordered a blockade of the Cuban coast around Havana, and Congress authorized him to call for volunteers from the states for the army; for on or around that date Sherwood may have telegraphed Captain Gillett, asking again "to be notified when the company was called out." But Anderson was certainly back in Clyde by April 25—the day that Congress formally declared war on Spain—to be enrolled for service, to enjoy the acclamation of his hometown for coming to his country's defense, and to find that Bertha Baynes had become engaged to Clarence Whittaker, the watchmaker in Sanford's jewelry store who subsequently married her. That Monday evening of the twenty-fifth, Sherwood probably had to escort Stella to the hall in Terry's Opera House where "the ladies of Clyde . . . had prepared a magnificent banquet to which the soldier boys and their parents, wives and ladies were invited, over 150 plates being laid."

> After the banquet the tables were taken out of the hall and the reception and speech-making began. Addresses were made by the local clergy and attorneys. The hall was crowded to its fullest capacity and hundreds were unable to obtain admittance. The scene was one long to be remembered, and several ladies were overcome and had to be carried from the hall.
> Later on, when the crowd had mostly gone home, the floor was cleared for a dance, and many of the boys remained until a late hour to indulge in this pleasure with the ladies.

Except for the lack of Bertha at his side, Sherwood must have felt that his dramatic imagination was for once equaled by reality, for during the banquet the "long expected and anxiously awaited call to arms came to the boys of Company I. . . ."[10]

The excitement and the feverish glamour continued for several days, and the experiences of the McPherson Guard were probably representative of the other state units that were being frantically and confusedly called up by an unready national government. Early on April 26, Sherwood and the fifty-odd other men of his company assembled at their armory and were escorted by the GAR veterans of Clyde—Irwin Anderson surely among them—through a wildly emotional crowd "numbering thousands" to the train that would take them to Toledo. Possibly, as he describes the occasion in the *Memoirs*, Sherwood took his revenge on Bertha for her engagement to the noncombatant Clarence Whittaker by turning his head away scornfully as he marched past her in the crowd; but considering the Whittakers' continued hospitality to Anderson on his subsequent brief visits to Clyde, none of the three could have felt permanently insulted.[11]

Arriving in Toledo, the members of Company I were quartered in the city's big castellated brick armory with some one thousand other men from seven counties in northwest Ohio making up the Sixteenth Regiment of the Ohio National Guard. That night the regiment held a dress parade, which was watched by many girls, and then the young soldiers, enthusiastic about everything except the crowded and uncomfortable sleeping quarters, sang and yelled late into the night, since, as one Clyde boy exclaimed, "there is nothing like a soldier's life." At 8:40 on the morning of the twenty-ninth, the regiment began its march out past the iron gates of the armory to the Union Station along streets crowded to the roofs of the flag- and bunting-covered buildings with people who had come in from miles around Toledo. The "unearthly, discordant" scream of tugboat whistles from the harbor joined with a band's blare and continuous cheers from the crowds, as the regiment, escorted by the city's police and G. A. R. veterans under Civil War battle flags, moved on "with that swinging step, with blanket-bags strapped in place, with canteens swung at the side, and with one thousand polished gun barrels glistening in the morning sun." When the regiment had reached that station and filed into two waiting train sections, the crowd surged into the train yard, covering the tracks, blocking the movement even of the switching engines, rushing toward the open windows of the trains. "Girls insist on bidding boys, whom they have never seen, good-bye; women bestow motherly blessings on acquaintance and stranger alike; men give all of them words of cheer." Promptly at ten o'clock the first section of the train, soon followed by the second, began pulling slowly out of the station, all the engine bells in the yard clanging, all the city's whistles shrieking, the crowd cheering, weeping, waving flags of their country and Cuba Libre. So "Patriotic hearts give expression to their feelings for the cause of liberty and humanity." Irwin Anderson's son must again have felt that reality was measuring up to fancy.[12]

All along the line from Toledo to Columbus people came out to cheer and wave at the troops, and when the men debarked from the trains at the capitol city in midafternoon of that April 29, they marched through streets lined with yet more shouting, flag-waving crowds. But then some of the other aspects of that most operatic of American wars began to appear. The new regiment marched six miles out of Columbus to Camp Bushnell and arrived tired to find no tents, no food, and a wet campground left in a mess by previous regiments. The colonel, William V. McMaken, fortunately an experienced and efficient National Guard officer, began winning his great popularity in the regiment by demanding and obtaining tents and straw for tick-beds by nightfall. Beginning the next morning, army routine closed in with three hours of drill a day, dress parade each evening, and a diet of beef, pork, eggs, and beans. Still, a sergeant of the McPherson Guard could write back to the *Enterprise* that "The boys of Co. I do their share of guard duty and other duties required of them without a murmur, and the new recruits are doing fine"; and on May 4, "A representative of the *Enterprise* visited Camp Bushnell . . . and found the boys all well and in good spirits." Loyally the representative asserted that "The Clyde company is one of the best on the grounds, and has excellent quarters which are kept in fine condition."[13]

Having learned from the Civil War the dangers of relying on the state militia system, the War Department had persuaded through Congress a volunteer bill that, despite major concessions to the state-organized National Guard, at least assured the buildup of the army under ultimate federal control. National Guard regiments, however, were taken into the army as units, and each man was allowed to choose whether to enlist for Federal service or to return home. At Camp Bushnell at the beginning of May, Company I was ordered to recruit eighty-four men for service, and Anderson, unwilling to go back to his dead-end job at the cold storage company and drawn by the adventure of soldiering, chose to enlist. Out of the company six men decided to return to Clyde as soon as they could be released. They were within their rights, but the feeling was so strong against the "quitters" that, as Anderson describes it in the *Memoirs,* they were mobbed by their comrades and painfully beaten, Sherwood joining in the assault but then in self-recognition discovering that "It was the first time I knew how cruel men in the mass could be."[14]

On May 11, 1898, the first American casualties of the war occurred during a daring raid to cut the telegraph cables at the entrance to Cienfuegos Bay—into which Company I would sail eight months later for its landing in Cuba—and on May 12, Sherwood Anderson, age twenty-one, and the rest of his company lined up at Camp Bushnell, held their caps across their chests with their left hands, stretched their right hands straight up, and were sworn into the United States service. Anderson was now a private in Company I of the Sixth Regiment Ohio Volunteer Infantry. The regiment retained its National Guard officers and its very casual democratic discipline, based partly on the Guard organization and tradition, partly on the fact that most of the companies were in each case made up of men from small Ohio communities who had known each other for years and would presumably have to live in the same town together after the war. "I was a soldier," Anderson recalled in the *Memoirs,* "and I had picked the right war. . . . I had got what I wanted. After my experience as a laborer the drilling seemed to me play. We were well fed. We had warm clothes."[15]

On May 17, the regiment entrained at Columbus and headed south through Cincinnati into "a glorious mountain country," as Anderson remembered it, "small town boys, farmers' sons seeing the great world." Women and girls flocked to the railroad stations to bring baskets of food and throw kisses as in some romantic novel. The Sixth was headed for

Camp George H. Thomas in Chickamauga National Park in the north-west corner of Georgia, the chief concentration point for all new regiments, where, as Walter Millis writes in *The Martial Spirit,* "over forty-four thousand men were dumped . . . in the last two weeks of May." Arriving at Chattanooga, Tennessee, on May 18, the regiment moved across the Georgia line to Rossville that evening, and on the following morning marched the twelve dusty miles to Camp Thomas through hot southern weather. The Sixth Ohio was better equipped than some of the National Guard regiments pouring daily into the disorder of Camp Thomas; but cooks were as scarce in the camp as medical supplies, Anderson and his fellows had to eat hardtack instead of bread and butter, and water was in such short supply that each regiment had to guard its ration. Although groves of trees shaded the tents from the sun, those groves would prevent the ground from drying out when heavy rains flooded the camp in July, and as a result typhoid and dysentery began to break out.[16]

From the references to Anderson in reports to the Clyde *Enterprise,* however, it is fairly clear that the war was not going badly for him despite the drill, the disorganization, and the monotony. He was detailed to guard a man in the Fremont company who had been arrested for sleeping on guard duty, and "Sherwood seemed to enjoy it"; another report shows him happily horsing around in time-honored military fashion: "Joel Elliott said the other day that he was not afraid of a lizard, but when Sherwood Anderson wet his finger and put it on Joel's neck one night the boys thought he was going through the top of the tent. . . ." He and six other men went to Chattanooga at least on June 4; and, recalling the tales told by his father and other Clyde veterans, he may have gone with friends to view the fought-over ground about the city from which Sherman, with McPherson the former Clyde boy on his left flank, had taken off on his Atlanta campaign just thirty-four years earlier. Yet, as is so marked a characteristic in Anderson, he seems much of the time to have preferred one form of the imaginative life to actuality. Though the other men in Company I liked Sherwood and found him invariably good-tempered, they were amused by his constant and concentrated reading, a pastime that may explain the report in the Clyde *Enterprise* for June 30 that "Jobby Anderson puts in most of his time at the Y.M.C.A.," presumably since here books and magazines would be most available. Years later a Company I man recalled that

Sherwood was never very tidy about his personal appearance, and had the peculiar faculty of sitting or lying around our mess bunk (as we were bunked together) reading, and a dozen of our boys could be laughing and talking around the tent, and he would read never hearing a word we spoke, he was so interested in what he was reading, which many times would be a Dead Wood Dick, or some other adventurous dime novel.

Under this spell of reading, in fact, Anderson may have begun to think of becoming a writer himself; for when William Holst, a fellow soldier, managed to "pry him loose" from a novel long enough to propose a trip to Lookout Mountain and asked him, "What's the idea of reading?" Sherwood replied, "I like the stuff and some day I'm going to write books."[17]

Such a remark need not be taken too seriously, but in view of Anderson's ultimate career it cannot be ignored, and in either case his reading jag at crowded Camp Thomas is itself significant. Released from a Chicago winter into the lush warmth of late spring in the South, a region that later often attracted him, he was released also from a hard, pointless routine into an easier monotony that gave him little responsibility and considerable leisure. No wonder his comrades found him always amiable if often unmovable; he was practically on holiday. Set down, then, by an impersonal government in a place that invited mere loafing when one was off duty and where the very landscape was marked by the recent deeds of heroes, he chose to immerse himself instead in imagined lives. So even if his remark about some day writing books was only a casual one with little conscious meaning in it, unconsciously he was even then being readied for serious intent.

Still, despite the addiction to reading, Sherwood must have seemed a more than average soldier to Edward Rydman, the big, mustachioed National Guard veteran who succeeded Gillett as captain of Company I; for on July 1 Anderson was appointed one of the company's six new corporals. The only other record of him during that summer at Camp Thomas is the notation that he was "sick in quarters" from August 9 to 19, for which reason he would not have been able to participate in any celebration on August 12, the day when representatives of Spain and the United States signed the armistice protocol that officially ended the less than four months of hostilities between their countries. On August 27, two weeks after the armistice, the Sixth Ohio, still incomplete in its combat training but caught up in the Department of the Army's plans, was marched back to Rossville from Camp Thomas and sent by train to Knoxville, Tennessee, from which on the following day it was marched to nearby Camp Poland.[18]

Camp Poland was considerably better duty than Camp Thomas, though with an irony appropriate to this war the only losses that Company I sustained during its service were the deaths here of two men from typhoid weeks before the regiment landed in peaceful Cuba. (Corporal Anderson was one of the signers of the routine "Resolution of respect" sent home on the occasion of the first man's death on October 5.)[19] Unlike the overcrowded Thomas, Poland held only one other regiment, the First West Virginia; and the "Twin Regiments," as they were called, were encamped on either side of a narrow gauge railroad that went into Knoxville, train fare being only a nickel. Knoxville was hospitable out of patriotism and the desire for the soldiers' trade that, according to the *Memoirs*, had prompted the removal of the two regiments there through political influence. The Knoxville ladies had greeted the Sixth with tables of food spread over a great field, and Anderson had then met "the daughter of some prominent citizen of the town," he claimed in the *Memoirs*, a girl whom he courted romantically during his leave time in the city. William Holtz recalled that Anderson "was popular and could always get a girl. . . . He could go into any parlor or church. I never saw him drink. He was a gentleman in every respect." When he was not on duty or seeing his girl in the city, Sherwood remained plunged in the reading that fed his imagination. His taste for the adventurous apparently continued, for in mid-December he was reading Henryk Sienkiewicz's long historical novel of seventeenth-century Poland's wars, *With Fire and Sword,* a translation of which had appeared that year in a "Popular Edition."

Relationships between the Twin Regiments were friendly. On Thursday, November 24, the First West Virginia invited the Sixth Ohio to Thanksgiving dinner. Bugles sounded the call at noon, turkey stuffed with oyster sauce was served at long tables, and the afternoon was filled with "oratory, music and rhyme." But two days after Christmas the Sixth Ohio marched out of the winter quarters they had carefully built and entrained for Charleston, South Carolina. They arrived there on the morning of December 29, embarked on the U.S. Transport *Minnewaski* in the evening, and on the thirtieth sailed for Cuba. On the last day of glorious 1898, the troops were mustered for pay at sea, at midnight fireworks sparkled over the dark ocean to bring in the new year, and during the following night the *Minnewaski* rounded Cape Maysi, the easternmost point of Cuba. Passing Santiago, where the men saw the wrecks of Cervera's Spanish fleet still strung along that mountainous coast after the American naval victory of the previous July, the transport steamed at noon on January 3 into landlocked Cienfuegos Bay, about midway along the southern coast of Cuba. On the following day the troops disembarked, marched through the broad, straight streets of Cienfuegos between rows of cheering Cubans, and found white tents already pitched for them in ordered rows in front of a band of palm trees four miles beyond the city. For the first time Sherwood Anderson and other young men from Clyde, Ohio, were in a foreign land.[20]

The Sixth and other regiments had been sent to Cienfuegos to do "guardduty to keep order and try to establish government, and protect plantations," the city being the commercial center for huge sugar plantations in the hinterland. The duties were easy enough and at first consisted mainly of keeping an eye on the unconfined and friendly Spanish soldiers who were waiting to be repatriated, though Anderson mentions in the *Memoirs* an idyllic excursion against bandits, the detachment complete with major, major's wife and baby, and cow to furnish the baby's milk. If such an expedition did occur, it may have been while Company I was stationed at the smaller city of Sagua la Grande, directly across the island of Cuba from Cienfuegos, where from January 26, 1899, until its return to regiment on March 13 the company was encamped just outside the entrance to a Spanish prison. Upon returning to "Camp Sixth Ohio," Anderson and the rest of Company I went to Provost Guard Camp at Cienfuegos on March 26 and remained there until they left Cuba four weeks later.[21]

Soldiering was not all duty assignments, however. Perhaps Sherwood continued his reading, but a letter dated January 9, 1899, written by Company I's first lieutenant establishes him as having been on at least one sightseeing expedition near Cienfuegos.

The other day I went into an old Spanish fort a little way from camp for relics, and I found about a million. I was with Harry Sergeant and Sherwood Anderson, and when we came out Harry said, "What are those things on me?" I looked and told him that they were fleas. Then I looked at myself and I will bet I had a million on me.

Not all the sightseeing could have entailed such unpleasant consequences. Marching through Cienfuegos for the first time, the small-town boy from Ohio had been struck by "this new strange semi-tropical place" and by the "strange" buildings with "little balconies on which stood dark, and, to our eyes, very beautiful women." Cienfuegos, then a city of some thirty thousand people, had been settled as recently as 1819; but it had a fine cathedral facing a huge square, the Plaza de Armas, shaded with laurels and royal palms. The city itself was built on a peninsula projecting into the "shining water" of the long bay, and to the east rose the "graceful outlines of the Trinidad Mountains." Sagua la Grande in turn, was a smaller, older, cleaner city with "the usual Plaza de Armas," fronted by hotel, casino, "old yellow" church, and stores. The cafes and barbershops that filled Sagua la Grande bore un-Clyde-like signs: "Without Rivals," "Without Competition," "The Elegant," "The Golden Lion." In the *Memoirs* Anderson recalled taking "long strolls" through the exotically beautiful countryside: "Some of us had picked up a little Spanish. We went into houses. We talked to people. We hired little native ponies and rode through the country and into the hills." His friend Herman Hurd, who had stayed home in Clyde because of "heart trouble" (that is, he had married Jennie Baker only a few months before the war with Spain), remembered that Sherwood never talked much about Cuba after his return, but that he had seemed to enjoy the experience, for Cuban life was "just what he had liked all along." Anderson appears to have reacted as did L. W. Howard, a captain in the Sixth Ohio, who wrote in the regiment's *War Album* of his own "First Impressions of Cuba." Expecting to find a people "gloomy, unhappy and despairing" after years of oppression, Howard found them "something very different."

There is fullness of life in Cuba, with exuberance of animal spirits and light-hearted gaiety. There are few care-worn faces to be seen in the crowded streets, the busy arcades and spacious plazas. The cafes and restaurants are thronged day and night with a pleasure-loving, rollicking population, and there gathers nightly a motley concourse, joyous in mood and mercurial in temper, to listen to the feeble murmur of a Spanish band, or to laugh and chatter by the hour over frivolous jests. The times may be hard, but Cubans disport themselves with intensity of enjoyment.

The enchanted captain's "First Impressions" rises to a peroration that, despite stylistic differences, startlingly parallels Anderson's own praise in the early 1920s for the quality of life still to be found in the southern city of New Orleans.

Those who find the unceasing activity of American life wearing upon the nerves are refreshed by the contemplation of a race that neither hurries nor frets, but basks in the atmosphere that is not too enervating to be positively enfeebling. To watch a Cuban unroll and remake a cigarette and then deliberately light it and lazily smoke it is to get a new idea of the refinement to which the sweets of indolence can be carried.[22]

The first way in which the Spanish-American War experience was important to Anderson, then, was precisely the opportunity it afforded "to observe the languid, pulsating movement of life" in a society where tradesmen could sleep "indifferent to the chances for trade." Here was a country not subservient to clock time, not bound by industrialism with its dirt, noise, and disorder, its alienated workers, its production of interchangeable machine parts and standardized minds. Here was a people who held the notion of leisure as a form of art and art as a form of leisure that was to become one of the recurrent themes in Anderson's own subsequent discussions of art and the imagination. Here was a lucky moment in history where one witnessed, where one experienced, despite minimum military restrictions, the joy of freedom. In recalling the months in Cuba in the *Memoirs*, Anderson showed little or no concern either for the suffering of the Cubans in their struggle for independence or the efforts by both Americans and Cubans toward reconstruction after the War. Instead he celebrated the warm, drunken fraternization of American and Spanish soldiers the first night after the Sixth Ohio arrived in Cienfuegos and the "kind of universal embracing" that marked the "capture"—if, indeed, it happened at all—of the plantation village of Caratura by himself and two West Virginian soldiers. The best part of Cuba was the alternative way of life it offered to a young man divided in his desires but still, he thought, centered on the drive to a business success.[23]

Except in the *Memoirs,* Anderson wrote little about his army life and even less about Cuba; but both here and in *A Story Teller's Story,* he emphasized the second important effect of his Spanish-American War experience as a whole. This was the almost visionary insight it gave him into what he called in the *Memoirs* the "little understood impulse that is in all men to lose self in the mass," an impulse that has "a kind of relief in it, perhaps to the pain of living," an impulse that contains "something strangely noble, strangely mean," that produces both heroism and "unbelievably cruel acts," that is both "labor's greatest weapon" and "the strength of fascism." One such moment of insight, resembling though not attaining the classic instances of mystical experience in its combination of heightened, camera-sharp awareness of concrete detail and its intense melting sense of universality, came to Anderson on a mass training march before going to Cuba. Dropping out of the ranks with permission to remove a stone in his shoe, he sat hidden in a wood, watching row after row of men pass, weeping at the intense feeling of containing in himself the gigantic strength of "thirty thousand men," of being "in myself, something huge, terrible, and at the same time noble." He was himself, he whispered, and "something else too." Returning to camp, he went at once to his tent and cot: "I did not want to eat. I was a man in love. I was in love with the thought of the possibilities of myself combined with others."[24]

Correct in detail or not, the general truthfulness, the essence, of the account seems certain, containing as it does the germ of his novel *Marching Men,* an attempt "to create a great epic poem of movement in masses." In this book an inspired labor leader organizes American workmen into armies whose silent, undirectioned marching finds them all as one and terrifies the factory owners. At the end of the book one knows that the "Marching Men" will come to nothing, and Anderson himself came to realize that his attempt to create an epic poem in prose had failed. Yet, though he would not be able in this novel to move either intellectually or creatively very far beyond his basic metaphor for rhythmic, ordered oneness, his quasi-mystical vision of separate selves merged into a group would recur in other forms in his life and his art. It would continue to balance against, or rather with, his admiration for democratic individualism

84

and his recognition of individual aloneness. With rare exceptions even his most painful tales of human isolation would imply a larger context, as though these desolate instances were momentary breaks in a magnetic chain, which, felt or not felt, links together all humanity with its mysterious charge. The community of Clyde, Ohio, had prepared him for this insight, as that of Winesburg does George Willard, but it was the military experience that seems to have brought it into sharp focus.[25]

Sherwood may have been consciously pondering such meanings while completing his tour of duty, but probably he more often thought about what to do after being sent home. On April 21, 1899, the Sixth Ohio went aboard the U.S. Transport *Sedgwick* and the next day sailed for Savannah, Georgia, this time rounding the western tip of Cuba and passing Key West. Arriving at the mouth of the Savannah River, the troops disembarked at the disinfecting station there, went through fumigation, and were taken by lighter to Detention Camp on Daufuskie Island, off the shore of South Carolina. On May 2, the regiment went by train from Savannah to Camp MacKenzie, Augusta, Georgia, to await mustering out. At some point during a three-weeks wait at MacKenzie, Anderson presumably participated in a scheme of all the enlisted men to honor the regiment's popular colonel. By prearrangement the men formed a hollow square, and each of the regimental musicians began playing a different tune. When McMaken came to investigate the disturbance, he was seized, taken into the square, addressed by a sergeant with words of praise, and then presented with a "magnificent" sword made in Cincinnati for $500, the hilt "studded in diamonds, emeralds, turquoises and rubies." It was a splendid conclusion for the Sixth's minor and belated part in what Ambassador Hay in London had described to another colonel, Theodore Roosevelt, as "a splendid little war." On May 24, just over a year after being sworn in Sherwood Anderson was mustered out of infantry service at Camp MacKenzie and paid the sum of about $100 due him as a corporal. Then he and the rest of Company I entrained for Clyde.[26]

The Clyde *Enterprise* tells the story of the return of the McPherson Guard from the wars. Early on the morning of the twenty-sixth, the populace began decorating the town with bunting and flags, people crowded in from the countryside, a welcoming committee boarded the train at Tiffin, twenty miles south of town, and the train pulled into a Clyde railroad station that was surrounded with a cheering, shouting, flag-waving throng.

. . . as the soldiers alighted from the train they were immediately surrounded by relatives and friends, and such kissing and handshaking has not been witnessed for many a day. Dinner was waiting in dozens of homes and travel stained soldiers were soon enjoying a square meal at mother's table.

85

Since Karl and Stella were both in Springfield, Ohio, Stella having gone there with young Earl in the preceding February to work in the office of the *Woman's Home Companion,* Sherwood may have had his first square meal at the table of Herman and Jennie Hurd with whom he stayed on his return. On the "torrid" evening of June 6 the town celebrated the return of the heroes with a homecoming banquet and reception marked, according to the *Enterprise,* by "an immense crowd, and exhibition of genuine patriotism, a lavish display of the stars and stripes, and a magnificent supper and flow of oratory." The Spanish-American War could now be considered officially over.[27]

3.

Unofficially also the war was over for Anderson. A fellow veteran of Company I later recalled that "Sherwood had a peculiar make-up and would never speak of the Spanish War and always felt indifferent about it all." There had been no heroics for Company I, of course, and possibly Sherwood was the less inclined to play the patriot because his father had, so to speak, been doing it for him. From about 1896 on, "Major" Anderson had been combining what his former commanding officer called his "great interest in army organizations" and his "considerable dramatic talent" into the active preparation of "entertainments for various Grand Army Posts." His chief contribution to the defeat of Spain had been his direction of a "war drama," the quality of which may be guessed from its name, *Old Glory in Cuba*. On November 17 and 18, 1898, while his son's regiment was still in training near Knoxville, Irwin had successfully staged this piece of patriotic art at Terry's Opera House, "having drilled the members of the cast to a high degree of excellency" and himself being "very effective" in the role of the villain. During December and January he had "drilled" other local amateur groups and had presented the drama in several nearby towns. Irwin's success in this sort of effort would hardly have resulted in a closer bond between the father and his estranged son or in the son's wishing to exploit his own share in a war, which was over before he got to it.[28]

The Anderson family had broken up now that Stella was no longer in Clyde to hold it together. Irwin Anderson soon dropped out of his children's lives altogether; in late 1900 or early 1901 he moved by himself to Connersville, Indiana, where on March 13, 1901, he married a recently divorced lady named Minnie Stevens, had a son by her, and continued his trade as painter and paperhanger, entirely content, it would seem, to be quit of Clyde forever. But Sherwood, at loose ends after his return from Cuba, had an even greater problem than the disintegration of the old Clyde bonds; he had to decide on his own future, and it may well have been his deep concern over the decision that most accounted for his unexpected silence about his part in the war. Both his work in the cold-storage warehouse and his military experience, the latter of which had shown him the limited lives faced by most of his fellow soldiers, made him gradually determine on further education as a ladder over the wall of a blind alley. He talked little about his resolution to the Hurds, but on June 7 he went to Springfield for a month to get advice from Stella and Karl, who found him "very thin, all skin and bones" and troubled about his future. Sherwood must now have been regretting both his refusal of Superintendent Ginn's offer of help and his failure to complete high school, for his lack of training narrowed his chances. He now had two choices left. Either he could return to Chicago, where brother Irwin was succeeding better than Sherwood had, and attend the Lewis Institute, where Irwin had just completed two terms in accounting and arithmetic; or he could stay in Springfield and prepare for Wittenberg College with a year at Wittenberg Academy, the college's preparatory school.[29]

In either case Sherwood needed money, and still undecided, he returned to Clyde in the first week in July, where he found summer work on the farm of Wallace Ballard, a friend of Karl's, of whom he was to write in "City Plowman." Sherwood soon showed his limitations as a farmer. Much to the distress of Ballard, he plowed, not in straight furrows, but in "wigwag lines" and was promptly put to other tasks. Later in the summer he took a job with a threshing outfit owned by Frank J. Wertel. With Wertel, his sons, and another man, Anderson traveled slowly about the countryside between Clyde and Sandusky in a caravan including a water wagon and a huge steam tractor that pulled the heavy grain separator from farm to farm where the harvested wheat was stacked in the fields. According to Wertel, "For one not particularly accustomed to this work he did well. He did feeding and cutting and traveled with the rig." Anderson later recalled that part of his job was also to haul coal from Sandusky and water from anywhere to keep the steam tractor supplied. Since that summer was unusually dry, he had to drive the water wagon and team of horses miles to find a well or go to the bay and then pump strenuously to fill the big boxlike tank for the tractor. Once in an effort to save himself work he drove the wagon into the water of the bay, hoping that the tank would fill itself; but the wagon floated away from the shore, dragging the horses off their feet and forcing him to dive to cut them free. "With the help of some neighboring farmers I finally got all clear but I still remember the heels of the horses swishing past my head as I dived to get them loose." Driving about the farms back from Sandusky Bay, sleeping at night in some farmer's hayloft, working with the land, horses, and men, Anderson stored up the acutely remembered sense of landscape and weather that were to give his subsequent tale "An Ohio Pagan" its mythopoeic quality of nature metamorphosed by the protagonist's imagination into the human.

Perhaps the sustained tone of that minor masterpiece, at once concrete and dreamy, tranquil and intense, derives from the fact that this summer of work in the open air was the last Anderson was to have before the cities closed in on him prisonlike for years.[30]

Early in September, Anderson was back in Clyde making preparations to leave it for the last time in his life except for brief visits. One part of the past to finish was his connection with the McPherson Guard, to which he had been returned on his discharge from U.S. Army service in May. On September 7, a few days before his twenty-third birthday and some six months before his original five-year enlistment would have been up, he received his honorable discharge from the Ohio National Guard "by reason of his own request by reason of Service in the U.S. V[olunteer]. War with Spain," his discharge paper describing him as "5 feet 9 inches high/fair complexion/black eyes/black hair" and of "Excellent" character. On September 11, he left for Springfield to see Karl again, still undecided, according to the *Enterprise*, "whether he will attend Wurtemburg [sic] College, Springfield, or at the Lewis Institute in Chicago." By the sixteenth, when the school year began, he had decided to enroll at Wittenberg Academy on the campus of Wittenberg College.[31]

In 1899, Springfield, Ohio was a city of thirty-eight thousand people, a city proud both of its major industries—publishing and farm implement manufacture—and of its large number of churches. Wittenberg College, Lutheran in origin, firmly Christian in orientation, and at the time insecure in finances, was a circle of some half-dozen buildings on a rolling, wooded campus overlooking the city from its northwest corner. A dozen blocks to the south, at what is now 341 South Wittenberg Avenue, stood a long two-story brick home, originally a farm house, which had been built up to with city buildings, but which retained, as Anderson accurately recalled in the *Memoirs* (1942) "a great stretch of lawn, trees, a big barn." Here at The Oaks, Mrs. Henry Folger ran an inexpensive boarding house, where Karl had already been living and where Sherwood now roomed with him, earning his board and lodging by doing house chores, such as mowing the lawn or shoveling snow from the walks and tending the fires in the big coal base-burner stoves placed in each room. (The Oaks had neither central heating nor inside plumbing.)[32]

Anderson was much older than the other academy students or "preps," and was determined to get as much as possible out of what would prove his last year of formal education. In three terms he took fourteen courses in the college preparatory curriculum: English, German, Physics, Latin, and Plane Geometry. His record shows that he made straight As in the first three subjects throughout the year, while he received Bs in courses in the last two, or a total of eleven As and three Bs for the year. A classmate, J. Fuller Trump, later remembered him as "'a very likable chap with a dry sense of humor that added to his popularity,'" but as essentially a "'lone wolf,'" who was involved in few of the academy's extracurricular activities. Trump summed up his memory of Anderson with a by now familiar image: "Reading with his back against a tree on the Wittenberg campus seemed to be his principal occupation." Although Anderson had at first seemed to Trump, who was only twelve at the time, "somewhat difficult to know, and . . . drawn pretty well into himself," the two became friends. Trump later recalled that he "spent many hours with a small group of youths who made their headquarters Anderson's room in 'The Oaks.'" The conversations were lively.

We talked about everything under the sun. He did most of the talking. He had a genuine sense of humor, but never was there anything malicious in any of his conversations. . . . His trend of thought was along a line that I can best describe as tending to indicate that he had much greater respect for one's intelligence, as compared to one's pocketbook. In other words, Sherwood would have been right in "Seventh's Heaven" sitting in a circle of acquaintances who came out of the slum area but who had intelligence, rather than to find himself the center of the Country Club crowd.

Still, Anderson never seemed to Trump to be particularly radical in his thinking. Other classmates recalled him as energetic, enthusiastic, eager to learn, while a freshman woman in the College remembered him as "retiring, goodlooking, slender" and studious. Yet another "prep" boy, who used to sit beside Anderson in their English and mathematics classes remembered him as "very much a gentleman, soft spoken and a little reserved," so reserved in fact that the boy never learned that Sherwood was a "Spanish American War Veteran" and "five years older than I was." In Springfield as in Clyde, Anderson refused to play the military hero.[33]

Despite his chores and his studies Anderson did find time to participate seriously in one extracurricular activity, and symptomatically it was a verbal one. Public speaking and debate held such great importance in the student life at Wittenberg that only the previous year a part-time instructor in public speaking had been employed after continued insistence by the men and women of the college. Most of this forensic activity was still carried on in the college by three student literary societies, while in the academy the Athenian Literary Society prepared the prefreshmen students for membership in the college organizations. From October 14, when he was enrolled in the society, Anderson was an active Athenian. On Saturday, November 4, he took the affirmative, and lost, in a debate on the question, "Resolved, That England is in the Right in Her War with the Transvaal"; on November 24 he was elected to the society's office of "Critic"; in December he gave a declamation, "The Defense of Dreyfus"; in March he read his essay, "The Mormons." Concerning the content and literary merit of these efforts no record survives, but in his Athenian Society activities Anderson may well have been following on his own initiative the advice to college men by Robert C. Ogden, then manager of New York's Wanamaker Store, as summarized in the college's weekly newspaper, *The Wittenberger:* "No business man has ever made a great fortune by manual labor. Large fortunes are obtained by severe mental application. Other things being equal, the man who has the most mental training, will succeed in business."[34]

But the imaginative side of Anderson was being developed as well as the "Jobby" side. Even more important than Wittenberg Academy in the education of the artist was The Oaks itself, which had developed into a warm little community of what Karl called "people of quickened mentality." The center of this community was Louisa Folger herself, in Sherwood's phrase "a small alert young old figure," remembered by a former boarder, then thirteen-year-old Margarete Hochdoerfer, as having given "charm and a kind of elegance to an inconvenient old home." A "wonderful manager," she was "practical, pleasant but firm" and beloved by her boarders. She delighted in the charade nights they held and though "an excellent housekeeper . . . did not object to tearing up the living room" at such times. She was kind to all her help both black and white, but she took a special liking to her chore boy, and Sherwood remembered long talks full of motherly advice in her room of an evening. Another part of this varied but harmonious community was made up of people in publishing and newspaper work. Karl, of course, did illustrations for the *Woman's Home Companion*, the offices and plant of which were only three blocks away, and another boarder, Frederick McCormick, was completing his fourth year as that magazine's art director before leaving in the summer of 1900 for China and a career as a foreign correspondent and writer on current affairs. Harry Simmons was the enthusiastic advertising manager of the Mast-Crowell-Kirkpatrick Company (later the Crowell Publishing Company), which then published out of Springfield the *Woman's Home Companion* and *Farm and Fireside*. Simmons, who was locally famous for having the picture of his baby in the advertisements for Mennen's Baby Powder, soon started Sherwood off on his business career. Two men often at The Oaks became lifelong friends of Anderson's. George Daugherty, who followed him into advertising in Chicago, was then editor of the Springfield *Morning Press;* while Marco Morrow, who lived near The Oaks with his wife Mary, was editor of several papers and magazines owned by the local publisher Arthur Hosterman. Morrow, a slim, dark-haired, rather elegant man, wrote poetry while also engaged energetically in business. By the end of 1899 he had left for Chicago to join the Frank B. White Company, the advertising agency in which Sherwood was shortly to be employed through Morrow's influence; but during his first few months of acquaintance with Karl Anderson's younger brother he too had become fond of him and considered him promising.[35]

Yet another group of boarders was engaged in teaching. Karl F. Richard Hochdoerfer, professor of modern languages at Wittenberg College since 1891, and his wife Hettie, who later became head of the College's French Department, lived at The Oaks with their daughter Margarete during the year Sherwood was there. Hochdoerfer, who had been educated at Leipzig and at Harvard, where he took his PhD, became a scholar of some distinction and, as an admiring sketch later put it, "possessed wide knowledge and such cultural development as to make him highly appreciated wherever educated people gathered." This kindly German pedagogue with his black beard and heavy eyeglasses took an interest in Sherwood and, as Margarete positively recalled, "did influence him to get more formal education since"—the reason is significant—"he wanted to write." Anderson's ambiguous thanks for Dr. Hochdoerfer's encouragement may have been the rather unfriendly portrait of the "Chicago University" professor in *Marching Men* (pp. 166–68), who is hopefully aware that "'The world is full of unrest . . . ; men are struggling like chicks in the shell,'" but who enrages the semi-inarticulate hero for talking rather than acting his ideas. Another person in education, who probably took her meals at The Oaks, was the very able principal of Central High School, a few blocks to the west. With her Anderson was to remain close through occasional visits and frequent correspondence until his death. A "tall, middle-aged Amazon woman," as Karl recalled her, Trillena White loved equally golf, books, and talk. She and Sherwood often went on walks together in the evening, Trillena, ten years older than he, discussing with him the books that she was advising him to read and in many cases lending to him. Whether or not she directly encouraged him to begin writing himself, her influence—at that time and in the later visits that they exchanged—made him aware of the importance of literature, particularly that written by the traditional masters, in whom Anderson was to be better read than he, the experimentalist, was ever ready to admit. It was Trillena White, he later commented, who was "the first person to really introduce me to literature, for which she had a very fine feeling." Aspects of his relationship with this "friend and advocate for his future" may very well have gone into his portrayal of George Willard's with Kate Swift in *Winesburg, Ohio;* for Margarete Hochdoerfer, who at thirteen did not care for Trillena, was to recall her as "much older than Sherwood, a rather masculine woman, very aggressive, who became interested in her talented students—especially the boys."[36]

All of these boarders, George Daugherty remembered, "liked Sherwood . . . as he went about the leisurely performance of his duties" at The Oaks, "tending the stoves, filling the kerosene lamps, going on errands.

He was respectful to his elders. . . . He had wit, original viewpoints, no bumptiousness—a certain magnetism." Karl Anderson later felt that the whole atmosphere "had no little to do with his deciding to become a writer." Karl seems to have been right in his unspecific way. Although Sherwood had never expressed to his young friend Fuller Trump any desire to be a writer, Margarete Hochdoerfer would later recall such a desire on his part at the time. The stimulating experience of The Oaks apparently came at a critical point, for within a year and a half after leaving Wittenberg he had published his initial piece of writing. First, however, he had to have a job, and one came to him in unexpected fashion.[37]

By the end of his year at the academy, Anderson's funds were low, he still was ready academically to begin at Wittenberg College only as a freshman, and Karl had decided to leave Springfield to study art in Europe. On June 4, 1900, sitting rather strangely among his twenty-five teenage classmates, he went through the academy's commencement exercises in the Wittenberg Chapel. He had been selected as one of eight orators on a lengthy program and for days had been preparing a speech on "Zionism," getting it "all out of books" in the college library. Young Margarete, present in the audience as an academy pupil, was pleased that he delivered his oration "with great enthusiasm" and that it "received much applause." She was much distressed, though, that one trouser leg had caught in the top of his boot when he got up to speak and stayed there throughout his speech and she "so wanted to pull it into place!" A newspaper account of the commencement spoke well of all eight orations on the program but singled Anderson out for praise as

certainly the orator of the class. His deep flexible voice and winning manner completely captivated the audience. The oration was a plea for the Jew, and a finely worded, scholarly address.

The speech and the applause moved Harry Simmons's "warm and impulsive nature" so much that this advertising manager went up to congratulate Anderson after the ceremony and on the spot offered him a job in the Chicago office of the Mast-Crowell-Kirkpatrick Company as an advertising solicitor. Here was Sherwood's chance. With his last formal education behind him, he went off immediately to Chicago, this time not as an unskilled day laborer but as a white-collar man with a white-collar future of rising status and pay.[38]

4.

When Sherwood arrived in Chicago in the early summer of 1900, he took up residence at 1036 (now 2518) West Adams, where he became unofficial head of the family, his father about to go his unconcerned way to a second marriage. Stella and the two youngest brothers, Ray and Earl, had already joined young Irwin in Chicago in the spring of 1899, while Karl at some time during the second half of 1900 left his safe job as illustrator on the *Companion* and on his savings went off to Paris to study drawing and design at the Colarossi Academy. While Stella kept house, Irwin continued his work as either "assistant superintendent" or "bookkeeper," probably at a Chicago meatpacking company, Ray attended school, and Earl studied art. Sherwood began work as an advertising solicitor for the Crowell company under the direction of Joseph A. Ford, the "Western advertising manager for the magazine," who according to the *Memoirs,* was not pleased to have the inexperienced Anderson given the place he had been holding for another man. If, as seems likely, Anderson was describing his own first summer's experience with the firm in a sketch he was to publish four years later, he nevertheless quickly gained a raise and a reputation for ability to sell advertising when a manufacturer-client, disregarding the young solicitor's nervousness and lack of experience, merely corrected a stenographic error in an original order and gave him the true, much larger one.[39]

It is instructive to compare the first version of this experience, published as "The Solicitor" in 1904, with the account in the *Memoirs* written much later. In the 1904 story, "the boy" is

a newcomer in the advertising field, a bright young fellow, fresh from school, who was trying hard to break into the business. He had been dashing about for three months. It was hot summer and things were dull and the boy discouraged.

He is sent by Bradley, his office head, to get a thousand lines of advertising from "Curtis" in Springfield, an unpleasant man whom neither Bradley nor even his superior has had success with. After much nervous hesitation, "the boy" goes to Curtis's office and blurts out his mission "to try and get that thousand line order the other fellows couldn't get." Surprised and amused, Curtis tells him that he is a modest boy and that an order for five thousand lines is already made out. Returning to the Chicago office, the boy starts to tell Bradley "all about it," but the latter says he is "altogether too modest" and raises his salary. In the *Memoirs* Anderson likewise emphasizes his own extreme nervousness, but he pointedly characterizes the client who corrects the stenographic mistake as "very kind, very good natured." Furthermore, writing long after he had rejected business for literature, Anderson asserts, as seems to have been the case, that instead of waiting to tell Ford he exploited his good luck by wiring the fact of an increased order to Harry Simmons in Springfield, who in turn wired Ford to raise his new employee's pay. The central difference between the two versions, however, is not in detail but in tone. Whereas the *Memoirs* account insists that Anderson very early learned the art of cynically manipulating others, the 1904 version earnestly concludes that along with the raise the boy "got the name of being a good solicitor, which perhaps he was. At any rate, he is now, and that's all the story."[40]

Judging solely by his contemporaneous "The Solicitor," one might assume that in his first years in the business world "Jobby" Anderson accepted that world uncritically at face value; judging by the *Memoirs* account, he appears to have learned very early what he later described as "foxiness." As will shortly be seen, his actual attitude was less simplifiable in either direction. Meanwhile he was not, in fact, very happy with the Crowell Company because of his dislike for the job of selling advertising space and for the monotony of office routine when he was not on the road traveling. Probably at some time during the second half of 1901, Marco Morrow, his friend from The Oaks, brought him into the Frank B. White Company, an advertising agency with offices at that time high on the seventeenth floor of the Fisher Building at 279 Dearborn Street. The White Company specialized in handling the advertising of firms manufacturing farming equipment and supplies. Morrow was in charge of the "literary and catalog departments" and was associate editor of a monthly trade periodical called *Agricultural Advertising*. Anderson came into the firm, Morrow later declared, "primarily as copy writer, with traveling and solicitation on the side."[41]

The new job fitted Anderson like one of the new suits that his skill with words soon allowed him to buy. Morrow recalled that he "early manifested a tendency to kick over the traces and to do things in his own way. He wrote good copy, sometimes too original to appeal to the conservative advertisers. But he made good despite the fact that he really saw through much of the bunk that advertising men talked in those benighted days." His knowledge of farmers and farm ways, if not of plowing, and his verbal gifts combined to make him particularly effective in writing copy for mail-order catalogs, and his reputation and salary increased together. Like a character in a Dreiser novel he bought new clothes as a conspicuous sign of success. In evening clothes he could now go to expensive restaurants and the theater; in morning clothes he could attend a fashionable Sunday morning service in the Loop. Apparently at this time also he adopted the long-held habit of occasionally wearing, not a necktie, but a strip of some brightly colored cloth, held together at the throat by a large finger ring. Subsequently when he left business for literature, he would more regularly wear clothes with an arty touch, at once flamboyant and beautifully colored.[42]

Soon after his coming to Chicago as an advertising man, he renewed his friendship with the Harkness Lay family. As before his departure for the Spanish-American War, he talked with Bessie Lay about the state of the world, and he now told her of his current girl friends, including the wealthy girl on the North Side whom he seems to have met while teaching American history to boys at a West Side settlement house and whom he courted briefly and then rejected for her humorless airs as described, with some fanciful trimmings of the episode, in the *Memoirs*. Among the new members of the Lay circle was Elizabeth Van Horne, a woman in her late twenties now living with the Lays while she worked as the organist of an Episcopal church not far away on the West Side. Years later she could remember Anderson's gleeful good humor during his calls on the family, his "wonderful brown eyes," and his tales of his "trips here and there in getting ads." As long as Sherwood had someone to talk and tell stories to, he "could talk all night." Though the constancy of the traveling may have irked him, his trips throughout mid-America pleased his restlessness and gave him a panoramic experience of persons and of places to add to those afforded him by his jobs in Clyde and elsewhere; but whereas while a boy he tended to tell tales gleaned from reading books, the origins of *Winesburg* developing in him from his surroundings unconsciously, now his imagination was more engaged with reality, with the kind of work he was doing, the nature of it and of the other people engaged in it. Within a year and a half after coming to Chicago, this rising young advertising man was using words not only to increase the sales of his firm's clients but also to express himself.[43]

The opportunity to get into print came about through Marco Morrow's position as associate editor of *Agricultural Advertising,* "a little journal," as its masthead read, "devoted to the art of Agricultural Newspaper Advertising, published each . . . month, by the Frank B. White Company." Anderson's first known contribution to this magazine, and his first published work, was a one-page article in the February, 1902, issue titled "The Farmer Wears Clothes," a piece distinguished only by its author's shrewd awareness of what his probable audience wished to hear. "Some of the big, general advertisers seem to be grasping the fact that the agricultural press is tucked up close to the hardest reading, best living class of people in the world, the American Farmer." He may also have been the author in the same issue of "Letter of an Advertising Solicitor to His Wife at Home," in which the solicitor writes of his unhappiness at having failed to complete a sale and his resolution to learn from his failure; for the article is signed "Bert Sherwood," which looks suspiciously like a pseudonym for Sherwood Berton Anderson. Certainly he was the author of "A Soliloquy" by "Anderson" in the April 1902 issue, a piece asserting that the "golden key . . . to advertising success" is probably not genius but "good, hard plugging early and late"; he again defined the road to success conventionally in "Not Knocking" in the December issue by rejecting the envious explanation for one advertising man's achievement as the result of "bluff" and "a gift for gab" rather than of the man's "belief in his work and in the good of his work." Only the one other contribution in 1902, that for November, "Writing it Down," in any way suggests the future story-teller. In it we read that one should write down at once any of those "best thoughts," which always "come to us at odd moments" lest they be lost.[44]

Beginning in January 1903, Anderson's contributions became a regular monthly feature of the magazine. This in itself indicates his increased status at the Frank B. White Company, but the two series of eleven short pieces each, one in 1903, one in 1904, are of extraordinary importance as Anderson's tentative entrance into what was to be his true career. The first series in *Agricultural Advertising* was presumably to run under the general title of "We Would Be Wise," which was used in the January 1903 issue; but Anderson or someone else apparently found another title more catchy, for the ten contributions appearing from February onward through the year (except September) are titled "Rot and Reason," an alliterative phrase that just possibly echoes the *Clyde Enterprise*'s occasional joke section, "Pith and Point." Typically each of the "Rot and Reason" series is made up of two or three brief informal essays centered on a main theme. "Rot and Reason" for March, 1903, for example, sympathetically discusses under the subtitles "The Lightweight" and "The Born Quitter" two kinds of men who fail in business; while "Rot and Reason" for the Harvest Home issue of August, 1903, praises the modern farmer as "rather a fine article" ("The Golden Harvest Farmer"), warns manufacturers that the farmer is now more independent and can be wooed only by more sophisticated advertising ("The Golden Harvest Manufacturer"), and decries dishonest attacks on one agency's farm advertising by any "Eddy Scalper" from another agency ("The Golden Fake"). In addition, all but one of the 1903 contributions include at the end some brief, random, often epigrammatic comments in the manner of such current newspaper columnists as "B. L. T." (Bert Lester Taylor) of the *Chicago Daily News:* "Hands were made to work with and not to hit heads with," which sounds like some adumbration of the *Winesburg* tale, or "A man's saying that he believes in the world does not necessarily mean that he is a credulous fool."[45]

The "Rot and Reason" series is not distinguished either stylistically or intellectually, nor, on the other hand, is it inferior in either to what a hundred other intelligent young businessmen with a facility for words might have been able to write. The significance of the individual pieces lies primarily in their statement of the public thinking of this particular young businessman at this point in his life; yet granting that the essays are conscious attempts at the literary, that they were written by a man with an advertiser's professional awareness of his audience, that the ideals asserted are often parallel to, if not echoes of, what his superiors were publicly thinking, still these pronouncements begin to provide a sense of the private man as well.

As would be expected, one of the major themes of the series is that business, particularly the business of advertising, is a great and noble game, which quite properly demands the best efforts and loyalties of the individual. The self-pitying man who changes jobs because his half-hearted work for the firm does not bring him the desired advancement in his first employment is ridiculed in the February issue, and the employer's right to "require that every man earn his salary" is upheld without question. In a passage in the May issue echoing Thomas Carlyle—whose *Sartor Resartus* and *Heroes and Hero-Worship* Anderson had read by this time—work is affirmed to be a positive good in a world of shadows, and the man who believes in and loves his work is said to throw about it "all of that glamour that comes to any place where a strong man works." Perhaps the most eulogistic words come in "Fun and Work" in the July issue, where a young advertising manager is quoted as proclaiming to the writer:

Give me the man who thanks his God when a day begins rather than when it closes, who goes eager to his office, who gets as much fun and knowledge out of to-day's failure as from to-morrow's success. I want to love my work because it supplies me with bread and butter, I want to laugh and sing and fight and win and lose, and I want to get a lot of good fun out of the whole business. The point is that doing the work well that you love isn't work, it's fun, the best sort of fun, the very meat and kernel of life. (p. 23)[46]

Quite as expectedly the American businessman is praised in the June issue (pp. 54, 56) as "the very front and center of things American" and "the man on horseback in our national life." Anderson refers admiringly to William Allen White's recent "brilliant series of articles in the *Saturday Evening Post*" showing that "a little group of brainy business men rule the senate and house of representatives," and adds with a satisfaction that in a decade would be deeply ironic for his career: "The business man rules the stage; our literature is moulded to his needs and 'good business' brings to us and keeps on our shores the great European musicians."

And what manner of man is he, this American business man? Is he a better, cleaner and braver man than the warriors and scholars who have cast their big shadows in the past? You can be sure he is. He may have occasionally a bad dose of dollarism, but he takes care of his family; he educates his sons, he loves one woman, and he usually knows that honesty is as a solid wall, and truth as a shining light. (p. 56)

Greatness did not die with Caesar and Lincoln (the juxtaposition of the names is startling and illuminating); every age produces "its truly great individuals," and the place to look for them is among business men," who will "quietly and firmly in good time" settle "the negro question, the labor question, and other things that do ripple the surface of things. . . ."

One would like to glimpse a flicker of irony beneath such passages, some of which read like quotations from Lewis's *Babbitt,* but the prose is utterly opaque. There also appears to be no irony in the occasional praise of the probity of the average advertising man, though as a contributor to a trade magazine Anderson could hardly be expected to maintain otherwise than that "the agency fellows" are "mighty near as square a lot of men as you will find" (July, p. 23). Yet one would more readily suspect these various uncritical announcements to be a mask concealing a more skeptical face if it were not that Anderson quite openly objects to some aspects of business while in the main rejoicing, in an image which would in a few years express dismay and loathing instead, that "We are part of the machine, part of the office force, workers in the big mill called America" (July, p. 26). The advertising man's work is "as hard as the day is long" (February, p. 14), and the end of a day always shows work unfinished in spite of morning hopes. "In the first waking sickness of it," Anderson writes in "Unfinished" (May, p. 20), "how many the good men who have felt like dropping the whole thing and going out to find a healthy, reasonable job as end man on a sewer contract." The great game is worth it, he concludes, but only when he has also admitted that the advertising man "Day after day, week after week, year after year . . . faces his own failures. . . ."

Even more characteristic of the Anderson that was to be is the frequent concern of this successful young businessman for the failures of others. "The intense strain of America's pellmell business life is breaking down the weak men and is, no doubt, the direct cause of many a fairly good man's downfall," he asserts in the March issue (p. 18), and he finds the "saving fact" to be that there are some men, and there should be more, "quick, hard, strenuous fellows who don't take much stock in 'the survival of the fittest' proposition" and who are willing to help the average man, the "lightweight," up instead of striking him down. Developing the metaphor of the horserace, though rather mixing horse and rider, Anderson defends "'Poor old Johnson,'" the "born quitter," who has been treated roughly by an "equal, the man who ought to be a brother." After all, he argues in an image that sounds like an early dramatization of his own overcome past, "Johnson . . . was born of a surly sorrel in the winter time and the wolves snapped up his mother's soul one night in his yearling days."

Let's reconsider Johnson and this smashing business. Not but what we ought to ride hard and whoop things up—that's what's making winners of us—but when we're away back there in the dark and the crowd is listening to the band and the judges can't see, and there isn't a soul looking, let's just smash Johnson over the rump instead of the nose. (p. 19)

This feeling for the failures and the misfits, the despised and neglected, which was to be one of Anderson's most attractive personal traits, obviously was not submerged by his push toward success. Already adumbrated in this first series, too, is the theme of human intercommunication, which was to become a central concern in his later writings; in fact, "We Would Be Wise" in January 1903 deals with the need of "Talking it Out," not only because one's plans can thereby be helped by a listener's critical analysis, but because one's own courage and convictions will be strengthened. "Every forward step in knowledge of ourselves," reads an epigram in June, 1903, "must lead toward charity for others." Already, also, Anderson was drawing on recollections of his boyhood for little homilies on conduct in the business world. "Rot and Reason" for April describes the quarter horses of "small towns of Ohio and Kentucky twenty years ago" that could "beat anything living" on short races into town but couldn't do "a decent whole mile." In the same issue a separate, unrelated paragraph reads like a quotation from the posthumous *Memoirs*:

There was an old fellow at home that hoed corn. He was grim, grey and silent, but because he pleased my boyish heart I was glad to hoe beside him for the dignity of his presence. One hot day when we had hoed to the end of a particularly long and weedy row and were resting in the shade by the fence he put his big hand on my shoulder and said, "Don't the corn make you ashamed, Sherwood, it's so straight?" (p. 14)

It is a flash from the future *Ohio Pagan*.

Though Anderson tended to beat the big drum of business in the "Rot and Reason" series of 1903, the undertones, the reservations, clearly showed that he was not an uncritical booster. Where the 1903 series is primarily valuable for its evidence of his conscious beliefs, however, the 1904 series is of central importance in seeing what was going on beneath the psychic surface of this businessman. During the late summer of 1903, Frank E. Long, president of the Frank B. White Company, and Major Elmer E. Critchfield, who among other duties was editor of *Agricultural Advertising*, organized the Long-Critchfield Corporation, which took over the business of the earlier company. The new agency continued the White Company's rapid growth, one sign of which was an expanded magazine. The back cover of the January, 1904, issue announced that "during the year 1904, every issue . . . will contain a number of special articles by writers of national prominence" and went on to say that "Sherwood Anderson, whose 'Rot and Reason' articles have been widely copied, begins in this number a new series titled 'Business Types.'" Though "national prominence" was straining it for Anderson, the rising young advertising man was clearly coming into his own in a rising young company. It is all the more significant, then, that the new series should be of the nature that it was.[47]

Of the eleven pieces in "Business Types," five of them, mostly at the beginning and end of the year, are of the essay genre of "Rot and Reason." Bunched together in the spring and summer, from March through September (except for the April issue, which contains another essay) comes a sequence of six pieces, however, that are clearly attempts at fiction, being either dramatized sketches or actual short stories. It is as though one were seeing Anderson the storyteller taking shape before one's eyes. Quite as significant as the new genre Anderson now writes in is the shift in attitude that these fictional pieces imply or explicitly state. A comparison of a piece in "Rot and Reason" with one in "Business Types" will make the shift clearer.

The one instance of a complete narrative in the former series is "Packingham," which appears in the April 1903 issue. (It may or may not be significant that "Packingham" appears between the homily on quarter horses and the paragraph on hoeing corn; it is at least conceivable that the writing of fiction and his boyhood life as a major source for this fiction were unconsciously becoming linked for Anderson.) With an open irony and in parable style Anderson tells the tale of "one Packingham," a man so "foolish" in his loyalty to his firm that his work meant more to him "than anything else in the world" and who, though he was "good to Mrs. Packingham," spent day and night on his job. When he invented a machine "which worked just like Packingham" and "enabled his firm to capture the market and sell something for two dollars that had formerly cost six or eight," a trust lawyer and "one Wescott, a very dear friend and earnest adviser of Packingham . . . together . . . descended on the silent man of work" with an offer of an enormous increase in income "if he would desert his firm" and come into their newly formed one. (The situation in part resembles Steve Hunter's descent on Hugh McVey in *Poor White*.) "And Packingham's salary was just five thousand a year. And Packingham laughed and went home and told Mrs. Packingham and she laughed. Wasn't he a fool?" It does not take a knowledge of Anderson's usual admiration in the essays of both "Rot and Reason" and "Business Types" for the "Silent Men" of work to see that the open irony of "Packingham" is mainly directed against those who would question Packingham's wisdom in rejecting wealth and in maintaining his loyalty to his firm and his adherence to an all-demanding "religion" of work.

A year and a half later, in September, 1904, Anderson published in the "Business Types" series a tale titled "The Hot Young 'Un and the Cold Old 'Un," which pays conscious, though not always effective, attention to setting and character and uses speech and dialogue for development by scenic method instead of the parable-like summary narrative of "Packingham." Bunker needs a western representative for his "big Monthly," *The Herald,* and must choose between two candidates, the clean-cut, forceful young Cartwright, who is backed by many "bold, clearheaded men of affairs," and an unnamed "old man, grown body-worn and watery about the eyes from hard service," who has written a "simple, straightforward" letter of application that Wright, editor of *The Herald,* calls "literature" because "he don't stick to dollars and cents and he don't tell what he has done, but he touches a fellow's heart. . . ." Bunker arranges to have each candidate present his case before himself, Wright, a third member of the firm, and two "dummies," a barber and a stone-deaf tobacconist, dressed up to look impressive. Asked to "'speak right out'" by the tobacconist, young Cartwright loudly proclaims his past achievements and his willingness to give "my brains and my strength and my love" to the magazine, concluding, "if you hire me I want you to know that I will be your man, body and soul."

The old man, who has been smiling to himself and "looking off across the housetops to where the lake lay, cool and green, with the cloud shadows fleeting across it," begins his presentation by saying in a merely conversational tone that Cartwright should be hired; for he himself has failed many times in the past, would spend his evenings at home by his own fireside, and, having heard the young man's energetic speech, doesn't want the job anyway. Cartwright, the old man concludes,

is ready to do all he says he will do for you. He has a wife, possibly, but he will walk the floor at night thinking of schemes to advance your business. He has memories of the quiet days when he was a fellow at school, and wandered out in the woods in the summer afternoons and feasted his soul on a good book, but he has heard of other American hustlers who forewent everything pleasant and quiet and hammered through a long hot life on the trail of dollars and he is ready to do that for you. Gentlemen, it would be very foolish of you not to take him on. (p. 26)

The old man quietly leaves the room, followed by Cartwright and the two "dummies," who speechlessly refuse Bunker's demand that they stay. Wright asks Bunker which candidate gets the job, and the story ends: "'Neither of those two," growled Bunker, 'one is too hot, and the other is too blame cold!'"

The denouement of the story is a surprise in the O. Henry manner, but the climax comes in the reversal established at the beginning of the old man's speech, and the length of the speech emphasizes that what he says is the true focus of the tale. Business as a way to make one's living is not basically repudiated in "The Hot Young 'Un and the Cold Old 'Un," nor is the rightness of loyalty to the firm really rejected; but the distortion of legitimate business energy into an all-demanding religion of hustling is very seriously rebuked, as it had not been so rebuked in "Packingham." Perhaps the most fascinating aspect of the tale, moreover, is the role of the deaf tobacconist, a constant reference point throughout the story. Described by the author as "born for director's duties, and compelled by fate to sell five-cent cigars to clerks having to catch morning trains," he enjoys his momentary and spurious importance and looks, as Bunker whispers to Wright, "'a bit like the pictures of Napoleon at Austerlitz.'" It is to this parody of Carlyle's strong silent man at work that Cartwright especially directs his loud words, leaning "far over the table toward the tobacconist, and looking deeply into his eyes." The old man, on the other hand, opens his quiet speech with an apology that he is "'a bit too old to shout'" though "'one of your gentlemen cannot hear.'" At first this appears simply another O. Henryish touch of rather obvious irony until one realizes that in having Cartwright address mainly to the tobacconist his pledge of total self-dedication to business Anderson is imaging a lack of communication almost as grotesquely absolute as naked Alice Hindman's crying out to the deaf man on the dark, rainy Winesburg street at the end of "Adventure." One understands then that even as early as 1904 Anderson was, tentatively and not without conscious retractions, questioning the greatness of the business "game," a game that must have losers as well as winners, costs as well as prizes. Even young Cartwright, who had had no "flaw in his business record," is victim rather than victor, and quite appropriately he follows the old man from the room "as though he would speak to him."

If "The Hot Young 'Un and the Cold Old 'Un" were an isolated piece of literary evidence, one might well ignore the serious implications beneath its fictional trickery, but it is not an isolated instance in the "Business Types" series. "The Solicitor," as we have seen, ends in a triumph for "the boy," but the triumph comes by good luck and misunderstanding rather than by merit, and at the beginning of the tale much is made of the fact that the more experienced businessmen act morally only when they are prevented from acting otherwise. "The Discouraged Man" (July, 1904) consists mostly of a harangue by an advertising solicitor to a "discouraged man," a storekeeper in a stagnant small town. The solicitor tells the storekeeper that Brown, the local manufacturer whom he has just seen, is about to make the town nationally famous; yet in the brief last paragraph, addressed only to himself, the solicitor regrets that he didn't land the Brown contract after all, and the "snapper" ending lets the reader understand that the solicitor's ebullient harangue has been merely a reflex action to his own discouragement. Still, the implied criticisms of business in these two tales are gripes against the job, not attacks on the system, and are softened by humor and the surprise endings. "The Man of Affairs," published in *Agricultural Advertising* in March, 1904 (pp. 36–38), and the first of Anderson's contributions to be entirely an attempt at fiction, is something else again. Here there is no need to interpret; the meaning is overt and forthright. Just the preceding month, moreover, in the essay "Silent Men" Anderson had praised Thomas Carlyle by name for describing "the quiet man of work" and praised business for providing heroic modern Napoleons: "And as it was the silent, earnest men who gripped a mad world then and turned the fierce energies of a people to the orderly carrying of muskets, so now it is the silent man of the business firm who moves it with orderly force along the lines of success." After this eulogy of the silent man of power—here one glimpses yet another part of the genesis of *Marching Men*—the tale of "The Man of Affairs" comes as even more of a surprise than does the parody of Napoleon in the person of a tobacconist, for the tale is no less than a repudiation in fiction of what the essay has just affirmed.

In "The Man of Affairs," Anderson tells in summary narrative with no attempt at scenes the story of Peter Macveagh, a healthy, cheerful country boy who leaves an Indiana farm for Chicago "because he wanted to mix with men, and stretch his mental muscles." At his boarding house he is liked by "sad-eyed little Mrs. Thomas, the landlady," but she has to send him away because he disturbs the other boarders, who are very ordinary people, by getting up early, "washing his body awake," and reading "Keats and Shakespeare aloud in a voice trained to call the cows." Peter leaves gladly, for he is reaching the conviction that "in this world there are many people who are stupid and incompetent, and many more that are unclean pretenders," though he believes that the building of the great city must be directed by "another kind of man; his kind; clean, stout of heart, clear of mind, square and vigorous." Such men do exist, his old family minister tells him by letter, reassuring him that "The men who made and are making Chicago, were just the sort of boys you are, Peter, and after a time when you deserve to know these men you will." So Peter works and makes money and becomes rich and powerful.

At this point the author-as-narrator comments that there is no use in stopping here with Peter's story as the articles frequently published now do, summing up this or that businessman as, like Peter, clean, frugal, moral, and, "having made money," successful. "To us Americans," Anderson goes on, throwing down the challenge in 1904 almost as flatly as he would a decade later, "this much seems to be taken for granted and the thought that Peter Macveagh, (strong, rich and powerful), may be a failure, never seems to occur to us." It was easy for Peter to rise above common people like the boarders or us, who "are not thoroughly awake once in a year," for they and we do not seize the "wonderful opportunities" America affords strong men to rise to wealth and power. Yet—and here the challenge is extended to Carlyle himself—the successful Peter, like other men come to power, "is not the Peter of old days." Now he despises men for having the weaknesses he plays on, and "all men hate and fear him."

Peter Macveagh is a product of the times and the opportunities. His lust for power is satisfied because most of us are asleep. Mere living is so simple a matter for a man of average energy and intelligence that Peter, with no more effort comparatively, becomes rich and works his own ruin, for if we pay for our stupidity and drowsiness, Peter also pays for his title, Man of Affairs. (p. 38)

Reading "The Man of Affairs," one realizes that Anderson, the still apprentice businessman, had articulated in crude form a central theme in his whole later body of work as writer, indeed a theme that was already beginning to work its way toward the center of twentieth-century American fiction: the coupling of outward, materialistic success and inner, spiritual failure. Here was specifically a first awkward version of the rise of Sam McPherson in *Windy McPherson's Son*. Though it is an overstatement, it is not an untruth to say that the career of Anderson the storyteller really began in 1904 even though he was himself to set it at a later time. So early a date is in general corroborated by the recollections of Marco Morrow, whose executive abilities brought him election to the board of directors of the Long-Critchfield Corporation in September, 1904, but who did not let this new position interfere with his continued close friendship with Anderson.

He came into the office one day just before leaving on a two weeks' trip and told me he would decide while he was away whether he would become a millionaire or an artist. Any one can become a millionaire if he decides that he wants, above all else, to make money. He cited a number of our clients who were notoriously stupid men, but who were rapidly massing great fortunes. "What sort of an artist?" I asked. "Well," he said, "I think I am an artist. I don't know what medium I shall use. I may paint; I may sculp; or I may write—probably write." Well, he began writing—on the train, in country hotels, nights and Sundays. He produced reams and reams of manuscript which few people could read, serving a hard apprenticeship under his own teaching.

Although the whole process of career change, of life change, would extend over the next decade and was hardly a steady, straightforward development, by 1904 the thought of becoming a writer had begun to turn for Anderson from a wish to an option.[48]

What made him want to be a writer? Fundamentally, perhaps, the question is unanswerable for any artist, but at least some of the reasons can be given in Anderson's case. Part of the explanation certainly was his consciousness that within the years of his adolescence and young manhood an unusual number of experiences, significant less in themselves than in their sum and variety, had crowded in on him. Within only a few years he had finished growing up in a small, rural, midwestern town and had experienced industrialism at the lower levels, had joined others of his generation in a large-scale military venture and thus lived briefly in another, different section of his country and in a foreign land, had been accepted by an attractive group of older, educated people who encouraged him at the critical point in this life when he became intensely aware that to live by one's brain provided an escape out of the dead end of living by one's unskilled hand, and had established himself, a "hungry fighter," in the highly competitive world of business, the quintessential mode, he was daily told, of twentieth-century America. It is too grandiose to say that at this point he felt himself to be, more than other people, an embodiment of the replacement of the nineteenth century by the twentieth, though an awareness subsequently grew in him of how his experiences had charted this replacement, an awareness that later drew him strongly to *The Education of Henry Adams,* that autobiography of a far different, far subtler person prepared to live in an eighteenth-century world and forced to live in a nineteenth-century one.

But many people have varied, representative experiences without feeling a need to articulate them; so another part of the explanation was Anderson's long-held curiosity about the lives of individuals that he had touched or failed to touch, his resort to his imagination to satisfy this curiosity, and his propensity for rearranging reality, negatively as an escape from it and positively as a restructuring of it. Such a propensity appeared both in his pleasure at merely telling to friends stories of what had happened to him and his pleasure at reading books to see what happened to others there. His continued absorption in reading while also making his first experiments with writing is, in fact, demonstrated by two personal essays in the Robert Louis Stevenson manner that appeared under his name in late 1903 in *The Reader,* a literary magazine published by the Bobbs-Merrill Company, and that are noteworthy as his first publications outside *Agricultural Advertising.* In the first, "A Business Man's Reading," the author rebukes a representative young businessman who scorns reading and prefers arguing of an evening with the author of the essay.

And you had thought you could not fight with Stevenson nor take issue with Socrates? That Shakespeare spoke only the truth and Johnson was invincible? Where all that bravado with which you strutted away after your conquest of me? Where all that fire and logic? Here are fellows to shake you. Why not rush at Carlyle's conclusions as you did at mine? Lay a trap for Browning's unshaken faith. Say for me the things that Shakespeare neglected. Leave me at peace with my pipe and my book. The bookshelf is there.

Grappling with the "truths" of such writers, Anderson advises, will make the businessman reader "a better man in the marketplace. . . ." A similar utilitarian argument, that literary reading makes the businessman "a better man in his work," appears in the second article, "The Man and the Book"; yet Anderson does describe here a commercial artist whom reading transforms into an "artist full of earnest love of his work" and another man who controls strong sexual lust by reciting Shakespeare, "both being instances of the way in which men call upon their friends among books in their hour of need." Americans may be devoted to making money, but, Anderson adds, "there is much of the music of words in them." Probably with the advice and encouragement of Trillena White, Sherwood had broadened his reading to include some of the traditional figures in English literature, and they too by example urged him to write, to set down on paper what he was telling directly to people like Elizabeth Van Horne or what his own imagination, as it were, was telling him on those certain exhausting days when he walked Chicago's streets and "just a glance at a passing face was like reading the whole life history of some man or woman."[49]

Yet a third reason for Anderson's wanting to write resides where it has rarely been looked for—in his advertising work. This is not to argue that the writing of advertising copy had as formative an influence on him as writing for newspapers was to have on the young Ernest Hemingway, but it is to suggest that though he came to detest the work, it had positive as well as negative effects on him. For one thing, it was customary both within the agency and outside to refer to members of the copy and art departments as writers and artists as well as businessmen. To be sure, the agency fostered a lofty conception of successful creativity in order to make that creativity more efficiently serve business ends; but it is revelatory that when Sherwood came quickly into fame as a composer of advertising copy and contributor to the company's trade journal, he began to affect by turns the clothing of the young executive and that of the bohemian artist. It is of some consequence also that his specialty was the relatively new field of mail-order advertising, which involved not only the preparation of newspaper and magazine advertisements, but even more of catalog copy and systems of "follow-up" letters in response to queries from individual farmers, letters designed to "pull" and elicit sales. Much was made in the pages of *Agricultural Advertising* at the time Anderson was contributing to it regularly of the need by the copywriter for empathic feeling: "Put yourself in the other fellow's place and think what would best serve to arrest his attention and secure his interest in your line." Coldly manipulative as such advice was, Sherwood succeeded by employing it in his own copy. His gift for empathy did not end with controlling Economic Man, however. Both his fictional and nonfictional contributions to *Agricultural Ad-*

vertising show his concern for and understanding of the losers as well as the winners in the business game, and the later contributions show an increasing sympathy for other human beings, even the Peter Macveaghs. In his essay "The Traveling Man" (April, 1904) Anderson first recalls the "savage tug" given his heart in boyhood by the sight and sound of trains bearing people to far-off wonderful destinations and his early dream of visiting "many strange cities" and then making his fortune by shining shoes in Cairo, Illinois, "land of promise, key of the golden west." But he now knows that the true traveling man is a "Hungry, lonely, story telling" wanderer, "doomed forever to uninteresting Saturday nights in lonely hotels a thousand miles from home," an insight and a sentence that shows Anderson unconsciously reaching for, if not yet grasping, the *Winesburg* tone.[50]

It is doubtless laying too heavy a critical burden on the half-dozen beginner's stories in "Business Types" to suggest that the publishing conditions of *Agricultural Advertising* tended to make Anderson think from the very outset of his writing career in terms of the short tale, or that his assumption of the advertising world in which at least five of the six tales are set may have prepared him for the discovery of the Winesburg setting as one of his organizing principles in that masterpiece of his maturity. It is more certain that a unifying theme of the "Business Types" tales is a pervasive concern with words, the materials of the literary artist as well as of the advertising copywriter. Discrepancies between the words that describe reality and the reality described are emphasized in "The Man of Affairs," "The Discouraged Man," "The Solicitor," and "The Hot Young 'Un and the Cold Old 'Un." In addition, the mildly amusing tale, "The Liar—a Vacation Story," (June, 1904) describes a walking trip undertaken by a "liar" and five other men who become annoyed by the liar's presumption of knowing the inside facts about everything, set a trap for him by starting an argument over the painting of bicycles, and become the biters bitten when he describes in elaborate and exact detail the entire process of manufacturing bicycles, ending with "fifteen busy minutes in the enamelling room" and "a short sermonette on prices and selling methods." One suspects here a union in Anderson's mind of memories of the Elmore Manufacturing Company in Clyde and of the verbalizers at Long-Critchfield, including himself; in any case, truth is spoken by a "liar," and the five men are vanquished by words. The dramatized sketch "The Undeveloped Man" (May, 1904) is explicitly focused on the skilled use of language and furthermore not only paraphrases a comment from *Huck Finn* and catches something of Twain's tone, but adopts, and adapts, the frame structure of such humorous oral narratives as "The Celebrated Jumping Frog of Calaveras County," whereby a "literary" speaker is contrasted with a "dialect" one for comic verbal effect. Both an "advertising man" and a Texas

107

"cow man" admire the gifted swearing of a railroad brakeman. The latter asserts that the brakeman should go to Texas where he could improve his natural talent for cursing, but the former insists that the brakeman is an "undeveloped advertising man":

He knows the value of words, that fellow does. . . . He knows how to use words and that's why I think he'd make an advertising man. How to use words, and say, Mr. Cowman, that's what advertising is, just using words; just picking them out like that fellow picked out his swear words and then dropping them down in just the right place so they seem to mean something. . . . He's a word man, that brakeman is, and words are the greatest things ever invented. (p. 32)

Words, as his advertising work was proving daily to Sherwood Anderson, had almost magical properties. Symbols put on blank paper or uttered into the insubstantial air, they could, when dropped down in just the right place, control the real world and create in palpable detail what had not been there before—money, primarily, and more clients for the firm, new suits, good food, the sleek feel of the comfortable life for the inventor of the words. Words were like divine invocations, like efficacious prayers; they gave you what you wanted, made you powerful over your own life, powerful over the lives of others. They were, as Anderson would later assert again and again, lovely things but tricky things too. They gave understanding of others, but they could be used for contradictory ends. They could stimulate sales, make American business hum, even satisfy real needs and wants; they could also manipulate people, make them want what they did not want, pervert their desires, violate and distort their personalities. From such contradiction arose in Anderson's feelings one of the profound tensions that within a few years would give a radical redirection to his life.

But their contradictory uses aside, words and writing had to be considered with some degree of respect by any copywriter, as the issues of *Agricultural Advertising* at this period indicate. In February, 1904, appeared, for instance, a reprinting of "How Should an Advertisement Be Written?," the "leading editorial in a recent issue of the Chicago *Evening American*." The conscious striving for style, the editorial argues very sensibly, usually spoils a writer's natural ability, for "Style in writing has no value unless it expresses the natural thinking process of a naturally interesting mind, with concentration and care added." Good advertising writing must be "interesting, convincing, businesslike and practical," and terse "without being dull and colorless"; in fact, it is foolish for a "literary person . . . to consider the writer of advertisements as necessarily inferior to the writer of other literature," since in the best advertising writing the "English is good, the thought is novel, the style is original, *because the thinking processes are original*." Above all, "every advertising statement should have for its foundation *truthfulness*. Nothing will last that is not based on truth." Anderson's own scattered comments on advertising writing in *Agricultural Advertising* indicate that he accepted this advice, prided himself on his originality, and, whatever his reservations, came out publicly for truth and honesty. If, as seems likely, the "S.A." who signed the brief article "Concerning Testimonials" in the September, 1904, issue of the magazine was Sherwood Anderson, then it was he who defended the use of testimonials in agricultural advertising on the grounds that a majority of people use good sense in buying. "These people will recognize a fraudulent testimonial, and they will be influenced by a straight, honest testimonial from an honest house published and put out by an honest advertiser." One Freeman Kueckelhan, another company writer, whose skepticism about testimonials in the preceding issue had occasioned "S.A."'s reply, in turn replied to him in the October issue: "Assuming that absolute probity pervades the whole advertising campaign of an advertiser, it is well-nigh impossible for him to fail, provided of course he have a popular, meritorious article but honesty is not, unfortunately, an universal policy, and it is not to be found more commonly in the field of publicity than in the realm of politics."[51]

Although one may find Kueckelhan more persuasive than Anderson, the most significant aspect of this exchange is that the latter, writing non-fictional prose, takes a position that suggests a complete commitment to business values yet contributes "Concerning Testimonials" to the same issue of *Agricultural Advertising* in which appeared the last of his series of fictional pieces, most of which in some way question these values. Obviously he had reservations about his advertising work and sometimes stated them in his essays, but it is especially striking that his criticisms were more emphatic, his questionings more fundamental when he expressed them in the form of fiction. Fiction, it would seem, allowed him to deal with subjective materials, with uncertainties, objections, protests, with reactions against and desires to escape from the pressures of business that he could not fully name in open argument. These could safely appear in a story, however, since fiction by definition prepared the reader for make-believe and since the reversal ending of a tale gave the reader a shock of surprise, which diverted him from what the tale was really saying. Paradoxically it was in fiction that one used words most respectfully to tell the truth. The two kinds of contributions Anderson made to *Agricultural Advertising,* the essays and the apprentice tales, are finally so central to an understanding of him at this time because they show how he continued to function effectively in his businessman's world by compartmentalizing his feelings. Part of him, the part that wrote the essays, still believed, so to speak, in Horatio Alger; the part of him that wrote fiction questioned the dream of material success and sought for another, profounder myth.

Two incidents occurring in the first half of 1905 suggest the conflicts already forming in Anderson. Early in that year, as Marco Morrow recalled much later, Sherwood's contributions to *Agricultural Advertising* "attracted the attention" of Cyrus Curtis, head of the Curtis Publishing Company in Philadelphia, which published the enormously successful *Saturday Evening Post* and *Ladies Home Journal.* At a time when Sherwood happened to be out of town, Curtis called in person at the Long-Critchfield office to inquire about the author. Shortly afterwards, George Horace Lorimer, editor of the *Post,* wrote Anderson "asking him to submit a story to the *Saturday Evening Post,* a story with a background of business life." He submitted a story, but though it did not "click" with the *Post*'s editors, Lorimer invited him to Philadelphia for an interview at the magazine's expense, "an important consideration at that time." In Philadelphia he "learned that what the editors wanted was a series of fiction glamorizing and glorifying American Business with a big B," but "he was *not* interested." To Marco Morrow, looking back after his friend's death, this was "one of the most significant episodes in Sherwood's career." If, as seems likely, Morrow was correct about Anderson's reason for refusing his first big opportunity for national fame as a writer, one can only assume that refusal to be another indication of the depth of his feeling about such persons as Peter Macveagh, the "Man of Affairs," whose failure was not one of too much innocence but of too much experience.[52]

Ironically, this early refusal to sacrifice his integrity as a storyteller appears to have received its reward at a second event, not in heaven, but very much in this world. On the evening of May 1, 1905, he attended a banquet for department heads and assistants at Long-Critchfield held at the Palmer House and was the final, climactic one of twelve speakers to address this select assemblage of thirty-six advertising men. The title of his speech, "Making Good," sounds like something out of Horatio Alger. What he may have said about his subject is not known, though since he was presumably not speaking through the mask of fiction, one can guess.[53]

5.

Behind every successful man, according to the management manuals, is a woman. When Sherwood spoke at the Long-Critchfield banquet, he had been married for almost a year to Cornelia Platt Lane. Cornelia had been born in Toledo, Ohio on May 16, 1877, the oldest of three children of Robert H. and Kate Pepple Lane. An energetic businessman, Robert Lane had purchased in 1885 the oldest wholesale shoe company in Toledo "and extended the trade over considerable portions of Ohio, Michigan, and Indiana," his specialty being the supplying of shoes and rubbers to stores in small towns. He was well-to-do by the day's standards—when he died in 1928, his estate was valued at over $100,000—and was "a pillar of the First Baptist Church." Strongly individualistic, he was very thrifty despite his income and a social position that would later make the activities of his children—Cornelia, Robert, and Margaret—of interest to the society columnist of the *Toledo Daily Blade*. He habitually wore old clothes, usually unmatched jackets and trousers, and even into his last years he saved money and obtained exercise by riding his bicycle to work. Despite her well-trained good manners, Cornelia learned individualism early and developed a tolerance for unconventional behavior in others so long as it was an honest expression of personality.[54]

She grew up in the Lane home, a large three-story house still standing at 2428 Robinwood Avenue, then a quiet upper-class street lined with wide lawns and rows of maple trees. A rather small girl with clear blue eyes and a fair complexion, she became good-looking though not beautiful. At some time while she was young a slight stroke had paralyzed one side of her face, and as a result one eyelid and one corner of her mouth drooped very slightly. She was rather self-contained, was not a good conversationalist in the ordinary sense, had the "Lane characteristic" of putting out words abruptly and then stopping; but when she did speak, her remarks were perceptive, pointed, and often witty or humorous, and she was absolutely firm about telling the truth. Years later she became an unusually capable high school teacher of Latin, and a younger friend would recall that she was by temperament very much an intellectual, one who characteristically thought "abstractly" like a linguist rather than "visually" like a novelist.[55]

She was educated in the public schools of Toledo. Though her mother died in 1892 just after she finished her first years of high school, it was not necessary for her to take over the family as Stella Anderson had had to do, and she graduated from the Toledo High School three years later. After a year at Shepardson College (later merged with Dennison University in Granville, Ohio), she entered the College for Women of Western Reserve University in Cleveland in 1896, where she was a "good but not excellent" student concentrating in English, history, and Latin. A college roommate would remember her as "intelligent, witty, fun-loving, a person of fine integrity, and a leader in her class." As a senior she was, in fact, president of "Student's Association," presumably the student government organization. Significantly for her relationship with her husband-to-be, her extracurricular activities centered on two major interests, current events and literature. She was a member of both the Present Day Club and the Browning Club, was a literary editor of the college annual of 1899, and in her last year at Western Reserve contributed to the college literary magazine a research paper on "The Development of the Mask in English Literature Until the Beginning of the Seventeenth Century."[56]

After graduating in June 1900 she stayed at home until in June 1901 she embarked, at first in a chaperoned group of five young women, later on her own, on a grand tour of Europe. Arriving in Antwerp on July 6, she went on to Paris for a few days and then for the rest of the summer visited cities in Switzerland, Italy, Austria, Germany, and the Netherlands. She spent September in London, where she read at the British Museum and visited various literary sites, and from early October until mid-February of 1902 she lived in Paris, studying literature and art at the Biblioteque Nationale and probably the Sorbonne. By March she was back in Toledo where she was living at home in the spring of 1903 when she and Sherwood Anderson met for the first time.[57]

Appropriately the meeting came about through a Clyde connection. A Clyde girl named Jane ("Jennie") Bemis, a friend of both Sherwood and Bessie Lay, had married a man from Chicago named Charles Weeks, and the couple had settled in Toledo next door to the Lane house. Jennie and Cornelia became good friends, and once when Bessie Lay visited Mrs. Weeks in Toledo, Cornelia gave a birthday party for the visitor. Around May, 1903, while on one of his advertising trips, Sherwood stopped off in Toledo to see Jennie Weeks and was introduced by her to her friend Cornelia Lane.[58]

After his return to Chicago, Sherwood began corresponding with his new acquaintance, and presumably he made other visits to Toledo over the following months. There is some evidence that Mr. Lane did not approve of marriage between them; but any objection must eventually have been overcome or silenced, for on March 6, 1904, Sherwood wrote to brother Karl's fiancée, Helen Buell, wishing her happiness in that approaching marriage and telling her of his own wedding set for May. The public announcement of Sherwood's marriage was made in the social column of the *Toledo Daily Blade* for April 25, 1904. On May 7, a Saturday, Sherwood was in Toledo for an "informal evening" honoring Cornelia and him, given by Cornelia's friend Eunice Alexander and attended by fifteen other couples. "Miss Chapman and Miss Farmer gave pleasure with music," the columnist reported, "and old fashioned games were enjoyed. White ribbons and sweet peas were used in the artistic dining room decoration."[59]

However one measures the distance, it was a long way from Piety Hill to Robinwood Avenue, and for the most part one must conjecture how the emotional distance was traveled by this man of twenty-seven and this woman who was to become that same age on her wedding day. Cornelia could not have been primarily attracted to Sherwood for his still moderate financial success; she was used to having money, and in fact she was not particularly interested in it, though she was probably impressed that he had been capable of rising from boyhood poverty to his present position. Certainly she responded to what she later termed the "charm and warm personality" that "were so much a part of him" in his "early years," and she liked his enthusiasm, which made him able to "convince you of anything," though she may not have learned until after the marriage that his enthusiasm could be as short-lived as it was intense. Attractive to her also would have been his knowledge of many kinds and classes of people, his sensitivity to their individual moods and needs, his humorous but sympathetic awareness of what went on beneath the surfaces that they presented to the surfaces of life. Like her he was much given to reading and, though intuitive where she tended to be logical, much interested in discussing the ideas he found in books, as well as in talking about what was going on in the great world of affairs. He was not simply another young businessman, too, in his growing desire to write things less utilitarian than advertising copy, and she knew that by the time she met him he already "had a lot of stories he'd written." Whatever his ability, he was trying to express himself in literary form, and literature was something she gave her allegiance to. Finally, she must have been attracted, as other women were to be, to his physical vitality, a frank aura of the flesh, expressed in his intense dark eyes and in a sort of negligent crudity beneath the slightly flashy clothing. All the evidence is that she fell deeply in love with him.[60]

On his part Sherwood must have felt as though the dream of success was coming true. As in the novels, he was marrying the equivalent of the boss's daughter, and he would have responded sensuously to the upper-class air of Robinwood Avenue, the feel of a home where, despite the father's thriftiness, the latent power of money could be brought instantly into play. As far as marrying wealth and status went, of course, a completely ambitious young businessman might have done better in Chicago; but Anderson was not completely ambitious, and he had already given up one chance to wed a really rich girl. Besides being a good-looking woman, Cornelia was attractive in other ways. She was an educated person, and Sherwood was always to respect education for its own sake, to regret his lack of it, rather to envy those who had gone through the forms that ended in possession of this intangible thing—and also, simultaneously and ambivalently, to suspect and resent both the forms and those who had passed through them. Here was a mature woman, however, who was less interested in being feminine in the usual sense than in intently discussing books and ideas, one who enjoyed listening to tales of his experiences and who responded with a sense of standards that were neither dogmatic nor rigid to his efforts to write. Perhaps he was attracted most of all to qualities in her that were like those his mother had had. Though not talkative, Cornelia had wit, perceptiveness, honesty. What she may have lacked in passion was balanced by integrity of mind and coherence of personality. All the evidence is that, at the time, he fell deeply in love with her.

Cornelia Lane and Sherwood Anderson were married on May 16,

1904, at eight o'clock in the evening at the Lane home. Assuming that all went as announced by the society editor in that day's *Blade,* the wedding was a small one but traditional in form. The pastor of the First Baptist Church performed the ceremony, and Eunice Alexander at the piano played "the Lohengrin and Mendelssohn wedding music." Margaret Lane, Cornelia's sister, "attired in white," was the bridesmaid, while the best man was Marco Morrow. Karl came from New York and Stella from Chicago to represent the Anderson family; among the few other guests was, quite properly, Jennie Weeks, who had in a way been the cause of it all. Cornelia's gown was "a handsome creation of white chiffon," and after the wedding supper that followed the ceremony, she changed to "a dark blue tailored costume," since later that evening "Mr. and Mrs. Anderson" left "for a wedding journey."[61]

6.

In the spring weeks before the wedding and in anticipation of it, Anderson had been putting down in a notebook five essay/sketches quite separate from the "Business Types" series he was currently writing.[62] Of these, two are of little consequence; the other three, however, deal in some way with a new theme—womanhood. In the first, "[Tramp killed by train found by girl]," a little girl on her way to school discovers the already decaying body of a tramp killed by a freight train, but she is not disturbed and merely informs a trackman. "I believe you," comments Sherwood, referring to Cornelia, would have been as composed as that girl, who in some spring "with sap running through the veins of the trees" will pay back God's demand for the life given her by marrying and becoming "the mother of a race of men." In the second, most fictionlike piece, "The Red Haired Woman," the "I" narrator visits the home of a friend, John, whose "clear-minded" wife Kate, uses "words in unexpected ways." As he reaches their house, a woman with red hair is leaving and startles him by looking straight into his eyes. That evening John shows him things the woman has written, the sentences unconnected but filled with "richness of phrasing," which only Kate understands. Neither John nor the narrator understands "this stuff," but returning home "I" thinks the world would be better "if there were more Kates who understood" this extraordinary woman. The third piece, "The Can Factory," linked in its ending to the first, is an outraged moral attack on an aspect of industrialism. The narrator, again "I," is being shown by a friend around a factory where many "marvelous machines with wonderful precision" for making cans are operated by "long rows of crooked backed, tired faced girls." The obtuse friend cannot understand why "I" is angered by this misuse of women, made deformed by this horrible drudgery. Now in spring when "the earth shakes with joyous birth pains," they are unlikely to respond to God's "command to woman kind" to marry and bear children. Taken together, these three pieces suggest that the expectant bridegroom's attitude toward womanhood was at once conservative and advanced. God has ordained that women's primary function is to bear children, a belief that comes rather strangely from a young man who had shown little interest in formal religion and may instead represent Cornelia's Baptist influence. Human procreation, however, has its biological link to the whole rebirth of nature in spring, an emphasis suggestive of Anderson's lifelong responsiveness to seasons and natural beauty; the ideal woman, then, is to be conceived of as representative of nature itself. Further, she should have certain personal qualities—composure and fearlessness, straightforwardness of manner, the gift for vivid language, and sympathetic, perceptive understanding. It is an ideal subsumed in what he would shortly call his bride—"Great earnest woman." Taken together, these pieces also demonstrate that though Anderson in the spring of 1904 was dedicated to success in business, he was also devoted to writing as at least an adjunct to that career but not yet a parallel one to it. Such a subsidiary interest explains why he decided to keep a "Honeymoon Journal," a daily commentary on the wedding trip.

Now Mr. and Mrs. Anderson, they took an evening train to Cincinnati, stayed at the elegant St. Nicholas Hotel, explored the city the next day, and on the eighteenth went farther south by train to the little town of Oakdale, Tennessee, on the Emory River some forty miles west of Knoxville in the Cumberland Mountains. Presumably Sherwood had admired the natural beauty of the area when he had passed through Oakdale with his regiment in 1898 or perhaps later on a business trip but had not been fully aware that it was a railroad town. They put up at the one hotel, the Babahatchie Inn, which he described in his journal as "a great barren breezy place given over to the feeding and housing of trainsmen." They agreed that the Inn was "southern," that is, somewhat slovenly; but since the bed linen and the dining room were clean, they decided to stay for the week they had allotted. Fortunately, they were very much in love and spent most of their days wandering along the banks of what they called "the little river Babahatchie," the original Indian name ("bubbling water") for the Emory, rejoicing in the hills and mountains, reading Browning to each other, talking much about themselves and their future together. "Cornelia has decided," he wrote in the journal, "that she is a woman of great common sense while I have put in my word for the fanciful and the unreal. I dare say that will make a great combination." Perhaps because she had already assessed her husband's temperament, it was she who, at the end of "a long talk over realism in literature," asserted that "It's a good thing to let the other fellow do." It was a prophetic remark, for Anderson would in fact spend a sizeable amount of his writing career searching for ways to get beyond realism.

Both feeling their "right . . . to be sentimental when you are young and on your wedding trip," Sherwood resorted frequently in his journal to an elevated style, especially to the apostrophe, in this case the personification of the inanimate, and other formal rhetorical "ornaments" in the current vogue of the sentimental personal essay. "Little river Babahatchie," he declares, for an instance, ". . . How gallantly the red boat sits upon your dancing body. The hills they are for truth but you little river you are for sentiment." He had apparently begun testing out any mode of language through which to express accurately inward states of feeling, as he would continue to do with varying success throughout his literary career.

Very likely it was during their week at Oakdale that he tried other experiments in three brief but very serious and revealing pieces he wrote about his and Cornelia's relationship. For the first he develops and surprisingly applies an extended simile.

A woman is like a river, she laughs and hurries along in the plains between the grassy banks, but put her among the hills in big serious places of life and see how different her tone. She goes forward so much more bravely than would a man but she is the very river and the hills in her earnestness.

She is completely the river among the hills when her honest eyes seek out in her husband any deceitful thought about her. In the second piece, built on a packed, consistent metaphor of sea voyage, he casts himself, not as "I," but as "the young man" at the beginning of the wedding. As "the woman in the white gown" stands poised on the last step of the staircase, he thinks of the journey through life they are about to take. When "this woman with the beautiful shoulders and fine eyes" comes toward him, however, the "beating notes" of the orchestra become, synaesthetically, like waves on a shore, and he wonders if she knows "the profitless shores all his journeying had come to in the past" and "the barrenness of his cargoes," that is, the emptiness of his previous relationships with women. He feels that he should tell her of them, but then love "surges back into his heart," and, completing the metaphor, he "cries in his heart," "Great earnest woman . . . it is for you to mark the voyage of the ship and I shall be your crew to work for you."

The last of the three pieces is an unexpected one, a first poem by Sherwood Anderson, or as he puts it "a speechless poet" writing in "this blank way." Nearly half the lines are indeed in rigidly iambic blank verse, the rest for the most part in rigidly iambic shorter or longer lines, the sort of form a reader of Shakespeare but an unskilled versifier might attempt. But "this blank way" can and very likely does have a second meaning, a psychological one; for the poem is written by a disturbed Sherwood, aware of his "many little weaknesses," certain that he understands a distressed Cornelia, but baffled and helpless to communicate that certainty to her, yet through this poem, "grimly trying" to succeed, "to sing to you and make you happy." What could be the nature of their mutual distress? The answer, to the extent it can be given, would seem to reside in certain key lines of this unexpectedly dark poem.

> I know the struggle in your heart,
> The sweet submission in your voice,
> The tender wishing that your man do right
> Dear journeying woman of my heart.
> So tender and so strangely unprepared.
>
> It is the spring dear heart you feel.
> The trees feel so
> and we stand by and call it beautiful.
> I think they suffer just as you do now.

It seems likely that Cornelia, loving and tender, was "so strangely unprepared," either was uninstructed about sexual intercourse or was unready for it but, trusting her husband, submits to it. The act is painful for her, but her suffering is to be understood as part of insemination and birth, a natural process. Although Sherwood conflates the beginning and the end of procreation, as at the end of "The Can Factory," he argues that the trees producing leaves from buds "suffer just as you do now." It is unlikely that this fanciful notion could be of any comfort to commonsensible Cornelia; but it *is* likely that, since the speaker "sees the rivers and the towering hills" (of Oakdale), some degree of sexual incompatibility was continuing between the couple, Sherwood certainly passionate, Cornelia less so, still submissive, still hurting. Perhaps, considering the two previous pieces, she may also have queried him searchingly about his previous experience with women, or he may as one of his "many little weaknesses" told her without her questioning, so adding to her hurt. There is no doubt, however, that they continued to be loving and, mostly, happy, but one suspects a dark area underneath their happiness, one which did eventually help bring the unhappy ending to this marriage.

"It was at the river we looked longingly," Sherwood wrote in his journal of their departure from Oakdale on May 25, "for it was the river had saved the place." Almost entirely he now dropped the formal embellishments in his account of their first honeymoon week and for the most part wrote in direct informal prose of their subsequent travels. They took the train to Chattanooga, where they spent the first evening observing the carnival spirit of the city's "Seventh Spring Festival" and the next day examined the Civil War sites of Lookout Mountain. The twenty-seventh was "a journeying day" on a slow train following the Tennessee River through Tennessee and northern Alabama to Memphis, Sherwood remarking on such signs of "the genuine south" as, at Tuscumbia, "the ragged negroes and the long legged listless whites." Arriving in Memphis too late for their intended upriver steamboat to St. Louis and their destination, its World's Fair, they registered for three nights at the fine new Gayoso Hotel near the Mississippi. Possibly being so close to Mark Twain's river he was encouraged to write more often in his journal with a simplicity and concreteness as though unconsciously reaching toward his more mature style: "Our room looked out upon a little roof garden with a fountain in the middle and over beyond that lay the big moving river, very silvery and quiet in the moonlight." They were happy in Memphis. On Saturday they sailed up the river and back a few miles on a freight steamer, dined in a fine restaurant, talked in a little park of "our life together," and "walked home with a great deal of peace and understanding between us." Sunday they attended church, where he thought the "clear sweet voice" of the soloist more beautiful and memorable than the sermon. That last evening in Memphis they went to another little park where, he would record, "we talked of big things and a man and woman's right attitude toward certain great problems of life." Apparently they had arrived at their accommodation with each other.

Embarking on May 30, they were three nights and most of three days on the passenger and freight steamboat *Ferd Herold,* bound for St. Louis. For the most part it was a quiet trip. The berths were comfortable enough, the meals "well cooked." The Andersons watched the occasional freight or passenger stops, noted the changing landscapes on the shores, talked with a few other passengers, spent an evening on deck together discussing Robert Louis Stevenson and Carlyle, and one afternoon were much entertained by the mate with "brisk little stories" about local inhabitants along the way. One morning the ship's barber did persuade Sherwood to have a haircut, although even then as later he disliked having it done; and one night he had a violent stomachache, from which he recovered when a lady passenger supplied "a hearty dose of paregoric," that opium-based painkiller then available over drugstore counters. In a morning rain they disembarked in St. Louis on June 2, registered as scheduled at the Planters Hotel, picked up their mail, one letter containing a check for Sherwood— welcome since they had spent most of their honeymoon funds—and set off for their first day at the huge, ornate Louisiana Purchase Exposition, the official name for the famed St. Louis World's Fair. With a summary of the sights they saw or would see and exclamations over the fair's "glory and beauty," Sherwood ended his journal. How long they stayed in St. Louis or when they went to Chicago, their honeymoon journey completed, is not known.

In Chicago the Andersons took an apartment on the South Side at what was then 5854 Rosalie Court between Jackson Park on the east and the university on the west. This was a convenient location, for Cornelia studied at the university for six weeks that summer, as she was to do the following summer, and registered for a year of French in 1904–5, while Sherwood could easily commute by the Illinois Central or the "El" to his office in the Loop. By summer of 1905, however, the couple had moved to Riverside, a suburb then at the western fringe of Chicago. They lived there and possibly, after yet another move the next year back to the South Side, at 6126 Jackson Park Avenue until they left for Cleveland and a new job for Sherwood in the late summer of 1906.[63]

A pleasant vignette of the Anderson's life together at Rosalie Court is given in a recollection of a friend.

> At the time of Anderson's first marriage, he lived but a short distance away from us on the south side of Chicago, and we went over there quite frequently. Mrs. Anderson was a charming hostess, and most of us felt that she did as much to take the "country" out of Anderson as any one. Games were seldom played, but we all were fond of reading, it usually happened that some choice bit was retained for evenings when we were together. The Andersons had a fireplace in their apartment, and were extremely fond of a log fire. Usually it was about the only light in the room, and we and the other guests often did the Abraham Lincoln stunt of reading by the light of the fire.

When this circle of friends, which also included Marco Morrow, tired of reading, they could always discuss books and ideas. Years later Cornelia recalled the "*good* fireplace" and the discussions, especially "the battles that used to rage over Shaw," that iconoclastic playwright in whose favor "Sherwood always took up the cudgels."[64]

Later, too, Sherwood recalled once speaking of death at that time in a way that unintentionally hurt Cornelia; yet all other indications are that in these first years they were happy together. And here a final point must be made about Anderson's contributions to *Agricultural Advertising,* those essays and stories that in effect initiated his career as an author. Because of the sketchiness of the evidence one cannot say flatly that his and Cornelia's decision to marry coincided exactly with his abrupt shift in the "Business Types" series from the essay praising Carlyle's strong silent men in February 1904 to the fiction dispraising them in "The Man of Affairs" in March. Yet there is at least a close chronological correlation between the publication of his tales and sketches from March through September of 1904 and the climax of his courtship, his wedding, and his first married months with Cornelia. It would seem likely that the speech of the old man in "The Hot Young 'Un and the Cold Old 'Un," published in September as the last of the stories, was composed by a writer who through an imagined character was calling into the most serious question a life so bound to business that it excluded both personal development and a full relationship with another, one's wife. But this would not be simply the dramatized complaint of the newly married husband. Seen over the long view, this and his other fictional questionings are prophetic of Anderson's future rejection of business as quite literally life-denying and his embracing of art as quite literally life-fulfilling. Women would always be in some way essential to his artistic creativity. Often ruthless, often rewarding to them as persons, he nevertheless felt a direct link between successful physical love and the successful covering of sheets of paper with words. His relationship with Cornelia Lane would not continue to be a happy one, but obscurely, complexly, powerfully it helped drive him toward becoming the artist he became.[65]

4

The Dream of Success

1.

Although Anderson may have written in 1905 the story that had failed to
"click" with the editors of the *Saturday Evening Post,* for the most part
that year and the next few his pieces were nonfiction ones. His "Business
Types" series of 1904 had ended with two personal essays, the last of
which defended the "man sitting calmly looking out a window" against
the presumptive charge of idling, since, absurd as it may seem to the "average business man," that person "may be working with his brain." In
1905 Anderson published only two essays in *Agricultural Advertising,* one
of which indicates the contradictory feelings he had developed about his
present work since it is concerned with the faults of business at the same
time that it continues to preach its virtues. The second of these essays,
"Advertising A Nation," in the May issue, simply praises President
Theodore Roosevelt's ebullient talk of the Square Deal as a mode of "good
advertising," which implies "good goods, good intentions, making good."
The first, however, on the "Sales Master" in the April issue, shows Sherwood in the role of business prophet proclaiming a loftier professional
function for the advertising man than the present one.

There are, in this country, many firms, that because of their size and limited
capital, cannot afford a high-priced organization man to handle and develop new
ideas for exploiting their goods, therefore the question arose, "Why should there
not come from the ranks of American Advertising Men a class of business physicians who can walk into an office and lay their hands upon diseased spots in the
selling system?"

Like the ideal medical physician, the Sales Master must be honorable,
must be free from "the lust of money," must love his profession, and must
be a "quick and sure judge of human nature." If the body of the article

suggests that Anderson saw himself as potentially fulfilling such a "noble" conception, an anticlimactic ending shows a more immediate irritation on his part with the agency practice of paying its personnel on a commission basis. Sherwood, one may guess, was finding that two persons could not really live as cheaply as one.[1]

What impelled him to take his next step seems to have been a combination of the desire to make more money, the ambition for a higher and more highly regarded place in business, and a sense that he had talents that could develop better if he were independent. In the *Memoirs* he was to claim that additionally he feared he was becoming "too slick, too plausible" in the manipulation of language and of other people's minds, though the job that he was to move to required just as much slickness and plausibility. Perhaps in his enthusiasm over the concept of the Sales Master he most of all wanted to show that Irwin Anderson's son belonged to the élite of the "business physicians." At any rate he temporarily turned away from thoughts of being a writer, ceased publishing not only fiction but essays as well, and began to look for a way to make a living at business outside the Long-Critchfield Corporation.

One of the corporation's, and Anderson's, specialties was preparing advertising copy for mail-order firms. Marco Morrow, for example, had himself handled the copy for the Kalamazoo Stove Company, which, according to an adulatory article reprinted in *Agricultural Advertising* for November, 1904, from the national advertising magazine *Printer's Ink*, was "doing a mail-order business of half a million dollars in what is practically its second year of business." As a contributor to *Agricultural Advertising* and friend of Morrow, Anderson would certainly have known about this "remarkable success," and it was not long afterward that he saw his chance to duplicate the Kalamazoo's achievement in the activities of a small Cleveland firm, the United Factories Company.[2]

United Factories had begun business on January 1, 1905, under the management of George A. Bottger, who had been an employee of one Edwin D. Cray, head of a Cleveland firm that dealt mainly in hardware for carriages. A resourceful and enterprising young man, Bottger was given encouragement and financial backing by Cray to start a mail-order firm, which at first sold only buggy tops and seats; the head of the agricultural advertising department of the Lord & Thomas advertising company in Chicago had advised Bottger to offer only a limited number of items. United Factories set up business in offices that occupied only part of one floor of one section in a five-story, five-section building, the "Whitney Power Block," near the center of Cleveland's business section—though an impressive engraving of the entire Block blandly labeled "Offices and Factory of the United Factories Co.," was used as a frontispiece to Bottger's 1905 catalog. Buggy tops and seats turned out not to be profitable by themselves, however, and the firm began to make changes. It brought in more items for mail-order sale, and in late 1905 or early 1906 it switched its advertising account to Long-Critchfield, which, being strictly an agricultural advertising agency seemed better fitted to handle it. At Long-Critchfield, Sherwood Anderson was assigned to this account.[3]

Bottger was impressed by Anderson. For one thing Sherwood knew something of the art of living and was "quite a gourmet." Once while Bottger and Cray were in Chicago, Sherwood introduced them to snails at DeJonge's, a famous French restaurant on Monroe Street, mentioned in *Windy McPherson's Son*. There was one order of four snails for the three men, and though Bottger did not like his one snail, Anderson insisted that they all draw lots for the fourth. More importantly, "Sherwood was a dreamer," Mr. Bottger recalled years later, emphasizing that he did not mean "dreamy." Like his own "Sales Master," and rather like Irwin Anderson, Sherwood could visualize the possibilities of a situation and see bigger and better things to come. Bottger recognized not only his enthusiasm, energy, and imagination but also his ability to write convincingly on any subject without knowing much, if anything, about it. At some time in the first half of 1906, Sherwood proposed to Bottger that he join United Factories to handle the firm's advertising and promotion, the agreement being that if he increased the business by a certain percentage within a year's time, he not only was to be made a partner but was to receive a bonus at the end of the year. Anderson showed that he was sincerely enthusiastic about his new prospects by accepting a lower salary than he had been receiving at Long-Critchfield and by insisting, against Bottger's more realistic skepticism, that "We'll each be drawing $25,000 a year." Although United Factories was unincorporated and had no definite officers, Bottger continued as manager, while Anderson became president because it would "look good in the advertising." Sherwood was so excited by future possibilities that when he and Cornelia moved to Cleveland on Labor Day, September 3, 1906, he went right to work in the company office on that holiday.[4]

The basic structure of the United Factories Company had already been established before Anderson came into the firm. Mail orders for a variety of products manufactured by a variety of firms involved in the arrangement were to be solicited from and be sent in to the central office of the company in the Whitney Power Block. The central office sent the orders out to the individual factories, which shipped product to buyer under the United Factories label but from their own warehouses. By October 1, 1906, the firm was handling seven different kinds of products—"vehicles, buggy tops and repairs, stoves, incubators, agricultural implements, . . . paints," and roofing materials. Two of the new president's duties were to write the copy for the advertisements that the company

123

placed in various agricultural publications, and to prepare or revise the catalogs for the kinds of products offered for sale. Mail-order houses like the Kalamazoo Stove Company and the United Factories Company had made it a practice to emphasize in their catalogs not only the superior quality of their merchandise, but also the firm's impeccable honesty and the savings that could be passed on to buyers by the "direct from the factory to customer" system, which eliminated the "middle man's" profits and the expense of maintaining traveling salesmen. Anderson's special contribution was to liven the flat prose of such arguments in the United Factories catalogs with a disarmingly personal, conversational tone. The "Roofing Catalog" of 1906 contained a signed statement, "My Word to You" beneath a reproduction of the picture of Sherwood used to illustrate "The Undeveloped Man" in the "Business Types" series, one that made him look handsome, clean-cut, firm-chinned, and well-groomed.

I promise as a decent man trying to be square that every man, rich or poor, small or large, shall have a square deal from my company.
Every word of this book was written under my supervision, and for it I am responsible to you.
As you and I may never meet face to face I give you my word now that what is written in this book is true in spirit and in fact.
I stand ready to do what is right by you, the buyer, and if you at any time buy anything of the factories whose goods are sold through our catalogs, and if you are not satisfied, you can feel free about taking the matter up with me personally, and I promise you that I will not delegate the matter to a clerk or pile up words to confuse you, but will satisfy you with what you have bought or return every penny of your money no matter what we lose by it.

Beyond the way Anderson does curiously pile up words in that last, paragraph-long sentence, it is impossible to gauge the sincerity of this message; yet judging by his gift for enthusiasm and his criticism of business practices he had observed, one may guess that he mostly meant what he said in this effort to persuade buyers. In any case, he was shortly forced to mean it.[5]

In addition to writing mail-order copy, he had other promotional duties. Both he and Cray put in much time traveling about the Midwest trying to interest still more manufacturers in the United Factories scheme. Henry Wick, head of the profitable Fox Furnace Company in the nearby small city of Elyria, for example, was invited to join. He "royally entertained" Cray, Bottger, and Anderson at his Elyria home; but Fox Furnace retained its independence, and the only positive achievement of the negotiations was to help acquaint Sherwood with the city in which he would soon try another business venture. "Anderson had some very big ideas for a factory combine," Bottger recalled, but he had limited success, for many companies, like Mr. Wick's, preferred to sell under their own names. And the success he initially had with one company turned out to be a financial and personal disaster retrieved only by the extent to which it may have been preserved in the amber of one of his finest tales.[6]

During their year in Cleveland, the Andersons lived first at 9711 Lamont Avenue and later at 8310 Cedar Avenue, both residences being old houses in middle-class neighborhoods on Cleveland's East Side. They especially liked the Lamont Avenue house, though as soon as they had moved in and "got it fixed up artistically," they discovered that the roof leaked badly. Fortunately the United Factories sold a heavy preservative roofing paint, which sealed the leaks; so for the first time "Roof-Fix" came profitably into their lives. Each of the two houses had a "pleasant atmosphere," according to their new friend, Edwin C. Baxter, who was then assistant secretary of the Cleveland Chamber of Commerce and who shared their love of reading. Cornelia was "a casual housekeeper," Baxter was to recall, "the intellectual side perhaps dominating the domestic a little." George Bottger, who occasionally saw the Andersons outside business hours, found their "home relationship" to be "very pleasant" and Cornelia to be "well-educated, a fine woman, always gracious." She was interested in improving both Bottger's and her husband's education and at one time started teaching them French, but they were too busy with company affairs to do the necessary studying. Bottger later insisted also—though Cornelia denied it—that like a proper young business couple the Andersons were active in church work and, however casual the housekeeping, outdid the Bottgers in formality of attire at Sunday service, Sherwood once even appearing in morning suit and top hat. Unlike her husband Mrs. Bottger met Anderson only once, when he umpired a baseball game at Willow Beach Park at one of the huge Bottger family reunions; yet she remembered him vividly as all "*brown*"—dark complexion, dark hair, dark eyes—and as a fast-moving, "bird-like, jumpy, alert" person. He was of medium height and, in those days, slender. What impressed her most was his "piercing" eyes, eyes so intense that "it was as though he used them for understanding."[7]

During the year he spent in Cleveland, however, Sherwood appears to have been mostly all business. Although he impressed Bottger with his exceptionally fine advertising copy and told him many incidents from his earlier life, he never expressed to him any interest in any other kind of writing. Cornelia kept up with her husband's work. "Sherwood gave her credit at that time at least for helping him with his writing," Bottger remembered. "I believe she edited some of his stuff, for he was not well-educated." At first he enjoyed his work, judging by how pleasantly the United Factories secretary would remember him.

He dictated easily and seemed to know and like his work. A neat dresser, he seemed well-read and well-educated, always used good language, never forgot to be "gallant." A "good-looking, dark, mature" man, he always had a smile, no matter how hard the work was. In fact, his pleasantness always made the secretary feel willing to work for him. He had a good, hearty laugh; he laughed when other men smiled. "He'd always kid with you when you came to the desk."

The heartiness and the laughter could not have lasted many months. Anderson never did develop the skill of organizing his office routine, and in the winter and spring of 1906–7 much more serious trouble of a different sort unexpectedly arose.[8]

While still with Long-Critchfield, Sherwood had become acquainted with one J. W. Miller, who manufactured chicken incubators in Freeport, Illinois, and had an advertising account with the agency. Trusting the manufacturer on the basis of this acquaintance, Anderson arranged in the fall of 1906 to have a new kind of Miller incubator marketed through United Factories. Under the stimulus of Sherwood's advertising copy the incubators sold in great quantity; in fact, they sold unfortunately well, for beginning in January a serious defect in the larger-sized machines began to develop. "One unversed in such matters"—the narrator says in that heartbreakingly funny tale, "The Egg,"—"can have no notion of the many and tragic things that can happen to a chicken." The Miller incubator was a hot air machine rather than a hot water one, the latter being preferable; and heat was supplied, during the twenty-one days it takes for an egg to hatch, by a lamp. The 60-egg size worked very well, but the 120- and 280-egg sizes did not: the lamps in the larger sizes had insufficient heating capacity, and, knowing this, the manufacturer, in order to increase the diffusion of heat, had made some holes, concealed from view by a casing, in the pipe designed to carry heat to the incubator and the lamp's fumes to an exhaust vent. In operation, some of the fumes leaked through these holes into the incubator and smothered all life in the eggs.[9]

The complaints that the mail began to bring daily to the United Factories office were many. Letter after letter came in, angry letters, sorrowful letters, and Anderson, as he had promised in "My Word to You," had to answer them all. Even George Bottger, who had not made the original arrangement with Miller or written the seductive advertising copy or composed the apologetic replies, could still after half a century recall those letters, especially a letter from a one-armed woman who had washed clothes for a living and had hoped to make some money with her incubator. Not only did Anderson have to reply to some six hundred such letters, which continued to come in for months, but also it was he who by the mistake of trusting Miller was the cause for the firm's losing thousands of dollars. Ultimately some of the loss was recovered when United Factories brought suit against Miller, who settled out of court. First, however, all their purchase money had to be refunded to the unhappy buyers, a sizable burden for a small company; yet how could one repay, for example, the one-armed washerwoman for the loss of her time and hopes? "In later life," says the narrator of "The Egg," "I have seen how a literature has been built up on the subject of fortunes to be made out of raising chickens. . . . It is a hopeful literature and declares that much may be done by simple ambitious people who own a few hens. Do not be led astray by it. It was not written for you."[10]

The anger and sorrow of the letters became too much for Anderson to take. An employee in the firm had noted "the pace Anderson was going," his heavy smoking, his extreme nervousness, and had predicted to himself that "that fellow would not last five years"; actually Anderson's breaking point came much earlier. He experienced a catastrophic psychological reaction to his accumulated anguish in, apparently, the summer of 1907, possibly about the time that his and Cornelia's first child, a boy named Robert Lane after his Toledo grandfather, was born on August 16, 1907. Certainly his business worries of the winter and spring, the frustration, anger, guilt, dismay he presumably felt about the incubator disaster, would have been reinforced by concern for his wife's first pregnancy and the pressure of an approaching new family responsibility, a "final triumph of the egg." Deeply disturbed, Anderson then had some kind of temporary nervous breakdown. For awhile, George Bottger emphatically recalled, Anderson disappeared from home and office and was finally found "wandering around in the woods." It is possible, indeed, that Sherwood may have had this breakdown in mind, rather than his later, more famous one when, some years later, he told his Chicago friend Margaret Anderson during a discussion of the significance of change that

> Change is a fine thing. . . . It's bad to grow static. If you can make a change consciously it's very good. I have never found the courage to do this. I used all the subterfuges of the unconscious; I have found myself lost in the woods after a day and night of wandering simply because I wanted to change the current of my life and didn't know how to do it. The getting lost amounted to a sort of conscious aphasia.[11]

Whatever the crisis of 1907 involved, Anderson appears not to have required hospitalization; but Bottger as general manager of United Factories had to "pick up the pieces" of the incubator fiasco, because the president of the firm was in no condition to do it. By the end of August, when the trial year was up, the arrangement between the latter and the company was not renewed, though there is disagreement over what actually happened. Sherwood later told his brother Karl that "By hard work he had increased the business 400 per cent, but the owners reneged on their agreement." On the other hand, though George Bottger could not recall years afterward the steps by which Sherwood left United Factories, he was sure that the departure was a voluntary one resulting from the breakdown; the two men remained good friends, and Bottger subsequently went over to nearby Elyria to help him organize his new business there. Whichever is correct—and Bottger's account seems far more dependable—the Andersons did move to Elyria, presumably in early September, where Sherwood had an opportunity to establish a business of his own.[12]

The significance of the Cleveland venture does not lie in its being a check to what the narrator of "The Egg" sardonically terms the "upward journey through life" for the Andersons, though Sherwood might well have uneasily feared that he was about to repeat his father's humiliating failure in Caledonia and Clyde to fulfill his own dream of success. Rather, the significance lies in what must now be accepted as fact, that he experienced a breakdown in the summer of 1907, a breakdown that anticipated the more serious and decisive one yet to come. This earlier crisis seems to have reinforced and confirmed in Anderson a psychological pattern in the face of distress that was observable in the petty episode from his Clyde years when he abruptly stamped on his own new straw hat: acutely mounting pressures from the conflicting obligations of a given situation, an abrupt collapse of resistance to the pressures, an eruption of behavior self-destructive in appearance but self-preservative in end. To be sure, such a pattern is to some extent "normal" in any human being; it is the overreactive nature of the response that is significant in Sherwood. The reaction of the adult Anderson was far more catastrophic than that of the young Anderson because, obviously, the conflicting obligations were more complex, important, and threatening. The Cleveland episode set in him a pattern of hysteric behavior under stress, of withdrawal from an overwhelmingly problematic situation through physical flight. It can be surmised that in 1907 the pattern was evoked from profound anguish before the requirements of survival in the business world, and recovery was made possible relatively simply by a move from one plan to another, one business to another. When the pattern reasserted itself much more urgently in 1912 in Elyria, the conflicting obligations had become yet more complex and demanding, but Anderson would have learned meanwhile that the terms of the conflict in themselves provided a door out of the psychic trap.

2.

Looking at it now, one might say that Sherwood Anderson went to Elyria as to an appointment in Samara; for when the Andersons moved there, probably in early September of 1907, they entered a community designed, as it were, to intensify the emotional conflicts Sherwood had been under-going. Not that this small city was an Ohio Gopher Prairie. For one thing, it was attractively situated some twenty-five miles southwest of Cleveland in level country but at the confluence of the two branches of the north-flowing Black River. Around the falls on each branch an extensive city park was already being developed through an unusual combination of private generosity and public foresight. Cascade Park with its river gorges, rock formations, woods carefully left in their wild state, and winding paths only a few minutes walk from the business center gave the citizens a right to their pride in "picturesque Elyria," and Anderson would enjoy taking solitary strolls there. During most of the nineteenth century, after its founding in 1817 by well-to-do New Englanders, Elyria had been kept mainly a residence town with "broad shaded streets and beautiful homes," though some manufacturing had come in with the railroads after the Civil War; but just a few years before the Andersons arrived, the city began expanding rapidly.[13]

This explosion of industrial and population growth had begun with the opening in 1895 of the great U.S. Steel factories of South Lorain, only a fifteen-minute commuting ride by interurban train from Elyria. By the early 1900s the city's "dominant spirits," as a current promotional book put it, had "caught step to the music of 'expansion' and were working, through the Chamber of Commerce, and every other legitimate source to emphasize Elyria's superior advantages as a manufacturing city." The ef-forts of the Chamber, which Anderson later joined, were so successful that within a decade and a half industries employing hundreds of workers and producing such varied objects as the Worthington golf ball and the Gar-ford automobile settled in Elyria. The population shot up from 8,791 in 1900 to 14,825 in 1910, a population, as the promotional volume phrased it, "Not of the floating variety but of people who have come to stay and to enjoy . . . the solid, substantial atmosphere which has ever character-ized the city's business features, keeping clear of reckless inflation and fic-titious estimates." Here, in the "all-pervading atmosphere of home life and stability," was presumably the right place for a man making a second try at business. All he needed to do was to impress people as a "live wire" and then to see that his company kept up with the city's fast industrial growth.

And if Elyria was not Gopher Prairie, it was not entirely on the way to being Zenith either, though Anderson used details from Elyria in portray-ing the industrialization of Bidwell in *Poor White*. The local "boosters"— the word was current in the city's newspapers at least by 1911—certainly measured progress in terms of Elyria's population statistics and the number, size, and variety of its businesses, in terms of its busy railroad lines and paved streets, its electric lights, gas, steam heat, and water and sewer system, that quantifiable complex "which stands for the life of a typical American city." To be sure, also, every bookkeeper and stenographer who graduated from the Elyria Business College could "secure employment," and the Elks Club, which Sherwood joined and where he enjoyed playing pool, was not only "One of the largest and most influential lodges in the city" but was said to have "the finest lodge rooms in Northern Ohio." The city was also proud of its progressive public school system, its many churches, its large free public library, its municipal hospital, which opened the year after the Andersons arrived, and even its spacious "Old Ladies Home," the founding of the latter especially testifying to the energies of some "public spirited women." The city's leaders took quite seriously the new doctrine of community "service."[14]

The biographies of civic leaders in local histories are of course suspect for their unremitting praise, but this theme of service runs through the accounts of the lives of many of Elyria's prominent citizens of the time. One instance must suffice, that of Dr. Philip D. Reefy, on whom Anderson was probably to draw for the Dr. Reefy of "Paper Pills" in *Winesburg, Ohio.* Born, like Irwin Anderson, in 1845, Reefy idealistically enlisted in the Ohio Volunteer Infantry in 1861, rose to captain for his bravery and leadership, subsequent to the War studied medicine, and in 1868 began a decades-long practice as a "true family physician" in Elyria, leaving only briefly for further study in hospitals in Vienna and Berlin. Unlike the Dr. Reefy of Winesburg, he married at thirty-two and had two children, and lived in some magnificence in a large stone house complete with castellated tower. An enthusiastic home gardener, he also owned for years a fifty-acre farm, much of it, the reader of "Paper Pills" might note, "set out in a cherry, pear and apple orchard." People would remember him affectionately as a "character," a big, energetic, bluff-mannered man, who swung his arms and whistled as he walked Elyria's street and who told "inimitable stories." Like Winesburg's Dr. Reefy, though public rather than private in expression, he was "strictly independent" in politics and religion and acted "on the impulse of his own opinion, caring little for the conventionalities of society or their influence." Twice, before the Andersons arrived in the city, the real Dr. Reefy had been elected mayor; nevertheless, "His public spirit was not manifested alone when in office, but he was constant in exercising his influence either personally or by the wielding of a vigorous pen toward any betterment which he was convinced was necessary for the city." His career, one factual-eulogistic account emphasizes, showed "individual and personal service" to be "at least coequal in importance with vested property and material rights and privileges."[15]

Not all of Elyria's leaders lived lives of such open civic virtue, and one may smile knowingly when the promotional volume *Picturesque Elyria* asserts that here was "a community containing high standards of intelligence and morality, with enough of puritanism introduced by its founders to warrant enforcement of law." Behind such self-serving prose one can sense, and rightly, that this prosperous, expanding community was under the tight control of a rather small power group knit together by economic, social, and personal relationships, a group to which, fatefully, both Sherwood and Cornelia were admitted. The more one learns of Elyria in that 1907–13 period when the Andersons lived there, the more one understands that the people who controlled the community were for the most part not hopelessly reactionary, and that the quality of the community's cultural life was less limited than Anderson's rebellion against a businessman's existence might have led one to suppose.

Although the majority of Elyria's citizens were safely Republican in politics, one of the most respected persons in town was Dr. Reefy's equally civic-minded brother, Professor Frederick S. Reefy, a former school teacher turned editor of the *Elyria Democrat* and frequent candidate for civic office on the Democratic ticket. By 1907, furthermore, the other two newspapers of the city, the weekly *Republican* and the daily *Evening Telegram,* were under the managership of a man who became Anderson's best friend in the community, one Perry S. Williams, liberal Republican city treasurer from 1902 to 1920 and representative to the National Progressive Convention of 1912 that nominated Theodore Roosevelt for the Bull Moose Party. In September of that year of the New Freedom, six thousand people assembled in Elyria to honor the Progressives' nomination of Arthur Garford, local automobile manufacturer and Chamber of Commerce leader, for state governor. Nor was interest restricted to the politically acceptable. In 1911, Emma Goldman, feminist and anarchist, denounced capitalism before "two hundred curious" Elyrians who "came away with an admiration for the woman," while in the same year the local Socialist Party brought to a good-sized audience a series of five nationally known lecturers who provided "a thorough exposition of the materialist philosophy."[16]

More significant of Elyria's general progressiveness was the widespread interest in "current issues," an interest that matched both Sherwood's and Cornelia's. As early as 1908 a Political Study Club was founded by some thirty women, many from Elyria's first families. Initially the objective of the club, to which Cornelia was elected at least by March of 1910, was to inform women of their legal status and to press for women's suffrage; but as the club grew in membership, it began to concentrate also on the improvement of the city's schools and on other social matters. In March 1912, for example, the Political Study Club arranged an open meeting "for the people of Elyria" at which a Cleveland social worker discussed "the needs of delinquent children," and Florence Terry, high school history teacher and close friend of the Andersons, spoke on abuses in adult penal institutions. Even more explosive issues than social-ism, suffrage, and penal reform were sometimes addressed to an extent surprising only to those who accept Anderson's account in his *Memoirs* as the full story of Elyria. Early in 1907 the *Democrat* reported a meeting of the Board of Health at which "Venereal disease was discussed at length," including its prevalence and "the prevention of its spread among young people." In February of 1912 the intrepid, upper-class women of the Po-litical Study Club held "One of the most interesting discussions ever con-ducted" by the club on whether the prevention of venereal disease should be taught in Elyria's public schools, while some months later an attentive male audience at the Chamber of Commerce luncheon heard a Cleveland physician attack "with utmost candor" the failure of parents to teach chil-dren by the age of four "the physiology of procreation." This is not to ar-gue that Elyria was at the spearpoint of modernity, but rather to empha-size again that the group of people at the top of the city's power structure, the group into which the Andersons were received, was not solely preoc-cupied with material progress, though Sherwood was to learn the limits of the group's tolerance in more subjective matters.[17]

Elyria, finally, was not even a cultural desert. Elyrians could, and did, go by train to Cleveland in forty minutes, not only to conduct business or shop but also to see *Peer Gynt* or to hear *Tannhäuser.* Only nine miles to the southwest was Oberlin College, where interested townspeople fre-quently went for musical events such as the concert by the Cincinnati Sym-phony under Leopold Stokowski's direction that Cornelia Anderson and "quite a number of the music lovers of Elyria" attended on the evening of March 20, 1911. Under Perry Williams's literate management, the *Evening Telegram* devoted more than a column to Mark Twain's death, called attention to the founding of a new magazine in Chicago named *Po-etry,* and in editorials praised *Pilgrim's Progress* for its "terse and graphic style," Dickens and Twain for their "universal appeal," and William Dean Howells, "the educated man's novelist," for the exactness of his language and his "supreme gift of making commonplace people interesting." The city contained a number of clubs for women interested in music or litera-ture, including the socially prestigious Fortnightly Club, to which Cor-nelia was elected, said to be "the oldest women's club in Ohio and the first purely literary club in the state." As Mrs. Anderson later commented, "We were all yearning for culture." The yearning existed whatever its level of sophistication.[18]

So Sherwood's rejection of a business career that climaxed his Elyria period cannot be understood as a reaction against a totally insensitive, to-tally antagonistic environment. The nature of the city in many ways actu-ally encouraged his personal development, but once encouraged, Ander-son proceeded to go far beyond socially permissible limits. This process was long and complex, one constant in it being that it worked itself out in a community far smaller than Chicago or Cleveland, a community where, because of the position conferred on him in the social hierarchy, Anderson was highly visible. It was this visibility that made his journey to Samara seem then so dramatic and now so inevitable.

3.

After their arrival in about September 1907, the Andersons appear to have settled readily enough into the life of the small but growing city. Their first place of residence was The Gray, a four-family red-brick apartment house at 401 Second Street, only a few blocks from Anderson's place of business. Sherwood's youngest brother Earl came to live with them there, and now with Robert nearly a year old and Cornelia again pregnant, the family presumably needed more room than an apartment afforded. Sometime in the late spring or the summer of 1908 the Andersons moved to a two-story frame house at 229 East Seventh Street where they lived for the remainder of their years in Elyria. It was a pleasant residential street. Directly across from them lived the Wilfords, with whom they became good friends. Frank Wilford, an Oberlin graduate, was already known as a capable young attorney in one of Elyria's leading law firms, and his energetic, very Baptist wife was full of good works. Right beside the Andersons lived the family of Angelo Delia, of whose love of gardening Sherwood wrote in his *Memoirs,* though he fancifully transformed this Italian immigrant from the expert stonecutter he actually was into a restaurant owner. It suggests Anderson's orientation at the time toward Elyria's Anglo-Saxon Protestant upper class that he looked down on Delia as a foreigner and a peasant, and, as he later confessed, "never made a neighbor" of this next-door resident, even though by 1912 Delia had sufficiently prospered that with his brother-in-law he could buy out the monument business of his former employer.[19]

Sherwood set up his own business in one of the brick buildings of the "Old Topliff & Ely plant" on the bank of the East Branch of the Black River, just across Depot Street from the Lake Shore Railroad Station and very close to the center of Elyria's business section. Despite its name the Anderson Manufacturing Company at first manufactured nothing. Solely a mail-order business in the beginning, its one commodity was "Roof-Fix," a name invented by Anderson for the heavy preservative roofing paint which United Factories had sold and which his folksy advertisements now guaranteed would "put any old, leaky, wornout, rusty, tin, iron, steel, paper, felt, gravel or shingle roof in perfect condition, and keep it in perfect condition for 5c per square foot per year." As Mrs. Anderson later said, "Roof-Fix carried us to Elyria." For a while Sherwood continued to buy Roof-Fix in bulk from a Cleveland manufacturer, poured it into one-and five-gallon tins of the sort used for putting up maple syrup, and sold it at forty cents a gallon often to farmers for barns and sheds, at first "direct from the factory," later through hardware and paint dealers.[20]

The Roof-Fix business prospering—United Factories had sold it for five times its cost of manufacture—Anderson looked about for new sources of profit. In September 1908 he purchased a locally invented knife sharpener and began "pushing it on the market," and subsequently added other household items. By August of 1909 the *Evening Telegram* could remark that Anderson had "already made his name known from one end of the country to the other as the Roof-Fix Man of Elyria," and on August 18 of that year he took his first major step toward expansion by acquiring the "plant and good will" of the Wilcoxson Paint Company, a firm in nearby Lorain that manufactured ready-mixed paint and sold it "direct to you at the Wholesale Price." Although L. L. ("Daddy") Wilcoxson and Waldo Purcell, his general manager, moved to Elyria to oversee the actual making of the paint, their business was reorganized as the Anderson Paint Company; by mid-January 1910, the Wilcoxson manufacturing equipment had been moved into the Topliff & Ely plant. Since now Wilcoxson paints and Roof-Fix as well were being made under his factory roof, Anderson could truthfully enough advertise himself as a paint manufacturer as well as mail-order supplier, though in the *Memoirs* he would more exactly write that he was "a salesman who had got control of a factory." With characteristic enthusiasm he announced to a local newspaper that he expected "to make a world wide reputation for paints made in Elyria."[21]

About office procedure and the management of a business Anderson knew only what he had observed in his advertising company experience and what he had learned from his year at United Factories. It may have been only a gesture of self-congratulation when he invited Burton Becker, his former Clyde employer at the Elmore Bicycle Company, to go into business with him, much to the latter's great hilarity at the suggestion; but he did get help from George Bottger of United Factories, who, feeling that Anderson lacked business sense, obligingly came over to Elyria several times to help him organize his procedures. When, long after Anderson's departure from Elyria, William Sutton interviewed Frances Shute, who had been Sherwood's secretary, and other office workers, he found some difference of opinion concerning Anderson as an employer. To one stenographer he had seemed simply an ambitious, hard-driving man who expected his employees to keep exact hours and to work hard themselves. To other employees, however, he was a "swell fellow," a "grand man" to work for, a considerate and kindly person who "had an understanding way with a beginner." Cornelia subsequently wrote to Sutton of her pleasure that most of Sherwood's employees in Elyria had thought him a fine person. "Mr. Anderson," she commented with her unfailing generosity in public statements on her ex-husband, "was good for people, and they were the better for contact with him." Significantly Anderson remembered himself in the *Memoirs* in the image of the driving businessman who "hurried to an office, sat at a big desk, rang bells, got suddenly and sometimes nastily executive," for in his later career as writer he wished to repudiate all aspects of his business life. By some combination of charm and drive he was able to obtain financial backing for his developing business ventures from the National Bank of Elyria, where he conducted his banking affairs. Further investment support came from John Emerson (formerly Clifton Paden), his old friend of Clyde days, and from Walter Brooks, a director of the National Bank and one of the city's leading businessmen. Indeed, one suspects that Anderson's later portrait in *Poor White* of Steve Hunter, the glib, grandiose manipulator of the wealthy men of Bidwell, is partly a self-recriminating image of himself in Elyria.[22]

Whatever self-image Anderson had when actually an Ohio businessman, certainly a large aspect of his real self was that he continued to be a man of ideas. At about the time, late 1909, when he took over the Wilcoxson Company, he initiated a scheme called "Commercial Democracy," which his associate Waldo Purcell later described as a "selling plan," the "idea being to sell small blocks of stock to dealers" in Anderson's paint products. In October 1909, Anderson began advertising in the *Rural New-Yorker* that he wanted to furnish "one sincere, earnest man in every town and township" with "the capital and advertising" to start in business; and with the November 20, 1909, issue of the weekly he began requesting "Farmers, Mechanics, Builders, Small business men, any one anxious to improve his condition," now to write to "Commercial Democracy." Initially "Commercial Democracy" seems to have brought him some commercial success, though one may wonder if he was reporting exact facts when only four months later, in March 1910, he expansively asserted that he now had "a thousand agents"—his dealers, apparently—who were "co-partners" with him and "shared in the profits of the business" of selling Wilcoxson paints and shipping Roof-Fix "into every state and territory in America, to Japan, Europe, South America, and Alaska." The last advertisement for "Commercial Democracy" in the *Rural New-Yorker* was in the issue for November 12, 1910. As late as March 1911, however, their neighborly "Paint and Roof-Fix Man" could advise Elyria's citizens that by buying from "our home town" paint factory they could save money because "We run our business on a co-operative basis," and despite "an increase of over one hundred per cent in business over last year we still have no travellers on the road." Nevertheless, the *Rural New-Yorker* advertisements suggest that the year from

November 1909 to November 1910 constitutes the life of the specific idea of Commercial Democracy.[23]

Karl Anderson's recollection, confirming Purcell's, was that his brother's plan was primarily "a new method of approaching dealers in paint throughout the state, in which the storekeeper shared in the profits of the product," but there is contemporary evidence that the scheme had for Anderson wider ramifications. In the *Memoirs* he wrote deprecatingly of Commercial Democracy as springing from a naive early interest in socialism and the "cooperative commonwealth." Although in context these terms seem to be synonymous merely with profit-sharing, in Elyria in 1910 he claimed more for his plan and claimed it seriously, seriously enough that his friend Perry Williams, with whom he often talked over his ideas, could discuss Commercial Democracy in an editorial in the issue of the *Evening Telegram* for February 2, 1910 (p. 4). Under the heading "Is Commerce to be Re-organized?/Sherwood Anderson is Doing His Best and Here's Luck to Him," Williams wrote that "Interest and good wishes of Elyria people and people outside Elyria will follow Sherwood Anderson in his effort to put his paint and roofing business on the plane of a commercial democracy." Although Americans enjoy "democratic public institutions," the editorial continues sympathetically, businesses are run

on a pretty thoroughly monarchical basis. In principle, the many exist for the benefit of the few, instead of each existing for the benefit of everybody else.

Anderson says that this despotic way of running business is all wrong and that it is thoroughly practicable to make a business entity out of every worker, just as every voter is a political entity.

We hope he is right about it. It is undoubtedly depressing to the average worker to feel that he is on about the same plane as a machine. Strikes universally reflect the instinctive feeling of semi-proprietorship that comes to a good workman who has labored loyally and earnestly for an institution.

Although that final paragraph may reflect Williams's own attitudes as much as his friend's, both men obviously had been discussing Commercial Democracy in terms, not just of paint dealers, but of factory workers to whom profit-sharing might be the means to a national cooperative commonwealth. In its concern over one mode of depersonalization of the worker, furthermore, that final paragraph of Williams's prose is, obliquely, both reminiscent of Anderson's own earlier factory experience and suggestive of the state of mind out of which, while still in Elyria, this businessman could write the first draft of a novel titled *Marching Men* and dedicated "To American Workingmen." Part of Anderson's desire to write was his intense desire to express certain ideas about American life as he saw it, a desire he had manifested even as a young workingman himself in the Chicago of the late 1890s.[24]

Writing of a semicreative sort was in fact associated with the profit-sharing plan, for in support of his scheme Anderson produced some kind of publication, itself titled *Commercial Democracy*. Although he referred to it in the *Memoirs* as a magazine of several issues that he wrote entirely himself, the recollections of others more strongly suggest that *Commercial Democracy* was probably an advertising pamphlet or series of pamphlets in which he described his "new plan of retailing, cooperation between manufacturers and retailers." What is particularly significant about this publication is the inclusion of material that appears to resemble some of Sherwood's contributions to *Agricultural Advertising* in 1903–4. According to Karl Anderson, his brother "wrote some semi-autobiographical sketches which he had printed up in pamphlet form and distributed as advertisements," while Cornelia recalled for Sutton "articles in *Commercial Democracy* using a picturesque fictional character based on 'Daddy' Wilcoxson, the paint-maker, as a 'mouthpiece for Sherwood's philosophy.' The Wilcoxson character 'used words with too many syllables in them, etc.'" Limited as Karl's and Cornelia's remarks are, they clearly suggest that around late 1909 or early 1910 Anderson was again, as earlier when he was an advertising man in Chicago, linking creative writing with his business interests. It is not too much to assert that at this point his future career was again beginning to develop symbiotically out of his present one.[25]

Whether, as Anderson claimed, Commercial Democracy actually did increase his business by "one hundred percent" between March 1910 and March 1911, he was becoming sufficiently successful that in the latter year he could obtain financial backing from some of Elyria's leading citizens to form a new company combining profit-sharing with more conventional business features. On November 20, 1911, at his instigation, the American Merchants Company was incorporated in the state of Ohio. Under this new name the Anderson Manufacturing Company and the Anderson Paint Company were to be merged—though in fact newspaper advertisements continued to run under the names of the original companies—for the purpose, as before, of manufacturing and selling paints, Roof-Fix, and other materials related to the paint and roofing business. The company was capitalized at $200,000 divided into two thousand shares of stock for which seventeen local investors subscribed $24,000, the remainder to be sold to local dealers "the country over and thus interest them especially in the sale of the company's products through their receiving a portion of the company's earnings." Anderson, whose name does not appear among the five persons signing the Articles of Incorporation, subscribed to no stock himself but was allowed $25,000 in common stock as president and general manager of the firm, an arrangement that provided him considerable potential profit at no cost of investment.[26]

In *Poor White* the shrewd, ambitious Steve Hunter, who intends "to become a manufacturer . . . to make himself a leader in the new movement that was sweeping over the country," parlays a contract with the investor Hugh McVey into two stock companies by cleverly bluffing a banker, a rich farmer, and the banker's assistant cashier into believing that he was "a man who could handle men and affairs," thus exploiting both inventor, who is ignorant of financial matters, and the investors, whom Steve knows he can handle simply by creating "the notion of money to be made without effort." One suspects, as has been suggested, that Hunter is in part a retrospective self-portrait of the author as businessman, avid to become "the one great man of the community" and willing to cheat and lie in order to obtain financial control of an invented machine the practical purpose of which he does not understand. The extent to which, in November 1911, Anderson may have secretly regarded himself as such an unscrupulous manipulator cannot now be known for certain; yet if fictionally the industrialization of Bidwell reflects the process by which Clyde, Ohio, turned into Elyria, still fiction is not reality. Anderson's backers obviously must at this point have had grounds for confidence in his abilities. One of them, a successful physician, later declared that he and others had invested in the American Merchants Company because they believed with the money-wise banker and businessman Walter Brooks that they "had a world-beater. We were going to put Sherwin-Williams out of business." These investors were not unshrewd, inexperienced men however they were represented in *Poor White*. Besides the doctor and Brooks, the investors included a well-to-do druggist, the cashier of the National Bank of Elyria, and one Charles H. Buttenbender, secretary of a highly successful local construction and insurance firm, and currently the president pro tem of the City Council. In retrospect one sees that the faith of these influential citizens in a man whom the *Democrat* straightforwardly praised as a "hustler" was misplaced, ominously so, but at the moment it must have looked from the outside as though Anderson had a sure future in the little world of Elyria.[27]

4.

In the autumn of 1911, Sherwood's fortunes seem in fact to have been at their height. By this time not only had the formation of the American Merchants Company solidified his position as one of Elyria's promising businessmen, but both he and Cornelia, though they had not become exactly prominent, had made a name for themselves in the community's social life. They had long since been significant enough in this city of now fifteen thousand that the "Personal and Social" columns of the local newspapers reported visits to them by, for instance, Sherwood's younger brother Irwin, now in business in New Orleans, or Cornelia's unmarried sister Margaret, or by out-of-town friends such as Edwin Baxter, vice president of the Cleveland Chamber of Commerce, or Trillena White, Sherwood's schoolteacher friend from his Springfield days. The newspapers also reported at least some of their occasional departures—Sherwood on business trips to northern Ohio towns or "the west," or all the Andersons to visit Cornelia's family in Toledo. Likewise the papers announced the births of two more Anderson children. A second son, John Sherwood, was born on December 31, 1908 at the Maternity Hospital in Cleveland, and nearly three years later, on October 29, 1911, a daughter, Marion, was born at the Elyria Memorial Hospital. Since Anderson, by choice as well as the pressure of business affairs, left the care of the children while they were very young mainly to his wife, it was not until late 1909 and after that Cornelia began to be active in the Fortnightly Club and to attend concerts at nearby Oberlin, sometimes with her husband, sometimes with other music-loving ladies.[28]

Where Sherwood's interest in music was less than Cornelia's, he very early in the Elyria years developed a passion for golf as a way of relaxing from business demands. In April 1908 he was among the men "elected to family memberships" in the Elyria Country Club. The club, situated on the southern outskirts of the city along a branch of the Black River, provided a golf course, tennis courts, canoeing, and dining facilities, and was a focus of social life for the more well-to-do Elyrians. (Shortly after her election to the Fortnightly Club, Cornelia entertained the other members there.) Placed among the Class B golf players, Anderson actually won the cup in his class tournament in July 1909 but, though his score had improved from much practice, he merely tied for second place two summers later. It is a measure both of his almost obsessive devotion to golf and of his increased status in the community that in February 1911, his year of particular business success, he was appointed to the Greens Committee and elected one of the club's directors; hence there is possibly a psychic and certainly a dramatic rightness to his account in the *Memoirs* of breaking off a golf foursome because of his first sickening moment of self-doubt as to his life goals.[29]

Such self-doubts as Sherwood may have had up through 1911 would not have been manifested widely, and the newspapers continued to announce the Andersons' participation in the ceremonial life of the city. They attended the Annual Charity Ball in May 1910, the "Social Event of the Season," held as a benefit for the Memorial Hospital, and the Anderson Manufacturing Company provided one of the two hundred floats in the Fourth of July parade that summer. Likewise in May 1910, Sherwood received reflected honor when the newspapers carried the announcement that brother Karl had just been awarded the second medal and a prize of

$1,000 at the Carnegie International Exhibit in Pittsburgh for his painting "The Idlers," which, according to one art critic, "places Mr. Anderson in the front rank of our younger artists." The *Telegram* jokingly commented that "Sherwood will probably claim that the picture was done in 'Wilcoxen' paint," a remark that suggests the Roof-Fix man's reputation for aggressive salesmanship. One may guess, however, that the public acknowledgement of Karl's success at this particular time may have strengthened Sherwood's interest in writing and in an artistic career of his own.[30]

Cornelia's position in Elyria was becoming even more secure than her husband's, as is indicated by her being one of those asked to pour tea—a marked social distinction according to the code rigidly governing such occasions—at a lawn party given in June 1911 at the home of one of the city's first families by the Women's Auxiliary of the Memorial Hospital Association. Certainly such an honor resulted in part from her having been an active member since September 1909 of the Fortnightly Club, her membership having been sponsored by a college friend in town, Helen Bowen. A number of the members seem to have been, like Cornelia, college educated, but there is no way to determine the level of the literary discussions. The regular newspaper announcements of the Club's twice-a-month meetings suggest a seriousness of interest in literature approaching both Cornelia's and Sherwood's. Coherent programs were planned for each year's sessions, and in the spring after Cornelia joined, the group discussed such unconventional writers as Ibsen, Walt Whitman, Tolstoy, and "several" other Russian authors, Mrs. Anderson herself contributing a paper on "Social Conditions in Russia." Since Anderson had by this time almost certainly begun to write fiction and since husband and wife frequently discussed their reading together, it is worth noting that in both the 1910–11 and 1911–12 seasons of the Fortnightly, Cornelia was involved in the club's sequential study of the development of the English novel from its beginnings up through George Meredith and Robert Louis Stevenson, concluding with a single meeting on "A Group of Short Story Writers." The program for the 1912–13 season, planned by Cornelia and another member, concentrated on Shakespeare, "the development of his mind and art through six typical plays," a fact which probably had something to do with the content of the so-called Amnesia Letter Sherwood sent to Cornelia during his crisis late in 1912.[31]

Despite having to care for two, and later three, young children, Cornelia Anderson found time for membership, from at least early 1910 on, in the highly active Political Study Club. Although she made fewer formal contributions to this group's meetings than to the Fortnightly's, the title of a discussion she presented at the meeting of March 9, 1910, "Why English Women are Militant," suggests that she was already an advocate of women's rights. That Sherwood was an advocate as well is indicated by his dropping business for a day to accompany her on June 27, 1911, to the statewide rally of the Ohio Equal Suffrage Association at Cedar Point, the resort near Sandusky where he had occasionally gone in his Clyde days. Support at that time for votes for women involved women and men with a considerable range of political outlook, but it had become known in Elyria that both the Andersons held advanced beliefs generally.[32]

In addition to Perry Williams's editorial comment on Commercial Democracy, the Elyria newspapers afford yet another glimpse of Anderson the man of ideas in their reports of his speech to the Teachers' Club of Elyria on the evening of January 20, 1911. As "the head of one of Elyria's growing industries," he spoke on "Women in Business," his talk being "the outgrowth of personal observation and association with women in the business world." This speech was a direct statement of the situation, much of what has proven undesirable being attributed to the wrong ideas underlying the education of girls and young women. He declared in favor of young women of whatever station in life, being prepared for the practical things in life. Permitting young girls and young women to indulge in the reading of romances and letting their minds dwell upon the impossible, unfits them for actual living. They should be trained to a common sense view of the future. Mr. Anderson took no stock in the oft-expressed fear that a business career unfitted women for the home. Rather he saw that such training made for better homes and better firesides. Because of his ideas and "very pleasant manner" Anderson's "clever address was enthusiastically received."[33]

The most interesting aspects of the talk, as reported, are Anderson's public stance as the thoroughly practical business man and his specific rejection of a form of literature that might encourage daydreaming, part of the imaginative life of human beings that he was later to examine much more sympathetically in his fiction. The enthusiastic reception of the talk by a professional audience suggests that the ideas were hardly revolutionary, though Sherwood's support of business careers for women precisely on domestic grounds was obviously not a widely held position at the time. But that same enthusiastic reception could only have encouraged him to be even more the man of ideas.

Meanwhile he and Cornelia had already acquired a less public and less passive forum where they might question ideas in more thoroughgoing fashion. Both were active members in and may well have been among the founders of the Round Table Club, a discussion group for young to middle-aged people, mostly married couples, that sometime in 1910 began meeting twice a month in each other's homes. Judging by what little is known about the club's membership, it included a high proportion of professional people. The Wilfords across Seventh Street from the Andersons belonged, as did Dr. John Rankin; Nellie Lewis, a high school teacher of German; and William Comings, the genial, progressive superintendent of schools. All were interested in civic improvement and in ideas in general, and each meeting consisted of presentations by two members, one amusing, the other "Something worth thinking about," Comings, for example, once reading a paper on "Nature and Instinct" and yet another member leading the discussion on it.[34]

By all accounts Sherwood was the most vocal member of the club. Throughout his life both attracted to those with more formal education than he and suspicious of them as over-intellectualized, he tended in the discussions to oppose the ideas of others and to take extreme positions. The Wilfords, who were to side with Cornelia in the emotional crisis that developed between her and her husband, felt that he was too "modernistic" in his views; Mr. Wilford suspected him of believing in "free love," while Mrs. Wilford thought him an advocate of socialism. Both she and Nellie Lewis, furthermore, considered Sherwood extremely conceited, though other members of the club did not, and Lewis was much offended by his lack of taste in discussing openly such matters as sex "that were not ordinarily spoken of in mixed groups." Although the memories Elyrians retained of the Andersons were markedly colored by Sherwood's actions before he left the city, several members of the Round Table felt that he was intellectually inferior to Cornelia but that he tended at club meetings to brush her opinions aside. Not only did Cornelia have a superiority in formal education, she had also a sharp, clear, logical mind, a devotion to telling the truth, a great respect for individual liberty, and views on literature and social questions that were as advanced as Sherwood's. In addition she had great tolerance toward new ideas and those who held them, and possessed a gentler, more refined manner than did her husband, who in fact struck at least two women at the time as unpolished to the point of being rather "oafish." Sherwood tended to take over a conversation, and he impressed a number of people who knew him then as being primarily and intensely interested in Sherwood Anderson and his own concerns.[35]

Among the most important of these concerns, Mrs. Wilford sharply remembered years later, was his writing; for Anderson had seriously begun working on, not simply essays and sketches for business-related purposes such as he had published in *Agricultural Advertising* or those pieces in the "Wedding Journal" notebook, but actual short stories and soon even novels. Just when he began writing fiction in and for itself can probably never be known exactly, exasperatingly so since such a beginning point is obviously crucial for understanding the life of any artist. According to Marco Morrow's informed testimony, of course, Sherwood had decided to be a writer back around 1903–4, before his marriage, when he was a new young advertising man. Still the demands of his job and his dis-

satisfaction with it in his last years at Long-Critchfield, the pressures during the disastrous Cleveland year, and the need to become established in
Elyria may well have deflected him. In his later years he did not refer to the
early fiction in *Agricultural Advertising,* now so clearly seen as apprentice
work for the future writer; that was put behind him as, presumably, the
work of a quite different Sherwood Anderson. Cornelia later recalled that
"his development as a writer was random rather than planned," a statement that accords with what has been seen of his career. Still, evidence
points fairly certainly to very late 1909 or more likely early 1910 as the
time when—as nearly as such a conscious conviction can be fixed chronologically—Anderson began to think of himself, not as writer secondary to
business man, but as engaged simultaneously in two equally demanding
careers, possibly even to think of himself as ultimately destined to be a
writer though presently supporting himself and family through a business.
Such evidence needs to be briefly reviewed.[36]

Anderson's lack of interest in, even willful disregard for, exact dates
needs little reiteration; the several statements in the *Memoirs* as to when
he "began to write" during the Elyria period are typical examples, being
both vague and contradictory. But a statement made much nearer in time
to the Elyria experience, and therefore inherently more dependable, appears to be more precise than usual for him. Writing to his close friend,
Marietta Finley, "Bab," on December 8, 1916, Anderson began his letter
with a remark reminiscent of Joseph Conrad: "For nearly seven years now,
ever since I began writing—and I count any happiness I have had in life as
beginning when I began to scribble—. . . ." Reckoning back from the letter's date brings one to very late 1909 or early 1910 as the time when he
felt he was beginning to be a writer. Anderson characteristically blunts his
apparent precision by going on to state that "In my second year here [in
Elyria] I began to write," a remark that could push the date back earlier
in 1909 or even into 1908; but Karl Anderson's testimony helps confirm
as reasonable a later rather than earlier dating. Referring, though not by
name, to Commercial Democracy, first specifically announced in November 1909, Karl recalled that the competition Sherwood's successful
scheme evoked from other paint manufacturers forced him to concentrate
more heavily on his business affairs, and Karl concluded circumstantially,
"Quite vividly do I recall his annoyance at this, as it interfered with his first
attempt at writing a novel, a project that he had been encouraged to undertake by our younger brother Earl." Finally, Anderson's business associate Waldo Purcell recalled that "while we were together he spent much
of his time writing short stories—none of which were accepted until after
he left Elyria." Since Purcell and Wilcoxson were settling their business affairs in Lorain and moving to Elyria during the last months of 1909 and
were definitely manufacturing paint in the Topliff & Ely building by late

January, 1910, Purcell's recollection again indicates that, surprisingly, Anderson can probably be trusted when he implied to Bab that the winter of 1909–10 was the time when he began to write for the sake of writing and to seriously consider the possibility of a career as artist. He was not yet ready, of course, to leave business for literature. After all, he had a family to support.[37]

As has been suggested, his writing had heretofore had a symbiotic relation to his business activities. Certainly for the essays and sketches published in *Agricultural Advertising* and apparently for those in *Commercial Democracy* he had drawn on personal memories and on observations of people around him as illustrations of ideas and attitudes that he wished to express. Yet in this business-connected writing he was not simply the absorptive ego. Even in composing a paint circular designed to increase sales and bring in more money, one searched, as the *Memoirs* declare, for "some sort of entrance into the confidence of the other man and so, even in such a crude approach to the art of writing, you thought, not of the thing of which you were presumed to be talking, but of the man addressed. 'How can I win his confidence?' you thought. . . ." In short, such writing in its limited way required that Anderson follow, not simply the business-oriented advice furnished by *Agricultural Advertising,* but also that more widely applicable advice that his fictional character Kate Swift, the Winesburg school teacher, gives George Willard when she talks to him of "the difficulties he would have to face as a writer": "The thing to learn is to know what people are thinking about, not what they say." Throughout his life Anderson was to be adept at learning "what people are thinking about," of winning people's confidence, though not always retaining it, and their confidences. Like his father, he could draw out feelings and experiences from friends, acquaintances, even the most casually met stranger. "Sherwood never went on a bus or anywhere," Cornelia said, "that he didn't come home with the life story of some acquaintance. All these later came out in his stories." Furthermore, the travels about the country enforced on him by his involvement with United Factories and the Anderson Manufacturing Company added to his store of knowledge about all sorts and conditions of men and women already gathered while he was laborer, race track swipe, soldier, and advertising copywriter. Although he was to turn almost violently against his career as businessman, especially for the gross and subtle corruptions he felt such a career inevitably engendered, the fact remains that in a real sense Anderson reached his literary career by going through his business one.[38]

Well before he was to leave Elyria, Anderson was giving much time to his writing. His secretary, Frances Shute, recalled that in 1911 and 1912, along with the usual business letters, she typed up manuscripts of stories dictated by her employer into his Dictaphone and prepared them for mailing out in an effort by him to achieve publication, an exact recollection supported by Cornelia's own that he was "sending manuscripts 'every-where' in his effort to publish." (One wonders at the possible relation such dictation of stories may have had on his development of an "oral" style.) He was engaged on more ambitious works too, for Frances Shute remembered that she "typed his first two books"—that is, drafts of *Windy McPherson's Son* and *Marching Men*—"and corrected his spelling." Rollin Reefy, successor to his father as editor of the *Democrat,* read *Marching Men* in manuscript, while Sherwood himself read aloud from a manuscript of *Windy McPherson's Son* to the Anderson's high school teacher friend Florence Terry and her mother until they told him "they could stand no more and advised him the reading public would not accept it." Other friends have testified to knowing that Anderson was writing; indeed, the fact of his writing must have been widely known, for when newspaper accounts of his breakdown appeared in early December 1912, he was referred to as both manufacturer and author.[39]

That Anderson was openly known to be writing and submitting manuscripts for publication makes at least suspect his own subsequent assertions that he began writing secretly and primarily for therapeutic reasons to resolve inner conflicts. Intense conflicts did develop in Sherwood, certainly by 1912, his last full year in Elyria, and no doubt he then found in the act of writing as well as in the subjects of which he wrote both an escape from acute unhappiness over his problems and a means of coping with these problems more "realistically" by "objectifying" them in fiction. Yet the "Rot and Reason" essays of 1903, and even more the "Business Types" fiction of 1904, had openly declared some years earlier a quite conscious tension within his own thought and feeling between an earnest dedication to rather conventional business attitudes and a recognition of the moral and psychic costs of business life. Judging by *Marching Men* and *Windy McPherson's Son,* it would appear, rather, that one very strong motivating force for their creation was a desire by Anderson to express his ideas about American life more honestly and dramatically and to a wider audience than he could through the limitations of a paint circular, a desire in all seriousness to gain people's confidence and "sell" them these ideas, now embodied in imagined lives, as a far more valuable commodity than Roof-Fix could ever be.

For whatever the initial drafts of *Marching Men* and *Windy McPherson's Son* may have been like—and these are the only works we can know for certain to have been completed by Anderson in some form before he left Elyria—they must have described alternatives to the way things then were in the United States. Seen in the context of what is known of Anderson's life in Elyria, *Marching Men* would seem to have been his first attempt at the novel form, though it was published after *Windy McPherson's Son* and hence has usually been assumed second in composition as well. Ideologically, *Marching Men* appears related to the period of Commercial Democracy running roughly from November 1909 to November 1910, the period when, according to the implication of Perry Williams's newspaper editorial of February 1910, Anderson was specifically interested in workers as well as in his paint dealers, and in envisioning a society in which each exists "for the benefit of everybody else." Like other romances of the future, such as Sherwood's boyhood favorite, *Looking Backward*, the book is a vehicle for the author's ideas, a fact that helps to explain its curiously abstract quality, as the probability of its being Anderson's first novel may explain its other weaknesses as fiction. Likewise *Windy McPherson's Son*, which obviously fictionalizes Anderson's doubts about and approaching abandonment of business career and first marriage, attempts to assess the effects of the business ethic not only on himself, through the persona of Sam McPherson, but on his fellow Americans as well. This is not to dissolve Anderson's acute personal problems into mere public concerns but to suggest instead that he felt his very real psychological conflicts to be a microcosmal reflection of sociological ones. It could not have been mere chance that, as his fellow Round Table members recalled, Sherwood was a great admirer of Ibsen, who in his dramas brought into single focus his corrosive analyses of both the individual and the social psyches.[40]

Nor would Anderson have been forced to write in secret because he had only self-encouragement to rely on. Actually at least three individuals in Elyria appear to have significantly supported his interest in writing. The first of these was Perry Williams, managing editor of the *Evening Telegram*. Williams, a "warm and friendly" handsome man, a bachelor and rather a rake, had been born in Toledo of Welsh descent but spent most of his life in Elyria. About Sherwood's age, he began his careers in both newspaper editing and local Republican politics in 1900, became manager of the Republican Printing Company, "the largest local and foreign printing business in Lorain county," and in 1907, the year that the Andersons settled in Elyria, founded the *Telegram*. Like Sherwood he was a member of the Elks, the Chamber of Commerce, and the Country Club—he had joined the Masons and Eagles as well—and thus constituted one of Anderson's closest links to the ruling class of Elyria. The friendship was a genuine one, and the two men enjoyed each other's company. One summer together with a third Elyria man they took a Stevensonian inland voyage by canoe up the west branch of the Black River beyond Oberlin in imitation of the Indians of an earlier time. According to Williams's account, Anderson on the trip was "an habitually early riser" who at "4 A.M. thought it was about time to get under sail again and incidentally commenced to tell us about some adventures he had down in

Clyde, when he was a boy . . . ," a comment suggesting that, like his father, Sherwood had achieved a local reputation as autobiographical raconteur. Williams, who, according to the *Memoirs* "had, vaguely, some notion of someday being a writer," loved to walk and talk about literature and ideas, and Sherwood "was always quoting him" to Cornelia. There is a tradition in Elyria that Williams once flatly asked Anderson, "Why don't you drop business and write?"; and the tradition may be tentatively supported by Anderson's account in the *Memoirs* of "Luther Pawsey," an admitted pseudonym for the rakish owner of a print shop and hence very possibly a figure based on Williams himself. Pawsey knows Anderson's dissatisfaction with business, sees from occasional sentences in the paint company circulars Sherwood gives him to print that he has talent, demands that he accept fully the aesthetic responsibilities of art, and is "perhaps the man who first suggested to my mind the idea of being a writer." For several reasons the Pawsey episode appears to be a highly fictionalized one, including the overtones in a purported print shop conversation of the scene in *Lord Jim* in which Marlow consults Stein concerning Jim's case and is told that the young man must in the destructive element immerse. Yet Anderson's method in the *Memoirs* of wrapping his fancy around a nucleus of reality does not obscure the certainty that in Williams, whether the latter be "Pawsey" or not, he found an Elyrian who supported his desire to become a writer.[41]

A second person who influenced him in the same direction, according to Sherwood's memory, in this case corroborated by that of Karl Anderson, was their brother, Earl. This youngest of the surviving Anderson children had grown up a tall, shy, odd, absentminded young man, a drifter and a loner, obsessed with the feeling that from birth he had not been wanted by the rest of the family. Just when he came to Elyria, apparently at Sherwood's invitation, is not certain, but by 1908, when he was twenty-three, he was definitely living with his brother and sister-in-law in their apartment in The Gray, and he seems to have stayed with them until at least the spring of 1911. At some time after that he left to visit brother Irwin, who was working for the American Can Company in New Orleans, and shortly afterwards disappeared again into his drifting life, not to be reunited with Karl and Sherwood until early 1926. For the three years or so of Earl's being in Elyria, Sherwood employed him as a shipping clerk in the paint company, partly out of affection and family loyalty, partly because of Earl's intense feeling for nature, his insight into the subjective qualities of people, especially "low-life" ones, and his strong, if largely ineffectual, desire to be, like Karl, an artist. Anderson felt later that as a result of long walks and talks together, brother Earl "had a great deal to do with my becoming a writer and understanding a little the impulses and purposes of the artist man"; and Karl, too, was convinced that the association with

Earl had helped stimulate Sherwood to write, specifically to undertake his first novel.[42]

That the companionship of Williams and Earl with Sherwood encouraged him in his writing seems certain even if their exact influence is not measurable. Perhaps as important was Cornelia's role in her husband's artistic development. One must treat as very dubious Anderson's own recollections of a wife who from the beginning resisted his desire to write. A profound conflict did develop in their marriage as their divorce in 1916 indicates; but there is sufficient proof that in later years Sherwood allowed his fancy to play with personal facts, as many divorced husbands might, and his several accounts probably reveal less about Cornelia than about his subsequent desire to justify himself as artist and ex-husband. Set against his own imaginative, after-the-fact perception of the situation, is the clear testimony of several people who knew both Andersons in the Elyria years that Cornelia did not oppose his writing but rather accepted it, even actively encouraged him in it. Mrs. Wilford, the Andersons' neighbor, who was very close to Cornelia, emphatically recalled that she helped her husband with his writing; and Cornelia's sister-in-law, who married her brother Robert in October 1912, insisted from equally direct knowledge that Cornelia not only was not opposed to Sherwood's writing, but actively "supported" his doing so. Despite her refined manner, Cornelia did not at all object to her husband's intense interest in people, especially "low-life" people, for what they actually were. She approved his being a "realist" about them, Robert Lane's wife declared; in fact she would have opposed only his falsifying a story and by temperament would have supported him in telling the truth about human beings as he saw them. The fullest and most exact testimony is that of Florence Terry. This very good friend of both Andersons stated that "it is certainly untrue that she ever discouraged Sherwood's writing efforts, but on the contrary, did all she could to help and encourage him." According to Miss Terry, Cornelia's actual assistance was stylistic, with such elements as "diction, rhetoric, and so forth," with his "*manner*" of expressing ideas rather than with the ideas themselves; and, Miss Terry affirmed, Sherwood "expressed great appreciation of his wife . . . for her help" in such matters. As for Cornelia herself, her remarks in later years to persons outside the family were few and guarded on this point. She told Sutton that the "'whole idea of Sherwood's writing was satisfactory'" to her and that it fitted with their mutually adventurous attitude toward life; she also told him that "she did not think she ever helped her husband with his writing." Possibly this remark merely denied "helping" him with his "ideas," for to her future daughter-in-law, her son John's wife, who was to know her intimately, she confided that, contrary to Sherwood's published accounts, she had supported his desire to be a writer and had in fact helped him in his writing, presumably in the way described by Florence Terry. In sum, the weight of evidence is that in his published accounts Anderson was largely fabricating a resistance to his writing on his wife's part. Perhaps in these accounts he wished to dramatize further the impediments that the American artist must overcome. Perhaps, too, Cornelia was at the time less complimentary about the quality of his apprentice efforts as novelist than he would have liked, he himself, according to Florence Terry, "being confident of his ability to write successful novels." Although Cornelia never criticized her husband's writings or ideas to the Terrys even when they did to her, she once remarked to Sherwood's secretary that a book Cornelia liked "isn't anything like those things Sherwood's writing," though such a remark might have been intended to describe rather than to evaluate. Certainly if Cornelia had not liked, say, Sherwood's first draft of *Marching Men,* she would have told him so in her characteristically truth-speaking way. But just as certainly Cornelia along with Perry Williams and brother Earl encouraged him to put down on paper what he saw and what he felt.[43]

5.

It now seems likely that up until near the end of the Elyria period the Andersons lived in reasonable harmony together; the discrepancy that Sherwood perceived between the ideals and the actualities of business life, though troubling, had not yet taken on the aspect of personal threat. Just when mental discomfort over his role as businessman became mental pain cannot now be fixed exactly; indeed, one might assume that only over a period of time did Anderson accumulate the profound sense of self-disgust he came to feel because of the cheating and misrepresentation he found endemic in his own and his friends' business practices, in his facility for using language to manipulate other people to his own profit. (Perhaps he really was made sick with such self-disgust during the playing of a golf foursome—if an actual experience, then best dated in the summer of 1911 when presumably he was already beginning to plan the launching of his last and most ambitious enterprise in the fall.) What is certain is that during 1912 intense psychic pressures built up in him, channeled themselves into the pattern set in his youth and reinforced by his Cleveland collapse, and burst out in the mental and emotional crisis that he ever afterwards was to view as having been decisive in his whole exterior and interior life.

One of the causes of mental and emotional strain during this last crucial year was the plain disagreeable fact that the American Merchants Company, which Anderson and his financial backers had set up with such great expectations in November 1911, did not achieve the desired success. It may have been only a symptom that the County Commissioners, who had purchased some $50 worth of labor and materials from the Anderson

Manufacturing Company in the 1909–10 fiscal year, purchased less than half of that amount in 1910–11 and nothing at all in 1911–12. But it was a cause as well as a symptom of financial trouble that "Daddy" Wilcoxson, whose paint company Sherwood had absorbed back in 1909 and who had served him as superintendent of his paint-making department, not only resigned from the Anderson firm on March 1, 1912, but in May with the backing of a number of local investors set up in Elyria a rival company for the manufacture of paint. In mid-August, Anderson, as "president and general manager" of the American Merchants Company, announced grandiosely to the *Evening Telegram* that his company was "making great plans for the extension of its business this fall" and that "the plan to establish a great factory in Elyria is meeting with the approval of the hundreds of retail merchants all over the country who are the owners of the company." If Anderson had been openly concerned before by the discrepancy between business pretense and business practice, he must have been privately far more disturbed now. Despite his assertion that his "strictly co-operative concern" was successful, his business was declining, he was probably overextended on credit from the National Bank of Elyria, he was certainly endangering the investments and the loyalty of friends who had trusted him, and his own financial situation was deteriorating to the point where he and his wife and three small children were approaching actual poverty. However he might try to deceive himself as well as others with the language of optimism, even bravado, the present lack of cash receipts meant that Irwin Anderson's son faced a repetition of his father's failure to achieve success as defined by his society, a failure made even harder to accept to the extent that the son may have retained some faith in profit-sharing as an ideal and not simply a marketing device. As his actions were to suggest, Anderson was aware of the disparity between his "tricky little words" about "great plans" and actual reality, and the result would have been to intensify sharply his feelings of guilt, self-hatred, and resentment of others.[44]

Part of Anderson's response to his increasingly desperate business situation was to devote himself even more to the interest that was supplanting the sale of paint. He spent "long days at the office of his paint factory," while in his evenings at home he "toiled over his writing." Apparently he had already begun his practice of secluding himself from his family during these evenings in a room he had boxed in as a study at the rear of the attic of his house. Here he could read and write, perhaps revising *Marching Men* or working on short stories to be typed up and sent off to magazines the next day by Frances Shute or even thinking about a novel, to be titled *Windy McPherson's Son,* about a successful business man who marries and becomes dissatisfied with marriage and business. The room over-looked the area behind his neighbor's house, which Angelo Delia, an enthusiastic gardener, did in fact cultivate. From his study early one spring morning in 1912 Anderson could well have watched this Italian immigrant, who had satisfactorily combined stone carving and business, preparing the earth for planting, and could have contrasted Delia's closeness to the land and to his family with his own increasingly isolating self-absorption. By this time Sherwood was finding in writing an escape both from business and his own sick self. One of his financial backers, the druggist Harry Crandall, seems to have become concerned at the way Anderson's nighttime activity was encroaching on daytime affairs. Years later Crandall recalled that "Anderson was a dreamer and did a lot of writing. He wrote volumes of stuff instead of tending to business. There was usually a sheet of manuscript on his desk."[45]

Early in the summer of 1912, according to one newspaper account of his later breakdown, Anderson, having already written "a quantity of magazine fiction," began a novel "which was to climax his work," setting himself this task, it will be noted, shortly before he was to proclaim his grand plans for further developing the American Merchants Company. Despite warnings from Cornelia and, very shortly, his own doctor, Sherwood began to drive himself even harder than usual. Occasionally in the evenings he would break off from his writing at Cornelia's insistence and play with Robert and John on the lawn, but usually he worked into "the early hours of the morning." Forced from his attic room by the summer heat, he "built a large screened porch at the back of the house and arranged lights so that he could write outside." Sometimes when he had written until well after midnight, Cornelia would go to persuade him to come to bed and find him "trembling with fatigue"; yet "at eight o'clock he would again be at the office, wrestling with the problems of manufacture."[46]

Torn between his "'duty to be in business and support a family and . . . his inclination to write,'" as Cornelia later analyzed the situation, Sherwood was also hurried toward serious crisis by the increasing strain between himself and his wife, a strain hardly improved by his absorption in writing to the further injury of his precarious business affairs and by the added care for Cornelia of a third child, one not yet a year old. Nellie Lewis, fellow member of the Round Table Club, later insisted that he was "never very nice to his wife" and that they "drifted apart during their stay in Elyria." Even allowing for Miss Lewis's intense, long-standing dislike for Anderson, the existence of stress between husband and wife is inescapable. Probably it had always had some basis in sexual incompatibility, as evidenced by his poem to her in the "Wedding Journal" back in 1904; for at least two people who knew Cornelia well and admired her greatly nevertheless felt that she was not physically so passionate as Sherwood definitely was. Still there is no doubt that she loved her husband very deeply, a fact that made their eventual separation extremely hard for her to bear despite the stoicism with which she did bear it. Some highly significant testimony of a different sort concerning the husband-wife relationship is that of Mrs. Robert Lane, Cornelia's sister-in-law, a shrewd judge of persons who knew Cornelia well. Although she was acquainted with Sherwood only during 1912 and even then met him but a few times, she was convinced that he felt profoundly rivalrous toward his wife. Drawn to her in part precisely because of her education, her intellectual acumen, and her enthusiasm for ideas, which was as intense as his own, he wanted the education that he had missed and felt sharply the lack of, and resented her having so much. This sense of competitiveness could manifest itself in apparently trivial but revealing ways. During one evening that she spent with the Andersons, Mrs. Lane became aware of Sherwood's great interest in words, the use of them by himself and by others as well. That night he was vying with Cornelia to find words that he knew but she did not. He began rushing about to dictionaries and encyclopedias to see if he could win the "word game," found a word only he knew, and was "delighted as a child" to have gotten ahead of his wife. Mrs. Lane vividly recalled Cornelia's tolerant look at the triumphant Sherwood as though at "a child with a new toy," the wife's question as to whether he was going to use that word (presumably in his writing), and the husband's assertion that he certainly was going to use it.[47]

This sense of competitiveness spilled over into his attitude toward Robert, John, and Marian, or "Mimi," as the little girl was called. Not particularly interested in the children when they were young, he left the care of them mostly to Cornelia. He did make a habit of putting them to bed at night himself, and the Wilfords across the street were aware that early evening was a raucous time over at the Anderson house, the noises seeming like those of circus animals to Mrs. Wilford, who was less tolerant of such bedtime antics than her husband. Significantly for a businessman turning writer, Sherwood's romps with his children were ways of "acting out imaginative scenes with them." At other times he would take the children on his lap, tell them stories, and ask them what they would "do with" these stories. In short, his main interest in the children when they were young was to "teach imagination" to them. Admirable though this part of his relationship with his children was, the major part of the responsibility for them fell on Cornelia, who may have had her own ideas as to what should be required of the New Woman in a marriage; Mrs. Lane recalled Sherwood's once telling her, entirely seriously, that this arrangement gave him a chance to get ahead of his wife in his reading and learning. Although he loved and within limits was even interested in his children, he appears to have felt at this point that they were hostages to fortune who hampered him in the assertion of his personality that his consuming desire to write had become.[48]

Not surprisingly, a man's relation to children, and to a woman as mother of them, is of considerable consequence in the two novels that he wrote first drafts of while in Elyria and later revised. In *Marching Men* the protagonist, Beaut McGregor, listens one Sunday afternoon to the tirade of a boardinghouse acquaintance, a barber, who had left his wife and children behind in an Ohio town and has come to live anonymously in Chicago in order to fulfill an artistic purpose, the making of violins. The barber describes children as a subtle stratagem employed by women to hold their husbands and to center their husbands' attention on themselves. Furthermore, in the melodramatic confrontation at the end of book 5 between the two women who love McGregor, a decision between a man's fathering children or continuing his work becomes central, though very unclearly resolved. In *Windy McPherson's Son,* Sam McPherson is temporarily deterred from concentration on moneymaking by a commitment to his wife's ideal that they devote themselves to the training of their future children, an ideal that may well include in its fictionalization of reality the fact that, in this critical autumn of 1912, Cornelia was reading Maria Montessori's newly translated *The Montessori Method* with its assumption that a new pedagogy for children will make them liberated adults. In the arbitrary and inconclusive ending of the novel Sam returns to his wife and three children, specifically adopted from a careless mother and not even his own—two boys and a girl, one older boy practical, the younger artistic, a constellation of age and temperament closely resembling that of the real Robert, John, and Mimi.[49]

This mesh of conflicts—the deteriorating business with its looming threat of personal financial disaster and betrayal of the confidence of others, the driving urge to write as a way both to feel "clean" through the act of writing and to fundamentally redirect his life, and the exhausting effort to be at once businessman and artist; the day-to-day, night-to-night tensions between husband and wife, and the sense of family obligations as barrier to the thrust of his profoundest desires—all this closed tighter and tighter within Anderson. Outwardly, at least in part, he was able to conceal his desperation—Mrs. Robert Lane had not at all sensed it during that critical year—or he appeared only to be overworking, though at least some friends knew that he was having business worries. Inwardly he must have felt jerked and hauled at as though by angry hands. Only a few years later he recalled hating Cornelia as a jailer bent on preventing his escape "out of marriage into life," and having night dreams of killing her. Such mingled feelings of guilt and hostility drove him to anguished solitary walks at midnight and to the self-destructive acts he wrote about in the *Memoirs* with an honesty that, ironically, few readers have focused on. With his womanizing friend Perry Williams and other local businessmen, who may well have been as harassed as he was could one see beneath the surface of their lives, he began to take trips to nearby Cleveland for bouts of drinking and promiscuity, very probably, as rumor soon came to have it in Elyria, joining with his friends in maintaining a room in a hotel in that city as a place for their frenzied holidays from daily routine.[50]

It is an ugly picture, relieved only by one's compassionate realization that the drunkenness and promiscuity on Anderson's part were attempts, useless and damaging to self and others, to cope with tormenting stress, and by, it appears, his refusal at that time as well as later to conceal the nature of these excursions. Such openness may of course have had an element of boasting in it, but one may speculate whether the scene in *Windy McPherson's Son* in which Mike McCarthy defiantly shouts out his sexual conquests to the men assembled that rainy evening outside the Caxton jail may not achieve its vividness from being obscurely yet truly based in the author's own life as well as in his observations of others. Whether Sherwood confessed his infidelities directly to Cornelia or whether they came to her first as rumor, her husband's behavior upset her so terribly that she finally broke through her composure and confided her troubles to Mrs. Wilford. The latter took up her cause; in fact, even half a century later loathing and horror at Anderson for the treatment of his wife could pour out from her in a rush of words at the unexpected mention of his name.[51]

Again Anderson seems to be writing in *Marching Men* directly out of personal experience when Beaut McGregor's acquaintance, the Ohio barber, comments on his desertion of wife and children: "'The town hates me. They have made a heroine of her.'" For several reasons many citizens of Elyria besides Mrs. Wilford came to dislike Sherwood and to keep his name unpopular in that community for decades after the Andersons left it, but his disregard for Cornelia's feelings was a compelling one. The ruling group of that city, which had taken in this promising couple, continued to admire Cornelia—and rightly so—but concluded that Anderson was "letting the side down" not only in defying community mores but in defying them so openly, sins of the flesh being more readily forgiven, or at least tolerated, if indulged in with a proper secrecy. Whatever momentary release from his troubles Sherwood may have obtained from drinking and sexual activity, whatever bitter satisfaction he may have taken from his refusal to be a hypocrite, he could hardly have avoided the ruling group's growing dislike of him, their new coldness in social relationships now being added to all his other conflicts and frustrations. According to Anderson's established psychic pattern, at some point the accumulated tensions had to break out abruptly and drastically. That point came late in November of this crucial year.[52]

6.

Although November 28, 1912, was Thanksgiving Day, Sherwood and his employees went to work as usual that morning. Cornelia noticed nothing peculiar about her husband before he left the house, though her parents from Toledo and their other children were visiting the Andersons for a family party that day and plans for the special dinner may have distracted her. When Anderson came into his office, however, his secretary, Frances Shute, noted that for the first time in her four years of work for him he "acted queerly."

He opened his mail, noted the small amount of money in it, and went to stand by a gas heater. He said, "I feel as though my feet were wet, and they keep getting wetter." Then he wrote a note to his wife, and leaving it with Shute, he said he was going for a walk and did not know whether he would be back or not. He walked along the railroad tracks which went past the office.

Crossing the nearby railroad bridge over the Black River, Anderson walked on eastward in the direction of open country and Cleveland.[53]

Concerned about her employer's odd behavior, Miss Shute phoned Mrs. Anderson and then delivered the note. "There is a bridge over a river with cross-ties before it," the note appears to have read; "When I come to that I'll be all right. I'll write all day in the sun and the wind will blow through my hair." But Anderson was not all right in the conventional sense, for he did not come home Thanksgiving afternoon or evening nor on Friday or Saturday or Sunday, nor did he telegraph Cornelia as he was accustomed to do daily when away from Elyria on a business trip. Advised by Walter Brooks, Mrs. Anderson did not notify the police. There was nothing else for her to do but call "upon friends to locate him" and endure the anxiety of waiting. Monday morning, December 2, the Andersons' Cleveland friend Edwin Baxter telephoned to tell her that the previous evening he had taken her husband to the Huron Road Hospital in Cleveland and that Sherwood had been admitted there suffering from some kind of nervous exhaustion. Cornelia left Elyria at once to be with her husband.[54]

What had happened to Anderson during those four days can be partially reconstructed. He later told Frances Shute that "he had amnesia and could not remember effectively things he wanted to do, such as call his wife. He would think of something he wanted to do and then forget it before he could do it." Dazed, fearful of other human beings, his head hurting, he wandered on foot at least part of the twenty-five miles to Cleveland, although later in the hospital he had a vague memory of at some point traveling in an interurban electric car. Though the weather was fair, it was cold at night; yet he seems to have slept out in the open at least two nights, once in a lumberyard, once in an open field. For food he took apples from an orchard, presumably the twisted ones the pickers had rejected, and munched on these together with the hard kernels from ears of corn, and once he dared to buy a loaf of bread in a village store. At least by Saturday, the third day of his absence, he was in Cleveland; for in an envelope postmarked from that city at 5 PM on November 30, he mailed to Cornelia seven pages of handwritten notes—the so-called "Amnesia Letter"—on his experiences since he left Elyria.[55]

Thereafter he wandered about wretchedly yet another day in the eastern suburbs of Cleveland, significantly enough the general area where he appears to have wandered during his earlier, briefer breakdown resulting from the United Factories catastrophe. Shortly after 5 PM on Sunday, December 1, he entered J. H. Robinson's drugstore at East 152nd Street and Aspinwall Avenue at the northeast edge of the city. He was haggard and unshaven, and the trousers of his bedraggled "dark grey business suit . . . were splattered with mud to the knees." Seeing that he looked ill, the store pharmacist, Fred Ward, offered him a chair. Anderson sat down and after a long pause announced vaguely that he did not know where he was, where he had come from, or even what his name was. On being told that he was in Cleveland, Anderson took out a pocket notebook and asked Ward to see if it gave his name and the name of any Cleveland person. From the notebook Ward identified Anderson and, finding Edwin Baxter's name, phoned him. Baxter came to the drugstore, and since Sherwood still appeared mentally confused, he had his friend taken to the Huron Road Hospital. Here Anderson was examined by physicians and "found to be suffering from a nervous exhaustion which apparently had been induced by worry of some kind or overwork."[56]

No direct comment by a physician on Anderson's condition and its causes has ever been found, though the newspapers, presumably on the basis of some kind of information at the hospital, reported variously that he was "suffering from nerve exhaustion" or from "severe mental strain" brought on by "overwork" or by "work and worry." In his four-day escape from Elyria and its agonizing conflicts, however, Anderson was clearly undergoing what psychiatrists now classify under the general term "dissociative reaction," a state in which, clinically speaking, certain "incoming, stored, or outgoing" mental information "is not associated or integrated with other information as it normally or logically would be." According to Karl Anderson, Sherwood told him, apparently not long after the incident, that a hospital doctor had advised him that he had suffered from amnesia. This is, of course, the term Anderson used when speaking subsequently to Frances Shute, and in *The Road to Winesburg* William Sutton accepts this diagnosis. Such evidence and informed opinion notwithstanding, the more exact term for Anderson's psychological state would seem to be "fugue," since, as the word indicates, fugue is specifically characterized by flight and since a standard clinical definition precisely fits Anderson's experience: "From a stressful life situation, the individual wanders off, perhaps in a daze or confused mental state, often with a complete amnesia, sometimes without care for his person or for his surroundings."[57] (On the basis of the sketchy evidence available, "fugue" would seem to describe the 1907 breakdown as well, since in that incident too he left home and office and was found "wandering around in the woods.") There is no question that Anderson was at least intermittently amnesiac, as is proved by the newspaper account of his memory loss in the Cleveland drugstore; yet what is involved in the question of specific diagnosis is not a mere terminological quibble but the most meaningful reading of the so-called Amnesia Letter, which Sutton rightly asserts supplies the "best evidence of what was happening to Anderson psychologically."[58]

First it must be said, however, that the degree to which Sherwood may have deliberately, or at least consciously, entered his fugue state is a less-settled question than has usually been assumed in more recent years when his account in *A Story Teller's Story* has been recognized as fanciful, that account of how he slyly and deliberately feigned insanity to his secretary and walked out on his paint business forever in a single, willed gesture. Writing to Bab in his confessional letter of December 8, 1916, he declared that his life in Elyria had "ended in a convulsion that touched the edge of madness," a statement that seemed accurate if not precise; but he went on to assert summarily that "One morning my mind became a blank and I ran away from Elyria." To Karl he insisted that "there was nothing deliberate in the act," that he merely "'rose from my desk and walked through a door,'" and that thereafter his "'mind was a blank until I found myself in a ward of a Cleveland hospital.'" One need not revert to accepting the *Story Teller's* version to see that these earlier accounts too are marked by the evasiveness that would characterize all his known discussions of the event, that these accounts also are "stories." Very possibly he remained evasive because he literally could not reconstruct what caused him on that particular morning to "act queerly," though it seems doubtful that, as the stress on him had mounted during the past months, he could have repressed all memory of the fugue he had experienced when the pressures of the year with the United Factories had become too much for him. There is also the provocative fact that the issue of Perry Williams's *Telegram*, published for the evening just before that fateful Thanksgiving Day, carried on its front page the news that a young musician of nearby Lorain, one Harry

O'Connor, who had collapsed in Cleveland the previous week, was now recovering physically at the Huron Road Hospital, but who "has absolutely no memory of what has occurred for nearly a year" after his mother had died. The appearance at that time of such a report about an amnesiac artist might well be an unconnected coincidence; nevertheless, it is possible that Anderson read the account and that, consciously or unconsciously on his part, it triggered the following day's "convulsion" that resolved his psychological bind. Perhaps he had something of this sort in mind later when, assuming that he was referring to the 1912 rather than the 1907 breakdown, he told Margaret Anderson of how he "had used all the subterfuges of the unconscious" to effect a change in his life he had not the courage to make consciously. Of course, with these words Sherwood may have been fictionalizing the event somewhat in response to an interesting conversational point, or Margaret Anderson, whose gifts were more appreciative than analytic, may have misremembered the conversation, as her use of the word "aphasia" rather than the expected "amnesia" might suggest. On the other hand, perhaps for once Sherwood was speaking, and Margaret Anderson listening, fairly accurately. Although it is certainly a question how one might *use* "all the subterfuges of the unconscious," the fact remains that at this point Anderson wanted desperately to "change the current of his life." If he did not know how to make the change, he knew what change it was he most wanted to make.[59]

Certainly the Amnesia Letter is the work of a person suffering severe mental and emotional stress; yet elliptic, dissociated, even surreal as are these seven pages of notes, they represent a conscious, even to some extent controlled use of language to describe that stress and to deal with it. The envelope itself is correctly addressed to "Cornelia L. Anderson" in "Elyria O.," though titling her as "Pres." of the "American Striving Co." is a tantalizing slip; the three references to Cornelia and two to Robert, the oldest child, are in appropriate context; and there is, as we will see, a coherence underlying the disconnected recollections. Certainly, too, the letter reveals that its writer was in a state of acute anxiety, but it is impossible to judge from the document how much of this anxiety originated in Anderson's fear of external hostility, how much, by the device of projection, in his concern to control his own hostile and destructive impulses. Children cry, for example, filthy dogs howl, the writer's head hurts constantly, he hides from a man with a gun, and when he tries to drink a beer, a roomful of men appear threatening to him and he runs—this last suggesting a possible autobiographical origin for some of the psychic tension Anderson would describe so brilliantly in one of his best fictions, "The Man Who Became a Woman." Yet again, the notes, not only by their very creation but by what they create, represent a successful dealing with anxiety in an at least temporarily nonamnesiac period during those first three days.[60]

Considering the concern of the young protagonist of "The Man Who Became a Woman" over his sexual identity, it is tempting to follow Sutton in his scrupulously tentative analysis of Freudian symbolism in the notes. Thus, as he argues, the dirty howling dogs would refer to male sexuality, while "so many long streets filled with dirty houses" would refer to female sexuality, the unpleasant, disturbing quality of both images representing the rejection by Anderson of both sexual role and sexuality itself. Possibly so, though a cautious psychoanalyst recognizes that a written document is not the exact equivalent of dream-work and that symbols may have differing, particularized meanings for individual persons. But neither the particularized meaning nor the symbol pattern is sufficiently clear for a reading of Anderson's own sexual problems, such as they might be, especially since every reference to Cornelia makes her appear as the opposite of hostile, as being trustworthy and protective, much like the Jessie in whom the middle-aged narrator of "The Man Who Became a Woman" has found refuge long after the shattering events of his late adolescence.

More revealing in Anderson's letter is the overt pattern formed by two themes embodied in two repeated words. Throughout the notes runs first the writer's fear of being hurt by a physical blow. Not only does Anderson record that he ran from a roomful of men "who would have hit me," but the letter opens with a reference to "Mrs Lenard-Lenard-Elyria," who on page two "had a book in her hand and tried to hit me with it." The verb "hit" appears ten times in the seven pages, eight asserting the threat of the act or the act itself, one admonishing the writer against hitting any person, and only one admitting, "They didn't mean to hit you," though in fact "they" had hit him. Anderson writes that he fears asking questions of people, for "if you ask the people they will hit you," just as they hit one "T Powers," an unidentified person whose name is mentioned four times and whose head, like Anderson's, "hurt also." Except for Cornelia, his fellow sufferer "T Powers," and Robert, to whom in fatherly fashion he wishes to give a "Piece of corn—tell him how it grows," most of the few people he encounters are hostile or potentially so, and most of his experiences are ugly, painful, distressing.[61]

Also running throughout the notes is a second theme and word counter to the first. Meeting Mrs. "Lenard" as the letter opens, he immediately tells her that he is going to "Elsinore" as, he here implies and later confirms, his alter-ego T Powers did. "Elsinore" is a name he invokes eighteen times, at one point writing the word almost in incantation ten times in nine brief lines. What Elsinore means is partly explained by the statement on page five: "Go to Elsinore. Hamlet-Elsinore." The reference is, of course, to the castle in Shakespeare's play. But surprisingly, at first, Anderson does not in any way suggest that he resembles Shakespeare's hero, whom he mentions only the one time, although Hamlet has become the type of the sensitive person torn indecisively by conflicting obligations. Rather Elsinore is a place, a goal, where one like "T Powers" who is hit and whose head hurts should go, as Powers did, to find sanctuary. Nor does Elsinore seem a metaphor for death. It seems instead to be a state of being, resembling in character the act of writing; for, as Anderson asserts, shortly after commanding himself to "Think of Elsinore," "Writing don't hurt your head. It's just being hit with things." Elsinore, synechdochic for literature as a whole, would appear to symbolize the life of the creative artist that Anderson seeks.

The so-called Amnesia Letter, then, is the account of two journeys, an inner and an outer one, the emotional one embodied in the physical. Leaving Elyria, the author-narrator tells the woman who threatens him with a book (perhaps literature seen in its aspect of established reputations and conventional values) that he is going to "Elsinore," that is, he is going to be a writer. But though he has left the immediate world of business, Anderson must deal with his own sick self, with its guilts, fears, pains, and with a reality that is unpleasant, threatening, and hurtful. Along the mean streets past howling dogs and crying children he goes, fearful of hostile men in town and countryside. It is "cold at night," but "Think of Elsinore"; and he comforts himself with the precious knowledge that though "being hit with things" hurts, "Writing don't hurt your head." He must "Get to Elsinore," as "T Powers" did, Powers whose head hurt, who was hit by "One after another," whose name "They put . . . on a wall—near Elsinore," but who nevertheless arrived at that good place. Anderson may prepare to teach his son about the ear of corn, may confide his secret whereabouts to his wife by sending her this account, but on his journey he must talk to no one. After awhile, "your head wont hurt"; he must "Walk and keep still" and "Go to Elsinore." But despite the "dirty houses," the man who "growled like a yellow dog," the man whose chewing of tobacco "made his mouth nasty," and the "they" who hit him, the artist is not born solely out of suffering nor from a rejection of reality. Not only must the double journey be recounted in painful and frightening, if disconnected, detail, but it is a sudden glimpse of the commonplace, a man with "his mouth full of dry crackers," that enables Anderson actually to get beyond the last dangers. This mundane image amuses him, and though he "Thought it made my head hurt," the sixth page concludes climactically, "I laughed to Elsinore." By re-creating reality—by subjectifying and reordering it but not abandoning it—the author-protagonist has survived his ordeal and has come into his kingdom, a conclusion supported by the almost blank seventh page of the notes, containing only a juxtaposition of elements reasserting the distance he has traveled: five numbers of from two to five digits, representing, it would seem, the business world of abstract calculation and of material profit, then the single final word "Elsinore." He is released from the past and can begin a new life.

Viewed in relation to Anderson's later work, this account of a double journey has certain striking similarities to some of his fictions. There is a guiding, "speaking" narrative voice; objective and subjective experience now flow together, now separate indeterminately; the "plot" develops indirectly rather than sequentially; the repetition of word, of proper name, of theme provides as much structure as does the ordering of events; the seventh page ending is not unlike that of the famous tale "Hands" in the way it concentrates and resolves discordant elements. Without making too much of the document one can see in it a faint foreshadowing of some of the *Winesburg* method. Even more, however, the letter suggests a primitive first draft of *A Story Teller's Story*. Anderson's "fancy" works on autobiographical material and produces an initial version of the major recurrent theme of his future work: the liberation of the self from a hostile world and from psychic pain, a liberation here achieved symbolically, indeed literally through the act of art. What the letter fundamentally records is not just the fright and pain of a profoundly distressed self but that self's resolve to "go to Elsinore," to turn from the deathly existence of the business man to the life of the writer. No wonder Anderson thought this resolve worth communicating to Cornelia. Here was proof that once he had crossed the "River at Elsinore./Bridge at Elsinore" and could "write all day in the sun" he really would be "all right," whatever psychological torment still had to work itself out within him.

7.

The people of his city first heard what had happened to this "Elyria clubman, manufacturer and author" from the newspapers on Monday, December 2. Accounts told how Mrs. Anderson had gone to him in the hospital and how he had at first recognized her only with difficulty. After a few hours sleep, however, he had "regained his mental faculties," was surprised to find himself in a hospital, and talked with her. Although he could not "remember exactly when his memory failed him," he did recall wandering about East Cleveland, and he was "inclined to consider his four days wandering a joke." By Tuesday, December 3, he had already improved so much from rest and quiet that he could expect release from the hospital on the following Saturday.[62]

While recovering, Sherwood followed the advice of the doctors on his case, "'who told him,'" as Cornelia put it much later, that "'if he'd just lie there in the hospital and think through the whole experience, he would not have to fear recurrence.'" Two brief pages of notes dictated by Anderson to some unknown person while he was in the hospital probably are part of the result of this "thinking through." These notes confirm certain details in the Amnesia Letter—that he ate corn and apples, that his head hurt, that "Dogs kept coming up" (perhaps, Sutton has suggested, in the mysterious manner described in "Death in the Woods"), that he was some of the time in the country, some at least close to a city, presumably Cleveland. They also add new details, for example that toward dark one evening he realized where he was, thought he'd "go home in daylight— and struck off into country for home." Yet the dictated notes mostly record fragments of things done and seen during his wanderings; they reveal almost nothing of Anderson's anxieties, have no structure, work toward no triumphal conclusion but simply stop, and appear to be facts only. These two pages must be only part of the process by which Sherwood did "think through the whole experience" and, according to Cornelia, "did finally get every link," a cryptic remark that rather contradicts her description of her husband's wanderings as an "amnesia trip," since, unlike the usual amnesia victim, Anderson thus appears to have been able to reconstruct the essential events of his four-day flight.[63]

Cornelia also subsequently explained that a purported interview with her and her husband, printed on the front page of the *Elyria Evening Telegram* for Friday, December 6, and datelined from Cleveland, was actually only the interviewer's interpretation of what she had told him together with "fantastic nonsense" the interviewer himself had said to her, he not having had access to Sherwood at all. It may have been merely the interviewer's notion that Anderson's ordeal began when he "through deep thought threw himself into a trance"; yet Cornelia herself is quoted as saying that, "He knew who he was, what he was doing, where he was going and what he wanted to do . . . but he could not tell any person or do what he wished." Not only do her remarks correspond closely to what Anderson told his secretary on his return to the paint factory, but they also tend to confirm a reading of the Amnesia Letter, not as amnesiac but rather as a literal-imaginative record of his resolve to become an artist once he was again able to act in the real world. "Yesterday," the interview appears to comment on Sherwood's thinking-through process, "he recalled the last thing that happened during that strange adventure." Anderson "will write a book of the sensations he experienced while he wandered over the country as a nomad," the article asserts, and it ends with his purported words that, "It is dangerous, but it will be a good story and the money will always be welcome. . . ." Fantastic nonsense or not, the fact is that Anderson did draw on "the sensations he experienced" when he came to revising the Elyria draft of *Windy McPherson's Son*. Sam McPherson's flight from the hospital where he believes his wife lies dead in childbirth describes a dissociative reaction strikingly similar in some specific details to what the author reported of his own fugue, including the specific sensation of having wet feet just before the onset of the state, as confirmed by what Anderson told Frances Shute that Thanksgiving morning and as reiterated in the account in *A Story Teller's Story,* the latter illustrating how his artistic imagination characteristically "fed," as he was to put it much later, on reality.[64]

By Saturday, December 7, Sherwood was judged to be recovered enough to return to Elyria, where Cornelia cared for him. Although the recollection is otherwise unconfirmed, a woman who knew them recalled Cornelia's pushing "her husband around in a wheel chair everyday." By the following Wednesday Anderson was "so far recovered from his recent disability" that he and Cornelia left town for a week's rest at her parents' home in Toledo, her younger sister Margaret coming to Elyria to help with the children. On December 19 the two Andersons returned from Toledo. As a result either of slow convalescence or lack of interest, or even of active distaste for the life he had led, Anderson did little about winding up his business affairs. As had happened after the 1907 breakdown, others mostly picked up after him. Apparently his one contribution was the sale of "the Roof-Fix Business" to the G. E. Conkey Company of Cleveland, this transaction being announced in the March 21, 1913, issue of the *Telegram* along with word of the sale "at a great sacrifice" of the American Merchants Company's remaining stock of house and barn paint. The Purcell Paint Company soon listed itself as successor to American Merchants, and Anderson's great scheme for a business triumph legally ended on the following September 20 when the stockholders met and dissolved the American Merchants Company.[65]

By this time, however, Sherwood had long since departed from Elyria. By early 1913 he had obtained assurance that he could return to his old job at the Taylor-Critchfield Advertising Company in Chicago, from which he had gone with such expansive hopes of business success nearly seven years earlier. He left for Chicago by himself on February 7, 1913, returning to Elyria once for a weekend visit with his family at the end of March. Cornelia and the children stayed on in the Seventh Street house, Cornelia handling the uncertain period of separation with her usual dignity. At the February 20 meeting of the Fortnightly Club she even read a paper on "The Stage of Shakespeare" and listened to a reading of *King Lear,* with what thoughts of Lear's wanderings on the blasted heath one can only imagine. Although she had apparently planned to follow Sherwood to Chicago with the children, the final decision was for her, the children, and Margaret to spend the rest of the spring and summer in a cottage owned by Sherwood's sister Stella at Little Point Sable, a tiny community halfway up Lake Michigan on the Michigan shore. Sending some of the furniture to Chicago, where Sherwood had only a room, and leaving some behind, they left Elyria on April 21 for Chicago, met

Sherwood, and then went on to Little Point Sable. Anderson visited his family on weekends, but the family was not to be reunited in Chicago, though husband and wife were still attempting to preserve a marriage soon to end in separation.[66]

So ended Anderson's attempt to become, as he would recall in the *Memoirs,* "a success in the American business world of that day." He left behind him in Elyria a widespread bitterness among the town's elite for what they saw as his irresponsibility toward the investments and personal trust of friends, for his suspicious-sounding breakdown, for his running away from Elyria instead of staying on and fighting back to prosperity again in the accepted manner. There was bitterness, too, for his careless, arrogant behavior toward a faithful wife whose own behavior had been admirable throughout, and especially for the brazen openness with which he had violated the taboos against infidelity and dissipation, taboos that should be violated, if the flesh was insistent, only surreptitiously; bitterness, in short, because the elite group had taken up the Andersons in good faith and Sherwood had in every way let the group down. One can understand the grounds for anger, but Anderson was repudiating the grounds themselves. It is not necessary to admire all aspects of his conduct in Elyria in order to understand also that, whatever the exact relationship of causes that produced his breakdown, the four days he spent near "the edge of insanity" at Thanksgiving time in 1912, days when he touched psychic bottom, were for him an essential, life-saving crisis. Although he was to continue writing advertising copy until his final rebellion ten years later against that use of language as well, these four anguished days remained permanently as a central, pivotal experience in both his real and his imaginative life. Again and again in the tales he would write, the protagonist seeks to break out, sometimes does break out, from a constricting existence into liberation, seeks freedom to express the self whatever that self may be, no more asking where this freedom and expression should lead to than does, say, the leaf breaking through the constriction of the bud, seeking only to be. What Anderson now knew he must *be* was a writer.

5

New Man in a New World

1.

Anderson could not have returned to Chicago at a more fortunate moment. Renting a drab room in a cheap lodging house on Fifty-seventh Street on the South Side near the university, he resumed his familiar tasks in the copy department of Taylor-Critchfield, since after all he still had a family to support despite his decision to be a writer. Only six weeks after his return, however, the International Exhibition of Modern Art, as the famous "Armory Show" of 1913 was officially titled, opened at the Art Institute, and the Modernist era burst upon the city. What nearly two hundred thousand Chicagoans saw during the three and a half weeks from March 24 to April 16 was a much smaller display of oils, water colors, prints, drawings, and sculptures than had just previously filled the huge armory of New York's Sixty-ninth Regiment, but the artists represented in Chicago included the most advanced of the French and American Post-Impressionists. For most of the spectators who now filed by some or all these 634 pieces it was their first encounter with Cézanne, Van Gogh, Gaugin, Redon, Matisse, Picasso, and the Cubists, as well as with contemporary American Realists and Avant-Gardists; and they reacted with delight or, much more often, amusement or indignation to the distortions of line, the violent, discordant colors, the geometrized substitutes for natural images, the unrecognizable nude descending the unidentifiable stairs. There was a carnival spirit about the Chicago exhibit as well as much outcry over the threat of some of this art to public decency, but the show had its defenders. Floyd Dell, the precociously successful editor of the Chicago *Evening Post*'s *Friday Literary Review,* managed to turn a front-page notice of a book he had not read into an enthusiastic discussion of Post-Impressionism at the Art Institute. Harriet Monroe, who had founded the monthly magazine *Poetry* only the previous October, argued in her art column in the Chicago *Sunday Tribune* that radical extravagance in art was an understandable "revolt of the imagination against nineteenth century realism" and against the "too pallid, nerveless, coldly correct, photographic" conservatism of much accepted American painting. Disturbing as "the new spirit" might be, she asserted, its "deeper meaning" signified "a search for new beauty, impatience with formulae, a reaching out toward the inexpressible, a longing for new versions of truth."[1]

In his *Memoirs* (1942) Anderson recalled that he went to see the show every day it was in Chicago. "Every day" may have been one of his exaggerations, but he probably did view it a number of times. He could hardly have escaped hearing of the show as the talk of the newspapers and the town, and the show's motto, "The New Spirit," would have appealed powerfully to one who had just completed a revolt against conventional life. By temperament he would have sympathized with what advanced critics perceived the show to represent as going on in the arts at that time: the impulse toward change as valid in itself, the assumption that art should not represent an object but should express the artist's individual, emotional reaction to it, the belief that art was more instinctive than rational in its nature, the conviction that the artist must have the courage to express himself truthfully even if he appears mad to the conventionally sane world. Since these tenets largely reappear in such aesthetic as he was subsequently to formulate, it seems likely that he was intellectually as well as emotionally stimulated by the show.

He had in addition a specific reason for visiting the exhibition frequently—brother Karl was involved in the Armory Show. Karl had been one of the charter members of the Association of American Painters and Sculptors, which had sponsored and mounted this collection of the contemporary, and had served on the show's Reception and Publicity Committee. Further, he had exhibited six oils in New York's Armory, and one of them, *Woman Drinking a Glass of Water,* which had been among the pieces selected to be "reproduced and sold in postcard form," was hung in Gallery 54 at the Art Institute among the other pictures by Americans. Sherwood would hardly have passed up the chance to see one of his successful brother's paintings, but Karl himself was there in Chicago to conduct him instructively through the show. He had come to stay with Sherwood at that time on a visit occasioned not only by the International but also by a concurrent one-man exhibit of fifteen of his recent oils at the Thurber gallery, nearly opposite the Art Institute on Michigan Avenue. Karl's show had in fact attracted the attention of the influential Harriet Monroe, whose article on the "new spirit" was dominated by a single illustration, Karl's *Woman Drinking a Glass of Water,* and who picked him out for praise as "a painter who will take high rank among modern artists" especially because of "a certain elusive quality of feeling, of poetic inspiration, in some of these recent works."[2]

Once more, as in Elyria in 1910, Sherwood lived in the excitement of his brother's fame. It was with Karl that he went again and again to see the International, and both found in it, the younger brother remembered, "a new approach to nature in art. Color was speaking in its own tongue." From Karl, whose gift was as a colorist, Sherwood could learn in detail modernist principles in art, principles that correlated with and therefore helped to confirm his own still evolving feelings about his writing at a time when he needed both support and guidance in the career he had chosen at great psychic and material cost to himself and others. From early in his writing career, then, Anderson saw writing as in some ways simply another mode within modernist art in general. This attitude helps to account in part for his tendency as a writer to infuse the representational with the imaginative, the objective with the subjective, and for his conviction that words rightly placed in relation to each other possess both "music" and "color." More specifically, he would certainly have read Harriet Monroe's praise of Karl's paintings and may well have noted her conclusion that "beyond these qualities of color and arrangement is a deeper beauty of feeling, a sense of poetic harmonies in form and color, which begins to express itself with delicate subtlety," for that description startlingly resembles some of his own subsequent statements as to qualities he tried to achieve in his writing.[3]

Karl's visit had another, more immediate consequence in his younger brother's life. Going to the Thurber gallery one day in late March or early April together with a Chicago Post-Impressionist painter, B. J. O. Nordfeldt, Karl was introduced by his companion to Floyd Dell's wife, Margery Currey, who was covering Karl's show as a reporter for the Chicago *Daily News*. During the conversation Karl mentioned that Sherwood had piles of unpublished manuscripts on his writing table, including a novel called *Windy McPherson's Son* that he was still working on, whereupon Margery asked Karl to get the typescript so that her husband could read it. Reviewing *Windy* on its publication three years later, Dell recalled picking up the typescript, "idly, a little cynically" as just one more "yarn," beginning to turn the pages, "and then before I knew, I was reading, with a curious and growing excitement." Feeling "curiously shaken" by the power and energy of the book, Dell wrote, he "went out to look for its author." More likely, as both Sherwood and Karl wrote in their several accounts, the hospitable Margery Currey brought the author to Dell. It was through her, Anderson always remembered gratefully, that he gained entrance into the group, or set of groups, that was then creating the Chicago Renaissance in the arts, that "Robin's Egg Renaissance," as he was to name it in the *Memoirs*, nostalgically imaging both its fresh brightness and its subsequent departure from the Chicago nest.[4]

The Chicago renaissance of the 1910s was emerging out of a happy concatenation of persons and institutions. In part a local response to aspects of the national climate—Progressivism, reformism, feminism, various shades of radical thought and action, a general rebellious stirring under the social crust of town and small city—it came to a focus in this time and place. The major city of the Midwest had long attracted not only workers looking for jobs and young businessmen looking for the big money, but also aspiring artists, musicians, writers, many of them young and poor, drawn to Chicago from smaller communities in hopes of finding other persons of similar interest and room to live independent, liberated lives. They found certain institutions already in place as a manifestation of late-nineteenth-century wealth and civic patriotism—the Art Institute with its art classes, the Chicago Symphony, the new and already major University of Chicago, Hull House, which combined a minor interest in little theater production with its major interest in social work, and the Fine Arts Building on Michigan Avenue just south and across from the Art Institute with a stage for traveling drama, a bookshop, and many studio rooms for the more prosperous musicians and artists.[5]

By 1910 the practitioners of the arts had reached some degree of mutual visibility, even a sort of tiny critical mass, and within a very few years around this time appeared certain other institutions that helped to give them cohesiveness and a voice. Just a few months before Anderson's return from Elyria, Harriet Monroe had founded *Poetry,* which was alert to new movements in verse whether the poets were local, national, or foreign. Only weeks after that first issue of *Poetry* was out, Maurice and Ellen Van Volkenburg Browne, in early November of 1912, opened their Little Theatre in a remodeled storage area, the miniscule "fourth-floor-back" of the Fine Arts Building. For the next five years the "repertory and experimental art-theatre," as the Brownes called it, would be primarily dedicated to the production of "poetic and imaginative drama." The most immediately influential institution had appeared earlier, however, and was still thriving. Traditionally, and as accurately as such cultural developments can be assigned a beginning, the renaissance is dated from the establishment of the *Friday Literary Review* as a weekly supplement of the daily newspaper, the *Evening Post,* its first issue appearing on March 5, 1909, under the energetic and literate editorship of a young Irishman, Francis Hackett. Hackett's assistant was that other *Evening Post* staffman, Floyd Dell, recently arrived in Chicago from Davenport, Iowa, with a Socialist politics, a socially oriented aesthetics, and an omnivorous interest in new ideas matched with a facility for talking and writing about them. Under Hackett's editorship the *Review* stood generally for anything considered individually liberating, and hence in literature it praised the innovative, the nongenteel, the unconventional, the cosmopolitan, praised it within, and sometimes beyond, the limits allowed by the management

of an otherwise relatively orthodox newspaper. When Hackett, dissatisfied with those limits, left for New York after a little over two years, Dell
succeeded him as editor with the issue of July 28, 1911, and continued the
policy of favoring the new in literature and ideas.[6]

When he became editor, Floyd Dell had just passed his twenty-fourth
birthday. Two summers earlier he had married Margery Currey, a warm,
charming, independent woman a dozen years older than he but as youth-
fully adventurous. Although she was then teaching school in nearby
Evanston, she had energy left over to work for women's suffrage, to keep
up with her husband's intellectual interests, and to maintain in their North
Side apartment a kind of salon for the artists and writers of the renaissance. By the time Anderson settled in Chicago again, however, the Dells'
marriage was beginning to break up, primarily as a result of Floyd's love
affairs with other women. Intent on being modern about their marital
problems, the Dells signified the new stage in their relations by moving in
late April or early May of 1913 into separate though contiguous quarters
in the one clearly definable art-bohemia locale in the city.[7]

The Jackson Park art colony was on Chicago's South Side not far from
the University and Anderson's rooming house. Just before the World's
Columbian Exposition of 1893, twenty-six one-room, single-story stores
were built on both sides of the very east end of Fifty-seventh Street and
around each corner onto Stony Island Avenue, which ran along the western edge of what was first the Exposition fairgrounds and afterwards Jackson Park. Designed as temporary restaurant and souvenir concessions,
these frame buildings could be rented cheaply after the Exposition closed,
and very shortly their single large rooms were taken over as homes and
studios by various artists, craftsmen, and lovers of the bohemian life. Two
of these studios became vacant, and Margery Currey moved into the more
comfortable one on Stony Island Avenue looking out on the green park
and the old Palace of Fine Arts of the Exposition (now the Museum of Science and Industry), while Floyd took the more Spartan one just around the
corner on Fifty-seventh Street, their back doors adjoining companionably.
Between these two studios was the corner one, itself about to be vacated
by the Paris-bound B. J. O. Nordfeldt, Karl Anderson's acquaintance,
who had flattered Dell by painting in "bold Post-Expressionist style" a
portrait of him as decadent dandy. Margery now transferred her Sunday
evening dinner gatherings to her Stony Island apartment, and it was to one
of these that Sherwood was invited.[8]

Anderson's recollection of the Jackson Park art colony and the Dells'
presence in it was to remain an especially vivid one. It is even probable that
his own account in the *Memoirs* of how he met the Dells is essentially correct. Receiving an invitation from Margery to attend one of her parties
shortly after the Dells were settled into their separate studios, Sherwood

went to Stony Island Avenue that Sunday evening but lingered outside the street door of her apartment, listening to the people talking gaily inside but not daring to enter and join the party for fear that he would be rejected as uneducated and pretentious, a mere advertising man. (Though his fear of entering may now sound like a later invention, it should be remembered that Anderson was then still recovering from an extremely disturbing emotional crisis, his written record of which had emphasized his fear of potentially hostile people.) A week or so later, however, Anderson ran into Margery Currey by chance just outside of her studio, and the two went for a walk in Jackson Park and got acquainted. Immediately thereafter she began to bring him into the Dells' wide circle of friends, and Anderson felt that suddenly a new life had opened up for him.[9]

Never before had he been close to people so deeply involved with creation in the arts and with talking about the arts, to men and women so intent on discussing, arguing about, living in accordance with new ideas. Evenings and weekends during the late spring and the summer of 1913 in this small but pleasantly unconventional-looking area, he became acquainted with all sorts of people such as he might have longed to have known in Elyria. The Dells themselves he felt closest to. Margery had read the manuscript of *Windy* also and had praised it to him. She was by nature companionable and encouraging toward anyone struggling to achieve something in the arts, and her pain at the growing separation from her wayward husband, whom she continued to love very deeply, perhaps made her especially sensitive to Anderson's uneasiness in his own marital situation. He and Margery were often together at parties and outings that summer in a happy comradeship, but he and Floyd saw much of each other as well. To Floyd, Sherwood seemed robust and carefree, "an extremely handsome and attractive figure, tall and broad-shouldered, with dark eyes and a mass of black hair; he had a gentle and friendly manner." As a result of subsequent estrangement, Dell would decide that his friend's "deceptively robust air . . . masked an inward state of doubt and gloom and anxiety," but in these first months of acquaintance he found Anderson "very likeable and companionable." They frequently "loafed and talked together" in Floyd's studio, Dell often breaking off from his reading and his editorial duties performed at home for discussions with this man older in years and experiences of the world yet younger in his knowledge of literature, especially that which was breaking new ground. Anderson on his part carefully listened to Dell expatiate in his rapid, incisive, graceful manner on the latest in books and ideas; in fact, this youthful critic became for awhile, Sherwood was later to declare in the *Memoirs*, "a kind of literary father" to him.[10]

In the Jackson Park art colony studio around the Dells lived painters, metalcraft workers, sculptors, such as, for example, Lou Wall Moore, in whose sculptor's studio during the previous year Maurice Browne had directed rehearsals of *The Trojan Women.* Other persons connected in some way with the arts came to Margery Currey's parties, and Anderson now met poets, college professors, newspaper people with literary aspirations. Arthur Davison Ficke, lawyer and poet of Davenport, Iowa, would drop in on one of his frequent visits to Chicago to buy Japanese prints or attend Little Theatre performances, Eunice Tietjens, who wrote poetry while working on the small staff of Harriet Monroe's magazine, might appear. From the University of Chicago came Robert Morss Lovett, who was to review a number of Anderson's books, or the iconoclastic George Burman Foster, professor of the philosophy of religion and exponent of Nietzsche's ideas. Through the Dells or their friends Anderson probably met in this summer of 1913 Ben Hecht, then a cocky nineteen-year-old reporter on the *Journal,* who volubly admired the French and British Decadent writers, and Carl Sandburg, who was still trying to establish himself in journalism and had not yet published *Chicago Poems.* He certainly met among other bohemians Michael Carmichael Carr, a man as flamboyant as his name, a scene designer, painter, and art instructor, who wore a pointed red beard, a black cape with a silver clasp, and, sometimes in summer, flowing robes.

Evenings after work groups would gather at Margery's studio or in some other person's room for long arguments or for walks and talks in Jackson Park. Often on weekends twenty to thirty people connected with the colony would take a train to Union Pier, a small Michigan town in the still-wild sand dunes area at the south end of Lake Michigan, where on some nearby isolated beach they would swim, men and women naked together as they felt free spirits should be, and then sit around a beach fire, talking far into the summer night about literature and art, about new configurations of ideas such as those of Freud or Nietzsche, about new social orders, about less barbaric relationships between the sexes. During these months Cornelia Anderson presumably was confined by the children most of the time to the tiny summer settlement at Little Point Sable, miles away up the Michigan shore; and while Sherwood may have visited his family on an occasional weekend, he appears to have been, and probably felt, largely on vacation from them. With the Dell group he was among new and exciting friends who were attempting to collapse the barriers between art and life, questioning accepted values, and seeking more workable ones. It was an atmosphere in which Anderson could flourish both as person and as writer.[11]

Exhilarated by what he would happily remember as this "rather wonderful new world," Anderson somehow found time and energy to write at his big manuscript-laden worktable in his Fifty-seventh Street rooming house. He had already received encouragement from two of his best friends from Taylor-Critchfield, for one Sunday in the spring of 1913 Marco Morrow and George Daugherty had sat in a room at the Sherman Hotel, listened to him read from his manuscript of *Marching Men,* and told him that it was "good writing." He worked also on *Windy McPherson's Son,* the typescript of which Margery Currey had obtained through Karl for Floyd Dell to read; indeed, he must have found time to write on it intensively, since it was apparently unfinished when Dell read it yet was in sufficiently completed state to be sent off, probably during that summer of 1913, to Alfred Harcourt, then an editor at Henry Holt and Company, for possible publication. Perhaps Dell had urged Anderson to submit the manuscript to Harcourt, for his excitement upon reading *Windy McPherson's Son* in manuscript was genuine and strong. Surveying the new fall books in the issue of the *Friday Literary Review* for September 5, 1913, one of last issues he edited, Dell generously praised the unpublished *Windy:* "And this impression of the forwardness of the younger generation is made all the stronger by the fact that I have seen in MS. recently an unfinished novel by a yet unpublished writer which if finished as begun will overtop the work of any living American writer."[12]

Although he had not been referred to by name in this first literary notice of his work, Anderson's reaction on reading it was to prance up and down his room with delight, perhaps being extra pleased by Dell's associating him with the younger generation despite the fact he had nearly reached his thirty-seventh birthday. But Dell did even more in his generous desire to spread the word of Anderson's promise. In the studio just across Fifty-seventh Street from his lived two young women, Ernestine Evans and Elizabeth Titzel. In his autobiography, *Homecoming,* Dell was to recall Ernestine as "a beautiful apple-cheeked girl . . . eager and buoyant" like the heroine of *Ann Veronica,* H. G. Wells's most recent novel. She had graduated from the University of Chicago in 1912, wanted to write, and wished to live in the city of Chicago, as her guardian allowed her to do on condition that she have a roommate, who very conveniently became her university classmate, Elizabeth, a doctor's daughter, who was secretary for the Little Theatre. Ernestine had heard of Anderson as a man with two unpublished novels, and when Dell asked her if Sherwood could give a public reading from *Windy McPherson's Son* in their studio, she and her roommate at once said yes. Among those gathered in a party atmosphere for that reading was Robert Lovett from the university, who several times afterward recalled in print that Anderson had come dressed for the part and the occasion in paint-stained workmen's clothes. Anderson was fond of reading aloud in his baritone voice with its customary drawl, and the performance went on practically all night. However others may have reacted to the marathon event, Dell continued to believe enthusiastically that this advertising man was writing "like a great novelist." Like Anderson a small-town midwesterner in origin, and, after high school, largely self-educated, Dell continued to feel strongly that he was "in the presence of a powerful mind, with a magnificent grip on reality, pouring itself out in a flood of scenes—a mind vivid, profound, apparently inexhaustible in its energy. A mind full of beautiful, intense, and perilous emotion." When Dell left for New York in October of that year, he proved his intense admiration of *Windy McPherson's Son* yet again by accepting Sherwood's request that he take a copy of the manuscript with him and try to place it with a publisher.[13]

On another occasion that summer, this time in Margery Currey's studio, Anderson was more spectator than performer. One of the audience at his reading from *Windy* was an extraordinarily beautiful, extraordinarily rebellious young woman named Margaret Anderson, who had escaped from her well-to-do family in Columbus, Indiana, after three years of college. In Chicago she had lived at the YWCA, at first reviewed books for and then was the hardworking literary editor of a religious weekly, had been drawn by elective affinity toward the Dell group, and had already been a contributor to the *Friday Literary Review*. Energetic, rapturous, impetuous, she had been searching for a way to focus her intense commitment to Art, Newness, and the Liberation of the Self. Waking one night in that summer of 1913, she realized in a flash that she must edit a magazine, and the next day she set about interesting people in and outside the Jackson Park art colony in her project. Later in the summer some thirty artists, writers, reviewers, professors, newspaper people crammed into Margery Currey's studio one evening to hear Margaret Anderson describe her plan to publish "the best art magazine in the world" and to help her select a name for it, though after a long debate over suggested titles it became clear that she had already determined to call this monthly magazine *The Little Review*. The most famous member of the audience that evening was Theodore Dreiser, already a hero to the others for his battles against censorship as much as for his novels, but he arrived late, looking even more monumental than ever because of a large bandage wound around his neck to cover a boil. Karl Anderson, again visiting Sherwood, was there and Sherwood himself. Though the latter seems to have had little or no chance in so large a group to speak to Dreiser, whom he would always admire as a liberator of American literature, the evening had important consequences. By founding *The Little Review*, Margaret Anderson provided for Sherwood one of the few early outlets for the new kind of writing toward which, under the stimulus of his new world, he was feeling his way. She had not, as she later put it, been quite so "passionate" about *Windy McPherson's Son* as Dell, but she recognized that this middle-aged, as yet unpublished writer was involved like herself in a search for self-expression, she liked the special way he talked, not by discussing ideas directly but by telling stories, and she asked him to contribute a piece to the magazine's first issue. So again Anderson was fortunate in coming to Chicago in 1913. When the brown-covered initial number of *The Little Review* came out the following March, it contained his first published article in his career as writer rather than businessman. With the founding of this magazine, dedicated as it was to beauty, intensity, rebellion, truth, and the priority of feeling over thought, the wave of the Chicago renaissance was beginning to crest, and Sherwood Anderson could feel himself lifted in that wave.[14]

Encouraged in their various ways by such friends and by the magic opportunity, outside business hours at least, to live the artist life as he had imagined it to be, Anderson grew in confidence that his decision to be a writer had been not only necessary but right, even providential. There remained from his former career, however, the problem of his relationship with his wife and family. In the early fall of 1913 George Daugherty, who had returned to advertising writing after a business venture in Michigan, moved into a rooming house with Sherwood near the Jackson Park art colony, perhaps the same one Sherwood had been living in on Fifty-seventh Street. Then Mrs. Daugherty joined her husband, and Cornelia brought Robert, John, and Mimi there after the summer in Little Point Sable. Now Cornelia accompanied him to Margery Currey's parties at the Stony Island studio nearby, and in her tolerant, intellectually curious, if somewhat reserved, way she got along with her husband's new friends in Chicago as easily as she had with his former ones in Elyria. Floyd Dell met her at one of the parties in September or October and recalled her as "a slender, delicate, self-contained, warm and understanding person who wore what someone called 'her sole recognition of evening dress,' a Dante wreath about her hair" and who "talked to me of her three children." Cornelia and Margery Currey began a long friendship; both were college-trained, intellectually lively women, both were committed suffragists, both were in the midst of marital difficulties. At yet another of the studio parties the Andersons became acquainted with a woman Margery had met the previous summer when Chicago suffragists marched in a parade for the Progressive Party's candidate, Theodore Roosevelt. This was a tall, graceful, elegantly dressed teacher of music and dance named Tennessee Mitchell, whom Cornelia liked and would remain close friends with even after Tennessee eventually became Sherwood's second wife.[15]

Another sort of complication arose during this early fall of 1913, however—the matter of Anderson's health. Very likely he had been under pressure at Taylor-Critchfield to prove that in this work he disliked he would "produce," despite his half-dozen years away from the agency; at the same time he had been excitedly trying to crowd much into his hours free of the office, both to work intensively at his writing and to play, as he would put it, just as intensively with his new friends. He had not yet fully recovered from the strains that had culminated in his four days of wandering and exposure that chilly previous November, and his health remained unsteady. Somewhat shadowing his delight in that summer may have been internal warnings of an emotional relapse, for some years later when his newspaper friend Harry Hansen was gathering information for *Midwest Portraits,* Anderson told him that his "'real reason'" for leaving Chicago temporarily at this time was "'to recuperate from a nervous breakdown'" and to "'get my strength back.'" There is also evidence that he was showing symptoms of incipient tuberculosis, the disease officially recorded in 1895 under the name of "consumption" as the cause of his mother's death.[16]

One may surmise that at this point a doctor advised Anderson to get out of Chicago and away from his job until he regained his health. Another, seemingly more cheerful event would have coincided with such advice. Around October Alfred Harcourt, to whom Anderson had sent *Windy McPherson's Son,* accepted the manuscript for publication by Henry Holt and Company on the condition that certain revisions be made in it by a "professional writer," a condition that the author, eager to have his novel published, agreed to. Ebullient over what then appeared to be a final arrangement, perhaps together with a publisher's advance of money or the expectation of it, Anderson again quit his job at Taylor-Critchfield, this time in order to be free to concentrate uninterruptedly on his writing. Cornelia, who recalled that she "'hadn't a practical hair on my head,'" readily agreed with her husband's decision. Perhaps she agreed so readily for another reason, the need both husband and wife urgently felt either to become reconciled to their marriage or to reach some decision as to its future.[17]

In early or mid-November Anderson went to New York alone to visit Dell, probably to discuss his publishing prospects with his "literary father." Dell, who had only recently arrived in New York himself, was sharing an apartment on the south side of Washington Square at the edge of Greenwich Village. Anderson arrived "in a suit such as a well-dressed Chicagoan should wear," but at night he slept, on a couch in the apartment, not in pajamas or nightshirt but in what Dell recalled as hilariously patched and baggy underclothes. Hurt and angered by Dell's amusement at his "disreputable drawers," Anderson later explained to him that

His mother, whenever any members of the family went on an overnight journey, had insisted that they wear their best underclothes, freshly laundered—so that they would look respectable if there was a train wreck. Sherwood, rebelling against this maternal tyranny and defying the American ideal of respectability, had formed the habit of traveling in old patched drawers which he kept for such occasions. Thus he symbolically established his spiritual freedom.

Possibly so, though one suspects Anderson's storytelling (or Dell's later malice) at work on what may well have been a means of economy for a just-resigned advertising man with a family to support. During his visit Sherwood found Greenwich Village enchanting, and he entered into its joyous spirit by acting a minor part in *St. George in Greenwich Village*, a play satirizing modern ideas, which Dell wrote for the housewarming of that gathering place on Macdougal Street, the Liberal Club.[18]

Despite its attractions New York was no place for a person in shaky physical and emotional health. Shortly after Thanksgiving Day—both Sherwood and Cornelia must have had unpleasant recollections of what began on that holiday only a year earlier—the Anderson family left Chicago by train for a quite different destination—Hooker, Missouri. Hooker was a backwoods settlement of some dozen houses in the south central part of the state in the Ozarks uplands close to where the Piney River empties into the Gasconade. Here the Andersons had been lent the use of a cabin about a mile from the settlement. As Cornelia remembered it, the cabin

had three rooms, two downstairs and one up, with a porch. It had the Little Piney River in front and a "branch" at the side, crossed on stepping stones. On that side was a better house owned by our landlord, who used it during the hunting season. We were given the key and Sherwood withdrew there to write.

It was wild hill country, barren now with winter approaching, though the dull red leaves that the oak trees kept gave a touch of beauty to the otherwise cheerless landscape. For his health Sherwood spent many afternoons tramping about the countryside in heavy, high-laced boots or hunting small game, at which he proved a good shot. On one expedition he nearly drowned when the boat in which he had just crossed one of the rivers slipped out from under him and left him hanging onto a bush he had just grasped on the riverbank, Occasionally he would walk to Hooker to get provisions at the general store and to sit around talking with the men, who, he later told Harry Hansen, were ignorant and circumscribed in their existence, but who had "good hearts," a good "grip on life," and "a genuine feeling for human beings."[19]

Probably he found talking with the men a relief from the situation back at this temporary home. Not long after settling into the isolated, winterbound cabin, the Andersons found themselves acutely poor. The Elyria venture had ended in financial disaster, Sherwood had not been back at his copywriting job long enough to have put much of his salary aside, and soon it turned out that there would be no money from Henry Holt. *Windy McPherson's Son* was not going to be published after all, either because Holt had finally rejected the manuscript or because, when the revised version was sent to Anderson for his approval, he was enraged to find that the reviser had, in Floyd Dell's words, "thoroughly tamed the wild beauty of the book," in consequence of which Anderson withdrew the manuscript himself and asked Dell to seek another publisher. If the latter version is correct or even partially correct, it suggests Anderson's conviction as to the worth of his work and his courageous dedication to his art under difficult circumstances. Real poverty, not just limited finances, would have been especially disturbing for him, considering his memories of the frightening winter he had lived through as a child early in the Clyde years. Now with a wife and three small children of his own—by the end of 1913 Robert was six, John just five, and Mimi only two—he faced under primitive conditions the kind of responsibility that his own father, to Sherwood's lasting contempt, had shirked or failed in.[20]

Even more harrowing for both husband and wife was the obsessive problem of their marital relationship. Only four years later Anderson would write a friend that during this winter in the Ozarks "together the woman and I went through poverty, hatred of each other, and all the terrible things that can come from such a situation," and that the conflict began to lessen only when his wife "came to the conclusion that I was not mentally sound" and hence needed mothering. As earlier, the conflict probably involved what Anderson termed to the friend "the difficulties and complications of sex," and whatever these may specifically have been, whatever needs and limitations existed on either side, Cornelia did conclude long after this winter that "what a genius needs is a mother and not a wife." It would be easy on the basis of such statements to categorize Anderson as a classic Oedipal case, too easy, perhaps, for the apparent substitution of a "son-mother" relationship for the husband-wife one could have been on both sides no more than a pragmatic solution to an emotionally exhausting impasse. Certainly Sherwood associated Cornelia with his abortive business career and recent painful rejection of it, associated her with it too much, fairly or unfairly, to allow significant place for her in the artist's life, which he had now tasted and to which as a result he felt all the more drawn. Significantly, there was not, at this point, another woman involved; Anderson wished simply and irrevocably to be free for a new kind of life. He appears to have been aware of the self-centeredness, even the selfishness of the wish, he recognized the possibility that his new direction could end in a failure more devastating than a merely financial one—"No one," Cornelia would later comment, "had fewer illusions about himself than he did"—and he felt as guilty about giving up his family as one might expect of a son who had disliked a father, even though the father had been, if anything, less irresponsible toward his family than he himself was determined to be. Looking back objectively and generously over many years, Cornelia would remember for both of them "a long period . . . not free from mental agony," but Sherwood was resolved on a break. The outcome of these agonized months of tangled conflict was not reconciliation but a more or less settled decision by husband and wife to separate.[21]

There is some evidence that Anderson actually lived apart from his family that winter in the house where he wrote, but in any case his writing and his tramping about would have taken him away from them much of each day. Writing, especially, would have been a way of shutting himself off for hours at a time from the all too pressing problems embodied in wife and children, the only other human beings nearby; it would have been a way also to "objectify" some of these problems through fiction. For the most part it is a matter only of conjecture what Anderson wrote during these months of freedom from the daily harassment of advertising work. Since Floyd Dell in New York was trying to find another publisher for the "untamed" version of *Windy McPherson's Son,* perhaps Anderson in Hooker, Missouri, tried revising *Marching Men,* adding such material as the barber's diatribe against the family and the community he had left behind in Ohio. More likely, given his enthusiastic nature, he turned to new projects. Some years later he told Harry Hansen that he wrote a novel during this winter in the Ozarks but on the train returning to Chicago threw the manuscript out the window; yet this was probably a dramatic way of saying that he was not satisfied with what he had written and had simply put the manuscript away for later attention. He could well have worked at this time on one, or possibly both, of two novels which he eventually completed drafts of but never published, *Talbot Whittingham* and *Mary Cochran.* To describe through the semiautobiographical Talbot the development of a young man into a writer, a "master artist," could have seemed to Anderson during this difficult winter a way to locate and affirm the sources of his present deep drive toward freedom and artisthood. More likely, considering his summer's experience, it was *Mary Cochran* that he worked at during his mornings. If so, the writing went very well indeed, for despite some awkward passages *Mary Cochran* is so well-conceived and shows so much sympathetic understanding of its woman protagonist that it is surprising Anderson remained dissatisfied with the completed novel and reworked from it only the two Mary Cochran stories of *The Triumph of the Egg*—"Unlighted Lamps" and "The Door of the Trap."[22]

Mary Cochran describes the growth of a New England village girl from uncertain adolescence into independent adulthood as one type of the "new woman." Offspring of a brief incompatible marriage between an introverted doctor and a vaudeville actress, Mary combines her father's quiet reserve and her mother's magnetism and self-reliance. The father, with whom she has lived, dies when she is sixteen, and she then attends a small denominational college in Ohio, where, though terrified by their

sexual advances, she attracts one of her professors and an awkward student poet. After graduating, she goes to Chicago and takes an office job as
head of mail-order correspondence in the Yetter and Hunnicutt washing-
machine factory. She almost marries Duke Yetter, her boastful, money-
seeking employer; but she has meanwhile become acquainted with
Sylvester Hunnicutt, Yetter's well-to-do partner, who has rejected a business career, has separated from his practical-minded wife, and, a
"dreamer," spends his time emphatically observing the lives of the city's
people. Challenged by him to realize her potentialities, Mary breaks with
Duke and her job and goes off with Sylvester for a two-week walking tour
in Wisconsin. During the tour Sylvester talks eloquently but makes no advances toward her until Mary, now passionately in love, insists on a physical relationship. Since she is as frightened by the possibility of sexual initiation as she is determined on it, their attempts at lovemaking fail, and
Mary eventually goes back to her New England village to sort out her
emotions. Here, two middle-aged sisters who run a successful printing
business urge her to devote herself to work rather than to love. Encouraged, she returns to her job in Chicago and begins working energetically
with Duke in a nonsexual relationship of equals to improve the business.
Meanwhile Sylvester has been stirred by his admiration for Mary to begin
writing a book "glorifying a new type of woman" and developing "the
idea that the hope of the world lay in its quiet, obscure working women of
the Mary Cochran type" who would "look upon work as an end in life,"
not as a way "to drive a better bargain in the marriage market." United
into an intuitive sisterhood, these women would feel "a horror of selling
out at any price and a passion for independence." In the concluding chapter of *Mary Cochran,* set two years later, it is revealed that Mary and
Sylvester have been married for six months very happily but have chosen
separate residences so that Sylvester can continue his writing at odd hours
and Mary can concentrate singlemindedly during the day on making the
Yetter and Hunnicutt business both honest and successful. By having been
willing to accept life without love, Mary realizes, she can now meet love
unafraid with a man.

The separate residences arrangement between Mary and Sylvester suggests that between Margery Currey and Floyd Dell in their adjacent studios, and there are other elements in the novel suggesting that Anderson
had his new friends in mind. In Chicago, Mary Cochran—whose initials
may only by chance correspond with those of Margery Currey—lives like
Margery in an apartment on Stony Island Avenue facing eastward onto
Jackson Park; and Mary finds independence through work as Margery,
whose marriage was ending rather than beginning, had maintained hers as
schoolteacher and newspaper reporter. There are even physical resemblances between Mary and Margery—the "small trim figure," the "bold

brown eyes"—though the mutual straightforwardness of manner in the fictional character and the actual person has differing sources in Mary's quiet, Margery's gregarious charm. Even more important is the consideration that in his depiction of a "new woman," Anderson makes his own interpretation of the feminism that had been so much of a topic of conversation within the Dell group. Almost certainly he had recently read, perhaps at Floyd's urging, Wells's *Ann Veronica,* the story of a young woman's liberation and marriage told, like *Mary Cochran,* primarily through the woman herself as a center of consciousness. And he could hardly have been unaware at the time that in April Floyd had published his first book, *Women as World Builders,* a collection of "Studies in Modern Feminism" he had originally written for the *Friday Literary Review;* in fact, Anderson seems to have read this little volume as well as talked with its author about its subject. In her rejection of Duke Yetter's desire to make her a pampered sex object in marriage, Mary is repeatedly characterized as being of the "worker," not the "courtesan type," a distinction Dell emphasizes in his introductory chapter; at a bohemian party a young painter, who resembles Michael Carr, warns, very much as Dell's book does, that when "the real free woman comes" she will "raise hell with the little game" men have played; and the conclusion of the novel virtually dramatizes Dell's comment that "The woman who finds her work will find her love."[23]

Yet while Anderson's account of how one woman achieves freedom in a man's world appears to have been shaped by his experience with the Dells, it also represents an attempt to work out through fiction an answer to the tangled emotional problem currently being lived by himself and his wife. Especially in her quietness, possibly in her initial fear of sexuality, Mary resembles, not Margery Currey, but Cornelia; and except for his wealth Sylvester the dreamer markedly resembles Sherwood in his abhorrence of the chicanery of a mail-order business, in his aspiration before his marriage "to become a writer of tales," and in his getting pleasure "from the faculty he had of seeing the tiny, inexpressible turns of human experience and from trying to think through the muddle of modern life into something like peace and contentment." Then, too, as Sherwood knew, Cornelia had her own interest in feminism. Sometime in that unhappy fall or winter she wrote for the first issue of *The Little Review,* at Margaret Anderson's request, a brief article about Ellen Key's book *Rahel Varnhagen,* an admiring portrait of the early nineteenth-century German feminist. Rahel, Cornelia asserted out of her own painfully complex situation, was "a true feminist and looked toward liberation through development and self-expression," though Ellen Key was right, Cornelia agreed, that as biological creator woman best expresses her individuality through the bringing up of her children, sacrificing everything to the central task of

helping the child "to learn to listen to its own inmost ego. . . ." Children
do not complicate the situation between Mary Cochran and Sylvester, and
like the Dells the Andersons were moving toward separation rather than
the union achieved by the fictional couple. Just as the anguished, honest-
minded Cornelia would have to admit to her husband's as well as her own
right to "development and self-expression," so Sherwood, creating fiction
from his side of the experiential conflict, might well have been suggesting
to his wife the necessity that she have goals in life apart from his. Significantly, Sylvester, repelled by his first wife's bursts of anger against his
dreaming ways, bought a poultry farm for Mary to manage, as she had
wished, lived separately from her for most of their married life, and eventually persuaded her to divorce him. Within a year Cornelia, living with
the children apart from her husband, would in fact be preparing herself
for an independent career.[24]

As for other writing Anderson may have done in those months in Missouri, it is fairly certain that early in 1914 he wrote the first two articles
published during his career as artist—"The New Note" and "More About
the 'New Note,'" brief pieces that appeared in the first and second issues
of *The Little Review,* those of March and April 1914. Perhaps during this
winter too he wrote, or revised, and sent off his first true short story to be
published, "The Rabbit-pen," which astonishingly, given the other aspects
of his early writing career, appeared in the July 1914 issue of *Harper's
Magazine.* According to the *Memoirs,* the seventy-five dollars he received
for the story would have seemed like a minor fortune to the Andersons at
this point.[25]

It had been a trying winter, relieved briefly at Christmas time by a visit
from the colorful Michael Carmichael Carr, who usually headed for
Chicago during his vacations from teaching art at the University of Missouri in Columbia, some eighty miles north of Hooker. He brought steaks
with him for broiling, Anderson happily recalled, and the latter would
have delighted to be once more, if briefly, in the company of a man learned
in art who had an "endless flow of talk." It was perhaps in imitation of
Carr that he let his own beard grow.

Despite the sharp tensions between husband and wife, Anderson's
physical health seems to have improved from outdoor exercise and the release from the advertising agency grind, but by late March of 1914 the family was so near the end of its funds that Sherwood was obliged to return to
Chicago and ask for his job back at Taylor-Critchfield. Bearded and with
trousers tucked into his boots, he pretended he was Karl, "telling his lady
friends that Sherwood had sent his love" and giving a kiss to such office
beauties as Colette, the receptionist. He needed all his real or feigned good
spirits to win reinstatement from the company heads, already twice burned
by the resignations of their talented but restless copywriter. Somehow he

persuaded the man in charge of the copy department to let him assist with *Agricultural Advertising*. Within a week or two, George Daugherty remembered,

he was asked by the head of the copy department to help with a rush job that had just come in, so he dropped the special arrangement with the magazine and turned to the new job. Some ten days later when the magazine executive said, "Sherwood, the boys are accusing me of hiring you back. I can't remember whether I did or not," Sherwood answered stoutly, "You certainly did." "Well," said the executive, "I guess I'll have to face the music."[26]

Whatever reservations the people at the agency may have felt about having Anderson back, Daugherty remembered his friend as having done "good work for years" thereafter as an advertising writer. Another copywriter, Donald M. Wright, later eulogized him for his outstanding ability "to execute some well-planned advertising with something in it to attract people to a product and to lead them to buy it." An advertising writer, Wright asserted, was supposed to produce "ideas" and ought to be a salesman as well.

Anderson was both a producer (of everything from layouts to sale policies) *and* a salesman. During his early years in the business he was even a high pressure salesman, though he later developed into a *subtle* salesman, disguised as copywriter.

No matter what Anderson was supposed to be, at any one time, his hunches were worth a dozen surveys; his insight into the vagaries of human nature was demonstrated no less cunningly in his apparently naive plans and copy than in his novels and short stories.

Sherwood had a habit, Wright remembered, of "waking up a too-solemn conference by, well, *hearty* stories," and "whenever a jam was on Anderson could clear the air with a few tonic guffaws and, nine times out of ten, solve the 'problem' . . . by a leisurely exhibition of plain advertising horse sense—usually throwing in free the hysterically demanded slogan."[27]

Anderson's usual public manner was to appear much relaxed and at home in the agency. Toward his fellow workers on the job, George Daugherty would remember, he was "jaunty, smiling, 'kidding.'" With "a long lock of his tousled hair hanging low on his forehead, his black eyes glittering," he "would be making suggestions on some advertising account in a long deliberate drawl, or taking a strong position in an argument, punctuated by chuckles rising to a high cracked pitch." Still though never appearing busy, "he turned out an astonishing amount of work." Both skilled and casual-seeming as he was at his copywriting, privately he continued to regard the way he was once more forced to make his living as occasionally interesting in its revelation of human character, more often boring at best, at worst deeply vicious and corrupting for its misuse of language to manipulate human desires, and always a frustrating impediment to his true vocation. Released from the winter's bondage to wife and family, however, he poured his time free from his hated job into working on various manuscripts, quite openly talking about them to the other copywriters and wryly referring to himself as "the greatest unpublished novelist in America." An early riser, he would sometimes be at the office an hour or more before the regular 8:30 AM opening in order to write, and he even worked more or less surreptitiously on his fiction during moments stolen from the daily office routine, like, as he once said, "the schoolboy who set his big geography up in front of him and drew caricatures of the teacher behind it." He was to continue this practice throughout his remaining several years at the agency. Picking a day in 1919 as typical of the "old Critchfield" firm, Sherwood's fellow adman Donald Wright described him at work in the copy department, incidentally revealing how sharply Anderson had cut himself off from his years in Elyria.

Sherwood Anderson is presiding over two piles of "copy-writers' yellow." The top sheet of one of the piles is an ad on golf clubs which has been assigned to Sherwood, perhaps because he not only does not play golf but actively dislikes golf and golf-players as such. The top sheet of the second heap of paper is blank, but the reverse side of that sheet is covered with practically illegible writing in pencil—the last paragraph or two of the first and final draft of a little story Anderson has just finished, called "The Triumph of the Egg." The author has been doing it this afternoon instead of the assigned golf club ad, now only four days past closing. One of the more conscientious lads . . . comes in and whispers, "Gee, Mr. Anderson; we just lost the golf club account." Anderson, in his actor's baritone, says loudly: "Well, *that's* good—now I don't have to write the goddam stuff!"

Anderson himself was to recollect specifically for a friend that his story "I'm a Fool" was "written at the copy desk one morning while I was presumed to be writing copy for a gas engine."[28]

Once more drawing a salary, Anderson could send money, rather irregularly, to his wife and children, who probably remained in the cabin near Hooker until summer when they moved to Union Pier, Michigan, the pleasant little beach town where in the previous year the "Dell group" had begun holding its weekend revels. Although they had separated, husband and wife had not yet decided on divorce; but out of sight was very likely out of mind as far as Anderson regarded his family. He lived now for the hours or stolen minutes when he was writing, and soon he must have taken pleasure in proving to both his copy department associates and his Jackson Park friends that he was a published author if not a published novelist. The two essays on the "New Note" were brief, and his story "The Rabbit-pen," despite characteristic motifs, represented a kind of writing he was trying to go beyond; but there they were in the March and April issues of the exciting new *Little Review* and the July 1914 issue of the staid but nationally circulated *Harper's*.

For all their brevity the two articles, especially the second, suggest the psychic terrain Anderson had set himself to explore. In one sense the new note is not new at all, the first article asserts; rather, it is ancient as well as modern, for it rejects the standards of commercial publishing in favor of "the older, sweeter standards of the craft itself," which have always been "truth and honesty." At the same time this note "is the voice of the new man, come into a new world, proclaiming his right to speak out of the body and soul of youth, rather than through the bodies and souls of the master craftsmen who are gone." Young poets and novelists are "soldiers of the new" just as are "ardent young cubists and futurists, anarchists, socialists, and feminists." Although the new tends always to become the conventional, the new note constantly recurs afresh like a repeated phenomenon of nature; "it is the promise of a perpetual sweet new birth of the world," only this time the note is sounded by both men and women, or as Anderson puts it with quaint dignity, "the youth and the maiden dancing together," creating not a half but a whole new world.

"The New Note" story was not only appropriate for the initial issue of *The Little Review*; it was, one guesses, a personal manifesto. Associating himself with youth, since as writer he was young whatever his chronological age, Anderson accepted from the past only its practitioners of a true and honest craft, rejecting all else old, all else past, as inhibiting, and dedicated himself to a future of "craft love" whatever hardship this might bring him. Obliquely he was telling Cornelia that she was part of the inhibiting past that he must reject.

In "More About the 'New Note,'" Anderson showed that he had already begun to work out, if not always clearly, a major tenet of the essentially Romantic aesthetic creed he came to hold throughout his writing career. A corollary of "craft love" is now, and always has been for the master artist, he asserts, "the spirit of self-revelation." To the extent that a writer "looks outside of himself for material," he fails, as did, for example, Howells and Zola; on the other hand, "Whitman, Tolstoy, Dostoevsky, Twain, and Fielding"—some of his permanent literary admirations—succeeded because the writings of each "'revealed the workings of his own soul and mind.'" Paradoxically, the writer to be great must understand other persons and convey that understanding to his readers; yet in order to "record truthfully the workings of other minds," he must first be able to record "simply and truthfully the inner workings of his own mind." It is, Anderson warns, "the most delicate and the almost unbelievably difficult task to catch, understand, and record your own mood"; but if one puts one's self to the constant practice of such recording, then "a kind of partnership will in time spring up between the hand and the brain of the writer." In his imagination he will "in truth" *become* the other person of whom he writes, and his hand will be guided by that imaginative identification. Inevitably a writer suffers "barren periods" when brain and hand do not coordinate, at which times the writer should return to recording the workings of his own mind until, in some unexplained way, coordination returns. Such recording of self, Anderson concludes, has been a help and a delight to him.

One source for these ideas, oddly enough, may have been Ellen Key's *Rahel Varnhagen,* the portrait of the German Romantic feminist that Cornelia seems to have been reading, writing, and talking to her husband about back in Hooker at about the same time he was writing his two articles; for he closely resembles Varnhagen in insisting on the rightness of an author's turning "in upon himself, trusting with childlike simplicity and honesty the truth that lives in his own mind." But such an idea is, of course, of long standing in critical doctrine, as exemplified by Sidney's and Tennyson's injunctions to the poet to look into the heart and write. Yet another source, considering Anderson's reference to it, might well be the example of the Armory Show with its pervasive theme that the modern artist abandons representation of an object in favor of expressing his subjective reaction to that object. Such an approach to writing would fit generally with the impulse of the whole Chicago renaissance toward liberation of the self, and specifically with the psychological needs of a man who lacked both the support and the hindrance of much formal education, who had only recently gone through a profound emotional disturbance and lifestyle reversal, and who needed both freedom and a validation of that freedom. Yet this doctrine, self-centered as it may seem, is by no means aimed at artistic solipsism. One turns in upon one's self in order to turn outward, to enter imaginatively into other lives. The subjective and the objective, the self and the not-self, the individual and the "world," the lyric mode and the realistic mode, as it were—all of necessity exist symbiotically. This would remain a fundamental assumption in Anderson's theory and practice as a writer. He never formulated, never pretended to formulate, a systematic aesthetics; he did, however, sense what some of the aesthetic problems of the act of writing are, and he came to grips with them as well as he could. But most of the time out of a combination of conviction and defensiveness he preferred to be the storyteller rather than the theoretician.[29]

His first published tale is closer than most of his subsequent work to what he condemned in "The New Note" as "the standards set up by money-making magazine and book publishers." Understandably so if he was substantially telling the truth in the *Memoirs* when he claimed that he had written "The Rabbit-pen" as the result of an argument with Trillena White over Howells, whom she admired but who, Anderson had asserted, left "too much of life" out of his writings, especially the "tremendous force" of sex. During the argument Anderson boasted that he could write a story *Harper's* would print, and he now carried out his boast. Perhaps he did deliberately aim, "rather with my tongue in my cheek," at what he considered to be the *Harper's* tone. Fordyce, the story's Jamesian center of consciousness, is a successful novelist; his friend Harkness, ex-newspaper man, lives comfortably off his wife Ruth's fortune and his business directorates; much of the action takes place at the Harkness summer home, "Cottesbrooke." This upper-class world is emotionally flaccid, however, vitality being supplied it by a young German housekeeper, "the free-walking, straight-backed Gretchen," who in the opening scene efficiently assists a mother rabbit, who is furiously protecting her newborn litter from being killed by the buck, by snatching the "huge fellow" out of the pen. Just as efficiently Gretchen disciplines the two small Harkness boys whom the gentle Ruth cannot handle. Throughout the rest of the summer the passive, bookish Fordyce self-indulgently daydreams of Gretchen as his wife. During a visit to Harkness's city office the following February, however, he learns that Ruth, distressed by Gretchen's hold over the children, had tried to buy their affection at Christmas time with expensive mechanical toys and then had burst out hysterically against the housekeeper. Devoted to his wife, Harkness dismisses Gretchen, who, Fordyce belatedly learns to his dismay, is no longer available to him, she having married Hans the Harkness stableman and gone off, leaving the Harkness parents as incapable of handling their unruly children as before.

"The Rabbit-pen" is a minor story, which Anderson never reprinted in any of his collections of tales. Its manner is imitative, its style is formal, its carefully structured plot moves toward a modified form of the surprise ending. Nevertheless it foreshadows important aspects of Anderson's later fiction. The contrast between the emotionally immature upper-class characters, overdependent on the externalities of wealth and possessions, and the competent, vital lower-class characters points toward *Dark Laughter* and other pieces. The symbol of the rabbit-pen, perhaps too obviously announced at the beginning, gradually accretes implications as the story progresses, as does, to take only one example, the symbol of the two tree stumps in "Brother Death," one of Anderson's finest late tales. And despite the decorousness of the language the story clearly manifests the power of sexuality, particularly in the way it can in subtle, indirect fashion cripple the relationships within a whole family group, a group bearing some resemblance to the Andersons themselves. Perhaps because of its imitativeness Anderson was offhand about the story in his later years, but its other qualities were sufficiently marked that he would have had a right to feel pleased about it in the summer of 1914 and not just because for the first time thousands of Americans would see his name in print.[30]

2.

If Anderson now lived most intensely in those free hours and snatched minutes during which he was covering sheets of fresh paper with his rapid pencil scrawl, he lived next in degree during the evenings and weekends he spent with others who shared his interest in artistic creation. By the time Cornelia and the children had settled as summer boarders in the home of the hospitable Edwin and Eva Leatherman in Union Pier, he had already become attracted to a woman whose mode of existence more nearly fitted his conception of the untrammeled artist's life. This was Cornelia's and Margery Currey's friend, Tennessee Mitchell.

Like Sherwood, Tennessee was a midwesterner who had been drawn in her youth to Chicago, worked hard to make a living, and developed artistic inclinations. She had been born in the small city of Jackson in south central Michigan on April 18, 1874, the eldest daughter of Jay P. and Mattie Stockham Mitchell. Her father, a comfortably off postal clerk and house builder, was markedly undemonstrative toward her and her two younger sisters; but her mother was warmhearted and given, much to young Tennessee's embarrassment, to defending unpopular causes, such as antivivisection, her own father being a freethinker who came out for spiritualism and other "advanced" ideas. Robert Ingersoll sometimes visited in the grandfather's house across the street from the Mitchell home, and as a little girl Tennessee would sit in the lap of the Great Agnostic for hours as he told her stories. Just before Tennessee was born, her grandfather had had as house guests Tennessee Claflin and Victoria Claflin Woodhull, the beautiful and flamboyant sisters who were then scandalizing the nation by their stock market speculation, muckraking journalism, advocacy of socialism, and unconventional love lives. According to Tennessee Mitchell's autobiographical account, her mother had "an especial affection for the charming and spirited Tennessee Claflin" and herself a "gentle feminist," on a neighboring woman's dare gave her firstborn daughter the name of a "rampant" one. At that time Tennessee Claflin was signing herself "Tennie C. Claflin," the "C." standing for the missing syllable of the first name and for her middle name Celeste; so the new baby was named Tenne C., the middle name being Content.[31]

Tennessee, or Tennis as she would call herself for many years, had nevertheless a conventional enough girlhood, but she had to seek independence earlier than usual. Her mother bore two more daughters and then died when Tennessee was about sixteen, whereupon Jay Mitchell soon married a second wife, who took a violent dislike to her oldest stepdaughter.

Tennessee finished high school, where she had been a good student and had developed a talent for piano; but after her stepmother had tried to kill her by poisoning some little cakes left out for the girl after a dance, she went to live in Chicago in the early or mid-1890s, subsequently sending for Amber, the younger of her two sisters, then about six. The two girls lived in poverty while Tennessee, who had an unusually accurate ear for musical pitch, learned the profession of piano tuning; her difficulties as a woman in obtaining instruction from male teachers helped confirm her growing feminist convictions. Around 1900 Amber contracted scarlet fever. Tennessee "walked the streets all day" trying to find a hospital that would take her sister in, but was unsuccessful. She nursed Amber herself as well as she could, but the girl died in her arms. Deprived now of her last source of close affection, Tennessee went through a five-month nervous collapse. Recovering, she returned to her profession, but by 1906 she had begun teaching piano to children, eventually including instruction in "rhythmics," a mode of individualized dancing designed to teach music through bodily response to rhythm. Gradually she developed a clientele among the rich and well-to-do on Chicago's North Side, but she became widely acquainted also with the artists and writers who were gathering there and elsewhere in the city just prior to the renaissance.[32]

During the next few years the independent girl from Jackson, Michigan, developed into an attractive, sophisticated individual. "Tall, spare, and positive," she was a "spirited" person with "lots of style." Her hair was medium brown with a reddish tint, and she wore unusual hats with a special flair; her clothes were striking and stylish. With her willowy, if flat-chested, figure and her deliberate, flowing rhythmic movements, she "knew just how to wear that smock that didn't look well on another girl." Not beautiful but not plain either, she was elegant, poised, graceful. Even-tempered and somewhat withdrawn in outward manner, she was not at all cold in personality—and in fact craved more affection than that manner appeared to admit. She was quietly jolly, calmly but fully interested in whatever was going on around her, and wittily amusing about herself as well as others. Most people who knew her were struck also by her courage, her basic self-reliance, her good critical mind, her responsible-ness, her ability to listen carefully to another's problems and then give sensible advice.[33]

The poise and evenness had not been won easily, however. She had often felt insecure, had often been economically insecure especially in her early, struggling years in Chicago. She found men and sexual relationships rather "confusing," too, though by the time she met Anderson she had had at least some sexual experience. At first attracted particularly to men on the periphery of the arts, she became acquainted by chance in the summer of 1909 with Edgar Lee Masters, who at forty was already frustrated and embittered by his drudgery at law, an unsatisfactory marriage, and his failure as yet to find an audience for his poetry. Masters writes of an ensuing affair with Tennessee in his autobiography, *Across Spoon River,* writes of it and her with extraordinary venom, portraying her as "Deirdre," the deceitful and designing woman who kept him in sexual slavery and writhing nerves until he managed painfully to rid himself of her as of a poison. Although Master's tone of self-pitying recrimination makes his account unpleasant and suspect, Tennessee's version of the relationship as an intellectual one only is not a wholly convincing part of her fragment of autobiography either; her apparent denial of a sexual aspect to the relation is given in uncharacteristically evasive language, and at least one other person who knew her very well accepted as fact that she and Masters had been sexually involved. A year later the relationship ended in bitter hatred on his part, intense aversion on hers. For a long time afterward the chance sight of Masters on the street would affect her "like physical danger" and send her into actual hiding until he had passed.[34]

It is very likely an indication of Anderson's great warmth and magnetism in initiating relationships with other people that Tennessee responded to him despite the ugly conclusion to her recent experience with Masters. How Tennessee dealt with the fact that the man she was attracted to was still married to a woman she considered a good friend can only be guessed at. Probably all three persons involved felt that the awkward situation must be handled, at least outwardly, in as "civilized" a manner as the Dells had handled the breakup of their marriage the year before. But it was a difficult time for Cornelia, coming as it did as a culmination of several years of domestic unhappiness. Fortunately she liked and trusted the Leathermans with whom she and the children were rooming and boarding at Union Pier. Ed, a hard-working, dependable man, was a teamster who did general hauling and also drove a taxi. Eva, whose one child, a little girl, had died, loved the three handsome Anderson children as though they were her own and took good care of them. Cornelia was willing to discuss the developing situation with her husband. As she recalled, they "talked pretty frankly. We had been separated for a long time and he had other interests. . . . We knew perfectly well that we weren't going to live together," but at that point neither wished to take the final step of a divorce.[35]

"Theoretically," as Cornelia later put it, her husband was to come to Union Pier weekends to see her and the family; but in actuality, as Margery Currey recalled, the wife was long since "out of it." Instead Sherwood usually came out from Chicago on the local train Saturday afternoons, not alone but with a group of as many as twenty-five or thirty of the old Dell crowd, including Margery, Michael Carr, Ben Hecht, and Tennessee, who this summer was the one Anderson kept close to as the previous summer he had kept close to Margery. The whole band would stay at Camp's

Cottages at the edge of the wide, white, fine-grained sand beach and have a weekend frolic. In the daytime they lolled in the sun or, going to a deserted part of the beach, would bathe in the nude. Everyone dressed for self-expression during the day. Once Sherwood was observed running through the main hall of the Cottages' central building, dressed in trousers rolled to the knees, a red shirt, a bandanna around his neck, and on his head a beat-up old hat with two red feathers sticking out of it. As he ran, he seemed unconcerned that sand was scattering over the floor from his bare feet. Nights the whole group would again go to a wild part of the beach, build a big fire, and gather around it. They especially enjoyed dressing up for ceremonials such as impromptu plays or pageants; Margery Currey remembered that once Sherwood and Tennessee were decked by the group in outlandish but attractive robes, she looking particularly elegant and lovely, and with great fanfare crowned king and queen of the revels. Day or night Sherwood was at the center of things, always the leader, which shows how much this artist-advertising man had been accepted into the group of which hardly more than a year ago he, the uninitiate, had stood in some awe.[36]

The townspeople of Union Pier tended to be shocked by what they considered the wild behavior of "The Nudist Club," as they called the weekend visitors from the city. Eli Camp, the owner of Camp's Cottages, rather enjoyed the carryings-on, as well he might since they were so profitable to his business in addition to being high-spirited; but when two local men became involved with women in the group and their marriages broke up as a result, a move grew to get rid of the visitors. Nothing came of it, however, and as the season ended, the group ceased coming to Union Pier. Not only the two jilted wives but the tolerant Cornelia herself was profoundly hurt by what developed that summer. Rarely did she criticize Sherwood to anyone, for the refinement so many noticed in her was reinforced by her abhorrence of what Rahel Varnhagen had called "coercive marriage" and by her conviction that her husband must be true to his own inmost needs. Yet once more, as in the Elyria crisis, the hurt was so sharp that she broke through her reserve and confessed to a neighbor, Della Garland, who had become a close friend, that Sherwood was "mixed up with," another woman, unnamed but almost certainly Tennessee. Now to Sherwood's desire for freedom from his family to write, a desire Cornelia felt bound to honor, was added his attraction to a woman whom, despite the pain of the immediate situation, Cornelia would always regard as a "very dear friend." What would develop, she must have realized, was not one of the brief sexual encounters her husband had almost frantically indulged in just before his Elyria breakdown but something more lasting, which would cut off any possibility of reconciliation between them. Years later Della Garland, having gone through an exceptionally distasteful first

marriage and divorce, remembered vividly how very hard Cornelia took
the finality of the separation, however composed she may have been outwardly. Noting that Mrs. Anderson's hair turned gray early, she believed
that this resulted from her anguish.

Probably admitting to herself at last the likelihood of eventual divorce,
Cornelia determined to take care of the children primarily through her
own efforts and to develop in her own way. At first she decided to prepare
for social work. Leaving Robert, John, and Mimi with the Leathermans,
she studied in Chicago from January to August 1915 at the School of
Civics and Philanthropy, found both that she did not care for a career in
social work and could get no job in it anyway, and with relief accepted a
position as a first grade teacher in the Union Pier school. Here she taught
from 1915 to 1917, her son John being in one of her classes.[37]

After the weekend excursions to Union Pier had ended with the coming of fall, Anderson, as though to emphasize the break with his family,
moved to another rooming house, where he lived for the next two and a
half years and where he wrote many of the tales collected as *Winesburg,
Ohio*. This house, a long, narrow, three-story rundown brick residence,
was at 735 Cass Street (now North Wabash Avenue) at the northeast corner of the intersection with Superior Street. George Daugherty, his friend
at Taylor-Critchfield who roomed with him briefly, recalled that the landlady was "Ma" Lindsay, "good-humored and sympathic, but keen on
collection of room rent." Probably Anderson moved there because rent
was cheap, and he could take the nearby streetcar or walk to his advertising job in the Loop; but the homelike office of *Poetry* magazine, five blocks
south on Cass at No. 543, added to the literary air of the neighborhood,
and Tennessee's apartment was only a dozen blocks north on Stone Street.
As Daugherty remembered it,

Anderson's room . . . was spacious enough, but dingy and furnished only with bare
essentials: a rough worktable jammed against a wall and loaded with a row of
books, a basketful of lead pencils of all lengths, a stack of yellow copy paper and
another stack of sheets covered with his almost undecipherable scratches, a bare
light bulb suspended over the table. Sherwood's bed, built for him by an old carpenter, stood near a window where he could command the prospect of Michigan
Boulevard, the street traffic, the lights and the lake while he meditated—life.[38]

From the window of his third-story room under the steep-pitched roof,
Anderson indeed might have been able to glimpse Michigan Avenue (then
Michigan Boulevard) only two blocks to the east, and over the roofs of the
buildings running south along Cass Street he could certainly have observed and meditated on the skyscrapers thrusting up in the Loop, visible
monuments to architectural imagination and business enterprise. He had

a different sort of prospect within the house. Although some clerks and other workers in the city lived there, many of the roomers were youthful aspirants in the arts; in fact, Anderson may have been especially attracted to the house for that reason. Max Wald, for example, who during the day taught music in a studio in the Fine Arts Building, where *The Little Review* had its office, worked evenings in his tense way on songs for a light opera he was composing. William Hollingsworth painted portraits, including one of Anderson himself. Others wrote poetry or painted or acted in the Little Theatre or existed as bohemians at the fringes of the arts. Some simply lived their lives, like Mary, the beautiful "born courtesan" whose room was next to Anderson's; or the fat, mannish woman who, agonizingly in love with Mary, would put on a man's suit and, looking funny with her great breasts bulging the jacket, would wait for her with desperate honesty in the hall; or "Jack," the odd young man whom Anderson used to think of as an egg in its shell, apparently because of his combined self-containment and potentiality, and who one December midnight in 1914 was dragged back unconscious along Cass Street to No. 735 by two huge policemen after they had found him dead drunk from an experimental binge. Most of the artistically inclined people were in their early twenties, poor, ill-fed, ambitious for fame, returning to the rooming house in the evening from stopgap jobs to crowd into one or another's small room and talk excitedly far into the night about "the day's dominant themes in art." Sometimes they held holiday feasts in Anderson's room. They tended to look up to him as an older, more experienced man and a producing artist, and would pause in their talk to hear "the long, easy drawl of his comment." In turn, Anderson, now in his late thirties, regarded them paternally as rather remote from life, turned in on their own little worlds of artistic interest, for the most part rather tepid in their sexual urges. He was fond of them, curious about them, both delighted and amused by the happy seriousness with which they discussed art. Though he talked with them by the hour, he felt them to be, as he came to phrase it in the *Memoirs,* the Little Children of the Arts. Often he pondered to himself their linked and individual lives.[39]

He was taking his own art seriously enough, though during the year and a half after the appearance of "The Rabbit-pen" in the July 1914 *Harper's* to that of the far different short piece, "Sister," in *The Little Review* for December 1915, he published nothing. "Sister" is a significantly new kind of writing, puzzling in its mixture of the defined and undefined. A semifantasy sketch with a semirealistic tale embedded in it, "Sister" has no plot but moves fluidly from present to past to present again within the consciousness of a narrator who, like that of the much later "Death in the Woods," explicitly wonders how he can know with such certainty the details of an event he did not witness, thus emphasizing the deliberate confusion in the piece between the real and the imagined. The unnamed young woman of the title is the artist-sister of the narrator; the narrator has sided with her against their authoritarian father and, like her, lives alone in a room in the city. On a symbolic level the brother and sister might be understood as parts of a single psyche, perhaps of Anderson himself, the brother being a kind of superego, "the worker in the world, the sister a kind of ego, "the artist right to adventure in the world." Earlier the father had beaten the sister with a buggy whip when she asserted her sexual independence as an adolescent, and now, like the father though with verbal punishment only, the narrator displays an incestuous anger against her on the occasions when she visits him in his room and tells him of her adventures. He thinks his sister "the most wonderful artist in the world" and "a little" understands her right to adventure.

It is tempting to try to define "Sister" in terms of Freudian psychodynamics, for it is indeed highly probable that, as he writes in the *Memoirs,* Anderson had become acquainted with the elements of psychoanalysis through Floyd Dell in the summer of 1913, and he had written a striking dream sequence into his story of another woman, Mary Cochran. Still, Mary's apocalyptic dream seems closer in symbolic method to those in Dostoyevsky or the Bible than to programmatic Freudianism, and in "Sister" Anderson the storyteller may well have been relying less on a psychological schema than on, as "More About the 'New Note'" had put it, "the inner workings of his own mind." "Sister" could in fact be read as a fanciful rendering of his unresolved relations with the independent Tennessee, whose puzzlement about sex had included not only a recent devastating adventure with another literary man but, as she recalled in her autobiography, the "deep impression" made on her by a spanking she had received from her father as a child along with the admonition that "men distrusted and despised females" for their lack of courage.[40]

"Sister" is simply too ambiguous for a single consistent interpretation, and perhaps Anderson preferred it so. But to compare the ordered revelations of "The Rabbit-pen" with the spare, shifting inconclusive psychodrama of this piece is to see a writer leap directly into the modernist era with its concern to find appropriate forms for rendering subjective experience. Evidence strongly suggests, however, that the leap did not just happen but was from a specific springboard—Gertrude Stein's *Tender Buttons.* Because Anderson would later write of her book's awakening influence on him, this evidence must be briefly summarized.

Published in New York in May, 1914, *Tender Buttons* quickly became for both admirers and detractors, especially in a Chicago then in full literary renaissance, the quintessence of modernism. At least four Chicago newspapers reviewed it that summer with varying reservations, the *Herald* review even containing a now tantalizing comment: "'Am I insane,

O *sister,* or has the printer gone insane before me? Be comforted, *brother,* the lost wits belong neither to you nor the printer . . .'" (author's emphasis). It is extremely likely that Anderson did read in the November 1914 issue of *The Little Review*—"Sister" would be published in the December 1915 issue—Ibn Gabirol's piece, "My Friend, the Incurable," with its admiring comments on Stein's book, which read rather like a description of "Sister" itself. The book gave Gabirol

rare pleasure to witness the first attempt to revolutionize the most obsolete and inflexible medium of Art—words. The author has endeavored to use language in the same way as Kandinsky uses his colors to discard conventional structure, to eliminate understandable figures and forms, and to create a "spiritual harmony," leaving to the layman the task of discovering the "*innerer Klang.*"

However he heard of it, a copy of *Tender Buttons,* Anderson wrote in *A Story Teller's Story,* "had come into my hands. How it had excited me!"

Here was something purely experimental and dealing in words separated from sense—in the ordinary meaning of the word sense—an approach I was sure the poets must often be compelled to make. Was it an approach that would help me? I decided to try it.

So, seeing Stein's words set before him like a painter's color pans on a table,

after Miss Stein's book had come into my hands I spent days going about with a tablet of paper in my pocket and making new and strange combinations of words. The result was I thought a new familiarity with the words of my own vocabulary. I became a little conscious where before I had been unconscious. Perhaps it was then I really fell in love with words, wanted to give each word I used every chance to show itself at its best.

Anderson had of course long been in love with words but not in Stein's fashion. Her book had so powerful an influence on him as to be most probably the impulse toward "Sister" and, eventually, the reason why he sought Stein out in Paris in the spring of 1921. Anderson formed a lasting friendship with her, and two decades after reading *Tender Buttons* acclaimed her as "a genius" for teaching him the vitality of word-color and making him recognize the "poet-writing person" within himself, that person who created "all the more beautiful and clear, the more plangent and radiant writing I have done."[41]

The concern he showed in "Sister" to find an appropriate form for rendering subjective experience is reflected, though with quite different results, in *Talbot Whittingham,* the unpublished novel on which Anderson appears to have concentrated his major energies from, roughly, the spring of 1914 to early summer 1915. Even more than the sketch, the novel helps reveal his development as a writer in the crucial and still obscure period just before he began creating the Winesburg tales.

3.

Even into the 1920s and 1930s Anderson would "play" in his imagination from time to time with the figure of Talbot Whittingham, producing a number of manuscript fragments concerning a person by this name, the large amount of such material suggesting that his character had some special significance for its author. That significance may be readily surmised. Whereas, when published, *Marching Men* described the development of a largely invented labor leader and *Windy McPherson's Son* that of an only partially invented businessman, *Talbot Whittingham,* the one full-length novel among the Whittingham manuscripts, traces the growth of a writer, one who despite obvious difference in external life seems often a projection of his creator's inner existence.[42]

Although the brief book 1 of the *Talbot Whittingham* manuscript is missing, some of its events can be reconstructed from references in the remaining four books and from a reader's report, which Anderson's friend Bab (Marietta Finley) prepared in "about 1916." Talbot, son of an "umbrella-thief" father and a musician mother, spends his childhood in "a stuffy little apartment in New York," where the mother tries to create a salon from "an indiscriminate lot of art hangers-on" and achieves only an "abnormal, sickly atmosphere." One night the boy listens intently as a drunken youth urges him to be an artist, explaining that it is the artist alone who, though he may not understand "the law of life," knows that there is such a law, which orders the mystery of existence. (Only Jesus of Nazareth, the omniscient narrator comments, would have understood this law, though a sense of it comes at times to the artist "in flashes" because of his desire to communicate with others through artistic "form.") When Talbot is twelve, his father disappears, and his mother, having discovered "her affinity in the person of a wealthy Breakfast Food man," commits him to the care of her former patron, Billy Bustard, a shy, middle-aged baker in the small Ohio town of Mirage, a name in keeping with the sardonic tone in which book 1 appears to have been at least partly narrated.[43]

Book 2 describes in a series of episodes Talbot's life in Mirage from age twelve to eighteen as he begins to develop toward what he eventually will become, a "master artist." Talbot, the narrator explains, has a "double nature." On the one hand, he is self-centered, arrogant, and manipulative of others, especially of Billy Bustard, who supports him in a lazy life with a large monthly allowance; on the other hand, he is imaginative, inquisitive and sensitive about life, and sometimes insecure inwardly despite his outward self-assurance. Thus he embodies in surrogate form the conflict between the success-seeking and the dreamy Anderson of the author's Clyde years. Through his relationships with various inhabitants of Mirage, Talbot begins to mature. Bruce Harvey, a man totally devoted to horses and harness-racing, urges him to be hard and relentless as a driver in the race of life. With a strong, imaginative girl named Jeanette Franks he vies as a teller of wild adventure tales until she enters sexual maturity, becomes pregnant by the local barber, and is forced into marriage with him, much to Talbot's puzzled distress. Another girl, Lillian Gale, provides him with his first sexual conquest, and Kit Donahue, a tough, virginal waitress, gets drunk with him one night while "they were trying to get at an understanding of each other and, through each other, of all men and women" who must live in the "modern world." Then Billy Bustard's brutal old father, Tom, returns to Mirage, rather like Huck Finn's Pap to St. Petersburg, demands money from his son, and tells Talbot to get out. Frightened by the man's threats, Talbot borrows Bruce Harvey's revolver, deliberately kills Tom, is exonerated on the false grounds that he was defending his benefactor, and with a gift of $1500 from the embarrassed Billy leaves Mirage on the advice of the town's one Socialist, who shrewdly perceives that secretly the boy regards the murder as his "passport to manhood."

Books 3 and 4 detail the sequence of experiences in Chicago, which over several years leads Talbot further toward an artist's career. On the train from Mirage to Chicago he meets and is attracted to a frank, courageous young woman who has left schoolteaching in an Indiana town for a try at becoming a painter. Once in the city, Talbot, living on Billy's gift, forgets her and responds to his double nature, satisfying his aggressiveness by acting as a sparring partner at a boxing academy and his curiosity about human beings by standing "at street crossings and looking at people," the latter being a "passion with Talbot all of his days" and "his way of going to school." Soon he begins the daily practice of writing down some of his thoughts, and in a dark street one rainy night he has a visionary experience. Suddenly "all the men and women he had ever known seemed to press in about him" and "with their eyes and their hands" to plead with him to be their voice: "'Do not think of your own life but lend your brain and your young courage to us. Help us that we may make ourselves understood; that all men and women may make themselves understood.'" Shortly thereafter, however, he joyfully beats two men in a fight over a dancehall girl but by chance again meets the woman from Indiana. She explains to him bitterly that she has failed as an artist both because the modern woman is still too hampered by her traditional social role and because women will perhaps always be prevented by their biological role from achieving what the male as true artist can achieve, even if his dedication destroys him—the expression through himself of "the very spirit of his times and people."

Despite these steps on the way, however, Talbot's journey toward becoming a master artist is not direct. Through an acquaintance named Billows Turner, a gifted if eccentric advertising man, he drifts with the moneymaking spirit of the times into the advertising firm of Lester & Leach. Here he is financially successful, but he soon begins seriously to question "the meaning of his life." He becomes involved at the office in a long-standing quarrel between an exponent of Christ's teachings and a disciple of Nietzsche. The former insists equally on Jesus's "idea of infinite pity" and his tough-minded saying (from Luke 9:60), "Let the dead bury the dead"; the latter dismisses Christianity as sentimentality and, briefly taking Talbot on a drinking spree before hurrying nervously home to his wife, lectures his saloon audiences on the necessity of an "army of individualists," of "natural men" dedicated to following their instincts, whether to become artists or murderers. Continuing the spree on his own, Talbot late that evening wildly accosts six separate people and attempts to make each perceive that he or she is a "grotesque," having been made so by the ugliness and deadness of life. Then he stalks a drunken merchant through the streets of Chicago's North Side with the purpose of killing him, obscurely feeling that this extreme act will somehow clarify his own confusion. About to assault the businessman, however, he suddenly conceives of another bizarre way by which he can objectify to his maddened satisfaction Christ's "terrible saying," "Let the dead bury the dead"; and he at once goes to Turner's house to obtain his assistance in the scheme, a mass sale of inexpensive cemetery lots that will let Talbot view crowds of the living paying money toward their deaths. When carried out, the sale is very profitable for Talbot, but paradoxically it also softens the hatred he has developed against human beings as physically ugly and spiritually dead.[44]

Book 5, set eleven years after Talbot's first coming to Chicago, consists solely of two contrasting meetings between him and a woman. In the first he dines at a restaurant with Adelaide Brown, a wealthy dilettante more interested in artists than their art, who, as Talbot has told her, has "never done anything bold and beautiful" in her life. Just as he has cruelly forced her to admit that she does not have the courage to enter an affair with him, he catches sight of the Indiana woman, now named for the first time as Lucile Bearing, entering the restaurant with a little foreign-looking man as escort. Talbot sends Adelaide away and turns to Lucile, who, his artist's nature recognizes, has been defeated by life and yet has had the courage to accept that defeat. Seating her at a restaurant table and ignoring her angry escort, he describes to Lucile his frequent daydreams of seeing her enter a long room out of a misty night, lovely of feature and with droplets of mist in her hair and on her coat that sparkle in the flames of the fireplace. The three people leave the restaurant, and as they walk toward Lucile's apartment through a misty evening, the escort becomes increasingly enraged, suddenly draws a revolver, shoots her, and runs off. Though wounded—fatally, it soon appears—Lucile continues to walk with Talbot to her apartment. Talbot insists on entering the apartment first, finds it, as he had hoped, a replica of the setting in his daydream, and, when the dying Lucile enters, perceives this woman who has accepted defeat to be as beautiful in actuality as in his fantasy. Then as the fireplace flames dance on the droplets of mist in her hair, Lucile, appearing to have "grown suddenly younger, taller and straighter," smiles at him for a moment and falls to the floor dead.

Such a summary of the book's action suggests why Anderson seems never to have submitted the manuscript to a publisher. As he himself presumably recognized, the novel has serious flaws. Not only is the ending contrived and melodramatic, but Lucile Bearing, who is given only three scenes in the narrative, functions largely as a mechanical device for charting the development of Talbot's understanding as an artist, her unselfish death being apparently so placed as to balance out in both the novel's structure and its ethical concerns Talbot's selfish act of murder. Almost as mechanical is the Jesus-Nietzsche debate. The values ascribed to Jesus in a series of references throughout the manuscript are affirmed at the end when Talbot links his perception of the beauty hidden in defeat with his recognition that Christ wanted men and women to live in the present, not the past; but Anderson's handling of concepts is simplistic and obvious, as would too often happen, in fact, when he attempted to discuss ideas directly in his fictions, and the "defeat" of Nietzscheanism is an easy, even unfair one. Perhaps the major defect of the novel is the uncertain presentation of the protagonist. In the long second book, set in Mirage, Talbot's double nature is awkwardly reflected in an inconsistent tone. Instead of being a coherent, though complex, personality, Talbot is at times described, sardonically, as one who exploits Billy Bustard, contrives a leadership image of himself among his fellows, and murders Tom Bustard with no sense of guilt, while at other times he is described, sympathetically, as one who is sensitive toward others and puzzled about life. In the Chicago books the tone shifts again as the narrator moves waveringly from a detached, somewhat condescending attitude toward Talbot, as he comes closer to his creator's age and condition, to an open approval of him, exemplified by pronouncements like, "Such men as Whittingham know everything. They confound us with the strength and insight of their glances."[45]

Talbot Whittingham reveals much, perhaps more than intended about Anderson's feelings and attitudes at this point in his life. The explicit assignment of a double nature to Talbot suggests how aware Sherwood was of having been inwardly divided in his Clyde years and later; the psychic melodrama of such scenes as Talbot's stalking of the merchant or his sale of the burial lots is probably a gauge of the frenzied hatred of self and others that seeped over Sherwood from time to time in reaction to his advertising job. The "argument" of the novel, too, reflects Anderson's own conviction that entering the artist's vocation could resolve divisions, conflicts, frustrations within the self; yet in the form in which he embodies this argument there is a curious ambivalence that seems to result as much from uncertainty of concept or attitude as from the inadequate technical skill of an apprentice novelist.

Overtly, the argument of the book resembles that of his *Little Review* article, "More About the 'New Note.'" The artist is connected with others, shares a common humanity with them, indeed can create his art only out of their lives and his understanding of their lives. This is what is asserted in Talbot's visionary moment in the Chicago night when all the people he has known seem to plead with him to be their voice, in Lucile Bearing's anguished admission that a man, if not a woman, can express the very spirit of his times and people, and in Talbot's ultimate penetration into the meaning of the grotesque. It is implied also in the series of admiring references to Jesus running through the novel and in the rejection of the Nietzschean view. This admiration of Jesus as one whose sayings and life were works of art is not only Talbot's or the omniscient narrator's, it was Anderson's as well. George Daugherty recalled that while Sherwood was living at 735 Cass Street his "passing interest in Nietzsche . . . awakened" and that "he bought a New Testament, applied himself to it, and informed the copy department that he 'was sold on Jesus Christ.'" Daugherty's memory of Anderson's interest in Jesus at that time is confirmed by the fellow lodger Jack, whose drunkenness first from liquor and then from life itself would prompt the story "Drink" in *Winesburg, Ohio,* and who later reminded Sherwood that in their Cass Street days he had "personally told Jack that Jesus was a great poet."[46]

But there are elements in *Talbot Whittingham* that contradict overt intention. Talbot's deliberate murder of Tom Bustard is closer to Nietzsche's will to power than to Jesus's infinite pity, and far from ever feeling guilt for his act Talbot instances it to Adelaide Brown in his mature years as a "bold and beautiful" thing to have done. And if he treats Adelaide Brown with what the narrator calls the "strange cruelty that is a part of such natures" as Talbot's, certainly his disregard in the book's concluding scene for the dying Lucile Bearing would appear, in realistic terms, self-regarding to the point of inhumanity were not that scene so obviously a maneuver by the author to provide Talbot and the reader with a climactic revelation. Especially noteworthy in a novel ostensibly asserting the closeness of artist and other men and women is Talbot's actual isolation from others. Such family ties as he originally had are permanently broken when he comes to Mirage at twelve; he establishes few close relationships among the townspeople and even these are abruptly severed by his act of murder; he forms no more than acquaintanceships among the men he works with in Chicago; his attitudes toward most of the women he meets in the city—the dancehall girl, a woman at his Cass Street-like rooming house, Adelaide Brown—vary from mere tolerance to contempt, and that toward Lucile Bearing appears to the reader essentially exploitative, however Anderson might have wished it to be regarded. Perhaps Talbot's isolation reflects Anderson's own intense desire to be free of family and business impediments in order to devote himself to writing, but in terms of the "meaning" of the novel it is as though the author of *Talbot Whittingham* were caught between competing conceptions of the artist. On the one hand, the artist is a being beyond good and evil in his personal life, the "master artist" whose gifts set him apart from other human beings; on the other hand, the artist is one who, in Lucile Bearing's words, must "give his life" in order to "make the world understand in him what there is in all men and women and what, in their own persons, they cannot understand." Perhaps Anderson himself recognized the warring impulses in the book as yet another reason for his dissatisfaction with it, but a conception of the role of the artist in relation to his society would continue to have its problematic elements for him, as one may have guessed by the unexplained leap taken in "More About the 'New Note'" from recording one's own moods to entering those of one's fellows. At any rate, *Talbot Whittingham* would not be submitted for publication, and in practical terms Anderson was faced either with finding an approach and a form that would reveal the essence of his artistic development more successfully, or with abandoning this subject.[47]

Actually what he was looking for was there, almost realized, not yet recognized, in the unpublished and unpublishable manuscript. The chief significance of *Talbot Whittingham* is its attempt to handle materials that would eventuate in two of his best books. Early in the 1920s Anderson would return to the characters in the manuscript as the basis for some of the tales that would make up *Horses and Men* (1923). The bold imaginative girl Jeanette Franks foreshadows the attractive and pathetic May Edgely of "'Unused.'" The Bruce Harvey scenes, with their emphasis on the satisfaction that "horse talk" and harness racing provided townsmen in Anderson's youth, look toward "I'm a Fool," while a few details, such as Talbot's desire to be with horses in a barn on a stormy night reappear in that highly personal tale "The Man Who Became a Woman." Particularly obvious is the resemblance of the final scene in *Talbot Whittingham* to its more successful reworking as "The Man's Story." This last tale

would remain one of Anderson's favorites and suggests that his unpublished novel had indeed a psychic value for him much exceeding its aesthetic achievement. That psychic value is especially manifested in the striking relationships between the Mirage section, significantly the longest by
far of the five books, and *Winesburg, Ohio,* the various tales of which
would begin almost to flood from his imagination only a few months later
in the fall of 1915.[48]

There is, to begin with, the close similarity of setting. Although the
name "Mirage" is satiric rather than, like "Winesburg," evocative, it
refers to the same kind of small town in the same part of Ohio. Mirage is
a rural community connected to the outside world by trains but with an
essentially pre-industrial economy. There are a town hall, a Main Street, a
hotel for travelers, a fairgrounds, a cemetery; just outside the town begin
the fields, meadows, patches of woods. As Winesburg would, in fact, Mirage much resembles Clyde in its geography. Though Clyde has no Pennsylvania Street, it has, as does Mirage (and Winesburg), a Buckeye Street;
the Main Streets of Clyde and Mirage slope downward from the town hall
to the railroad tracks; in each case the cemetery lies beyond the tracks in
the north part of town. The inhabitants of Mirage, furthermore, bear
Clyde names in many instances and some exhibit Clyde characteristics.
Barley Miller, son of the Mirage butcher, presumably received his first
name from Barley Mann, son of the Clyde butcher, and his last from such
a Clyde citizen as Harkness Miller; Salty Adair, Mirage's shoemaker, may
get his name from "Body" Adare, in whose saloon young Sherwood used
to sell off his last newspapers for the day; Bruce Harvey—the real Frank
Harvey was a partner in Harvey and Yetter's livery stable—habitually
howls out an Indian war cry in the excitement of a harness race as did
Clyde's George Crosby. So close is the Mirage milieu to remembered folk-
ways that, as though his reader were a fellow townsman, Anderson could
refer to fictitious community landmarks without bothering to describe
them, simply to "Turner's Grocery" or "the alley that turns out of Main
Street by Nichols Tailor Shop." Only lightly masked by invented names,
his home town stood in the eye of Sherwood's memory, a background
against which to move the part imagined, part remembered character of
Talbot Whittingham.

Occasionally the distance between townsman author and townsman
character narrows suddenly in the manuscript. At one point the omniscient narrator drops his intermittently sardonic tone and, as though he
were writing a first draft of *Sherwood Anderson's Memoirs,* asserts that
Talbot's boyhood in Mirage "was for him the great romantic epic of his
life, the period about which he was never afterward effaced" (p. 84).
Thereupon the narrator interrupts his narrative with an essay in praise of
the American village, beginning with the statement that Talbot "was, in

later life, like most of us who live in cities, a man who looked lovingly back upon his days in an American small town." With Whitmanesque expansiveness Talbot's individual experience becomes generalized, since men from Michigan, Pennsylvania, Vermont, and Ohio and "western fellows who have looked out over the prairies" share in common the townsman past: "'Tis a thing in the blood of Americans, this memory of village life." Then suddenly the abstract essay turns into a single lyric scene which in its selection and composition of detail, its diction, even its sentence rhythms is fully in the yet-to-be-achieved *Winesburg* manner.

The young and vigorous looking man we see walking before us in the street and who is going in at the door of the great store there, half running forward, working his way through the crowd, was such a fellow and walked with such a girl but five short years ago. On an evening he went with the girl along a street over a hill and a bridge into a country road. With the girl he climbed over a fence into a field. There was a pile of brush and he set it afire. The dew wet his shoes and made a dark band at the bottom of the girl's skirt. The fire did not burn well and the young man tramped it out. With the girl he went to lean against a fence. When a team passed on the road they crouched, hiding. There was no reason for concealment but they did not want to be disturbed. They were silent, their minds alive and filled with vague thoughts. The young man thought he would cut a noble figure in the world. His thoughts were vague, now they are quite definite. Next year he thinks perhaps he may own an automobile and have a beautiful woman to live in his house. His thoughts have lost color. They are now the thoughts of a thousand young men we shall see going in at the store doors.

The stylistic manner is maintained only momentarily; yet in other ways as well the long Mirage section of *Talbot Whittingham* shows that, unbeknown to himself, Anderson was going toward *Winesburg, Ohio*. The novel as a whole traces into early middle age the development of a writer, and that second book shows how a town and its people influence the writer's adolescent years. Foreshadowings of particular *Winesburg* tales occur in other books of *Talbot* besides book 2: out of her defeat is born in Lucile Bearing what a drunken young man, apparently borrowed from the missing book 1, prophesies in "Tandy" for Tom Hard's little daughter, "the quality of being strong to be loved," and Talbot's vision in Chicago of "all the men and women he had ever known" pleading to him to interpret their lives resembles the old writer's vision in "The Book of the Grotesque," the prefatory tale of *Winesburg, Ohio*. But in the Mirage section, significantly episodic as it is in structure, appear several meetings with individual human beings that help shape Talbot as similar meetings in Winesburg will shape George Willard. Though Bruce Harvey is not an isolate like *Winesburg*'s Wing Biddlebaum and though his message differs from Wing's, each is fond of the young protagonist of his respective book and seeks to guide him; and Talbot's relationship with Kit Donahue will share with that of George Willard and Helen White in "Sophistication" a common interest in how men and women may understand each other in the "modern world." Most strikingly of all, the chapter describing Talbot's sexual initiation with Lillian Gale prefigures that of George with Louise Trunnion, although the superiority of the tale over the chapter reveals how much Anderson was about to learn of his craft.

A final aspect of *Talbot Whittingham* points directly toward *Winesburg, Ohio*—Anderson's concern with what he was already calling the "grotesque." Although he twice uses the term in the Mirage section, only midway into book 4 does he begin to attach a special meaning to it. Significantly, that special meaning appears during his night drinking spree when he runs through the Chicago streets distraught with the conviction that he is "trying to live in a dead world filled with dead men and women." Life, Talbot believes, has "twisted and maimed" the minds and personalities of the six people he accosts, making them "grotesques," mere reflections of the world's own deadness and ugliness. The only one of six to be described at length is a woman who works in a restaurant where, persecuted by male customers, she has become obsessed with a single desire, literally to "beat down men" with an iron bar in order to begin life anew, "to stand for something," to "make her protests felt and understood." This Chicago woman would have been at home in Winesburg. Talbot's confrontation with her and the other five "grotesques" saves him that night, the author asserts, "perhaps from insanity": for in his agitation he senses that by roughly touching the six persons, each of whom he tells is "alive but . . . not beautifully alive," he will be able to find and restore "Something sweet and precious that has gone out of the world." The full meaning of grotesqueness only comes to Talbot much later, however, when by perceiving the courageous beauty Lucile Bearing exhibits beneath her outward defeat, he understands that "Everything is grotesque and the beautiful is beyond the grotesque." It is the duty of the artist to break through the grotesque, which Talbot now likens to a wall surrounding each person and thing, and to discover the beauty behind it. Grotesqueness, in sum, is a universal but outward condition of the world which both defeats men's dreams and separates them as individuals; beauty is a universal but inward condition which exists beyond defeat, binds individuals into a community, and when liberated by the artist's insight, emerges out of defeat in the form of art.

In *Talbot Whittingham*, then, Anderson had told the story of an artist much resembling his inward self, had reawakened and set down memories of his home town, and had worked out a theory of the grotesque all apparently by the late spring of 1915. It is not surprising, therefore, that on some evening taken off from writing he would be stirred by a book published at this time by Edgar Lee Masters, whom he knew little about except as an embittered former lover of Tennessee's. Shortly after Masters's *Spoon River Anthology* appeared in book form in April, 1915, Max Wald, one of the Little Children of the Arts, purchased a copy, read it, and praised it to his fellow lodger. Wald would later recall how "Anderson, after remarking that Tennessee Mitchell knew Masters, took the book to his room and returned it in the morning, saying that he had stayed up all night reading the poems and that he was much impressed by them." It is easy to see what could have impressed him about the *Anthology*. A Midwest small town, that "thing in the blood of Americans," was recreated in this book too, the setting emerging, because of the monologue form of the poems, not from passages of realistic description but as Mirage did—and Winesburg would—by the slow accumulation in the reader's mind of scattered details. Within this setting the inhabitants spoke from beyond their graves revealing what their inner lives and actual relations to each other had been behind the walls of external appearance. Very many of these human beings had been twisted and maimed by life, but out of their defeat the poet, however filled himself with frustrations and deep resentments, had managed to create something beautiful that united him with his readers. Anderson could well have felt that Master's book validated what he had already attempted in an early part of *Talbot Whittingham*. Rather than suggesting a new direction for Anderson, the *Spoon River Anthology* would have confirmed him in the direction he had already taken in the Mirage section of his novel. That direction, he soon knew, was the right one for him.[49]

4.

By early July of 1915 Anderson appears to have completed *Talbot Whittingham,* and he went off to lie in the sun for two weeks on "a long yellow beach," where he thought nothing, read nothing, swam until he was tired, then slept until he was rested. Tennessee had gone east for the summer to Lake Chateaugay in the northeast corner of New York State where Alys Bentley, head music teacher in the schools of Washington, D.C., had purchased Camp Owlyout and established a summer program in which girls and young women could learn the approach to music through "rhythmics," or rhythm dancing. The following summer Sherwood would take his vacation with her at that camp on the shore of the blue, hill-surrounded lake; but for further relaxation this summer he had to content himself with the final weekend excursions the Fifty-seventh Street group would make to Union Pier.[50]

Back on his job at what was now the Taylor-Critchfield-Clague Company, Anderson wrote to Floyd Dell on July 27 requesting that he return the manuscript of *Marching Men,* which (sometime prior to the preceding May 10) Dell had persuaded the Macmillan Company to consider for publication. Although the manuscript had been rejected and Sherwood's own direct negotiations with Macmillan were "temporarily suspended," perhaps the rejection letter contained some encouragement. Anderson wrote Dell that since he could "think clearly again" after two weeks at the beach, he was "ready to do some patient sustained work" on this manuscript that would "make it do." Presumably he spent some of his free time the rest of that summer of 1915 revising *Marching Men,* but in addition he seems to have resumed his fanciful play with the figure of Talbot Whittingham, attempting to use him now as an even more direct means of self-examination. He started but did not progress far with a novel titled *The Golden Circle,* the very first page of which confirms the intensely personal significance of the Whittingham persona for his creator. Talbot is first seen standing "at the window of a room on the second floor of a frame house in the town of Winesburg, Ohio." So the evocative name has already replaced the earlier sardonic one; and the close relationship of the fictional Winesburg with the real Clyde, of Talbot Whittingham with Sherwood Anderson is drawn tighter when the description of the frame house and its setting is seen exactly to tally with 129 Spring Avenue, where the Andersons lived from 1889 on. In Winesburg there is even a big beech tree in the front yard with a spring at its foot. A neighbor child had drowned in the spring, and a white-faced Mrs. Whittingham had pulled the body out. Anderson here was openly relying on his own psychic past, for in a clear-sighted but sympathetic way he portrays seventeen-year-old Talbot as one who continues to envy another Winesburg boy his skill at baseball while turning for compensation to the reading of books and to flamboyant daydreams so intense that they take on the vividness of actuality. Having jumped backward in a second chapter to the earlier life in Cincinnati of Talbot's doctor-father and his meeting with the young Winesburg woman who was to become Talbot's mother, Anderson may have sensed that *The Golden Circle* was losing its focus, though he would save this second chapter in some other manuscript form and draw on it ten years later in the writing of *Dark Laughter.*[51]

Another attempt to search the author's self by means of the Talbot persona was the likewise unfinished *Talbot the Actor.* Here Whittingham is introduced as a young man on the last evening of his year-long stay in Springfield, Ohio, during which he had lived at a boarding house run by an older woman much like Louisa Folger of the Oaks, had attended the local college, had given a speech at Commencement exercises on the Jews in modern society, and had so held the audience's attention that a man as enthusiastic as the real Harry Simmons had offered him an advertising solicitor's job on the spot. So many other events prior to Anderson's own

Springfield year are so direct from memory that they recall what Talbot's former army friend Bert had told him, that Talbot "was always an actor." This last evening in Springfield, while he waits until time to meet a passionate town girl with whom he is having an affair, Talbot as usual is absorbed in thinking of himself, of the contradictory impulses making up his "subconscious life," impulses that he visualizes as separate people conflicting within him in a kind of psychodrama. One person is "a white bearded old man," always sternly and honestly judging others and Talbot himself, but a "laughing lustful thing" within Talbot struggles with this puritanical judge and always comes out victorious.Although the stern old man remains aware of Talbot's trick at parties of unobtrusively but intently working to fix the attention of any strange young man on himself and then, when he had succeeded, trying the same game on the next young man. ("'You work as hard to attract men as you do women. You are a kind of wanton,' a stern voice said. 'Do you want everyone in the world to love you?'") But there are other contending persons within the "big easy body" of Talbot. A very real-seeming one is the "poet" person, whom Talbot significantly visualizes as resembling the young Sherwood Anderson, a handsome, slender youth with "black hair and burning eyes," a youth always "running, through the world, among people, through streets of towns, over hills," though to what goal Talbot does not know. Sometimes, however, this "white and pure" youth, dancing like a white streak through the world, turns abruptly into "a grotesque ugly thing." Such a metamorphosis had happened in the terrible period just before Talbot had gone into the army when for two years he had been "a young laborer in factories" and had devoted himself to hating people. Talbot likes to think, and knows that he likes to think, of the poet rather than the grotesque ugly youth as his true self, though "One could be quite satisfied if the poet was within him occasionally." Yet other persons exist within the "highly organized" Talbot, who, the narrator comments, is becoming a type in the modern world: one is "the figure of a small white faced woman hurrying with quick frightened footsteps through life as though wanting to escape from it quickly and another of a general, very pompous and empty headed; he continually strutted before people."

This self-analysis by the fictional Talbot Whittingham is striking, since seen in the closely autobiographical context of the novel fragment it confirms Anderson's capacity for both imaginative self-dramatization and for a ruthlessly honest introspection. It also confirms his interest just prior to beginning the Winesburg stories, in dealing, as he did in "Sister," with the inner life of a character and in discovering fictional devices for expressing that inner life. In addition the person's self-analysis suggests how closely Anderson's observation of his own psychic mechanisms was related to the creative act itself. So Talbot's emphasis on the youthfulness of his poet-self points back to the boyishness, which repeatedly characterizes the mature artist in *Talbot Whittingham,* and points forward to the young woman artist of "Sister" and the "young thing" within him that saves the old writer in "The Book of the Grotesque," the introductory tale of *Winesburg,* all of these instances expressing Anderson's sense of being, in terms of his own writing career, as still a youth. In such ways both *The Golden Circle* and *Talbot the Actor* fragments show him groping toward his master work.

Anderson's several versions of how he wrote the first story of *Winesburg* conflict with each other in details and even with obvious facts, including his specific reference in most versions to the first story as being "Hands," actually the second written after "The Book of Grotesque"; but most of the accounts agree in suggesting that at the moment he was feeling especially harassed by his advertising job. He may also have been feeling frustrated by his and Dell's failure as yet to place one of his longer works with a publisher. It would be reassuring when Ben Hecht, writing anonymously in the October *Little Review,* praised Dreiser as "the only real, uncontaminated genius of these States" and added "and I pray to God that my friend Sherwood Anderson will hurry up and get published so that there will be two of them"; yet even public praise was hardly the same as word that a publisher wanted one of his novels. Anderson had begun or was about to begin the excitement of getting magazine acceptances of some short pieces such as "Sister," but it could well have been dispiriting that, though he had been writing steadily through the summer and into the early fall, so much of this writing did not appear to be getting anywhere. Putting aside the inconclusive experiments with Talbot Whittingham, he had started a story about a George Bollinger and an Alice Hassinger who, though each is married to another, fall desperately in love; but he could not get them beyond the point where they admit what is happening between them. Adding the pages of this failed effort to the growing pile of discarded sheets, he next drove his pencil across some thirty-three sheets of yellow paper in an effort to tell about a Trigant Williams, who as a boy in an Ohio river town lacked the courage to approach a promiscuous little girl from a rural slum, but who, with the town "fixed" in his memory even in adulthood, later became "a pagan." The Trigant Williams material suggests some of Sherwood's current and future preoccupations in his writing; for as omniscient narrator Anderson could enter his tale to attack those who try "to separate the sex instinct from all other human impulses," to liken men and women to houses that may be slovenly or neat and "cold," to compare the beauty of sun and wind on a cornfield with the backbreaking labor that went into creating that "strange and lovely sight," and to assert explicitly how like a phallus, "that most pagan of living things," is an ear of corn.[52]

Since the Trigant Williams story appears to have been intended as an account of the sexual development of an artist, its explicit eroticism may have its origins in Anderson's own urges or in the current general intellectual interest in the psychology of sex or even in a desire to emulate Dreiser's *The "Genius,"* published early in October, 1915, which, considering Anderson's admiration for that novelist, he may have already read. Perhaps he felt, however, that he could not join so much overt sexuality with the theme of artistic development, for he abruptly dropped Trigant Williams and tried another approach to the subject. Here he described the boyhood of a Paul Warden, who rejects formal Christianity because it lacks the sense of the erotic and mystical that, Paul feels, Christ himself must have had, and who in high school shows sufficient skill at drawing that a teacher encourages him to "protect your imagination." Yet the Paul Warden story did not seem to head in the right direction either, and Anderson broke it off on a final page containing a single sentence: "Paul was in a house in the city of Chicago."

That sentence may have been the last push to his imagination that he needed; for one evening in the fall of 1915 he came back wearily from the advertising office to his room in Cass Street and was seized with yet another story idea, which—by conscious or unconscious design—would unite the fixed, present image of an old writer in a house in Chicago with the moving, past image of a young man developing his artistic imagination in a small Ohio town named Winesburg. So the inner conflicts of the three Talbots—of *Talbot Whittingham, The Golden Circle,* and *Talbot the Actor*—together with the other rejected artist protagonists could be fused with an "external" world of remembered hometown and observed boarding house; the fancied could become the real, the real become the fancied. Turning over on his work table the big pile of discarded sheets, Anderson took the top one—on its reverse was that sentence, "Paul was in a house in the city of Chicago"—and, after putting down the word "Grotesques" and crossing that out in favor of "Book of the Grotesques," began to write about an old writer in a room like his own whose mind was filled with a procession of people, all the people he had ever known, all of them grotesques, who had helped a young artist to maturity and kept an old one young. He began to write *Winesburg, Ohio.*[53]

6

The Dream of Failure

1.

Through the late fall of 1915 and into the winter months of early 1916 Anderson wrote at the Winesburg tales. Sometimes they came out of him on consecutive nights, sometimes there would be days in between stories, sometimes he stole minutes from his advertising chores to scribble at them. With the writing of the introductory tale he had a working title, "Book of the Grotesques," soon "The Book of the Grotesque," which he would retain over the next two or more years for this growing collection of fictional lives. With the writing of the first of these, "Hands," the story of a "poor little man, beaten, pounded, frightened by the world in which he lived into something oddly beautiful," he must have known intuitively that he was succeeding where the various Talbot Whittingham attempts had failed. The solution was one he had announced in "More About the 'New Note'" at the time he probably was applying it in the writing of *Mary Cochran*, not simply to move more and more deeply into his own self but to use this increasing understanding of himself and the meaning of his experience to make the imaginative leap into the being of a quite other person, one who would exist in his or her own person if only through the words on a page. It was the writing of "Hands," most of Anderson's several retrospective accounts agree, that moved him profoundly and convinced him he had for certain found his vocation. Later his memory, or his imagination, would trick him into declaring that he never changed a word in what he had written straight through that autumn evening, despite the manuscript evidence of considerable revision. Yet surely the declaration meant that with "Hands" he knew the essential rightness of what he was doing. It was for this reason that he felt, perhaps actually with the tears of joy he remembered shedding, that this tale put down on paper was *there*, solid and rocklike.[1]

The following autumn he wrote his new friend Waldo Frank that he had "made last year a series of intensive studies of people of my home town, Clyde, Ohio" under the name of Winesburg. The studies were indeed intensive, but the evidence is that to create his characters, he played in his fancy with many persons he had met in many places, though the hometown setting was a fundamental imaginative necessity for him. Perhaps half of the studies were written in an initial spurt perhaps lasting into the early months of 1916, but no more than fifteen out of twenty-four stories were completed by mid-November, 1916, at just about which time he set down on paper one of the finest of them all, "The Untold Lie." This last he had apparently conceived barely three weeks earlier when, riding on a train, he saw before him "a long stretch of fields and in the distance a town" and suddenly imagined, as though a scene were being enacted, a middle-aged farm hand with muddy boots and a torn overcoat tramping across the fields and then beginning to run in order to reach the town and board the train, Sherwood's own train, before he lost the courage of his decision to desert his wife and children.[2]

The writing of the Winesburg tales went on, then, over many months, in fact over two or more years, and was interrupted by other projects. About the time he wrote "The Untold Lie," for example, his fanciful playing with the character of the little girl in "Tandy" turned briefly into an impulse to develop a trilogy about her, an impulse possibly springing from his reading of Arnold Bennett's Clayhanger trilogy, the first volume of which he recalled as "marvelous." For another, rather surprising example, it was somewhere near this same time, mid-November, 1916, that Taylor-Critchfield was selected to handle the advertising and Anderson assigned to prepare the copy in a campaign to introduce and market Frank Lloyd Wright's visionary and carefully planned venture of American System-Built Houses. As the subject and the ebullience of his prose indicates, Sherwood for once must have been happy to write advertising copy. Designed by Wright to be both beautiful and economical, livable and lasting, variable in shape and size according to family income, the houses were to be constructed from carefully engineered, quality materials, assembled by franchised local builders, "generously equipped with furniture that is a unit with the structure itself," and sold according to size at prices ranging from $2,750 to $100,000. An essential point Anderson—and Wright—emphasized was that the design was not some borrowed, foreign one, good in its own country, but in its simple, unornamented, "swift, straight lines" was "a genuine expression of our national feeling," a reflection of "our life, mode of living and character." In words reminiscent of his praise for Dreiser, Anderson declared that Wright was "The greatest architect America has known. . . . Today, there is an American Architecture. An architecture as brave as the country. It is a pioneer work. Frank Lloyd Wright has cut fresh trails as did the early American. He has forgotten the time-trodden roads of the older orders." Considering such a story as "The Untold Lie" and other *Winesburg* tales, Anderson may have been inspired to feel that in architecture Wright was already doing what he by parallel was trying to do in his book—to create an American style of fiction. It is not clear how well the two men may have become acquainted at this time beyond business conferences, but in a diary entry twenty-four years later he would write: "Went to see Frank Lloyd Wright's exhibition at Modern Museum. Frank not changed—same kingly man. Exhibition beautiful."[3]

Along with the *Winesburg* stories done in the initial spurt of late 1915/ early 1916, he was also writing other short pieces, and with the appearance of "Sister" in the December 1915 issue of *The Little Review* he began to place something month after month in magazines. Sometime probably in the fall when he wrote the first Winesburg stories, he had finished a quite different kind of tale called "The Story Writers," describing satirically the efforts of two men to disregard the real lives being lived around them in a city slum in order to compose romances about exotic persons improbably motivated to far-fetched actions. "The Story Writers" resembles "The Rabbit-pen" in its attack on the author who keeps aloof from common, passionate experience, but differs in its mocking tone; and just as the earlier story may have been consciously designed for *Harper's,* so the later one may have been aimed at *The Smart Set,* the "Magazine of Cleverness" that H. L. Mencken and George Jean Nathan had recently assumed joint editorship of in New York. Aimed or not, the tone was right, and "The Story Writers" was published in *The Smart Set* for January, 1916. As literary critic for the magazine over several years, Mencken had already built a national reputation for his hilarious savaging of sentimental or romantic literature and for his forthright advocacy of writers as different as Joyce, Conrad, Gorky, and Dreiser, of any writers who in his view were trying to reveal the "naked reality" of life. Now as editors he and Nathan were vigorously printing a number of the talented new fictionists, along with many more who were merely light and "sophisticated." Recognition by Mencken was a heady kind of honor.

Encouraged by the acceptance of "The Story Writers," Anderson very late in 1915 sent off to *The Smart Set* one of the Winesburg stories, "'Queer,'" a fact which suggests that he may have completed drafts of as many as a dozen of the tales in that first spurt. "'Queer'" did not fit *The Smart Set*'s tone of cleverness, however, and Mencken sent it back. On January 4, 1916, Anderson replied to Mencken's rejection letter, saying that "I hadn't much sense of the magazine world and so have to offer the stories blind and have had no success with New York agents," but also asserting politely that, "Of course, it should not be true that *Smart Set* readers are limited in their outlook and if a story is close enough to life it should be good enough for any magazine."[4]

Fortunately another magazine was available for stories close enough to life. This was *The Masses,* one of the liveliest magazines ever published in the United States. Cooperatively owned by a talented, rambunctious group of artists and writers, imaginatively edited from 1912 on by the outspoken Max Eastman, and attractively designed and illustrated, *The Masses* announced itself as "A Free Magazine" with a revolutionary outlook and a "frank, arrogant, impertinent" willingness to print "what is too naked or true for a money-making press." Although Anderson did not adhere to the left-wing Socialism declared by *The Masses,* he had come, as *Talbot Whittingham* showed, to despise the wealthy and the society-conscious almost as strongly as did the gifted *Masses* artists with their bitingly funny drawings attacking big business, class snobs, and moral puritans. He may have observed that the magazine's fiction tended to be realistic rather than explicitly revolutionary in tone, and disheartened or annoyed by Mencken's rejection of "'Queer,'" he may have decided to send some of his first-written Winesburg stories to this rebellious periodical as one of the few publications that might be sympathetic toward his new and unconventional sort of writing. But Floyd Dell had been serving as Eastman's able associate editor since late 1913, Sherwood had been sending his "literary father" manuscripts for criticism from time to time, and Dell may have decided on his own (or in agreement with Sherwood) to bring these stories to one of the monthly sessions at which the artist and writer owners of *The Masses* wrangled out the contents of the next month's issue. Dell himself had apparently already begun to feel that, by comparison with *Windy McPherson's Son,* Anderson's stories showed "a lessening of conscious control and a more and more indulgent use of unconstrained fantasy." Perhaps because "Hands" touched on the forbidden subject of homosexuality and because "The Book of the Grotesque" might introduce other similarly bold stories, the decision was to accept both. *The Masses* thus became the first magazine to publish any of the Winesburg tales. "The Book of the Grotesque" appeared in the issue for February 1916, "Hands" in that for March.[5]

If Anderson was delighted, as he must have been, over appearing in *The Smart Set* and having two stories accepted by *The Masses,* he was overjoyed to learn in mid-January of 1916 that *Windy McPherson's Son* might actually be published. It had been a long, involved, frustrating effort by several people, chiefly Floyd Dell, to reach this point, an effort that had begun back in late 1913 when negotiations with the Henry Holt company had broken down. At that time Sherwood had asked Floyd to find another publisher for the novel, an unrevised typescript of which Dell had taken with him when he left for New York in October. Dell first submitted *Windy* to Macmillan, who turned it down as they would later turn down the manuscript of *Marching Men.* Then Dell, persisting in his friend's behalf despite the demands of his own writing, his complicated personal life, and his job as associate editor of *The Masses,* tried several other publishers, all of whom, he recalled, "kept it a long time and were reluctant in passing it up." Meanwhile he had been praising Anderson to New York literary people, one of these being his Greenwich Village neighbor, Theodore Dreiser. In the spring of 1915 Dreiser brought Anderson's name to the attention of J. Jefferson Jones, managing director of the New York branch of the John Lane Company, the enterprising London publishing house. The Lane Company had dared to issue Dreiser's latest novel, *The Titan,* and at the novelist's urging Jones wrote Anderson in May, 1915, inquiring about the manuscript of *Marching Men,* then being read by Macmillan. Anderson and Jones corresponded briefly, but even after Floyd Dell informed Jones that Anderson's negotiations with Macmillan "were, at least, temporarily suspended," Jones for some reason made no further move. Dell had become discouraged because American publishers now told him that "a serious long novel like *Windy McPherson's Son* had no chance in wartime," and that summer he sent the manuscript across the submarine-infested Atlantic to Grant Richards, the English publisher who a year before had finally brought out James Joyce's *Dubliners.* Richards wrote Dell that he would like to publish *Windy* but could not because of wartime conditions. Dell sent the bad news to Anderson, who, probably at his friend's suggestion, wrote Richards on October 18 requesting that the manuscript be delivered to the John Lane Company in London.[6]

While the manuscript was still with Richards, Anderson had had a copy of it typed in London at his expense and returned to him. After revising this copy— how extensively is not known—he sent it on to Dell in preparation for a final assault on the American branch of John Lane. In his letter to Mencken of January 4, 1916, the one deploring rejection of "'Queer'" for *The Smart Set,* Anderson thanked Mencken "for the interest you are taking in my stuff" and asked him to read the revised manuscript of *Windy* in hopes that, if Mencken thought it "first class work," he would recommend it to Lane of New York. Six days later he wrote a similar request to Dreiser, respectfully urging that he had written four novels but published none, was growing weary of writing while also holding a business job, and hoped to be published so that he could get on to other projects. Fortunately for these generous but busy men, Frederic Chapman, the learned and influential literary advisor of John Lane himself in London, finished reading the original manuscript delivered by Grant Richards, felt that it "showed promise," and sent it off to Jefferson Jones in New York with a letter "in warm praise" of the book. Finally on January 17, Jones, recalling both his earlier correspondence with Anderson about *Marching Men* and Dreiser's insistent urging of his name, wrote Anderson about the recommendation in Chapman's letter that "while [Chapman] could not advise Mr. Lane taking up this story for England alone, if it were published in New York by the John Lane Company, he should certainly advise Mr. Lane taking an English edition." Jones promised a careful reading of the manuscript before Anderson should come to New York in February to discuss publishing through Lane. Anderson promptly wrote the good news to Mencken and Dreiser, adding that he was relieved they would not have to do the favor he had requested of them and explaining to Mencken that he wanted Jones to read the revised manuscript that Mencken held, not the one Chapman had sent on from England.[7]

With Dell, Dreiser, and Chapman favoring it, and probably Mencken as well, Jones's acceptance of *Windy McPherson's Son* for publication was now assured. Anderson did go to New York as planned, very likely staying with Dell. On February 28, 1916, a publishing contract was drawn up between him and the John Lane Company of New York, stipulating delivery of the manuscript of the novel in final form on or before April 1, setting royalties at 10 percent of the book's retail price on sales up to five thousand copies, and binding the author to offer his "next three full length novels" to Lane, which would have the right of first refusal of them, or option to publish, for thirty days after the delivery of each manuscript. This last clause would subsequently have some effect on the relations between Anderson and the John Lane Company, but by the end of February 1916, Sherwood could begin to think of himself excitedly as one who would soon have whole books bearing his name.[8]

Perhaps to announce this developing self-image, Sherwood arrived for this New York visit dressed with a touch of the aesthetic, Floyd Dell rather waspishly recalled. Anderson sported the same kind of high collar and black stock that Floyd had worn in Chicago for self-advertisement as aesthete and had quickly abandoned in New York for the expensive but proletarian-looking blue flannel shirt, which he considered more suitable for an associate editor of *The Masses*. Then or later Dell decided that Anderson's adoption of this dress consciously symbolized his taking over of Dell's discarded aesthetic role and an ending to the period when the older man had regarded the younger as literary father. Very likely it was during this same New York visit that Anderson read to Dell one of his new Winesburg tales, "Loneliness," and was annoyed when Dell told him that the story didn't go anywhere. At that time or soon after he would be further annoyed when, under what he probably wrongly suspected to be Dell's influence, the editorial board of *The Masses* decided to accept only one more Winesburg story, "The Strength of God," which appeared in the August issue. The February visit certainly marked some kind of watershed in the relations between the two men. Thereafter, Dell would state many years later, he "didn't have to worry about Sherwood's literary career, nor give him advice, nor read every line he wrote, nor minister with the balm of praise to his suffering soul, so easily hurt by a harsh word." Although the acerbity of his comment probably reflects the accumulated disappointments of his later life, Dell had reason in 1916 for resenting the rapidity with which Anderson turned against the friend who had in fact advised him privately and praised him publicly, had spent hours reading his manuscripts, though hardly "every line he wrote," and despite repeated discouragements and the cost to his own time had been the person most responsible for securing the publication of his first book. Anderson was demonstrating his capacity for tiring of and turning against people who assisted his career, a capacity that existed in him side by side with a generous willingness to help other writers, especially the new, struggling ones.[9]

By mid-1916 Anderson must have felt that his own struggles were being rewarded at last. Stories by him had appeared in the nationally know *Smart Set* and *Masses,* and *Windy McPherson's Son* was scheduled for September publication; in addition he had a sketch or tale, including a Winesburg one ("The Philosopher," later renamed "Paper Pills") in each of the five issues of *The Little Review* that were published from January to July. The two sketches among these five pieces suggest how his self-confidence was growing with public recognition. In serious contrast to the satirical "The Story Writers," "The Novelist" describes how an author wishes to tell a tale based on the experience of an actual woman who had been unsuccessful in all she did yet who had had a spirit that, "but for the muddle of life, might have become a great flame." The dream of the novelist is to make others understand that spirit, perceive "the reality of the woman who failed"; and, wanting to explain himself as well, the novelist puts himself into his story in disguised form, in this way expressing his love, not only for the woman's essential being, but for himself as well. Writing a novel is, in fact, a way of making love to the ego and its world. Since certain details in "The Novelist" are only lightly masked autobiography, one may read it as, among other things, Anderson's commentary on his projection of self into Talbot Whittingham in relation to Lucile Bearing. The assertion of the author's self-love in this sketch need not, of course, be interpreted too literally as egotism; but in "Dreiser," the second sketch, Anderson manages to combine self-confidence, even boastfulness, with his admiring praise of the older man: "In the books we write [after Dreiser is gone] there will be all the qualities Dreiser lacks"—humor, "grace, lightness of touch, dreams of beauty bursting through the husks of life"—though only because the heavy feet of this literary pioneer have made a path through the American wilderness.

The two non-Winesburg stories in *The Little Review,* however, show little cause for boasting. "Vibrant Life," a clumsy attempt to deal with the theme of sexual force, tells how a passionate middle-aged lawyer is attracted to the "magnificent blonde" nurse of his and his beloved wife's children while he and the nurse quite improbably sit up with the corpse of his younger brother, an adulterer who has been killed by a jealous husband. Stirred by the picture of a great stallion in a magazine, the lawyer tells the nurse that all the men in his family have in them a stallionlike "vibrant, conquering life." He then pursues her about the room and seizes her. As they struggle, the coffin containing the corpse falls from its stand, and the body with eyes staring rolls out melodramatically on the floor. Wisely Anderson did not republish "Vibrant Life" in any of his story collections, but "The Struggle," which appeared in the May 1916 number of *the Little Review,* he later included in *The Triumph of the Egg* under the title, "War." The tale is of some biographical interest as the first evidence of any concern by its author with World War I, now in its second fearful year; it is of some aesthetic interest as an early attempt by Anderson to use a first-person narrator's reaction to an unusual natural setting as a means of guiding the reader into the mood of a psychically intense event, in this case an exchange of "souls" or personalities between a German soldier and the Polish refugee woman he guards. Much adapted, this device would eventually help Anderson to get "Death in the Woods" fixed in final form, but of "The Struggle" one can only say that it is somewhat better than "Vibrant Life." Neither story has the skilled simplicity of the Winesburg tales he was writing at the same time.

Anderson placed one more non-Winesburg story in a national magazine in that breakthrough year of 1916. "Blackfoot's Masterpiece," published in the June *Forum,* is directly based on the tragic career of Ralph Blakelock (1847–1919), the American landscape painter, whose first mental breakdown in 1891 and later insanity in 1899 were both immediately caused by his inability at times of great family need to sell a fine painting at the modest price he asked, but whose pictures ironically began to sell well soon after his commitment to the New York state asylum for the insane. Anderson probably first heard of Blakelock from brother Karl in the spring of 1913, since a group of paintings by George Inness, Alexander Wyant, and Blakelock had been on exhibit at a Chicago art dealer's gallery at the time Karl was in town for his own exhibition and the Armory Show; but the Blakelock references of the story are so open that a date of writing can almost be pinpointed as March 1916. In fact, the event that was clearly the genesis of the story occurred in New York between the twenty-first and twenty-fourth of February, by which time Sherwood was probably in the city to negotiate the contract for *Windy McPherson's Son* with the John Lane Company. In company with Karl, who was one of the "Fifty" contemporary American painters concurrently exhibiting at the Montross Gallery on Fifth Avenue, he may even have attended, as the story's narrator purports to have done, the auction at which Blakelock's

"The Brook by Moonlight," for which the painter had originally asked $1,000 of a wealthy merchant and had received about half that sum, was sold for $20,000, at that time the highest price ever paid for a painting by a living American. If Sherwood did not actually witness the bidding on this luminous picture, he would certainly have learned of the sale from Karl or the newspapers, which were turning the discovery of the artist's impoverished life and present institutionalization into a sensation in the American art world, a sensation that produced special Blakelock exhibits at New York's Reinhardt Gallery in early April and at three different Chicago galleries in early May.[10]

In "Blackfoot's Masterpiece" a sensitive first-person narrator, who says he wishes to hurt his listeners as he was hurt by the auctioning off of the great picture for $20,000, recalls how Blackfoot, living with his poverty-stricken family in Greenwich Village, creates the painting and proudly sets its price at $1,200. An art dealer offers successively smaller sums for the picture, each being rejected by Blackfoot until in desperation he accepts four hundred dollars in cash for it. Driven insane by this outcome, Blackfoot creates a living masterpiece that night when in front of his wife's eyes—as Ralph Blakelock had himself once done—he burns in the fireplace most of the bills the art dealer gave him. Just as Anderson may in part have been exploiting a current cause célèbre, so *The Forum* by accepting the piece for its June number may have hoped to do the same; indeed, the story, which was never republished, is aesthetically inferior in its heavy-handed use of repeated motifs, a technical device Anderson had already experimented with more effectively, because less obtrusively, in the Winesburg tales. But the relative speed with which he wrote the story and sent it off suggests also that the real Blakelock, his work and fate, had a special meaning for him. (A woman who knew Sherwood during the ensuing summer could date her recollections a half century later by the fact, impressed on her at the time, that "He had just sold a story . . . and it was about a painter, based on Blakelock, who was not a success until he died and the dealers reaped the harvest.")[11]

Since Anderson obviously had picked up a good deal of information about Blakelock's career, he may have been struck by certain parallels between it and his own. The painter had had only a little more formal schooling than the writer, and each was largely self-taught in his art. At a time when young American artists went to Paris if they could, Blakelock had chosen to travel for some years in the West and had found in the United States, not Europe, subjects for his highly individual, antiacademic, at first unpopular kind of experimentation. Having almost certainly seen some of Blakelock's paintings, in 1913 if not 1916, Anderson perhaps found a sympathetic correspondence between the artist's preference for twilight settings and his own preference for them in the Winesburg tales. He must have observed, on his own or with Karl's help, how Blakelock regarded the external world only in part as a surface reality to be reproduced, sometimes with great exactness, but more basically as a collection of forms and colors through the painterly organization of which he could express his own mood or emotion, in this way, like Anderson in the Winesburg stories, suffusing the commonplace with magic and mystery.

Anderson may not have been aware of all these comparisons, but as the story makes clear through its overinsistent motifs, he certainly intended to project his own values into "Blackfoot's Masterpiece," to make it, in fact, a parable of the artist in America. Forgetting his poverty in the excitement of creation, the painter, or the writer, devotes himself wholeheartedly to his art; and in his moments of achievement, as when Blackfoot paints his masterpiece, he makes "Order out of disorder." This order has a personal value and potentially a social one; nevertheless, most people understand only the values of the marketplace, reduce art to one more commodity, and aim solely for financial success. (In one major motif of the story the successful ones admonish the artist figures to "Breathe deeply and keep your shoulders straight"; rigid physical fitness is another sign of the social norm.) Deprived of all but the meagerest reward for his labors, Blackfoot as representative artist is driven mad. As he slips into a dehumanizing insanity, however, he makes the final assertion of his artistic and human values. Striding about in torn pajamas yet sporting the cane that has become symbolic of his creative virility, he burns the money paid him by the dealer, an act "as fine as the painting of the great picture." By repudiating the disordered values of, not a healthy, but a sick society, he makes of defeat a triumph.

2.

The gathering proofs of literary success in the spring of 1916 probably strengthened Sherwood's desire to change other personal relationships besides that with his "literary father," Floyd Dell. Especially he wanted to formalize his separation from Cornelia. The two of them presumably talked over his wish now to be free to marry Tennessee and agreed on what had to be done, for on April 8 Cornelia L. Anderson of Union Pier, Michigan, filed in the Circuit Court for Berrien County a Bill of Complaint against her husband for deserting her "in the last of March, 1914 . . . without any reasonable cause" and persisting in the desertion for two years. Although Sherwood was now earning $50 a week, averred in 1916 to be "large sums of money," he had been very irregular in sending amounts to support the three children, now aged nine, seven, and four, with the result that "this plaintiff has been obliged to teach school for her own support and to help support the children." Accordingly the plaintiff prayed that a divorce be granted and that she "be awarded such sums of money for the support of [her] and her children . . . as may seem just and right to this honorable Court." On April 17, Circuit Judge George W. Bridgman issued a chancery summons, which was served on Anderson on the nineteenth. Anderson not responding, Judge Bridgman on June 19 ordered that "testimony be taken in open court." On July 27, 1916, the case was heard, and the judge found for the plaintiff. The divorce was granted as of that day, and since the defendant was regarded as "an unsuitable person to have the care, custody and maintenance of the children, the plaintiff was awarded custody of them "until each shall become fourteen." Surprisingly, given the Bill of Complaint, Judge Bridgman decreed that Cornelia should "not be entitled to, or receive from the said defendant . . . any alimony, maintenance or support." One can only guess that in her testimony in open court Cornelia had, characteristically, been more generous toward Sherwood's irregularities than the necessary legalisms of the Complaint had implied.[12]

The defendant had not been present in court on July 27. At some time earlier he and Tennessee had already left Chicago for a summer at Camp Owlyout in the extreme north end of the Adirondacks, she in the previous summer having prepared the way for his coming there. It was to be a memorable vacation in a nearly idyllic place. Alys Bentley's camp was on three acres of lakefront land close to the hamlet of Merrill, New York, at the northern end of Upper Chateaugay Lake and looked southward over the three-mile long lake with its little island in the middle standing out against the blue water. On almost all sides around the lake hills rose into low, wooded mountains. Anderson, whose love of natural beauty was always intense and absorptive, loved the lake by day or by night when the darkness of woods and mountains showed the occasional flare of a small iron foundry. Alys Bentley and her assistant Edith Westcott were at Camp Owlyout itself, a big roomy lodge near the lake shore with a screened-in dining porch that could seat the sixty woman campers who lived in tents around the lodge. Farther up from the shore was The Outlet, a cottage owned by Leta Bentley, Alys's niece, a mothering, winning, artistically sensitive woman in her late thirties who during the rest of the year was a gifted teacher of reform school boys in Washington, D.C. She was also a fine cook, and Sherwood and Tennessee took their meals at The Outlet along with a small, trim, handsome young woman named Sue de Lorenzi, who lived by herself just above Leta's place in a camp named Killoleet after the white-throated sparrow. So close to Killoleet that the occupants could easily shout over to each other was the Tenthouse, part frame building, part tent, which was where Sherwood stayed.[13]

Alys Bentley, now forty-eight, was an extraordinary woman. Brilliant, dynamic, "indomitable," she had a tremendous ability to attract people, and to use them. This included her niece Leta, who worshipped her and whose willingness to work was cruelly exploited by the older woman. In camp and sometimes on city street Alys wore a Grecian robe and sandals and no hat; her white hair stuck straight up on her head, and one of her characteristic gestures was to run her hand vigorously up through it. One of the first Americans to teach rhythmic dancing as a way to learn music and to express the total self, she poured her vitality, her sensitivity, her salty, earthy humor into running her summer camp, grandly refusing to worry about money matters, which were left to Edith Westcott to manage as well as she could, and autocratically demanding that her students, whose lives she tried to dominate, express their inner selves. She had "theories about everything." Her powerful personality made Camp Owlyout a center for various people in the arts who had their own summer places at the lake—Louis Untermeyer and Geraldine Farrar and other writers, singers, actors.

The Bentley System, originating in part from her work as director of music in the Washington, D.C. public schools, was designed to restore to adults, especially but not solely those with artistic inclinations, the spontaneity of the child, who in singing used unconsciously the natural muscular rhythms of its whole body. By rediscovering these coordinated bodily rhythms and responding to them the individual could achieve non-self-consciousness and thus be led not only to physical but to ethical and aesthetic regeneration within a serene society of similarly regenerated individuals. Every morning at camp there were exercises on the dance green overlooking the lake or, on rainy days, in The Shack, an assembly hall near Killoleet and Anderson's Tenthouse. Unperturbed at being the one man among so many women, Sherwood would do the exercises along with Tennessee and Sue—the bicycle motion with sixty-odd pairs of legs going in the air or "taking the frog position." Then he would go off to the Tenthouse to write for the rest of the morning. Afternoons were free for all the campers, and Anderson, his writing stint done, especially liked canoeing out on the open lake or over to the Narrows, where the Chateaugay River began flowing northward to Lower Chateaugay Lake on its way to emptying into the St. Lawrence. Sometimes he and Tennessee would lie out in the sun on Leta Bentley's beach or walk in the woods and hills or down the road that led from Merrill past Camp Owlyout and southward along the lake. Sherwood was sharply aware of the natural setting around him even as he talked. Sue, who had quickly fallen into a younger sister-older brother relationship with him, later pictured him walking along, casually picking up a flower or weed, and looking at it intently in his hands as he walked. Had she come up to him at such a time, he would have made some acute observation about it. Though to her he seemed big, burly, robust, very masculine, he seemed also very sensitive and perceptive.[14]

Late each afternoon just before sunset Alys would send out word for all the campers to assemble again on the dance ground, which was kept smooth as a putting green with its close-cropped grass. Each girl now wore a floating Grecian robe, simply cut but hand-dyed to the person's taste. Years later Sue happily remembered hers, which started with sapphire blue at the shoulder, became navy blue, then turned gold at the bottom of the skirt. The women, who had worn sandals all day as Alys required, danced barefoot to classical music furnished by a Victrola or an old piano, which was unfortunately always out of tune. Each dancer sought to express the music as she felt it, and any group dancing was informal only, though in a favorite such grouping a tall girl would show with her hands the falling of water in a fountain, a small one crouching below as if to catch the water, others posed around them to form the fountain itself. The dancing was a lovely sight, all the girls in their bright robes moving rhythmically against the sunset and on into the afterglow that sharply outlined the mountains to the west. Sherwood was always there to watch, and sometimes he too would join in the dancing. Wearing sandals, knickers, and a hand-dyed, burnt-orange, open-collared shirt with a big steel ring in one ear, he was quite a sight. On the whole he and Alys got on well enough as she surveyed her students at their sunset dance, even though she tried to govern his life as well as the lives of even the more mature women among them. In one of the dances she insisted that he take a humble attitude. "I'll be damned if I'll be humble!" Sherwood exploded, whereupon she flashed back, "You'll be damned if you won't." Sherwood remained very much his own man at Camp Owlyout, but in the dancing even he generally followed the Bentley command to the tense mind and body, "Let Go." After the rhythmics, as though lapsed back into boyhood, he would regularly go off with the young women, whom he regarded as beautiful sisters, and play softball down by Leta's cabin in the twilight.

Obviously he was happy that summer. Florence Becker, another camper, who yearned to be a writer but was too diffident to tell him so, remembered him clearly half a century later: "The brooding tone of Anderson's writing is not what he conveyed when you met him. He seemed to have enormous zest and appetite for life—to be a warm and hearty person, with quick and delicate perceptions and rugged good humor." He had, she recalled, "a rich, warm voice, and his laugh was something to remember." Tennessee too was intensely, if more quietly, happy that summer she and Sherwood were together. Unlike him she followed the whole Bentley program, the morning exercises, the rhythmics at sunset. Graceful and deliberate always, she moved smoothly with the others on the dance ground. If she could not "get" how she wanted to express herself in motion, she would go off calmly to the edge of the green, stand there concentratedly thinking out what she should do, then come back and do it in her physically elegant way. Very much in love, she and Sherwood were pleasant to everyone in camp and showed in their dress, as it were, how in almost Jungian fashion they complemented each other's self. Just as Sherwood did not appear feminine but wore sandals, dyed shirt, and massive earring at the dancing, so Tennessee, without appearing masculine, always wore her hair in two long braids and crowned it with a man's wide-brimmed velour hat. Sherwood spent his mornings by himself writing, but Tennessee was always accessible. Girls came to her with problems of camp living—she was, after all, much older than most of them—and after listening carefully and quietly, she would suggest sensible solutions in the never excited, always calmly interested way habitual to her.[15]

While Sherwood and Tennessee were living their summer idyll, waiting until they were free to marry, Cornelia's suit for divorce was going forward. After the divorce was granted on July 27, a Thursday, Anderson's copies of the official papers were put in the mail. He must have been kept apprised of the scheduled court hearing, probably by the cooperative Cornelia, for Sue de Lorenzi could see that over the weekend he became extremely nervous about the possibility that the papers would not arrive. By the morning of Monday the thirty-first he was almost frantic and could not wait for old Mr. Merrill to drive over as customary to get the mail at Lyon Mountain, another hamlet three miles to the south on the railroad from Saranac to Plattsburgh. He went over and got the papers from the mail himself. Then, doubtlessly greatly relieved, he returned to Camp Owlyout where Tennessee awaited him together with Alys Bentley and Edith Westcott, who had agreed to be marriage witnesses. The four of them drove north by car some thirteen miles to the town of Chateaugay, the place where Alys had been born and the nearest community of any size. Here they picked up Justice of the Peace M. J. McCoy and headed west by the state road that ran through woods toward Malone. The mood of the party must have been a carefree one that afternoon, for Sherwood and Tennessee wanted to be married in some attractive spot outdoors rather than in a church. A short distance outside Chateaugay the state road bridged the Chateaugay River, and looking down, they saw that the forest opened out into a sunny green pasture beside the flowing water. Here, under an apple tree, was the right place for the wedding for two free spirits. Mr. McCoy, perhaps to maintain what of tradition he could, used a regular marriage service. His beard waggled ironically as he spoke, and just as he had announced the words, "If any man know ought why this couple should not be joined in holy matrimony, let him speak now or forever hold his peace," a horse in the pasture neighed, convulsing everyone, including the Justice, with laughter. It was a splendid ceremony.

All this the newly married couple hilariously told Sue after they had left Mr. McCoy in Chateaugay and returned directly to Owlyout, though they probably did not tell her that in supplying the information required for the marriage record Tennessee had given her age as thirty-seven rather than her actual forty-two—one wonders if her husband knew she was two and a half years older not younger than he—and Sherwood had unaccountably set back the date of his divorce to June 19. Sue herself had been busy that afternoon helping Leta Bentley prepare the wedding supper, a big affair to which, apparently, the whole camp was invited. During the supper the bride and groom, both laughing a great deal, again described the wedding ceremony. Afterward they rowed across the lake to Split Rock, a cottage owned by Alys Bentley, for a few days honeymoon.[16]

The west side of the lake was the wilder one, unlike the east side, accessible only by boat or canoe, though there were a few other cottages scattered along the shore. Right beside Split Rock, in fact, Trigant Burrow, the psychoanalyst Tennessee had met the previous summer, was building a bungalow which he and his wife had appropriately named Lifwynn, an Anglo-Saxon word meaning "the joy of life." From 1916 on Dr. Burrow and his family with a growing group of psychoanalytic associates and students would spend the summer there; and by the time Sherwood and Tennessee honeymooned next door Burrow, already launched on his active and distinguished professional career, had probably begun keeping up his private practice at Lifwynn, meeting with his patients, as was his habit for some years, on a rustic bench by the shore of the lake. The Andersons and the Burrows had a chance now to talk at some length, and Sherwood and Trigant began their custom, continued more frequently the following summer, of taking long walks through the woods and conversing about their mutual interest in, though differing approaches to, the complexities of human nature. Sue de Lorenzi would later recall Burrow, with whom she too got along well, as a slender, rather "pretty" man, who loved to wear a cloak and who had a good deal of the feminine component in him, she felt, though he was not at all effeminate. The two men were markedly different in appearance as in backgrounds and careers; yet they hit it off well together this summer, and Anderson began to get from this trained, sensitive, professional person a more informed acquaintance with Freudian doctrine than Floyd Dell had been able to provide three years before.

The honeymoon at Split Rock seems to have been happy if brief. Back at Owlyout the couple lived at the Tenthouse, which Sue had helped Sherwood fix up for two. He and Tennessee continued to be pleasant to everybody and to laugh a lot, but the great summer was drawing to a close, and probably toward the end of August they had to get ready to go back to the noise, dirt, and rush of Chicago. They had already agreed on another mode of social rebellion. When they returned to Chicago, they planned to live as husband and wife in the modern manner, in separate residences.

3.

They did live in separate residences in Chicago a good part of their married lives. By October, Tennessee had left her Stone Street apartment and had moved to 12 East Division Street, just to the east of State Street and only two and a half blocks from the shore of Lake Michigan. Here she would settle down for the next half dozen years. Sherwood would also move to 12 East Division for awhile beginning in May, 1917, but for now he returned to his room at 735 Cass among The Little Children of the Arts. Tennessee had a bed for him at her place, and sometimes she would visit his room at the lodging house. Like the Dells earlier and like Sherwood's Sylvester and Mary in *Mary Cochran,* they spent many of their nonworking hours together, but they were determined to keep themselves free to follow their separate occupations. Tennessee continued to teach music at her studio in the Fine Arts Building; Sherwood daily turned out advertising copy at Taylor-Critchfield-Clague on the tenth floor of the Brooks Building at 223 West Jackson Boulevard just outside the Loop, and fought for time in which to live in the storyteller's world of his imagination.[17]

He was now all the more intent to do so, for on September 1, 1916, *Windy McPherson's Son* was issued, and he was at last started on his career as a published novelist. The John Lane Company of New York printed *Windy* in a first edition of twenty-five hundred copies, one thousand of which were sent in unbound sheets to the parent firm in London; and an advertisement for the book, acclaiming it as a "forcefully, earnestly written tale . . . that holds out unmistakable promise," appeared in the *Chicago Daily Tribune* as early as September 2. The designer had made the book a decorative object with its rust-colored binding, the author's name in black letters on the front cover at the bottom, the title in gold across the top, and, beneath the title, black stylized art nouveau cornhusks scrolled back to reveal an upright ear of corn stamped in gold. It was an appropriate treatment for a novel dedicated affectionately "To the Living Men and Women of My Own Middle Western Home Town."[18]

Only book 1, the first third of the story, is actually set in "the little corn-shipping town of Caxton in Iowa," yet that dedication implies much about Anderson's close relation to his fictional material. This opening third, the most solidly realized portion of *Windy McPherson's Son,* neither predicts what would soon be termed "The Revolt from the Village" nor follows the opposing tradition that sentimentalized the American small town in the manner of Zona Gale's popular Friendship Village stories. Instead, Anderson presents the Midwest town as he had experienced it with its good and its bad, though basically its good. From the viewpoint of one of its more flamboyant inhabitants, Caxton is a "Cesspool of respectability," a remark within a striking episode that may have led a few reviewers to compare Anderson's Caxton to Masters's *Spoon River*. The little town has its full share of narrow, mean, hypocritical men and of a class of women "the thought of whom paralyzes the mind," as the author describes them in one of his essaylike intrusions, women who sell themselves into marriage as Mary Cochran refused to do, who without vision or ideals "live lives of unspeakable blankness," obtaining emotional release only through vicious gossiping. Yet the town has as well its attractive individualists, among them the group of middle-aged men who enjoy each other's outspoken company and who have assumed "a kind of common guardianship" of Sam, the village newsboy and son of Windy McPherson, Civil War veteran, drunkard, braggart, liar. Caxton contains preachers of a dead, because institutionalized, Christianity, but it also contains the handsome Mike McCarthy, who has bedded the wives of twelve respected citizens, who understands how sexual energy is distorted into moneymaking, and who calls for "a modern Christ with a pipe in his mouth who will swear and knock us about" until people "understand that we have only this, our lives, this life so warm and hopeful and laughing in the sun." It contains John Telfer, dandy and admirer of *Looking Backward*, who failed as an artist because he too much loved the admiration of women, yet who as surrogate father to Sam encourages him to seek a goal by summoning up for the boy a vision of the growing corn, not merely as a food to fatten steers for the market, but as both "a vast river of life" and, in its long straight rows, an ordering force within the chaos of nature. And Caxton contains women to whom Sam can respond with the intuitive understanding of which he is capable: his silent, deeply loved and loving mother, Jane McPherson; Banker Walker's dark-skinned daughter, whose kisses awaken Sam's strong sexuality; the school teacher, Mary Underwood, who in her fostering love for her former pupil becomes a surrogate mother for him during Jane McPherson's final illness.

In sum, Caxton offers Sam what Clyde offered his grateful creator, a deep sense of community to offset the humiliation of being their fathers' sons; and later, during his first years in Chicago, Sam happily recalls "the essential goodness of the town amid the cornfields." What Caxton cannot provide forcefully enough for young Sam, as Clyde could not for young Sherwood, is an alternative to moneymaking through which, in addition to repudiating his father, he can release the dreamer part of himself, that part which responds almost lyrically to wind and rain and which yearns blindly for some larger purpose beyond devotion to material success. Because of this lack of alternative goal the dreamer part of Sam McPherson is forced to express itself, now and in later life, more through the intensity than the object of his self-dedication, though it manifests itself indirectly in his lifelong contempt for hypocrisy, "windiness," lies.

Like Mirage and Winesburg, then, Caxton is a fictionalized version of Clyde, which set its impress permanently on "Major" Anderson's son. Underneath the fictionalized surface lies experiential truth. That truth is to some extent of fact but even more of feeling. Sherwood had been one of Clyde's two newsboys, for example, and as such had pitted himself for sales against John Emerson (formerly Clifton Paden), the other, though the novel's finely conceived opening scene much transforms the actual circumstances of the rivalry. Again, the character John Telfer is certainly modeled in some part on the real John Tichenor, the Clyde artist who had taught and encouraged Karl and was a friend of Sherwood. Most obvious of all renditions of essential truth is, of course, the savage portrait of Irwin Anderson under the name of Windy McPherson, the importance of whom as negative incentive for Sam's dedication to moneymaking is indicated by Anderson's choice of a title for his novel. A bitter recollection of the drunken housepainter will at crucial points reinforce Sam's desire to rise in the business world and then to leave that world in a wandering search for Truth. Significantly, Sam's mother is given little attention as a positive motivator for his future careers, though the son's love for her repeats Sherwood's love for Emma Anderson. As Sam grows up in Caxton, he develops an understanding of the quiet Jane McPherson, which, the author once states, gives "a seriousness and purpose to the ambitious plans he continued to make for himself." But *Windy McPherson's Son* is not, like Lawrence's *Sons and Lovers,* the story of a young man emotionally obsessed with his mother. In contrast to that summary statement concerning Jane's influence, Anderson elaborates at length the roles of the surrogate parents in shaping Sam's future. Designated explicitly by the author as a "formative influence," Telfer, who had once shown Sam the vision of the corn, impetuously and ambiguously voices the town's advice to him: "'Make money! Cheat! Lie! Be one of the men of the big world.'" Mary Underwood, on the other hand, appears to subsume, at least in her intellectuality, the Trillena White of Springfield who discoursed to Anderson of the classic English and American writers and Superintendent Ginn of the Clyde schools who by offering to help young Sherwood go to college might have made him, as Mary hopes to make Sam, "a scholar, a man living his life among books and ideas" rather than "a money-maker" living "his life among men." So Caxton sends Sam into the great world as Clyde sent Sherwood, with a memory of communal affection and a goal incommensurate with his personal needs. Appropriate to the truth of the author's feelings about his "Own Middle Western Home Town," book 1 ends in an sequence of emotion-laden scenes in which Sam almost kills his father in a rage of hatred and contempt, his mother dies of a wasting illness, John Telfer honors her memory, Mary Underwood comforts Sam in his distress, and the McPherson family disintegrates even more rapidly than the Anderson family had done shortly after Emma Anderson's death in 1895.[19]

The remaining three books of *Windy* contain autobiographical truth too, but autobiography even more masked, displaced, distorted, fantasized; and accordingly this last two-thirds of the novel is generally more compressed as to events and more intermixed with traces of Anderson's reading of other writers. Still, in the account of Sam McPherson's young manhood and early middle age, one can perceive how Anderson, this man from a midwest American small town, was trying to work out problems that had puzzled and disturbed him during his more recent career as artist.[20]

Driven by his desire to make money to prove that he is not another Windy "failing to blow the bugle before the waiting crowd," Sam the ex-newsboy goes at the beginning of book 2 like a Horatio Alger hero (or like Sherwood himself) to make his fortune in the city. The Alger analogy persists even to Sam's marrying his boss's daughter; yet as far back as 1904 Anderson had questioned the Alger values in his sketch for *Agricultural Advertising* of Peter Mcveagh, "The Man of Affairs." Now fabricating freely on the basis of knowledge gained from his own experience as advertising copywriter and small businessman, Anderson much expands that sketch by detailing Sam's rise from produce buyer in Chicago's South Water Street Market to buyer, treasurer, head of the Rainey Arms Company, then power behind a national consolidation of firearm companies, and eventually chief of the "McPherson Chicago crowd" of stock market manipulators. Sam's subsequent departure from business quite reverses Alger and goes beyond the sketch of Peter Mcveagh; but if Anderson needed models here in addition to his own fantasized experience, he could have found them ready to hand in the protagonists of a well-established type novel, one which described a businessman who seeks wealth and power then becomes disillusioned with both, and which had already provided figures like Howells's Silas Lapham, Frank Norris's Curtis Jadwin in *The Pit*, and William Allen White's John Barclay in *A Certain Rich Man*.[21]

In his attempt to make Sam representative of the late-nineteenth-century American drive toward the concentration of economic power, Anderson is as insistent but no more innovative than other writers of this type novel. More original is his treatment of Sam's marriage to Sue Rainey, daughter of the pompous, ineffectual Colonel Tom Rainey, president of the arms company, though the events of this fictional married life are told too often in the language of popular romance. Just as Sam's repression of the dreamer aspect of himself and his dedication to the external world of material success is a projection of Anderson's memory of his own youth, so the rendition of the marriage, which is seen almost entirely from Sam's point of view, projects Sherwood's sense of his troubled relationship with Cornelia. Several times the point is explicitly made that Sam has been attracted into marriage less by sexual need than by his conversion, for a period, from the goal of moneymaking to Sue's ideal of service for the world's future, her conviction that as husband and wife they must devote themselves fully and selflessly to the children they expect to have. The marriage is devastated, however, when Sue becomes pregnant three times and each time is delivered of a dead child. Although it would be too pat to see the stillbirths as a symbolic rejection by Anderson of his own three children, one glimpses beneath the fictional mask such elements of the real marriage as the tensions and antagonisms of two persons with differing social backgrounds and emotional needs, sexual maladjustment, Cornelia's intellectuality in contrast to Sherwood's greater intuitiveness and sensuousness, her strong and his much weaker devotion to the actual Robert, John, and Mimi. Anderson may also have been drawing, indirectly, on painful memories of marital discord when he attributes to Sue's third failure to bear a live child Sam's surprisingly intense reaction, a temporary breakdown that, as has been noted earlier, simulates many of the elements of his own "dissociative reaction" in the late fall of 1912—the physical sensations of onset, extreme disorientation, feelings of anger, guilt, and fearfulness, aimless wandering in and outside a city, a blow which makes Sam's face hurt (as Sherwood's head had hurt him), railroad tracks, a drugstore, a night spent out of doors in the countryside, loss of memory, hospitalization, the presence of the wife at the hospital bedside as the husband recovers.[22]

It must have been with acute discomfort that Anderson recalled, as he obviously was able to, detailed particulars of his Elyria crisis and reorganized them into a scene, which he makes a critical one in the development of his semiautobiographical hero. Perhaps it was the acuteness of that discomfort as much as narrative design that encouraged him, in some postcrisis revision of the novel, to an act of psychological displacement, which had more than literary implication. To make Sam's breakdown result from marital difficulties and biological chance alone, rather than also from business concerns as in the author's own case, may have been required by the characterization of Sam as one of the new American "Captains of Finance," but in terms of narrative probability Sam's reaction is an effect too great for its cause. Still, the displacement of cause and effect had its emotional value for Anderson in dealing with his personal problems in fiction. Throwing the blame for Sam's breakdown primarily onto Sue's unrealistic devotion to an ideal inflicted, if only in fiction, a kind of vicarious punishment on the highly principled Cornelia, and it exonerated Sherwood, though again only in fiction, of any incompetence as businessman. The breakdown as a sign of the destroyed marriage is blamed also, in the novel, for both Sam's reawakened decision to give "the Chicago world a display of that tremendous energy that was to write his name in the industrial history of the city as one of the first of the western giants of finance," and his increasing resort to a magnified version of the chicanery, lies, and personal betrayal that Anderson felt had marked his own experience with the business world.

But there was another matter involved in that psychological displacement. Ruthlessly Sam consolidates all western and eastern firms into a national firearms trust—one recalls the grandiose plans for the American Merchants Company—and destroys Colonel Tom's authority after a tense business conference at the end of which he finds that he has unconsciously written over and over the sentence, "The best men spend their lives seeking truth." After Sue leaves him because of his betrayal of her father, he becomes more and more corrupt in his financial manipulations, and more and more gross in body and "sick" in mind. Shocked by word of Colonel Tom's suicide, however, he abruptly decides to "follow the message his hand had written" and "try to spend his life seeking truth." Whereupon at the end of book 2 he deliberately "walks out of the office, again a free man." There may be a question at this point in the narrative as to whether an effect is again greater than its cause, for though Sam unhappily realizes the connection between his betrayal of Colonel Tom and the suicide, the Colonel has been carefully portrayed from the first as another Windy McPherson of boastfulness and ineptitude whose death deserves the contempt Sam feels along with guilt. There is no question at all, however, of the way in which the author was putting to use here his original psychological displacement. By having Sam walk out of his business office so abruptly and so deliberately, Anderson was already preparing for the equivalent scene in the fanciful autobiography *A Story Teller's Story* he was to publish eight years later, that scene in which he consciously pretends to be insane and deliberately walks out abruptly and forever from his paint business. Fiction, as here in *Windy McPherson's Son,* was not only a means by which he could try to solve personal problems or even alter unpleasant past reality to quite literally suit his fancy; it was a means by which he could try to create and test out a series of personas to present to others and the world.[23]

Since Sam McPherson is not destined to be an artist, Anderson instead sends him in the episodic book 3 wandering on foot among people in a physical search for truth. For the settings of Sam's several adventures and some of the persons he meets Anderson may well have drawn on observations during his train travels as advertising writer and businessman; but this section of the novel, in effect a series of tales connected by a single character, appears to derive its form from the author's reading as well as his experience. As Sam walks the American land during a cycle of seasons, "backtrailing," it may be noticed, from the Midwest to the East Coast, he enters not only towns and villages but also the realm of the picaresque as compounded from such favorite writers of the author's as the Henry Fielding of *Tom Jones*, George Borrow of *Lavengro* and *The Romany Rye*, and Robert Louis Stevenson of, among other "open road" volumes, *Travels with a Donkey*. Perhaps the episodic journey structure reflects also his reading of *Pilgrim's Progress;* for though they have no allegorical and hardly any other cumulative design, Sam's adventures on his vagabond year represent successive attempts to find Truth—never defined and always elusive. Each adventure ends, however, in this modern pilgrim's disillusionment with some program or ideal for a better America—with Socialism and civic reform, with institutionalized religion, with unionization as a means of helping workers, with the vague faith that "American men and women" can readily learn "to be clean and noble and natural, like their forests and their wide, clean plains," disillusionment with almost any vision of life except, as Sam momentarily comprehends, that of the artist, who wishes simply to record the real story behind individual lives. It is with something of the artist's impulse that one night Sam picks up a prostitute on a city street, takes her to dinner, listens to her plain story of a bad marriage and the need to support a child, and finds in her "a quality of honesty that he was always seeking in people." Afterward, refusing to go to her room, he remembers McCarthy of Caxton calling out for a new Christ, and Sam himself calls out on God to ask, "'Have you left your children here on the earth hurting each other?'"[24]

At this point in his novel, as in his life, Anderson could not envision more clearly how to reconstitute a corrupt, disordered, but potentially vital America. To conclude his book and Sam's quest, which has in effect reached its limit with this troubled cry, he went to an old device, an apparently happy ending presumably drawn from his reading but also from an almost parodic reversal of his and Cornelia's last unhappy effort to save their marriage. It is an ending with a sting concealed in it, however. During one of the debauches to which he has reverted in despair of finding truth, Sam meets on a St. Louis riverboat a dissolute but independent woman who takes him to her home overlooking the Mississippi River, which, the author twice emphasizes, hinting at his past reading and his present design, is the one Twain wrote of in *Huckleberry Finn*. At home they find the woman's three children, who in sex, temperament, and order of birth, though not in exact age, are analogues of Robert, John, and Mimi. After seeing and talking with them, Sam has the sudden revelation that what men and women want is children, any children if not their own, a revelation that has struck most commentators on *Windy* as arbitrary and inadequate. Paying off the woman, Sam takes the three children with him, reading them *Huckleberry Finn* as they journey East on the New York flyer back to Sue.

One of the devices Anderson had been trying to bring to full power in this apprentice novel is a motif linking "the force of sex," as he forthrightly calls it, with such elements of natural setting as storms and "water moving in great masses." Considering both the thrust of this motif and Anderson's view of Twain as the crude, vital frontiersman who went East and was tamed, there is a special irony in Sam's return to Sue that the author seems consciously to be preparing. Since her embittered departure from Sam, Sue has been living, not in brawling Chicago on great Lake Michigan or along the mile-wide Mississippi, but in a village on the Hudson River, a moving mass of water but Eastern, merely named in the book, never viewed or described. She lives in a well-appointed house with a book-lined study and writing room, two black servants, a "well-ordered garden," and pastoral surroundings through which—Anderson skillfully modulates his motif—"a little stream ran down over stones toward a small lake, the falling water making a persistent, quiet note in the stillness." In all ways a diminuendo is being effected in this final scene. With a surprising lack of surprise Sue accepts the children, and husband and wife conduct a sentimental dialogue of reunion ending with Sue's shyly loving confession, "I never did let you go."[25]

Read uncritically, the ending seems an almost embarrassing surrender to all the genteel conventions of literature and life; read more carefully, it reveals that Anderson is quietly manipulating the conventions to a different end and that his apparent naïveté—the phenomenon was not limited to his fiction writing—is full of hard knowledge. While the man who betrayed her father and caused his suicide had been "'seeking and being defeated,'" Sue has been waiting for him in her house "'like a sailor's wife.'" She has read books, done "'what I called perfecting myself,'" has even "'written articles about life and conduct and had them published in magazines'"—as indeed Cornelia had published an article on Rahel Varnhagen in *The Little Review*. But she is ashamed, she confesses, of the pettiness of her life; and later that evening, standing alone outside the house in the darkness, Sam also wonders "if he had found the way or if life with Sue and the children would become petty as the big life of affairs had become brutal." Sam then makes the choice that Sherwood had brutally and, for him, necessarily rejected. Repressing an "impulse to run away into the darkness, to begin again, seeking, seeking," Sam instead enters the house, which had seemed vaguely familiar to him "as though he had lived in it before," and prepares "to try to force himself back into the ranks of life."[26]

In context that final image is a claustrophobic one, which shrinks to a petty tightness beside John Telfer's forgotten vision of the wideflowing river of life in the Midwest cornfields. It is the image of a constricted, diminished future such as Sherwood could have predicted for himself had he resumed life with Cornelia and the children. "I never knew how to end a novel," he wrote to Waldo Frank of the latter's review of *Windy McPherson's Son,* thanking him for his "slap at my ending of the novel." But the apology was an assertion too, for he would continue: "Always feel as though I were just at the beginning when the thing has to be wound up and put aside." Considering the dreamer part unquietly buried in Sam's nature, the real ending of his story might well be the reassertion all over again, at some time in the future, of his need to go seeking; but by undercutting the happy ending Anderson brings his book to a rest and remains true to its title. At this moment the son of Windy McPherson is as defeated as his father had been, as little able to "blow the bugle before the waiting crowd," by comparison with what he had desired and quested for hardly less ridiculous. The failure in the ending, rightly seen, is that of Windy McPherson's son, not of the skill or conviction of his creator, who had tried to tell honestly the real story behind his book and his life.[27]

4.

Shortly after the publication of *Windy McPherson's Son* someone on the *Chicago Daily News* staff—presumably Ben Hecht or the paper's highly literate news editor, Henry Justin Smith—invited Anderson to contribute a statement about his novel and his "literary ideas and ideals." From the length and tone of his reply, printed in the *News* for October 4, it appeared that he was delighted at the chance to get his ideas before a mass audience. Dismissing "all this talk concerning the technique of novel writing" as just talk, Anderson insists in his letter that a novel must be judged as good or bad depending on whether "the characters seem real, living and vital" to the reader or only "puppets to serve the purpose of a tale." The English masters like Borrow and Fielding he argues, rather circuitously, achieved form in their books mostly "by disregarding what we have come to think of as the proper form of the novel" and instead merely wrote for the "fun of writing and for the healthy exercise of their ability as writers"; they "didn't think of happy endings and the solving of problems." Contemporary American novelists like himself, on the other hand, are faced with special difficulties. The novelist's art is a "reflective" art; yet the "terrible state of social disorder" in which Chicagoans live allows "no feeling for the reflective mood among us." Then, too, people "do not want to face truth," and instead demand of novelists only "a rigid and unflinching sentimentality." The question of what the novel should be is yet further complicated by the popularity of the short story, which "won out" over the novel because it is "a more or less rigid, definite art form like the sonnet," provides a single impression, and in its fixed pattern is readily "understandable." Conquered by its rival, the novel today is "no more than the prolonged short story," though when the two forms are compared ideally, the latter is only "a solo by the second cornet," whereas the former, which attempts to "carry into the mind not one impression but a mass of impressions" is "a piece by the full orchestra." What novelists must now do is to "release" the novel form in accordance with the contemporary world movement for the release of all art form. *Windy McPherson's Son*, Anderson modestly concludes, does not sufficiently provide such release. It isn't "loose and disorderly enough to reflect modern American life," and his characters "are not enough alive . . . are not enough American." Perhaps the other books he has written and will write can "do the job."[28]

This statement, by turns dogmatic and ingratiating, is an interesting one. It is Anderson's first direct public attack on what he would come to call the "poison plot" story, though he has not yet made an author's willingness to force his characters into preconceived fictional patterns—the test, as he would come to make it, of that person's fundamental morality or immorality. That the attack on the formula story came so early in his career is not surprising, considering the number of Winesburg tales he had written by the time he sent this letter to the *News*. What may surprise for the same reason, however, is his ranking of the short story in relation to the novel as to his mind "always a quite secondary art form." One of Anderson's real achievements, an achievement that by itself would give him a permanent place in American literary history, was actually to be his release of the short story from the prison of the pattern. At the moment, of course, he had been asked to discuss *Windy*, but this early comparative ranking of novel and tale suggests that he had already become fixed on the novel as the form more crucially needing "release," an attitude that helps explain why he continued almost to the end of his career to write and publish novels, even though it became more and more evident, to others if not himself, that in the writing of tales lay his greatest talent and his best use of creative energy.

Hecht's review in the September 8 issue of the *Chicago Evening Post* was the first that *Windy* received and in its rambling, impressionistic, overwritten way said for the most part what the novelist wanted to hear. For the admiring Hecht the characters had the sense of life and movement that, according to Anderson's letter to the *News*, made a novel good. The "greatest secret of Sherwood Anderson's style," is, Hecht declared, his "love of his people and love of life," arrived at by years of "pondering and dreaming," though to Hecht's mind Anderson "is a stylist first and a thinker afterward." He is "a poet. The soul of man as he has found it in America is his theme." Although *Windy McPherson's Son* is "a prelude passionate and quiet" to the "Iliad of America" and not that Iliad itself, in its pages "lies the promise of a new human comedy and a new, fresh, clean and virile spirit in American literature."[29]

Hecht's friendly excitement must have helped offset the less warm reception of the novel in Chicago's largest newspaper, the *Tribune*, though two different reviewers commented on the book in two successive issues late in September. One Gordon Seagrove began by finding that Anderson "has written his first novel better than many men have written their last" but ended with the complaint that there was too little incident to make the reader believe in Sam's rise; and Fanny Butcher, who was already conducting a weekly "Tabloid Book Review" and would always have reservations about Anderson's work, thought the first half of *Windy* a less realistic imitation of Dreiser but felt the "paragraphs" which merely "chronicled the reactions of Sam McPherson to life" were "convincing." But even Fanny Butcher was kind compared to Margaret Anderson's associate editor on *The Little Review*, the strong-minded Jane Heap, who flatly condemned *Windy* as one more awkward attempt at the Great American Novel. (Sherwood remained friends with her, but would refer to her years later as "an arbitrary one, that same Jane.")[30]

As would be expected, Anderson seems to have watched for the reviews published outside his city, and he must have been encouraged that the national response to his Midwest novel was so often, though not invariably, favorable. That popular academic William Lyon Phelps, writing from Yale for *The Dial*, attacked the book as unreal in characterization and lacking in structure, though he admitted its vitality and promise; but a large majority of reviewers, while judging the first half of the book superior to the last and most often objecting to the ending, admired the picture of the small town, the seriousness of Sam's search for the meaning of American life, and the author's poetic force, a force that some reviewers compared to that of Dostoyevsky. The first of two enthusiastic critics for *The Nation* selected *Windy* as "perhaps the most remarkable of the year" among first novels, and the unsigned review in the influential *New York Times Book Review* concluded its praise of this "epic of modern life" by calling it a "rare and exceedingly fine book" and declaring that "Whoever desires to keep abreast with the best in current literature cannot afford to let it go unread." Presumably on the basis of such reviews the "book began to sell," as Jefferson Jones recalled, "and cheered by the growing demand we put another edition of one thousand copies on the press in February, 1917." But after Lane of New York "had sold a little over eighteen hundred copies the demand stopped abruptly." The novel must have begun to sell by December 1; for on that date Anderson wrote to Mencken, who in *The Smart Set* had both commended and criticized the work: "'Windy' is going pretty well, as well as it deserves, I fancy." Then he cautiously dismissed his novel as one "written several years ago and . . . to my mind, a long ways from being a hell of a book. I've got some better ones."[31]

From one review in particular he probably took great satisfaction, and from another he certainly did. In the first, in the November issue of *The Masses,* Floyd Dell, still generous toward Sherwood despite their estrangement, recounted his excitement upon reading the manuscript of *Windy* and meeting its author, praised the portraits of the Caxton townspeople, "too real ever to have got into American fiction before," and specified the most important thing about the book to be "the profound sincerity, the note of serious, baffled, tragic questioning" of why American life is what it is. As Anderson developed away from the realistic tendency of *Windy,* Dell became increasingly unsympathetic toward his work as toward the man, and this assessment in the November *Masses* was already a voice from an important past relationship. The other review, Waldo Frank's enthusiastic piece in the opening issue, also November, of the magazine *The Seven Arts,* was titled "Emerging Greatness." This voice prepared the way for an important new relationship.[32]

5.

In almost every possible way Waldo Frank was Sherwood Anderson's opposite. Born in 1889 and hence nearly thirteen years younger than Anderson, he had grown up in New York, the son of a father who was a successful lawyer and a mother who was a talented musician. Close to but arrogantly rebellious against his family with its upper middle class, German Jewish, Europeanized cultivation, Frank went on to be a brilliant, enormously well-read student in high school, at a preparatory school in Switzerland, and at Yale, from 1907 to 1911, where he majored in French literature, wrote drama reviews for the New Haven newspaper, was a fine amateur cellist, and in four years graduated Phi Beta Kappa with both a bachelor's and master's degrees. After working in New York as a newspaper reporter, he lived much of 1913 in Paris, writing and further absorbing French culture. Late in that year, however, he returned to the United States determined to help bring to birth in America a new national self-expression in the arts, comparable to but not imitative of what he had witnessed in France. For the next two years this "short, nervous, articulate, and self-assertive" young man, as he later described himself, with his uncombable mass of black hair and intense dark eyes, lived in Greenwich Village and wrote plays, stories, and critical articles, most of them unpublished, to further the American cultural rebirth of which he took Walt Whitman to be the prophet.

Early in 1916 he met James Oppenheim, then in his middle thirties, at a small party in Manhattan. Oppenheim, a Whitmanesque poet and popular novelist, wanted to start a monthly magazine of the arts and had already obtained financial support from Mrs. Annette K. Rankine, a wealthy lady who, like Oppenheim, was undergoing Jungian psychoanalysis and who "needed something to do with her surplus and her time." Oppenheim needed an associate editor, and after his first talk with Frank he knew he had found his man. The two set up an office at 132 Madison Avenue and assembled an Advisory Board, which included poets Robert Frost and Louis Untermeyer and literary critics Edna Kenton and Van Wyck Brooks, the latter to be listed beginning with the fifth issue of the forthcoming magazine as another associate editor. Only a few months before, Brooks had "struck the note of the new day" with his *America's Coming-of-Age,* but as he remembered, it was Frank who was "the real creator of *The Seven Arts.*" During the spring and summer of 1916 Frank threw his burning energy into creating what he would regard, not as just a magazine, but as a "living organism," which would protest by its presence the rising war spirit in the country. That summer an appeal for contributions was sent out to American authors, an appeal that would be reprinted in the first issue as a statement of principle. Americans are living, the statement grandly declared, "in the first days of a renascent period, a time which means for America the coming of that national self-consciousness which is the beginning of greatness." Recognizing these "new tendencies," *The Seven Arts* aimed to become "an expression of our American arts that shall be fundamentally an expression of our American life." With no regard for tradition or for "current magazine standards" it was to be "not a magazine for artists, but an expression of artists for the community."[33]

Anderson seems not to have been sent a copy of this statement, with which he would have been at once in accord; but Edna Kenton, who had been a newspaper reporter and freelance writer in Chicago and kept acquainted with the literary scene there after moving to New York, advised Frank of "an unknown 'bright Chicago advertising man,' named Sherwood Anderson, who wrote stories and novels in his spare time." Probably about the time Sherwood and Tennessee returned newly married from their summer at Chateaugay Lake, Frank sent him a request to look at his writings. For some reason Anderson mailed back only the Winesburg story "'Queer,'" but he must have asked Jefferson Jones to get an early copy of *Windy McPherson's Son* to the busy associate editor of the forthcoming magazine. Frank, by nature both intensely intellectual and intensely emotional, was excited by what he received. Out of the Midwest was coming just such new American expression as he and the statement had been looking for. He accepted "'Queer,'" which Mencken had turned down for *The Smart Set,* for the second issue of *The Seven Arts,* and set space in the first number, that of November, for his review of *Windy*

McPherson's Son, titling it in echo of the statement "Emerging Greatness."

The review was itself a kind of manifesto. American writers, Frank asserted, have either abstracted themselves, literally or figuratively, from American experience or have lost themselves in it, have been pure, isolated artists or blind worshippers of fact. Anderson's significance was to have escaped both extremes and presented life "shot through with the searching color of truth, which is a signal for a native culture." Frank found the section on McPherson's quest as awkward and improbable and as truthful as passages in Dostoyevsky, for in his quest Sam "is America today," a "clear symbol of America groping." Only the last chapter of the book was really bad, for "it slams the door on the vista of passionate inquiry which the book unfolds." But despite the book's faults and the author's age there was hope for his growth. Already Anderson was pointing beyond Twain and Dreiser, and "Genius in America," as witness Walt Whitman, "rises slowly." In the emerging greatness of Anderson, Frank implied without saying, was symbolized the emerging greatness of the new American literature.

Understandably Sherwood was stirred by such praise. In the first of the letters he began writing to Frank in early November, he thanked him for the "intelligent discussion" of his novel, denied, most improbably, that he had even heard of Dreiser or Dostoyevsky when he wrote it and then, both artist and advertising man, began reinforcing Frank's image of him as symbol of American expression. Frank had associated him in the review with Twain and Whitman, who, he now told Frank, he had "always believed . . . belonged among the two or three really great American artists." He himself, he declared, was trying to do what Romain Rolland in the opening issue of *The Seven Arts* had urged American writers to dare—"to express themselves freely, sincerely, entirely, in art." Frank warmly replied that he was certain his enthusiasm for *Windy* had not been misplaced and asked to see some of the author's most recent work. Anderson immediately mailed off "The Untold Life," which he had just finished, and then on November 14 offered to send all fifteen "intensive studies" in the Winesburg series, since "they, as a whole, come a long step toward achieving" what Rolland had called for and since when "published in book form they will suggest the real environment out of which present day American youth is coming." Frank showed his very real editor's gift by happily accepting "The Untold Lie," because of its "extreme limpidity through which one senses the profound," but also by raising practical questions about handling the whole series in the magazine in such a way that its "composition . . . as a single organism" would not be destroyed. It would be better, he felt, to publish the best of the stories "in sufficiently quick succession . . . to suggest at least the scheme of the whole." Subsequently, too, he would be firm about rejecting some of the Winesburg tales, which Anderson had decided to send a few at a time, and some of the non-Winesburg pieces. But though Anderson might grumble as artist at the rejection of such tales as "Loneliness" or "Drink," or as business man at having "you fellows" pick the best stories and send only the customary $40 check—"the writer occasionally has the foolish dream that he ought to get a little money out of his work"—he could have no doubt about Frank's personal enthusiasm and the genuine desire of both editors for him "to think that the 'Seven Arts' is properly your home."[34]

Thus, long before the March 1917 issue of *The Seven Arts,* in which he was publicly hailed in the notes on contributors as "one of the significant new men out of the West," Anderson was receiving personal praise, his work was being published in a "quality" magazine, and he could foresee closer friendship with a group of literary men who, trained in looking east to Europe, were capable of looking west across America as well. It was a recipe for the euphoria he often demonstrated during these months. But buoyed up as he was by the excitement of literary recognition together with the long, restoring summer recently past and his present happiness with Tennessee, he could nevertheless have days when the amused detachment he tried to keep toward the advertising grind would turn temporarily to frustration at how it was costing him "dearly in fine moods destroyed, rare projects gone wrong because of lack of strength to get on with them." Sometimes the frustration would turn to rage and horror at what a materialistic life seemed to do to people. "At times," he wrote to his friend Marietta Finley late in November,

there comes over me a terrible conviction that I am living in a city of the dead. In the office dead voices discuss dead ideas. I go into the street and long rows of dead faces march past. Once I got so excited and terrified that I began to run through the streets. I had a mad impulse to shout, to strike people with my fist. I wanted terribly to awaken them. Instead I went to my room and shut myself in. I drank whiskey. Presently I slept. When I awoke I laughed.

The extremity of language in this letter is a sign of how emotional a time it now was for Anderson. By nature he was always one to shift from mood to mood anyway, but in the months just after he had proven himself an artist by publishing *Windy McPherson's Son* and entering the pages of *The Seven Arts,* the shifts became unusually frequent and sharp, apparently because, at least in part, the beginnings of success were forcing him to clarify his sense of artistic mission.[35]

The correspondence between Anderson and Frank tells something of what was going on in Sherwood's excited consciousness toward the end of 1916, but much more may be learned, or guessed, from the remarkable series of letters he had begun writing to Marietta Finley beginning on September 26, significantly within four weeks after *Windy* had appeared. She and he had first met in Chicago in late 1914 or early 1915, shortly after he had moved to 735 Cass Street. Long after their correspondence ceased in 1933 she could recall his physical appearance in detail, that he was of middling height, "at that time not too heavy," and she particularly remembered of him "Black eyes—dark brown hair, smooth shaven,—and a contagious kind of laugh—more of a giggle." At the time they met, she was working as a manuscript reader for the Bobbs-Merrill Company in Indianapolis, where from 1916 on he would occasionally stop off to visit her on trips to see advertising clients in Kentucky; and he trusted her professional judgment enough to ask her, somewhere around 1916, to write reader's reports for himself, not Bobbs-Merrill, on the manuscripts of *Mary Cochran*, *Talbot Whittingham*, and *Marching Men*. Little is known about their relationship, but Sherwood felt close enough to write frankly of himself as person and artist in these letters.[36]

He wrote frankly, but not entirely frankly; for if he poured out to her what he thought and felt, sometimes almost from day to day, by the time of his November 23 letter he was already proposing that he write, not "personal things, a cold in the head, etc.," but "my observations on life and manners as they present themselves here and now." If Marietta, or "Bab" as he habitually called her, would date the letters on receipt and type them up with a carbon copy, in a year or less "we will see if we haven't material for a book that would be of interest to others." His main reason for the proposal was his own special character as writer, a character that he is honest in describing.

Perhaps no man writing has had to meet just the peculiar difficulties I have. With me writing has never been in any sense a science. There are days when to save my life I could not write a good sentence. I have really no knowledge of words, no mastery of the art of sentence construction.

And then a mood comes to me. The world is of a sudden all alive with meaning. Every gesture, every word of the people about carries significance. My hand, my eyes, my brain, my ears all sing a tune. If I can get to pencil and paper I write blindly, scarcely seeing the sheets before me.

At such times the terrible feeling of the utter meaninglessness of life passes. I am carried along through hours and days as by a great wind. I am happy.

If in one of these moments of exaltation, he is called to an advertising conference, he is filled with anger or laughter, and the major mood is broken. Many times, however, he may "scribble little notes" about the men he sits with at the conference, or on street cars his mind "plays with little notions about things and people." The act of expressing "these things in even a fragmentary way gives me satisfaction" and hence is of value to him if not to others. These letters, then, can express the "little moods" if not the major one. Incidentally, the letters may also be of value to Bab if they "extend or enlarge your own horizon."

Accordingly, the letters are not just personal communications but a conscious literary workshop as well. In a direct sense, of course, his life was the basis of his art, and the letters reveal this fact again and again. On December 7, 1916, he wrote a long letter about a three-hour visit to Clyde the previous day, a visit that had overwhelmed him with a flood of memories of people and events, memories so vivid and warm that halfway through the letter he suddenly asserts that he is now physically "here" in "the little hotel office," watching the townspeople pass outside and, with his hand shaking from excitement, writing "of my people and the strange things that have happened to them." He concludes with the story of Maria Welling, former "keeper of a house of ill repute," who married a gambler and with her husband came to Clyde, where they ran very respectably a little hotel (actually the Empire House). Maria had frankly warned her waitresses against the temptation to become prostitutes, and one night after the boy Sherwood had delivered the daily newspaper to the hotel's kitchen door and had probably eaten a wedge of her delicious pie, she affectionately but bluntly explained to him "what she meant by her talk with the girls" and warned him never to give money for sex. The event may well have happened much as described; yet Anderson in his letter to Bab calls the woman "Maria Welling," as though she were one of the Wellings of Winesburg, rather than "Julia Welker," which was her real Clyde name. The author's remembered experience is beginning to turn into literature before the reader's eyes. Again, in another extraordinary letter written the day after the one about Clyde, he tells Bab how, in order to change trains on this same trip back into Ohio, he had had to wait briefly the previous evening on the platform of the Elyria railroad station just across from the factory that had for five years housed the Anderson Manufacturing Company, and how, as he kept in the shadow of the station lest he by chance be recognized, the "soul within me was weary with old memories." He sketches the torment of his final years in Elyria, his writing of *Windy* and *Marching Men*, which "saved me from insanity," the tensions with his wife, the sympathetic understanding of his secretary who typed the fiction he was writing. Then he concludes with a description of his breakdown, that "convulsion that touched the edge of insanity," telling how he wandered blank-minded in the fields for several days, how "my mind came into my body" again, how "I dragged myself . . . into a hospital in a strange town and slept, and how he woke to the touch of his secretary's "honest hand." It is a well-told tale, as close to the facts of his breakdown as the comparable scene in *Windy McPherson's Son,* and not much closer.

If one looks for essential rather than the not-always-dependable factual truth about the author in these letters to Bab, what can be made of his assertions about his nature and its relation of that to others, especially to Tennessee? As with marriage so with friendship, he writes, neither must be taken too seriously; let either "become a necessity and you are in danger of losing it." He himself must retain a sense of freedom in life, and he asserts that "In marriage I am a guest and in love too. I cannot conceive of myself as permanently anything." Since he is inwardly less secure than he may outwardly seem, he never goes "into Tennessee's house but I go a little timidly, questioning," ready to "run away" if she should not want him. This last was written on January 12, 1917; yet just a week later he sent Bab a fanciful sketch titled "Masculinity," in which naked women with shining eyes creep from behind curtains in a long hall toward a man lying back in a dentist chair. As each woman reaches him and kisses him, he slaps her and, laughing, says that it has been and always will be so. Then one week after that he wrote of having been in a "grey" mood for weeks, although now that he is back in Chicago with Tennessee after an unpleasant advertising mission to Minneapolis, "things are better." Still,

I do not dare approach too close to her, make her too close a part of my life because I do not want to take into her life my greyness but to be where she is means everything.

And even this is misunderstood. I live away from this woman I have married. I go often to walk alone, to be alone. This also is misunderstood. Rumors run about. The woman is condemned because of the loneliness of my life. She is made to seem hard, cruel and indifferent when she is only big. No want of mine is left unsatisfied. In her love she, like others, is willing to give all. I will not take it. Often I shut the door and go away. And she is condemned for that.

Taken together the statements are a mixture of acceptance and denial, need and rejection, an ambivalence that gives and takes away and suggests, through it cannot prove, that the second divorce may have been implicit in the second marriage despite its present satisfactions. If there was any "note of distinction" in him, he had written to Bab at the beginning of the correspondence, it lay in "a certain power" he had to dare to shut doors on completed experiences as well as to open them on "new and wonderful possibilities." Whether or not his words may have been intended for Bab, they would eventually have an application for Tennessee.[37]

The feelings in the letters are more consistent one with the other on more specifically literary matters, though even here the comments on his current writing projects show sharp fluctuations of interest. On November 23, the day on which he proposed to put into his letters his "observations on life and manners," he was involved in "a big piece of work" (the

Tandy Hard trilogy) into which he was blindly pouring "myself and my character Tandy," though in fact only about two weeks earlier he had written the brief tale, "The Untold Lie." A month later he liked "the intensive things I am trying to do now rather than attempts at long novels"; yet by mid-January he already had "a splendid senses of grip" on a novel with many characters to be titled *Immaturity* from its "broad, real, sturdy" theme of "the terrible immaturity of America." Although this last project was in turn shortly pushed aside for yet another, Anderson held much more firmly in the letters written to Bab in late 1916 and early 1917, to two matters closely connected with the theme of *Immaturity* and with each other: the relation of American artists generally to America and, more specifically, his conception of himself as writer. If his views on these matters show more strong feelings than reasoned convictions, are expressed more in poetic images than in logical discourse, they can nevertheless be abstracted into a fairly coherent and highly revealing statement.[38]

To begin with, the writer, and all other Americans, needs to love the American land itself, not what men are doing to it, but the sense one gets on trains of the land's "vastness of possibility," for "If we can love *that* we can love America." At present Americans have scarred the beauty of the land with factories, and the pursuit of materialistic goals has made their lives mechanical, aimless, dead. Lacking the "courage . . . to embrace deep emotions," fearful of "bodily injury, sexual adventures, misunderstanding," of the damnation preached by conventional religion, men and women everywhere build "death walls" around their individual selves. Yet, unrecognized and unrealized, life flows on beneath these walls, and beauty lies hidden "in the night of industrialism." Both beauty and life can be discovered, but the professional artists do not know how to search for them, being hampered by traditional notions of beauty and art. Such artists fall into amusing or contemptible types: "the small store keeping artist, the artist who keeps a little garden and produces say, imagist poems for the early spring market, the artist who is smart and sharp . . . who is professionally funny for the Chicago Tribune." Or they think to be artists simply by indulging the bohemian lifestyle, or like Whistler and James—Anderson almost certainly is thinking of the first paragraph of Frank's "Emerging Greatness"—they do "not dare face America." The real American artist must accept the crudity of an industrial age and look through and beyond it. They must be courageous enough—and here Anderson is certainly thinking of *Huck Finn* as well as himself—"to start on the road to art by saying to God, 'All right then send me to hell. That is your affair. It is my affair to try and find out and to express what I really feel.'" Anderson sums up his lesson for the American artist in a comparison both odd and characteristic.

One morning . . . I could not sleep and so arose and went out on our new long Municipal Pier. The pier extends far out into the lake; it extends magnificently. The long rooms running away into the distance are like the cornfields of Kansas and Illinois. The whole structure is long, orderly, breath taking. It expresses something of what American lives should be, it is the kind of thing Americans can do, should do. It points a way. The Municipal Pier is calling to American artists, telling them what to be like.

The Municipal Pier, Anderson continues, is like Twain and Whitman who achieved their purposes despite the limitations of their time and place. They are the true pioneers of American writing.

I think we will have an American art unlike any other art in the world. When men, like my [friend, a manufacturer], who makes fence, become artists that will happen. The art they produce will be sustained, magnificent. It will be like Whitman's "Out of the cradle endlessly rocking" and like this great pier on which I now sit. It will be like the cornfields.[39]

Like all literary credos this probably tells more about the author's view of art than about art itself, but again Anderson shows that he was working out a coherent, if not always precise, conception of himself as artist, a conception that fits thematically, as the appeals to the Midwest cornfields suggest, with the only just published *Windy McPherson's Son*. Basic to this conception is the thought that, he claims, was born in him when he first began to write in his Elyria days: "I want to try to remember the relation of myself to my time and place." This means, on the one hand, that he thinks of his experience—small town background, independent business career and departure from it, present involvement out of necessity in a money- and success-oriented business organization—as representative American experience; it means, on the other hand, that this experience is not something to be repudiated or avoided but rather to be accepted as subject matter. Acceptance of it as subject matter does not, of course, imply acceptance of either its appearance or its values; quite to the contrary, he is one of those "damned souls, condemned" to try and break through the crudity, ugliness, deathliness of an industrial and business civilization to see the common and beautiful life beneath. "What lies to be done," he proposes for himself as well as other writers, "is to understand and see more and more intensely our life here," for "Everywhere is life with its story that aches to be expressed." His most succinct and eloquent statement of his artistic mission comes on January 15, 1917, in a letter—he sent a copy of it to Bab—addressed to a woman in Hollywood, California, who had given "*Windy* a laudatory notice in a newspaper" but who, though living "in American in these intense times," had advised him that she "would like to have me write like Dickens and Hardy:"

It is inevitable I suppose that people who like some of my work will not like the rest. I have never written two books in the same mood. I hope never to do so.

Now I write intensively. I see life so and express it. I have lost hope in the broad foundations of things and turn to the intensive human things.

That is natural. To my mind it is inevitable to one who opens himself to life. We are in the midst of the terrible age of industrialism. If for beauty I, who live in this ugly, ill-smelling Chicago must go into the past, if I must write of old times and places then I am not a man of my times.

I embrace my times. I go with my own people. If they are ugly I shall be ugly. I shall strive for the tortured and trusted beauty of my own time and place.

Such an assertion of determination and purpose accords with a reading of *Windy McPherson's Son* as a story that ends in apparent success and real failure; for the truth Sam quests after is surely that he must embrace his times and people, and he fails because he cannot achieve and sustain that embrace through the one possible way, the development of the artist's vision.[40]

Anderson's own desire somehow to embrace his times and people was one, though only one of the motivations behind a sequence of five letters to Bab compacted into a half-dozen days in mid-January 1917, a sequence of both psychological and literary significance. Just before the sequence begins he had written enthusiastically to her about the "possibilities" of *Immaturity,* the development of which would set John Hardy of Winesburg (in the tale "Surrender") against a background of that town's industrialization, a background he would eventually adapt into the novel *Poor White.* Since, however, this is the last reference to *Immaturity* of any consequence for a long time in the letters to Bab, one infers that the novel did not develop as foreseen. Sherwood's enthusiasm seems to have died rather quickly. On January 14, a Sunday and hence a day free for fiction writing, the sequence begins with a long letter with a quite different subject and mood. Almost elegiacally he describes one by one the inhabitants of his Cass Street lodging house, from which he feels he must (and would) soon move away. It is as though he had begun a "warm-up" letter—later in life he would often dash off several short letters in preparation for his daily stint of writing—and then had become engrossed in thinking about The Little Children of the Arts rather than about his fiction. On the sixteenth, no longer in a quietly sad mood, he writes of going out at night "into a madness of snow," of running and dancing by the icy lakeshore in "the mad confusion of snow flakes," of then more calmly resolving on the difficult task of achieving "purity in the midst of modern life": "One only succeeds occasionally, at odd moments, when one writes fervently, when one runs in the snow, when pure physical love finds natural expression, when one maintains friends in the midst of difficulty and misunderstanding." By the following day his mood has become more tense; he is assertive but with an edge of contempt for others and for himself. Drawing on ideas expressed in *Talbot Whittingham,* he discusses the close relation between religion and art. In contrast with modern writers, including himself, who rush to turn every experience into words, Jesus "alone is the master artist," for only he "dared to let his soul grow, asking no reward, seeking none of our silly modern goals, money, comfort, fame, an established place in a distorted world." What Americans must learn is that "art is the great, the true religion. It alone satisfies."[41]

Then finally two days later come two letters, both dated January 19, which complete the sequence of five and appear to be attempts to project aspects of the self into literary form. One is the fanciful sketch, "Masculinity," which in the context of the other letter can be read as an oblique retort to Bab, who has just written charging him with never having known the experience of giving things up. Directly and angrily in this other letter he rejects the charge, laying it on her instead and asserting with self-pitying exaggeration that "every word I have ever written that has any semblance of truth and beauty has been wrung from me" through sacrifice. Then, aroused by this dramatization of himself as sufferer and creator, he begins an explicitly Whitmanesque passage.

This morning I walked to work saying words. Like Whitman I gloried in words. Ohio, Illinois, Kalamazoo, Keokuk, Tennessee, Missouri. I thought how beauty had lived on here in the face of industrialism and made a foundation for beauty.

Some day the strong race will come. Men will suffer and be unafraid. I went along praying. "My destiny is new," I said to myself. "I can believe in beauty in the midst of this hubbub. Down the wind comes the call of the new men. It plays in the corn, in my corn, in the long corn fields."

Thereupon he launches into a prose hymn to the cornfields, which "shall be the mothers" of the strong men to come, the new men whom he, "a little child," thinks of as he runs cold and weeping through the street. It is a prose dithyramb that, within a matter of a few weeks, he would with only a few revisions put into free verse form as "Hosanna," one of the poems to be collected in his third book, *Mid-American Chants.*[42]

The psychological significance of this short, self-contained sequence of letters emerges when, on January 22, Sherwood quietly writes to Bab that he has just had "two days of real illness," brought on, he has the notion, by the circumstance that "I get [people I like] so keenly it does me up." The ascending curve of emotional intensity described by the letters, the climactic outbreaks of anger and self-dramatization, and then the abrupt physical collapse are in their very minor way an analogue to the Elyria crisis, and the recurrence in miniature of this psychic pattern during a period of relative success rather than failure is predictive of further emotional difficulty in the future. But there is another significance here, related to the first but going beyond it in terms of Anderson's literary development at this time. Over the four or more months since the publication of *Windy McPherson's Son,* Anderson had been unsuccessfully seeking a subject of some scope that he could fix on and work steadily at. Given this uncertainty and given also the impact of Frank's review and Anderson's experience with *The Seven Arts* generally, he seems to have felt the urgency of defining more clearly for himself and others his role as writer. He must and would, he had concluded, embrace his times and people, subsume them into himself as representative American, and thus through expression of his individual self express the larger whole. It was a grandiose concept, to be sure, though one sanctioned to Anderson's thinking by the example of Whitman. There was one more step to take, however, and judging by the very first letter sent to Bab back in late September 1916, he had in effect already taken it with his enigmatic declaration that "the whole secret of reality in writing depends on acknowledging the necessity of failure as a writer." Now, in the exaggerated, overwrought language of the angry letter that climaxes the mid-January sequence, he takes the step unambiguously. In the images of a "new John the Baptist crying in the wilderness" for people to give things up and a cold, weeping child thinking of new strong men to come from the cornfields, he presents himself as a precursor, a sacrificial leader, a sort of culture-hero, whose task it is to build a bridge to the American future by his continued willingness to risk and to accept the failure of his own art so that later writers can be assured of success. His mission as artist would be to embody in his life and work the parable of "Blackfoot's Masterpiece": failure would be his subject, the triumphant gesture in defeat would be his theme, the renovation of America would be his goal.[43]

To state Anderson's sense of his artistic mission in this way is to risk sounding as hyperbolic as Anderson himself in this climactic letter to Bab, a letter that was personal because written in angry reaction to her charge and impersonal because it also sought a literary form for other emotions. During the late winter and spring of 1917, similar highly charged ideas and language would reappear in an outburst of free-verse poems; but in his daily life that unsettled January he went on with his advertising job, he wrote calm letters to people, he had "grey," and probably no-color, days as well as days hectically colored by emotion. Still, that he was capable of conceiving of his artistic mission in so grand a fashion at this time explains why in letters to another person he should so flatly repudiate a specifically political role for the artist. Upton Sinclair, then famous as Socialist novelist and activist, had written him urging that he create fiction from an explicitly political point of view. On December 12, 1916, Sherwood responded, with a copy to Bab, that his wife was a Socialist and he voted Socialist himself when he did vote, but that "there is something terrible to me in the thought of the art of writing being bent and twisted to serve the ends of propaganda." Here, he emphatically declared, "is all America teeming with life that we haven't begun to really cut into or to understand." Rather than drawing apart into various political positions, writers should "stay in life" and be "something of brother to the poor brute who runs the sweatshop as well as to the equally unfortunate brutes who work for him." Writers should "leave politics and economics to the more lusty throated ones and run away, one by one into the streets, the offices and the houses—looking at things—trying to write them down."

Clearly it was a long time ago and in another state of mind that Anderson had invented and propagandized for Commercial Democracy. Sinclair restated his argument in a second letter, and Anderson responded again late in January of 1917. In a more conciliatory tone he assured Sinclair that he sympathized with revolutionists and even wished them success, but he could not write "propaganda" since neither as artist nor even as citizen did he have political remedies to suggest for an ill society.

My conception of an artist's attitude toward life about him is that he shall at all costs keep himself open to impressions, that he shall not let himself become an advocate.

To me there is no answer for the terrible confusion of life. I want to try to sympathize and to understand a little of the twisted maimed life that industrialism has brought on us but I can't solve things, Sinclair, I can't do it. Man I don't know who is right and who is wrong.[44]

Anderson's conception of the artist's function, whether stated rhapsodically or less so, as here, helps explain also his changing attitude toward the war in Europe, now well into its third exhausting year. His story "The Struggle," which had been published in May of 1916, had used the war merely as convenient background for a psychological conflict, and rarely thereafter would the First World War enter his fiction in any but tangential fashion. The Spanish-American War had been "his" war, and as a man now of forty with three children to whose support he contributed, if irregularly, he escaped the direct experience of European combat afforded the next generation of writers. He was kept aware through the newspapers of the massively bloody battles that had begun at Verdun in February of 1916 and on the Somme in July and still ground horribly and inconclusively into the autumn; but in all the extant correspondence, admittedly incomplete for most of 1916, there is no reference to the war until November 20, two days after the Battle of the Somme had officially run out, when he sent to Waldo Frank at *The Seven Arts* "a little war thing you may like." The nature of the "thing" may be guessed at from his first discussion of the war, which occurred in a letter to Bab dated November 27. Women especially, he had told Tennessee the previous evening, tend to "get too close and personal a view of men at war." Presumably recalling from 1898 his own near visionary experience of the giant rhythm of soldiers on the march, he insisted that before a battle the individual man would have no courage himself but would suddenly get it from the mass of his fellows. "In some one of my books," he writes, "I have worked it out." (The curiously magisterial reference is to *Marching Men,* which he could quote from easily enough for Upton Sinclair, and to the authorial essay on pages 155–56.) Trains bring thousands of "strong bright-eyed young men" into Chicago "from the cornfields," but once in the city, though they live physically, they die spiritually. "I should prefer my sons to die in the war and terror of a Verdun." But if the European soldier survives the war, he will return to his native village, where he and other veterans will talk "over and over their wonder stories," passing on to listening boys "a new heritage of beauty"; for, as Anderson puts it in the manner of the narrator of "The Untold Lie": "Boys, you know, are right when they are thrilled by the tales of war and are not thrilled by the tales of the stock-exchange." After all, when the war is over, which will be soon, the world will not collapse in "ruin and anarchy."

Trust instead the lesson men have got. I tell you that youth will run all through the old places. Poets and thinkers will arise, and the old world will be sweetened by the storm, the very air will be purer. It is inevitable.

Such trust in the power of poets to be unacknowledged legislators may now seem incredibly self-deluding, though Anderson's optimism as such was not unique at that time even among less poetic Americans who felt that Verdun and the Somme might have bled the European antagonists to stalemate and a negotiated peace; and anyway his optimism did not last. He would continue to view the war from one of the standpoints open to the artist, but the assurance expressed in that late November letter almost disappeared within a few days when on January 31, 1917, Germany announced that unrestricted submarine warfare would begin on February 1, and when on February 3 the government of the United States severed relations with the German government. On this last date Anderson wrote to Bab that war would bring hatred, and "all truth and beauty" would die "amid a jumble of words." On February 4 he wrote her of an obsessive mental picture: "the sea, the long, black dreary wintry sea. The sea is too pitiless and now has become the hunting place of pitiless men, our men and theirs." Once he himself had run to enlist, and he still thought it "more noble to thus adventure than to lose your soul in commerce"; but the war now has no glamour for him: "I smell the stench of wounds that may not heal." Probably thinking of the promise of *The Seven Arts,* he writes: "In my country something had begun to shine out. Now will come darkness." On February 5 his anguish reached a kind of climax.

Of course you must know that if war comes it will mean the practical death of all pure effort here in America just as it has meant that on the other side. Perhaps our best men here will be blighted just as their men have been. Hatred and prejudice will be in the saddle and we will have to wade through a more hopeless muddle of words and sentimentality than has been brought on by industrialism. This kind of war, is I suppose, industrialism gone mad.

I had some dreams when the war began. I saw in fancy men marching shoulder to shoulder and doing great deeds. Instead, as you know men have gone into the ground and there is only the horrible, mechanical guns and the deafness and the stench of decaying bodies.

Well, I wont go on! Thinking of it has driven me near to madness.

The war had come home to Anderson at last, turning excessive optimism to more realistic, though still excessive, despair. The dream of failure, which implied a better future, was one thing; the nightmare of failure, which negated the artist's hopes, was another.

Yet his despair was about to swing back as quickly to something like exaltation. During this January when he passed through so many moods, he and Waldo Frank had been getting further acquainted in preparation for an approaching face-to-face meeting. Now on February 2 he wrote Frank that he would be in New York for a week beginning Monday the twelfth and could be found at the office of the John Lane Company at 120 West Thirty-second Street. Although no record of the transaction has been discovered, he was probably going to New York to discuss and sign a contract for the publication of *Marching Men*. While he was there, he was certainly planning to meet the men around *The Seven Arts*. Whatever his expectations may have been, the reality of that meeting would exceed them. Going to New York at this point was as momentous and fortunate a journey as had been his return from Elyria to Chicago just four experience-crammed years earlier.

7

The New York Attraction

1.

On Monday morning, February 12, 1917, Anderson met Jefferson Jones at the New York office of John Lane Company. Since *Windy McPherson's Son* was selling into its second printing, author and publisher must have had little difficulty in agreeing on the contract, presumably made at this time, for the publication of *Marching Men.* Sometime during that day, business over, Anderson phoned Waldo Frank at *The Seven Arts,* and from then on through the rest of the week New York became one exciting whirl of people, talk, sensations. Sherwood looked up Alys Bentley, then in the city, and doubtless visited Karl, Helen, and their two children at their place in Westport, Connecticut; but the really memorable meetings were with Waldo and the other men around the magazine that had become a home for his new writings.[1]

These men saw different things in their midwestern visitor, and to more or less extent each saw rightly. To Frank, who admitted the figure was exaggerated, it seemed Anderson had "come out of the West with a cornfield in each hand and a wide open sky in his brow." Van Wyck Brooks, small, shy but with warm blue eyes above a bristling little mustache, was less grand in speech but glad to meet a writer who appeared to embody many of the artistic impulses Brooks felt were needed to bring American literature of age; and he was much struck by Anderson's naturalness, his "fresh healthy mind and his true Whitmanian feeling for comradeship." The more businesslike James Oppenheim was also very friendly, but when Waldo and Van Wyck brought Sherwood into his editor's office, Oppenheim was surprised to find, not the self-effacing Winesburg grotesque he had expected, but "an up-and-coming ad man, with a stiff collar, and a bit of the super-salesman air." The writer from Chicago was taking no chances until he learned what the New Yorkers were going to be like.[2]

He soon found that he could relax into his easy outward manner with them, though underneath he was intently eager for each meeting and experience. It was, he would subsequently write Bab, as if he had been temporarily "lifted out" of his Chicago life and were "running to meet and to know new people." He was warmed and grateful at his reception by the *Seven Arts* men, who responded to what Brooks would call "his beautiful humility, his lovely generosity" with affectionate praise of his work and a willingness to listen to his theories of art and his stories of Midwest people. As much as they had time for, which seemed all too little, he and Waldo walked the New York streets together and talked, or sat and talked at the magazine's office or in the Thirtieth Street apartment where Frank lived with Margaret Naumburg, the experimentalist in children's education whom he had married only two months earlier. Years later Frank remembered Anderson's physical appearance at that time, describing him rather floridly as "a large man with a great surf of hair on his impressive head. His features were broad, crude-cut like the not quite finished work of a genial woodcarver, yet exaggeratedly, almost femininely tender, and his eyes had both an animal distance and a depth of human subtlety and candor." Anderson's eyes, memorable to so many people, were recalled by Paul Rosenfeld, sensitive appreciator of the "newness" in music and the other arts, who was giving much of his time to helping Waldo on the magazine. A few weeks earlier Rosenfeld had read *Windy McPherson's Son* straight through in one enthralled day's sitting; and having met Sherwood at the Franks's apartment, he took him one noon to the Yale Club where, over a lingering lunch, Rosenfeld talked with this "broad-chested kind of individual whose wavy-haired, bullety-cheeked head and warm eyes, color of iodine, by turns resembled those of an actor, a racetrack-sport, a salesman, a Shelleyesque poet and half the population of rural America." Writing of this occasion shortly after Anderson's death some twenty-five years later, Rosenfeld recounted the impact Anderson made on him that day in early 1917.

With an elbow on the cloth, one paw supporting his head while the other occasionally and delicately plucked at some grapes, my guest regaled me first with the tale of a female Falstaff up in Michigan, then with a strong recent impression of Randolph Bourne, "the only man whose political talk ever had interested him." I began telling him about another brilliant young fellow, the pianist and composer Leo Ornstein; of his conception of universal sympathy as the possible goal of existence. "Still, how are you going to feel in sympathy with policemen?" suddenly I asked, only half jocose, glancing through the window across coppery rooves at the emerging image of something beefy on a sidewalk, wooden in its blue uniform, harboring readily inflammable brutality. Hatred of those physical brethren, "New York's finest," was one of the apparently irreducible remnants of a childhood.

Anderson leaned back, laughing, "Oh!" he drawled, "I see them when they reach home at night. I see them taking off their boots. Their feet hurt them."

Thereupon Rosenfeld had a flash image of a Chicago policeman kneading his shoeless foot in the kitchen of his tenement home and became "sharply aware of the presence of an amazing force in the peasant-like and highly civilized being over the table, and its amazing mode of operation." Fueling that force in Anderson, he decided, was "a life-long uninhibited approach to ordinary people and a phenomenally keen faculty of observation."[3]

James Oppenheim and Anderson would never get beyond the brief acquaintance stage. As for Brooks, Sherwood much admired his incisive, adventurous mind and for a few years wrote to him occasionally; yet with mixed diffidence and resentment he acutely sensed something withholding on Brooks's part in personal relationships. Rosenfeld he grew close to, especially in the early 1920s when that small, sad-eyed, sensitive man repeatedly proved his generous spirit toward him and other trail-breaking artists; but with Waldo Frank, the man who had "discovered" him for *The Seven Arts,* Sherwood made a mutual discovery of friendship. For Frank the meeting with Anderson and their subsequent association would be of emotional and ideological importance, emotion and ideas being in him closely linked. To the younger man, an easterner who actually knew Europe better than most of what lay west of the Hudson, "Sherwood Anderson was America; the discovery of him was an exhilarating part of my discovery of my own country." Frank admired Anderson, though not uncritically, as an older, more experienced person and as a dedicated artist, but even more he admired him and his "luminous prose" as the embodiment of what he had been seeking for through the magazine. In this personification of "Mid-America" Frank found a needed complement, as their frequent correspondence and occasional meetings over the next two or three years would indicate; shortly they began to address each other as "brother."[4]

Looking back during the next few months on that magical week in New York, Anderson had a complex reaction to his whole momentous experience. Immediately after his return to Chicago on or around February 18, he was still almost overwhelmed with the excitement of having met so many new people who openly expressed admiration for what he had achieved as artist and confidence in what he would achieve; and he wrote Bab that he would "probably go to New York to live one of these days" to be near "the busy intellectual life that goes on there." He felt immensely grateful for the "good and wholesome" sense of a sustaining affection these people had for him, a "world of love" that filled him with a mountain-top kind of gladness and made him want to "write madly, joyfully, opening new veins of life and experience." Along with this renewed self-confidence and artistic stimulations, however, he had, as he wrote Frank on his return to Chicago, "an odd feeling of reverence and humbleness" of the willingness of the *Seven Arts* men "to listen to my provincial point of view." Very deeply, if only in part of himself, he did feel provincial— not just as the midwesterner on the easterner's home ground, but provincial as the relatively uncultivated, middle-aged businessman with a small-town background, little formal education, and no particular gift for analytic thought, a provincial thrown by lucky accident with men who were from a secure social class, who were well educated, articulate thinkers, and who, though years younger than he, could already speak with an authority based mostly on immersion in European cultural traditions, on first-hand acquaintance with the international stir toward new art, and on a commitment as strong as his own to discovering the true soul of America. Even a year or so later he would humbly retain the feeling that Frank and Brooks were "more civilized" than he, more "fixed and real" than his "wavering and uncertain" self. Referring specifically at this later time to Waldo and Tennessee but including Brooks as well, he would confess to sometimes feeling, "in view of the affections" all three gave him, that he was "like a crude woodsman that has been received into the affection of princes."[5]

But if Anderson felt rather apologetically that he was the humble, immature provincial before the sophisticated eastern intellectuals, he at the same time felt genuinely and strongly that in ways he was superior to them and that they had quite rightly deferred to him during his visit. If he was older, less educated, less traveled than they, he was more experienced in and thus more representative of American life. It was he who had written *Windy McPherson's Son;* other reviews besides "Emerging Greatness" had praised him as a spokesman for Mid-America. Even before coming to New York he had revealed his combined defensiveness and self-assertion when he wrote to Frank that "I want to know many little subtle things you know and that I do not know, and I want to tell you things, make you feel things concerning life and writing that I have felt and that you have not felt." If he had something "rank and vulgar" in himself that Frank had escaped, there was "something reeking and vulgar about life" that the younger man hadn't got at. It was apparently during the February visit that an incident had revealed to Waldo the ambivalent attitude of this new friend who had shrewdly observed that both of them needed "growth, but in what different directions."

And to him, his New York friends . . . represented *le grand monde* of intellect and culture. Nevertheless, although respectful, he was reserved; although impressed, he was suspicious. I recall walking up Fifth Avenue with him, one sunny day; as the throngs of shoppers tided over us, he suddenly broke his silence, "All these people," he said, "simply *do not count.*" He was comparing them, unfavorably, in his mind with the lost and fumbling men, the frantic girls, the inarticulate mothers of his stories.[6]

In January, Anderson had felt a pressing need to settle on a more definite subject matter and a clearer self-image as writer. The February visit to New York was catalytic. Under the stimulus of his exciting and gratifying reception there and the tension of this dual response of humbleness and pride, he did begin to open up "new veins of life and expression." Immediately upon his return to Chicago around February 18, he suddenly and for the first time in his career began composing free-verse poetry. By the twenty-sixth of that month he was writing Bab that he could not tell her "how deeply this inclination to song has taken hold of me," and he either enclosed with this letter or had already sent her copies of some of these "songs." Feeling "like one who has been climbing up a steep hill and has got out upon a broad wind-swept place," he poured out the poems. Soon he began to refer to them playfully in the correspondence he had resumed with Frank, though the chief literary matter discussed by the two men in the final days of February was the best way to handle a group of ten or a dozen essays on the task of the novelist, which Sherwood had previously written and five of which would be published in the May issue of *The Seven Arts* under the title "From Chicago." By March 5 Anderson had completed "about twenty" of his songs, he wrote Frank, and he sent along typed copies of two for his friend to look at. Shortly he mailed off a second group of songs, this time submitting them for possible acceptance for the magazine. By April 5 he had written about forty poems in all. The American declaration of war on Germany the next day spurred him to begin a group of five songs about the war, culminating in the long "Mid-American Prayer," which he wrote on the morning of April 19 and sent off to Frank "hot"—that is, unrevised—from his Brooks Building office later that day. This poem, a plea that the suffering of war might cleanse the spirit of America and bring forth a greater sense of brotherhood, he liked so much that he urged Waldo, before publishing it in the magazine, to have it printed as a *Seven Arts* pamphlet and sent out to subscribers and the newspapers and "spread over the country." Thereafter the poetic outpouring quickly slowed, the last poems dating from late April or perhaps early May. Within a space of about two and a half months he had written some fifty "songs," a speed of composition that suggests the push of creative energy behind them.[7]

As the songs themselves evidence, this push was associated with his adoption of a role, that of prophetic bard. Well before his New York visit he had been searching for appropriate ways to express his time and place, and at least two of the seventeen poems he wrote first clearly relate to that earlier search. "Song of Theodore," echoes a December 1916 letter to Bab in describing the writer as one who, by the act of putting words on paper, achieves both self-purification and a symbolic lovemaking with all the men and women of America; "Hosanna," of course, merely revises into free verse form that prose hymn to the cornfields, which had been part of a January letter to her. But his fully conscious adoption of the role of prophetic bard was more immediately a result of the New York visit and his reaction to it. Such a role was encouraged in him by his new friends— if they regarded him as the voice of Mid-America, then the voice of Mid-America he should and would be. As bard, furthermore, he could display some of his best qualities—his intuitiveness, his quick, deep rapport with people, his sense of having lived the American experience—and could minimize his limitations as he perceived them—his lack of formal education, his provincialism, his tendency to be uncertain rather than fixed and determined. The public role of bard was also a private means of coping constructively with the intense, conflicting emotions evoked by the whole New York experience, the mingled humbleness and pride, uneasiness and self-confidence. A number of these earliest poems relate almost explicitly to Anderson's ambivalent reaction to the *Seven Arts* men. "Chicago," for example, expresses the humble aspect of his response, for in the poem the singer himself personifies the city, rising up among the cornfields both as "a confused child in a confused world" and as an old man incapable of song. On the other hand, in "Manhattan"—the title is explicitness itself— the poet self-confidently embodies Mid-America:

I am of the West, the long West of the sunsets. I am of the deep fields where the corn grows. The sweat of apples is in me. I am the beginning of things and the end of things.

From "the place of the cornfields," the poet declares, he had gone into the city, where men and women had received him affectionately. For all their affection, however, he sees that the men are old, weary, and in pain; and bearing their weariness easily with him, the robust poet returns "laughing and singing" to the cornfields.[8]

Confused child, impotent old man, or culture-hero could be temporary guises from poem to poem of the same thing, the prophetic bard, who could incorporate them into a single style, the elements of which lay ready to hand from Anderson's own reading. Untrained and uninterested in using conventional poetic forms, he turned quite spontaneously to free verse, finding his models less in the free verse experiments going on around him than in the Bible and in Whitman, his own and Frank's and Brooks's favorite American poet. The Bible he drew on for a few echoes of Genesis and the Song of Solomon, for an occasional reference to the

Christ story, for the prose rhythms and some of the language, and for the prophetic tone generally. He drew on Whitman for the long, unrhymed lines, the occasional catalog of names, and a diction that combined the declamatory, the colloquial, and the lyrical, though in his word choice he tended toward the general, the abstract, and the vague where Whitman would more often have been specific and concrete. He took also from Whitman the notion of the multiple person behind the "I" of the poem, which included the poet himself, the representative of America, and the inspired seer—child, old man, culture-hero—who articulates the nation's past, present, and future. This notion of the many-personed bard he arrived at very early. In "Song of Cedric the Silent," which is among the first seventeen poems written, "Cedric" speaks of himself as "The Son of Irwin and Emma I am, here in America, come into a kingship"; prophesies that "Into the land of my fathers, from Huron to Keokuk, beauty shall come—out of the black ground, out of the deep black ground"; and concludes, "Cedric . . . Give your life, give your soul to America now." There is no doubt who Cedric is in the poem nor that he speaks as bard and prophet.

Role and style suited what Cedric-Sherwood had to "give" in this late winter and spring of 1917 after his intense conversations with the *Seven Arts* men, who like him looked toward a great national renewal provided the United States could keep from being drawn into the European conflict. Although the poems are for the most part undistinguished as poetry, their major themes develop consistently, if unsystematically, a set of ideas making up a species of myth about America, a myth that Anderson would draw on from time to time in his writing over the next few years. Generalizing in bardic manner from his own experience, he gives his myth a quasi-historical dimension by envisaging three stages of national development. Nostalgically the bard recalls a former American golden age of small town life, a patriarchal period in the Midwest when "Our fathers in the village streets / Had flowing beards and they believed." This was the "quite biblical" time when the old craftsmen were close to the soil, "talked of old gods" to listening youths, and passed on the lore of craft and land to succeeding generations, a time furthermore when the inhabitants of each small town lived together in secure, unconscious harmony. This age or stage was destroyed by the "terrible engine" of industrialism, which has produced the bard's city, "Chicago triumphant—factories and marts and the roar of machines—horrible, terrible, ugly and brutal." Here is modern life emblemized, a cityscape of "disorder and darkness," where men and women are corrupted by money or bestialized by lack of it, where any sense of community is lost in vicious self-interest. The war is an intensification of industrialism's antihuman qualities; it is "industrialism gone mad." In "We Enter In," presumably written sometime from April 6 on

and hence among the last of the songs, the prophet-poet accuses himself
and his countrymen directly:

> Do we not know that we ourselves have failed?
> Our valley wide, our long green fields
> We have bestrewn with our own dead.
> In shop and mart we have befouled our souls.
> Our corn is withered and our faces black
> With smoke of hate.

Now America must go through the darkest spiritual death before it can
hope to emerge, as it may, into a new golden age, a third stage in which the
unrecoverable order of the past and the inescapable disorder of the present are transcended by that order of the future in which community and
love will prevail.

Like the visions of more gifted prophet-poets, Anderson's is more concerned with prophetic images than with such prosaic matters as accurate
history or social dynamics. In this he agreed with the *Seven Arts* men, who,
as the existence of the magazine demonstrated, believed that America
would be transformed by a national change of heart, by a great spiritual-
cultural awakening prompted, not by political action but by the urging of
artist and thinkers. What Anderson needed for his role as prophet-bard
was an appropriate major image that would embody his message to America. Almost as soon as the "inclination to song" took hold of him, he
found that image in a master symbol, the Midwest fields of corn; and as
the poems flowed from him, he developed, though again unsystematically,
a variety of meanings for that symbol. On the simplest level the cornfields
merely differentiate Mid-America from the East as a section of the nation,
but, as in "Manhattan," they also stand more complexly for those cultural
differences between the sections that Anderson sensed and which Frank
did as well when he exaggeratedly wrote of his friend's coming to New
York "out of the West with a cornfield in each hand." Beyond this, however, the cornfields took on for Anderson a semireligious meaning, as in,
for instance, "The Cornfields," one of the very earliest of his songs and the
one he would later select to open *Mid-American Chants*. Here, in a mixture of Old and New Testament language, the prophet-bard describes
himself as having by the power of his song broken the chains that bound
him and that still bind the people of his time because, gathered in cities,
they have forgotten "the long fields and the standing corn." Dying to his
old life, he is reborn through the corn itself and resolves to "renew in my
people the worship of gods" by setting up in the cornfields the "sacred
vessel" of his song, which would bring "love into the hearts of my
people." Thus through the theme of death and rebirth, a theme obviously

implicit in the corn's natural cycle of growth out of the buried seed, Anderson could suggest the power of art to transform a nation.

Having found his major symbol of the cornfields, Anderson used it frequently in the poems he wrote in March and April of 1917. As one who had written in his first novel about "the force of sex," he might occasionally refer to the cornfields within a sexual context, but such references are generalized and diffuse. He was concerned with social, not individual, passion; the planting of corn seeds in the earth would stand, not for the physical act of sex but for the impregnation of minds with the message of rebirth. This much one might, so to speak, expect of a prophet-bard; but one might not expect that in his repeated images of the cornfields he would almost wholly disregard most of the physical, sensory aspects of corn and emphasize a single element—the orderly planting of the cornfields and the growth of corn in straight, deep, even endless, orderly rows. "Spring Song," for example, one of the best of the poems and presumably written in response to the actual planting season, speaks of

> Spring. God in the air above old fields.
> Farmers marking fields for the planting of the corn.
> Fields marked for corn to stand in long straight aisles.

Again, in "Song of the Middle World," probably one of the last to be written, the poet has "been to the Dakotas when the fields were plowed" and has seen "Promise of corn, / Long aisles running into the dawn and beyond / To the throne of gods." The implied meaning of this orderliness is clear enough; the physical order of the cornrows is analogous to a metaphysical order of "the gods," who represent the essentially religious harmony of the community-to-be of human brotherhood and love.[9]

But Anderson's repeated, almost exclusive emphasis on the symmetry of the cornfields seems to be more than a poetic device for conveying a social message; it suggests rather, or in addition, that order had an obsessive value for him reflecting his deep personal need for a stability of self he lacked. Writing to Van Wyck Brooks a year later, shortly after he had published his songs as *Mid-American Chants,* he himself confessed as much.

In the chants I reached into my own personal muttering, half insane and disordered, and tried to take out of them a little something ordered. You should see how I clutched at the ordered cornfields, insisted on them to myself, took them as about the only thing I could see.

By assuming the role of prophet-bard he met the immediate emotional situation in which he found himself on his return from New York; but paradoxically, had he been fully self-secure at the time he wrote his songs, he need not have made so direct a response to that exciting and unsettling visit, need not have adopted the bardic role at all, need not have deflected even momentarily into experiments with poetry a talent better suited for experiments in prose. At best the bardic role provided him no more than a temporary solution to his basic problem of how to survive as a steadily creative writer, that condition which alone represented order for him, when his outer and inner lives threatened his creativity with so much disorder.[10]

2.

In the midst of songwriting and bursts of activity at the advertising agency Anderson began planning a three-month summer vacation back at Alys Bentley's camp on Upper Chateaugay Lake. Since Tennessee had to stay in Chicago until July 1, he in early March began urging Frank to come spend some time with him in June, offering the beauty of lake and mountains and the chance for long walks and talks. They had much to talk about, Anderson increasingly felt later in the spring after *The Seven Arts* had turned down two more of the Winesburg tales along with a story called "Impotence," which Frank had already refused once before, and all of the "songs" offered the magazine except "Chicago" and "Mid-American Prayer." Waldo was too analytic in his thinking, Anderson wrote him; he needed to learn to be more relaxed, more intuitive about life, less given to pronouncements about prose and poetry, especially the pronouncement that prose was Sherwood's true "road," not mythic poetry like the songs. What did it matter if the poet wrote the poems only for himself? "I have opened the door of failure a thousand times. I know that road. It doesn't frighten me." Despite his own pronouncement, however, he would not refuse to publish some of the songs when he had a chance to do so.[11]

Early in May, shortly before he left the Cass Street lodging house for good and moved in temporarily with Tennessee at 12 East Division Street, he ceased writing songs completely and plunged into a final revision of the manuscript of *Marching Men* before it was due at the John Lane Company. Nevertheless something of the singing impulse carried over consciously into his present view of the novel. By May 12 he was well into the revision, and he wrote Bab how the book "aroused and stirred" him. "In a way," he told her, "the whole big message of my life is bound into that volume," for working on the book took him back to the time when he was trying to write it, "crudely and brokenly." It had been "a great song" to him then, "a big terrible song," too strong for him to hold; but now "the story is beautifully simple and will start a song in many hearts." By May 25 the revision was complete and the novel sent on to Jefferson Jones in New York.[12]

A few days earlier, on the evening of May 19, Sherwood and Tennessee had been invited to a small dinner party at the North Side home of Burton and Hazel Rascoe. The hardworking, quick-tempered Rascoe, who held several posts simultaneously on the *Chicago Tribune* and would soon become literary editor, commented afterwards at length in his diary on his special guest. In honor of the occasion Anderson wore "dinner dress" in the conventional manner, but he impressed his host with his less formal qualities, as "a man with a marvelous softness in his voice, kindly, contemplative eyes, an intense emotional capacity and a calm manner." After dinner an argument over basic personal attitudes arose among Rascoe, Anderson, and the third man present, Lewis Galantière, then head clerk at a Chicago bookstore and a good friend of the other two. Mainly to draw Anderson out, Rascoe argued in favor of a "modified Nietzscheism," and, as he recorded in his diary,

Sherwood said I intellectualized life too much, that I sought causes and traced effects, that I did not "lie fallow" enough. "My whole philosophy of life is made up," he said, "of the contention that two and two do not make four, that the mathematician's idea of life is wrong. You believe that two and two make four and act on that principle."

Rascoe felt that Anderson had a great unconscious vanity and expected everyone to talk about his work, yet at the same time had

a beautiful idealism, a great depth of poetic feeling; he is more religious than I have been, even though he has never been to church. He said, in fact, that he believed he was an old-time Christian, that "Christ was righter than any man I know of." "What we need in this country is more sorrow, more prayer, more reliance upon something outside ourselves," he contended.

The conversation had got partly onto the war, and Anderson seems to have been, in effect, quoting to the group from his "Mid-American Prayer."[13]

When the revised *Marching Men* was off to the publisher, however, he had no desire either to brood on the war or to go back to writing songs; his mind went toward future projects, not past ones, and he was mainly concerned with winding up affairs at the office before the long summer. He had already arranged for Waldo to come up to the camp in the Adirondacks for the week of June 10 to 16, advised him to bring some warm clothes along with his bathing suit because it might be cool there so early in the season, and had given him explicit instructions about sending word as to his time of arrival so that Sherwood could get over from Merrill to Lyon Mountain to meet his train. On Monday, May 28, during his remaining week at the office he took to lunch a young revolutionist who asked for advice about the war. Reluctant to advise, especially when he was not certain how he felt himself, Anderson spoke first of how war threatened "the sacred old things—the dreams of love and orderly movement forward," then of how inflexible of principle the leading radicals had become. "In embracing their truth," so positively, Anderson said with his Winesburg people in mind, "they have become grotesque." Writing about the incident to Bab, he went on to assert:

Now I hold it to be true that no truth is the exact truth that is not also a lie. All of life lies in the gesture. Nothing must become so precious that it cannot be thrown away. To kill men's bodies seems to me the last thing. There is something physically and morally nauseating in the thought.

But here the matter lies. My brothers are in this war. It is a disease, a terrible thing. Would one refuse to go into a hospital and serve because millions of men lay in the hospital suffering from some horrible disease?

It was no advice to the young revolutionist, Anderson realized, to say, as he did, borrowing a figure from "We Enter In": "My brothers are in the flood and I give my soul to them. I fling it into the black water." But the young man could have understood that the older one had now come to accept the war as an evil condition to be lived through rather than actively opposed on principle, as Waldo Frank, who was of draft age, had courageously, even if "grotesquely," long since determined to do.[14]

For the most part, however, the war seemed far away during that second summer in the Adirondacks. When Anderson arrived alone at Chateaugay Lake around June 4, the weather was still cold and wet, and mornings were uncomfortable in the unheated Tenthouse. Sue de Lorenzi was already at Killoleet camp close by, fortunately, and after his usual early morning walk Sherwood would beg her to let him come into her snugly built, shingle-sided cottage to get warm. He would sit by the fire, his big wet mackinaw steaming, until he felt thawed out and would then go over to her desk in the corner by the entrance door and say that he wanted to write. She liked to keep some inspirational poems and mottoes—Kipling's "If" and others—on the desk and around it. With a lordly gesture of his arm he would say, "Take them all away, Sue;" and when she had as usual taken them away, he would sit down and lose himself for the rest of the morning in his writing. The relationship they had established the previous summer continued for the most part amiably, and the big brother could wheedle help from her by casually exerting his charm or by merely expecting assistance. One day toward the end of that first month he shouted over to her from the Tenthouse: "Sue, come over here. Bring your hammer and screwdriver." When she appeared, he told her he was supposed to put up some shelves in one corner because Tennessee was soon coming. Where should he put them? Advice led to more advice, and soon the small, feminine, capable Sue found herself helping her big, strong neighbor put up his shelves.[15]

Before Tennessee arrived, however, Waldo Frank came for his week's stay with Sherwood in the Tenthouse. It was a week of almost uninterrupted talk. Mornings they might walk the country roads in the hills overlooking the lake with its little island in the middle. For meals they ate, as customary, at Leta Bentley's camp, The Outlet. Each afternoon Sherwood, Waldo, and Sue would go down to the beach beside Leta's boat landing, where Sue would dream in the sun paying no attention as the two men talked or read Sherwood's writings aloud in storyteller fashion. Conventional in her literary tastes, she had once told Sherwood that she just couldn't read his stuff, a judgment that had not seemed to disturb him in the least. Usually after one of the lakeside readings Sherwood and Waldo would "experiment" on her by asking her opinion of the story, and she would respond out of her inattention that it shouldn't be published. Once, however, the two men broke through her self-possession when she proudly told them about the elegant Victorian neoclassic mansion that her wealthy Uncle Martin and Aunt Susie Beiger had built in Mishawaka, Indiana, where Sue had grown up. Her uncle had died before it was fully completed, and shortly after his death General Lew Wallace, author of *Ben-Hur* and an acquaintance of Aunt Susie, called on the widow. Aunt Susie told Wallace how she was going to have a painter come from Chicago— as she in fact did—and paint scenes from the life of Christ as murals along the tops of the walls of the library, the scenes to be as described in Wallace's novel. When Sue finished her account, much to her chagrin Sherwood and Waldo burst into great laughter and then began to argue hotly as to whose story it would be. "Now, it's going to be my story, Waldo." "No, it's mine. I'm going to use it." Both thought it absurd, she realized, for a well-to-do person to have paintings of Christ's life in her home.

Anderson's reaction in particular struck Sue as typical of his "socialistic" attitude toward the rich, his scorn for them, and his sympathy for workers and poor people. Later in the summer he would scold her for not working herself and for living easily on an allowance from wealthy Aunt Susie. Sue would do more good, he insisted half-seriously, if she walked the country roads selling artificial flowers for farm girls to wear in their hats; and once in the manner of one of his songs he exclaimed, though she did not know what he meant: "Oh, Sue, if only I could take you in my arms and fly up to the top of a mountain so that you could talk with the gods." His censure of her did not hurt their friendship more than momentarily, however, nor, when "jeweled" Aunt Susie bought Sue a car later in the summer, did it prevent him from enjoying rides in it with her. Their friendship even survived a yet more unpleasant situation that developed during Frank's week at Camp Owlyout. Waldo, physically attracted to Sue despite her conventional views on money and literature, made advances to her in her camp. Sue, who had expected that Waldo would treat her as a sister in Sherwood's way, told him that she considered him a gentleman and that if he didn't have respect for her, he should at least have respect for his wife. Waldo replied that he and Margaret had agreed to leave each other free for affairs. At this point a friend of Sue's (who had approached within hearing of Camp Killoleet) decided that she had better knock at the door, and Waldo left immediately. Both he and Sue spoke to Sherwood separately of the matter, Frank telling him that she had acted like a schoolgirl. Anderson, siding with him apparently on the belief that a sexual relationship would have been good for Sue, hurt her feelings by saying that she had acted stupidly. She refused to see Waldo again, and he, contrite, picked a big bouquet of flowers just before he left, took it to her door, and asked forgiveness.

Whether she then forgave Frank or not, she would remember him as he was one day when he and Sherwood together with herself and two other young women campers had sat out in the sun in front of her camp talking and she had taken a snapshot of them. In the photograph Frank wears unpressed trousers and a beat-up fedora, but his shirt, though open at the neck, is a white dress one, the combination of clothing and the intent eyes in the round unsmiling face suggesting the essentially city intellectual a bit out of place in the Adirondacks. Sherwood in the snapshot is as Sue would remember him in one of his serious moods. Sitting on a deck chair a little apart from and above Waldo and the two women, he is staring at a cigarette held loosely in his left hand with its big ringless fingers like those of a manual workman. His dark rumpled hair falls over his eyes, and his wide mouth is also unsmiling in his still firm-cheeked, rather oblong face. He wears a tweed jacket, corduroy trousers, and a sport shirt with a silk polka-dot scarf knotted around an almost Byronic collar. On his feet he wears, not high-laced shoes like Waldo's, but Bentley-style sandals. He is relaxed, comfortable, and at the moment quite gone inward into his own thoughts.

For Sherwood, if not entirely so for Sue and Waldo, the latter's visit had been a heartwarming success. He was somewhat put off by Frank's egotism in assuming himself to be one of America's important men and by his tendency to dominate life with his sharp, quick mind rather than letting it "flow" into him, but at the same time he admired Frank's intellectual acuteness and generous spirit. "Surely," he would write his friend soon after Waldo had taken the train for Plattsburgh and New York, "we will never grow so very far apart." With Frank gone he turned only desultorily to his writing, preferring instead to have a complete change from the pressures of the preceding winter and spring in Chicago. He loafed about, canoed on the lake, and spent whole afternoons merely lying on his back gazing at the water and the mountains. He liked being by himself, feeling himself into the landscape, and one day, as he wrote Bab, in an ecstatic moment

I ran into the woods. . . . I stretched myself out on the grass and sobbed like a woman for the glory and quiet of this place. Deep in the ground my roots and my gods lie, They are whispering to me.

Nevertheless toward the end of June he was gladly looking forward to the arrival of Tennessee for "her quiet, dignified companionship and for the thing in her that understands these hills and these soft quiet nights better than I." Even before she came, he had not been entirely idle; for he had begun doing the exercises and dancing three or four hours a day under Alys Bentley's domineering direction, and his body was rapidly toughening.[16]

Between Frank's departure and Tennessee's arrival, Dr. Trigant Burrow and his entourage returned to Lifwynn cottage across the lake from the Bentley camp. Burrow was unhappy to have missed Frank, for he had been reading Waldo's recently published first novel, *The Unwelcome Man*, and he had been much excited by its use of Freudian concepts. Several times in late June and again in early July after Tennessee had come, Sherwood with or without her would canoe over to Lifwynn for a Southern-style breakfast of sausages and waffles with the Burrows, after which the two men would go off to tramp the country roads for long talks about human lives as viewed by the scientist and the artist. One morning apparently near the middle of July, Sherwood paddled over by himself, and after breakfast Mrs. Burrow put up a lunch for him and her husband. This time the men took the two-and-a-half-mile hike to Rocky Brook. "We sat there beside the brook," Burrow would recall years later, "and talked the livelong day, and our talk was entirely along psychoanalytic lines. It was a delightful midsummer day and I have thought back upon it many times." He could not have looked back upon the talk without some unhappiness, for it became a day-long argument that brought an end to such meetings between the two men for the rest of the summer.[17]

Part of the difficulty lay in Burrow's proposal to "sike" Anderson, that is, to psychoanalyze him, but Anderson's resistance seems to have been less the usual one of the prospective analysand than the result of a fundamental difference between the two men as to the function and goal of psychoanalysis. Each man would use that day's "rather hectic talk" in one of his characteristic writings, Anderson sometime after his return to Chicago in a subtle, intricately structured story, "Seeds," and Burrow nearly eight years later in a scholarly paper titled "Psychoanalytic Improvisations and the Personal Equation." In his paper Burrow summarizes the disagreement "as to the merits of the psychoanalytic aim" that had so divided the scientist and the artist that bright summer day.

Anderson argued that human life was not a thing to be delved into with surgical probes—that it was not to be got at that way. Needless to say, I argued as stoutly that the surgical probe was the most wonderful of all human inventions and that it was the only way to lay open to health and growth the sick personalities of our human kind.

What Burrow first came to understand over the intervening years, as he continued to develop from a fairly orthodox Freudian to a more indepen- dent investigator of the "social neurosis," was that in their quarrel each man had been impelled to argue as he did because of the "personal equa- tion," that is, every individual's "private predilections. . . . Each of us was out for himself. I in my egotism was out for understanding life and help- ing humanity (God help it!). Anderson was out for "many marriages" and for helping himself."

What Burrow further came to believe, however, was that though artist and scientist still would differ as to the possibility of curing the neurosis of an individual or a society—both together making up the "universal ill- ness," as the narrator of "Seeds" puts it—the psychoanalyst, unless he de- velops the objectivity of the laboratory situation, merely meets his pa- tient's neurotic improvisations with improvisations equally dependent on his own personal equation, "improvisations of unconscious artistry" essentially no different from those "of the admittedly creative artist." In this view, Burrow concludes in 1925,

the positions of Mr. Anderson and myself were really the same. Anderson was as bent on understanding life and on the service of man and his personal relationships as I, and I was bent on the sheer experience of life and on helping myself to such personal relationships as custom doth not stale in their infinite variety as was Mr. Anderson.[18]

Perhaps the most extraordinary aspect of Anderson's story "Seeds," is that within only months after that July day, Anderson had thought his way through the experience and come out to a conclusion very similar to Bur- row's, although until the two men reestablished a friendly relationship through later letters, he had been "a little sarcastic," as he would write Burrow, in his thoughts of him.

My difficulty lay in the fact that I continually thought of you as one who thought they had found truth. What I thought to be your truth I could not accept for my- self and perhaps I was angry at the thought you could accept it. I have thought of the science to which you have given so much of your life as one that would very well do wonders in making life and its difficulties more understandable but that one person could in any way cure the evils in life for another seemed to me impossible.

In "Seeds," there is no doubt that the author agrees with the first-person narrator when, as he and the psychoanalyst walk a country road in hills above a lake, the narrator declares that "It is given to no man to venture far along the road of lives" and that the "universal illness" the psychoanalyst pretends to cure cannot be cured. Yet though the narrator is right in this way, he is not right in others, being in fact for the most part as imperceptive and dogmatic as any grotesque who seizes on a single truth. Though the psychoanalyst may be wrong in maintaining that "'What you say can't be done can be done,'" he is right in crying out at the narrator

You think you understand, but you don't understand. . . . You cannot be so definite without missing something vague and fine. You miss the whole point. The lives of people are like young trees in a forest. They are being choked by climbing vines. The vines are old thoughts and beliefs planted by dead men. I am myself covered by crawling creeping vines that choke me.

That the psychoanalyst is right in this analogy for psychic repression is confirmed when later in Chicago, LeRoy, a mediocre painter but potentially a fine writer because of his "understanding," tells the insensitive narrator of the "strange and terrible fate" of a young woman he has briefly helped after she had been made desperate for a man's love by too feminine an upbringing. "'The living force within [her] could not find expression,'" LeRoy sympathetically explains, paraphrasing Freud, and hence her sexuality manifested itself neurotically in both a desire to exhibit herself and a terror of being physically touched. When the narrator suggests that LeRoy could have become the woman's lover, the painter repeats the psychoanalyst's charge that the narrator misses the point by being so sure of himself, and describes the young woman as a young tree from whom a climbing vine "had shut out the light."

She needed a lover and at the same time a lover was not what she needed. The need of a lover was, after all, a quite secondary thing. She needed to be loved, to be long and quietly and patiently loved. To be sure she is a grotesque, but then all the people in the world are grotesques. We all need to be loved. What would cure her would cure the rest of us also. The disease she had is, you see, universal. We all want to be loved and the world has no plan for creating our lovers.

Then, having reasserted the difference between psychoanalyst and artist, between Burrow and Anderson, LeRoy asserts their identity by echoing the psychoanalyst's words and recognizing the all-pervasiveness of the personal equation.

I am myself like the woman. I am covered with creeping crawling vine-like things. I cannot be a lover. I am not subtle or patient enough. I am paying old debts. Old thoughts and beliefs—seeds planted by dead men—spring up in my soul and choke me.

Identity, not difference, is the concluding note of the story. Just as the psychoanalyst, wearied by the universal illness, had wished "'to be a leaf blown by the wind over hills,'" to die into the landscape and then be reborn clean, so the equally wearied LeRoy, who has been talking to the narrator in a park by Lake Michigan, "'would like to be dead and blown by the wind over limitless waters. . . . I want more than anything else in the world to be clean.'"[19]

Although "Seeds" was yet to be written, it retrospectively reinforces the conclusion that by the summer of 1917 Anderson had absorbed at least a layman's knowledge of Freudian theory. A steady reader, he nevertheless probably gained little of this knowledge from direct contact with the works of Freud, who was, after all, one of those analytic thinkers he tended to be suspicious of; in fact, Burrow, who was in a position and qualified to know, later asserted categorically, "I can say very definitely that Anderson did not read Freud." Like other writers, however, Sherwood always learned through his ears as well as his eyes, and the talks with Burrow leading up to the day-long argument, as well as the argument itself, would have been highly informative. Though "Seeds" is one of his few stories to reflect a specific acquaintance with Freudian psychodynamics, Anderson had of course demonstrated from the outset of his writing career an intense interest of his own in the conscious and unconscious workings of the human mind and in what he had called in *Windy* the "force of sex." Burrow would subsequently praise him, generously but genuinely, as "like Freud, a genius in his own right" and "a man of amazing intuitive flashes" and "uncanny insight." As late as the year before his death in 1950 Burrow, while agreeing that the writer might have been influenced by the talks with the psychoanalyst, could loyally reassert his conviction "that Sherwood Anderson was an original psychologist in his own right and, if he profited by any insights of mine, I also profited in no small measure by the exceptional insight of this literary genius."[20]

Retrospectively "Seeds" would also suggest the outline of a new artistic development shaping in Anderson in the summer of 1917. The songs of the preceding spring had been only the first of a series of literary experiments triggered by his meeting with the *Seven Arts* men. When he became caught up in writing again in August, he would increasingly explore the possibilities beyond the selective realism of *Windy McPherson's Son,* beyond even the minimal realism of the Winesburg tales, onward toward writing that was symbolic in form, subjective in content, mythic in implication. He would still write realistic pieces during the next few years, and he would never fully abandon realism, believing as he did throughout his career that the imagination must feed on reality or starve; yet now he would intensify his search for new ways in which the imagination might deal with the actual. So in "Seeds," for example, he would create a structure that would depend neither on chronology of event, as in *Windy McPherson's Son,* nor on a fluid movement back and forth in time until the story could suddenly stand still in some revealing moment, as in "Hands," but rather a structure that would depend on a subtlety elaborate web of corresponding scenes, recurrent motifs and symbols, verbal refrains that, like some of the more sophisticated ballads, echo without fully repeating. Reality is observable under or through the web. The psychoanalyst, the artist LeRoy, the sex-tormented woman, even the narrator are believably sketched fictional people; furthermore, their actions take place in actual, if barely suggested, settings—country road in the hills, Chicago lodging house, park by Lake Michigan. But a doctor and a painter linked only by separate acquaintance with a third person would obviously not speak with such similar words in "real life," and the settings function almost entirely to extend the theme, not to make one visualize the action but to make one feel the universality of the "universal illness." Because of this structure the story would approximate a self-contained, aesthetic object, did it not force one constantly to extrapolate its meaning inward upon the self and outward upon others.

In July of 1917, however, Anderson was writing little, instead letting such new creative developments, as was his custom, gestate slowly within him. He continued to let the days drift by. There were the small crises—a cow lay down in the garden he had helped to plant and flattened it, a fire broke out in the Tenthouse and some of the manuscript of the Winesburg stories, which he had brought along, was scorched. Traces of scorching were on the manuscript of "The Thinker," which he sent to Waldo, who accepted it for the September issue of *The Seven Arts.* Around the first of July Anderson wrote Frank the good news that *Poetry* would publish "a group of my western songs" in the August issue. It is not known when Harriet Monroe had become interested in his poems, nor whether he sent her some on his own initiative or at her request; but late in June or very early in July she had written him suggesting that *Poetry* print six poems in one issue—"Song of Stephen the Westerner," "American Spring Song," "Evening Song," "Song of the Drunken Business Man," "Song of Industrial America," "A Visit"—and offering $75 for the group. A few days later Anderson replied, agreeing to the amount of payment and to her selections, which "suits me very well for my debut as a singer." She should call the sequence "West Winds." He was not satisfied with that title, however, and on July 9 he sent off a postcard to tell her, "I really prefer *Mid-American Songs,*" though she should use her own judgment as to title. Miss Monroe would, in fact, give the second title to the group when it appeared, but on or about the ninth she wrote that the poems must wait for the September issue. Anderson at once responded that he hoped they would come out then for a particular reason: "I may issue a book of songs soon and would like ground broken by publication through such good channels as Poetry as early as possible." Already he was considering the possibility that his third work with the John Lane Company would be, as he wrote to Miss Monroe in mid-September, a "book of verse or 'emotional prose' or whatever it may be called. . . ."[21]

As the July days drifted away, Sherwood danced, loafed about, recalled the talks he had had with Waldo, and looked forward to the latter's promised visit to Chicago, perhaps at Christmastime. His novel *Immaturity,* abandoned back in January, began to grow again in his mind, though for awhile he made no move to start writing. Then "scenes and situations" formed more and more in his imagination, and by mid-August he had suddenly begun working on the novel each day. Rather like a pregnant woman, he at last wrote Frank, he went about "scarcely speaking to people," his mind filled with "Scenes, incidents and conversation." By late August *Immaturity* had turned away from describing the industrialization of a small town toward depicting that town's pastoral past. What Anderson now wrote would not lead toward his future novel *Poor White;* instead, two chapters of it would, apparently, be adapted as the first two parts of the four-part Winesburg tale, "Godliness." Having probably borrowed the Bentley name from Alys and Leta for one of his major characters, he was working in a mood that combined his present existence with the bardic image of his songs.

As I have loafed and danced and waited in the sun up here this summer, a peculiar thing has taken place in me. My mind has run back and back to the time when men tended sheep and lived a nomadic life on hillsides and by little talking streams. I have become less and less the thinker and more the thing of earth and the winds. When I awake at night and the wind is howling, my first thought is that the gods are at play in the hills here. My new book, starting with life on a big farm in Ohio, will have something of that flavor in its earlier chapters. There is a delightful old man, Joseph Bentley by name, who is full of old Bible thoughts and impulses.[22]

Working on this new narrative and writing to Waldo Frank, the conscientious objector to the war, made him think of the effect American military mobilization was having on artists and artistic expression. Frank's situation was far worse than his, he felt, for if the younger man were drafted, it might mean jail, where, to be sure, "the best men of our time" ought to be rather than to take part in the slaughter. Still Anderson showed special concern about art and the threat that it faced from the propagandists, who were corrupters of language like advertising men simply selling patriotism. Men like himself and Frank must stick to their art despite the distractions and dangers.

By the end of August, Anderson was half dreading, half anticipating his return to Chicago. He detested the thought of going back to writing "advertisements for plows, horse medicines, etc.," but even in the clamor of wartime, Chicago would also provide the stimulation and companionship of other men interested in the arts. Tennessee was staying on for a few weeks; she loved the Bentley camp and the lake, and had even tried unsuccessfully back in July to buy a little frame house with a porch up in the hills as a permanent summer place for the two of them. On the last day of August, Sherwood received the distressing news from Margaret Naumburg, who had been vacationing with her husband at an oceanside hotel near Gloucester, that Waldo had just had a serious operation. When on Sunday, September 2, Sherwood said goodbye to Tennessee and any remaining campers and caught the train at Lyon Mountain for the first stage of his trip back to Chicago, he was concerned about the coming year and about the health of his hospitalized "brother." At least he himself, as he rather tactlessly wrote Frank, was "in splendid physical shape" and would soon have some more stories for *The Seven Arts*. Then, too, advance copies of *Marching Men* would be along any day now. He was determined to make the coming winter a creative one.[23]

3.

Returning rested and energetic to Chicago, Anderson once more took up his advertising tasks, but during all his free moments he drove at writing *Immaturity*. Once again he was surprised and delighted to find, as he wrote Waldo, "that I always work better and most freely when conditions for working are the worst." Perhaps this was because the whole advertising firm busied itself with such utterly trivial matters under such constant deadlines that to preserve one's mental balance "one is compelled to create and sustain in his own mind a world of people who have significance." Daily, as he worked at his novel, this imagined world came to seem more definite and real to him, "to have height, breadth and thickness." Here, he lectured his slowly convalescing friend, was an illustration of how one could depend on imagination and intuition, as one could not on the merely rational, for right responses to life.

I have on several occasions heard you curse your own education and I begin to understand why. I suppose, for the most part, education consists in gathering confusing facts. These facts divert and occupy the mind. They prevent a man's falling back on something buried deep within himself.

If, instead of trying to dominate life, one let it simply flow into one, then the war and all the other outside forces antagonistic to the artist would only succeed in throwing the self more firmly back onto its "true level."

You see the real mind, the thing that is buried away in us must be a wonderful thing. I sometimes think that our minds really record every little thing we see and hear in life and that we only confuse and perplex ourselves by not trusting absolutely the knowledge that flows in to us.

Perhaps he was "talking like a fool," but the "weary trivialities" of the office were not touching him since because of *Immaturity* "I wake and sleep and dream in a world full of significance."[24]

Briefly he managed to sustain his work-absorbed mood, and by mid-September he had completed five chapters of *Immaturity* that were solid and satisfied him. Then his imperviousness to the growing war spirit in the country and to the "unclean" demands of his advertising job began to erode. One cold, gray September day with Tennessee still in the Adirondacks, he was struck, as he would often be, with "the universality of loneliness" and, wanting companionship, wrote Waldo of his sense of a war-distorted world: "A great city filled with misunderstanding, a world in which men and women live turning constantly toward hatred and misunderstanding." Before October was over, he had gone through a week of feeling "in a futile time and a good deal depressed," a bad spell from which in his emotionally changeable way he would shortly rebound into such high spirits that *Immaturity,* as he wrote Waldo, began in its "naive, gaudy splendor to ramble and stroll and stop to loaf and chatter about the most absurd and unexpected things in the world." Despite his expressed delight, however, he could not have been wholly easy in his mind that again the novel was headed nowhere.[25]

He had another reason for so rapidly losing the self-confident energy that the summer's rest had given him—the reception of his newly published work. The September issue of *Poetry* containing his six "Mid-American Songs" had "created some stir out here" and, he complained to Frank, "everyone abused me." He was particularly irritated that a newspaperman, amused by the line, "See the corn. How it aches," had called him "the chiropodist poet." Then on September 14 came the publication of *Marching Men.* Since *Windy* had sold very badly in England, the John Lane Company refused to chance an English edition of this second novel and put out only an American one in twenty-five hundred copies, of which one thousand would eventually be purchased, a number barely more than half that of the first novel. One cause of the relatively poor sales may have been the warning printed in red near the bottom of the dust jacket, "N.B.—THIS IS NOT A WAR NOVEL"; but many kinds of books are read during a war, and the copy on the front of the jacket tried for timeliness by announcing that, "Although dealing with a time of peace, [the novel] is a study of the war spirit as applied to civic life." A more likely cause for the limited sales was the generally unenthusiastic, sometimes hostile, tone of the reviews. To be sure, the commentator in the widely distributed weekly, *Life,* wrote in the October 11 issue that *Marching Men* added to its author's earlier reputation as a "coming man"; and Burton Rascoe featured the novel in his Saturday book column in the *Chicago Tribune* for September 22, praising it for its "intensely subjective" conception, its dramatic love story, and its inclusive picture of Chicago life. Anderson was in fact so pleased by the review that he wrote Rascoe to thank him for the "bully piece of critical writing . . . one of the most seductive, persuasive things I ever read." But he had little reason to thank most of the other reviewers. An anonymous critic in the *New York Times Book Review* briefly dismissed the novel as "disappointing"; the ex-Chicagoan Francis Hackett, writing in *The New Republic,* could find nothing to praise in the book except "its apprehension of the great fictional theme of our generation, industrial America"; and while H. L. Mencken in *The Smart Set* admired the small town setting of the first part, he condemned most of the book for its "dubious sociological ideas." Even Ben Hecht used his review in the *Chicago Daily News* to poke fun at Anderson as well as praise him, and asserted that though he had read the last three chapters of *Marching Men* twice, they were "totally unintelligible" to him.[26]

Sometime in November Anderson wrote Bab that "I have recovered from the depression that came with the inevitable pawing over of Marching Men and am clear of it," but he never entirely forgot the disappointing reception of a book that remained one of his favorites. If *Marching Men* was, as seems likely, the first novel he ever wrote, then he might have been unreasoningly fond of it, and especially unhappy about the reviews, because of that priority and because this novel was the one in which he discovered the writing of a long fiction as the way to objectify personal problems and preoccupations and to reach for psychic health. Certainly he remained fond of the book for what he felt to be the poetic quality of its conception. When he was writing the first draft of *Marching Men,* he had told Bab in May of 1917, "It was all a great song to me then, a big terrible song"; and as late as the *Memoirs* he would conclude that the book should have been put into the form, not of a novel, but of "an epic poem." Perhaps, too, he would remember his revision upon revision upon revision of the novel as a kind of record of his intellectual and emotional development over the early years of his artisthood, and he may even have recalled with perverse satisfaction the creative energy he had expended on the original Elyria draft to give it what artistic excellence he could. That expenditure had been enormous. Burton Rascoe began his favorable review by reporting Anderson's comment to him that he had "subjected [the first draft] to revisions so infinite that he had a month's fuel supply of it in manuscript before he finally dispatched one that pleased him to the publishers."[27]

The surviving manuscript proves that Sherwood's humorous comment was not wholly an exaggeration. It is impossible to say now whether the typescript that forms a basis of the manuscript is the one prepared possibly as early as 1910 or 1911 by Frances Shute, Anderson's secretary in Elyria, from her employer's scrawled pages, or whether it is a later fair copy prepared by a typist in Chicago from revisions he may have made in the summer of 1915 after requesting the manuscript of the novel back from Floyd Dell. This "original" typescript seems to have been the one that Bab read and wrote a report on around 1916, but presumably in response to some of her suggestions as well as to his own dissatisfaction with the novel, Anderson subjected it to yet more of those "infinite" revisions he would wryly mention to Rascoe. He continued to make changes as late as May of 1917 just prior to his having a fair copy of the novel typed up and sent to the John Lane Company. It was apparently in or shortly before May that he almost completely rewrote the concluding chapters, discarding some which Bab had objected to and even a final one she had praised, and in this way substantially altered the implications of the book's ending. It was almost certainly around May when, having just poured out his poems, he added the descriptions of the Marching Men Movement as the "great song" of labor and when he inserted as the "one bit of written matter from the leader McGregor" a free verse poem titled "The Marchers," making his protagonist, like himself, temporarily a Whitmanesque bard.[28]

Since Anderson had worked on *Marching Men* off and on for some six years, years during which his life and attitudes changed critically in many ways, the novel is by no means so coherent and focused an expression of his thoughts and feelings as the quickly written songs had been. At the time he began *Marching Men*, he would later tell Paul Rosenfeld, he "did dream of a new world to come out of some revolutionary movement that would spring up out of the mass of the people"; by the time he was making his final revisions, he had certainly concluded, as the songs show, that fundamental social change would be created by the artist rather than the labor leader or the radical politician. His repeated revisions of the manuscript were therefore attempts, not simply, if at all, to follow editorial advice, but to reshape the original direction of his book to accommodate this shift in belief. He had written and revised *Windy McPherson's Son* over

several years also, but Sam McPherson and his career were more intimately related to himself and his crucial life change. Beaut McGregor, the
protagonist of *Marching Men,* is far more an invented character. Anderson occasionally drew on personal experience, usually much fantasized, in
creating McGregor, he voices through him some of his own ideas and feelings, and he clearly considers McGregor admirable in many ways; yet
more firmly than is at once obvious he was able to dissociate himself from
his creation.[29]

Despite a very generalized similarity between Anderson's and McGregor's careers—a boy grows toward manhood in a small town, goes to
Chicago and achieves success, then rejects success in favor of an ideal—
the differences in detail are of course sharp. McGregor is the loving, not
the antagonistic, son of a half-crazed yet heroic coal miner; he grows up
to be a huge homely young man in Coal Creek, Pennsylvania, an ugly mining town little resembling Clyde, Ohio; he passionately hates town and
townspeople and leaves them gladly; after his obscure early years in
Chicago he become a lawyer, gains fame by winning a hopeless case, and
then, inspired by a vision of "Old Labour's" power, organizes a movement
called the Marching Men. Some of his experiences were originally those
of his author. Like Anderson, for example, young McGregor briefly takes
a job in his town's livery stable, where as a practical joke his fellow workers make him ill, as Sherwood's had made him, with doctored beer; or
again, his first job in Chicago is as an unskilled laborer in a produce warehouse on the Near North Side, and he attends night school in order to rise
in the world. Whereas in reality, however, Sherwood appears not to have
resisted the domineering German foreman at the Western Union Cold
Storage Company, in the novel he replaces his memory of powerlessness
with a fantasy of aggression. McGregor beats his German foreman with
his fists and soon takes over the man's position.[30]

Author and protagonist come closer together in their possession of certain common attributes. The labor leader is enraged by meaningless talk
and lying words; and his humiliation of "talkers" and even physical attacks on them seem to be fictional manifestations of the strong dislike Anderson had already developed by his Elyria years for corrupters of language. Even more frequently—and at all perceivable stages of manuscript
revision—McGregor expresses in word and action Anderson's abhorrence of the disorder that he had increasingly come to believe over the
years was characteristic of present-day American lives. Sometimes indirectly through McGregor, sometimes directly in his own comments as author, Anderson sketches a fictional analysis of American development very
like that proclaimed in the songs. As McGregor, in going to Chicago, has
abandoned not only his hometown but the Edenlike green valley his father
had shown the boy beyond the hills around Coal Creek, so the disorder of

industrialism has separated Americans from "the stately order of nature." As McGregor learns by observing the purposeless existence of people at many social levels in Chicago, industrialism has likewise deadened in Americans both their individual imaginative lives and their capacity for community. Through a recovery of the sense of community, order will appear out of disorder, McGregor discovers, and it is in the mode of this discovery that he and his creator touch most closely.

Beaut has grown up to have contempt and hatred for the miners of Coal Creek, who "shuffle" aimlessly through their daily lives, and has admired only the ordered marching of the uniformed soldiers twice sent to town to break strikes. His widowed mother, however, has always sided with the workers. When he returns to Coal Creek from Chicago after her death, he sees the miners spontaneously fall into ordered step in her funeral procession and suddenly comprehends the capacity of individual workers to merge themselves into a coherent mass, to march together as a single force, to become a "giant." At that point McGregor experiences a fictional equivalent of Anderson's own ecstatic moment on the army training march in 1898 when he was overwhelmed by a semimystical sense of unity with thousands of his fellow soldiers, the sense simultaneously of being part of something giantlike and of himself containing the giantness. Returning to Chicago, the inspired McGregor begins to plan and eventually to organize the Marching Men Movement, wherein factory workers march silently together under drillmasters at times when they are not on the job, achieving in this disciplined action a sense of ordered unity to replace the former disorder of their lives and filling their employers with consternation as to what dread force may be gathering outside their control.[31]

The movement is destined to fail; indeed it could hardly do otherwise since, though Anderson celebrates the élan of the movement, he provides no further program or goal for it beyond McGregor's one vague assertion that out of their experience of communal order the workers will develop a kind of communal brain. From the vantage point of the 1930s, Anderson would half-seriously suggest in the *Memoirs* that his vision of "labor armies" had been put into perverted practice in Nazi Germany, though he would more soberly point out that the loss of self within the mass might be either beneficial or harmful depending on the end toward which the power of the mass under a charismatic leader was directed. He had been naive, he would admit, in assuming in *Marching Men* that it would be inevitably directed to a good end by a noble leader.

Some critics of the novel have questioned whether Anderson might not have unconsciously exposed an authoritarian side of himself in celebrating the movement, which, with its essential mindlessness, its latent capacity for violence, its lack of clear purpose beyond the mere experiencing of mass power, is potentially fascistic. Anderson's generally favorable presentation of McGregor is suspect to these critics too; it is certainly anomalous that a novel dedicated "To American Workingmen" and ostensibly favoring working-class revolt should, almost without exception, depict individual workers as unattractive and their lives as unremittingly aimless, should have as its protagonist a man whose fierce hatred and contempt for workers is transmuted by his visionary experience, not into a personal love and respect for them, but into an abstract identification with the power residing within them as an ordered moving mass. *Marching Men* does appear to reveal contradictory elements in tension with each other because its author was unclear about and unsettled in his impulses over a period of time. Looked at one way, the novel is a violence-tinged fantasy of power by a man who in fact distrusted the intellect and relied on the emotional and intuitive, one who had directly experienced working-class powerlessness, had struggled successfully to escape into middle-class security, and at the time he wrote his first draft was already questioning middle-class goals. Looked at another way, the novel is an extended metaphor, a "song," about the sense of community, intensely experienced by the author under circumstances that set the terms of the metaphor, a community available to his fellow Americans despite the sterile loneliness of their lives. Looked at yet a third way, it is primarily an expression of a profound desire and need for psychological order at first within a businessman torn between conformity and rebellion, later within a writer finding that financial insecurity, personal isolation, lack of recognition, and recurrent dark moods might be the lifelong price exacted in return for the joy and satisfaction of putting stories on paper. In short, *Marching Men* is several things besides a novel of working-class revolution.[32]

To concentrate on a basically political reading of *Marching Men* is to miss other aspects of the novel, each of which shows the author consciously qualifying his approval of McGregor and his movement. If Anderson was projecting through his protagonist some of his ideas and feelings including his growing dissatisfaction with business and industrialism, in the character of the wealthy David Ormsby he appears to have originally extrapolated himself from head of the Anderson Manufacturing Company to head of a national "plough trust" without, as with Sam McPherson, including his own misgivings. Ormsby has come from a small town, has organized a company along lines resembling Commercial Democracy, has prospered swiftly, and regards his devotion to business as "an end in itself." Now Chicago's "plough king" and a professed individualist, he represents industrialism, which is responsible for the pervasive disorder of contemporary America; yet Anderson makes him personally a highly attractive figure. Like his businessman creator, this fictional businessman privately considers himself "capable of a broader culture than most of his daily associates." If Ormsby is successful, he is also cultivated; if urbane in manner and aristocratic in attitude, he is also honest and perceptive about himself and others; if shown briefly as willing to be ruthless in maintaining economic power, he is shown at length to be sensitive to the emotional needs of others. Ormsby and McGregor are obvious antitheses: handsome, cultivated capitalist against homely, crude proletarian, conservative against revolutionary, believer in the power of individuals against advocate of the power of the mass. But if the antitheses are obvious, the balance between them is more nearly even than might be expected. In pitting Ormsby against McGregor, it seems certain, Anderson was creating a crude, ambitious mode of psychodrama, dramatizing clashing aspects of his own personality, his actual and perceived roles, and his feelings about them, with the intent of understanding himself as troubled person and as an individual arena for basic conflicts in American society.

In the one confrontation between Ormsby and McGregor as representatives of opposing powers, Ormsby attempts to persuade McGregor that the strong men of wealth "are responsible for the march of the world" and is effectively answered when the labor leader silently points to a body of workers swinging past them in a rhythmic moving mass. Thereafter, at least in the revised version of the book, the two men do not meet, nor, as would be expected in the true revolutionary labor novel, is there any kind of clash such as a strike or a confrontation, as in the Haymarket Affair of Chicago's history, between police and Marching Men. Instead, Anderson begins deliberately to dissociate himself as storyteller from McGregor, through whose consciousness he has told much of his novel. First, as author he categorizes the Marching Men Movement as a "madness," which can be viewed as either "big and inspiring" or as a hopeless outbreak of rebellion by a working class incapable of rebellion. Next he describes the emotional turmoil within Ormsby's daughter, who has loved McGregor but let him go, and finally he concentrates on Ormsby's thoughts and words as the capitalist sets about persuading his daughter that McGregor and the movement will fail.

His shift away from McGregor is of more than technical significance. Whether it was the first or a later draft of *Marching Men*, the version that Bab read and criticized concluded with a chapter showing McGregor married, "a father, owner of a small farm and outwardly content but with the old love of battle strong within him," this conclusion being "a clever contrast to his former stirring existence." Evidently the movement has failed, but McGregor remains at heart the revolutionary dreaming of social change. In the last chapter as finally revised, however, the failure of the movement is clearly implied, but more importantly the significance of McGregor's life and cause has been altered. It is Ormsby the capitalist who, in attempting to win Margaret away from McGregor's continuing influence, asserts what Anderson himself was asserting in 1917—that the essential role of the mature man is to undertake "the struggle for living beauty in everyday affairs." For this reason, Ormsby argues, McGregor has failed. But in the last paragraphs of the book both father and daughter have begun to doubt whether after all—and the book ends on the unresolved question—McGregor may not have enacted the role Ormsby has defined. Beauty comes, not from success but from failure and defeat, not from accomplishing a goal but from turning one's life, as did Blackfoot the painter, into a gesture. If McGregor knew that the movement would fail yet courageously persisted, then he created beauty, thus transforming himself from labor leader into artist.[33]

Anderson's finally revised ending to *Marching Men,* declaring the achievement of beauty through failure, was in accord with one of the themes that had preoccupied him at least from around 1915 when he completed *Talbot Whittingham* and began the Winesburg stories. It was in accord too with the "argument" of the songs that the artist, not the political leader, is the true agent of social change. The theme grew naturally out of the Winesburg materials, and the bardic nature of the songs allowed for such visionary pronouncements; but Anderson's subsequent admission that *Marching Men* should have been an epic poem, not a novel, appears a tacit admission that despite all his efforts at revision he was not successful in making his book change as he had changed. In one other aspect, however, his flawed work was consistent, within itself and with other of the writings he had produced. Like *Windy McPherson's Son, Marching Men* examines sex as a basic force in life and, like *Windy* or the Winesburg stories, views it as almost invariably distorted in its manifestations. Working-class husbands are brutal to their wives; upper-class women subtly rob their men of their virility. Even David Ormsby is emotionally estranged from his wife, herself a sexual fantasist, and has an unconsciously incestuous relation with his daughter, a pattern repeated at the middle-class level by an acquaintance of McGregor's. Most such instances could be taken as part of Anderson's continuing attack on the perversion of sexual force by the pursuit of money were it not that he consistently emphasizes an equal if different distortion of sexuality in McGregor himself.

Although highly attractive to women from his youth onward despite his homeliness, the forceful McGregor finds sex confusing and disturbing, and for years he admits only protective, nonsexual relationships, first with a pale, sickly, older woman in Coal Creek, then in Chicago with Edith Carson, a frail, shy, colorless, and likewise older woman who runs a millinery store. He falls in love for the first time only when he meets the beautiful and independent Margaret Ormsby, who, because she has at last found a man who can dominate her, returns his love. While recognizing sex as a powerful force, McGregor fears it as a threatening and disruptive one as well because it deflects men from their goals; he now realizes that his love for Margaret is interfering with his developing conception of the Marching Men. Nevertheless he determines to marry her but is forced by the situation to become aware of what he has refused to recognize before, that Edith Carson has long loved him silently. He then brings the two women together in the Ormsby home in a melodramatic confrontation. With brutal directness he declares his love for Margaret and his desire to have children by her, whereupon the usually quiet Edith asserts defiantly that her own colorless beauty is greater than Margaret's since it has courageously endured defeat. Margaret is frightened by her rival's fierce self-defense, and McGregor abruptly decides that though he physically desires Margaret, he loves Edith and will take her and "'go back to work.'"[34]

The phrasing of McGregor's decision indicates that he separates sexuality and affection and that he now believes himself free from the complexities of physical desire. At the conclusion of the earlier version of the novel he has married Edith and is at least outwardly content with her and their child; in the two remaining books of the revised novel Edith does not reappear, a marriage can only be assumed, and McGregor, to the extent that he himself appears, is wholly immersed in his work. But he can no more be thought of as having escaped the complications of sex than Sam McPherson or any other confused businessman; for, as the author of *Windy McPherson's Son* knew, a conscious attempt to repress sexual force or to sublimate it into an ideal of service, or of power, is as much a mode of distortion as an unconscious repression of it for material ends. That Anderson, struggling with repeated versions of *Marching Men*, could evolve so subtle and damaging an insight into his protagonist's character reveals as much about his artistic gifts as his inability to turn an immature work into a fully mature one.

4.

While the disheartening reviews of *Marching Men* were coming in, Anderson received another piece of dismaying news—the death of *The Seven Arts*. After the United States had declared war back in April, the magazine continued its opposition and even intensified it by printing the antiwar articles of Randolph Bourne. Bourne, whose sharp mind and tongue in a shockingly misshapen dwarf's body had made him a close friend of Frank, Brooks, and Rosenfeld, had been contributing political commentary to *The New Republic* but broke with that magazine's editors when they announced support of the war. Thereupon Oppenheim invited him to write for *The Seven Arts*, in the June 1917 issue along with Anderson's "Mid-American Prayer" appeared "The War and the Intellectuals," the first of five incisive attacks by Bourne on the war spirit that were published in successive months. These and John Reed's journalistic piece, "This Un-popular War," in the August issue alarmed the nervous and politically con-servative Mrs. Rankine, whose money was subsidizing *The Seven Arts* and whose relatives and friends began to criticize her bitterly as unpatriotic. From August onward she threatened the editors with the withdrawal of her financial support if they did not cease their public opposition to the war. Brooks had from the first favored keeping political discussion out of a cultural magazine, but Oppenheim and Frank refused to abandon their anti-war stand, and late in October Mrs. Rankine turned her threat into a formal action. Already, however, an insert in the front of the magazine's October issue had announced that the subsidy had been withdrawn and that friends of *The Seven Arts* must keep it alive with contributions if it were to be kept alive at all.

Sherwood, out in Chicago, was only dimly aware of the ensuing con-flicts among the editors about possible reorganization with other financial backers, and urged Waldo, still ill from his operation, to try to find some way of keeping the magazine going. But that October issue, with an ad-vertisement for *Marching Men* prominent on its back cover, was the last issue of *The Seven Arts*. Generously Anderson recognized that the real blow had fallen on Frank and Brooks, for whom the magazine had been a focus of their lives, and in mid-October he wrote them to express his sym-pathy and encouragement. Nevertheless he realized that he had a share in the misfortune. No longer would he be warmed by such praise in the monthly "Notes on Names" as, "Sherwood Anderson, more perhaps than any other novelist, represents the new generation in the West." Now Frank could not hail his new novel with another review like "Emerging Greatness." Worst of all, one of the few outlets for his tales and essays was gone.[35]

October was mostly a bad month, though it improved toward the end as he recovered from his emotional depression over the reviews of *March-ing Men*. Enthusiastic as always about new projects, he was briefly inter-ested when around the end of October representatives of the Curtis Pub-lishing Company, owners of the hugely popular *Saturday Evening Post, Ladies Home Journal,* and *Country Gentleman,* approached him with the proposal that he "do some country town stories for them." He explained that he "couldn't write to order," especially for mass-circulation maga-zines, but made the counterproposal that the newly established *Country Gentleman* send him "on a two years literary pilgrimage to the cornfields" so that he might wander about among the midwestern farmers and towns-people, writing stories and articles concerning them as he might feel in-clined. Nothing came of the unbusiness-like scheme, but his desire for such a two years "walk" was one of the signs of his increasing restiveness about having to live in Chicago and support himself by writing advertisements. Fortunately, that fall it was necessary for him to travel about the Midwest by train to work in various towns with clients of the Critchfield firm. The late October countryside was lovely now, he wrote Waldo Frank, with its "red splashes of wood and the long fields filled with the dry crackling corn." He was hoping Waldo would come to visit him and Tennessee in Chicago, but Frank, the struggle to maintain *The Seven Arts* being lost, had rented a room in downtown Manhattan to write in and had gone headlong into a second novel as his own way of escape. He did take time to write his Chicago "brother," warning him that though the arrangement for a "literary Odyssey through the West" might initially appeal to the Curtis people, "your gospel of defeat, your golden discovery of unfinancial gods, your subtle revolutionary visions would give them the creeps if they began to catch on."[36]

At least the traveling got Anderson out of Chicago, which was more and more oppressing him as a symbol of "the shrillness and emptiness of our times." Somewhat restored by the countryside, he wondered to Frank, in one of the letters they were frequently exchanging, why so few modern Americans could "shake off the success disease," could "really get over our American mania for 'getting on,'" that mania brought on by industrialism; and in a pastoral mood he created for his friend in New York a myth of an earlier half-animistic midwestern land.

A curious notion comes often to me. Is it not likely that when the country was new and men were often alone in the fields and forests, they got a sense of bigness outside themselves that has now in some way been lost? I don't mean the conventional religious thing that is still prevalent and that is nowadays being retailed to the people by the most up-to-date commercial methods, but something else. The people, I fancy, had a savagery superior to our own. Mystery whispered in the grass, played in the branches of trees overhead, was caught up and blown across the horizon line in clouds of dust at evening on the prairies.

I am old enough to remember tales that strengthen my belief in a deep, semi-religious influence that was formerly at work among our people. The flavor of it hangs over the best work of Mark Twain. That's what makes it so moving and valuable. I can remember old fellows in my home town speaking feelingly of an evening spent on the big, empty plains. It has taken the shrillness out of them. They had learned the trick of quiet. It affected their whole lives. It made them significant.

Six months before, he would have immediately struck the more self-conscious, more declamatory bardic note. Now he was to move quietly and in a natural tone of voice toward a kind of mythopoeic vision of the relation between Americans and their physical land, a vision he would give substance to in some of his writings over the next several years.[37]

Still, Anderson, quite as comfortable in his serener moments as Whitman at containing contradictions, was publicly urging immersion in the industrial age at almost exactly the time that he was privately hoping to withdraw from it. Just as he had refused to write stories to order for the "Curtis crowd" and then for his own amusement "began doing some small-town stories in a semi-light vein" that might sell, so in early November while he was musing on the American land, he published in the Chicago literary magazine, *The Dial,* one of his best-known essays, "An Apology for Crudity," which insisted that "we shall never have an American literature until we return to faith in ourselves and to the facing of our own limitations." Twain and Whitman "wrote out of another age, out of an age and a land of forests and rivers"; the modern writer must write out of an age of industrialism "as ugly as modern war." He must abandon "objective writing and thinking" and follow the "subjective impulse," which will lead him "deeply into modern American industrial life." As Dostoyevsky in Russia "lived and . . . expressed the life of his time and people," so the American writer must "live as the men of his time live . . . must share with them the crude expression of their lives." The credo was a characteristic one for Anderson, stating as it did ideas he had begun shaping in rough form a year earlier in the letters to Bab, but the feelings he was expressing in his letters to Frank were characteristic also. The contradictory pulls toward city and land, toward acceptance of a wide and ugly urban present and return to a quiet pastoral past, remembered from youth or somehow preserved in reality, would appear repeatedly as themes in his writing and even as modes of physical living. Almost rhythmically throughout his life he would feel driven from city to countryside, then drawn back from countryside to city. Without conscious intention he lived the great rural-urban tensions of his time, and his writing would often be at its best when these unconscious feelings took on conscious design.[38]

It was a sign of his growing status as a public literary figure, a "Chicago writer," that "An Apology for Crudity" was picked up and reprinted on the book page of the *Daily News.* He must have been pleased when on November 28 the *News* reprinted the titles of "the thirty-three outstanding fiction works of the last year" as selected by *The Dial,* a list that included *Marching Men* but with the somewhat qualified comment, "A sincere attempt to handle American life in one of its most significant aspects." As fall drew into winter, perhaps the accumulation of those compliments helped, along with the business travels, to restore to him some of the emotional poise he thought he had brought back from the summer in the Adirondacks. Temporarily he felt able to take the long view of things, a view encouraged by his spurt of reading in the histories of the combatant nations as "an antidote to the War." The war itself he now managed to put into some personal perspective. Although he admired

Waldo for his continued resolution to refuse military service if called up, he had decided that he himself would merely accept the life of his time and people and, in the remote chance that he had to serve, would go with his fellows into the "stupidity and horror" of war. Meanwhile he assured his friends that art would after all continue despite the war. Death and horror characterized an industrial civilization even in peacetime; and since civilization was always opposed to the artist anyway, the latter should simply disregard "war and government," keeping instead to the search for beauty and accepting the "great truth" that beauty enters life "only . . . at odd moments and in quite unexpected ways." He could even view his own artistic career with some detachment. "As for myself," he wrote Frank, using seriously a somewhat absurd figure,

you know something of what I have dreamed. At my best I am like a great mother bird flying over this broad Mississippi Valley, seeing its towns and its broad fields and peoples and brooding over some vague dream of a song arising, of gods coming here to dwell with my people. At my worst I am a petty writer not big enough for the task I have set myself.

On other days he was less solemn, was even exuberant. He was working on *Immaturity* again after his period of depression, he told his New York friend, was taking his own time with it, and was only delighted that it had "gone insane; a really delicious, garrulous, heavy, lame fellow with shaggy eyebrows is writing." Since the world was drab and ugly, he was restoring truth to it by quite literally giving it color, by sticking bright little feathers in his hat or by wearing the golden yellow scarf or the purple and yellow socks which the understanding Tennessee was buying him.[39]

The careless gaiety following depression suggests that he was in a period not of true emotional poise but of emotional instability, a period of fluctuating moods outwardly marking some continued inner concern, but he did have in mid-December a real reason for being ebullient. Back in black October, with *Immaturity* not far along, with neither of his old novel manuscripts, *Mary Cochran* or *Talbot Whittingham*, in anything like satisfactory shape, and apparently with even the Winesburg stories not quite as he wanted them, he had sent off to Jefferson Jones at the John Lane Company his collection of poems, to which he had finally decided to give the title *Mid-American Chants*. Unlike *Marching Men,* of course, this was not one of the "next three full length novels" specified in his original contract with Lane for *Windy McPherson's Son*. He was resentfully aware that the six pieces published in the September *Poetry* had brought him critical "abuse" and that Frank, who had refused all the songs except two for *The Seven Arts* because he thought them vague and formless, advised that his third book be fiction, but Sherwood was determined to see the *Chants*

283

published. To risk failure was "part of my creed," he insisted confidently to Waldo, though he privately hoped that the book of poems would not fail. For some weeks he had worried whether Jones might "lose his nerve" and reject the manuscript, but that particular worry was over. Despite the poor reviews and weak sales of *Marching Men,* Jones accepted the poems, and on December 14 Anderson contracted with the Lane Company for the publication of *Mid-American Chants* in both American and English editions. Given even wartime printing schedules, he could expect to maintain his record of publishing a book a year in addition to carrying a full-time, demanding advertising job. Perhaps he could somehow manage to continue doing both.[40]

5.

Sherwood and Tennessee began 1918 by joining "many of the city's literary and artistic people" at the annual New Year's Day reception given in the Fine Arts Building by the Cordon Club, an organization of well-bred Chicagoans friendly toward the arts—provided that the individual artists and art works were not too shocking. What observance the Andersons may have made of the Christmas just past, with or without Cornelia and the children, is not known. Probably they had made little or none; for each of them disliked the holiday, apparently because of childhood feelings of neglect on that occasion, and this year Sherwood was especially struck by the irony of a nation at war celebrating the birth of Christ. "The very thought of Christmas fills me with pompous phrase," be wrote Bab on December 26. "Don't you suppose that Christ on his cross laughed at the follies of men?" It was the last letter he would write her until the following April; in fact, he who liked to write letters as a way of reaching out toward other persons wrote almost no letters during that winter. Although it was often bitterly cold and frequent blizzards paralyzed Chicago under feet of snow, he had to keep "hopping in and out of town like a wild man, trying to make a living," as he wrote in a note to Burton Rascoe in mid-February, congratulating him on having just been made literary editor of the *Tribune.* Despite the flurry of business he was able to write a brief foreword for the *Chants* and to contribute a short article to the *Chicago Daily News* for February 20, "Chicago Culture," which reads as though he were making a virtue of his current necessity. Unlike New York writers, who waste their time and talent among groups of mutual admirers, the men and women writers of Chicago, Anderson loyally asserts, remain "intensely individual" because most of them "have to make a living under rather hard circumstances" and hence are forced into daily contact with a workaday world of factory and business. This situation has the great advantage, however, of preventing Chicago writers from gathering in groups of mutual admirers and thereby killing the chance for a "distinctive middle western literature" by talking it to death. "Chicago Culture," however, was only a kind of occasional piece, expressing a part (but merely a part) of Anderson's feelings. It did not mention his sense of lonely isolation from his "brothers of the East," and one would not have guessed from it that his note to Rascoe referred to having had lunch with the literary editor of the *News* and invited Rascoe to lunch as well. Even individualists liked company, and Anderson could work up an idea for a newspaper as readily as for an advertising client.[41]

When he found more time for writing toward the end of the winter, he did not take up *Immaturity* but had another brief spell of writing poems, stimulated perhaps by his reading of printer's proof for the forthcoming *Chants* and by hearing from Frank the welcome news that he was feeling better after his long illness and could come to Chicago in the spring if Sherwood and Tennessee still wanted him to. Unlike the *Chants,* however, these "songs" were not bardic utterances but "lyrical things," as Anderson wrote to Harriet Monroe near the end of March in response to her inquiry about the possibility of printing another group of his poems in *Poetry.* He sent along to her six of the free verse lyrics, which indeed did "strike . . . a new note" for him, as one of them, "Oblivion," made clear in its expression of a desire to escape from one's time and place rather than a determination to accept them. Both Harriet Monroe and her associate editor, Alice Corbin Henderson, read the six poems, together with a seventh, "Spring Song/For the Fields" that Anderson sent on in late April. They liked some sections of the poems, felt that other sections needed revision, and ultimately returned the whole group to him unaccepted. Not until 1939, two years before Anderson's death, would any of these poems be printed.[42]

While Waldo and Sherwood were trying to arrange the best time for the spring visit, Waldo sent confidential word that Brooks, Bourne, Rosenfeld, and he might be starting a new magazine to succeed *The Seven Arts,* that, if it did come into existence, Anderson "must *be* the magazine in Chicago," and that the first number might feature the serialization of *Immaturity.* Anderson's insistence in reply that he had something for the magazine "more real and human than any novel" may be a reference to his new poems; but clearly *Immaturity* was thoroughly stalled, and he was turning to other projects, such as a story called "The White Streak," which he sent off to *The Smart Set* on March 12. Mencken asked him to trim down its length and to let him, as the experience-wise editor, make certain changes to avoid censorship difficulties. Anderson cheerfully agreed to both requests, and Mencken accepted the tale. Then, too, by late March Anderson was at work, as he enthusiastically wrote Mencken, "on the best story that I have ever written in my life which I am going to call the Pagan Christian," a "crackerjack thing" though it would probably run too long to be printed in the usual magazine. Two weeks later, with equal self-confidence, he wrote Frank that if the story—now called "The Pagan Jesus"—"comes out clean it will do in a swift tale what [H. G.] Wells wanted to do when he wrote 'God, the Invisible King.'" The author of *Marching Men* had, outwardly at least, fully recovered from that book's bad reviews.[43]

The possibility of a new magazine soon disappeared, but Anderson was even more excited by the information, presumably also supplied by Frank, that Brooks was considering doing a full-length book on Mark Twain as an example of failure in the American writer. This news prompted Anderson in late March or early April to start a memorable correspondence with Brooks in which the midwesterner showed his desire to "sell" Twain to the easterner. A good part of what Sherwood wished to sell had been, as it were, bought by Van Wyck already; and in *The Ordeal of Mark Twain,* eventually published in 1920, Brooks would often agree with Sherwood's sketch of the "river man" who could write despite a crude, cheap frontier background but who went East, was partly tamed by marriage to a "good woman," and got in "with that New England crowd, the fellows from barren hills and barren towns," who did their barren best to curb his creative spirit. In Twain's frustrated career, which, Anderson cautioned, must be sympathetically understood, was mirrored the tragedy both of the American writer and of his times. Yet—and here the Mid-American slipped back into the bardic tone—Twain did write one book, *Huckleberry Finn,* where he got beyond the "cultural fellows" and the "rather childlike" pessimism he adopted in order to escape their influence.

> Now, Brooks, you know a man cannot be a pessimist who lives near a brook or a cornfield. When the brook chatters or at night when the moon comes up and the wind plays in the corn, a man hears the whispering of the gods.
> Mark got to that once—when he wrote *Huck Finn.* He forgot Howells, and the good wife and everyone. Again he was the half-savage, tender, god-worshiping, believing boy. He had proud, conscious innocence.
> I believe he wrote that book in a little hut on a hill on his farm. It poured out of him. I fancy that at night he came down from his hill stepping like a king, a splendid playboy playing with rivers and men, riding on the Mississippi, on the broad river that is the great artery flowing out of the heart of the land.

Van Wyck would remember that remark about Twain's "proud, conscious innocence" and apply it to Sherwood himself after the latter's death. Whatever other effect the bardic pronouncement may have had on Brooks, however, it did not change his decision, one he later publicly regretted, to minimize the importance of *Huckleberry Finn.* Perhaps he suspected his friend's judgment of the novel as too self-serving, for Anderson's sense of kinship with Twain showed directly and indirectly through-out the correspondence in such a shorthand remark as that, like himself, Mark Twain was a "factory child," or his claim to understand Twain be-cause he himself was living in a crude and cheap environment and admit-tedly lacked "background," as Brooks and Frank did not, or the implica-tion that a midwest novelist so aware of another midwesterner and his times might be capable of writing in his own crude, shrill time another *Huckleberry Finn.* Again, as a year earlier, Anderson was revealing his am-biguous reaction of pride and humility before the author of *America's Coming-of-Age,* the eastern intellectual whom he sought to instruct on Twain, whose clarity of mind he admired, whose criticism he requested but whose approval he more deeply desired. "What I want to ask you," Anderson wrote, half annoyed, half pleading, "is why you do not sympa-thize with me in such expressions as my essay 'An Apology for Crudity' or my *Chants?* Where do I hit wrong?"[44]

Unfortunately, Brooks was in every sense too remote, but when Waldo finally came for his visit, he was as much Sherwood's "brother" as he had been at Chateaugay Lake nearly a year earlier. He arrived in Chicago somewhere around the middle of April and stayed for about two weeks. Apparently Anderson's amiable landlady at the lodging house at 59 West Schiller Street had held a room for Frank to sleep in, and during the day while his host was at the advertising agency, Waldo worked on his nearly completed novel in Sherwood's room at his big table, which held both can-dles and typewriter. Evenings they sat by the fireplace in Tennessee's large living room with its piano on which Waldo was free to play at any time, or they walked for hours about Chicago so that the visitor could get a sense of the loose, disordered life of the midwest city. Sitting or walking they of course talked, Waldo intensely voluble, Sherwood soft-voiced and drawling, Tennessee, when she was with them, observant, then witty and direct.[45]

Toward the end of Waldo's visit, perhaps on the evening of April 27, the Andersons gave a dinner party at Tennessee's place in his honor, though they may or may not have warned him that they were preparing a practical joke on two of the other men invited. Since early April in the Sat-urday book pages of the *Tribune,* Burton Rascoe had been acclaiming the literary achievement of the Virginia novelist James Branch Cabell and an-grily battling Cabell's detractors, including Ben Hecht, who delighted in verbal duels with the high-strung Rascoe and who with much amusement had proceeded to attack Cabell in the Wednesday book pages of the *Daily News.* To present Waldo with and to a spectrum of Chicago's literary people and to have fun, Sherwood and Tennessee invited to the dinner Carl Sandburg, Llewellyn Jones, then the editor of the Friday book pages of the *Evening Post,* and also Hecht and Rascoe without letting either of the last two know that the other was coming. The guests assembled, at some point during or after the dinner Hecht made an unfavorable remark about Cabell, Rascoe exploded, and for an hour Hecht and Rascoe went into a wild, vituperative shouting match that delighted all the Chicagoans, astonished Waldo, and, paradoxically marked the beginning of a warm friendship between the combatants. According to Rascoe, Frank "was forced to be content with one utterance: 'I did not know that such excitement about literature existed anywhere in the United States.'"[46]

However Waldo may have felt about the dinner party, his visit with the Andersons was a happy occasion. When he returned to New York, he left with them, Sherwood assured him, "a flavor of affection and understanding." As one of Anderson's various efforts to "get the Midwest" into his friend, the two men had talked in Chicago about Twain and about Brooks's visceral distaste for the "dreadful cheap smartness, the shrillness," which, they agreed, characterized Twain's time and spoiled too much of his work. They talked also of another midwesterner, Abraham Lincoln, and Frank gave Anderson a copy of Lord Charnwood's recent biography. Sherwood did not get around to reading it until Frank had left, but as soon as he had begun, he felt it to be in ways a study of himself and the midwestern temperament, its alternation of cheap looseness and ability to "rise to exalted occasion." Fascinated anew by Lincoln, he began reading everything he could find on the man and was soon including comments on Lincoln along with those on Twain in his letters to Brooks. The gift of the Charnwood biography was a fateful one, for when he finally got back to work on the *Immaturity* material later in 1918, his preoccupation with Twain, Lincoln, and the midwestern character would lead him to a different and more successful approach to the industrialization of an Ohio county town.

Anderson and Frank could hardly have avoided talking also about *Mid-American Chants,* for Lane brought it out on April 12, and Hecht and Llewellyn Jones reviewed it in the *News* and the *Evening Post* while Waldo was in Chicago. The author would already have received his six free copies; and since he mailed one off to Mencken, whom he barely knew, and presumably, sent another to Brooks, as well as giving a third to Tennessee with the curiously formal inscription, "To Tennessee Mitchell/ Sherwood Anderson," he would certainly have given one to his "younger brother," especially since Waldo Frank had considered the poems to be a deflection of his "older brother's" true talent as a fiction writer. Anderson stubbornly continued to insist that they had brought him "a greater satisfaction than anything that I have ever done," and his stubbornness may have had its effect. Waldo, reading the poems aloud some weeks later, conceded that though most lacked sufficient "solidity" of form to sustain their vision to the end, "I also see through the interstices a lovely upright spirit that means more to me than academic accomplishment. I want you to work hard at your stuff—harder—but I am not going to shut my eyes to the beauty you are bringing to life and to work."[47]

Anderson needed all the praise Frank could give and all his own stubbornness, whether it came from defensiveness or conviction. As the few reviews of *Mid-American Chants* trickled in during the spring and summer, they confirmed his expectation that the critics would again abuse him. Even the local newspaper reviewers, even Ben Hecht, were cool toward the book, and those elsewhere condemned the poems as the obscure expression of vague feelings, not poetry but the material out of which poetry might have been made. Most of the reviewers also quarreled with the book's foreword, which Anderson had written back in busy February and which, a variation on "An Apology for Crudity," lacked that essay's self-confidence. "Immersed as we are in affairs," the argument ran, "hurried and harried through life by the terrible engine—industrialism," midwesterners have not "come to the time of song." Poetry belongs to civilizations with a longer past; hence midwesterners, hungering for maturity and poetic expression but faced with the ugly reality of city and factory, can only "mutter and feel our way toward the promise of song." These chants—not "poems," not "songs"—are only expressions of the hunger for a "beauty . . . not yet native to our cities and fields" and should be judged only as standing "stark against the background of my own place and generation." Like Anderson's earlier decision to change the title from "Songs" to *Chants,* his foreword seems a wary attempt, despite what Frank had called his "gospel of defeat," to forestall defeat at the hands of the critics. The critics were not forestalled. The chants, they felt, were stark enough, but how did the foreword explain the recognized poetic achievement of such other midwesterners as Vachel Lindsay, Edgar Lee Masters, and Carl Sandburg?[48]

Only one reviewer, Alice Corbin Henderson in the June issue of *Poetry,* praised *Mid-American Chants,* finding virtues where others found defects. Accepting the "songs as musical improvisations with recurring themes and motives," she argued that the crudity of the book was intentional and "expressive," and that the poems were therefore effective as both a protest against "the burden of industrialism" and a "prayer that we may get back to the lean life of the growing corn at last." Linking Anderson positively with Lindsay, Masters, and Sandburg, she found that the expressing of "local consciousness" by all four was the means by which they would achieve "national expression." Understandably, Anderson felt that Alice Henderson alone understood what he had been trying to do. Writing to Bab, he showed his irritation with the other critics by rejecting as "smug, slippery and dishonest" the review in *The Dial* by Louis Untermeyer, formerly poetry editor of *The Seven Arts.* He presumably was irritated too at Ben Hecht, who in his review of *Mid-American Chants* in the *Daily News* for April 17 found many poems obscure and explained the obscurity on the grounds that Anderson was "neither a poet nor a thinker, but . . . a mystic, singing of corn fields as mystics once sang of the Virgin's eyes." But if, as seems likely, Sherwood was the "J. Smith" whose letter to the literary editor was published in the *News* on May 1, he had shrewdly decided that humor was the best means to defend and advertise the *Chants*. Mark Twain was on his mind, and using many of Twain's humorous devices—the assumed pose of the naive, forthright observer, the colloquial tone, the occasional malapropism—Anderson, if it was Anderson, created a plainspoken workman who talks rather like a grown up Huck Finn. Smith understands "only things that are wrote out straight" and thinks the author of "Mid-Western Chance" no mystic according to "my daughter Fanny's pocket Webster . . . Remote from or beyond human comprehension." Smith figures instead that Anderson "is just a plain hoss like me that works his eight hours and smokes stogies and eats over at the automatic." The poet may have copped some of his lingo out of the "St. James version" of the Bible, but there "ain't none better" as a place to steal from, and besides in the poems "Every word was just like the fellows in my shop . . . uses, only put together different." Smith thinks the poems good, "barring what the printer done, not making the lines come out even," and to prove his point he quotes from two of his unnamed favorites, "The Cornfields" and "Song of the Mating Time." Anderson's poetry makes Smith "feel sort of gingered up," and incidentally, "there wasn't a word in the book I had to look up in the dictionary. That's more than I can say of Hecht's article." When Anderson gets his next book out, Smith concludes, the literary editor should reprint it in full in his newspaper.[49]

The letter, again assuming that it was Sherwood's, was yet another illustration of a vein of humor that he not only drew on often with his friends orally, but had worked in his writing as early as his sketch, "The Undeveloped Man," in the May 1904, issue of *Agricultural Advertising* and would work again at the end of the twenties when he became editor of two country newspapers. "J. Smith" was a clever invention, but the free advertising could not have been very successful. The American edition of the *Chants* sold less than two hundred copies, and Anderson must already have begun to worry whether the John Lane Company would contract to publish the collection of short stories, now titled *Winesburg* instead of *The Book of the Grotesque,* which he was preparing to send off to the affable but businesslike Jefferson Jones.[50]

Around the beginning of April, Anderson's efforts at Critchfield had gained him the status of having his own secretary. "The firm have the wild notion that they can thus make me work," he rather deprecatingly had written to Frank. Now early in May he was working both himself and the secretary hard so that he and Tennessee could get away from Chicago to see the Kentucky Derby at Louisville's Churchill Downs on the tenth and to enjoy a week's automobile tour of the state at the invitation of his client and friend, Davis T. Bohon, whom he had helped to enrich with his schemes for the mail order business, which the "brainy shrewd" Dave and his less capable brother Hanly had set up in the small town of Harrodsburg. While it lasted, the trip to Kentucky was a great success. Both Sherwood and Tennessee thrilled to the "fleet beautiful thoroughbred horses" and enjoyed staying at the Bohon estate in the Bluegrass region. Sherwood found Kentuckians "the most beautiful people I have seen in America," and he fell in love with the hill country where sheep and horses grazed on the hillsides and men and women worked in the fields along the river bottoms. It was a land untouched by the war, as pastoral as Biblical times or, he may have thought, as the Ohio of patriarchal Joseph Bentley in the story "Godliness" in his Winesburg manuscript. He returned to Chicago in mid-May, temporarily rested and at peace with himself. He had "a scheme on foot" to leave Chicago and live and write for two or three years in a small, quiet Kentucky town, supporting himself by working on his own with some of his advertising clients.[51]

Here was another version of escape like the walk through the Midwest, and like the walk it came disappointingly to nothing. As had happened after the summer at Chateaugay Lake, the feeling of quiet strength given by the Kentucky countryside dissipated very quickly; and for several days early in June he became so ill, surely psychosomatically, that he consulted a doctor, who told him that he was "full of nerve fatigue" and warned him that he might not be able to keep up both a business and a writing career. In similar form the conflict of his Elyria days began to repossess him, so insistently that for apparently the first time since the fall of 1912 he was willing to admit in a public context, not simply in confidence to brother or friend, what had then happened. Responding on June 3 to Burton Rascoe's request for biographical information, he gave a "simple" condensed summary of his life with a conclusion serious in meaning if jokingly put.

About the biography matter. It is simple enough. Born at a place called Camden, Ohio, September 13, 1876—I nearly wrote 1776—Spend most of my youth in the village of Clyde, Ohio, near Cleveland. Town poor family, village news-boy peddling papers, cheating people out of change etc.—all that stuff.

Came to Chicago at eighteen—no work—common laborer until the Spanish War broke out. Went into that.

Stumbled into advertising, writing and have been there ever since except for five years when I got the great American idea of getting rich. Started a factory— got all my friends to put money in—bright young business man, etc.

Scheme didn't work. Went nutty—had nervous break-down—slight suspicion have been nutty ever since.

Started writing for the sake of the salvation of my soul and except for one or two slips—when I fancied I might by some chance hit on a popular note—have been writing for that end ever since. Don't know whether I'll make it or not.[52]

Whether he would make it or not may have been a rhetorical flourish to end a letter; in this June of 1918 it was also a doubt to be faced daily. Heavy and listless in body and mind, deeply worried as to how he was to support himself and to help support Robert, John, and Mimi, uneasy about the fate of the *Winesburg* manuscript now in Jones's hands, he deliberately gave up writing for perhaps as much as two weeks even though, as he wrote Waldo, reading again in the Charnwood biography suddenly made him want to do "a novel about the figure of Lincoln." But denying himself writing merely made him fear the loss of his creativity and feel more painfully the excruciating drudgery of his advertising work.[53]

Then by good fortune a door to the trap opened. During Anderson's years as independent businessman, his friend of Clyde days John Emerson/ Clifton Paden had been rising in the New York dramatic world as actor, stage director, and producer. Brought to Hollywood in 1914 by D. W. Griffith, the tall, dark, handsome, hypochondriacal Emerson became a writer and producer of motion pictures with such stars as Douglas Fairbanks, Constance Talmadge, and Mary Pickford, for whom the witty, petitely beautiful Anita Loos, his future wife, was writing scripts. In 1918 John and Anita were working together in New York where, as the talented heads of Emerson-Loos Productions, they wrote scripts for and John directed and produced films released by Paramount Pictures and Artcraft. John and Sherwood had kept up their friendship over the years. Now at John's suggestion after Sherwood's plea, the latter took a brief trip to New York on June 17 and 18 to talk over business affairs with his boyhood friend. In the joking and casual way he performed all such generous acts, Emerson offered him a position as a publicity man in Emerson-Loos Productions at a salary of seventy-five dollars a week with a minimum of duties. The opportunity to live in New York and have more free time for his writing restored Sherwood's good spirits almost immediately. He returned to Chicago and on June 25 drew up a "memorandum of resignation" addressed to Bayard Barton, his friendly superior at Critchfield, mock-seriously urging that either Barton or himself fire Sherwood Anderson. This Anderson fellow was "an ornament to our organization" if only for his "long and mussy hair," which "gives an artistic carelessness to his personal appearance that somehow impresses such men as Frank Lloyd Wright and Mr. Curtenius of Kalamazoo when they come into the office"; but he "is not really productive" because "his heart is not in his work."

Anderson should leave on August 1. "He is a nice fellow. We will let him down easy but let's can him." Barton, who liked his gifted and wayward copy writer, went along with the resignation.[54]

July was as happy a month as June had been devastatingly close to emotional smash-up. With a new job to look forward to in a city where he had thought for over a year he might sometime live, Sherwood first took a two-week vacation with Tennessee in Michigan and then spent the last two weeks in and out of Chicago cleaning up his affairs at Critchfield. He was joyful at the thought of New York, he wrote Van Wyck Brooks, enclosing a copy of the memorandum of resignation with self-satisfaction: "I want to wander about, readjust myself, get the weariness out of me and see if I cannot face life anew." Waldo Frank was writing from California, where he had gone to start work on *Our America,* a book of impressions to be directed at a French audience; but Anderson hoped to see Brooks and Rosenfeld in New York and other people whose company would cut through the "fog of loneliness" that he felt surrounding him in Chicago.[55]

He may have learned by now that Lane had turned down *Winesburg,* and though this would have been disappointing, the Lane association was another of the ties to the past he was breaking. Besides, some of his more recent work was at last beginning to appear in magazines after a space of half a year when nothing had appeared there. *The Little Review* had published a Winesburg story, "The Man of Ideas," in its June issue—in December it would print "An Awakening," the last to have magazine publication—and by July must have accepted the early sketch, "Senility" for its September issue; but it was in the July number of *The Little Review* that his new kind of tale, "Seeds," appeared. With "Seeds," "Senility," and the earlier story "The Struggle" (to be retitled "War") he had the beginnings of a new book of tales. Furthermore, Mencken included "The White Streak" in *The Smart Set* for July. Appropriately, the story told of an old commission merchant in Chicago's South Water Street Market who as a young man in his father's business had almost revolted against a dull job, a dull wife, and a dull existence but did not, and who as an old man is successful at selling poultry, butter, and eggs and at accepting job, wife, existence. With changes in detail it was the story of what might have happened to its author had he decided to stay in Elyria—or possibly, he may now have felt, had been forced to remain in Chicago.[56]

Anderson's gaiety and relief over his approaching escape probably set the tone of one last piece published in July, a brief literary self-portrait "written especially for The Daily News" and printed there on the tenth under a stern-faced caricature drawn "from life" by Quin Hall. The drawing emphasized, along with a conventional collar and tie, his thick mass of hair, his heavily defined eyebrows, his penetrating eyes, and, now that he had reached his early forties, his definite double chin. Playing lightheartedly

with verbal paradoxes, Anderson portrayed himself as having the "extraordinary vanity" of all writers, who can never tell the truth about themselves because they see their lives as drama.

> With this preface I would—did space permit—be delighted to go on and tell
> you a thousand things concerning myself. I would tell you touching tales of my
> early poverty, my heroic struggle to acquire learning, my keen sympathy with the
> men and women who, like myself, are caught and held in the trap of industrial life.

But such "hours and days and months" of talk about himself would only
feed his "lustful vanity"; they would not be true. The truth is, he concludes, simultaneously affirming and denying, "I am a hero to myself" and
will remain so "in the future by refusing to read criticisms of my books."[57]

A hero to himself, he prepared to leave Chicago for New York on August 1. He would return to his midwest city and sooner than he may have
expected. Increasingly, however, he wished to live elsewhere, and future
departures would be more frequent, last longer, take him farther away
from that place where he had become a published novelist, a literary figure, a sometime bard.

8

Achievement

1.

Anderson arrived in New York on August 3, 1918, during a heat wave, left his things in the apartment of John Emerson and Anita Loos on Fifth Avenue at Fiftieth Street, and went away with them to the country over the weekend to cool off. On the fifth, a Monday, he was back in the city, lunched pleasantly with Van Wyck Brooks in a restaurant with a garden, and began several days of hunting for the right "hole" to work in. Finally he found just what he wanted in the old Chelsea section on the West Side above Greenwich Village, the Village not meeting his need for a quiet, secluded place where he could write. Number 427, West Twenty-second Street was an old, high-ceilinged house owned by Rose McCarron, a neat, devout, unmarried Irish woman of sixty, whom Anderson would shortly celebrate by adapting her name for a fictional character. He had a big room at the back away from street noises, though at night he could hear the steamers crying hoarsely from the nearby Hudson River. The room had a fireplace and two cots. Tennessee, it had been arranged, would be spending September with him.[1]

Quickly he fell into a routine. His landlady, whom as usual he had charmed, got up at dawn to attend daily Mass, then returned to bring him a breakfast of coffee, toast, and fruit at 7:30. After a morning cigarette Sherwood would sit down in an old dressing gown and write steadily until noon. He would then shave, dress, and go out on the streets. Usually he would check in at the movie studio to sit around for awhile and chat with whoever was there or to dash off in a few minutes one of the newspaper publicity stories for Emerson-Loos Productions by which he was making his living. He might snatch a half-hour's talk with the hard-driven John and then have a leisurely lunch by himself at some little restaurant. Afternoons he would stroll about the city or drop in on an acquaintance for more talk. Occasionally he would dine with John in the evening or go off on Sundays with him and Anita to the countryside along the shores of Long Island Sound where he, the midwesterner, especially enjoyed swimming in the salt water.[2]

He and Anita liked each other's company from the beginning, and he was with her more than with John. Tiny and trim herself, she thought of "Swatty," the nickname she and John invariably addressed him by, as a "lion-faced man" with a striking resemblance, because of his big, rugged frame and thatch of tawny hair, to one of the stone lions in front of the New York Public Library. With his loose build, big hands, and genial manner, he seemed at other times simply like a countryman, but a countryman with an incongruous air about him of Greenwich Village. He dressed in rather loud, "arty" clothes, favored blue shirts and colorful neckties and scarves, and, she decided, was in fact as arty as he was bluff and genial. Priding herself as the wryly witty sophisticate who saw through all human foibles, she considered him hopelessly naive and romantic about people, even literary about them; she accused him, seriously, of learning about people from Dostoyevsky and of making them fit his own writings. She and Sherwood very comfortably amused each other.[3]

The satisfying routine of this life went on through August, though Anderson broke it one weekend by taking the train to Washington to see Paul Rosenfeld now drafted into the army and stationed at nearby Camp Humphries. Paul, who detested military life and in addition was often hospitalized by illness, had begged his friend to visit him and offered to pay the railroad fare, but Sherwood would have gone anyway to cheer him up as one man of the arts to another. Rosenfeld, he could see, was desperately eager for talk about writing and ideas, for reassurance that he had not been forgotten by his friends out in civilian life.[4]

Although Sherwood had been distressed to see Rosenfeld so physically and emotionally miserable, most of the time he himself was supremely happy. He vacillated about settling in New York permanently; but it eased the ache of cultural isolation to be able to talk directly with such men as Brooks who lived and worked for a resurgence of the arts in America. He was attracted by what he felt as "a certain definite sharpness and shallowness" about New Yorkers in general, liking them, as he knew he would like Parisians or beautifully dressed aristocrats, despite his sense of being rather an outsider among them. He still retained some of his uneasy feeling of being the provincial. To Bab he wrote of being impressed by a certain New York atmosphere that sprang "from the fact that a great many real men of vast significance in America have walked and thought thoughts in these streets"; and Anita Loos later remembered with amusement a confidence that he made to her "soon after he arrived: 'Nita, I'm not going to let New York get me down. When I walk along the streets, I brace myself to look everyone right in the eye!'"[5]

Provincial or not, Anderson maintained his confidence in himself as writer, and here he was at his happiest. It was "paradise" for him, he wrote to Bab soon after settling in, to have the unbroken daily time for his writing; and a sense of ease and accomplishment pervaded him during those morning hours. He wrote of this also to Waldo Frank, who, by ironic chance, was spending August in Carmel, California, trying to get started on a book of his own designed to tell a French audience about the new America, which was struggling to be born out of the old. "Do you realize," Anderson asked him in a letter of around mid-August,

what it means to me to arise and have an unbroken, uninterrupted morning? Even letters are not opened. Already there creeps back over me the sense of power to handle long unbroken rhythms as when I worked on my long books. If this truly comes back and I can work in the old mood of unlimited power, carrying into it also the sense of a greater subtlety of understanding gathered from these years of living and of association with such men as you, things may yet be done. I was beginning to be afraid. Now courage comes surging back.

The writing went steadily. He turned out a short story called "The Dancer" and apparently worked for a good part of August on a piece, perhaps an unfinished novel, titled "The Romanticist," his term for anyone who refused to face cultural and sexual realities. It was now, or later in the fall, that he wrote one of his finest stories, "The Triumph of the Egg," that tale of American aspiration for success, of absurd failure, of human communication coming out of failure, a tale told just halfway between tears and laughter by a narrator who knows the comical pathos of lives, such balance and poise of tone suggesting how art and time had enabled the author to distance himself from the wholly painful experience years earlier in Cleveland with the defective mail order incubators. This story, resembling the Winesburg tales in its use of a singleminded, unworldly grotesque as protagonist, was set in the town of Bidwell, Ohio, or rather in the nearby hamlet of Pickleville grown up around a pickle factory and the Bidwell railroad station, the two buildings a synecdoche for the coming incursion of the industrial age into the towns of the Midwest. "The Triumph of The Egg" showed something of what was beginning to take shape in Anderson's mind, stimulated by the talks he now could occasionally have with Brooks about Mark Twain and Lincoln. On September 9 he resorted to a letter, though Brooks was still in New York, to tell him about a new long tale called "The Poor White." He had already written ten or fifteen thousand words and had even prepared an outline, which he could show his friend. This work, he felt, ought to interest Brooks, for it concerned one Hugh McVey, "a Lincolnian type from Missouri," Twain's home state. Anderson was moved to "live with him in his impulses and among his people and show if possible what influences have led him to be the kind of man we are puzzling about." Here, unlike "The Romanticist," was a work he would eventually finish and publish as his third novel, *Poor White*. It would be, on and off, one of the centers of his creative life for nearly two years.[6]

The conversations with Van Wyck had another, quicker result. Toward the end of August just before the publication of Brooks's *Letters and Leadership,* Anderson wrote Burton Rascoe to ask whether he would let him review for the *Chicago Tribune* this collection of essays mostly reprinted from *The Seven Arts*. Within days he sent off to Rascoe his statement about what he felt to be an important book by an important man, one who was not "smart and clever" like the popular writers but who instead tried "to get down to the bedrock." Rascoe ran the review, "Our Rebirth," in the *Tribune* for September 14. *Letters and Leadership,* the review declared, continued the call that had been sounded even before the war broke out for "a distinctive culture rising out of the need of Americans." Such a reawakening was and must be a spiritual, not a religious, one that had little to do with economic or social or political reform. It had even less to do, on the one hand, with the manufacture of popular fiction to be consumed like breakfast food or, on the other, with the "aping of the Europeans." It was, rather, a reawakening of faith in the possibilities of life as led by Americans who "work and laugh and grow a little to like and understand each other." In his scholarly, clear-sighted, unsentimental way, Brooks was voicing in *Letters and Leadership* "the hopeful young spirit growing up in American life and literature."[7]

The enthusiasm of the review suggests the middle-aged reviewer's youthful zest for his own living and writing. Around September 1, Tennessee ended her vacation in the Michigan countryside and came East to be with her husband for the month. Sherwood kept his work routine unbroken in the mornings, but in the afternoons and on weekends the pair did the city like tourists. They went on sightseeing trips, took the elevator to the top of the Woolworth Building, rode the ferries, sailed up and down the harbor, went swimming in the Sound, and ran out "to look at pieces of New England." One weekend they spent at the farm owned by their former Chicago friends, the painters Jerome and Lucile Blum; and Sherwood concluded that Jerry, who was exploring Post-Impressionist techniques, was "the best American painter I have found, his spirit is braver, his impulse more direct and real." Jerry might be "to painting here what I may some day be considered to writing." By mid-September Waldo and Margaret Frank had returned to New York, and the two couples occasionally met for further excursions and for hours of talk about the books the two men were deep into writing. As autumn came to the city, the very air seemed to Sherwood "like wine."[8]

As a way of organizing his experiences, he planned long letters to his children, and he began setting down more formally "a book of notes covering the impressions of a western man in this town"; he even wrote two more short stories, "delicate things" unrelated to the themes of *Poor White,* and sent them to a typist. But during most of those happy September mornings he wrote steadily and rapidly at his new novel in "a detached impersonal mood" that came from his certainty that he had found a way to get at the subject he had failed with in *Immaturity.* The new book, he confidently wrote to Bab, seemed to him "to have something of the sweep of *Marching Men* without the tendency of that book to subvert the human element." Very likely he had already brought his Lincolnesque protagonist from childhood and youth in a dismal settlement along Twain's great river eastward in space and to adulthood in time, an adulthood coinciding with that historical moment when, like the river rising to flood, industrialism begins to sweep in on the Ohio town of Bidwell. Sherwood asserted that the book "will lead me I hope into deep structural impulses in our civilization and cut deeper than anything I have ever tried to do before." Very likely, too, he was sustained by his conviction that this novel would prove him to be the "great artist" Brooks had called for in *Letters and Leadership* when extolling "the poetic view of life" and insisting that "poets and novelists and critics are the pathfinders of society; to them belongs the vision without which the people perish." The great artist, Brooks had declared, "floats the visible world on the sea of his imagination, and measures it, not by its own scale of values, but by the scale of values he has himself derived from his descent into the abysses of life." In the creative drive of those mornings in Chelsea, everything, the city and all its people, seemed remote to Anderson, quite outside "the present strong drift of my impulses."

Even the problem of finding a new publisher seems not to have disturbed him more than fitfully. In the *Memoirs* he would recall sending off the manuscript of *Winesburg* to several other book firms after John Lane had refused it as a financial risk early in the summer of 1918, each of these other firms rejecting it in turn. He could not have had time to send it to many, for shortly after he arrived in New York, he was being advised by a number of his friends, presumably Brooks among them, to look up B. W. Huebsch, who ran a small, enterprising publishing house under his own name. Around August 22, Anderson had written Huebsch a note asking when he might drop by to introduce himself. The publisher had already learned about the author from their mutual friend Francis Hackett, the literary editor of *The New Republic* who had so enthusiastically reviewed *Windy McPherson's Son,* and on August 23 he replied to Anderson's note, inviting him to come to his office at 225 Fifth Avenue on Saturday the twenty-fourth so that they could have lunch together. Considering the cordiality of Huebsch's reply, which suggested lunch "anyday next week" if the twenty-fourth were not possible, it seems likely that author and publisher had at least met before August was out. When Anderson told Huebsch that the John Lane Company was ready to release him, Huebsch scrupulously telephoned Jefferson Jones, who said that though he himself liked the Winesburg stories, Frederic Chapman at the London office had decided Anderson was "too gloomy" and that, since his three-book contract with Lane had been fulfilled, Huebsch was at liberty to sign him up. Sometime in the fall Anderson gave Huebsch the manuscript of the Winesburg stories to read. Perhaps since the previous spring he had become uncertain about the best title for the collection as a whole, for it would subsequently be Huebsch's settled conviction that the stories came to him without any overall name, that he read them, saw "what they were about," and eventually gave the book its title, *Winesburg, Ohio.* At any rate Huebsch liked the stories and, supported by Hackett's recommendation of them, offered to publish them as a volume. At least by December 2 Anderson had accepted the offer.[9]

All things considered, Sherwood's friends had advised him well in steering him toward his new publisher. Born in New York in the same year as the author, Benjamin W. Huebsch was the son of a rabbi who had immigrated to the United States from Germany. Ben was brought up in a home where the arts as well as learning were respected; in fact, he had studied both painting and the violin, and as a young man had been music critic for the *New York Sun.* He was especially influenced by his Uncle Samuel, who ran a print shop although his real love was for literature, philosophy, and the study of languages. Huebsch set up his own printing establishment, did well at selling annual diaries, and by 1902 was already advertising himself as "B. W. Huebsch, Publisher." Starting with a few nonfictional works of "advanced" thought, he soon added novels to his list, and in 1908 began publishing translations of books by such contemporary European writers as Gorky, Strindberg, and Gerhard Hauptmann. A man willing to take risks on new writers of promise, he published Brooks's *America's Coming-of-Age* and *Letters and Leadership,* advertised in 1916 three books by D. H. Lawrence, including *The Prussian Officer and Other Stories,* and in December of that year brought out James Joyce's *Dubliners* and *A Portrait of the Artist as a Young Man,* the latter in the first edition issued anywhere. In addition he had already established himself both as a well-known figure in the American Booksellers' Association and as a crusader against militarism and in defense of civil rights. He had sailed on Henry Ford's "Peace Ship" in 1915–16, and subsequently in 1920 he would become a member of the organizing committee for the American Civil Liberties Union, of which he would serve as treasurer for some three decades. A big-framed man with a large nose and wide mouth, he was soft-spoken, tolerant, but determined. Neither by temperament nor by principle was he to be deterred from publishing a book he liked no matter how unconventional its style or content. After all, he enjoyed being a publisher because, as he used to tell his friends, quoting Goethe, "A man can stand almost anything except a succession of ordinary days," and there were no ordinary days in publishing. He liked *Winesburg* and its author and was ready to risk backing both.

When publishing arrangements were settled, Anderson was as pleased by the new relationship as Huebsch was. "It is so delightful," he would write Ben on December 2, "to have a publisher you can have as a friend also." That *Winesburg* was to be published was the finishing touch for what he now realized must be only a New York interlude. But the interlude had not been as happy throughout as at the beginning and end. Taking John Emerson's money for writing brief publicity bits had begun to make him feel guilty, especially so since he came to understand that being a show business press agent called for a particular advertising talent he did not have. Considering how closely linked always were his moods and his physical condition, it is possible that feelings of guilt began to break in on him early in October when he came down with the Spanish influenza, which was epidemic in the United States and the rest of the world during the last autumn of the war. Tennessee had barely gotten back to Chicago at the end of September when she too fell ill. Even in mild cases this strain of flu, which killed over half a million people across the country, was seriously debilitating, and Sherwood recovered slowly. Frequently now he would take the bus up to Central Park and sit for hours on a park bench in the sunny air—sunlight and rest were cures widely recommended in the current newspapers—writing or merely watching people flow past and playing with them in his fancy. His illness seems to have made all his thoughts more somber. To Bab, who had come to New York for a vacation only to become ill herself, he tried to be sympathetic and encouraging. She was being forced by her responsibilities of caring for her aging parents, he wrote her, to face the test of maturity that every man and woman had to face whether they were aware of it or not. "And what is maturity beyond a realization that life is a trap into which we are thrown and no one knows the way out." This sense that "we are all so apparently caught in a trap" had persisted and would persist throughout his adult life. Normally it was offset or relieved by his sharp delight in physical sensation, his pleasure at putting words down on paper, his concomitant belief that life, looked at another way, consisted at its best of the moments when one felt most intensely. But such moments stood out from intervening spaces of emotional blank like bright sparks in the night, and the darkness or the sense of entrapment was always there as the backdrop against which lives were performed or, more exactly, simply happened.[10]

As the fall deepened toward winter, he remained depressed. Presumably he shared in the nationwide explosion of triumph and relief at the news of the Armistice; but most of November was darkened for him by his realization that he must return to the prison of his advertising job, provided that yet once more he could undo his resignation from it, and this concern over his personal affairs was mingled with his conviction that people in general would soon become bitterly disillusioned at how they had been tricked by patriotic words into the profitless "years of killing and ugliness." By early December, however, his black mood began to lift momentarily, in part because he had Huebsch's assurance that *Winesburg* would be published, and once again the writing of *Poor White* went steadily and the novel had "power and meaning" for him; in fact, he hoped to finish it by the time he returned to Chicago for Christmas. Meanwhile he had become friends, through Waldo Frank, with Jacques Copeau, director of the experimental Théâtre du Vieux Colombier in Paris, who with his troupe was in the second season of a two-year stay in New York. The friendship with Copeau may have increased his desire to visit France and may eventually have helped lead him to his own writing of plays, but at the moment he was particularly heartened by the Frenchman's enthusiasm for *Marching Men* as a picture of America and his offer to arrange for French translation of that novel and of the forthcoming *Winesburg*. The possibility of an international audience as well as the completion of a new novel would be signs of a New York interlude well spent.[11]

If he was pleased to find a new friend in Copeau and to strengthen his friendship with Paul Rosenfeld, now free of the army and back in the city, he found his relations with Waldo Frank coming to a crisis. When Waldo had visited Chicago the previous spring, he must have told Sherwood something about his nearly completed second novel; for when he had finished a first draft of it in May, he had appealed to Anderson for suggestions for a title, an appeal that had sent the latter "grouping," as he almost invariably spelled "groping," in the Old Testament for an evening on an unsuccessful hunt for inspiration. Frank did not, however, send on the manuscript to his "brother," very probably because he felt that the novel needed a thorough revision. By November, however, he had reworked the manuscript and now showed it to Rosenfeld, who thought it seriously flawed and who without Frank's knowledge let Anderson read it. Sherwood agreed that the book was wordy and overwritten. He had already become irritated in his talks with Waldo by the latter's increasing insistence on his own greatness as an international literary figure. One day Anderson blurted out to Frank all his accumulated criticisms of him as person and writer, and Frank, who had his own accumulated resentments against the older man's occasional tendency to put him down, was profoundly hurt and angered. Sherwood would later apologize affectionately for being "too big brotherly" in his preachments, but the incident shadowed all the meetings of the two men during the last few weeks of Anderson's stay in New York. For another two years they would keep up a comradely correspondence and on a few occasions visit each other in old friendship, but that angry interchange in New York would prove an omen of their gradual drifting apart.[12]

By mid-December, Anderson was in a final flurry of engagements, lunches, trips out into the country, and even the pleasant obligation of showing New York to the volatile Ben Hecht, who was en route from Chicago to an assignment as foreign correspondent for the *Daily News* in postwar Germany. On December 18 he met with Ben Huebsch for an important occasion, the signing of the agreement to publish *Winesburg, Ohio*. It was a standard contract, though the terms were somewhat more favorable for Anderson than Lane had agreed to with Sherwood's first book. The meeting was a happy one for both men; their personal and business relationship made him "feel right," the author wrote Huebsch gladly.[13]

That same week he said his last farewells to his friends, including Rose McCarron, and a few days before Christmas he took the train to Chicago. By the twenty-third he was definitely resettled in Chicago and already at work again on the still unfinished *Poor White*. By then someone had wired him from New York the sad news of Randolph Bourne's death from pneumonia just a day earlier, and Anderson wrote to Paul Rosenfeld to express his sorrow. Presumably he did not know that Rosenfeld had shown his devotion to Bourne by being one of the four people who helped care for the sick man during his last hours; otherwise Anderson might not have written so vaguely that "I have a feeling he was in a very real way your friend." Characteristically he was concerned less with death than with life and particularly with his own life; most of the letter concerned his plans for completing *Poor White* at his own pace now that the New York sojourn had deeply rested him and given him "courage and strength to keep on in the face of the dullness of the daily grind for a year or two." Somehow, presumably through Bayard Barton's long-suffering regard, he had managed quietly to go back to his old job at Critchfield. Art must go on, but he had proven once more that life was essentially a trap. His first attempt to escape from Chicago had ended.

2.

Despite the confidence he had displayed to Rosenfeld, Sherwood was for a time deeply depressed at having to reenter the prison, as he now would repeatedly term it, of business. Soon after his return from New York he had two long-ulcerated teeth extracted and had momentary hopes of feeling better. But his problem was psychological rather than physical. He did recover from his initial black mood, made some progress in January of

1919 on the concluding chapters of the *Poor White* manuscript, which he knew would require extensive cutting throughout when a first draft was finished, and had days, even weeks at a time when he again felt rested and encouraged. He had to work at his advertising chores unusually hard to reestablish himself in his job after nearly five months of freedom, and having been daily at the office from eight to five-thirty, he had fewer free moments and less energy for concentrated writing. As the winter wore on, he gradually ceased trying to finish *Poor White,* and the black moods periodically returned to cut across the times when he felt well and wrote freely. The taste of freedom made him long for more of it, and the longing exacerbated the inevitable frustrations of his job.[14]

Respites from his sense of imprisonment were welcome. One January Sunday he and Tennessee spent a satisfying day in Michigan City, Indiana, with Cornelia and the three children, who had settled in a small frame house at 123 Detroit Street. Sherwood was delighted by the puppet show that Robert gave at twilight in a theater the boy had constructed. John was a quiet pleasure; Mimi was less babyish, more the little girl; Cornelia, who was now in her second year as a teacher of English and Latin at the nearby Isaac C. Elston High School, seemed happier and more able to "handle her life." It must have taken all of Cornelia's habitual composure to keep the day so pleasant for the man she still loved and the woman, his wife, with whom she generously maintained affectionate friendship.[15]

More important for his writing than the visit to his first family was Sherwood's reading at this time of *The Education of Henry Adams,* issued in its first public edition just the previous fall and already selling heavily across the nation. To Van Wyck Brooks he revealed by letter in just how personal a context he regarded that autobiography.

I . . . feel tremendously its importance as a piece of American writing. New England can scarcely go further than that. It must be, in its way, very complete. We do, I am sure, both live and die rather better in the Middle West. Nothing about us is as yet so completely and racially tired.

When you get at your Mark Twain (I suppose you already have) you must do a chapter on the American going East into that tired, thin New England atmosphere and being conquered by its feminine force.

As though to emphasize by contrast the rich, vital, masculine force of the Midwest—a force which in these unsettled weeks he could more assert than feel—he concealed under a metaphor his actual failure to finish *Poor White:*

I came West with my new book, *Poor White,* about laid by, as we out here say of the corn crop in early October. It is in shocks and stood up in the field. The husking is yet to do. I will not attempt it for a time, as the proof on *Winesburg* should be along most any time.

Back in Chicago after giving up the "moving picture dependence," Anderson would claim for Brooks's benefit that "I almost feel able to say that I don't care if I never travel again. The place between mountain and mountain I call Mid-America is my land. Good or bad, it's all I'll ever have."

Anderson may well have used the bardic touch because it was Brooks to whom he wrote; yet this conscious comparison of his Midwest self with New England's Henry Adams would become one of the impulses behind the writing of his fanciful autobiography, *A Story Teller's Story,* some four years later, when he had physically left Mid-America.[16]

Over the next months Anderson restlessly considered several schemes for financial independence, but he could not yet find a door out of the prison that at moments drove its prisoner to playing with the thought of suicide as an escape, though, as he admitted to Frank, "that would not help and there is so much eager life I want to find my way into." For day-to-day living he had to content himself with the company of Tennessee, who was tired by the long hours she spent in teaching music and dance in the Fine Arts Building, and with mostly casual contacts with various kinds of friends like his fellow copywriter George Daugherty, who too had plans for novels, or like Pascal Covici, who with an ex-priest named Billy McGee had established a mid-Loop bookstore that became an informal rendezvous of Chicagoans interested in literature and art, or like the persons met at two institutions of the "literati" that had fairly recently been established in the city.[17]

The first of these was the Dill Pickle Club, one of the "bright spots in the rather somber aspect of our town," as Anderson commented when he wrote about it and its founder in "Jack Jones—The Pickler" in the June 18, 1919, issue of the *Daily News.* John Archibald Jones, who tended to keep his past to himself, was a Canadian of Anderson's age. Radicalized by working as a metal miner in the West, he had become an organizer for the Industrial Workers of the World, married Elizabeth Gurley Flynn, "The Rebel Girl," soon separated from her, left the IWW in 1912, and for several years was a left-wing member of the Painters Union in Chicago. (Sherwood and Jack greeted each other as "Brush," since each had at one time worked as a housepainter.) In 1917 he established the Dill Pickle Club as a public forum that would bring together radicals, hoboes, college professors, artists, writers, and mere dwellers in Bohemia. The Club was a reconditioned stables at 18 Tooker Alley, a narrow, cobblestone lane that connected Dearborn and State Street on Chicago's North Side just south of "Bughouse Square," or Washington Park, renowned for its soapbox orators. On Sunday nights just before eight o'clock, one entered through the orange door of the Club into a large, comfortable main room with brightly painted chairs and benches, counters along the side where coffee and sandwiches were sold, a small stage—one-act plays were occasionally presented—and a lectern for the night's speaker. Jones, a thin-faced, blue-eyed, smiling man habitually dressed in a lumberman's jacket, had a gift for showmanship, and with his invariable question to anyone, "Are you a nut about anything?," always found someone to try out his or her ideas before an audience of "Picklers" highly skilled at heckling. By early 1919 Jones had succeeded in attracting the interest of intellectuals and artists, like Sherwood himself, and the Sunday nights might feature a poetry reading or a defense of Nietzscheanism as well as a discourse on the necessity of free love or of social revolution. Anderson himself talked at least one Sunday evening, joining a line of speakers that over the years included radicals like Big Bill Haywood, Emma Goldman, Eugene Debs; poets and novelists like Carl Sandburg, Ben Hecht, Alfred Kreymborg, and the Bohemian's Bohemian, Maxwell Bodenheim; local or national figures like Clarence Darrow, Aimee Semple McPherson, or Yellow Kid Weil. Shortly before Anderson published this description of the Pickle and its owner, Jones had initiated a regular Thursday evening dedicated entirely to the arts and was planning to establish a *Pickler* magazine; the article amiably suggested that Jones, with his alert showmanship and his ability to make everyone laugh, might possibly "make a home for the arts among us" as more serious-minded entrepreneurs had failed to do. But the Sunday evenings, half test runs for new ideas and bizarre notions, half verbal roughhouses, would be the times best remembered by the Picklers themselves. What some celebrity said in Tooker's Alley of a Sunday evening, they felt, might make news in Monday morning's newspapers.[18]

The goings-on at the Dill Pickle tended to be on the hilarious and rowdy, if stimulating, side, and Anderson was often not in the mood for them. For months before his New York interlude he had already been participating in the quieter, if not always more serious, weekly discussions of literature and life at another bright spot in somber Chicago, Schlogl's restaurant on Wells Street in the Loop close to the *Daily News* building. Over some thirty years Schlogl's had developed a reputation for good German cooking as well as for occasional more exotic dishes like eel in aspic and, it was declared, "owls to order." During the war newspapermen had gone there when payday made them willing to accept the restaurant's rather high prices, and slowly a custom had grown up whereby once a week, usually Saturdays, the more literarily inclined of them preempted the large round wooden table in one corner of the smoky, black walnut paneled dining room for a leisurely lunch and for talk that might last well into the afternoon. Many of the men—it was an entirely masculine atmosphere, including Richard the "Literary Waiter," who took care of the round table—were from the *Daily News,* including Henry Justin Smith, the quiet, capable news editor who encouraged any creative writer on the staff, Ben Hecht, Carl Sandburg, Keith Preston, a professor of classics who contributed a witty column on literature, poet-reviewer John V. A. Weaver, Henry Blackman Sell, founder in 1916 of the *News's* Wednesday book page, and Harry Hansen, reporter, book-lover, and subsequently, in March of 1920, successor to Sell as manager of the book page when the latter went off to New York to be editor of *Harper's Bazaar.* Although Burton Rascoe was a *Tribune* man, he had become a Schlogl's regular partly by virtue of his editorship of that paper's Saturday book page, as had the more conservative Llewellyn Jones, who since 1914 had been literary editor for the Friday edition of the *Chicago Evening Post.* Very likely it was Hecht who had originally brought Sherwood into this group, but all of Anderson's books had been reviewed in both *Daily News* and *Tribune,* and he had published a piece in each newspaper in 1918. Indeed, his presence at the weekly lunches may have been used as an added lure when Sell or Rascoe invited to the round table, as in their capacities as book page editors they often did, some American or foreign writer passing through Chicago on a visit or a lecture tour.[19]

It could not have helped stabilize Anderson's fluctuating moods in the early months of 1919 that some of the regulars were missing from the weekly talk fests. Hecht was in Germany, Hansen was covering the Paris Peace Conference, Rascoe was so harried by his multiple jobs on the *Tribune* that he could attend only infrequently; yet Sherwood could and did maintain the connections he had developed with the editors of the various book pages. He especially liked Burton Rascoe, though he was amused by Burton's explosive intensity of manner. Rascoe was more widely read than the handsome, enterprising Sell, who was as much promoter of books as critic; but unlike Llewellyn Jones, whose taste and manner were more restrained, both Rascoe and Sell were personally and professionally alert to the exciting new developments in postwar American literature, eager to risk supporting them rather than the merely orthodox and popular, and delighted in confronting Midwest provincialism with praise of European novelists, poets, and thinkers. Neither man, nor Sandburg or Hecht for that matter, could give Anderson the companionship he had found in New York with Brooks and Rosenfeld or in the less irritating moments with Waldo Frank. Still the Schlogl group did associate him with persons who found the literary life superior to business and who, Rascoe and Sell particularly, in their opinion-making positions were helping to create an audience for his writing and for experiment in literature generally. Perhaps, as Anderson had argued a year earlier in "Chicago Culture," the best way "to kill the growth of a distinctive middle western literature was to talk about it," but the round table sessions were a respite for him at a time of recurring frustration and dissatisfaction.

Looking back only three or four years later, two members of the Schlogl group would not remember a moody, intensely frustrated Anderson but one utterly, though quietly, assured of what he was doing as an artist. Writing of the weekly round table talks in his *Midwest Portraits,* Harry Hansen gave a picture of Sherwood breaking in on one of Hecht's tirades with his usual "low, delighted chuckle."

Anderson leans forward and smiles across the table. His eyes are big and gentle and there is always a sort of friendly look about them. His hands are clumsy and soft but active; you get the feeling that he must hold a pen clumsily, that he must pound a typewriter mercilessly. He is the only man of whom one can say that he speaks caressingly. He rarely argues. He never expounds. He merely chuckles a bit to himself, tells a story when he has been prodded long enough, preferably an anecdote about somebody he knows. He and Ben Hecht are old friends. Back in the old salad days . . . when Ben was a cub reporter reading the "Arabian Nights" between assignments and Sherwood was the world's greatest unpublished author, reading his manuscripts aloud by candlelight in studios, in the back rooms of saloons, in forlorn lodging houses, the two men met and learned to respect each other's gifts. For years Ben predicted a big writing career for Sherwood Anderson. For years Sherwood Anderson looked with kindly eyes on Ben's ripening powers. "He thinks I am the greatest writer living," said Ben once, "that is, next to himself."

Rascoe, who in 1921 would follow Sell to New York, took with him a recollection of Sherwood's "gorgeous vanity," a vanity implied by Hecht's remark, but "gorgeous" because Burton found his friend on the surface modest, deferential, willing to listen to others, but at bottom imperturbably convinced of his worth, firmly believed in by Rascoe also, as "the phenomenon that is Sherwood Anderson, a great and original figure in American literature." Anderson's belief in himself as "the greatest writer living," Rascoe goes on to comment with a flick of the satirical whip, is not entirely hidden either.

His vanity peeps out, like those atrocious socks he wears with red and black checks in them, each block of color two inches square. Most people are not likely to notice these socks, because his suit is usually a quiet and comfortable tweed. They are not likely to pay close attention to the violent multicolored muffler he wears, because his overcoat is a decorous raglan. They are not likely to notice the guinea feather in his hatband, because his hat is cleverly chosen to show off his head most effectively and unostentatiously. They are not likely to notice that his hair is trimmed more often than a movie star's because it looks so unkempt, unwieldy and romantic. They are not likely to observe that he is fastidious, because he so adroitly conveys the opposite impression.

Being basically interested in himself, he is willing to listen with an appearance of sympathetic interest even to some "windy old fraud backed up to a building on the busiest street in Chicago," and there is in fact "something about him that makes people want to recount their life histories to him."

He is the confidant of enterprising businessmen who tell him their dissatisfaction with life, their secret aspirations, the difficulties they get into over their sweethearts. Hard-ups and frustrated geniuses, neurotics and racehorse touts tell him all about themselves. Give Sherwood twenty minutes in the corner with a married woman and he knows every blessed grievance she has against her husband, from his habit of wearing nightgowns to his silly preferences in women, from his humming idiotic snatches of song in his bath to his shallow lies, petty trickeries and empty vanities.

Anderson's reward for his listening, Rascoe asserts, is an intuition of "amazing accuracy" about the nature of human beings, a talent acquired—and here the satire drops wholly away—"by a persistent and patient interest in people, by an insatiable curiosity, by an early Christian belief in the profound significance of all human life." This the reward, together with, of course, material for more novels and stories.[20]

Granted that Hansen's and Rascoe's are literary performances, that they reflect a knowledge of their subject's artistic development subsequent to 1919, they suggest, when juxtaposed against the unhappiness he was then revealing to his closest correspondents, a disparity between Anderson's outer manner and inner life. It was a disparity that he noted in a letter to Waldo late in the winter of 1919:

To the men about me in the office here I present myself as a strong swimmer. Hardly a day passes that some business man or woman does not come to me asking a question.

How do you remain so calm and quiet?-they ask.

I laugh. It is because I love God-I say.

The men and women are baffled. They are angry at me. They love me. I cannot explain to them that I also am tumbled and tossed out.

I am too much like them.

Throughout his life some people, becoming aware of similar disparate selves in Anderson, would conclude that he was only a poseur, that while like many writers he sought an identity through the trying on of personalities, but unlike them his search was not an honest one, that he was essentially a showman of the self and little more. That he was a mixture of selves he himself believed; for example, he often confessed to being, as he would put it in the *Memoirs,* part artist, part "rather foxy man, with a foxiness which at time approached slickness." Yet everyone, he was convinced, was a mixture of selves, was one or more persons to the world while inwardly living constantly shifting "lives" in response to the mood of the moment and the restless activity of imagination.[21]

Such a conviction may have been especially strong in him during this unsettled winter and early spring; for with *Poor White* laid aside and with printer's proof of *Winesburg* read and returned to Huebsch, probably by late January, he began two writing experiments designed to further explore the inner life. That the first was to be a book of tales might have been predicted since, in no frame of mind for the extended effort of another novel, he could at odd moments of the day let his imagination play with some limited aspect of a person's life until he was ready to put words on paper and could then dash down a draft of the story at a single sitting. The book of tales, some already written, some waiting, as he would often say, on the doorstep of his mind, was to be organized around a single theme— the psychic injury done by the blocking of the individual's emotional, sexual, imaginative capacities, the very basis of the inner life. As he wrote to Trigant Burrow after he had unexpectedly reopened friendly communication, "You and I know that the big story here is the story of repression, of the strange and almost universal insanity of society." The organizing theme was to be, in a word, "Repression," as he also wrote Jane Heap, the associate editor of *The Little Review,* explaining that though he had submitted "The Triumph of the Egg" to her, he did not want it published at present since he intended to use it in the book. To be included in the collection also was a story he had just written in late winter or very early spring called "The New Englander," which, he told Jane Heap, "would curl your hair."[22]

Flawed though it is by stereotyped characterization and overly explicit symbolism, the story was indeed a bold one for 1919 and still retains a certain power. Elsie Leander, thirty-five-year-old virgin, has grown up on the rocky, mountain-surrounded Vermont farm owned by her repressed and repressive parents, a family group personifying that "tired, thin New England atmosphere" Anderson had recently complained of to Brooks as having marked Henry Adams's education. The Leanders leave their tiny, walled-in acreage for the open expanse of Iowa, where the surviving Leander son has settled as a village grocer, fathered several energetic children, and purchased for his parents a big unfurnished farmhouse, which stands like an island in a giant sea of corn. The timid Elsie is drawn to the long, tunnel-like rows of corn that, looked at from ground level, seem to her to be "mysteriously beautiful . . . warm passageways running out into life." Slowly she half awakens to what she does not understand are her own sexual needs. While her brother's family are visiting the farm one hot August afternoon, an approaching thunderstorm begins to turn the sky black, and Elsie is filled with a confused, urgent desire "to get out of her life into some new and sweeter life she felt must be hidden away somewhere in the fields." Rushing into the vastness of the corn, she accidentally tears her dress so that her "tiny breasts" are exposed, and throwing herself on her back she lies for some time quiescent in one of the warm, close corn-tunnels. About to return to the house the "distraught woman" sees her brother's sixteen-year-old daughter kissing a young plowman, and in blind, lonely arousal she grasps one of the cornstalks and presses her lips into the dusty ground. The storm breaks, water pours over her recumbent body, and she "abandons herself to a storm of grief that is only partially grief." Through the sound of the rain she occasionally hears "the thin voices of her mother and father calling to her out of the Leander house."

"The New Englander" is almost a paradigm of Anderson's view of certain cultural-geographic differences in the United States and of the emotional damage done by what in the 1920s he was not alone in stigmatizing as "Puritanism," defined as that pervasive spirit of intolerant, joyless moralism, which was especially antagonistic to any expression of the power of sex. This was hardly a new theme for him, as that first published story of his, "The Rabbit-pen," had attested; but his own anti-Puritan attitude, based on temperament and lived experience, had recently been reinforced by his talks in New York with the more analytical author of *America's Coming-of-Age* and by his own very personal reading of *The Education of Henry Adams*. In one of those flashes of ruthless self-insight of which he was often capable, he had pointed out to his brother Karl that neither of them had much intellect, of the rigorously analytic sort, that is, and that "What we have got to do is to feel into things." As though to confirm his insight, the weakest aspects of "The New Englander" are just those where the tale cannot be trusted because the teller demands that his premises must be trusted first; the strongest aspect is the picture of an unawakened woman slowly being invaded by blind sexual longing.[23]

But the notion of a book of thematically organized tales was not, so soon after he had returned the proof sheets of *Winesburg,* a particularly fresh kind of experiment, and simultaneously Anderson was attempting another, more original investigation of the inner life. Two years earlier he had returned from a short visit to New York so stimulated by admission to a new world that, though he had apparently written only one poem before, the sad one to Cornelia on their honeymoon, an outpouring of bardic chants seemed his only appropriate expression. Memories of his recent, longer stay in New York combined with his conscious anti-Puritanism and his subjection to erratically swinging moods now impelled him to begin what he characterized to Waldo Frank as "the Mid-American Chant thing carried on—is out on the edge of madness but earthy too." This new experiment was not, however, in poetry but in prose "by way of design in words and feelings," as he cryptically wrote the devoted Bab when he sent some of the experimental pieces to her to be typed fair with an original and a carbon copy.[24]

These pieces he intended to collect into a book, which at first he called *Industrial Vistas,* probably in imitation of Whitman's *Democratic Vistas,* because it was "written out of the jangle and ugliness of industrial life." It was to be, he explained in another letter to Burrow, "the autobiography of a man's secondary self, of the quiet, unnamed fancies that float through his brain, the things that appear to have no connection with actualities," or, more succinctly, "the autobiography of the fanciful life of an individual," through which microcosm, as with the bardic persona of the *Chants,* Anderson predicted he could analyze the macrocosm of America. Sometime prior to the end of March he wrote Jane Heap at *The Little Review* that he had found a better title, one with obvious religious overtones—*A New Testament.* The individual testaments "propose to be," he told her, "a sort of autobiography of unreality—of the life within that exists because it doesn't exist." Enclosing the first of them in his letter with the assurance that "they are insane enough to satisfy anyone," he suggested to her that they be published as a series, one to an issue of the magazine. Having started to write them in February or March, he continued to pour them out, as two years earlier he had the *Chants,* until some time in May when the "mood" temporarily left him after he had finished "about eighteen or nineteen." By mid-June, Jane Heap had accepted thirteen of the testaments, presumably all that he sent her, for serial publication, and the June 1919 issue of *The Little Review* announced that the series would soon begin to appear.[25]

Not until eight years later would Anderson publish a much enlarged *New Testament* in book form, and thereby puzzle and irritate reviewers as to its form and purpose; yet the series of thirteen that ran in *The Little Review*—at first one or two a month beginning with the issue for October 1919, but straggling to an end with that for January–March, 1921—makes up a comprehensible unit and indicates something of what was occupying the author's inner life in the late winter and spring of 1919.[26]

There can be no doubt that *A New Testament* began as an experiment in prose. Although some of these short pieces have the tone and cadence of Anderson's favorite King James Version, especially of the prophetic books, others more exactly resemble his own semifantasy sketch "Sister" in the December 1915 issue of *The Little Review,* except that a narrative element appears only infrequently. The series breaks roughly into three groups according to prose form. The first four are for the most part meditative essays spoken to "you," the reader, though they proceed not only by a clear argument but by a mode of free association and even at times dream logic. Testaments 5 though 10 are pieces of poetic prose close to the less rhythmical of the Chants, a form appropriate to the quasi-religious prophetic visions several describe. The final three testaments are mixed in form—part meditation, part fairly realistic narrative, part highly subjective fantasy. This rough division by form corresponds generally, though not precisely, with a division by dominant theme, the sequence of themes in turn implying a development backward in the chronology of Anderson's life and downward, as it were, in layers of consciousness.[27]

That *A New Testament* was partly "an extension of the mood of the chants" is suggested in the very first of the testaments when the "I"-person who speaks the twelve numbered ones, quite openly Anderson himself, announces a "patriot" conviction: "I have a feeling that the great basin of the Mississippi River, where I have always lived and moved about, is one day to be the seat of the culture of the universe." The bardic note and the bardic view of American history recur intermittently—"The words of old time men have been reborn in the factory towns of my country" (Testament 5)—yet the emphasis in the first four testaments is on the speaker's lack of interest in the life led at the surface level "by my conscious self," his concern with "the hidden thing in myself," and his desire to make loving contact by way of his fanciful thoughts with the imagination that sleeps in all persons like the seed buried "in the winter of time." Not surprisingly in this context, Anderson refers at length to Chicago North Side room where he "came near achieving complete happiness"—almost certainly a reference to the room at 735 Cass Street where he began *Winesburg, Ohio*, the book Huebsch was at that moment preparing to publish—and he ruminates on how these testaments of his hidden fanciful life may fertilize what is hidden in others, may bring out the creative self in them. The way to true sanity, he asserts, is by way of what is usually called insanity, that is, by way of the fancy, which makes exist that which does not "really" exist; the way to truth is by way of the lie. Through this method of indirection the speaker is making "love to all the men and women of a city."[28]

For a writer, such lovemaking must by definition be carried on, however indirectly, through the instrument of words, and in Testament 5, the first of the group in poetic prose form, the speaker proclaims his book to be a "hospital" where he will mate barren female words and male ones crippled by an industrial age. Nevertheless the theme that dominates this second division within the testament series is, paradoxically, the failure of the speaker to communicate with others. Whereas the prophet-bard of *Mid-American Chants* had released his people from bondage with his visionary words, the speaker of Testaments 8, 9, and 10, a self-styled Jeremiah, is in one episode a "dumb man" who writes crudely with a stick in the sand by a stream but who lacks the "sweet words" to tell his tale and whose writing in the sand is washed away by the water. In a second prophetic episode the speaker has gone into the mountains and prepares to speak to the "millions of men and women who live in the valley of the Mississippi River" and have gathered "into the plains" to hear him; yet when "I tried to say the word . . . my tongue became dry and hard like a stone." Leaving the mountains, abandoning the role of prophet, he resolves instead to run at night through towns and cities.

Such running is not, as in the first testaments, a figure for the imaginative touch of others but a mode of escape from them. Escape as a minor theme had been introduced at the beginning of Testament 6 when the speaker stated forebodingly that the "idea of escape long ago attacked the seat of my reason" and that he was "one who has walked out of a tall building into the streets of a city and over plains into a forest that fringes a river." In the final group of testaments that speaker is no longer the prophet but simply one who walks "far out, at the edges of life" and who, when afraid, runs "crazily in wider and wider circles." For this person the notion of escape has become obsessive. It is at this point that Anderson's "autobiography of the fanciful life of an individual" becomes most autobiographical; for masked though it is, what follows in Testament 12, the last of the numbered pieces in the series, is a reenactment of that traumatic Thanksgiving Day event some six years earlier. The speaker visits a woman who sits at a desk in an office in Chicago; but what he tells her resembles what Anderson actually said to his secretary at her desk in an office in Elyria and remarkably resembles what he would soon report himself as saying to her in *A Story Teller's Story:* "I told her my feet were cold because I had spent my life walking in the bed of a river." Although the speaker then recalls a *Winesburg*-like episode of passionate lovemaking with the Chicago woman in a field at night, his thoughts soon return to the moment of escape with a comment that indicates Anderson had already in 1919 worked out the elements of his account in the fanciful autobiography of 1924, that account which would establish so firmly the legend of how he left business for literature. "It is my own belief the whole plan was matured in advance. It is my own belief that I took hold of insanity as, in a crowded city street, one takes hold of the hand of a child." Insanity, the speaker muses, perhaps adapting a figure from the third paragraph of "The New Englander," is "a slow moving liquid in a cup" that changes color as one looks at it. Had he, he concludes, been asking the woman "to drink with me out of the cup of insanity" in order to lift her out of her life, or had he only been attempting to escape by himself from the dreary domestic fate of being "one who breeds in the beds at night?"

Taken as a self-contained whole, the series of testaments published in *The Little Review* becomes a revealing document. Though it is not one of his major accomplishments, it demonstrates, for one thing, his refusal to rest in his own, or anyone else's, formulas. In ranging from the spare, simple-appearing Winesburg tales to such intricate, self-contained stories as "Seeds" to a novel like *Poor White* where a central figure must appear both representative and individual, Anderson had been trying "constantly to push out into experimental fields," as he wrote Brooks with honest pride, had been asking and attempting what could be done in prose that had not been done. His reward for putting "so much emotional force" into these attempts was the "adventure" of the thing itself and the knowledge that he gained "a little colorful strength in my everyday writing." In *A New Testament* he deliberately set out on yet another new road, accepting the possibility of failure as a condition of the journey.[29]

Nor were these testaments mere finger exercises for a writer between books. When he returned to "making testament" late in 1919, he would insist on how much the making meant to him privately, however others might regard the results. Coming in that self-troubled spring of the year, the first thirteen testaments confirm that private importance through the themes with which they deal, the doubts they express, the willingness shown by their author to work back and back into increasingly painful psychic material. The first group in the series elaborated a conviction. That the true self in any human being resides in his or her imaginative relation to outer reality, not in the immediate confrontation with that reality by act and word, resides in the hidden "seed" not the visible "husk"—this had been and would remain one of Anderson's fixed beliefs, together with its corollary that the writer through his art can touch other true selves with his own in a transcendental communion that is religious in quality, but unsupernatural in substance. In the middle group of "prophetic" testaments Anderson courageously posed the possibility that his writing so far had failed to bring about this communion, not because of some lack in language itself, but because of some lack of skill on his part in the use of language. In the third group, therefore, he probed the circumstances of his becoming a writer; and if through the voice of the speaker he might be seen as preparing a legend about a crucial incident that he never fully understood himself, he was not afraid of questioning the motives he had at the time it happened.

Since he had gone this far back in his "autobiography of the fanciful life," both the aesthetic requirements of form and the psychic requirements of making testament, of giving witness to his inner self, seem to have forced him to go back even farther in the last testament in the series, the only one without a number, the only one with a title. The speaker of "The Man in the Brown Coat" is still a persona for the author—he represents himself as a college-trained historian who has written three books and now is writing yet another "history of the things men do." Against a refrain concerning generals who have gone into battle, a symbol of the great events of history, the speaker visualizes the division between himself and his wife, a division pathetically like that which had existed between Sherwood and Cornelia Anderson. (This testament is, in fact, the most compassionate view of that marriage he would ever publish.) The wife "cannot come out of herself" and does not know him; although he sometimes hears "the voices of her mind" talking, he cannot come out of his brown coat, his husk, and does not know her. Sitting in his locked room, symbol of a self "as alone as ever any man God made," he asks himself why he has "never been able to break through the wall to my wife," though he can picture his face "floating" into her mind as other faces float into his. He has written hundreds of thousands of words, but are there, he asks, "no words for life?" Someday, he concludes, "I shall make a testament unto myself." Thus Anderson neatly rounds out the structure of his series. The historian of the past returns the reader of the testaments to the artist in the present, all three faced with the challenge of making, through the instrumentality of words, one imagination reach out and touch another, since that is the only way people may meet in their essentialness.

3.

On May 8, 1919, B. W. Huebsch published Sherwood Anderson's *Winesburg, Ohio*. For years before he died Anderson was to have a fixed conviction that when his best-known book appeared, it "was widely condemned, called nasty and dirty by most of its critics." As he would remember it, most reviewers took *Winesburg* as "the work of a perverted mind . . . in review after review it was called 'a sewer' and the man who had written it taken as a strangely sex-obsessed man. . . ." As he also remembered it, for months his mail was filled with abusive letters from people who could not accept the honest revelations in his tales of "obscure and often twisted lives," and hence projected their own repressions onto him in "a spewing forth of something like poison." Probably he did receive some letters, long since destroyed, resembling the one to the *Chicago Tribune* from a Miss D. H. of Los Angeles:

I consider Sherwood Anderson's "Winesburg, Ohio" both disgusting and dull. . . . It seems to me a distillation of the sort of leering gossip one would expect to find bandied about by male scandalmongers chewing tobacco on cracker barrels in a dirty cross-roads grocery store. . . .

I suppose this book will be "hailed" by a few Dreiser devotees and some impressionable reviewers will admire it as "strong." It is so strong it ought to be buried without delay in the nearest public sanitation.

Perhaps a friend of Sherwood did witness the public burning of three copies of *Winesburg* by the thin-faced library board of a New England town, though one wonders incidentally why a library board should have had more than one copy for its bonfire. Certainly the *Sunday Republican* of Springfield, Massachusetts gave the book only a brief notice, which ended, "Some of his sketches . . . have an underlying significance and real beauty of feeling, but more of them are descriptions somewhat boldly naked, of the commonplace without a spark of life or creative feeling." The second review to appear, that in the New York *Sun,* was titled "A Gutter Would Be Spoon River," charged that "Mr. Anderson has reduced his material from human clay to plain dirt," and condemned "his very bad English." Again, the reviewer for the New York *Evening Post* warned that none of the stories was an "artistic interpretation of life" and at least half were "of a character which no man would wish to see in the hands of a daughter or sister." That Anderson should recall only such stings suggests that, in his later years in the 1930s, he was reacting defensively to the erosion of the fame *Winesburg* helped to bring him, for he much exaggerated the amount of hostility his masterpiece had to overcome. That there was widespread hostility to the "new literature" among the postwar American public, especially when sexual taboos were questioned, was as much a fact of the 1920s as the appearance of the new literature itself, as the decade's legal battles over censorship would attest. But the actual response to *Winesburg* had been much different from what its author would fabricate long afterwards.[30]

If he had received many letters from outraged Puritans, he would have complained of them, or ridiculed them, when writing at the time to Waldo Frank, but he made no such reference. On the contrary, when he did write on May 27 to thank Waldo for his excited praise of *Winesburg,* he remarked that the book "has only been out a few days but already I have had several letters of very deep appreciation of it"; and five months later he would boast, again to Waldo, that "I get constant and beautiful reactions from Winesburg." About the reviews of *Winesburg* he thoroughly misled the future readers of the *Memoirs.* Between May 31, when Heywood Broun praised and criticized *Winesburg* in the New York *Tribune,* and September 21, when John Nicholas Beffel unreservedly praised it in the Sunday magazine section of New York's Socialist daily *The Call,* at least twenty-one reviews appeared. Of these, the *Sun* and *Evening Post* reviews alone damned it completely—at the time Anderson wryly suspected that the *Sun* reviewer was a woman who needed "someone to gratify her choked up desires"—and only two others found that the defects of the book outweighed its virtues. Of the rest, nearly a third were very favorable in their judgment; more than half, including that in the *Boston Transcript* of "tired, thin" New England, were unqualified in their praise. Writing to Trigant Burrow in September of 1919, Anderson could say proudly: "The book has been getting rather remarkable recognition even from

those who have fought me before. In another year it will no doubt get publication in France and perhaps in other European countries." That later in
life he should have remembered otherwise tells much about the power of
his fancy to shape reality at need.[31]

Overwhelmingly the reviewers were just the opposite of hostile. If
many of them made the obvious comparison between *Winesburg, Ohio*
and *Spoon River Anthology,* the comparison was usually in Anderson's
favor. If half a dozen linked Anderson and the Russians, particularly
Chekhov and Dostoyevsky, he was usually acclaimed their equal. If H. W.
Boynton in the conservative *Bookman* charged that the author had "too
freely imbibed the doctrine of the psychoanalysts" and conversely Floyd
Dell in the radical *Liberator* charged that he, like Dreiser and other naturalist writers, had imbibed too little, Dell concluded that Anderson was
"more of an artist" than they, while Boynton concluded that, "Always he
seems to be after the true morality that so often governs men and women
when they are at odds with, or merely conforming to, conventional morality." As for Sherwood's friends at Schlogl's round table, they supported
him to a man. John Weaver announced in the *News* that he had done for
America what "Dostoyevsky, Andreyev, Gogol have done for Russia. . . .
If the great American novel ever arrives, he will bring it." Llewellyn Jones
praised the book for its skill and humanity; Burton Rascoe ranked its author "with the most important contemporary writers in this country."[32]

Not only were the reviewers mostly hospitable to *Winesburg,* some
were perceptive as well. Several saw that Anderson used commonplace
material but that, as Boynton put it, he "illuminated it from within, so that
we perceive its reality shining through the dull masks of convention and
humdrum." Not one reviewer objected that the stories were formless. On
the contrary, Jones pointed to Anderson's control of the "significant
episode," and "M.A." in the *New Republic* declared that, "as a challenge
to the snappy short story form, with its planned proportions of flippant
philosophy, epigrammatic conversation and sex danger, nothing better has
come out of America than Winesburg, Ohio." Individual tales were picked
out for particular praise—"Hands," "Paper Pills," "Mother," "The
Strength of God," "The Teacher," and "Death" were the favorites—but
several reviewers remarked on their unity in what H. L. Mencken in *The
Smart Set* admiringly called "a continued picture of life in a small inland
town." From the standpoint of Anderson's developing literary reputation,
the most valuable accolade was this by Mencken, who despite some reservations concluded that "what remains is a truly extraordinary book, by a
man of such palpably unusual talent that it seems almost an impertinence
to welcome him." *The Smart Set* had a national circulation, but Mencken
was even willing to praise Anderson in his own city. Under the heading
"Anderson Great Novelist, Says Mencken," he announced in an early July

copy of the *Chicago American* that *Winesburg* "embodies some of the most remarkable writing done in America in our time." "Here, indeed," Mencken continued with his usual gusto,

is a piece of work that stands out from the common run of fiction like the Alps from the Piedmont plain. Nothing quite like it is to be found in our literature. It lifts the short story, for long a form hardened by trickery and virtuosity, to a higher and more spacious level, and it gets into that form something of the mordant bitterness of tragic drama and something of the reflective detachment of epic poetry.[33]

The most perceptive review of all, however, was that of Burton Rascoe. Like several other reviewers Rascoe compared *Spoon River Anthology* and *Winesburg, Ohio,* but only to emphasize the difference between Masters's "bitter, reproachful, and removed" attitude toward the dead of Spoon River and Anderson's sympathy for the living of Winesburg, his "fraternal pity and . . . homely tender feeling of participation in human destiny." Perhaps profiting by a talk with the author over the round table, Rascoe also described the form of *Winesburg* as

something of an innovation: [Anderson] has, with much the continuity of a novel, written a series of complete short stories in which the same characters recur at different times. As a result, we have the fluid illusion of life, together with the heightened drama of it, the revelation of character in crucial flashes instead of by arduous development, the selection of incident without the detail that is part of the method of the novel, a group portrait of a community in an interwoven series of vignettes.

Then, in one of the most acute summaries ever made of Anderson's technique in the tales, Rascoe pointed out that he

frequently suggests rather than depicts; that he respects the imaginative faculty of his reader by refusing to be explicit where overtones of emotion are already invoked in the reader; that he is selective, indefinite, and provocative instead of inclusive, precise, and explanatory. He, one of the most personal and subjective of writers, has in these stories achieved a fine effect of impersonality.

At the same time, Anderson responded happily to all his praise. Perhaps recalling Mencken's rejection of "'Queer'" for *The Smart Set* several years before, he had a hunch that Mencken would not care for the book of stories, but now in response to the *Chicago American* review he could gratefully write: "I'm damn glad you like the book and it was bully of you to say so in such a convincing way. I may sell a few copies." His note to Rascoe was a grateful one to a friend who had understood a fundamental part of his attitude toward life and the people of his art.

What ever may be the truth about a lot of the fine things you have said concerning Winesburg there is one thing very true and I cant help being glad you said it. Whatever is wrong with the people in the book is wrong with me. I detest the damn paternalism of the writer who patronizes life.

Another letter would go later to a stranger, one Hart Crane, who in a review in a little magazine named *The Pagan* had expressed "intense gratitude" to the author of *Winesburg,* praised the book for its "sustained inner illumination and bloom" and its "flawless" style, and proclaimed in tones that must have spoken directly to the Anderson of *A New Testament:* "America should read this book on her knees. It constitutes an important chapter in the Bible of her consciousness." Anderson supposed that the circulation of *The Pagan* was hardly more than a dozen copies, but so ecstatic a review deserved thanks. "Dear Mr. Hart Crane," he wrote on October 1:

Some friend has sent me your review of Winesburg, Ohio, in The Pagan.

How can I hope to express my appreciation of your generous words. Surely it is to the minds of such men as yourself the American workman in the arts must look for new fuel when his own fires burn low.

Again I thank you for your good words.

In this way the forty-two-year-old Anderson and the twenty-year-old Crane began an acquaintance that would run over several years.[34] One other letter specifically about *Winesburg* Anderson wrote on a hot day late in June while on a business trip to Kentucky. Rereading *Letters and Leadership,* he was reminded that he had not yet sent a copy of his new book to Van Wyck Brooks, and he quickly wrote him a note promising to do so, commenting in his usual half confident, half humble way with this friend that

My mind is a little hopeful that in Winesburg and in future novels that come from my hand you will find a real refusal to accept life on the terms it is usually presented. If that is true the result is not a conscious effort on my part but is in fact the way life has come to look to me.

The growth of that point of view is I take it what you were seeking when you wrote those remarkable papers. I do hope you will find some realization in Winesburg.

Brooks, intent on finishing *The Ordeal of Mark Twain,* would not tell Anderson for several months that he thought *Winesburg* "the most beautiful prose fiction of our time."[35]

Only one aspect of the reception of *Winesburg* would Anderson remember at all accurately in his last years, that the book "was more than two years selling its first five thousand." Sales started out well, and in mid-June Burton Rascoe could tell him that during the second week of that month his book was a best seller in Chicago. McClurg's big bookstore had sold seventy-five copies in a single morning, the elated author reported to Jane Heap, and the purchasers were "either joyful or as mad as the devil." Realizing that *Winesburg* was selling better than any of his previous books, Anderson joked to Huebsch that they "might make some money. Ruin is staring me in the face." On August 21, Huebsch informed that the book was selling "in the fashion that suggests a continued demand." The first printing of eighteen hundred copies was not yet exhausted—even in Chicago it had been a best seller only that one week—but the publisher wanted to get ready for a second printing, apparently of a thousand copies, and asked Sherwood to send him as soon as possible the list of corrections he had begun to collect. The second printing was run off in December, but third and fourth printings would not be needed until January and December of 1921. Eventually Huebsch's records would show that the book sold 2,154 copies during its first year after publication and 914 during its second, for a total two-year sale of 3,068 copies. Sales translated into royalties, of course, and these were only tantalizing for an author desperate to find a way outside of business to support himself for further writing. For its first year in print Anderson received about $320 for *Winesburg, Ohio* and for its second about $160, for a total two-year income of just under $480. It was not much for what, as the years continued to go by, others besides himself would come to call "an American classic."[36]

4.

It is probably impossible, except impressionistically, to isolate the essential quality of any work of art, but Hart Crane may have come close to isolating that of *Winesburg, Ohio* when in another context he wrote of Anderson himself that, "He has a humanity and simplicity that is quite baffling in depth and suggestiveness." Leaving the matter of "humanity" aside, one is indeed struck on first reading the book by its apparent simplicity of language and form. On second or subsequent readings, however, one sees that the hard, plain, concrete diction is much mixed with the abstract, that the sentence cadences come from George Moore and the King James Bible as well as from ordinary speech rhythms, that the seemingly artless, even careless, digressions are rarely artless, careless, or digressive. What had once seemed to have the clarity of water held in the hand begins to take on instead its elusiveness. If this is simplicity, it is simplicity—paradox or not—of a complicated kind. Since *Winesburg* constantly challenges one to define the complications, it will do to examine a few that perhaps lie closest beneath the surface of the book and the life it describes.

It has been often pointed out that the fictitious Winesburg closely resembles Clyde. Even now the visitor to the two communities can see that
Winesburg and Clyde are both "eighteen miles" south of Lake Erie;
in both, the central street of the town is named Main, and Buckeye and
Duane branch off from it; both have a Heffner Block and a Waterworks
Pond; both lie "in the midst of open fields, but beyond the fields are pleasant patches of woodland." To be sure, the wooden Gothic railroad station, from which Sherwood Anderson and George Willard took the train
for the city and the great world, no longer stands; and on the hill above
Waterworks Pond, where George walked with Helen White on the darkened fairgrounds, grounds and racetrack have long since been built over.
Modern Clyde is perhaps half again as large as the town that the future
author of *Winesburg* left in 1897, but the growth has shown itself princi-
pally in housing development on the periphery. The central village is basically unchanged, and even now to walk through the quiet old residence
streets with their white frame or brick houses and wide lawns shaded by
big maples—the old elms are gone now—is to walk uncannily through a
fictitious scene made suddenly real.

The more one learns of the town as it was in the 1890s, the more one
sees the actual Clyde under the imagined Winesburg. Of course the correspondence of the two communities does not have a one-to-one exactness;
nevertheless the correspondences become striking, particularly as one sees
that in many instances Clyde names of persons and places appear only
faintly disguised in the pages of *Winesburg*. Anderson wrote about Win
Pawsey's shoe store, Surbeck's Pool Room, and Hern's Grocery; in the
Clyde of the early 1890s there were Alfred Pawsey's Shoe Store, Surbeck's
Cigar Store, and Hurd's Grocery. Wine Creek flows through Winesburg
instead of the real Raccoon Creek of Clyde, but the former follows the latter's course; and beyond the Wine rises the fictitious Gospel Hill in the
same place as the actual Piety Hill, where the Anderson family lived for a
time. Sometimes the disguise is somewhat less casual, though it may turn
out to be merely a transfer of names. The owner of one of the two livery
stables in Clyde was Frank Harvey, but there were Moyers in town, from
whom Anderson borrowed half the name of Wesley Moyer for the livery
stableman in Winesburg. Clyde personal names, it must be noted, are used
almost exclusively for the minor characters, and except for one or two de-
batable possibilities no character, either major or minor, seems to be recognizably based on an actual resident of the town. The important matter,
however, is that the "grotesques" of the several tales exist within a physical and social matrix furnished Anderson by his memories of Clyde.

That he should have visualized the locale of his tales so closely in terms
of his hometown is not surprising, and the reader may dismiss the matter
as merely a frequent practice of realistic writers. Yet Anderson was not a

realistic writer in the ordinary sense. With him realism was a means to something else, not an end in itself. To see the difference between his presentation of "reality" and the more traditional kind that gives a detailed picture of appearances, one needs only to compare the drugstore on the Main Street of Sinclair Lewis's Gopher Prairie with that on the Main Street of Winesburg. Twice over, once as Carol Kennicott, once as Bea Sorenson sees them, Lewis catalogs the parts of Dave Dyer's soda fountain. Anderson, like his own Enoch Robinson preferring "the essence of things" to the "realities," merely names Sylvester West's Drug Store, letting each reader's imagination do as much or as little with it as he wishes. As with the drugstore, so with many other landmarks of Clyde-Winesburg. As he repeats from tale to tale the names of stores and their owners or refers to such elements of town life as the post office, the bank, or the cemetery, there emerges, not a photograph but the barest sketch of the external world of the town. Perhaps even "sketch" implies too great a precision of detail. What Anderson was after was less a representation of conventional "reality" than, to keep the metaphor drawn from art, an abstraction of it.

Realism was for Anderson a means rather than an end, and the highly abstract kind of reality found in Winesburg has its valuable uses. The first of these is best understood in relation to George Willard's occupation on the *Winesburg Eagle*. (Clyde's weekly newspaper was, and still is the *Clyde Enterprise*, but Sherwood was never its reporter.) It has been suggested that the author may have made his central figure a newspaper reporter in order that he could thus be put most readily in touch with the widest number of people in town and most logically become the recipient of many confidences; yet Anderson's point is that exactly insofar as George remains a newspaper reporter, he is committed to the surface of life, not to its depths. "Like an excited dog," Anderson says in "The Thinker," using a mildly contemptuous comparison, "George Willard ran here and there," writing down all day "little facts" about A. P. Wringlet's recent shipment of straw hats or Uncle Tom Sinnings' new barn on the Valley Road. As reporter, George is concerned with externals, with appearances, with the presumably solid, simple, everyday surface of life. For Anderson the surface is there, of course, as his recurring use of place and personal names indicates; yet conventional "reality" is for him relatively insignificant and is best presented in the form of sketch or abstraction. What is important is "to see beneath the surface of lives," to perceive the intricate mesh of impulses, desires, drives growing down in the dark, unrevealed parts of the personality, like the complex mass of roots that, below the surface of the ground, feeds the common grass above in the light.

But if one function of Anderson's peculiar adaptation of realism is to depreciate the value of surfaces, a corollary function is constantly to affirm that any surface has its depth. Were we, on the one hand, to observe such tormented people as Alice Hindman and Dr. Parcival and the Reverend Curtis Hartman as briefly and as much from the outside as we view Wesley Moyer or Biff Carter or Butch Wheeler, the lamplighter, they would appear as uncomplicated and commonplace as the latter. Conversely, were we to see the inwardness of Moyer and Carter and Wheeler, their essential lives would provide the basis for three more Winesburg tales. (The real lamplighter of Clyde in the early 1890s was a man named John Becker. It may well have given him the anguish of a "grotesque" that he had an epileptic son, who as a young man died during a seizure while assisting his father in his trade.)

Yet a third function of Anderson's abstract, or shorthand, kind of realism is to help him set the tone of various tales, often a tone of elegiac quietness. Just how this is done will be clearer if one realizes that the real Clyde that underlies Winesburg is the town, not as Anderson left it in 1896, but the town as it was a few years earlier when, as he asserts in "An Awakening," "the time of factories had not yet come." The Winesburg tales he conceived of as for the most part occurring in a preindustrial setting, recalling nostalgically a town already lost before he had left it, giving this vanished era the permanence of pastoral. Here, as always, he avoids the realism of extensive detail and makes only suggestive references, one of the most memorable being the description in "The Thinker" of the lamplighter hurrying along the street before Seth Richmond and Helen White, lighting the lamp on each wooden post "so their way was half lighted, half darkened, by the lamps and by the deepening shadows cast by the low-branched trees." By a touch like this, drawn from his memory of preindustrial Clyde, Anderson turns the evening walk of his quite ordinary boy and girl into a tiny processional and invests the couple with that delicate splendor, which can come to people "even in Winesburg."

If Anderson's treatment of locale in his tales turns out to be more complex than it seems at first, the same can be said of his methods of giving sufficient unity to his book so that, while maintaining the "looseness" of life as he actually sensed it, the tales would still form a coherent whole. Some of these methods have a point in common: they all involve the use of repeated elements. One such device is that of setting the crisis scenes of all but five of the tales in the evening. In a large majority of the stories, too, some kind of light partly, but only partly, relieves the darkness. In "Hands," "Mother," and "Loneliness," for example, the light is that of a single lamp; in "The Untold Lie" the concluding scene is faintly lit by the last of twilight; in "Sophistication" George Willard and Helen White look at each other "in the dim light" afforded, apparently, by "the lights of the town reflected against the sky," though at the other end of the fairgrounds a few racetrack men have built a fire that provides a dot of illumination in the darkness. Finally, many of the tales end with the characters in total darkness. Such a device not only links the tales but in itself implies meaning. *Winesburg* is primarily a book about the "night world" of human personality. The dim light equates with, as well as literally illuminates, the limited glimpse into an individual soul that each crisis scene affords, and the briefness of the insight is emphasized by the shutting down of the dark.

Another kind of repeated element throughout the book is the recurrent word. Considering the sense of personal isolation one gets from the atomized lives of the "grotesques," one would expect a frequent use of some such word as "wall," standing for whatever it is that divides each person from all others. Surprisingly that particular word appears only a few times. The one that does occur frequently is "hand," either in the singular or the plural; and very often, as indeed would be expected, it suggests, even symbolizes, the potential or actual communication of one personality with another. The hands of Wing Biddlebaum and Dr. Reefy come immediately to mind; but to name only a few other instances, George Willard takes hold of Louise Trunnion's "rough" but "delightfully small" hand in anticipation of his sexual initiation, Helen White keeps her hand in Seth Richmond's until Seth breaks the clasp through overconcern with self, in the field where they are working Hal Winters puts "his two hands" on Ray Pearson's shoulders and they "become all alive to each other," Kate Swift puts her hands on George Willard as though about to embrace him in her desire to make him understand what being a writer means. Obviously the physical contact may not produce mutual understanding. The hand may in fact express aggression. One of the men who run Wing Biddlebaum out of the Pennsylvania town at night "had a rope in his hands"; Elizabeth Willard, who as a girl had put her hand on the face of each lover after sexual release, imagines herself stealing toward her husband, "holding the long wicked scissors in her hand"; Elmer Cowley on the station platform strikes George Willard almost unconscious with his fists before leaping onto the departing train. Nevertheless, the possibility of physical touch between two human beings always implies, even if by negative counterpart, at least the possibility of a profounder moment of understanding between them. The intuitive awareness by George Willard and Helen White of each other's "sophistication" is expressed, not through their few kisses but by Helen's taking George's arm and walking "beside him in dignified silence."

As for George himself, one can make too much of his role as a character designed to link the tales, unify them, and structure them into a loose sort of bildungsroman; on the other hand, one can make too little of it. Granted that Anderson tended to view his own life, and that of others, as a succession of moments rather than as a "figure in a carpet," that his imagination worked more successfully in terms of the flash of insight than of the large design, that his gift was, in short, for the story more than the novel, still through his treatment of George Willard's development he supplies a pattern for *Winesburg, Ohio* that is as definite as it is unobtrusive. This development has three closely related aspects, and each aspect involves again the repetition of certain elements.

The first aspect is obvious. Whatever the outward difference between created character and creator, George's inward life clearly reflects the conflict Anderson had experienced between the world of practical affairs, with its emphasis on the activity of moneymaking and its definition of success in financial terms, and the world of dreams, with its emphasis on imaginative creativity and its definition of success in terms of the degree of penetration into the buried life of others. The conflict is thematically stated in the first of the tales, "Hands." Wing Biddlebaum's hands are famous in Winesburg for their berry-picking (hence moneymaking) skill, but the true story of the hands, as told by "a poet," is of course that they can communicate a desire to dream. Wing declares the absolute opposition of the two worlds by telling George that he is destroying himself because "'you are afraid of dreams. You want to be like others in town here.'" The declaration indicates that George has not yet resolved the conflict, and his irresolution at this point is reinforced by his ambivalent attitude toward Wing's hands. Unlike the other townspeople he is curious to know what lies beneath their outward skill; yet his respect for Wing and his fear of the depths that might be revealed make him put curiosity aside. The conflict between practical affairs and dreams is again made explicit in the third story of the book, "Mother," where it is objectified in the hostility between Tom and Elizabeth Willard and the clash of their influences on their son. *Winesburg* is not a book of suspense, and thus early in the tales the conflict is in effect resolved when George implicitly accepts his mother's, and Wing's, way, the way of dreams. From this point on both the conflict and George's resolution of it are maintained in a formal sense by the opposition between the "daylight world" of the minor characters and the "night world" of the major ones, the grotesques. George continues to run about writing down surface facts for the newspaper, but his essential life consists in his efforts, some successful, some not, to understand the essential lives of others. From these efforts, from the death of his mother, from his achievement of "sophistication" with Helen White, he gains the will to leave Winesburg, committed, as the final paragraph of "Departure" asserts, to the world of dreams.

The second of these closely related aspects of George's development is his growing desire to be a creative writer and his increasing awareness of the meaning of that vocation. George's interest in writing is first mentioned approvingly by his father in "Mother," but Tom Willard, Anderson makes clear, assumes that his son wants to write, not about dreams but like a "newspaper man" about surfaces. His interest is not mentioned again until the book is half over, when, in "The Thinker," it appears to have been an interest that he had had for some time. He talks "continuously of the matter" to Seth Richmond, and the "idea that George Willard would some day become a writer had given him a place of distinction in Winesburg. . . ." At this point his conception of writing centers on externals, on the opportunities the writer's life offers for personal freedom and for public acclaim. In a remark that suggests a reading of Jack London, George explains to Seth that as a writer he will be his own boss: "Though you are in India or in the South Seas in a boat, you have but to write and there you are." Since writing for George is at this stage mainly a matter of fame and fun, it is not surprising to find him in "The Thinker" deliberately, and naively, planning to fall in love with Helen White in order to write a love story. The absurdity, Anderson suggests, is twofold: falling in love is not something one rationally plans to do, and one does not write thus directly and literally out of experience anyway.

Actually Kate Swift, in "The Teacher," has tried to tell George that the writer's is not "the easiest of all lives to live," but rather one of the most difficult. In one of those scenes where physical touch symbolizes an attempt to create the moment of awareness between two personalities, Kate has tried to explain the demanding principles by which the true writer must live. He must "know life," must "stop fooling with words," must "know what people are thinking about, not what they say"—all three being principles Anderson was to insist on himself as the code of the artist. That George is still immature both as person and as writer is signified at the end of "The Teacher" when he gropes drowsily about in the darkness with a hand and mutters that he has missed something Kate Swift was trying to tell him. This needed maturity comes to him only at the end of *Winesburg*. When, sitting beside the body of his dead mother, he decides to go to "some city" and perhaps "get a job on some newspaper," he is really marked already for the profession of writer, whatever job he may take to support himself, just as Anderson supported himself by composing advertising copy while experimenting with the Winesburg stories. In "Departure" the commitment of George Willard to writing unites with his final commitment to the world of dreams. For both George and his creator the two are indeed identical.

The third aspect of George's development provides another way of charting his inward voyage from innocence to experience, from ignorance to understanding, from apparent reality of the face of things to true reality behind or below. Three stories—"Nobody Knows," "An Awakening," and "Sophistication"—have a special relationship. They all center on George's dealing with a woman, a different one in each case; they contain very similar motifs; they are arranged in an ascending order of progression. The fact that one comes near the beginning of the book, one about two-thirds of the way through, and one at the end indicates that Anderson had his own subtle sense of design.

The first story, "Nobody Knows," is in all ways the simplest. In it George Willard enters traditional manhood by having, with Louise Trunnion, his first sex experience. In relation to the other two tales in the sequence, the most significant elements of the story, besides the fact of actual sexual conquest, are George's lack of self-assurance at the outset of the affair, his bursting forth with a "flood of words," his consequent aggressiveness and failure to sympathize with his partner, and his action at the end of the story when he stands "perfectly still in the darkness, attentive, listening as though for a voice calling his name." The sexual encounter with Louise has been simply that. It has brought him physical satisfaction and a feeling of entirely self-centered masculine pride. His expectation of hearing a voice, however, would seem to be a projection of guilt feeling at having violated the overt moral code of the community even though "nobody knows."

In the second and third stories these elements, or their opposites, appear in a more complex fashion. In both "An Awakening" and "Sophistication," George's relation with a woman is complicated by the involvement of another man, though, significantly, Ed Handby in the former story is laconic, direct, and highly physical, while the college instructor in the latter is voluble, devious, and pompously intellectual. In both, too, the final scene takes place on the hill leading up to the fairgrounds, close, incidentally, to the place where Kate Swift tried to explain to George the difficulties that beset the dedicated writer. Yet the two stories have quite different, if supplementary, conclusions.

As George and Belle Carpenter walk up the hill in the final scene of "An Awakening," he feels no more sympathy for her, has no more understanding of her needs, than he had for Louise Trunnion; but before this last walk he has experienced an exaltation that keeps him from any fear of masculine incompetence. Earlier that January night a kind of mystical revelation has come to him when it seems as though "some voice outside of himself" announced the thought in his mind: "I must get myself into touch with something orderly and big that swings through the night like a star." Unlike the situation at the end of "Nobody Knows," George actually "hears" the external voice, and the voice is now the positive one of inspiration, which has replaced the negative one of conscience. Thereafter he talks volubly to Belle, as he had to Louise; but when in "An Awakening" his "mind runs off into words," he believes that Belle will recognize the new force in him and will at once surrender herself to his masculine power. Of course an insistence on the necessity of universal order—"'There is a law for armies and for men too,'" George asserts—was a characteristic of Anderson's own thinking particularly as expressed in *Marching Men* and

Mid-American Chants; yet George makes this concept ridiculous at the moment because of his intense self-centeredness about his inspiration. As Kate Swift would have said, he is still playing with words, a destructive procedure for the artistic personality as well as for the nonartistic one. Holding the quite uninterested Belle in his arms, he whispers large words into the darkness, until the passionate, nonverbalizing Ed Handby throws him aside, takes Belle by the arm, and marches off. George is left angered, humiliated, and disgustedly disillusioned with his moment of mystic insight when "the voice outside himself . . . had . . . put new courage into his heart."

Where "An Awakening" records a defeat, "Sophistication" records in all ways a triumph. Though Anderson presents the moment in essay rather than dramatic form, there comes to George, as to "every boy," a flash of insight when "he stops under a tree and waits as for a voice calling his name." But this time "the voices outside himself" do not speak of the possibilities of universal order, nor do they speak of guilt. Instead they "whisper a message concerning the limitations of life," the brief light of human existence between two darks. The insight emphasizes the unity of all human beings in their necessary submission to death and their need for communication one with another. It is an insight that produces self-awareness but not self-centeredness, that produces, in short, the mature, "sophisticated" person.

The mind of such a person does not "run off into words." Hence Helen White, who has had an intuition similar to George's, runs away from the empty talk of her college instructor and her mother, and finds George, whose first and last words to her in the story, pronounced as they first meet, are "Come on." Together in the dimly lit fairgrounds on the hill overlooking the town of Winesburg, George and Helen share a brief hour of absolute awareness. Whereas his relationship with Belle Carpenter had produced in George self-centeredness, misunderstanding, hate, frustration, humiliation, that with Helen produces quite the opposite feelings. The feeling of oneness spreads outward. Through his communication with Helen he begins "to think of the people in the town where he had lived with something like reverence." When he has come to this point, when he loves and respects the inhabitants of Winesburg, the "daylight" people as well as the "night" ones, the way of the artist lies clear before him. George Willard is ready for his "Departure."

9

In the Trap

1.

On the day *Winesburg, Ohio* was published, Anderson was just about to leave Chicago on a business trip to Owensboro, Kentucky, going by way of Louisville, where on May 10, 1919, he watched the thoroughbred Sir Barton run a muddy track to victory at the Kentucky Derby. By the following day he was in Owensboro, then a small city of some seventeen thousand on the Ohio River, had checked in at the old Rudd House, the leading hotel, and was ready for a week's work on the advertising needs of the Owensboro Ditcher & Grader Company, manufacturers of the Martin ditcher-terracer and road grader. The account of the Owensboro firm with Critchfield had been assigned to him because he got along well with W[illiam] A[lexander] Steele, the firm's well-to-do president and general manager, who admired Sherwood's ability to write "stories," by which he meant the ads and circulars he could turn out so effectively. Not a "book-learned" man, Steele never read any of Anderson's nonadvertising works. Sherwood nevertheless felt at home with the businesslike but kindly Steele, his wife, and their three daughters so that the visits to Owensboro were a far greater pleasure than most of his frequent business trips about the Midwest. After a day's stint of advertising work in the factory the two men, who had become good friends, would drive together into the country along the yellow and gold waters of the Ohio for hours of talk, or they would spend the evening with the whole family at Green River, the Steeles' farm home, where Mrs. Steele, with the help of black servants, maintained a huge rose garden. Anderson would remember the home as beautiful, the whole setting by a deep ravine on the Green River as idyllic. When the firm's advertising needs were taken care of, he would often prolong what he considered almost a vacation by taking one of the small river steamers some miles up the Ohio, crossing to the Indiana side, and riding an interurban trolley car back down to Evansville, where he would catch a train for Chicago, regretting always that he had to leave Owensboro with its pleasant, tree-shaded courthouse square in the heart of the town and the lovely, hospitable home of the Steele family. Such trips relaxed him mentally and physically, and this "reaction into laziness" always helped him to endure the rush and clatter of Chicago for a little while after his return.[1]

On this May visit he stayed for about a week, working on advertising material in a room upstairs in the Ditcher & Grader factory across from a schoolyard. Here, Anderson watched an Army sergeant put the boys through military drill even though American troops were arriving home from France by the thousands daily. "Militarism has evidently come to America," he wrote disgustedly to Bab. He had read the terms of the Versailles Treaty as presented on May 7 to the German delegation to the Peace Conference, and though he had no particular regard for Germany, he was horrified at the demands imposed on the defeated country. It was cowardly of the Allies, he felt, like hitting a man when he was down, and he especially disliked the thought of going back to Chicago where the war spirit still flamed. Perhaps his fondness for the Steele family and the quiet Ohio River town combined with his revulsion against "civilization" to give him the notion that he might leave Critchfield, set himself up independently in a small, quiet office with the Owensboro account and a few others he had worked on, and thus both free himself from the constant distractions of the big, noisy copy room and gain more time for his writing. Even if the scheme may have occurred to him earlier, it now grew rapidly in his mind, and he began to tell friends about it.[2]

Sometimes on the way to or from Owensboro or Harrodsburg, where he continued to manage the Bohon account, he would stop off in Indianapolis for a visit with Bab. This time he did not stop, for he had to be back in Chicago by the evening of May 16 to prepare for a guest far different from any of his Kentucky business clients. Jacques Copeau had written that he was coming briefly to the Midwest to visit Sherwood, give some lectures, and sense life in the American Heartland. He arrived on the seventeenth, and Anderson took him to the small, one-bedroom apartment that he maintained separately from Tennessee. For a week Sherwood mostly stayed away from work in order to entertain his guest. Wherever they went, Copeau attracted attention. Tall, thin, nearly bald, with dark luminous eyes and a great swooping beak of a nose above a wide full mouth, the director -actor was a distinguished presence. Both Andersons were delighted with him, admiring his sophistication, his combination of tenderness and sensitivity underneath, in Waldo's phrase, "his intellectual imperiousness and executive cunning"; and they enjoyed his zestful insistence on walking or riding on streetcars all over Chicago seeing the working class and slum sections as well as the Gold Coast, the whole stir of the American city's life. Sherwood was especially amused that this intensely

Gallic person had purchased a corncob pipe and smoked it even on the streetcars. When conductors objected, Copeau would suddenly lose his excellent command of English, and his friend would straightfacedly explain to the conductors that in France it was the custom to smoke on streetcars. In New York, Copeau had picked up an early copy of *Winesburg,* read it eagerly, and now insisted that the two of them must at once begin a dramatization of the book. They did not get far with the project, being too busy seeing Chicago, lunching with Rascoe and the others at Schlogl's round table, or traveling over to Michigan together, Sherwood to do business for Critchfield in Detroit, Copeau to lecture at the University of Michigan at Ann Arbor.

The visit was framed by Copeau's two lectures in Chicago. In the midafternoon of Sunday, May 18, he spoke before the Bryn Mawr Club of Chicago on the work of his experimental Theatre du Vieux Colombier, which he had organized in Paris in 1913 and had brought to New York in 1917, while on the evening of the twenty-third at the Arts Club he discussed, or rather excoriated, the rest of the modern French theater as containing "nothing living, nothing true, nothing authentic," merely "affectation pure and simple." Copeau always spoke his mind, but perhaps the energy of his attack reflected his dismay over a quite unrelated catastrophe that had struck him on some evening between these two days. Along with the corncob pipe and a copy of *Winesburg* Copeau had purchased in New York a whole wardrobe of luxurious clothes including a yellow astrakhan overcoat, elegant suits, dozens of expensive ties, shirts, pairs of shoes, together with enough pigskin suitcases to pack them in, the whole representing most of his savings from the two years during which the Vieux Colombier troupe had been presenting its plays to New York audiences as a goodwill gesture between Allies. Copeau had displayed these magnificent garments to Anderson, who admired their colors and textures as much as their owner did, but unfortunately the Frenchman left them lying about the bedroom in full view of the window, which opened in this ground-floor apartment onto an alley. One evening Anderson invited Carl Sandburg to the apartment to play his guitar and sing American folksongs for the visitor. After Sandburg had left, Anderson and Copeau entered the bedroom and discovered with horror that during the singing someone had opened the window from the alley and had made off with every beautiful piece of clothing and luggage. Anderson would always remember the comi-tragic scene that followed—Copeau's eloquent laments to "Sherwoodio" over his loss, the casual questioning by two phlegmatic policemen, the despairing realization by host and guest that two years' savings and the objects themselves were irrevocably gone.[3]

Except for that distressing incident the visit had been a joyous one. Between both Andersons and Copeau there had grown up a quick friendship, which strengthened the desire of the Americans to experience Europe at first hand, to see Copeau in his native country. Besides his attractive personal qualities, Copeau, as Anderson had learned from Frank and Rosenfeld, was a leader of the "new generation" in French cultural life; and it was very satisfying to Sherwood to find that Copeau, with his own groundbreaking, antirealistic theories of the theater, could immediately perceive how a fictionist was also seeking to get at essences rather than surfaces. For weeks before Copeau arrived Sherwood had been living an alternating pattern of "several days of feeling almost normal and then several days when I am rather dragged out and weary." The cause, or at least a major cause, for the symptoms had of course long been obvious to him. "The whole matter is, I am sure," he had written Waldo shortly before Copeau's visit, "half physic," by which he assuredly meant "psychic . . . it has its base in the fact that my whole being is in revolt against business and I am bound to it. Now I am groping for some way to find release." Copeau's exciting and flattering visit helped turn groping into active resolve.[4]

The resolve had two results. Within days after his guest's departure Anderson had set September 1 as the date when he would open his own office where, without having to punch a time clock, he could "take care of two or three clients and make enough money to earn my bread and pay my secretary." In addition, his mood for the Testaments having dissipated, he plunged again into a long-term project, the revision of *Mary Cochran,* "my woman's novel," he called it in a letter to Jane Heap, "which I hope to make a real book." The whole month of June seems to have been a cheerful and cheering one because of the attention he was receiving as a writer. Very early in the month one "George Gordon" (Charles C. Baldwin) published in Moffat, Yard's American Writers Series a book titled *The Men Who Make Our Novels,* composed of brief biographies, often in their own words, not only of such figures as William Dean Howells, Booth Tarkington, and Harold Bell Wright, but other more controversial ones such as Dreiser, Sinclair Lewis, and Sherwood Anderson. If Anderson did not see this volume, he at least had the satisfaction of knowing he was being included as an American novel-maker; and a condensed version of his entry—the entry was a reprint of the 1918 John Lane brochure, *Sherwood Anderson Writes of Himself*—had just appeared in the *Tribune* on May 31 in a "Who's Who" series. Then, too, *Winesburg* was selling at its best in June, so well that without resentment he could start a list of his "bad use of words" as they were pointed out by "these educated chaps" like Rascoe, Frank, an unnamed friend of Huebsch's, and the anonymous reviewer in the New York *Sun.* If sales justified a second printing of *Winesburg,* he would send the list to the publisher. He was even amused rather than upset when he received a long letter from one of the citizens of the actual Winesburg, Ohio, near Canton, angrily protesting his use of that village's name and enclosing snapshots of its street to show their real existence. Just why Anderson had picked that name, he never knew or never fully explained. Perhaps, as he would suggest in the *Memoirs,* he had seen it during his travels, and it had sunk into his unconscious until needed. Now the matter was largely a joke on himself that he could tell to his friends at Schlogl's.[5]

June was a good month also because he could look forward to practically the whole of July on vacation in the quiet little resort town of Ephraim, Wisconsin, near the tip of the Door County peninsula, where he was counting on a couple of weeks visit from Waldo and Margaret Frank. Meanwhile he willingly took another business trip in late June to Owensboro, where the heat of the Ohio River valley was offset by the Steeles' hospitality. This time he did stop off in Indianapolis to see Bab. During a long evening's conversation they discussed their own relationship and Sherwood's with Tennessee. Unfortunately, the letters he wrote Bab immediately afterwards leave much unclear, but they do indicate that she found him temporarily acquiescent to her desire to hold him by one means or another, and he did then begin accepting occasional gifts of money from her, as he had not before, because of his driving desire to be free of the business world. The first check that she gave him could not have been for much, and while he might be able to accept such a gesture if it were performed "splendidly and beautifully," she must know that he was not, as she seemed to think that evening he was, "one capable of becoming the property of another person." His basic loyalty was not even to Tennessee, Bab must realize. "While I am the man I want to be," he wrote in blunt, open recognition of his feelings at this time, "I shall never belong to anyone. I shall try to belong to the moment and the new day." Bab, impatient for freedom from demanding, aging parents and for release from "the house of pain" in which her sometimes ill body shut her, must be content with Sherwood's "attempt to hold you in the right place as in many ways my dearest friend," whatever that qualified statement might or might not mean. Eventually she would have a freedom like his own; now she must courageously endure. "We are all destroyed," he wrote her, "but some there are who do not meet a cheap defeat."[6]

One senses going on here some subtle, undefined shift in the relationship between these two human beings, the woman needing the man, the man continuing to a much less extent to need the woman, satisfied with seeing her occasionally, at other times using her as the recipient of his letters, some of these being among the most eloquent, most personally revealing, but not personally "giving" that he would write to a woman. But whether this was specifically an adulterous situation, Sherwood's insistence on his ultimate inner freedom suggests that the constant weariness Tennessee herself was now feeling may have been not simply the result of overwork but of her quiet recognition that her three-year-old marriage had lost its original warmth. Admittedly there is more conjecture here than evidence; yet in less than three more years the husband would be walking out on his second marriage, and long before then there would be other signs that it was more than the prison of business Sherwood was restlessly seeking to escape.

Nevertheless he was genuinely troubled at this time by Tennessee's poor health. She had never fully recovered from the effects of the Spanish flu in the fall of 1918 and had had periods of illness ever since. Sherwood went ahead to Ephraim for the first week in July, then returned for a few days to catch up on business matters at Critchfield and to persuade her to start her vacation with him at once. He returned also, apparently, to meet Waldo and Margaret at the train. Chicago was hot, and at Sherwood's insistence the two men purchased "creamy white pongee suits," which they wore about the city, Sherwood being delighted at the flamboyance of the dress, Waldo being more self-conscious but determined to keep up with his older "brother." After seeing Chicago briefly the two couples went on to Ephraim, probably by the Lake steamer *Carolina,* which regularly put in at Anderson's Dock at the center of the village.[7]

Ephraim, a Door County village of about two hundred permanent residents and many summer ones, was a cluster of white frame buildings at the foot of Eagle Harbor, a deeply curving bay edged with wooded hills and opening out to the long Green Bay of Lake Michigan. Tennessee's friends, the Walkers, had for years maintained a summer home there, partly out of a liking for the townspeople, mostly Norwegian Moravians, who were so honest that, as Judge Walker would say, if you dropped a wallet in the road before you left in the autumn, it would still be there the next spring. From 1910 on Tennessee had occasionally made summer visits to the Walkers, but this July the Andersons and Franks had the use of the large Norwegian-style log home of Dr. Charles F. Millspaugh on "University Row," a road close to the lake where a number of university professors had summer homes.

The vacation must have been a quiet one for the two women, who were bone-tired by their year of teaching, Tennessee with her piano and rhythms pupils, Margaret with the children at her highly progressive Walden School. Sherwood, however, felt at once relaxed in the rural atmosphere, and Waldo had bounced back from the frenzy of finishing the manuscript of *Our America* in time for Copeau to sail for France with a copy to be translated and published there. For much of the week or ten days still left to the visit, the two men had a boisterous good time together. Probably using Dr. Millspaugh's own guide to edible fungi, they would go off to hunt mushrooms, bring home quantities, cook them, and sit around eating them and watching to see if the other died. Waldo had brought a banjo, and, much taken with the "indefeasibly lovely" Mrs. Walker and daughter Carolyn, he once, perhaps on Carolyn's twentieth birthday, wound a piece of vine with its leaves around his head and serenaded the Walkers on their porch steps. Part of the time, however, Anderson was less talkative than usual, being preoccupied with worries over Tennessee's health and the difficulty of fleeing the advertising world.[8]

Mornings he put in on his writing. Going over the *Mary Cochran* manuscript, he felt that he could greatly improve it but that it would require almost complete revision. He began that; then, under the stimulus of conversations with Tennessee and Margaret about guiding children toward their full potential while avoiding too much or too little direction, he became briefly interested in writing a children's book, not one full of "asinine sentimental nonsense" like most such, but "a series of tales of country life at the edge of a middle-western small town.—Little pictures of the actual life of the boy, the farm hand, the dog, the cow etc." He went so far as to write Huebsch and ask if he would be interested in publishing such a book, but he shortly dropped the project even though Huebsch later encouraged him to turn the pieces into a connected narrative in order that he would not be typed as a writer solely of short stories.[9]

After the Franks left for New York, a few more days of July vacation remained. Tennessee was feeling better, but Anderson often went off by himself on long walks or swam in the cool water of Green Bay. One afternoon he climbed a cliff to a moss-covered ledge where he could look down on what he thought of as "the sea." He felt renewed and at rest and wished that he could stay on at Ephraim for months, but almost symbolically factory smoke from a town miles away across the bay faintly discolored the sky. If he could only "give up the superficial battle for a living," he wrote Bab that evening, he would have strength this coming year "to do things more subtle and difficult than anything I have ever done."

Chicago, when he returned on August 1, made him psychically ill by contrast with the woods, hills, and harbor at Ephraim. The city people, even the children, looked old and weary to him; the lines of the buildings were ugly. For the five days just preceding, Chicago had in fact been convulsed with race riots during which gangs of marauding whites had invaded the Black Belt and thirty-three people, twenty black and thirteen white, had been killed and over three hundred injured. Even on this first day of sullen calm Anderson sensed tension and hatred still thick in the air. It remained risky for blacks to be in white neighborhoods, and Sherwood, who had become acquainted with several black men who worked nearby, now out of revulsion at white violence gave them a key to his small apartment so that for some nights they could sleep on the floor of his living room, uncomfortable but at least safe. He had become acutely sensitized to the reality of pain by Tennessee's and Bab's illnesses and even at

Ephraim had seen pain "in the fishes taken from the sea, in the writhing of the worms by which the fishes were caught, in the eyes of cattle in the field, tortured by flies." Returning to the hate-filled city and to the demands of business was like being afflicted with a terrible disease.[10]

Fortunately the practical demands on his time brought him through his initial days of shock. He had to make final arrangements about leaving Critchfield with the accounts he would manage independently, to find a secretary, to locate an office. For this last he found a room on the twelfth floor of the Provident Building at 226 South La Salle Street in the Loop. Then he had to see his clients personally, which meant a trip to Harrods-burg and Owensboro late in August and another to the Illinois State Fair at Springfield, where he happily spent a day with a client admiring the farm animals in the exhibition sheds and watching the harness races from the grandstand. While he went about his business affairs, however, his mind was busy scheming ways to get out of them completely. One plan that momentarily interested him enough so that he wrote Waldo about it was to buy a piece of wooded land in Door County and to start a summer camp for both children and adults. Under the guidance of a carpenter and a farmer, the children and many of the adults could have the practical ex-perience of building log cabins, clearing the land, raising crops. Tennessee with her "genius with children" could help—he himself could "handle the grown ups"—and she would thus be freed of the strain of teaching, while six months outdoors would strengthen him and support him financially for another six months of writing in a room in New York or Chicago. Per-haps John Emerson might finance such a project initially. Waldo, aware of how such "fancies" took hold of his friend and then "evaporated," rather reluctantly approached Emerson in New York and got nowhere, but even before then Sherwood had realistically rejected his plan on the grounds that he knew he could not be responsible for "a lot of middle class, dis-satisfied people. . . . The impulse toward the camp scheme, when coldly looked at came only from the fact that I realize I must get back to the quiet of out of doors life more and more if I am to survive."[11]

As so often happened, however, Anderson was able to snatch a few hours here and there for his writing even when he was most harried by business if some outer event or inner fancy precipitated a story. Such an event might have been the news in the sports pages of August 10 that on the previous day the thoroughbred Sun Briar had won the Champlain Handicap at the races at Saratoga Springs, New York, and set a new track record. Around the record-breaking winning of Saratoga's "Mullford Handicap" by a stallion named "Sunstreak" began to accrete in Ander-son's mind one of his finest stories, "I Want to Know Why." It was told in the first person as a reminiscence by a fifteen-year-old boy from a small Kentucky town who, though the son of a lawyer, was crazy about racehorses and had perhaps picked up from the people who worked with them, people outside conventional middle-class society, a mode of speech rather like Huck Finn's. The narrator recalls how the previous summer he and some other boys had stolen off by freight train to see the races at Saratoga, in the "East," had been taken care of there by a black racetrack cook named Bildad Johnson from their hometown of Beckersville, had seen Sunstreak and the gelding Middlestride, both horses from farms around Beckersville, come in first and second in the Handicap, and then returned home to take the expected punishment from their parents, though the narrator boy's father understood his love of horses and barely scolded him. As the boy is telling his adventure the following spring, however, he is still troubled by something he alone saw at Saratoga, the one thing he didn't tell even his father.[12]

So with many digressions about his joy at watching thoroughbreds working out at the Beckersville training track early on spring mornings, about the beauty, honesty, and courage of the horses, about the superior decency of "niggers" over most white men where boys are concerned—digressions that both build up a world of rapture and reveal the boy's reluctance to get to the event that destroyed it for him—he tells how, with his gift for intuiting whether a horse is going to win, he watches Sunstreak being saddled for the Handicap, catches the eye of Jerry Tillford, the horse's trainer, and loves the man as much as the horse because he knows from Jerry's look that the trainer too has sensed Sunstreak's resolve to win. After Sunstreak's victory the boy wants to stay close to Jerry and secretly follows him and some of the other men from Beckersville to a farmhouse where, he discovers, there are "ugly mean-looking women." Watching through an open window, he hears Jerry brag that Sunstreak had won only because he had trained him. Then when Jerry looks at one hard-mouthed whore in the same way he had looked at the boy and Sunstreak at the saddling and kisses her, the boy is enraged, creeps away, and persuades his friends to leave Saratoga for home. The repulsive fact that Jerry could watch Sunstreak run and kiss a bad woman the same day has stuck in the boy's mind for months and is now spoiling his joy in a new spring, in the laughter of the track Negroes, in the morning run of the thoroughbreds. Why, he wants to know, should such things have to be?

"I Want to Know Why" has been read in many ways—as a variation on the Genesis myth of the fall from innocence to experience, as a representation of the ambiguity of good and evil in the world, as a psychological study of a young male's concern over sexuality—but in the context of Anderson's emotional situation at the time he was probably writing the story in the late summer of 1919, an immediate, personal reading also emerges. Part of what he was transmuting into this fiction was his direct experience of the racetrack milieu, and bits of that assimilated reality stand out. Very possibly he had seen the thoroughbreds race at Saratoga in the August of 1916 or of 1917 when he was not far away at Chateaugay Lake; but certainly from his visits to Harrodsburg, Kentucky, he had all he needed to know about "Beckersville," since both were near Lexington in the Bluegrass region and in both there was a "Banker Bohon." For the lyrical descriptions of the morning sights, smells, and sounds of the training track, he had only to recall nostalgically his boyhood mornings at the track at the Clyde fairgrounds. The names and characteristics of the thoroughbreds required little invention. "Sun Briar" was readily converted into "Sunstreak," of course; and he could draw on his recent memory of watching Sir Barton's five-length win over Billy Kelly at the 1919 Derby for his conception of a horse that before a race was outwardly composed but was "a raging torrent inside." Yet he may have drawn as well on reports concerning a new two-year-old, Man o' War, who was driving the Saratoga fans wild that August with his speed, stamina, and utter will to win; for just as Sunstreak is owned by "Mr. Van Riddle of New York" who has "the biggest farm we've got in our country," so Man o' War was owned by Mr. Sam (Samuel D.) Riddle, a wealthy Pennsylvania textile manufacturer who had both the Glen Riddle Farm near Philadelphia and the huge Faraway Farm near Lexington. As for the awkward-looking but powerful gelding "Middlestride," Anderson had seen him win at Churchill Downs in 1918 under his real name Exterminator, a gelding well-known for his many victories and his gaunt, unprepossessing appearance, which gave him the affectionate nickname of "Old Bones." The name Middlestride Anderson may have adapted from Midway, a thoroughbred who, the newspapers reported, had won the Kentucky Handicap at Churchill Downs back in late May, 1919.[13]

Horses and Negroes would have been much on Anderson's mind in August of 1919, not only because of the Saratoga thoroughbred meets but also of the Grand Circuit harness races that were moving from Ohio to the East and back to Ohio, carrying with them an intense rivalry among three great drivers—Walter Cox, Tom Murphy, and Anderson's longtime favorite, Pop Geers, the Silent Man from Tennessee, who unlike Jerry Tillford never boasted that it was he, not his trotter or pacer, who won a race. The horses themselves one could depend on; they were embodiments of beautiful motion, courage, a clean honest devotion to the challenge of the race. One could depend too on some, if not all, of the men who worked with the thoroughbreds and hence took on their best qualities. Especially one could depend on the track "niggers" like Bildad Johnson, who intuitively understood horses and horse-crazy boys, and of whom one could say, comparing them with whites: "You can trust them. They are squarer with kids." When "I Want to Know Why" was published in *The Smart Set* in November after that summer of frenzied race riots, it was as though Anderson were declaring publicly which side he had been on.

The praise of blacks might also have been prompted by some memory of Burt, the black groom Sherwood had known in Clyde; but the chances are good that Bildad was in part suggested by Nigger Jim in *Huck Finn,* for *Huck* would have been on Anderson's mind that August also. Off and on for over a year he had been talking and corresponding about Twain and his masterpiece with Van Wyck Brooks, who was at the moment writing about that Westerner's ordeal in the East. A Huck Finn cast to the boy's speech—why else his use of the odd word "fantods"?—would be fitting, given a Bildad Johnson who was as comical and admirable a figure as Huck's black friend and given the picaresque atmosphere of the racetrack world, which was as much a refuge from conventional society as was the Mississippi River. As much and no more, for just as life on the raft was vulnerable to invasion by all sorts of human ugliness, so was life at the track. Only a few weeks earlier Anderson had been planning a group of children's tales, not the usual "asinine sentimental nonsense," as Twain might have put it, but pictures of actual "country life at the edge of a middle-western town"; and "I Want to Know Why," concerned with someone just beyond childhood, was not conceived as sentimental nonsense either. Like Huck Finn of St. Petersburg, Missouri, the fifteen-year-old boy from Beckersville, Kentucky, is no innocent. He knows a good deal about adult nastiness already—a horse can be "pulled" in a race by a crooked jockey, one can hear "rotten talk" around a livery stable, a "bad woman house" can be found near any race track—but he can submerge such knowledge in his sheer joy at the thoroughbreds and the aura of dedication, beauty, and sensuous delight they cast around themselves. He can submerge it up to the point, that is, when the world of corruption breaks massively in on him.

Such a point is reached, of course, with Jerry Tillford's perceived betrayal of Sunstreak and the communion that the horse created between Jerry and the boy. The betrayal occurs in a sexual context; yet as happens so often in the Winesburg tales, something does not symbolize sex, sex symbolizes something. Fundamentally the boy is right to question why things are as they are. What he protests against is not adulthood, sexual or otherwise, nor even moral ambiguity as the condition of existence. He (and his creator) already knows that some adults are "good," others "bad," most are a mixture of both. Although the father of one of the boys is a professional gambler, he alone refuses to enter the "rummy-looking farmhouse" where the women are as unbeautiful as they are unvirtuous; although the boy's own father is middle-class by professional status, he understands his son and allows him his lowlife associations. Rather, the boy despairingly protests that spoliation of a shared moment, though he would not himself see the analogy, is equivalent in intensity and function to the artist's imaginative creation of an art work and to the observer's imaginative experience of it.

Such spoliation, Anderson knew intuitively, comes from two directions. There is the corruption always threatened by the conventional world, represented here neither by the boy's father nor by the professional gambler, but by those minor characters, some of them Beckersville citizens, all of them, incidentally, white, who follow the thoroughbreds but cannot intuit their inner natures and who view the racetrack as a milieu licensing the satisfaction of their lusts, for money or for sex, in no matter how squalid a fashion. One such person, to take a real-life example, might be Dave Bohon, businessman son of Banker Bohon of Harrodsburg, whose visits to Chicago required of Anderson and other Critchfield employees that they pander their brains for his advertising needs while Dave alternated an evening at the Chicago Symphony with sordid debauches of drink and women. More terrible even than the corruption from the outer world, however, is that which threatens spoliation from within the self. Jerry Tillford shares the moment of communion at the saddling, yet debases it doubly—not so much through sex as through ugly sex, and not by ugly sex alone but specifically through slander. He uses words to defame Sunstreak, the ultimate source of the shared moment; he uses words to lie with—as indeed Anderson with self-loathing felt himself doing daily in his advertising work and thereby defaming the material with which he should be building his art. Instead, words should be used as the boy uses them, to tell truths no matter how bitter the truth or how embittering the telling of it—as indeed Anderson used words in this story. The personal meaning of "I Want to Know Why," then, is that it affirms the value of intuition and communion, which Anderson saw as the very ground and function of both art and life, but acknowledges the almost overwhelming destructive forces arrayed against them. The extreme unhappiness of the boy is a measure of how, "more than ever before," as Anderson wrote Bab, he felt and understood in that August of 1919 "the reality of pain."[14]

2.

Even the move into his own private La Salle Street office around September 1 and a week's escape to his Kentucky clients did not at first relieve Anderson's dark mood, for he had to drive himself hard to get his new business arrangement working. Writing advertisements made him feel ill with the illness of spirit that seemed to him to afflict people in Europe as well as the United States in the aftermath of the war. "Nothing seems healthy," he wrote Bab, "but the out of doors, the corn growing in fields and the silent strips of woodland." Feeling himself "no fit company for anyone these days," he continued to long for a quiet place out of the city in which to live and work, and he even spent a weekend walking with Tennessee through some of the prairie towns near Chicago hoping to find a small house at the edge of one of them where he might live and she could visit him and rest from the increasing demands on her as a gifted private teacher. Perhaps, he wrote Trigant Burrow, he could find a patron who would be willing to assure him an annual income of $2,500 to $3,000, nearly half to go to the support of his children, so that he could be free to do the "more and more delicate and subtle work" he now had developed the skill to do. The money had to come on his own terms. Later that fall, though, he would be offered $5,000 for writing a series of articles attacking the Nonpartisan League, that Midwest populist movement which conventional politicians were then vilifying as part of a "Red" plot against America. The sum would have provided him two years of freedom, but he would not be able to bring himself to take it. The very unworkableness of his own schemes for freedom merely disheartened him the more. On September 25, returning to Ben Huebsch the corrections to be made in the second printing of *Winesburg,* he confessed that his revision of *Mary Cochran* was "moving very slowly as I am seldom in the mood for writing these days."[15]

As much as anything, a series of letters from Frank with a series of requests began to lighten the weight of his despondency. On September 25 Frank hurriedly mailed him in a form letter a translation of Romain Rolland's "Declaration of Independence of the Mind," an appeal to intellectuals in all countries, the "Workers in the realms of thought," to cast off the war-enforced bonds of nationalism and declare an international solidarity honoring "truth alone, free, without frontiers, without limits, without racial or caste prejudices" in order to hasten unity among humanity. Since Rolland's appeal fitted Anderson's antipolitical convictions, if not his nationalistic ones, he willingly wrote to the French writer stating his support of the appeal. But Frank had another, more immediate concern. His *Our America* was to appear shortly, and both Frank and Horace Liveright, the publisher, were uneasy that in Chicago the book might fall into the hands of newspaper reviewers unsympathetic to its particular vision of the country. Sherwood at first tried to arrange with Sell and Rascoe that Carl Sandburg would do the review for the *Daily News* while he himself would do that for the *Tribune;* but Sandburg excused himself on the grounds of ignorance, and his own "review" eventually took the form of a letter about Frank, which he sent to Rascoe in mid-November but was never published.[16]

Through October his mood gradually brightened as a result of his efforts to help his "brother" and, in addition, his relief that Tennessee's health was steadily improving. What the business life was doing to him, he now realized in a more detached way, was "blurring . . . the vision" that held him to his craft as artist. When he was himself, he wrote Waldo, he could with his "inner eye" see "something unattainable."

Writing is like cutting and nailing on steps by which one attempts to reach some unattainable height.

One has to do it because he is so made that he cannot just stand gazing into nothingness.

That he could articulate even so vague a vision was a good sign that he was recovering from the access of horror that had come over him when he returned to Chicago from Ephraim.[17]

Then toward the end of October he received an advance copy of *Our America*, read it happily, and knew at once what he would say in his letter about it to the *Tribune*. He would recall how when he first "found" Frank in New York, they had walked the streets together and how Frank's talk "glowed, how it fused the city into understandable life." Now in the written words of *Our America* Frank was doing for the nation as a whole what he had done in spoken words for New York. Anderson had reason to like *Our America*, for its author had made him by far the most important figure in his central chapter, "Chicago." (Perhaps Rascoe did not publish the letter on the grounds that it might have appeared self-serving.) In his highly charged prose Frank was declaiming a variation on Brooks's theme in *America's Coming-of-Age* and *Letters and Leadership*. An older generation of writers, for example Dreiser and Masters, had rebelled, though without hope, against American materialism and morality, the double heritage of Puritanism; and a new generation, for example Sandburg and Anderson, were continuing the rebellion but with the hope that by finding and releasing its buried life America as a whole could "create her own salvation." Summarizing Anderson's career as paradigmatic, Frank declared that it was in the "magical" stories of *Winesburg* with their "true aesthetic form" that one best finds the "consciousness of life and love which must create for us the America of to-morrow." Together Anderson and Sandburg and lesser figures like them, the chapter concluded,

disclose the luminosity of American materials. Against the American doctrine of success with its subsidiary Puritan morals, they bring their gospel of Failure. Meaning only this: that the material ends to which we have reduced the largess of our lives are shoddy falsehood, and that the glory of truth is but the glory of *being*. An ancient gospel that gleams with the fierceness of its need in the American night.[18]

Such praise would have heartened even a less moody person than Anderson. "You know," he wrote to Frank at the end of October, "that I love [*Our America*] so that it is hard for me to talk of it." Now in late October, although he had been concentrating on business affairs so intensely that on some days his body twitched with weariness and he feared that he might be catching the "neuritis" that had afflicted Tennessee, he felt a renewed quietness of self and was writing again. Encouraged in part by the appearance of "Testament 1" in the October issue of *The Little Review,* he started to compose further Testaments; and perhaps prompted by Waldo's praise of *Winesburg,* he began a new kind of revision of *Mary Cochran,* which, in its biographical form, had never quite satisfied him. By November 12 he could write to Ben Huebsch much more confidently than he had been able to do a month and a half earlier.

One of these days I shall be able to give you the Mary Cochran book. It has tantalized me a good deal but is coming clear now. In its final form it will be like Winesburg, a group of tales woven about the life of one person but each tale will be longer and more closely related to the development of the central character. It can be published in fact as a novel if you wish.

It seems to me that in this form I have worked out something that is very flexible and that is the right instrument for me. The reason will be plain. I get no chances at all for long periods of uninterrupted thought or work. I can take my character into my consciousness and live with it but have to work in this fragmentary way. These individual tales come clear and sharp. When I am ready for one of them it comes all at one sitting, a distillation, an outbreak.

No one I know of has used the form as I see it and as I hope to develop it in several books. Damn man I wish I had time to work.

For days at a time now, he felt the harmony of self that he sought for in order to write and which the actual process of writing could then reciprocally strengthen. "I am writing again," he told Bab,

and when I do much goes over my head. Suddenly things thus begin to coordinate for me. All staleness in life floats away. I find myself vitally interested in everything. I live and am strong.[19]

It was at this time that he must have written "The Door of the Trap," a tale apparently adapted—the relevant pages are missing from the manuscript—from chapters 2 or 3 of *Mary Cochran,* dealing with Mary's college years. Presumably also he finished at least a draft of "Unlighted Lamps," which concentrates on the relationship of Mary and her father at the time of Dr. Cochran's death, the climax of chapter 1. "The Door of the Trap" is perhaps most significant for its title, which would have come readily to the mind of a writer himself seeking escape, and for its picture of a loveless prison of a marriage, obviously an interpretation by Sherwood of his marriage to Cornelia. Told mainly through the consciousness of Hugh Walker, a professor in a small Illinois college, it describes his emotional involvement with his student Mary Cochran, and his deliberate liberation of her from the prison of his life that she might herself mature.[20]

There are only suggestions in *Mary Cochran* as to the extent to which the circumstances of "The Door of the Trap" may differ from those in the novel, one being the change from New England setting to midwestern one. "Unlighted Lamps," however, shows dramatically how rapidly and in what direction Anderson had developed artistically in the half dozen years since he had written his unpublished third novel. Granted the necessary differences between a short story and the first chapter of a novel, it is clear that he knew now how to reject extraneous material and to concentrate on the essentials of an action. Except for the general situation—a small-town doctor unable to communicate with the young daughter left him from a mismatched marriage—only the climactic scene of the doctor's actual death from heart disease comes from the novel's first chapter, most of the events of the short story having been newly invented to emphasize the tentative efforts of both father and daughter to reach each other through an habitual wall of separation. Even more striking is Anderson's addition of the motif of flickering light—a fire by a riverbank, a dropped match, a swinging lantern, moonlight on flood waters, a held cigarette—not only to link the parts of the story but to symbolize both the potentiality for emotional communication and the frustration of that potentiality. Nor is the symbolism intellectualized or schematic; indeed, two instances of flickering light connecting man and nature have the indefinable quality Waldo Frank had termed "magical." In the novel Dr. Cochran had merely taken Mary in his buggy to see a river so flooded as to look like a lake and to threaten a wooden bridge across it. In "Unlighted Lamps" Anderson adds to the dangerousness of the flood the mysterious night beauty of moonlight dancing on the lake's little waves. Just as Dr. Cochran, moved by the "dancing lights," is about to reveal to Mary the secret of her mother's and his brief married life, the timbers of the bridge begin to crack, the horse drawing the buggy is terrified, and in regaining control over the horse, the doctor reassumes "his diffident silent nature." What he might have revealed to Mary, but failed to do, was his earlier failure to express his love to his wife toward the end of a particular summer day during the first year of their marriage before she left him. At a farm the doctor's wife had been given an unused mirror she had admired. As she drove the buggy home, the doctor holding the mirror on his knees beside her, she told him she was pregnant. Now years later the doctor recalls how the "mirror on his knees caught the rays of the departing sun and sent a great ball of golden light dancing across the fields and among the branches of trees," while he, though "stirred as never before," remained silent at the announcement because, in his introverted way, "he had thought no words he could utter would express what he felt." Anderson had learned, in short, that symbols should not be imposed on a story but should develop out of the story it-self and help it to function; they should also, at their Andersonian best, be at once commonplace and unusual.

But beyond "The Door of the Trap" and possibly "Unlighted Lamps," he did little, or nothing, more with his intention to recast *Mary Cochran* "into the Winesburg form, half individual tales, half long novel form." Unlike *Winesburg,* there was no single setting to provide focus and unity, and the strongly linear biographical form of the novel resisted being bro-ken down into a series of tales told through a variety of central con-sciousnesses, not simply through Mary's. By early December Anderson was in effect admitting to Frank that he had reached another stalemate with the book, using, as he often did, a metaphor that confessed more than it said outright.

The tales that are to make the Mary Cochran book are waiting like tired people on the doorstep of the house of my mind. They are unclothed. I need to be a tailor and make warm clothes of words for them.[21]

For the Testaments he showed a somewhat more sustained interest. Returning to them again in late October, half a year after the initial out-break, he recognized that he could no longer call them an experiment in prose but rather, as he explained to Frank in mid-November, "a grouping [groping] after expression of my own faith, songs, chants, speculations." Enclosed with this letter of explanation was a copy of the prose "Testa-ment I" from the October *Little Review,* but he now was "making the tes-tament" out of what he described to Frank as a "mood of poetry." Adding the new, lyrical pieces to those written in the spring, he had "some twenty" Testaments by this time; and he bought a notebook so that he could carry them with him on his business trips, since they were not parts of a project he could work at steadily but "a peculiarly personal thing that leaks out of me anywhere, any time."[22]

As with *Mid-American Chants,* Anderson's impulse toward poetry had a connection with his relationship to Frank, this time not only that Waldo had praised him so highly in *Our America* but also that the younger man had announced to him his intention to get out of New York for a while. After seeing *Our America* through the press in October, Waldo did go off late in the month to absorb more of the nation he had just written about. Originally he had planned to "embrace vagabondage," as Sherwood put it, by taking a boat to New Orleans; but since a longshoremen's strike was keeping ships from running out of New York harbor, he returned to the plan he had been mulling for nearly a year and instead took a train for St. Louis and went on to wander about through towns and cities in Kansas, immersing himself in "brother Sherwood's" Midwest. Shortly after mid-

November he settled in the central Kansas town of Ellsworth, where for some three weeks he lived with a family named Amos and worked as "jack of all trades" on the local newspaper before going on to attend the populist Nonpartisan League's national convention in St. Paul, Minnesota, in early December. While in Kansas he wrote emotional letters to Sherwood declaring how through having known him he was able to feel a loving brotherhood for the Amoses despite their pinched lives and to sense the beauty of "this stupendous, this passionate flat land." In turn, Sherwood took vicarious delight in Waldo's escape from the city, wrote warmly of how in his imagination he companioned him in his wanderings, and enclosed in a series of letters several of the new poetic Testaments to show his "honest love" for his "Good brother—neither big nor little but brother walking up and down. . . ."[23]

Brotherhood in wandering was, in fact, the theme of the first of these Testaments, "Here Is a Testament I Have Made for You," which in somewhat shortened form would be printed in *A New Testament* of 1927 under the title simply of "Brother." Anderson sent it off to Frank in a letter of November 18 or 19 from an Evansville, Indiana, hotel—he was apparently returning from one of his business trips to Owensboro—after a night on the Ohio in a little riverboat when, "the whole land out here being so little removed from its savage state," he had imagined "in the darkness the stars and the country waiting for men to come." The bardic note was there, but in the rest of the letter, as in the Testament itself, it was modulated from what it had been in the *Chants*. For the first time, Sherwood confessed, he had just read all of Waldo's articles in copies of *The Seven Arts* he had had bound, and he had been struck by "how often you have voiced the gropings of my dumb years, do yet voice my dumb days." All three of the poetic Testaments addressed to Frank himself were, not prophetic pronouncements as in *Mid-American Chants* nor self-lacerating doubts about the bardic role as in some of the original Testaments but, instead, explicit attempts to reach out for companionship with a fellow artist.[24]

He could not find such companionship with another poet, a New York friend and admirer of Frank, who had come to Chicago the previous summer at Harriet Monroe's urging and who had become an associate editor of *Poetry*. Emmanuel Carnevali was a slim, thin-faced young Italian immigrant who had won a Young Poet's prize in *Poetry*'s annual awards of 1918 when he was only twenty. Waldo had written of him to Sherwood, that he was a "man of remarkable power" of personality, passionately receptive to life but immature and as yet directionless. "You will find him delightful, exciting, at times irritating, but always worth while," Waldo had concluded. Sherwood found Carnevali both exciting and irritating when the young man spent an evening with the Andersons and "talked violently, at times beautifully." The two men went out for a walk that evening, Anderson wrote Frank, and "Suddenly Carnevali began to speak of his marriage to an Italian girl and told me a lovely tale of strong young lovemaking." At some later time, Carnevali would himself vividly remember, Sherwood and "his wonderful wife" visited him when he was ill, bringing him "a magnificent grapefruit." Overcome by gift and givers, Carnevali talked hysterically, all the time realizing that the Andersons were silently dismissing him as "melodramatic and a play-actor." Anderson's combined attraction to and withdrawal from the excitable young man showed in the Testament he wrote to Carnevali toward the end of November, a Testament in which the Italian girl is turned fancifully into a goddess who "wears heavy gold wristlets and in her hair is a chain of finely wrought silver."[25]

In his new mood of poetry Anderson felt closer to Hart Crane, whom he had still met only through letters; but when Crane sent him a copy of his poem "My Grandmother's Love Letters" for criticism, Anderson, admitting to having "so little knowledge" of poetry, wrote back on December 3 that the letter accompanying the poem had conveyed to him more of Crane's "reality . . . as a man," the conveyance of self to others being what he was himself trying to "work out into expression in my New Testament." Then as an example he quoted for Crane the statement made to him by a businessman when the two had been at lunch the day before. In a "moment of frankness" the man had said:

> "I was at my prayers
> And the lust for women
> came to me."
> That was to me a perfect poem. I went away and put it down as a Testament out of his life to all life.

Finally, in another letter to Crane, on December 17, Anderson summed up the new emphasis the Testaments had taken on since the original series of the previous spring.

> In a way I like the structure and mood of the *Testament* thing better than anything I have found. In it I hope to express much of the vague, intangible hunger that constantly besets me, as it must you. One doesn't hunger to defeat the materialism of the world about. One hungers to find brothers buried away beneath all this roaring modern insanity of life.[26]

The original Testaments had begun as a self-confident assertion that the speaker of them could in fact communicate with all other human beings through the imagination, but as that series developed, Anderson had made his "autobiography of a man's fanciful life" probe more and more deeply into his own barely conscious desires, motives, and memories. The more obviously lyric Testaments he was now writing represented a recoil, as it were, from what the probing had revealed and expressed, a felt need to link up his own self with the selves of others. The intensity of his need was implied in the Testaments but came out most clearly in the paradoxes of that December 17 letter to Crane. Because of the vastness of the American land, he resignedly wrote, "We must remain like seeds planted near each other in a field. No voice any of us may raise will quite carry across the spaces." Nevertheless, he insisted, "In the *Testament* I want to send the voices of my own mind out to the hidden voices in others, to do what can't be done perhaps."

Despite such doubts he was himself hearing the voices of other minds. Early in November he read D. H. Lawrence's *Sons and Lovers*. "By god it is a book," he wrote Huebsch, thanking him for having sent a copy of *Winesburg* to Lawrence. Whether he had previously read *The Rainbow* and *The Prussian Officer and Other Stories,* published by Huebsch in 1915 and 1916, is not known, but his admiration for the English author was thereafter both deep and lasting. He was more intimately affected by a lesser novel, which he read and recommended to Bab probably later this same November.

> You must read a book called *The Moon and Sixpence* by Somerset Maugham. A striking story that will I am sure make you understand a great deal in myself. It is a story I have often thought of writing and will yet. When I do write it, will lay it down without explanation or all the talk Maugham indulges in.[27]

A novel suggested to Maugham in general outline by the career of the French Post-Impressionist painter Paul Gauguin, *The Moon and Sixpence* tells through a narrator, a minor novelist, of one Charles Strickland, a London stockbroker with a conventional wife and two children, who in his mid-forties abruptly leaves his family and goes to Paris in order to fulfill a demonic urge to paint. Befriended by another artist, a second-rate painter but one capable of recognizing genius, Strickland rewards the man by seducing his wife and, in painting a nude portrait of her, breaks through to a new, strange, and extraordinary artistic manner. When the woman becomes possessive toward him, however, he brutally rejects her, she commits suicide, and he, quite unmoved by her death, goes off first to Marseille and then Tahiti, where his painting genius flowers. Out of physical convenience he lives with a native girl who remains faithfully with him even after he contracts leprosy. Horribly ravaged by the disease, he nevertheless lives long enough to paint directly on the four inside walls of his shabby house his masterpiece, terrifying, obscene, passionate, and beautiful.

Obviously Anderson had no intention of dying of leprosy, but clearly

he saw Strickland's break from a conventional career and marriage as imaging and validating his own; and, though he could not in living fact
match it, he would have admired Strickland's simpleminded indifference
to family, fame, money, love, and the loneliness that, as the narrator puts
it, shuts up each human being almost incommunicado "in a tower of
brass." Strickland's artistic aspirations, as voiced by the narrator, sometimes closely resemble what Anderson had himself voiced in "An Apology
for Crudity" or the *Chants* or, in some moods, in his personal letters. The
painter "saw vaguely," the narrator fancies,

some spiritual meaning in material things that was so strange that he could only
suggest it with halting symbols. It was as though he found in the chaos of the universe a new pattern, and were attempting clumsily, with anguish of soul, to set it
down. I saw a tormented spirit striving for the release of expression.

Strickland's complete escape from the complexities of modern society and
his success in effecting "a revolution in art" by following unswervingly
"the vision that obsessed his mind" were what Anderson was at that moment dreaming to achieve himself. That the book spoke to him powerfully
is indicated by his direct identification with Maugham's artist in the letter
to Bab. Immediately following the paragraph in which he asserts that
through Maugham's story she will "understand a great deal" in himself,
he abruptly and with a transition not logical but psychological states an
attitude toward women echoing that expressed by Strickland: "Am often
startled in the presence of a woman on a fine evening to see how the mystery of trees, silence, colors, and life goes over her head. It is because what
is so vital and necessary to her is necessarily a passing thing to the man."
Reading *The Moon and Sixpence* would help Bab to understand his attitude toward her, he wrote. His own reading of it helps explain why within
months he would begin writing *Many Marriages*, which eventually turned
into a version of his and Strickland's story.[28]

Other, more direct voices came to him unexpectedly. In the same mail
on the morning of December 15 he received letters from the long-silent
Van Wyck Brooks and Paul Rosenfeld with the news that *The Ordeal of
Mark Twain* and *Musical Portraits* were finished. He was particularly
anxious to see the Twain book and immediately wrote to Van Wyck; for if
it "will not have the passionate flaming thing in it that Waldo's book often has," Brooks "must realize what an inciter to flame in others you are."
For example, his own Testament experiment was "A passionate attempt
to get poetry into the thing you have expressed time and again and that
you and Waldo have together made me a little conscious of." As always
with Brooks he was both assertive and deferential.

When in speaking of *Winesburg* you used the word adolescence you struck more nearly than you know on the whole note of me. I am immature, will live and die immature. A quite terrible confession that would be if I did not represent so much.

I am conscious I do represent much, and often I feel like a very small boy in the presence of your mind and of Waldo's too.

What is true of me is true of Sandburg, but we are different. He is submerged in adolescence. I am in it and of it, but I look out. Give Sandburg a mind, and you perhaps destroy him. I don't know whether that would be true of me or not.[29]

For weeks now Anderson had been planning a few days in New York between Christmas and New Year's to see various friends and to talk with Scofield Thayer and James S. Watson, Jr., who at the end of November had assumed control of *The Dial* and were turning it into a monthly magazine with an emphasis no longer on politics but on art and literature, including the publication of some fiction. Nevertheless, Rosenfeld, probably to celebrate the completion of *Musical Portraits,* came to Chicago on December 22 for a brief visit with Anderson. The visit was one of the joyous spots in what Sherwood had summarized in his reply to Paul's letter as "a year of long blank, black places illuminated by periods of not too much weariness with business to turn to other things." The enthusiastic Rosenfeld praised *Our America* and predicted, clear-sightedly on the eve of the 1920s, that "there is going to be a turning to the Americans—that the men who have not sold here will sell." One of those Americans ought to be Sherwood Anderson, both men could hope, for by now they would know that in the Holiday Book issue of the *New York Times Book Review* for December 7 an anonymous critic, surveying at length "The Year's Achievement in Books" had pronounced *Winesburg, Ohio* one "of the six best American books of fiction of the year" even though, like Dreiser, its author's "place in literature is a matter of bitter controversy." *Winesburg,* the critic commented,

is a collection of short stories which, coming from Russia, would have been given the lip service of the literati. They delve into the subconscious in the most approved Freudian manner.[30]

Such national recognition of *Winesburg* as an "important landmark of 1919," despite the question about his "place in literature," should have kept Sherwood ebullient for weeks; yet hardly had he seen Paul off on the train for New York when his good spirits dropped away. He had already determined that he must somehow get out of business during the coming winter, and even before Paul's arrival he had revealed a degree of desperation by reviving, in a letter to Bab, his rejected notion of a summer camp for children and adults. Time and strength were steadily running out on him, he had the skill now for better work, he remained caught in the trap. Here was a year almost gone in which three of his closest friends had completed books, while as for him *Poor White* lay unfinished, the Testaments had no foreseeable conclusion, and the revision of *Mary Cochran* had very quickly run to a dead end. The "Christmas psychosis" from which he annually suffered hurled him into what he described to Waldo as

two days of terror—such days of terror as sometimes come when the whole world gets dead black and turns into dollar grabbing insane men. At times the writing of one little advertisement becomes a terrible thing—like striking a child.

The worst of the seizure passed with the passing of Christmas, and, "sane again," he took the train for New York, headed, though he did not yet know it, for a second, more distant escape from his life in Chicago.[31]

10

Experiments in Prose

1.

As always New York excited him. There were old friends to see again, new friends to meet, art exhibitions to visit, constant talk, walks in the throng-ing city, which by now he had come to feel familiar with. Brooks and Frank were still out of town, but he saw Margaret Naumburg Frank again, met the English novelist Gilbert Cannan, who had enthusiastically reviewed *Our America* and admired *Winesburg,* and visited with Paul Rosenfeld, who invited him to a concert one evening in delighted thanks for Anderson's having sent him a book of selections from the Greek An-thology. He saw new paintings by Georgia O'Keeffe and photographs by Alfred Stieglitz, leaders in the modern art movement whom he had met through Rosenfeld perhaps as early as his February 1917 visit to New York. As for business, he talked at length on January 3 with *The Dial's* new editor, Scofield Thayer, whose slim, pallid appearance and cultivated manner annoyed him. Thayer had an "interior decorator's soul," Sher-wood decided; and when Thayer commented that he was offering Sand-burg only five or ten dollars for his poems, Sherwood angrily told him to his face that with his wealth *The Dial* could afford to pay writers at more than that absurd rate. Feeling like a labor leader, Sherwood immediately wired Sandburg to ask $25 per poem and subsequently wrote both him and Frank urging that they hold out for proper payment. He himself in-sisted on $200 for a story—though when he did shortly sell two stories to *The Dial* he accepted $200 for the two.[1]

The two-week trip to New York helped him to clear his mind, and he returned to Chicago around January 11 even more resolved than ever to get out of the "damp, dark cellar" of business. But the demands of busi-ness kept him in a whirl during the next few days, and he had to travel to Ohio and Kentucky to see to the affairs of his clients. Then overwork, the tantalizing glimpse of freedom New York had briefly given him, and a despairing conviction that the whole world was ill in spirit helped send him to bed for ten days with a bad siege of the flu. Remembering how long it had taken him to recover in the fall of 1918, he decided that he must use his savings to find recovery in a warmer climate. Around February 1 or shortly after, he took a train going south to the Gulf of Mexico.[2]

Someone seems to have told him about the Single-Tax community of Fairhope, Alabama, on the eastern shore of Mobile Bay; for he went there first, apparently stayed a very few days at the much-verandahed Colonial Inn, found the town and townspeople unattractive, and around February 9 took the little side-wheel steamer *Apollo* across the bay to Mobile. This quiet, untouristed Southern city was just what he was looking for. Quickly he found a place to hole up in, an old rooming house at 351 St. Michael Street inhabited by dockworkers from the nearby wharves on the Mobile River. For only $3.50 a week he had a large, low-ceilinged room with "quaint little windows and a fire place." As he would recall it, that first evening he walked about the city streets in a warm, gentle rain and by luck found a wallet with $140 in it and no indication of its owner. This, added to his savings, was the key to a long stay in the South. Walking on through a Negro section, hearing the quiet voices of the blacks in the soft night, he felt the tensions of Chicago and the business whirl leaving him. The North was like this, he told himself, making a hard fist; the South was like this, he said aloud, letting his hand "lie open and relaxed." For the first time in months he felt fully happy.[3]

He had brought some advertising work with him, and though he had not yet completely recovered from the flu, he first took care of business affairs. Then he turned eagerly to finishing *Poor White,* the novel he had worked on so steadily in New York in the fall of 1918. Once again the words flowed, and his spirits were even more improved by the fact that *The Dial* had purchased two stories, "The Egg," which he considered "one of the best I have ever done," and the Mary Cochran story, "The Door of the Trap." Now he rose gladly each morning, made his own breakfast, and wrote undisturbed by anyone until ready to stop for the day. Afternoons he walked about Mobile, which he thought charming with its fine old houses and its sleepy air. He also had located someone in the city to talk to, a painter named Anna Mitchell. One evening in Chicago, Anna had gone to the Dill Pickle and met Jack Jones; unexpectedly she and Jack had fallen in love with each other, but though he approved of her being a painter, she was not sure that she would be the right kind of wife for him. She had come South to Mobile to paint and to think out her personal situation, and Jack now wrote Sherwood to look her up. Sherwood found her a small, plain, aristocratic-looking person with, he felt, a remarkable painting talent and a fineness of spirit, which must have been the quality that had so attracted Jones. Sherwood liked her immediately.[4]

It was apparently Anna who suggested that, since Sherwood still wanted to be out of doors as much as possible until his flu was entirely gone, he should move back to Fairhope but to a house on the beach. A day's excursion there by the two of them decided the matter for him. From a Mrs. Nichols he rented a small, furnished beach cottage, and by February 28 he had recrossed the bay on the *Apollo* and moved in just as a three-day blow of cold north wind began.[5]

The town of Fairhope was on a plateau set high enough about the bay that on clear evenings the lights of Mobile could be seen fifteen miles to the northwest across the water. From the plateau the land dropped in rugged bluffs to a long, narrow sand beach, these bluffs being deeply scored by steep, red-clay gullies. Sherwood's cabin stood in the dense growth of hardwoods that edged the beach, and the blue and green waters of Mobile Bay were only thirty feet from his door at high tide. By day he could see ocean-going ships passing out in the bay, and at night the sun went down behind the distant, low-lying western shore in flames of color that turned both sky and water red as blood. After a rain, red clay washed down from the gullies onto the white sand of the beach, where wind and tide mixed clay and sand into shifting colored patterns. Along the beach, which stretched north and south for miles, were scattered great tree stumps, cast ashore and bleached by years of sun; when he walked the beaches on moonlight nights, the stumps assumed strange, constantly changing shapes. It was a new world of form and color, a fantastic world.[6]

For the first time in his life, or at least since his days in Cuba, Anderson experienced a true color shock, which would shortly lead him to try his hand at painting, an adventure encouraged by the fact that within a week after he had settled into his little cottage he was invited to dinner by a painter, Wharton Esherick, and his darkly beautiful wife Letty. Esherick, a tall, bony, energetic, earthy-humored Philadelphian of thirty-two, was then teaching art at Fairhope's School of Organic Education, a progressive, child-centered school founded in 1907 by Marietta L. Johnson, where painting was one of the many "self-prompted, creative" activities whereby the children's bodies, minds, and spirits were to be developed simultaneously, that is, "organically." Through Esherick, Anderson was able to visit the school, meet Mrs. Johnson, and observe the effects on the children of an educational system, which, to his approval, emphasized the development of the individual's imagination. He found Mrs. Johnson "remarkable" and the children happy, and concluded that the school was "a real force"; but he continued to despise the town above the beach as physically "hideous," the townspeople as "middle class resorters, the sort who give themselves to mild reforms like Single Tax in these times of revolutionary movements"—not that he had become at all interested in politics or the philosophy of change or indeed in abstractions in general. What

interested him was something at once simple and complex. As he had written Hart Crane just after moving to Fairhope beach,

I am in truth mighty little interested in any discussions of art or life or what a man's
place in the scheme of things may be. It has to be done I suppose but after all there
is the fact of life. Its story wants telling and singing. That's what I want—the tale
and the song of it, I suppose.[7]

At the moment the tale that most wanted telling was *Poor White,* and
in the soft days that followed the three-day storm the book continued to
come out of him in a rush. Even before moving from Mobile to Fairhope
he had begun the fifth of six planned "books," or sections, of the novel and
had predicted to Huebsch that he would be finished by the end of March.
Urging Ben to use his influence as publisher of the new magazine *The Freeman* to have *Poor White* printed there in serial form—purchase of serial
rights by *The Freeman* might bring him "some real money"—Anderson
described his book in a way that showed still his original inspiration for
the protagonist in the combined figures of Lincoln and Twain-Huck Finn.

It is really the story of the development of an American town into an industrial center and the effect of the coming of industrials on the people. It is not of course
propaganda for anything but is the story just as I see it. The central figure is an inventor, one Hugh McVey, son of a Mississippi River raftsman and a descendent of
Poor Whites of Kentucky. The story itself is I believe a rattling good one and the
novel moves.

Again he had settled into a steady, productive routine of writing in the
morning, then doing his few household chores, walking in the afternoon
along the beach or in the pine woods surrounding Fairhope, or swimming
or fishing for sheepshead and saltwater trout in the bay, and reading and
lounging about by himself in the evenings.[8]
　　Almost at once to his dismay and concern, however, he was "jerked
out of solitude" by word from Chicago that Tennessee had gone "to pieces
nervously" and badly needed his help; so on Sunday, March 7, with a draft
of *Poor White* frustratingly within days of completion, he was on a train
heading north, his plans for the future in momentary disarray. Back at 12
East Division Street he found his wife so worn out that he was able to persuade her to give up her teaching job immediately and to return with him
to Alabama, where in the freedom, warmth, and quietness she could regain her strength. He must have lured her also with excited descriptions of
the shapes and colors he had found there, for before leaving Chicago
around March 20 he purchased a supply of watercolors, brushes, and
paper to take south with them. [9]
　　The next two months were for Sherwood and Tennessee a golden time

in what he repeatedly called a golden land. Within days after the return to Alabama he had finished a draft of *Poor White*. Writing some three years afterwards of those days of happy concentrated work, he would remember "how I sat in the back room of a small bootlegging establishment at Mobile, Alabama, one afternoon . . . and while three drunken sailors discussed the divinity of Christ at a near-by table wrote the story of little, tired-out and crazed Joe Wainsworth's killing of Jim Gibson in the harness shop at Bidwell Ohio." Once the draft was finished, it took him only two or three weeks more to complete what he described in a letter to Bab as "the harder labor . . . the slow laborious correction of my always sketchy manuscript." By mid-April *Poor White* was done, the fleshed-out and corrected version typed by a friend of the Eshericks, and the whole manuscript bundled off to Huebsch in New York. Sherwood was free now for other impulses.[10]

Even before going north to Chicago to rescue Tennessee, he had been aware that spring was coming to Alabama; as March progressed, the land around Mobile Bay glowed all colors with blossoming azalea, wisteria, jasmine, dogwood, the shrubs and flowers now adding intensity to blue water, white sand, green trees, red gullies. Color mad, as he put it, Sherwood passionately exchanged the inward eye of the writer for the outward eye of the painter. At first he went for guidance to Wharton Esherick, but Esherick, formerly a pupil of the academician William Merritt Chase, expected him to learn some of the fundamentals first. Sherwood rebelled. Scornful of classes and lessons, convinced that if one wanted to do anything expressive hard enough, one could do it intuitively, he plunged into the "tremendous experience" of "playing with colors." The experience opened up for him "a vast new field for the sight of his eyes." Eventually he would conclude that painting might "count most" by giving "more color and a sweeter roll to the old boat I call my prose"; but coming directly to painting in that Alabama spring was an enormous excitement. To him it was "as though a savage were to come suddenly out of the forest into the presence of beautiful music."[11]

His paintings, always in watercolor, were less of things that were there than of what he felt were there. His subjects might be anything or nothing, expressionistic experiments merely in laying one gaudy color against another. Sometimes he attempted a partly representational piece, such as the face of a singing Negro with the teeth sharply white against black skin, full red lips, and red mouth; but the nostrils of the flat nose flared exaggeratedly, and the face was a disembodied plaque on an intense pink background. Another time he simply tried to catch on paper the dark red of the bay at sunset. It may have been at this time that he did one of his best paintings, a cross section of a log, showing "a core of brown, green and red concentric rings," with "fifteen light bars" extending outward from the outermost ring, the bars "slightly tilted and trailing streamers behind them, making the log seem to be moving rapidly clockwise," the whole effect being of "a saw blade superimposed on the image of the log." It was obviously at this time that he lavished so much cobalt blue on the sketch which he tore up in resentment at Esherick's admiring kidding.[12]

Despite Wharton's insistence on the necessity for basic artistic training, Sherwood enjoyed the artist's lively company and his store of hilarious dirty stories, and the two men often went off on painting walks together. By early May, Anderson told Bab that of his many pictures he now had, "four that stand up and remain beautiful." Asserting rather proudly that his painting—certainly interesting but amateurish when objectively considered—"will have to make its way against all the prejudice of that craft," he nevertheless felt that "it, like poetry is something I have always wanted. One feels as though the doors to the spiritual house were slowly coming open." Ecstatically he wrote to Karl to tell him of his painting and to urge his brother to come down and share in the simple, economical life he and Tennessee were leading, since the "riot of color" would make Karl "paint like mad." Karl might even want to do a portrait of Sherwood, something of which the younger brother had "long dreamed."[13]

Tennessee too was responding to the color and warmth of land and season. As her health steadily improved, she first at Sherwood's insistence tried painting but then turned to working with the colored clays that lay about. Like her husband without any formal training but with a sense of fundamental form and rhythm given her, she believed, by her disciplined training in music, she toyed with a lump of clay one day until, to her amazement, it became a rough but recognizable likeness of Jacques Copeau. Suddenly, modeling in clay assumed for her "the terrific and delightful importance of a new game with life." She began molding figures that were characterizations of people, often heads of imaginary persons such as she and Sherwood invented and talked about. The heads were very small, realistic in detail but sometimes slightly distorted in wittily satirical or wryly sympathetic manner to emphasize some dominant personality trait. Sherwood admired them so much that when in the following year he published a story collection, *The Triumph of the Egg*, he included photographs of seven of these "Impressions in Clay" as an introduction to his own "Impressions from American life in Tales and Poems." Later in the 1920s Tennessee would so develop her unexpected talent that she attained at least a local fame in Chicago as a sculptor working in clay, plaster, and bronze. But in that spring of 1920, modeling in clay began to give her a sense of health and emotional freedom similar to Sherwood's.[14]

As though the two of them were not happy enough already, in early April they discovered the river boats. Probably on Saturday, April 3, they and the Eshericks crossed the bay to Mobile in time to catch the excursion steamer *Peerless,* which left that afternoon for a two-day trip up the Alabama River to Selma, some three hundred winding miles through green forests flecked with white dogwood. Here they went ashore for an "interesting day" in the city that, as a young Federal cavalryman, Sherwood's father had helped to capture just fifty-five years before. By April 8 the *Peerless* brought them downriver to Mobile again in time to catch the *Apollo* back to Fairhope. Sherwood was so enchanted with the trip that within two weeks he took passage, apparently without Tennessee, on the *John Quin,* a freight steamer plying the Tombigbee River between Mobile and Demopolis, Alabama. On the *Peerless* trip he had probably taken along the manuscript of *Poor White,* then in its final stage of revision. On this trip, a kind of self-reward for having got the novel off to Huebsch, he brought his watercolors and, privileged as the only passenger aboard, spent much time on deck, painting. Unlike the *Peerless,* the *John Quin,* a working boat, dirty, the food heavy and greasy. The discomforts did not bother him, however. He had provided himself with a basket of fruit to offset the regular fare, and the week-long trip gave him not only the opportunity to chat with the white officers and to paint but also to observe the black stevedores, whose body rhythms and endurance fascinated him. Sitting by his stateroom door one "unspeakably quiet and lovely evening," he was moved to write to Bab of how he had discovered "the niggers" the "sweetest-souled people in America and no one knows it."

I am writing in the dark. The niggers are singing. The white mate swears but they sing on and on. They haven't stopped singing and dancing for days although they've moved unbelievable quantities of freight and have worked day and night. That makes me feel small.[15]

Sensitized to blacks by his revulsion against the Chicago Race Riots just the previous summer, he had been drawn to their soft-voiced ways from that first night in Mobile. Writing to Hart Crane on February 29 just after the move to Fairhope, he declared: "The negroes are the living wonder of this country. What a tale if someone could penetrate into the house and the life of the southern negro and not treat it in the ordinary superficial way." Part of the attraction of blacks for Anderson was purely aesthetic, his delight as a painter in what he rapturously described to Waldo Frank as "the greens, the blues, the golden yellows, the vivid living red of their tawny skins." Part was his admiration for a people who, despite their being kept, at times violently, at the bottom of American society, "know failure but no defeat." Part was his perception of blacks, essentially excluded as they were from industrialism, as having retained a capacity for the spontaneous, the intuitive, the emotional, the imaginative, those qualities which, he had long insisted, had atrophied in most whites because of their devotion to money-getting and conventionality. Blacks were at one with the Southern land. "My notion," he would write Jerry and Lucile Blum at the end of the year,

is that the American Negro is a thing apart from the Negro in Africa or anywhere else. It is a subject race, and yet a strange thing has happened. One isn't long in the Southern states without realizing that the land, the rivers, even the cities belong to the blacks and that all the whites are outsiders there. Perhaps that's what makes the Southern white so unnecessarily vain and casually brutal. It is the brutality of the small man who by a trick has got the better of the bigger thing.

You see, I've a notion that the black is really powerful—"The Terrible Meek."

Once again Anderson was siding with the humiliated and despised, for the blacks and the artists were alike in being the outcasts of America, the outcasts, however, to whom Anderson really belonged.[16]

To a considerable extent Anderson's view of blacks must be recognized as romantic and primitivistic; it must be recognized also as being, to use a harsher term, unconsciously racist to a certain degree. He rejected as "silly" the efforts of "reformers . . . to make [blacks] conscious, fight for their rights and all that." From the standpoint of Anderson the artist, it was better that there continue to be black stevedores shouldering the heavy loads along the gangplank in that dancing lope while the white mate swore at them steadily and as ineffectually as though he were swearing at a phenomenon of nature; their burdened bodies as well as their mouths carried a song of "life," the song being inextricably rooted in, and apparently sufficient recompense for, their subject state. Yet despite his primitivistic notions, in part an expression of his own unconscious sense of white superiority, Anderson knew that whites did in fact oppress and degrade blacks, he felt genuinely humble before the blacks' endurance of their lot, and he was convinced that "the American nigger"—the term came as easily to him as "negro" or "black"—had "something absolutely lovely that's never been touched." He wanted to return to Alabama, he would tell the Blums at the end of this year, and write, "not about the American Negro, but out of him. . . ." The distinction here, not "about" but "out of," was significant. Rather than exploiting blacks as artistic material, he wanted to grasp and to absorb, if he could, the "essence" of blackness and then to let that essence power his writing. "To my mind" he told the Blums, "there is a thing to be done as big as any of the great masters ever tackled." If the limitations of Anderson's attitude toward blacks now seem clear, it should be equally clear that he had a sympathy, admiration, and respect for them and also a desire to understand them far exceeding that of most white Americans in 1920, including most artists and writers.[17]

Color of land, softness of season, presence of blacks, brightness of paint—these together with Tennessee's returning health and his own bodily well-being after the January illness kept Sherwood in a condition of almost constant delight. It was for him as though he had entered a state of pagany. Wharton Esherick would always remember vividly how a woman came to see Sherwood and, despite Tennessee's presence and Sherwood's lack of interest, showed openly her desire to seduce him. Wharton, Tennessee, Sherwood, and the woman went over to an island and began walking across it to a beach on the other side. On the way the woman became very attentive to Anderson, and he, irritated at her, strode ahead of the group. When they finally caught up with him, he had reached the beach. As he walked toward the water, they saw him stripping off his clothes, dancing gaily along, and flinging the clothes from him. Stepping into the waves, he paused to remove his underwear and then plunged naked into the water.[18]

"Quiet warm days," he wrote Bab early in May, "with thunder clouds always lurking in the distance and a sense of bells ringing over fields and hills for the joy of life." He had just come back from a walking trip by himself down through the fishing villages along the eastern shore of the lower bay. Crossing the long spit of land that half cuts off Mobile Bay from the open Gulf, he came to the Gulf shore itself "and had a swim on a long silent milk white beach in a sea of strange purple. Such blinding light and no man within many miles of me." One night he slept on the beach—and was bitten "unmercifully" by sand fleas. Another night he slept in the home of a fisherman's wife, "a tall gaunt woman much like my own mother," with whom he had a long talk. Then he sailed back up the bay to Fairhope in a fishing smack, the whole "marvelous adventurous time" having cost him "practically nothing." Practically nothing, that is, except a fiercely itching skin infection that attacked his "belly and balls." Walking by "a yellow sea at dawn," he had picked and eaten blueberries; but little poisonous vines grew beneath the berry vines, and when he scratched his sand flea bites, the poison on his fingers infected them. For several days after his return he lay out on a cot on the porch of the cottage with his inflamed genitals wrapped in lotion-soaked cloths, a condition he described with anguished hilarity in a letter to Waldo.[19]

Despite this brief affliction, he was living, as he had written Bab from the deck of the *John Quin,* "in a profound rush of events and emotions these days and sometimes my body is racked and shaken I plunge along so many new roads." At least since mid-April he had been making Testaments again; in fact, he found painting and writing poetry to be, as he told Van Wyck Brooks, "much alike in me—mystic, vague impulses" that expressed his inner self however bizarre others might regard the resulting pictures and poems. Of the "many poems" he wrote at Fairhope, only one finally to be published in *A New Testament* ("The Visit in the Morning") was certainly written there although three others probably were, since two—"The Red-Throated Black" and "Singing Swamp Negro"—describe black song emerging from suffering, while the third—"Negro on the Docks at Mobile,

Ala."—is spoken by a black who has "surrendered" but whose soul remains "sweet." In "The Visit in the Morning" Anderson was again in the prophetic mood. Reminiscent of section 6 of Whitman's "Song of Myself," it asserts that God came to the poet "in a glaring light" as he lay on his belly by the sea in "the yellow sightless sand." Made "alive" by God's loving caress, the poet feels himself part of the air, water, and earth, feels himself to have become "you," the postulated reader. The poem is, as it were, an expansion of the vatic and exuberant side of Anderson's letter to Frank, which detailed in more earthy language than customary for their correspondence the origin of his affliction: "One has been bitten on the belly and balls by little sand fleas as he lay thinking of God in the eyeless yellow sand."[20]

That letter was exuberant despite Sherwood's physical misery at the moment, for he was about to plunge along yet another road. He had a "delicious impulse," he told Waldo in this early May letter, to write a new sort of book rather than return once more to the often-postponed revision of *Mary Cochran.* It would be

a book full of rascals, men and women. It shall reel and stagger with the multitude of people I shall put into it, rascals all. There shall be flat nosed patent medicine venders, fake clap doctors, heavy handed horsemen, gamblers, profane men, lovely old bearded rascals who smell of fish.

The impulse continued, and by May 15 he could write both Burton Rascoe and Van Wyck Brooks that he had begun

a rollicking Rabelaisian thing called Many Marriages that I hope will keep me happy and satisfied in a writing way for months. It will need good health and spirits to keep the thing up but I have hungered to do just some such a thing and will probably never be in better shape to at least begin it.

Through that whole glorious spring Sherwood's exuberance had also been fed by signs that his work might be finding some of the acceptance abroad that he had long been hoping for. One sign had been an article devoted to him in the *Christian Science Monitor* for March 24 by C. Lewis Hind, an English journalist acquainted with artists and writers, whom Karl had known years earlier in England and whom Sherwood had met in Westport through Karl. Hind praised all four of Anderson's published books, sketched, somewhat inaccurately, his life, and placed him, in opposition to the English-oriented "New England school," as being in the tradition of Whitman and Winslow Homer, those "two dynamic forces" who with their successors "symbol the America that is to be." Hind ended his article with a recollection of the last time he had seen Sherwood. It had indeed been in Karl's studio in Westport.

The talk about art and life was fierce. Sherwood was restless because he wanted to read us a short story he had just finished. At a late hour we succumbed. It was a fine story and he read it wonderfully, hammering the points at us, standing. I reflected that the authors I know in Hampstead, Middlesex, never read their stories aloud. They endeavor to convey the idea (this is camouflage) that their stories are not worth reading and hardly worth writing. That is the way of authors in Hampstead, Middlesex. In Winesburg, Ohio, authors are different.

Anderson saw Hind's article soon after it came out and, pleased, asked Karl to thank "our English friend."[21]

Other signs came more directly from England. On April 28 Grant Richards, the London publisher who had turned down the manuscript of *Windy McPherson's Son* because of wartime uncertainties, wrote Anderson that he was interested in discussing "the possible publication in this country of your future work." Richards's letter had been occasioned by one of the literary events of 1920, the publication in the London weekly *Nation* of April 17 of a special "American Literary Supplement" with articles describing the present hopeful situation in American poetry, criticism, philosophy, and fiction, and concluding with H. L. Mencken's proclamation of Chicago as "The Literary Capital of the United States." Just when Sherwood actually saw the Supplement is not clear, but Richards's letter mentioned Francis Hackett's article on "The Recent American Novel," in which *Windy McPherson's Son* "is referred to as an important addition to American fiction." When he did get to see the Supplement, he was undoubtedly happy to find that Hackett had praised him as "a naturalist with a skirl of music haunting him," and even more pleased that Mencken had included his name among those of the Midwest novelists and poets whose original and "absolutely American" work had placed "the gargantuan and inordinate abattoir by Lake Michigan" ahead of "timorous" New York as "the real capital of the United States."[22]

At the moment, Richards's letter would have been exciting enough, especially when added to the continuing possibility that a translation of *Winesburg* would be brought out in France by the publisher Gallimard. These portents of an international fame may have offset Huebsch's financial statement on May 1 that *Winesburg* had sold only four hundred copies in the previous six months for a royalty income to Anderson of $59.18. The best news of all, however, came in the form of a "glowing letter" from Van Wyck Brooks announcing that Huebsch had given him the manuscript of *Poor White* to read and that he thought it "the finest and most sustained thing" Anderson had done. Tennessee had given him the same judgment, but praise from Brooks's "clear, fine mind" made Sherwood ecstatic.[23]

Nevertheless, the time had come to end the golden days at Fairhope.

Sherwood ground up bags of red clay to take back to Chicago for him and Tennessee, who was by now almost completely well and had acquired a "new joy in life" from sculpting. He took one more river trip on a freight boat. In mid-May he hired a horse and ramshackle wagon and drove bareheaded "through this golden land looking at brown soft-eyed negroes and at the color and wonder of the country where I have been more free, more alone and at the same time closer to all people than ever before in my harried life." The gods had been good to him. Now he had strength, he wrote Bab, "for new adventures and new paths." Around May 24 he and Tennessee left Fairhope for good and went over for a few days to New Orleans, where he was delighted by his first experience of the old French Quarter. Then Tennessee left directly for Chicago while he went north by way of Kentucky, where he had business to attend to in Owensboro with Mr. Steele. He reached Chicago on June 1 at about the time Tennessee headed for Ephraim, Wisconsin, with the Walkers.[24]

On June 2, on the instigation of *The Freeman*, Anderson joined Dreiser, Edwin Arlington Robinson, and several other writers in paying their literary respects to Thomas Hardy in England by cabling him congratulations on his eightieth birthday. Then suddenly it was as though Sherwood had never left Chicago at all. The city appeared to him "unspeakably hot, crowded and dirty." In the two weeks or so he was there, he was driven distraught trying to collect money a client owed him so that he could pay for his own summer at Ephraim. Worried, unable to sleep, he had one of his "damned psychic lesions," which affected his body "in the shape of a terrific cold in the head." Since that new strength he had gained in Alabama had dissipated so abruptly, it was utterly clear to him that he could no longer live in the midwest city, literary capital of the United States or not. Probably on July 18 he escaped eastward to New York. "My peep back under the lid at Chicago," he grimly wrote Bab from the train,

convinces me that the industrial, capitalistic age is slowly choking itself to death but its death will not be a cheerful or inspiring sight. The truth is we shall probably live out our lives in the midst of intensified political and industrial ugliness.

The more reason for an intensification of the effort for real spiritual growth now. There is promise in America and it must not go the way of trickery, Christian Science or some other second rate manifestation.[25]

2.

Reaching New York, Anderson went on to Westport, Connecticut, to stay with Paul Rosenfeld, who had taken a house there for the summer. In Paul's voluble company he began to recover his spirits, and he quickly finished some final revisions of *Poor White* before the manuscript went to the printer. Then he visited friends in the city, walked in Central Park with Waldo, and showed some of his watercolors to Stieglitz and O'Keeffe, who praised several of them as being "well realized." This was a particularly welcome compliment from O'Keeffe, whose painting he admired. She had liked Anderson on first meeting for his pleasantness and warmth, but in her direct manner she had made "some unpleasant remarks" about *Winesburg, Ohio,* a book she "never could get through completely." Anderson would have been convinced that she was, of course, wrong about *Winesburg,* not only by his own faith in the book but also by his learning in New York of the flattering pronouncement by one Vincent O'Sullivan in the *Mercure de France* that this "novel" was "perhaps the best appearing in any country since the Armistice."[26]

On a Sunday, probably that of June 27, Brooks came out to Westport, and he, Paul, and Sherwood spent the warm, pleasant afternoon in what Paul remembered as a "hilarious walk" full of exuberant conversation about the books each was going to write and about books that ought to be written by others, such as psychological studies of the Business Man, the Intellectual, and the Magazine Writer, or an examination of the Decline of New England and "the parallel rise of the intellectual life of the West," or a "novel showing the artist as hero . . . in American conditions." This walk was the source of a tag-phrase about Sherwood that he resented—a "phallic Chekhov." It was apparently Brooks, walking along sedately in coat and vest despite the day's heat, who coined the phrase, though Rosenfeld would shortly use it jokingly in a letter to Anderson; and Sherwood added to his already complex attitude toward Brooks a rankling suspicion that the easterner, more radical in his literary ideas than in his lifestyle, covertly regarded him as being obsessed with sex. Later that summer Sherwood's resentment exploded in an angry letter to Brooks, and despite a quick remorseful apology, he henceforth felt that for all his intellectual emancipation Brooks, New Jersey-born though he was, at bottom harbored much of "the inner cold fright of the New Englander."[27]

Late in June, Anderson returned to Chicago but almost immediately took a train north to Ephraim, where Tennessee had rented for them a small cabin standing in deep pines just above a rocky beach, close to the Millspaugh house that they had occupied the previous summer. Again away from cities he was filled with a "flowing Quiet." Throughout July he wrote steadily, and, until writing absorbed all his creative energy toward the end of the month, he painted steadily too, completing among some unsuccessful experiments four watercolors that he considered worth keeping. During the stay with Rosenfeld he had worked at *Many Marriages,* trying to realize, as he had written Jerry and Lucile Blum, "an idea of a new novel form floating about in me, something looser, more real, more true." Presumably he was not achieving that form in his *Many Marriages* manuscript after all; settled peacefully at Ephraim, he began instead to put together a book of stories to be ready in the fall for spring publication and, as one of them, took up a tale he had started but left unfinished a year or more earlier. As he worked on it, he saw the "yarn" expanding first to a short novel and then to a full novel to be called *Ohio Pagans*. It was, he wrote Bab,

a highly personal tale of a girl named May Edgley of Bellevue Ohio—daughter of a teamster whose two sisters "went on the turf" and Tom Edwards, a Welsh boy, grandson of Twm O'r Nant a Welsh poet. It is full of working people, laborers, farmers and ice cutters and fishermen of Lake Erie—near my own home country.

Although he never could find a way to bring together the individual lives of May Edgley and Tom Edwards—the two narratives would be published as separate stories, not in his next collection but in the one thereafter—each was indeed near his own home country. May's story is told by a narrator who recalls it from the time when he worked as a boy for a large, meticulously neat doctor, as Sherwood had for Dr. Harden; and it is set in Bidwell, another name for Winesburg-Clyde, and the Sandusky area, including an actual Dewdrop Inn on the shore of Sandusky Bay where the leader of the band at a dance has the real Clyde name of Rat Gould. "'Unused,'" as the story of May would be called in *Horses and Men,* is the tale of a young girl who reaches out for physical and imaginative experience in hope of feeling herself "a part of all life," yet whose acts are misinterpreted by those around her and who in fear and despair half intentionally drowns herself. Tom Edwards of "An Ohio Pagan" in *Horses and Men* is a God-seeker, not a life-seeker, for whose story Anderson draws heavily on his own youthful experiences. For awhile Tom works as a groom for a "sporting farmer" named Harry Whitehead, as Sherwood had for the similarly huge Tom Whitehead, then is an unskilled laborer in grimy factories, and finally, like Sherwood after his return from Cuba in 1899, becomes a teamster on a threshing outfit moving from farm to farm over the countryside south of Sandusky Bay during a summer of lovely days. Introducing Tom as the grandson of the actual eighteenth-century Welsh dramatist and poet Twm O'r Nant ("Tom of the Dingle"), who had made his living as a teamster, Anderson was drawing on the story of Twm as told in *Wild Wales,* the account of a walking tour through that country by his much-admired George Borrow. Yet where Borrow presents Twm as a gifted yet thoroughly human person, the Twm of "An Ohio Pagan" is exaggerated into a figure of mythic powers in order that his fictitious grandson be capable, in the reader's eyes, of a final religious-erotic vision of the land about the bay as a gigantic naked woman enticing him with her body just as, the dreamy, sex-aroused, sex-puzzled Tom believes from his one attendance at a church service, Jesus had been enticed by Mary Magdalene.[28]

Tom Edwards's metamorphic vision of the land, one of Anderson's most astonishing achievements in fiction, came partly from the author's reading, partly from his imagination, partly from the extension into much of that Ephraim summer of his own exalted mood of the Fairhope months. Sherwood felt himself to be an Ohio pagan, living close to nature, fetching fresh milk each morning from where it had been left in a fishing shed, rowing out in a boat to catch "little barred perch for breakfast," writing until weary, then swimming, walking through the woods, painting, picking raspberries, quietly watching the "sea" from the cliff behind the cabin. A neighbor, David Stevens, a professor of English at the University of Chicago and a regular summer resident, saw him at eight o'clock one morning walking up the lane along the top of the cliff, his shaggy head crowned paganlike with a wreath of field flowers—though Anderson broke the effect by muttering disgustedly to Stevens as they passed in the lane, "She didn't bring the milk!" Working so concentratedly on his "novel of country people and their efforts to find God," then going at will into the nature awaiting him just outside the cabin door, he sometimes experienced intensely the oceanic feeling his May Edgley sought and his Tom Edwards achieved. "I get you and others keenly," he wrote Bab early in August. "At times moments come when it seems to me I know the whole thought of the world, every emotion, desire. I am often shaken by these moments."[29]

Occasionally matters connecting him with the outside world intruded, some pleasant, some not. Toward mid-July he sent off to Ben Huebsch the clipping from the *Mercure de France* containing Vincent O'Sullivan's praise of *Winesburg*, and Huebsch replied with word that he was using it in an advertisement for the book in *The New Republic*. Very likely Huebsch sent him a copy of that advertisement, and though it ran once only, in the July 21 issue, Sherwood would have been delighted by its summation of signs of his growing fame.

This book marks the event of our literary coming-of-age, for America is here at last writing her own literature. . . . No current comment on our literature is without allusions to Sherwood Anderson. See the London *Nation*'s recent American supplement; see the N. Y. *Times*'s choice of six best books of 1919. A writer in the current *Mercure de France* speaks of it as "the best fiction to appear in England or America since the armistice."

On July 30 galley proofs for *Poor White* arrived at Huebsch's office, and Ben sent them off to Sherwood special delivery, urging him to return them by the end of the following week. He read the proofs at top speed and got them into special delivery again on August 6 with the reminder that Huebsch not forget the dedication: "To Tennessee Mitchell Anderson." Much less pleasant than these intrusions, however, was another, the necessity of composing some advertising layouts for the Owensboro Ditcher & Grader Company that would combine, as Anderson put it, slipping into his best copywriter manner, "the proper dignity with sufficient punch to make them stand out no matter where they are placed in the paper."[30]

Perhaps resentment at the reminder of how he must still support himself was added to the cumulative weariness he suddenly began to feel from having gone at *Ohio Pagans* so hard "head down," together with the burden of rapidly reading galley proof of *Poor White* and making final changes. At any rate, whereas he had for a whole month lost himself in writing and become "like a rock or a tree—an impersonal thing," abruptly he switched to feeling as helpless as "a bug on its back in the bottom of a bowl." For a few days in mid-August he was low in spirits, and his hand trembled when he unsuccessfully tried to write about the lives of May Edgley and Tom Edwards. It was at this point that he wrote the angry letter to Van Wyck Brooks and to whom he had recently sent one of the Testaments, "The Man in the Brown Coat," for possible publication in *The Freeman,* and who had returned it unaccepted. Part of Anderson's anger came from the refusal of the Testament and his frustration at the lack of outlets for his work beyond *The Little Review* and *The Dial,* both of which he contemptuously, and ungenerously, dismissed in his letter as "immature, undignified, pretentious, asinine things." The basic causes of his anger, however, were two. Someone, he claimed to Brooks, had told him that Brooks disapproved of *Winesburg* as a "sex book"; and was it true, as was his "secret belief," that Brooks regarded its author's "reactions to life" as being "at bottom . . . well, not nice"? Further, Anderson had been reading and rereading the just-published *Ordeal of Mark Twain* "like a Bible or Shakespeare's sonnets"; but—and here he merely hinted at a deep resentment—for what Anderson felt but did not openly express in his letter was that, since Brooks knew how much Anderson identified his situation with Twain's, in condemning Twain as an American writer who under pressure had failed to fulfill his creative possibilities, Brooks seemed indirectly to be condemning him as well. Thus depression bred suspicion, suspicion bred further depression. His anger discharged, the letter sent, Anderson felt even lower in spirits from shame at what he had written. "You see," he wrote to Waldo abjectly, "I am in no mood to understand why any man should love me." Physically and emotionally ill now for several days, he could only wait for the "cloud of weariness and distraction" to pass and "the machinery of his imagination to set itself going again."[31]

Then as quickly as the depression had fallen on him, it lifted, probably as soon as he had received Brooks's soothing reply of August 15, denying any charge of sex-obsession except what he may have spoken directly to Sherwood "in conversation only," praising *Winesburg* and "The Triumph of the Egg," but admitting that he didn't "get" his friend's poems or paintings, "There are many things about you . . . I don't understand. . . . You are a new kind of animal in literature. . . ." On August 22, almost symbolically a "clear beautiful Sunday morning" after a storm the day before, Anderson replied, apologizing for his outburst and amiably excusing Brooks for "not knowing sometimes what I'm driving at" since he didn't always know it himself and simply felt himself "often an instrument to adventure in flights along strange paths." Once again words flowed easily from his hand. Writing also to Bab on the twenty-second, he expressed confidence in himself and his work like one indeed just recovered from a brief but severe illness.

> In a sense, and that you understand, all my work and my relationships too are aimed to the realization of life in myself, to teach myself that in any muddle, under any circumstances life can be lived.
> It is a terrific hard lesson and the harder when one has to fight illness.
> To me the arts are tools, instruments to the end suggested above. One transfers from the perplexing baffling fact of life into them. . . .
> There is enough of life. Single men and women do not control life. It runs on regardless. All a man or woman can do is to live life.
> You see my thesis. On that philosophy I chose to live.[32]

Perhaps he so explicitly reiterated his long-held belief that art was his own therapy and guide in the muddle of life because just the day before, the day when a severe storm had driven him in from the lake, he had had an instance of the muddle thrust in front of his eyes in the persons of his friends Jack Jones and Anna Mitchell. After Anna had left Fairhope in the spring for her home in New York City, she had decided to marry Jack as soon as he could obtain a divorce from Elizabeth Gurley Flynn, from whom he had long lived apart. The divorce went through in July, and, because of objections by Anna's parents, the couple eloped and were married on August 13. Jones, a man of several skills and of great self-confidence, had earlier built a boat, an eighteen-foot sailing dory with auxiliary motor. For a honeymoon trip the couple decided on a cruise in the boat, which Jack had painted green in honor of his Dill Pickle Club. They headed out from Chicago bound for Ephraim, apparently invited there by Sherwood and Tennessee, ran into the storm of August 21, and, with the engine disabled and the boat half swamped, just made it into Ephraim harbor. After staying a few days with the Andersons, Anna painting, Jack fishing with Sherwood, the guests sensed that they had worn out their welcome in the small cabin and camped out nearby in their tent for several more days.

Then, much against the advice of those who knew the lake, Jones with arrogant self-confidence insisted on continuing the honeymoon cruise, and Anna, despite her memories of the terrifying struggle against the storm, loyally accompanied him. It was the last time the Andersons would see her.

What shortly happened made headlines in Chicago and New York newspapers. After camping out for a period on Washington Island at the entrance to Green Bay, Jack and Anna headed back toward Chicago again. Early in the evening of Saturday, September 11, they found themselves six miles out from Racine, Wisconsin, the motor dead, and the boat helpless in yet another wild storm. When the boat capsized, Jack managed to secure themselves beneath it so that they could with difficulty breathe in the trapped air space. For eight hours that night, Jack managed to keep Anna alive before she drowned and her body was swept away by the waves. He himself hung onto the boat, was able to right it when day came, and that Sunday afternoon he was rescued by a fishing tug and taken shore to a Racine hospital, his body raw and bruised, his mind temporarily confused by the ordeal. News of Anna's death and Jack's survival was headlined in the Chicago papers at about the time the Andersons were getting ready to leave Ephraim. Sherwood angrily blamed Jack for, in effect, taking Anna's life through his arrogance and misjudgment. Succumbing to the muddle of life, the artist in Anna, he would conclude, had surrendered to the egotism of the male.[33]

Meanwhile during the remaining few weeks of his Ephraim vacation, Anderson became so absorbed again in *Ohio Pagans* that daily he wrote until he felt weak. There was one break of several days in the routine. On August 29 he returned to Chicago and spent the following day catching up on business affairs and on correspondence over arrangements made by the French publisher Gaston Gallimard, after an annoyingly long delay, for a translation of *Winesburg* to be prepared for publication by a French admirer of Anderson's work, Madame Marguerite Gay. On the thirty-first he went on to Owensboro, Kentucky, for a discussion of advertising projects with W. A. Steele. (Earlier that month he had written in his copy-writer persona, "That is one thing I have always tried to get into [advertising brochures]—readability and then the sense of conviction of what he is talking about on the part of the writer.") Coming back by way of Indianapolis on September 2 or 3, he stopped off for an afternoon with Bab. They had a long walk and comradely talk, and Sherwood was glad to find that, despite her painful illnesses over the years, she continued never to speak with "that note of spiritual tiredness that expresses itself in cynicism and that is so universal in America." It was her persistent "faith in life," he would subsequently write her from Ephraim, that made *Ohio Pagans* "closer allied to the spirit of you than any other I have written." Whatever Bab may have hoped concerning any future relationship between her and

Sherwood, she must by now have realized that it would continue only as friendship. The artist in Sherwood would never surrender to any other person met in the muddle of life.[34]

3.

Vacation over, the Andersons reluctantly returned to Chicago in mid-September. After the months outdoors in clean places, Sherwood fancied wretchedly that in this dirt and turmoil everybody's disease germs were crawling through him. His mood was further darkened by Anna Mitchell's needless death; and the daily revelations by the newspapers of "ball players turning crooked"—the Black Sox Scandal was breaking—seemed to him "true to the note of the age." He might be compelled, as he now was, to rush about the city on the odds and ends of advertising accounts that supported him, but for some days he put all his free time into searching the small towns around Chicago for a place where he could be free of noise and crowds. Then one weekend late in September he found what he had been looking for in the village of Palos Park.[35]

He had been attracted by the romantic-sounding "Palos"—according to local tradition the name had been taken from the Spanish port from which Columbus had set sail in 1492—and as soon as he had reached the village, he knew that he wanted to live there. Twenty miles southwest of the Loop, Palos Park was in an area that thrust itself up out of the flat prairie into hills covered with great oak groves and thickets of wild crabapple. Scattered along unpaved roads were the inexpensive houses of artists, musicians, university professors, Chicago businessmen, and retired persons who had discovered the quiet beauty of the rolling countryside and the lively but unpressured sense of human community that the village offered; yet the Loop was only an hour away by the Wabash Railroad, which picked up commuters at the little Palos station at 7:15 in the morning and returned them by the 5:30 train each evening.

Someone had suggested to Sherwood that he look up Felix Russman, a painter who lived with his poetry-writing wife Helen in the house formerly occupied by the sculptor Lorado Taft. Russman was in the midst of shaving when he answered a rap at his door and found there a "soft-spoken, easy-spoken" man who introduced himself as Sherwood Anderson, said he wanted to live in Palos Park, and asked if he knew of a place to rent. The artist guided the newcomer down narrow Ridge Road south of the village to a small house owned by Mary Madernach, a retired vaudeville dancer, who also owned a "little box" of a cottage about a hundred yards away. It did not take much time for Miss Madernach to show off the cottage, which was soon to be vacated by its present occupants. Hardly as large as two medium-sized rooms overall, the little box was cut up into a kitchen, a bedroom, and a dining-living room. In front there was a screened-in porch; by the back door there was a deep well with delicious cold water tasting of iron; a little way down a path behind a clump of crabapple was a privy and beyond that a large oak forest. The rent was only $12.50 a month. Delighted by the Palos area, by his chats with Felix and Mary, and now by the box of a cottage, Anderson spoke for it at once. Just after October 14 the occupants moved out, and he moved in. It would be his home base for nearly two years thereafter.[36]

Except for an occasional brief spell of depression, he was almost as happy in Palos Park that fall of 1920 as he had been in Fairhope in the spring. Tennessee had gone back to her music and rhythmics teaching in Chicago, but she usually came out from the Division Street apartment for three-day weekends. Soon after he moved into his cottage Anderson felt obliged by friendship to go to a literary gathering in Milwaukee one Sunday with Carl Sandburg, he to speak, Sandburg to play the guitar and sing folk songs; yet the engagement brought him a welcome small fee, and it may have led him to begin viewing lecturing as a not very pleasant but more honest way to make money than writing advertising. As a rule he needed to take the Wabash into Chicago no more than one or two days a week to clear up business at Critchfield—he seems to have closed out his own office away from the company as a needless expense—and to lunch at Schlogl's with Hecht, Harry Hansen, and other friends. He conducted most of his business affairs from his cozy little house. Mornings he could again put in on his writing, and whenever he wished, he could take walks along the winding roads of Palos Park or through the oak forests. The forests, now bright with autumn, excited his eye made even more sensitive to natural beauty than usual by his months of trying as painter to catch "the flow of lines, forms, in moving color." Once he walked a whole day through a countryside "awash with color," as he wrote to Bab in mid-October,

feeling like one swimming in a gorgeous sea. There was something light and at the same time sensual about the feeling I have been having. . . .

I have walked all day, or rather floated in this sea of color. The air is warm and soft. Little flames of color dart out of the midst of the dense color of trees. The sumac is a living pulsating red.[37]

It was not only the countryside that delighted and rested him. With his gift for quick acquaintance he found the village to be as full of odd and interesting people as Clyde, or Winesburg, had been, lovable grotesques like an old, gruff farmer named Wilson, who lined up different colored beans on his dining table and treated them almost as persons to talk to, or Miss Underhill, a mildly demented spinster who lived alone with her cat in a house that was, to Sherwood's great amusement, literally built into the underside of a hill. He became particularly fond of Mary Madernach, about whom he would write in the *Memoirs* as "Old Mary." Now in her seventies, gray-haired, stout, untidy, she preserved the independence and disregard of public opinion that had characterized her younger days when she and her sister had danced in the saloons of Western gold rush towns and then had gone on to be chorus girls on the burlesque and vaudeville circuits. From those days Mary had kept her habits of swearing "like a cowboy" and of smoking cigarettes, which she rolled expertly with one hand. Throughout her gaudy career she had wanted to retire to such a small town as this so that she could watch birds and wildlife, keep chickens, dig in the earth of a kitchen garden. (When a friend of Sherwood's first met her, she was squatting in the dirt road in front of her house intently watching tumblebugs roll bits of horse manure out of the road into their holes at the edge.) Nevertheless, she read Flaubert, Balzac, and Shakespeare frequently and intelligently and had an original imagination. She adopted Anderson and Russman as "her boys," cooked pies for them, gave them wine in utter scorn of the Eighteenth Amendment now in force, and told them endless stories out of her past, such as the time she was in New Orleans with a man who liked to spend money. At four in the morning the two were in the market section, and Mary said she wanted some strawberries; they bought a chamber pot at a nearby stand, filled it with strawberries, and walked on eating them out of the pot unabashed. Sherwood thought the story both funny and admirable. Old Mary was a character out of Rabelais in real life.[38]

With Felix Russman he struck up a close friendship. Although Felix felt that Sherwood knew little about painting, he encouraged him to continue his watercolors as a means of self-expression. Sherwood was fascinated, as he would later describe in *A Story Teller's Story,* with the 144 pans of color in Russman's palette, which Russman and George Bellows had earlier worked out together, and he was astonished that the artist had two hundred brushes in addition to the many pans. All he himself needed for writing, he pointed out, was fountain pen and paper. The two men talked frequently of painting and writing, and Russman later insisted that he taught Anderson much about abstract art, using as text the fifth chapter ("About Faces in Japanese Art") of Lafcadio Hearn's *Gleanings in Buddha-Fields,* a book Anderson read and liked. At some point in their acquaintance the artist even painted an abstract portrait of the writer, now unfortunately lost.[39]

Perhaps through Russman it was arranged that the Walden Bookshop in the Chicago Loop would show some dozen or more of Anderson's watercolors, and just before the one-man show opened in late October, Felix went in with him to the shop at 307 Plymouth Court to see that the pictures were hung to best effect. Thereafter, at least for awhile, Sherwood kept away from the exhibition of what he called "my adventures in line and color"; but as it went on through November, he began to report to his friends that the pictures were "creating some stir." Out of loyalty and curiosity a group from the Critchfield office attended the show in a body, most, though not all, being hilariously unimpressed by what they took to be another of Sherwood's bids for attention. He himself felt that the paintings "hit some people hard" and others not at all. On November 12 he wrote to the Blums in amused satisfaction that "there is a good deal of discussion as to whether I am insane, decadent, or a new note," while the day before he had told Rosenfeld that the show occasioned "much wondering what about and some flashings of real intelligence. I want to sell some of them and am at the same time afraid I will." While the show was on at the Walden, his fears were probably unjustified. Perhaps there was "a strange woman, from Denver," whom, according to the *Memoirs,* he never met but who purchased two paintings for seven hundred dollars and left him a note saying "They make me feel as I would like to feel"; but more likely he was remembering giving two paintings to Bab, who, because his advertising accounts were bringing in little that fall, sent him money in mid-November as a friendly gift.[40]

Local notoriety over what was after all a secondary mode of expression for him was, however, of less long-term consequence than wider recognition of his writing. Around mid-October he received a letter from Edward O'Brien, editor of the annual *Best Short Stories* volumes, requesting permission to include "The Other Woman" in the forthcoming 1920 volume and to dedicate the collection to him "since the stories you have published this year seem to me from every point of view the finest which I have read." Such praise would have "at least . . . some publicity value," Anderson wrote Huebsch rather offhandedly, but as a sign of his growing national reputation it must have been very satisfying to him.[41]

By the time he received O'Brien's letter, he had dropped *Ohio Pagans* and returned to his earlier project of a collection of short stories as his next book publication. From this time would come several of the tales that would appear in *The Triumph of the Egg.* One of them, "Brothers," is a classic demonstration of how his creative mind worked, being rooted in reality but significantly changing it. Unlike many of his stories, the composition or at least first draft of this one can be dated precisely. On a rainy Monday, October 25, he started a letter to Bab to tell her "something about a very strange old woman here. Then the old woman became an old man and the letter," as he put it, "became a story." The old woman was Miss Underhill, whose pet cat Anderson changed to a pet dog in presenting a strange old man for the masculinely titled story. Little change was necessary, however, for the borrowing of an old habit of Miss Underhill's.

Having lived alone so long, she had become, Felix Russman believed, mildly insane from the lack of human contact and would insist to the two men that the persons she read about in the newspapers were all her relatives. When the famous Italian tenor Enrico Caruso came to Chicago to sing, as he in fact had just done for a well-publicized single concert before "a huge audience" at Medinah Temple on October 3, she claimed kinship with him, as does the old man of "Brothers." Very likely she claimed kinship also, as does the old man, with Governor James M. Cox, Democratic candidate for the presidency, who was completing the campaign that ended on November 2 in the landslide election of Harding; but Anderson could have drawn this bit of real life from the current newspapers himself. What he certainly drew from real life were the exact description of the location of his little "house in the country" in the opening paragraph, and the description in the second paragraph of the autumn leaves outside his window being beaten earthward by the rain and denied "a last golden flash across the sky," whereas on a bright October day the wind might carry them "out over the plains . . . dancing away." So the story begins in the facts of the letter and of reality.[42]

For the central event of the story Anderson drew on but changed much in his fancy another piece of reality, a murder and a murder trial, which, as the I-person narrator correctly states, "the Chicago newspapers . . . have been filled with." This was the case of Carl Wanderer, as romantic-sounding a name for attracting Sherwood's attention as "Palos." On the night of the previous June 21, twenty-five-year-old Wanderer, a butcher's assistant on Chicago's South Side, had taken his twenty-one-year-old pregnant wife to the movies. Returning to their apartment house, they were followed into the darkened hallway by a ragged stranger, who, as Wanderer told it afterward to the police, started shooting at them. Wanderer, who was carrying a pistol, returned the fire, and in the melee both stranger and wife were fatally shot; but the circumstances looked suspicious, and on July 9 he confessed to the police that he had hired a tramp to stage a fake holdup and that he had shot his wife and the tramp. Shortly it came out that he had been in love with seventeen-year-old Julia Schmitt, a petite, dark-haired stenographer who lived across the street from the butcher shop, whereupon he promptly admitted to having killed his wife in order to free himself for Julia. Placed in "Murder's Row" in prison, Wanderer decided that, in his words, "Life is sweet," and repudiated his earlier confessions as having been forced from him by police brutality. His trial on the charge of killing his wife began on October 4, and during the days just before and after Anderson moved into his little house, both the *Daily News* and the *Tribune* carried daily stories, sometimes with front page headlines, about the proceedings. On October 19, after the prosecution had stated its case, Wanderer again repudiated his confessions, and his court-appointed attorneys began presenting the paradoxical defense that their client was innocent, that his final confession had been elicited by third-degree methods, and that even if not innocent, he was not guilty by reason of insanity. By Sunday, October 24, the day before Anderson began "Brothers," the newspapers reported that the defense had completed its case and that final arguments and addresses to the jury would begin the following day. On the twenty-ninth a puzzled and weary jury found Wanderer guilty of killing his wife but, divided on the question of his sanity, rejected the expected death penalty in favor of a twenty-five-year prison sentence.[43]

In writing "Brothers" Sherwood manipulated sordid, titillating reality so that his "tale ran something like this." The unnamed man on trial of murdering his wife is a silent, stolid foreman of a bicycle factory who falls in love with a young stenographer whom he can see from the window by his own desk through the window by hers. He dreams of her as "the most beautiful woman in the world," lovely, pure, and remote as a star. The stenographer senses his infatuation, but uses the figure of the heavy, middle-aged man with large, always-grimy hands as the basis for dreams of the handsome rich young man she longs to meet and marry. At home in his apartment with his pregnant wife, their two children, and helpful but ever present mother-in-law, the man finds his life as ugly as his grimy, shapeless hands; and one night as he returns with his wife from the movies, the momentary furtive appearance of a man from an alleyway and the lack of light in the entrance hallway to the apartment house prompt him to stab his wife to death with a knife. At first he maintains that the man from the alleyway had followed them home, and in the struggle the wife had been accidentally killed; but as soon as he is arrested, he confesses to a deliberate killing, though he says nothing about the stenographer and leaves the newspapers to try fruitlessly to "discover the motive for the crime."

In the conclusion to "Brother" the narrator once more meets the loneliness-crazed old man, who carries the little dog in his arms. It is early "Yesterday morning," and a heavy fog covering the village makes the old man's face "indistinct," makes it move "slowly back and forth with the fog banks of the upper air and with the tops of trees"—and prepares the reader for the hallucinatory climax to follow as the old man wildly and repeatedly protests that he and the man on trial in the city courtroom are sons of the same father.

In the fog the slender body of the old man became like a little gnarled tree. Then it became a thing suspended in air. It swung back and forth like a body hanging on the gallows. The face beseeched me to believe the story the lips were trying to tell. . . . The spirit of the man who had killed his wife came into the body of the little old man there by the roadside. It was striving to tell me the story it would never be able to tell in the court room in the city, in the presence of the judge. The whole story of mankind's loneliness, of the effort to reach out to unattainable beauty tried to get itself expressed from the lips of a mumbling old man, crazed with loneliness, who stood by the side of a country road on a foggy morning holding a little dog in his arms.

In the intensity of his desire to tell the two stories, the old man squeezes the little dog until it cries out in pain. The narrator tears the tightened arms away from the dog, and it drops, perhaps fatally injured, at the old man's feet, where he stares at it as in that dark hallway "the worker from the bicycle factory had stared at his dead wife." The two men are indeed "brothers," as are, Anderson implies, all human kind trying to reach out of loneliness toward unattainable beauty. They are, as the reiteration of house and forest in the final paragraph restates, like the bright oak leaves, which the rain now beats heavily, brutally down instead of being allowed "a last golden flash across the sky," as the October wind might carry them dancing away over the plains beyond the hills of Palos. So Anderson demonstrates how the writer's imagination may metamorphose sad, ugly reality into the sad beauty of the shaped art work, this self-enclosed story that at its climax convincingly escapes reality.

4.

Two days after the first writing of "Brothers," on October 27, 1920, *Poor White* was published. The seeds of this novel are apparent first in Anderson's framework, sketched in *Mid-American Chants* of three and possibly four stages in the socioeconomic development of the United States, and then in his talks and correspondence with Van Wyck Brooks in New York about Twain, Whitman, and Lincoln during the late summer and fall of 1918 when he wrote much of a first draft of this novel, his most ambitious and, despite weaknesses, his best. Referring to one of the two major story lines of the book, he subsequently emphasized how he "tried to dramatize" through the microcosm of a Midwest town—not unlike Clyde or Winesburg—the processes and results of late-nineteenth-century American industrialization; in fact, he would insist that the town itself was "the hero of the book rather than the people of the town." Considering his emphasis throughout this novel on the deleterious, sometimes disastrous effects of this development, "hero" would seem an odd term to use, and it ignores the book's second major story line, the "man-woman thing," as he often called it, concerning the "poor white" Hugh McVey, who as an unwitting agent of change is the male protagonist of the book, and Clara Butterworth, who is a seeker for love in the modern age. One of Anderson's several achievements in this novel is his intertwining, in large and small ways, these two story lines.[44]

Book 1 of the five "books" composing the novel serves as prologue. Hugh is born in 1866 in "a little hole" of a river town on the Missouri side of the Mississippi derisively called "Mudcat Landing." His mother having died soon afterward, he is brought up in squalor and laziness by his drunken, ne'er-do-well father, who is very much like Huck Finn's pap. The boy likes best to lie for hours dreamily on the bank of the great river. By age fourteen he has become Lincolnesque in stature, very tall, gaunt, and unusually strong, but is awkward and slow of thought. He is taken in to live and work with Henry and Sarah Shepard, Henry, the railroad stationmaster—already industrialization has begun to change America— teaching him various duties, Sarah, rather like the Widow Douglas with Huck, determined to "sivilize" him. Soon, however, she develops a motherly feeling for the slow, gangling boy, gives him good home schooling, and impresses on him three lessons, which shape his life for years: that he comes from humiliatingly worthless, "poor white" stock; that he must stop his lazy dreaming and instead work hard at any assigned task since in this way he is certain of material success; and that in the settled East from which she came there are beautiful towns full of people whose lives are beautiful. A year or so after the Shepards go back East, leaving Hugh as stationmaster; he, now at age twenty, turns over the station to another man and begins a three-year eastward and northward journey through a series of hard work jobs. At the beginning of this journey Anderson takes a narrative risk, which few other writers at this time would have taken. Having reached Iowa and a bluff overlooking the Mississippi at night, Hugh slips back into his half-awake, half-sleeping world of dreaminess and has an apocalyptic dream-vision in which his mind seems to go up among the clouds and stars, then looks down on the river suddenly flooding over the land, uprooting forests and towns and drowning people, whose "white faces" look up into his "mind's eye."

The clouds of which he felt himself a part flew across the face of the sky. They blotted out the sun from the earth, and darkness descended on the land, on the troubled towns, on the hills that were torn open, on the forests that were destroyed, on the peace and quiet of all places. In the country stretching away from the river where all had been peace and quiet, all was now agitation and unrest. Houses were destroyed and instantly rebuilt. People gathered in whirling crowds.

   The dreaming man felt himself a part of something significant and terrible that was happening to the earth and to the peoples of the earth.

This terrible "cloud dream," which recurs to Hugh from time to time during his three-year journey through small Midwest towns, is indeed prophetic in its symbolic way of things to come; but his daylight hours are spent in overcoming dreaminess by performing his jobs and using up any spare time in many small, meaningless tasks. Although he wants to find, he tells himself, "the right place and the right people," it is difficult for him to communicate with others, to feel at home anywhere because of shyness, a habit of silence, and self-disparaging memories of his poor white origin.

Book 2 begins with an extended description of life in the north-central Ohio town of Bidwell, to which Hugh will come. Bidwell has already emerged from its pioneer past into its second stage of development, the golden age of the small town, when

> In all the great Mississippi Valley each town came to have a character of its own, and the people who lived in the towns were to each other like members of a great family. The individual idiosyncrasies of each member of the great family stood forth. A kind of invisible roof beneath which every one lived spread itself over each town. Beneath the roof boys and girls were born, grew up, quarreled, fought, and formed friendships with their fellows, were introduced into the mysteries of love, married, and became the fathers and mothers of children, grew old, sickened, and died.
>
> Within the invisible circle and under the great roof every one knew his neighbor and was known to him. Strangers did not come and go swiftly and mysteriously and there was no constant and confusing roar of machinery and of new projects afoot. For the moment mankind seemed about to take time to try to understand itself.

This expository essay is followed by a sample gallery of town characters— the tailor Peter White, who once or twice a year gets drunk and beats his wife, the community understanding his behavior because she is always "jawing at him"; Allie Mulberry, the "half-wit," whose skill at whittling objects is admired by everyone and is later useful to Hugh; Jane Orange, wealthy, stingy widow who to the town's delight is caught shoplifting; old Judge Hanby, who in another of Anderson's foreshadowings describes the coming of the factories, where workers feel "like being in prison," who predicts "a long, silent war between classes, between those who have and those who can't get," and who suggests, in one of Anderson's intertwining of story lines, that "Tom Butterworth the rich farmer send his daughter away to school"; and finally an opposing figure to Tom, Joe Wainsworth, harnessmaker "of the old school," whose hostility to factory-made harnesses will lead to his violent revolt against industrialism. At the end of Book 3, a little more than halfway through the novel, Anderson will balance these preindustrial "types" with a panel of Bidwell persons psychologically damaged by the third stage of development, industrialization, "the new forward-pushing impulse in American life."

At age twenty-three in 1889—Anderson is more specific with ages and date in this novel than usual—Hugh arrives in Bidwell to take up the job of telegrapher at a semi-isolated railroad station a mile away in the hamlet of Pickleville, so named after the abandoned pickle factory nearby, the physical isolation indicating that he is not yet included under the invisible roof of Bidwell. From an idealistic desire to free people from backbreaking hand labor, this Lincolnesque man from the West begins making possible the assault on Bidwell of industrialism, this "terrible new thing, half hideous, half beautiful in its possibilities." After watching Ezra French driving his sons and daughters like slaves, like grotesquely crawling animals at the hard, monotonous task of spring cabbage planting, Hugh teaches himself mechanics, conceives of a plant-setting machine, and dreaming now only in "wood and iron," begins to work out the machinery by imitating planting motions with his own angular body, so symbolizing the reduction under industrialism of the human to the mechanical.

Rumor of what he is inventing comes to young Steve Hunter, just back to Bidwell from business college and eager for money and power in the community. An unprincipled schemer intent "to become a manufacturer, the first one in Bidwell, to make himself a leader in the new movement that was sweeping over the country," this "man of affairs," as Anderson calls him, presumably with that "Business Type" from *Agricultural Advertising* in mind, decides to put Hugh and his invention under contract and involves in his scheme the banker John Clark and Tom Butterworth. Bluffing to them that he already has the contract, he easily persuades Hugh to sign it after approaching him at the telegraph station, himself fearful of failure, "as excited as a village girl in the presence of a lover," and with "an air of one about to ask a woman to become his wife," figures illustrating Anderson's insight into the perverse eroticism of money. Hugh has no interest in money, only in the solving of mechanical problems; but he is exhilarated that a Bidwell person should want something from him, the first one to start bringing him under the town's invisible roof. Steve and his fellow schemers, on the other hand, see Hugh as someone to exploit, a bargain at the twenty-five-dollar-a-month salary Steve now pays him. They form a promotional company, The Bidwell Plant-Setting Machine Company, to "launch the first industrial enterprise in the town," the construction of a factory for the manufacture of plant-setters, with Steve as president, the company officers to purchase stock and stock to be sold to townspeople. Steve rents the old pickle factory for temporary work space, Allie Mulberry whittles the various parts of the plant-setter machines-to-be, Hugh continues to solve mechanical problems. Already in the first paragraph of Book 2 Anderson has introduced his frequently used device in this novel of forecasting future events—Bidwell "is a busy manufacturing town now and has a population of nearly a hundred thousand people"—as reminders that industrialization and its discontents is an ongoing present process. Now after describing some months of activity on the plant-setter, Anderson announces that the company was formed in "1892 . . . and in the end it turned out to be a failure." When Hugh after nearly two years of work tells Steve that the machine is impractical, the unscrupulous Steve insists that Hugh and the company officers must keep this failure secret so that the sale of stocks could continue, since in the time-dishonored expression, "'It's a case of the survival of the fittest.'" Then as was happening all over the Midwest, "A vast energy seemed to come out of the breast of the earth and infect the people." Anderson continues:

Thousands of the most energetic men of the middle States wore themselves out in forming companies, and when the companies failed, immediately formed others. In the fast-growing towns, men who were engaged in organizing companies representing a capital of millions lived in houses thrown hurriedly together by carpenters who, before the time of the great awakening, were engaged in building barns. It was a time of hideous architecture, a time when thought and learning paused. Without music, without poetry, without beauty in their lives or impulses, a whole people, full of the native energy and strength of lives lived in a new land, rushed pell-mell into a new age.

Stock is bought all around Bidwell, even by Joe Wainsworth, who invests his life savings. One night this "man of the age of flesh and blood" goes to Pickleville wanting "to walk in the presence of the man who belonged to the new age of iron and steel." He would like—the Biblical reference is clear—to "touch with his finger the hem of Hugh's coat," to pray before one of the machines; but on the way home he hears a devout but doubting neighbor praying for Hugh and the success of his invention, and Joe's "new-found faith" is destroyed.

That Anderson does not introduce Clara Butterworth until Book 3, about a third of the way through the novel, caused one reviewer in 1920 (and a few critics since) to object to his bringing in so late a major character, one insufficiently connected, it is asserted, with the theme of industrialization. They seem not to have observed that Anderson has made her ten years younger than Hugh, hence only thirteen when he arrives in preindustrial Bidwell, and that from the first sentence of Book 3 on there are frequent connections, intertwinings of her life and Bidwell's development into its third stage. So, "When Clara . . . was eighteen years old she graduated from the town high school," and since her father, already deep into Steve's scheming, sends her to Ohio State University in the fall, the reader recalls that Tom does so on the prophetic advice of Judge Hanby, while some pages later it is noted that she goes in the year Steve's first company fails. More extended connections appear throughout this Book.

Growing up a tomboy on her father's extensive farm close to Bidwell, Clara at seventeen is "a tall, strong, hard-muscled girl, shy in the presence of strangers and bold with people she knew well," feels closest, her mother having died, to Tom and an old farmhand, Jim Priest. That summer she begins to experience confusingly vague sexual feelings, has an ongoing quarrel with her "intensely possessive" father when he falsely accuses her of an affair with a young farmhand, begins to wonder about the nature of men and marriage. The following year when she is driven to the train for college, not by her father, who is shortly seen as instead conniving with Steve to purchase the new factory building at a cheap price, but by Jim Priest, she is much touched by his "rough gentleness" in giving her a fatherly kiss on the cheek. Lying in her berth on the train that night, however, she has a terrifying hallucination out of "her deeply buried unconscious self" parallel to Hugh's cloud dream though less overwhelming in its prophecy.

It seemed to her that the walls of the sleeping-car berth were like the walls of a prison that had shut her away from the beauty of life. The walls seemed to close in upon her. The walls, like life itself, were shutting in upon her youth and her youthful desire to reach a hand out of the beauty in herself to the buried beauty in others. She sat up in the berth and forced down a desire in herself to break the car window and leap out of the swiftly moving train into the quiet night bathed with moonlight.

It is prophetic of her first two years at the university. She attends to her studies "passably well," but lives with her aunt Priscilla, who had married wealthy businessman Henderson Woodburn. In a prison of routine he brings home each evening business papers, which rustle as he works at them; her knitting needles click loudly as she knits hundreds of pairs of stockings, supposedly for poor children but which never leave the house, papers and knitting needles being, Anderson states, "the trivial by-products of the age's industrial madness." The young men who occasionally call upon Clara are equally dull and routinized. In her third year with the Woodburns, however, she meets two more interesting people: a young man who briefly attracts her with his restlessness and his dissatisfaction with his life, which match her own, but has "nothing to urge upon her except the needs of his body"; and Kate Chanceller an independent thinker, a socialist, and a lesbian, who loves Clara but resolutely refuses to try to turn her from her desire to find a man to marry, provided that, as Clara puts it, she can "find somewhere a man who respects himself and his own desires but can understand also the desires and fears of a woman." Clara decides that her classes have nothing to offer her and she will not go on for a fourth year, but as Anderson puts it with one of his forecastings, "During all the rest of her life she thought of those last weeks in Columbus," weeks of intense talk with Kate, "as the most deeply satisfactory time she ever lived through."

When she arrives home in June, her father meets her at the train; and since, as during the mild industrialization of Clyde, "Main Street was torn up for the purpose of laying a brick pavement and digging a new sewer," they bypass this first sign to her of new development and head out into the countryside. As they rise out of the valley in which the town lies—a scene to be echoed in Book 4—Tom stops the horse to point out the new factory he and Steve are having built for the manufacture of Hugh's new, successful invention, a corn-cutter, the first factory built, the one for the failed plant-setter, being too small and now sold at Tom and Steve's profit to a bicycle maker. Industrialization is visibly on its way in Bidwell, Tom boasts to Clara, and he, not Steve, is "'the man who has done the most . . . I'm the big man in this town. It comes pretty near being my town.'" Her annoyance at his boasting turns to anger when in referring to her marrying someone, he speaks of her "as though she were a possession of his that must be disposed of." By contrast, when Jim Priest welcomes her back at the farm, she does not mind his saying kindly, "'I guess you'll get married pretty soon now . . . You're one of the marrying kind'" who will do it on her own.

"If many things had happened to Clara," since she left Bidwell, begins the last chapter of Book 3, "things had happened to the people" there to make them seem different to her; and though the omniscient narrator describes the changes, it is as though she were aware of the changes. Ben Peeler, the friendly carpenter, for example no longer builds things but instead makes money as head of a construction firm and makes "a swinging profit" on his lumberyard business. Having become nervous and irritable, he stays awake the night after he finds three men sleeping on boards in the yard, thinks of going back there with a shotgun to drive them away lest they carelessly set the place on fire, finally falls asleep. He has a horrible dream of guarding the lumberyard with his gun, blowing half the head off a man advancing toward him in the dark, and, discovering that the face of the dying man is that of his long dead brother, wakes up screaming. The dream is surely one of guilt springing from an unconscious sense of self-murder. Again, Ed Hall, once a poorly paid carpenter's apprentice, is now a foreman in the corn-cutter factory, feeling superior to his former fellows because of his higher pay, "feeling very keenly the importance of his new place in the community." Later he will trick workers into a speedup, which provokes an unsuccessful strike. The worst change of all is in Joe Wainsworth. To keep up with the demands for new harnesses or the repair of old, broken ones by the increasing number of workhorses needed to haul materials for the increasing construction of business buildings and houses, Joe has had to hire a journeyman harnessmaker, Jim Gibson, who turns out to be a drunkard and a believer, not in the craft but in quick profits, and who bullies Joe into accepting him as master of the shop, even to purchasing and selling cheap, factory-made harnesses. Through such individual sketches Anderson has charged industrialism with destroying the age-old sense of craftsmanship, the urge to shape materials into beautiful-because-functional objects, and with opening manifold opportunities for greed, which deforms individual character and personality, and tears apart the social fabric.

Book 4 centers on the uneasy relationship and uneasy marriage of Clara and Hugh. Hugh has the possibility of a prior relationship with Rose McCoy, a schoolteacher, but mutual reticence and Hugh's conviction that as a "poor white" he hasn't "the right" to her keeps them apart. Clara, however, is more determined. He first sees her and she him when she visits his workshop accompanied by Tom and a schemer from New York named Alfred Buckley, who has very formally asked her to marry him but is interested only in talking with her father of ways to outwit Steve and get control of Hugh's future inventions. Buckley reminds her unpleasantly of "a greyhound in pursuit of a rabbit," while Hugh, whom Buckley has called "a backwoodsman with a streak of genius," she thinks of as "an honest, powerful horse, a horse that was humanized by the mysterious hungering thing that expressed itself through his eyes." Unlike most men she knows in Bidwell he is not a schemer but "a creative force" who "works, and because of his efforts things are accomplished"; he is the man she wishes to marry. To Hugh, this beautiful, beautifully dressed woman is arousing but too far above a "poor white trash" to do more than dream about. Tom has encouraged the rumor that Clara and Buckley are to marry, but when the man is arrested as a "notorious swindler," he is furious at her for bringing "disgrace on my name." Hugh sees his chance when he overhears an ugly rumor about her, which she denies; he goes to the farm one evening, abruptly asks her to marry, is astonished when she accepts, and remains astonished as the two of them hitch a horse to a buggy, and with Jim Priest's silent approval Clara drives off with Hugh south toward the county seat to get married.

At this point Anderson demonstrates his skill with the minor but apt "echo" detail. As the pair reach the crest of Lookout Hill, "the highest point in the county," she stops the horse and looks back down the hillside.

Below lay the lights of her father's farmhouse—where he had come as a young man and to which long ago he had brought his bride. Far below the farmhouse a clustered mass of lights outlined the swiftly growing town.

There in two sentences are the agricultural past and the industrial, electrified present still far away but beginning a swift encroachment upon it, as implied when Tom points out to her from just above the town the second factory in swiftly growing Bidwell, and as reiterated when Clara looks down again "at her father's house and below at the lights of the town, that had already spread so far over the countryside, and up through the hills toward the farm where she had spent her girlhood. . . ." Returning married to the farm, Hugh and Clara face troubles—a wedding feast summoned up by Jim Priest and Tom, which both bride and groom for different reasons dislike; a wedding night in which Hugh runs away from the farmhouse without consummating the marriage because, he tells himself, "'I'm a poor white . . . It isn't fitten I should marry the woman'"; and another week of living together without consummation. Then comes a day represented by Anderson both realistically and symbolically in two conflicting patterns of repeated images—Hugh's habit of "thinking in iron" and his seeing as he walks to work "a trivial thing."

A male bird pursued a female among the bushes beside the road. The two feathered, living creatures, vividly colored, alive with life, pitched and swooped through the air. They were like moving balls of light going in and out of the dark foliage. There was in them a madness, a riot of life.

That night Hugh overcomes his fear and self-contempt, and the marriage is consummated.

Book 5 begins three years later, in about 1900. The marriage of Hugh and Clara has continued, though there are many times when she still feels a wall between them. Tom has bought the first automobile in Bidwell, and he is taking them on a drive in the evening when Joe, whom Jim Gibson has forced to buy eighteen sets of machine-made harness, cuts Jim's throat with his harnessmaker's knife, methodically cuts all those sets into small pieces, and then runs from the town into the countryside. Ed Hall, now factory manager, pursues and captures him in a road as, most fortuitously, Tom drives up and, with Ed guarding the half-crazed Joe, drives to the police station. Just before he is arrested, this man of the past attacks Hugh, man of the present, and is torn away from him by Clara, who, to the dismay of many of today's readers, ceases from then on to be a thinker and becomes only the mother.

The concluding chapter begins four years later, during which time Clara has borne her first child. Hugh has been designing a hay-loading machine, discovers that an Iowa man already has a patent on such a machine, is urged by Tom to "get around" the patent somehow, and, thinking of the Iowa man as a fellow human being, is reluctant to do so. Halfheartedly he has taken business trips to look for possible machine parts, first to Sandusky, where walking on the bay shore he picks up some brightly colored stones, and then to Pittsburgh, where waiting for the train home he takes out the stones and watches their colors flashing in the light. For a moment he becomes "not an inventor but a poet." He wishes that ugly industrial towns scattered across the land could glow colorfully like the stones and begins to dream vaguely of a stage in American life beyond that of industrialism, one in which people understand themselves, relate themselves with the life about them, one in which the "invisible roof" of each town might, as implied in *Mid-American Chants,* be extended to cover the entire country. Reaching home, he is greeted happily by Clara, now pregnant with their second child. The "disease of thinking that was making Hugh useless for the work of his age" has made him at last at ease with her. Putting his arms around Clara, Anderson's symbol for human communication, he goes with her into the farmhouse accompanied by present reality, the "whistling and screaming" of Bidwell's factories announcing the night shift. Together the pair head toward the uncertain future.

5.

By early November, Sherwood was so certain that he wanted to stay in his little house in Palos Park that he spent several days whitewashing ceilings and painting the walls in bright colors. Old Mary lent him an ancient steamer chair on which he could stretch out snugly by his stove, writing and occasionally looking out at the oak leaves, brown and gold against the first snows. On the afternoon of November 12 as a kind of housewarming, he invited Felix and Old Mary over to help entertain an unlikely visitor, Theda Bara, the movie star famed as The Vamp. Bara was interested in Anderson's stories, seeing them as possible dramatizations, for she was making a courageous but inadequate attempt to establish herself as a stage actress and was then appearing at Chicago's Garrick Theatre as the lead in a melodrama titled *The Blue Flame.* Bara and another woman came out to Palos Park by car that afternoon. Old Mary, who greatly admired the star and had prepared a kind of feast for tea, was deeply hurt when Bara completely ignored her and gave all her attention to the painter and the writer. "You fellows are mighty lucky living in a world like this," Bara told them, apparently thinking of the exploitation she had encountered in Hollywood and the critical savaging she was receiving from Boston, New York, and now Chicago reviews of *The Blue Flame.* Sherwood, who had seen enough of the movie world in his brief stint with John Emerson, agreed that Hollywood was a "machine" he never wanted to "tie up to" and was pleased that Bara liked his tiny house; but he was both angry and sad that she would not talk with Old Mary as one actress to another, and soon after the visit he concluded that she seemed "an impossible ass of a woman."[45]

He felt mixed emotions too in a quite different matter. Just before he settled in Palos Park, he had read Waldo Frank's new novel *The Dark Mother,* a copy of which Waldo had sent him. He thought it lifeless and too explicit in its psychoanalysis, and wrote Waldo as tactfully as he could to say that he "felt a lack of conviction and reality in the book." If the writer's self, he wrote with what would become an increasingly strong belief,

really gets lost in the wonder of life, wonder will grow out of it. Often . . . it has. To me in this book it doesn't. I want life to be, in the artist, the glowing thing, I want self forgotten. Hell you know old brother & I may be all wrong.

To Bab he could express his dislike of the book more bluntly.

I expect your reactions to Dark Mother are very like my own. It is of course all right to write a book about the mother complex and to involve it with other complexes. Life is surely so involved. The point is that Waldo should have told his story simply, straightly—as a story of life, leaving us to figure out the motives involved. There is something too paternal and involved in all this repeated emphasis. It is as tho he were afraid we would not know he knew what he was doing.

   One cannot be too humble before human lives. They are the only things in the world worth being humble about and he isn't humble.

He became defensive about Waldo, however, when Paul Rosenfeld began writing him concerning a review article on *The Dark Mother* he was preparing for *The Dial,* an article in which he would psychoanalyze Waldo's psychoanalytics and, though it might well cost him Waldo's and Margaret's friendship, would for once publicly point out how Waldo's "novels are the confessions of a passionate and energetic and even powerful person who has never been able to care for any one but himself, and therefore has no feeling for reality." It was his aesthetic as well as public duty to make such a public statement, Paul declared, for this might possibly awaken Waldo to that dangerous flaw in his "rich dynamic temperament" and force him to come to terms with it. Despite their agreement both on the weakness of *The Dark Mother* and on Waldo's consuming need to be recognized as "a great man," when Paul sent Sherwood the completed article in mid-November to get his judgment on it, Anderson, noting his "sense of brotherhood" to both Paul and Waldo, commented in one abrupt, one more careful response that he thought the article "a little too much" elaborated upon Waldo's flaw and hence seemed revengeful. In turn defensive, but about the article, Paul rejected the suggestion of revengefulness, yet admitted that he had already cut some passages in "bad taste" and asked his friend to read the revised version. Sherwood seems to have decided that he had done all he could to tone down Paul's article, for there is no record of further objection. When in mid-October Frank wrote him for advice on where to go in the South for some weeks of rest, Anderson urged him to go to both New Orleans and Fairhope and added warmly, "I'm feeling you very deeply and constantly"; but he must have realized that his friendship with his "Brother" was inevitably moving toward a close. From now on going to New York would mean seeing primarily, not Waldo, but Paul.[46]

Money was the key to such mobility. The postwar slump in business was now affecting his income since some of his few remaining clients were cutting back on their advertising budgets. The unnamed sum Bab had sent him in mid-November he had gratefully put away for an intended trip to New York in January, but at the moment a business trip to Kentucky was essential. Leaving Chicago on November 20, he stopped off in Indianapolis for a brief, happy visit with Bab and then went on to Owensboro, where he stayed until the following Thursday. Financially the trip was a success. Not only did he plan further advertising for Steele, but the latter introduced him to William H. (Pete) Moberly, president of the Green River Tobacco Company, who needed advice on a mail-order campaign for his Old Kentucky Homespun pipe tobacco. In addition, the public-spirited Steele wanted him to write a series of six newspaper editorials supporting a campaign the businessman was leading for approval of a school bond issue to pay for new school buildings in Owensboro, and for a day the two men visited one crowded schoolroom after another in the dilapidated buildings in the city's racially segregated system so that Anderson could observe the situation at first hand. Being with businessmen again, even the likeable Steele, and away from the quiet of Palos Park wearied him and made him, as he wrote Bab just before leaving Kentucky, "understand and love" the black schoolchildren more than the white. Was it because "at bottom I feel myself like them secretly alien, an outlaw?" Weariness, however, was a universal phenomenon now. It was weariness that turned people into "romanticists," those who closed their eyes to anything ugly in life.[47]

Very likely Sherwood's own brand of "weariness" had begun even before he left for Kentucky. Probably Huebsch had sent him the first review of *Poor White* to appear, an anonymous one—it was actually by Ludwig Lewisohn, novelist and critic—in *The Nation* for November 10 as a depressing single paragraph conclusion to a review mostly praising Sinclair Lewis's *Main Street*, judging Anderson's novel as inferior because of its "structural looseness and a diction that alternates between the pretentious and the mean," its comparative lack of "fire and edge, lucidity and fullness." Certainly he had seen by November 12 Mencken's review in the December *Smart Set;* writing to the Blums on this date he commented that "Mencken was out with rather fulsome praise of *Poor White,* and Huebsch says he's going to push it; so maybe . . . I'll have money enough. . . ." He must have been using "fulsome" in the mistaken positive sense, for he had written Bab that it was "a well thought out, dignified article." Surveying Anderson's work, Mencken asserted that although his first two novels showed him split between artist and social reformer, *Poor White* showed the artist dominant and the social reformer relevant in the description of "the demoralizing effect of the introduction of the factory system into the rural Middle West." Anderson must have glowed at this influential critic's extraordinarily high, and prescient, praise of *Winesburg, Ohio* as a total victory of artist over reformer.

The result was a book of high and delicate quality, a book uncorrupted by theories and moral purposes, a book that stands clearly above anything of its sort in latter-day American literature, saving only Dreiser's "Twelve Men." It will be appreciated at its true worth, I believe, in the years to come. At the moment its peculiar excellencies are obscured by its very unusualness—its complete departure from all the customary methods and materials of prose fiction among us. Study it, and you will get some smell of the fiction of the future.

Presumably he had also seen his friend Llewellyn Jones's very favorable piece in the *Chicago Evening Post* pointing to the novel's keen description of industrialization's effects and its fitting ending. Certainly, however, he had read Francis Hackett's criticism of *Poor White* as having a "hopelessly shambling" narrative and showing "a small sense of the values of form," for he had referred to it in a letter to Bab from Palos Park dated November 16. He must have been particularly vexed and "wearied" by this review, for in the letter he characterized it as "spiritually tired," and he described to her a kind of vision that had troubled him all the previous night.

A boy is given a golden goblet containing a strange liquid. The liquid is love. He runs through the world sprinkling it on people, begging them to put their lips to it.

At first the eyes of the boy are clear but they become troubled. As the lips of the people touch the magic liquid in the goblet they are transformed. Many become hideously ugly, others remain beautiful but suffer terribly. The boy runs less and less swiftly, he looks at people doubtfully, his eyes become more and more troubled and when at last the goblet is empty he finds himself suddenly become an old man and lies down to die.

Quite manifestly the "vision" had been about himself and the hope, self-distrust, and fear of failure he felt as writer.[48]

Not surprisingly, after returning from Owensboro on the twenty-fifth he at once went to bed for several days with a severe cold. Then, his body and mind rested, he quickly put together advertising materials for Steele and Moberly and was soon gratified to learn that to the Owensboro Ditcher & Grader account he could now regularly add that of Green River Tobacco. In addition he was able to put together for Steele six editorials strongly urging passage of the Owensboro school bond on the economic ground that to delay would increase the cost and the moral/social one that the school children as future citizens deserved the best training in the best environments. In the Owensboro election on January 22, 1921, the bond was "overwhelmingly approved." For Anderson, the November financial pinch was over.[49]

With some irritating exceptions the commentary and reviews of *Poor White* were also encouraging over the next few months. Out of twenty-eight reviews twenty-one, three-fourths of them, would be highly or on balance favorable; only seven would be mostly unfavorable. In the *Chicago Daily News* Harry Hansen recommended the novel as "The Book of the Week" on the grounds that it was "A truthful, well written study of the middle west," while on December 5 Fanny Butcher, along with an ecstatic review in the *Chicago Tribune,* listed *Poor White* as third among the best sellers in the city area. A few days earlier the *Tribune* had quoted FPA's (Franklin Pierce Adams) comment from his "The Conning Tower" column in the *New York Tribune,* urging Americans "despondent over the low state of novel writing" to read *Main Street, The Age of Innocence, Poor White, Youth and the Bright Medusa,* and *Miss Lulu Bett* and then "throw away their inferiority complex" about American as opposed to English writers. Heywood Broun, book reviewer for the same newspaper, probably would not have included *Poor White* in that list, for he objected that, "The book ranges from miraculous insight and beauty to muddled sentimentality and not a little crude and tired recourse to mere blood and thunder invention." Constance Mayfield Rourke in the New York Evening Post's *Literary Review,* however, praised the "flexible naturalism" of *Poor White,* called it "a poetic novel," and placed it "close to Whitman" for its "hold upon certain large pulsations of American life." Anderson's University of Chicago friend Robert Morss Lovett found the ending unsatisfactory but commended the author's "easy mastery of Middle Western life, and his power to touch it with significance." Astutely Lovett noted that, "Mr. Anderson's formula is realism, enlarged and made significant by symbolism." Toward the end of November Sherwood received a letter from Hart Crane, who had been fascinated by *Poor White* as much as he had by *Winesburg.* Crane especially admired "the simplicity of [Anderson's] great power of suggestion," his "uncanny intuition into the feelings of women," as a number of women had told Crane, and his strong sense of nature that "colors his work with the most surprising grasp of what 'innocence' and 'holiness' ought to mean." Gratefully Anderson wrote to say how especially pleased he was by the praise, for "you know how to take a story naturally and simply and how to read naturally and simply."[50]

So much appreciation from so many quarters made Anderson reach out confidently to two other writers who had just published books. He had already written Mencken to thank him for the *Smart Set* review, "the sort of criticism that gets somewhere," and to say that he would like to see him on the trip to New York he was now planning for January. On December 1, he sent off a note to Sinclair Lewis to tell him how glad he was that Lewis had written *Main Street,* which, published four days earlier than *Poor White,* was already a best seller. Lewis promptly replied, exclaiming that he was "a rather ardent booster for *Winesburg*" and looked forward to reading *Poor White,* ending with the suggestion that they two and other American writers and reviewers ought to "get together—in a savage place without constables—have a week together, & fight & roar." Anderson in turn replied, professing to prefer Gopher Prairie to such an intimidating meeting but hoping that "everyone in every small town in the country reads *Main Street.*" In expressing this hope Sherwood was being more his advertising self than his artist one, for already he had written Rosenfeld of his desire to write an article on *Main Street,* Floyd Dell's *Moon-Calf,* and a third novel asserting the limitations of the first two despite the extravagant praise of them by many reviewers. He was especially angry at Lewis for satirizing in his novel the American small town and most of its inhabitants. In actuality, he would have been happier if no one read *Main Street* rather than the many thousands who were doing so.[51]

Equally irritating was the fact that the increasingly large sales of *Main Street* and *Moon-Calf* were being announced by frequent advertisements in the Chicago papers, while Huebsch ran few ads for *Poor White* and the book sold far less well. Nevertheless, Anderson warmly wrote Ben that he was "the descentest best publisher that any perverse crab like myself ever found." He was generous, if not wholly honest, in an interchange of letters with Floyd Dell. Sherwood had begun reading *Moon-Calf* almost as soon as it was published, like *Poor White,* on October 27, and even before finishing it wrote to Floyd to praise its "clear straight writing" and to say that it "makes me love and understand you as I never have before." Dell gratefully replied at length, explaining apologetically that his antagonism to the element of fantasy in Sherwood's books, even in *Poor White,* "in many ways your finest," resulted from his own clinging to straight realism, lest he be swept away by his actual fear of reality and great love of the fantastic. Sherwood immediately wrote back explaining that, disliking in himself his instinctive skill at manipulating people in business, at being "a smooth son of a bitch," he had turned to writing as "curative"; writing "helped me face myself, helped me tell myself things," helped give the poet in him "breath and life." Dell ended the friendly exchange by urging that, as perhaps he should not fear the poet in himself, Sherwood should not fear the part of him that was the business man with a firm grip on reality. But Sherwood was not interested in changing his "impulse toward the strange and beautiful impulses" in himself. He seems not to have finished reading *Moon-Calf,* and the correspondence lapsed.[52]

Probably the personal praise of *Poor White* that he wanted most to have would be Waldo's and Paul's. In the elaborate manner in which he paid compliments, Paul wrote that Sherwood was "making beautiful things," while Waldo with his just as characteristic expansiveness exclaimed that in this "amazing . . . beautiful work" Sherwood had "swept the life of half a continent into a form, sprawling, halting, at times, yet in its fidelity to its own life indefeasibly sure and even swift." Perhaps remembering his friend's criticism of *The Dark Mother,* however, Waldo found a major fault in *Poor White.* The first two major sections tracing the early separate lives of Hugh and Clara were "full of luminous color" and had "real form," but the couple's relationship after marriage had been abruptly told rather than shown in its fullness, made to *"live,"* to be "luminous and singing . . . to glow and throb," the result of this failure being to damage the "entire foregoing structure of your novel." Still, *Poor White* was "American expression" and surpassed the "entire contemporary English novel" in its "livingness." As when he discovered Anderson in 1916, Waldo still saw his friend as symbolic of the America he himself longed to embrace.[53]

Around the first of December, Bab came to Chicago for a brief visit, during which Sherwood took her to see his pictures, which were hanging for a few more days at the Walden Bookshop. Despite a lingering illness her spirits were good, perhaps because she had fully come to accept their relationship as only the warm friendship Sherwood had long wished it to be. As usual he found in her a willing listener to his ideas. Although neither of them, he told her, could hope to enjoy the "newer sweeter life that is to come," that newer life would be made possible by people like themselves who, when faced with a "wall," refused to turn inward in frustration but turned outward, accepting life as it is and growing from any experience it offered. Relieved and gladdened by her new poise, her "fine dignity of living," convinced finally also that his next book should be a collection of short stories, Anderson in early December quickly wrote the tale "Why There Must Be a Midwestern Literature" and on the thirteenth sent it off to *Vanity Fair,* which accepted it for its March 1921 issue. (When printed in his story collection *Horses and Men,* it would be retitled "Milk Bottles.") Soon he was deep into another tale he first called "Out of Nothing Into Nowhere," which, he wrote Bab, "Should be a strong lovely singing story" and which by early January he would tell her "is such a delicately adjusted thing that I am uncertain whether I shall be able to pull it off." By January 14 he had pulled it off and was finishing what he would retitle "Out of Nowhere Into Nothing."[54]

The first of these two stories seems now one of his weaker ones, for the motif of half-filled bottles of milk that have gone sour throughout the city of Chicago because of stifling summer heat appears with manipulated frequency, and the point of the tale is too obvious and pat. On a hot August night an advertising writer sets down a long romantic vision of a beautiful Chicago built by "brave adventurous people," which he reads to the narrator because he thinks it "real stuff"; but, weary from a hard day at the office, he had first written and discarded a brief angry piece about smashing half-filled bottles of sour milk, a piece which to the narrator really does present the lives of Midwest people as they are. The vision, as the narrator tells the reader, is "lifeless," whereas the angry outburst "frightened you a little but there it was and in spite of his anger or perhaps because of it, a lovely singing quality had got into the thing." Obviously the writing of the romantic vision had been a way of turning inward away from the ugliness of life, whereas turning outward and embracing that ugliness had, paradoxically, created its own beauty. Anderson's first appearance in *Vanity Fair* showed him far from his best.

"Out of Nowhere Into Nothing," on the other hand, shows him at his experimental best. As in the earlier story, he was trying to give fictional life to some of the ideas he had been expressing to Bab and other friends that fall; but even the open statement of these ideas at certain points in this long story grows naturally out of the gradual understanding by the woman protagonist, not a writer herself, of what Kate Swift, the Winesburg teacher, had told George Willard the writer must learn, a basic lesson that Anderson himself in actual life would insist on to persons who wrote him asking how they might become writers. As Kate Swift had put it, "The thing to learn is to know what people are thinking, not what they say"; or as Melville Stoner, middle-aged, birdlike bachelor of Willow Springs, Iowa, tells Rosalind Wescott, the strong-bodied young protagonist, "In every human being there are two voices, each striving to make itself heard"—the voice that says words, which too rarely express "living truth," and the voice that consists of feelings, thoughts, the play of the imagination, which sometimes makes itself "heard" through facial expressions or sudden, almost accidental outbursts of "truthful" words but must more often be simply intuited by a sensitive other person. Anderson, with the resources of his craft that he was developing, uses words to express the inner voices of Rosalind and of Walter Sayers of Chicago (and unnamed Palos Park), her well-to-do, married employer with whom she has fallen in love and who loves her instead of his possessive wife. Because the story is told omnisciently, the thoughts and feelings of Rosalind and Sayers are given directly, but the fictional structure supplies a kind of "second voice" for the story itself. Anderson achieved this effect partly by his inconspicuously deft control of time. The present action is carefully carried through a few critical hours in Rosalind's life, but flashbacks and flashbacks within flashbacks provide a cumulative sense of how her past experience impinges on and shapes her present state of mind. A second aspect of the structure is its intricate network of "cross-reference" details, episodes, daydreams, fantasies, motifs, and symbols linking the past and present lives of the two lovers, a network of comparisons and contrasts that not only re-creates the complex impulses conflicting within Rosalind but supports the author's further statement about individual lives and man-woman relationships in America more generally. Since the reader only gradually becomes aware of the extraordinary intricacy of this network, the effect is not, as in "Why There Must Be a Midwest Literature" and even to some extent in "Brothers," one of mechanical manipulation by the author but of his revelation of a rich, subtle web of psychic actuality.

For six years, one learns, Rosalind Wescott has escaped in Chicago the dull routines by which her parents and most of the other inhabitants of her small Iowa town have repressed their longings and desires. Chicago has been ugly and lacking in the contact with the earth and growing things that a country town makes possible, but it has made possible first Rosalind's awareness of books, music, and painting, then through her closeness as secretary to the gentle, unhappily married Sayers, their falling in love, her slow awakening to her sexual and emotional needs, and finally the development of her childhood gift for fantasy toward more meaningful visionary moments, such as—to take one of the many recurrent motifs—her perception that the gulls from Lake Michigan, when they swoop down gracefully to feed on sewage in the Chicago River beneath her office window and rise again into the air, unite ugliness and beauty in that process. Resolved to give herself physically to her lover, Rosalind has come back to Willow Springs in the August heat to tell her mother of her intention, in hopes that her mother for once will speak her real feelings to her as woman to woman. Now on the third and last afternoon of her visit she still has not spoken her resolve to her mother; but on a walk into the flat, hot countryside she meets the next door neighbor Melville Stoner, and recognizes him as isolated from the drab townspeople by his intense absorption in the processes of nature and by his uncanny penetration into the private thoughts of others, including hers. Through the brief contact with Stoner there flashes upon her the meaning of a recurrent mental picture in her girlhood, that of broad steps descending between strangely carved marble walls and a procession of people going down them and away. These men and women, she realizes, were going "down into the hidden places in people, into the hall of the little voices." She has comprehended the lesson of the two voices.

That evening after the routine of supper, her mother as always putters about the kitchen. Her father, about to go "up town" as always to sit silently with other men of the town in Emanuel Wilson's Hardware Store until bedtime, comes upon Rosalind unexpectedly and, actually looking at her, perceives the sense of life radiating from "this lovely daughter of the cornlands," as Anderson puts it, fitting the detail into a motif in the story drawn from his old theme of the corn as symbolic of the cycle of birth, decay, and rebirth. Made uncomfortable by his sudden perception, the father quickly escapes up town; but sensitized by her talk with Melville Stoner, Rosalind wonders, in one of Anderson's finer and most characteristic sentences, whether for a moment her father might not have felt as, she has realized, Stoner sometimes does: "Did loneliness drive him to the door of insanity and did he also run through the night seeking some lost, some hidden and half forgotten loveliness?" Then her mother at last comes out from the kitchen, Rosalind abruptly tells her of her intention to give herself to her lover and is horrified when the older woman savagely rejects sexuality and satisfies the "passion for denial within her" by calling out into the darkness: "'There is no love. Life is a lie. It leads to sin, to death and decay.'"

Shocked at the death-in-life existence of her parents, unable to bear home and town longer, not even pausing to pack her bag, Rosalind leaves the house and starts walking toward the next town to the east in order to take a night train back to Chicago and her lover. Stoner accompanies her as far as the town's last streetlight, and she understands that by making her perceive the thoughts of others and face her own, he has shown her, as the gulls have, how to achieve beauty through the experience of ugliness, how death conquers life but life conquers death in an unending cycle. Beginning to run through the hot, dark prairie night, she envisions herself as a "creator of light" running "on forever, through the land, through towns and cities, driving darkness away with her presence." Title and conclusion coalesce in Rosalind's vision, the story, not the author, asserting what in fact the author believed: life comes "out of nowhere" and goes into the nothingness of death yet, repeating this process endlessly, achieves value according to its degree of intensity within the individual. In "Out of Nowhere Into Nothing" Anderson gives firm and palpable expression to one of his strongest, if vaguest, convictions, that, as he had put it abstractly, if vaguely, to Waldo Frank, "life should be, in the artist, the glowing thing."

6.

"Out of Nowhere" occupied most of his creative attention through the rest of December and the first three weeks of January, for it had developed into a longer story, almost a novella, than he had at first expected. He was happy about the story. It was, he wrote Bab, both intricate and delicate: "In a way I think it the best story I have ever written, having more beauty in it." He wrote steadily at it even though yet again depression was settling down heavily on him, and he was beginning to feel a constant physical tiredness that was more than the "spiritual" weariness he felt so prevalent among people.[55]

The depression and to some extent the tiredness, though for the latter a physical cause would be discovered the following March, was strongly linked to the season. Predictably he was enduring his old "Christmas psychosis." Going into Chicago on a snowy December 21 to catch up on business affairs at Critchfield and then to rush about doing belated shopping for gifts for his children, he momentarily saw the city as "white and very ghostly and lovely"; but for the most part he felt Chicago to be ugly, ugly as the nasty, hate-filled letters strangers would send him—so he wrote to Bab—whenever he published a book, calling him "a beast, a stupid egotist, a bad writer, a fool to see people as I do." How many such letters he had actually received it is impossible to say; but in the grip of depression he could have been moved by only one to "sketch in" a story just before Christmas "to fix the mood of it," a tale, as such never published, to be called "The Man Who Sat In His House" dealing with an author's feeling that strangers who wrote hateful letters were like real people coming into his workroom and making a "mess on the floor."[56]

Christmas itself, however, was an unexpectedly "lovely" day. Sherwood and Tennessee with Bob, John, and Mimi (now thirteen, eleven, and nine) had dinner at a restaurant and then went to see Sherwood's paintings, which were now hung at the Arts Club. Sherwood gave a talk about them to his little audience, and later, probably at Tennessee's Division Street apartment, the children entertained in turn. Taking parts that revealed something of the boys' developing temperaments, they

had a mock trial and charged me with being a Bolshevik and writing literature that was against the government. Robert was the government lawyer. John wanted to defend me but it was more fun to convict. I got twenty years.[57]

The warmth and happiness of Christmas Day did not, unfortunately, linger afterwards. "Weariness," as Anderson wrote Rosenfeld at the end of the year, "has a thousand hands that can be laid upon one's shoulder." On a cold, windy afternoon he went for a long walk in the snow-filled oak woods around his little house, came home to sit by his fire, and watch the black tree trunks standing out against the white snow until the sunset faded into darkness. Felix and Helen Russman were away for the holidays, and he kept the fires going in their house. Late that night he would, as usual, "go through the wood, past a deserted house, up a hillside to their door. The trees crackle, shadows play about, my ears tingle in the cold." Possibly it was on this evening that he began casually to play in his fancy with the figure of a woman, old-looking at middle age, who, carrying too heavy a burden on her back, lay down in the snow, went to sleep, and never awoke. Possibly, but if so, it was more likely driven out of his mind for the moment by a revulsion he had just recently begun to feel against his Midwest, its cold winters, its ugly factories and factory towns, its raw newness. He

wanted to flee, to escape, to walk in old European and African cities, see the colorful beggars on the streets of Rome, visit all old places.

That I have always and will always live in the middle west, in a raw new civilization, that I shall perhaps die not having seen old places made me ill.

Staying in his own land between mountain and mountain and writing beautifully-told stories was not enough. He wanted to escape across the ocean into beautiful experience. As though dream had created actuality, his wish was shortly to be granted.[58]

11

To the Old World, and Back

1.

For Christmas 1920 Paul Rosenfeld had sent the Andersons a copy of
D. H. Lawrence's just published *Women in Love,* "gotten up to look like
the Holy Bible" in its fifteen-dollar subscription edition, so issued to avoid
censorship. Beginning to read it after the holiday, Sherwood was at first
struck by the sophistication of its manner, which suggested to him that
Lawrence might have been touched by the universal postwar weariness of
spirit that he himself was feeling. Finishing the novel on January 14, however, he decided that *Women in Love* was "tremendous . . . like a storm I
once lived through" when everything about shook and trembled. Lawrence's appearance on the literary scene, he would tell Harry Hansen some
weeks later, was "one of the great events of our decade."[1]

Still, he detected a kind of strain in *Women in Love* that he tried to
avoid in his own writing. The matter was so important to his thinking and
his art that he kept coming back to it in a series of letters to Bab in early
January. In *Women in Love,* he argued, Lawrence had "tried to formulate
a thing I've often spoken of—the putting of sex into its right place—not
by suppression or repression but by realizing that sex is not love—any
more than another hunger." But out of spiritual weariness Lawrence had
resorted too often to sexual symbolism, thus intellectualizing feeling
rather as Frank had done in *The Dark Mother.* Overemphasis on sexual
symbolism was destructive in fiction. "For example," he told Bab, "had I
written thus of the woman in the story "Loneliness" I should have been
impelled to explain her—work her out into expressed symbols. The story
would have been ruined."[2]

The matter had an immediate personal as well as an aesthetic application for him. When Bab, he warned her, used sexual symbolism in her letters, she did not reach his real self. "It is not that sex is not a part of me also.
The point is that I do exist in myself—aside from my hungers." To make

the matter clear he wrote more explicitly, and more revealingly, about his own sexual nature than ever before in their surviving correspondence.

The impossibility of beauty in personal relations when those relations are too much talked of one sees everywhere.

Most women simply frighten me. I feel hunger within them. It is as though they wished to feed upon me.

As a matter of fact I am very strongly sexed but hard work, constant thinking, saving my strength for flights into my imaginative world. . . . All of these things consume strength that might otherwise go into sex expression.

Sexually hungry or starved women are made angry by what therefore seems a perversion of the ends of life to them. The more noble among them do not give way to the feeling. It is however there.

More and more the critics who write of my work discuss, rather than the work, myself—what I am striving toward, what I would accomplish.

The significance of this passage should not be missed. Anderson was indeed "strongly sexed," though the evidence indicates that, except for such an episode as the debauches in Cleveland when his first marriage was breaking up, he could not be characterized as promiscuous. What he feared was not women as such, but rather their capacity, as he perceived it, for possessiveness, for making sex the center of a relation and thus impeding him from his goals. The apparent shift in the last paragraph from sex to the literary critics was not in actuality discontinuous. He was bluntly emphasizing that preserving his artist's self was more important to him than meeting the sexual needs of another or maintaining intimate relationships generally. This was not just a conviction, it was a dictate of his being; and others besides Bab would see him act in accordance with it.

Women in Love thus drew him to articulate some of his deepest feelings and perhaps express them in another medium than words. In early January he got out his watercolors again after months of ignoring them, for one thing painting in "warm rich colors of earth" a bowl, from the mouth of which rose "more intense floating colors." But his brief return to painting may also have been prompted by the fact that the pictures he had shown at the Walden Bookshop were again placed on exhibit and that to prepare viewers for these "color impulses," as he now called them, he wrote and framed a short description of their origin. Through most of January the pictures hung in the hall of the Arts Club of Chicago at 610 South Michigan Avenue, where, Harry Hansen announced, they caused "much excitement." They caused puzzlement and amusement too. Writing of them at length in her weekly column for January 23, Eleanor Jewett, the art critic of the *Tribune*, found them moderately interesting but opaque to interpretation. After summarizing Anderson's account of how he had been excited into painting at Fairhope one day after "a tropical storm had brought down a great deal of red earth upon the beach sands" and "the waves and wind, the flow and ebb of the tide tossed and turned the sand into various shifting colored patterns," Jewett rather helplessly concluded:

It is hard to know what to add to this tale that he tells about them. They are queer, a round of color, a chaos of design, a grotesque checkering, binding the seams of a writer's fancy with the thread of a painter's trade.

Less politely, Gene Markey, newspaper caricaturist and professional wit, commented that "the exhibition . . . can be interpreted by no one (including Mr. Anderson): 'one of 'em looked like the interior of a rhinoceros's throat infected with tonsillitis.'" Nevertheless, two of the pictures were sold for two hundred dollars apiece, and Anderson had the laugh on Markey.[3]

Paul Rosenfeld's Christmas gift had been one way of indicating his affection for Sherwood. In addition he had been making arrangements for a New York exhibit of the watercolors at the Sunwise Turn, a "modern" bookshop in the Yale Club Building at 55 East Forty-fourth Street, the show to be set up as soon as possible after the Arts Club one ended. Then on January 20 Paul manifested his affection even more generously by sending his friend a telegram that suddenly made a reality of Anderson's dream of escape to older civilizations: "Will you go to Europe on May Seventeenth will Pay your Passage both ways have reserved berth for you & me. . . ." Anderson did not receive the telegram until the evening of January 23. With no hesitation he wired back an acceptance, and on the twenty-third he poured out in a letter his joy at the invitation. "Of all the men I know in America," he told Paul ecstatically, "it is you I should have picked to go with to Europe." His plans for a New York visit in February were all off. He must stay in Palos Park in order to save money for the European trip, get his advertising accounts in order, and finish putting together the book of stories for Huebsch. He had completed "Out of Nowhere Into Nothing" at last, he added as an excited afterthought. Would Paul read it?[4]

Suddenly the world was expanding on all sides. The January issue of *Vanity Fair* was out with a page of six captioned photographs of "American Novelists Who Have Set Art Above Popularity," and though Edith Wharton's picture was the large central one, there was Sherwood's together with those of Dreiser, Cather, Cabell, and Hergesheimer. Anderson's caption, though presenting a limited view of his aims, was nevertheless flattering as an eastern recognition of a midwesterner:

Foremost among those who are using the novel as a means of criticizing American civilization. His new novel, "Poor White," presents with an uncompromising fidelity the life of the industrial towns of the Middle West.

Then, too, he had just discovered a talent in his favorite son, the quiet, affectionate John. Writing to Bab on January 23 to rejoice in Paul's "splendid" gesture, he told her that after speaking to his children on Christmas Day about his watercolors, he had sent John some paints. Now John had sent him a painting the boy had done "that is one of the finest things I've seen—ever." Even, the proud father declared, John Marin,

the best watercolor man in America would not be ashamed to sign it. The boy has that god given thing—a real color sense and to say that of a painter is to say the same thing as saying a singer has a voice. Nothing has made me so happy in months.

Exultant that John was certain to be "a big painter," Anderson saw not only himself coming into fame but his son carrying on the creative spark.[5]

On January 27 Paul wrote a letter full of details about the trip. A fifteen-hundred-dollar mortgage, which he and his sister owned was being paid off in a lump sum, and it was his share that would cover round-trip steamer fare for the two men. Sherwood must not expect to travel in luxury, for Paul had booked passage on the French Line's *Rochambeau,* an all second-class ship. The liner would sail from New York on May 14, not the seventeenth as the telegram had stated, and land at Le Havre, from which they would go by train directly to Paris. After three or four weeks in France, Paul intended to go on to London to look for an English publisher, as Sherwood might also wish to do, and would be returning around the first of August, with Sherwood if that suited the latter's convenience. Because of Sherwood's acquaintance with Jacques Copeau, he should have a "bully time" in France. "I am sure you will be introduced all around, especially since you are being translated, written up by Catell in the *Mecure,* and, I believe, lectured on at the University of Montpellier."[6]

After his acceptance letter, which, like the telegram, made no reference to Tennessee, Sherwood had apparently become concerned as to where she might fit into the picture and within a day or so had queried Paul about her. This was a perplexing matter, Paul continued in his January 27 letter. He would love to have Tennessee come along, but his share of the mortgage money was too small to cover her fare also. One can only speculate whether Tennessee might have decided not to come along, as at first she did, out of some resentment at having been left out of the original invitation. Still, Sherwood was genuinely concerned about how worn down she was becoming by "the grind of teaching in Chicago" and had made her promise not to continue beyond the present year. Between them they decided that she too should have an extended holiday in Europe even if Paul were not paying her way.[7]

Paul ended his long letter with other matters. Because of his review of *The Dark Mother* and a misunderstanding over who was to evaluate a

French translation of "Hands" that Marguerite Gay had made and sent to Sherwood and Sherwood had sent to Paul, Waldo Frank had become estranged from them both. The Sunwise Turn would definitely exhibit Sherwood's paintings, and he must ship them at once. Finally, Paul wanted to read "Out of Nowhere" but did not like the title Sherwood was now considering for the book of stories, *Some Americans*. "The Triumph of the Egg was ever so much more colorful."

The Arts Club show ended on January 27 or 28, and Anderson hurried to get his paintings crated and off by express on February 1 for the New York exhibit. So January ended in a flurry of excitement, but for all of February his emotional pendulum swung far to the other side. He had to busy himself with advertising chores and in his free moments was often too tired to write. The feelings of weariness had been accumulating for months, and, grown "glum as hell," he finally decided that the cause must be at least as much physical as "spiritual." He consulted several doctors, including a woman one who, sometime around the first of March, detected that for months his sinuses had been infected and had been poisoning his whole body. Possibly, he wrote Bab, this long-term infection had "a good deal to do with my occasional long periods of depression." As March progressed, he went to the physician's office three times a week for a three-hour treatment each time. It was boring and costly, but the treatment was restoring his energy, and he could take more interest in literary affairs.[8]

On some business trip late in February he had stopped in Cleveland for a few hours one evening, hoping to see his young admirer Hart Crane, who had sent him a draft of a new poem, "Black Tambourine," describing the position of the black man in America's "cellar." Unable to locate Crane in Cleveland, Anderson wrote him on March 4 to say, characteristically, that something "intellectualized" in two lines prevented the full realization of the poem, and to rejoice, equally characteristically, that the poet had discovered Dostoyevsky.

It is delightful that you should also have picked the two books I care for most, *Karamazov* and *Possessed*. There is nothing like *Karamazov* anywhere else in literature—a bible. You will like *The Idiot* and the prison tales too. However, one doesn't like this man, one loves him. I have always felt him as the one writer I could go down on my knees to.

When Crane shortly sent back a revised version of the poem, Anderson approved it, though he tentatively questioned Crane's assumption that "the American negro is quite lost in mid air between Africa and our stupid selves. Sometimes I think he alone is not lost. I don't know."[9]

To Crane, Anderson had complained on March 4 that despite much talk about it, *Poor White* had sold far less well than *Main Street;* yet on the same day he sent off a jocular note of thanks to Sinclair Lewis, "you Babe Ruth among boosters," for Lewis, currently on lecture tour, had spoken in Chicago on the merits of American fiction and had praised Anderson along with Dreiser and others. But if *Poor White* was still only occasionally a weekly best seller in Chicago bookstores, Anderson had good luck with "Out of Nowhere Into Nothing." Paul had read the typescript and had submitted it to *Pictorial Review,* which found it too unconventional for its readers, and then to *The Dial,* where Thayer accepted it for serial publication in the July, August, and September issues, and paid its author five hundred dollars. At least that would cover his doctors' bills, Sherwood ruefully decided.[10]

Paul had liked "Out of Nowhere" for its "wonderful picture of the messiness of America" and its "fine lyrical bits," but he had been confused and annoyed by Anderson's fluid use of "cut-backs" that made him lose the chronology of the present action and produced, for him, a serious problem of form. Still, he concluded, "I know you are a big man, from that tale, and every bit a better man than Chekhov. I think that, with all its faults, the story marks a new period in your work." On March 10, Anderson replied, questioning Paul's "strictures regarding form," that element of fiction which so many reviewers of *Poor White* had shown so much concern about. Confidently he asserted his refusal to be bound by that concern.

[Francis] Hackett always attacks me by saying my sense of form is atrocious, and it may be true. However, he also commends me for getting a certain large, loose sense of life. I often wonder, if I wrapped my packages up more neatly, if the same large, loose sense of life could be attained.

In the matter of form, Paul, I have so much to say to you that we shall have an opportunity to say this summer. One thing I would like you to know is this: as far as I am concerned, I can accept no standard I have ever seen as to form. What I most want is to be and remain always an experimenter, an adventurer. If America could have the foolish thing sometimes spoken of as "Artistic Maturity" through me, then America could go to the devil.

Now that he was feeling better, Anderson went ahead in March with a final selection of stories for his *Book of Impressions from American Life in Tales and Poems,* as his subtitle would finally have it. There were to be twelve stories including two long ones, "Out of Nowhere" and "Unlighted Lamps." There were to be four poems, three not previously published, one preceding the half-title page, one preceding the first story and one following the last, the fourth inserted so as to divide the first six stories from the second six. Just before the contents page were to be seven pages of illustrations, photographs, one to a page, made by the Chicago photographer Eugene Hutchinson of seven of the clay heads modeled by

Tennessee. Up to and even beyond March 24, when Anderson sent off the typescript to Huebsch, he was uncertain about a title for the collection. The one Rosenfeld had disliked, *Some Americans,* he had reworked into the subtitle; but he wrote to Huebsch that he would call the volume either *The Triumph of the Egg* or *Unlighted Lamps,* and as late as April 2 he wrote the Blums that the book would have the latter title. Huebsch put his foot down flat. *Unlighted Lamps* sounded "too much like O. Henry," whereas *The Triumph of the Egg* "sounds like nothing else, and is a most arresting title." Huebsch's good judgment settled the matter.[11]

That Anderson had wavered among three such disparate titles might suggest that he had little conception of an overall structure for the collection; nevertheless, the arrangement of the stories into two groups of six does present, if "loosely," a developmental structure emphasized most clearly by the carefully placed poems. In the untitled poem, which constitutes the first page of printing in the book, the speaker is "helpless" to clothe the tales that, like people, sit "freezing on the doorstep of my mind"; and in "The Dumb Man," the poem preceding the first story, the "wordless" speaker similarly concludes "I have a wonderful story to tell but know no way to tell it"—a fateful line for Anderson to write since in later years hostile critics would often quote it as a conscious or unconscious confession by the author himself of artistic inadequacy. Yet "The Dumb Man" is succeeded by "The Man in the Brown Coat," the poem that separates the first six stories from the last six. Here the speaker admits that the thousands of words of history he has written do not "lead into life," but he also asserts that "Some day I shall make a testament unto myself." There is a movement, then, from helplessness and dumbness toward a mode of speech profound if solipsistic; and this movement culminates in "The Man with the Trumpet," the poem with which the book ends. This final speaker is triumphantly articulate, not simply to himself, but to many others, including the readers of the book.

I threw my words at faces floating in a street.
I threw my words like stones, like building stones.
I scattered words in alleyways like seeds.
I crept at night and threw my words in empty rooms of houses in a street.
I said that life was life, that men in streets and cities might build temples to their
    souls.
I whispered words at night into a telephone.
I told my people life was sweet, that men might live.

This development from dumbness to prophetic speech—a development implied as well by the epigraph from *Mid-American Chants* Anderson chose for his title page—has also a relation to the themes of the first six stories as compared with those of the last six. With varying degrees of seriousness the first six deal with the destruction of innocence ("I Want to Know Why"), with the entrapment of personality by old belief ("Seeds") or by a not fully satisfying marriage ("The Other Woman"), with grotesque defeat ("The Egg"), non-communication and death ("Unlighted Lamps"), and fantasy gone futile ("Senility"). In the second group of six, though these also usually deal with locked-in, thwarted persons, there is always some kind of ultimate, if limited, release. The trapped Hugh Walker helps Mary Cochran to escape through the door of the trap; loveless Elsie Leander abandons herself to a storm of feeling until then denied her by an emotionally starved New England upbringing; strength to do or to accept comes to characters in those slight sketches "War" and "Motherhood." Even in "Brothers," balanced as the initial tale of the second group against "Senility" as the last of the first group, the lonely fantasies of both the old man and the murderer are understood by yet another "brother," the narrator, who knows that gold October leaves can be carried dancing away by the wind as well as beaten straight down by the rain. The real "triumph of the egg"—that is, of life itself in its universal onward surge—is of course embodied in Rosalind Wescott's running through the prairie night, paradoxically running toward love and life as well as toward her individual death. "I Want to Know Why," the first tale in the book, declares that the sensitive can not break through the wall of life; "Out of Nowhere Into Nothing," the last tale and by far the longest, declares that the sensitive can.

Such juxtapositions of the themes of imprisonment and escape might seem simply Anderson's way of imaging in the structure of his book an actual ambivalence in his mind, alternating according to mood, as to the fate of the individual in the modern world; yet the progress of the two groups of stories is from imprisonment to escape, not the reverse, the second group has the emphasis of much greater length, and the development of the poems is pointedly from inarticulate failure to successful communication. The words of the prophetic last speaker are like the seeds through which life continues and triumphs; the message he whispers into the telephone is that life is life, and is sweet. Anderson most definitely was not Henry James, but he understood that structure helps to provide meaning. If his instinct for form was by no means infallible, it was stronger, and more subtly expressed, than Rosenfeld had given him credit for.

2.

Meanwhile preparations for the European trip went forward. As directed by Paul, both Sherwood and Tennessee obtained passports and Sherwood the required proof that he had paid his 1920 income tax. He urged Ben Huebsch to get galley proofs of *The Triumph of the Egg* to him by May 1 so that he could read them while on the boat. He exchanged letters with his friend Alfred Kreymborg, who was assisting Harold Loeb in preparing the first number of *Broom,* a new "little magazine" that would be published in Italy, where the cost of fine printing was relatively cheap, but which would emphasize American writing and actually pay for contributions at a penny a word. Kreymborg hoped that Sherwood had several stories to contribute that were of the quality of "Brothers," a "masterly piece," and early in April Sherwood mailed off at least "The Contract," which would be included in *Broom*'s first issue in December. On April 5 he sent the story "Unlighted Lamps" to Mencken, who promptly accepted it for the July issue of *The Smart Set;* and he arranged to stop off in Baltimore on his way east for dinner and the evening of Sunday, May 1, with this man who had done much to build his rising fame. Also around the first of April he had made plans to sublet his Palos Park house for the summer to Donald Wright, a fellow Critchfield employee, and then moved back in with Tennessee at 12 East Division so that he could more readily settle his business affairs before the voyage. Probably he went to Michigan City on Sunday, April 10, for a farewell visit with Cornelia and the children, and on the twelfth he entered the hospital to have his tonsils "dug out" so that, he hoped, he could be rid forever of his nose and throat infections. On the twentieth, recovered from the operation, he took a last trip to Kentucky for several days of conferring with Steele and Moberly. As usual, he stopped on the way back to Chicago for a visit with Bab.[12]

Throughout this busy April he was buoyed up by the excitement of preparations, by anticipation of the voyage, by the good news of stories accepted and of future outlets for others. Through a fortunate coincidence, furthermore, the Londoner Jonathan Cape, having recently set up his own publishing firm, had visited New York back in February, been given copies of Anderson's books by Huebsch, and was now, as Huebsch wrote, offering to become his English publisher. Sherwood should not be too hopeful of income from the English editions; but Huebsch favored the offer because Cape was "intelligent, energetic and ambitious" and because, bluntly, his was so far the only offer made by a British publisher. Pleased that he could now go to London with Rosenfeld, not to hunt for a publisher but to talk with one already committed to him, Anderson agreed to accept. That his reputation was beginning to spread from the United States abroad buoyed his spirits still further.[13]

One person who was much impressed by that reputation was an intense, ambitious young man named Ernest Hemingway, who was currently supporting himself by writing large sections of a monthly cooperatives magazine published in Chicago, but whose real and driving desire was to become a novelist and short story writer. Early in January Hemingway's friend Y. Kenley Smith, an older man with Critchfield connections, had invited him, Don Wright, and several other young men likewise eager to become writers to move into a large apartment Smith had taken in the Belleville, an elegant apartment house at 63 East Division Street. Now that Sherwood was a close neighbor to two lively Critchfield associates, both of them interested in literature, he and sometimes Tennessee began to drop in frequently in the evening at the Kenley Smith "Domicile," Sherwood talking by the hour about his revolt from business or telling "tales of the mythical inhabitants of Winesburg." For the most part Hemingway listened quietly and admiringly, though not uncritically, since he was already far more bent toward realism in his writing than Anderson was; but the older man had been convinced from their first meeting, probably in early April, that Hemingway was "going to go some place." Generously Anderson encouraged the young man to follow his own talent, to write of his Midwest experiences, as Anderson had written of his, even though their styles and attitudes might differ. Despite nearly twenty-five years difference in their ages, each man admired the other's dedication to his craft, and at least over the next few years Hemingway repaid Anderson's kindness to him during those April evenings of talk by praising Anderson's books to others and on occasion even imitating his style. A quite other mode of payment was yet to come.[14]

In mid-April Paul wrote to send the Andersons their steamer tickets and their railway tickets from Le Havre to Paris and to ask whether Sherwood planned to do any writing while abroad. Sherwood replied that

> I have no definite plans for work this year, but I am taking with me the novel, *Ohio Pagans*, and a play that I am at work on. I am also hoping to do some short stories that are in the back of my mind, but I am not telling myself definitely that I will do anything except look about and enjoy you and Tennessee.

The idea of writing a play was a recent one. When Raymond O'Neil, director of the Cleveland Play House, had written the previous summer to ask if Anderson had done anything about dramatizing some of the *Winesburg* stories, as he and Copeau had discussed in Chicago, Anderson replied vaguely that he had occasionally thought of doing so but had not, "although the frame work of several plays are in the back of my head." In the fall he had had a brief correspondence with Rollo Peters, who, though only in his twenties, was achieving fame in the New York theater as a set designer, a founder of the Theatre Guild, and a talented actor. Despite what he called "your evident distrust and dislike of the Theatre," Peters hoped to persuade Anderson either to dramatize *Winesburg* himself or to let Peters try it, and he had invited Anderson to visit him when in New York to discuss possibilities. Under Peters's repeated urgings and his own post-Christmas euphoria Anderson, back in January, had begun thinking seriously of writing a play, though apparently not a dramatization of *Winesburg;* but he had made little, if any, progress with it before the project was interrupted, first by his illness and depression, then by the rush to get his story collection to Huebsch and to clear up business before sailing. For the first time, however, he had begun to think seriously of drama as a new mode for his restless desire to be the experimenter with forms.[15]

The last days of April were a final whirl of preparations, but Sherwood felt "splendid." On the twenty-sixth he went out to Palos Park, perhaps then taking his new friend Hemingway with him, to clean up his house and to have a last look around. It was a rare spring day, and he felt intensely "the half veil of mystery over the land" he was about to leave. Then it was back to Division Street to do the final things before packing. He sent some of his more recent Testaments to Harriet Monroe—who did not take them for *Poetry*—and dashed off a note to John Cournos, an English novelist who had written to praise Anderson's work, to tell him that he would look him up in London. Anderson had planned to leave Chicago on April 29 by himself, he and Tennessee having arranged that she would go to New York just prior to the date of sailing; but it was not until late on the thirtieth that, weary from the final push but happy to be in motion toward Europe, he finally caught a Baltimore and Ohio train for the East.[16]

Arriving in Baltimore at 6 PM on Sunday, May 1, he took a taxi to Mencken's town house at 1524 Hollins Street and within half an hour was amiably drunk on the cocktails Mencken served him in hearty defiance of Prohibition. The two men had dinner at Mencken's club and spent the evening pleasantly discussing, as the critic typically put it, "the loftiest themes of aesthetics." Anderson had long been grateful for Mencken's support of his work, but he came away from this first meeting with the man somewhat disappointed. Mencken, he decided ungratefully, was "a rather naive stupid man after all. One can't take him really seriously."[17]

The next day Anderson went on to New York. Dropping his heavier baggage at Paul Rosenfeld's apartment, he almost immediately went off to the country to Rollo Peters's home to talk playwriting for two or three days. He returned to the city for a day to lunch and dine with various people. This "riot of personalities" was exciting but distracting, and he realized that he would have to wait until on shipboard to sort out his swiftly crowding impressions. The weekend of May 7 and 8 he spent quietly in Westport with Karl and his family, and again he was back in New York, staying with Paul, giving himself to a "debauch of people" until the eleventh and twelfth, which he spent walking with Waldo in the Westchester hills along the Hudson. The usually intense Waldo was, for Waldo, rather subdued. Hurt by the destructive reviews of *The Dark Mother*, including Paul's, he seemed to Sherwood "less the aspiring great man and more the quiet worker." The two days were happy ones, and Sherwood felt that he and Waldo had put their relationship on a new and better basis.[18]

Back in New York just before sailing, he lunched with John Emerson and renewed that old friendship, talked, either then or earlier, with Loeb and Kreymborg about possible further contributions to *Broom,* and even took time to visit the office of *The Bookman,* the editor of which, like Kreymborg and others, had thought "Brothers" to be a "great" work. The office personnel were surprised to find Anderson not "someone a little wild" as expected, but "a very gentle middle-aged fellow, with rather piercing dark eyes."[19]

At some point in the exciting confusion of the New York visit he went to see his watercolors, which had been on display at the Sunwise Turn since late February. Paul had thought that the more recent ones were "up to the standard" of those done in Alabama and all of them in their unconventional way "the work of some one who has felt, and has been able to communicate his feeling. . . ." Conscientiously he had kept Sherwood informed about the plans by Mary Clarke, the bookstore owner, to send out invitations to the exhibit and by the editors of *The Little Review* to give it a write-up, although Margaret Anderson and Jane Heap had instead published in their January-March issue Anderson's own brief "Adventures in Form and Color," a statement about his painting revised from "Color Impulses" and emphasizing his "faith that an impulse needs but be strong enough to break through the difficulty of lack of technical training. In fact, technical training might well destroy it." Georgia O'Keeffe, Paul had reported, had been "whole-heartedly taken" by the watercolors. Now Sherwood could admire his works again in their new setting and learn to his great satisfaction that four more of them had been sold at "an excellent price."[20]

The income from these pictures assured him extra funds for the trip abroad, much needed since Huebsch's May 1 statement of royalties on sales of *Poor White* and *Winesburg* for the previous six months was hardly encouraging. *Poor White* had sold 3,213 copies—very little compared with *Main Street,* which in March was advertised as having sold over 130,000—and *Winesburg* only 1,113. Subtracting the price of copies of each book Anderson had had sent to other people, the amount payable to him was $888.23. Of this amount a check for $478.23 was sent to his account at the Corn Exchange Bank in Chicago, while the remaining $410 was to be held by Huebsch until February 1, 1922, to cover his purchase from the John Lane Company of the plates and unsold copies of Anderson's first three books. Huebsch also agreed to issue a new edition of *Windy McPherson's Son* with a revised ending that Sherwood was contemplating. Since neither Ben nor Sherwood expected much income from the sales of the Lane publications, this arrangement was primarily a goodwill gesture by the publisher toward an author in whose work he had faith. In addition, by pushing his printer hard Huebsch had managed to get proof for *The Triumph of the Egg* back in time for Sherwood to take it with him on the *Rochambeau*.[21]

The agreements with Huebsch were reached only a day or two before sailing date. Tennessee had just arrived, and on May 13 she, Paul, and Sherwood got their baggage to Pier 57, where their liner was berthed. On the morning of May 14 the three went aboard the *Rochambeau*, which sailed at eleven o'clock. For the first time in their lives Sherwood and Tennessee were headed out to open ocean and toward Europe.

3.

For the first two days the *Rochambeau*, a slow ship, plowed on under clear sunny skies over a sea that Anderson described as "a splendid sparkling thing," and out on deck he felt irresistibly impelled to face eastward away from his native land toward a France that was growing "huge" in his imagination. Then a cold, damp mist shut down, and he fell into his usual pattern of writing in the smoking lounge each morning and, in the afternoon, reading or walking the deck with Paul and Tennessee and observing the other passengers. Often the three were joined by a young Chicago friend they had spotted on board, Ernestine Evans, who had lived in a Fifty-seventh Street studio across from Floyd Dell's in 1913 and was now on her way to observe famine conditions in the Soviet Union for the magazine *Asia*. She was to see the Andersons and Paul frequently in Paris and became Tennessee's usual sightseeing companion there.[22]

Catching up on his correspondence during these lazy days, Anderson wrote first to Ben Huebsch to tell him of his dismay at getting out the proof for *The Triumph of the Egg* and finding that the printer had muddled the job. There was neither proof nor manuscript for several stories, and the title story was included in manuscript only, unset. He read what proof there was and had the whole miscellaneous package ready to ship off to Huebsch as soon as possible after landing. His disappointment was all the greater because he had hoped to have *The Triumph of the Egg* appear early in the fall rather than late, as had *Poor White*, the delay of the latter having, he was convinced, adversely affected sales. Near the end of the voyage he also wrote Waldo reaffirming their old friendship and encouraging him in his new more humble resolve of "buckling down to the work" of creating beauty.[23]

On May 23 the *Rochambeau* docked at Le Havre, having come through the English Channel in a chilly fog that had given Sherwood a severe head cold; but he hardly noticed it on the train that immediately took the party to Paris through the flowering French countryside. Sherwood,

Ernestine would remember, was "delighted at everything" he saw along the way, delighted also to see the small, elegant figure of Lewis Galantière welcoming him at the Gare St. Lazare in Paris. Lewis, whom he had known in Chicago as an employee of Kroch's bookstore and who since 1920 had been working in Paris with the International Chamber of Commerce, had generously appointed himself the Andersons' chief guide around Paris during their stay, and now saw them to the small, clean, inexpensive Hotel Jacob et d'Angleterre at No. 44 on the narrow Rue Jacob close to the Seine on the Left Bank. There for the sum of ten francs a day, or about eighty cents American, the Andersons took a big comfortable room with a bay window overlooking the street, while Paul had a room close by. At last Sherwood was in Paris, the city he had dreamed about since he had picked up in a secondhand store a copy of Eugene Sue's *The Mysteries of Paris* and had begun picturing Paris as a metropolis of wide avenues, beautiful women, and palaces set beside dark, violent tenement streets filled with, as he had then told Galantière, "'thousands of simple people wondering what it's all about—and not realizing at all that they're living in a place most of us would give our eye-teeth to get to.'"[24]

During his six weeks in Paris, Sherwood remained for the most part delighted by the city and the people. On their first full day there Paul took him and Tennessee on a preliminary tour of the sights. A little to the south of the Hotel Jacob was the Luxembourg Garden with its trees, walks, and central pool; five minutes stroll to the east lay the Ile de la Cité like a huge ship in the Seine, the square towers of Notre Dame dominating over the far end; just to the north on the Right Bank of the Seine with its side quays and its bridges, only ten minutes walk from the hotel, was the long gray bulk of the Louvre facing west toward the Tuileries Gardens, the Place de la Concorde and, beyond, the broad tree-lined Avenue des Champs-Elysées rising toward the Arc de Triomphe, which loomed in the distance at the center of the Place de l'Etoile. The city vistas under the pearly skies were almost too much for the midwesterner. Paul would later tell of

Anderson's first glimpse of the Place du Carrousel near the Louvre. [Paul] saw Anderson rubbing his eyes, and thought he must have acquired a cinder, in memory of Chicago days. Not so; Mr. Anderson was weeping, and he continued to weep through lunch; for, said he, "It is so much more beautiful than anything I had imagined."[25]

One of his few less-than-happy experiences, a first meeting with Gaston Gallimard, who still delayed with publishing translations of his work, occurred a day or so later. Accompanied by Sylvia Beach, proprietor of the Shakespeare and Company bookshop, who had agreed to act as interpreter, Anderson went to the publisher's office at the *Nouvelle Revue*

Française and was kept in the waiting room so long that, in Sylvia's words, he "got angry and threatened to break up the place." Fortunately Gallimard did finally see him and mollified him with assurances that some of his books would be published as soon as they could be properly translated. On the other hand, Sherwood's earlier meeting with Miss Beach had been entirely satisfactory. He had dropped in at Shakespeare and Company, not too far away from the Hotel Jacob, his eye caught by a copy of *Winesburg, Ohio* in the window display of books in English. Sherwood introduced himself to the proprietor as the author of the book and, his sense of liberation at being in Paris calling up memories of his liberation from business, told her almost at once a version of that wrenching episode, "how he had suddenly abandoned his home and a prosperous paint business, had simply walked away one morning, shaking off forever the fetters of respectability and the burden of security." Warmly responding to him as a man of "great charm," Miss Beach nevertheless saw him as a complex person, "a mixture of poet and evangelist (without the preaching), with perhaps a touch of the actor. Anyhow . . . a most interesting man."[26]

Past and present liberations were much on Anderson's mind in Paris. The journalist William Bird met him with Tennessee in a cafe one day, heard Sherwood say he was "homesick" for some Bull Durham tobacco for the cigarettes he rolled himself, and invited them to his and his wife's apartment, where he gave Sherwood a pound of it. Over drinks the two couples talked; or rather Sherwood did most of the talking, Bird later recalled of his guest with his "shaggy hair" and rough "prominent" features, talking mostly about how he left business. He had been worried about the business, had not been doing well financially, and one night he had an inspiration to "pack his bag and just walk out on" the business. The next morning he did so and—this he emphasized to Bird—felt wonderful and relieved to depart so abruptly. Here was another version that the storyteller was testing out on another audience.[27]

Through Galantière, Copeau, and Rosenfeld, Anderson at once began meeting a series of French writers, literary critics, and university professors interested in American literature. One of the critics even dressed in morning coat and striped trousers for the occasion and was brought into the hotel room by Paul for formal presentation to the American author, who stood by the marble-topped table and chair in the bay window. Anderson spoke almost no French, and communication, unless it could be in English, was limited, but he enjoyed being lionized to such an extent and was especially gratified by the attention of Charles Le Verrier, critic and college president, who wanted to, and eventually did, review some of his books. Anderson probably met André Gide at this time, but at any rate he reported, as he doubtless had been told by his friends, that among French writers Gide was "the most powerful in himself and in his influence. . . ."

He certainly met Léon Bazalgette, translator of Whitman, who was enormously widely read and, much to Anderson's pleasure, knew and admired some of his Ohio tales. After their first long talk in the hotel room, Anderson and "this man with the gray, pallid skin and the kind eyes" met several more times over bottles of wine in sidewalk cafes to discuss writers and writing, Bazalgette filling him in on the contemporary French literary scene. This man, Anderson felt, was the first real "cosmopolitan" and "European man of culture" he had ever met. Possibly Bazalgette's comments had something to do with the unexpected criticism of France and French writers that Anderson set down as the second entry in the notebook that he began keeping as a kind of journal on May 28.

There is something in the air of present day France, a kind of death. Before the war one felt something growing here. Now there is a kind of bitterness. I am sure it is affecting, will deeply affect French artists. Men who before the war were searching, hungering, striving, have fallen to scolding. The men I have so far met give me no sense of something growing. For example it does not seem to me that present day France could now produce a figure as naive, honest, sweet in his outlook on life as our Sandburg.

As for Jacques Copeau, he could still be charming over wine in a cafe, but he and his Théâtre du Vieux Colombier, Anderson felt, had become too much the successful center of a dramatic cult. One night soon after their arrival in Paris the Andersons and Paul had gone to see Copeau's troupe do a production of *Twelfth Night,* a disappointing experience since the translation and delivery were for them too declamatory.[28]

One of the English-speaking expatriates Anderson met in Paris disappointed him even more. Around the end of May, Ezra Pound hospitably called on him at the Hotel Jacob, but Sherwood thought him "an empty man with nothing to give." Meetings with two other literary celebrities were much more satisfying. Perhaps urged on by Ben Huebsch, who had published *Dubliners* and *A Portrait of the Artist,* and by Sylvia Beach, who had just decided to publish *Ulysses,* Anderson wrote James Joyce on May 28 requesting the privilege of calling on him. Almost as soon as he received the note, Joyce instead called on Sherwood, Tennessee, and Paul. Sherwood found him "a long, somewhat gloomy, handsome man" with—the observation was characteristic of the author of *Winesburg*—"the most delicately lovely hands I have ever seen on a human being" and with an Irish wit and smile that offset the gloom. "Among all modern writers," Anderson wrote in his notebook, which he carried everywhere, "his lot has perhaps been the hardest and it may well be that his Ulysses is the most important book that will be published in this generation." Clearly Sylvia Beach had been proselytizing on behalf of Joyce and his novel—so successfully that Anderson paid her the $12 prepublication subscription price for a copy of *Ulysses,* prepared for her a list of possible American subscribers, and sent "a personal note with the prospectuses" for the book.[29]

It was Beach also who readily agreed, at Anderson's request, to introduce him to Gertrude Stein, that "great master of words," as he spoke of her. Apparently on a Friday evening in early June, Sylvia took Sherwood and Tennessee to the already famous apartment at 27, rue de Fleurus, with its walls lined with pictures by Picasso and other contemporaries. While Alice Toklas, as she did with all visiting wives, frustrated Tennessee's determined attempts to enter the conversation, Gertrude and Sherwood talked together like immediate old friends. He told her simply and deferentially that he admired her use of words in *Three Lives* and *Tender Buttons* and that these books had influenced his own development as a writer. Stein, hungry for literary recognition, was "visibly touched" by his praise and told him that he was "really the only person" who understood what her writing was "all about." Though Anderson would later admit to another individual that actually he did not understand much of her recent writing, he had sincerely appreciated her attempts to freshen language; and now meeting in person this "strong woman with legs like stone pillars," he recognized a fellow oral narrator, one who could "tell stories with an American shrewdness in getting the tang and kick into the telling." He returned to the rue de Fleurus at least once that June to introduce Galantière, and perhaps other times. The lifelong affectionate, though never close, friendship between Stein and Anderson had begun.[30]

But Paris was not just a place for meeting literary figures. After a few overcast days, the weather turned comfortably cool and bright day after day so that mornings Anderson could sit under the great trees of the Luxembourg Garden or in a favorite spot he had discovered on a terrace overlooking the Tuileries Gardens. Here, perched above the life of the boulevards, he found it "very quiet like being in a shell while the wind blows outside." He sometimes rented a chair for a few centimes and, with the broad flat terrace wall for a writing desk, entered random impressions of Paris and the French in his notebook; or simply sat pleasuring in a city, which, unlike American ones, he felt, put no barrier between himself and "the imagined beauty of life." Part of that beauty came from the fact that Paris was a city of painters and painting, and frequently in the afternoons he went with Paul to see the Old Masters in the Louvre or the Cézannes and the Impressionists then in the Musée du Luxembourg or, at least once, a current exhibit by Picasso, the painter in whom he decided, perhaps with Stein's assistance, "the strength of the revolutionist movement is pretty well centered." Having been mainly interested in contemporary painting and long suspicious that the great painters of the past had been overrated by second-rate living ones he had known, he rejoiced to find that Rembrandt, Leonardo, and others actually were "great because of simplicity, directness, wholeness." These were qualities he wanted for his own painting.[31]

Ernestine Evans, who thought that children's playgrounds might be as informative about a country as its museums, accompanied the two men on only one of their visits to the Louvre and was amused rather than shocked to hear them seriously and often in "sexy" terms discuss how the painter must have felt when painting each picture. In one of the longer entries in his notebook, however, Anderson described in other, though as imaginative, terms two of the Rembrandts that he and Paul returned to again and again. In the first—"a golden and brown mass of figures, horses, wild half-mystical scenery"—"Everything was suspended movement. Here was all life and none of it—something out beyond life, mystic, wonderful, caught in paint." The second was of a "little old man lying in bed . . . in a sea of cushions," beside the bed "a queenly woman, past youth, in full splendor of womanhood."

> The old man had already slipped away, he sank into gorgeous dreams. Nothing human of him was left, just the sense of the dreams. Rembrandt had painted into the picture his own, half barbaric, splendid, mystic conception of death.

These two paintings—one of life, yet suspended life, one of death—were the only ones by any artist Anderson described in his notebook. Clearly they had tremendous impact on him, an impact that, perhaps linking up with that winter walk in Palos Park months ago, might well have stirred within him an obscure creative impulse toward a story he would soon attempt to write.[32]

All Paris was a kind of museum, one "without walls," to be experienced in the same intense but leisurely way that the hardworking but relaxed Parisians seemed to conduct their lives. Anderson was constantly enchanted by the physical beauty of so many of the buildings, the truest beauty, he felt, showing marks of its origin in medieval times, when artists inspired by religious faith had anonymously set stone on stone; yet these buildings, patinaed with age, were inhabited unselfconsciously by the living. After dining one evening soon after their arrival, in a little eighteenth-century cafe on the Left Bank overlooking the Ile de la Cité, the Andersons and Paul walked to Notre Dame and sat for a long time before its "delicate and massive beauty," Sherwood pleased that the cathedral's gargoyles, those "sensual grotesques," looked down on prostitutes drifting past and on a drunken couple "laughing and wrestling under the shadow of the church." In the Gothic mode the medieval artists had accounted for all aspects of human nature.[33]

Daily Anderson immersed himself in Paris. With Paul, sometimes with Tennessee, most often alone, Sherwood would put a few francs in his pocket and "plunge" into the city of an afternoon or evening to find what he could. During the day he might observe the Seine and its quays with the life of the barge people and women washing clothes at the river's edge, or a sudden street battle near the École des Beaux Arts between two rival groups of young painters, or the exhibition of his skill by a juggler in one of Anderson's favorite little restaurants, the Rendezvous des Mariniers in the port district of the Ile de la Cité, frequented by fishermen and river-boatmen, or best of all, the teams of uncastrated stallions pulling great-wheeled carts loaded with sacks of grain or hogsheads of wine. Were he to live in Paris, he would like to be a carter cracking his long whip over six of these splendid horses, for here was a life "more noble than anything machinery has yet achieved." Sometimes at night he would go alone, as he wrote to Bab,

into old Paris. There are streets where one may almost touch the walls on each side. Slinking figures go past. Little prostitutes shout at you. Up the narrow old stair-ways is the rank smell of life.

Generally, he found, French people treated him well, contrary to what he had been warned to expect, perhaps because he mostly kept away from those parts of the city where the many Americans, tourists or expatriates, tended to herd together. (That he occasionally wandered into such a part, however, is shown by the fact that he first met young John Dos Passos over a glass of beer at one of the American-frequented cafes around St-Germain des Prés.) He even obtained from a French barber for the equivalent of fourteen cents a non-American haircut that left his hair "somewhat long" as he vainly preferred it.[34]

One night in early June a particularly "lovely thing" happened, an incident he set down in detail in his notebook like a moment of community in one of his own tales.

My hotel is in a narrow street in the midst of the old city of Paris. Last night I awoke as a clock somewhere in the neighborhood was striking three. The whole city was silent. Suddenly from far off a nightingale began singing madly. It flew into our street and for a long time sat perched on some building near at hand. The clear lovely notes rang thro the narrow street. I heard window shutters opening. Others in the street were awake—listening. The lovely bird had united all of us. For ten minutes all in the street listened carried out of our self by the sweet song of the bird. Then it flew away, its song growing fainter and fainter as it floated away over the roofs of the city.[35]

There were the trips outside Paris. On the memorable Sunday of June 5, Galantière took the Andersons, Paul, a young French poet and the poet's girlfriend to Provins, a market town some forty miles southeast of

Paris. Sherwood was in an ebullient mood. As the train was pulling out of the Gare de l'Est, Lewis remembered,

Sherwood stared at the enginemen and wipers and switchmen in the wide and dirty yard. "You wouldn't think these little Frenchmen could do things like running railroads, would you?" he said. He was very pleased with his remark, and chuckled.

Reaching Provins, the party walked from the "new "town, built in a valley in the fourteenth century, up the hill to the twelfth-century "old" town on top. After wandering about the narrow streets among houses "whose old beauty," Sherwood wrote Bab, "makes the tears come," the six of them went into a trellised arbor in a garden behind a cafe, were brought wine and flowers by an attractive, broad-mouthed peasant girl, and sat around a table for a long time happily chatting and admiring the view. Sherwood began to read from his notebook a Testament he had recently written, probably a Whitmanesque one celebrating the "invisible cord" that connects the poet with his dreaming self and that self with the men and women he sees in the rush and clamor of a modern city. While listening to his "grave and sweet" voice, Lewis noticed a bent old woman standing at one end of the arbor, also listening. When he spoke to her, Lewis translating for Sherwood, she told him that she liked the man who was reading even though she didn't understand his words. Lewis asked her for something to eat for the party, but the old woman said that this cafe never served food; yet when Sherwood smiled at her, she persuaded the cafe family to produce some of their own food—an omelette, sardines, some cold ham. Then while waiting for the food to be brought, the old woman, "walking beside Sherwood and not quite daring to take his arm," showed him every part of the fruit and vegetable garden. This midwestern American, Galantière concluded, might be naive in his genuine amazement that "these little Frenchmen" understood trains and ran them efficiently, but he nevertheless was charmed by the French and in turn charmed them. Essentially without their language, he won the French with his smile and friendly chuckle, his obvious readiness, perhaps not to understand them but to appreciate and accept them.[36]

Sherwood loved Provins as much as Lewis did and called the whole visit there "a very happy time." On the following Sunday, the twelfth, the excursion was to Fontainebleau, where Anderson's delight in the palace was partly marred by the sniggering jokes of the guide about the kings' mistresses. He would have preferred to see the palace by himself without even an intelligent guide's commentary. "One does not receive the caress of beauty thro the intellect," he wrote in his notebook. "It creeps upon you or flashes down on you like a stroke of lightning." Still, one of his pleasantest memories would be of drinking "beer with men and women you

love, in a cafe, under a giant tree, in the forest of Fountainbleau." Beauty
flashed down on him on two other excursions, to Chartres Cathedral on
Sunday, June 19, and to Amiens Cathedral on the twenty-third. Very
likely, as his various comments on medievalism and Gothic architecture
suggest, he had prepared himself with a reading of Henry Adams's *Mont-
Saint-Michel and Chartres* or had listened to Paul discoursing on Adams's
theories; yet he was sincere in praising Chartres to Bab as "the final last
word in beauty. It is almost all poetry in stone and the glass is the most
lovely radiant moving mass of colors and light conceivable." Three years
later he would climax his *A Story Teller's Story* with the day at Chartres,
"that cathedral that had made me more deeply happy than any other work
of art I had ever seen."[37]

Almost certainly on the evening of June 11 he had another kind of experience, which also remained in his memory. Three days after the Andersons had arrived in Paris, Ernestine Evans had accompanied them to a
party for Americans where he had met her friend Rose Wilder Lane,
daughter of Laura Ingalls Wilder. Lane, a novelist and freelance writer,
was living in Paris and sending daily reports of her activities to the *San
Francisco Bulletin*. Although she had found *Winesburg* "disgusting," she
invited the Andersons to a party in her apartment the evening of the
eleventh after she had arrived home that morning from the all-night orgy
of the annual Quat'z Arts Ball. An adventurous, liberated woman, she had
nevertheless observed rather than participated in the sexual license of the
Ball but at her party was quite willing to talk frankly about what she had
witnessed. Anderson was so fascinated-repelled by her account that he
recorded in his notebook that the Ball "is a sex orgy that would be impossible in an Anglo Saxon civilization but nevertheless I am quite sure
that many of the participants, perhaps a majority of the men present were
English or American." Although at her party Lane found Anderson an un-
likable poseur, she more than once invited him and Tennessee to join other
Americans in Paris for a weekend at a small house, Les Lilas, she had
rented at Barbizon, weekends where, she noted with weary acerbity, there
was endless talk about food and sex but no indulging in the latter. These
contacts with Lane, whom he apparently did not care for either, would go
into Anderson's memory, later to be transformed by his imagination into
the Paris episode central to the development of *Dark Laughter*, the novel
he would write in 1924–25.[38]

So many impressions were crowding in on him that around mid-June
he stopped setting them down in his notebook and began merely storing
them up in his memory for recollection. He was doing other writing during those mornings in his perch above the Tuileries Gardens but, he now
admitted to Bab, not very much, mainly work intermittently on a revised
ending of *Windy McPherson's Son* for the new edition Huebsch had prom-

ised to bring out. By June 24 this revision was "about completed." Soon after June 11 the rest of the printer's proof for *The Triumph of the Egg* finally reached him, and for the next week or so he concentrated on reading it and getting it into the mails as soon as possible. He continued to correspond with Huebsch on other matters as well. While he was still on the *Rochambeau,* Ben had written him the good news that Boni and Liveright wanted to issue *Winesburg* in its Modern Library. Scrupulously fair as always, Ben had given arguments about the offer pro and con, pointing out that although a Modern Library edition "would be in direct competition" with the Huebsch one, it would open up a new market for the book. Given a choice to respond yes or no, Anderson consulted with Galantière and on June 9 cabled yes, then wrote Huebsch to request that the Modern Library edition include a list of all his published books, including *The Triumph of the Egg.* There was also the matter of the cover for *The Triumph,* a suggested sketch for which he had left with the publisher before sailing. Ben had hoped to carry out the suggestion, but a conversation with the book designer convinced him that such a cover would be both expensive and nondurable, a conclusion Anderson accepted without protest. On June 24 he received Huebsch's June 10 letter describing the more serious matter of new delays in publication resulting from current "labor troubles" in the printing and bookbinding businesses.[39]

Yet another kind of delay had developed with Gallimard's projected French edition of *Winesburg.* Both Copeau and the publisher, who had a slight reading knowledge of English, had long objected that Madame Marguerite Gay's too-literal translation of the stories was taking the "flavor" away from them, and now they decided that it must be done over. In this matter Anderson was generously more concerned for the Frenchwoman's disappointment than with his own, for he had grown fond of this sensitive, thirtyish banker's wife. Back in February at his request Galantière had called on her and had written of her as "a small homely person with short legs, a big nose, a lisping, fluent and earnest speech," with a "whole-souled appreciation, accurate insight into your meaning and honest, deep enthusiasm for your work." Simply as a labor of admiration she wished to preempt any hack translation with a conscientious French version of a book, which, as she told Galantière, had "completely bowled [her] over by its freshness, its freedom from affectation and (as she says) 'literariness' and its sincerity." Now that the author himself was in France, Madame Gay, on or around June 13, invited him and Galantière to tea at her home at 20, avenue Rapp, near the Eiffel Tower. Galantière would always remember how startled and shaken she was upon seeing Anderson for the first time, for, as she excitedly whispered to Lewis, the "artist" looked exactly as she had often envisioned him in her "mind's eye" while she was translating his stories. Sherwood's more amused recollection of his visit to this "upper class French home" was of his getting down on the floor and trying to explain to the gathering the game of baseball. "It was just such an evening," he wrote in his notebook, "as one might have spent in the home of a well to do banker in Iowa."[40]

For some unexplained reason Copeau and Gallimard reversed themselves late in June on the quality of Madame Gay's translation, perhaps because it had been commended by Hélène Bousinesq, a friend of Bazalgette who taught English and had done the French version of Frank's *Our America*. Sherwood wrote Madame Gay the good news before a final visit to her at her country home in the Paris suburb of Ville-d'Avray on July 2 or 3, just before his departure from the city. That visit was a perfect conclusion to the Paris adventure. The Gay estate was on a small lake, and a garden sloped to the water's edge. There "in the garden amid the flowers" author and translator, together with another admirer of *Winesburg*, a M. de Marabray, talked away "a delightful afternoon," Anderson urging Mme. Gay to "feel free in your work," that is, to follow the spirit of his book, not the letter.[41]

Before going on to England as planned, Sherwood, Tennessee, and Paul left Paris, probably on July 4, for the Channel town of Cabourg, some twenty miles across the bay of the Seine from Le Havre. The little Hotel du Nord with its garden, set among the gaily painted houses and many rose gardens of the town, cost only about $2.40 a day for both room and "good fare." Here for several days the three caught up on the sleep they had missed during their last weeks in Paris, swam in the ocean, sunned on the beach, and reflected on their French experience. Paul, Anderson wrote to Bab, had at last developed into a fine companion. Intense, hypersensitive, possessive, he had at first wanted to wander Paris alone with Sherwood—as Ernestine Evans had privately observed also—but when Sherwood had bluntly told him that he often wished to go off by himself, Paul had eventually accepted the situation with grace. Of Tennessee, Sherwood continued to have almost nothing to say in his letters back to America, nor had he made any reference to her in his notebook; and she had more often seen the sights with Ernestine than with him. The Andersons seemed to Galantière to be very happy together in Paris; yet it appeared that for Sherwood the Paris visit had happened to *him,* not to *them.* His concern was with his own reactions as artist—and here, reflecting further on how "skillful . . . about life" the Parisians had been and how even the town life in France was "half joyous" and lacked the American oppressiveness—he felt that his real roots were nevertheless in his own land. Even early in his stay in Paris, when walking one day in the Garden of the Palais-Royal, he and Paul had agreed that "while American cities were all comparatively ugly nothing could tempt us to come away to live permanently in a European city. We agreed that it was in some way a man's part to play the hand fate had dealt him in life." This conviction would grow increasingly strong in him during his last few weeks abroad.[42]

In the restfulness of Cabourg he got back briefly to work, writing in his notebook again after some three weeks of entering little or nothing. Now he turned from recording brief impressions of France and the French to trying pieces that were longer and about Americans. Apparently it was at this time that he began but did not finish a portrait of Gertrude Stein, summarized but did not elaborate a story, "A Woman's Evening," about a Mary Cochran-like person's relation to men and other women, and then sketched out in some detail a frame tale in which the first-person narrator, on a train trip to Kansas to write about "the life of a man who manufactures incubators," falls in with another man who tells as his own life story what Anderson obviously intends as a parody of a Western romance. Very likely it was this last piece, "The Story of a Day," that he was referring to when he wrote Huebsch on July 5 that as soon as he had finished it, he would "get busy on the novel," that is, *Ohio Pagans,* which he had dropped months earlier and which he would not in fact get busy on until after his return to the United States. He promised to send on the revisions of *Windy McPherson's Son* as soon as he could find a typewriter to put them into fair copy, but his main purpose was to request that, since the title of his forthcoming book was *The Triumph of the Egg,* the title of the story be changed to simply "The Egg," a change he would later explain as showing that the book was not printed for the sake of that one tale.[43]

Presumably the Andersons and Paul took the two-hour train trip to Le Havre on July 9 in preparation for a night crossing of the Channel; for on the bright Sunday morning of July 10 they landed at Southampton and went by train to London, where they engaged rooms at Cranston's Kenilworth Hotel, 97 Great Russell Street, close by the British Museum. That same day Anderson sent notes to John Cournos and to Thomas Moult, poet, novelist, editor of the little magazine *Voices,* whom Raymond O'Neil had urged him to look up, to see when he might meet them. Then the three Americans went out for a first walk in what Sherwood felt to be a dignified, solid, endlessly vast city.

They had arrived in London at a fortunate time for visitors. England was in the midst of one of the longest droughts on record, and the authorities worried that the Thames, London's main water supply, might be drying up; but though the weather was unprecedentedly hot, the skies, as they had in France, remained sunny and clear. Sherwood did little of the usual sightseeing, though he several times viewed the Old Masters at the National Gallery, saw the Elgin marbles at the British Museum, and went to the Tate especially for the Turners and Blakes, for color and the visionary. Much of the time, however, he walked day and night in different sections of the city, in the "smart streets" of the West End and in the "poor streets" of the East, "seeing the crowds, looking at them, thinking of them and of America too." By the fourteenth he had given himself a stomachache from evenings of drinking ale in East End pubs, where he talked for hours with the regular customers and compared their English speech and attitudes with his American ones. He liked London, he wrote Bab, yet "I'll be rather glad to go back. The trip here has taught me how much I am American, how much I want for America." And he added, significantly: "I do not write much but I gather impressions—not so much concerning all these people over here as concerning the people at home, the people of my own mind."[44]

London was more deserted that usual because of the heat, but he was able to meet a number of persons who interested him. Thomas Moult gratifyingly arranged to publish in the autumn issue of *Voices* three poems from *The Triumph of the Egg,* the opening and closing pieces and "Motherhood." When Sherwood and Paul called on John Cournos at his home a day or two after reaching England, Sherwood took an instant and permanent liking for this rather retiring Russian Jew who had lived in the United States and hated its mechanization. Cournos would remember vividly that Sherwood was wearing that day a very beautiful shirt, blue and of a soft fabric, a two-guinea shirt on sale for one guinea, which he had already found time to purchase at an expensive shop in the Haymarket. Cournos openly admired the shirt and was profoundly touched when later that day Anderson returned to the shop and had a shirt of the same color and fabric sent to him as a gift. The gesture was typical, Cournos felt, both of Anderson's generosity and his real love of fine fabrics, which he would sometimes go into a shop just to touch. Anderson was one of the few people Cournos ever met of whom one could say that one knew him as soon as one met him. Very outgoing and understanding, he combined masculine strength and a great feminine sensitivity toward others.[45]

Another person he met was a young American black woman, Ruth Anna Fisher. In a subsequent correspondence between them she at first resented a letter from Anderson gently accusing her and "all other intellectual colored people" of assuming in advance that no one could understand them, but later thanked him for that letter, "one of the kindest . . . I have ever had—one which has made me, as near as it is humanly possible to do so, forget race consciousness and loathe the propaganda which goes with it." Yet another person he saw was an American, Harold Stearns, just arrived in London after having completed his editing of the ironically titled *Civilization in the United States* on the day he sailed from New York. Sherwood told him that he "was really 'European'—and didn't know it," speaking with "a curious earnestness" that may have come from Sherwood's growing desire to return home and from some concern that it was this "queer bird," in flight from America, who had been commissioned to write an introduction to the Modern Library *Winesburg.*[46]

Anderson's most useful meeting in London was with his new English publisher, Jonathan Cape. Cape assured him that he would issue *Poor White* in September and *Winesburg, Ohio* the following spring. It was apparently Cape who arranged for him to write for *The Saturday Review*, at a fee, his impressions of England and the English, these to be stated forthrightly even if hostile. Less helpful, it would turn out, was Anderson's meeting, probably through Cape, with a young man named Andrew Dakers, who had left the Curtis Brown literary agency to form his own business and who, by September, charmed Anderson, much to the annoyance of the astute Huebsch, into a year's unproductive employment as his literary agent for selling magazine rights to his stories.[47]

The *Saturday Review* fee, however, helped Sherwood and Tennessee, together with Paul, to go up to Oxford to escape London's heat and to provide Sherwood with a quiet, less expensive place in which to work, By July 21 the three were settled in at The Golden Cross Inn at Oxford, "one of the most lovely towns we saw that summer, or any summer." That night they dined with Edward O'Brien, who had dedicated *The Best Short Stories of 1920* to Anderson and who lived in Oxford. O'Brien and his mother continued to be hospitable to the Americans throughout their two-week stay in Oxford, and Sherwood came to enjoy this "girlish gentle man with colorless blue eyes" who so strongly praised his fictional art.[48]

Afternoons he usually walked the countryside around Oxford; on July 22 he amusedly wrote Bab that the following day he was "to play golf with the director of the Moscow Art Theater, a hindu prince and an Englishman." He had obtained a typewriter in a little shop in town, however, and every morning he wrote in his large comfortable room or in the courtyard of the inn, breaking off work from time to time for a pint of "the best ale I have found in England." By Sunday the twenty-fourth he had at last typed up for mailing to Huebsch the revised ending of *Windy McPherson's Son*. Then he turned to the *Saturday Review* article, which he titled "'Hello, Yank: What About England?'" The article was a kind of summing up of his brief but active encounter with the English. Admitting that he is a "typical American," a midwesterner, not a New England "Yank," Anderson attempts to define the American attitude toward England and the English. Americans love England and like individual Englishmen, yet resent their smug and mistaken assumption that, because of the common language, they understand America. But, first, there is little English blood left in polyglot America, and second, a struggle is going on in the United States to produce a new culture which even a typical American like himself cannot yet understand, hence much less can the English.[49]

Subsequently Anderson commented that his politely blunt plea for a more accurate understanding of his country "stirred up a little fury" of English response after it was published in the August 6 issue of *The*

Saturday Review. He was essentially saying in his own way what the journalist C. E. Bechhofer had just been asserting in his "Impressions of Recent American Literature," a series of letters to *The Times Literary Supplement* arguing that this literature, "which holds extraordinary promise," could only be understood as a revolt against "Puritanism" or whatever one wished to call the present dominant, English-oriented standards of American culture. Cape might have shown Anderson this series; for on June 23, Bechhofer named him, along with Dreiser, Masters, Cather, and Lewis, as the "most interesting" Middle West prose writers, and on June 30 had praised *Poor White,* though with some reservation, "as an example of the newer and better strain in the Middle-Western writing." Such timely praise, even if qualified, encouraged Anderson to hope that his work might make "a deeper impression" in England than at home, a hope that was strengthened when he learned from Huebsch that Somerset Maugham had recommended *Winesburg,* in a current interview, as a description of "what Middle West America really is" and as "a collection of stories which suggest Chekhov in their subtlety and realism."[50]

Now that the European trip was drawing to an end, it was America, not France or England, that was growing huge in Anderson's imagination. In what time he had left after completing "Hello, Yank," he returned to writing in his notebook "concerning the people at home." The meeting with Ruth Fisher put him in mind, in "A Forbidden Friendship," of his Fairhope experience with blacks, whose singing had sent him to seek something that "was very elusive, is very elusive." Leaving this tale of reminiscence unfinished, he set down a second Testament, which mixed nostalgia and hope: "To see all America in the leaf that dances before the nose as you sit in a cafe in a village in France or in a park in London."[51]

It was time to go home. On August 2 the Andersons and Rosenfeld returned to London and the Kenilworth Hotel, from where on August 5 Sherwood wrote a last grateful note to the hospitable O'Brien, telling him that, "It has been a great experience for me—this coming to look at Europe, not the less great because I have a new and stronger faith in America and Americans." Paul seems to have taken passage home alone about this time, perhaps because he preferred first-class accommodations to the all second-class ones of the *Rochambeau.* Considering what happened to the passengers on that ship, he was certainly better off.

Probably on August 9 the Andersons left London for Southampton to take a Channel boat back to Le Havre, for the *Rochambeau* sailed from the French port on the tenth. Since all its passengers were either second-class or steerage (the class to which immigrants to the United States were assigned), a year-old American law ranked both classes together and both were required to submit to vaccination against typhus and smallpox before embarkation lest these diseases, still widespread in postwar Europe, be transmitted to the United States and become epidemic. The second-class American passengers were outraged at being "treated like immigrants," and became even more furious when the overstrong vaccine from the U.S. Public Health Service gave a number of passengers painful reactions. It was not a happy voyage. The day after the *Rochambeau* arrived in New York on August 19, the *New York Times* ran a page two story describing how, "as they went down the gangway from the liner," the "275 wrathful Americans, among them the Harvard Glee Club and . . . Sherwood Anderson, the novelist," loudly protested the "crime" perpetrated against them. Judging by his unfinished description of the vaccination incident in his notebook under the title "Embarkation," Anderson had sympathized in Le Havre more with the immigrants than with his humiliated fellow passengers. Whether he himself subsequently had a painful reaction to his vaccination is not known, but an immediate cause for anger was the fact that Tennessee's vaccination "took" just as the *Rochambeau* was reaching New York, making her so ill that they both went at once to Karl's home in Westport so that she could recover. Perhaps the *Times* account at least gave Sherwood the satisfaction of seeing that he had become "newsworthy" in his role as writer.[52]

Ultimately far more satisfying to him would be what he had written during that troubled voyage home; for it was probably then that he entered in his notebook an unmistakable, though unfinished, version of one of his finest stories, "Death in the Woods." This untitled version, one of several he would write over the next few years, begins with a description of the nightmares suffered by "Mother Winters," who at thirty-six "had got suddenly old" and whose body aches agonizingly. One of her frightening dreams is of being trapped, unable to breathe, in a great building filled with many domestic animals, all of them disturbed and crying out. She tries unsuccessfully to lift the "heavy iron bar" that fastens the door and imprisons her and the animals so that light and air may come in. Although the final version of "Death in the Woods" would begin quite differently with the establishment of a relation between a young-old woman and a semiautobiographical narrator, already in this early draft Anderson seems to have been linking himself to the woman imaginatively since, despite differences, Mother Winters' nightmare shows striking resemblances to the one the author would assign to himself in Note 3 of *A Story Teller's Story*, that in which he thinks himself to be dead and buried in a marble sepulcher, or standing in "the great cathedral at Chartres," or dead and standing in spirit in "a large half-ruined and empty factory." Struggling half-awake, fearing the onset of a depression so severe that all the muscles of his body will ache, he lapses again into the dream where he waits terrified in a "great empty place," unable to breathe, while a "great iron bell" (here a symbol of industrialized America) swings silently over him in darkness, then drops and imprisons him. Both nightmares, furthermore, appear to have certain roots in the reality described in Anderson's note-book piece, "Embarkation," which begins suggestively, "A woman of thirty five in a great shed like building at Havre." Without transition the sketch shifts to describing first the second-class passengers, who, confined to the building for vaccination, are disturbed and complaining, and then the immigrants who stand in "a long roped in place . . . like cattle in a pen." Since the fragment thereupon ends with the tantalizing sentence, "An idea came to me," we never learn what happens to the "woman of thirty five"; but Mother Winters' aching body has at least its analogue in those vaccinated passengers whose "arms and limbs," as the *Times* put it decorously, "had become inflamed five days after leaving Havre," who had "suffered much pain," and who as a result might well have had night-mares, a condition which, given the general temper of the voyage, would have been known to the other passengers.

In the remaining half of the "Mother Winters" piece the similarities be-tween her story and that of Mrs. Grimes in "Death in the Woods" become much more direct, even to some of the phraseology—the decaying Grimes house, the violent husband, the woman's feeding of the farm animals, a dog who follows her, even the beginning of a flashback in which her hus-band-to-be gets her, a kind of "bound girl," away from the household of a German farmer. Perhaps the most significant aspect of the notebook ver-sion, however, is the way it seems to have sprung creatively, like "'Hello, Yank'" but at a far deeper level, from the impact of Anderson's recent European experiences on his American materials. Even in this unfinished version the young-old middlewestern country woman appears designed to reveal, like the old man in Rembrandt's painting, Anderson's "own, half barbaric, splendid, mystic conception of death."[53]

The Anderson's return to New York, as the *Times* story indicates, was not exactly as planned. Tennessee's illness delayed for several days her de-parture to Lake Chateaugay and the Bentley camp. By August 23, Sher-wood had returned from Westport to New York, putting up at the Hotel Algonquin and expecting to see friends for the next ten days. Word came, however, that he was in danger of losing his "bread and butter" Owens-boro account. Since he had returned to the United States "about broke," he hurriedly left for Chicago on the twenty-fourth, the European adven-ture now only a glorious memory.[54]

Anderson children, seated from the left: Sherwood, Ray, Earl, and Irwin. Standing: Stella and Karl.

Sherwood as a young boy in Clyde.

Busy Saturday in Clyde, 1906.

Early photograph of railroad station in Clyde.

Anderson family, 1899, left to right: Karl, Earl, Sherwood, Stella, Irwin, Ray.

Sherwood as soldier.

HOME OF ROOF-FIX
(CURE FOR ROOF TROUBLES)

Just a Word in Your Ear

JUST SUPPOSE you were going to buy a new roof this year. You would expect to pay anywhere from $2.00 to $4.00 per hundred square feet, wouldn't you? Now, the interest on $3.00 at six per cent is 18 cents per year. So the cost of the new roof would be 18 cents per square per year, not counting repairs, cost of putting on, or anything.

Well, we have proven to thousands of cases that with ROOF-FIX you can keep the old roof in perfect condition at five cents per square per year. Think it over. It's a dollar and cents matter. Buy ROOF-FIX and keep the price of the new roof in your pocket. Catalog free. Write for it.

THE ANDERSON MFG. CO., Elyria, Ohio

An ad for Anderson's business in Elyria, Ohio.

Empire Hotel, believed to be the Willard House in *Winesburg, Ohio*. Note man in right corner sitting on rail at railroad station.

The print ship at Marion. Anderson lived for a while in an apartment on the second floor. (Sherwood Anderson papers, the Newberry Library, 108/3451)

The cabin (or one like it) where Anderson lived at Fairhope, Alabama, in 1920. (photo by David Spear)

Ripshin under construction, 1926. The X at the top right is Anderson's mark for the location of the writing cabin. (Sherwood Anderson papers, the Newberry Library, 109/3500)

12

Arrival and Departure

1.

Chicago was hot, dirty, and ugly, and on arrival Anderson had to set about at once saving his financial "scalp" by "jollying a fat businessman"; but the glow of the European trip was still with him, and in spite of everything it made Chicago mean more to him than it ever had. "In an odd way," he wrote Paul gratefully, "the summer has given me more than I have ever got from any other adventure, a sense that I can adjust to my own life, that I do not need ever to leave my life and my story." Since the sublease of his Palos Park house ran until September 1, he settled temporarily in a friend's house in the city, got hold of a typewriter, and, having quickly rescued his Steele and Moberly accounts, plunged into the unfinished novel *Ohio Pagans*, hoping to tell it and other stories waiting on the doorstep of his mind "so they'll be understood, sometime, by somebody."[1]

All through September after he got back to Palos Park, the novel went steadily along. "It will be different from anything else I have ever done," he wrote Huebsch confidently, "more personal and with the social significance if it has any more hidden away." By the end of the month he had written around eighty thousand words, perhaps two-thirds of the projected book. During much of this time he was so deeply immersed in the lives of his imagined people that actual men and women seemed far away, but occasionally the actual ones intruded on him. He wrote Huebsch frequently, impatient to learn when *The Triumph of the Egg* would be out. In mid-September he received from Waldo, in Paris, a letter expressing hurt and resentment over one Sherwood had written him from London criticizing a piece Waldo had published in the *Nouvelle Revue Francaise* for what Sherwood had mistakenly thought to be a heroicizing of Sinclair Lewis. This was simply another instance of Sherwood's hostility beneath declared friendship, Waldo charged bitterly. Sherwood replied that Waldo needn't kick him downstairs, that "I'll get out of your house without violence until you want again the companionship I'm always at bottom eager to give you." Waldo wrote back somewhat mollified, and toward the end of October Sherwood expressed the friendly hope that "it wont be too long before we have a chance to walk and laugh together." But the breaking point had arrived. Sherwood had for too long been irritated by Waldo's thirst for fame, his intensities, his hypersensitivity to criticism; Waldo had for too long resented Sherwood's objections to *The Dark Mother,* his tendency to be the older brother putting down the younger, his insistence on such points of personal dogma as that, in Waldo's exaggerated words, "the less one knows of an art the more likely one is to excel in it." When *The Triumph of the Egg* appeared, Waldo would write to say "beautiful things" about it, and Sherwood would reply warmly, but the end of the year in effect brought the end of the friendship. Thereafter each would go his own way, rarely corresponding or meeting in person.[2]

At the same time that Sherwood was parting with Waldo, he was unexpectedly rejoining a former friend. Tennessee had returned from Alys Bentley's camp around September 11 with the astonishing news that Trigant Burrow, the psychoanalyst, had for some time been questioning Freudian principles, had dismissed his patients "just at the time when, after years of struggle he had begun to be financially successful," and had completed the manuscript of a book describing his new theories. Anderson at once wrote Burrow excitedly, asking about the book and offering to alert Ben Huebsch to it. Trigant replied that the thesis of his book, *Our Common Consciousness,* was "inherently identical" with that of *Marching Men,* and Sherwood immediately wrote Ben urging that Rosenfeld and Brooks see the manuscript as soon as possible. As it turned out, Ben did not accept it for publication, but Sherwood was of course impressed by Burrow's rejection of financial success in favor of his new beliefs, and in a warm letter on October 14 welcomed him to what he hoped was becoming "a real brotherhood" of Americans "who have at bottom the artist's point of view" and who might "make with their bodies and spirits," as Rosenfeld had put it, "a kind of fertilizing element in our soil." Burrow should not be turned aside by any interest in social movements, for artists were more important than social reformers; and he must be proud at being "a man coming into his kingdom" at last. "No man in America," Anderson asserted proudly, "ever really becomes anything until after forty."[3]

The circumstances of the letter also gave Anderson a chance to tell Trigant why he wanted Huebsch to look at his book.

Let me say a few things to you about him. He really at bottom, I suspect, doesn't know what a good book is or how to sell books, but he is a fine fellow; and at any rate you wouldn't have to, with him, go through the wearisome business of having some smart publisher tell you what to do to make your book sell. There is somewhere hidden away in Benny a real altruistic streak. In practice it takes itself out in radicalism. As you know, he is also publisher of the *Freeman*. Besides which he is a single-taxer, a Socialist, and I'm not sure what else.

As you know, my own books do not sell much, but I suppose a smart publisher could sell twice as many; at least several have come to me with the proposition that they would undertake to do something like that if I would only come to them. I've stuck to Ben because my years as a businessman cured me so effectually of any desire to make money that there is almost a satisfaction in some of Ben's inefficiencies as a publisher. You will know what I mean by that.

Quite aside from overstating the degree of Huebsch's "radicalism" and understating his literary taste, the characterization was somewhat disingenuous, considering Anderson's frequent inquiries to Ben as to when *The Triumph of the Egg* would appear and start making money. Still, it showed an appropriate gratitude toward the publisher who had put the resources of his small firm into helping build, if not Anderson's fortune, at least his reputation as a serious artist.

There were increasing proofs of how high that reputation had reached. Sherwood must already have seen the July issue of *Vanity Fair*, in which he was nominated, along with Madame Curie and Louis Untermeyer, for the magazine's "Hall of Fame," the caption under his photograph praising *Winesburg* and *Poor White* and their author's gift for "setting down in an unmannered prose the wild glamour and the intensity of beauty which American life at moments preserves for him." Now on October 12, Harry Hansen reported to the *Chicago Daily News* that he was finding on a visit to New York "tremendous interest in the growing literary consciousness of Chicago" and that "Sherwood Anderson has a host of followers." At about the same time Anderson received Edward O'Brien's request for permission to reprint "Brothers" in *The Best American Short Stories of 1921*. Already Ben Hecht had given him an advance copy of his first novel *Erik Dorn*, and although Sherwood found Ben's style too flashy, he presumably was pleased to see himself portrayed for the first time, and to a large extent favorably, as a fictional character, Warren Lockwood, middle-aged midwestern novelist, who, though naive about the arts and politics, understands people and events with "vivid simplicity."[4]

The most significant proof of his rising fame, however, came on or just before October 19 when Gilbert Seldes, managing editor of *The Dial*, notified him that he had been chosen to receive the first annual Dial Award to "acknowledge the service to letters of some one of those who have, during the twelvemonth, contributed to [*The Dial*] by the payment to him of two thousand dollars." The award was designed to provide both recognition of achievement and a year's freedom for further creative work, and Anderson followed an immediate telegram of acceptance with a letter of gratitude for the honor and the leisure time. Because of "the general business depression," he explained, "I am making practically nothing, and this money coming to me at just this time would give me freedom to do work I very much want to do." Seldes asked him to keep the award secret until the public announcement on December 20, and he was glad to comply; but a jubilant letter from Paul Rosenfeld informed him a week later that the editors of *The Dial* had "betrayed their secret" (at least to Paul) when they asked him to write a major article on Anderson, which was to appear in the January issue of the magazine along with a review of *The Triumph of the Egg* by Robert Morss Lovett, Anderson's University of Chicago friend from 1913. Paul hoped that Sherwood could send him a copy of all he had completed of "the New Testament" so that he could "live with it" while writing the article. He also passed on word of a talk with the publisher Alfred Harcourt, who in a roundabout way was trying to find out if Anderson could be hired away from Huebsch. Paul was pleased that Sherwood's writing was going well, whichever novel it was, asking the question "Marriages or hosses," suggesting that *Ohio Pagans* might have been intended to develop the racetrack world of "I Want to Know Why."[5]

Although denying the intention, Sherwood replied with a long letter obviously designed to shape Paul's article through an analysis of the Testaments and of his career as a writer as he now saw it. In his New Testament, "a purely experimental thing," Paul should observe that he was

trying to get at something that I think was very beautifully done in some parts of the Old Testament by the Hebrew poets. That is to say, I want to achieve in it rhythm of words with rhythm of thought. Do I make myself clear? The thing if achieved will be felt rather than seen or heard, perhaps. You see, as the things are, many of them violate my own conception of what I am after. In making this book I have felt no call to responsibility to anything but my own inner sense of what is beautiful in the arrangement of words and ideas. It is in a way my own Bible.

Paul must understand that Sherwood had grown up in an atmosphere like Mark Twain's, a different one from that of Paul, Brooks, and Frank where ideas and culture were taken seriously. From the time he began writing, as a way to achieve psychic health in the midst of his businessman's lies, he had conceived the Midwest, his "Mid-America," as "an empire with its capital in Chicago." His conception was at first unclear but even then, as still, he wanted "only not to lose the sense of life as it is, here, now, in the land and among the people among whom I live."[6]

His first two novels, he continued, had been a reaction against the business world back to his earlier working-class one, a reaction involving a sentimental "dream of a new world to come out of some revolutionary movement that would spring up out of the mass of people." But a new conception came to him, as recorded in *Mid-American Chants* and the first of the Testaments, an acceptance of the present because of its possible future.

I take these little, ugly factory towns, these big, sprawling cities into something. I wish it would not sound too silly to say I pour a dream over it, consciously, intentionally, for a purpose. I want to write beautifully, create beautifully, not outside but in this thing in which I am born, in this place where, in the midst of ugly towns, cities, Fords, moving pictures, I have always lived, must always live. I do not want, Paul, even those old monks at Chartres, building their cathedral, to be at bottom any purer than myself.

Slow and stupid unlike his friends in the East, he must nevertheless not be mistaken as one who lacks respect for "the old masters of my craft" or for words in themselves, for he fears and dislikes the ability of men like Mencken and Hecht to "rattle words like dice in a box." Rather his slowness and stupidity are proof that at present

culture is not a part of our lives out here in Mid-America. We are all, businessmen, workers, farmers, town, city and country dwellers, a little ashamed of trying for beauty. We are imprisoned. There is a wall about us. You will see, as you get into the spirit of the *New Testament,* how that wall has become a symbol of life to me. More men than you and I will ever know have become embittered and ugly in America, Paul. The flush-looking, hearty, go-with-a-slam-bang businessmen and others, what we have come to think of as the up-and-going American, are not so up-and-going. They are little children. Immaturity is the note of the age, and immaturity is a wall too.

And so in my inner self I have accepted my own Mid-America as a walled-in place. There are walls everywhere, about individuals, about groups. The houses are mussy. People die inside the walls without ever having seen the light. I want the houses cleaned, the doorsteps washed, the walls broken away. That can't happen in my time. Culture is a slow growth.

But then, Paul with his quick mind will have known all this; he simply must not be "fooled by my crudeness or . . . be led to believe that I am not, in my own way, trying to live in the old tradition of artists."

Sherwood's letter—he liked it well enough to send a copy of part of it to Bab—would have its influence on Paul as he wrote the article; but there was little to be done about the reviews of *The Triumph of the Egg* except to wait while Huebsch pushed the book with all his determined, if limited, resources. Sherwood did ask Ben to send review copies to Hecht and Sandburg at the *Chicago Daily News* and to Burton Rascoe, who that spring had moved to New York to edit *McCall's Magazine.* The book was finally published on October 24, while he was still in the first excitement over the Dial Award. When he at last saw a copy, he wrote Ben happily that, though

439

he did not care for the traditional cover design, "the inside is as nifty a piece of book making as one could want." Huebsch had provided a first printing of three thousand copies, about half of which had been taken in advance sale, and was ready to run off a second printing as quickly as needed. Both men had a hunch that at last a book of Anderson's might sell reasonably well, especially when the news of the Dial Award was made public. Mindful of the advantages of such publicity Huebsch met with Seldes to lay plans and persuaded him to move up the announcement to December 1.[7]

Through much of October the weather in Palos Park was "a march of lovely days," and *Ohio Pagans* marched with them. As the forest leaves turned gold and started to fall, however, Sherwood began vaguely to dread the coming winter and to think of escape to a warmer land after Christmas. By the end of the month he had fixed on Mexico City as the likely place to go. Meanwhile Tennessee had bought a Model T Ford sedan, and Sherwood began learning to drive it, with the result that, as he wrote Karl amusedly, "I spend a part of each day in the ditches here abouts. The Ford is still all there although somewhat banged." Now at the wheel of a car he could feel that he was "truly a modernist." Only occasionally did he have to go into Chicago on business, as when on the twelfth he had met his Owensboro friend Steele at the Fort Dearborn Hotel to talk about the Martin Ditcher and his European trip. Then, late in the month, his writing spell was broken in on by a letter from Steele saying that he was needed in Kentucky for several days to work on the Owensboro company's advertising. He went to Kentucky on November 1, made "a little money by writing some advertisements—pimping for an agricultural tool," and was back in Palos Park Saturday, November 5, having stopped over in Indianapolis on the way home for a "peaceful, quiet day" of talk with Bab.[8]

For a few days after his return he slipped again into the lives of his Ohio Pagans; then the week back at business hit him with a "violent readjustment," the weather turned wet and cold, and for a day both he and, it seemed to him, the dead countryside became "infinitely, sad," he "futilely . . . trying to remember what good work has been accomplished." On that day he decided to move back into Chicago and write in an unoccupied office at Critchfield, but though his sad mood quickly passed, the "rhythmic march within himself" that had carried the novel along so steadily had been broken. From mid-November on he could work only in scattered fashion at what was now an almost completed first draft of the novel.[9]

Apparently he was becoming edgy at the slowness with which reviews of his new book were appearing and at his own uneasy sense that he might be at some turning point in his life. On October 25 Huebsch had sent him a check for $45, representing the author's half of Cape's advance royalty on the English edition of *Winesburg, Ohio* "less the agent's commission of

10 percent," and on November 7 Huebsch sent another check for $120, again the author's half, by contrast, of Horace Liveright's advance royalty on the Modern Library issue of that book. On the one hand, the amounts were welcome, for the award money was some weeks away, and Tennessee, as well as her husband, was feeling the contradictory demands on her time. As he explained the situation to Waldo, when the latter praised her photographed heads in *The Triumph of the Egg,* she

is unfortunately married to a man who can't support her so she has to make her own living. Therefore, she doesn't get much time to work when she isn't tired. In other words, having found the impulses of an artist within herself, she is meeting the same situations that practically every American artist meets.

Huebsch, however, had indicated that by contract he was retaining half of each advance, and Anderson felt that such an arrangement was unfair. His irritation deepened when his friend Francis Hackett, the literary editor of *The New Republic,* came to Chicago on November 17 to lecture and had lunch at Schlogl's with Anderson, Hansen, and others of the regular literary group. The matter of contracts came up in the conversation, and Hackett insisted that the new Authors' League contracts cut the publisher entirely out of any share in foreign rights and, on Sherwood's questioning, that he thought it unjust for a publisher to take a "50 percent split" on a Modern Library edition. The following day, in the first such letter he had ever sent Huebsch, Anderson poured out his whole resentment over the contract provision for equal sharing since "what a publisher has done to deserve any such advantage, I can't figure out and will never be able to figure out." Huebsch, who had been busy working on plans to promote sales of his author's works at the announcement of the Dial Award, took several days to get his facts confirmed, and then wrote Anderson a diplomatic letter explaining that Hackett had been wrong about Authors' League contracts and the practices of other reputable publishers, the "fifty-fifty" clause being invariably the standard agreement. Anderson's immediate response was to apologize for his "bust out," but he was still not fully reconciled to equal sharing on the Modern Library edition, and wrote Huebsch so. The publisher had generously offered to reconsider that contract clause with him, but Anderson did not push the matter further. He did not, however, forget it, and it would be one of the complaints about his connection with Huebsch that would accumulate over the next few years despite their strong personal friendship and Huebsch's continued efforts to promote his books.[10]

For the moment the matter disappeared under the excitement of the reviews, which toward the end of November were at last beginning to appear. Among the first were those of Ludwig Lewisohn in *The Nation,* of Robert Morss Lovett in *The New Republic,* and of John Peale Bishop in

Vanity Fair, all three, Anderson joyfully felt, "the best and most intelligent I have ever had." Lewisohn praised the "bitter power" with which Anderson described "that repression and crippling of natural instinct which is so obvious a mark of our life" and concluded, "In these episodes and stories there are pages as memorable as have been written by any contemporary American." Like Lewisohn, Lovett admired the artistic unity of the book, and he compared Anderson's fiction with Chekhov's drama since in both "the action is centrifugal; it diffuses attention and carries it beyond the trivial action of the stage to remoter implications of a life that is unrevealed but none the less present and significant." In this new collection Anderson showed

a great advance in resourcefulness and technique over his earlier books. Just as his stories have opposed qualities of meticulous, immediate reality and vague, remote suggestion, so his style has a double aspect, a stark, determined, forthright mode of statement, which wavers into rhythms that lead the mind outward and far.

It was John Bishop's essay-review, comparing D. H. Lawrence and Anderson that gave Sherwood the greatest satisfaction. Neither writer is basically interested in ideas, Bishop wrote; both approach life and art emotionally and are concerned with "the amazingly difficult and vital business of human relationships"; both share a "mythopoeic faculty" that appears in their common understanding of "the physical ecstasy and contentment that would come of belonging utterly to the dark rich life of the earth and moving with the ancient rhythms of light and dark, of green and sterile seasons, of dayrise and nightfall." Still, they are unlike as well. Both are interested in the "private struggles of the soul," but "where in Lawrence this struggle is almost always between the cruel aloofness of the male and the tender devastating pervasiveness of the woman, in Anderson it is between some dream of impossible loveliness, which the dreamer wishes to attach to the body of the beloved, and the inane fecundity of life." Furthermore,

where the Englishman piles words upon words, approximating his meaning by a rich welter of words, Anderson is so sparing in statement as to be almost inarticulate. There is at times in his books an unbelievable and glamorous beauty, but it is the beauty of things seen with delight or known in an intensity of emotion, haltingly recovered and scarcely set down in words.

These qualities, Bishop argued, are at their clearest in *The Triumph of the Egg,* which despite defects—a "confusion in the element of time," a "choppiness in movement"—shows its author's considerable gain in craftsmanship. They are qualities of "that passionate imagination which from the first marked him apart from the other American realists."[11]

Upon reading this last review Anderson sent off a letter of gratitude to

Bishop. Objecting only that it was not Lawrence but Dostoyevsky, "always . . . the one great master to me," who had "opened my eyes to what the possibilities might be in the development of my own vein," Anderson felt that Bishop had done "more than justice" to himself, perhaps less than justice to Lawrence. Nevertheless, he thought it "an amazing article" that made him "feel as one might feel sitting in his house in a lonely place in the country and having someone he thought a long ways away suddenly open the door and walk in." The figure was, in fact, an apt summary of the sense of artistic and personal breakthrough that the generally favorable reviews were at last providing him. Writing Bab from his Critchfield office—being there temporarily was "like visiting a prison in which human souls are confined"—he spoke of the reviews as

unlike anything I have had before. One feels real minds, coming as out of grey shadows and saying "I understand." During these years I have been saying something over and over as into a black night. "These twisted ones have souls. Beauty lies asleep in them."

No one responded. There was the clatter, about sex obsession, about dirt and ugliness.

And now, out of these bitter winds, comes something like a sweet wind.

In some way the clatter and the vulgarity doesn't so much matter now. One finds new brothers to add to a few, who long ago sensed what I have been grouping for.[12]

Such a pitch of delight made it even harder for him to work at *Ohio Pagans,* and it was still harder to do so when the news of the Dial Award was announced. Harry Hansen, eager to be first in reporting an honor to a Chicago author, prematurely revealed the secret in his weekly book column in the *Daily News* for November 30, a column featuring Anderson and his career. The official announcement by Gilbert Seldes appeared in the *New York Times Book Review* on December 4 preceding a review of *The Triumph of the Egg,* which, somewhat awkwardly for the award statement, found the book drably truthful but lacking in idealism. Editorially *The Nation* praised the selection of Anderson as the first recipient of the award since, despite lapses, he "is original, powerful, experimental," "his career is full of admirable promise," and in *The Triumph of the Egg* "he has brought beauty and passion and reflection together and given them masterful form and outline." To those interested in the literary scene Anderson had become a public figure, and while such notice was gratifying to him, it was also disturbing. Daily life became a "jumble," as he wrote Bab, that made further work on *Ohio Pagans* impossible. Suddenly being a celebrity threw him, as he put it, off his center. For one who had preached, even if inconsistently, a gospel of failure, success was as hard to adjust to as it was sweet. He needed quiet to do "ever more difficult and delicate things"; yet he had to face a future in which, he complained, "I shall not be as much a man by myself as I have been." And yet, he also wrote her of the reviews and the award, "There is a kind of loveliness in a message said over and over in dark streets and rooms, said persistently—when it strikes something into fire in others." And yet Francis Hackett had hit the point by sending him "a little drawing he had made called 'Celebrity—or The Price of Fame.' It is illuminating and shows me with a worried look fleeing from fat men in dress suits."[13]

During these exciting and disturbing weeks Sherwood took time to assist his young friend Ernest Hemingway, now married to Hadley Richardson. Earlier in the fall the Andersons had had the Hemingways to dinner, and Sherwood had talked enthusiastically about how the young couple should go to Paris rather than Italy as they had planned. The city was beautiful, the French wonderful, the living cheap, the Left Bank full of writers and artists. The Hotel Jacob was small, clean, inexpensive, conveniently situated, and the Hemingways could stay there until they found an apartment. Ernest and Hadley were easily persuaded and by the end of November had booked passage for France. As he had offered to do, Sherwood wrote Galantière on the twenty-eighth, sincerely praising Ernest as "a young fellow of extraordinary talent" who "will get somewhere," and Hadley as "charming." Lewis would find them "great playmates." Then early in December he wrote notes for the Hemingways to mail in Paris as introductions to the other persons he thought they most ought to meet—Beach, Joyce, Stein. Hemingway, each note read, was "an American writer instinctively in touch with everything worth while going on here" and the couple "delightful people to know." The night before they left Chicago, Sherwood would recall in the Memoirs, Ernest showed his appreciation by appearing at 12 East Division Street with a huge knapsack on his broad shoulders. It was full of canned goods that the Hemingways would otherwise have had to leave behind. Sherwood was touched by the gift of so much food from one "scribbler" to another.[14]

Now that the Dial Award had been announced, all sorts of mail began to flood in to him each morning. He was invited to be a Non-Resident Member of the Authors Club in New York, and accepted. Elizabeth Prall, manager of the Doubleday bookshop in New York's Lord & Taylor department store, wrote to ask for a photograph to display in her shop window—and in this minor, businesslike way the woman who was to be his third wife entered his existence. Ben Huebsch had a supply of photographs for booksellers and magazine editors, and took care of Miss Prall's request. He sent Sherwood clippings of reviews of The Triumph and notices of the award as they came to him, and he also sent him a copy of a one-page promotional statement about the author's work as a whole, "Of Beauty and Pity," which Ben had almost certainly drawn up himself and which, while quoting various critics, showed his own insight into the "sensitive" and the "epic" sides of Anderson's writing. Most satisfying of all, Sherwood wrote Bab, were the letters from young American men and women, eager to be artists, who were not asking for "personal attachment" but only wanted to tell him "'we'll try to keep the faith and seek the truth.'" It was a spontaneous expression of love which moved him and gave him hope that someday American artists would be like European ones, who did not live "isolated as we do here."[15]

The mails also brought word of the developing plans for an award presentation dinner in New York. At first there was an absurd misunderstanding on Anderson's part. Originally the dinner was set for December 14 at the Civic Club, and it was only the week before when Anderson realized that, in the confusion of his days, he had mistakenly assumed the Civic Club to be in Chicago and that it would be awkward for him to get to New York by the fourteenth because of his and Tennessee's plans to have an early Christmas celebration with Cornelia and the children on the eighteenth. Huebsch and Seldes managed to postpone the dinner until the twenty-first, but even though the children already felt cheated enough that their celebration was moved to the week before Christmas, it was moved up yet another week to the eleventh. Sherwood usually considered his own concerns before those of his children; indeed, he admitted as such when he wrote to Paul just after the celebration to thank him for his "very beautiful" article on Anderson in the new *Dial,* an article that astutely and prophetically recognized "the escape from the dominance of women and children" as among the "other subtle things . . . I did not know you knew." In many ways Tennessee was more considerate than he to Robert, John, and Mimi (now fourteen, twelve, and ten), even though they were not her children, and she remained closer to the self-contained Cornelia.[16]

Around December 14, Sherwood and Tennessee left Chicago to spend a few quiet days with, he wrote Bab, "a friend in the country in Pennsylvania" so that he could prepare himself for the ordeal of the dinner and his acceptance speech. He had already warned Huebsch that he wanted as little public dining and speechmaking as possible. He didn't know what to say, and the whole notion of honoring him for achievement

has nothing to do at all with what I really want to do.

Achievement is all right, but how much is achieved? I have written a few stories that are like stones laid along the highway. They have solidity and will stay there.

And what is this in a life? what I mean to say is that there is old age and death in accepting the idea of achievement. Not what is done, but what is to be done.[17]

On December 18 the Andersons came to New York to stay for some days with Jerome and Lucile Blum, who lived just above Greenwich

Village. Tennessee was to remain until New Year's Day and then go back to Chicago, but Sherwood was planning to be in New York a little longer and then head south by himself. He had hoped to have time during the visit to talk painting with Jerry Blum, to explain how he had little desire for representational work and hungered "for more poetry and fantasy to be brought into being by line and color"; but from the nineteenth on when he first met with Huebsch, his waking hours became a "rather mad jumble of people—faces." He survived the Civic Club dinner though he seems to have been embarrassed and awkward about speaking. If the gossip of his former friend Floyd Dell can be trusted, Anderson had early in his career memorized a formula first line for such painful moments, a formula surely expressive of no more than humility: "I am not really an author—I am a businessman." When "called upon for a few remarks," Dell maliciously reported, Anderson

hitched himself out of his chair, and began with his customary "opening." One of the editors of *The Dial,* who was present, was observed to frown and bite his lip. Turning to his neighbor, he said in an agonized whisper: "We didn't award the Dial prize to a *business man!*" [18]

The following evening, the twenty-second, was most likely much more pleasant, for Huebsch and his wife had a dinner for the Andersons at home with only two other couples, Louis Untermeyer and Lawrence Gilman both well-wishers, and their wives. Untermeyer had praised *Poor White,* and Gilman, editor of the *North American Review,* would write of *The Triumph of the Egg* as his Book of the Month and "An American Masterwork." At least one more quiet occasion was Christmas Day, which Sherwood and Tennessee spent with brother Karl and his wife Helen in Westport. During the rest of the New York visit, however, seeing so many unfamiliar people became "a kind of violence," as he put it in one of his hasty, half-complaining, half-boasting notes to Bab. There were interviews with newspapermen "with their sharp cynical eyes," more dinner invitations, constant questions from the curious asking him to explain his works. It was distracting and exciting.

One might so easily get the most absurd and childish sense of power here.
One goes out to breakfast and a crowd of literary people gather about. There is a rapid fire of talk. Quick enmities and friendships are made. Vast possibilities open and close quickly again.
People think you have something they want. You say something and it is repeated, distorted too.

He couldn't stand it much longer and would simply have to run away. But it was not until some days after Tennessee left for Chicago that he would finally run, toward New Orleans where he hoped to "be alone, work, think and feel for a time."[19]

2.

Anderson took a train out of New York around January 9, heading first for Lexington, Kentucky, where he conferred for two days with Dave Bohon of Harrodsburg about advertising. Free of New York's kaleidoscope of persons, he had time to sort out his impressions, realize that he had enjoyed much of the literary talk, and decide that something had begun to happen in America—writers of standardized fiction were being shaken by the challenge of those who, like himself, were trying to write more honestly about people's inner lives. But such thoughts made it even harder than usual to concentrate on the immediate concerns of his business client, to follow what Bohon was saying about moneymaking schemes. He kept wanting to break in and tell him, "For God sake man drop it. You have a little money, go play, learn to love someone or something." On the night of the eleventh, as a relief after the talk of business, he drove over back roads in the moonlit Kentucky hills with a man running illicit whiskey, Sherwood listening to the man talk of racehorses and relishing the chance both took of landing in jail.[20]

On the morning of the twelfth he left Lexington, arrived that evening in New Orleans, and stayed the night at the Hotel Lafayette on Lafayette Square. The next day he found the perfect room to settle into in the French Quarter, to which he was drawn because it reminded him somewhat of the French town he had loved. The room was on the third floor of the LaBranche Buildings, then a rather dilapidated complex of rooming houses, at the corner of Royal and St. Peter streets—his entry was at 708 Royal—the buildings then, as now, a landmark because of their two rows of lacelike cast-iron balconies wrapped around the two street sides and attractive to Anderson for their delicacy and flamboyance of oakleaf-acorn design. His room was large and rather bare; but it had a big table on which to work and a fireplace with, as he wrote Jerry Blum, "a picture of the Virgin over the mantle and beside it two glass candle sticks, in the form of crosses with Christ on the Cross in bronze on them," a piece of "good catholic" decor that would soon find its way into his writing. Windows ran from floor to high ceiling, and by stepping through them out onto the balcony, he could walk back and forth delighting in the life of the street below. He arranged with the landlady, a strong, handsome young "French Creole," that she or her husband would bring him coffee and toast in the mornings so that he could at once begin his favorite routine of writing until noon and "loafing" in the afternoons and evenings.[21]

That particular afternoon of the thirteenth, or the following one, he sought out the office, on the third floor of a commercial building at 204 Baronne Street, of *The Double Dealer,* the little magazine started the previous January by several well-to-do young men who wanted to bring the new spirit in literature to what Mencken had contemptuously called The Sahara of the Bozart. Julius Friend, one of the editors, recalled that when Anderson dropped in from the street to introduce himself, he "was wearing a wool coat with leather buttons, a loud tie gathered in below the knot by a paste ring. He had on a velour hat and carried a blackthorn walking stick." Flamboyant as the ironwork of the balconies outside his room, he looked to Friend like "a burlesque show idea of a racehorse character," but almost immediately the editors forgot his flashy clothes because of Sherwood's warmth and vitality and their own excitement at having a distinguished literary figure call on them so casually, telling them that he had seen some copies of their magazine, liked what "you fellers" were doing, and wanted to contribute things and do anything else to help. The magazine, they felt, was "made." Over the next few weeks, off and on, Anderson saw much of the *Double Dealer* group, especially of Friend, a tall, gentle, soft-spoken man, of the short, lively Albert Goldstein, who after a spell as associate editor of *The Double Dealer* became a reporter on the chief New Orleans newspaper, *The Times-Picayune,* and of John McClure, who had come from Oklahoma and with his wife had started a bookstore in the Quarter. Years later Friend remembered that Sherwood never posed as "a great writer."

He met everyone on a personal level never the official. No one felt that he was young or old, famous or unknown, while in contact with him. The extremely vivid relationship which S. A. assumed with nearly everyone was an experience having value in and for itself. One felt himself living more vividly. The best way I can express it is to say that he had a talent for living in the present and dispensing with all the usual props used to sustain amour-propre. Consequently everyone was enthusiastic about him and concluded that Sherwood was especially interested in him or her. This was true during the contact.

Then in his memoir Friend added from the hindsight of years of acquaintance, "But Sherwood, I believe, cared for only a few people and none to the exclusion of his interest in his work—wives and children not excepted."[22]

This first meeting with the *Double Dealer* group showed Anderson that, as he soon wrote Mencken, this "crew was as pleasant a crowd of young blades as ever drunk bad whiskey." The editors eagerly presented him with a copy of their July 1921 issue, which contained Hart Crane's appreciative article on his work from *Winesburg* onward, an article that he had not seen, the one which praised him for his honesty, lyricism, sense of nature, and "a humanity and simplicity that is quite baffling in depth and suggestiveness." Very likely it was this same afternoon that Sherwood agreed to let them have the first of three Testaments, which the *Double Dealer* would print in their next few issues, and he may then have promised an article on the city and the magazine.[23]

As for New Orleans, he almost at once fell in love with it, particularly with the French Quarter, the Vieux Carré. After a morning's work at the big table and lunch, often with Julius Friend, he would roam the old streets of the Quarter, then a largely working class, French-Italian area, rundown and colorful, where cheap rents had produced a small bohemia of local artists and writers, and where tourists had only begun to come. Just a block or two away from his room was green Jackson Square, faced on one side by the Spanish-style Cabildo and the plain-fronted St. Louis Cathedral, on two other sides by the long, graceful facades of the Pontalba Apartments, and open to the east toward the markets, warehouses, and wharves along the busy Mississippi. Evenings he could spend over a dinner in talk with the *Double Dealer* group at some restaurant where red wine was obtainable in casual defiance of Prohibition, or he could wander along the wharves or walk in the ramshackle Negro section, as he had done in Alabama, loafing, watching, listening to the voices and the laughter of the blacks. Concerning them he wrote to Jerry Blum,

The one thing they constantly do for me is to rest something inside me. I've really been going like hell and sometimes at night can't chuck it and sleep. Well I go where the niggers are at work and watch their bodies and my own body gets rested. There aren't any other people in America know anything about physical work. They have the key to it, the secret to it.

Don't know whether or not I'm romancing, but I've a notion they know I have a somewhat different attitude toward them than most of the whites. There is a kind of something in their eyes, both men and women, something like surprise and pleasure.

Whatever the degree of romantic self-deception Anderson half recognized in himself, he was genuinely drawn to blacks as he was to the raffish characters of the Quarter, to the French and Italian workers, to any other persons and groups outside conventional middle-class society, like the bums and flashy people who hung around the New Orleans racetrack, where he sometimes went more to talk than to watch the races. New Orleans, this half-foreign city at the southern "lip of the continent," at once excited and soothed him with its color, its culture, its slowness of tempo and its warmth in contrast to cold and frenetic Chicago, with the eagerness of so many of its peoples to be individuals, as the homogeneous French had impressed him as being nevertheless individuals. On one of his most memorable days—it was January 28 and sunshine brought the temperature up to about 60 degrees—he wrote all morning, after lunch watched Mike

Algero of the French Market win the world's championship at oyster shucking before a crowd of thirty thousand in Lafayette Square, in the late afternoon walked along the docks on the river front "among singing negro laborers," and with Albert Goldstein that evening "under the stars in an open air arena," saw Panama Joe Gans, Negro middleweight champion of the world, knock out Oscar Battiste, Negro middleweight champion of the Midwest, in the second of fifteen scheduled rounds. It was a day to write about, and he did so both in a joyous letter to Karl and in his article, "New Orleans, The Double Dealer and the Modern Movement in America," for the March issue of the magazine.[24]

On the way down to New Orleans he had already decided to put the almost completed *Ohio Pagans* aside again as unsatisfactory, and instead he went immediately into a new work he had begun in one form late in his Fairhope stay and had been actively thinking about again at least since the Paris visit, when his escape from business had been so often on his mind. At first he was not sure whether he was writing "some long short stories or short novels," but he did know that in structure they were to be interconnected, somewhat in the *Winesburg* manner, and that they were to be written in "a quick nervous prose that will have in it something of the intense nervousness of modern life while it, at the same time, strikes at what seem to me the diseases of modern life." Just as the "new designs of color and emotions" in *Mid-American Chants,* he explained in a letter to Rosenfeld, had led him into *Winesburg, Poor White,* and *The Triumph,* so now the "new, more complex, nervous prose" of his Testaments was leading him into this new book, or books, which by early February he had already named *Many Marriages.*[25]

Day after day the words rushed out of him. Usually he kept to his regular schedule of writing only in the morning, but sometimes he was so seized that he wrote all day until he was "almost too weak to walk." By mid-February he had written fifty thousand words and had nearly completed what he saw as the first of a two- or three-volume work. The whole work, he explained to Bab, whom he had been too preoccupied to write to for weeks, was "an effort to go deeper into people and show their processes of thought and the effect of their thoughts, unexpressed, on their lives—a very interesting, delicate and difficult thing to do." The book was an effort to break through that wall which had become the obsessive symbol of the Testaments. In a letter to Huebsch he described the "thought back of the book" more fully and precisely, so precisely in fact that either he was paraphrasing a passage he had already written or he later adapted into the book part of what he had written to Ben.

There is within every human being a deep well of thinking over which a heavy iron lid is kept clamped.

Some thing tears the lid away. A kind of inner release takes place. In other words the man cuts sharply across all the machinery of the life about him. There is in the old Christian phrase a rebirth.

Is this man in his new phase sane or insane? He does new things, says new and strange things and his words and actions fall with strange illuminating power on those about him. To some they are sentences of death, to others invitations into life.

What I aim to do you see is to show step by step the process of this rebirth in a man and its effect on those about him.[26]

As the writing went on, two literary considerations occasionally concerned him. First, since he was deliberately dealing with the world of the fancy, he felt bound by realism even less than heretofore and hoped his intention would not be misunderstood. After reading Mencken's praise of *The Triumph* in the February *Smart Set* as being "full of a strange beauty and an unmistakable power," he wrote to thank him and to take exception to Mencken's assertion that the "primary purpose of the author is plainly realistic."

My purpose is realistic you say. It isn't, man. I care as much for realism, as realism, as I do for wornout underwear. I'm only using it to try to peg something down, keep it close to the ground.

He meant what he said. Writing to Seldes at *The Dial* a few weeks later, he would exuberantly call *Many Marriages* "a hummer of a tale. Down with realism. A bas naturalism. Up with fantasy."[27]

The other consideration had to do with method of publication. On February 3, he warned Huebsch that *Many Marriages* was "infinitely more bold and daring than anything I've ever done" and suggested that to escape censorship it might have to be printed in a limited subscription edition. Huebsch's response was characteristically both principled and practical.

I am leaving the most important thing for the last, and that is your new book. The various publishers who have been bringing out limited editions at robber-baron prices have pretty nearly worked the subscription graft to death. To issue a book in that manner is to stamp it as pornography. This new feature in bookselling has resulted in the creation of a class known as book-leggers. They sell books with a wink and a leer. If the book happens to be a work of art they handle it with slimy fingers. For you to bring out a book in that manner means to limit its reading to one or two thousand persons interested mainly in the collector's value, or the obscenity value, and to withhold it from your real audience, ninety-eight per cent. of which consists of people who can afford to pay only the normal market price of books.

My advice to you is to walk the straight path with your head high. I do not think that anything that you may say will cause your book to be pinched unless, of course, you want to invite the lightning by using unnecessarily bald terminology. With regard to the use of words, though I do not advocate compromising with the vice societies, I believe that in most instances a work of literary art can be presented without employing a style or vocabulary offensive to the great many people who have not yet abandoned the Victorian tradition.

I have not covered the case, by any means, but I have said enough to indicate my attitude, and I hope that you will ponder it. I want you to write for the great public, and not for the furtive-eyed erotomaniac.

Ben's remarks about "greasy fingered book-leggers" gave him the fantods, Sherwood replied, accepting the advice as "dead right," and for the moment that matter was settled. When *Many Marriages* was finally published in book form, however, Huebsch would have the chance to put his beliefs to the test.[28]

In his novel, bold in subject for the time though decorous in "vocabulary," Anderson was writing for "the great public." In one sense he was presenting his version of Somerset Maugham's *The Moon and Sixpence,* that story about a man who rejects conventional life for a vision of a new art, which back in November 1919 Anderson had urged Bab to read because it would explain to her so much of himself. At the age of thirty-seven or thirty-eight, a Wisconsin washing machine manufacturer named John Webster, who has crushed his tendency to "dream" in order to be a successful American businessman, abruptly falls in love with his stenographer, Natalie Swartz, and resolves to run away with her from his factory, his town, and his dull wife, Mary. Purchasing a picture of the Virgin and "two glass candlesticks, made in the shape of crosses and with little gilded figures of the Christ on the cross upon them," he begins a nightly ritual of walking up and down naked before them in his bedroom. One evening Mary and their seventeen-year-old daughter Jane, puzzled by the sound of his walking, come from their own bedrooms into his in their nightdresses, whereupon, as a means of guiding Jane to a mature attitude toward life, he tells her at some length the story of her mother's and his first meeting when by odd chance both were naked, of their courtship by self-deceiving letters, and of their marriage and their first sexual relations, made unhappy then as subsequently by the shame of the flesh inculcated in both through their puritanically repressive upbringings. The agonized Mary Webster, grown ugly and heavy-bodied since her youthful beauty, can endure to hear only part of this story, but Jane listens and is filled with love for her father. Webster concludes by giving Jane a bright-colored stone as a talisman for her to carry against the conventionally minded world, and by telling his wife that he is leaving her. Mary commits suicide, but Jane is awakened to a new sense of self-respect and independence. In the final scenes of the book Webster, that "weaver of designs out of threads of thought," goes off with Natalie to take a train for Chicago where he may become a writer. (Anderson's conception of this book as containing the first of three to five "episodes" suggests that subsequent volumes, had they been finished, might have described Webster's finding himself as a new kind of writer, just as Strickland in *The Moon and Sixpence,* after the suicide of a mistress he had deserted, finds himself as a new kind of painter.)

Thus baldly summarized, *Many Marriages* might sound, as most reviewers would later decide, like merely the recounting of a sordid, commonplace enough affair, made even more unattractive by a father's exhibiting his nude body to an adolescent daughter; in fact, even now commentators on this oddest of Anderson's novels tend to find the "exhibitionism" either distasteful or preposterous, so much so that for one thing, they fail to observe that Webster remains naked only briefly while telling Jane the first part of her mother's and his chance meeting when naked, a meeting that "was really our wedding moment." Just as his present nakedness parallels that original nakedness, so Webster tells the rest of the long story of a potentially beautiful, actually shameful marriage after, appropriately, he has clothed himself. In order to understand what Anderson was attempting in *Many Marriages,* one must focus, not on the "exhibitionism" nor even on its short rather than long duration, but on the parallelism Anderson set up, through the metaphor of nakedness, between two moments of direct communion, two "marriages," between a young man and a young woman and between a middle-aged father and his daughter. As with "Seeds," Anderson did not create the form of his novel primarily through its chronology of events but rather through its intricate pattern of parallel actions, repeated motifs, recurrent symbols, a pattern resembling the ordering of poetry almost as much as of prose. In his two-month creative burst Anderson wrote his own version of what is now called the "lyrical novel."

It was his own version, not some adaptation of Maugham's rather thin realism nor of D. H. Lawrence's impassioned prose, and he was at least generally aware of what he was trying to do to the novel form as soon as he began. In his letter to Hart Crane of January 15, he commented on his projected "long short stories or short novels":

It may be indeed that I will come up to my feeling and conception of the novel in this way, something more nervous, exciting and intense than our accepted novel form. Anyway I shall be working toward that.

He had in fact been working vaguely toward this form since his abortive first try at *Many Marriages* in the late spring and summer of 1920 when there had been "an idea of a new novel form floating about in me, something looser, more real, more true," but the idea now assumed appropriate shape in him from an earlier and other kind of writing. However he may have exaggerated in asserting to Rosenfeld that *Mid-American Chants* led into *Winesburg, Poor White,* and *The Triumph of the Egg,* he was right in saying that his experiments with the Testaments from the spring of 1919 onward led directly into *Many Marriages.* Like them the novel deals with "the autobiography of the fanciful life of an individual," asserts that sanity and truth may be reached through "insanity" and "lying," and by such indirection allows a man both to find "the hidden thing" in himself and to make love to, have many marriages with, other persons. To a striking extent the seed of the novel had already been planted in Testament 12; for in that Testament the "I" person speaks words associated by Anderson with his own "insane" escape from business and an unsatisfactory marriage, makes love to a woman in a field one night as John Webster makes love to Natalie, and wonders, as Webster wonders at the end of the novel, whether he may not be using a woman simply as a means to self-liberation. So "woven together" in Anderson's mind were his "New Testament" and the novel that in mid-February he suggested to Huebsch that they might be published simultaneously: "The complicated rhythms and the rush of imagery I have worked for . . . would be better understood after reading the same impulse in prose and the prose would be better understood in the light of the Testaments."[29]

In writing *Many Marriages,* then, Anderson was extending one kind of experimental writing into another kind, creating in the process a "lyrical" rather than a realistic novel. The distinction needs to be emphasized lest the novel be misread. Where the realistic novel traditionally, as the critic Ralph Freedman has put it, "separates the experiencing self from the world the experiences are about," the "lyrical novel, by contrast, seeks to combine man and world in a strangely inward, yet aesthetically objective form"; indeed in the latter case,

The writer aims for the effect of lyrical poetry: to use whatever scene, characterization, action in time, and corresponding techniques are the *donnes* of the novel within which he works, not in the development of a fictional world, but in the rendering of objects, sensations, even ideas, with immediacy.[30]

Many Marriages gains its immediacy as much through its patterning devices as through narrative. Event, real or imagined, echoes event after event. For example, early in the book Webster sees piles of bright yellow boards in his washing machine factory and imagines their source in the logs that singing black men collect on a southern river. As he "watches" this imagined scene—an actual or fanciful memory from Anderson's Fairhope experience—a strong young black woman appears in a boat by herself, paddles vigorously past the admiring workers, and disappears

around a bend in the river. Shortly afterwards Webster returns to his office and sees the strong young body of Natalie Swartz (that is, "black"?)
outlined against a pile of yellow boards outside the window behind her,
and for the first time admits he loves her. Near the end of the book Jane,
Webster's daughter, resolves to accept her future as one moving along "the
river of life," achieving the self-reliance and self-respect which, by implication, the imagined black girl had embodied. Events echo others by contrast as well as by comparison. When John Webster and Natalie become
physical lovers, the act occurs in a field at night and is mutually exalting
because there is no false modesty on either side; when John and Mary first
have sex relations after marriage, the act occurs in daylight in a field above
a river yet is mutually unsatisfactory because of puritanical inhibitions on
both sides. Obviously one act is in accord with "nature," the other not.

Parallelism of event is reinforced by repetition of motif. As Webster begins to revolt against his life of dull routine, he finds a small jewel-like
green stone along a railroad track (as toward the end of *Poor White* Hugh
McVey finds some brightly colored stones on the shore of Sandusky Bay).
He fantasizes that "a tall strong fair woman" stands on a hill above a river,
pointing with a finger on which is a ring with a green stone set in it. By
later giving the stone to Jane, he is passing on to her what he fancifully
calls the "Jewel of Life," which Jane clutches while imagining, as is actually occurring, the scene of her mother's suicide. Again, lamps illuminate
scenes both "real" and imagined. A street lamp faintly illuminates Webster's office when he and Natalie cling to each other; telling his story of the
past by the light of the candles set before the picture of the Virgin in his
room, he describes to Jane how a lamp once illuminated the naked bodies
of himself and the youthful Mary; at one point he imagines a serene house
in a future city of beauty and community, a house containing a lamp that
may be carried on a finger like a ring containing a precious stone, lamp
and jewel-stone motifs thus merging.

As motifs recur and combine, so various symbols weave in and out of
present actuality, remembered past, and fantasied scene. Walls and rooms
may separate as husband, wife, and daughter sleep in separate rooms; yet
walls between people may be broken down by the power of the imagination or by direct communication, and rooms, repeatedly likened to the
lives and bodies of people, may be cleansed and entered. Besides the pictured Virgin, who seems in Henry Adams fashion to embody love as a
physical and nonphysical force, three other symbols are of special importance for the "argument" of the book. One is, of course, the river of life
which Jane must be awakened to and enter. The second is the symbol of
the well, explicated both in the book itself and in Anderson's letter to
Huebsch as somewhat resembling the Freudian unconscious, into which
each human being pushes forbidden thoughts, both ugly and beautiful,

covering them tightly with the iron lid of repression. Yet at times the lid may somehow be lifted and the repressed material—shameful desires, "dreams," imagined beauty—may be released, and psychic health may thereby be gained. The most ambivalent of the symbols, however, is that of the sea. Mary Webster, repressing her fear of sexuality into the well, enters a sea of silence, a mode of death-in-life leading to actual death; but John Webster, releasing from the well both an uninhibited sexuality and his imagination, the "creative . . . healing thing" within himself, becomes "a great little swimmer in seas," that is, in life. Life and death—one recalls Anderson's attraction to the two Rembrandt paintings in the Louvre—struggle for domination within each person, as the Freudian pleasure principle struggles with the reality principle. Human beings plunge into the sea, or the river that empties into it, and either swim or, as most people are intent to do, drown, since "in general mankind had preferred . . . death."

In his insistent use of symbols Anderson either forgot or ignored his criticism of Lawrence's use of them as "intellectualizing" his fiction, for one purpose of *Many Marriages* was, clearly, to make an argument against the "Puritanism" of American society and not simply by the choice of a bold situation. In the midst of his two-month creative spurt he received a letter from one Lewis Chase, a teacher at the Government University in Peking, China, asking for material for "a course of lectures on contemporary imaginative literature." Much interested by Chase's opportune request, Anderson took the trouble to write to the Modern Library, Huebsch, and *The Dial* to ask that works by or about him be sent to Peking, and then responded to Chase with one of his most explicit critiques of American civilization, a critique no less urgently felt because similar in concept, though not in its hasty expression, to those of Brooks and Frank, whose books he recommended that Chase read. American civilization "is made up of many undigested elements," he told Chase, across which

has been shot Puritanism and Industrialism. As the effect of the most obvious thing is first felt, the man in revolt first began thinking politically. There was here, as you know, a great deal of dependence on that. We talked pretty big of Freedom, Democracy, etc.

Now some of us believe a second movement is begun. There is a striking at Puritanism too. Young men are growing up here who begin to think of lives lived for something other than Progress, Material Growth, being the biggest thing on God Almighty's earth, etc.

Naturally, in a civilization such as ours, the first thing necessary is a deep criticism of the present standards of life. . . . At any rate what seems to me the living work here now is all at this job of tearing the veil. It may even seem to you that we are trying to rape the Puritan Virgin—not a bad idea that, either.

Against Puritanism, Anderson concluded, stands a new breed of artist.

> What I should call the most important phase of what we have come to think of here as the new writing is the escape from trickery to get dramatic effect, the effect to be got instead from the imagery, the power of analysis, the insight into lives, the sheer fine handling of prose and poetry.
>
> Forgive me man I'm an ungodly bad speller.

As is usual with authors, Anderson's description of the characteristics and purpose of the new writing remarkably resembles what he was reaching for himself.[31]

Putting the Chase letter and *Many Marriages* together, one sees that Anderson's definition of puritanism was not in fact a matter of what some of his reviewers would call sex-obsession. For him, as for Brooks, puritanism had developed historically to include both sexual repression and the industrial system as a whole, a double force constituting the iron lid on the well in human beings, inhibiting both their instinctual and their imaginative lives, and, by perverting all their energies outward onto material objects, turning human beings themselves into objects rather than subjects, death-seekers not life-seekers. Such is an essential part of the "message" of *Many Marriages*. The pattern of symbols, motifs, echoes among events was designed, quite as much as the story of one man's rebirth "in the old Christian phrase," to make the novel a kind of modern Pilgrim's Progress from the City of Destruction to the Heavenly City, but a lyrical exemplum not a carefully worked out allegory.

Many Marriages thus represents Anderson's continued search for a new aesthetic form through which to express ideas and attitudes as well as to see into human lives. One may object to Webster's lapses into didacticism, or one may find that the author takes his protagonist too seriously— though this is to overlook Anderson's several deprecations of Webster's acts and ideas—or, more impressionistically, one may argue that the realism and the fantasy do not mesh well in the book; but one should not demand of a lyrical novel what it was not designed to give. True, Natalie is not a clearly defined character, Mary Webster's suicide is not sufficiently motivated in the usual sense, it is unlikely that, in the early 1920s at least, a father would appear naked in front of his daughter while telling her of his and her mother's first meeting; but these objections on the basis of "realism," made by several reviewers on the book's publication and by some critics still, are in fact irrelevant to Anderson's purposed and actual achievement: to use realism only as a means of keeping "close to the ground" his depiction of the inner life of a man who is in the process of being awakened to his emotional and imaginative self. Though the book does seem awkward and mannered at times, objections on the basis of re-alism tend to obscure, not only the complex and controlled patterning, but also the lyricism, in concept and language, of certain of the retrospective scenes. Chief among these are the moment when naked young woman "swims" upward to naked young man "out of sleep like a swimmer out of the sea," that moment of their "real wedding" recollected separately in the book by John and Mary Webster, and the long scene in the field above the river before their unhappy first sexual union, except for this conclusion one of Anderson's most remarkable presentations of delicate pastoral beauty. These and other scenes show his ability to perceive and express what John Webster thinks of as "the poetry of the actual."

However flawed or successful *Many Marriages* may be aesthetically or ideologically, the book must finally be seen as a revealing psychological document. The echoes of Anderson's escape from Elyria are clear enough. Although he changed the event in many ways, his protagonist, who closely resembles the author in physical description, rejects a stultifying business career, breaks with his wife, leaves his small city and conventional social position, and moves toward the world of the imagination. The antagonis-tic portrayal of Mary Webster presumably was colored by recollections of the strained relationship with Cornelia as Anderson perceived it in 1912; yet the cruelty of that portrait almost certainly had its source less in mem-ories of a past marriage than in thoughts of a present one. The suggestion is not arbitrary, for three months after he completed the first draft of *Many Marriages* Anderson left Tennessee permanently. One need not assume that she had become physically unattractive like Mary Webster to see that Mary's suicide expresses a fairly overt fantasy on Sherwood's part, if not of Tennessee's actual death, certainly of the end of marriage to her. Since late in the previous fall it had been understood between him and Tennessee that after the New York visit he would go south without her to escape the Chicago winter, but his significant decision was to drop *Ohio Pagans* and to plunge into the sea of *Many Marriages,* "the book I had on my chest," as he phrased it expressively in a letter to Lucile Blum, "when I left New York." The recognition accorded him by the Dial Award and the accom-panying adulation, the pleasure of being in a colorful, friendly, leisure-loving city with no financial worries, the deep satisfaction of having free time to write and the excitement of risking an experiment he felt ready to make—all these coming together enabled him to tear the iron lid off his own inner well, letting the ugly and the beautiful impulses emerge into full consciousness and so onto the page. *Many Marriages,* which is about a man's liberation, was itself an act of liberation for its author.[32]

The concerns of the book were much on Anderson's mind even when he was not at his writing table, and "real life" tended to flow into and feed his imaginative life, as when the picture of the Virgin and the candlesticks in the room before his eyes became part of his hero's nightly ritual. Julius Friend recalled that during Anderson's two-month stay in New Orleans he "talked a good deal about Freud," though Friend was "sure he never read the books and that he got Freud second hand. . . ." Judging by Anderson's description of the "great well of silent thinking" in each person, it would appear that his view of the Freudian unconscious and the means by which its contents may enter consciousness was, if secondhand, also modified to fit his own notion of the imagination and its health-giving capacities; but his active concern with Freud suggests again how much *Many Marriages* was an exploration of his own psychic depths as well as those of American society as he saw it. Further, Anderson had met and often walked and talked with one of his main characters in the novel, or rather with the young woman who was clearly the real-life prototype of Jane Webster.[33]

This person was Adaline Katz, the small, dark-eyed daughter of a New Orleans banker and a very Southern lady, "who wanted a butterfly [as a daughter] and got a grub." She had graduated from Sophie Newcomb College, had taken an MA at Columbia University in 1920, and in the fall of 1922 would go north to study for a PhD in English literature at the University of Chicago. Meanwhile, she lived in her parents' home, but rebelliously would "sneak away" to the Quarter whenever she could, dropping in often at the *Double Dealer* office, probably the place where she first met Anderson. Years later she remembered herself as being then a very dull, withdrawn, walled-up person whom Sherwood perceived as one of the "waifs and strays" who needed to be brought out from behind the wall; so he concentrated on her out of everyone else in the Quarter and by their relationship helped greatly to bring her to emotional self-awareness. Naive, repressed, but as obscurely eager for life as a girl in an Anderson story, she was at once deeply drawn to this man old enough to be her father, a famous writer, a man physically attractive with his heavy shoulders, ruddy complexion, tousled hair and "wonderfully soft" brown eyes, an exotic even in the Quarter with his battered brown tweed suits and the blackthorn stick. Like his stories, she felt, he was a "conductor of warmth," giving out warmly to others, making "them the sponges rather than being one himself." By mutual consent there was no sexual affair, though with characteristic honesty she later admitted that such would have been fine and rewarding, very good for her. But though no physical sex was involved, this platonic relationship had otherwise all the emotional quality of a sexual affair. Thoroughly masculine in his psychology, he was "an emotional stallion, not a physical one." Like John Webster with his daughter Jane he wished "to penetrate the spirit, not the body" in one of many marriages; and like Webster with Jane he made a much more self-confident, outgoing person of her.[34]

Sherwood and Adaline sometimes lunched or dined together at Guy's, a little French restaurant with a cheap table d'hôte on Royal Street near his rooming house; and when she took a room in the attic of the Pontalba Building, for five dollars a month, a room that had been inhabited by an Italian family who had kept chickens and a goat there, he cheerfully lugged up bucket after bucket of water and helped her scrub the floor clear of droppings and clean the windows. In return, Adaline copyedited the manuscript pages of *Many Marriages,* correcting Sherwood's uncertain spelling and punctuation but never changing his writing in any other way since she knew that he loved both words in general and the words he had written. But most of all the two had an "ambulatory relationship." Both loved the river and walking on the levees day or night. They knew and enjoyed talking with the bums who sat on the benches in Jackson Square or lived in shacks by the levees, and they happily watched the black stevedores singing and laughing in contests at unloading ships.

On their rambles Sherwood talked much to her. He talked often of writing, what he had written that particular morning and writing in general. He talked frequently about the importance of love in human lives, and he talked sometimes about the one thing that was disturbing his present happiness, his troubled relationship with Tennessee. He had married his second wife, he impressed on Adaline, because he felt that, like Adaline herself, she needed to be brought out, fulfilled emotionally; but she had now grown possessive of him, even desperate to hold him, so desperate in fact that in her letters she was neurotically threatening to kill herself. Thus again "real life" flowed into the fiction of *Many Marriages* where Mary Webster, rejected by her husband, commits suicide. The talk too went into the novel; for the relationship between Sherwood and Adaline was reflected with remarkable emotional accuracy in that between the fictitious John Webster and his daughter Jane, the middle-aged man instructing the young woman in the necessity for honest, "naked" communion between persons, encouraging her to self-reliance, awakening her to "the poetry of the actual." Both valued the relationship. He gave her a copy of *Mid-American Chants* in which he had written new poems and his own copy of *Winesburg, Ohio,* which he had filled with notes, and during the year after he left New Orleans, he wrote her enough letters to fill "a large carton" together with "some unpublished poems and the unfinished manuscript of a novel." She would treasure these and the memory of one of the most alive and aware men she would ever know.[35]

Over the many years to come, Julius Friend "never saw Sherwood so radiant and vital as he was that winter in New Orleans." As always when his writing was going well, Anderson could feel the words flowing steadily from his mind down through arm and hand onto sheet after sheet of paper, a literal sensation that gave him physical and emotional well-being. He had friends to play with, black and white dockworkers to watch, the whole warm lazy life of the Quarter to step into at will. The Quarter had not been overwhelmed by industrialism as in the cities of the North; it was "surely the most civilized spot in America," he wrote Karl, urging him to come for a visit. Word of his literary fame kept coming in from the outside world to heighten his satisfaction; he "already had more recognition than expected in a life time." He had read Paul Rosenfeld's "beautiful" article on his work in the January *Dial* before going to New York, but the thought of it still filled him with gratitude for its understanding and love. The last few reviews of *The Triumph* were appearing, all strongly favorable. Lawrence Gilman in the *North American Review* called it "a great book, a very great book," and Bechhofer told the English that it was "the most important American publication of the latter half" of 1921. *The Triumph* was even selling, Huebsch wrote him, not tremendously but "spreading out—orders are coming from all quarters." A second printing had been required in December and now a third in February. The Modern Library edition of *Winesburg* was going into a second printing in March, and Sherwood told Karl that this edition had sold in a month as many copies as the Huebsch one had in its first year. Late in February, Huebsch brought out *Windy McPherson's Son* with the revised ending. Anderson's "I'm a Fool" in the February *Dial* had begun to attract the interest that would eventually make it one of his most popular tales. The time in New Orleans was, in sum, a condition of happiness. Sherwood felt of himself that "surely few men have been so blessed of the gods."[36]

The happiness spilled over into three nonfiction pieces he found time to write while working on *Many Marriages*. The first was "My Fire Burns," a piece for the general weekly, *The Survey,* which, beginning with a description of the ugliness of the coal mining towns among which the author had once "lived for nearly a year," proceeds to attack the national ideal of coal-consuming Industrial Progress for failing to bring "anything at all of light or beauty or meaning" into the lives of Americans. Nostalgically Anderson recalls the preindustrial small towns of the Midwest when there was leisure, a "recognition of the rights of the individual to his idiosyncrasies," and a deep if untutored respect for poetry and learning. Love of country and a desire for beauty are qualities of the true citizen, but how can one love and find beauty in the ugly restlessness of industrial cities? For his own part, he declares, "It has long been my desire to be a little worm in the fair apple of Progress." Things are ordered better in the French Quarter of New Orleans, where one's landlady, hearing the street cry of a ragged Negro coal seller on a cool winter afternoon, has him bring up a basketful to the writer's room and dump it in an old iron washtub by the fireplace. Now Anderson can humble King Coal by burning his bones for warmth. Perhaps increasingly others will withdraw their fealty to the King and to Progress.[37]

Probably Anderson had completed the *Survey* article by early February when he received a letter from Gertrude Stein asking him, as he had earlier agreed to do, to write an introduction to her *Geography and Plays,* a book of samples of her experimental work from 1904 to 1921, which the Four Seas Company of Boston was publishing in the spring. "I have never had more genuine emotion," Stein wrote, "than when you came and understood me and it is a great delight to me to know that it is you who is to present me." Sherwood cordially replied at once that the introduction was "a literary job I'd rather do than any other I know of," and, as promised, got at it soon enough to send copies of his introduction around mid-February to Edmund Brown of the Four Seas Company and to Stein. Soon afterwards he decided to submit a copy of the review to Jane Heap, who accepted it for publication also in the forthcoming spring issue of *The Little Review.*

Brother Karl, Sherwood recalled, had introduced him to *Tender Buttons,* commenting on how "It gives words an oddly new intimate flavor and at the same time makes familiar words seem almost like strangers." Since then Anderson had talked with Stein in Paris and to his "surprise and delight" found her, not the languid decadent, which stories about her had led him to imagine, but "a woman of striking vigor, a subtle and powerful mind, a discrimination in the arts such as I have found in no other American born man or woman, and a charmingly brilliant conversationalist." Her writings, he long since concluded, are "the most important pioneer work done in the field of letters in my time"; for she extended the limits of the writer's medium by using words that in themselves have touch, taste and smell and create in the reader's mind "a whole new world of sensation." Her books "in a very real sense re-create life in words." As soon as she received the copy of the typed draft he sent her, Stein wrote to say that she was "very much touched and more than delighted with the preface."[38]

Anderson's third nonfiction piece was "New Orleans, The Double Dealer and the Modern Movement in America." Written in late February and early March, it was a hail and farewell to the city he had come to love. Within his own lifetime, he writes, the United States has accepted a "standardization of life and thought" unknown in his father's day or even now among the individualistic French. Against this standardization, mirrored in the technically skilled but empty stories of the mass magazines, is set the Modern Movement, which "is really no more than an effort to re-open the channels of individual expression." Are our American lives, dedicated as they are to the merely quantitative goals of "progress," worth living? Only if America begins "to turn more of its natural vitality into the Arts, and if we begin to think more of quality than of quantity and more of living than of accumulating. . . ." Here in the "Vieux Carré," the "Old Quarter," this Modern knowledge has, paradoxically, been a traditional one; and *The*

Double Dealer, which proclaims the Modern Spirit, merely reasserts the real meaning of culture: first of all the enjoyment of life, leisure and a sense of leisure; . . . time for a play of the imagination over the facts of life; . . . time and vitality to be serious about really serious things and a background of joy in life in which to refresh the tired spirits."[39]

Anderson's conclusion that "the Modern Spirit" means "putting the joy of living above the much less subtle and . . . altogether more stupid joy of growth and achievement" came to him naturally after the climactic event of his stay in New Orleans. Mardi Gras fell on February 28 that year, and though the weather was gray, the streets were filled with maskers who, Prohibition being little observed, were "properly gay and at least half abandoned to fun." Leaving his desk early, Anderson wrote Bab, he

went . . . to play with the crowd and at noon met some friends. We went off to the old French Market to an Italian restaurant and ate, drank and danced all afternoon. The party went on no doubt half the night but at dusk I lit out to go into the negro section and walk there.

It is because of the negroes, the French and the Italians that there is play to be had here.[40]

The party was over, and Anderson had to head back to the winter-bound industrial North with the first draft of *Many Marriages* essentially complete. Leaving New Orleans around March 4, he set off for Chicago via Louisville, Kentucky, where he was joined by Dave Bohon, eager for business deals and a wild carouse in the city. By the thirteenth at the latest Anderson was again at Critchfield, that "prison" of "human souls."

3.

Chicago, after "openhanded" New Orleans, was like a "tense closed" fist, he wrote a friend on his return. He had his advertising accounts to catch up on, since he would still be much dependent on them for income, even though Huebsch had just mailed him a royalty check for $731.61; but in all the time he could steal from business commitments, he drove at revising *Many Marriages,* the first draft of which in some fifty-five thousand words he had "written . . . through" before March 13. Replying to a query from Gilbert Seldes as to whether he had some short pieces to submit to *The Dial,* he suggested that the magazine might want to serialize this new novel. What he was "striking for" in this revision, he wrote to Bab, was "a new, a more intense prose. To write whole novels that will drive forward without a break, as I have in the past written short stories." Into the projected four or five novels of which *Many Marriages* was to be the first, he could, he felt, "crowd the whole expression of my own impulse toward life," and shutting Chicago out as much as he could, he was "stripping [himself] like a soldier entering a long campaign."[41]

His life was not to move so single-mindedly forward, however. Tennessee had been informed that by April 1 she must vacate her apartment at 12 East Division, where Sherwood was staying at the moment, since the building was to be torn down or completely remodeled inside. On the first of the month she moved into the tiny house in Palos Park with him, but the confinement to so small a space merely exacerbated the tension between them.

Throughout the spring that tension could occasionally be eased for the moment by the buffering presence of guests. On the morning of May 22, for instance, Sherwood took Hi Simons, an aspiring young writer, for a "flivver-drive" in his Ford, purchased back in mid-March, before Simons had lunch with the Andersons. The year before, Simons's wife, Bernardine, had left him and the *Chicago Evening Post* for a newspaper job in New York, and he was reexamining his life, including his desire to be a writer. It was hard, he suggested to Anderson as they drove over the Palos hills, for a young writer to make a living out of writing. "That's one of the problems that's existed since the beginning of time," replied Sherwood.

Why, God damn it! any young man can get a hearing. But he can't make a living out of his writing. That's the trouble in this country: art's got all mixed up with the matter of earning money, and really they have nothing to do with each other.

I'm able to write and earn a living, both, now. But it's only because I've got something of a reputation as an advertising writer. It took me twenty years to do it, and I'm forty-five now. I don't make anything from my books—don't expect to. But I earn my living—not very much—we live very cheaply—and do my writing in the time I might make more money in.

The real problem for Simons, Anderson continued, hesitating lest his words hit the young man too hard, "is, you're interested in being a writer instead of writing." After a stunned moment, Simons agreed and asked Anderson how he knew. "Oh, without guessing," he laughed. "I could tell by the books you ask about and what you ask about them." After all, "the only reason for writing," he concluded, "is because you can't help it." So impressed was Simons that he would note down what else Anderson commented on that day—on the need to be humble, as Dostoyevsky supremely was, and "simply let the story tell itself" rather than getting "in the way of it ourselves"; on Dreiser as "a really heroic figure" for his unyielding resistance to censorship, though that resistance had robbed him of "tenderness" and "reverence"; on what Europe offers the American artist, who must go there to see it:

Chartres!—You can read about it and see pictures of it, but actually to sit in front of it, see it yourself—there's nothing you can get like that in America . . . And nobody built Chartres to make a living, to get rich! How humble they must have been![42]

Anderson's own humility was being tested, for in this spring of 1922 there were signs, though mixed ones, that his fame was spreading to a wider public abroad and at home. Early in May, Hart Crane wrote to him of a German poet's desire to have exclusive rights to translate *Winesburg, Ohio;* Huebsch, when Anderson consulted him, warned him against tying himself "hand and foot" to someone who might not actually do the translation or find a publisher for it if done. At about the same time came appropriately ironic news from France. Madame Gay had recently finished her translation of *Winesburg,* and prior to book publication, as Galantière explained the situation in his "Paris News Letter" in the *New York Tribune,* newspaper rights were sold to "Le Gaulois," the organ of the Mondaine Royalist party, and several of the stories duly appeared therein. Suddenly, after three or four of them had been published, they ceased to appear. The last tale published was "Hands" and this, it seems, was so offensive to readers of "Le Gaulois" that no others were inserted.

Huebsch sent a clipping of Galantière's column to Anderson, who dryly replied:

It is always rather nice, when one gets swatted by the moralists, French or Anglo Saxon to have it done stupidly on our own best battle ground.

It is always one of the best and finest things, and the cleanest too, they manage to tackle us on.[43]

The most important indication of his wider fame was an article, complete with his photograph, in the mass circulation weekly magazine *The Literary Digest* for April 1, 1922. As usual with the *Digest,* the article, titled "An Exponent of the New Psychology," consisted largely of extended quotation, in this case from the English critic Rebecca West's review of *The Triumph of the Egg* in a recent issue of *The New Statesman.* Despite Anderson's tendency to be indifferent to "the superficies of existence," West considered all his stories "profound" if uneven in quality. "I Want to Know Why" was "momentously good," and "The Triumph of the Egg" succeeded "prodigiously." She had reservations about the extent to which "his excessive preoccupation with the new psychology strikes deeply at the root of his talent," but she pronounced him "one of the most interesting personalities writing in English to-day" and "of all the younger American writers . . . the one we have most reason to envy." Anderson, flattered, commented briefly to Huebsch that this *Digest* article "might help" in publicizing his work, but his chief interest remained the question whether *The Dial* would serialize *Many Marriages*.[44]

So concerned had he become and so restless that he "couldn't wait for spring in Chicago any longer," and sometime in the week of April 3 he went off for a few days in New York, where the trees were already beginning to show green. Here he saw much of Paul Rosenfeld, visited with Karl, had lunch with the painter Arthur Dove of the Stieglitz circle, and on April 10 dropped in on Burton Rascoe, who had just been appointed literary editor of the *Tribune* and who noted in the first appearance of his regular column "A Bookman's Day Book" that "Sherwood is enthusiastic about New Orleans, where he says people have a good time and aren't always trying to do things in a hurry." Most importantly, he settled with Seldes that *The Dial* would serialize a shortened version of *Many Marriages,* installments to begin in the late summer (actually with the October number) and to run over into the early issues of 1923. Since Huebsch would hold off book publication of the complete version until the installments had appeared, he was indulging himself in 1922, Anderson wrote a New Orleans friend, in a first "year of innocence" when he did not publish a book after six years of publishing one each year.[45]

On April 14 he took the train back to Chicago. Clearly there had been more on his mind in New York than the slowness of the Midwest spring. On the fifteenth he dictated to a Critchfield secretary a reply to a request from one Newlin Price of the Ferargil Galleries in New York for information about Karl's early years to be used in an article Price was preparing on Karl's artistic development; and Sherwood then wrote his brother, apologetically asserting that he had not been able to provide Price with the "little flashing adventures of life that make up that part of our own lives upon which we later feed and live" because such adventures are not told to each other by brothers. Then after praising Karl as a painter with "the gift of loveliness and of fragrant delicate color" and asserting his own interest now in fantasy, "the god of Naturalism . . . dead" for him, he hinted for the first time in the extant correspondence that he was contemplating a change in his personal life. As far as he was concerned, any artist was "better off unattached" to another person, perhaps should never make permanent attachments at all. "Of that," he concluded darkly, "no more. One has enough of a job whoring after the gods of beauty."[46]

Beneath this veiled language can be perceived Anderson's growing determination to separate from Tennessee, though in the next few days he must have put her mostly out of his mind since he had job enough cutting his nearly revised manuscript of *Many Marriages* to the shorter length agreed on for *The Dial*. By April 24 he could exuberantly write to Seldes:

I've come very near taking every word out of this story, have washed their little faces and pressed their pants.

Also I had the counting machines at work and the whole thing has been gone over by a public accountant.

You will see yourself that every undesirable citizen, of this corrupt city of my fancy has been jailed, sand-bagged, thrown out of town.

With the cut version of *Many Marriages* dispatched to *The Dial,* Anderson turned to completing his revision of the full-length book, which he got into Huebsch's hands around May 15, and to starting its sequel. By the nineteenth he was deep enough into the second novel in the projected series that he had set aside entirely another project he had contemplated, a book to be titled *Threads* made up of "satirical comments on American literary life." Perhaps, he admitted to Huebsch, his notion of doing such a book was only a "fancy to play with," for it did not really seem to be "my note."[47]

Any writing, however, soon became impossible, for the tension between him and Tennessee had reached the breaking point. That for some time he had, to her dismay, been drifting away from her had been indicated, of course, by his physical absences—his going to Fairhope in 1920 at first by himself, his move from her Division Street apartment to the small house in Palos Park, his initial agreement to go abroad only with Rosenfeld and then his tendency to explore Paris either with Paul or by himself, and, most obviously, his two jubilant months in New Orleans. Bernardine Simons, who remained a close friend of Tennessee yet was also very fond of Sherwood, later maintained that his reason for leaving her was that he had become profoundly resentful of her "brilliance." He had habitually given her "everything to read as he was writing it," Bernardine recalled,

and she would make suggestions, and damn-it-all they were all such wonderful suggestions. And I think it got to the place where he felt that she was participating too much in his writing, and he began to resent that a *woman* should be that smart and that bright and be able to criticize and help and aid him that much.

Even more than Cornelia, whose mind had tended toward the abstract, Tennessee had the creative artist's insight, and with her wit and her direct force and honesty she may well at times have made her suggestions or criticized her husband's writing too bluntly. But tactfully or untactfully made, her suggestions and criticisms could cumulatively imply to Sherwood that he was not fully the master of his craft, he who regarded his vocation as artist with a seriousness approaching the religious and who was far more sensitive to adverse criticism than he would usually admit.[48]

There were other reasons as well to explain his subsequent admission that in Tennessee's "presence" he had been "assertive, combative, egotistical." He had come to regard what her friends saw to be her admirably strong personality as, rather, a dominating one, the desire to dominate coming partly from jealousy of his artistic success, partly from a neurotic possessiveness, a feeling-state she had manifested at least as early as 1920 when he had gone off to Fairhope by himself only to be called back to Chicago when she had the nervous collapse from which she recovered so dramatically after he brought her back with him. She had certainly remained in love with him, as even he must have recognized at times, held by the warmth and charm he intermittently displayed and by her self-confessed deep need for "thought and affection," which lay beneath her independence and self-sufficiency. Her increasingly desperate attempts to hold him as he drifted away became, however, confirmations to him of her desire to possess and dominate; and when she had written him in New Orleans threatening to commit suicide, he had symbolically allowed her to do so in the person of Mary Webster, his fictional cruelty a measure of his real life antagonism. However much and for how long his and Tennessee's sexual life had deteriorated, as had John and Mary Webster's, may only be guessed at as a cause and sign of their present disharmony; but certainly Tennessee had disorganized his emotional life. When not "combative" with her, he felt passive, "empty," uninvolved with others and his surroundings. Grimly he analyzed her struggle in "the fight," he confided bitterly to Bab, "of the one who by the circumstances of life has become an invert. There is this terrific fight to bring the one outside ones self within the circle of the individual's life."[49]

As with Cornelia ten years earlier, too, Sherwood associated this second wife with a specific place and stage of his life that he must break free from, if possible transcend. The Dial Award and its attendant publicity and, most recently, the recognition in *The Literary Digest* were making him nationally known; he was beginning to be regarded, not as a leading Chicago writer but as a leading American one. Chicago had "lowered over" him, he would soon write Rosenfeld, "like a great beast ever since I came from New Orleans," and he was resolved this time to leave it for good and Tennessee with it—or as he put it guardedly, but at last unmistakably, in a May 9 letter to Hart Crane, to make "some permanent changes this summer in the mechanism of my life."[50]

To resolve to act and to act were not the same, however, and for some weeks he remained sunk in depressed indecision as just how to proceed. At night he slept fitfully; by day he shrank fearfully away from friends. Sometime in late May or early June, remembering how being among blacks in Mobile and New Orleans had soothed him, he rented a room in a "negro house" in the great black ghetto of Chicago, evading decisive action by a retreat into anonymity and the past. As he wrote Bab,

I go there in the evening and sit in my room. Well it is hot and uncomfortable but I do not mind the physical discomfort. About me are the voices of people who do not know me, whom I do not know. I do not cut down across the realities of their lives at all. The low murmur of voices arise. There is always low laughter.

I sit until darkness comes and then go into a negro restaurant to dine. I am, for the time, far away from my own people, in a strange place. Here I am nothing. I am myself as I was when I was a boy. I look out at life wonderingly.

Now I want a great deal of this sort of thing. It is a kind of pilgrimage back into the realities of life I am going to undertake now. There is something I want to accomplish. It may take me a year. It may take ten years.

Although he would never make love to a black woman—as he revealingly put it, "a civilized man must love a civilized woman"—he preferred living among blacks "more than with any other people I have found in America. There is more laughter, more real sense of life and oddly enough—more unconscious sense of beauty."[51]

Briefly the weeks of indecision were broken in on by a trip to Owensboro, where through several days of sultry mid-June heat he sat at a desk with sweat rolling off him and wrote advertising copy for Steele's farm machinery, wishing in his revulsion that "everyone for whom I work would go broke." Too upset to visit Bab on the way, he returned to Chicago and around June 21 poured out his wretchedness to a sympathetic Paul Rosenfeld, declaring that he must get out of Chicago and wanted to visit Paul in the East. Paul's warm invitation that he come early in August for a month or more and stay in Paul's new house in Westport seems to have helped him to act. He prepared to leave Chicago, quietly going about among a number of his friends to ask that they keep a kindly eye on Tennessee. He could not bring himself to face her with the flat statement that he wanted a divorce and instead merely told her that he was going to tour the country in his Ford. As he had done before, he was resolving a crisis by literally escaping from it. When subsequently she learned of Sherwood's real intent, Tennessee, still much in love with him, would grieve most over a sense of her personal failure, that, in Bernardine Szold's words, "having always believed in an honest and noble communication, she had in some way made it impossible for Sherwood to tell her straight out that he was off for good." But that was to be some weeks away. At the end of June he had packed his car and driven away from Chicago and Tennessee. He never saw her again.[52]

13

A New Life

1.

"I am going to drive to Ohio," Anderson told Harry Hansen, "and maybe New England. If I get the feeling that I ought to write I'll sit down and write and may be I'll do a book." Drifting eastward, he decided first to go back to where he had been a boy, to Clyde. He spent July 5

with a group of my boyhood friends, now become lawyers, grocers, laborers, doctors, mechanics. We had a big feed out of doors on the shore of Sandusky bay—with wine and song. It was really charming of them. They had a notion I had done something but weren't very sure what it was, so they got up this feast to celebrate anyway. One of them said, "We are proud of you. We don't know what for but we are proud of you anyway."

The brief return to his roots stirred memories that would shortly issue in that autobiographical tale, "The Sad Horn Blowers"; but, restless, he drove on the following day to Cleveland, found lodging in a "hot little room," and settled in for two weeks of impatient waiting for Seldes at *The Dial* to send proofs of the serial version of *Many Marriages*.[1]

The monotone days of driving had helped him to sleep better than during those last unhappy weeks in Chicago, but he still felt "in a rather tired bedeviled mood," a mood probably alleviated only a little by a royalty statement from Huebsch indicating that from November 1, 1921, to April 30, 1922, *The Triumph of the Egg* had sold 4,446 copies. He had a novel, "or rather the sense of one floating about . . . like a fog seen through a window," he wrote Rosenfeld, but the "creative machine inside me hasn't set to work yet." Paul had earlier written him in Chicago that a "general rottenness" had made the spring miserable for everyone they knew; yet Sherwood wondered whether his own "going to pieces" may not have been "as usual . . . all my own fault." Success and public attention had come to him too abruptly.

> What I think is that I have allowed people to make me a bit too conscious of myself. A certain humbleness toward life in general, that has always been my best asset, was perhaps getting away from me. One begins to be taken up by people of little or no intelligence and soon cannot discriminate. I have thought the remedy to be a long period of being unknown—even if necessary losing my name.

Even with Paul, however, he was not yet ready to refer to the real cause of his unhappiness, the break with Tennessee. This was a matter he presumably discussed only with Bab, whom he arranged to meet in Detroit on July 10. Their talk must have been painful for each, if for different reasons, since he would have wanted to unburden his own troubles on her rather than give her hope for a revival of their relationship now that he was definitely leaving his second wife.[2]

On the second day after his arrival in Cleveland he had informed Hart Crane of his presence there, and Crane, then living in the city with his mother and grandmother, had excitedly invited him to dinner at their home on the tenth, an invitation Anderson had to refuse because of his trip to Detroit to see Bab. He did not try again to meet Crane for some days, partly because his depressed mood made him "hunt solitude," as he later explained to Crane, and partly because he had learned that Crane currently had as house guest a close friend, Gorham Munson. Munson was not only was writing a book praising Waldo Frank, but he was the opinionated "Director" of the little magazine *Secession*, which in its first number, distributed in mid-April, had contained a vicious attack by Munson on *The Dial*, on Paul Rosenfeld, and particularly on Anderson as an incompetent writer who, middle-aged and well-off financially, had not fitted the criteria for, hence had not deserved, the first Dial Award. Probably reluctant to see Crane in Munson's company, Anderson instead spent his afternoon at the country racetracks around Cleveland watching the trotters and pacers. Evenings he often walked and talked with another friend of Crane, Richard Laukhuff, to whose bookstore in Cleveland's Taylor Arcade Anderson had his mail addressed. Laukhuff, son of a Bavarian organ builder, had himself worked as an organ builder for some time after emigrating to the United States until, offended by American inexpensive manufacturing methods, he had opened his bookstore, stocking it with classics, books by contemporary Continental and American authors, and even some of the current little magazines. Since Laukhuff loved fine craftsmanship, the two men got on well; and when some weeks later Anderson wrote a tribute to Stieglitz which was published in *The New Republic*, he praised

Laukhuff as yet another craftsman-artist opposed to the shoddy ugliness of the Machine Age.[3]

It was not until July 17 or 18 that Anderson finally telephoned Crane, whereupon Crane invited him to dinner at a restaurant and to his home afterwards. During dinner Crane was charmed by Anderson and talked enthusiastically about the possibility of a German translation of the older man's work and about the many paintings he had hung in his room at home by two Cleveland artists, William Sommer and William Lescaze. When later at home Crane led Anderson and Munson to his room to show the paintings, Anderson liked them, though Munson, hardly an objective observer, would later recall being "annoyed by the way [Anderson] walked around the tower room, looking at the paintings. He'd look closely at a painting, pace back a few steps, admire it for awhile and then praise the color: 'What color!'"[4] Crane, who was especially trying to spread Sommer's reputation, was pleased when Anderson offered to show some of the paintings to Rosenfeld if Crane would ship them to him via Huebsch in New York. Unfortunately for the evening, Munson tactlessly began to disparage Rosenfeld, which angered Anderson, and to praise Frank, which angered him further. To Crane's distress his two guests began to quarrel bitterly, and it was all he could do to quiet them.

On July 20, the day before he left Cleveland, Anderson wrote Crane apologizing for his "stupidity in being drawn in to a literary argument" and for his failure to see more of him, and again offering to show a selection of Sommer's pieces to Rosenfeld. Crane could not have known that Anderson was indeed in a "super sensitive" condition while in Cleveland, and so concluded that Anderson not only had deliberately avoided him but was "fibbing" about a "tired bedeviled mood." Feeling himself insulted, Crane apparently did not reflect that, though he had known Munson's attitude toward Anderson and Rosenfeld, at the least from having read the attack in *Secession,* he had brought the two men together and hence had made a quarrel likely. Instead he sided entirely with Munson. When, shortly, he learned that Anderson in New York had spoken unfavorably of Munson to some of the other contributors to *The Dial,* he dismissed him as "nasty" and "just another fool." Nevertheless, though expecting nothing under the circumstances, Crane on August 5 did send twenty-seven of Sommer's watercolors and drawings to Anderson, who dutifully showed them to Rosenfeld and two painters, and then in mid-August reported to Crane that all three had rejected them as having "No distinct personal note." By mutual unexpressed consent the older writer and the younger one thereupon ended their correspondence. Their first meeting in person had been their last.[5]

The evening of July 19 was a much pleasanter one for Sherwood, for he was taken on an outdoor picnic by two "delightful women," Margaret

Lane and a friend. Margaret (Peg), sister to Cornelia Lane Anderson, had been a highly regarded anesthetist at Cleveland's Lakeside Hospital but had for some time been living and working in New York. She was tall, dark-haired, beautiful, vivacious in dress and manner, and very adventurous. Despite Sherwood's divorce from her sister, she and he got on well together, and he found both women "great fun."[6] He agreed to look Peg Lane up in New York.

The proofs for *Many Marriages* still had not come, even though he stayed on an extra day beyond his original intention. On the morning of July 21 he again began his slow drift by Ford toward the East. Either in Cleveland or during some stop on the way to New York he composed a farewell to Ohio to be published in the August 9 issue of *The New Republic* as the ninth in a series titled "These United States." Done in the satirical style of the discontinued *Threads* pieces, "Ohio: I'll Say We've Done Well" ironically praises his native state for having so quickly managed to destroy its natural beauty through building so many ugly, noisy, dirty industrial cities. In a pastoral mode as striking as Mark Twain or Huck Finn describing the Mississippi, he sketches what the Ohio must have been like when the explorer La Salle first saw it.

I remember that an old man I knew when I was a boy told me about seeing the Ohio River in the early days, when the rolling hills along its banks were still covered with great trees, and what he said I can't remember exactly, but anyway, he gave me the impression of a sweet, clear, and majestic stream, in which one could swim and see the sand of the bottom far below, through the sparkling water. The impression I got from the old man was of boys swimming on their backs, and white clouds floating overhead, and the hills running away, and the branches of trees tossed by the wind like the waves of a vast green sea.

Now that we Ohioans have been able to "lick the poet out of our own hearts and then . . . lick nature herself," any citizen with a "little more push, a little more zip and go . . . can lead a decent life."

He can get up in the morning and go through a street where all the houses are nicely blacked up with coal soot, and into a factory where all he has to do all day long is to drill a hole in a piece of iron. It's fine the way Ford and Willys and all such fellows have made factory work so nice. Nowadays all you have to do, if you live in an up-to-date Ohio town, is to make, say, twenty-three million holes in pieces of iron, all just alike, in a lifetime. Isn't that fine? And at night a fellow can go home thanking God, and he can walk right past the finest cinder piles and places where they dump old cans and everything without paying a cent.

Obviously material drawn from his experience as young man and as middle-aged man looking around him was beginning to coalesce toward

473

the making of "The Sad Horn Blowers." His "creative machine" was beginning to work again, and the lively tone of the article suggests that he
was beginning to recover from his depression. Certainly such a recovery
would have been speeded up as soon as he saw or learned about the "Letters and Art" feature in *The Literary Digest* for July 22, a long article entitled "America's Literary Stars." For all his desire to live temporarily "obscure," he could hardly have objected to the announcement that a poll of
literary editors and reviewers had placed him third among "the five leading American literary stars that have risen above the horizon in the past
ten years," with the now largely forgotten Joseph Hergesheimer first and
Eugene O'Neill second, Willa Cather fourth, and Robert Frost and James
Branch Cabell tied for fifth.[7] It must have pleased him too to see that he
placed well ahead of both Edgar Lee Masters and Sinclair Lewis. And he
must have rejoiced at Mencken's judgment that "We are in the midst of a
shifting of standards. The dominant critical opinion of the United States,
once strongly Puritan, has become anti-Puritan, and it has, to some extent,
carried the more enlightened sort of public opinion with it."

Anderson had not, however, fully recovered emotional health when, at
least by August 7, he reached New York and holed up in Ben Huebsch's temporarily vacant apartment at 14 Mt. Morris Park West. By selling "what
was left" of his Ford he had enough money to support himself for the next
few months. Still not able to tell Paul Rosenfeld of his break with Tennessee
until they met face to face, admitting that he was "a fighter gone a little stale
perhaps," he begged off writing a piece for a Stieglitz publication on the
grounds that "You both know I cannot write without feeling with my whole
being the thing I write about." Yet finally unburdening himself to Paul, being away from Chicago with its distractions and in New York with few distractions beyond those he wished, he suddenly began "writing like a mad-
man," working each day until exhausted and then walking for hours about
the city. Within the next month he made several false starts on a novel but,
in addition, wrote five short stories and a long poem.[8]

Four of these five tales can be identified with fair certainty, and they
suggest some of his current concerns.[9] "The Sad Horn Blowers," of course
came out of his visit to Clyde, which had awakened, among happy memories, unhappier ones of a detested father (who had died as recently as
May 1919), a youthful departure (as he had again departed) from a familiar milieu into an uncertain future, and a period of loneliness and disorientation (such as he had been painfully going through for weeks) in a
city. The father Tom Appleton, whose wife has recently died, has long embarrassed his sons and daughter by his boyish "lack of dignity." He plays
the cornet only a little better than Windy McPherson had the bugle, boasts
of his skill at housepainting, hints at wild, secret carouses, and through his
own foolishness scalds himself badly as Irwin Anderson had done eight

years before Emma died. Having thus punished his father again in his fiction, Anderson concentrates on his remembered misery as his persona Will Appleton leaves the security of Bidwell (Clyde) for factory work in Erie. Here he endures loneliness in a grimy boardinghouse and alienation at a job where all day he stands at "a machine and bores holes in . . . little, short, meaningless pieces of iron." Nevertheless he finally comes to terms with his fear that he is "a thing swinging in air" with "no place to put down his feet" through accepting the friendship of his landlady's timid, dominated husband, a grotesque who yearns to blow his cornet loudly at night but dares sound only a few soft notes.

The theme of feckless husband and dominating wife is repeated in "There She Is—She Is Taking a Bath," a slight tale about a fussy, hypersensitive businessman who suspects his wife of adultery, hires a detective to spy on her, and then hires a second detective to make sure that the first reports his wife to be innocent, thus leaving himself in continued doubt as to his wife's faithfulness. Unlike "The Sad Horn Blowers," however, the tone of this story, told in the first person by the suspicious husband, is entirely satiric, Anderson having apparently decided to test further the skill that produced "Ohio: I'll Say We've Done Well." The self-revealing monologue of the husband markedly resembles that of one of Turgenev's "superfluous" men who expend their lives in useless, self-contemptuous talk and connect only ineffectually with reality, in this instance illustrated by the husband's nervous dropping of his shaving brush or spilling of his dessert at dinner.

The assumption that Anderson was yet again rereading his favorite *A Sportsman's Sketches* to speed up his "creative machine" is strengthened by the two remaining stories. Despite obvious differences between them, "The Triumph of a Modern: or, Send for the Lawyer" has strong points of similarity to Turgenev's "Tatyana Borissovna and Her Nephew." In both satiric tales there is a nephew who has no competence as an artist but who likes the notion of living "the life painters lead"—one recalls Anderson's characterization of Hi Simon back in May—and an aunt who is emotionally and financially exploited by him. Anderson seems to have liked this trivial story, in which an orphaned nephew writes his dying aunt that he wishes he might find refuge from life by laying his head on her "breasts," deliberately using the plural since he is "a thorough modern and full of the modern boldness" and thereby winning from her a deathbed change of her will making him her heir. Or perhaps the author was just being "foxy" when on August 23 he wrote Edmund Wilson, the new managing editor of *Vanity Fair,* to praise "a very charming and amusing thing" he had written, "a satirical comment on modern writing in the form of a tale" which "I fancy you might just eat . . . up."

The Turgenev echo is even stronger in the fourth, and much more

consequential, story Anderson wrote that August; for its title in book publication, "A Chicago Hamlet," clearly comes from "The Hamlet of the
Shtchigri District," and, as in that tale from *A Sportsman's Sketches,* a
first-person narrator reports the reminiscences told him by a "superfluous
man," who, Hamlet-like in Turgenev's definition of the type, unpacks his
bitter, frustrated heart with words.[10] To create the protagonist of this
story, first titled "Broken," Anderson drew on memories of his Critchfield
friend, George Daugherty, here the big, awkward self-analyst who, the
narrator says, "has given me the most material for stories," just as the big,
awkward Daugherty, Anderson would later assert, had been his own best
"feeder" of story material.[11] Unlike Turgenev's self-hating provincial
gentleman who volubly recounts his wholly "unoriginal" life to the listening Sportsman in chronological sequence, Tom, the Daugherty figure,
tends to let fall for the listening storyteller "fragments, . . . little illuminating bits of his personal history," of his early years of hardship before
he became a weary, disillusioned writer of advertising copy, a dull Hamlet
trapped in a dull, ugly Chicago. In "a fragmentary way" echoing Tom's
own narrative manner, the storyteller gives Tom's account of the enmity
between him and his father, a "dislike," which on Tom's part "took the
form of contempt," that after the boy's mother had died, the father, a fanatically religious farmer, had married a slovenly "poor stick" of a woman
with four children of her own. One day when Tom is nineteen, he abruptly
leaves home for good out of revulsion at seeing his father on his knees at
prayer in the fields, his bare feet blackened by dirt at heel and toe, his in-
steps oddly and unpleasantly white. After wandering as a casual farm laborer through southern Ohio, Tom takes work on the farm of a German
couple where one "silent, hot, soft night," as he sits sleepless by the barn,
the young wife unexpectedly comes to him in her nightgown. Unable to
speak each other's language, Tom and the woman embrace, then face each
other for long moments but have no further physical relation. Theirs is "a
union of two people that was not personal, that concerned their two bodies and at the same time did not concern their bodies." The following
morning Tom leaves the farm, feeling that he has possessed the woman in
a way her husband never can; and thereafter he frequently sees in fancy a
woman walking away from him across a treeless countryside he has never
seen in actuality, a strong woman walking vigorously though her limbs
and body are "broken things."

Typically, in this story, Anderson seems to have started with pieces of
"reality"—memories of George Daugherty and of his own detested father,
his present reaction against Chicago and his life there, his current reading
of a Turgenev tale—and to have combined and reworked such fragments
into a story, which, through a series of careful digressions, climaxes in a
pastoral lyric of silent communication between a man and a woman. Just

as Tom's fragmented manner of telling his story to the narrator is an analogue of Anderson's own storytelling manner, so Tom's fanciful picture of
the woman who walks strongly with broken body is an analogue of the
story itself, fragments but a whole "shaken loose and fallen . . . as a ripe
apple falls from a tree in a wind." That Tom's reminiscences are presented
through a narrator allows the latter, a transparent mask for Sherwood Anderson, to comment explicitly and memorably on the art of storytelling.

> In telling this tale I have an advantage you who read cannot have. I heard the tale
> told brokenly by the man who had the experience I am trying to describe. Story-
> tellers of old times who went from place to place telling their wonder-tales had an
> advantage we, who have come in the age of the printed word, do not have. They
> were both storytellers and actors. As they talked, they modulated their voices,
> made gestures with their hands. Often they carried conviction simply by the power
> of their own conviction. All of our modern fussing with style in writing is an at-
> tempt to do the same thing.

Now that Anderson could fuss so insistently with his style, clearly he
was becoming himself again after a bad time.

One further reason for his burst of writing may have been the renewal
of his feelings about the work of Gertrude Stein, happy memories of her
having been awakened by a photograph she had sent him early in August.
On August 9 he lunched with Burton Rascoe and Edmund Wilson, on
which occasion, according to Rascoe's account in his "A Bookman's Day
Book," Anderson talked at length of how Stein "was, somehow, back of
this whole movement in literature toward a new method of expression."
He did not think, Rascoe reported him as saying, that

> she will ever be anything to readers but I think that she is a big event in literature,
> that she is of the utmost importance to writers. She gives them a new sense of word
> values. Expression had been formulated and cut to precise patterns that were old
> and without life and Gertrude Stein comes along and jumbles words all up and
> gives combinations of them new emotional values and meanings.
>
> She has resigned herself apparently to being made the butt of a joke . . . but all
> the time she is doing work which will, some day, be known to have a tremendous
> influence upon literary expression. A thousand years from now writing will be
> vastly different from what it is now, and I believe that it will be seen that these ex-
> periments by Gertrude Stein have been back of it all, just as the experiments
> Cezanne made and threw or gave away are back of the whole modern movement
> in painting."[12]

Since his praise of Stein was genuine, if expansive, Anderson might
have been pleased to see it in print on August 20; unfortunately, however,
in beginning his report Rascoe had apparently confused the frequent
ridicule *Tender Buttons* met on publication with the more favorable

attitude of Karl Anderson, who had introduced his younger brother to the book. Sherwood said at that August 9 luncheon:

I was at a house one night . . . when my brother, Karl Anderson the painter came in laughing his head off over a book he had in his hands called *Tender Buttons*. He began reading it aloud to us as a joke, and everybody laughed and had a good time over it; but I got up dazed and left the room. I felt as if a door to a new world had opened for me. I walked about alone for half the night turning this new experience over in my mind. She seemed to me like a woman who played with words in the same way another person might toy with precious stones, admiring and being thrilled by them and letting them fall through her fingers to catch their changing color and radiance.

Much annoyed, Anderson wrote to Karl on the twenty-first to apologize for making him appear "a somewhat boorish gentleman" laughing at *Tender Buttons* when Karl had actually been interested in its use of words, while to Stein he wrote denying responsibility for any of "this glib and trite transcript." Fortunately she replied that she had not seen the *Tribune* account and in any case would never doubt that he understood her.[13]

Throughout August he remained mostly hidden away mornings in Huebsch's apartment, where he was working his "phool head off," he wrote Edmund Wilson on August 23 in high spirits. A special reason for his ebullience was that by this date he had been approached by the literary agent Otto Liveright, brother of Horace (the publisher), with the proposal that he handle the sale of Anderson's work now that Anderson's fame was established and the large circulation magazines, even the *Saturday Evening Post,* wanted to publish his stories. Anderson need only continue to write in his own way, and within a year such magazines would "surrender" and, not daring to demand that he write "as they wish," would be paying him high prices, "not because of admiration of his work but as an answer to the criticism that has been directed against them." Anderson should no longer "bother" himself with marketing his writings but should leave that to Liveright. "It will be the proudest moment of my life," Otto told Sherwood, "when I make some of the big magazines pay you, as they are now paying inferior men."[14]

Pleased at the prospect of financial reward at last and of relief from having to deal with magazine editors, confident that his creative machine was working well again, Anderson by August 23 had agreed that Otto Liveright should be his literary agent. Thinking over his new arrangement with Liveright, he wrote to Bab early in September of yet another decision.

And while I am at it I shall quite separate myself from the advertising business too. The other morning I walked, thought it all out, bowed my head before the gods and took the oath that I would write no more drivel about plows or breakfast foods. Enough is enough. I am forty-six next week. As the matter stands I shall be very comfortable for a year and I shall work more steadily.[15]

A new phase of his life was definitely beginning.

2.

Since he was through with his advertising and Chicago years, and wanted to remain for the present as hidden away as possible, he located a small apartment in New York and moved in on September 16. This one-room apartment, which he shared with the original renter, a young professor at Columbia University named Burdette I. Kinne, was in the basement of a narrow, three-story, red brick building at 12 St. Luke's Place in Greenwich Village. The two windows of the apartment looked south at sidewalk level onto a school playground just across the narrow street. Much of the day the neighborhood was quiet, and it probably attracted him by its pleasantness, as it probably did Theodore Dreiser, who moved in at No. 16 a month later. By early September, however, Sherwood had a more compelling reason for moving to St. Luke's Place—its nearness to the brownstone house at 51 Charlton Street, four blocks to the south, owned by the woman he had, unexpectedly for both, fallen in love with.[16]

Elizabeth Prall was a small, slender, black-haired, delicate-featured woman of thirty-eight. Born in Saginaw, Michigan, in 1884, she had grown up a quiet, gentle, self-contained member of an individualistic but close, loving family. She attended the University of Michigan, where she majored in Latin and Greek, talked books and music with her classmates, and acquired a love of horseback riding. After successfully surviving a year of high school teaching in an isolated mining village in Michigan's Upper Peninsula, she went to New York and entered the library school of the New York Public Library. She enjoyed learning about the operations of libraries, but beneath her reserved manner was a bent toward the exotic and adventuresome, which led her to buy the house on Charlton Street in the Village. Each floor was an apartment. She lived in the one on the top floor and rented the other apartments to various Village inhabitants, some staid like the "group of earnest women who embroidered church vestments," some less so, such as, for awhile, Floyd Dell. In 1916, because of her excellent work in library school, she was selected by the publisher Frank Doubleday to manage the large and busy Doubleday Doran Bookstore in Lord & Taylor's department store on Fifth Avenue at Forty-third Street. One of the few women at that time to hold so responsible a position, Elizabeth Prall fitted well into the genteel atmosphere of the store; but she knew how to sell books, kept up with current literature, was not afraid to criticize the popular but worthless or to praise the new and unpopular, and displayed a talent for managing her many clerks.[17]

One of these had been the young William Faulkner, whom another Oxford Mississippian Stark Young had persuaded to come to New York at about the time in mid-October 1921 when he himself left Amherst College, where he had been teaching, for a career as drama critic in the city. Young had met Elizabeth Prall through her younger brother David, who had recently taught philosophy at Amherst; and now Stark rented the small basement apartment at 51 Charlton, which Faulkner shared with him until he could find a room of his own. When Elizabeth met Faulkner, she was immediately impressed by his "very elegant and distinguished appearance," took him on at the bookstore, and found him to be an excellent salesman, even if he did not bother to keep his sales accounts straight. With his charming and intimidating Southern manners, Faulkner would load down the lady customers with the many books he advised them to read instead of "the trash," as he would tell them, they had intended to buy. Elizabeth was appalled by his heavy drinking off the job and both shocked and amused by the lurid tales he would invent around his experiences; but she and he became good friends in the few weeks he worked in the bookstore, and she missed his colorful ways when he returned to Mississippi after the Thanksgiving rush. He had invariably addressed her as "Miss Elizabeth," a name that suited her quiet manner and that stuck with her thereafter.

She was becoming interested in Stark Young, however, and friends such as Peg Lane, who was at this time sharing her third-floor apartment, felt him well suited to her. Not handsome, Young nevertheless "Dressed with great elegance and carried himself grandly," was far more sociable than she, but was "entertaining and gallant" and learned in the theater and the arts. Then Sherwood Anderson entered her life. Margaret had already told her about this former brother-in-law whom she had just recently seen again in Cleveland and who had promised to look her up in New York; and from Peg's stories Elizabeth had begun to conceive of him as a "great, free spirit of the Midwest, my own territory."

Anderson did come to see Peg soon after settling in at Huebsch's apartment, took her and Elizabeth out to dinner, and subsequently began coming to the apartment less and less to see the handsome Peg and more and more to see Elizabeth. At first she was a bit afraid of him, of his burliness, his flamboyant clothes, his habit of telling "extravagant, unlikely stories in which he dramatically acted out all the roles." Both were all too aware that he was not yet divorced from Tennessee, but they began to have dinner together occasionally in small out of the way restaurants Sherwood had discovered. After a drink—though he never needed liquor for stimulus, Elizabeth quickly understood—he would talk to her endlessly about himself, his artistic goals, or what the characters had done that day in the stories he was now writing so rapidly. For a book-oriented person like her it was exciting and flattering to be close to a famous writer, and his appearance, especially his very dark eyes, began to attract her more powerfully than any other man she had met. "I had come to realize," she recalled,

that Sherwood was a man who was unlike anyone I had known before. He was both impressive and impressionable, exciting and excitable. It was impossible to tag him with a label,—he was never the same person from day to day. He had to be accepted for the mood he happened to be in at the moment, and slowly I was beginning to accept him. It was a grudging process, for I did not want the order of my life to be shattered.

Disturbed at how he was disrupting her pleasantly satisfying existence at the bookstore, she stopped seeing him briefly; but by the end of August she was helplessly in love with him and seeing him constantly.

Just why he should by then have fallen in love with her is less easy to understand. That he had not even begun divorce proceedings against his second wife did make him wary at first of involvement with a possible third one; but just as women generally were attracted by him, he was attracted to women, in fact felt that he wrote best when he was in love, his present surge of writing clearly being linked in his mind to his developing relation with Elizabeth. Then, too, he was attracted, as with Brooks or Rosenfeld, to college-educated, cultivated persons who had the trained intellect he obscurely resented not having himself, but who nevertheless fed his need for self-worth by admiring his intuitive insights and the Americanness of his art. Rosenfeld at this time said flatly to him concerning Elizabeth, "There's the kind of woman you ought to marry," a mature, cultured one, that is, independent but not dominating like Tennessee; and at this unsettled point in his emotional life he was especially vulnerable to this friend's advice. He perceived, furthermore, the taste for adventure and now the sexual stirring beneath Elizabeth's reserved, gentle manner. Even more than the youthful, inhibited Adaline Katz in New Orleans, she was someone very much worth drawing out. It was warming and reassuring to him that this obviously stable and intelligent but unawakened woman of thirty-eight was falling in love with him, as he at forty-six with her, and showing the eagerness of, in her words, "a teen-ager" to run away from a settled existence into an unknown, exciting future.

Tennessee, meanwhile, was trying to hold her husband. Through friends in New York she learned his phone number and repeatedly tried to reach him, but Sherwood wanted no more contact with her. The obliging Kinne "helped by telling [her] that he was not in when he was & that he had left town when he hadn't. Simultaneously [Anderson] was receiving the woman who afterwards became Miss Mitchell's successor. . . ." One need not read into Kinne's words that Anderson and Elizabeth Prall had at this point entered on a sexual affair, for they probably had not; but for weeks they preferred to tell no one about their love except Elizabeth's brother David, Sherwood's friends Jerry and Lucile Blum, and then Peg Lane and Stark Young. David, who became good friends with Sherwood, and the Blums approved, while the latter two felt that Elizabeth was making a serious mistake. By this time, however, the middle-aged couple were beyond taking advice from anyone, and they began going about together openly though cautious to appear as no more than friends.[18]

Buoyed up by the relationship, Anderson continued to write furiously on several projects. At about this time he began preparing in final form the manuscript and then the typescript of *Many Marriages* for Huebsch, who was scheduling an early 1923 publication of the book. He probably added a new ending to the original version, and he certainly went through the whole novel making a final rewriting. At least by September 13 he was definitely planning a new collection of tales, and by the twenty-second, when, "resplendent in his black stock tie and his bushy aureole of sandy hair," he went to the opening night of *The Exciters,* a play starring Tallulah Bankhead, he could tell Burton Rascoe during the intermission that "he was working very hard on some short stories." Just that day he had finished an article for *The New Republic,* "Four American Impressions." In this four-part piece, published in the October 11 issue, he generously praised Gertrude Stein for "making new, strange and to my ears sweet combination of words"; Ring Lardner for giving "new life to the words of our everyday life"; and Paul Rosenfeld for being "a real aristocrat among writers of prose" and "the American . . . who is unafraid and unashamed to live for the things of the spirit as expressed in the arts." Only Sinclair Lewis among these handlers of "our speech" he criticized, as a "man with a sharp journalistic nose for news of the outer surface of our lives" whose "dreary" prose reveals little awareness of the beauty that lies beneath the barrenness and ugliness of "our American towns and cities." To admit at the end of this attack that a few such moments of awareness did fleetingly appear in the recently published *Babbitt* seems a curious way for Anderson to thank Lewis publicly for having just sent him, as Sherwood wrote Bab, a copy of the novel with an apology to him "written on the flyleaf." His private comment to her had been as ungenerous: "It is really amazing how sincerely the men who have devoted their lives to material progress are now apologizing to such men as have not done so. . . . How much better that Lewis be at the business of squaring himself with his God and not with me."[19]

One suspects that Anderson disliked Lewis not only because of the texture of his prose and the objects of his satire but because *Main Street* had sold so much better than *Poor White*. He was himself entering a stage of his career where his commitment to art would slowly but increasingly come into conflict with his desire to make money from that art. On the one hand, he could write triumphantly to Karl that

> I . . . rather think that the swing of the pendulum has begun. The material age has had its say and has said nothing. What we all are now is partly due to life in the time in which we happen to have lived. You and I will not live into an age that may come out of the growing disgust with life's emptiness, that is to say, an age when the spirit may again breathe and live. . . . Well, after all, that terribly abused word "love" is at the bottom of all the decay. When men do not dare love, they cannot live, and the men of our day did not dare love either God or their fellow men.

On the other hand, he was understandably delighted when his new literary agent Otto Liveright sold "The Sad Horn Blowers" on September 26 to *Harper's Magazine* for $500 (less $50 for the 10 percent commission) and "There She Is, She Is Taking Her Bath" on October 19 to *Pictorial Review* for $750 ($675 to Anderson). Triumphantly he wrote Jerry and Lucile Blum that, "Since I've been here, I've got more for two stories than I ever got for all the stories I've written these years." Then he added, self-justifyingly,

> There'll be a howl. I've sold out, I suppose. It doesn't matter. My bread and butter struggle is probably at an end. There'll be another and more intense kind of struggle with all the things I want to do.

The bread-and-butter struggle was not at an end, but whether he knew it or not, his growing fame and the prices magazines would now pay for his stories were providing him the chance to test his belief that popular success was a mode of failure.[20]

All this good fortune did not ward off his customary physical afflictions. Early in October he caught a bad cold, which became so much worse that around the thirteenth he left the city for Karl's home in Westport and went to bed for several days. Being out in the country seems to have prompted him, on partial recovery, to invite himself and Elizabeth to be weekend guests at the Mt. Kisco home of Jerry and Lucile Blum. He had hoped that the Blums would like "my gentle little woman," and he was not disappointed. The excitable Jerry had for long detested Tennessee, whom he regarded as a gifted but dominating woman bent on destroying Sherwood as man and artist, and he and Lucile took to the quiet, undominating Elizabeth in a way that made Sherwood glow with happiness. The Blums' frank, easy acceptance of their guests as "a man and woman whose love was very sweet," Anderson wrote Lucile gratefully after the country weekend, especially since in pious, censorious, unloving New York, as the city seemed to him at the moment, the loving couple must be circumspect about revealing their affection.[21]

By October 23 he was back at his desk writing, but he still had not fully recovered from the cold, and he decided to try "looking at people in strange places where I'm not known." Recalling how well he had felt in the South, however, he took passage on a coastal steamer, the *Momus*, scheduled to leave New York on November 4 and arrive in New Orleans on the tenth. The voyage down was a great success. The first officer was himself an aspiring young writer, "spotted" Anderson, and gave him the use of his own cabin on the upper deck mornings. By the third day out the *Momus* was far enough south into the Gulf Stream that Anderson could work on a new story at the officer's big desk in his shirtsleeves "with all doors and windows open." He was lucky also in his cabinmate, "an old sport of 65" who "turned out to be a veteran racetrack gambler and horseman" with three pals of the same interest aboard. The group, Anderson with them, "had great times talking horse" or watching the old gambler act out racetrack lore such as "how a foxy rider can throw a horse off stride right under the nose of a judge."[22]

The week's stay in New Orleans was only partly successful. He finished the story he had worked at on the *Momus* and started a complex one called "Fragments," which fascinated him, he wrote the Blums, with its subtlety, its "shades and lights." His pleasure at watching the black stevedores came back to him strongly, and he half-considered spending the colder months of each year in New Orleans so that he could write, not describing blacks directly, but getting into his tales "their abandonment to feeling, their rhythmic sense of life, skies, the river here. Everything at moments seems in them, and they in it all." When he went to the *Double Dealer* office, he was delighted to find these qualities in a story manuscript called "Avey," which a young black writer named Jean Toomer had sent in to John McClure, one of the editors, and which confirmed his earlier excitement on reading Toomer's piece, "Nora," in the magazine's September issue, an excitement that had then prompted him to write Toomer a note of praise. Except for Julius Friend and McClure, however, the white people he had enjoyed the previous winter now seemed "all messed up," purposeless, uninteresting. Having his portrait painted by Ronald Hargrave, a local artist, perhaps pleased him as a sign of his new fame; but much had happened since he had come to New Orleans some months before to escape from an unhappy marriage. Now he missed Elizabeth "horribly" and felt "a growing constant hunger" for the woman he was "most completely in love with."[23]

One week in New Orleans was enough this time. Around November 17 he apparently headed back by boat to New York, where he arrived at least by the twenty-third in time to have Thanksgiving dinner with Elizabeth and Stark Young at 51 Charlton Street. Temporarily his urge for travel was assuaged by the voyage south, and now back with her he felt physically "well and happy." Determined to escape from the telephone calls and visitors distracting him at St. Luke's Place, he found a room "no one knows of but me and God" for his mornings of writing. "I am working," he wrote Bab early in December, "and only perhaps when I am working do I live at all fully." Finishing the last revision of *Many Marriages,* he felt that his clear break with realism in this novel would lead American literature to a similar new phase. "Surely," he declared to her "our writing must take wings a little, not sit forever like an old hen on her nest of china eggs."[24]

Around mid-December his writing took wings in a way he would never forget. One evening as he was walking back to St. Luke's Place, there came clearly to him at last the right way in which to turn the conclusion of his unpublished *Talbot Whittingham* into a short story. When he got to his apartment, he sat down, wrote until three AM, slept for four hours, and then early in the morning, still obsessed with his story, wandered to 51 Charlton Street and rang Stark Young's doorbell at about eight. Young was just going out, but he provided the paper and pen Anderson asked for and also a bottle of whiskey. For the next seven hours Anderson wrote "in a heat," scattering the numbered sheets of manuscript about Stark's apartment in his haste and staving off his weariness by drink after drink from the bottle, which might have contained coffee for all he noticed. By mid-afternoon "The Man's Story" and most of the whiskey were finished; the story was "fixed" as he wanted it, "the swing and rhythm of the prose" fitting the theme exactly. The hours of absolute and completely sober concentration had been one of those "glorious" creative moments he would always remember, and as he wrote the last word, he suddenly was exhausted and drunk. He staggered to Young's bed and fully clothed collapsed onto it in a dead sleep. Stark, coming home that evening, found him there still sleeping and so pale that he thought at first his friend was ill. When Stark woke him, Sherwood declared that he was drunk now but had succeeded finally in writing that "beautiful" and "significant" story he had tried and failed at "a dozen times" before.[25]

Later in his life he would regard "The Man's Story" as his favorite among favorites, a judgment that now seems more understandable on psychological than on aesthetic grounds. Obviously the circumstances of its composition had much to do with that judgment, for in describing them in a "Note" written in the mid- or late thirties, he would conclude, "I have a kind of faith that something of the half mystic wonder of my day in that apartment still lingers. . . ." He had "lived fully" in these hours, salvaged the last four chapters of an abandoned manuscript, and expressed indirectly through one man's story his own devotion to art and his new happiness with a loving woman. Symptomatically he incorporated into his tale two Testaments purporting to be poems by the protagonist, one an entry into people's lives through the exertion of superhuman power, the other an entry through fruitful love. As with *Many Marriages,* these prose poems, whether written that day in Young's apartment or inserted later, would be associated for him with his continuing impulse to attempt new modes of writing, new experiencings of life.[26]

Whatever its limitations as fiction considered, apart from Anderson's fondness for it, "The Man's Story" does show how he could now solve some of the technical problems that had flawed *Talbot Whittingham* seven years or so earlier. He had long since learned the varied uses of a narrator within a story, and for this version of the ending of *Talbot* he discarded the omniscient voice for a teller within the tale, a not-too-scrupulous or perceptive newspaperman who is just scrupulous and perceptive enough to validate certain hardly believable events. Where the artist, such as Talbot is to become, had been described in the discarded manuscript inconsistently, now man of egotistical power, now man of all-enveloping love, Edgar Wilson of "The Man's Story" consistently combines both aspects and, already a poet, expresses the paradoxical combination of cruelty and tenderness in his acts and in the paired poems quoted by the narrator. Lucile Bearing, the defeated woman artist who appears only intermittently in *Talbot,* is here transformed into an unnamed woman who leaves her dull, small-town husband to live in poverty with Wilson in Chicago, devotedly taking a job in "the world of fact" so that he may be free to inhabit the world of poetry, of the imagination.

Wilson's poetry, we are shown as well as told, is obsessively concerned with images of walls between individuals and wells into which each individual has sunk, and with efforts by the poet to overcome separation and create a felt unity, first with the body and mind of his beloved and then with the bodies and minds of all human beings. Walls and wells, separation and loneliness are, in fact, recurrent motifs and themes in Anderson's story as well as Wilson's poems, but both story and poems emphasize more the themes of community and communication. Wilson's desire to break through the grotesqueness of the world into the beauty and harmony beyond is understood by the woman and constitutes the grounds of her devotion to him. That desire is intuited also by a minor character, an impoverished hunchbacked girl who for a time rents a bare bedroom in the Wilson apartment, spies on Wilson alone or in silent harmony with the woman, and feels satisfied afterwards as though Wilson had made physical love to her. Herself a grotesque, she thus dramatically embodies an idea, which in *Talbot* had been asserted too abstractly.

More skilled now at communicating as writer to reader, Anderson much reworked the melodramatic ending of the manuscript novel, even though the climactic event of the story remains melodramatic. As the woman is walking home one night with the poetry-absorbed Wilson, she is shot by a theater stagehand crazed with passion for her. Not admitting a mortal wound, she survives long enough to reach the apartment, where she lights some trash in the fireplace, "making a little flare of beauty at the last," walks lovingly toward the man, and, as at the end of the novel, dies at his feet. Yet the story continues with the newspaperman's description of Wilson's odd unawareness of the woman's death, his gradual awakening to it, and then his compulsive talking about the woman. Before he had met her, he had been "sunk far down into a deep sea of doubt and questionings," and the woman's love had brought him up "to the surface of the sea of life," where, buoyed up by her, "he had floated . . . under the sky, in the sunlight." Deprived of her, he feels himself sinking again like a drowning man. The partly puzzled but wholly sympathetic narrator concludes by saying that, moved by Wilson's despair, he has been impelled to tell the man's story in the hope that, by understanding it fully himself, he may become strong enough to drag the drowning Wilson to the surface again.

That Wilson is a fantasized double for Anderson is obvious. Anderson too, as he saw it, had rejected the world of fact for that of the imagination, though his resulting poverty had hardly matched Wilson's, and he was presently counting on being released from money cares through Otto Liveright's good offices. He too had only recently been sunk far down in the sea of "doubt and dumbness" and was now pulled to the sunlit surface by a woman's love; and if by some mischance this love were taken from him, he could well imagine himself drowning again. Only a little less obvious is what the doubleness further tells—and might have told, perhaps did tell, Elizabeth. To Wilson-Anderson the woman is important to the extent that her love, and incidentally her wages, helps maintain the man within his imaginative artist's world. Wilson, the narrator reports in puzzled reproof, at times acts cruelly, at her death even inhumanly, while he is absorbed in his poetry. He subsequently regrets his cruel acts, is tender toward the living woman, seeks her forgiveness; and the woman understands his being both "casual and brutal . . . tender and sensitive," comforts him, sees nothing to forgive. The self-sacrificing woman is thus essential to the man's happiness and sense of direction in life, but though it is she who dies after putting her last strength into a beautiful gesture for him, it is the man whom the narrator pities. What is truly important, then, is the creation of art. An art concerning the necessity of love for all other persons is of greater importance than any actual human love. This valuation of the artist and his art must at bottom be why Anderson thought his tale "a beautiful, a significant" one and why he came to regard it as his favorite among favorites. Probably Elizabeth saw herself as exempt from any warning she may have perceived in her man's story, but ultimately she would have reason to perceive it.

3.

Along with his bouts of writing and illness and his developing relation with Elizabeth, Anderson found time in the fall of 1922 to meet other people in the arts. On September 7, for example, he went to a supper in honor of Marie Tempest, the British comic actress, who was currently performing with Leslie Howard in *A Serpent's Tooth*. A month or so later Frank Crowninshield, editor of *Vanity Fair,* gave a party in Anderson's honor at the Coffee House, a party attended, according to "The Gossip Shop" in the November *Bookman,* by various writers and critics "and Mr. Anderson himself, hesitantly acknowledging the honor thus paid him. His *Many Marriages* appearing in *The Dial* is already attracting much attention."[27]

His hesitancy was a sign of his pleasure but also his uneasiness in the unaccustomed role of literary lion, and he was usually more at ease with individuals or with the small groups he could hold under the spell of his storytelling. In August and September he lunched or dined a number of times with Edmund Wilson, whom he persuaded to accept two of the Testaments for publication in the October *Vanity Fair* as "Pages From a New Testament." Writer and editor got on well together. Anderson thought Wilson "a fine sensitive man," while Wilson, who had judged *The Triumph of the Egg* to be "about the best thing in current American fiction" and had praised Anderson's "seriousness about life and . . . gift for making a local story seem of universal significance," also much enjoyed "the humorous racy quality" of his talk. (After the writer's death Wilson would recall him as "one of the most agreeable men I have ever known.") At one of their meetings around mid-September, Anderson described the whole of *Many Marriages,* and Wilson concluded that "it is one of the damnedest things ever written. It is a sort of wonderful erotic nightmare full of strange symbolic scenes reared on the old circus ground of American life."[28]

On a bright day early in October, Sherwood was invited to lunch by the current celebrities Scott and Zelda Fitzgerald amid the expensive elegance of the Plaza, where they had taken a suite while househunting on Long Island. John Dos Passos had also been invited and later recalled Anderson somewhat ambivalently as

an appealing sort of man with curly graying hair and strangely soft wrinkles in his face. [He] had large shadowed eyes and prominent eyebrows and a self-indulgent mouth. He had put on a gaudy Liberty silk necktie for the occasion. When I told him how much I admired his writing all the wrinkles in his face broke into smiles.

During lunch "Sherwood got talking about his writing" and afterwards left for an engagement. Subsequently Fitzgerald, who seemed to Dos Passos "a born professional" in his literary comments, "talked about Sherwood's writing, admiringly but critically." Presumably Fitzgerald had already reached the judgment he was to express to his editor Maxwell Perkins some three year later.

There is an impression among the thoughtless . . . that Sherwood Anderson is a man of profound ideas who is "handicapped by his inarticulateness." As a matter of fact Anderson is a man of practically no ideas—*but he is one of the very best and finest writers in the English language today.* Tom [Thomas Boyd] could never get such rhythms in his life as there are on the pages of *Winesburg, Ohio*—. Simple! The words on the lips of critics make me hilarious: Anderson's style is about as simple as an engine room of dynamoes.[29]

Apparently Anderson had some difficulty becoming acquainted with his neighbor Theodore Dreiser. Admiring Dreiser as he did for "making a path for us . . . through the wilderness" with his "brutal heavy feet," as he had stated it in *The Little Review* back in 1916, he seems to have been uncharacteristically shy about calling on the older man, but sometime in November he got up enough courage to ring his neighbor's doorbell. Dreiser opened the door, stared at him when he gave his name, replied "Hello," and closed the door in Anderson's face. Sherwood rushed off to explode in rage to a frightened Elizabeth, who had never before seen him angry; but returning to his St. Luke's Place apartment, he found a note from Dreiser apologizing for his rudeness. He had simply been embarrassed by Anderson's unexpected call. Subsequent meetings between the two men were still somewhat stiff despite Anderson's admiration for Dreiser's accomplishment and Dreiser's feeling that Anderson was "like his books," through which shone his "groping, artistic, sincere personality." On one occasion, Anderson wrote to Mencken, he

went into see Dreiser but I think he suspected me of being a government agent or a Jew. "I am going to get out of the city and let the Jews have it" he said. I thought perhaps he was offering it to me and hurried away.

Because of the imitation Menckenese Anderson usually adopted when writing Mencken, it is impossible to know his real reaction to Dreiser's anti-Semitism, but it would be a decade before the relationship between the two men in practice would match their regard for each other's work.[30]

The stiffest meeting of all involved several men and became famous in literary gossip. In the week before Christmas Dreiser gave an evening party to celebrate the publication of his *A Book About Myself,* inviting a dozen or so well-known critics, essayists, and novelists including Anderson, Mencken, Burton Rascoe, Ernest Boyd, Llewellyn Powys, and Carl Van Vechten. Dreiser received them in the long, bare living room of his apartment, where, Rascoe recalled in the most circumstantial of several eyewitness accounts, "the chairs were arranged around the walls as though there were going to be a dance." Unaccustomed to literary gatherings, Dreiser had not realized that many of the men actually did not know each other, made no introductions, and had provided no liquor to loosen his guests' tongues. Conversation was lagging dismally when the doorbell rang, and Dreiser, who had been standing silently in the middle of the room, answered it. The new, uninvited guest, was a very drunk Scott Fitzgerald, who had heard about the party, had long wanted to meet Dreiser, had purchased a bottle of champagne, and now presented it to Dreiser "with an eloquent speech of homage." Dreiser accepted the champagne and invited Fitzgerald in; but he put the bottle unopened in his kitchen icebox, and the memorably dull party soon broke up.[31]

Fortunately Anderson found easier relationships elsewhere. His earlier note of praise to Jean Toomer brought just before Christmas a grateful response, delayed because Toomer had been working on his book *Cane*. He had read *Winesburg, Ohio,* Toomer wrote from Washington, D.C., just before going to Georgia where *Cane* had been conceived, and while there he had read *The Triumph of the Egg*—a statement that suggests the combination of poems and stories in the *Triumph* and that book's developmental organization had as much influence on the form of *Cane* as did *Winesburg*. In fact, Toomer declared, "*Winesburg, Ohio,* and *The Triumph of the Egg* are elements of my growing. It is hard to think of myself as maturing without them." He went on to praise effusively the "golden strength" of Anderson's art, his "clean, glowing, healthy, vibrant" images, his gift for finding life's possibilities "deeply hopeful and beautiful." Pleased, Anderson replied almost immediately, offering to help Toomer find a publisher for *Cane* and to write an introduction.

> Your work is of special significance to me because it is the first negro work I have seen that strikes me as really negro. That is surely splendid. I wanted so much to find and express myself something clear and beautiful I felt coming up out of your race but in the end gave up. I did not want to write of the negro but out of him. Well I wasn't one. The thing I felt couldn't be truly done.
>
> And then McClure handed me the few things of yours I saw and there was the thing I had dreamed of beginning.

Toomer responded that in "Out of Nowhere Into Nothing," despite the "unreal" Negro minor character, Anderson had worked "an emotion, a sense of beauty that is easily more Negro than almost anything I have seen.

And I am glad to admit my own indebtedness to you in this connection." He explained that Waldo Frank was trying to place the book with Horace Liveright and was writing the introduction, and that to aid "the budding of the Negro's consciousness" he himself would like to start a magazine dedicated to the "negroid ideal." Early in 1923 Anderson sent two letters urging Toomer to stick to his writing and not have his time taken up by a magazine. Thereafter the correspondence languished, and by the time Toomer was again in New York, Anderson had left.[32]

All fall he had been renewing his friendship with Alfred Stieglitz and Georgia O'Keeffe. The small, fragile-looking, intense Stieglitz he especially admired for his craftsmanship with the camera, sharply focused as it so often was on common American scenes and objects, and for his years of relentless effort through exhibitions in his now-defunct small gallery at 291 Fifth Avenue to spread an acceptance of modern art and of a specifically American modern art among his fellow Americans. Back early in the year Anderson had contributed three Testaments to the February 1922 issue of *MSS.*, the first number of a little magazine put out for some months by the "Stieglitz Group"; and late in September he completed for the fourth, the December issue, an essay in praise of Stieglitz, which the latter allowed him to publish first in *The New Republic* for October 25. Traditionalist and prophet, Stieglitz fights passionately, Anderson wrote, against our "ugly and ill-smelling" mechanical age and for the "old male love of good work," for "man's old inheritance—the right to his tools, his materials, and the right to make what is sound and sweet in himself articulate through his handling of tools and materials."

And perhaps that he is a photographer is significant too. It may well be the most significant thing of all. For has he not fought all of his life to make machinery the tool and not the master of man? Surely Alfred Stieglitz has seen a vision we may all one day see more and more clearly because of the fight he has made for it.

Early in 1923 Stieglitz's return tribute was to take four close-up photographs of the writer now entered on his years of greatest fame. In each the dark eyes stare intensely at the viewer from beneath heavy eyebrows and a forehead half covered with tousled hair; the eyes are pouched in a face still square but just beginning to show the lines and wrinkles of middle age; the wide, full mouth, slightly turned down at the corners, is set, unsmilingly, sad. The least well-known portrait, that showing the largest amount of muffler and overcoat, and some of the dotted tie with teardrop-shaped stick pin in the knot, was pronounced "*Perfect*" by his friendly but uncowed apartment-sharer, Burdette Kinne, who went on to note with amusement:

The tousled locks were carefully arranged in their touseled condition before leaving the house, and were never touched again. The muffler was in shades of nausea green, very ugly (I thought) very heavy woollen material & very long. It was *always* worn.

Anderson's favorite among the portraits was the one that has become best known, the one taken closest up so that the slightly tilted head fills most of the frame, though he would not see it until some half a year later when Stieglitz sent him prints of three. On the same day he received them he wrote his thanks.

The turgid head of Anderson I hadn't seen, even in reproduction. It is surely a great piece of work. In that one thing you make me respect myself. That is the man who has done anything good Anderson has ever done.

The two others are in a way terrible but wonderful to have about. They are to me the man disintegrated, gone to pieces, fallen down before the ugliness in himself and others. I'll look at them on certain days, when I dare perhaps.[33]

The Christmas season of 1922 was a pleasanter one for Sherwood than usual because of Elizabeth, though he deeply missed his children. On the day itself the couple shared their happiness by sending a telegram of good wishes to Otto Liveright and his new wife Bernardine Szold, whose divorce from Hi Simon had just recently been declared. Parties were being given by "nice people . . . right and left," and to avoid them without giving offense Anderson took refuge the day after Christmas in the handsome country house of the liberal lawyer Dudley Field Malone on a hill with a striking view of the Hudson River. He had house and view to himself except for a servant and "worked steadily," first finishing a short story and then "plunging into a new novel." It was around this satisfyingly busy time that he wrote the second of two long letters to Harry Hansen, who was preparing his *Midwest Portraits,* a "Book of Memoirs and Friendships" with Chicago writers. In the first, dictated from Ben Huebsch's office on November 29, he had given, somewhat inaccurately, certain biographical details, minimized "the Russian influence," listed "all" of George Barrow and the Old Testament as the books he had "read most consistently," and named "The Egg" as "the best thing I have ever done." Now in the second, "a long winded scrawl," he described the recent writing of "The Man's Story" and declared, as he often did, that "I love passionately the mechanics of writing, the blank sheets before me, the smell of ink." Only with *Winesburg* had he become "an individual writer," for his earlier books had been "too deeply influenced by the work of others," and the essential quality of any individual writer must be "first class straightforward story telling." Then in one of his longer comments on his craft he fumbled toward and finally defined his functional notion of style.

You see Harry—where most writers fail—and this is not clearly enough understood—is because they aren't, at bottom, story tellers. They have theories
about writing, notions about style, often real writing ability but they do not tell
the story—straight out—bang.

You see after all Harry style—well the devil—its like the dress worn by the actor—the way he walks across the stage etc. etc—important to be sure—

But—if the man is thinking too much of these things—and isn't feeling within
himself the part he is to play.

Well what I am trying to say is that style should naturally grow out of the content of the thing itself.[34]

Back in New York after the holidays he wondered to Bab what the new
year would hold for him. One thing that "seemed fairly safe" at last was
his literary reputation, he wrote, although his books still did not sell well.
He had in fact become safely institutionalized in a small way by *The Bookman,* which had included him, along with Willa Cather and Zona Gale's,
on the Committee on Contemporary Fiction as part of the magazine's
study service to women's literary clubs, and had also included him, along
with Fitzgerald, Gale, Floyd Dell, and Cather, as one of five "outstanding
figures" of a "Younger Group" of fiction writers who "Within the past ten
years have come prominently into notice in America." Such prominence
would help Anderson to find speaking engagements with women's clubs
when he went on his first lecture tour two years later, but now he took
greater immediate satisfaction with Burton Rascoe's report in his "Bookman's Day Book" column on January 21 that Rascoe, Mencken, and
George Jean Nathan had agreed on "the high qualities in Dreiser and the
work of Sherwood Anderson." Probably the most exciting news in January came from the Soviet Union in a letter from Peter Ochremenko, a
translator working for The All-Russia State Publishing Department in
Moscow, stating that he had already put a third of *The Triumph of the Egg*
into Russian and would like to have copies of the rest of Anderson's books
for translating. "Such kind of literature [as *The Triumph*]," he assured the
author, "appeals to Russian mind and soul." Anderson, "highly pleased
and flattered," wrote back that he would have Huebsch send copies of all
his other books; and shaping his letter to his correspondent, as he so often
did, he maximized, rather than minimizing as with Hansen, how "deeply
indebted" he was "to your Russian writers."

May I say that, until I found the Russian writers of prose, your Tolstoy, Dostoyevsky, Turgenev, Chekhov, I had never found a prose that satisfied me. In America we have had a bad tradition, got from the English and the French. To our tales
that are popular in our magazines one goes for very clever plots, all sorts of trickery and juggling. The natural result is that human life becomes secondary, of no
importance. The plot does not grow out of the natural drama resulting from the

tangle of human relations, whereas in your Russian writers one feels life everywhere, in every page.

When he "came to your writers,"

A door opened. I saw at last that the art of prose writing might spring into life directly out of an impulse of sympathy and understanding with the man beside you.[35]

The pleasant distractions of the literary life were always there to be gone to or not as he wished. Despite a blizzard on the evening of January 3, for example, Anderson, Van Wyck Brooks, Dos Passos, Rosenfeld, and others made their way to a party for Gilbert Seldes. The party went on until three o'clock the following morning when, the snow having stopped, all went off to continue the festivity at an East Side restaurant. Most mornings, however, and sometimes whole days he spent writing furiously in his rented room or in Elizabeth's or Stark Young's apartment at 51 Charlton, "hidden away like a crab in his hole at the edge of the sea." He finished two "rather fine" stories, worked at his new novel, "a departure from anything I have done," he wrote Bab, and was full of schemes such as doing for one of the monthly magazines "a series of papers I would call 'The Note Book of a Modern.'" Ebullient at being on the artist's committed quest "toward the unatainable," he dismissed, for the moment, his lack of popular success.

I'll tell you a great secret. The critics sometimes write of my work saying I express the soul of America. It really isn't true. America is as yet a child, thinking of getting rich, owning automobiles, etc. I am writing, have always written of an America not yet born.
The result is that two hundred years from now I will be understood as I am not now.
Its true and can't be helped. That is why I am not popular as a writer and yet, as a person interest people profoundly. They see in me themselves unborn.[36]

His old energy and gaiety were returning, not only because the writing went well, but because he was free at last from the cloud under which he felt he had lived during those last months with Tennessee. "The central fact," he wrote Bab in mid- or late January,

that Tennessee is one who of herself cannot believe in life becomes more apparent.
The dark moody terrible thing always lurking there. Poor child—I know now she came toward me as toward something warm and in the end I grew tired and myself wanted warmth outside myself.
There are these things in life, one can't account for or dare not account for. Relations poison or make well.

Elizabeth's "gentle aristocracy" had made him well, he confided to brother Karl, and he hinted at an action finally decided on by remarking that he might "drop out of the scene unexpectedly" and go to the West where things were quiet. Such hints were all that he provided most people; only a necessary few, like Ben Huebsch who would forward his mail, knew that he was in fact going to Reno, Nevada, where at that time a divorce could quickly and easily be obtained, to begin the six-months state residence requirement for a divorce from Tennessee.[37]

Early February was packed with preparations for departure, one of the more crucial being the matter of money. On February 8, with the assistance of Otto Liveright, he settled on a contract with Harper and Brothers for a book of "Autobiographical Essays," described also as "articles" and "stories." He was to receive $1,000 (less 10 percent agent's commission) as an advance payment for two "stories" to be published in *Harper's Magazine* and then, at the *Magazine*'s option, an additional $1,500 for four more, the six to be collected as the book. This somewhat awkward arrangement subsequently created difficulties; but it gave him funds for the stay in Reno, and it indicated that he was already thinking of dropping the hardly begun novel for the "Autobiographical Essays" volume that would eventually appear, under Huebsch's imprint rather than Harper's, as one of Anderson's best books, *A Story Teller's Story.* On the eighth he must have felt as though one of Liveright's predictions had come true, that the established magazines would be paying him for his stories. As further proof, the February issue of *Harper's Magazine* was out with "The Sad Horn Blowers" as the opening piece, a colored illustration of the tale facing the first page, and a note on the author as having "taken a conspicuous place among American novelists who have broken from the traditional literary manner." It was not yet nine full years since his first published story had appeared in *Harper's.* "The Rabbit-pen" had been written in the style of other writers; "The Sad Horn Blowers" had been written in his own.[38]

There were other matters to be attended to. Henry Seidel Canby, editor of *The Literary Review,* was anxious to meet Dreiser; and Anderson arranged to stop by his neighbor's apartment at about one o'clock on February 8 to pick him up for lunch at the Players Club at Canby's invitation, symbolically a member of the Establishment again accepting the literary rebels on their own terms. Anderson had a last visit in Westport with Paul Rosenfeld, who was in on the secret of the trip to Reno, and "carried off" Paul's "Herman Melville," presumably *Moby-Dick,* which he promised to return. Paul was to see that all went well with Elizabeth, who was to remain temporarily in New York. In addition, Sherwood found time to drop in several times on O'Keeffe's exhibit of a hundred pictures, which had opened at the Anderson Galleries on January 29, and out of his $900 advance for the Harper's book he purchased one of her paintings. In the last flurry before leaving, he wrote her a friendly note on February 10 to apologize for not having cared for her work before and to admit that her show had been "a tremendously education thing for me." He was "off for the West," he concluded vaguely.[39]

His decision to leave was, as usual, a sudden one. Presumably Elizabeth saw him off on a westbound train on or just after February 1. He went first to Michigan City for a glad reunion with his children. After the divorce was granted, he hoped to have one or more of them live with him and Elizabeth. "They are getting old enough now," he wrote Karl, "to make it important and worth while to them and me." Then from Chicago he settled down for the days-long train journey to Reno, a "tremendous experience" for one who loved the American land and who was now for the first time seeing the Rockies and the mountain states beyond. "Anyway I feel that life is suddenly better in America," he had written Rosenfeld from the train the first day out from New York, "and that a man has a better chance to work out his problems." So he was running away from as well as toward. As had happened before, he was solving problems of the past and present by escaping into the future.[40]

14

Reno

1.

Well before dawn on February 19, Sherwood got off his Southern Pacific train in Reno, registered as S. Anderson at the Hotel Overland, and walked up to the campus of the tiny University of Nevada to see the sun rise on a part of the American earth that was strange to him. Reno, then a small city of some twelve thousand permanent residents, lay in its nearly mile-high, pan-shaped valley rimmed by hills to the east and the abrupt slope of the Sierras to the west. The city itself was unimpressive; but the buildings, unlike the smoke-blackened ones of the industrial cities Anderson had lived in so long, were white, the sparkling Truckee River ran through the middle of town, the streets were tree-lined, and the air was exhilaratingly thin and clear. Just outside Reno the sagebrush desert began, stretching for miles toward the hills and mountains, on which sunlight played and shifted constantly. Within a few weeks he would be painting again, trying excitedly to catch the elusive, rapidly changing forms and colors under this light. That first day in Reno, however, he was pleased to find the sun warm even in February, the pace of life unhurried and easy, the westerners friendly and ready to chat.[1]

Conscious of how "shattered" his nerves still were from the events of the previous year, he at first slept badly, but he felt himself relaxing. Within a day or so after his arrival he was into his routine again, writing all morning from eight to twelve, walking about the city or out into the desert in the afternoon, dining alone or with some casual acquaintance he had gotten into conversation with, and in the evening often reading books found in the surprisingly good public library. He was relieved at being away from the East and the "row" he expected with the publication of *Many Marriages,* and his quiet, isolated life would have been fairly satisfactory for the moment except that he missed Elizabeth desperately. He wrote long letters to her almost daily, pouring out, she would recall, "all his miseries, his passions, his poetry in pages and pages of scrawled, almost illegible handwriting" and thereby deepening both her own misery at the separation and her conviction that she could provide him with the "peace and a feeling of security" he so obviously longed for and needed.[2]

Despite his loneliness for Elizabeth the writing was going well. He had begun work on the semiautobiographical "Modernist Notebook" for *Harper's Magazine,* as he wrote Bab on February 22, would afterward pull together a collection of tales for which he already had the title, *Horses and Men,* and then get back to the novel, presumably *Ohio Pagans,* which he had "written through" once but then dropped because "too many terrific outside things happened." Encouraging news about the sale of *Many Marriages* was coming from Huebsch; book orders required a second printing on the day of publication, February 20, and a third would follow in March. Anderson was eager to see a copy of the book, though for some reason one would be weeks late in reaching him; but, uneasy about the reception of his fanciful novel, he asked Ben not to send him any reviews: "They often just disturb me and not one in a hundred teaches me anything."[3]

There was more reason than usual for him to be uneasy about the fate of *Many Marriages.* On February 5, before Anderson had left the East, New York's Supreme Court Justice John Ford announced, as the *Times* reported the following day, that "a circulating library had placed a copy of D. H. Lawrence's *Women in Lov'* in the hands of his daughter," and, outraged at what he considered obscene passages in it, he intended to prosecute the publisher, Thomas Seltzer, and to urge the state legislature "to put teeth into the present law against books likely to impair morals." On the sixth, Justice Ford joined with John S. Sumner, secretary of New York's active Society for the Suppression of Vice, in a drive "to stop the sale of filthy and scandalous publications." On the tenth, Lawrence's telegraphed denunciation of Ford was made public— *Women in Love* "wasn't written for the Ford family," he stated contemptuously—and Ford and Sumner conferred on a "new method" for legal prosecution of publishers. Previously courts had held that the alleged obscenity of a book must be judged on the basis of its entire contents; now Ford and Sumner hoped for legislation that would allow prosecution solely for one or more "immoral and objectionable passages" without regard to the whole. Huebsch and Otto Liveright's brother Horace were certainly aware of the threat this "new method" held for themselves personally and for their attempts to publish books such as *Many Marriages,* and almost certainly Ben or Otto had alerted Sherwood to this danger before he left New York; indeed a reluctance to be directly involved in the row may have been one reason why he left the city so suddenly.

It was a sign of Huebsch's loyalty to Anderson and to literature that, despite the growing possibility of prosecution, he brought out *Many Marriages* as scheduled on February 20. Ford and Sumner meant business. The Sunday *Times* for February 25 contained, along with a disparaging review of *Many Marriages* in its book section, a front-page story on a large meeting called by Justice Ford at the Hotel Astor the previous day to launch a "crusade" against "publishers and sellers of books alleged to be immoral" and in favor of new, restrictive legislation to make prosecution more readily successful. The following day the *Times* editorialized that if such legislation were passed "and taken seriously by the courts, about half the masterpieces of all literature would have to be thrown on the junk heap"; but such opposition did not prevent Ford and Sumner from forming the Clean Books League on March 8, with Ford as president, and drafting a Clean Books Bill, which was introduced on March 22 into the state assembly and senate. The most pernicious part of this bill, as the *Times* explained, was

a clause under which it would be possible to segregate a word, phrase or sentence which to a jury might appear objectionable from its context in a book written for an entirely laudable purpose and make it the basis of conviction that would carry with it suppression of the book and fine and imprisonment for author and publisher.

Nevertheless, the bill was rushed through the assembly but was finally defeated by a 2–1 vote in the senate on May 2. Horace Liveright, with little backing from other publishers except for Huebsch, Seltzer, and a Dutton representative, led the testimony against it at an April 18 hearing, and the dapper senator James J. Walker opposed it on May 2 with a speech, which included his famous remark that "No woman was ever ruined by a book."[4]

Probably Anderson out in isolated Reno knew little about the skirmishing over the Clean Books Bill, but he did learn from Huebsch early in March that the Watch and Ward Society in Boston had succeeded in having a local bookseller arrested and fined for selling a copy of *Many Marriages*. The book would run into more such difficulties, but into the spring Huebsch continued to be encouraging about sales figures, reporting as of May 1 that between February 20 and April 30 a total of 9,195 copies were sold. The sales, which brought Anderson royalties of $2,758.50 for this brief period, must have resulted in part from his new fame as a writer, in part from the word that the book was as sex-obsessed as its title implied.[5]

In fact, such was one of the themes of the many hostile reviews, which, for his tranquility of mind, Anderson had wisely asked Huebsch not to send him. Out of nearly thirty reviews that appeared over a few months after publication, two-thirds attacked the book, sometimes as being simply sordid, more frequently as being both sordid and dull. It was on these grounds that the reviewer of the *New York Times* savaged the book; but two editorials in the *Times,* one in March, one in April, used *Many Marriages* as a means of opposing the crusade of the Clean Books League. Anderson's real offense was not that passages of his book "may seem to be mere grotesque obscenity," but that the book was solemn and pretentious: "If Mr. Sumner tries to suppress this book, or others like it, he will merely bring a piece of pompous flatulence to the attention of people who will like it for the very reason that makes Sumner dislike it. . . ." A very few reviewers, like Llewellyn Jones in the *Chicago Evening Post,* praised the book unreservedly as a poetic achievement and "the best thing [Anderson] has done so far"; a few either praised the book as having a healthy-minded attitude toward sex or, like Mencken, found scenes and details good but the novel as a whole formless and talky, much inferior to the short stories. Whether a reviewer liked or disliked *Many Marriages,* however, it was clear that the book was regarded as a sexually daring one.[6]

During March some word about the reception of the book did come to Anderson. He learned that Burton Rascoe was "thumbs down on my novel" and wryly sent him a letter he had received from one Henry W. Fisher, whom he had dined with at Rascoe's home in the previous fall, who had spent "the whole time trying to tell us some nasty tales," and who had now written with malicious delight that various New York reviewers were calling *Many Marriages* a dirty book. Fisher's spiteful letter was offset by a generous one from the young novelist Thomas Boyd, praising the novel for having what Rascoe accused it of lacking—form. Then one of Anderson's brothers sent him a copy of Scott Fitzgerald's enthusiastic review in the *New York Herald* for March 4, which described Anderson's method as his "accustomed transcendental naturalism," his book as not immoral but instead "a rather stupendous achievement," his reputation as being as solidly "first class" as that of James Joyce. Anderson gratefully wrote Fitzgerald to say that he had read the review "with delight," and Fitzgerald warmly replied that

I like *Many Marriages* much more fully than I could express in that review—It stays with me still. It's a haunting book and, it seems to me, ahead of *Poor White* and even of the two books of short stories.[7]

Anderson may have felt that on balance, as far as he knew, *Many Marriages* was doing well, but in any case he was getting his nerves back in shape, and it was up to Huebsch to take care of censorship problems. It was better for himself, he wrote Ben, "to stay as far as possible from the squabble concerning the book." When, however, as one of the forty-five "men of letters" and publishing personnel queried by *The Literary Digest* in a survey letter of May 19, 1923, as to their stand on censorship in literature and the arts, he responded bluntly.

Surely I do not believe in censorship in the theater, literature, or in any of the arts. No censorship has ever worked. But then, you see, I do not believe in Prohibition either. . . .

The Anglo-Saxons have a passion for making laws and breaking them and already the bootlegging of forbidden books is assured. Presently we shall have a tribe of pornographic writers, catering to a market what censorship we already have is building up.

The whole notion is, I am sure, absurd.

Through March he worked each morning on the "Modernist" manuscript, which would eventually become *A Story Teller's Story,* and by the end of the month he could write Otto Liveright that the book "is going to be pretty good size" and would fall into three "periods—Book 1—Youth, Book 2—Life—Book 3—Reaching—let us say—toward Maturity." Book 1 would "break nicely into the six installments" contracted for with *Harper's.* "I'm full of stories," he continued, "but I'm hot on this book and shall stay with it." By very early April, Book 1, "some 40,000 words," was "written . . . through the first time," and he would outline the projected volume to Rosenfeld in more detail.

As I see it now the book will separate into three sections—
1 Youth—the call of the material world—the call of the life of the imagination—
2 The period of the attempt to go out to the world—to take it at its own valuation—the muddle of sex—etc. etc.
3 The beginning of the realization of surfaces—the significance of the artists life etc.
I think of calling the book "Immaturity"—a protest—The writing runs along in comments—narrative—observations etc as one would talk to a dear friend.[8]

Every moment he could spare from his writing during these weeks he spent outdoors in the mountain air. He bought a Dodge Roadster for a little over $100 from a divorcee leaving Reno, but he also tramped about on foot in the sun and wind and was "getting strong as a bull." One day while hiking along a road in the hills he was given a ride by a young man in a Ford, and the two became companionable. The young fellow was naive and had no interest in writing, but he loved outdoor life, was skilled in it, and was filled with good health and good spirits. He had a cabin up in the hills, and Anderson found it relaxing to go up there in the afternoons for trout fishing in the streams. He was beginning to find Reno amusing, he confessed to Rosenfeld in April.

Such a place you have never dreamed of. Some 700 to 1,000 divorcees, many lawyers, small hotels, Indians in gaudy blankets, flappers with dogs—pretty girls on horseback, cowboys, gambling houses, bootleggers, sage brush deserts, trout fishing and the snow clad hills looking down and grinning at it all.[9]

By now his joyousness came from Elizabeth's at last being with him in Reno. Disturbed by the rumors spread by Tennessee among her New York friends that Elizabeth was the cause for Sherwood's wish for a divorce, and unhappy at his distance from New York, Elizabeth had by mid-March decided to resign from Doubleday Doran and sell her house in the Village. On March 31 she took the train west to visit her family in California, stopping off briefly in Reno to see Sherwood before going on to Berkeley, where the Pralls had settled after the father's death. Brother David had been appointed to the Philosophy Department of the University of California in 1921, sister Margaret was teaching music at Mills College in Oakland, and both lived with their quiet, elderly mother at 1420 La Loma Avenue in the Berkeley Hills overlooking San Francisco Bay. Sister Dorothea, an accomplished translator from Russian and Polish, and her learned husband Max Radin, a law professor at the University, lived at 2597 Buena Vista Way, the intersection of the two streets making them next door neighbors and the two houses forming a "compound." On Friday, April 6, Sherwood took the train to Berkeley to meet Elizabeth's family and to give her support in her decision to return to Reno with him. His visit could not have been an easy one, for the other Pralls were shocked to learn of the decision and strongly advised against it, but the quietly strong-willed Elizabeth was resolved to be with Sherwood while he waited out the divorce from Tennessee.[10]

By April 10 the two were back in Reno living together in what Elizabeth would recall as "a hideous little cottage" at 33 East Liberty Street. There began a happy period for both. Sherwood talked to her by the hour about his life from childhood onward, and Elizabeth concluded that she

knew what Sherwood wanted and needed. He needed to be managed, not dominated. He wanted someone to make his world right for him, to cook his meals, clean his house, to love him without demanding. I had been independent all my life and I thought I could provide him with all of this. His other wives had tried to change him. I would try to adapt myself to him.

She had found, at least for the time, the right tone for the relationship, and Sherwood responded with an outburst of creativity. For some two weeks after they had settled in, he worked steadily on the revision of Book 1 of the "Modernist" manuscript, which he was soon to call, tentatively, *Straws*. He completed the revision, and putting it aside to await a "final reading" before sending it off to Otto Liveright, he at once "lit into" the stories that were crowding his mind for the *Horses and Men* volume, to be published in October.[11]

First, having decided to abandon *Ohio Pagans* as a novel, he worked sections of that manuscript into two long stories. One was "'Unused,'" in effect "a short novel" about May Edgley, "a bright sensitive young girl born into the family of a drayman and with all her brothers and sisters low-brows," as he described this "very beautiful" tale to Otto. Even before sending off a fair copy of "'Unused'" to Otto Liveright on May 7, he had finished or nearly finished revising a second section into the long tale "An Ohio Pagan," which recounted the early life of Tom Edwards and climaxed in Tom's metamorphic vision while overlooking Sandusky Bay. The telling of his own life to Elizabeth while putting final touches on the semiautobiographical material for *Harper's* had flooded his mind with memories of his "own home country"; for by May 9 he had finished a short Ohio tale with "a real pastoral flavor," and a day or so later he had given final shape to "a new long tale—about 15,000 words," clearly "The Man Who Became a Woman," one of his most remarkable achievements in fiction. On May 14 he mailed to Otto final copy of "the matter for the Harper serial," which should, he felt, "just about run nicely in six numbers of the magazine." Then on May 16 he sent to Huebsch "copy for the new book of tales—HORSES AND MEN," in his cover letter urging a quick setting of the book in type so that he could read proof on it before getting "into a new novel for next year that is already eating at me." Probably in no other single month in his entire literary career did he produce so much work and of such high quality.[12]

The intensity with which he worked was fired not only by his daily happiness with Elizabeth and by the surge of his past into active memory but also by the emotions associated with those recollections. When the short "pastoral" tale was first published, in *Horses and Men,* it served as part 1 of the two-part story with its Turgenevesque title, "A Chicago Hamlet," part 2 being, with minor revisions and some slight transfer of background material to part 1, the story "Broken," just out in the March issue of *The Century.* As in "Broken" there is a first-person narrator, who tells how he and the protagonist Tom dine together one cold rainy fall evening in Chicago, the city where at such times all its inhabitants sag with weariness at its "almost universal ugliness." Tom, often weary and dull because of his "dreary meaningless living," suddenly puts his hand on the table, closes his fingers into a cup, and announces that he once held his own life in his cupped hand and could have died simply by opening his fingers. Thereupon he tells of an incident on his father's rented farm in Ohio, which occurred when Tom was eighteen, the year before, as described in "Broken," he left the farm for good. After a cold day's work with his detested, fanatically religious father, Tom refuses to eat the supper prepared by the slovenly stepmother. Later that evening he decides to kill his father while the inept man is kneeling in his dirty nightgown at one of his interminable prayers, but Tom is saved from the act by his revulsion at the sight of his father's work-soiled bare feet. He scrubs his own body clean, returns to his bed, lies awake for some hours feeling that he holds his life in his cupped hand, and finally resolves not to let his life slip away by loosening his fingers. Cleansing his naked body has given him a sense of self-worth.

The tale may have been based on one of George Daugherty's recollections "fed" to Anderson, but the emotional overtones coincide with the author's several other fictional attacks on his own father. There are the hostility toward the father's sexuality indicated by Tom's disgust with the father's marriage to an unattractive woman with sickly children after the death of his first wife, Tom's mother; the murderous anger of the son toward the father for the latter's ineptness at farming and self-delusion with prayer; the son's revulsion at the sight of his father's dirty feet and his compulsive self-cleansing, a sign of his psychic separation from the father, which in part 2 becomes a physical one. Significantly, Elizabeth would especially recall from Sherwood's "long hours" of telling her his life that his father had been "a charmer, not a worker," whose "reputation as a clownish ne'er-do-well humiliated him." Tom's bitter resentment of his father is exactly the resentment of the humiliated.

Another surge of disturbing emotions expressed in and brought under control by aesthetic form appears to account for "The Man Who Became a Woman." For the setting of this extraordinary tale Anderson turned once more to the racetrack milieu of "I Want to Know Why" and "I'm a Fool," that world of sensuous happiness among the horses available in its fullness only to a youth who has temporarily abandoned conventional values for the liberating low-class ones of the swipes and other track followers, yet ultimately a world of loss, of lost communication between boy and man in the former story, of lost love between boy and girl in the latter, losses that bring devastating unhappiness to each youth. But in this last return to that milieu Anderson would describe the passage of a late adolescent from sexual confusion toward greater emotional maturity, a passage presented in terms of and made possible by the milieu yet ending in a transcendence of it.

Certain autobiographical elements are discernible in the tale. Most obvious are the youthful Anderson's summer as a swipe on a harness-racing circuit, his acquaintance with the black groom Bert Ellison (the "Burt" of the story, who cares for a black pacing stallion named O My Man, who seems based on Tom Whitehead's prize-winning black trotting stallion, Solarion), and especially a curious psychic episode that Anderson would describe in the *Memoirs* as undergone by himself during a period of bodily weakness in early puberty, specifically at a time when "the body of the female begins to have a strange significance" to a boy. During that episode he felt that his life, which like Tom in "A Chicago Hamlet" he seemed to hold "in the palm of his hand," slipped from him, flew away like a bird until it became a speck in a blue sky, then "with a rush" came back into his body, whereupon he fell into a dreamless sleep like that after coitus. In the story a similar experience, briefly described, is assigned to the narrator, Herman Dudley. Yet another aspect of autobiography appears in the opening section of the story in the figure of Herman's friend, young Tom Means, who has become a swipe "to bring a kind of flourish . . . into his life," but whose real ambition is "to write the way a well-bred horse runs or trots or paces," and who subsequently does become a writer.[13]

Other autobiographical details appear, but the significance of the story comes more from the overt process of narration. With a startling resemblance to the narrator of Dostoyevsky's *A Raw Youth*—a copy of which Tennessee had given Sherwood in December, 1916, and which he may have been rereading in Reno—Herman announces in the course of his tale that he has been led to write of a deeply troubling experience of his past, not because he is trying to be literary but because he is "forced, by some feeling inside myself," to tell it as a means of feeling clean again. He has "often dreamed" about this bizarre experience, he confesses, and has sometimes "screamed out at night" even after, ending a long bachelor-hood, he "married Jessie and was happy." Writing the story, then, is a way to exorcise something that "has been on the chest" of this middle-aged narrator, who is otherwise so self-secure as to recognize, for example, the fear of most American males of admitting that a man can love another man in a nonsexual sense. In describing his feelings, the narrator explicitly is not "claiming to be able to inform you or to do you any good," but rather to make you, the reader, understand him, the tale-teller, "as I would like to understand some things about you, or anyone, if I had the chance."

Quickly Herman sketches his drab middle-class life in a Nebraska small town up to age nineteen and then his period of seeing the world as a tramp, a period during which his "most delightful experience" was traveling as a racehorse swipe through a series of Pennsylvania county-seat towns and enjoying the "gaudy undependable" people around the race track—"about the best liars I've ever seen, and not saving money or thinking about morals . . . an independent, go-to-the-devil, come-have-a-drink-of-whiskey, kind of crew." While Tom Means also travels along with this crowd as another swipe, Herman is happy, grooming a gelding named Pick-it-boy and taking long evening walks with Tom, listening to him talk about writing but mostly about racehorses, their courage and fineness, and about fresh, lovely mornings on the racing circuit with no women present and the only sexual expression that of stallion for mare. When Tom leaves, the owner of Pick-it-boy buys the stallion O My Man, who is groomed by the black swipe Burt. Herman gets to be friends with Burt, but not close friends as he and Tom had been, and in his loneliness Herman begins to have a bad time. Extremely shy about approaching the "fly girls" who are always hanging around racetracks, he dreams of women's bodies at night and during the day is tired and "mopey" and subject to recurrences of his creator's youthful psychic episode. Burt covers for him with the boss and helps him with his grooming, and Herman spends much of his time cooling out Pick-it-boy after a run, walking the gelding slowly around the track, going "round and round and round" in a daze, feeling— "maybe negroes would understand what I'm trying to talk about now better than any white man ever will"—a curious sense of inter-identity with the horse, sometimes even wishing that "he was a girl . . . or that I was a girl and he was a man."

Then comes the season's last race, which is to take place at a fair-grounds situated on a hill above a Pennsylvania coal mining town as ugly as that where Beaut McGregor grew up in *Marching Men*. The country-side is "wild and untidy and ragged," filled with "stones sticking out of the ground" and stunted trees; the fair is postponed for a week because of a steady rain, and close to the back stretch of the muddy track stand the still stinking ruins of a slaughter house with the bleached bones of animals lying about it in a field. Only the miners, Herman thinks, could put up with living in such a hellhole of a town. When the other swipes go down into the town Saturday night for liquor and women, Herman promises to keep an eye on all the horses; but after walking about in the dark and rain and mud, dreaming, not of "some cheap woman," but of such a slender, flowerlike one "as I thought then I should never find in the world," he becomes so lonesome and restless that he breaks his word and, feeling "sick as a dog inside myself," walks halfway down the hill to a saloon.

Inside the dirty room where a dozen miners are sitting at tables, he self-consciously orders a whiskey at the bar, looks into the cracked mirror behind the bar, and nearly drops his glass when he sees looking back at him not his own face but that of a lonesome and scared young girl. In consternation he has a second and then a third whiskey, though he has no head for liquor, thinks that the miners are laughing at him, then realizes that they are laughing at a huge, red-headed man who has just entered with a big, red-headed child in his arms. The man, whom Herman still has wits enough to perceive is "one of the cracked kind" found in any town, seats the child on the bar and, muttering to himself, drinks six cheap whiskeys in quick succession. One of the miners meanwhile shows off to his fellows by strutting up and down behind the man singing a song "about the crack getting bigger in the old tin pan." The big man shoves Herman toward the child, quietly tells him he'll kill him if he lets the child fall, strikes the show-off to the floor with one blow, and stomps his shoulder so hard that

Herman, sickened, can hear the bones crunch. Then he knocks Herman aside, takes the child, and, still muttering to himself, tramps out of the saloon.

Herman quickly slinks out and returns to Pick-it-boy's stall at the track, where he tries to forget the doubly horrifying scene in the saloon by thinking of beautiful, queenlike women and then by running his hands over the horse, feeling as though he were touching the body of a lovely woman. Calmed, he climbs into the loft above the stall and taking off his wet clothes goes to sleep naked in a pile of horse blankets. He is soon awakened by two black swipes, who because of their color could not have been served by the town's white prostitutes. Drunk and sexually hungry, they either mistake the white, naked Herman for a young girl or, the middle-aged Herman now understands, perhaps pretend to mistake him so merely as a joke. He escapes from them and runs frantically out into the stormy darkness, trying to scream to them that he is not a woman but, for some reason he even now does not understand, unable to utter a sound. Convinced by the noises of the wind that they are still after him, he runs terrified along the track and into the field around the slaughterhouse. Here he stumbles and pitches forward into the white skeleton of a horse lying on its back, his hands clutching the horse's ice-cold cheekbones, the white rib cage wrapped around him. Thereupon he is swept with "blind terror," which "like the finger of God running down [his] back" burns him clean of "all that silly nonsense about being a girl"; and at last able to scream, he is wholly restored to himself. He creeps into a haystack where some sheep are sheltered and goes to sleep with the animals.

Waking to a clearing day, he realizes that the other swipes will laugh to see him naked in daylight. They do laugh, but Burt, furiously brandishing a pitchfork, shouts them into silence. Herman, crying, not with shame but with pleasure to hear Burt "sling language" so well, gets his clothes, kisses Pick-it-boy goodbye, and runs off down the hill "out of the race-horse and the tramp life for the rest of my days."

Whether Anderson may have earlier sought and failed to find the appropriate form for his tale is unknowable, but in this period of exuberant creativity he obviously did discover it. On the simplest level he organized the story into three sections of almost equal length and of increasing emotional intensity for both narrator and reader: (1) Herman's early life, relation to Tom Means, and onset of sexual confusion in which he wishes he were a girl and Pick-it-boy, the emasculated male, a man; (2) his perception of himself in the saloon as a girl and his witnessing of the big man as both the "maternal" protector of the child and an image of brutal male power; (3) the actual physical threat to him as "woman" by the black swipes, his flight from them, and his abrupt transformation into adult maleness resulting from a symbolic death within the skeleton of the horse.

But this traditional technique of ordering a tale is supplemented by a more complex organization through echo details and repeated motifs, which, as in *Many Marriages,* unexpectedly connect different parts of the story into patterns of meaning. Near the beginning of his account Herman speaks of physical nakedness in relation to cleaning a room (that is, the self); near the end he, naked within the horse's skeleton, is cleansed of his sexual confusion by overwhelming terror. Again, the big, violent man in the saloon at first seems more horselike than human; yet he has thick lips "like negroes' lips," while both his eyes and those of the two black swipes who threaten Herman are like the scary eyes of little animals "gleaming out at you" by lantern light in a wood at night "from a dead wall of darkness." Other motifs and themes are introduced, dropped, and picked up again throughout the story, providing what might loosely be called a "musical" structure and expanding the social as well as psychological implications of this Dostoyevskian fiction. In a succession of apparently random comments, the mature narrator firmly identifies undergroups in American society: the "cracked" or retarded, whom the "normal" treat unkindly; women, who "aren't so much to blame as men" for the ugliness of living since "they aren't running the show" and who may be "generally . . . lonesomer than men"; and blacks. Burt is as kind and capable as Bildad Johnson of "I Want to Know Why" and rages loyally in Herman's defense against black and white swipes alike; yet he and the two sexually frustrated "buck niggers" in the hayloft and even any college-bred "young negro man" get "'the messy end of the dung fork'" when they want many of the things whites have. If the middle-aged Herman Dudley still has an unresolved psychological problem when he begins cleansing himself through this confessional story, his glimpses of life from the swipe's underclass point of view have taught him that white-male-dominated American society is emotionally immature and oppressive.

As the storyteller weaves his tale, the reiterated motifs and themes begin to fall into antithetical pairs: men/women, horses/human beings, loyalty/disloyalty, black/white, violence/kindness, loneliness/community, silence/speech, reality/illusion, death/life. Such pairs suggest that Anderson was using them not only to give formal shape to his tale but to dramatize a view of human experience itself as consisting of contrarieties. Still, the basic movement of the story is psychological—the charting of Herman's passage from a state of fearing women and full masculinity to one of mature, integrated selfhood via an experience so frighteningly disruptive of the self that it remains a psychic threat until the act of writing about it tears away the "heavy iron lid," which, as Anderson had recently described the process of repression in *Many Marriages,* has been "kept clamped" over the "deep well of thinking" that exists within Herman as "within every human being."

The act of writing, then, is therapeutic, and to this extent Herman is a direct projection of his creator, one of whose original impulses to write fiction had been thereby to deal with psychic burdens. But if "The Man Who Became a Woman" is to be read as autobiographical, its key is most likely to be found, not literally in Herman's youthful sexual confusion, which no evidence suggests that his creator had suffered from in his own adolescence, but in what that confusion and especially its terrifying climax may represent from Anderson's more recent experience, specifically his deeply disturbing break with Tennessee less than a year before. That break had been preceded and followed by a period of debilitating and disorienting distress, which he had found "impossible to speak plainly about" even to such a close friend as Paul Rosenfeld. It was a period when he was unable to function as a writer, that is, in his own eyes to function as a man, and when he took refuge among Chicago's blacks, his ill spirit sought nurture from association with the humiliated and despised. He had slowly groped his way out of depression, though not without painful relapses and a nagging fear that his recovery was fragile even after he had begun writing again and had found Elizabeth, surely the Jessie of the story, "slender and like a flower and with something in her like a racehorse too," such a woman as he (like his confused Herman) "thought then he should never find in this world." Going to Reno had been to recover nervous health as well as to obtain a divorce, and as recently as his first lonely days there, he could write to Bab Finley, to whom he did not reveal his exact whereabouts, that

As you know the last year has been a shattering one for me and I am not yet through the valley of ghosts. To one who like myself lives upon life Tennessee did a dreadful thing. She filled my house with the ghosts of death and it will take long in quiet places and in the sun to cure me.[14]

Here in this melodramatic, anguished passage lies the key. However variously one may interpret in story terms Herman's terrifying, liberating fall into the skeleton of the dead horse, it is in autobiographical terms an encounter with death, not mere physical death, which is the ignominious end of even such noble creatures as racehorses, but a psychological death, a psychic disintegration within a nightmarish externality of ugliness, darkness, and threat, such a death being a fictional representation of what Anderson had referred to as "the dark moody terrible thing always lurking there" in Tennessee. Now that Elizabeth was constantly, reassuringly with him after their unhappy weeks of separation, when Tennessee would inevitably have troubled his thoughts, he could look back on the emotional devastation of the previous year and feel—with relief—that the psychic terror, which had shaken him, like Herman, "to the very bottom of me, to

509

the bottom of the inside of me," had burned him clean of disorientation and terror and rendered him reborn. Having reached this point of new beginning, he could safely fictionalize the whole recent experience, disguising it as a long-past one, which troubles a middle-aged man until he exorcises it, as Anderson was himself strikingly doing, by writing of it.[15]

When he soon thereafter began Book 2 of *Straws,* he would almost at once describe in a quite different tone his youthful experience as a swipe among the colorful "sporting fraternity." He watched the "beautiful temperamental" horses working out on the track, then afterward "rubbed their legs . . . and walked them slowly for miles, cooling them out," dreaming as he walked of being a successful racing driver, but knowing that, as a "track negro" with whom he worked told him, he was "too excitable, too flighty" to become one, and so giving up that life although he "loved it well." There may be some fiction in such memories as there is much in "The Man Who Became a Woman," but the mood of them comports with what he had written Paul Rosenfeld shortly before finishing, as he would succinctly describe it to Ben Huebsch, the "Bold but rather fine" tale. To Paul he wrote with the joyful relief of one who had come through: "Something dark, afraid—is gone out of my life." Cleansing his mind of the dead, ugly past had restored his sense of self-worth.[16]

2.

As had happened back in the spring at Fairhope, Sherwood's happy creativeness spilled over in early May into a fit of painting "cubistic stuff." Almost every afternoon he and Elizabeth wandered in the Dodge across the desert and up into the mountains, occasionally stopping for him to try, half in delight, half in exasperation, to catch in watercolor the elusive "spirit of this country." You "might have done something with it," he wrote Karl:

It wants a light, facile hand, a kind of strange upper fairyland of changing form and color. The South with the Negro and slower, more lusty rhythms of life is more to my own rather heavy hand, I fancy. Time and again I have fairly wept tears trying to get the feeling of a line of hills, strangely suggestive, and then have gone back to reinforce my impression, and what I saw at first wasn't there at all any more.

By the time his fit had passed in early July, he had some twenty paintings but only one that he was satisfied with, and he gave that one away. Perhaps, he characteristically decided, he could catch those ever-changing forms and colors "when I am gone away from their presence and when they are a fixed dream in my fancy."[17]

Just driving or walking about with Elizabeth was hugely satisfying. Although the sand and sagebrush desert at first looked dead, one could spot "under the brush hugging the ground closely the most lovely brilliant little flowers," many "no larger than a pinhead," and this "under delicacy" would sometimes flame forth into color. The drive on May 30 was especially memorable to the pair. Taking one of the narrow dirt mountain roads, which at first Sherwood was scared to drive but now took casually, they found themselves "in an upper grassy valley amid the pines." Many years later Elizabeth would happily recall that

we ran into a heavy snowstorm and the snow was piled up on the windshield and hood. As we drove back down, the snow gradually changed to sleet, then rain, and finally a warm rain was pattering down on the roof of the car. It was like being able to choose the season we wanted and then driving into it.

Even Reno itself afforded an occasional delight. From June 9 on, for a month there were horse races, and the pair "haunted" the track. Although they won their "expenses and about fifty dollars" in bets, Sherwood exulted primarily in watching the "noble bearing" of the animals "all the flesh of the body quivering with desire to run." Elizabeth more coolly concluded that living "so very much in his mind and imagination," he actually knew less about horses from direct experience than he thought he did, but "would throw himself into such interests and soon find out enough to pass as an expert."[18]

During the months that they lived in Reno, Elizabeth slowly became aware that Sherwood, being "so much wrapped up in his own thoughts and emotions, . . . was quite oblivious to many of the more ordinary aspects of everyday life." Once when they were walking in the city, he angered her by stopping and talking at length with the driver of a parked car, a pretty young woman he had met earlier, leaving Elizabeth standing alone and unintroduced on the sidewalk. It irritated her also that he "could not be bothered" to ever comment on how she looked or what she was wearing, but these were petty matters in face of the basic fact that being with him made life exhilarating. He "lunged at everything he did. Others might eat an apple; Sherwood *experienced* it." He was, she recognized, "a man of intense moods. When he was happy he was irrepressible, bubbling over like a boy, and when he was depressed, gloom hung over him like a pall." Most of their time in Reno he was happy, "far less aggressive and self-assertive than he had been in New York" and she responded with equal gaiety.[19]

The writing was, of course, going well. Having sent off in mid-May fair copy of part 1 of *Straws* to *Harper's* and of *Horses and Men* to Huebsch, Anderson began to work at once on part 2 of *Straws,* which was to cover that period of his early adulthood when he had attempted "to go out to the world—to take it at its own valuation." The book as a whole, he wrote Karl on May 31, would be "half narrative of experiences with men and women, half dissertation on life, and amid all this a good deal of pure fancy, in short, pure lying." Yet lying in the fancy was not really like lying in real life, as he had just intimated in a clear-sighted analysis of himself as a writer in response to a reader of *Many Marriages* who had objected to his use of the word "fancify."

May I make a frank confession to you? I am afraid I am rather an unschooled man and one who goes at writing depending upon a passionate desire to get something just expressed to a shade, rather than knowledge to pull him through.

The word "fancify," I confess, is coined, to get just a shade of meaning. I meant it to mean "conveying something over into the world of fancy, but doing it quite playfully and consciously." If you tell me it is bad usage, I shall not be surprised.

He continued to mull the problem throughout June, as almost every morning he pounded away at his first draft on one typewriter and inked in revisions while Elizabeth tapped out fair copy on another, correcting his spelling and punctuation as she went along. By this time he had well in mind the nature of "this semi-autobiographical thing" on which he was working. Linking it to his Testament, a "prose writer's experiments in rhythm—of words, emotions, thoughts," as he had recently described it to Harry Hansen, he wrote on June 30 to Alfred Stieglitz, to whom he planned to dedicate the book, that *Straws* was

thoughts, notions, and tales all thrown together. The central notion is that one's fanciful life is of as much significance as one's real flesh-and-blood life and that one cannot tell where the one cuts off and the other begins. This thing I have thought has as much physical existence as the stupid physical act I yesterday did. In fact, so strongly has the pure fanciful lived in me that I cannot tell after a time which of my acts had physical reality and which did not. It makes me in one sense a great liar, but, as I said in the *Testament,* "It is only by lying to the limit one can come at truth."

Part of his happiness in writing, then, was his feeling that *Straws* was "opening new vistas" of prose for him, that his fanciful lying would be lies like truth.[20]

Occasionally less pleasant matters interrupted his satisfying routines. There was the minor problem as to whether *Pictorial Review,* which had purchased "There She Is—She Is Taking Her Bath," would get it into an early enough monthly issue so that the story could be included in *Horses and Men,* indeed whether the magazine would publish the story at all. There were his painful visits to the dentist for extensive dental work. There was the good news from Ben Huebsch that he would follow the

Winesburg format, which they both liked, in making *Horses and Men;* but there was bad news from Ben that *Many Marriages* was in trouble.

New England has practically shut down on it because of the Boston Watch and Ward. A number of large book sellers in other parts of the country including New York City have been bitten by the morality bug and either refuse to sell it at all or only buy it on order from their customers, which is quite an effectual way of dissuading a customer. The Womrath Library with its many branches refuses to display the book and lends it only upon the insistency of the subscriber. During one month, it was the sixth best selling book of The Baker and Taylor Company, but they deliberately omitted it from their printed announcement on "moral" grounds. From these few items you will gather that I have not been having an easy time of it.

Ben promised to increase his advertising for the book somewhat, but, Sherwood continued to feel, censorship was his publisher's problem to solve. His own problem to solve was Tennessee.[21]

Earlier this year she had found a temporary focus for her life in cooperating with the director Raymond O'Neil in organizing a group of black actors in Chicago into the Ethiopian Art Theatre—ironically it was Sherwood who had suggested such a group to O'Neil—and in late April she, as press agent, and O'Neil had brought the troupe to New York for a series of performances of Oscar Wilde's *Salome,* a black folk drama, and a jazz version of *The Comedy of Errors.* Paul Rosenfeld reported to Anderson in late May that the actors had done well with *Salome,* "a detestable play," and that Tennessee was "much pulled together" and enjoying her job. Sherwood apparently felt this an opportune time to write her; he sent Otto Liveright a letter to be forwarded to her requesting that she appoint a Reno attorney to represent her so as to expedite divorce proceedings since his Nevada residency would be completed in some two and a half months. Tennessee refused on the grounds that she might be implicated in the divorce proceedings against Edgar Lee Masters, who had recently separated from his wife. Later in June, Anderson wrote her directly with the same request, and again she refused, now insisting that proceedings would be delayed "until such time as a divorce would not hurt her economically." Perceiving that a delay on these grounds could extend indefinitely, he resolved to use whatever legal action possible against this woman who, he wryly observed, had spent "a lifetime of scolding and storming" at people who refused to break up hopeless marriages. Whatever Tennessee's motives for delay may have been it is impossible now to know; Sherwood, hardly an unbiased observer, put them down simply as "just a kind of dogged determination not to face simple facts and an unwillingness to make the gesture that would be most gracious and fine." He decided not to repeat his request but foresaw that the legal proceedings would drag on beyond the mid-August termination he had hoped for.[22]

Very likely exasperation over Tennessee's opposition caused him to work more slowly in July on part 2 of *Straws,* which had gone so smoothly in June that he needed to write almost none of his frequent "warm up" letters. Then he learned early in July that *Harper's* had rejected Part 1 for serialization, though he was not greatly disappointed since he could always meet his contract with the magazine with stories, and if parts 2 or 3 should also be rejected, he could send the book as a whole to Ben and thus assuage some feelings of guilt for entering into the *Harper's* contract primarily for money. After all, he calmly wrote Otto, "You must know, knowing me— that I am not the sort of writer who works having the wants of magazines in view." But the main reason why the writing of *Straws* was taking time was that, as he wrote Bab, he had so much to write about.

A great wealth of material but the difficulty to get them to flow along a channel. Like trying to confine flood water.

You see I quite frankly threw facts overboard when I started on the voyage. What I wanted was to give something of the spirit of the life of a modern American artist without embarrassing any who had touched that life. Out go the real persons to be replaced by a troup of imaginary figures.

There are too many of them. O, how many men and women have influenced my thoughts and dreams. They are like the sands of the sea.[23]

Nevertheless, around July 19 he finished the second part of *Straws* and paused to read the first batch of proofs on *Horses and Men* and to write a brief statement in praise of Stark Young as a drama critic to be used in any way Young might wish for his forthcoming book *The Three Fountains.* This clear-sighted critic, he wrote, realized that the "personification of the world of fancy we call the theater must be approached with the same sincerity that life must be looked at if it is to be understood." The compliment was sincere, but it was also a way to thank Stark for picking up, at Sherwood's request, some antique jewelry as gifts for Elizabeth and Mrs. Prall during his summer vacation in Italy. Tennessee was in Italy, Anderson had learned, traveling with a wealthy older couple from Chicago. The uncertainty of her movements, he wrote Stark, had "kept me awake sometimes at night," and with grim humor he asked Stark to "kindly push her into a canal some dark night."[24]

After the pause he began work on the third part of *Straws.* In this section he had to deal first with his years as a businessman, years that in the final version of *A Story Teller's Story* would be largely telescoped into an evasive and fanciful account of his departure from his "factory" and his becoming a writer. This was still psychically dangerous material for him, and understandably, as he wrote Julius Friend at the end of the month, he was "having a tussle" with the book, going "to the mat" with it every morning. "Some days the book floors me and some days I get in a few good rabbit punches at the book."[25]

He was stimulated in his struggle with this section by briefly reestablishing contact with Van Wyck Brooks, the first installment of whose *The Pilgrimage of Henry James* he had at last read in the May *Dial.* Inspired by Brooks's piece, as he reported to his friend, he put in "some solid weeks of *James* reading" and concluded, not surprisingly given the immense differences between himself and James as persons and writers, that "I really can't care much for any character after he gets through with it." James, he felt, "did not dare love." Might it not be that he was "the novelist of the haters? Oh the thing infinitely refined and carried far into the field of intellectuality, as skillful haters find out how to do." As had always been the case in his relationship with Brooks, his attitude toward the man was a mixed one, combining admiration for Brooks's trained mind and "clear flowing style," a hunger for praise from this easterner, who seemed more of James's world—the world of intellectuals and haters, Brooks would have perceived Anderson as saying—as he felt himself to be more of Twain's world, and a resentful desire to obtain from Brooks the full sympathetic respect for his worth that Brooks always seemed to him to withhold. Taking on the Whitman tone as he so often did with Brooks as a means of simultaneous defense and attack, he insisted that in *Straws*

I am frankly daring to proclaim myself the American Man.

I mean by that to take all into myself if I can—the salesmen, businessmen, foxy fellows, laborers, all among whom I have lived. I do get the feeling that I, in a peculiar way and because of the accident of my position in letters, am a kind of composite essence of it all.

And actually there are days when people by thousands drift in and out of me. On a recent day here when I walked in the streets, this actual physical feeling of being completely *en rapport* with every man, woman, and child along a street wherein I walked became so intense that I had to go hide myself, to rest a little.

Apologetically, yet assertively, he hoped Brooks would be willing to read *Straws* when it was completed. Meanwhile he hoped that Brooks would treat James more sympathetically than he had Twain.[26]

Except for another pause to read the remaining proofs for *Horses and Men,* which he returned to Huebsch on August 4, he put all of August into "struggling" with the difficult third section of the book, discarding more unsatisfactory pages than he had done in the writing of any previous book; but by Labor Day, September 4, he had begun the long sequence concerning himself, "for the most part . . . a crude fellow with a hunger," in relation to the New York intellectuals, and felt that he was at last "in the homestretch." In order to improve the "surface" quality of his prose he was reading Turgenev "pretty steadily," and because Huebsch had sent him a prepublication copy, he read *Arlie Gelston* for relaxation, the first novel of a young assistant professor of English at the University of Pittsburgh named Roger Sergel. This realistic account of the troubled marital relationships of a very ordinary young Iowa woman reminded Anderson of Dreiser—"the same brutal honesty, the same deep sympathy for the people of whom he writes and the same lack of grace in much of the writing." With his usual kindness toward young truth-telling artists, Anderson wrote a letter of appreciation to Sergel and thus initiated what would soon become one of his closest and most enduring friendships. By coincidence, one of Horace Liveright's editors, Thomas R. Smith, wrote him in mid-August asking him to write an introduction to the Modern Library issue of Dreiser's *Free and Other Stories.* Anderson's brief tribute to Dreiser in the April 1916 *Little Review* was shortly to be printed in slightly revised form in *Horses and Men,* but he was glad to praise again the man whom he considered "the pioneer and the hero" of the "modern movement in American prose writing," the writer who had "worked so honestly and finely America is a better place for all workmen." Anderson celebrated his predecessor's honesty and courage, his refusal to resort to "trick writing" like the authors of plot stories, his "sympathetic understanding of life," his unshakable resolution to work in native materials when New England writers, "the children of a European culture," were giving "so little help to the Americans who are seeking masters to aid them in finding a life and a basis for a culture of their own." Such an introduction must have been easy for Anderson to write; he was presently discussing such ideas in his book.[27]

He was indeed in the homestretch with it, and now, he jubilantly wrote Karl, "the days march past in a kind of sun-washed splendor." By September 24 he had completed the first draft, finding as he did so the "inevitable" title. "I have called it simply *A Story Teller's Story,*" he wrote Otto, "and that is just what it is." By October 7, two weeks later, he could report to his agent that he had gone through the book twice for revisions and that the last of the fair copy was being typed. He was satisfied that he had achieved the right form and surface for his story, "not of a journey traveled, but of one begun, of long threshing about in a wilderness trying to find a path." Around October 14 he sent off the completed fair copy to Liveright.[28]

After the rejection of part 1 for serialization in *Harper's* he was puzzled whether the magazine and Harper & Brothers really intended to publish *A Story Teller's Story* in serial and book form. Sometime in August or early September he had talked in San Francisco with Henry Seidel Canby, editor of the *New York Evening Post Literary Review* and a literary adviser to Harper & Brothers, who had read the unrevised part 1 and told

Anderson that "it was about the most absorbingly interesting stuff he had ever come across." Feeling partly vindicated, Sherwood "half promised" Canby that he would let him read the completed book before it went to Harper & Brothers, and by mid-September Canby, who had yet to see the book, wrote that the firm wanted to publish it. Anderson now left the matter in Liveright's hands, suggesting only that if the magazine refused to take the six installments, Otto might try to interest Mencken and George Jean Nathan in serializing the book as a feature for the new magazine they were planning, *The American Mercury.*[29]

Equally puzzling but more dismaying was the unsettled situation with the divorce. By mid-September, Tennessee had returned from Europe looking "quite poorly," Rosenfeld reported, but she maintained her silence as to whether she would "stand aside" and let Sherwood "get things cleaned up." He fumed to Stieglitz that, "The woman has been a great feminist all her life. Oh for the freedom of women, etc., but doesn't seem to want to take her own medicine." Worried that she might get wind of how successfully he had been working on his book and take that fact as "proof that I have no immediate need of getting our situation cleared up," he decided to act without her agreement. On October 28, he and Elizabeth were to take the train west to visit the Pralls and Radins, and view the devastation caused by the terrible Berkeley fire of September 17, which had burned hundreds of houses around them yet by some quirk had spared their two houses. Before leaving Reno the twentieth Anderson, now a "bona fide resident of the county of Washoe," filed suit for divorce on the complaint that the defendant (Tennessee) had deserted him for "more than one year last past"; and since the defendant lived outside Nevada and could not receive a personal summons, he made affidavit that the summons be published in the *Nevada State Journal.* The Order for Publication was signed by District Judge George A. Bartlett, and it was probably at this legal proceeding that Anderson first met the man who became his best friend during the months he would still have to reside in Reno.[30]

As if *Harper's* and Tennessee were not puzzles enough, there was the odd behavior of *The Dial,* which had given him its first award, had serialized *Many Marriages,* had recently purchased "The Man's Story," though paying for it at the regular rate of two cents a word rather than the highest rate, and now published the tale in the September issue. They, however, immediately preceded the publication with what Anderson rightly considered an "ill-natured and ill-mannered" attack on his whole work by Alyse Gregory, a regular reviewer, soon to be the magazine's managing editor. Gregory charged that Anderson's writings "Never, no never, touch for more than a fleeting second that subtle art of restraint and aesthetic arrangement which we have come to associate with the most distinguished writing," and that where Dreiser had prepared the ground for a more liberal treatment of sex in American literature, Mr. Anderson, nervous and mystical, follows along like the anxious white rabbit in Alice in Wonderland, clasping instead of a watch the latest edition of Sigmund Freud.

Anderson complained to Brooks that "I could have written so much sharper and cleaner criticism of myself" than was contained in "so evidently incompetent" an article. Particularly among New York intellectuals, he felt, "there is so often just a superficial slinging of some smart saying at the head of a man, when understanding or the inclination to try to understand fails."[31]

The unpleasantness of the Gregory article was offset by other news, which convinced him, as he wrote Karl, that "The literary world seems to decide about once a year that I have committed literary suicide but they always get over the notion after a while." A young French university professor and literary critic named Bernard Faÿ requested permission to translate several Anderson short stories. A check came in from a sixth printing, in the Modern Library issue, of *Winesburg, Ohio,* a small check but a sign that the book was still in some demand. Otto Liveright reported that he couldn't resist reading the typescript of *A Story Teller's Story* and was finding it "extraordinarily fine," and that people were speaking enthusiastically about "The Man's Story," which Edward J. O'Brien intended to include in his *Best Short Stories of 1923,* a form of recognition that Anderson nevertheless regarded mainly as useful advertising. Then there was the publication on October 25 of *Horses and Men,* the format of which pleased him with its orange-colored covers, though after *Many Marriages* he was uncertain about the book's critical reception.[32]

It would be well into December before he would learn from Huebsch's semiannual royalty statement that, whereas the sales of *Many Marriages* had dropped to only 1,021 copies during the six months from May 1 to October 31, 1923, *Horses and Men* sold 2,121 copies in its first week, bringing him $1,045.85 out of his total net royalty income of $1,175.16. As for the reviews, which Ben on Anderson's direction did not send him, there would be only half as many as for the scandalous previous book, but several reviewers, including Mencken, announced that the author had redeemed himself after that lapse. Of the fourteen reviews that would appear over the next half year, nine would in fact be either wholly or mostly favorable, five mostly unfavorable, and only the *Boston Transcript* would object that the tales were "overloaded with sex." The reviewers were obviously correct in their assumption that *Horses and Men* was a collection of stories, not a structural group of them, and by present-day standards they would seem to have chosen the best tales for special mention: "I'm a Fool," "'Unused'"—which also had its detractors—and "The Man Who Became a Woman."

Two reviews Anderson certainly saw. In his friendly but not uncritical remarks in the March 1924 *Dial,* Robert Morss Lovett judged Anderson's work as uneven, his novels as "ambitious failures," his approach as intuitive rather than intellectual. The stories in *Horses and Men* were mostly successful, but all expressed their author's "fundamental belief in the futility of conscious art or any other form of intelligence to achieve the deepest truth." Anderson was enough upset by the review to write Lovett a response, but a polite one, denying that writing about emotional themes implied his sacrifice of a "guiding intelligence," that his novels "seemed to me to do what I wanted them to do" and that Lovett might be judging them by some kind of formula for the novel, that he wrote about what Lovett called "mussed up" people because "the general mess [of life] reacts on the lives of all sensitive people."[33]

The other review evoked in Anderson the same unqualified delight that caused Huebsch on November 22 to make an exception and send Anderson a copy of it before its appearance in *The Freeman,* the weekly periodical Ben was busily publishing. Early in December, Anderson wrote Huebsch to thank him for "the Newton Arvin article," explaining happily, "Great God, he is intelligent, isn't he? He gets what I am driving at." As Frost undertakes to interpret New England, Arvin wrote, so Anderson has assumed the task of interpreting "the deep human truth" of his Middle West,

the task of depicting a life so clumsily organized for human intercourse, so sterile in the values of personality, so poverty-stricken in what makes for humane conviviality, so hostile (as a consequence) to the integrity of the individual soul.

With a kind of "passionate puritanism" Anderson describes the resistance of the intensely individual self to "a life that in some sinister way threatens the purity" of that self, threatens "spiritual deformity" in the one who goes among "fellow-beings" only to find that "the contacts which should be cleansing are for the most part smirching, and the experiences which should be joyously shared have to be joylessly withheld." Like "a certain sort of puritan," too, Anderson

is more interested in the inner life than in anything else; indeed, "this vain show of things" seems to him but an aspect of the inner life, and he is not too curious about the line that divides material from spiritual. This is what gives his fiction its curiously poetic quality, and, in details, accounts for the seemingly unpremeditated beauty of many of his figures. . . . If the word had not too many dusty connotations, one would say that Mr. Anderson was a symbolist; he is at any rate a symbolist without the doctrine, a sort of congenital symbolist: to him the myth is not a theory but an irresistible mode of expression. It will not do to quarrel with him for not being a "realist." Mr. Edmund Wilson objects that none of the personages in *Many Marriages* has a persuasive reality; that they are consistently incredible as washing-machine manufacturers and housekeepers. But surely it should not need to be pointed out that reality exists on several planes; that the reality of *Babbitt,* valid as it is, is but one kind of reality; that John Webster is not a washing-machine manufacturer, in any special literary sense, but the man who has walked part way down the road of death and has come back to walk the way of life. The employment of this mythopoetic reality is Mr. Anderson's special forte, and it can be vindicated on the solidest artistic grounds; it gives form and color to fables of subtle subjective experience which would otherwise be too unsubstantial for artistic treatment. The fiction of the inner life would hardly be possible on any other terms.

Anderson, Arvin concluded, cannot properly even be termed a novelist in any traditional sense. Rather, he

is attempting—more or less unconsciously, no doubt—to fill the role of a kind of bardic poet; to put into simple and beautiful forms the vague and troubling pains of a bewildered people, to personalize a rather mechanical life, to give new values to a world that has discarded its old ones as invalid. And that, as the teller of "The Man's Story" says, "is I suppose what poetry is all about."[34]

3.

With the fair copy of *A Story Teller's Story* sent off, Anderson turned to working on several tales, which, he wrote O'Keeffe, "have been in my head for years but never would come straight, couldn't just get the tune." These would include a ten-thousand-word murder story that he dashed off "at heat" in two days at the end of November but which no more than the others did he finally "ink in," that is, revise to his satisfaction. He did satisfactorily rework the first thirty-two pages of *A Story Teller's Story,* a self-contained introduction to the book, into the short story "Caught," which Liveright sold for $175 to Mencken and Nathan for their second issue of *The American Mercury,* February, 1924.[35]

Anderson felt, correctly, that these editors would like "Caught," for it depicts the artistic and personal frustration of a successful magazine writer. Conceived by Anderson back in New York when he, Rosenfeld, and Brooks had called one afternoon on a painter whom he felt to have "something fine and at the same time cheap in him," the story describes a meeting between the first-person narrator (in the original version named "Anderson") and another writer who, distraught, has sought out the narrator in order to tell his life story. The man had been born in America of an Italian immigrant father who had prospered, anglicized his name, and sent his son to college, "wanting to make a real American of him." Mediocre on his college football team, the son achieved his first success by

writing a magazine story in which a young "Wop" substitute player wins
the important game. The writer then marries one of the popular women
at college, settles in New England, acquires an automobile and a daughter
who now attends Vassar, and continues to write football stories to popular magazine formula for high prices. Actually an artist by nature, sensitive both to the "surface" of life and the "more subtle life going on below,"
he forces himself to write only of the "outside of things" and hence has become simply "a man of business" producing standardized object. He realizes that he is caught in a trap, is sickened by that realization, despairs
of ever escaping. The narrator meanwhile has been interweaving his own
reactions to the man's tormented confession with glimpses into the inner
lives of the New England townspeople, which the man describes to the
narrator but cannot put into his stories. In short, with several relevant digressions the narrator tells an Anderson story about inward failure mas-
querading as outward success.[36]

Quite possibly the editors at *Harper's* had been influenced in their rejection of part 1 of the book manuscript, where this exemplary tale of
course came first, by so open an attack on American assumptions of success, on magazines as accessory to those assumptions through their demand for "clean healthy" patterned fiction, and on the very pattern of that
fiction by a fiction, which defied the pattern. Quite possibly, too, this initial reaction had something to do with the decision by Harper & Brothers
early in December not to take six magazine articles from the completed *A
Story Teller's Story* and hence not to publish the book despite the urging
of Henry Seidel Canby. Canby had written Anderson encouragingly on
November 15 that he had read the complete manuscript, liked the first two
parts, but felt that the third could be improved by being broken into
two parts and made "more precise and specific." Anderson agreed and began combining work on short stories with revising and cutting part 3, but
by December 8 he learned of the final rejection by *Harper's* and at once
wrote Ben Huebsch asking him, to the latter's relief, to publish *A Story
Teller's Story*. Anderson's one regret was the loss of the money that would
have come to him had the six installments been taken, and he occasionally
worried that he might be broke by the end of the year; but he had increasingly felt the contract with *Harper's* to have been a betrayal of Huebsch.
Now he could rid himself of a feeling of guilt, would have the book published, and in addition would not jeopardize the uniform edition of his
works he had begun contemplating by having to omit one volume under
Harper copyright. He was further pleased to hear from Canby that the latter had argued strongly against the Harper rejection on the grounds that
though the manuscript might need tightening and might provide only three
rather than six "first-rate magazine sections," still "the breath of life is in
it." Canby felt "like the devil at seeing that ms slip from my fingers."[37]

By the time Canby's second letter arrived in mid-December, Anderson was not only busy cutting part 3 of *A Story Teller's Story* but was two-weeks deep into a new novel, for which suddenly he had "at last got just the swing, feel etc" he had wanted, as he wrote a young Harvard graduate student in English named Whitney Wells whom he had met through the Pralls. The novel, tentatively titled *The Golden Circle* and never completed, was an outgrowth of his semiautobiography and dealt with a writer's feeling of being "lost in a huge empty place" like America, of having to cope with a country so "spread out that men at work do not see each other." Revising part 3 of *A Story Teller's Story* was putting him even more than usual in mind of his craft, for that part concerned the period of his life when, as Joseph Conrad had put it in *A Personal Record,* he began truly to live because he began writing. The storytelling craft was sufficient in itself, Anderson asserted in his morning warm-up letters; the aim of the storyteller was to make the reader "feel what he felt," not to give his tale "social-implication"—this despite the open lesson of *A Story Teller's Story* that the American writer should work with native materials and should recognize that, as earlier writers like Dreiser had made it easier for Anderson to work, so he would provide for later workmen "a greater stretch of room for individual development in the craft."[38]

A letter from Huebsch outlining the plan by the critic Frances Newman for what would become her anthology *The Short Story's Mutations* (1925) gave Anderson the opportunity to name his own best tales. He was uneasy at the suggestion that Newman wished to "explain" any of his stories, and he felt that she was quite wrong in selecting "The Other Woman" for her proposed anthology, as Edward O'Brien had been in choosing it for *The Best Short Stories of 1920.* That story, "so decidedly French in technique and spirit," he had written "partly with my tongue in cheek . . . to show the mutts I know this damn technique." At the top of his own list, which still proves a generally sound self-judgment, he placed "The Egg" as his "best shot" with "The Untold Lie" next, "a tale overlooked—solid as a rock." To these he added in sequence of publication "Hands," "I Want to Know Why," "Out of Nowhere Into Nothing," "I'm a Fool," and "The Man's Story." (Newman eventually chose "I'm a Fool" for her anthology, did not "explain" it, and praised the author's "beautiful kindness to his characters" and his "perfection of simplicity.") He was "much more conscious of technique etc than the critics think," Anderson insisted to Huebsch, adding, "It's pretty childish to think an artist gets results without knowing what he is doing." Writing to Liveright to ask him to turn the manuscript of *A Story Teller's Story* over to Huebsch without trying to place parts of it in a magazine market he recognized as "pretty limited" for his work, he described his present literary status realistically.

It seems to me that I may at present be going through one of my regular literary eclipses. You know the literary world is always deciding I am either a great man or a flivver and I am neither but a damn good workman.[39]

His self-confidence about his work at this time came from the steadying influence of Elizabeth. "Seems to me," he told Rosenfeld,

I have got hold of something—its hard to explain but has its basis in E. Her presence satisfies me, leaves no questions, doubts. It is a long time I have been seeking that feeling.

He had eagerly begun planning to have each of his children, starting with the oldest, Robert, live with him and Elizabeth for a year after they finished high school; and this December the depression, which usually descended on him "like a disease" as Christmas approached, came but went quickly. Without Elizabeth he would by now have found Reno almost unbearable after these months of waiting in uncertainty over what Tennessee might demand next. Both had in fact become "bored dreadfully" with the small city with its transient hundreds of divorcees and its population of "cowboys, ranchers, gamblers, etc." who now struck Sherwood as "rather crude, noisy, brutal children." Early in December he had gone on a long automobile ride with four other men southeast to mostly deserted Goldfield, once a wide-open, violent mining town. The mountain country was marvelous with its great sweeping vistas and its incredibly clean air; yet his companions spoke mostly of gold, then "relaxed out of that into rather unclean talk, whiskey, rank cigars," each trying to outdo the other "in vulgarity to seem manly." He and Elizabeth missed the companionship of writers and painters. With most people in Reno, Sherwood complained in one of his frequent letters to Paul Rosenfeld, "One has to restrict every conversation to anecdotes, never say quite what one means."[40]

The couple's increasing irritation with their surroundings was exacerbated by continued uncertainty as to what Tennessee might yet do to obstruct the divorce. Their hope that they might be able to leave Reno by Christmas had dwindled as it became clear that Tennessee would drag things out, at least until spring. She refused to talk with Clarence Darrow, whom Sherwood had retained in Chicago to handle his suit, and in her infrequent letters to Sherwood repeatedly raised new objections, though her major one was her fear of publicity. By early December, however, she had finally agreed to let the situation be arbitrated by a mutual friend, Ferdinand Schevill, a scholar of European history at the University of Chicago. A specialist in the Italian Renaissance, Schevill used all his fairness and finesse to propose to her that Sherwood delay his divorce suit until April 1, 1924, in exchange for her signing over to L. D. Summerfield, a leading

Reno lawyer, a power of attorney for him to represent her interests in court on or after that date so that she need not appear, together with her signing of a note to Summerfield, also dated April 1, stating that she would not contest the divorce. Tennessee agreed to this arrangement, and around December 21, Sherwood sent Ferdinand the power of attorney paper and a suggested wording of the note, both documents when signed by Tennessee to be held by Ferdinand, then mailed to Summerfield on April 1.[41]

With final negotiations thus left in Schevill's hands, Sherwood and Elizabeth set off for Berkeley on December 23 to spend the Christmas holidays with her family, taking with them for gifts the collections of antique Italian jewelry and boxes which Stark Young had picked up for them during his summer in Italy. Their visit was a great success. The Pralls and Radins received them warmly, Sherwood found the quiet, gentle David especially good company, and he admired and felt somewhat awed by Mrs. Prall as "a very delicate beautiful old woman of seventy and one of the most thoroughbred aristocrats I've ever seen." The weather was summerlike after Reno, and the great fire, which had spared the two houses and even their gardens and trees, had left an unobstructed view of the East Bay cities and of San Francisco and the Golden Gate across the water, with, at night, "thousands of lights stretching away for miles down below." One day Sherwood and David went over to San Francisco to lunch with a student of David's named Ralph Church, who turned out to be as enthusiastic about George Moore's writings as Sherwood had long been. Sherwood found all these people very alive in their ideas and talk, and he realized even more sharply, as he wrote Whitney Wells, what an "intellectual desert" Reno was compared with this "marvelous feast" of mind and senses.[42]

Returning to Reno on the twenty-sixth, he went at once into the final cutting of part 3 of *A Story Teller's Story* by some three thousand words to speed up the movement of the book, and by the thirtieth, in the midst of a three-day snowstorm, he mailed the revised part 3 to Ben Huebsch. Then, propelled by a telegram from Schevill at the very end of December, he plunged joyfully into *The Golden Circle* again, trying to grasp its "very elusive and exciting" theme. The telegram, followed by a letter, had announced that Schevill now held the two documents signed by Tennessee, and by the third day of the new year Anderson wrote his friend to express his everlasting relief and gratitude for Schevill's intersession. But in the weeks to follow, his and Elizabeth's growing impatience finally to be free to marry kept the novel's theme elusive, and he later admitted that in his remaining mornings in Reno he wrote some thirty thousand words toward the book just to keep his mind occupied.[43]

Other distractions crowded in. At Berkeley he had begun reading Jean Toomer's *Cane*, which Horace Liveright had just published, and became so excited about this "real American negro book" that he praised it to his friends and wrote Huebsch asking him to ask Van Wyck Brooks, literary editor of *The Freeman,* to let him review the book for the magazine or do an article on its author. Before he learned from Huebsch that *Cane* had already gone to a reviewer and that any article would have to follow a review, he wrote Toomer to praise him as "belonging" both to black men and "us moderns" and his book as "very very fine." The last story in *Cane,* "Kabnis," he would especially pick out in a later letter as simply "wonderful." He was much pleased to receive praise himself from Theodore Dreiser, who wrote on January 10 to thank him for the foreword to *Free* and the "Dreiser" piece in *Horses and Men,* and to tell him that he liked "all of your stories" and *Many Marriages.*[44]

Before Dreiser's letter reached him, he had had a sharp attack of the flu, which kept him from even busy work on the novel. By mid-January he was well enough to write a brief statement, printed as a broadside, for an exhibition at the Weyhe Gallery in New York of the paintings of his friend Alfred Maurer, "one of the really great modern painters," he asserted, and one of whose paintings of young street girls he had bought and brought with him to Reno to remind him of "the unextinguishable charm and reality of life." At this time also he agreed to write, for $50, a foreword to Volume 6 (*Maggie* and *George's Mother*) of the Knopf collected edition of the works of Stephen Crane in order "to help . . . get now a belated audience for so sincere a craftsman."[45]

He was looking for ways to make the time pass until April. As winter set in, Elizabeth had taken to sewing, at which she was skilled, and now set about making blue linen shirts for Sherwood to "bring out the intense Italian brown of his eyes." Delighted with them, he rented a sewing machine and had her teach him how to make shirts, and they spent hours together in their tiny dining room cutting and sewing the blue linen. He liked being able to do all sorts of things, Elizabeth had concluded.[46]

The snow and cold increased their sense of isolation in a small city with "no cultural impulses," Anderson complained to Stieglitz, "the talk endlessly on food and hunting." Invited to the university one evening, he found that among modern writers the "intellectuals of the college" had heard, and only slightly, of Sandburg and of no others. "It was a little like talking to the people of Mars," he wrote Paul Rosenfeld, as indeed it must have seemed in a time when the teaching of contemporary American literature was still rarely a part of any college curriculum. Being Anderson, he had made a number of acquaintances in Reno, including reacquaintance with Dr. B. H. Caples, who had been a boyhood friend of his and John Emerson's back in Clyde; but it was not until around the first or second week in January that he came to know George Bartlett, the district judge in whose court he had filed for divorce back in October.[47]

Bartlett, seven years older than Anderson, was a small, energetic man with sharp, humorous blue eyes. He had grown up in Nevada mining towns, taken a law degree, served as a district attorney and as attorney for several mining companies, and, renowned in his state as an orator, represented Nevada in Congress from 1907 to 1911. Then he turned to divorce law and, as an attorney and soon judge, became locally famous for his humane wisdom and advanced ideas. After presiding over some twenty thousand divorce cases, including Sherwood's, he would in 1931 distill his ideas and experience into a well-received book, *Men, Women and Conflict: An Intimate Study of Love, Marriage, and Divorce,* which would argue that marriage was a man-made institution and was changing, that divorce was a sensible solution to mental economics, and sexual incompatibilities, that adultery might under certain conditions promote marital happiness, that birth control should be encouraged, that affection and sympathy between partners was essential, that men should understand women better and women should better understand marriage.[48]

Such a tolerant, eager-minded man was a real find for Anderson in the Nevada desert and especially so since, as judge in the divorce court of Washoe County, Bartlett might hold Anderson's freedom from Tennessee in his hand. After their first evening of exuberant conversation Sherwood worried that out of excitement in finding a real friend he had been too "chesty in statement," and he wrote Judge Bartlett a note of apology.

I wonder if I was a little rude last night. It is such a delight to again find myself talking with a man who likes the play of ideas that perhaps I go too far, like a drunken man. For example my attacks on political thinking. In reality I know that a man who works directly with people, as you do, has to be conscious of prejudices.

After all, he explained, he could himself write about as he pleased and had "no illusions" that he was "doing or trying to do anything of too much importance to others." He ended his apology by recommending the "intensely human" *Education of Henry Adams* and George Moore's "delightful" *The Brook Kerith* to Bartlett and to "Monte," or Margaret, the younger of the Judge's two teen-age daughters. The lively and outgoing Monte with her aspiration to be a writer had been even more taken with the evening's guest than her older and quieter sister Dorothy. During his remaining weeks in Reno Anderson would spend hours with Bartlett walking about the city or sitting in the Judge's chambers in the courthouse or in his "lovely old fashioned library" at home evenings, talking of men, women, and books. Although Monte would later become a more frequent correspondent, her father was Sherwood's "only close friend" in Reno.[49]

Barely recovered from his first attack of the flu, Anderson succumbed to another, recovered, tried to pick up the "shreds" of *The Golden Circle,* went instead late in January through "a bad fallow time," which he thought might come from exhaustion of "nerve force" after long work on *A Story Teller's Story,* and had a second relapse with the flu in early February. Otto Liveright wired him on January 21 that he had sold a chapter of the *Story* to *The Century* magazine for $350 (less Otto's ten percent fee) and on the twenty-third wrote of an inquiry from *Phantasmus,* a little magazine soon to be published in Pittsburgh, about the possibility of serial rights to the rest of the *Story;* but as he often did when his nerves were bad, Anderson worried about his finances—Huebsch informed him for income tax purposes that he had received $3,620.49 from the publisher in 1923—and on January 29 he wrote to Ben asking, for the first time seriously, about lecture agents who might arrange some lectures for him in the fall. Although he could write to Ferdinand that Tennessee now was to him "but as an illness passed through," he was restive about waiting for the early April divorce, disliked the thought of Chicago, which he connected with "the whole TM period of my life," and longed to carry out his and Elizabeth's decision, made back in mid-December, to settle in New Orleans, "the city that charmed me more than any other American city I have ever been in."[50]

It was an in-between period for him in all ways. Work on *The Golden Circle* not going well, he began thinking in mid-February about a book to be called *Father Abraham,* "an attempt," he wrote tentatively to Huebsch, "at an intimate and sympathetic study of the development of Lincoln's fine soul." It had been for him "a buried treasure dream," he explained to Rosenfeld, not to attempt the usual "life" but "to make felt the final opening out of that strange, grotesque, sweet man" who "did, I am sure, at the last mature, come into being." He had been reading toward this project for a long time and while in Reno, he now told Paul, had "soaked myself in every scrap of Lincoln I could come by." But at this point he did no more than "scrawl" a little on *Father Abraham;* for as April drew closer, he and Elizabeth, while happy together, were both "a bit on edge" from the wait.[51]

March was largely a month of tense unsettledness for them; but midway in the month Sherwood received a copy of Rosenfeld's just-published *Port of New York* with its essays in praise of him as well as of Stieglitz, O'Keeffe, and others, and he wrote at once ecstatically to thank his friend.

Paul there are essays in this book so keen, so close to some inner thing in myself that I shall never be able to read them without the same impulse to tears you once saw break out in me before the Louvre.

. . . This book dear Paul will place you as nothing else ever has. Wish I were rich. I want every young artist in the country to have it.

Then within a few days Anderson received a letter from Otto Liveright with the exciting news that *Phantasmus* had purchased for a promised sum of $3,875 the serial rights to all of *A Story Teller's Story* except for the two parts bought by *The American Mercury* and *The Century*. The combination of tension and excitement was too much; Anderson simply stopped writing until the divorce was final.[52]

At almost the last minute Tennessee wrote Summerfield in Reno, seemingly to impose new financial demands, and on March 31 Sherwood desperately telegraphed Schevill for immediate help. Schevill phoned Tennessee, learned that she did not intend the demands as obstacles to the divorce, and wired Sherwood that, as agreed, he would mail her signed power of attorney on April 1. When that document arrived on the morning of April 4, Summerfield and Anderson went to the court house to arrange a date for the final proceeding, whereupon Judge Bartlett decided to hold the hearing in his chambers "then and there." Sherwood testified that some two years before Tennessee had "refused to live with him" in the Palos Park house, preferring to live in her Chicago apartment and "to follow her music." After the months of waiting, Judge Bartlett quickly granted him a decree of divorce. He and Elizabeth hastily packed, caught an afternoon train, and by evening were in the Prall compound in Berkeley, free to marry.[53]

15

"The Most Cultural
Town in America"

1.

Since the Bay Area newspaper reporters were eager to cover the speedy re-marriage of the author of *Many Marriages*, David Prall arranged that his sister and Sherwood avoid publicity by being married on April 5, not in Berkeley but at the Congregational Church in the little town of Martinez, some twenty-five miles away, with only Mrs. Prall and himself as witnesses. Sherwood had obtained a marriage license but had not bothered with a ring, and Elizabeth had to buy one for herself. After "a brief, almost curt, ceremony," the newlyweds foiled the reporters again by escaping for their honeymoon to Carmel for a weekend, after which they registered at a San Francisco hotel under an assumed name and for several days loafed about seeing the Bay Area sights. By the end of a week they were back in Berkeley, and Sherwood was at his desk again.[1]

The desk, a broad one, was in a separate little round house at the foot of the Pralls' hillside rose garden, a setting Anderson would soon adapt into his next novel, *Dark Laughter*. The Pralls, who were fairly well off financially, had turned the little house, Margaret's studio when she was not teaching, into a "luxurious" study for him with "a big comfortable couch, an open wood fire, a window looking out on the bay." Early in the morning he could come down to his "own hole," make coffee to go with a "bite" of breakfast, do his warm-up letters, and then go into the day's stint of writing.[2]

Deciding that *The Golden Circle* had indeed been only busy work, he put it aside and "plunged" into the Lincoln book, "a project close to my heart," he wrote Otto Liveright, adding that *Father Abraham* "is really the same theme under another and I believe more vital form." It would be, he informed Huebsch, "a novel really but not directly told as a novel." It

529

was not to be a conventional biography, and his continued reading in the many books about Lincoln—he now had "the run of the University library" and was "reading like a hound"—was to learn as much as possible of the people around this representative figure in American life, not to establish facts. Rather, his purpose was, as in his fiction, to let his imagination play with the person and life of Lincoln, who belonged to Anderson "an American story teller, as I to him," since Lincoln was to be understood as being fundamentally himself an American storyteller.[3]

Thus the long fragment, which is all that Anderson completed of *Father Abraham,* begins with references to Lincoln's telling "off-color" stories and quickly asserts the theme, frequently repeated thereafter in various ways, that he was "the story-teller from the beginning," one of Anderson's own sort.

> I mean that he had a certain gift not clearly understood by many people. When it appears, people tend to call it selflessness, but that is not exactly what it is. It is a certain ability to separate something deeply within yourself from the rest of you, put something deeply yourself out before you. You see yourself in a mental image. Seeing yourself in a certain situation makes you understand the motives and actions of people in that situation.

Not only is Lincoln's gift defined as Anderson had just recently defined his own in *A Story Teller's Story,* but there are other ways in which this interpreter of Lincoln may be perceived as putting what he felt to be deeply himself out before him. Like Anderson, Lincoln—according to William Herndon's biography, which Anderson too readily accepted as dependable—had a weak, shiftless father; he endured periods of deep gloom; he was a dreamer who "built his tales" at those times when he was "lost in dreams"; as a westerner he sensed the "vein of contempt" for his kind always present in the "men of the East, fellows who had advantages, who knew books, who had traveled, who were smart, keen, alert"; nevertheless, he the awkward, often puzzled westerner, not the easterner or southerner, represented America.[4]

To present this doubled image of the story teller, Anderson adopted a new style and adapted an old structure. As in *A Story Teller's Story,* the style is an oral one, but the sentences are not the smoothly flowing, conversational-narrative ones of that book. Here many sentences are short and declarative, many paragraphs brief and lacking transitions to the point of jerkiness. Occasionally there is a Whitmanesque, bardic passage, as in the hymn to the "Mid-American empire," which opens the fifth of the fragment's nine numbered sections, or, especially in the long Ann Rutledge sequences, a passage of lyric prose, and at the beginning of section 7 a free verse poem is inserted as in *The Triumph of the Egg;* but the overall effect is of the development of a few selected events in Lincoln's early life, or rather a reiterative circling about those events, by associational shifts or quick jumps in thought. The style, then, is simple in its elements yet constantly shifting in focus to accord with the picture of a Lincoln who when young did not understand himself or others, was not conscious of a purpose to his life, was—the terms are singularly Andersonian—"a questioner, a groper."

The stylistic effect is emphasized by a constantly shifting, nonchronological scheme of events. In section 1 Lincoln is abruptly placed in the still frontier village of New Salem, Illinois, where he actually settled at age twenty-two, with only brief, random references to his parentage and childhood. In New Salem he becomes acquainted with an Ann Rutledge straight out of Herndon's romantic legend, and one night he gets sick-drunk. In section 2 he becomes sober and stands outside Ann's bedroom in the tavern where both are living but does not dare enter. (Here as in his physical description the ungainly, self-doubting Lincoln closely resembles Hugh McVey in *Poor White,* as Hugh had earlier been partly based on Lincoln.) At the beginning of section 3 Lincoln is riding a horse to Springfield in the spring of 1837—the first and one of the few dates in the fragment—but he arrives there only near the end of section 5, the intervening pages being primarily a flashback to the scene of Ann's death (in 1835) in New Salem and to Lincoln's partial recovery from despair at her death during some months at Bowlin Greene's farm. (To Herndon's romantic tale of love, death, and agonized despair Anderson adds his own lengthy embellishments.) In Springfield, Lincoln becomes a lawyer and marries Mary Todd, but twenty pages later in section 9 the night of wild despair over the death of his one true love, Ann, is described again and in greater detail, whereupon the fragment ends. As in Anderson's fiction, the time scheme is fluid but here unusually so.

The most surprising and most successful part of *Father Abraham* comes in the twelve pages constituting section 8. In the previous section a group of men gather in a Springfield hotel for drinking and talking on the evening after Ward Hill Lamon, lawyer for the prosecution in a rape case, has secured the conviction of a young German farmer who had brutally and permanently injured a "bound girl" of fourteen on his farm while his wife was in town getting supplies. Only Lincoln among the men broods over the facts revealed in the courtroom; and being "just the story-teller studying his materials, accepting all life as his materials," he becomes in his imagination simultaneously the strong, lustful, determined man, the "thrifty, scheming" wife, and the "frightened, overworked little bound girl" who must feed all the farm animals and is entering the lonely confusion of puberty. In section 8 Lincoln emphatically experiences what in Anderson's imagination happened to the adolescent "Ma Winters" after the abrupt breaking off of the partial draft of "Death in the Woods," which Anderson had entered in his Paris Notebook ("PN") three years earlier. In the tale that follows, Lincoln and his interpreter are no longer doubled as storyteller; they are one.

The barely adolescent, bound girl—"Abraham's own mother, Nancy Hanks, might have been, at fourteen, just such another"—works so hard feeding the animals that her legs ache, as Ma Winters's body aches; she is feverish with uncomprehended urgings in her developing body; she is frightened of her employer's new notice of her. The farmer waits his chance to possess the girl and keep her as both worker and sexual partner. The childless, hardworking wife perceives her husband's intention and accepts it, knowing she can eventually get rid of the girl without having to "give her that money when her time as a bound girl is over." One summer afternoon the wife drives off to town for supplies, and the farmer tries to entice the girl into his and his wife's bedroom, but terrified she runs to the barn, the farmer in pursuit. When she tries to climb a ladder into the hayloft, he catches her leg "and down she came and fell across the tongue of a wagon." So aroused that he does not see that she is hurt, he tears open her dress and rapes the girl whose back is already so injured by the fall that she may never walk again.

This tale of troubled adolescence and adult ugliness, so like in that sense to several of the stories Anderson had written in Reno the year before, is interrupted only once. Just as the wife drives away toward town and the climactic scene is about to begin, there is a one-page return to "a tall, troubled-looking" Lincoln, "who found relief for his own intense inner thoughts and feelings by telling stories" and who, sitting silently among the talking men, is still in his imagination wife, farmer, girl. The single interruption is a skillful link between the story of Lincoln and this story within a story, but the tale itself is otherwise compact and powerful, moving steadily toward a conclusion known to be horrifying but even more horrifying when reached. After such a tale, only a retelling of Lincoln's night of despair subsequent to Ann Rutledge's death would seem to have afforded a means to equal intensity of feeling. One guesses that Anderson may have left *Father Abraham* a fragment partly because he had made his point about Lincoln as storyteller, had shown why "he is the figure closest to my heart," and could find only in the far-off Civil War years material of sufficient depth to warrant continuing after the sections on the death of a young woman whom the Lincoln figure had deeply loved and the brutalization of a girl, which Lincoln/Anderson had deeply imagined.

There were, of course, other reasons he cited variously to friends why he did not complete the fragment. At least by midsummer he learned that Carl Sandburg was at work on *Abraham Lincoln: The Prairie Years* (published in February, 1926), and he thereupon dropped his own attempt, he wrote Carl, because "I've a hunch you'll do the job better." By midsummer, too, he had concluded in a reaction to Lincoln that, as he wrote Paul Rosenfeld, "There was something wrong with the man, and unlike Brooks I cannot feed myself on other men's failures. Perhaps Lincoln was too far from my own time, impulses, feeling." Most importantly, he notified Huebsch as early as May 21 that he was "working along pretty steadily—every day—pushing forward both the Lincoln book and the novel. It isn't at all unlikely that the novel will get the upper hand and be finished first." Probably the novel was one of the "several starts" leading toward *Dark Laughter*, but in any case the writing of *Dark Laughter* would soon get the upper hand, and *Father Abraham* would remain unfinished.[5]

It was Sherwood's habit, Elizabeth recalled, to talk to her each day about what his characters had done in the pages he had written that morning. To one as gentle and humanly sympathetic as she, it may have been somewhat disturbing to see the extent to which her husband could imagine brutality; and certainly she was aware that her kindly but much more gentle mother, uneasy about her daughter's marriage to a twice-divorced man, found Sherwood to be fun in his happy moods but also "somewhat frightening" because she "was not at all accustomed to the kind of emotional violence" that Anderson might generate. David Prall admired Sherwood's writing, and the two liked each other very much despite their striking differences, which a colleague of David's in the Philosophy Department later described—David, thin, short, intense, a "perceptive aesthetician of delicate sensitivity"; Sherwood, "large" in personality and physique, looking "like a man who had had and liked sense experiences—food, drink, love—but had never lost his sense of discrimination in these matters." But when the two got into a discussion

it would soon turn into an argument, with both Sherwood and David expounding their views furiously—almost fanatically. . . . [Sherwood's] total absorption in his passion of the moment affected others as well, for if David wanted to disagree with Sherwood, he had to do so violently or he would not even be noticed.

For his part, Sherwood was "in love with the entire family of Pralls," he wrote Ferdinand Schevill, and "as there is in the whole house an atmosphere of gentleness and fineness I am very happy," despite his usual mixed admiration for and resentment against the evidences of much formal education in this highly intellectual, close-knit family, so unlike the one he had grown up in. Yet Elizabeth knew that it would be unwise, given her mother's love of quiet and her husband's earthy, restless nature, for her and Sherwood to live in Berkeley permanently. Since *Father Abraham* was going well at the moment, they planned instead to stay on in the compound through the spring and then, on the serial rights money from *Phantasmus* ($3,487.50 after Otto Liveright's fee), take a summer trip to Europe before settling in New Orleans.[6]

Meanwhile they were drawn into Bay Area activities. Almost certainly they went in to San Francisco on April 22, first to hear Rebecca West, who had praised Anderson's writings in England, lecture that afternoon on "A Woman's View of Life's Problems," and then to attend a PEN dinner that night. There was an "emotional" evening at the Radins' when two of the dinner guests, a painter and an etcher, attacked the modernists as "a lot of fakers," Sherwood attacked the two as dogmatists of tradition, and, after the upset guests had departed, Elizabeth wept "because people could be so easily hurt and could be so deeply hurt by beauty as by ugliness"—and possibly because her much-loved husband had again displayed his "emotional violence." There was the day early in May when Anderson, "in a weak moment," agreed to be photographed by Imogen Cunningham, an admirer of Stieglitz. She arrived at ten AM after he had been four hours at his desk, "and stayed," he complained to Stieglitz, "following me about and pointing her box at me until 5 PM." One of the best-known camera portraits resulting shows Anderson wearing tweed jacket with, instead of a necktie, a piece of variegated cloth drawn up under his collar through a large jeweled ring. His right arm is crossed against his chest, his right hand holds a cigarette between the first two fingers, the other two fingers are partly covered by Elizabeth's delicate hand. Beneath his slightly disheveled bangs his intent dark eyes look downward, and he half smiles. It is a portrait of the artist and of hands, but mainly of the artist.[7]

An equally characteristic, less "arty" picture from a different angle would be drawn orally years later by the university's English professor Benjamin H. Lehman in recollecting "a wonderful evening at the Warren Gregorys"—Gregory was a well-known lawyer and Regent of the university—"at which Sherwood Anderson and his wife were the guests of honor, a really good evening. The residue settled in your spirit for a long time." The impression Anderson left on Lehman was of

His kindness, his utter kindness, and, when things were discussed that brought it into play, his compassion—I think of kindness as being to people present, compassion with respect to the understanding of people whose predicaments were described. He was very handsome in a dark, brooding way, I remember, very quiet, not much gesture, but ready to talk about anything. I do not remember that he talked about his own works, and I specifically remember that someone commended him, a few nights later in my company, for having not talked shop that night. As a matter of fact he was talking shop, because he was talking about people, and people are a novelist's shop, but what my interlocutor meant was that he didn't talk about how you wrote.[8]

While Anderson worked at *Father Abraham* during that spring, Huebsch was going ahead with his author's affairs. As Anderson had requested, Ben sent the typescript of *A Story Teller's Story* to Rosenfeld early in April for a critical reading. He would have the typescript copy edited as soon as Paul returned it, he informed Sherwood, and then give it at once to the printer. Any cuts advised by Paul or still desired by Sherwood could be made, not as usual in the typescript, but in the galley proofs. (That Huebsch took this relatively expensive alternative suggests that he may have heard rumors concerning schemes by other publishers to lure his favorite author away from him, and wished to forestall them by getting the book into print quickly.) Ben also arranged to have an agent try to place "The Man's Story" and "Caught" in English magazines, negotiated the rights for a Swedish translation of *Poor White* with Tidens Forlag in Stockholm for a fee of $100 (to be divided equally between him and Anderson), and worked out an agreement with the prestigious Insel-Verlag in Leipzig to publish German translations of *Horses and Men, The Triumph of the Egg, Poor White,* and *Winesburg, Ohio,* terms of payment to be $100 for each book as advance payment against an 8 percent royalty. Not much money was involved in any of these transactions, but Anderson was pleased to see European interest in his work, an interest further suggested by Ben's report of a conversation with the German publisher and diplomat, Count Harry Kessler, who on visit to the United States had just told Huebsch that "The big things that impressed him in America were its architectural development and S. Anderson!"[9]

But by mid-May money had become an increasing concern for Anderson. So far he had received only one payment of $500 from the owners of *Phantasmus* although they had printed the first installment of *A Story Teller's Story* in their initial, May issue. Both Huebsch and Liveright had thought the magazine to be well backed financially, but now at Anderson's request each began to make discreet inquiries. The results became more and more disturbing. On May 26 Otto wrote that he was having "an awful time" trying to collect payment from the owners, Ella G. and James Edmonds; and since Anderson was obviously so concerned about money, Otto for the first time revealed that his brother Horace

has been after me persistently about your books. He wants to be your publisher. He thinks he can do very much better than Huebsch. I have nothing whatever to say in the matter. It is entirely up to you but I do think that if you at any time intend to leave Huebsch Horace is the best publisher for you.

So began Horace Liveright's ultimately successful campaign to add Anderson to his already outstanding publisher's list, though Anderson's immediate response to Otto around June 8 was at this point that if he wanted to leave Huebsch, he would talk to Horace first of all.

And I've no doubt more of my books could be sold by vigorous merchandizing.
But on the other hand Ben Huebsch stuck to me when I wasn't worth salt as a
property and he'd have to give me a pretty raw deal of some sort before I'd ever
quit him.[10]

By early June Anderson had decided that *Phantasmus* was "a smoke
. . . a mere fly-by-night adventure"; and in fact though one more installment of *A Story Teller's Story* was printed in the June issue, the magazine
thereupon folded, and no more payments were forthcoming. More bad
news came in Huebsch's letter of June 10 with his announcement that Anderson's royalty statement from November 1, 1923, to April 30, 1924
showed only $500 from sales of all his books. (The statement, sent on June
16, showed sales of only 1,094 copies of *Horses and Men* and four hundred of *Many Marriages* with a net income from all sales of $487.34.)
Shocked and dismayed, Anderson at once wrote Huebsch on June 16 that
on such an income he could not support either himself or his children. This
bringing in of his children was obviously a sign of his degree of desperation, more than of a true sense of obligation, since actually he had contributed only irregularly toward his children's support. Although it was
"rather like cutting off a leg" for painfulness, he wrote, he must withdraw
A Story Teller's Story from Ben and offer it to another publisher. Too disturbed to wait out the five days it usually took for transcontinental mail
to arrive, he wired Huebsch on June 18 again requesting withdrawal of
Story for offering to another publisher. "ITS THAT OR STARVATION FOR
KIDS AND ME," the telegram concluded, Sherwood perhaps stirred to
melodrama by his knowledge that in a few days his son Robert would be
appearing at the Prall compound for his year's stay with father and his
father's new wife.[11]

Even before sending the telegram Anderson had offered *A Story
Teller's Story* directly to Horace Liveright and indirectly, through H. L.
Mencken and Henry Seidel Canby, to Alfred Knopf and Harper & Brothers. Huebsch, "quite bowled . . . over" by the telegram and in a rush to
prepare for a month's selling trip to the Midwest, waited until Anderson's
letter arrived and then on June 21, the day before leaving on his trip, took
time to write a long, carefully considered reply. Admitting that another
publisher might sell more of Anderson's books, Huebsch reminded him
that "you have always deliberately written as you wished and never with
a view to popular applause" and that he himself had "abetted you in this";
however, "you must be willing to pay the price of such independence."

The men whom other publishers boost into popular success cooperate to find the
common denominator of public taste; that's why they sell stories to the *Saturday*

Evening Post and the like. I am not complaining, or criticizing you: I admire you for what you have done, and I can't help slightly admiring my own attitude too. Now, all these people who made you promises are ready to take the fruit of these slow years in which you have proved that a man can make a reputation as an artist and yet preserve his integrity. I don't say they won't fulfill their promises and, even at this juncture when I ought to make out a strong case for myself, I won't insist that I am the ideal publisher for you. Frankly, I think that in the long run you are and will be better off with me than with almost any of the others and, unless you cherish the belief that your books are potential "best sellers," you may agree with me, on further consideration.

In his own defense Huebsch asserted that he had helped build Anderson's reputation, not through conventional advertising but through "more assiduous press-agenting than any contemporary author gets. No publisher had devoted himself so singly to an author as I have devoted myself to you. . . ." Anderson should know that just as there is a "smug crowd" of reviewers, the best-seller market, who "make it almost a business to pound you," so "there are booksellers who would almost rather not sell your books than sell them."

If you knew what I had to contend with, (on *Many Marriages,* for example), you might be astonished. The largest shop in Rochester, to take one instance, insisted upon returning their entire consignment after their first customer for the book came back and told them about it. My stand in the matter jeopardized the account, for I stood by you and the book regardless of how it affected their attitude towards my line. The letters that I received, (both anonymous and signed) reproaching me for the book, were many, and some were from decent people whose good opinion I was reluctant to lose even if they made asses of themselves about the book.

Finally, Huebsch pointed out that *A Story Teller's Story* was already at the printer's with the first batch of proofs "promised for next week," that it had been widely announced as the leader of his list of fall publications, and that it would be the "principal item" on his selling trip. "I don't want to be too proud to mention that my prestige demands that I go through with this." [12]

On receiving this letter Anderson replied at once, explaining apologetically that he had thought the typescript of *A Story Teller's Story* had not yet gone to the printer and that he had written other publishers because he "got scared for my children's bread and butter." Now he would like to go to New Orleans by way of Chicago early in July, he urged Ben, so that the two could meet during Ben's Midwest tour and clear up any remaining misunderstandings, Elizabeth and Robert to go to New Orleans directly from Berkeley, Then Anderson got off letters to Otto Liveright and Mencken to apologize for unintentionally offering *A Story Teller's Story* to Horace Liveright and Knopf when he didn't have it to offer because Huebsch already had it in production. Despite the awkwardness of the situation he nevertheless felt better, he explained to each man, for he had hated being disloyal to a publisher with whom he had been associated for so long.[13]

He still faced the bread-and-butter problem, but a solution neatly presented itself when he was invited to speak on "Modern American Writing" at the University of California Summer Session on June 27. "There was nothing melodramatic" about the occasion, the reporter for the student newspaper subsequently commented,

but there was something just a little bit inspiring to the audience that listened eagerly to a pleasant-voiced man in neatly pressed gray tweeds (obviously suffering at first from stage fright) who bade the world go its way and let the artist go his.

Giving "the impression of sincerity," Anderson told his listeners what he had long been asserting and what his present situation was reconfirming to him, that

in an industrial age like this conscientious craftsmanship will not be rewarded, that a certain meretricious cheapening and insincerity is the demand that the social system makes upon the creative worker. [Anderson] advises craftsmen of genuine integrity to do their real work without hope of much reward, and to plan to make their living at some other "job" that will occupy only part of their time.

However, he concluded, with a public cheerfulness that contrasted with his private dismay,

it is easy to make a living in America; a man can make enough to live on in half his time, and there are, after all, publishers of books (though not of magazines) who can and will find some kind of a market for sincere, uncompromising writing.[14]

Possibly drawn by his billing as the author of *Many Marriages* and "one of the most discussed novelists in America," the audience in the university's Wheeler Hall was so large even on a late Friday afternoon in summer that Anderson could soon boast about it to Stieglitz.

Although my books had not sold much out there, 1,500 people came to hear me talk. They could not all get into the hall; so I had to give the lecture twice in one afternoon. Over 300 people waited 1½ hours for me in a nearby hall.

Since, as he wrote Mencken, the university paid him "more for this stuff than you do for a story like 'Caught'"—*The American Mercury* had paid $175—lecturing would be his "half-time job." He wrote Stieglitz that he would provide the opportunity to tell audiences what the modern artist was doing:

> While the people do not buy my books, I am in some odd way a figure in their minds. I stand for something. They wonder vaguely what it is. They will, I believe, crowd to hear me talk.
>
> And I shall talk well and straight. I'll give them something worthwhile for their money. I shall not go around, recite a few poems, sing a few songs, read a story. I'll tell them what men like you have been up to all their lives. I'll have a chance to tell them of real painters and real writers. In two months, perhaps, I shall be able to earn enough to work the rest of the year.[15]

Buoyed up by the success of his lecture, he left Berkeley at the end of June for Chicago where he met with Huebsch at the Congress Hotel on July 3 for a thorough discussion of their publishing relation. Huebsch changed the percentages on income author and publisher were to receive on translation rights from 50 percent each to 75 percent for author, 25 percent for publisher. He also showed Anderson some of the outraged responses to *Many Marriages,* and heading south to New Orleans, Anderson felt a revulsion against the publishers who had promised to make him a best-selling author. They were "greasy, vulgar people" who talked of "artistic merit" but meant that their authors should pander their talents—like the tormented supplier of football stories in "Caught."[16]

2.

Back in his beloved New Orleans, Anderson moved at once into a three-room furnished apartment, which had already been taken for him by Lillian Friend Marcus, sister of Julius Friend and manager of *The Double Dealer.* The apartment, at 504 St. Peter Street, was a second-floor, corner one on the "uptown" (toward Canal Street) side of the block-long, red-brick Pontalba Building bordering Jackson Square. He had expected to be joined by Elizabeth and his son, but a telegram announced that they were still in Berkeley and that she was nursing a very sick Robert. The gangling sixteen-year old, wild for "experience," had hitchhiked across the country from his mother's home in Michigan City, Indiana, and what was first thought to be diphtheria turned out to be a bad throat infection, probably from desert dust. Disturbed by the boy's illness as well as by the addition of doctor's bills to his other financial problems, Anderson quickly arranged for the energetic Mrs. Marcus, who also managed The Modernist Lecture Bureau from *The Double Dealer* address, to set up speaking engagements for him; and dropping *Father Abraham* completely, he began writing three lectures, which he entitled "Modern American

Writing," "The Modern Movement in the Arts," and "America—A Store-house of Vitality."[17]

When Bob was well enough to travel, Elizabeth and he left Berkeley and reached New Orleans around July 15 on the same day that galley proofs for *A Story Teller's Story* arrived. Mornings now, Sherwood immersed himself in reading the proofs, while in the afternoons and evenings all three joyously immersed themselves in the sights, sounds, smells, tastes of the Quarter with its narrow, noisy streets, Creole restaurants, delicate or flamboyant ironwork balconies, bright semitropical flowers and palm trees, the French Market, the levees and loading docks along the Mississippi. Elizabeth was "immediately enthralled" by the city, which Sherwood declared "the most cultural town in America," one where people "know how to play a little." The weather was moistly, drippingly hot now in the early summer, but at this point none of them minded the heat, and Sherwood even claimed that like an old horse he went better in it. By July 24 he had finished reading proofs, made cuts in the concluding book 4 where the prose needed tightening and where some initial references to Waldo Frank and others could be eliminated, and finally decided to include the story "Caught" as an epilogue since it "so perfectly sums up the whole book." On that day he returned the proofs together with wording for the lengthy subtitle of the book and the dedication: "To Alfred Stieglitz, who has been more than father to so many puzzled, wistful children of the arts in this big, noisy, growing and groping America, this book is gratefully dedicated."[18]

Three days later on the morning of Sunday, July 27, having gone back to working on the lectures, he "suddenly shot off into a novel theme," which "poured" from him "like a flood . . . something like 28,000 words in 10 days." He was reacting to his sense about *Father Abraham* that "Lincoln was too far from my own time, impulses, feeling" and more generally to his irritation at the tendency of some literary people to assume that, as he had written the poet John Gould Fletcher a month before, because he wrote sympathetically of adolescence, he must himself be "an eternal adolescent." ("It doesn't seem to me," he had rather tartly told Fletcher, "that if I were that I could ever be on top of my subject enough to write of it.") Possibly he was prompted by some fierce and friendly argument with David Prall to assert in dramatic form convictions about the "immaturity" of America and Americans that he had long held, and certainly he was affected simply by being again in New Orleans, where *Many Marriages* had poured out of him in a similar rush. At any rate, what he quickly was "going like hell on" was not exactly a novel but, as he wrote brother Karl, "a kind of fantasy of modern life—the War, sex reactions in America, artists, labor, factories. Am trying to make them all dance to slow music." It was, he wrote in other warm-up letters as the work progressed, "unlike anything I've done . . . all 'here and now'"—an attempt "to get and give just the slow after effect of war hatred on the emotions of people," the characters to be, not the "more or less naive simple people" he had "always written about," but people, "neither simple or naive," who were being affected by postwar "European moods" of cynicism and sophistication. The theme was so complex and "elusive" that he had "to work into a new style to fit it." As for title, he quickly rejected *The Golden Circle,* tentatively tried *The Lovers,* and by early September had settled, temporarily, on *Love and War* or "perhaps 'War and Love.'"[19]

One aspect of New Orleans that he especially liked and which was soon working its way into the book was the life of the blacks, at least as he perceived it.

You walk a block to the Mississippi. Big ocean steamers are coming and going. The niggers are working, laughing, sweating and singing. They have the real flare for physical things. One of them rolls a heavy barrel up and down a sharp incline. He plays with it as a cat with a ball—never letting it quite get out of hand. In all handling of heavy loads in difficult places they are as clever as a good boxer. The load never quite gets the upper hand. When it is on their shoulders or heads there is a remarkable play of the body muscles, giving to the load—controlling it. Often a negro with a heavy load walking on a narrow plank does a little dance step to show he has the upper hand. . . . I have come to have a real feeling of nearness—not to any particular negro but to them all. They rest me, playing with life as they do.

His "feeling of nearness" to blacks as a kind of concrete abstraction indicates how explicitly primitivistic his attitude had become; in his book the Negro would not be a personality but a symbol of what whites now lacked. "What one gets down here, at least I do," he wrote John Gould Fletcher around late July

is a kind of impersonal touch with life. What we whites seem so to have lost, the power of doing—the power of feeling, sensing each other . . . the blacks seem to have. Perhaps their animal suffering in the past has done it. They laugh, rub shoulders with each other, love like healthy animals, are no neurotics.

What whites had lost was, of course, a sense of the self as an integrated whole. Asked in late August for his "philosophy" by V. F. Calverton, Marxist editor of *The Modern Quarterly,* Anderson reiterated his old conviction about the psychic disfiguration resulting from industrialism and suggested a context for his "fantasy" of postwar America.

As for my philosophy—Lord man—that's a large order. I've a sort of notion that men—in our day—having—because of the coming of the machine—got rather far away from their own hands, bodies, eyes, ears—having rather depended too much upon intellectual development, have got into a jam. There is partial development or none. Men remain immature. Immaturity is no doubt the note of our own American civilization.

Still, the place for Americans was America, "with life as it is, here and now," and he outlined succinctly for Calverton one of his clearest statements of the relation, as he saw it, of art and life.

> Like all the so-called moderns, I would take the fact into myself, color it with my own thinking and feeling, and get it out of me again through the fingers, in words, color, line. You get my drift. I think the arts—practised—are a sort of cure for the disease called living. Living becomes a disease when you remain immature mentally and emotionally after the years when your body comes to physical maturity.
>
> It is rather a question, isn't it, of attempting to live fully, all over, with the mind, the emotions, the body.[20]

Yet another element he was writing into his book was the postwar expatriate experience, a kind of life that he decried to an interviewer from the *Times-Picayune* shortly after his arrival in New Orleans. The American expatriate is "an unhappy creature" whose vehemence of attack on "the turmoil of life in this country" betrays his regret at exile. Ironically, expatriates can find most of what they are looking for in New Orleans, "the only city in American which the factory has not spoiled with grime and dinginess" and with "the futile 'gogetter' spirit which spends itself in hustling around, accomplishing nothing." America "is the place for Americans to live, whether they are artists or not," but New Orleans, Anderson insisted enthusiastically to the receptive interviewer, "offers the greatest field for the writer and painter of any in the United States."[21]

It was all falling together as he could wish—heat, blacks, the city, the "rich find" of love with a woman "not afraid of herself . . . the first woman who has had always something to give," "the dance of the book," "Often 3 or 4,000 words a day . . . until I could not sit at the desk any more and all my body trembling." Huebsch might not be selling his books effectively; but he had confidence that when *A Story Teller's Story* came out in October, it should go well and his nagging money worries be eased. Meanwhile he had just had comforting proof that other publishers were eager to take on his work, and interest in translating him into foreign languages had spread, he now learned, to Japan. The Women's Club in New Orleans refused to engage the immoral author of *Many Marriages* for a lecture; but his literary fame warranted the *Times-Picayune* interview, and—a sign that at least New York was recovering from the shock of that book—the August issue of *Vanity Fair* could carry Samuel Hoffenstein's "Love in Lettuce, Ohio," a light-hearted spoof of small-town sexual complexes "Re-counted in the Manner of the Realistic Middle-Western Novelist," illus-trated with a cut of Anderson, the "most widely discussed" of this realis-tic school.[22]

There was no doubt about his fame among the writers, artists, and in-tellectuals who centered around the Quarter, *The Double Dealer,* the *Times-Picayune,* and Tulane University. Elizabeth retained a sharp, if composite, memory of certain evenings with Sherwood that summer and ensuing months.

It was a social and congenial time, with clusters of people meeting to eat at one of the less expensive restaurants, such as Galatoire's, dining on hot, spicy foods which were complemented by cold wines. Later, everyone would move over to a place called Max in the Alley, a newspaper hangout, with a large ceiling fan that languorously revolved, stirring flies into brief action and casting moving shadows on the walls. It is a scene that is still vivid in my memory, with all the men dressed in rumpled, messy seersucker suits, patched with perspiration and giving the curi-ous effect of a group of people sitting about in white pajamas. There would be William Spratling, looking as slight and dark as a Mexican, with his jutting jaw and eyes that squinted half defiantly at the world; Franz Blom, the anthropologist, with lank brown hair drifting casually over his high forehead and his light-colored eyes staring as if in interested amazement; Oliver La Farge, thin and spindly, all head and thick glasses; Roark Bradford, looking preoccupied and harassed as if all the news of all the world filtered through his active mind into the *Times-Picayune,* which he edited; Hamilton Basso, lithe and handsome with a flashing grin that was startlingly white against his dark tan; Lyle Saxon, who looked aristocratically re-mote even in a seersucker suit that dared not rumple when worn by him. . . . And there would be Sherwood, massive and burly as a bear, with his light cotton jacket twisted and wrinkled impossibly. Sherwood was the only one of them who had an established literary reputation in those days and the younger writers gravitated to him and usually deferred to him, even in the matter of seating, for he was the cen-ter of the conversation, always.

Although this composite memory would be written down many years af-ter the collapse of Elizabeth's and Sherwood's marriage, it is significant that her focus is on appearances, especially clothing, Lyle Saxon's ele-gance, much like that of Stark Young's, and Sherwood's dishevelment. She recalled also how, when New Orleans debutantes came to visit Sherwood's favorite cafes, "he thought nothing of unbuttoning his shirt and grabbing one of them to dance with him." Already she was recognizing that her new husband, "an impulsive and generous man," was "inclined toward ex-travagant gestures" and that she must tactfully "temper his rashness" when she felt that he "was going too far." Her own impulse toward or-derly management would later come increasingly to bear on and irritate him, but mostly this summer was intensely happy for them both.[23]

If Anderson was always the center of conversation during their social evenings, it was not simply that others deferred to his status as a writer, but also that they provided a constant, enraptured audience for his stories. James Feibleman, then a twenty-year-old would-be poet long before he became a professor of philosophy at Tulane, recorded in his memoirs one of the few extended descriptions of Anderson's storytelling manner, though the biographical details (some in Anderson's tale not entirely accurate) come from a later period in the lives of both.

Sherwood and Bruce [Manning] are the only two men I have ever known who could tell a story properly. They employed the same method, as a matter of fact. It consisted in the technique of the bedtime ghost story for children, applied to the commonplace, an atmosphere of great mystery applied to the most trivial of events and thereby transforming them into something greatly meaningful. The effect was tremendous; for the present, everything in the present: the room in which we were sitting, the furniture, the glasses in our hands, the fire in the fireplace, even the sounds outside, became invested with enormous significance. You felt as you sat there that you were being let in on some event of tremendous importance, that you were the only one being made acquainted with happenings which were capable of changing the whole course of history.

"You know, Jim," Sherwood would begin, "I only made lots of money one time and that was on a book called *Dark Laughter*. I bought a big farm in Virginia with the royalties, a place with a large stone farm house. Well, I decided that I could not write in the house, so I had a little stone cottage set up away from the main building." He leaned forward in his chair, his voice dropped, and his eyes looked away. "In the cottage there were two stone tables, and I was to write on one of them." He was on the edge of his chair now. "You know, Jim, what happened? I went down to that cottage every morning and sat there pencil in hand and paper before me." Here he looked around the room apprehensively, as though to catch the murderer himself in the act of eavesdropping. I could hardly understand the hoarse and furtive whisper spoken very slowly: "Well, I sat there and never wrote a god-dam word."

Other storytellers could produce suspense by introducing supernatural elements, mystery or magic. Sherwood needed only the ordinary circumstances of the everyday life of ordinary man.[24]

The constant availability of such attention was yet another reason why the summer of 1924 was an emotional peak in Anderson's life. Because of the intensity with which he worked on *Love and War* through a steamy August, he had one of his "little bad times" at the beginning of September; but the depression was a brief one, and he was soon back creating "a new free form" for his book and even taking notes toward a series of sketches on the tone of life in the present-day South for a book to resemble Turgenev's *Annals of a Sportsman*. At midpoint in September *Love and War* was about half done, and he drove so hard at it in hopes of finishing by fall before his lecture engagements began that by the twenty-third, with occasional tropical rains bringing cooler days and nights, he was two-thirds through the first draft and hoping to finish in October.[25]

As usual, domestic details intruded. Elizabeth found young Bob undisciplined, and the boy found her too disciplinary, but they had slowly warmed to each other. Bob wanted to be a writer, he wanted to be a prize fighter, he wanted to be a painter, and by mid-September, taking painting materials with him, he had shipped out as a mess boy on a freighter bound for Hamburg, Germany. On or about September 15 Sherwood and Elizabeth moved from their first apartment to one being relinquished by the impeccably dressed Lyle Saxon, a feature writer on the *Times-Picayune,* who was leaving the city in order to be in a quiet place for his own fiction writing. It was on the third and fourth floors of the Pontalba Building, 540 B St. Peter Street at the corner of Chartres. Now they faced onto green and flowering Jackson Square with the austere, three-spired front of St. Louis Cathedral at their left, Clark Mills's prancing equestrian statue of General Andrew Jackson in the center of the Square at their right. From their windows they could look down on the Square, the Quarter, the city, the curving river. It was "the loveliest view in America," Anderson insisted. At last they could hang their paintings and unpack their books. Saxon let them use what Sherwood called his "magnificent" furniture rather than putting it in storage, and Sherwood bought a huge old carpenter's bench, covered it with green billiard cloth, and had a desk big enough to spread out his writing projects on. After a week's flurry they were settled in, even to finding a black cook, a feisty little woman named Josephine, who kept the apartment in "shining" order when she was not preparing rich, spicy Creole dishes.[26]

All this social living cost money, however, the rent of $110 a month for the new apartment alone being nearly double what they had been paying. Early in August, Anderson had warned Huebsch that he must soon request an advance of $1,000 against future royalties on *A Story Teller's Story,* and in mid-September he did request and receive it. There were smaller amounts coming in as well—$225 from Insel-Verlag and $120 from the reprint of the Modern Library *Winesburg*—but by the end of September the Anderson finances were being stretched. Lillian Marcus had at last arranged half a dozen lecture engagements, but these were mostly for late fall and early winter, and in any case Anderson could not command the top prices of the professional speaker, settling instead on a fee of $100 a lecture plus expenses or $150 if he paid his own expenses. "Lordy," he wrote Huebsch about October 4, "I wish I had this financial problem off me. Its a pest."[27]

At this point Elizabeth resolved that she must somehow help out. Among the new friends the Andersons had made were Marc Antony and

Lucile Godchaux. Lucile was a lively, liberated woman whose wealthy family had repudiated her because she was living in the Quarter with Marc before marriage. Neither writers nor intellectuals, both much admired Sherwood, and Lucile had got in the habit of taking long afternoon walks with him around the Quarter or sitting on the levee with him while he talked about the characters in *Love and War* as though they were living people. "Do you know," he would begin, "what kind of trick that [naming a character] did today?" Now Elizabeth and the Antonys decided to start an interior decorating shop. Elizabeth had had her bookselling experience, and Lucile was a fairly accomplished painter, but unfortunately neither they nor Marc understood the decorating business. When they opened the Leonardi Studios at 520 St. Peter Street around early October, they ran it "along languid, leisurely lines," having fun and meeting new friends but making no money. By the end of October, Sherwood had resolved that if *A Story Teller's Story* sold, he would "insist she get out."[28]

Everything, it seemed, depended on the sales of the book. *A Story Teller's Story* was published on October 15 in a first printing of three thousand copies, Huebsch thinking it "good policy to be able to announce a second [printing of three thousand] very soon." Ben was putting all his available resources into his most extended advertising campaign ever, and by end of the month 2,631 copies had been sold and the second printing run off. Anderson began to hope for sales up to twenty thousand, but by mid-November a slackening of the book business as a whole began to affect *Story*. Despite Huebsch's continued efforts to promote the book through placing advertisements in newspapers and sending window display cards to bookstores, it went into just one more printing in December and in the six months from November 1, 1924, to April 30, 1925, sold only 3,548 more copies for a total of 6,179. After deducting the $1,000 advance, Huebsch could report a mere $334.29 due the author at the end of October 1924 for all his books. Clearly everything really depended now on the lecturing.[29]

Anderson was particularly hopeful and then concerned because, with very few exceptions, the reviews were favorable, the strongest any of his works had received. Since Huebsch felt that as a publisher he would "sink or swim with this book," he changed his usual practice and jubilantly sent the first reviews to Anderson as soon as they appeared, beginning with Lloyd Morris's in the *New York Times Book Review* for October 12—"a book which should be read by every intelligent and reflective American"— and not one but two in Lawrence Stallings's book column in the New York *World*—"a document of first importance for those interested in the growth of American letters." Of the dozen or more reviews that appeared within the first six weeks after publication of the book, all praised the book with complete enthusiasm, as did John McClure's in the *Times-*

Picayune and Stark Young's in his *New York Times* drama column, or, with only minor reservations, as did Sinclair Lewis's in the *Herald Tribune*. Eventually more than three dozen reviewers would discuss the book including Ernest Hemingway and Gertrude Stein, both of whom praised it in *Ex Libris*, the English language periodical published in Paris; and only three, only two of any consequence, were primarily unfavorable. Fanny Butcher, the decorous editor of the *Chicago Tribune* book page, who had thought *Many Marriages* "disgusting," admitted that *Story*, while a "total failure" as autobiography, was not "sexy" and in only one place descended into Andersonian vulgarity; Llewellyn Powys maintained the ambivalence of *The Dial* toward Anderson by objecting to the book's self-consciousness and slipshod style. But almost unanimously the other reviewers praised the book's flowing style, its character portraits, especially that of Anderson's father, its opposition to the ethos of materialism in American life, its defense of the craftsman's values, its repeated instances of Anderson's gift as a teller of tales. One of the earliest reviewers called *A Story Teller's Story* "the most significant book of the year"; one of the latest, Carl Van Doren in *The Century*, declared that "There can never be too many such books as 'A Story Teller's Story,' and there will never be many."[30]

In the context of the literary history of the twenties, one of the more extraordinary signs of the book's impact on the critics was a speech made in New York on December 11 before the august American Academy of Arts and Letters by Stuart P. Sherman, formerly a rather conservative professor of English at the University of Illinois, recently elected to the Academy, but now in his first months as literary editor of the *Herald Tribune* and more in touch with contemporary American literature than his fellow academicians. Under the headlines "S. P. Sherman Calls This Great Literary Period/Herald Tribune Critic Praises Sherwood Anderson as Explorer Lighting New Vistas of Human Experience," the loyal *Herald Tribune* reporter outlined Sherman's speech, which "twitted the academicians and institutions of learning in general with being custodians of cold candelabra rather than of torches burning with living fire." Just as the nineteenth century had its now classic writers from Cooper and Melville to Emerson, Thoreau, Whitman, and Twain who were "emotional discoverers" of America, so the woods of this present "great and fascinating period . . . are full of lighted torches; are full of men and women bent on exploring and reporting the truth as they see it, and nothing but the truth, and great areas of repressed truth about their own lives and the lives of the American people." In concluding his own account, the reporter quoted Sherman on the significance of *A Story Teller's Story*.

Of the incident that started Sherwood Anderson on his literary career—when he stopped in the dictation of a letter to his stenographer, and renounced the business world in favor of the "discovery of himself"—Mr. Sherman said, "Fifty years hence, I think, the literary antiquarian will point to this passage and say, 'There is one of the historic moments in American literature.'"[31]

Many more than fifty years hence one sees that Sherman was accepting too literally Anderson's brief and ambiguous account of his departure from business, was too readily falling in with the author's own construction of a legend that did much to make him briefly in the mid-twenties a culture hero of his time; yet Sherman was recognizing this departure— however extended rather than momentary it in fact was—as an essential event in the often blind struggle of one American into self-realization as an artist. The storyteller's story is, of course, that of his education, an education much unlike that of Henry Adams, to which Anderson several times indirectly alludes and then directly quotes, yet in certain ways much like, indeed, that rereading the *Education* half a year later he could say of Adams, "that man is nearer to me than any other American." Differing in background and social class, in intellect and training, in temperament and cast of mind, in opportunities, career, historical times, in almost every way, both men nevertheless record attempts to understand an American culture and civilization in which they have not been adequately prepared to live, with major elements of which they are profoundly unsympathetic, within which they seek to find both work that fully expresses the self and an inner order that effectually defends the self against outer chaos. But the intellectual, philosophic, skeptical Adams depends on ironic analysis to record successive defeats, failures, and a final despair; the intuitive, emotional, "groping" Anderson depends on tale-telling to record defeats, failures, hard-won successes and a final hope. *A Story Teller's Story* raises some of the questions, but by no means all, raised by *The Education of Henry Adams;* its answers in effect are, or at least are intended to be, an affirmative rejection of Adams's denial.[32]

A Story Teller's Story should be seen as one of Anderson's finest achievements in the art that conceals art, conceals it so well that some critics even now more readily perceive the book's faults than its perfections, or simply evade the book altogether. Discount as one will the enthusiasm of the reviewers for the new, still they understood fairly well the implication of the book's lengthy subtitle, recognizing that this was indeed the "tale of an American writer's journey through his own imaginative world" as well as "through the world of facts," that Anderson's aim was explicitly not to compile a "record of fact" but "to be true to the essence of things."[33] That he describes his mother as dying at thirty on a "wet dismal fall day" rather than at forty-two on May 10, 1895, proves that his true interest is not in the actual but in the emotional weather of his tale. That he gives two-thirds of the volume (book 1 and 2 out of four books in all) to his childhood, youth, and very early manhood, and says little of his later years as advertising copywriter and businessman (and again copywriter) shows both his conviction as to which part of his life was important and his desire that *A Story Teller's Story* have, not a chronologically ordered "plot," but rather "form," which, he explains, grows "out of the materials of the tale and the teller's reaction to them." Only the last third of the volume (books 3 and 4 and the epilogue) deals with his rejection of business and his conscious search as writer for the place of the artist in American life, but the longer first two books set in conflict themes that are resolved only in the shorter last two. The chronological asymmetry of the book—twenty-two years covered in the first two-thirds, at least that number in the last third—turns out to be an artistic symmetry.

Individual words, Anderson asserts near the beginning of book 4, are "the surfaces, the clothes of the tale," and as writer he has sought to use the "little native American words" rather than the more formal, bookish English of the schools, a declaration that suggests Anderson's contribution to the fundamental divergence between American prose of the nineteenth century and that of the twentieth and, in the twentieth, between English and American prose. On this surface of words each of the books tends to seem a loosely organized, at times even rambling, collection of reminiscences and tales interspersed with commentary by the now self-realized storyteller; but buried deep beneath that surface in each book is a firm structure, consisting always of two contrasting major themes, which govern the selection of reminiscences and tales.

The major themes in book 1 are fact and fancy. Usually their story manifestations place them in opposition, though there are hints that, properly regarded, fact and fancy are linked though separate. Thus Anderson's talkative father is introduced immediately as one for whom "there was no such thing as a fact," while his silent mother, introduced next, is fact-bound by the terms of her existence but connected with the fancy—when she does speak, "her words . . . filled with strange wisdom," and when she soothes with melted fat the chapped hands of her sons at bedtime, she is wordlessly "making love" to them. Fancy is too strong in the boy Anderson's younger brother in their imitative play drawn from *The Last of the Mohicans,* for the brother sinks himself totally in the part of Uncas even to hurling a hatchet at a neighboring boy's door. Fancy, in the form of expectation by the townspeople of quick wealth, is defeated by fact when the hole drilled for oil, a symbol of encroaching industrialization, gushes forth only water and mud. The absurdity of fancy quite unrelated to fact is demonstrated best and at greatest length in the episode of the father's wildly romantic narrative of Civil War adventure, told one evening in a farmhouse where he and his assistant, Aldrich, are staying while on a tour presenting a magic-lantern show in neighboring towns.

For some fifty pages (almost an eighth of the whole volume) Anderson tells this tale, and tale within tale, in complex fashion. There is his immediate story of Father and Aldrich in the farmhouse with the farmer, his wife, and Tillie, the wife's middle-aged unmarried sister. There is the story that Father, "the showman," tells at length, ostensibly autobiographical but patched together out of the most hackneyed stereotypes of romantic fiction about the War Between the States. Intercut with the romantic tale are entrances into the mind of Father, his recognition of the haunting beauty that semidarkness and intent listening bring to Tillie's face, or his quick decisions as to how to shape his tale to his attentive audience; briefer entrances into the mind of Aldrich, guesses by Anderson as to what may be going on in Tillie's mind. Most revealing are the further intercut comments of the author—a flashback to Father's early life, sardonic remarks on the cliches of romantic fiction and especially of the movies, ironic attacks on received attitudes ("The purity of a southern woman is unlike any other purity ever known to mankind."). At one point the intricately told tale is interrupted by Anderson's apparent digression into the Cabbage Story, still sometimes accepted as an autobiographical account of how Mother tricked boys at Halloween into throwing many cabbages at the family door, but actually a hilarious satire on the stereotypes of literary influence, Anderson's similarity to the Russian novelists being explained as springing from the "fact" that, like them, he had lived so much as a boy off cabbage soup.

The complex method of narration has complex ends within the book. The overt and implied attacks on stereotyped fiction and the standardized minds it helps to induce in its readers prepare for Anderson's youthful "first tale of the fancy," his preposterously romantic account of an alternative father and mother near the end of book 1, for subsequent attacks throughout the volume on "poison plot" stories in themselves and on their destructive effect on the American imagination, and for the summarizing exemplum of the epilogue. Further, the narrative method enables Anderson to portray his father with the vividness of fiction and to make that fiction simultaneously favorable and hostile. On the one hand, Father is said to be, unconsciously, an artist before his time and "the bearer of lovely things to obscure people"; on the other hand, his absurd, if audience-enthralling, tale illustrates at every point the specious use of the fancy quite unrelated to reality, so that Anderson's several assertions in the volume that he is his father's son actually emphasize his sharp difference as storyteller from his father, his true personal animosity beneath the genial mask being "safely" generalized into direct and indirect attacks on dishonest modes of fiction. Then, too, into Father's flow of romantic cliches Anderson at a key point inserts, rocklike, the condensed Winesburgesque tale of Tillie's one brief, genuinely romantic encounter as a young woman, thus illustrating the coexistence of the commonplace "fact" Tillie on the outside and the lovely "essence" Tillie living inside. So, in an artfully controlled paradox, Anderson uses the episode of Father's bogus fancifulness to assert the value of the true fancifulness, uses Father's "showmanship" to assert the value of the serious artist in America. Seen in their interconnectedness, then, these story-told hints of subsequent themes in *A Story Teller's Story* form a kind of midstructure connecting the discursive surface of book 1 with the fundamental themes of fact and fancy.

The "argument" of book 1, like that of the other three books, is clinched, not by explicit statement, but in Andersonian manner by a climactic story. Anderson's youthful "first tale of the fancy" is told within the context of a housepainting job on which, as a boy, he is his father's assistant. A prosperous farmer has had a new house built close to the road to town in order to display his wealth; the house had "instinctively run out to meet the coming automobile and the interurban car," to announce "blatantly" that it was big, new, and cost money. The boy Anderson sees this new house, which he and his father must first cover with an ugly priming coat he detests, as belonging to the menacing world of fact. He is drawn in the world of his fancy to the farmer's older house, far from the road, hidden by trees, a log house built when the land was first settled, one "in which long lives have been lived, in which men and women have lived, suffered and endured together." But drawn though the boy is, as was Henry Adams, to the security and certainties of the past, the times are hurrying him into the new, confusing industrial world, where as a young man he must deal with the fact that, as everyone tells him, "money will count big."

Book 2 is as intricate in design as book 1, but its two fundamental opposed themes are clearly embodied in contrasting characters. At first the themes of fact and fancy appear to be central again; for in the part factual, part fanciful account of his days as unskilled laborer, first in a city like Erie and then in Chicago, Anderson describes how he uses fantasies of power to alleviate the drudgery of the factory and the grime of cheap boardinghouses, and how he tries to impress a young chambermaid named Nora by his imagined skill as a boxer in a fight, which he loses ignominiously. But the Erie period contains an extended account of a man who at the time, Anderson claims, much influenced him, one Judge Turner, who is intellectually keen and witty, yet filled with antagonisms and destructive desires, and given to cynically advising that "money-making is the only sure method to win respect from the men of the modern world." A homosexual, Turner has sought affection but has been rebuffed and tormented until in defense he has grown a carapace of ironic contempt for self and others. It is the ultimate self-centeredness that Anderson the storyteller deprecates in the Judge, not his unconventional sexual needs; and indeed Turner is no more "perverted" than the young Anderson is when for self-satisfaction he plays with the emotions of Nora, who is engaged to marry a sailor, or when later in Chicago he seduces the reluctant wife of another worker.

In the narrative design of book 2, Judge Turner represents love turned inward, emotional needs thrust down in the "deep well" of being where they corrupt and corrode the self. In a tough Chicago saloon Anderson one night rescues a sick and drunk young man, Alonzo Berners, from being robbed and beaten, takes him to his father's home in an Illinois town, and spends a week there sometimes listening to the father's praise of a trotting stallion he had once owned but mainly talking with Alonzo. Because of a nervous illness Alonzo lives "in the dark house of pain" and occasionally goes on drunken sprees for momentary escape, but unlike Judge Turner he is a "giver" not a "taker." When talking with another, he always "entered into the man's thoughts, understood him, gave him what he apparently wanted, sympathetic understanding without sentimentality." Under Turner's influence young Anderson, like Talbot Whittingham, has contemptuously divided men and women "into two classes containing a few shrewd wise people and many fools"; now in the person of Alonzo Berners he is faced with a new morality, for Berners embodies an outgoing, unasking love for others, a power surpassing "the power of intellectual force" or the lust for money or greatness. One night before the end of his visit, Anderson walks out of town on a moonlit country road and, ridiculing himself as a sentimentalist while doing so, kneels in the dust in a quasi-religious effort, not at the attainment of belief in a nonexistent God, but "at the rediscovery of man by man."

This conflict between the embodied themes of inward-turning, perverting love of self opposed to outward-turning, health-giving love of others is partly resolved in book 2's symbolic summary, the climactic episodes of Anderson's experience as a young man in the Spanish-American War. He recognizes the antidemocratic, brutal aspects of his army life, its conditioning of men toward the "machine-like and impersonal" standardization of the World War; yet as he marches with his fellows "across a great open field," he realizes that "No man is a single thing, physical or mental," and he is swept with an oceanic feeling.

One was afloat on a vast sea of men. There was a kind of music on the surface of the sea. The music was a part of oneself. One was oneself a part of the music. One's body, moving in rhythms with all these other bodies, made the music.

This rapture of community is itself momentary and can on occasion seem ridiculous, but it points toward one of the conditions of art, that the artist turns outward from himself and unites himself with a body of others.

In book 3, the shortest of the books, the demands of business are put in opposition with the impulse toward art. Instead of describing directly the Elyria years and their cumulative tensions, Anderson recounts a brief night stopover in Elyria between trains, two years after he left that city. During these few hours he guiltily fears that he will be recognized as the man who had foxily persuaded several citizens to invest in his business and then had lost their money in a failed "effort to conform to the standard dreams of the men of my times." Convinced suddenly, as Anderson now states it, that buying and selling were corrupting him and that he was "in my whole nature a tale-teller," he resolved one day simply to walk out of the door of his factory office. Acting from conscious craftiness or from temporary insanity—eleven years after the event Anderson will not, cannot, or prefers not to decide—he announces to his amazed secretary that "My feet are cold wet and heavy from long wading in a river. Now I shall go walk on dry land." Thinking, ambiguously, that "you little tricky words . . . , not myself, have lifted me over this threshold," he walks out of town and, as his Herman Dudley had put it, "out of that phase of my life." So in that deviously forthright way a culture myth is told, not in its full factualness, but in its essence as myth.

Anderson has begun book 3 by praising the craftsman of words who through "the force of the imagination" can penetrate other personalities, feel "all of the life within" them, and in the moment of creation can lose consciousness of self in consciousness of others. Having stated the theme of art and then opposed it with the theme of business rejected, he shows art triumphing over business by telling a story from his advertising years. As he sits, bored, in a conference between "some six or eight" Critchfield executives and officers of a plow company, whose sales campaign he is to write the copy for, he notices that the company treasurer has on one cheek a long scar partly concealed by a beard. Thereupon he recollects an incident he witnessed one night years earlier when, as a young laborer riding the rails of a freight train, he is thrown off by the brakeman in an Indiana town. Hidden in a dark field between two houses, he observes a struggle between two brothers and a third man whom they have discovered making love to their sister in the field. The third man flees, is caught and slashed on the cheek by a knife, but escapes being killed by agreeing to marry the sister that night. This "scene" having played itself out in his fancy as he sits in the conference room ignoring the talk of plow sales, Anderson now "in fancy" talks privately with the bearded man, who tells how on that wedding night he and "Molly" did not undress but simply lay side by side on the bed until morning "holding fast to each other's hands," in loving community.

To what extent, if any, is the incident in the dark field, is the advertising conference itself, an actual autobiographical recollection or a creation? And of what importance, if any, would a factual answer to such a question be in either the storyteller's story or the present story of Sherwood Anderson's life? The proper question concerns the truth of the essence of the thing, and the answer is that there the truth is absolute. As far as the "argument" of *A Story Teller's Story* goes, Anderson has not proved but demonstrated the superiority of art over the world of buying and selling. One reviewer was moved to judge this skillfully told episode to be "one of the great short stories of our generation."[34]

After so fine a symbolic summary for book 3, book 4 except for its ending is a disappointment. The fundamental structure is recognizably there; one theme is the midwestern artist's search for self-identity and for greater mastery of his craft, while the other is the lure of the cultivated American East and of the much older European culture. Yet the midstructure of narratives is almost entirely missing. Instead, for the most part Anderson states his opinions on such matters as the standardization of American life, theorizes briefly on the nature of art, pays tribute to Stein for awakening him to consciousness about "the words of my own vocabulary," praises Brooks, Rosenfeld, Stieglitz, and other easterners. He tells rather than shows. Thus he explicitly decries the "Poison Plot" story and its "pasteboard world" rather than showing dramatically, as in Father's tale in book 1, how the stereotyped plot turns human beings into manipulated objects. Likewise, he quotes from *The Education of Henry Adams* the passage on the American unawareness of the religio-sexual energy embodied in the Virgin—"An American Virgin would never dare command; an American Venus would never dare exist"—and counters Adams's "accusation that an American could neither love nor worship" simply by asserting that this might apply to "New England men" but not to midwesterners.

As the mingled praise/rejection of *The Education* suggests, Anderson's double attitude toward the men of the East reappears in book 4 almost unchanged from *Mid-American Chants*. He goes East, he maintains, to learn what more cultivated men can teach him about his craft and to overcome "the feeling of separateness from the life about" him. Yet he goes committed to "the background of my tales, the Middle West of America"; he already knows that tales must have form, not plot; he understands that it is "the artist's business to make [the moment of experience] stand still . . . to fix the moment, in a painting, in a tale, in a poem"; and he is aware that the feeling of separateness is "common to all Americans." He is humble and proud, awed and self-secure; he wants to know and he does know. This ambivalence of attitude, unlike the creative ambivalence of fact and fancy in "the dark field" tale, muddles what he says about Middle West in relation to East. But of course the muddle was the true essence of Anderson's feelings about this relation. He made friends among the easterners, men like Frank, Rosenfeld, and Stieglitz who were deeply committed to a new expression of America; but contrary to the charge, made then and still, that like Twain he was somehow corrupted by the East, *A Story Teller's Story* proves by its very existence that the easterners confirmed rather than changed his resolve to tell in his own way "the tales of my own people."

There is nothing muddled about the symbolic scene that concludes book 4. Anderson on his European visit sits with a loved friend (Rosenfeld) "on a bench before the little open space that faces the cathedral of Chartres," the creation "that . . . made me more deeply happy than any other work of art I had ever seen." He and his friend watch a "little drama" played out unconsciously before the cathedral door by the actions of an American man and two women, one American and one French, and from this hint out of real life his fancy begins to construct a tale. Like Hugh McVey near the end of *Poor White* with his handful of colored stones, Anderson thinks of this "little drama" as yet another of the colored stones, another of the "many flashes of beauty" that have dropped into his hands "out of American life." It is up to him, he realizes, "to carve the stones, to make them more beautiful" if he can, and he knows that his carving of native American materials must be done, as was the stonework of Chartres, in his own land.

Such is likewise the import of the epilogue, the cautionary tale published as "Caught," now serving as the symbolic scene summarizing the whole book. Instead of holding the colored stones that every day drop into his hands and devoting himself at whatever cost to making them more beautiful, the writer of the one-plot football story has chosen to throw them away, thereby destroying the true function of his craftsman's hands. But he has sold out more than his craft and his imagination; he has sold out as well the American life that goes on around him in its crude, simple, intensely human way, that always goes on beneath the disfigurement inflicted on it by industrialism, by the standardization of machines and minds, by the fever to buy and sell and to be new and rich and big. This is the point of the storyteller's story, and it compresses into dramatic form the education of a representative American up to his forty-eighth year. Quiet rightly Anderson felt that this book marked the end of a period in his life.

16

Turning Point

1.

In the gray, warm, early October days Anderson kept at *Love and War*, on the sixth day at last getting down "boldly and delicately enough" in a three-hour push a difficult scene he had "been waiting for." Then on the eighth he broke off from his "fantasy of modern life" long enough to write out in an article, "A Note on Realism," his thoughts about the relation of art to life, of imagination to reality. It is a mistake, Anderson argues, to confuse the "life of reality with the life of the fancy," for the two are separate. Certainly "the imagination must constantly feed upon reality or starve"; artists must not, like Irwin Anderson, be simply romancers, for then their imaginative lives and their art will not be "significant." But the writers and painters who attempt simply to reproduce the exact picture of life, the realists, likewise produce bad art. The true artists

are not trying in the novel and the painting to give us reality. They are striving for a realization in art of something out of their own imaginative experiences, fed to be sure upon the life immediately about. A quite different matter from making an actual picture of what they see before them.

The life of reality is without order or clear purpose, whereas "in the artist's imaginative life there is purpose. There is determination to give the tale, the song, the painting Form—to make it true and real to the theme, not to life." As for the people and events the writer creates in his imaginative world, he has the moral obligation not to "tell lies" about them, not to "fake them." He must have the courage to let his imagined people "really live," but live within his tale not in "real life." This would be one of Anderson's best formulations of the grounds for his literary experimentation, and it was a sign of his current fame that Otto Liveright was able, in the real world, to sell the article almost immediately to the *New York Post*'s *Literary Review* for $60, "more than they have paid anyone before."[1]

For four days in mid-October he broke off from the novel again to go along with Julius Friend on a cotton-buying trip to Natchez and other Mississippi and Louisiana towns. Then, rested and buoyed up by Lloyd Morris's complimentary linking of *A Story Teller's Story* with *The Education of Henry Adams* in the *New York Times Book Review* and by his pleasure at holding in his hands a first copy of *A Story* designed with Huebsch's "characteristic good taste," he went back into the novel, now temporarily called *The Lover*, and by October 26 had finished it and "put it away for a bit of seasoning." Huebsch notified him regularly of the enthusiastic reviews of *A Story* and reassured him on the twentieth that the second printing of three thousand was ready, and a third would be at "the first intimation that the public is coming across intelligently." Now Anderson felt ready to go energetically into some short tales.[2]

The inspiration for the first of two appeared literally at his door in the person of Elizabeth's former bookstore salesman, William Faulkner. With the financial help of his friend-mentor-manager Phil Stone, Faulkner had recently contracted with the Four Seas Company for the publication of his first book, *The Marble Faun*. Writing poems seems to have been one of the occupations interesting him far more than tending to his duties as U.S. postmaster at the University of Mississippi. Keeping up with contemporary literature interested him more too, and he had been particularly impressed by *Horses and Men*. Except for Conrad's *Heart of Darkness*, he wrote his friend Ben Wasson, "I'm a Fool" was "the best story he knew." Apparently in late October he visited Wasson at his home in Greenville on the Mississippi, and while the two sat on the grassy levee one afternoon, Faulkner read the Anderson story aloud. When he finished reading, he told Wasson emphatically that he would like to meet the author, and Wasson urged him to go to New Orleans, see Elizabeth again, and through her be introduced to her husband. Fortunately Faulkner's career as one of the least dutiful postmasters in the history of the postal service was officially ended on October 31 after an investigation of his office by an appalled inspector; and much relieved at his release from a job he detested, he left within hours for New Orleans.

When he called on Elizabeth in the Anderson apartment, almost certainly on the afternoon of November 1, a Saturday, he had not expected to meet Sherwood; but the author was at home, the two men liked each other at once, and the Andersons invited Faulkner to dinner, for they had generously gotten into the custom of having impoverished writers and artists of the Quarter in for a Saturday meal. Another guest that evening was Hamilton Basso, who at twenty was still studying law at Tulane but was bent on becoming a writer. Rather awed by the twenty-seven-year-old Faulkner, Basso listened to his talk of the northern Mississippi South and admired "his beautiful manner"—Faulkner was clearly on his best behavior for the Andersons—"his soft speech, his controlled intensity, and his astonishing capacity for hard drink." Basso later recalled that dinner in an article memorializing Faulkner after his death, an article also briefly memorializing his host, the "Royal Personage" among the young painters and writers of the Quarter.

We owed him much. All of us were young enough to profit by example, and Anderson's example, leaving aside the example of the artist, was basically that of benevolence. What he had, he shared. What was his to give, he gave—his time, his patience, his attention, and, rather like a canopy spread over all of these, the hospitality of his house.³

In his carefully detailed biography of Faulkner, Joseph Blotner has filled in a part of the contemporary social history of New Orleans that Anderson would very shortly draw on for his tale about a young man named David, who is Faulkner after Anderson's fancy had played over the real-life person. In a house on Chartres Street, only steps away from the Anderson apartment, there lived one Aunt Rose Arnold, a tall, ample, red-haired woman in her sixties, who years earlier had been a news service telegrapher in Chicago but who had moved to New Orleans and prospered as the owner of a gambling house where prostitutes or amorous couples could rent upstairs rooms. She was a shrewd business woman but motherly and generous, and Sherwood had become acquainted with her since, more than Elizabeth did, he enjoyed talking with the "low-life" of the Quarter, the rumrunners, whores, cardsharpers, bums. In the story, "A Meeting South," she appears as the "Middle Western born and bred" Aunt Sally, "a motherly soul" long since retired from her business ventures. The unnamed Ohio-born narrator first meets the young Mississippi poet David in the narrator's apartment, notices his limp as they go out to spend the evening together (a limp such as Faulkner would assume when he was role-playing), is impressed as they sit on the river's docks by David's "gift for drinking," and listens to David's tale of his serious injury while flying in France with a British squadron during the war. Because of the injury David lives so constantly "in the black house of pain" that he has difficulty sleeping and, to manage his suffering, drinks heavily of whiskey made by a black on his father's run-down plantation. The narrator takes David to Aunt Sally's house, where the three sit talking on her brick-paved, flower-scented patio. Aunt Sally likes David at once, understandingly furnishes him with whiskey, and listens happily while he talks of his north Mississippi country and of the blacks there. Relaxed by her presence, David lies down on the bricks and is able to go to sleep. "'We used to have some good men come here in the old days too.'" Aunt Sally comments quietly, and the narrator goes out into the "soft smoky" New Orleans night, thinking of midwesterner Aunt Sally and the pain-wounded young southern poet as both aristocrats.

It is pleasant and fruitless to speculate how much of this tale came from Anderson's fancy, but it is certain that Faulkner's own imagination supplied the yarn about a flying injury in a wartime France where he had never served. Ironically, Anderson seems to have transcribed this directly from what he thought to be "real" life, for later he would tell Ben Wasson that he was extremely upset to learn how Faulkner had lied to him about his war service. Bur this knowledge would come to him subsequently. The significant qualities of the tale are several: the controlled casualness of the oral narrator; the sensuous feel for the Quarter at night; the quiet intimation that "aristocracy" is a personal characteristic manifesting itself less often "above" than "below," at any rate outside, a convention-bound middle class; and of course the proof in fiction that Anderson and Faulkner did hit it off at first meeting. After a very few days Faulkner left for Oxford, but his visit had been so happy for him and the Andersons that he knew he was welcome back. As for the story, Anderson wrote it quickly, in time to get a typed copy—he now had a part-time secretary—in the mail to Otto Liveright by November 8, only a week after "David's" first appearance at the Pontalba.[4]

The second story Anderson wrote in that first week in November, "The Return," is less impressive. A successful middle-aged architect, who had lived carefully in all ways and taken no personal chances, decides to drive back from New York to his home town of Caxton, Ohio, to see the friends of his youth and especially Lillian, who, except for his care to "observe the rules," would have given herself to him years earlier just before he left town for the city. Arriving at Caxton in the evening, he falls in by chance with a dissolute group of younger townspeople and learns that Lillian, after an unsuccessful marriage, has become "a little nervous and queer; has lost her looks a good deal." Unwilling to meet the advances of a cheap woman in the group, he suddenly wants to get out of town that same night without seeing Lillian and drives off at top speed on the highway toward the East. "The Return" is one of Anderson's weaker stories, for what it "says" is muddled. One should not, like the architect, fear life, fear breaking "the rules," as Aunt Sally and David and the narrator of "A Meeting South" manifestly do not; yet the architect's one weak attempt at unconventionality puts him in so sordid a situation that his flight is justified. It is a comment on just how far magazines were willing to go—even at that point—with an Anderson story; within two months after receiving "The Return" on November 12 Otto Liveright had sold this weaker, more circumspect tale about a circumspect man to *The Century* for $400, but that it took him twice as long to sell the much better "A Meeting South" with its uncircumspect characters and structure to *The Dial* for $90.[5]

These two stories out of the way, Anderson at once "plunged" into a new novel with the "corking" title of *Another Man's House*, the theme to be

almost entirely the relations of two men—each in fancy living a part of his life within the other man—that is to say seeing or trying to see life through another man's eyes. The theme grips and fascinates me.

Within a week, however, he was deflected from this project by rereading a typed copy of *Love and War*—or was it to be *War and Love?* After wrapping copies to send to Otto and Ben, he did not mail them. Pondering the book on a long evening walk, he decided that "the last two or three chapters were not right," and in an all-night session he rewrote them. Still uneasy about the book, he warned both Ben and Otto in mid-November that he might hold their copies for yet another week. Around November 22 he finally sent off the copy to Otto, though not the one to Ben; but instead of going back to *Another Man's House*, he excitedly started a short novel with the "lovely" title *Come Again Man*, to be the story of "the adventures of an imaginative man for a day among unimaginative people—his mind and emotions during the day." After writing about twenty thousand words, he began thinking of yet another book of a related sort, *The Man of Business*, "the tale of an imaginative man's life in the world of affairs," which would cover the years he had left out of book 3 of *A Story Teller's Story*. Predictably, as a climax to all this vacillation among projects, he took to his bed for several days at the end of November with a bad cold.[6]

As usual his body was responding to his state of mind. Chiefly he was worried about finances. Although he lectured on November 17 at Monroe, Louisiana, before the state convention of women's clubs and the next week pleased an audience at Brookhaven, Mississippi, he had no more engagements lined up until January, and Lillian Marcus was turning out to have been an unfortunate choice as lecture agent since she seemed, he felt, "to have the faculty . . . of offending everyone she writes and generally bungling things." Then, too, despite the encouraging reviews, he was soon concerned about the sales of *A Story Teller's Story*. The New Orleans bookstores were stocking few copies, and despite Huebsch's reassuring letters, he wondered whether Ben was supplying copies to the stores efficiently and advertising effectively. Huebsch's word in mid-November that the book business was generally dull was discouraging, as was the six-months royalty statement showing only $334.29 for all of Anderson's books. Further, Otto Liveright was unable to sell "A Meeting South" and "The Return" immediately, and "confused" by his reading of the new novel, Otto was undecided as to what magazine might serialize it. Beginning with its August-September issue *The Double Dealer* was running one of the Testaments in each number, but there was little or no payment for these. Finally, though, Anderson's son Bob, back from his voyage, now had a job as a newspaper reporter, Elizabeth's decorating business was not going well and promised to go no better. About December 1, Anderson, just recovering from his illness, wrote to Huebsch to request $300 as an additional advance, saying discouragedly:

> I hate to try to work with the shadow of financial worries over me but they seem to stay there like a ghost all the time. I used to have the feeling always that next year would be better but I begin to loose that a little. To tell the truth I suppose I have hoped that A Story Teller's Story might be such a success that it would take the shadow away for a long time.
>
> Maybe it will yet.

By return mail Huebsch sent a check for $300.[7]

Ben was a generous man, but he was also astute enough to know, after almost losing *A Story Teller's Story,* that his favorite author was vulnerable to enticements from other publishers. In fact, to Anderson's financial worries had been added the tension of such an enticement by Horace Liveright. Brother Otto began the campaign for Horace with his October 22 letter to Anderson asking "where [that is, to what publisher] the novel is to go?" and asserting that he himself had "no other feeling except that you have a right and a necessity to earn as much money as possible through your books." A week later Otto criticized Huebsch's advertising as "perfectly ridiculous from a sales standpoint" for not making use of quotations from the many favorable reviews, as "every decent publisher" would and thereby "undoubtedly further the sale of the book." In reply Anderson agreed that Ben might not be an aggressive business man but asserted that he had "something else" such a man often lacks.

> As for Ben—after I prepared to leave him last year I felt like a dog. When all is said and done he published my *Winesburg* when no one else wanted it. Then came *Many Marriages.* I believe there is no other publisher who would not have balked at the book. You know the experience I had with Harpers. They coldly turned down *A Story Teller's Story.* Ben has never quibbled with me in any way. Perhaps there are others who would not quibble with me now but he gave me a free hand when the others did not want me.
>
> I have, you see, a lot of sentiment about it. It may be foolish but I guess it goes pretty deep and the chances are all that I shall now stick to Ben to the end of the story.

He was "never going to be a hell smashing money maker for anyone," Anderson admitted, and then proudly: "I'm too experimental as an artist for that."[8]

Horace Liveright's next move was apparently to send an emissary directly to Anderson in mid-November. This was Konrad Bercovici, Romanian-born New York reporter and prolific author of gypsy tales, which Otto as his agent sold easily to magazines, and two volumes of which had been published by Boni and Liveright. Bercovici told stories out of his wanderings as readily as Anderson did, and during his two-day visit the two men talked steadily, one subject almost certainly being Horace's ability to sell his authors' books. Then on November 18 Horace himself wrote Anderson, declaiming "I'm your man" because "In a short time I have built up the best book publishing organization in the country." If Anderson wanted to discuss a contract, Horace would come to New Orleans to talk it over. Sherwood's reply was essentially the same as earlier to Otto, that Horace was "probably correct" about his superior ability to sell books but that he himself "would just find it too hard and uncomfortable . . . to make a change."

. . . I got out of business some years ago. Things like sticking to old friends have really got bigger to me than anything else. While Ben never sold my books much he has been very very fine with me in other ways. There never has been any lack of moral support. He published me and gave me his support when no one else wanted me.

Still, though there could be no talk of a contract, it would be fun for both of them if Horace could come to New Orleans for a visit.[9]

That Anderson nevertheless had private reservations about his position is clear from the letter he wrote to Huebsch on November 22 even before answering Horace. Using Horace's letter rather freely as a means of pressuring Ben to push *A Story Teller's Story* harder, he began:

At least we have the other publishers thinking the book is a great success. They are even asking to come down here and see poor me. I'm telling them not to come.

He went on to quote passages from half a dozen admiring letters just as a "sample" of those he was receiving daily; and most significantly, he told Ben that he was holding back the novel "a little for a few more corrections," though in fact he had just sent or was about to send a typed copy of it to Otto. Despite his protestations of loyalty to Huebsch, he was keeping his future options open.

Into this time of worry and tension came a letter from Bab Finley after a long silence during which she had been painfully learning to live with the fact that, once divorced, Sherwood had married, not her, but another woman. He had recently responded to an unexpected note from her with a letter she characterized as "splendid in its straightness and fineness." Now she wrote to say that of necessity her "physical need" of Sherwood "had been disciplined a great, great deal," and she wished only to help him "in times of stress." Beginning in January she was "offering to send you a hundred dollars a month for as long as we both shall live." Further, she was "planning to start an educational fund for Mimi and John"; for, she insisted, "quite frankly you and your children are the reality and the meaning of my life." Despite his money worries Anderson's reply was apparently a harshly worded refusal of both her financial offers; but now that the correspondence with her had been reopened, he began as before his marriage to Elizabeth to use letters to Bab as an outlet for his feelings.[10]

As December advanced, these feelings became progressively gloomier. Paul Rosenfeld had confirmed that *A Story Teller's Story* was not "going so well"—"The most American thing of the century, and not going so well?" Paul exclaimed—but more than money worry was burdening Anderson now. "It seems to me," he wrote Bab on the eleventh,

that I am in a state of transit. I feel about. Many stories and novels are started and few finished. Some of the driving impulses of the past are lost and others are being born.

Three days later he was "in a strange state of uncertainty," as Bab knew he always was after publishing a book:

And there may be a real and basic change going on in me. Now days I dream of clothes, much very much. I mean a kind of clothing for myself. The inner self it will perhaps be more and more difficult to give to others in any direct way.

By the eighteenth the sense of a possible new self had left him, and he felt "in a stalemate." Perhaps only because of "tired nerves," he was beset by "images" for tales and poems that "break off and disappear"; there seemed a "chaos" in his brain, an "inner confusion." The following day he admitted to Bab that he was in a "time of depression" and felt "a strange deadness and lassitude."[11]

There were happier matters, which might have dispelled his gloom. In mid-December David Karsner, reporter for the *Herald Tribune* sent him the account of Stuart Sherman's praise of Anderson and *A Story Teller's Story* before the American Academy of Arts and Letters, and he continued to receive enthusiastic letters about the book, sometimes as many as six a day, from "writers, painters, musicians," including one from author Rebecca West. For a month now engagements for Anderson's coming lecture tour were being busily scheduled by a New York lecture agent, W. Colston Leigh. Leigh was new to the business and still operating out of a bedroom, but he was energetic and enterprising and intent on handling Anderson's lecture affairs well since, as he later said, Sherwood was the agent's "first big catch." As one result, Anderson could look forward to an increasing number of speaking engagements at an average fee of $150 and to a visit with Bab in Indianapolis between other Midwest engagements. (Bab soon helped to arrange a lecture there for January 19.) Because of Elizabeth's "gentle aristocracy" he continued to feel himself, as he wrote Stieglitz, "really married for the first time in my life," though this did not prevent her from sharing in his depression, intensified as customary by the approach of Christmas. "The other evening," he confided to Stark Young, "we both sat down and had glooms about it." The ebullience of the summer just past was dissipating.[12]

Emotional relief came with the arrival on December 21 of David Prall, with "his sharp face—small alert delicate body," rather like that of the young poet in "A Meeting South." Before David went on for a meeting of professional philosophers, he and Anderson had four days in which they mainly walked about and talked steadily, Anderson feeling sharply how much he had been shut off from a vigorous mind by being mostly among southern men perhaps made "lazy-minded," he hazarded, by the long southern summers. Then David went on to his meeting, leaving Sherwood to walk the New Orleans streets alone unable to write. "New impulses— themes come flocking," he had told Stieglitz,

come too fast to be really a part of me.
Much has happened that I begin slowly to realize.
The absorption in sex as a theme has passed. I am after something between men and men. Elizabeth has profoundly changed me.
I get a whole sharp new angle but do not get it clear enough yet.
I walk and think. Flocks and flocks of tales—themes—all not quite the thing yet.
The itch not yet down at the finger tips.

So he marked time in the last days of 1924 before rushing into the pressures of his first lecture tour.[13]

2.

On January 2, 1925, Anderson began the tour, setting off by train from New Orleans to Cleveland, where on the morning of Sunday, the fourth, he spoke at the Jewish Center Forum on "America—A Storehouse of Vitality." Of his two lecture subjects, this was the one designed for a general audience. Though it was the less literary one, he still spoke out for the new writers of the twenties: "When the American reads more of the literature of America, he will find that honest art is more interesting than any false art of the past and he will want to live in the present day." This initial lecture, he felt, "went over with a bang"; but he had caught a severe cold on the way north and was glad to go on to Chicago, where he was staying with George Daugherty, his "feeder" of stories, and could get a day's rest in bed. It would be one of the few respites he would have during the tour.[14]

In the week or so he was in the Chicago area he was cheered to receive from Otto Liveright a check for $360 for the sale of "The Return" and a fan letter from Julia Collier Harris together with a copy of her enthusiastic review of *A Story Teller's Story* in the *Columbus Enquirer-Sun,* the newspaper she and her husband Julian, son of Joel Chandler Harris, were running in the small city of Columbus, Georgia. The review was, Anderson gratefully replied, "the best written, most clear and logical review of the book I have seen," and so a useful friendship began. Further, Huebsch, casting about for ways to keep Anderson with his firm, let him know of a large-scale literary luncheon he was planning in honor of his author when Anderson reached New York. Otherwise Anderson found Chicago, where he lectured twice, to be "horrible." He had forgotten, he wrote Bab, "how noisy, dirty and tense it could be." It was probably a relief for him to give his "America" lecture on the evening of January 12 to the Beth El Social Center in Hammond, Indiana, since he was the houseguest there of Dr. and Mrs. H. A. Kuhn (Mrs. Kuhn was a niece of Alfred Stieglitz).[15]

By the sixteenth he was in Topeka, Kansas, where in the evening he again gave the "America" lecture at the Washburn College chapel under the auspices of the Saturday Evening Reading Club of the Central Congregational Church. Since his old Critchfield friend Mario Morrow was now assistant publisher of the Capper Publications in Topeka, Morrow probably saw to it that the local newspapers had been creating interest in Anderson—"the most significant voice now heard in America," according to the *Daily State Journal;* a "shocking realist," according to another paper—and some people had to stand in the packed audience to hear him announce, apparently without the stage fright that had afflicted him at his Berkeley lecture the previous June, that "As the American man becomes more and more an imaginative man he will pour his energies out more and more in channels of beauty." A reporter was sufficiently impressed by Anderson's appearance to describe him as having "heavy features, black hair just turning gray, a subdued rainbow tie draped unconventionally, and burning black eyes. . . ."[16]

From Topeka he cut back to Indianapolis, where Bab had arranged for him to lecture on "Modern American Writing" in the evening of January 19. John Farrar, editor of *The Bookman,* happened to be in Indianapolis that day, met Anderson in a bookshop, and was so dazzled and amused by his dress—"a rough brown coat, a brown suit, brown spats, a wide and very bright blue tie drawn through a ring studded, I think, with garnets, or possibly rubies"—that he passed up a prizefight in order to hear the lecture, which he thought unconventional in argument and, to his conservative way of thinking, mostly unpersuasive, though Anderson, who "talked with effect," made his points "clearly and cleverly."[17]

The argument was that of his Berkeley lecture the previous spring; in fact, the Berkeley lecture would be handsomely printed as the booklet, *The Modern Writer*, by Ernest Grabhorn's private press in San Francisco the following August, and would be the first of Anderson's works to appear in a limited edition. Up until now, the argument runs, American writing has been dominated by the "rather cold and stony" New England culture with its demand that all the arts be "the servants of morality," and by industrialization and its attendant standardization, which produced the mass-circulation magazine and its demand for the safe formula story, a commercialization of art that makes assenting authors popular, wealthy, but untruthful about life. Life is "a complex delicate thing," and writing should grow "naturally" out of human lives, not out of formula plots and cheap technical tricks; "there are no plot stories in life." The Modern Movement is an attempt by the writer and other artists to return to the honesty, truthfulness, and skill of the individual craftsman, who seeks to express "some need of his own inner being" and dares to actually touch people's lives." The Movement is growing, New England Puritanism "is pretty well licked," and young men and women now must "put money making aside" and find their "real reward" in honest craftsmanship, "in the work itself."[18]

The best part of the Indianapolis stopover was the time he could take to walk and talk with Bab about the tour. The hours with her "will stay in my consciousness for the rest of my life," he wrote her from Pittsburgh. Here on January 22 he lectured "splendidly," he felt, on "America—A Storehouse of Vitality" to the Quill Club of the University of Pittsburgh, and stayed at the home of a quiet, serious, warm-hearted couple, Roger and Ruth Sergel. Roger, a young assistant professor in the university's English Department, regarded Anderson as "one of the outstanding figures of American Literature," who through his tradition-breaking tales had given life to "the 'poor folk' of American literature" before then treated as "merely effigies filled with sawdust." At the Sergels' insistence Anderson stayed on at their home the following day relaxing in the "sweetness" of these "gentle . . . real people," as he would call them in a heartfelt thank-you letter. By the time he left for New York the evening of the twenty-third, he and the Sergels had begun a very close friendship that would last the rest of his life.[19]

New York would be "one mad jumble." John Emerson, then in New York with Anita Loos, generously paid for a comfortable room for him at John's club, The Lambs, on West Forty-fourth Street, where he could snatch a few hours of sleep during kaleidoscopic days and nights of lectures, visits, talks with people, and parties. On the twenty-fifth he gave his "America—A Storehouse of Vitality" talk at Cooper Union, and on the thirtieth he gave the first of three weekly lectures at the Rand School of Social Science, all four lectures having been arranged by Lillian Marcus. Otherwise, from February 1 on he was under contract with Colston Leigh, Anderson to pay his own traveling, living, and advertising expenses, much of this last handled by Huebsch, and to remit 20 percent of his fees to Leigh, who set up engagements for him and a week in advance gave him each week's speaking schedule. During his four weeks in New York he would leave to lecture in Boston and Philadelphia, but most of the time he found himself a literary lion in the city, an experience that, he complained to Bab, was a "half ugly rather exciting thing" since some days it seemed as though "half the city wanted to see and talk with me all at once."[20]

The high point of the lionizing was Ben Huebsch's literary luncheon for him in a private dining room of the Brevoort Hotel at noon on Thursday, January 29.[21] Huebsch had sent out invitations to at least sixty-eight reviewers, literary critics, and writers acquainted with Anderson or his work, and only thirteen were unable to attend. Counting several spouses, at least sixty-four guests along with Huebsch's staff came to honor Anderson, including Louis Bromfield, Kenneth Burke, Henry S. Canby, Floyd Dell, Waldo Frank, Harry Hansen, Joseph Wood Krutch, H. L. Mencken, Burton Rascoe, Stuart P. Sherman, Carl, Irita, and Mark Van Doren, and Edmund Wilson. "Few authors would call forth such an aggregation of literary ladies and gentlemen as greeted Sherwood Anderson recently in Manhattan," John Farrar, another of the guests, would subsequently exclaim in *Time* magazine. Although Huebsch, who could ill afford the cost of such an assemblage of literary opinion-makers, had hoped to keep all things smooth, an initial tension rose when Mencken openly refused to meet Stuart Sherman, whom he detested, and pointedly chose a table separate from all the New York "vermin." Anderson, Mencken noted sardonically,

showed up wearing a navy blue shirt with a soft collar and a flowing necktie to match. His tweeds, at least three quarters of an inch thick, were yellow shot with brown. In his necktie he wore a ruby at least an inch in diameter.

The tension increased at the end of the lunch, when Sherwood, perhaps because Ben's invitations had specified "no speeches," refused to speak, whereupon Huebsch quietly asked Hendrik Willem Van Loon to say something in order to get him started. Van Loon began with a few comments and then asked jovially: "and will you tell us Mr. Anderson how you have managed to keep on good terms all these years with that ogre Huebsch and continue to publish with him?" Van Loon had expected his question to prompt "an outburst of pleasant things" about Huebsch from Anderson, but the guest of honor obstinately remained silent. Presumably the gathering soon broke up.[22]

From the conflicting recollections of several guests at the luncheon has arisen the legend that Anderson had already signed a contract to go with Horace Liveright and that all the persons present except Huebsch knew it, but the legend is only legend. It was then generally known in the publishing world that Ben had almost lost *A Story Teller's Story* to Liveright or some other publisher, and for that reason many persons there did feel that Van Loon's attempt at humor was rather gauche; but in a note thanking the Huebsches for the luncheon, Anderson apologetically explained: "I could have told them why I have Ben Huebsch for publisher but there aren't a lot of them would know just what I was talking about." Huebsch felt Anderson's note to be "affectionate" in tone, and generously explained his refusal to respond to Van Loon as probably resulting from shock at "the abruptness and form" of the question and from a sensitive surmise that "I would regard it as indelicate for him to say nice things about me to a crowd of people with me present."[23]

Anderson did see something of Liveright at this time. Somehow by early February he managed to read for Horace the manuscript of a collection of stories titled *In Our Time,* which had recently come in from Ernest Hemingway. Sherwood liked all the stories, urged Horace to publish the book, and promised to write a blurb for its dust jacket. Horace may have renewed his overtures to Sherwood then or at a party he gave in February in his elaborate office, but if so, the overtures failed; Anderson was disgusted by the unfeeling sexual encounters men at the party and in the New York publishing and theater worlds generally had "with women and young girls as casually as rabbits." After seeing something of Knopf and Liveright "at close hand," he would write Bab, the more he was "pleased that I am with Huebsch. Quality counts."[24]

Pleasure and disgust continued to be mixed during the weeks of his stay in New York. Despite the tensions that marred the literary luncheon, he felt himself to be "temporarily a sort of man of the hour," to be looked on by floods of people as "an exceptional man," though he refused to think of himself as exceptional and was glad only at the signs that he had "made a place" for himself "in American life." People in New York seemed tired, older, disillusioned; many were "clutching people" who seemed to be "pleading for some vague thing—life perhaps—for the most part offering nothing in return." Since being in New York before going to

Reno he had learned to be less sensitive to such persons, but still they exhausted him. Paul Rosenfeld, whom he had hoped to see much of, was emotionally troubled by being unable to choose between two women in love with him; so instead he saw much of Stieglitz and O'Keeffe, recently married and now preparing to open a group show of contemporary artists, "Seven Americans," at the Anderson Galleries for three weeks in March; and Sherwood, excited by a preview of paintings, watercolors, and photographs by Charles Demuth, Arthur Dove, Marsden Hartley, John Marin, Paul Strand, O'Keeffe, and Stieglitz, wrote a free-verse poem included in the exhibition catalog. The seven Americans were "Seven Alive" bringing "moments of life" through their art to the "very tired" people of the city.[25]

Equally exciting was to find himself desiring "passionately" to write for the theater. Earlier Otto Liveright had urged him to turn "There She Is—She Is Taking Her Bath" into a three-act farce, but the immediate cause for this sudden new fascination was probably the three-week run at the Provincetown Playhouse on Macdougal Street of a double bill, Eugene O'Neill's *Diff'rent* and Raymond O'Neil's dramatization of Anderson's tale, *The Triumph of the Egg*, with John Huston successfully playing the part of the father. On opening night, February 10, Anderson had to be in Philadelphia giving a "contributor's" lecture under the auspices of the little magazine *The Guardian* to a large, eager audience; but after his return to New York on the eleventh, he saw the production of his play and was pleased by the moderately favorable reviews. He began spending his evenings at various theaters, studying the acting to see which of his stories he could dramatize. Although the season seemed thin, he was especially impressed by the Theater Guild's production of John Howard Lawson's Expressionist *Processional* and by Paul Robeson's performance in *The Emperor Jones*, acting so "extraordinarily fine" that he hoped someday "to write a play in which he will consent to star." In anticipation of the opening of *The Triumph of the Egg*, he had already written Raymond O'Neil in Chicago in care of Tennessee to suggest an acceptable royalty arrangement and to urge that the two men talk together about the theater. (Tennessee opened the letter and wrote her former husband, apparently angrily, to protest the arrangement.) O'Neil now replied encouraging a dramatization of *Winesburg*, though cautioning that "the thing you have to give would be very difficult for the American theater to do."[26]

After a month of seeing more "not . . . quite human" people, Anderson left the city on the morning of February 21, spent a day with Henry Canby in New Haven, and then headed west for Chicago. Here, as arranged, Elizabeth met him, and after they had visited with the Schevills and Sherwood had spoken—very woodenly, Elizabeth felt—at a large Jewish temple on the South Side on the twenty-fifth they went on to

Urbana, where on February 29 he gave "Modern American Writing" at the English Journal Club of the University of Illinois as the last lecture of his tour. He too felt he had had a dull night in Chicago, but the Urbana lecture, he wrote Leigh, "went off with a great bang." Weary from the tour but pleased with the financial results, he traveled with Elizabeth by slow train to Natchez, then "a charming, sleepy place" on its bluff overlooking the Mississippi for a couple of days rest. By March 2 they were back at 540 St. Peter Street in New Orleans.[27]

3.

Feeling at the moment "very fine and fit" after his return, Anderson by the sixth had cleared his desk of accumulated correspondence and written an enthusiastic review of Nathaniel Wright Stephenson's *Lincoln: An Account of His Personal Life,* which, he admitted, he had read in one of his recent "psychic illnesses" and by which he felt "betrayed" because, though Stephenson was "a perfectly proper college professor," he had "gone at his job as an artist goes at it" and produced, not the expected dull compilation of facts but a "beautifully written, beautifully imagined . . . true life story." Anderson was pleased to learn from Peter Ochremenko, Soviet translator of *Winesburg, Ohio* and *The Triumph of the Egg,* that these two books had been "more praised in our press than [those of] any other foreign author" and that a cooperative publishing house, Field and Factory, had decided to publish translations of his complete works in a uniform edition. Now Ochremenko would like a copy of *A Story Teller's Story* to translate, and Anderson wrote Huebsch requesting that a copy of the book go to him. Otto Liveright, to whom Sherwood mailed the review of *Lincoln,* sent him the second of three checks for $20, each a royalty on a week's performances of O'Neil's *The Triumph of the Egg,* and a check for $81 for the sale of "A Meeting South" to *The Dial.* Apparently at some time during the hurly-burly days in New York, Otto had also brought him together with Gertrude B. Lane, on the editorial staff of *The Woman's Home Companion,* with whom he had discussed the possibility of his writing a "Childhood book" suitable for serialization in that mass-circulation magazine; and attracted both by the nature of the project and the chance for a considerable payment, he was already at work on the venture.[28]

But in Natchez, Elizabeth had recognized how the lecture tour had tired him and became concerned to protect him from unnecessary intrusion, one form of it being young Bill Faulkner. After his short November visit to New Orleans, Faulkner had returned to the city in early January two days after Anderson had left on his lecture tour. Since he had little money, Elizabeth generously let him stay in the extra room in the Anderson apartment while Sherwood was away, providing him daily with breakfast and dinner. Here Faulkner began writing his early sketches for the *Times-Picayune*, found the writing of prose more suitable for him than poetry, and planned his first novel with the working title *Mayday* (published title *Soldier's Pay*). He was well into the writing of it by late February, made a brief visit to Oxford while Elizabeth was off meeting Sherwood in Chicago, and again returned to New Orleans the day after the Andersons got back, apparently hoping to continue his stay with them. Protectively Elizabeth felt that the apartment would be too crowded, and Sherwood suggested that Bill instead rent an inexpensive ground-floor room in the house behind St. Louis Cathedral where William Spratling, then a bohemian professor of architecture at Tulane, had a little apartment at 624 Orleans (now Pirates) Alley. Sherwood may have himself taken a room in the alley a few doors from 624 as a working hideaway, but in any case Faulkner would be nearby in the Quarter but not under foot. Faulkner took the room, the Andersons lent him a cot and bedding, and he went back again into concentrated work on *Mayday*, in his spare time joining the close friendship already established between Spratling and the Andersons.[29]

It was well that Elizabeth had not let Faulkner move in with them. Despite the good news Sherwood was receiving, he quickly came down with an attack of the flu as an aftermath of the strain of the lecture tour, and though he was soon back at his desk, the flu triggered a weeks-long period of emotional ups and downs. On better days, as on March 9, he could write an ebullient piece for *The Nation's* series of responses "by American writers of the first rank" to the question, "Can a literary artist function freely in the United States?" His answer in "Living in America" was that the artist can, provided that he maintains "sufficient reserve nerve force" to avoid "the rush of all modern American life" and to see the many stories going on about him. Or on "up" days Anderson could scrawl a long letter about the teaching of writing to Professor Ruth Kelso of the University of Illinois, who had sent him a plan for her writing course. "Doesn't it really come down," he told her,

> to a question of whether the student wants to write as an easy amusing way of making a living or whether he wants to approach writing as an art.
>
> The arts are as you know intangible challenges to the whole of life. There is this queer thing called "the imagination." What may not be done with it.

Perhaps students may be taught "that there is no good art without giving, giving, the best of yourself—all of yourself. The relationship with an art should be like the relationship with someone you love." Or on such days he could resolutely reply to a query from George Sylvester Viereck, editor of the *American Monthly*, that no "organized plan for endowing men of talent would really work." Consider his own situation, he declared.

I have set out on a certain road, knowing full well that what I want to do will not bring me much money. If I were to spend my energy in another direction, I might get money aplenty.

Very well. I plan to get something money will not buy. It evens up fairly well.[30]

Yet there were things money could buy, and Anderson wanted to buy them; in fact, the nagging want for money was one of the major causes for his emotionally worse days. There were problems with seventeen-year-old Bob, who was developing the same kind of "slickness" he had seen in himself, and who, his father would soon decide, might be helped by going to college, where the raw youth would be among "gentler people" than the inhabitants of the Quarter. There was the approaching problem of a college education for John, age sixteen—when Sherwood was troubled about money he worried more than he usually did about his children's welfare—and, later, for Mimi, age thirteen. There was his "passion" to own a house, he "never having had a home of his own," and Elizabeth's passion for one of the old houses in the Quarter was as strong as his. Significantly, the gentle Elizabeth was firmly set on shaping her husband—Marc and Lucile Antony would be convinced—into a cultivated man of letters like her admired Stark Young, and a house would be a more appropriate setting than the Pontalba apartment. By March 20 they had engaged to purchase "a little sweet old wreck of a place" at 628–630 St. Ann Street with a two-hundred-year-old brick wall around a tiny courtyard garden and were preparing to go into debt to buy and refurbish it, the money to come, if necessary, from Sherwood's continued lecturing if not from his writing. There were the costs of frequent dining out even in the cheap, excellent restaurants in the Quarter and of the weekly dinner at home for the young artists and writers; and there were Sherwood's impulsive grand gestures he was subject to making, especially that when he hired the yacht *Josephine* for a weekend pleasure cruise with friends on March 14 and 15 out on Lake Pontchartrain.[31]

The gesture was to be in honor of his pert, witty friend Anita Loos, who had just come down to New Orleans at Sherwood's invitation to stay with the Andersons, but who because of her "many trunks, dresses, maids, cosmetics" moved instead into the St. Charles Hotel as a quiet place where she could work steadily at *Gentlemen Prefer Blondes*, just beginning to come out as serialized episodes in *Harper's Bazaar*. Sherwood had invited all the other guests for the cruise before mentioning the honor to Anita, who apologetically but firmly declined to come because she was working against a deadline for the next episode; so the party sailed off without her. Among those on the cruise were Julius Friend, Lillian Friend Marcus, the

Antonys, a young poet named Samuel Gilmore, Hamilton Basso, Spratling, Faulkner, and, as Elizabeth would recall, "several young girls Sherwood had casually asked along." Unfortunately, the weather was drizzling, the expanse of the lake gray, the area on the north side of the lake around Mandeville, an intended port of call as a resort town, swarming with mosquitoes. There was nothing to do as they sailed aimlessly about on Lake Pontchartrain for two days except sit around the main cabin eating the cook's bad food and talking as they would have done more comfortably every evening back in the Quarter. Sherwood as usual told stories, when he was not simply responding, as he would write Bab, to the "slow rhythm of waves—slow thoughts coming and going." The cruise was uneventful; most of the "events" would subsequently be supplied by Faulkner's imagination when in his second novel, *Mosquitoes*, written the following year, he would satirize his companions and others in the Quarter by bringing them together for a four-day cruise on Pontchartrain on the *Nausikaa*.[32]

Anderson, portrayed in *Mosquitoes* as the jovial, burly, middle-aged "successful novelist" and tale-teller Dawson Fairchild, would receive relatively light flicks of Faulkner's satirical whip, in part because of the closeness that quickly grew up between the two men that March. Mornings both worked at their writing; afternoons, when Faulkner was not still furiously working away at *Mayday* or more *Times-Picayune* sketches, they would often meet, wander the Quarter and talk, Anderson doing more of the talking to the deferential younger man, telling tales, recounting his experiences, speaking of the craft of writing, declaring the necessary commitment of the artist to art and to America rather than to the nation's material success. At least some of Anderson's talk would be imported into *Mosquitoes*, though it is a question, for example, how much was Anderson's narrative art and how much Faulkner's. In having Dawson Fairchild tell Anderson's tale about his own "college experience" in *Mosquitoes*, was Faulkner only beginning to formulate his late dubious conclusion that "the great tragedy of [Anderson's] character" was that he "expected people to make fun of, ridicule him"?[33]

One subject they both talked about apparently interminably on the *Josephine* and certainly at night parties in the Quarter was Al Jackson, the web-footed "fishherd" whom they invented out of their mutual delight in tall tales. In an exchange of letters after the *Josephine* cruise, Anderson claimed that he had first learned of this "biggest man in the fish industry" from one Flu Balsam, a cowpoke who "couldn't sleep much nights, and so he traded his horse to an easygoing, restful kind of a Texan, and an expert sleeper, for a night's sleep" and then "herded fish under Al for almost two years." In two letters to Anderson, Faulkner supplied many of the details he would subsequently have Fairchild elaborate on in *Mosquitoes*. Al

Jackson got his start by raising sheep in a swamp up the Tchefuncte River, but the sheep took to the water, grew scales in place of their wool, and had to be caught by Al's son Claude, a wild young man, who himself took to living in the water in order to chase the sheep down and slowly turned into a shark attracted to blonde women bathers on Florida's beaches. Anderson contributed the information that when Al went from sheepherding to herding fish off the Florida coast, he branded his fish by notching their tails. The storyteller agreed that many fishherds develop webbed feet, which they conceal by wearing congress (ankle-high) shoes; but though Anderson denied that Al was a descendant of Andrew Jackson, Faulkner insisted that he was, proof being that the equestrian statue of Old Hickory in Jackson Square shows him wearing congress shoes. Besides, Andrew Jackson had won the Battle of New Orleans, fought in a swamp, because he had webbed feet himself and had the special support of "two battalions of fish-herds from Florida swamps, half horse and half alligator they were."[34]

In 1953 Faulkner would recall that Anderson scolded him for not making a first version of his first Al Jackson letter as good as he possibly could, then in effect praised his second version when the younger man admitted he was not satisfied with it, but it was "the best I know how to do." Satisfied with the second version himself, Anderson may have planned a collaboration with Faulkner on a whole book about Al Jackson, but any such project was abandoned in the press of other matters. Faulkner was pushing hard on *Mayday* and would soon contribute an Andersonesque story, "Cheest," to the *Times-Picayune;* in a burst of energy Anderson had by March 20 again taken up the "Childhood" book. On March 25 he mailed to Otto Liveright a "childhood tale," first of "a dozen or more" he expected to finish in the summer and from which Gertrude Lane could select to her purpose. Along with the story he sent a letter, which Otto could show to Lane to give her "a feeling of the tone of the tales. They should be gentle and whimsical and yet with plenty of dramatic force to carry the reader forward." Much of the letter outlined a second story, not yet written, about the child's complicated reaction to "a fire in a small Ohio town at night." This story would not in fact be included in the published *Tar* and would only appear, much truncated, as an episode early in the *Memoirs,* the meager factual account by comparison showing how, as usual, Anderson's imagination had in his outline greatly changed and developed the actual event. Enclosed with completed tale and letter was a cover letter for Otto's eyes only, saying in Anderson's advertising tone,

The tales are going to be corking stuff for Lane's purpose, I believe. It will be fun doing them.

If Miss Lane likes them do try to get a $2,000 advance for me. I am going to need it.[35]

His felt need for money was so acute on top of the strain of "intensive work" on the tales that in the last days of March, as he would write Bab, he "died. About 5 or 6 days of death—every nerve aching—sinking and sinking into slack depression." About April 1 he took a step he would have turned from in disgust only a month earlier: he wrote to Horace Liveright, saying that he "was open to a proposition" about changing publishers if Liveright wanted to make him one. Even before such a proposition could be made, he had asked John Emerson for a $600 loan for a down payment on the house in the Quarter, and had asked Huebsch for an estimate of the royalties, which would be coming to him from sales of *A Story Teller's Story*. (Ben's estimate would be "about $1200" to date. When on August 1 Huebsch sent the statement of royalties due from November 1, 1924, through April 30, 1925, the net amount after $500 in advance Ben had given Sherwood in New York, would be $1,154.39 on a sale during this period of 3,548 copies of the book for a disappointing total sales of only 6,179 copies.) Since Liveright and his wife, Lucile, were at this point taking a trip south, they at once arranged to come to New Orleans, and on April 5 publisher and author "verbally closed their deal." On signing the contract Liveright would begin paying Anderson $100 a week for five years as advance on all of his books sold during that period; Anderson, it was subsequently agreed, would furnish Liveright at least one book each year. Together with other provisions—15 percent royalties after deducting the advance, a possible uniform edition of Anderson's complete works, all royalties to Anderson from foreign editions—the agreement was a generous one, but too generous, some of Liveright's editors felt.[36]

The editors, it eventuated, would be right for both contracting parties; indeed, Anderson's decision to leave Ben Huebsch for Horace Liveright, would prove a major turning point in his literary career. It was a decision based in large part, not simply on the Andersons' immediate need for money, but, understandably, also on Sherwood's long-held hope that he could make his living from writing and not be forced into hated advertising work or into continued lecture tours beyond the one he was committed to for 1925–26, tours which, he admitted, satisfied something of the actor in him but were physically and emotionally draining. The "strain and uncertainty" of his financial situation had disturbed him off and on for years, and financial worries in the past and now had affected his ability to write, he believed, at his best. Although he regarded Liveright and most other publishers as "a bad lot," suspected Horace's gambler's nature, and had been revolted in New York by his wild party, Sherwood knew of his fights against literary censors, his willingness to take risks on new, talented writers, his impressive publisher's list, his large-scale book operation, his financial success. Anderson was of course a writer of proven talent, but Liveright's flatteringly generous offer was of necessity a gambler's risk too; yet Liveright was taking it in all sincerity and, most importantly, was both guaranteeing to push the sales of Anderson's books vigorously and assuring him freedom from financial worries for an extended time, freedom to do the kind of writing he felt capable of doing.[37]

Huebsch, on the other hand, was a kind, decent man, but more interested, Anderson felt, in economic reform than in literature despite his publishing Joyce, Lawrence, and Anderson. Further, he had a small editorial staff and especially a small sales and distribution organization, or so Sherwood, with his author's sensitivities, had long felt, and as the insignificant sale of *A Story Teller's Story* (despite strongly favorable reviews) indicated. Anderson had stuck by Huebsch longer than had Joyce and Lawrence, turned down, several times, tempting offers from other publishers, given Ben repeated chances to push his books as aggressively as Liveright promised to do and could do, chances Ben had been unable to exploit. Nevertheless, Ben had dared to take Anderson on when no other publisher wanted him and had stood by him faithfully even during the uproar over *Many Marriages*. To leave Ben, as Anderson keenly felt, was an act of personal disloyalty whatever Ben's limitations as a publisher might be. "The Huebsch matter is complex," he wrote to Bab around April 12, deploring Ben's incompetence: "It is hard for me to decide between the immorality of bad hesitating slovenly methods and competent rascality."

But he had already opted for the competent rascal. As part of the oral agreement on April 5, Liveright was to draw up the contract as soon as he got back to New York on the eighth and submit it to John Emerson for approval prior to Anderson's signing. On the April 6 Sherwood and Elizabeth had lunch with Horace and Lucile in a private room at Antoine's. As to the contract Horace insisted only that it "should definitely call for a book a year or . . . it would not be a contract at all," and Sherwood agreed to this point. Then the table talk may well have turned to other books and writers. Urged by Anderson and by John Dos Passos, Liveright had contracted to publish Hemingway's *In Our Time* with his usual option on this promising young author's next two books. It was either at this luncheon or on the previous day that Sherwood gave Horace the enthusiastic comment that would appear on the book's dust jacket with blurbs from five other admirers of this collection of stories interrelated somewhat in the *Winesburg* manner: "Mr. Hemingway is young, strong, full of laughter, and he can write. His people flash suddenly up into those odd elusive moments of glowing reality, the clear putting down of which has always made good writing so good." Almost certainly it was also at the luncheon that Anderson brought up the name of William Faulkner as a writer to watch and sign up; he had read a chapter of his *Mayday*, thought it "good stuff," and hoped to persuade Liveright to give Faulkner an advance on the unfinished novel. Now that Anderson had decided to leave

Huebsch for Liveright, he was eager to help his new publisher-to-be in other ways.[38]

Still the luncheon was a somewhat uneasy one for him despite Antoine's superb food, uneasy because John Emerson had yet to approve the contract, because Sherwood did not like the thought of an annual deadline "hanging over" him "to hurry . . . sometimes when an extra month or two might make the difference between a good and a bad book," and because he sensed that Liveright did not fully understand how devoted he was to his art. Then, too, he had committed a blunder with Lucile the day before. When he and the Liverights had met by chance on a Bourbon Street corner, Horace had introduced the beautiful Lucile as his wife. Recalling Liveright's reputation as a womanizer, Anderson had unwisely wisecracked, "Oh, yeah?" Fortunately the Liverights were leaving for New York that evening.[39]

In letters on April 5 and 6, Anderson gave John Emerson the details of the contract, apologizing for imposing on his busy time and asking him to reassure Liveright that the required books would be written and be good ones. The next few days were up and down for him. He finished a second "installment" of the "Childhood" book and most of a third, and wrote a short story, "Moonshine," in which a manipulative older woman, by telling a repressed younger one of a wholly imagined affair with a man, destroys the possibility of marriage for the younger to him, an added implication being that a writer likewise "lies for the sake of the lie" and would be "a dangerous criminal" were not his purpose to "create beauty." The tale, he wrote Otto Liveright, was "amusing but somewhat naughty" and "might catch on with some of the smarter women's magazines, like *Harper's Bazaar.*" But, as the subject of "Moonshine" suggests, he felt sad and guilty about what he was doing to Ben, who meanwhile was writing him faithfully of his efforts on Sherwood's behalf and of other news. Ben had earlier informed him that E. Haldeman-Julius had paid $200 ($100 to Sherwood) to publish about half of the *Winesburg* tales in two of his Little Blue Books, and that terms for a Spanish translation of *Poor White* had been agreed to. He now wrote that he and his employee Marshall Best had worked hard to prepare a not "commonplace" advertising circular for Sherwood's next lecture tour, which would soon be out in "tasteful typographic form"; the London publisher Jonathan Cape had signed the contract for the English issue of *A Story Teller's Story* (Cape would bring this out in August); Newton Arvin, the young Harvard man who had reviewed *Horses and Men* so perceptively, might write a first critical book on Anderson; Ben had been told "of the interest in your work expressed by . . . 'Her Majesty, the Empress Hermine' . . . wife of the one time well-known German emperor," and was amusedly sending her two of Sherwood's books. Anderson's psychosomatic reaction to the situation was to complain to Otto Liveright that he had been "rather knocked out for two or three weeks," and to have a thorough physical check-up by a doctor, who prescribed a medicine that quickly "straightened" him out.[40]

At least equally effective medicine was a telegram from Horace Liveright on the morning of April 11 stating that the contract was in the mail, his letter of that date confirming that Emerson had gone over the contract as arbitrator. On the twelfth Emerson wrote that he had approved the contract with a somewhat more generous arrangement for Liveright on movie and drama rights, and the contract itself arrived on the fourteenth. On the fifteenth Anderson signed the contract and mailed it to Liveright, and the deal was complete.

There remained the task Sherwood had been dreading, the letter to Ben announcing his decision. On April 13 he had dictated to a part-time typist a noncommittal acknowledgement of Ben's letters. On the fifteenth, along with letters to Emerson, and Horace Liveright, and to Paul Rosenfeld, thanking him for sending a copy of his new *Men Seen: Twenty-Four Modern Authors* and dedicating it to Anderson, he dictated a long letter to Huebsch. He had returned from his lecture tour, he explained, weary and deeply discouraged about his finances. In the past he had turned down "flattering offers" from other publishers in order to stay with Huebsch out of a "personal feeling" for him; but now that he could no longer "see my way through" financially, he had written to Horace Liveright, who proceeded to make him a proposition that Sherwood knew Ben could not match. So he had signed a contract with Liveright, who would be publishing his novel next fall. "This whole matter," he insisted, "has given me sleepless nights but it is over and done now." As for the advertising circulars Ben had prepared, he would be glad to pay for them himself. "Ben," he concluded unhappily,

I might write volumes to you in this matter but you know what I personally feel towards you and about what my situation has been. If you have some feeling of resentment I can't blame you. On the other hand in fairness to myself I think I have only done the best thing for me and my work. I am very, very sorry.

4.

Now that the letter to Ben was off his chest, the thing to do was to go back to the novel he had been uneasily revising the previous November, a project he and Liveright had certainly discussed along with the contract. The "Childhood" book was barely begun, *Love and War* was nearly completed and could quickly fulfill the requirement of a book for the contract's first year, and Horace was particularly adept at marketing novels, especially a somewhat experimental one dealing with contemporary themes.

On April 11 Anderson had written Otto Liveright that he was "going to turn back to the novel soon" and have it ready for fall publication, leaving late spring and summer for the "Childhood" book and the fall for the dramatization of "There She Is—She Is Taking Her Bath." In a cover letter for the signed contract on the fifteenth, he predicted to Horace that he would get the complete novel to him "early in June." The problem of the right title was still unsolved; but Horace had thought the title should be *Deep Laughter,* and that might be best, although the word *Deep* seemed "a little pretentious." By the seventeenth he was well into his revision of the novel and did not want to be interrupted by writing a review for the *New York Evening Post* of his friend Alfred Kreymborg's autobiography *Troubadour,* a Liveright book, which he had anyway found often dull. In exchange he would like to review *In Our Time* when it came out in the fall. Already he was contemplating changing *Deep* to *Dark* in the title, and on April 22 he had decided definitely, he wrote Horace Liveright, on *Dark Laughter* for the novel on which he was working "night and day" and which should be in Liveright's hands by May 15.[41]

He was feeling and working better than he had in months. His obsessive worry over finances was fading, for the arrangement of weekly payments from Liveright seemed to trigger other money. On April 17, Otto Liveright wired him that *The Woman's Home Companion* had agreed to buy six installments of the "Childhood" book for $6,000 with at least $1,000, perhaps $2,000, as an advance. Lesser amounts were coming in from Otto too—$135 for Anderson's share from the sale of "Betrayed" to *Golden Book* and $54 from the sale of a piece on lecturing, "When the Writer Talks" to the *New York Post*'s *Literary Review.* Sherwood and Elizabeth could now afford to get away from the coming heat of the New Orleans summer for perhaps six weeks and meanwhile to have repairs done on their house on St. Ann Street, which they hoped to take possession of by mid-May after the remaining "weak spots in the title . . . cleared up."[42]

Buying the house proved that Sherwood, and Elizabeth, wanted to settle down, and why should he wish to settle in New Orleans, asked an interviewer from the *Times-Picayune,* preparing for Anderson's "first public appearance" in the city, a lecture to be given on the night of April 23. Because, he answered, the spirit of New Orleans is

restful, unruffled and sympathetic. Here a writer can withdraw from the turbulence of modern life, and find relaxation after the strain of creative work. Here he can feel a certain cultural security and live in the old tradition of European civilization without losing touch with the youthful energetic life of this country.

It was about creativity and energy that the "leader of the modernist movement in this country," as the interviewer termed him, spoke on the evening of the twenty-third to an audience of "several hundred Orleanians" in the Athenaeum as he gave a version of his lecture, "America—A Storehouse of Vitality." Starting "like a neighbor instead of a lionized author," according to the *Times-Picayune* reporter covering the event, Anderson praised the "beautiful oldness" of New Orleans, which preserves its old buildings more than any other American city and should not hurry to let the house-wreckers "modernize" it. Because of its regard for beauty New Orleans is, paradoxically, ready for the change rapidly occurring in America, this country, which has "vitality in the very name." The "coming American man is a gigantic figure" who is bringing "about us an intense spiritual activity." As a writer Anderson wants to understand this man; as an American he himself wants to be "a part of America."

The tone of American life has been physical, something new and strange in the world. Take distances, for instance. Under any other circumstances America would have been a dozen countries, with a dozen languages. The mere fact that the nation needed binding together called for heroic character, the "man of action" type. Now that the binding job has been done something has changed, we are beginning to ask where we are going. The need for the man of action has passed. There will soon be so many automobiles that there will be no place to go, so many radios that nothing will be worth listening to.

The coming American man will be "the dreamer and creator of beauty," who will prepare us for "emotional, imaginative lives." This change in America is "already . . . very definite," as is evidenced by the fact that "poets, writers, artist are bolder. Their imaginations, instead of straying to London Society or to the mythical lives of mythical cowboys in a mythical west, are 'staying home.'" Focusing their creativity and vitality on their native land, these bold young writers and artists are transforming American society.

The imaginative life has a practical value, too. . . . Without it there would be no art, no religion. The function of the imaginative man is that of the tailor who provides clothing for our lives. We are flowing into channels of beauty.[43]

Three days later, the Sunday book page of the Dallas *Morning News* carried an assessment of the lecturer's own work by one of the bold new generation of writers. In his essay "Sherwood Anderson," William Faulkner showed not just admiration for his older friend but also independent judgment. Working out an extended metaphor of the land—"I prefer to think of Mr. Anderson as a lusty cornfield in his native Ohio"—Faulkner separates what he considers to be the "lesser ears and good ears," Anderson's "lesser books and good books." *Windy McPherson's Son* and *Marching Men* are lesser because in both there is "a fundamental lack of humor," and *Many Marriages* lesser because it "gets away from the land" and also lacks humor. On the other hand, *Winesburg, Ohio,* which Faulkner mistakenly considers Anderson's first book, is a remarkably good ear because of the author's "self-effacing" manner—"one of the first attributes of genius"—and his sympathy for his fictional people; in *Poor White* Anderson "gets his fingers and toes again into the soil"; *Horses and Men* is "reminiscent of 'Winesburg,' but more sophisticated," and "I'm a Fool" is "the best short story in America." Perhaps Anderson's true medium, Faulkner suggests, is the short story. Apparently he had not yet read *The Triumph of the Egg,* for he does not refer to it, nor to *Mid-American Chants,* but he comments at length on *A Story Teller's Story,* which to him seems "two distinct books." The first, good half "is really a novel based upon one character—his father," who is pictured with "keen humor"; in the second, lesser half, however, the author abandons self-effacement for opinionizing and assumes "an elephantine kind of humor about himself," characteristics that make *A Story Teller's Story* "not his best contribution to American literature." Anderson has and has always had a sense of humor, but "only recently has he got any of it into his stories." The lateness of this development shows that "he has not matured yet, despite his accomplishments so far."

Anderson's reaction to the essay, which presumably he read in typescript or tear sheet, was never recorded and can only be guessed at. He had himself already come to regard his first two novels as lesser works, and he must have been pleased by the praise for *Winesburg, Poor White,* and *Horses and Men.* He almost certainly would have thought, perhaps irritatedly, that Faulkner had misread *Many Marriages* and the second half of *A Story Teller's Story,* and he might well have bridled at Faulkner's dictum that Anderson had not yet matured and at the suggestion that the short story, not the novel, was his medium. Given his own use of land and cornfield as metaphor and symbol, he could not have resented being called a "field of corn with a story to tell and a tongue to tell it with," nor, given the context, would he have resented Faulkner's halfway comment that Anderson "is American, and more than that, a middle westerner, of the soil: he is as typical of Ohio in his way as Harding was in his." Indeed the author of "Ohio, I'll Say We've Done Well" could have made the comparison-contrast remark about himself. Considering Anderson's own Al Jackson letter to Faulkner with its tale of Flu Balsam's trying to trade a horse for a night's sleep, one wonders more whether Anderson did actually have such a "funny dream" himself and tell it to Faulkner the next morning during "a week-end on a river boat" on the Mississippi—the *Josephine* on Lake Pontchartrain?—or whether Faulkner elaborated the Flu Balsam tale as his concluding proof that Anderson was purely American as a writer and not derivative "from the Russians," an assertion

Anderson would have firmly, and rightly, agreed with. On balance, then, Anderson should have been pleased, with reservations, by Faulkner's essay. In any case, the essay did not put him off the reading of fifty thousand words of *Mayday* and approving them. Faulkner was clearly a coming young writer, and Sherwood was generously supportive of such.[44]

Besides, he was at the moment ebullient. On April 24, Otto Liveright had telegraphed him that *The Woman's Home Companion* would pay $2,000 rather than $1,000 advance. The very satisfying doubled sum made more acceptable Otto's letter, just received, politely criticizing the first half of *Love and War* (*Dark Laughter*) as too slow moving and needing much cutting, though the second half "is superb and needs not a pen stroke." After a long illness Otto had only now gotten around to reading the first version of the novel Sherwood had sent him back in November, but after a couple of weeks of intensive work Sherwood could write Anita Loos on the twenty-eighth that a much revised version of the newly titled *Dark Laughter* was "being rapidly whipped into shape." Among many other changes, he had presumably by this time deleted a lengthy section, which Otto had rightly objected to as superfluous, that concerning a young, emotionally immature American soldier, Billy West, who has contracted syphilis in Paris soon after the war and worries how to confess the fact to his proper American wife who is about to join him in France. By May 6 the revision was almost complete and a fair copy being typed.[45]

Meanwhile Anderson could allow himself a brief vacation starting on April 28. For $25, including round-trip fare, stateroom, and meals, he had passage on an old river packet, which took eight days to steam up the Mississippi to Vicksburg and back, picking up freight and passengers at towns and plantations along the way. He had tried to get "the regular Mississippi and Ohio River swing" into *Dark Laughter,* he was thinking about writing "some Southern stories," and the trip would give him a greater feel for the South. It was a slow, plodding trip up the river, first through flat country stretching wide on either side, then through green hills around Natchez, the river "so majestic, so strong" yet sadly idle of traffic, "like a Samson blind." Riding in the pilot house, however, he listened to an old riverman telling him "tales of the grand old days—when being a river pilot was something"; and he returned to New Orleans on May 5 fired up to do a nonfiction book on the history of the river, the "strange romance and interest and excitement" of the years before and during the Civil War and the slow decline afterwards. Horace Liveright, whom he had at once written to about it, would soon reply agreeing with his editor T. R. Smith's opinion that the subject had already been covered and that any book about it by Anderson should be fictional instead.[46]

Anderson had probably hoped that a reply to his April 15 letter to Huebsch would be waiting for him when he returned from his river trip, for with combined guilt and hurt he complained to Stieglitz on May 6 about Huebsch's silence. Ben's reply of May 5 was already in the mail, however. It was a dignified, generous letter, which, Ben explained apologetically, he had delayed in writing until he felt sure that his more considered reaction was the same as his immediate one. He assured Sherwood that though his going to another publisher was "the last thing that I should have cared to have happened," he felt no resentment, no sense of grievance, no unfriendly feeling; for Sherwood was right to choose "whatever course permits you to do your best work most freely."

> I can only wish you well under the new arrangement. I think that you are at the threshold of your biggest achievements and, if I cannot share in them, I may at least have the satisfaction of remembering that we joined forces when the Lane firm lacked the vision to go on with you and that I served your needs usefully during a period that was more or less experimental.

Ben's one objection was that he had learned "that your new publisher's office was gloating over its new acquisition before I had word from you"; but that "sour note" was irrelevant to the main matter, he declared, and he ended with "every good wish that you may find happiness and satisfaction in the new arrangement." Years later Huebsch would still feel hurt, however, that Anderson had not told him of Liveright's offer and given him the chance to do something to help him financially, though he might not have been able to afford as much as Liveright was willing to pay. Horace, he had continued to believe, was a "flashy" man of the "tinhorn gambler" sort, to quote the future Mayor La Guardia. Admitting Liveright's successes, Huebsch would characterize him to the biographer W. A. Swanberg in more careful language as "a good showman rather than a good publisher, but then I have often asked myself whether my instinctive dislike for him was not in part due to envy." Although Anderson would not know it, his going to Liveright would be one of the major reasons why Huebsch very shortly joined his firm with Viking Press, which had just been formed in March and of which he became vice-president and part owner, the second reason apparently being his feeling that, as Anderson had complained, he was indeed not very good at actually selling books.[47]

Sherwood's defensive reply to Ben on the tenth was to insist that he had written "as soon as I had quite made up my mind I had to do it"—the fact being that he had made up his mind to accept Liveright's offer as soon as it was made, provided that John Emerson approved the contract. He had to choose, he declared, between "getting money or going back into business." Leaving Ben had "been about the hardest thing I ever had to do." As for the "finely done" circulars advertising Anderson's fall lecture tour, for which Ben in a separate letter had felt Sherwood should pay "only the actual cash outlay and nothing for the preparation of the circular and seeing it through, or for overhead," Sherwood agreed he should pay that amount.

To lose one's self in work was the best way to deal with lingering feelings of regret and guilt at leaving Ben. *Dark Laughter*—after consultation with his staff Liveright had agreed to the title—needed final polishing, a process that went on furiously for two more weeks. By May 20 Anderson had made his final revisions, and fair typed copy went off to Boni and Liveright a day or so later. A month earlier as he had begun revising, he had exuberantly outlined the novel to Horace Liveright.

This whole novel was written in a heat last fall. I went through the whole thing in about two months and have never been so absorbed in a job before. It is the story of the present day, of postwar life in America now and in particular of postwar life in the Middle West.

The three central figures of the book are a young man who has come home from the World War to find his father dead and himself at the head of a large manufacturing plant in the Ohio River Valley in the town of Old Harbor, Indiana. In France he has married a young woman, the daughter of a prominent Chicago lawyer, whose brother and fiance were both killed in the war. Her marriage with the young manufacturer was the result of war fever and emotionalism brought on by conditions in Paris just after the war.

These people are living in the Indiana town, facing the Ohio River, after the war and have no children. To them comes a man of thirty-four, disillusioned by a bad marriage and seeking the romance of life by going backward over his boyhood trail. After they meet, the story intensifies and becomes a struggle for the love of the woman.

The book has in it many strange side lights. Its setting embraces the Middle West, the Ohio River Valley, the Mississippi River, and New Orleans. In it there are lazy, dancing Negroes, a description of the Quat'z Arts Ball in Paris shortly after the Armistice, and an intense love story. I believe the book is even more intense than *Many Marriages,* but is even broader and has a greater swing to it. It is going to be by far the best novel I have written.

In two two-week periods of concentrated work, "pruning and cutting," filling in "sags and holes," carrying through "the whole swing of it," he had added some twenty-two thousand words to a first draft of around eighty-two thousand and deleted about eight thousand. The hard work improved all aspects of the novel from the strengthening of individual passages and scenes, and in some cases the rearrangement of their order, to the addition of new episodes and the deletion of unnecessary ones. The most important change was in the novel's conclusion. In the original version the struggle between the husband and "the man of thirty-four" ends with the husband shooting the lover; in the revised version the wife and the lover leave together despite the husband's attempts to prevent them, a conclusion better emphasizing the book's basic theme of the superiority of the uninhibited life to the inhibited one.[48]

Even during those last two hard-driving weeks of revising there were outside interruptions. In the first week Frederick O'Brien, author of the popular travel-adventure book, *White Shadows in the South Seas,* came to New Orleans, and in their talks Anderson urged him to consider Otto Liveright as his literary agent. Then around the seventeenth, George Daugherty, Sherwood's old "feeder" friend from Critchfield days, came for a few days visit. Meanwhile Elizabeth made a six-hundred-dollar-check deposit on the six-thousand-dollar property she and Sherwood had picked out at 628–630 St. Ann Street. (A "splendid value" he was told, worth a loan from the Peoples Homestead Company of "80 percent of purchase price.") There were also, as it were, internal interruptions. Conversation with O'Brien, who had published two more books of his adventurous life among South Pacific islands, probably set Anderson off on starting "a straight adventure book" based on Mississippi River life, even though Sherwood was still in the last revisions of *Dark Laughter;* and on other mornings his "nose was buried in my desk" with several "Childhood" pieces, only one of which

was worth typing up. He did not get far with the Mississippi book, but with the manuscript of the novel off to New York he drove hard at yet other "Childhood" episodes, working daily "to the point of exhaustion" in his hideaway room in Pirates Alley but feeling for the moment that the book was beginning to come alive.[49]

By June 1 Liveright, whom Anderson still half distrusted as "an eager rather corrupt . . . child," had sent telegrams enthusiastically praising *Dark Laughter,* Hemingway had written a grateful note of thanks for Anderson's help in getting *In Our Time* accepted, and, Faulkner having now finished *Mayday,* Anderson suggested that Liveright might want to look at this novel by "the one writer here of promise" to become "a real writer." But then, baffled in his efforts to express the "strange intangible thing" of childhood, overeager to finish the serial episodes in order to collect the remaining money, haunted by what he had done to Ben, wearied by the forced draft revising of *Dark Laughter,* he pushed at the book too hard, began to feel that it "danced like a shadow just out of reach," and predictably went "down, down" into a "bad time." Over the next few weeks Elizabeth somehow managed to drag her husband up from the depths; it was wearying work, and she realized that they must get away for awhile from New Orleans to escape the heat and to give both of them a rest.[50]

Just where to escape to was a problem. Fortunately Julia Harris, coeditor with her husband of the Columbus, Georgia, *Enquirer-Sun,* had recently sent Anderson a copy of her article "The Spirit of Revolt in Current Fiction," which praised him as "the most talented of the younger school," and more recently another article on educational conditions in Georgia. Because of the Harrises' knowledge of the South, he wrote her around June 12 telling her of his wish to write a southern novel and to talk with them about the South, not, he would later write, "the surface life as just the buried thing." In conclusion he asked her whether she knew of some place in the southern mountains, perhaps in Virginia, where one could fish and "live economically." By chance she had just received a letter from a Mrs. John Greear of Troutdale, Virginia, saying that she would like to have summer boarders; and replying to Anderson, Harris suggested several summer places but particularly recommended Caroline Greear's home. The Andersons would not leave for their mountain vacation for nearly a month, but when they did leave, they would go to Troutdale.[51]

In the meantime Sherwood remained sunk in what he called his "half insane" slump, which blocked him from effective work on the "Childhood" book, the block in turn driving him deeper into the slump. In the enervating wet New Orleans heat he found some escape in reading. Both he and Elizabeth enjoyed Julia Harris's *Life and Letters of Joel Chandler Harris* and looked forward to her sending them John Wade's *Augustus Baldwin Longstreet,* Longstreet's *Georgia Scenes,* and a book of Joel Harris's rural tales, all these recommended by her for Sherwood's interest in Southern culture. He was much less happy with D. H. Lawrence's *Studies in Classic American Literature.* "As for Lawrence," he wrote Stieglitz, "when he tells a story, he is fine; when he lays down his principles, I think him a pretentious fool. He dreams of being the great, dark animal. It is, after all, a neurotic wish. To me his whole book lacked reserve, good feeling, delicacy." Another escape continued to be through letters to the faithful Bab, though when she wrote him a letter touching on sexuality, his reply was curiously evasive and betrayed a deep unease. Sex was "all and nothing." He had been trying for a long time to "get up into consciousness" what he felt about it. "As usual with me"—it was the fictionist speaking—"to express what I feel I shall have to transpose it out of myself into another. I have in mind a hulking old man, a thinker, a book man, living an isolated life, away from people of culture. This old man has lived in my consciousness a long time. I want some day to write a book about him." (Such a book would have been another storyteller's story; for in a letter to Stieglitz of about the same date Anderson, reader of books, complained of feeling "isolated," far away from cultured people.) The old man—this protective mask for Anderson—would be "a little frightened and glad," frightened—and glad?—that Bab suffers what "most people think they rather suffer alone." What do sensitive people want amid others who "want to hurt one another like malicious monkeys? Really gentleness. Just that. . . . money is nothing, power is hurtful. What is left. Real gentleness, if one can get it. I can think of nothing else."[52]

Behind the mask, the evasions, this is a cry from one who, "when at all well," tries "to think of himself as a passing guest in a strange place." For such a sense of alienation there was another possible escape, change of place. A friend at the *Times-Picayune* arranged a free trip for him on a tugboat towing a fleet of big barges up the Mississippi to St. Louis and return, leaving New Orleans around June 27 for two weeks on the river. There being no regular accommodations for passengers, Anderson slept nights on a cot on the deck, ate with the captain and his officers, and was occasionally allowed by the pilot to take a turn at steering. The boat ground slowly along, but this was what he liked, for he needed to think only of the "power and strangeness" of the river and its possibilities for a future book. The ever-changing yellow water sliding by, he confided to Bab, was "in some way the key to something I want."[53]

Before leaving on the trip he had managed to read galley proof on *Dark Laughter* and even to make further revisions in it, including a much more effective final chapter to replace the one he had already revised from the original draft. (As late as July 7 a Boni and Liveright editor acknowledged receipt of two new chapters to be incorporated into the galley proof.) So that was out of the way, and back in New Orleans on July 10 he approved the dust jacket for the volume and agreed to the deletion of the titles he had assigned to each of the eight "Books" into which he had originally divided the chapters of the novel and which at the galley proof stage he redivided into twelve. Despite his quiet days on the river, however, he dejectedly wrote Paul Rosenfeld that various projects were still "fighting inside me" and that "a real grasp of something I want in word values" constantly eluded him. Recognizing that he was still in a nervous state, Elizabeth insisted that he telegraph Mrs. Greear to see if they might come to Troutdale at once. Mrs. Greear wired back that they could, and in the evening of July 11 they took the Norfolk and Western out of New Orleans, bound for the small city of Marion in the southwest corner of Virginia. Here, Julia Harris had written them, they would take a little "switchback" railroad up through "the most superb mountains" to the village of Troutdale. They could not have known it at the time, but they were headed for their future home.[54]

17

Speaking of the
Modern Movement

1.

As the crow flies, Troutdale is only a dozen miles south of Marion; but since both city and village lie among the hills and mountains rising into the Blue Ridge on the east, the logging train (the Marion and Rye Valley Railroad) with one passenger coach crawled as usual on July 13 up steep grades, zigzagging from switchback to switchback for four hours. Sherwood, dressed in his version of city clothes with white linen suit, bright blue shirt, crimson tie, and soft white panama hat, could well have felt that he was returning to a remnant of the American past. Before World War I thousands of acres of virgin forest had been clear-cut in Grayson County, where Troutdale was situated, and the mountain men among the loggers had gone back to their one-room cabins scattered along the valley sides. In the hard times after the war, Troutdale's single furniture factory and one of its two small banks had failed, the other bank barely survived, and this once-thriving lumber town was now hardly more than a hamlet stretched out along a winding dirt street. It was like going back to a tiny dying Winesburg.[1]

The Greear farmhouse on a hill above the village, however, had a view of tumbled mountains and valleys from every window, the weather at three thousand feet was pleasantly cool, and board, room, and laundry were only a dollar a day for each Anderson—to Mrs. Greear's amazement that Mr. Anderson would offer so much, to his that she would gladly accept so little. John Greear, a gentle man rather like an "old fashioned American," Sherwood felt, had been cashier at the bank and part owner of the factory, the failure of both being unfairly blamed on him by many villagers and leaving the family frighteningly poor. Caroline Greear, trained as a practical nurse, was the stronger of the couple, very capable, hardworking, hospitable, and talkative. There were six children, an older girl and five boys ranging from seven to early teens, all of them, especially David, the next to youngest, delighted by the visitors. Sherwood charmed the whole family at once—Elizabeth would remain pleasant but reserved—and Caroline would never forget from his first appearance his voice, "the gentlest, kindest and most musical" she had ever heard, and his eyes, "very black, soft, but penetrating, as if they were a sort of X-ray, making a picture of the person before him." The six children adored him, and he was to spend hours with them, playing card games and horseshoes, having, their mother remembered, "many quiet talks with each of them, but particularly with Dave," living in their children's world until "he knew more of what went on in their minds" than the parents did.[2]

Being in a new place with wide mountain views and among the worshipping children quickly broke him out of the block he had worked and worried himself into with the "Childhood" book. In an isolated corn patch about a mile from the house, the Greears had an unused cabin, which the boys swept out and furnished with a small desk and chair for him; and mornings after an early breakfast—he would take Elizabeth coffee and toast in bed—he would go along a woods trail to this workplace where he wrote until weary by the open door, visited by "flies, wasps, bees, humming birds" and looking out on corn patch and high Pine Mountain. Feeling in touch with nature, he conceived the notion of from time to time reading parts of what he wrote to the growing corn, its soft rustling reminding him of the great Midwest cornfields he lived among in his youth and so being linked with his subject, childhood, just as the flow of the Mississippi would, he hoped, be linked with his projected book about the river. In this way a suitably *Chants*-like title came to him: *A Mid-American Childhood*. The work, he gratefully wrote Julia Harris, was "going well," so well that by the end of his five-week stay with the Greears he had written perhaps fifty-thousand words.

Afternoons when he was not with the children, he was off with Elizabeth or alone exploring the countryside for miles around on foot or by an old mare and buggy, feeling the country "taking a hold on him," talking with people he met along the way, like the man who offered him a drink from a quart jar of moonshine and urged him to "Go ahead and keep the rest of it. I've got another quart for the foot washing," Anderson learning to his great amusement that the man spoke of the Primitive Baptists' custom of washing each other's feet in an annual meeting, at which the men drank moonshine freely while awaiting the ritual. Evenings Elizabeth would go to bed early, but Sherwood and the Greears would sit up for hours on the porch while he kept the family spellbound with tales out of his life or accounts of his afternoon's adventures. He gave them, in Caroline Greear's words, "new 'eyes for seeing' the common everyday things of day to day living." Then there was the great day when the Mighty Haag Show was performing at Mouth of Wilson fourteen miles beyond Troutdale, and Anderson, learning of the family's hopelessly desperate desire to see this small circus, hired the only two automobiles in Troutdale and took them all to one of the most exciting experiences in their recent poverty-pinched lives.

The outside world did come to this mountain idyll. Anderson's mail, Caroline Greear exclaimed, "was a sight to behold." Fortunately Sarita, one of the two Cuban girls also staying at the farmhouse, knew typing, and Anderson began paying her "spending money" to type his business letters. Early in August he received proof to be read for the little book reprinting his Berkeley speech, *The Modern Writer,* handsomely designed by Edwin Grabhorn for The Lantern Press of San Francisco. Very possibly he may have received around this time a copy of the August 1 issue of the *Saturday Review of Literature* containing Virginia Woolf's lead article, "American Fiction," based in part on the English issue of *A Story Teller's Story* and making extended comparison of the specifically American qualities of Anderson and Sinclair Lewis, these two being of "all American novelists the most discussed and read in England at the present moment." That in *Story* and *The Triumph of the Egg* Anderson is "resolutely and defiantly American" is the source of some of his work's defects—its formlessness, its vagueness of language, "his tendency to land his stories softly in a bog"—but paradoxically it is the source of a strength beyond nationalism.

> Mr. Anderson has bored into that deeper and warmer layer of human nature which it would be frivolous to ticket new or old, American or European. In his determination to be "true to the essence of things" he has fumbled his way into something genuine, persistent, of universal significance, in proof of which he has done what, after all, very few writers succeed in doing—he has made a world of his own.

Whenever Anderson did read this essay, he must have been more pleased than otherwise by Woolf's conclusion that he had "gained more than he has lost by being the spokesman of a new country, the worker in fresh clay."[3]

A bothersome intrusion of the outside world was the necessity that Elizabeth return to New Orleans in late July or early August to see to "some affairs." Presumably these had to do with her decorating shop, but they may also have involved matters of housing. For some reason the Andersons decided around this time not to have their St. Ann Street property renovated and instead sold it for a profit. Since their lease of the Pontalba apartment would run out on September 30, Elizabeth may have wanted to oversee the sale and to start hunting another house in the Quarter. But an additional plan appears to have been forming in Sherwood's mind, as he accompanied her on the logging train down to Marion to see her off and returned to Troutdale the next day to stay on for awhile where the writing was going so well.[4]

He had fallen in love with the countryside, its high rolling hills and rounded mountains like the breasts of women, he would later declare, the deep-cut valleys with their springs and streams, the tiny corn patches hacked out of still dense woods and clinging to the sides of mountains. In the countryside around New Orleans "everything, the grasses, weeds, wild flowers, vines, trees and bushes" were "strange." Everything in Virginia, even "the insects and crawling things," were ones he had known as a boy. He liked the hill people, too, with their Anglo-Saxon Protestant names such as Anderson and Smith, who might have been his forebears. He disliked their fundamentalist Methodist or foot-washing Baptist religiosity and their sectarian quarrels, and some of the mountaineers, he unsentimentally knew, were sullen, mean, full of scarcely repressed violence; but many were kindly, generous, in his term of highest praise "very sweet," though even for him some were difficult to get acquainted with since, as he gradually learned, his exploration of the countryside had at first made them suspect that he might be a revenue officer sniffing out their illegal stills. He especially respected their independence and quiet dignity within hardscrabble lives, qualities he was to describe in a number of his later stories, and he found most of them susceptible to his gift, in Caroline Greear's admiring words, for getting "everything out of people there is in them," for "inviting strange confidences," for drawing out in a few minutes from people she knew more about their lives and often terrible "troubles" than she had learned over several years. Above all it was here in the mountains and among a family of children that he was writing well. "Country life," he would soon write Bab, "will be better for me now. I shall have enough to do writing the unwritten stuff in me."

Perhaps I shall find it better to spend more time with nature. A little farm off in these hills might be the best thing. I can spend a few months a year with people then I must have nature.[5]

He at last found what he had been looking for in his explorations. One day he took the Laurel Creek road out of Troutdale and a few miles from town got into a rough "wagon road" that led into a narrow valley among hills where the Laurel and Ripshin Creek joined, the valley being called Ripshin, Mrs. Greear explained, "because it was so hard and steep it was hard to get about without skinning one's shins." By a log bridge crossing Ripshin Creek there was an old apple orchard and the cabin of a widow-woman with many children, who owned the thirty-one-acre, run-down farm lying up the valley from the bridge. The view from the hills enclosing the valley was spectacular, however, and he knew that this was the place he wanted. He asked the widow, Barbara Miller, if she would sell. She replied that she might, but in mountain fashion, she would not be more definite. By this time Anderson had become acquainted with William Wright, head of the remaining Troutdale National Bank, who was to become one of his best friends in the community. When he told Wright that he wanted to buy Mrs. Miller's farm and asked if he thought she would sell it for a thousand dollars, Wright assured him that she did want to sell and was asking for less than that price. Anderson, Wright admiringly recalled, did not want to cheat people and insisted on offering Mrs. Miller $1,450. Without consulting Elizabeth he did so. Mrs. Miller still did not finally commit herself to sell, but agreed that if she did, she would sell for that amount. Shortly after returning to New Orleans and presenting a surprised but not very pleased Elizabeth with his decision—she would have preferred to live in a larger town but yielded to his characteristic enthusiasm—Sherwood sent Mrs. Miller a check for fifty dollars drawn on the Troutdale bank, where he had set up an account, this sum as earnest money on his offer, the remaining $1,400 to be paid when the property was transferred to him. Not until September 15 would he receive a letter from Barbara Miller at last agreeing to sell. On September 30 he sent to Bill Wright a check for $700 made out to Barbara Miller and an offer to pay the remainder by November 15. Now he was assured of hearing repeatedly, as he had expansively written Bab, "the call the old Greeks heard—the growing corn, apple trees, birds nesting," nature having become "more and more my goddess." Already he had persuaded Elizabeth that they should build "a little stone house" at Ripshin and "live there in the mountains about seven or eight months a year."[6]

Reluctantly he left Troutdale and the Greears on August 14 and returned to the "poison" heat of New Orleans on the sixteenth to face an accumulation of mail on his desk, the necessity of more work on *A Mid-American Childhood*, the impending success or failure of *Dark Laughter*'s publication, and the knowledge that his second lecture tour was less than two months away. He and Elizabeth sent a thank-you gift of phonograph records to the Greears, including the Volga Boat Song and Negro spirituals, and Sherwood wrote John Greear to ask about a local contractor who could build a spacious log cabin on a hilltop looking up Laurel Creek toward the distant mountains, the cabin to be his writing workshop for the following summer if he got the Miller farm. John recommended a Mr. Marion Ball, who would eventually build not only the cabin in the late winter of 1926 but also, during the ensuing summer, the fine fieldstone house named Ripshin to which the Andersons would move from New Orleans. Ben Huebsch, who had earlier sent Sherwood a check for $109.13

as his 50 percent share in the royalties paid by Jonathan Cape for the English issue of *A Story Teller's Story*, had written on August 5 about his position with the newly formed Viking Press, which would free him from business matters for editorial ones, and, as proof that despite "the altered business relations between us" he still had "your interest," informed him of favorable English reviews of *Story* in the *London Evening Standard* and the *Manchester Guardian*. The Viking Press, Ben assured Sherwood, would promote with "greater vigor" the sale of his books done with Huebsch alone. On the seventeenth, just back from Troutdale, Anderson wrote Ben "all kinds of good luck to the new firm," but first wired him asking whether the royalty statement of August 1, not yet received, had been mailed. "I need the money," he wrote, presumably thinking of his hoped-for purchase of the Miller farm but revealing also how money-conscious he had become.[7]

There were other matters to clear up over the next few days. He agreed to sign the fifty extra copies of *The Modern Writer* to be printed on vellum by Edwin Grabhorn and the 370 copies of a limited edition of *Dark Laughter*, these being the first two instances of special signed editions in his publishing career. With amused gratitude he thanked William S. Hart's publicity director for sending him (at the cowboy film star's request) an inscribed photo of Hart because Anderson had referred to him in *A Story Teller's Story*, only partly ironically, as a beloved "national hero": "There has been something of a crime wave in New Orleans and I feel safer with [the photo] in my room." He assured Faulkner's friend Phil Stone that Horace Liveright would read *Soldier's Pay* and decide between the two readers who were enthusiastic about the novel and the third who was less so, and that if Liveright wanted, he would be glad to write a blurb for the book jacket since he "certainly admired Bill's talent." When some days later Liveright wired him that he would publish Faulkner's novel, he wrote Horace of his pleasure: "I have a hunch this man is a comer." He arranged to repay with interest the six-hundred-dollar loan John Emerson had gotten for him and told John that he had put Anita into *Dark Laughter*, where her name appears among those of other writers of "good books."[8]

From the time of his return to New Orleans he had been working hard at *A Mid-American Childhood* with the hope of finishing it before he had to begin his lecture tour. Remembering his talks with the Greear children, he was trying "to get inside kids a little," he told Julia Harris, but those children had more been a powerful stimulus to his writing of childhood than models for the Moorehead children in the book. Soon he would confess to Bab the autobiographical base of what he wrote: "It is really my own childhood dramatized and lived in the person of one Tar Moorehead." Significantly, two months later he would focus the true subject of the book in its more individualized final title, *Tar*. The subtitle *A Midwest*

Childhood would come afterwards. Despite the fact that the "life of the children in the Moorehead household absorbed" him, he was willing to break off from it briefly early in September to comply with a hurried request by Donald Freeman, managing editor of *Vanity Fair,* to write for a fee of $100 a comment on a photograph of the portrait painting "Mr. and Mrs. Philip Wase" included in New York's Metropolitan Museum Memorial Exhibition for the recently deceased George Bellows. What was the artist telling his viewers through his depiction of this ordinary working-class couple?

What you realize, what every man dimly realizes, is that what a man feels toward his work, he is. We have all in the end got to square ourselves with ourselves if we can.

The challenge is always there. "Get a little closer. Give more of yourself. Be more impersonal before the possibilities of the materials you touch with your fingers. Love more."

That chore done, Anderson returned to work on the less impersonal semi-autobiography of *Tar* until toward the end of September he went to bed for a week with a fever.[9]

He could pass this illness off to Horace Liveright as "my regular yearly attack of Flu or Grippe"; yet the circumstances suggest something less automatic. Originally he had set October 1 as a tentative completion date for *Tar,* then had told Otto Liveright that he might not finish by October 15 since he had rejected "about half" of what he had written in Troutdale as "not quite up to what I wanted." By September 15 he was insisting to Otto that he didn't want to feel hurried about *Tar* and that the book "is perhaps about two-thirds done," but his estimates tended always to be on the optimistic side. The more realistic Elizabeth flatly wrote Julia Harris that "it's only a little more than half done now." Not only was there a question in Sherwood's mind as to when *The Woman's Home Companion* needed the completed manuscript for their publication deadline, but he was clearly writing for money as well as under pressure. It was "rather a wrong notion," he wrote David Karsner just before his illness, "this waiting for money in order to do good work. As well tell a girl to go on the street to get money to afford living with a man she loves." Much as he wanted the money from the *Companion* and from the arrangement with Horace Liveright, he as an artist had some squaring to do with himself since "what a man feels toward his work, he is." His week of fever pointed toward his slowly growing sense in the future that he might be in danger of compromising his principles, might in fact have done so already.[10]

There were other reasons for the illness too. Because their lease was lapsing on their Pontalba apartment, Elizabeth's plan for living while

Sherwood was off for months of lecturing was upsettingly vague at least until mid-September. Almost at the last minute by September 23, about the time his illness began, they found a house to rent in the Quarter. The one story, red brick house at 825 Bourbon Street fronted immediately on the "banquette" (the sidewalk) on the northwest side of Bourbon halfway between St. Ann and Dumaine streets. A gate in a wall at the right led into a longish, narrow courtyard with, at the rear, a two-storied brick former slave quarters, which Elizabeth planned to have renovated for her and Sherwood to live in, the house on the street then to be rented or used as a guest house. The only obvious inconvenience was that the toilet was situated in a small brick building in the courtyard, though when the November cold came Elizabeth would long for the heat of a furnace. But the house was suitable for living in at once, so that worrisome problem was solved, but Elizabeth had to supervise the move out of the Pontalba since Sherwood was barely out of bed by October 2.[11]

Over him, finally, had hung for weeks two disturbing questions. How would he stand the taxing two-part lecture tour Colston Leigh had scheduled for him, engagements on the two-and-a-half month first leg taking him to the South, the East, and the Midwest, those on the second leg taking him to the West Coast for three and a half weeks but with only ten days of rest back in New Orleans in between? And how would *Dark Laughter* be received by reviewers, and sell?

2.

Boni and Liveright sent out advance copies of *Dark Laughter* to reviewers and to Anderson in the third week in August, and the book was published on September 15. The first review, by Laurence Stallings in the New York *World* for September 11, was in Anderson's words "a fine send-off." Stallings hailed the novel as "a fine one, a better thing than his superb *Winesburg, Ohio*," as "the finest contemporary estimate of American life . . . since old Walt Whitman passed on," and as "a masterpiece, a book justifying [Anderson's] career." Two days later Liveright's advertising campaign began in the Sunday *World* with a box two columns wide and eight inches deep reproducing Hyde Man's etching of the author with a caption announcing that in *Dark Laughter* Anderson had discovered "a new centre in American life, the South, and, especially, New Orleans," and that in the novel "he makes known the enlargement of his vision and of his sympathies." Julia Harris immediately sent him a clipping of the Stallings review and shortly thereafter that of a largely negative one, V. F. Calverton's in the Baltimore *Evening Sun*, "Sherwood Anderson Not At His Best In His Latest Novel." He also saw the anonymous attack in the *New York Times Book Review* of September 20—the novel "is poisoned from end to end by that strange underevaluation of the human will which has descended like a blight upon the modern school in fiction"—for he dismissed it as the work of a "masculine old maid, who is afraid someone will steal his wife if you let out the secret that wives are sometimes stolen." Yet the fact that of the four other major reviews appearing in September, only one was positive and that one muddily written could well, if he saw them, have been another reason for his taking to his bed with flu and staying there. Clearly he could not expect with *Dark Laughter* the kind of widespread acclaim he had received with *A Story Teller's Story.*[12]

At the beginning of October things began to look up. Julia Harris praised *Dark Laughter* in the Columbus *Enquirer-Sun* on October 4 and sent Anderson a copy, and he knew by this time from her that H. L. Mencken thought the novel "a capital piece of work—the best book he has done" and would be saying so in *The American Mercury.* Even more reassuring, though Anderson would not see it until well into his lecture tour, was Stuart P. Sherman's admiring essay review in the October 4 *New York Herald Tribune Books.* Even now Sherman's "Sherwood Anderson's Tales of the New Life" seems a striking summary of Anderson's "gifts" when he is seen as a "whole" in relation to his time. He has, Sherman contends, a "white-hot zeal for craftsmanship" and "possesses the idiom of American colloquial speech beyond most living writers." He is "a natural born story teller, who has scornfully rejected standardized tricks and formulas and has steadily perfected and subtilized his art, and devoted it to expressing secret crises in the mind and in the feelings which only a delicate and subtle art can explore." He "is tremendously American and is glad of it," and he is "a passionate seeker for the meaning and purpose" in American life. He is, Sherman believes, "a genuine mystic" subject to moments of "almost ecstatic 'awareness' of common life transfigured into beauty." One does not, therefore, read *Dark Laughter* "or, indeed, any of his books as if they were ordinary 'realistic' novels attempting to picture the detail and circumstance of contemporary society"; for "Sherwood Anderson has always been a symbolist, feeling from the outset the necessity of storming sluggish sensibilities with a new set of images, strange, extravagant and grotesque, symbols of an experience otherwise untransmissible."[13]

Presumably Anderson saw or was told about other reviews, which appeared during his weeks on tour. He could take comfort from the praise of *Dark Laughter* by Henry Seidel Canby in the *Saturday Review of Literature,* by Robert Morss Lovett in the *New Republic,* and by Mencken in *The American Mercury,* for these were critics of stature and influence; and he could dismiss the shock at his "unclean ugliness" expressed by "K. S." in the *Boston Transcript* and Fanny Butcher in the Chicago *Tribune* as the usual puritanical moralism. The reviews asserting that *Dark Laughter* showed his increased control of the long novel form gradually outnumbered those asserting the opposite, even though many of the positive reviews raised minor objections. Probably the best news for the author at this point, however, was that as promised Liveright was selling the book. By the end of December it would be in its second printing, having sold some twenty-two thousand copies. For the first, and only, time in his career Anderson had a book that was an immediate, moderately popular success.[14]

Such success does not necessarily equate with inferior art, of course, and the weaknesses of *Dark Laughter* should not obscure its strengths. In composing this novel Anderson borrowed certain elements from his previous ones. Like Sam McPherson, the protagonist Bruce Dudley becomes dissatisfied with his life, abruptly abandons it, and wanders over part of America on a "voyage of discovery" of his true self. Like *Poor White* in structure, the first of three major sections of *Dark Laughter* (books 1 through 5) concerns this protagonist, who like Hugh McVey has a submerged artistic talent; the second (books 6 and 7) concerns a developing woman, Aline Grey; the third (books 8 through 12) brings man and woman together, though in this case Aline has been three years married to Fred Grey, a factory owner. Like *Many Marriages, Dark Laughter* was conceived of originally as a "fantasy," by which Anderson apparently meant here that it primarily dealt with the inner, imaginative lives of his three main characters. Further, two "marriages" beyond the ceremonial ones are emphasized in *Dark Laughter*. But in his extensive revisions Anderson had worked these self-borrowings into a form that united with considerable success many of his major concerns for the individual—liberation from sexual and social repression, the discovery of and fulfillment of the self, the awareness, rudimentary in Bruce, that the practice of the arts is "a sort of cure for the disease called living"—and in turn displayed these concerns against the sickness, as Anderson saw it, of national and to some extent international society, afflicted additionally now with a deep postwar malaise.

To tell his tale of "sophisticated" people in the "here and now" of contemporary life, Anderson had felt that he had "to create a style to fit it." Writing to George Daugherty on the day *Dark Laughter* was published, Anderson reiterated what he had told Daugherty on his spring visit to New Orleans about the influence on him of Joyce's *Ulysses*, that he "very frankly took Joyce's experiment as a starting place for the prose rhythm of the book." "Starting place" should be emphasized; Anderson does occasionally use a kind of stream of consciousness, largely in the long first section where Bruce's thoughts shift, sometimes associatively, sometimes abruptly, from the present to various points in his past and back to the present, so that only gradually does one learn why Bruce, a thirty-four-year-old

597

reporter on a Chicago newspaper, leaves his wife, a feature story writer on the paper, makes his way down the Mississippi for a several months stay in New Orleans, and, having changed his name from the original John Stockton to prevent recognition, now works in the Grey Wheel Factory in Old Harbor, Indiana, the small city on the Ohio River where he had lived with his parents as a boy. Yet such shifting about in time had already been one of Anderson's storytelling devices; and whereas in *Ulysses* the stream of consciousness occurs without authorial intrusion into the minds of individual characters, that in *Dark Laughter* usually filters Bruce's thoughts—"stream of consciousness" is largely confined to his section—through the mind of the authorial narrator, direct authorial intrusion being common. (For example, it is obviously Anderson, not Bruce, who essayistically lists among other writers of "good books" Van Wyck Brooks, Ring Lardner, and Anita Loos.) In addition to his much modified "technique of *Ulysses*," Anderson may have taken from Joyce's novel, or from *A Story Teller's Story*, the hint for occasionally inserting in the New Orleans section snatches of black folk songs, such as the repeated "Oh, ma banjo dog," which, he later explained, he had heard sung in 1920 by "the Negro stevedores on the old steamer *Peerless*, on the service between Selma and Mobile, Alabama." His frequent collecting of a series of separate descriptive items in short sentences seems less like a borrowing from Joyce than from Whitman's catalogs of impressionistic details and seems designed to make the book's prose, as he had told Paul Rosenfeld, flow "like a real river" in "a slow, fantastic dance of sounds and thoughts."[15]

Despite this stylistic experimentation, some of the best parts of the book are those in which Anderson simply tells tales. One of these opens the novel. Bruce, barely introduced, is dropped for a description of a fellow workman, the aging but feisty Sponge Martin, and his "fox terrier" of a wife. Sponge, who is modeled on the skilled painter B. M. Rice whom Anderson had worked under years earlier in the Clyde bicycle factory, is a craftsman, independent to the point of truculence—he had once offered to fight the first owner of the factory, Fred Grey's father, when Old Grey tried to make him skimp on a special job—and still sexually active with his wife. That on payday evenings the Martins sometimes go fishing in the Ohio, get drunk together on moonshine, and then make love on the river's bank seems to present them in an odd kind of digression simply as amiable Winesburg characters until it gradually becomes clear that, through this sketch, Anderson has by indirection initiated an important theme in the novel. Sponge is a type of uneducated but liberated, self-unified American man, a craftsman who has not "got rather far away from his own hands, body, eyes, ears" as so many other white persons have in the machine age, as Anderson had told V. F. Calverton back when *Dark Laughter* was first pouring out of him. Sponge is associated in Bruce's mind, as is explicitly

Mark Twain, with the great Mississippi-Ohio artery of Anderson's Midwest heartland. When Bruce leaves his wife and heads down the Mississippi by skiff and riverboat to New Orleans, a latter day adult Huck Finn lighting out from modern "sivilization," he unconsciously becomes a part, as Sponge and Twain are each a part, of what Anderson suggests is a life-giving myth of America's "lost youth" and of its possible future as well, a myth manifested in the abiding natural force of the river. One of the strengths of *Dark Laughter,* then, resides in Anderson's continued ability to lead the reader by such associative links into sudden awareness of the full implications of an only apparently simple, only apparently digressive tale.[16]

Anderson's attack on business and industry as a perversion of this American myth into a social ethos based on the drive for money and power will be embodied in Fred Grey later in the novel. In the opening Bruce section, Anderson primarily attacks the subsidiary world of the false artists as represented by Bruce's wife, Bernice, who beneath differences in detail is obviously a Tennessee Mitchell figure. Symptomatically, Bernice has been trying for some time to finish a psychologically false short story about a man who falls in love with the wax dummy of a woman in a store window, and she enjoys the company of the "talking artists," who in Anderson's view had made up so much of the now past Chicago Renaissance. Bruce, on the other hand, is bored by the talk of art and has become so contemptuous of his fellow reporters' manipulation of language that he has ceased to write his stories and only telephones in the information to a young Jewish "word-slinger" (Ben Hecht?) who adeptly writes them up. Nevertheless, Bruce has the true sense for news; he gets to the "heart of the matter," that is, to the Andersonian "essence of things," and he vaguely considers that he might become a writer, his one goal being, he later thinks, to be "more sensitive to everything going on about him than others could possibly be," Anderson's own goal as he had expressed it to V. F. Calverton a year earlier when he was well into writing *Dark Laughter.* Bruce and Bernice have long since tired of each other, and Bruce has only one friend, Tom Wills the city editor, who bluntly excoriates the "impotence" of the times, the spiritual weariness of people, the recent World War as "a sign of universal impotence, sweeping over the world like a disease." One day on impulse Bruce abandons his sterile, "impotent" marriage with Bernice, as Anderson had abandoned his with Tennessee, and begins drifting down the Mississippi to New Orleans.

The city Bruce lives in for a summer is not that of *The Double Dealer* and the bohemian artists; rather it is that of a "five dollar" bug-infested room among blacks where he luxuriates in the heat, the river activity, the lack of hurry: "A slow dance, music, ships, cotton, corn, coffee. Slow lazy laughter of niggers." The blacks with their easy, relaxed sensuality become associated in Bruce's mind with the flow of the Mississippi, with fertility, with the slow "dance of life"; thematically they become another aspect of the true myth of America. Significantly, it is in New Orleans that Bruce begins to write poems, his closeness as a projection of his creator indicated by the two poems he writes (which are inserted in the text, as well as the two he later writes), would be included with some revision in Anderson's second collection of prose poems *A New Testament*. Creativity is thus linked with the "dance of life" and by extension with the American myth initiated by the sketch of Sponge Martin the craftsman. Later, Bruce will wonder whether as a writer one could "use his own thoughts, his own feelings, his own fancies as Sponge could use a paint brush."

Interspersed in Bruce's mind with these memories of his recent past are linked immediate present and long past events in his life in Old Harbor. Leaving the wheel factory at the end of the working day, he and Sponge see Aline Grey waiting in her car for her husband, and for a moment Bruce and Aline's eyes meet. Bruce is dimly aware that a "marriage" has taken place; Sponge is alert to it at once, intuiting it as a craftsman "perhaps through his fingers," and tells Bruce that Fred Grey has not "really got" his wife and that Bruce might well be the man she is looking for. The momentary "marriage" with Aline immediately calls up in Bruce's mind an experience from his boyhood: "Another woman . . . sitting on a bench beside her boy looking at the moving face of a river in the evening light." In those years his father had been a school teacher, and the family had lived in the small hotel where Bruce now again lives. His mother, "a slender, rather small woman with a sweet, serious face," was usually "quiet and reserved"—like Anderson's own mother—but on rare occasions became "strangely alive and eager." One such occasion was a "marriage" Bruce had witnessed between her and a young man when she and her son had been sitting on the deck of a riverboat. Immediately associated with and paralleling Bruce and Aline's "marriage," this intricately organized climax to the Bruce section is the finest tale in *Dark Laughter* and among the finest in Anderson's work.

When Bruce was twelve, the Stockton family moved from Old Harbor by riverboat bound up the Ohio to Louisville. Soon after embarking, the father, as Anderson's would have done, is off talking with the captain, who boasts of how he exploits his black deckhands. Two young men have also boarded at Old Harbor, and Bruce senses that the slender one of the two and his mother, who looks young that day "like a girl," have felt some sudden emotional connection. That evening at the last landing before Louisville, Bruce is deeply affected by the singing of the deckhands unloading bags of grain. The blacks are "Word-lovers, sound-lovers," whose bodies are united in feeling by their song and their work, just as the red of the twilight sky is united with the reflected red of the river. On the shore sits a ragged, half-crazed man, part white, part black, his body rocking "slowly to and fro in the rhythm of the singing negroes"; on the boat the body of the slender young man, who is intensely aware of Bruce's mother though trying to converse with his companion, rocks "almost imperceptibly," and the mother's body also rocks. To the boy "the whole world, the sky, the boat, the shore running away into the gathering darkness" seems to rock with the voices of the singing blacks, and he sees that his mother has "turned her face toward the young man . . . as though she had suddenly consented to something—a kiss perhaps." In this long lyric passage where detail echoes detail linking sound, sight, and feeling into a momentary human and aesthetic "marriage," Anderson may well have been suggesting "the beginning of a kind of big continental poetry" such as, Bruce thinks, "Mark Twain had almost got and didn't dare to quite get"—as Fred Grey has not dared to quite "get" his wife of three years.

After this passage the Bruce section ends in a kind of reprise in which the adult Bruce echoes the note of *Mid-American Chants* by envisioning the "whole Middle American empire" as being swept by springtime, spends a Saturday evening with the self-reliant Martins, thinks of Joyce as a distinctly "European" writer whose realism was "something burning and raw like a raw sore," wants to be "partly" like Sponge in his self-assured maleness and craftsmanship, and returning to a present event is told by Sponge that when Aline passed them in the car with her husband, she again looked at Bruce. By bringing so many story elements and themes together, Anderson creates a frame for the Bruce section while pointing toward the Aline and Paris sections to follow. The leaps backward and forward in Bruce's thought now prove to have been more purposefully structured by Anderson than may have appeared.

Despite numerous flashbacks and flashforwards the Aline section, the shortest of the three divisions of the book's action, has a more traditional chronological development, which leads up to and circles about Rose Frank's half-hysterical account in her Paris apartment of the Quat'z Arts Ball and the aftermath of that account . . . the marriage of Aline and Fred Grey. Unlike Bruce, who is said in the most general terms only to be "young-looking and handsome," Aline is physically described in, for Anderson, unusual detail. Another woman thinks of her as "a prim, neat little figure of a woman, with good ankles, a small sharp interesting face, a good neck—the body graceful and fascinating too"—in sum, quite like Elizabeth Anderson—and she has slender hands and "slender feet, clad in expensive shoes," such shoes being one of her indulgences as the daughter of a wealthy Chicago corporation lawyer. Anderson's even more detailed analysis of her personality makes her one of his most complex women characters. She dislikes vulgarity, thinks sexual suggestiveness not "nice," and both acts and thinks of herself "as a lady"; yet she quietly wonders

"Was there something in her still to be aroused, awakened from sleep?" Despite her reticence she is honest with herself, as in recognizing that her amateur painting is clever rather than talented, and she has become fairly acute at sensing social relationships and the ulterior motivations of others. Her one childhood memory suggests a natural sensitivity beneath her conventional exterior. When a traveler told her father and her of how turpentine trees in the South were cut and maimed for their sap, she later wept in bed as she fantasized the trees as injured human beings, "Trees crying out . . . staggering about, bleeding." When her brother and her fiancé are later killed in the war, their deaths seem to her no nearer than the imagined trees; her relationships with both men had been, because of the conventional upbringing of all three, merely formal. "She had not touched them closely"—and she must learn closer touching in order to be awakened into full personhood.

Aline meets and marries Fred Grey in Paris in the summer after the war, that is, in 1919, when she is twenty-six. (Since she is specifically said to be twenty-nine when she sees Bruce, the "here and now" of the novel's time is the late winter to fall of 1922, despite an anachronistic reference to the Loeb-Leopold case of 1924.) She is accompanied to Paris by Joe and Esther Walker. Joe, who has painted a portrait of Aline's dead brother from a photograph, expends his talent for a considerable fee on portraits of the rich, and Esther helps him by snaring further wealthy subjects. This cynical husband and wife team functions thematically in the novel as another example of the false artists besides those Bernice associates with, while the bisexual Esther's unsuccessful attempt to seduce Aline during the transatlantic crossing reiterates, in Anderson's thinking, the impotence, sterility, and death-in-life, which for him characterize so much of postwar American and European society. In Paris, Aline tends to go about by herself. Like Anderson she recognizes in the Louvre the enormous talent of the old masters, admires that of such great moderns as Cézanne, is charmed by the French "matter-of-fact acceptance" of sexuality, observes the French men's maturity, so preferable to the immaturity of American men, but also their "inability to think or feel women as anything but flesh." Then the night after the Quat'z Arts Ball, the Walkers take Aline to a party in the apartment of Rose Frank.

When the American journalist Rose Wilder Lane reluctantly read *Dark Laughter,* she recognized herself as the basis for Rose Frank, "a plump strong-looking little American woman of perhaps thirty," and was furious at what she considered Anderson's misrepresentation of her and of her account of the Quat'z Arts Ball at her party in Paris on the evening of June 11, 1921. She had then talked "frankly" of the sexual orgy, which, according to her, she had observed with cool journalistic interest but which she had not participated in because she preferred to take her pleasure with a man in privacy. Rose Frank, on the other hand, talks compulsively, confessionally of the debauch, of her own "black, ugly, hungry desire" to go "the limit," of self-disgust at her "cheating" when she was repeatedly "saved" from coupling with various men by her young American male escort. Further, Lane declared Anderson "just plain silly" in presenting the Quat'z Arts Ball of 1919 as an outburst of the extreme revulsion felt by the men who had survived the war against the horrors of the trenches, and the "debauch of lying" by which governments, churches, writers, artists, and sentimental women fed the war fever. The men at the ball, according to Rose Frank, wish to punish women and, through them, punish a lying Western civilization by "muddying" them with sexual assault. The balls are "as routine a thing in Paris as the blossoms on the chestnut trees," Rose Wilder Lane angrily wrote a friend; Anderson "doesn't know what he is writing about."[17]

But Anderson did know what he was writing about, or rather tried to, and his failure was of a different order, not whether the 1919 ball was or was not routine. As always he had been looking for, not facts, but "the essence of things." Very early in his Paris visit in 1921 he had entered in his notebook his sense of "something in the air of present day France, a kind of death . . . a kind of bitterness" that the prewar feeling of "something growing here" was lost in the war sickness; and almost immediately afterward he had recorded that the "tired faces" of the people in America manifested what Tom Wills in *Dark Laughter* terms impotence, "a sense of something like hopelessness" because the "old belief in material progress is lost and nothing new had yet been found." True essences or not, Anderson had sought to express them through a scene, which would provide a total image of the war. Yet herein lies the first major flaw of *Dark Laughter;* for the scene and image he arrived at are not powerful enough and suggestive enough, as is indicated by his attempt to strengthen them by adding to the galley proof his authorial outburst against the war as a vast "debauch of lying." (Lane the reporter might better have criticized the novel's one vignette of trench warfare for being as vague and unrealistic an episode as Ernest Hemingway would declare it to be.) Anderson's failure, in expecting to compress the essence of the war into Rose's account of the Quat'z Arts Ball, was a failure of the imagination.

Unlike the reader, Aline feels at the end of the account that "Rose had given her the war, the sense of it—all in a heap—like a blow." At the party she has felt sexually drawn to a quiet man, a farmer workman whom Bruce will later urgently remind her of because each man has the air of being capable of "burning himself out . . . in some kind of work, or in the love of a woman." At the end of the party the man stays behind with Rose and is clearly her lover, and Aline leaves with Fred Grey, a wealthy young American whom Esther Walker has told that Aline would be the perfect wife for him. Fred has endured his share of the war's horrors, but he is shocked at the notion of men debasing women at the ball. To him in his "boy-man" innocence, women are like the white stone angels whom he and Aline see that night on the roof of Notre Dame and who seem to be "walking up into the sky." Anderson thus ironically continues the motif of the artificial versus the natural woman he had begun with: Bernice's never-completed story of the man who falls in love with the wax dummy. Deeply stirred by Rose's self-hatred, Aline is determined not to "cheat" on her own emotions and is ready to give herself to Fred, partly out of pity for his sufferings in the war; but Fred sees Aline as the safely American girl he wants to keep pure to marry. Not understanding their mismatched feelings toward one another, they are easily pressured by Esther into marrying immediately.

As in *Many Marriages,* Anderson provided *Dark Laughter* with what he described to Horace Liveright as "orchestration" by a network of repeated details, motifs, and themes and by a fundamental contact in the latter book between the

neuroticism, the hurry and self-consciousness of modern life, and back of it the easy, strange laughter of the blacks. There is your dark, earthy laughter—the Negro, the earth, and the river—that suggest the title.

Early in his journey of self-discovery Bruce begins to be healed of his white self-consciousness by the laughter of the blacks in New Orleans; and the title phrase itself occurs in the Aline section when Rose Frank insists on beginning her account of the Quat'z Arts Ball and laughs "a queer high nervous laugh—dark laughter that." Rose's laugh is ambiguous, for it suggests both the "strange feeling" that possessed her at the ball, in her words "something primitive like a nigger woman in an African dance," and her self-contempt that her feeling did not burst out in violent sensuality. In the final major section of the novel the dark laughter will be that of the two black servants in the Grey household, two barely individualized women who echo and thus balance the generalized blacks of the first section. But this symmetry will not prevent the concluding section from being, to some extent, a falling off from the rest of the novel.[18]

This section, which brings together Bruce, Aline, and Fred, begins with expert bluntness, "She had got him," meaning both that Bruce had been fully attracted to Aline and that she had broken through her social and personal constraints and brought him physically near her. No longer satisfied by his factory job, Bruce has been doubtful that he could find his life work in the arts, but he occasionally writes poems and wants "periods of rather intense emotional outpourings." Aline "gets him" by her contrivance of advertising for a gardener and selecting him from the applicants even though he knows nothing about gardening. Symbolically he leaves the world of machines and moves toward the world of natural things, learning from Aline's deft hands how to use his own "rather thick fingers, broad palms"—hands like Anderson's own—regaining the sense of the body and the power of feeling lost by most white men, Anderson had told Calverton, "because of the coming of the machine." His total divorce from the world of business is expressed in his feeling toward the fertile flat lands of Old Harbor along the Ohio, which he sees from the hill above them where the Grey house stands, that these are lands to be plowed and planted as, Anderson implies, the body of a woman is to be plowed and planted. In contrast, Fred's father, "Old Grey," banker and manufacturer, had recognized that this valley land was rich soil for crops, to be sure; but he had craftily foreclosed on the farmers who had borrowed from him and failed, had sent "an army of hired men" onto the land he now owned, and had it tilled as one massive operation from which he had "made money hand over fist," this trite expression gaining sudden vividness as a sign of the corrupted function of hands in the business world. By opposition, as Bruce observes the "caress" in Aline's hands when touching plants, a caress like that in Sponge's hands when holding a brush, he feels like "a painter at work on a vast canvas on which others were also at work." Nature and art link fruitfully, Anderson's dramatized argument goes, in opposition to the perverse abstracting of nature solely into the source of wealth. Anderson handles with much subtlety the slowly developing intimacy between Aline and Bruce. From the novel's beginning, contrary to the reader's expectations and assumptions, Bruce has been deliberately presented as a relatively passive figure, despite his sudden act of leaving Bernice. As is suggested by his repeated looking out of windows early in the novel, Bruce is the withdrawn, dreamy observer more than the active participant in life. Uncertain of Aline's feelings, he himself decides like a romantic youth that "If I do not love fully now, I shall never love." (In this context it should be clear that Anderson is being sardonic rather than sententious when he describes the endless generations of human lovers and comments: "A German scientist can explain perfectly. If there is anything you do not understand in human life consult the works of Dr. Freud.") Bruce considers his unarticulated love for Aline as "one of the adventures of life," life itself being, as Anderson himself saw it, a "series of adventures—little glowing moments, flashes in darkness, and then utter darkness and death." Yet at this point he is passively content that Aline should be the wife of Fred Grey. It will be Aline, the "stone" woman in the process of self-liberation, who will be the active agent in precipitating the affair.

The weakest figure in the erotic triangle and unfortunately the weakest creation in the novel is Fred Grey. By the logic of Anderson's "fantasy" of the interior life, Fred's thoughts must be given frequently in this last section, and these present him too much as Anderson's stereotype of the American businessman. Too often he is a cardboard figure, at times almost a caricature. He prides himself on owning so decorative a wife as Aline; but his real love is for the wheel factory, "the center of his life," and he takes great satisfaction in working with a "smart" Chicago advertising man on "a national advertising campaign on Grey Automobile wheels in the magazines." A "boy-man" American—"Most American men never get to be beyond seventeen—perhaps," the authorial voice has charged— Fred is emotionally immature and unable to face the reality of himself and others. Although he has suffered the destructive ugliness of war in France, he delights at home in marching in a parade to dedicate a memorial to the war, that "debauch of lies"; and, a private in the army but now "the richest man in town," he smugly congratulates himself for being willing to march in temporary equality "with the common soldiers." He is temperamentally unable to have close emotional relations with anyone, especially with Aline, whom he has idealized as being "like one of the small, old-fashioned white marble statues people used to set on pedestals among green foliage in a garden" and with whom he feels sexually insecure. In turn, Aline is often "irritated and bored . . . by his childishness, his obtuseness." Anderson subsequently commented succinctly to a friend on the couple's relationship: "Fred was simply incapable of being loved. He hadn't intelligence enough for her." The "mark of the highest intelligence," he noted, is "in reality a wholesome attitude toward the flesh." [19]

Fred does sense with vague unease the developing relationship between Aline and Bruce, but he is "afraid to know" of it and therefore refuses to know it. The two black women servants, however, watch the domestic drama with knowing laughter. Aline gradually admits to herself the feelings prefigured in her own earlier childish game of imagining herself a "tiny stone figure" in her garden but one who also feels "a part of the sky, of the ground, of passing winds" and is ready for a lover to appear out of nature and take her. The "stone figure" has become human, a strong, mature, self-aware woman ready to enter into the "dance of life." On the day when Fred is down in the city marching in the patriotic parade, Aline wordlessly communicates to the willing Bruce her desire that they become lovers. Their one act of love impregnates her, she is certain; but she accepts her husband into her bed after his return from the parade, and for weeks afterward, while Bruce has disappeared, she encourages Fred to believe that the coming child is his. One evening Bruce returns, Aline confronts Fred with the assertion that Bruce is the father of her child, and the lovers go away together despite Fred's distraught effort to bring Aline back. Later that evening Fred sits "upright and rigid in bed," sleepless and alone, hearing the "high shrill laughter" of the younger black woman, who stands "in the road before the house" with her companion and two black men and cries, "'I knowed it, I knowed it, all the time I knowed it.'"

This ending, which Anderson wrote into the galley proof in place of the revised one from the original, makes for an effective confrontation of the values represented in the book by black and white, of the easy, uninhibited "natural" as opposed to the stiff, conventional, machine-bound "civilized," the "dance of life" against a nondance of death-in-life. *Dark Laughter* thus achieves a dramatic closure of its action; yet Anderson obviously felt a need to deal somehow with the future of the lovers after their act of liberation. Aline, with what Anderson terms "a practical turn" of mind, is said to be confident that her father and even Fred will eventually forgive her and that some of her father's wealth will persuade Bernice to accept a divorce so that Aline and Bruce can marry; but otherwise the future is briefly disposed of with the authorial observation that the lovers "would be compelled to face new problems, a new kind of life . . . Bruce being a laborer perhaps, Aline without money to spend freely, without luxuries." Bruce, it is remarked, has found "a woman he could really marry, but that was only half of it. He wanted to find the right kind of work too." Yet he has already found factory work unsatisfactory, and the thought of being a professional poet is "rather dreadful to him." Given his desire to "handle words as you might precious stones," he might well, as is intimated of John Webster at the end of *Many Marriages,* become another kind of writer, a novelist and storyteller, say; but such is left unresolved. As with *Many Marriages,* originally conceived of as part of a multivolume work, it is as though Anderson knew he had finished the first volume of at least a two-volume novel but had been unwilling or unable to imagine what would be the substance of an implied sequel beyond one thing. Given the resemblances between Bruce and Sherwood, Aline and Elizabeth, even after the author's fancy has played with the real-life situation of himself and his wife, that sequel would almost have had to be more semifictionalized autobiography, and which had already been brought almost up to the present by *A Story Teller's Story.* In *Dark Laughter* Anderson's favorite subject of the escape of a man or a woman or both had simultaneously reached climax and exhaustion.

3.

Not yet fully recovered from the flu and "with little taste for the thousands I shall have to meet," Anderson left New Orleans on October 8 on the first leg of his lecture tour. On the ninth he spoke at Fort Worth, Texas, probably on "America—A Storehouse of Vitality," again his standard lecture for a general audience, and on the tenth he presumably gave "Modern American Writing" or "The Younger Generation" at Baylor University in

Waco, both lectures, he reported to Colston Leigh, "going off fine." Then he doubled back to Atlanta, where on the twelfth he registered at the Hotel Aragon and met there in person Julia and Julian Harris. He and they were instant friends, and they joyfully took the train with him to nearby Athens, where on the morning of the thirteenth he spoke on "Modern American Writing" to an overflow audience of students and faculty in the chapel of the University of Georgia. Again Anderson told an attentive audience that the "Modern Movement," which was replacing the culture of both England and New England, was simply the "effort to find out the truth." Popular writers could become rich because their standardized work was a reflection of the standardization created by the industrial age, and they were careful not to "actually touch peoples lives." The true Modern writer, on the other hand, is a craftsman who deals not cheaply but honestly with his materials, these lives.[20]

Regretfully leaving the Harrises, Anderson backtracked to Birmingham, Alabama, where he spoke in the evening of October 15 at the Allied Arts Club. He had already been interviewed for the Birmingham *News* by one Dolly Dalrymple, who, not having read any of his work, had decided to ask "frivolous" questions, to some of which Anderson gave serious, characteristic answers. He considered Ring Lardner "the greatest humorist today" and Eugene O'Neill "the greatest American dramatist" because he "knows life." *Processional* was the best play he had seen "in the last decade" because "[John Howard] Lawson has put more life in it than any other play I've seen." The Bible was "the greatest book" he had ever read "because it is the best written." Wearied by interview and lecture, he headed for his next engagement, in Nashville, but stopped for two days of rest and writing in the small town of Columbia, Tennessee, through which, as Sherwood may have recalled from his father's tales, Trooper Irwin Anderson had ridden south with his cavalry regiment after the Battle of Nashville sixty years earlier. Lecturing, Irwin's son now wrote Bab,

is tiring work. Each speech takes something out of you and then the people are very insistent and very greedy.

Well, there is another side. There is something to be said. The people have such childish notions about what artists are up to and some of them are really greedy to know something.

Leigh had cautioned him not to talk about sex in the South, and there seemed to be some absurd notion that since he wrote of sexual matters, he might suddenly perform a sexual act publicly; but southerners seemed to him like any other people, and with his audiences "I get on fine and people flock to hear me."[21]

Very likely urged on by enthusiastic preappearance articles and a flow-ery editorial in the morning Nashville *Tennessean*—"To hear Sherwood Anderson lecture is more than a literary treat. It is an adventure."—hundreds of people did flock to hear him on the afternoon of October 19, the hall of the Centennial Club being so crowded that extra chairs had to be brought in, depressingly, "From a nearby undertaking establishment." The lecture, "Modern American Writing" "went off with a bang," he wrote Julian Harris; and in a newspaper report Donald Davidson, poet and professor at Vanderbilt University, agreed that it "was one of the most successful lectures ever given in Nashville," though Anderson had at first looked, and had been, scared before so large an audience and had walked back and forth nervously on the stage. Slowly he had begun to speak "in an ordinary conversational tone, making his points with such earnestness and absorption in his work that nobody could help being attracted." Davidson agreed too that "Sherwood Anderson has something very definite and valuable to say to American people in lectures as well as in novels and stories." When speaking on the lecture circuit, Anderson was on occasion halting, rambling, dull according to his mood, but on his good days, as at Nashville, he could in his earnest, unflamboyant way lead his audience to understand, even begin to appreciate what many of the new writers of the twenties were "up to."[22]

After speaking at a noon meeting of the Nashville Exchange Club on the twentieth, he left for Troutdale for a few days to renew acquaintance with the Greear family and to talk about plans for his writing cabin, which he wanted built "for permanency . . . of the best material to be had." The highlight of his few days stay was a night possum hunt by the Greears and their friends, ending at the Greear home in a feast of possum meat, roasted potatoes, gallons of coffee, and stacks of thick-crusted pies, and in a square dance in the living room, all to Anderson's delight. Seldom, he told Caroline Greear, had he "felt so close to folks as I do you people." On the twenty-sixth he left for New York, where he stayed with the Emersons, checked his crowded lecture schedule and his accounts with Leigh, generously persuaded Otto Liveright to act as literary agent for the New Orleans writer Lyle Saxon, and learned from Horace Liveright that *Dark Laughter* had "gone over fine," news which he celebrated by getting "very drunk." Then, with New York as a base to return to from time to time, he dashed off again on a lecture run in New England—Attleboro, Massachusetts on October 29, Boston at the Women's City Club on the thirty-first, Hanover, New Hampshire, at Dartmouth on November 2. From the Hanover Inn he wrote exuberantly to Bab:

My last two books seem to have pretty well removed the old fear of me. It may be that just the weight of many books, many tales has removed the old fear of me. People no longer seem to think me unclean. The head of the English department of Wellesley introduced me in Boston. It is all hard work but there is something gained—a sort of feeling of many kinds of Americans in many places and under many different conditions of life. As a matter of fact am standing the grind pretty well—get a kind of strength out of the crowds.

Almost every where big crowds—many curious people.[23]

For the next ten days he was, as he wrote Karl, "running in and out of New York going like a race horse every minute." He had two engagements on November 4—Newark, New Jersey, in the day, Brooklyn in the evening—and two on the fifth—Baltimore in the afternoon, Hoboken, New Jersey, at night. At Sherwood's urging that this was their only time for a "decent visit," Karl took the train with him on the Baltimore trip, and the brothers made a splendid whiskey-flavored morning call on Mencken. The sixth was a day of rest, but Anderson apparently used it for writing; on the seventh, in addition to lecturing at the New School of Social Research, he sent off to Bennett Cerf an introduction for the forthcoming Modern Library edition of *Poor White* with its often-quoted claim that "The town was really the hero of the book. . . . What happened to the town was, I thought, more important than what happened to the people of the town." The well-to-do young Cerf had recently purchased the very profitable Library from Horace Liveright, set up The Modern Library Incorporated (later Random House) as his own firm, and hoped to repeat the Library's success with *Winesburg, Ohio* with another book by an author at the moment much in the public eye. Part or perhaps whole payment for the introduction was a complete set of Modern Library books, which Anderson had shipped to Mrs. Greear to hold until his writing cabin was built. His final stipulation to Cerf was that the original dedication of *Poor White* to Tennessee Mitchell Anderson should be omitted, as it was, in the new edition.[24]

One reason for Liveright's willingness to sell the Library may well have been that he needed money for, among other speculative ventures, a production of *Hamlet* done in modern dress, with Basil Sydney as the Prince. Between lecture engagements in Philadelphia and Ithaca, New York, Anderson was able to attend the opening night of the play on November 9 and was so moved by the performance and the applause and cheers of the audience that on the eleventh he wrote a protesting letter to the *New York Times*, whose drama critic, unlike most other reviewers, had treated the event only in "an academic way," ignoring the wild enthusiasm of the audience. The critic had missed what Anderson felt to be "the important thing about the whole production":

Taking off the trappings at once took something of the dead old strut out of the players. The players were close to us, and the tremendously important thing is that this beautiful old play suddenly became all alive again and seemed a part of our age.[25]

This protest of a modernist made, Anderson was almost ready to leave the "mad rush" in and around New York. On the evening of the twelfth, a night of driving rain, he was accompanied by a woman interviewer in the taxi ride to the Jersey ferry and on to Englewood for his last lecture. The following March, *Success* magazine published the results of her interview, "not one word of which," Anderson complained to Bab irritably, "is true." Actually, except for the usual lapses in biographical accuracy, no doubt his own, the interview seems remarkably "true"; for his reported opinions mostly fit with those expressed elsewhere—that a writer's "early environment . . . becomes the background of his tales"; that women who write are "neither one thing or another," merely "mules," a judgment the interviewer does not accept; that he admires the Old Testament for its "beautiful simple prose, the poetry and rhythm of it"; that Dreiser broke the ground for the new writers; that "the true history of life is but a history of moments, and it is only at rare moments that we live." Talking with the interviewer on the way back to New York, he comments provocatively of *Dark Laughter* that

I couldn't have written that novel if I hadn't lived in New Orleans. The plot of course, could have been used anywhere, but it is what happens to the story after you think and feel about it for a long time that is important. It is your reaction to the story that counts, not the plot. I think the form of *Dark Laughter* is complete. It functions all the way through.

After stating that he judges any other writer on "his grasp of form—does he really completely function in the materials that he is handling," he explains, here for the first of several times, why he writes novels as well as stories.

The novel is more fascinating and difficult than the short story, however. You do the latter in a rush, in one sitting, but with the novel you must carry the mood five or six months through all sorts of things that interrupt that mood. That is why we respect the novelist more than we do the writer of the short story.

The interview ends back in Pennsylvania Station in New York with Anderson "dashing for the train that was to take him West" and the interviewer exclaiming that "Now he is considered by many America's most interesting writer. Certainly he looks like a genius." Reading the interview later, Anderson may have bridled at "genius" as being, however flattering, a journalistic exaggeration, and he may have disliked appearing in a magazine called so crassly *Success*, but he could not have foresworn his opinions.[26]

He journeyed back to his own Midwest via engagements in York and Lancaster, Pennsylvania, Fort Wayne, Indiana, and Toledo. This last was home territory or near it, as evidenced by an article in the *Toledo Times* prior to the lecture date summarizing the "Toledoan" George Richards's recollections of "Job Lots" Anderson when he clerked in Richards's dry goods store years before in Clyde. "Anderson was a queer sort of a boy," Richards recalled in his kindly, generally accurate memories, "giving little promise of the genius which later flowered in his life. . . . He was industrious enough but sort of detached and different from other youths even at that age." This portrait of a dual Jobby the Dreamer was augmented by an interview published in the *Toledo Blade* on November 19, the day of his lecture that evening before the Women's Educational Club. "Jobby," was now a "calmly cheerful . . . 'just folks'" person, the interviewer reported, even though "one of the most talked about figures in the field of American letters." Anderson praised Dreiser, Mencken, and D. H. Lawrence ("a genuine genius") and responded firmly to a question whether he wanted to "uplift the world" through his own writings.

> "Have I, as an author, 'a mission to perform?' None that I can think of—except, of course, to be a story-teller. I'm interested in people as human beings and as material but I don't want to change them. I'd be afraid to, even if I could. When a man sets out to reform the world he should have something to offer which he is sure is better. And I haven't."[27]

He was in a genial mood for the interview because Elizabeth had arranged to meet him in Cincinnati on the twentieth, and he would have ten days respite with her from the lecturing grind. Coming west he had already begun relaxing by reading Van Wyck Brooks's recent *The Pilgrimage of Henry James* and had praised the book for showing "much more real sympathy with and understanding of your man than in the Twain"; his mood was heightened by his having received from Julia Harris clippings of Stuart Sherman's review article on *Dark Laughter* and an amusing column by Heywood Broun in the New York *World* suggesting that "Sherwood Anderson might live as the most important novelist of our day." Now he had time to work at preparing "a book of essays and fragments" intended for spring publication by Liveright under the odd title of *Wind and Water*, eventually *Sherwood Anderson's Notebook*. Probably on November 23 he and Elizabeth went to stay the rest of their time in Springfield, Ohio, where they visited Wittenberg College, arranged to buy two Currier and Ives prints at The Bookshop, and, best of all, began receiving word that their financial problems were over, at least for the present. *Vanity Fair* had purchased for two hundred dollars Anderson's occasionally funny parody of movie plots published in January as "Aching

Breasts and Snow-White Hearts: Being Some Fan Letters of Ezra Bone of
Elmore, Tennessee, to Gloria Swanson." Further, Donald Freeman of *Vanity Fair* wanted to have as soon as possible the piece on New Orleans Anderson had promised him in New York, and Freeman, alert to Anderson's
current fame as in *Vanity Fair*'s words, "one of the most promising of
American novelists," was also eager to have more articles by him. A few
days later a long wait was over when Otto Liveright mailed him a check
"for three thousand six hundred dollars covering the full payment from
Woman's Home Companion for *A Mid American Childhood*," which Anderson had just decided he would like to call *Tar* with *The Story of a Mid-American Childhood* as subtitle. This check, put together with the lecturing fees, the monthly one hundred dollars from the Liveright contract, and
Horace's assurance in New York that *Dark Laughter* would sell twenty-five thousand copies, showed that, as he wrote Stieglitz, he seemed "to be
riding a good horse."

Well, I intend to harvest if I can. Last year I was terribly in debt. This year I am
paying out, getting a little money ahead. I shall pay for the little Virginia farm and
have money to build a little stone house.[28]

Only three weeks were left on the first leg of the lecture tour, but they
were a whirl of engagements across the Midwest: November 30, Pittsburgh, where he presumably saw his friends Roger and Ruth Sergel; December 2, Indianapolis, where he certainly saw Bab Finley; December 3,
Detroit; December 5, Grand Rapids, Michigan; December 7, Columbus,
Ohio; December 9, Kansas City. A brief break during which he sent detailed instructions to John Greear in Troutdale for the building of the hilltop writing cabin by Marion Ball. Then on the road again: December 12,
Iowa City; December 14, in the afternoon Minneapolis, in the evening St.
Paul, at night houseguest of the University of Minnesota professor Joseph
Warren Beach, who was just then writing a perceptive discussion of Anderson's "imaginative prose"; December 16, Aberdeen, South Dakota;
December 17, again Minneapolis for a final talk at Ulrichs Book Shop.
That same night, weary of getting to "know no one" on his rapid tour, of
seeing "Faces pass like blown things before a window in a storm," he was
on the train for New Orleans.[29]

During the two weeks at home over the Christmas season Anderson
"spent most of the time," he complained to a Boston friend, "at the dentist's," and he did have two teeth pulled and two filled, and faced more
work on his poorly kept teeth in the near future; but he was busy with
other matters as well. He brought his accounts with Leigh up to date. For
his thirty-two lectures he had grossed $4,530 in fees at an average of
$141.25 a lecture. Less Leigh's commission of 20 percent he had earned

$3,624. Even deducting travel and living expenses he had done well. Despite his expressed disdain for authors who wrote for financial success, all this money coming in from various directions tempered his wry amusement that *Vanity Fair* was now willing to pay him much more for his pieces than formerly and that Mencken had solicited a contribution to *The American Mercury* on which Anderson could set his own price. As Mencken had recently written him: "You have come to such a position in a few years that not all the professors will ever be able to shake you out of it." He had, however, come some distance from the artist of "Blackfoot's Masterpiece" who, though poor, does the "lovely thing" of burning the few hundred dollars he had received from the sale of his greatest painting. Early in December, Otto Liveright had informed him that his "Notes Out of a Man's Life," written in the spring of 1924, had been liked "tremendously" by the editorial department of *Vanity Fair* but that the business department had "demanded" cuts of material—Anderson had written in one of spending a night with a prostitute—that might have an "effect upon certain advertisers and subscribers." Instead of indignantly withdrawing the manuscript, Anderson now accepted the cuts as "all right," and he was promised publication in the March issue of the magazine.[30]

Christmas Day he spent more happily than usual reading alternately in Amy Lowell's *John Keats* and Dreiser's *An American Tragedy,* just published by Boni and Liveright, and then writing a review of the novel for the *Saturday Review of Literature.* The Keats biography he liked for its "fine sensual love of words," precisely the quality, he emphasized, Dreiser's "heavy cumbersome sentences" have always lacked; yet Dreiser's "great human tenderness and his ability to create unforgettable people," make him "the most important American writing. More than that—the most important man writing English." Most of this two-week break, however, he spent in final preparation of *Sherwood Anderson's Notebook: Containing Articles Written During the Author's Life as a Story Teller, and Notes of his Impressions from Life Scattered through the Book,* the typescript of which, containing his original version of the *Vanity Fair* piece, he got into the mail on the last day of the year. He dedicated the book to "Two Friends M. D. F. [Marietta D. Finley] and John Emerson," since, as he wrote Bab the day before Christmas, "Surely this book—in an odd way belongs to you. There are in it so many little notes—half addressed to you when written—." It was a kind of Christmas present to the woman who over the years had had perforce to serve as confidante for so many of Anderson's "little notes." One wonders what she and Sherwood and Elizabeth said and thought when, in the last few busy days of 1925, Bab visited New Orleans, perhaps even staying with the Andersons, until January 2 when she left for Indianapolis and they for Los Angeles and the second leg of Sherwood's lecture tour. "It seemed very rotten," he did write Bab from his train, "that you should have been in New Orleans and that I got so little of you. Still there was the walk by the river. I am glad we had that without the others around." Elizabeth need not have been too concerned by the visit. She and Sherwood had decided that if they had money enough, they would spend next fall and winter in Europe.[31]

4.

The Coast tour was shorter, only ten or eleven lectures, though these were spread from Long Beach in southern California, where he had his first engagement on January 5, to Seattle, where he spoke last at the University of Washington on the evening of the twenty-eighth. In between he lectured in the Bay Area: Modesto on January 8, San Francisco on the eleventh, Mills College in Oakland on the fourteenth, and Stockton on the fifteenth. Then he took trains south to an engagement at La Jolla (January 18), back up to San Francisco (January 20), again south to Los Angeles (January 22), again north all the way to Eugene and the University of Oregon (January 25), probably to Reed College in Portland (January 26), and finally on to Seattle, where he addressed a sell-out audience of seven to eight hundred university students and faculty on "America—A Storehouse of Vitality," on Americans living "in an age of things, of physical facts, but even so . . . not quite sold on the things for which they sell their souls." The "Famed Author" was lionized in Seattle and enjoyed it despite arriving in the city the evening before with so bad a cold that he took to his hotel room bed at once and gave a newspaper interview in his flannel pajamas. "American literary appreciation," he cheerfully told the interviewer, has improved and now allows "greater frankness" in writing, adding, "I don't believe in dragging things into stories just to shock . . . but frankness does make it possible to bring the reader into closer touch with life." On the twenty-eighth before the lecture he was again interviewed, taken on a tour of the city and the university district, and honored by a student-faculty dinner at the Wilsonian hotel. The lecture, given in his "'story telling' manner" was one of his successes.[32]

On this second leg of his tour there was no New York rush to distract him, he could see something of Elizabeth, who was visiting her family in Berkeley, and he earned at least $1,260 after Leigh's commission but before travel expenses; yet the tour had been a strain. Trying wearily toward the end to sort out his experience with lecturing, he felt that the crowds had liked him and that he had some special "hold on the imaginations of the young"; but he also felt that "To attempt to influence any great number of people is to influence no one." Then, too, he had begun to notice in himself the public speaker's tendency to say things "for their effect—not for their worth." Lecturing had finally grown so "distasteful" to him, so contrary to his nature, that on the Coast tour he had "become ill every time" he had to speak. On balance he concluded that he never wanted to do a lecture tour again.[33]

On February 5 the Andersons headed home from Berkeley, apparently going roundabout through Montana, where Sherwood was too ill with his cold to meet a last-minute lecture engagement, and arriving in New Orleans on the tenth or eleventh. As usual, unopened correspondence was piled up on his desk, and on the fifteenth he and a secretary began cutting it down. To Mary Blair, actress wife of Edmund Wilson, he confessed only fitful interest in the theater.

I presume that the trouble with me is that I have never gone to the theatre much and my imagination has never played very freely within the confines of the theatre and when I am in New York and if I am lucky enough to see a good play or two, I get all stirred up again and when I come away the excitement oozes out of me. I get caught up by some novel or story and the theatre is quite forgotten.

He described his same problem with playwriting to Frederick O'Brien, now living in Italy, though he had thought of writing a play about Paul Robeson after he met the actor in New York and was "crazy about him as one of the few negroes I have seen who is able to be interested in the arts and live as an artist without a terrific self-consciousness." The journalist David Karsner, who in an article in the *New York Herald Tribune Magazine* was perpetuating the legend of Anderson's abrupt departure from business as a deliberate act, had written him concerned about a *Times* report that the manuscript of *Sherwood Anderson's Notebook* had been destroyed in a slight fire at Boni and Liveright's; Anderson could now reassure him that the manuscript had only been singed and was still usable.[34]

At about this time he also replied to a letter from Bab which, he said, he had been "turning . . . over in my mind all night." Possibly prompted by their walk together by the Mississippi, Bab seems to have told him that she was going to do more financially for the Anderson children beyond the monthly one hundred dollars she had been sending Cornelia for their support since about 1920, the increase perhaps to take the form of a separate fund for their college education. (In all, the three children received from Bab, through their mother, during the 1920s at least eight thousand dollars, perhaps more.) Sherwood advised Bab that she probably should not tell Cornelia of her intention and certainly not the children lest they "begin thinking of you in terms of their own interest—now or later." He expressed great gratitude for Bab's generosity, but made it clear that their own relationship remained unchanged; he "felt proud" of knowing beforehand that she had reconciled herself to not asking of him more than he was willing to give. It was not one of his more generous letters.[35]

Perhaps he was saving his generosity for current visitors. Ring Lardner and his wife came to New Orleans for Mardi Gras, which fell that year on February 16, and had what Lardner would call "two long and entertaining sessions" with the Andersons, at least one of them being a dinner the Andersons gave for Lardner and friends in a little French restaurant in the Quarter, an occasion so happy that Ring for the moment dropped his usual "solemn-faced" mask. A quite different occasion was a dinner given in Lardner's honor by wealthy New Orleans people, "a bunch of morons" who were "rushing" him, in Ring's acid phrase. The Lardners took the Andersons to that dinner, probably for self-protection, and Sherwood, Ring noted approvingly, "was very frank in stating his opinion of the host and local guests." Disgusted by the adulation of the wealthy, Lardner and Anderson apparently left the party and got drunk together.[36]

Another visitor was unintentionally one of the causes for a long-lasting break between Anderson and Faulkner. From at least February 15 to the end of the month, the Andersons' close friend Ferdinand Schevill was their houseguest. Learned, academic, conservative, Schevill was more interested in observing a Louisiana plantation than in exploring the Quarter's bohemia; but the Andersons wanted to have some of their New Orleans friends in to meet the distinguished historian from the University of Chicago. Among the party guests were the two Bills, Spratling and Faulkner. Faulkner had just returned from Europe and Oxford, Mississippi, for a few weeks visit to New Orleans and was staying in Spratling's attic apartment in a house on nearby St. Peter Street, newly leased by the Antonys for their decorating shop and their own apartment. (Apparently Elizabeth had turned her share of the business over to the Antonys because she was soon leaving the city.) Bill Spratling, who was teaching in Tulane's School of Architecture, was at this point making drawings for the fieldstone house the Andersons planned to build at Ripshin and was frequently at 825 Bourbon Street to patiently discuss the changes they were constantly asking for. He and Schevill liked each other and got on very well at the party and during the rest of Ferdinand's visit; but at the party, according to Elizabeth's account, Bill Faulkner "had been eyeing Ferdinand suspiciously because he distrusted anyone he regarded as stuffy or as a 'philistine.'" Elizabeth knew that he was "often difficult at parties" because he was "very sure of his own knowledge about certain things and was flatly outspoken about saying so." On this occasion he "set off upon one of his more improbable expositions, touching on an area in which Ferdinand was expert." The scholar corrected him, "perhaps somewhat pedantically," and was bewildered when Faulkner "lashed out" at him with an insulting reply. Elizabeth was so angry with Faulkner for being rude to a guest and older man that she reprimanded him sharply afterwards, but he stubbornly denied that he had been rude at all. If Elizabeth was angry,

Sherwood—made hypersensitive by weariness from the lecture tour and by an acutely distressing family matter he had just learned about—would have been furious at the insult and subsequent denial of rudeness, to one of his oldest, most loyal friends, who most recently had helped him through the difficult divorce from Tennessee. That Faulkner inscribed a copy of *Soldier's Pay* to Sherwood and Elizabeth on March 17, about the time he returned to Oxford, may have been not only a thank offering for Sherwood's recommending him and the novel to Liveright, but also an oblique apology for his behavior at the party.[37]

This event provides a context for a succeeding quarrel with Faulkner, which Anderson would recount four years later in his article "They Come Bearing Gifts," the relative closeness in time being some guarantee that he was reporting fairly accurately. One night, perhaps partly drunk, the two sat on the steps of St. Louis Cathedral "discussing the [sexual] cross between Negroes and whites"; and Faulkner obstinately argued in one of his "improbable expositions" that any resulting offspring like a mule "can't breed its own kind." When Anderson laughed at this absurd notion, Faulkner, who, Anderson felt, was "a Southerner of the Southernest" despite his superb critical insight into his region, angrily called the older man "a damn Yank, absolutely ignorant and stupid concerning all Southern things." Still quarreling, the two "separated, each walking off alone and each turning to swear at the other." Writing later in the 1930s in his *Memoirs,* Anderson would repeat Faulkner's assertion about a "cross" but omit the ensuing quarrel and would date the argument as taking place "when I first met him," an impossible dating since all other evidence indicates a continued friendship between the two at least through 1925. Further, the true content of this event is not Faulkner's assertion—he may have made it at first as a tall tale such as both men enjoyed—but rather the quarrel itself and Faulkner's lashing out insultingly against Anderson as he did at about the same time against Schevill, perhaps not incidentally another northerner. The angry swearing at each other would be Anderson's powerful general term covering a good deal of personal nastiness on both sides, and his stressed condition at the time would help make the younger man's nastiness, whatever it was, seem to him unforgivable.[38]

It has been suggested that Anderson may also have been angered at Faulkner by yet another incident, this one involving young Bob Anderson. From the attic apartment in the Antony house, Spratling and Faulkner at some time began the "diversion" of shooting with a BB rifle at the buttocks of passersby in the street below, scoring points for each hit on some painfully surprised person. Bob became so fascinated by the game that he took to visiting the apartment much too frequently, even interrupting Faulkner in his writing. To get rid of this "nuisance" the two older men one day pulled Bob's pants off, painted his penis green, and forced him out on the street. A problem with this suggested additional cause for the break is that, although Anderson may, or may not, have learned about the crude prank played on his son, the incident almost certainly occurred after Faulkner had returned to New Orleans in September, when the Andersons had been living for several months in Virginia well after the rupture.[39]

There may of course have been other causes for the break between Anderson and Faulkner, whose side of the story is not known, such as Elizabeth's vague subsequent statement in an interview: "Sherwood and Bill were too much alike. This probably caused the eventual coolness between them." But theirs was not the gradual parting of a "master" demonstrably at the height of his fame and a "disciple" certain of his own talent but not of its future recognition, two men and writers at least as different from each other as alike. Rather, it was a rupture, quick, sharp, definite; and the insult to Schevill followed quickly by the angry, vituperative quarrel in front of the cathedral seem sufficient causes for it.[40]

The rupture probably occurred around early March before Faulkner left for Oxford in midmonth. Sometime in the latter half of February the Andersons talked amiably with Bill Faulkner about *Gentlemen Prefer Blondes,* comparing Anita Loos with their new acquaintance Ring Lardner; yet on April 19 Sherwood wrote Horace Liveright again praising Faulkner even though "I do not like the man personally" and urging Horace to encourage him by writing him of this praise. "He was so nasty to me personally," Anderson would bluntly conclude, "that I don't want to write him myself, but would be glad if you were to do it in this indirect way, as I surely think he is a good prospect." The two former friends would rarely see each other in the years afterward, but Faulkner would graciously dedicate his first mature novel, *Sartoris,* "To Sherwood Anderson through whose kindness I was first published, with the belief that this book will give him no reason to regret that fact." On his part, Anderson despite personal antagonism never wavered in his admiration for Faulkner the writer. Even in "They Come Bearing Gifts" he could praise him perceptively for having "written a beautiful and sympathetic piece of work in the novel, 'The Sound and the Fury.'" Nevertheless, what Stark Young would later call the "unfortunate end" of the relationship, a phrase also suggesting an abrupt break, would leave Anderson with a sharp, long-enduring reaction against a man who had been one of his best friends, and the most gifted he had made in New Orleans.[41]

The distressing family matter, which darkened his feelings at this time and made him ready to react, even overreact, to any provocation, Anderson first learned about from a telegram he received from a stranger, Mr. S. N. A. Fyse, on February 16 stating only that his brother Earl was critically ill in New York City's Roosevelt Hospital. Sherwood at once telegraphed the news to Karl in Westport, who was away from home and did not receive the message until the morning of the seventeenth. On that day Sherwood and Elizabeth committed themselves to purchasing another house in the Quarter, a two-and-a-half story, red brick one fronting on the banquette of 713–15 Governor Nicholls Street, a house Elizabeth especially admired for its severely elegant facade and its restrained wrought iron balcony on the second floor. Meanwhile Karl in New York was seeing Earl in a Roosevelt Hospital ward for the "desperately ill," arranging his transfer to a private room, consulting doctors, visiting the lodging house in Brooklyn where Earl had been living for five years, and at the end of the day sending Sherwood a telegram and a letter. Karl explained that the long-disappeared Earl, now forty, had for four years been working as a baker's assistant in Manhattan, and on his way to work the night of February 15 he had collapsed on Amsterdam Avenue from a cerebral hemorrhage, which totally paralyzed him and left him temporarily speechless. According to Karl's later recollection, at the hospital a letter with Earl's Brooklyn address was found in his pocket, and the hospital telephoned his landlady, who knew that Earl had an author brother and who furnished the name of Liveright from a copy of *Dark Laughter* in her lodger's room. The hospital then called Horace Liveright, who in turn seems to have had one of his employees wire Sherwood. Karl's reply telegram and letter confirmed Earl's condition from the stroke as serious; the doctors' prognosis was a month's hospitalization and at best recovery of his left side from the paralysis. Karl and Sherwood would have to take care of hospital costs, though since Earl had served in the Navy during the World War, he might be eligible for admission to a marine hospital.[42]

Subsequently Karl had a sad day's task of returning to Earl's "nice . . . semi studio" room in Brooklyn, where his landlady said he had been happy but lonely, and sorting out the things to be thrown away and those to have sent to Karl's home for Earl's eventual move there. By now Earl could speak slightly, and he asked Karl to search out some of his baking earnings, which he had left scattered in bills through magazines and even behind loose wallpaper. Karl found the bills and copies of Sherwood's books, and under the bed he discovered something almost out of a *Winesburg* tale:

a stack of drawings illustrations—etc. which were remarkably fine, finer than most of the illustrations one finds in magazines—he had the ability to make a fine living and possibly great distinction [and] for years he had been mixing dough for a baker. What a tragic muddle—

Among the other belongings of this solitary, introverted "grotesque" of a brother that Karl took to Westport were a journal Earl had kept in recent years, which detailed his "antagonism against his family," an unsent letter to Sherwood, and a copy of *A Story Teller's Story* in the margins of which Earl had protested Sherwood's characterization of family members. The letter, apropos of his own "panning" in his brother's book, asserted that as a child he had received no affection from either parents or siblings and that his ego, "puny and anemic" at birth, had been made "more helpless" by "the hostility of the family."[43]

Knowing of Sherwood's actual affection for the younger brother and perhaps of his feelings of guilt for not having demonstrated it sufficiently in boyhood, Karl never showed him the journal and book, but Sherwood was already distressed enough by Karl's telegram and letter of February 17. He had "bad dreams at night, thought of little else all day," he shortly wrote to Bab. He sent a check to Karl to help with expenses, began planning to have Earl come to stay with him and Elizabeth at Troutdale as soon as the sick man could make the move, and was brought out of his obsession with his stricken brother only by the need to read proof for the forthcoming *Sherwood Anderson's Notebook* and to entertain his newly arrived guest Schevill by walking about on the levee. Then suddenly in the last days of Ferdinand's visit, perhaps prompted by his concern over Earl, he began to write Testaments again and was cheered by feeling that he was recovering his "nerve force," despite a series of painful trips he had meanwhile had to make to the dentist.[44]

By the beginning of March he had gone back to finishing a draft of the *Childhood* book and somehow made progress despite "an invasion of people" coming for visits, interviews, or brief meetings prompted by mere curiosity to see a famous writer, and interrupting his work. "Silly women bring flowers to my door—write me notes. The phone rings constantly." A more welcome visitor, however, was Edmund Wilson, who arrived for a month's stay in New Orleans about March 2 and on his first evening was taken by the Andersons to the midnight show for whites at the Lyric, the Negro theater, for a taste of the "marvelous dancing" and the "Rabelasian-Elizabethan" jokes. On their subsequent walks around the city Anderson found Wilson "likeable" but "very much the intellectual." It amazed him to see how the outside world came to Wilson, not directly as to himself, but through books. When Wilson wanted to see the river and Anderson took him there, Wilson did not observe it because he was absorbed in talking about the sea in Conrad's fiction. Later, Anderson felt, "he will read something about the Mississippi and will get it in his own way, through the mind of another." Still, Wilson consciously tried to react more directly, and indeed the contact with Anderson may have helped Wilson to achieve greater power of observation at first rather than second hand. In his "Reflections on Returning to New York from Louisiana," he could find the northern city gray but energetic, the southern one decaying but colorful, and could fill a long paragraph with recollected images.

Writing Anderson, he thanked him for being "so kind" to him in New Orleans: "if I hadn't found you when I went down there, I probably wouldn't have such a high opinion of the place."[45]

Anderson's growing impatience with incursions on his time is revealed in a *Times-Picayune* interview by his friend Lyle Saxon with him, Dorothy Dix, the paper's "advice to the lovelorn" columnist, and New Orleans author Grace King. Dix and King answer Saxon's questions seriously and at length; the answers of Anderson, said to be "the most widely discussed writer of our generation," are mostly unserious to the point of flippancy. He has "no idea what the trend of the times is," his advice to anyone starting out to write is "not to do it," what he likes best of his writings is "all my stuff." He admits that writing is "hard work"; but when he is asked, "Is success all that it is cracked up to be?" he rises, stands swinging his stick, smiles, his eyebrows raised: "Success? What do you mean—success? There isn't any such thing. It's a fool's dream." He sounds tired or not in the mood, eager to have the interview over.[46]

Or perhaps he was downcast by what he had written in a revealing four-page fragment headed "Note book Mar 5–1926" about his desire and failure to make his prose "sing," as true prose should.

The real rhythm of prose must be hidden away. It is a delicate, finely balanced thing. When it begins to sing to the tune of some popular song of the street or beats itself out with a slow monotonous rhythm you are lost.

"Every art of my life," he asserts, "every thought I have affects my writing." So when he begins a story, he may become distracted by "Katharine, my negro maid, dusting a chair" or by the memory of last night's conversation, with the result that the "minute nerve adjustment" necessary for making singing prose becomes a "maladjustment."

I am a boat that will not swing up into the wind. The rhythm of the sea of consciousness rocks me aimlessly. My sails flop about. The hand at the rudder trembles and is uncertain.

Continuing the image, he wishes his writing self to be a boat, not becalmed, but venturing constantly the sea of creativity.

There must be a feeling in the bodies of ships that make them love the sea. There is a strange sea of fancy, filled with weird crosscurrents, adverse winds, tides. I keep setting out from the shore wanting to sail for ever on the sea. There is some place to which I want to go.

Perhaps I seek Nirvana. I want to sit at a desk, my body filled with a cargo of thoughts, emotions, dreams and sail forever away into the sea of prose.

But though "Wanting that," the boat-self remains becalmed:

I lie near the shore, flapping about in the tired waves. The wind had died. My nose will not come up into the wind. My prose will not come into its proper rhythm. I shall write nothing of any account today.

Whether the failed voyage was for that day or others as well, this image was an ominous one. Less than a year later it would recur in more devastating circumstances, suggesting that it had lain like a sunken hulk beneath the surface of his activity.

Certainly a tiring visit was that by his next younger brother, Irwin (Irve), who arrived around March 26, briefly overlapping Wilson's sojourn in the city, for a two-week stay. Irve, the honest, resolute boy "Uncas" of *A Story Teller's Story* and now a tall man of forty-eight, had centered his life on his family and his job as a factory superintendent for the American Can Company in Baltimore. A hard-driving executive who out of economic necessity had forced down an obscure desire to be an artist like his two older brothers, Irve had had a "semi-breakdown" the year before and, fearful of further nervous illness, was bringing his "silent misery" to Sherwood for help. At least by April 1 Karl had brought the other afflicted brother Earl home from the hospital; but Sherwood, still concerned over Earl and occupied with finishing the *Childhood*, felt that Elizabeth, who herself was having trouble with her teeth, talked more freely and helpfully with Irve than he did. To Sherwood, who had, he wrote Bab, "to live immediately," Irve was by contrast one of the many victims of "modern industrial life," a man who felt defeated because his devotion to the job had robbed him of inner resources and because he had at last realized—the one hopeful sign, Sherwood thought—that he had always had "a queer inferiority complex." By the end of his visit Irve seemed somewhat better, but before returning to Baltimore and his job, he confessed that "After years of running a factory . . . he hated factories." Sherwood did feel that Earl's illness had brought into closer sense of brotherhood himself, Irve, and Karl, who had written sympathetically that he had once gone through a nervous crisis similar to Irve's. Sherwood, who had had his own nervous crises, may have been convinced at the moment that the "only way" was to live immediately and may have been able with his writer's insight to analyze Irve's conflicted state of mind; but it seems extremely likely that his near-simultaneous knowledge of his three brothers' emotional problems helped to push him closer to the emotional collapse that would strike him within a year.[47]

By the time Irve left, around April 9, life would indeed be lived more immediately. Despite an unusually cold, wet spring, the roses were gorgeous throughout the city that year, and the chinaberry tree in the courtyard at 825 Bourbon was about to put out bloom. Word came that Sherwood's writing cabin at Ripshin was finished. He had survived his many sessions with the dentist, and after Elizabeth had had four teeth extracted, she was feeling herself again. It was definite that, after their Spratling-designed stone house was built in the coming summer, they would be going to France, partly because Elizabeth had never been abroad, partly because, as Sherwood wrote Karl, "My own European vogue is just beginning. My appearance over there would help just now." Proof of the vogue came from Marguerite Gay, his French translator, who sent him a just published copy of the quarterly *Les Cahiers du Mois* titled *l'Homme Qui Devint Femme* and largely devoted to translations into French of three of Anderson's tales—"The Man Who Became a Woman," translated by Bernard Faÿ, French professor of American culture and friend of Gertrude Stein, and "Broken" ("Debris") and "The Man's Story" ("Histoire de l'Homme") by Jean Riviere. Also included were a laudatory introduction by Faÿ, an article on Anderson by Andre Berge, and an article by Faÿ on contemporary American literature praising Anderson as a poet who has invented "une forme originale . . . une melopee en frome d'histoire" (a recitative in story form). Writing to Madame Gay to thank her, he told her happily that Eugene Jolas, a young French poet summering in New Orleans with his Kentucky-born wife, considered the translation "very good." Jolas, he added, was translating an anthology of American poems for French publication and wanted to include several of the poems in *Mid-American Chants* and "A New Testament." As further proof of a French "vogue," Madame Gay had sent word two months earlier that, as contracted, she had turned in to the publishing firm of E. Rieder et Cie the manuscript of her translation of seven of Anderson's tales from *The Triumph of the Egg* and *Horses and Men*. The translations would appear in the spring of 1927 as *Un Paien de l'Ohio,* the first Anderson volume to be published in French. She may not have been aware that in addition Professor Regis Michaud was lecturing at the Sorbonne from February to May on "Le Roman Americain d'Aujourd'hui" and was giving his major attention to Dreiser, Cabell, and Anderson.[48]

"A man's life is his work," Anderson wrote Karl in early April, and on the whole the work was for the moment going well. Despite distractions he had by late March completed a draft of the *Childhood* Book, "adding several long chapters that are not in the Companion version," and had set it aside "to stew for a time." Then he had gone "like a crazy man" into a new novel his fingers had been itching to get at, a novel tentatively titled either *Another Man's House* or *Other People's Houses* with a theme, presumably the hidden lives of outwardly dull people, that "fascinated" him. For protagonist he had gone back to Talbot Whittingham, who was to be "an odd mixture" of a man, and as material he was drawing for the first time on his experience as an advertising writer and a businessman. Probably because the novel contained "a kind of real truth in it and a lot of rather bitter plainness," he made several false starts until toward the end of April he felt he had got "the mood, the tune, the rhythm of the whole," though he was not yet sure whether the characters, who interested him as people, really matched rhythm and theme. Unless they did he would have to begin all over again. As it turned out, he never would finish the novel, though he would subsequently go back to wrestle with it from time to time, and eventually settled for publishing short sections as separate tales. His aborted starts may well have resulted from the unpleasant, even upsetting memories his subject matter would inevitably have evoked.[49]

In between bouts with the novel, he quickly wrote two short pieces for *Vanity Fair* because their subjects "delighted" him. The first, "New Orleans: A Prose Poem in the Expressionist Manner," uses a semiliterate speaker to give images of the city's civilization, which "aint no intellectual civilization" but rather a colorful lively one "bedrocked in ships, in song, in the Mississippi River"—yet on the verge of being corrupted by "boomers" and investors. His own "investment" from this fragment was $100 less Otto Liveright's 10 percent. Then shortly before April 25 a telegram from *Vanity Fair* offered him $400 for a contribution to a special July issue celebrating the one hundred and fiftieth anniversary of the Declaration of Independence, and he "got right at it." "Hello Big Boy: An Inquiry into America's Progress During One Hundred and Fifty Years" rapidly surveys American history from the Revolution through Andrew Jackson, who "made the common man politically conscious," and Lincoln, the nation's one "poet in power," and into "the mechanical age," which, as Anderson had been saying on his lecture tour, "did away with much drudgery, but . . . tended also to destroy individuality" through standardization of minds as well as of things. Democracy itself standardizes life when, as with Prohibition, the majority makes the minority conform; but Anderson, who rejects being a reformer, whose "central interest is in human life," and who "believes also that I am a pretty typical American," is confident that the state's power to dictate what one should eat, drink, think, and say is weakening. Weakening also is the earlier imitation of British art and writing, now in favor in America of "artists who spring up naturally in a country, who get their inspiration as story-tellers, painters, singers and builders, out of the life of their own country and out of the people directly about them." In sum, "America is getting somewhere," and on this anniversary of the nation Anderson is "glad" to be an American.[50]

The appearance of "Hello, Big Boy" as the lead article in the "Sesqui-Centennial Issue" of *Vanity Fair*—the opposite page displayed "The Early

Stuart Portrait of Washington"—marked a high point in Anderson's reputation, at least among the magazine's sophisticated readers, and he was
honored further in that issue. A feature was a page of photography of
seven writers designated as "Signers of Our Literary Declaration of Independence . . . Some Important American Authors Who Have Founded a
Tradition of Their Own in Native Letters." Anderson's picture is in the
center in a wide, attention-drawing frame and is surrounded by pictures
in narrow frames of Lardner, Sandburg, Masters, O'Neill, Lewis, and
Dreiser. The caption beneath his photo announces smugly: "Sherwood
Anderson had to fight the dull incomprehension of an Ohio town to become an artist. He represents the revolt of New America from crude materialism and the great cult of bovine contentment." It was praise but in so
self-satisfied a tone that one hopes Anderson felt uncomfortable with it as
well as pleased, since his article, for all its breeziness, had seriously summarized his beliefs and attitudes toward American civilization.[51]

The Andersons' last days in New Orleans were busy ones. Early in
April they had started to pack books and small items, and by the twelfth
professional packers began crating their furniture for shipment to Troutdale. "Really hungering now for the hills," and a long summer's work in
his new writing cabin, Sherwood went "steadily along into the novel, writing at every odd moment," setting himself a fast pace, he wrote Bab, "like
a horse prepared for a race." But he soon had to drop out of the running.
On the twenty-first at Horace Liveright's telegraphed request he had
dashed off a brief statement concerning *Tar* for the firm's fall catalog. The
book, completed in first draft and to be revised after two months' work on
the novel, concerned a boy's developing consciousness of self, family,
neighborhood, town up to his adolescence. It was "of course partly autobiographical . . . but not written as autobiography," and, he emphasized,
"the book's value must be in the charm of the telling of the story."[52]

The odd moments snatched for the novel became fewer with the word
that Earl, who had been improving at home with Karl in Westport, had
had another stroke and had been rushed to a hospital in nearby Norwalk
where he might have to stay for some time. April 25 was final clean-up day
for letters. Sherwood sent off the bad news to Bab and to Cornelia, who
had been close to Earl in Elyria days. Irwin, too, he told Cornelia, remained unwell and discouraged, but at least son Bob was "doing splendidly" as a New Orleans newspaperman and had even written a poem. He
wrote to Karl's wife, Helen, expressing sympathy for the burden Earl's illness was placing on her and insisting that his brothers and sisters really
had loved Earl "more than we ever loved each other. We weren't a very
tender lot. Restless ambition seemed to drive us all on." He told Karl that
"there should be a portrait of me by you," perhaps to be painted that summer if he and Helen would come to Troutdale for a visit. He explained to

Otto Liveright about the article for the special issue of *Vanity Fair*—Otto would received his 10 percent fee—and he assured Horace that the theme of the new novel was "in a way the most comprehensive and intriguing . . . I have ever tackled and I do hope I will be able to pull it off." He regretfully told Gertrude Stein that the copy of her new *The Making of Americans* she had sent him had got packed off to Troutdale with his other books, but he would "dip into" it there. Just yesterday, he added, he had read Hemingway's story "The Undefeated" in *This Quarter:* "It was a beautiful story, beautifully done. Lordy but that man can write." Presumably Stein was no more aware than he that Hemingway's parody of both their styles in *The Torrents of Spring* would be issued by his new publisher, Scribner's, in just over a month.

Sherwood's last letter, dated April 28, 1926, was to D. T. Flynn, Agent authorizing him to collect rents on the house at 713–15 Governor Nicholls Street, which on the twenty-sixth Elizabeth had purchased for $2,750 cash. The Andersons were never to live in this house nor again in New Orleans. On the twenty-ninth, just as the first hot nights of spring were beginning, they left the city for more permanent residence in the far southwest corner of Virginia.[53]

18

Collapse

1.

When the Andersons arrived in Troutdale on May 1, the whole Greear family welcomed them happily. The boys were delighted to be pitching horseshoes again with Sherwood, and when he purchased a Star car, they were as proud as though they owned it themselves. The first motor excursion of Andersons and Greears together was an evening visit to what was now named Ripshin Farm to dedicate the new writing cabin. Built solidly of square-cut chestnut logs with wide windows and a great fieldstone fireplace, it stood on a hill alongside a mountain road with a forest at its back and, in front, a magnificent view of the farm below and of sensually rounded hills rising fold on fold beyond. Anderson opened a bottle of "some very old Italian wine," and they all stood drinking it and watching a violent thunderstorm flashing wildly over Pine Mountain. Within a day or two Anderson was driving regularly each morning over from the Greear home, where he and Elizabeth were temporarily staying, and up the hill to the cabin, admiring the dogwood and mountain laurel just coming into bloom around it in this cold, late spring, and sitting down at his built-in writing desk to work at his "strange intense novel," *Another Man's House.*[1]

Marion Ball was ready to work on another man's house too. Ball, who had overseen the construction of the writing cabin, was a huge mountain man in his sixties, with a face like that of George Washington in the Gilbert Stuart portrait. A former moonshiner, then builder of sawmills, Ball accepted as his first task the conversion of the old barn into a garage and a two-bedroom apartment, into which the Andersons moved early in June so that they could keep an eye on the building of the main house. Using Spratling's plans, local materials, and his own skills and those of neighboring hill farmers, Ball then began raising Ripshin, designed to be a two-story house of fieldstone with two one-story, squared-log wings in the rear connected by a screened-in porch. Since it was sited at the foot of the valley, as the original farmhouse had been, and its wide front would look up toward hillsides, the new house lacked the wide-ranging view from the writing cabin; but it was protected here from winter storms, and one end was close to Ripshin Creek just above where it joined Laurel Creek. Sherwood would love the sound of the stream that came to him, when the house was built, through the windows of the spacious master bedroom at that end of the first floor or through the glass doors leading out to a tiny balcony from the bedroom above, one of three bedrooms on the second floor. Next to the master bedroom would be a large living-dining room with fieldstone fireplace, and one would step out of this room by the front door onto a flagstone terrace running the whole front width of the house. Water would be piped in by gravity from a "bold" hillside spring—Anderson much liked the mountain word "bold," meaning strong, plentiful—and served the kitchen and the downstairs and upstairs bathrooms. The plumbing was installed by the same men who laid the eighteen-inch thick stone walls, cut and set beams and rafters, and plastered the interior walls, all work performed, Anderson noted incredulously, at "common labor—15 c to 17½ cents an hour—fairly skilled men 20 to 30 c. I should be shot but its good wages here." When completed, Ripshin would not be a mansion, but it would be a large, comfortable, strikingly handsome house, "a house," Ball prophesied self-confidently, "that will stand here until Gabriel blows that Trumpet."[2]

The cost of building Ripshin, even with inexpensive labor, was much on Anderson's mind. Royalties from *Dark Laughter* came in at $3,361.76 for the six-months period ending April 30, in May the novel went into its eighth printing, and he hoped that continued royalties would pay for his dream house; but he and Elizabeth wanted more reliable income besides the hundred-dollar check from Horace Liveright that appeared in each Monday's mail. In mid-May, Otto Liveright sent him $360 ($400 less Otto's commission), which *Vanity Fair* had paid for "Hello, Big Boy," and at about the same time he received a letter from Donald Freeman at that magazine proposing that he contribute a series of articles, the top payment for an article to be $250. In his circumstances the "foxy" part of Anderson's personality readily took over, and he wrote Otto asking him to tell Freeman he was interested in the proposal but to urge a price of $300 for each article. Otto was successful in his negotiations. Even though he had learned that $250 was itself "far in excess" of what other contributors received, on June 10 he reported that in order "to have Sherwood Anderson's name on our Contents Page" *Vanity Fair* had agreed to pay "$300 per article for twelve articles, six of which are to be non-leading articles of about 1700 words each and six leading articles of 2600 words each," *Vanity Fair* to suggest subjects or to approve any suggested by Anderson. By mid-June, before the contract for the twelve was signed, Freeman wired him the magazine's emergency need for an article on the South for the September issue, copy due by July 15. Anderson agreed to write it and now had assurance of thirteen months of steady income from *Vanity Fair*.[3]

Despite his need and desire for money, he was at first hesitant about accepting it from another source. Early in May he received a letter from Burton Emmett, who over a number of years would be a warm, kind, and generous friend. Born in Illinois, five years older than Anderson, Emmett had been a country newspaper editor and theatrical press agent, became an advertising copy writer, worked his way up in New York advertising firms, established with a colleague the successful Newell-Emmett Company of advertising agents in 1919, and, soon wealthy, built up fine collections in the graphic arts and first editions of modern American authors. Would Anderson, he inquired, be willing to sell his manuscripts? He had never thought much about it, Anderson replied, feeling some "shyness" concerning the matter; still, "if these sheets of paper will help run up the stone wall of my house why not let them." In a second letter he declared the idea of selling his manuscripts "a bit absurd," for he "ought to give them to anyone interested enough to want them." Still, "If I take money from you it is only because I so often need it. O Lord. I feel cheap about it, really." In the ensuing correspondence the two men would settle on a financial arrangement, but Anderson would continue to have moments of feeling shy and cheap about taking money for "the fragments of his efforts scattered about." It bordered on the commercialization of art.[4]

Mid-May brought another, very disturbing letter about money. It was from Elizabeth Graham, whom Anderson had known as Bess Van Horne, a friend of the Lay and Paden families met in his first year in Chicago. While in Elyria, Sherwood had borrowed twenty-five hundred dollars from her, in addition to sums from Elyria businessmen, very likely for his grandiose American Merchants Company venture of 1911–12. Conscience-stricken that he had lost Bess's money when he and the company collapsed—the other investors he could dismiss as business men who simply took a gamble and lost—he had long ago promised her that she would be the first one he "would take care of" as "soon as . . . books began to sell," and had at some time earlier sent her $250 in down payment. Now, however, she was living in Brooklyn, alone, desperately poor, and begged him to send her a thousand dollars. On May 21 he wrote an answer to her May 17 letter but did not send it for nearly a month; for she would not receive it until June 21 and only after she had sent him on June 12 a second distressed letter asking why he had not written and pleading in a way which must have cut like a knife that "altho I understand I have no legal claim on you, there are other things in the world, a fact which you have assured me many times." His answer pled the costs of Earl's hospitalization and, as usual, the support of his three children, and asserted that "I wake up in the night thinking" of her and of his "bad luck" over the years. There was "no use" trying to repay his debts to the businessmen, but would she be willing "to take a thousand dollars to be paid in cash within a year from date in full payment of the old score"? Still he did not send money for three days and then only a check for one hundred dollars, but she agreed to accept the thousand dollars instead of $2,250 owed her, she having let the interest "go by the board." In July he sent another small check, for which she was pitifully grateful (she had been seriously ill and it went toward paying doctors and nurses). Not until October 28 would she acknowledge the payment of the last installment of the thousand dollars, send him a final receipt, and wish him "all the good luck in the world."[5]

Anderson's own elaborate pleadings to Bess about his lack of money suggest a strong source of guilt, and that guilt probably brought back ugly memories of his business past to join with memories of his advertising years, which the subject matter of *Another Man's House* was calling up. As late as May 24 he was working every day on the novel until "so exhausted my hands tremble," he wrote Bab, but by the end of the month, in part because of such memories, he was beginning to put mornings in the cabin into short stories. He had already written Otto that he was thinking of doing brief tales about mountain men and women, some of then "uneducated, sweet people with plenty of character" who dropped by his cabin to visit out of curiosity, more of them like "country people . . . everywhere—a little more primitive, rude, violent" with their "rude emotional" religion and a mode of family life "primitive in a way you would hardly believe." Otto was also asking for short pieces for the magazine market, perhaps sections from the novel or extracts from *Tar* not taken by *The Woman's Home Companion* for its serial publication, which was beginning in its June issue.[6]

This last suggestion from Otto set Anderson to rereading—in the draft of *Tar* he had completed in April—the chapters he had then added to the early ones taken by the *Companion*, especially those dealing with Tar's awakening to girls and sexuality. The creative impulse for revising one excerpt seems to have come from his half-erotic response to the "sensual lines" of the folded hills before his cabin and to the mountain spring about him, blended with his growing awareness of the harsh yet admiringly self-sufficient lives of the hill people. Late in May he wrote Bab one of his most lyrical letters.

You become absorbed in the things of nature—the grass growing, trees in bud, then putting forth the first little hard nipples that are to become rounded fruit.
The insects that destroy, wild flowers, weeds. Trees become individuals.

How all important whether or not it rains.

I have written a short story of an old woman's death alone in the woods.

How hard and close to the ground the lives of people. One begins a little to see into lives.

The story was, of course, "Death in the Woods."[7]

For years he had tried to find the right way to tell this remarkable tale. In the earliest version yet found, one perhaps written as early as 1916 since it is typed on sheets the back of which he used in writing the *Winesburg* stories, a middle-aged newspaperman named Fred comes upon a pack of dogs in a clearing in a wood who are tearing a bundle of meat from the shoulders of a dead woman. The corpse "might have been saying" to Fred that she had always "'fed the animal hungers of man and beast'" and was still feeding them. Years later Fred recalls his sense both of terror and intense aliveness at the scene and would like to describe in words a poetic vision of life. From the first, Anderson had linked death, animal life, and the artist imagination as parts of some mystical whole; yet the emphasis here is on the observer far more than on the dead woman. In the abortive "Mother Winters" fragment in the "Paris Notebook," such a linking of animal-feeding woman and artist may be inferred, but the emphasis is on the cruelly hard life of the woman, the piece breaking off well before her death. In the episode included in the "Father Abraham" manuscript of 1924, the focus is entirely on the adolescent "bound girl" who is forced to feed animal hunger and male lust, identification being between Lincoln the story teller and the storytelling narrator in their joint empathy for the brutally used girl. The balance between the narrator and the life and death of the old woman might have been better adjusted had he completed and revised "The Death in the Forest"; but this undated manuscript recounts Ma Marvin's life and death briefly and, only incidentally, its relation to ongoing life in the small town. The piece breaks off with the narrator's statement that the narrator will now tell "the actual story of Ma Marvin's death." Very likely Anderson realized at this point that to go on would be repetitious.[8]

In the *Tar* version he came close to the balance and interconnectedness between woman and artist-observer he had apparently been groping toward. The semiautobiographical Tar is linked with the "nameless" old woman at the beginning and later in his life and his tales; the woman's brutalized existence as "bound girl" and then wife to Jake Grimes is fully detailed; her constant feeding of animal life, her trip to town with the dogs on a winter day, her death from freezing in a clearing in the woods on her return as the dogs run in a circle about her. Then, the discovery of her body, the hurrying of the townsmen—without the women included in "A Death in the Forest"—to the clearing, Tar's awed-erotic response to the woman's half-naked body, his dissatisfaction with his brother's account of the event, his slow recognition as he grows older that, "like music heard from far off," the experience required an understanding he did not have as a child—all these elements are there, united in a whole, even to the incremental suggestions of the uncanny in the circling dogs and of the terror and awe among the subsequent witnesses of this strange moonlit tableau in the snowy woods. Still, the *Tar* version lacks the final all-embracing understanding that the mature Anderson had not yet quite achieved, beyond the conclusion already recognized in the first version of the tale, that the life and "appropriate" death of the woman had been the feeding of animal hunger.

That final understanding came when, as he put it in a cover letter sent to Otto Liveright with the typed copy of the tale probably on June 5, he had "merely thrown [the *Tar* excerpt] into short story form." In addition to a number of minor changes in phrasing and the division of the text into five sections, the storyteller made three important revisions. First, he changed the third-person Tar to a first-person narrator, even assigning to the "I" the same childhood illness he would assign to himself in the *Memoirs*, thus bringing the whole story closer to his storytelling self. Second, at different points he added significant words in describing the body of the woman, old before her time. It now looks not simply like that of a young girl, but as a "charming," a "beautiful" one, and her frozen flesh is not only white but also as lovely in its resemblance to marble, so that the boy "I's" response now more emphatically combines the erotic and the aesthetic, his body now trembling "with some strange mystical feeling." Third and most important, in rewriting the ending Anderson discovered for himself and his readers the essential understanding he had sought for during years of failed attempts. The hard, lonely life of the woman, who suffers dumbly knowing no other possible life, indeed consists of feeding animal hungers, and she continues to feed them after death with a completeness of existence, which, the mature narrator now asserts, "has its own beauty," as all commonplace things do. Yet that completeness of her life and death involves also the continued lives of the animals, the revelation of the beautiful, girlish body, lovely as marble beneath the outward appearances of this despised and neglected person, the effect of her strange death on the community, which at last and too late takes her in by casting out her brutal husband and son, and the effect of her life and mode of death on a boy who repeatedly tries to understand the meaning of his experience, telling the story again and again until in its final telling he understands that the imagination complements and completes reality. "A thing so complete"—a life, a death, an understanding, a story—"has its own beauty."

In a comment revealing the taboos of many magazine editors in the

1920s, Otto Liveright replied to Anderson's cover letter: "Death in the Woods" is a fine story but one which I think all of the better paying magazines will reject because they will consider some of the relationships you mention as being illicit and, therefore, not pure as Ivory soap for their readers." *Harper's* did turn the story down, but Liveright soon sold it to a delighted Henry Mencken for *The American Mercury*'s September issue for $325. On the letter bringing news of this "very pleasant" transaction, a calculation in Anderson's hand shows that he would receive $292.50.[9]

"Death in the Woods" would be his finest accomplishment in an increasingly hectic summer, would be one of the finest in his literary career. He needed all of his conviction that he had at last told the story right, for he was receiving some blows against his confidence in his craft. Concerning *Sherwood Anderson's Notebook*, published on May 14, he wrote defensively to Gertrude Stein that it was a "rather slight thing"; yet he must have been disturbed, when he eventually saw them, that of the five reviews, which appeared in May, three were negative. Walter Yust and the faithful Julia Harris praised the book highly; but his old friend Harry Hansen politely questioned the pronouncements in this collection though admiring Anderson's "simple and well-placed words," and the critics for the *New York Times Book Review* and the *Boston Evening Transcript* were not even polite. The former found that the essays offered nothing new in ideas and were written with an "affectation of frankness," while the latter dismissed the author contemptuously as being a confused man "groping with the problems which confront most youths of eighteen and which are usually satisfactorily solved by the age of twenty-three," as being "troubled, like a boy approaching puberty," as "vainly crying in his child-like distress."[10]

As the title suggests, the *Notebook* is a "fragmentary thing," gathering together as it does ten essays or articles, one story ("A Meeting South"), and five sections labeled "Notes Out of a Man's Life," all, except for the last four sections of "Notes," published between 1917 and 1926. Yet the nonfiction pieces show a familiar consistency in Anderson's ideas over the nine-year period from "An Apology for Crudity" to "After Seeing George Bellows' Mr. and Mrs. Wase." The onslaught of industrialism has disfigured the American landscape, disrupted the American social fabric, focused Americans narrowly on money-getting, standardized American minds as much as the products of the machines. Nevertheless, despite the confusion of modern life the American writer must deal with that life, cease manufacturing standardized, formulaic writing, and recover the workman's honest sense of his craft and, in this way, revitalize America. ("Ahab had seventy sons in Samaria," runs the cryptic epigraph of the book, taken from 2 Kings 10:1, perhaps Anderson's "prophecy" of the end of an unregenerate America as the prophet Elisha had announced that "the whole house of Ahab shall perish," because of its worldliness and worship of false gods.) Likewise the "Notes Out of a Man's Life" are gatherings of fragments, brief commentaries, and sketches written during the New Orleans years, yet display recurrent themes—Anderson's preference for blacks ("the sweetest people"), workers, and the poor rather than the rich; the "difficult and puzzling" sexual relations between men and women; the demands of art and its importance in life. As he knew, the *Notebook* was not one of his major books, but the contempt of the *Times* and the *Transcript* reviews could not help but hurt him.

Someone at Boni and Liveright would almost certainly have sent him clippings of the reviews and also of Scott Fitzgerald's admiring review in the May *Bookman* of Hemingway's *In Our Time.* "How to Waste Material: A Note on My Generation" incidentally praised Anderson's "difficult simplicity" and the excellence of "The Egg," but condemned his lapses into "disorganization," praised his "brilliant and almost inimitable prose style" but asserted that he had "scarcely any ideas at all," and concluded that his "sentimental 'horse stories' . . . inaugurated his respectability and also his decline four years ago." Disliking *Dark Laughter,* Fitzgerald ignored his earlier liking for *Many Marriages* and thus casually wrote Anderson off as a has-been.

In this dismissive judgment Fitzgerald was following the lead of his new friend, Ernest Hemingway, who by attacking the man who encouraged his career had broken out of his contract with Horace Liveright and gone over, as Fitzgerald had been urging, to the latter's publisher, Scribner's, with its renowned editor Maxwell Perkins. When he was first in Paris, Hemingway had spoken highly of Anderson as friend and storyteller, and even as late as early 1925 he enthusiastically reviewed *A Story Teller's Story* as "a fine book" by "a very great writer"; but he had become increasingly annoyed by suggestions that he had been much influenced by Anderson, and he felt that *Many Marriages* and *Dark Laughter*—Sherwood had sent him a signed copy of the latter—were bad books, so bad that they deserved public ridicule. In a week at the end of November 1925 Hemingway wrote *The Torrents of Spring,* mainly a parody and satire of *Dark Laughter* intended, he boasted in a letter to Ezra Pound, "to destroy Sherwood and various others." Sherwood, he gloated, would never "be able to write again." Convinced that *Torrents* was "the funniest book since *Joseph Andrews,*" Hemingway insisted on reading it aloud to several different people. Hadley thought it a "detestable" attack; Bernardine Szold, friend of Tennessee and recently divorced wife of Otto Liveright, was "stunned" by Hemingway's gloating over what she considered a malicious, badly written book; John Dos Passos was amused by it but argued against publication. Backed, however, by Fitzgerald, Pauline Pfeiffer (who was intent on becoming the second Mrs. Hemingway), and his own dark need to "destroy" as well as free himself from a benefactor, Hemingway sent off the manuscript to Horace Liveright, who, as Hemingway expected, rejected it on the grounds that it was an assault on one of his chief authors and was less successful as parody than Hemingway declared it. Now that Liveright's refusal of his second book released him from his contract for two books beyond *In Our Time,* Hemingway took his manuscript to Perkins and Scribner's, who accepted it for publication as a means of acquiring Hemingway's not yet completed novel, *The Sun Also Rises.*[11]

As parody *The Torrents of Spring* hardly ranks with that minor masterpiece *A Parody Outline of History* (1921) by Hemingway's friend Donald Ogden Stewart, one of the originals for Bill Gorton in *The Sun;* but it has its amusing, if sometimes heavy-handed, moments, and the chief target of its satire is unmistakable. The opening chapter is an obvious take-off on that in *Dark Laughter,* starting as it does with one Yogi Johnson at a factory window and switching to Scripps O'Neil, who like Anderson's Sponge Martin enjoys getting drunk with his wife. As what passes for plot develops—Hemingway may or may not have understood why Anderson rejected the notion of plot—elements of Anderson's *Dark Laughter* style are ridiculed. There are passages of choppy sentences, sentence fragments, and self-questionings representing modified interior monologue, intrusive authorial comments, recurring tags ("that poet chap," "that critic fellow Mencken"), repetitious, absurd ones in *Torrents,* of statement or idea. Themes from *Dark Laughter* and *Many Marriages* appear. Scripps takes as wife an older waitress in a Petoskey beanery who reads literary magazines and who proclaims of her new husband, "'You are all of America to me,'" then leaves her for a younger waitress who entrances him with literary anecdotes, and at the end of the book contemplates leaving her too, these "many marriages" being accompanied by the "dark laughter" of the beanery's black cook. Yogi Johnson, feeling something stirring inside him when a naked Indian woman walks into the beanery, follows her out into the night, stripping off his clothes as he goes. Midway in the book, however, the parodic mask slips briefly, and the attack becomes direct. Yogi Johnson thinks contemptuously of "Fred Something" in "that fellow Anderson's book," who is haunted by the man he has killed in the war. "That was the way the soldiers thought, Anderson said. The hell it was," thinks Yogi, and in his own voice Hemingway begins an essay on wartime brutality and the steps in becoming "a good hard-bodied soldier," revealing the destructive brutality, which drives the whole parody. Any amusement *The Torrents of Spring* affords must be tempered by the recognition that the caricature of Anderson's writing is, as Horace Liveright told Hemingway in his rejection letter, "bitter . . . almost vicious."[12]

Ten days before Scribner's published *The Torrents of Spring* on May 28, Anderson wrote his young Berkeley friend Ralph Church, who was leaving for Paris before studying philosophy at Oxford. Generously he also wrote notes of introduction to Stein, Galantière, and Hemingway for Church to take with him. The note to Hemingway included an invitation to visit Ripshin if he should be coming to America and an expression of admiration for "the solid fineness of your stories." It must therefore have been a singularly unpleasant shock for Anderson to receive from his young friend, about the time *Torrents* was published, an uneasily self-righteous, sometimes confused explanation for the parody of *Dark Laughter.* Fellow craftsmen should not "pull . . . punches" with each other; if a good writer like Anderson writes something "rotten," a beginner like Hemingway is obliged to tell him so, and "the tougher . . . the better." Yet *Torrents* isn't meant to be "mean" or "personal" but "just a funny joke," though an "absolutely sincere" one. Admittedly the book looks like a case of repaying kindness with ingratitude, and Anderson may be hurt; but "Outside of personal feelings nothing that's any good can be hurt by satire."[13]

Anderson showed some of his personal feelings to Bab after reading *Torrents.* The parody was "Heavy and dull" and "didn't come off," unlike Robert Benchley's brief, "brilliantly" done ghost story in the Anderson manner. In a "rather patronizing" letter Hemingway had written that he didn't want to hit his friend but had to. Anderson could hit back if "so minded," he told Bab, but had got his "fill of hitting long ago." In his reply to Hemingway on June 14 he was blunt but not unfriendly. Is it the Paris literary life that has made all of Hemingway's letters so "patronizing," as from master to pupil?

> You speak so regretfully, tenderly, of giving me a punch. You sound like Uncle Ezra [Pound]. Come out of it, man. I pack a little wallop myself. I've been middleweight champion. You seem to forget that.
> Tell the truth, I think the Scribner book will help me and hurt you. Spite of all you say, it's got the smarty tinge. You know it. Fitz and Dos must have baited you.
> But in your turn now, man, don't get sore at me. If you are going to wallop, you've got to take yours. You started it. I didn't.

Anderson still liked Hemingway and his writing, and the invitation to come to Ripshin still held.[14]

Perhaps inadvertently the letter revealed deeper feelings, however. He *has been* middleweight champion, and in a postscript he asks, "D'you ever hear of Kid McAllister—the nonpareil—that was me." In other words, he is no longer champion and nonpareil, certainly a painful admission if intended; but the blows to his self-confidence were coming fast—the recent rupture with Faulkner and the hostility in the letter from Hemingway, two young writers he had befriended and encouraged; the dismissal into literary past tense of Fitzgerald, the acclaimed voice of 1920s youth; the unkind parody of *The Torrents of Spring,* and, as they continued to appear, its generally favorable reviews, praising Hemingway at Anderson's expense; to say nothing of the initial unfavorable reviews of the *Notebook* and his uneasy feeling that *Tar* had "charm" but needed another year's work to give it more solid qualities.[15]

Very likely it was in reaction to these troubles that around mid-June he fell briefly into what he described to Otto Liveright as "one of my periodical states of blues about my work"; but he was cheered by receiving a letter from Paul Rosenfeld after a long silence. Rosenfeld praised the *Notebook* in detail, urged Anderson to contribute to *The American Caravan*, a yearbook of experimental writing he would coedit, and hinted that his plans for the first part of the summer were not settled. To Paul's delight Sherwood and Elizabeth immediately invited him to Ripshin as their first guest, and Paul set July 3 for his arrival in Marion for a week's visit. Sherwood went back to writing short pieces, making final revisions of his *Tar* manuscript, and even on occasion working on *Another Man's House,* that "little city of lives," until exhausted.[16]

One of the short pieces, mailed at the end of June to Otto Liveright, was "Another Wife," a "rather nice" story, Anderson thought. It is, indeed, a nice enough story, though rather thin, and interesting in its way. A middle-aged, moderately successful physician, a widower, is spending a summer of rest in a mountain cabin and becomes attracted to a plump, unmarried younger woman who lives with her mother and two sisters in a nearby country house. A well-to-do "modern" woman, she has taken to visiting him in his cabin evenings, smoking cigarettes, and smiling at him with wise, worldly eyes. Although he is ten years older than she, he feels boyish and uncertain before her. One evening they go for a walk, and she tells him of an unhappy affair she had had when younger with an English novelist in Paris. "Without premeditation" he takes her in his arms, she returns his kiss, and "feeling foolish, feeling frightened, glad," he begins to realize that they both wish to marry, that he will have another wife.

This romantic little tale is interesting in part for its narrative method, its presentation largely through the thoughts of the man, "dancing through his head," sometimes images linked by association, sometimes "absurd notions" leaping abruptly, disconnectedly into his "fancy." It is a fusion of the freedom of storytelling with that of interior monologue. For setting, Anderson drew on his own writing cabin, near a country house and close enough to a country road that the mountain people passing by can "stare" into it. So for the first time in his fiction Anderson included, if only as background, "the people of the hills" among whom he now lived and about whose varied natures he was planning to write. They may seem "at the bottom clear and sweet" as the mountain streams, but the men get drunk Saturday night and talk coarsely about the "modern" woman. These bits of personal experience combined with the play of the man's fancy over, for Anderson, an uncharacteristically well-described woman, give the story a curious air as though of wish-fulfilling daydream by the author. And what could this daydream have been about? Considering how soon the relationship between Sherwood and Elizabeth would begin to deteriorate, it is not unlikely that the man's repeatedly feeling "glad and foolish and frightened" at the prospect of another wife may represent some as yet only half-conscious dissatisfaction by Anderson with his third marriage, some appealing, frightening wish to be free as a widower is freed by the death of his wife, some desire for a woman physically so unlike Elizabeth in solidity of body and sexually so experienced and responsive.

2.

On the whole Paul Rosenfeld's eight-day visit was the "great fun" Anderson had predicted, though it had its trying moments. Having spent his life in appreciative criticism of other artists, Paul had decided to be creative himself and at Ripshin worked all day each day on a novel, presumably *The Boy in the Sun* (1928). Very self-critical, he might labor a day on two or three paragraphs and if not satisfied with them would walk, irritated and despondent, up to the writing cabin, where Sherwood would have to encourage him. Still, the two friends had very satisfying talks on contemporary writers and artists, and for Anderson it was a "nice feeling" having Paul about.[17]

The feeling helped him to work intensely and speedily. During the visit he had made final revisions on *Tar*, outlined his first article for *Vanity Fair*, "The South," and even gone back into *Another Man's House;* and on July 13 he mailed off fair copies of *Tar* to Horace Liveright and of the completed article to the magazine. "The South," the first "Story of America" he had suggested as overall theme for his *Vanity Fair* series, reveals how living two years in New Orleans had changed some of his ideas about what he now defines as the "southern problem," the relation of white and black "races." As before, he asserts that the southern land is "really the Negro's land because he works it, sings of it, loves it,"; but the white man owns it, and, Anderson now asserts, properly so since the "blacks"— often Anderson uses the term "niggers"—"remain children" and are treated better in the South than in the North because in the South "injustice is often tempered by real affection." Northerners, especially those "hot on justice" make their "cheap, snap northern judgments" on the problem, which is actually "the most difficult problem in America"; but their attitude "has never helped much." Even granting that southern white men continue to father many part-white children on black women—Anderson is well aware of the sexual tensions embedded in the problem—still southern white men and women best handle the problem, which cannot be solved but must be faced. "Facing it," he concludes, "may be the one thing needed for the flowering of a truly southern art, a truly southern contribution to an American civilization." (Anderson's sentiments so suited Frank Crowninshield, editor of *Vanity Fair,* that he had the article prettily printed up on pale rose paper as a booklet with a brief introduction by himself emphasizing Anderson's Americanness.)[18]

Perhaps Anderson had been reconsidering Faulkner's charges of Yankee ignorance in their recent bitter quarrel, but certainly he was no longer experiencing what he here calls "the nigger craze," which marked his earlier Southern visits. Like "all sensible white men" he wants the *Dark Laughter* things, "a kind of closeness to nature, rivers, the earth—more primitive men have that men less primitive are all seeking"; yet he now admits that this is to "want to have the cake and eat it." The phrase "more primitive" is the operative one. In the years to come he would speak out against the many "second-class" southern whites who lynch blacks "down there, in the dreadful ugly little towns," he would continue to have his own genuine affection for blacks such as he ascribed also to "the southern people with class to them," and he would add to that affection some concern for justice not shown in "The South," where he admits but simply accepts the injustice done to blacks. Nevertheless, blacks would remain for him a sweet but relatively primitive people, an abstraction. He would rarely again show the enthusiasm for black writers that he had shown for Jean Toomer during his "nigger craze" period; indeed in "The South" he complains that now a "second rate Negro poet or artist always [gets] twice the credit of an equally able white man" as the result of "northern sentimentality." Black writers and artists should be thought of simply as writers and artists, he had suggested earlier in 1926 in another context. Besides, it would be whites, he clearly implies in "The South," who would produce the most significant American art. Anderson had left the Deep South, but the Deep South had not, would not, entirely leave him.[19]

July was the busiest month yet. Even before Paul Rosenfeld arrived, the foundations of Ripshin were being laid; and by the time he left, the walls were beginning to go up. In country fashion the men worked slowly but solidly, using, to Anderson's delight, native materials, collecting stones from the farm and from all the roads in the area, fitting each stone carefully in place, getting sand and water for the mortar from the creek. Bringing presents of wild fruit, the neighbors would come by to watch the local spectacle. Anderson was amused and touched by one old woman who told him, shaking her head: "I'm afraid you came to the wrong place to write books. You can't sell them here. We never buy books—have no money. Lots of us cannot read." Always tempted himself to watch the walls go up, he would tear himself away, climb the road to his cabin, and write ferociously at, as he told Bab, "poems, short stories, articles, a novel" sometimes until his arms and shoulders ached. On July 21 he sent off to *Vanity Fair* for its October issue "Chicago—A Feeling" as the second in the "Story of America" series, this one a personal impression of the ugliness, beauty, and vitality of the nation's second city. He liked to do these pieces ahead of schedule, he explained to Donald Freeman, adding a condensed statement of his writing method:

Let them soak in me a while. Everything with me comes through feeling.
　　Then a while to let them cook.
　　You will know what I mean.

At just about that same time he read proof for "Death in the Woods" and at one sitting wrote a story, "Not Today" (never published), about a man and a woman whose love, he told Bab, "grew in a world of fancy" but was killed when brought "into the world of fact."[20]

In his letters to Bab—he was as usual keeping up his correspondence with her and others along with all his other writing—he made it clear that "Not Today" was a kind of answer to a letter from her, apparently importuning him to give more in their relationship. It was long ago settled between them, he reminded her, that it was unsound "logic" for her to "lift what we are to each other over into the world of fact." She is related to his work, to his accomplishing it, but neither to his everyday self nor even to his fanciful self. "You—all who know and care for me—have to accept something. The logical cruel cruelty of the workman." As subsequently in the introduction to the *Memoirs,* he defines his particular workman's nature.

I am committed to the world of fancy. Am gone off into it for long periods.
What is real and what unreal in thoughts, moods, people, nature, I cannot tell.
Facts elude me. Truth is lost.
It does not altogether matter. Something real remains.

With a cruelty that may have struck Bab as more of the person than of the workman, he insists that it hurts him not to give her more when he has so much "taken you as part of my life," but more he could not give even were they to live together.[21]

Still, he was enough in touch with facts to analyze for her the sharp differences between his two sons, who on July 19 arrived for a three-weeks' stay in the now crowded garage apartment. Each was like one side of himself—John at seventeen "still and quiet—wise—big of body—conscious of people . . . uncertain what he wants to be" but content simply to be; Robert, almost nineteen, "self-conscious—not really nice to anyone because being so self-conscious he hasn't much time to think of others," speaking and acting "for effect" but not achieving that effect. It was "a rest to be with John—a job to be with Bob." Now that he at last had the chance to see something of John, he was lovingly drawn to him rather than to the better-known Bob to an extent that probably increased the latter's self-consciousness. Besides, John had already displayed talent as an artist, and the father could happily encourage him toward painting, his own favorite art after writing. It was more difficult to advise Bob, though as the father would soon carefully write him, "with your energy, your quick imagination, and your love of life you are bound in the end to go toward one of the arts." Storytelling would put him in his father's shadow; rather he seemed "a natural dramatist." The road to any art was long, but members of the Anderson "tribe" needed "a moral balance," and "There is and can be no moral balance like the long difficulty of an art." In any case, the father would tell his older son out of his own experience: "A man needs a purpose for real health."[22]

Family and family problems were on his mind along with his writing at several projects and with, as the walls of Ripshin grew higher, his "watching almost every stone that goes into the house." In mid-July, Karl wrote that Earl had suffered a third stroke and had fortunately been admitted to the United States Marine Hospital at Newport, Rhode Island, because of his service in the World War. Karl and Sherwood would no longer have to pay heavy hospital bills, but there was no hope for Earl's recovery, and he might die anytime. Absorbed in his writing, conscious that he would pay for this absorption with a "slump" sooner or later, Anderson with the cruelty of the workman delayed visiting the younger brother until August 9 when he took the train to New York and on to Newport. The shock of seeing how much the partially paralyzed Earl had failed over their years of separation was part of the "terrific experience" of being with him again, an experience leaving Sherwood exclaiming ecstatically to Bab that Earl, whose outward life had been so futile, was "the most beautiful man . . . the truest finest poet I have ever seen. . . . I think I loved him in that half day more than I have ever loved." He did not, however, return for a second visit and instead spent the rest of his three days in New York talking with Horace and Otto Liveright and members of Horace's editorial staff, especially Maurice Hanline, about various publishing projects. The movie director Cecil B. De Mille had telegraphed Otto earlier inquiring the price of rights to *Horses and Men*—nothing would come of this—and as Anderson often did when in New York, he became interested in the theater, this time in the possibility of having a dramatist turn "The Man Who Became a Woman" into a play. Before the crazily busy trip was over, someone at *Vanity Fair* "ran" him into Edward Steichen's studio to have photographs taken. The futile life of poor stricken, beautiful Earl haunted his mind, nevertheless; it was "satisfying completely," like, it would seem, that of a worn-out, lovely-bodied old woman dead in the snow.[23]

Back at Ripshin by August 13 or 14, he was delighted to find a check for $675 from Otto Liveright for the sale of "Another Wife" to *Scribner's* as part of the magazine's plan to publish in each of its twelve 1927 issues "a short story by a writer of the first rank who has won a distinguished place in contemporary letters." Emotionally worn but concerned to get more money for the fall and winter trip to Europe as well as to pay his workmen and repay Bess Graham, he plunged again into his writing, when he was not house-watching. But now his and Elizabeth's lives were complicated by more invited guests. Brother Irve, still not really recovered from his breakdown, and wife Anne arrived on the fifteenth to occupy the spare bedroom in the garage apartment just vacated by Bob and John; and by the nineteenth Karl had arrived and was put up in the writing cabin. Despite the uncomfortable crowding and ten straight days of rain, which isolated them on the farm because of muddy roads, they all had a happy time together.[24]

Sherwood had urged Karl to come down especially because the countryside was "tremendously paintable . . . full of sensual lines and color"; but Karl was equally taken with painting the house, the stone walls of which were soon all up, roof rafters in place, shingling begun. Then, too, he almost at once had decided to paint a portrait of his two brothers, deciding also to put Earl into the canvas later. *Three Anderson Brothers,* now at the Yale University Art Gallery, shows Karl's skill as a portraitist. In three-quarters view Sherwood and Irve are seated on a sofa. Irve on the right, arms partly folded, cigarette in right hand, stares abstractedly through round glasses off just to the right of the viewer. Earl, slumped in seated position on the left, is turned away in profile from his brothers, is partly hidden behind Sherwood's shoulder and the emphatic dark curve of sofa end, and gazes somberly out of the picture. Sherwood, burly in white suit, lounges slightly to the left of center and dominates the picture. One knee is partly crossed on the other, left arm stretches along the sofa back behind Irve's head but not on his shoulder, the face is oblong and firm, the mouth unsmiling, and the eyes engage those of the viewer darkly and intensely. He leans away from Irve so that his head is close to Earl's, but sofa end to the viewer's left and partly raised knee just off center to the right set him off from either brother. He is himself, at ease, self-confident and self-secure, arrogant even, as in a later dark time he would admit to Karl the painter had caught in him. What Karl did not catch in the portrait, though he would witness it in real life, was the beginning of that self-security's collapse.[25]

It began toward the end of August with the predicted "slump." He swung readily from a mood "close to poetry" at the beauty of Earl's futile life to one of distress. Plagued by memories of Earl's stricken body and by regret for lost opportunities in the relationship between himself and "the brother to whom I most clung," he began to write Earl, pleading for his love and telling him that he felt his illness in his own body, perhaps finding it easier to confess first to the physically sick Earl his own growing emotional sickness.

> I think of you every day, every hour of every day.
> Writing, writing, work. It is the only thing I can do that will keep something inside me quiet. Novels, stories, articles. I have tried to write an article about the Modern Great Factory. It does not satisfy me. Nothing does.
> Nothing will pay me back for things missed.

Elizabeth knew soon enough that work and workman went badly. Answering a depressed letter from Roger Sergel with an equally depressed one, Anderson admitted that he had undertaken too much with both house and novel and was feeling the consequence.

> Only last week me creeping to Elizabeth, tears in my eyes, saying all I had ever written was nothing, declaring I would never write anything really decent.
> A man plows on and then dies. God knows about it all. This summer I have destroyed 30 to 40,000 words of a novel twice.

> Rubbish piled up. The real flaw always eluding a man.[26]

Elizabeth must have felt herself beset with relatives to entertain and a husband to comfort, along with the confusion of a house being built nearby by unskilled mountain workmen who sometimes got drunk and fought among themselves and whom Sherwood somehow had to, and did, control. Irve and Anne left at the end of August, but Karl stayed on another week or two working at the portrait slowly and patiently, requiring frequent sittings by Sherwood and further interrupting his frustrating hours at his writing desk.[27]

During this first week in September, however, Anderson had a brief recovery from his slump. When, back in early July, Burton Emmett had sent him a check for two hundred dollars as a payment toward manuscripts, Anderson had written at once to thank him and genially added get-acquainted bits of literary comment. In his Critchfield days, he told the other advertising man, he had written "I'm a Fool" at his "copy desk one morning while I was presumed to be writing copy for a gas engine company"; the storyteller's "tool," his method, "must never become more important than matter"; Joyce is an important ground-breaker from whom he has "stolen" much; Stein "is something special." "She isn't a story teller—perhaps not an artist. She has given me a lot. An artist in phrase making, word combinations, something like that. She is a sort of tool maker."

Now writing to Emmett on September 6 he could affirm a sense of friendship with him and prove it by admitting bluntly that it was still "rather rankling" to have accepted his check since "the possession of money brings power and that power is corruption in itself." Nevertheless, it was probably in this week that, for money, he completed two pieces, successfully rewriting "A Great Factory" for the November *Vanity Fair* and dashing off an introduction to Stephen Crane's *Midnight Sketches* for Wilson Follett's edition of Crane's works.[28]

The introduction is a slight, rambling piece, recalling that Marco Morrow had introduced him to Crane's fiction when both were at Critchfield, asserting that Crane's individualistic writing "exploded" on a "pretty dead" time in American literature, calling attention to the experimental color of his prose. "A Great Factory," on the other hand, recalls personal experience as a factory worker to lead into one of his best summations of his attitude at this time toward industrialism. He and his fellow worker Harry admired the cleanness and order of their factory, the beauty and efficiency of the machines which produced "vast quantities . . . of very well made" goods, and the contribution the factory made to lifting "sheer brute, heavy labour . . . at least partly, from the shoulders of mankind"; and they had no use for reformers and radicals, since many of these were "ready to surrender individuality for the common good." Anderson claims to have had not "one political thought" in twenty years and to "have no scheme for changing anything in the social structure"; yet both he and Harry feared as well as admired the factory. Why feared? Because the factory—industrialism, standardization—threatened then and "remains a threat to the individualist, the workman." The artist, the worker, every man "deep down" wants more than anything else, not industrialism's production and standardization, but workmanship. All at base have Anderson the artist's great fear, that of "losing touch."

Fear of losing touch. With what?
Why, with wood, cloth, iron, stone, earth, sky. The line this pen makes on this paper as I write, the quality of the paper, the ink, with everything in nature my mind or body touches. My life is centered here. Life, to me, has always this universal quality. There is something the machine cannot do for me. When the machine makes my fingers useless it makes me useless. I am afraid of the impotency that comes with the losing of the workman impulse.

During this brief remission from emotional illness he received on September 7 a mildly upsetting telegram from the *New York Herald Tribune* explaining that Theodore Dreiser's poem "The Beautiful," published in the September *Vanity Fair* appeared to have been plagiarized from a passage in Anderson's *Winesburg* tale "Tandy." (On September 6, Franklin P. Adams had implied the charge by publishing, without comment in his "The Conning Tower" in the New York *World,* "The Beautiful" and the relevant section from "Tandy" in parallel columns.) Had Anderson given Dreiser permission to turn his prose into poetry? At once Anderson telegraphed back in defense of a writer he had always admired that he didn't believe there was plagiarism, since "'Mr. Dreiser is not the kind of man who needs to take lines from me or any one else. It is one of those accidents that occur.'" But he was puzzled by the incident and bothered by it for Dreiser's sake. To both Bab and Burton Emmett he gave his own private explanation that Dreiser may have turned Anderson's prose into poetry "as an exercise," had later forgotten his source, and had unthinkingly published the poem as wholly his own. The incident, he hoped, was now closed.[29]

Karl left Ripshin soon after the Dreiser affair, but at least by his fiftieth birthday on September 13 Sherwood's "nerves had gone rather to pieces," as he wrote his brother in a letter filled with self-accusing for never having realized before the visit that Karl's relationship to his work was "much purer and finer" than his own, though one suspects, he was feeling guilty for still not having sufficient brotherly regard for Karl as person and painter. (He had only recently written Earl that "Karl is in a strange way a shadow.") *Another Man's House,* he had already explained to Bab, "went wrong" because in spite of himself he had "made a scheme" for his characters who struggled against him "to be themselves." Sometimes confusing the persons and actions of the real world, with its mountain workmen and visitors, and those in the world of his fancy, he felt "like a man trying to cross Niagara Falls on a wire with a wheelbarrow—the wheelbarrow filled with squirming people." Fearing he had lost touch, he succumbed abruptly to an attack of his "own special kind" of psychic illness, in which

I go off suddenly, terribly. There is a kind of nameless sickness. At times I can scarcely lift my legs to walk. It is all inside. The sickness may last two weeks, a month, a day. While it lasts I am sunk so low it seems I can never again lift myself. The hills no longer have form. Books are meaningless. Words squirm and writhe before my eyes.

Words are nothing. I am nothing. The disease must simply spend itself.[30]

This time it was not a few days of slump but two weeks of wretchedness before the disease spent itself. Then another familiar pattern began, work and health interrelated. Some days he felt up, and the novel seemed "really alive"; other days he felt down, the novel eluded him, the characters struggling to lead their own lives against his will to control them, against what he now thought of as his preoccupation with "self" that had possessed him all summer. In an up period early in October he was able to write "A Criminal's Christmas" for the December *Vanity Fair*'s "Story of America." The tale purports to be, but is not, a reminiscence from his twelfth year, uses Clyde names, has a small-town background. Working at his grocery store job on Christmas Eve, the boy, "I," steals six dollars from the cash drawer and with two of the dollars buys presents for his mother and the five other children; but after taking the presents home he becomes fearful of being apprehended there by some detective, hides in a house where the family is away for the holiday, and spends a cold night fantasizing in Tom Sawyer manner that he has a pistol so that he might be mortally wounded in a shoot-out with a detective and expire at his mother's feet with a grandiloquent speech about having stolen the money "to bring a moment of happiness into her life." The day after Christmas he returns the remaining four dollars to the cash drawer, and his crime passes unnoticed. This minor effort has the "charm" of an episode from *Tar* but little else, except evidence of the persistence of a fixed configuration in memory and imagination, love for the mother, rejection of the father, who here is not even mentioned, and possibly a prompting of this Christmas tale by some combination of guilt, fearfulness, and aloneness as residues from his recent "disease." The voice of the reminiscent narrator, however, is pleasant, and amused, and no serious harm comes to boy, family, or community. When the tale was printed, *Vanity Fair* would flatter its author by placing on the page opposite its beginning a reproduction of one of the Steichen portrait photographs of him, together with a paragraph of praise from H. L. Mencken titled "America's Most Distinctive Novelist—Sherwood Anderson," in which Mencken declares him to be "one of the most original novelists ever heard of" and *Dark Laughter* to be "one of the most profound American novels of our time." Anderson would almost certainly see this encomium soon, but by then it could have cheered his spirits only briefly.[31]

On his up days everything excited him about the building of the house, which in its solidity already looked "as though it had grown out of the ground." He learned the "lovely" names for the parts of a house and delighted in the challenge of handling the mountain men.

A worthless man comes to work and I discharge him. He threatens me. The others stand aside to see what will happen. A new look at life—through the eyes of these simple men. I must be ready to knock a man down if that is necessary. It is not necessary. The man sees I am not afraid and that ends it. People try to cheat. The man who brings me wood for my fire tries to get the best of me. If he cannot I see the respect grow in his eyes. There is a simple code—the early American code. These men close to the soil. Every man must look out for himself. Back of it all real friendliness. "If you can take care of yourself I respect and like you."

The mountain women, he could shrewdly observe for later stories, are

in a peculiar position. It is like the Older Testament. The man of the house is the patriarch. The women are little better than servants. They work in the field, sit in silence when the men talk, are ordered about like children. They are however not weak. I see many resolute faces. That is the way life is. It is accepted.

His return to the soil was complementing and enlarging his city life. "After all," he wrote Bab, "to me everything must have the two values—the value of a life experience—the value of its relation to me as a workman."[32]

On his up days, too, he would enjoy the guests he had impulsively invited to Ripshin. His friend Charles Connick, stained glass designer from Boston, and his wife came for several days in late September; Lyle Saxon dropped by at the beginning of October on his way from New Orleans to, he hoped, literary success in New York; Maurice Hanline of Boni and Liveright would arrive a month later to discuss the possibility that the firm might publish the Testaments. Visitors helped lighten the weight of depression. Back in July, Hemingway had written a more coherent, more apologetic letter than his previous one; and Anderson had replied kindly, again inviting him and Hadley to Ripshin, complimenting him on his "sense of vitality," expressing his pleasure that the Hemingways were planning to return to the United States to live: "Whatever it is, it's our own mess. I rather like the whole show myself and I think you do." Midway through his September depression, Anderson received a third letter from Hemingway, now separated from Hadley but not mentioning it, complaining that the return was "shot to hell along with a lot of other things" and that he had "been living this side of bughouse with the old insomnia for about eight months now." But "we" would be glad to see Sherwood in Paris. On October 10, Anderson replied sympathetically, "My God man, I have always thought of you as a horse for strength. It shocks me to hear that you don't sleep. Aren't there any real huskies in the world?" The Andersons would be sailing, he wrote, "about December 1st" and "drifting into Paris along about Christmas."[33]

The European trip was definite by now, though Anderson occasionally worried about adding that cost to the cost of the house, and it was settled that John would accompany his father and stepmother. But December was a long time away for one who knew all too well that he was not one of the real huskies. Soon after writing to Ralph Church, probably on the same day as to Hemingway, and saying he was "Working steadily at the most difficult novel I ever undertook," he dropped once again into his black despondency, which lasted this time through the rest of October and most of November. Toward the end of October he went to see a doctor in Marion; but as he knew from long experience, the physical illness was psychic in cause, and the doctor could not help him. He felt "like a stone beside the road," unmoving, "hard, frozen."[34]

The worst part of this "terrible blank time" was that he could not function "as a workman," for to do so was for him, he lamented to Bab, "the key to Heaven—to personal dignity, good manners, everything." Work on *Another Man's House* effectively stopped. Somehow he was able to write two "Stories of America" pieces to get ahead for the January and February issues of *Vanity Fair.* Both were slight affairs. In "The Far West" he recalled in detail his automobile trip of 1923 from Reno to Goldfield, Nevada, with four coarse men, praised San Francisco's beauty, wrote off Los Angeles as "the very peak of everything industrial America means," and insisted on the Far West "sense of the rest of the country as something too far away." The second article, "Prohibition," relied on memories of Body Adair's saloon in Clyde and Anderson's subsequent development of a more discriminating taste in drinking to declaim that "Prohibition is the triumph of vulgarity" since people now drink inferior liquor; Prohibition has "in reality struck at the slowly growing culture of the whole country." The chatty combination of recollection and impressionistic comment in both articles suggests work performed simply for pay, the sort of work he had always decried so contemptuously; indeed, one of the reasons he remained sunk in depression was his frightening conviction that he had become a successful hack writer. His best hope now was to get to Paris where he might regain his joy in life and his sense of a burgeoning talent that had filled him there five years ago.[35]

He and Elizabeth planned to leave Ripshin for New York at Thanksgiving time, John to meet them in the city, and had booked passage on the *President Roosevelt,* embarking December 1. Early in September they had already hired (at the mountain rate of twenty-five dollars a month) a quiet, capable Troutdale woman, Mary Ball, to help with cooking and housework during the autumn and for the following year, and had arranged for Claude Reedy, an able young farmer, to live in the garage apartment and look after the farm and garden (at fifty dollars a month) while they were abroad. After several weeks when the plumbers, electricians, and plasterers swarmed about the house simultaneously, Ripshin was now finished except for odds and ends that Marion Ball had agreed to do over the winter, but did not get around to doing until spring. Exultantly Anderson wrote the Schevills that the cost of the house, including the farm itself, was "about $10,000," a third of the cost in a city according to Karl. Curiously, despite his eager absorption in the building process, certain of his persistent memories of it were in some degree humiliating ones. There had been the matter of assembling, not the great stone arch in the master bedroom behind which the bed would stand, but a less dramatic one over the door to the smaller downstairs bedroom. By himself a mountain man named Cornett skillfully assembled the stones, cemented them into place, and triumphantly chiseled his name crudely across the keystone. When Anderson furiously swore at him before the other men for defacing this fine stone, Cornett, his mountain self-respect offended, abruptly quit his job. Drawing Anderson aside as he left, he said he would return only once more, by himself, and cut his name off the stone. Then looking at his former employer, he asked him if he wrote books. When Anderson said he did, Cornett asked, "Well, when you have written a book you sign it, you put your name on it, don't you?"; then he walked away, again triumphant, leaving Anderson with nothing to say.[36]

There had been the matter of plastering the walls and ceiling of the last room. While the Andersons were busy elsewhere, the plasterers got drunk on moonshine in premature celebration of finishing their job and began happily throwing plaster about at the ceiling, walls, and each other until they were all covered with it and the floor was inches deep in the wet mess. When Anderson went up to the room to see what the maudlin shouting was about, he was too appalled to be angry. Drunkenly the men urged him to join the fun and threw some plaster at him, and he retreated with a lump of plaster on his shoulder to where Elizabeth was standing. When he explained "rather plaintively" what was going on, they simply looked at each other helplessly and walked silently away. The next day, sober, the men returned, cleaned up their mess, and plastered the room properly.[37]

And there had been another remark by the little old woman who had warned Anderson that some of the mountain people could not read. She and the other neighbors, she told him, were of course grateful that he had provided many men work and wages. "'But there is something else,' she said. 'We were all poor together in this neighborhood before you came.'" For the first time, apparently, Anderson fully realized how his coming into the hills and having a fine house built may "profoundly disturb a way of life that had had its own values." But if he had felt shame when the old woman had spoken to him so forthrightly, he could now take what satisfaction his dark despondency might allow him—that he had again and again passed the tests, which the reserved mountain people had put him to before admitting him to their friendship. In addition he had before his eyes, on such days as he could lift them, Ripshin itself, solid on the earth with its eighteen-inch-thick, stone-of-the-country walls, sheltered in its valley, close to the sound of the stream.[38]

3.

There was one more event before the Andersons left for New York—the publication on November 20 of *Tar: A Midwest Childhood*, copies of which had reached him a few days earlier. Reading it over in its brown cover with gold lettering, he was uncertain whether he liked it or not. It showed "in a certain lack of flow in the prose," he explained apologetically to Emmett when sending him a copy, "the effort of trying to do two things at once—build a house and a book." It was not, he told the Schevills, an "important" book. Of the two reviews he would have been able to read before embarking for Europe, one, Herbert Gorman's in the *New York Times Book Review,* was flattering in its praise for *Tar* as "a sensitively conceived, delicately handled expression of bygone youth," successful also because of its "simpleness of structure" and its "limpid and supple flow of language." The other, Rebecca West's in the *New York Herald Tribune Books,* was a sharp disappointment, especially since she had written favorably of his work before. West did begin by declaring *A Story Teller's Story* a "beautiful book" and *Winesburg, Ohio* and *The Triumph of the Egg* "two of the most interesting books of short stories ever written"; but she dismissed *Dark Laughter* and *Many Marriages* and ridiculed at length the wedding night scene in *Poor White.* Worst of all, she declared the portrait of *Tar* to be flat and "pale" and singled out only two episodes as outweighing the book's faults. It was the sort of review to reinforce Anderson's depression. The December reviews, even those in the *Boston Transcript* and the *Springfield Daily Republican,* were laudatory, but by then he had already sailed from New York and probably did not see them for some time. Thereafter, the positive reviews would slightly outnumber the negative ones, but even the favorable reviews contained criticisms, such as Mencken's objections that the "philosophizings" were "thin" and much of the material had been used, "sometimes much more effectively" in previous books, though certain chapters showed Anderson "at his very best—subtle, penetrating and incomparably romantic." For the first time a sizable number of the reviews, not just the book notes, would be brief, as though there was little to say or worth saying about the book.[39]

Things can be said about *Tar* besides its undeniably having "charm," some favorable, some unfavorable. Mencken was right in pointing out Anderson's reworking of previous material. As in *A Story Teller's Story,* *Tar* mingles fact and "fancy," though whereas in the former book the unwary reader may miss the implication of its subtitle, in the latter a foreword explicitly warns the reader at length not to expect "Truth," which is "impossible" for the author to arrive at either as man or as storyteller. Rather, as he puts it with deliberate ambiguity, he has "created a Tar Moorehead to stand for himself." Certain elements in *Tar* are identifiable "Truth." For example, Tar is born specifically in Camden, Ohio, but leaves there when still a baby; he is the third child in an eventual family of five boys and two girls, the younger girl, the only child given its actual name, dying in infancy; the family's economic fortune declines as the father, a harness maker and later a housepainter, moves his brood through a series of small towns until it comes to rest in one unnamed but having the geography of Clyde. On the other hand, the author makes the father, Dick Moorehead, a captain in the Civil War; Tar's older brother and sister, John and Margaret, are older in relation to him than Karl and Stella were to Sherwood; John works in the bicycle factory where Sherwood worked and which had not been established when Karl left Clyde, and so on.

Again as in *A Story Teller's Story,* and in *Windy McPherson's Son* and in reality, Tar loves his mother and hates his father. As before, Mary Moorehead is a quiet, caring woman who wears herself out for her family. Dick, who receives much attention as in *Story,* is a talker and boaster, a poor provider, a drinker and womanizer; the townspeople like him because he is entertaining, but they have no respect for him. Even the tales he enjoys telling, like those of the Story Teller's father, "never hold water." Though Tar claims to understand Dick much later in life, the portrayal of him under the thin layer of humor is as contemptuous and hostile as that of the father in *Story,* except that in *Tar* the attack is always direct, rather than complexly and self-revealingly suggested, through that long, preposterous tale of North and South.

Like the beginning sections of *A Story Teller's Story,* too, *Tar* is a portrait of the artist as a young boy; but the later book focuses on its protagonist's life from early childhood to preadolescence, a period only selectively touched on in the earlier book. Because he wrote with this focus and with the general audience of *The Woman's Home Companion* in mind, the structure of *Tar* unlike *Story* or *Dark Laughter* relies for the most part on straightforward chronology, episodic but tracing Tar's development through a series of stages. Occasionally the narrative is interrupted by flashforwards to Tar's later life as a storyteller in which he writes of commonplace people like those in this book and, on a visit to Europe, hungers for America. More frequently this storyteller, a persona for Anderson, comments with adult hindsight on the events of Tar's life, which are primarily seen through the eyes and mind of the growing boy. *Tar* lacks the amplitude of *A Story Teller's Story,* but its simpler structure and its narrative method provide it with greater concentration.

This method, combining present and retrospect, boy's immediate response and adult's greater understanding, has another effect. The major strength of *Tar* lies in its penetration of a child's, then a boy's psychology. In the first two of the book's five parts, Tar experiences a series of emotional states—resentment as a young child that a new baby is depriving him of his mother's attention, a sense of both abandonment and opportunity when he is taken to an outlying farm and left in a scary and enticing new world by his sister, fear of a bully in his early grade-school years and exultation at frightening the bully by an impulsive attack, fascination later with trotting horses, and nameless satisfaction while spending alone a "Wonderful Sunday," as *The Woman's Home Companion* titled this next to last of its serial installments, watching the horses trot at the track and then wandering through the countryside.

At this point, slightly more than halfway through the book, Anderson moves to a new stage in Tar's development, a stage not included in the *Companion*'s serialization, obviously because it deals with the boy's earliest responses to sexuality. The relatively brief part 3 opens with the next to last version of "Death in the Woods," which by its position here gives greater emphasis than the final version to Tar's first sexual awakening, and closes with a brief chapter on Tar's glimpses of "the world of older people" and their secret relationships as he makes his evening rounds delivering newspapers. Slowly his consciousness has expanded outward from parents, home, street, school, town, and now is expanding inward beneath the surfaces. His "alleyway" view of the town's and townspeople's night world is preparing him for his own experience with sexual urges. Part 4, the briefest one, is divided into two linked but contrasting chapters. The first shows twelve-year-old Tar smitten with unfulfilled yearning for a girl of the same age, the pretty, well-dressed Esther Farley, who stays briefly with her grandparents in the town while her rich parents are in Europe. One of the several lyric passages in the book describes Tar lying by himself in a grove of beech trees outside the town and fantasizing the slenderest tree as the Farley girl, whom he does not dare approach. Embarrassed by his lower social position in town, idealizing this "good girl"—who knows what a good girl may think about whatever this mystery of sex may be?—he becomes attracted yet repelled by Mame Thompson, a physically dirty girl of a social level below even his own. She invites him toward a first sexual adventure about which he is even more nervous than George Willard in "Nobody Knows," and which events prevent him from experiencing. The paired chapters show Anderson's subtle understanding of the links between sexual availability and social class, of a boy's unconscious sublimation of balked sexual desire into idealization, of the uncertain balance within a young boy between, on the one had, fear of violating the overt moral code of the town and fear of sexual incapability and, on the other, the desire to satisfy his curiosity about sexual contact and the desire to fulfill the covert masculine code of proving one's self a "man." Only "Nobody Knows" among Anderson's writings surpasses the handling of this particular mesh of fear and desire.

In the sketches and tales that make up the final part of the book, Tar, now about thirteen, learns more about adults and their ways, including adults from beyond the town's horizons. The picture often is not a pretty one for perceived or perceiver. Hating his father, eaten by "money hunger"—"Tar's hatreds were nearly all concerned with money"—Tar just before Christmas deceives an impoverished lawyer into giving him a dollar-and-a-half tip instead of a fifty-cent one, though afterward he feels ashamed of the deception. The boisterous family of his friend Hal Brown generously invite him to the "warm safety" of their huge dinners, so much in contrast to the skimpy meals his mother prepares, but more often adults exploit others, especially women and children, as his father has always done. A flashy young black man visiting his "Uncle Tom" father in town boasts of living as a pimp off of two women; a broken-down boxer cheats town boys out of boxing lessons they have paid for; a successful local lawyer, people say, "fools around with other men's wives." In a longer episode, a woman temporarily living in town has been set up in luxury there as the mistress, the gossip has it, of a man who lives elsewhere, and this "bad woman" is shunned by all the "good women." Tar, however, delivers her newspapers and befriends her. After she abruptly leaves town, he receives a note from her saying only, "Good-bye, you're a good boy" and enclosing a five dollar bill. Shortly afterwards a package of new clothes for Tar, his sister, and his brothers arrives. "The express," the sketch concludes with fine understatement, "was prepaid."

These sketches and tales are reminiscent of *Winesburg, Ohio,* but only one is their equal in suggestiveness. The repulsive Hog Hawkins, disliked by everyone, angers Tar by not paying for his daily newspapers and then gloating publicly at his petty victories over the boy. On a night of wild rain, the train bringing Tar's papers is delayed until very late. Margaret, Tar's sister. is aroused by the storm to a restless need of adventure—one recalls from *Winesburg* the rain's effect on the more mature Alice Hindman—and she insists on delivering the papers with her brother. Taking a shortcut through the town cemetery, the two Moorehead children almost stumble over Hog kneeling in prayer in the rain and darkness by the grave of his long-dead wife, the one person who had ever liked him. Beginning the next day, money-hungry Tar allows Hog to cheat him out of payment for his newspapers and to rejoice in his small triumphs.

Coming as it does after Tar's deception of Lawyer Whaley and before his befriending of the lonely "bad woman," the Hog Hawkins episode demonstrates that Tar's increasing expansion of consciousness outward and inward throughout the book has been Anderson's way of showing, unschematically, how this imaginative boy who "stands for" himself grows toward the human understanding required of the mature writer. This is, of course, a major theme in *Winesburg, Ohio,* and Anderson further links the two books by occasionally referring to inhabitants of that fictional town. The telegraph operator at the train station is the "grouch" Wash Williams, John Spainard (Spaniard in *Winesburg*) owns a tree nursery, a boy named Elmer Cowley is regarded as "too dumb." Most frequently appearing of all is Dr. Reefy with his "strange looking hands," who at middle age, as in "Paper Pills," married a young woman who lived only a year. As in *Winesburg,* it is Dr. Reefy who in the next to last chapter of *Tar* attends Mary Moorehead when she is dying and talks intimately with her. The parallel between *Winesburg* and *Tar* continues. In the former, the tale "Death" is followed by "Sophistication"; but since Tar is about thirteen when his mother dies, it would not be likely for him to achieve a moment of maturity with another as George Willard does with Helen White. Nevertheless, in the final chapter an equivalent recognition appears when Tar first longs for his own death after his mother's funeral and then resolves instead to go on doing his job as John and Margaret are doing—"Things had to go on." Grabbing up his bundle of newspapers, which the train has brought in, he races off to deliver them, not physically leaving his town as George does in "Departure" but "racing away out of his childhood."

So the ending of *Tar* reused elements of *Winesburg, Ohio* as its beginning reused elements of *A Story Teller's Story.* Much new material, the childhood and boyhood of the artist, came in between, but that was used up now. In the gloom-ridden fall of 1926, Anderson began to be convinced that he had written himself out.

19

The Door of the Trap

1.

The Andersons had planned to leave Ripshin for New York on Thanksgiving Day, November 25, but perhaps because Sherwood hoped that travel would dispel his gloom, they abruptly decided to leave a day earlier still wondering whether they could afford going to Europe. Ashamed, Sherwood had to confess to Karl that he could not pay him the money he owed him to help cover the previous costs of Earl's illness but would "probably" do so on returning from France in the spring. In New York the Andersons put up at the Chelsea Hotel, and Sherwood went on to Newport for a day with Earl. He managed to take his sick brother away from the dispiriting hospital to dine at a downtown hotel, but felt humble and useless at not being able to do more for this "terrific man."[1]

In the few days before they sailed, New York was "a kind of madhouse" for Anderson, leaving him with a "sense of confusion and of terrible futility." He had chance encounters with other writers, he discussed a brief series of post-France lectures with Colston Leigh, he saw Otto Liveright about selling any of his short pieces to be written abroad, and he talked with Horace Liveright, presumably making final arrangements about the publication of *A New Testament*. He visited the office of *Vanity Fair*, which he would tell a friend was like a "high-class whorehouse," a comparison suggesting how much he felt he was prostituting himself with his series for that periodical. A day or so before departure his son John arrived in New York accompanied, to Elizabeth's annoyed surprise, by his fifteen-year-old sister Mimi. Without consulting Elizabeth, Sherwood had written Cornelia suggesting that Mimi go with them to Europe; and Cornelia, uneasy about the crowd of "rather boy-crazy young girls" Mimi was currently going with, had agreed, stipulating only that she herself pay all their daughter's expenses for the boat trip and the stay in Paris. Perhaps to avoid rebellion on the girl's part she had taken her out of a class at school at the last minute to inform her that she was going to Europe. Whereas John had his mother's quiet reserve, Mimi, who looked like a feminine miniature of her father, had his outgoing eagerness for experience; in her school record the "Very Independent" category would be checked. Swallowing her anger—"Being angry with Sherwood's impulsiveness was like being angry with the color of his eyes," as she would later put it—Elizabeth accepted the situation, took Mimi shopping, and bought her an evening dress for dining on shipboard.[2]

At one o'clock in the early morning of December 1, the Andersons sailed for England on the S.S. *President Roosevelt* of the United States Lines. The boat was comfortable and the weather pleasant, but for the first few days Elizabeth was overcome with seasickness. Temporarily lifted out of his depression by changing scene, Sherwood read, explored the ship, talked with the crew members, and made the acquaintance of the gregarious Englishman Frank Swinnerton and his wife, the daughter of Arnold Bennett. The red-bearded Swinnerton, publisher's editor, literary reviewer, and prolific novelist, was as much a storyteller as Sherwood, and the two agreed to see each other in London during the Andersons' one-week stay there. Elizabeth finally recovered from seasickness only to be horrified to see that Mimi, impressed by the bobbed hair of smart New York women, had cut off, rather badly, her own long dark hair. Elizabeth hurried to the ship's hairdresser, who shaped the bob so attractively that her father was much taken with it and began to be pleased with his daughter.[3]

On December 8, the Andersons disembarked in England, went up to London, and settled in at Sherwood's old favorite, the Kenilworth Hotel in Great Russell Street. For the first few days they walked about the city seeing the sights; then Anderson wrote Swinnerton hoping to see him and continue the "great fun" they had had talking on shipboard. Swinnerton's reply was to invite him to lunch together with Arnold Bennett on the fifteenth at the Reform Club, Pall Mall, an event Bennett found worth recording in his journal.

Lunched with Swinnerton and Sherwood Anderson. The latter outrageously untidy and long grey hair, all over his eyes, etc., blue shirt and darker silk necktie in the arty style of the '90s, with a pink-stoned ring to hold the tie; still it looked rather nice—save for its evil arty associations. He had sound sense on lots of things, and I liked him.

Anderson's memory of the luncheon would be less complimentary. Although he had admired *The Old Wives' Tale*, he felt that Bennett's later work was simply "cheap romancing" and that the man was "hungry for money and position." Both Bennett and the club struck him as "ponderous," and with deliberate rudeness he reminded Bennett that authors were "all little whores," a remark which Bennett may have calmly accepted as only another example of "sound sense." Very likely at the luncheon Anderson was already coming down with the miserable cold that made him, on the following day, especially glad to leave England and the English for France and the Parisians.[4]

Arriving in Paris on the boat train in the cold, gloomy evening of December 16, the Andersons were relieved when Ralph Church met them at the station and helped get them settled at the Regnard, a small, inexpensive hotel at 4, rue Regnard just off the Place de l'Odeon, near the Luxembourg Garden. Anderson celebrated being in France by drinking so much that the following morning his hands shook, but he was able to respond characteristically to an interviewer from the Paris edition of the *Tribune*. In an hour this "novelist who has forged to the front rank in contemporary American letters" showed little concern for schemes to serve mankind, decried Prohibition, professed to be interested in maturity, not youth—he had "lost interest in Tar before the book was finished," he was quoted as saying—and of course announced that "Our greatest curse is industrialism . . . with its deadly concomitant standardization." Unlike the "purely mechanical writers'" who are essentially "factory hands," he declared, "I've never done standardized work of that kind yet, but"—and the unexpected last clause revealed one of the fears on his mind—"I'm not sure that I'm not going to." The interview appeared in the Paris *Tribune* on the eighteenth; on the nineteenth, under the heading "Who's Who Abroad," the paper printed a summary of Anderson's life and work by the young reporter William L. Shirer, who regarded the author as one of his "literary idols."[5]

Within a few days after this public welcome to Paris, Elizabeth entered Mimi in a private French girls school, and Sherwood placed John in a pension to pick up French and, at Gertrude Stein's suggestion, in the Académie Julian to study painting. The Andersons joyfully attended the Christmas party Gertrude had invited them to, Sherwood "as usual very handsome in one of his very latest scarf ties," she would later write. Immediately thereafter his bad cold turned into flu, his depression returned in dark force, and he took to his bed in his hotel bedroom for ten days. Elizabeth was certain, and would remain certain throughout her life, that he did not have the flu but was simply severely depressed; so she was irritated with him, and he, certain as was John and others that he did have the flu as well as depression, was irritated by her irritation and lack of sympathy. Clearly from the beginning of that winter in Paris the couple got more and more on each other's nerves; and when Sherwood finally was able to sit up to work, this growing rawness between them was yet one more reason why he was mostly blocked in his writing during the remaining two months of their stay, depression, recurring illness, irritation, and block reinforcing each other disastrously. On the back of a business card for the Hotel Regnard, Anderson would later scrawl, "I was very unhappy here all one winter."[6]

Around mid-January when he had recovered from the flu but had not yet regained his strength, he wrote despondently to Paul Rosenfeld that everything he did manage to put down "seems dead stuff" to be discarded. He was wading through a long swamp; he was "in a riverboat in the midst of the sea. I row in one direction thinking I may find a new promised land, then turn about and row in the other direction." (The image of the boat-self in "Note book Mar 5–1926" had surfaced in new and more hopeless form.) To Bab he confessed feeling that he had written himself out: "I am weary of restating the mere fact of my own defeat." To Burton Emmett and again to Bab he expressed fear of becoming "a hack" if he continued to accept the weekly checks, the advances, from Horace Liveright since their agreement required him "to grind out books" annually, the verb defining his state of mind as he sat down each morning before the blank white pages, which he had formerly loved to fill. Did Emmett think "some wealthy man or woman interested in American writing"—the appeal to Emmett himself was transparent—could "put up enough money to insure" for him as a kind of investment the unforced leisure he needed to continue being "experimental," not a producer of "cheap hurried writing." As though to prove his fear justified, apparently the single piece he wrote in France, around mid-January, and sent off for publication was one in the series contracted for with *Vanity Fair,* "Educating an Author," the title and content of which suggest that he had been reading in disgust Arnold Bennett's *How to Become an Author: A Practical Guide* with its assertion that "fiction is a lucrative profession." The piece satirizes the "national" impulse toward successful authorship among Americans, though "If you really want to succeed as an author in America, you should be born an Englishman." Despite this handicap for Americans, however, anyone "at the business" of becoming a successful author is advised to acquire "a simply huge vocabulary . . . of very hard words" and not to write "as simply and clearly as you can of the life immediately about you" but instead to "sink yourself into the life of books . . . by successful authors." Read every best seller, for from each "you will get something that will help you on your way." The barely concealed resentment in this rambling piece done for money suggests, almost as much as the letters to his friends, the depths of his daily frustration and despondency, not only at being unable to find success on his own terms but also at being hardly able to write at all.[7]

As usual, of course, there were happier moments. One day while he was still ill in bed, an American woman friend of the Andersons visited and at once perceived that he had the grippe and was bored and frustrated.

"How are you, Sherwood?" she asked sympathetically. "Well, I know one thing," he exploded. "There are 258 goddam baskets of flowers in this wallpaper." Even better, one afternoon during his illness Léon Bazalgette, his friend from the earlier stay in Paris, insisted on coming to his room, laughing in his animated way at Anderson's fear that he might catch the flu. Bazalgette, who had meanwhile published his book on Thoreau and become editor of the new cultural monthly *Europe*, again filled Anderson in on current writing in France and other European countries. As an associate of the publishing firm of Rieder, he could cheer Anderson at least temporarily with the word that Rieder would definitely issue Marguerite Gay's *Un Païen de l'Ohio* early in the spring. Then late in December, Victor Llona, a Peruvian-born novelist and translator living in Paris, came by with the heartening news that Gaston Gallimard would finally get around to publishing Gay's *Winesburg-en-Ohio* in 1926 and that her translation of the *Notebook* and his of *A Story Teller's Story* would soon appear. Probably it was he who assured Anderson that the 1926 translations of three of his stories from *Horses and Men* by Faÿ and Rivière had had, in Anderson's words, "a distinct literary success"; for Llona praised Faÿ while extolling Anderson as one of Paris's distinguished visitors in the January 1, 1927, issue of the weekly *Les Nouveles Littéraires*. On January 6, after a delay because of his illness, Anderson (with Sylvia Beach as translator) was able to call on Gallimard, who reassured him that *Winesburg-en-Ohio* would shortly appear, as it did on May 10. These signs of French interest served somewhat to offset the failures each morning in front of the white sheets of paper on the desk.[8]

While her husband had kept to his room gloomy from illness, depression, and inability to write prose "like the Mississippi going down to the sea" or indeed any satisfactory prose, Elizabeth, who spoke French, had been happily walking in the crisp, clean winter air all over the city with a young woman she had employed as guide, or occasionally with Mimi going about among the fashionable shops for the girl's education in high style. Stepmother and daughter grew to like each other, but Mimi would never become as attached to Elizabeth as she had been to Tennessee. As January wore on, Anderson too began to get out to see people. Paris was not the exciting adventure to "plunge into" it had been for him in the spring of 1921 and only rarely now in winter the base for glorious excursions into the country, but talking with others was a way to forget temporarily the frustrations of the morning writing stints. Twice he had "long, heady talks about writing and writers" with his admirer William Shirer, who found him "an immensely likeable man." Often of an afternoon or evening he would have beers at the Brasserie Lipp on the Boulevard Saint Germain with Ralph Church, on vacation from Oxford and visiting his mother now in France. Anderson loved Lipp's, Church would remember.

Until closing time at 3 AM, it was full of expatriate characters, most of them interested in writing.,The reason for the restaurant's popularity was that for thirty-six cents American, one could get a big plate of sauerkraut, two fat sausages, two boiled potatoes, and a "formidable" (a glass containing four-fifths of a liter) of beer. Here Anderson could feel relaxed and cheerful, talk for hours with Church, tell stories. The Hotel Regnard, for instance, was on the corner of a dark, dead-end alley with a name that delighted Anderson when it was translated for him: *l'Impasse des Deux Anges*, the Blind Alley of the Two Angels. On the other corner was an orphanage, which used to have coal delivered to it down a chute from the street. The coal, which came at least once a week, made a tremendous noise like an express train. Anderson loved the sound so much, he told Church, that he had written a story about the coal and the coal chute, and then thrown it away.[9]

Years later Church would reconstruct, from notes taken at the time, one or more conversations about Hemingway, whom he had met through Anderson's note of introduction and seen frequently in Paris and whose self-satisfaction over *The Torrents of Spring* had puzzled and appalled him. Anderson told him of Hemingway's first letter to him about the parody, a letter "so raw, so pretentious, so patronizing that in a repellant way it was amusing," and of his own reply, Ernest's letter apparently still rankling more than the parody itself. Then the conversation turned to what Church termed Hemingway's "anti-literature bias," an attitude Anderson felt to be healthy if what was distrusted were "the alleged values of Literature, with a capital l," but an "unhealthy" attitude on Hemingway's part. Anderson began by praising Hemingway as having "a very fine talent; but it's a talent for describing what he can observe. Hemingway is a master of episode. That's one reason why his short stories are so damn first rate," and why, Anderson felt, *The Sun Also Rises* wasn't a novel "in any genuine, growing sense"; it was only "a string of episodes," and its characters were all based on actual people the author knew. Hemingway's major limitation, Anderson asserted, was that he had little imagination; and since "most of the writing that lives is written out of imagination tutored but not controlled by the senses," Hemingway feared "his writing may not stand up in contrast to imaginative writing," and so in an unhealthy way he derided literature in 'a spiteful, ignorant kind of self-defense."[10]

By contrast, Anderson insisted, the imaginative writer develops his characters in his imagination, meanwhile "checking what you say about them against similar people you hear and see and dream about." Then when Church asked him how he went about developing characters, Anderson provided an insight into his creative method and indirectly into the cause for his continued inability to get on with *Another Man's House*.

Well, as a matter of fact, my characters usually begin by being proper names—proper names that fit the kind of story I want to write. You wouldn't call an Ohio Circuit stable boy Colin Chesterfield, but you might call him Sandy McPherson. Once the proper names begin to feel familiar, they begin to have conversations with each other. That's the beginning of growth; with those conversations the characters begin to take shape. They begin to have physical characteristics and personal idiosyncrasies. Pretty soon my characters are just about full-fledged. Then I sit down to write my story.

. . .

The plot is naturally dictated by how the characters feel, what they want, fear, hope for and want to do. That point is unavoidable. Otherwise you betray your characters. You adjust their natures, because you adjust their actions to a preconceived plot. And a writer, a story teller, can make no worse mistake than to betray his characters. O. Henry is a case in point. He made his people move in accordance with the dictates of a slick formula, not of their developing characters. That way he could always be sure he had an ending. It was usually a trick ending, though.

When at least by February Anderson learned that "Death in the Woods" had received second prize in the O. Henry Memorial Award Prize Stories of 1926, the name of the award may have had unfortunate ironies for him, though the $250 prize money would come in handy.[11]

He did also see the chief subject of his and Church's conversations, twice in fact before January 20, when Hemingway wrote to Max Perkins from Switzerland that he and Anderson had had "Two fine afternoons together" and that the latter "was not at all sore about *Torrents*," a remark suggesting that Anderson had concealed any soreness in order to maintain Hemingway's friendship. Anderson's references to having received $750 from *Scribner's Magazine* for "Another Wife," however, probably set Hemingway off to the boasting about himself and his accomplishments that the older man would in retrospect find so offensive.[12]

Likewise on further acquaintance with Joyce, Anderson interpreted the Irishman's reserve as a sign of self-importance. One evening when the Joyces took the Andersons to dine at the Deux Trianons, Joyce asked the Andersons if they would like to begin with oysters. Although he detested oysters, Anderson tried to dispel the initial awkwardness of the occasion by answering yes. Joyce ordered only one plate of oysters each for Sherwood and Elizabeth, and he uneasily and his wife calmly waited while their guests struggled through their servings. "The dinner was a failure," it would be reported, "so far as intellectual contacts were concerned, and each man left the table somewhat baffled and covertly annoyed." Sherwood's annoyance was so great that when again Joyce invited him and Elizabeth to dine, this time at the splendid Tour d'Argent, Sherwood pleaded a return of the flu, refused to go, but insisted that Elizabeth must, to her intense mortification since she knew that Joyce wished to talk with her husband, not with her. It was largely a silent dinner with Elizabeth ordering and eating one of the less expensive dishes and Joyce ordering and slowly sipping a glass of milk. The conversation between the Andersons on Elizabeth's return must have been anything but silent.[13]

Much more successful were Anderson's meetings with Eugene Jolas, the reporter and poet he had known in New Orleans, now city editor of the Paris edition of the *Chicago Tribune,* and the American expatiate novelist and *Tribune* literary editor Elliot Paul, who were finishing selecting material for the first issue of *transition.* He was delighted that the two had designed their magazine to encourage free expression and experimentation by American writers and writers abroad and, since the editors were translating into English all non-English contributions, designed also to make an American audience aware of new movements in literature and art. Anderson "enjoyed deeply," he told Church, "the spectacle of two newspaper men showing a critical prescience"—the word is surely Church's—"that would have seemed merely a nightmare to an English Professor." He was even listed in the first issue of *transition* as a future contributor, though his one brief contribution would not appear until 1938, when, in response to a query by Jolas as to whether a new language ("The Revolution of the Word") was needed for the expression of the imagination, he would reply: "No. There seems to me to be infinite opportunity, as yet untouched by me, in the language as it is."[14]

Happy also were his visits with or without Elizabeth to Sylvia Beach's Shakespeare and Company around the corner from the Hotel Regnard on the Rue de l'Odéon and to Adrienne Monnier's French book shop, La Maison des Amis des Livres, across the street at No. 7. He was grateful to the energetic, endlessly thoughtful Beach for her many kindnesses, such as inviting him and Elizabeth to evening parties or sending flowers unexpectedly to their hotel room. Out of admiration for *Ulysses* he gladly at her request put his name to the list of 167 writers around the world who were protesting Samuel Roth's unauthorized printing of sections of Joyce's novel in his New York magazine *Two Worlds Monthly,* the protest statement being released to the press on February 2. Through Beach he became better acquainted than in 1921 with her close friends the sturdily built Adrienne and her slender younger sister Marie, who was married to a portrait artist and illustrator, Paul-Émile Bécat. He relished Adrienne's chicken dinners and her pidgin English conversation, and at the Bécats' apartment he was enchanted as a lover of fine fabrics with Marie's needlework of embroidered silk panels, with "the play of light" upon them, "the changing, living radiancy of the colours." Enthusiastically he promised to write an article on the panels for *Vanity Fair,* an admiring piece, which he later did write but could not place with any magazine since no editor would then accept needlework as a form of art. Before leaving France he sat for and received as a going-away present a drawing of himself by Paul-Émile, which he told Adrienne was "charming" but which he later gave to Bill Wright in Troutdale because, he told Bill, it made him look too serious, "as though I ought to have a lily in my hand."[15]

Although he would later write Adrienne that Paris to him meant more than anything else her shop, Sylvia's house, and the Bécats' apartment, he felt most at home at 27 rue de Fleurus. Through Bazalgette, Llona, and Monnier he had met a gratifying number of French writers, scholars, and critics who knew his work or his reputation. At the Stein-Toklas place he more often met painters, such as Stein's current interest Pavel Tchelitchew, or writers, some French, more often expatriate British or American, like the young Oxford aesthete Harold Acton, who had just begun writing his second novel, or the cosmopolite Sisley Huddleston, who always insisted that Anderson's "poetical" language with its "subtle meanings" was more English or European than American and who considered Elizabeth "uncommonly alert and sympathetic." Yet Huddleston could report Anderson's newly ambivalent attitude toward France—"among all these evidences of a splendid and ancient civilization, there is a poverty that is far more killing and hopeless than the almost amusing poverty of my boyhood"—and could also report his fear that he would "have to go back to the [advertising] game."[16]

Acton, who liked Anderson despite their differences in temperament and background, felt that when among the many "very voluble and ultra-cosmopolitan" artists and writers who came and went in Stein's studio, Anderson tended to stand or sit rather silently "in the same place, musing and wondering and rather puzzled." The very best times for Sherwood were when—either alone or with Elizabeth—he could sit by the hour talking with Gertrude, meanwhile Elizabeth and Alice chatting amiably about their common interest in French and American cuisine. The talk between the American expatriate and the American visitor was often of things American. Stein had turned against Hemingway by this time, and to her sympathetic ear Anderson would have described with disgust and amusement the exchange of letters over *The Torrents of Spring*. (That he also told of the exchange to Archibald MacLeish, then writing poetry in Paris, at their one meeting confirms how much Hemingway's first letter continued to irritate him.) The two friends talked much about the Civil War, about Grant, whom both admired, and Lincoln, whom she liked less than he did. They enthusiastically planned a collaborative life of Grant but never carried it out. Anderson would record one conversation during which Stein held forth on her notion that since New York was the country's greatest city, it should also be the nation's capital. Once Sherwood and Elizabeth came to call after Alice at Gertrude's urging had cut off her companion's two long braids and cropped her hair short. When Alice asked Sherwood how he liked it, he said he did, that it made her look like a monk. Elizabeth was shocked at the remark, but Gertrude was delighted and wore her hair cut close thereafter. Despite Anderson's gloomy feeling that many things in Paris had changed for the worst, Stein for him was unchanged, as was the warmth of their friendship. Years later Toklas would write of this time to Anderson's fourth wife, "My memory of Gertrude and Sherwood together at the Rue de Fleurus is one of my happiest and most vivid."[17]

Anderson was less at ease with his two visits to the Friday afternoons of one of Stein's lesbian friends, the rich, bilingual writer, Natalie Barney who, though an American from Ohio, had established a famous salon at her pavilion at 20, rue Jacob. In the courtyard of the pavilion stood a small four-pillared Greek temple to Friendship in a garden where on warmer days concerts and poetry readings were held. On the first visit, the elegantly dressed Harold Acton went with "the shaggy tousled" Anderson, who was under the mistaken impression that the gathering was in his honor. Instead it was for the "burly" English feminist poet Anna Wickham, who read from her poems, each of which Barney translated, with commentary, into French for her audience. To Acton, Anderson seemed not to mind his mistake, but when Stein later asked Anderson about the event, he told her with humorous disgust that "it was a party for a big woman, and she was just a derailed freight car." Elizabeth recalled a second visit to the Barney salon. Gertrude and Alice invited the Andersons and Ralph Church, who had become well acquainted with Gertrude through Sherwood's letter of introduction, to attend another poetry reading in the garden. As a "tall, emaciated English lady with burning eyes . . . droned out her poetry," the Andersons and Church began to "shake with suppressed laughter" but managed to hold it in until the reading ended and they could get out on the street, where they "collapsed into great shouts of near hysterical, helpless laughter." The Barney salon was one of the "evidences of a splendid and ancient civilization" that was not for the American visitors.[18]

Sometime after the visits to 20, rue Jacob, perhaps early in February, Stein arranged a party in Anderson's honor so that many of her friends, some French, but a lot of them Americans, could meet him. Already the Andersons had been "much entertained and acclaimed by literary France," Sherwood would later write Karl with some pride: "Evidently my little hour has come over there." But although he had agreed to attend, apparently the prospect of meeting many adulating Americans brought back his despondency. When the time came to leave for the party, he refused to get dressed and go, despite Elizabeth's annoyed insistence that what he claimed to be a recurrence of the flu was actually depression. Extremely embarrassed, Elizabeth had to go to the party alone; but Alice tactfully explained to the American guests that Sherwood was too ill to come, Gertrude was shrewdly understanding, the Americans gradually drifted away, and what was left of the party turned out to be very pleasant. When Elizabeth returned to the hotel, Sherwood, she recalled, "was drinking whiskey and apparently having a good time all by himself, as if he had been able to exorcise his gloom by giving in to it."[19]

This act of self-indulgence may have had something to do with his beginning to write a little again. In the front of a small black notebook such as he could carry in a pocket to, say, the Brasserie Lipp, he printed his name and "Paris Feb 11–27." Inside, slight changes in hand suggest that at different times he had started to warm up by putting down thoughts or memories. A page asserting that he loves Christ as he was before Christianity became corrupt is followed, after a mark of separation by a series of erotic recollections: a blighted sexual affair with a woman named Edith, as a young man his keeping of a wooden figurine to be caressed, when he was despondent, but only at night and in the dark, his thrilled touching of a tree in Jackson Park in Chicago "once when I was in love and could not find a woman who satisfied me." There is a description of an hallucinatory night of "strange depression" in Cleveland when he awoke causelessly, certain that someone was being murdered in the house, is linked with an unpleasant personal experience, which at times has convinced him "that thoughts and impulses had by people in houses remain after the people go away." After pouring out these troubling memories from his past, Anderson asserts that the only thing worse for a writer than associating with money-oriented writers is associating with their "silly wives" who "chatter endlessly—always about writing." This passage, which sounds like a veiled comment on his own present situation or the future one he feared, leads to the longest part of the notebook, from page seven to the final page twenty-one, the draft of a story drawn from his hated advertising experience.[20]

The draft opens autobiographically with "Jim" having a nervous breakdown and going with wife and child to a wild stretch of country in the Ozarks because he "for years has been doing something he does not want to do," but it quickly shifts focus despite a kind of author's self-direction midway through the draft: "The thing to do is to get at Jim, tell why he went down to the Ozark mountains—what happened to him there." Instead, the body of the tale is a rambling, half essay, half narrative about four advertising copywriters, including Jim—four "little sick whores of business," one, the cynical Fred, calls them—who work with a dozen others in a big "rabbit pen" of a room "day after day—year after year to serve some obscure purpose with which they had nothing to do." Like the men who make money writing formula stories for magazines, these four get drunk frequently, "trying to establish something," talking and trying not to talk about their lives; for when "you" talk, you

take a long stick and stir up the mess of life. What do you find?
A stench eh—Green looking stuff floating up to the surface.
Let it alone.
For God sake let it alone.
You can't.

Then as though Anderson felt it too painful to go on specifically with Jim, the draft ends abruptly with a sketch of a fifth copywriter, "a quiet capable man very silent," who shoots himself at a desk in a hotel room, his head falling forward onto blank sheets of white copy paper: "Red blood rather than black ink all those sheets."

In that brief notebook Anderson put much that was pressing against his mind through images of corruption, long ago desire, loss, darkness of mood, inexplicable fear, all too explicable fear of a forced return to the loathsome abuse of language and spirit, destruction of self as person and writer, the suicide whose blood rather than his writing covering the white sheets of paper. This last was, indeed, not a symbol but an exact picture of the emotional state of the blocked writer and the severely depressed human being. He wrote nothing more except letters. "Paris is N. G. [no good] for me," he told H. L. Mencken. "I get nothing here but flu. Coming home in two weeks."[21]

That last thought carried him through a last attack of the flu in late February. God only knew, he had written in the notebook, how glad he was to escape from New York or Paris. There were still ends to tie up. It was arranged that Mimi was to stay on at her school until June 1, John at the Académie until September 1. At fifteen Mimi had been more interested in acquiring French and thinking about her school crowd back at Michigan City than in talking with Stein. John, on the other hand, who had expected to find Stein someone "arty with a long cigarette holder," had seen her several times and was much impressed by her "horse sense." After the older Andersons had left, John called on her frequently and became one of her favorites. She noted that upon his parents' leaving he at once changed from "an awkward shy boy" to an assured, handsome young man; decades later he would think of his whole stay in Paris as a young art student as "a golden time." Ralph Church had gone back to Oxford, but the Andersons had been seeing his mother often and were quite taken with her "infinitely fine quality" and concerned that she was at loose ends. On one of his "wild impulses," which Elizabeth "for once" agreed with, Sherwood wrote Ralph a long excited letter, urging him and his mother to buy the farm adjacent to Ripshin so that she could occupy herself building a house on it and being their neighbor. Given the tensions developing between the Andersons, one suspects that Elizabeth wanted a genteel woman nearby as companion, perhaps one to help her get Sherwood through his despondency, but nothing came of the proposal. [22]

There were good-byes to be said, for one to Hemingway, who was in Paris between bouts of skiing at Gstaad. He had already called on the Andersons at the Regnard and had had much fun scoffing at the shabbiness and inefficiency of the hotel until, to Sherwood's dismay, Elizabeth snapped back at "poor Ernest" with a deliberately rude defense of the Regnard as a place where they had been treated well. Very possibly Hemingway, his nerves raw from the divorce from Hadley he had precipitated, was offended, which would account for his brusque last meeting with Sherwood as the latter would recall it in his *Memoirs*. On the Andersons' last day in Paris, Hemingway came to their hotel room and to Anderson suggested a drink. The two men crossed the street to a bar, ordered beers, said "Here's how," and gulped their beers. Then without saying anything more Hemingway walked quickly away. The evening farewell was much pleasanter, for the Andersons dined with the Jolases at Lipp's. Maria, who was fond of Sherwood, had noted throughout his stay how frustrated he had been at not knowing French and being unable to communicate, as he had hoped, with French workers. Now she realized that he still could not even understand the menu, for when she asked him what he would have, he answered wryly, reading the words at the bottom of the menu, "I'll have Lavabo [Lavatory] Telephone." Nevertheless, they all chatted happily about the future of *transition* as a bridge between European and American experimental literature and about their New Orleans days together, and laughed at something on the expedition they, together with John, the Jolases' four-month-old daughter and the daughter's nurse, had taken to Colombay-les-deux-Églises to look at a house the Jolases thought of buying in order to get away from Paris. (They did buy it, lived in it for three years, and then sold it to a youngish French army major named Charles de Gaulle.) The peasant woman nurse became very suspicious of Sherwood and told Maria that Mrs. Anderson looked much too young to have had a son as old as John. Maria explained that John was the son of a former wife, that Mr. Anderson had been married before, in fact had been married twice before. "What," the nurse had asked suspiciously, "do the wives die of?"[23]

The next morning, March 4, the Andersons took the boat train from Paris to catch the Hamburg-Amerika liner *Cleveland*. It was a slow German ship, at first the sea was rough, and again seasickness kept Elizabeth in the cabin for two days. His spirits recovering because he was in move-

ment, Sherwood walked the decks in the cold, gray weather, read, and began writing thank-you letters to Paris friends. The Prussian captain, having read *Poor White* in translation, allowed him to stand on the bridge
with him; but Anderson decided that he did not "feel warm or close to either the English or Germans," as he very much did to the French. Looking
back on his Paris experience, he began to feel better about it since the
French had apparently taken his work up. Toward the end of this uneventful voyage over a mostly quiet sea, he began at last to sense that he
might be able to write again after the long barren months. He felt guilty
that the expense of the trip kept him from repaying his debt to Karl, but
he would do so, he wrote his brother, from one of the lectures on his tour.
Nearing Halifax, the slow ship was further slowed by dense fog and was
a day late in reaching New York. Early in the morning of March 16 the
Cleveland docked at West Forty-fourth Street, and the Andersons went
ashore just about the time, Sherwood would be shocked to learn from Karl
later that day, brother Earl had died at the Marine Hospital in Newport.[24]

New York that day and the next was even more a madhouse than before. Apparently Karl saw to having Earl's body prepared for burial, a coffin purchased, and preparations made for shipping it to Clyde for burial;
but he also went to Liveright's office with Sherwood, who among other
matters had to arrange to file his 1926 income tax a day late because of
the *Cleveland*'s delay. If Karl's later memory was accurate, his brother's income for the year had been $16,000, largely because of the success of
Dark Laughter; yet Sherwood needed more money. Elizabeth was to go directly to Ripshin, but Sherwood had to find out the itinerary of his lecture
tour, which began abruptly the following evening with a talk "somewhere
in New Jersey" and the next evening one in Brooklyn. Immediately after
the Brooklyn lecture, he and Karl took a train to Ohio with Earl's body in
its coffin riding in the baggage car.[25]

The funeral ceremony was conducted in Clyde on March 19, "a very
dour day, cold and dismal," Karl would recall, and Earl was buried in
McPherson Cemetery beside his mother. After the burial Sherwood started
at once for Memphis on his lecture tour, his frame of mind only to be wondered at since, curiously, he did not mention the interment in any of his letters of the time. On the way south he stopped in Springfield, Ohio, to visit
his son Bob, who seems to have taken a newspaper job there. While in
France, Anderson had been incensed by a book review Bob had written of
Martha Ostenso's *The Dark Dawn,* a review, he felt as "faky from start to
finish" as that melodramatic novel itself; and he had sent his son a harsh letter warning him against the slickness that he detested as also a part of
himself. By now John had clearly become his favorite son; the young art student had shown "some red flashes of talent" and unlike the cleverer Bob,

the father felt, was "straight with his own feelings." The visit was a pleasant surprise, however, for despite that review and letter he found Bob amazingly improved in his awareness of other people through the kind attention and counsel Bab had been giving him. From Springfield, Anderson went on to two evening lectures, "America—A Storehouse of Vitality" and "The Younger Generation," at the Goodwyn Institute in Memphis, doubled back north to talk in Detroit, and then spent Sunday, March 27, with Bab in Indianapolis, a day of "rest and . . . real joy" during which she urged that Bob should be given the chance to go to college. The following day he was in Chicago lecturing, taking his old friend George Daugherty and Cornelia to dinner, and greatly pleasing his first wife by reporting Mimi's fine progress at the French school. One good result of the Paris stay was that he had come to know his daughter better and to see her, no longer a child, as interesting and lovable, a person he could write letters to with fatherly advice.[26]

On March 29 in Madison, Wisconsin, in one of the university's largest lecture halls he gave his "The Younger Generation" lecture. His platform manner as well as many quotations from his talk were reported at length on the front page of the student newspaper by one of its desk editors, who, impressed yet observant, saw an aging but stimulating speaker.

A short thick-set man with a shock of iron-grey hair, Sherwood Anderson delivered himself of . . . a succession of pithy sayings last night, as he paced the platform of Music Hall and twisted his fingers in nervous absorption.

Speaking in a voice which oscillated between a throaty rumbling and an almost feminine shrillness, he condemned the writers of popular standardized literature and lauded the efforts of the younger generation of writers who are striving to see and express the realities of life.

Anderson had an additional reason for being in Madison, to discuss the possibility of a scholarship for John to the Experimental College, just founded within the university by Alexander Meiklejohn of the Philosophy Department, which might provide the unconventional sort of education that would suit his son. Meiklejohn was out of town, but President Glenn Frank, who came to see the famous writer in his hotel room, was encouraging and promised to speak to Meiklejohn, as did Kimball Young, the energetic sociology professor, a friend of Anderson's, who had sponsored his lecture. A college education might have its drawbacks, but his sons and daughter, Anderson had decided with his new interest in his children, should at least have their chances at it.[27]

Weary from the "ghastly exhibitionism" of the tour, he headed back to New York to do his final lecturing and to read proof for his forthcoming *A New Testament.* He talked with Herbert Croly at the *New Republic* about the possibility of scholarships from Mrs. Witland Straight's fund for both John and Bob; Bob, he felt, especially needed to be with people his own age. For pleasure he went to see a show of Karl's paintings at the Ferargil Galleries and visited his brother in Westport. Then he was free to return on April 6 or 7 to Ripshin and the quiet country life.[28]

2.

In the hills there was an unusually early and glorious spring, the apple, peach, cherry, plum trees already coming into blossom, violets blooming along Ripshin Creek, arbutus in the woods. "The second year in the same valley," Anderson wrote Stieglitz joyfully, "is like living with a lovely woman after the first fever of passion and when the little nice things about her begin to come out." Marion Ball had withdrawn the construction deposit from the Troutdale bank and had stayed drunk much of the winter, but he now had a few carpenters and painters, not the small army of them as in the previous summer, back at work finishing the last details of the house. One of the first things the Andersons did was to buy Elizabeth a riding horse so that they now had two, a gray and a bay, and they often rode together. They had decided to become "agricultural." Elizabeth bought three hen turkeys and a cock, three geese and a gander, and soon had the hens laying, while Sherwood put the farmer Claude Reedy to clearing four more acres for corn. John and Mimi wrote in high spirits from Paris. Mimi was making good grades, and Sherwood in his new fatherly affection sent her extra money for school excursions outside the city so that she could make the most of her remaining time abroad. With relief he was able to settle accounts with Karl. For some reason Earl had made Sherwood and Irve but not Karl beneficiaries of a one-thousand-dollar life insurance policy, and both of the younger brothers now made over their insurance checks to Karl as their share of expenses he had incurred in caring for Earl. As a result of all this welcome activity Anderson felt physically well for the first time in months and even began writing again.[29]

Cities, intellectuals, other writers, literary talk were not for him, he had decided—the thought of James Joyce made his "bones ache"—and instead he wanted to get inside the lives of the hill people, who in their reserved way were slowly admitting him to friendship. When he wrote about them, as he now began to do, developing in his imagination or even just recounting incidents picked up from them in chance conversations, he was the storyteller again and rapidly drafted a number of tales, which he put aside for ripening. One day he spent the whole afternoon talking with "a queer gentle little man" named Felix Sullivan. Sullivan was supposed to be building a stone wall for a sunken wildflower garden in front of Ripshin, and he later boasted among his friends that he had been paid by Anderson just for sitting and talking rather than lifting stones. When

Anderson eventually heard of the boast, he was amused that the joke was on Felix; for Felix had been spinning yarns about his experiences with a French family during the Great War, and Anderson had contrived out of them his first mountain people tale, which appeared as part of "A Note on Story Tellers," published in the August *Vanity Fair*. The three-hundred-dollar payment for the magazine piece seemed a pretty good return on a dollar or so to Felix for a few hours of "loafing." Many of the mountain people were skilled storytellers, he explained in that piece, because they could make each word in their limited vocabularies "serve many purposes," could fit each into the complete tale, give it its necessary "design, form."[30]

The mornings spent wrestling with *Another Man's House* were another thing. By the end of April he had to admit that the novel "broke and broke"; toward the end of May he had had a month of "sheer struggle" with it because he "kept superimposing myself on it"; late in June he was again deep in the novel, which had "started and stopped a dozen times," all the starts turning out to be "fakes." When the novel "goes," he confessed to Burton Emmett, "I am happy. When it falls to pieces, because the structure isn't sound, I have days of being miserable." A new cause for, or symptom of, the recurring days of depression stood out in his letters. The weekly checks from Horace Liveright and his obligation to produce writing in return continued to trouble him deeply; but in addition on his bad days he now felt a "deep sickness" over the fame he had encountered in Paris, his own and that of Joyce and Hemingway, and the "big feelings, self-induced" brought on by being considered a success, whatever that was. He had seen self-importance "popping" detestably in those other two writers and detested it in himself, detesting it all the more because his continuing failure to find the right way into his novel made him less and less likely to meet his own standards of success as artist. "The point of being an artist," he advised his now beloved son John in Paris, was not to produce "salable pictures" but to "live," and one truly "lives" through creating on paper or canvas: "The materials have to take the place of God." What one gets from creative work, he told John in another letter after a morning when he had managed to write until his hands were shaky, "is the power of losing self. Self is the grand disease. It is what we all are trying to lose." But on the days when he failed to write, his concern with self became obsessive. "I've had a bad six months, inside," he admitted to Paul Rosenfeld at the end of April, "and may be in for another."[31]

So the spring continued, Elizabeth not knowing whether her husband would be up or down in mood from day to day. Fortunately, she had come to love the farm almost as much as he did, and it was the activity of the farm and the delight both took in watching the spring advance around them that kept their winter's irritation with each other temporarily muted. In early May, as the dark purple rhododendrons blossomed, they were excited by the birth of a girl baby to Claude Reedy's wife and diverted by the first of the summer's visitors. The wealthy Lucile Swan, now divorced from Sherwood's painter friend Jerome Blum, came to stay for the summer, living first at Ripshin, then in a nearby house, painting and riding a black horse she had purchased across the countryside. By late May the white and red rhododendrons and the mountain laurel were out; the "whole country," Anderson wrote Bab ecstatically, was "a mass of color . . . and the air heavy with perfume." For the moment he seems to have been buoyed up also by reading the two volumes he had perhaps picked up in London of Julius Meier-Graefe's *Vincent van Gogh, A Biographical Study;* for it was through Van Gogh, he wrote Paul Rosenfeld, urging him to a long visit, that "I am getting a little straightened out . . . this time. . . ."

> Just now it seems to me Van Gogh was as near right as a man can be.
> I mean only my own efforts to get humanized here. To penetrate into the soil, plowed fields, people in little houses in hollows, to shake off, if possible, all smart-aleckness.

The way out was not Gauguin's to the exotic far away but rather Van Gogh's submergence in the land and life. Quite appropriately, "like peasants—land hungry" the Andersons began to think of adding a twenty-five-acre piece of high hill land, which Elizabeth herself purchased in August and had cleared as a meadow for sheep and more turkeys.[32]

By May 23 he had accepted an invitation to receive an honorary Doctor of Letters degree at the commencement exercises on June 5 at Wittenberg College in Springfield, Ohio, and on a rainy morning just before that date, he set off north over the mountains by car. He had mixed feelings about returning to the campus where over a quarter of a century before he had had his last year of formal schooling and from which he had gone, at first enthusiastically, into advertising, the now-hateful occupation he again feared he might have to resume. The degree was a form of recognition of him as a writer, but the recognition was from conventional society and thus another sign of success and fame, which now seemed "detrimental" to him. He had just learned, too, that Karl, who in Springfield days had barely begun his painting career, was having emotional trouble, having at fifty-three "come to a sudden and terrible realization of the futility of much of his life and his art." The tree-shaded college campus was "very lovely," he wrote Karl disconsolately on the way home; but the weather was hot—a photograph taken of him after the ceremony shows him in full academic regalia of cap, hood, and long gown—and the speeches and prayers were filled with references to God, "all of it as far away from myself as Mars." With both brothers it was "the same story. Perhaps as we grow older we realize more fully the terrible limitations of ourselves compared to what we want to do." Earl was much on his mind, that dead brother's life like any artist's life "so crammed full of disappointments and futility" that it was "a kind of living picture of all the more sensitive lives of our times." As for himself, he wrote these days "desperately. If—in what we want to do—there is not salvation where is it?" Karl should come to Ripshin in early July after Paul Rosenfeld's impending visit was over, he concluded, though he was "damned doubtful" that he had "something clear in me from which you could get some thing."[33]

Fortunately Rosenfeld arrived soon after Anderson's return home and stayed until July 4. Whatever the reason Paul had never been so easy to get along with, and the visit was "a great success." With Paul and his "razor edged" brain, Sherwood wrote Karl, this time cheerfully, "you have to pay for what you get but you get a lot." Then before Paul left, Margaret Prall, the violinist, arrived for a brief stay. She was Sherwood's favorite of Elizabeth's sisters, a "hard working and straight" woman, and she also got on well with Paul. Anderson still had his "miserable" days when *Another Man's House* resisted him, but by the end of June he had another mountain people story, "A Jury Case," ready for typing and final correction.[34]

During the spring he had managed to "grind out" his monthly pieces for *Vanity Fair* after missing the March issue completely because of his illness in Paris, substituting six pieces from the forthcoming *A New Testament* for the usual essay in the April issue, and having "Educating an Author," the one article completed abroad, printed in *Vanity Fair* in May. "On Conversing with Authors," a slight piece written in April judging by its subject and appearing in the June number, is a satirical attack on self-important authors, whose "whole purpose . . . is to live quite separated from ordinary people." "New York" in the July issue—an expanded version of a draft written "After an evening [drinking Prohibition liquor] in a night club"—is an impressionistic representation of the speed, noise, power, and "vast grim imperial beauty of our great American city." The tale "A Jury Case," however, was not aimed at *Vanity Fair;* rather, Anderson sent this "murder story" to Otto Liveright's agency for sale "at a good price to some popular magazine" or else to Mencken's *American Mercury.* The tale was proof that Anderson knew the darker side of mountain life, here the shooting of a mean whiskey-maker, Harvey Groves, by George Small, a weak man dominated by an even meaner roughneck Cal Long. With many short declarative sentences an "I" person narrator first describes Harvey's hard-bitten father, who could make whiskey out of "anything . . . potatoes, buckwheat, rye, corn," in order to give the reader the necessary moonshine lore, and then characterizes the hell-raising Harvey and the dangerous Cal before focusing on George, the "country neurotic," and his nervous, sickly wife. A storyteller within the story, Luther Ford, has told the narrator an ugly instance of how Cal likes to bully George physically and "spiritually too." Returning drunk from town late one night, Cal and George stand outside George's house, his wife, inside the house, sick with a pregnancy, and Cal eggs George on to join him in cursing her, George even "strutting like a little rooster as he cursed." The narrator takes up the tale, quickly telling how Harvey, Cal, and George buy a still, how Harvey steals it from the other two, and how Cal forces George to take his shotgun and go with him after Harvey, George to do the shooting. Then, skillfully adapting the scene in *Huck Finn* where a "long lanky man" acts out Colonel Sherburn's shooting of Boggs, Anderson has his narrator move into long complex sentences for maximum suspense as he describes how the "long and loose-jointed" Luther Ford, "who is something of a dramatist," depicts the scene of the killing by acting it out, Cal in this dramatization making the driven George shoot just by touching him on the shoulder. After the murder Cal skips the country, George is imprisoned, his wife goes "clear off her nut." Luther Ford and others who have known all three men predict that any jury in the county will return a verdict on George of not guilty. The narrator, not having lived as long in the county as the others, asks himself, "How do I know what I think?" and concludes both evasively and to the reader challengingly, "It's a matter, of course, the jury will have to decide." *The American Mercury,* which had published "Five Poems" from *A New Testament* in its May issue, wisely bought "A Jury Case" for its December number.[35]

Apparently Rosenfeld's June visit kept Anderson's "miserable" days to a minimum, and his presence must have been reassuring as Anderson waited for the reviews of *A New Testament,* published on June 15. He had reason to be uneasy about the reception of what he had termed to Paul back in October of 1921 "this purely experimental thing . . . my own Bible," which now appeared as a small book, its blue board cover stamped with title and author's name in gold Gothic lettering like a pocket New Testament. (The limited edition, bound in vellum and boards and boxed, had an even more ecclesiastical format including a blue silk marker.) These experiments, now brought together in a single volume, had been written at different times over seven years of personal and artistic change from early 1919 to early 1926 and so had expressed varying moods, attitudes, experiences, wishes, beliefs. In the initial series of thirteen published in *The Little Review* from 1919 to 1921, this "autobiography of the fanciful life of an individual" had been loosely but effectively organized into a three-part pattern in which Anderson had explored his consciousness, reaching back courageously into troubling depths. Later when he spaced four more testaments strategically through *The Triumph of the Egg,* tracing a putative storyteller's passage from speechlessness to prophetic utterance, again a pattern emerged, this one reinforcing the collective implications of the two sets of tales. As he continued to write testaments, however, they became, intentionally, more and more fragmentary records of the life of his imagination. In assembling *A New Testament* he broke up and redistributed the pieces of the two early patterns, seemingly at random, and did not create a new overall pattern for the book. So not only might, and did, several reviewers question the form of the individual testaments—were they to be considered poems, prose poems, pieces of lyrical prose, Zarathustran pronouncements, Bible-like psalms or parables?—such reviewers objected to the book's lack of structure. Presumably Anderson felt that the structurelessness and fragmentedness of his *Testament* represented the very nature of the imaginative life, his own and that of others.

Part of what holds the book together, very loosely indeed, is the recurrence of several themes among a number of individual pieces, though by no means all. Occasionally the bardic note of *Mid-American Chants* appears; for example, the "one who would be a priest" who speaks the four "songs" making up "Testament" proclaims in Whitmanesque fashion "a new song . . . an American song" and addresses a "you" whom the speaker has seen in a catalog of situations and occupations. The bardic note tends to include the theme of regeneration or resurrection, as in the lyric prose of the brief "A Poet," the note's best expression.

> If I could be brave enough and live long enough I could crawl inside the life of every man, woman and child in America. After I had gone within them I could be born out of them. I could become something the like of which has never been seen before. We would see then what America is like.

The speaker or speakers of the testaments rarely assert any specific midwesterness as in the *Chants,* however, and "Americans" usually is a term for all other human beings. The most frequently occurring theme in *A New Testament* is the imaginative entrance of the artist-speaker into others, with connecting themes suggesting a pattern at least within Anderson's mind. As in *Poor White* and *Many Marriages,* all individuals live isolated lives behind walls, sometimes the "stone and iron" one of industrialized cities, sometimes those of imprisoning selfhood. The artist-speaker reaches out toward these others, touching them through his words or through the sheer force of his creative vitality and liberating them into life. So in "Man Lying on a Couch," a title suggesting the act of fantasizing, the speaker declares himself in quite obviously psychosexual terms to be a tree growing toward the top of a wall, desiring to "drop blossoms and fruit" over it, to "moisten dry lips," to "caress with falling blossoms the bodies of those who live on the farther side of the wall."

Occasionally in a related theme another person enters the emotional

life of the speaker directly, as in "An Emotion: To E. P.," the initials indicating that this was a love poem written to Elizabeth before marriage.
Wrapped in a gold and silver gown, E. P. walks "softly in the dust of the
road, whispering words"; the speaker runs into the road, tears at her
gown, and "With a little whispering laugh she passed into me. I was drawn
into her and was healed." In several of the testaments, however, the reaching out toward others is balked; in fact, the concluding piece in the book,
the three-part "A Man and Two Women Standing by a Wall Facing the
Sea" explicitly affirms isolation and denies human communication. The
first woman cannot see through her narrow-slitted eyes "what life is like";
the man becomes "a holy man," that is, an artist, carrying his message
through countryside and city but is everywhere beaten and flayed by
everyone's hands; the second woman laments that though she is born into
"a wide colorful world," she sees herself as gray, colorless, and so is not
born after all.

It is possible, though not provable, that this concluding testament was
the last one Anderson wrote, back early in 1926, in reaction to the news
of Earl's stroke on a New York street; for in its confessions by imprisoned,
tormented selves it might well foreshadow Sherwood's notion in his recent
letter to Karl that the sad, thwarted life of their brother seemed "a living
picture of all the more sensitive lives of our time." The contradiction between this prominently placed testament and those with the more frequent
theme of the penetrating, liberating artist confirms that, ultimately, what
holds this book together is less recurrent themes than the obvious fact that
all these pieces are simply parts of Anderson's shifting, varied, intense "autobiography of the fanciful life," ironically a celebration of the "grand disease" of self, which in the summer of 1927 he was striving to recover from.
Some, perhaps many, of the testaments are as vague, even opaque in meaning as several reviewers would complain; others are startlingly clear, such
as the violent "The Ripper," that parable of hatred for death-in-life lives,
or powerfully imaged, such as the even more violent, surrealistic "A
Young Jew," with its phantasmagoria of a mother whose "breasts are
tipped with flame," a son burning his "flame out in an empty place," both
beholding a world "choked with smoke of burning men" likewise "burning out in an empty place." "The Ripper" and "A Young Jew" are both
less astonishing of Anderson when one remembers the physical and psychological violence in "The Man Who Became a Woman." *A New Testament* is a flawed, minor work, of most value to Anderson himself as a
record of how he released his imagination so that he might "grope" in the
first half of the 1920s with uneven success for new kinds of prose, new
kinds of fiction. Yet William Wright, his closest friend in Troutdale, could
remember how, as they drove home from a day's fishing, Anderson
stopped his car, got out a package of copies of *A New Testament*, which

his publisher had just sent him, opened it, took out one copy, inscribed it to Wright, told him it would sound foolish at first but that if he read in it from time to time it would take on meaning, as Wright later found for him it did.[36]

3.

The first reviews of *A New Testament* in June had been gratifyingly favorable, and in early July Sherwood could write Karl in one of his up moods that "The Testament has shot home well in the right places." His old friend Harry Hansen, for example, had praised him in the New York *World* as "one of the few authentic authors of our time" and his book as "bringing home many rich truths." The *Boston Transcript* had turned in the dissent—"This is not creative art, merely a very self-conscious artist allowing the public to see the turmoil inside his head"—but the *Transcript* had always been unfriendly, and what could one expect from cold New England, that wrong place?[37]

Things were going well generally. Paul had left for Maine on July 4; the pleasant Margaret would be at Ripshin through most of July, John's letters from Paris were "full of fine frankness," and it looked as though Bob might be entering the University of Virginia in the fall. The carpenters and painters had finished their work, the air in the rooms seemed sweet, and Anderson was drawn irresistibly to his own completed house, drawn down from his writing cabin since the "rich sensuality" of the surrounding hills was too much of a "direct challenge" for him. With Cornelia and Tennessee, he told Karl, "I always had to escape as far as I could from them to work at all," but now he wanted to work in his and Elizabeth's bedroom or where they sat in the evening, a sure sign that for the moment they were again happy together, and of course that the writing for the moment went well. Around early July on a day of discouragement with *Another Man's House,* he had written a note to Boni and Liveright "proposing that they farm me out to a minor league"—that is, stop sending the weekly hundred-dollar advance—but he had not sent the note since almost immediately the prose began to flow. Now at last the novel was getting "the earthy full feeling" he wanted, and he seemed to himself "contented"—a word he had not used for months—to stay at Ripshin and "work out my artistic problem here."[38]

His contentment seems to have lasted through much of July, through Margaret's stay and a ten-day visit from Max and Dorothea Prall Radin, who had been in Europe and had kindly accompanied Mimi from Paris back to New York. The previous summer, Sherwood noted with amusement, various Andersons had been looking him and Elizabeth over; this summer they were being looked over by the Pralls, who had almost certainly been privately alerted by Ralph Church to the tensions he had observed between the couple in Paris. For a long time Anderson had been considering what he had named to Karl as "the problem of relationships," and very likely prompted by the visits of various relatives, he broke off from the novel to write the story "The Fight" in the simple, straightforward prose of "A Jury Case." This slight tale exemplifies what Anderson called "the two voices," which a writer must be alert to in a person or a character. Earlier he had had the teacher Kate Swift explain the concept to George Willard: "The thing to learn is to know what people are thinking about, not what they say." Most recently the concept had informed one of the two epigraphs of *A New Testament*: "They talked and their lips said audible words but the voices of their inner lives went on uninterrupted." In the story two middle-aged professional men cousins, John and Alfred Wilder, have had "something wrong with their relationship" since childhood, some irrational antagonism, which had made them want to fight, though they never did. As a boy John, through whose consciousness the narrator presents most of the story, was compelled by his mother to give his beloved puppy to Alfred for a Christmas present; and as a youth he took a shameful joy in shooting the dog as a possible sheep-killer. Growing into mid-life in separate cities, the cousins continue to hate each other and to be elaborately polite in any communication. When Alfred on a business trip comes to visit John and his wife in their Chicago suburb home, the two men, now in their fifties, at last stumble into a fist fight in which John gets a black eye and Alfred a bloody nose. But the "fight had settled nothing." Alfred at once packs and leaves the house, to the dismay of John's wife since, as she tells her husband, she has become fond of his cousin. John gets "out of his wife's presence as soon as he can" and walks about the house, telling himself with satisfaction that he gave Alfred some good body punches that ought to make him sore the next morning.[39]

Needing money, Anderson sent off this tale of hostile family relationships to Otto Liveright to be placed elsewhere than in *Vanity Fair* but Otto was unable to do so, and it was printed as Anderson's contribution to that magazine's October issue. (He would have no piece at all in the September number.) Otto's lack of success may have been a disappointment to Anderson, but it was nothing compared with the devastation that struck early in August. While he was discarding "perhaps 200,000 words" of *Another Man's House* in July and "getting some of the old stuff on the ball" with yet another beginning, two more strongly unfavorable reviews of *A New Testament* appeared. In the *New York Evening Post Literary Review*, the poet Conrad Aiken praised Anderson's short stories but dismissed the *Testament* as "a mere welter of pictures, some bad and some good, but in the main meaningless"; and in a review titled "Betrayal" in the *Herald Tribune Books* section, another poet, Babette Deutsch, concluded that "It is difficult to believe that any man who respects the craft of writing should cause to be printed a bundle of utterances that read like the free monologue of a psychiatrist's patient whose reading matter has been limited to Whitman and Djuna Barnes." These were bad enough, but the review that hurt most excruciatingly was that by Lawrence S. Morris in *The New Republic* for August 3, 1927: "Sherwood Anderson: Sick of Words." In his early novels and tales, Morris began, Anderson wrote within a narrow range and in the "mood of adolescence," but he used "fresh words which had grown out of his own experience. He was minor and genuine." Soon, however, his writing degenerated into sentimentality and vagueness, and he began to "love [words] for their own sake" until "At last he had become a professional writer." Now his "posturing of pretty words, filled with vague emotion, is the double disease which has been consuming Anderson." In *A New Testament* he "has reached the place where he is content to put unreal emotions into unreal words." Then after quoting lines from "The Red-Throated Black," Morris concluded with the one-sentence, almost literal coup de grace: "The author of *Winesburg, Ohio* is dying before our eyes."[40]

In describing in mid-August the effect of the review upon him Anderson was the most open to the man he knew least well, had still not even met. To his friend Stark Young he admitted that the review had made him "sick for a day," because of Morris's "evident revengeful feeling, so much unconcealed joy in the death"; with bravado he told Stieglitz that he liked "thumping criticism" since the real champion must expect an occasional "mauling"; writing to Ralph Church he passed off the "roasting" with studied casualness: "It didn't affect me much." But sitting up in his bathrobe with a headache and stomachache on the morning of August 19, he confessed to Burton Emmett that

The article, when I read it, made me sick to my soul.
    I spent a couple of days in hell, trying to deny to myself what the man said. In fact I have hardly recovered yet. The fellow doesn't quibble at hitting below the belt. My present belly ache may be due to one or two punches he landed.

To all these four men he agreed with varying degrees of self-confidence that the Anderson of *Winesburg* was indeed dead and that the significant question was what new Anderson was emerging since, as he told Church, and himself, "the only fun is in trying to push on into something else." But Morris's "funereal" piece had contemptuously charged him as having degenerated into what he despised and feared becoming, "a professional writer." It would not have helped his darkening mood that Boni and Liveright was about to publish *Who and What: A Book of Clues for the Clever,* a book of 793 riddles, edited by Samuel Hopkins Adams "in association with many prominent people," including Anderson and many obviously professional writers, such as Alexander Woollcott and Kathleen Norris. Presumably Horace Liveright had paid well to bring together so large a group of the literary prominent.

By now the summer's visitors had all gone, Sherwood and Elizabeth were left together, and there could have begun only now the further grim days she would remember so unhappily. With *Another Man's House* going badly or not at all, Anderson sank into a deeper depression than ever. "Dissatisfied and ugly," as he would put it to Bab, eaten up by "self," he began to turn on his wife as the one who had wanted him to be a professional writer, as the one who was now the cause for his inability to write. He "began to be subtly cruel and hard," she would recall, and to her instance of this new hostility—the instance actually occurred a whole year later—the crude but clear-sighted Bill Wright could add another. Once after lunch the two men remained seated talking while Elizabeth went upstairs to change into riding clothes. When she came down past the dining table, Sherwood glanced at her and said, "You look just like Tennessee." Elizabeth, aware that his words were a slur, went angrily back upstairs and never wore that habit again. By mid-August the couple began taking, in Elizabeth's words, "long, terrible drives through the country" in the moonlit nights, "neither of us saying a word for hours, cloaked in bitter, choking silence." Feeling helpless to help him, she sometimes refused to go along, but he insisted "for a reason that became shatteringly clear to me."

We were driving along a deserted road, nearly in North Carolina. The road had a soft shoulder that fell away to a deep slope. Without any preamble, Sherwood said, in a strange blank voice, "I wish it were all over." With that, he twisted the wheel and we went over the edge.

We skittered and slid and nearly toppled over, but somehow the car remained upright until the slope flattened out and then the car simply rolled to a halt in the middle of a field.

It was a grim illumination for me. I had not dreamed he was desperate enough to try to kill us both.

After a long silence Sherwood began getting the car back on the road, and silently they drove home, never speaking of the incident afterwards.[41]

Although the experience must have been terrifying for Elizabeth and although at the following Christmas time Sherwood would admit to Bab that "Lots of times I said to myself—why don't you die," it would appear that this suicide-homicide attempt, though dangerous, was not truly life-threatening. After all, a "deep slope" is not a cliff, and by her account it was gentle enough that he was able to get the car back to the road without assistance. Rather, the attempt was a gesture, far more serious than the youthful stamping on his own straw hat as Herman Hurd remembered his friend doing, but characteristic in its pattern: resentment against a fancied hostility from another and an impulsive act of aggression against that person, but an aggression expressed symbolically through self-destructive behavior. One wonders whether Anderson had ever talked with Hurd about his marriages or whether Herman had profoundly intuited that the pattern was connected to his friend's "inability to stay with any woman long." Clearly, as Elizabeth understood, Sherwood was projecting his own self-hatred onto her, and though they continued to live together, the marriage began to dissolve from that point on.

4.

With this incident Anderson touched emotional bottom, and he might well have stayed there except for a chance encounter. The Smyth County Fair was held that year in Marion, the seat of the county just north of Troutdale's Grayson County, from August 30 through September 3, and on one of those five days the Andersons went to see the harness races since Elizabeth loved the trotters and pacers almost as much as Sherwood did. While sitting in the grandstand, Anderson got into conversation with a manufacturer in Marion named Denny Culbert, who told him that the two small weekly newspapers in Marion were for sale. As Elizabeth recalled it, Anderson was almost at once interested in becoming a country newspaper editor, they thereupon left the fair and went straight to the office of Arthur L. Cox, owner and editor of the *Smyth County News* and the *Marion Democrat,* and when Cox had explained "the setup," Sherwood told Cox "on the spot" that he would buy the papers. Possibly so; he could be very impulsive, as his wife had long known and would long remember. Yet the record indicates that for most of September he went over and over in his mind the question of whether he should and could buy the papers, a period of three weeks or more during which he, the constant letter writer, seems to have written no letters at all so concentrated was he in resolving the question.[42]

Assuming that he could find the means to purchase the papers, the venture was financially risky, and it did mean that temporarily at least he must abandon writing, "the only path," he had told Bab, "that makes life continually possible for me." Obviously his writing was sickeningly blocked anyway, and here was a way to deal with that fact, simply to evade it. But the most important reason for taking on the venture was that he was determined to give up the contractual arrangement with Horace Liveright whereby he received one hundred dollars a week for producing a book a year. From the beginning of the arrangement Sherwood had worried about this obligation, and now he had become convinced that, as he put it to Bab late in September, "I had got myself on the back of my own pen, was astride it, trying to ride it," so that he was "in these last two years in real danger of becoming a literary hack, hating the very paper on which I wrote." In the long letters he began writing the end of September to explain to his friends why he had decided to make the great change, this was the key point, that he desperately feared he was on the way to becoming a "professional writer," one of those contemptible persons he had consistently excoriated for having sold out their talent for fame and money. Somehow he had to support himself by honest work, and the only other work he could do, he told himself and then his friends, was at the dishonest trade of advertising. Were he to go back to that hated occupation, he would find it doubly distasteful, for now the head of any advertising firm would exploit the literary fame of his new employee. Buying and editing the papers might have its scary moments for him as a person untrained in journalism, but it would, finally, give him the chance to regain closeness to people, to real life, a closeness he felt he had lost in his months of being consumed by a destructive concern for self.[43]

The decision made, he began to feel more at peace with himself, the world, even his writing. Late in September, Henry Canby, editor of the *Saturday Review of Literature,* sent him a copy of the magazine containing an unsympathetic article on his work by Cleveland Chase condensed from Chase's short book *Sherwood Anderson* to be published in October. The article criticized Anderson's writings, except for a few short stories, as being marred by "great weaknesses," two of them being "profitless philosophic speculations" and "sentimental day-dreaming"; and Canby asked whether Anderson wished to contribute an answer. Although, Anderson replied, he especially disliked the feeling of the article, its "manufactured smartness," its "distinct pleasure" that he is "not a bigger and better man," he would not answer. If Chase knew so much about art and life that puzzled Anderson, why didn't he write a book "making it all clear" rather than attacking him? Besides, he was tired of being a public figure and would not add to his own publicity. (Late in November, enlivened by the fun of editing the papers, Anderson would in fact reply in the *Review* to Chase's attack, good-humoredly enlarging on points in his letter to Canby and suggesting that writers not sign their published work in order to end the current popular fascination with writers as personages. Presumably he was pleased when the *Review*'s reviewer of *Sherwood Anderson* attacked the book as lacking sympathy, "intellectual integrity," and understanding of its subject.) Evenhandedly, when N. Bryllion Fagin, a young professor of English at the University of Baltimore, sent him in October a copy of his book, *The Phenomenon of Sherwood Anderson: A Study in American Life & Letters,* a much more sympathetic critique, Anderson gently told the author of this second of the first two books entirely about his work: "In many cases of course our two points of view are not the same. How should they be?" Fagin had given his work "much more of his attention than it could by any stretch of the imagination deserve," but, he concluded, "I am grateful to you for being always kind to me."[44]

As for his own writing, it was probably in late September that he completed and sent off for the November *Vanity Fair* another tale drawn from his regional subject, "A Mountain Dance." Poly (Napoleon) Grubb, still a bit drunk from moonshine the morning after, tells the narrator about the dance of the night before. Stirred into a kind of craziness by the promise of snow in the wind that November evening and by the falling, dancing oak leaves, the young people of the area run silently as though by telepathic desire to a high hill and dance to a fiddler around a great bonfire all night, the men drinking whiskey steadily, the women not drinking but excited. Poly dances mostly with the strong, capable Stella Franklin, whom he plans to marry; but suddenly enamored of a loose mountain girl, he takes her into the darkness, then returns to dancing with Stella, who is aware of his being with the girl but, unconcerned, keeps on planning to marry him. In "A Jury Case," Anderson had shown that he knew some mountain people were dangerous but that most had an unconventional yet humane sense of justice; in this later tale he was explicitly correcting the popular "romancers" like John Fox, Jr. who "have done what they could to spread misunderstanding" of the mountain people. Miserably poor in their one-room cabins, they do not in their independence "feel poor" and so are not "really poor." Rarely dangerous, they are usually gentle and sensitive to the needs and desires of others even if their impulsive actions violate "normal" moral standards. As exemplified by the wild hilltop dance itself, they are also as deeply responsive to nature as the more sophisticated narrator, and as Anderson himself, and as capable of infusing with poetic imagination their outbursts of passionate emotion.

As always, Anderson received three hundred dollars from *Vanity Fair* for this piece, but in order to purchase the papers he needed far more substantial sums. To Anderson, the presumably wealthy man of Ripshin, the wily Cox named a price of $15,000 for the papers. The new owner would later learn that Cox had earlier offered them for $10,000, concealing also that they were $3,000 in debt. Cox would accept $7,000 in notes to be paid over three years out of profits from the papers and job printing operations, but the remaining $8,000 must be in cash. Of this, Anderson could raise $3,000 from a mortgage on Ripshin, but he needed $5,000 more. After his weeks of deliberation he decided that there was only one good possible source for this amount, and on September 27 he telegraphed Burton Emmett asking if he could meet him at his New York office on the morning of October 2, a Sunday. Anderson felt awkward about asking to borrow money from Emmett on the occasion of their first meeting, but Emmett was warmly gracious in New York and took him to his country home, Valley Cottage, in Nyack to meet his wife, Mary, and spend the night. The three got on so well that the time for Anderson seemed to pass "with unbelievable rapidity"; he could hardly believe that such nice people existed. Burton and Mary Emmett would in fact become long-term friends of his. Returning to New York the following day, he had sufficient assurance of a loan of $5,000 that, probably on the fourth, he arranged with Horace Liveright, to the publisher's surprise, to stop the weekly checks, the advances to date being, he optimistically calculated, about off-set by current sales of his books. He celebrated his new freedom by spending three hours at the Metropolitan Museum looking at prints and his favorite old paintings. At lunch together on Thursday, October 6, he and Emmett came to agreement on details of the loan as Emmett, business man and collector as well as friend, would specify. Anderson would sign two notes for $2,500 each, one to mature in four years, the other in five. In lieu of interest on the notes he would turn over to Emmett all his manuscripts, published or unpublished, as long as the two men lived and, where possible, would assist Emmett in obtaining memorabilia from other authors. The following day he left the city to inform Cox in Marion that he could purchase the papers. "The country or the small town is better for me," he informed Bab, adding cavalierly, "Fame is a whore and must be treated so."[45]

Back at Ripshin on October 9 among the "lovely" mountains, he felt assured and happy again. He had received a clipping of a long column by Harry Hansen in the New York *World* reporting that in Germany, Anderson was currently "the most interesting American luminary," but he now sent it to Emmett with the comment that it would be disastrous to take such announcements seriously. Elizabeth, hoping that the newspaper venture would keep her husband happy, agreed to "break in" with him as business manager. Admitting to himself that she had "some sense," he was willing to have a long, reasonable talk with her as to why everything he wrote should be "a subject of controversy," should evoke such antagonism as in Lawrence Morris's "Sick of Words" review, from which he had "suffered horribly." Bluntly she accused him "of being too greedy, of wanting the love of the whole world," and in his new equanimity he agreed, "It may be true." When Elizabeth's brother David arrived for a two-week visit, it was for both Andersons "a pure joy." One day the two men took a long walk among the hills, now in autumn "spread with a gorgeous carpet of color"; and Anderson tried to explain how a young man wants fame but that, when it comes, it can come in excess, giving him a corrupting sense of power, turning him into "a public character" too self-important to remain an artist. Time, Anderson wrote Emmett calmly, "will put me more nearly in the position of utter obscurity than you, dear friendly man, can realize."[46]

Quite possibly it was in this quietly accepting mood that he wrote "A Ghost Story" to meet the deadline for the December *Vanity Fair.* The tale is a pleasantly mocking one of a lonely school teacher in South Bend, Indiana, who is visited by a well-mannered male ghost, "low-brow" in life but now eager for culture in order to keep up with the cultured snobs in the spirit world. Each evening throughout a winter she reads to him "all of the moderns"—Joyce, O'Neill, Dreiser, Frank, Hemingway, Stein—until "their names and a knowledge of their works have given him *entrée* to the best and most exclusive circles" among the spirits, whereupon he deserts her without even the ghostly kiss she has yearned for, which, she comments, "just shows how a woman comes out when she tries to do something for a man." The repetition of Hemingway's name, along with those of Joyce and Dreiser, suggests that the piece was in one way a gentle rejoinder to *The Torrents of Spring,* amiable satire in return for the unamiable kind, an amused warning against literary snobbery.

On Monday the seventeenth, Anderson began driving daily down to Marion in order to learn about the craft of editorship and the mechanics of getting out weekly newspapers. Cox had purchased the papers in 1921 and then announced that he would make them "clean, newsy . . . devoted to the upbuilding of every material, moral and social interest" of the community. His uplift had included firm support of Prohibition and the efforts of law enforcement officers to search out and destroy the whiskey stills of the mountain men, and especially firm support in the 1925 Scopes trial of the state of Tennessee, William Jennings Bryan, and the Bible against the teaching of Darwin's dangerous theory of evolution. News had consisted mostly of "personals" from Marion and around the county, though he had among other items printed a dispatch from Troutdale recounting the establishment there in August 1926 of a chapter of the Red Cross with William Wright as chairman, Sherwood Anderson as vice-chairman, and Mrs. Sherwood Anderson as member of the Emergency Chest Committee. There was less advertising than might be expected, and large quantities of space were filled with syndicated material or other standardized boilerplate such as columns of information on Hawaiian pineapples sent free by the companies, which Anderson detested on sight. Cox had openly kept out of political fights in the town himself and had let the town's Republican postmaster contribute Republican editorials to the *Smyth County News,* the Democratic sheriff contribute Democratic ones to the *Marion Democrat;* but his political allegiance was indicated by the *Democrat's* four pages, the *News's* eight, and he tried to steer prospective subscribers to the latter. The *Democrat* appeared on Tuesdays, the *News* on Thursdays, but for the most part they shared the same contents. The papers were dreary enough and run simply to make money. In mid-August of 1927, Cox had cleverly announced a subscription drive for both papers to end

October 15, so that when Anderson took possession of the papers on November 1, Cox had already collected all likely subscription money for the following year. In addition he had allowed stocks of newsprint and job printing paper to run low. From the editing standpoint as well as price, Anderson was not getting a bargain; in equipment he was doing better. He would have "a five thousand dollar Lin-o-type machine, sufficient fonts of type, a job printing outfit, flat bed press and folder, a good enough little shop." In addition, he could rely on three experienced pressmen—Gil Stephenson, compositor, his son Joe, linotypist, and Jack Menerik, who did the job printing—while Zeb Petty, the "printer's devil" (apprentice), had the "makings then of a good printer." He particularly liked the sixty-year-old Gil, an old-school craftsman like his own Sponge Martin, who would accept nothing less than perfection in his trade.[47]

During the two weeks left in October, he began familiarizing himself more fully with the town of Marion, up to now primarily a place where he could catch the Norfolk and Western to New York. With a population of about four thousand, it was somewhat larger than the Clyde of his youth but resembled it as an agricultural commercial center with some light industry, including a large furniture factory. It was situated more dramatically than Clyde in the broad, fertile valley of the Holston River, shut in on the north by long Walker Mountain, on the south by a range of rounded hills. Running through the middle of the town was long, upward sloping Main Street with its stores, banks, and major hotel, its broad sidewalks lined by angle-parked cars, a busy street that, because of the connotations of Sinclair Lewis's novel, Anderson would regularly refer to in the papers as the Rialto. The print shop of the Marion Publishing Company, on the first floor of a two-story brick building, was a block and a half off Main on North Park Street and faced an eyesore of an open lot where the town dumped its road machinery. Near the top of Main Street were two centers of town life, the pale gray brick county courthouse with its Corinthian-pillared portico and the post office, both visible through a back window of the print shop. Two blocks farther up Main Street were the red brick and Corinthian-porticoed Marion Junior College for women; beside it and set back from the street by a wide, tree-shaded lawn, was a spacious, white, two-story frame house with a one-story colonnaded porch stretching across the front. This was Rosemont, the Copenhaver home; and Anderson admired its simple elegance so much that, strolling by one day, he walked up to the front door and introduced himself to the owners, the stolid Bascom E. Copenhaver, superintendent of the Smyth County schools, and his warmly outgoing wife Laura Lu, former English teacher at the college, writer for periodicals, and an active person in Lutheran church affairs. Clearly the Copenhavers were among the town's élite, part of its power structure, which along with other social relations he as yet could only dimly perceive. As for the "Winesburgness" of the town, the psychic life of its inhabitants, he knew that even less, but he hoped that his position as editor of the papers would help him to learn it.

Enthusiastic with his new venture but uncertain of its success, he had much to learn about the town, and the town about him. Back in early June he had been an "honor guest" as "famous author" at the evening banquet celebrating the opening of the remodeled General Francis Marion Hotel on Main Street. Now in his new role as editor-to-be, he was the speaker on October 25 at the annual Kiwanis dinner for the teachers of the Marion schools and the college, and the outgoing editor reported that his "very witty, neatly expressed address" on his reasons for liking south-western Virginia "charmed his hearers with his happy expressions" so that "by the time that he finished they all felt like he was an old-time friend. . . ." It was a comforting send-off. On October 31 he and Elizabeth were busy getting out the first issue of the four-page *Democrat,* which appeared on Tuesday, November 1, the day on which he took legal possession of the papers. The first issue of the *News* came out on Thursday the third, and the initial deadlines had been met, though he soon found out that unlike a daily newspaper, a weekly could "drift out" a day late without damage to anyone.[48]

In the rush of buying the papers he had had time to work out only a few notions of policy for them, and even in the eighth week of publication he would admit that "we have been feeling our way along." (More than three years later he admitted that he was still feeling his way along in this, for him, "educational experiment.") From the beginning, however, he knew that the aim of both the *News* and the *Democrat* should be "to give expression to . . . all of the everyday life of a very typical American community." In his "Our New Editor's Bow" on the front page of the first issue of both papers he announced that they were to be "intensely local"; and he asked for the help of his readers both in sending in news items and in writing letters to the editor so that the papers could become "a sort of forum" of Marion public opinion. Because of his own lack of interest in politics, he would leave political comment to the designated contributing editors, one Republican and one Democrat; instead he would speak editorially "on the life about me and on the life of the outside world." He would print things that interested him, he explained in early issues: poems, famous short stories, some of his own tales, and "things seen and felt, strange happenings in this and other communities. . . ." The function of a country weekly was not to give state and national news, like the city dailies, but to help bind "all sections" of a community together, to help its people to understand each other. A weekly "should have some life in it, fun, a serious streak, plenty of home news, some good solid reading." Whatever the papers became, they must escape the curse of most modern publishing of newspapers and magazines: they must not be mass-produced, standardized, impersonal, or dull.[49]

The specific changes that Anderson introduced were directed toward making the papers more personal and readable. As quickly as he could, he threw out the drab syndicated material, particularly on the Hawaiian pineapple, eventually keeping only the agricultural information that might be useful to the farmers of the area. Writing much of the papers himself except for the local items sent in from outlying communities—the material set up for the *Democrat* was mostly repeated in the *News*, thus saving time and expense of typesetting—he began at once injecting a personal note into the news stories. "Fire in the Mountains," on the front page of the first issue of both papers, was typical.

Fires have broken out in the mountains all over Smyth and surrounding counties. The long dry time has made even a spark of fire dangerous. Yesterday when the writer drove over the mountain from Troutdale fires were burning in many directions. It has swept through many farms, burning fences and endangering stock. Just east of Marion, beyond the red bridge, a whole mountain was afire. On last Saturday evening the writer drove out to Fairwood and the whole sky was alight. It was a gorgeous sight but not a welcome one if the fire is sweeping through your own land.

At Fairwood I was told that the fire had swept on into Government land and that the government fire fighters had been summoned and the next day as I drove over the road there they were, hard at it.

As long as the dry weather lasts be careful of your matches and cigarettes ends.

On the same front page he showed his readers that they could now expect some humor in the papers.

Fooled Again

Your new editor came into town Monday. Children prancing in the streets at night, dancing, song, laughter, cheers. Girls and boys in fancy costumes.

Fool that I am. I thought it was because all Marion was so glad the new editor had arrived.

It was only Halloween.

On any page he printed brief characteristic observations of his own to fill out a column: "If a great wind should suddenly tear off the front of your house, what would your life look like to people passing in the street?" Throughout the papers he scattered short and long editorials on things he had seen and felt—the beauty of an autumn maple tree or the fine lack of self-consciousness in dogs—while from the first issues a feature was his regular last page column "What Say!," a kind of running supplement to *Sherwood Anderson's Notebook*. Only occasionally, as when Hoover split the Solid South in the 1928 election, would he run a story on a national event, but in his dislike of Prohibition he derived great enjoyment out of Sheriff Dillard's raids on the stills of the mountain men, raids which he had a tendency to report as though they were pursuit sequences from the old Keystone Cops comedies. When news ran low some week, he might print a story by Chekhov or one of his own. As early as the last week in November he reprinted "War" from *The Triumph of the Egg,* for example, and in the following August he would celebrate the Smyth County Fair of 1928 by republishing "Sophistication," here subtitled "A Fair Story of Youth." Much space in the February 23, 1928, issue of the *News* was given over to an article by Laura Lu Copenhaver, which *Scribner's Magazine* was to publish in June. Mrs. Copenhaver's description in "Madame Russell" of this eloquent sister of Patrick Henry is somewhat more elevated in style than Anderson probably liked, but his printing of the article suggests that the two writers had by now begun their long close friendship.

On November 7, the Andersons moved into a room at the General Francis Marion Hotel, returning to Ripshin only for weekends in the fall, since the new job kept Sherwood busy, sometimes wildly so. "I get up at 6:30, eat, cut out to the office," he told Ralph Church. "All sorts of people drift in during the day—old farmers, people wanting a bit of printing, etc." Besides writing most new stories and all editorial matter, as editor he attended Kiwanis meetings, trials at the courthouse, sessions of the town council; and although he had refused to go back to an advertising firm, he must now solicit ads from the town's businessmen, often using his old skills in composing the copy himself. Then there was the matter of subscriptions, $1.25 yearly for the four-page *Democrat,* which he soon changed to eight pages for $1.50 to forestall the Democrats from starting their own paper, and $1.50 yearly for the *News.* Subscriptions to the *News* outside the county were $2.00 a year; relying without hesitation on his status as a sort of national public figure, a status that had revolted him back during the summer, he counted on these as his special market. Ascertaining the price from Emmett, he paid his benefactor to insert a twenty-nine-word advertisement under the lead "Grass Root News" in the *New York Times,* the *New Republic,* and the *American Mercury* to run from late November into January. Even by mid-November, however, because of the wide publicity his purchase of the papers was receiving, outside subscriptions were "coming in now, several a day from all over the United States." Alfred Stieglitz alone would request five.[50]

Getting out the papers, Anderson found at once was fun, though he had occasional "moments of terror" because of the newness of his situation, and after a month of issues he could exclaim to Emmett, "I never did anything I liked so well." Of necessity meeting all kinds of people, farmers, businessmen, housewives, professional persons, he realized that during his months of gloomy absorption with self he had missed constant direct human contact. Many of the people he met only casually, but besides Laura Lu Copenhaver he probably very early became acquainted with two men, lawyers, who would become his closest friends in the town. Burt L. Dickinson, a tall, trim man, was then mayor of Marion and judge of the Court of Juvenile and Domestic Relations, and Anderson frequently ran into him at the courthouse. Liberal in politics and intellectually inclined though not particularly literary, Dickinson was committed to observing legal ethics but also to using practical advice in settling the "welfare" cases, which as mayor, by Virginia practice at the time, he tried. Years after he would recall that Anderson was especially interested in welfare cases, and the two carried on an amiable running argument about Dickinson's handling of them, Anderson insisting that "good intentions" on the part of a lawyer and the defendants in a case were important, Dickinson holding that he himself was long enough on good intentions and that Anderson was short on fact. These two men were to drift apart in the 1930s, but Anderson remained close friends with the other lawyer for the rest of his life. Charles H. ("Andy") Funk was a big, craggy-faced man, a Commonwealth's Attorney (county prosecutor) feared by anyone on the witness stand for the defense, a person delighting in argument, given to rough humor yet underneath sensitive to others as well as perceptive about them, and a true craftsman in his hobby of cabinetmaking. Andy Funk had been drawn to Anderson some months earlier before he even knew who he was. On the evening of April 15, a man named Harry Gardiner, billed in the *News* as "The World's Famous Human Fly," had set out to climb the front of the Bank of Marion building before a crowd assembled in Main Street. Partway up, the Human Fly got temporarily stuck, tried to find a higher handhold, strained time and again unsuccessfully to pull himself up from a window ledge. Funk was watching the climber intently but couldn't help noticing a man standing just in front of him in the crowd, a middle-aged man of middle height with rather heavy shoulders. When the Human Fly strained upwards again and again to try to catch the next handhold, the shoulders of the middle-aged man strained upwards again and again. Tiring, Gardiner rested for a few minutes. The crowd below thought he had given up and began to jeer and whistle at him, whereupon the middle-aged man threw angry looks from side to side at those who were making fun of the Human Fly. Gardiner did reach the top of the building, and Funk eventually learned that the middle-aged man was Sherwood Anderson; but what had especially struck Funk at the time was that Anderson, though a member of the crowd, had completely identified himself, as the upward straining of his shoulders proved, with Harry Gardiner, had in his imagination *become* Harry Gardiner momentarily trapped on that window ledge with the jeering crowd below and no apparent way to get to the top of the building. When the crowd began to jeer, Anderson seemed to have sided instinctively with the trapped man, sided with the daring individual temporarily in trouble. This was a person Funk wanted to, and did, get to know.[51]

Being now "with the crowd" in his position as editor of the town's newspapers satisfied that part of Anderson which desired human contact, and especially so since he was, for the most part, freed by his necessary busyness from the lacerating fear of degrading himself into a professional writer, a literary hack—whereupon as he "suspected," he told Emmett, "the moment I had something else to do I began wanting to write." At first it was all he and Elizabeth could do to get their "hands in" with the paper; but later in November, when he was "busy every moment" with editing, he found time to write "America on a Cultural Jag" for the *Saturday Review* and one of his best mountain tales, "A Sentimental Journey" for the January *Vanity Fair*. On December 5 he could tell Emmett that he had "written an article 'On Being a Country Editor' for Vanity Fair this week and a rather long chapter to my novel." By the twelfth he had written two more articles on his new career for the New York *World* and *Outlook* magazines, adding his own efforts to what he described to Emmett as "a great deal of publicity for the venture."[52]

"A Sentimental Journey" is a tale of contrasts and parallels among perspectives. Again, as in "A Mountain Dance," a narrator from outside the hills tells in simple yet educated language of an experience a mountain man named Joe tells him, the narrator's purpose being again, though this time implicit, to correct the stereotyped image of mountain people as dangerous and unfeeling. This time the distance between narrator and Anderson himself, never great in most of his mountain stories, seems deliberately minimal as though to record fictionally the development of the author's own outsider understanding. The narrator's wife is named "E," the couple live in "a small log house . . . on the bank of a creek"—a curious premonition of Anderson's later having his writing cabin moved down from its hill to a position close to Ripshin Creek—and another outsider couple inhabit a more elaborate house, the whole interior of which Joe describes as "like one big grand piece of furniture," like Ripshin, one would say. When the narrator, out riding his horse on a lonely road, first meets Joe, also mounted, the man's fierce appearance frightens him, but they ride together to the narrator's cabin, where he invites Joe in to eat. At first he and his wife are nervous about Joe until Joe, a "talker" unlike the usual "uncommunicative" mountain man, begins to tell of how he had always wanted to go see "the outside world" though he admits, now to the couple's relieved amusement, that the prospect frightens him. Once as a younger man he did go out into the world one late fall, taking with him out of his fear of loneliness his oldest child, a boy of seven, and leaving his wife and their other five children in their mountain cabin. He found a job in a noisy, smoke-filled mining town on the plain; but his fellow workers, in the narrator's words, "seemed as strange and terrible to Joe and his son as these mountain people had seemed to 'E' and myself," and both longed for the hills, now covered with heavy winter snows, hills pure white unlike the ugly, dirty town. Collecting his pay one evening, Joe and his son, both "half insane" with homesickness, at once set out on their freezing, three-day and three-night journey on horseback back into the hills. Joe never once sleeps, but the horse and boy need food and rest. The mountain people along the way welcome them to their cabins, and only one time, when they reach the grand house, are they refused entrance by the owners, a "high-toned" city couple like others now beginning to build big houses in the upland valleys. When Joe forces the door, the frightened couple lock themselves in their bedroom. Joe builds up the fire to warm his son, feeds his horse in the stable, but because the couple are so "high and mighty," touches none of their food or anything else in the house. Reaching home cold and hungry but happy, Joe knows that the "desperate trip" has been "all sentimentality." It was "only the snow-covered hills that had called him back out of the world," as indeed it was the hills that had called the narrator-Anderson there too.

Foxily appreciating what *Vanity Fair* termed his "news value," Anderson emphasized different elements of his venture in each of the three articles about it. The piece in the December 18 issue of the Sunday *World* described the business and policy sides of the papers as condensed in the boxed "Grass Root News," which gave the yearly subscription rate "at a distance" as two dollars, an announcement that "brought us a new flood of subscriptions," he wrote Emmett. In "On Being a Country Editor" he self-deprecatingly stressed how his ownership of the papers made him "a power in the land." "Nearer the Grass Roots" in the *Outlook* sketched his earlier life and his editorial policy but gave special attention to the help being given him in writing the papers by "a young Virginian mountain man" who writes under the name of Buck Fever and "who promises to develop into something special."[53]

Here it is necessary to get somewhat ahead of the story. Buck Fever did develop into something special both for Anderson as editor, particularly during the following year, and for his town subscribers, who began to find Buck a major reason for looking forward to each issue of the papers. Writing to Ralph Church just before Christmas, Anderson explained Buck's genesis: "As I couldn't afford a reporter I invented one. I call him Buck Fever—a purely mythical being. Buck and I do all the writing." In another letter to Church some months later, he commented that there was "a kind of interesting experimental thing" about editing the papers: "I try to give the fancy a little play, create in the town imaginary figures of people and situations." Among such figures would be Mrs. Colonel Homing-Pigeon, a downy-bosomed southern lady whose son Sullivan was in the Diplomatic Corps, and the mysterious Black Cat of Chilhowie, a neighboring town, who had thirteen kittens and loped along the highway at a speed of thirteen miles an hour; but Buck Fever and the invented persons immediately surrounding him developed into an elaborate conception of a humorous character and a way of life. For the creation of Buck, Anderson very possibly drew on his garrulous neighbor Felix Sullivan who had entertained him with his World War experiences all one afternoon; but certainly Buck represented yet another way to look at the southwest Virginia mountain man such as Anderson had been writing about seriously in his hill country stories.[54]

The name Buck Fever—the term for the inexperienced hunter's nervousness on first sighting game—initially appears on the front page of the third issue of the *News,* that for November 17, signed to two brief news stories, but beyond a reference in one to his boyhood in a mountain town, Buck has not emerged as a created character, and the voice is still Anderson's. In the fifth issue (December 1), however, an anonymous front-page letter, dated from "Coon Hollow" and filled with misspellings, warns Buck against disgracing his family by becoming a newspaperman, while on the second page a similar warning is printed in a letter from Buck's mother, Malaria Fever. Paw Fever, Malaria goes on to say, is a mountain man, descendant of the ancient Virginia family of Fevers, and one-half of the firm of Fever and Ague, which runs a general store at the head of Coon Hollow. In this issue Buck is clearly on his way to what his mother considers a vulgar career, for he signs three stories and is referred to by the editor as the paper's Coon Hollow correspondent. (The fictitious Coon Hollow, it turns out later, is up near Troutdale in the vicinity of Ripshin.) With the sixth issue (December 8), Buck has come down out of the hills to Marion and inaugurated a front-page column, "Buck Fever Says," which appears with fair regularity in the following months.[55]

From this point on Buck gradually acquires a history and a character. He is a young man, too young to have been in the war; he went to school with Hannah Stoots, who writes letters about him to the Marion papers; now that he has come to town, he is dressing better, studying spelling and grammar, and clearly bound to rise despite Malaria's objections. Strong and handsome, he likes pretty girls and in turn receives mash notes— printed in the papers, of course—from Bessy Wish of Roanoke or Girlie Gravey of Groseclose; nevertheless, he is still unmarried and "has of course no children." Almost from his first appearance he has begun to ask "the boss" for a raise from his six-dollar-a-week salary, and Anderson's presumed reputation as an unrelenting tightwad becomes a recurrent target for Buck's sly abuse.

Bit by bit more of the Fever family and life in Coon Hollow are revealed. Like the usual mountain woman, Malaria does the work, while Paw loafs at the store and occasionally gets drunk on corn likker. Like the other Fevers, sixteen-year-old Spring can take care of herself; any man who gets fresh with her will have to accept the consequences. The Fevers are poor but honest. A cousin once shot a revenue officer, "but that, as you well know or should know, is no disgrace among decent mountain people." From Coon Hollow "Personals" comes word that Miss Holly Tawney, "grows one of the finest beards in Coon Hollow," that Miss Hyacinth Wormwood has just had a baby, and that Old Uncle Henry Wormwood, a good church-going man who made more whiskey than anyone else in the Hollow and was jailed only three times, has died at the age of ninety-four.

Anderson's main overt use of Buck would not be, however, as the center of a half-fanciful, half-realistic world, which appealed to the comic sense of his readers and also to the prejudices of town folk against country folk. Buck is a rustic, a backwoodsman sometimes boastful of the fighting and drinking abilities displayed up in Coon Hollow in the manner of Sut Lovingood or other frontiersmen created by the humorists of the Old Southwest; yet he is also acute and plainspoken, a shrewdly humorous reporter of and commentator on current events in Marion and Smyth County. In a style that does not rely on dialect forms or comic misspellings but rather on the vocabulary and rhythms of average southwest Virginia speech that Anderson's ear had become accustomed to, Buck slyly or raucously pokes fun at the eccentricities and foibles of the townspeople as he recounts the events of the previous week. Buck could say things or say them in a particular way that Anderson could not or preferred not to say them.

Doubtless Buck would often be identified with his creator. In the issue of the *News* for May 8, 1930, some months after son Bob had in effect taken over management of the papers, Anderson would write, on the way back to Marion from one of his trips to the textile mills of the Deep South, that he saw a Marion man at a gas station and rejoiced to hear the man call to him, "Hello, Buck." On the other hand, Joe Stephenson would insist years later that the townspeople "knew and they didn't know." The men in the print shop never let on, and when people would ask Anderson directly whether he were Buck, he would say, "Sure," in a way that would leave them still wondering. Whatever people knew, however, the important matter is Anderson's own conception of the relationship existing between himself and his created character within his real-life situation. That relationship was an intimate one: however Anderson may have regarded Buck at the beginning, the figure would become for him a kind of persona, an actual psychological necessity. Buck became a mask allowing him to speak out more completely from semiconcealment his complicated feelings toward his position as editor of the newspapers and therefore a leading town citizen.[56]

This position, he knew, was an anomalous one. He was living a paradox. As a lover of small towns and of human beings he desired community; as an intensely individualistic artist, one who had dared break with many conventions, he rebelled against community. He had bought the papers because he could no longer write, needed a way to support himself and Elizabeth, and wanted to regain contact with people; but he had also hoped that, as when he wrote advertising copy during the day and fiction at night, the busyness of editing the papers would release him into writing again, recreate him as individualistic artist. As early as the second issue of the *News* he described in his "What Say!" column the conflict in him between his need for "group feeling" and his love of privacy. But, as he suggests in other numbers of the papers, the public-private conflict is complicated by the fact that, though he likes both "good" and "bad" people, his quickest sympathies are with "The Despised and Neglected," and he cannot help identifying himself with even the most wretched criminals. In one issue he writes that he would like to set all the prisoners in the county jail free at Christmastime. Granted, society must be protected, but the townspeople should never elect him to an office of public trust because he is always on the side of the criminal, as indeed Burt Dickinson accused him of being in their arguments over welfare cases. In the issue of the *News* for January 3, 1929, he would specifically summarize the conflict and suggest its psychic cost.

> There are always two men struggling in me. One of the men appears to want to lead a plain, common-sense life. I am to be a good steady man, pay my debts, be moral.
> The other is a wild fellow. He roves restlessly over the world. He would as soon consort with thieves or prostitutes as good respectable people.
> These two men fighting in me. They exhaust me with the fight.

The antagonists are evenly matched, and the conflict is a continuing one.

Anderson would be, then, both in the community and not in it, even against it, given status by his editorship, liking that status, yet at the same time distrustful and scornful of it, just as some months before he had sided with Harry Gardiner the Human Fly against the jeering crowd. As he edited the papers during the ensuing months, "getting under the skin a little" of the town, seeing "where the local fights lie," he would not resolve the conflict, but he could alleviate it by certain psychological devices; and Buck Fever was one of the most important of these devices. Taking Buck with him, he could attend the weekly Kiwanis Club meeting or the wedding of two members of Marion's highest society—either event was enjoyable in its way—and then Buck could write the event up afterwards, poking fun at the entire proceedings. Sometimes Buck and his boss could, and did, publish two different versions of the same event on the same page, one comic, one straightforwardly factual. It was with considerable help from Buck Fever, then, that Anderson could continue to function in the ensuing months, despite the conflict within him between "the good steady man" and the restless "wild fellow."

The sharpening of the conflict was yet to come. Now in December of 1927 he was mostly the solid citizen editor, "determined," he wrote Emmett, "to make a go of these papers." Not interested in politics or in reform, he did very early take up a safe civic cause, boosting the band, the "corking good one" that, as George Babbitt might have said, brought "Life. Music. Zipp." to Marion. Through editorials and personal letters to friends and acquaintances he began in mid-November to solicit contributions to pay the twelve dollar annual dues of each band member. By Christmastime he could name H. L. Mencken, Horace Liveright, Alfred Knopf, and the financier Otto Kahn, who had sent one hundred dollars, as outside contributors. His effort was self-interested as well as altruistic, for he was hoping to bring the *News* to national attention. Already, he boasted to Emmett, "A great many editors of city papers are on our subscription list, presidents of five large advertising agencies etc." People out in Smyth County showed how much they liked the papers by sending in 150 new subscriptions in six weeks. One of the benefits of all this activity with the papers for both Sherwood and Elizabeth was that their personal relationship improved. Both were well, he declared to Ralph Church just before Christmas, "both leading much healthier and saner lives, being very busy."[57]

He would be writing again too, he told Church, "if it is in the cards. I've quit worrying about that." His books "keep going big in Germany," translations of *Poor White* were soon to be published in Sweden and the Netherlands, requests to authorize Polish and Danish translations had recently come in. His "vogue may grow stronger in Europe than here," he also wrote Emmett cheerfully. "There does not seem to be the same carping." As for his future writing, "Stories rumble in my belly"; and after he finished his novel, which as at last taking shape in his mind, he wanted to do a nonfiction book "on the American situation. . . . What happens . . . when a civilization is speeded up as ours is." Then to Emmett he added without resentment, with a certain pride, his wife's shrewd perception about her husband.

Elizabeth is inclined to think that thinking is not my field, that everything from Me is better when told in a story telling way. It may be true. Abe Lincoln and I may be alike in that.[58]

5.

Outwardly all seemed to be going well, but a long, disjointed confessional letter to Bab written out of his usual Christmas Day depression suggests otherwise within, suggests in part why in the coming year Anderson would need the mask of Buck Fever. The letter begins with the admission that the "holiday season has always quite stunned me." He can't bring himself to send out cards, buy gifts, to be "jolly and happy"—be the "good steady man," that is—so "I do nothing and am ashamed of that," of not being the good steady man. Belatedly he thanks Bab for her gift of "nice blood red peppers, with all their suggestion of the sultry south that I love"; and abruptly their suggestiveness brings up a memory which tantalizingly reveals and conceals.

Did I ever tell you of getting off a stalled train once in Arkansas. I got off and walked through a burned over forest.

At last I came to a yellow stagnant river. Something happened there. I shall write about it some day.

There was some queer sort of wedding between myself and the savages.[59] It has affected my whole life since.

My bag was in the train and the train went on without me. That night I walked ten miles through the soft night to a little town and slept there.

I did get my bag back the next day—or was it two days later.

All that is too long for a letter.

Exactly what he so momentously "wedded" can only be guessed at, perhaps some passionate encounter with backwoods whites or blacks or native Americans he witnessed or participated in, but the essence of the experience seems clear. As in an almost dreamlike archetypal journey he abandoned a symbol for modern mechanized society, temporarily broken down, moved like some pilgrim through a wasteland, and entered into a transfiguring relationship, intimate as sexual union, with representatives of the "natural," thus permanently confirming the "wild fellow" part of him. (Very possibly, too, one senses here the emotional, creative source for the uncanniness and power of "The Man Who Became a Woman," "Death in the Woods," and the riverboat scene in *Dark Laughter*.) Fulfilled by the "wedding" in a lasting way, he completed the journey, walked tranquilly through "the soft night" toward sleep, after which he returned at some uncertain time to the everyday life of recovered bags, running trains, and clocks.

From the event for an unwritten story Anderson understandably jumps in his letter to his present "rather comatose" life of "Work, work," which is at least better than his previous condition when he was as stalled as that train, and then jumps to his continuing commitment to art above any personal relationship.

Truth is no woman will ever be first with me.
    I would sacrifice any woman for the line of beauty when I can find it.

"What really happened" in his life, he goes on, "was 'I'm a Fool' and other things," meaning artistic accomplishment. As a result, critics in this "time of publicity," not of greatness, took him up as a "great man," made him "self-conscious" and "muddled inside" so that the "sweetness" went out of him and he often thought of death. Now he wants to take a step beyond where he has been or is. Dissatisfied, he wants, in an image frequently related to his sense of creativity, "a new youth deep down in me." Running the papers is only a way to make a living, has put him in debt, has linked him—the change in phraseology is startling—"cheek to jowl with little merchants, farmers, laborers small men"; indeed, "Its silly, a great deal of it," or as he shortly calls it "madness and much else." His "hand" as writer, however, is

coming up out of its lethargy. I am an unusual man in my age in this. My faith is in some way deeper, stronger—than most men's.
    In what?
    O, dear Bab. How can I put my hand on that?
    I do keep projecting a little, hoping waiting.

His sudden inconclusiveness at this crucial point is matched by the remark with which the letter soon ends. Speaking of the "madness" of working only "for bread and butter," he comments cryptically, "What ever the central thing is it doesn't show its face often to any of us." What does show its face in this revealing-concealing letter is his deep-lying dissatisfaction with his life as it recently has been, and is. He had begun to sense that, once again, the direction of his life and writings was about to make a major change.

Notes

In the interest of readability, many typographical errors in quotations were silently corrected. In a few places, *sic* or details such as names, places, or dates were added to clarify a point.

CHAPTER 1. A MID-AMERICAN BEGINNING

1. Except as noted, biographical information on James Anderson comes from Nelson W. Evans and Emmons B. Stivers, *A History of Adams County, Ohio* (West Union, OH: E. B. Stivers, 1900), pp. 504–5. This eulogistic but factually dependable two-page account was written by Evans, who was from West Union and had known both James and his son Irwin well. See also "III. One Who Enjoyed This Life," pp. 469–75 in William A. Sutton, *The Road to Winesburg: A Mosaic of the Imaginative Life of Sherwood Anderson* [hereafter *TRTW*] (Metuchen, NJ: Scarecrow Press, 1972). To Sutton's careful research all scholars of Anderson are deeply indebted.

2. Although most of the records of Adams County, including any information on Irwin's birth, were lost when the courthouse in West Union was destroyed by fire in 1910, the birth date assigned to him by Evans in *A History of Adams County* is confirmed by other documents, including Irwin's own statement on an information form submitted by him on Apr. 12, 1915, to the U.S. Bureau of Pensions. See his Pension File WC 880 555 in the Military Service Branch of the National Archives and Records Service.

3. Except as noted, all quotations in this paragraph are from Evans's biographical sketch of James. Letter to Sherwood Anderson from his older brother, Karl, Sept. 16, 1931. Unless otherwise noted, all letters quoted are in the Sherwood Anderson Collection in the Newberry Library in Chicago. The quotations are reprinted with the kind permission of the library and of the Sherwood Anderson Literary Estate Trust.

4. See the biographical sketch of Irwin Anderson by Nelson Evans, pp. 677–78 in *A History of Adams County*. Evans, three years older than Irwin, had been a schoolmate of his and was first lieutenant in the infantry company in which Irwin saw his first Civil War service.

5. Details on Irwin's and the 129th's service come from several sources: Company muster rolls and Irwin M. Anderson's Pension File WC 880 555; Evans and Stivers, *History of Adams County,* pp. 354, 677; *Official Roster of the Soldiers of the State of Ohio in the War of the Rebellion, 1861–1866* (Akron, OH: Werner Ptg. and Litho. Co., 1891), vol. 8, p. 537; Whitelaw Reid, *Ohio in the War: Her Statesmen, Her Generals, and Soldiers* (Cincinnati, OH: Moore, Wilstach & Baldwin, 1868), vol. 2, pp. 657–58.

6. Capt. R[ichard] C. Rankin, *History of the Seventh Ohio Volunteer Cavalry* (Ripley, OH: J. C. Newcomb, Printer, 1881), p. 23. In addition to this twenty-nine-page pamphlet, a firsthand account by the captain of Company E, the following chief sources have supplied details of the Seventh's nearly three years of service: Nelson and Stivers, *A History of Adams County,* pp. 356–58; *Official Roster of the Soldiers of the State of Ohio in the War of the Rebellion,* vol. 9, pp. 367, 385–87; Fletcher Pratt, "James H. Wilson: The Man Who Got There First," *Eleven Generals: Studies in American Command* (New York: William Sloane Associates, 1949), pp. 217–43; Reid, *Ohio in the War,* pp. 795–803; Theo. F. Rodenbough, ed., *The Cavalry,* vol. 4 of *The Photographic History of the Civil War,* ed. Francis Trevelyan Miller (New York: The Review of Reviews Co., 1911); William Forse Scott, *The Story of a Cavalry Regiment: The Career of the Fourth Iowa Volunteers: From Kansas to Georgia 1861–1865* (New York: G. P. Putnam's Sons, 1893); "Campaign in North Alabama and Middle Tennessee" and "Wilson's Raid from Chickasaw to Selma, Ala., and Macon, Ga.," *The War of the Rebellion: A Compilation of the Official Records of the Union and Confederate Armies* (Washington, D.C.: Government Printing Office, 1894 and 1897), series I, vol. 45, part 1, pp. 21–776 and series 1, vol. 49, part 1, pp. 339–506; James Harrison Wilson, *Under the Old Flag: Recollections of Military Operations in the War for the Union, the Spanish War, the Boxer Rebellion, Etc.,* 2 vols. (New York: D. Appleton and Company, 1912), vol. 2, pp. 1–379.

7. Muster and descriptive roll of a Detachment of U.S. Vols. forwarded for the Seventh Reg't Ohio Cavalry, dated Ironton, Ohio, Aug. 27, 1864. The Civil war files of Irwin M. Anderson, Company F of the Seventh, and his Pension File afford a number of details in the following paragraphs. The muster roll notes that he was paid $33.33 as the first third of the $100 bounty then given by the U.S. Government to any man who enlisted for a period of a year.

8. Scott, *Story of a Cavalry Regiment,* pp. 371, 425. Scott's regiment was in the same division as the Seventh Ohio, but in the division's other brigade.

9. Scott, pp. 443, 446. (Irwin was in Company F of the Seventh.) See *Official Records,* series 1, vol. 69, part 1, pp. 473, 500. For the action of the Seventh Colonel Garrard was officially "mentioned for bravery and efficiency" (p. 397) by his brigadier-general.

10. Scott, p. 474. Wilson, *Under the Old Flag,* vol. 2, p. 251. Rankin, then commanding the Seventh Ohio, implies that this regiment, mounted, was involved in this initial charge, but other accounts contradict him. The Seventh was in action at Columbus and presumably entered the city but subsequent to the important dismounted charge.

11. The muster-out roll shows that Irwin had previously been paid only once, on Oct. 31, 1864, a date that supports the assumption that he was in training during September and October and did not join his regiment until it returned from the Atlanta Campaign. Since a private's pay was only $11 a month, he would have received $22 on Oct. 31. On discharge he would have received $88.88 for the remaining eight months of service plus $66.67 as the amount due on his bounty, minus $3.52 due the U.S. Government on clothing and equipment, or a total discharge pay of $151.15.

12. Rankin, *History of Seventh Ohio Volunteer Cavalry*, p. 28. In his *Ohio in the War*, vol. 2, p. 803, Whitelaw Reid states that the Seventh was indeed galloping along the Andersonville Road "toward the 'prison-pen,' driving the enemy before them," but that when the flag of truce appeared, "the pursuit was at once discontinued." Despite discrepancies in both accounts, they agree that the Seventh had been sent to strike at Andersonville Prison.

    See Irwin's Pension file and WBR, ed., "Memories of Sherwood Anderson by His Brother Karl," *Winesburg Eagle* 16 (Winter 1991): 1–14. As the health of the aging Karl Anderson, Sherwood's older brother, deteriorated during the early 1950s, the late Anne Poor, his Westport, Connecticut, neighbor, kept a helpful eye on him daily and among other things took notes on his recollections of his family and especially of Sherwood. On November 14, 1964, Mrs. Poor read her notes into a tape recorder and most generously sent the unedited tapes to me: "It was [Karl's] wish that anyone writing of Sherwood should know these things." My research assistant Jon S. Reilly made a careful transcription of the tapes, which I checked and in instances corrected from my knowledge of Sherwood, and I sent a corrected copy of the transcription and the tapes themselves to the Newberry Library for the Sherwood Anderson Collection, where they may be consulted. To provide readers with readier access to Karl's information, the editors of *The Winesburg Eagle*, Charles E. Modlin and Hilbert H. Campbell, published a slightly shortened version as cited above. Reference will be to the *Winesburg Eagle* publication as "Memories of SA" or in a few instances to the transcription in the Newberry as "A/P Tapes." All Anderson scholars and readers are much indebted to Karl Anderson and Anne Poor. I wish to express my gratitude to her for her great generosity.

13. *Sixteenth Annual Catalogue of the Xenia Female College, for the Collegiate Year 1865–6* (Xenia, OH: Kinney & Milburn, 1866), pp. 11, 7. Information on the College has been taken from this catalog; from M. A. Broadstone, ed., *History of Greene, County, Ohio: Its People, Industries and Institutions*, 2 vols. (Indianapolis, IN: B. F. Bowen & Co., 1918), pp. 454–58; from Ray Higgins, "Xenia College Recalled by Excelsior Society Program," *Xenia Daily Gazette*, Nov. 18, 1964, p. 4; from the files for 1866 of the *Torchlight*, Xenia's weekly newspaper; and from a very charming description of the college by Helen Hooven Santmyer in *Ohio Town* (Columbus: Ohio State University Press, 1962), pp. 160–67. Miss Santmyer's maternal grandmother attended the college during the Civil War years, and her great-uncle Joseph Santmyer was a captain in the Seventh Ohio Cavalry.

14. One of William Sutton's infrequent errors is to argue that James Anderson might have sent his son and daughter to this college because "it was United Presbyterian," but in fact it had been under Methodist control since 1853.
15. Sutton points out the possibility about residence in *TRTW,* p. 489. Letter to WBR from Mrs. Earl Flora of Xenia, dated Jan. 19, 1965. Mrs. Flora reported that, on a visit to Xenia in the 1930s, Anderson informed Mr. Ray Higgins of the *Xenia Daily Gazette* that Irwin did run a livery stable.
16. "Commencement Exercises," Xenia *Torchlight,* June 27, 1866, p. 2.
17. Declaration for Pension under Act of May 11, 1912, sworn to and signed by Irwin M. Anderson on May 18, 1912, but filled out in another hand. The "traveling" period is listed as "1865 to '70," but in 1912 Irwin appears to have forgotten to add the Xenia year, 1865–66. The Declaration states that "from '70 to '77" Irwin resided in "Preble County Ohio." Sutton describes his father's loan in *TRTW,* p. 472. Considering the organization of cavalry regiments, to which full-time harnessmakers were attached, it is unlikely that Private Irwin Anderson learned harnessmaking during his cavalry service. In "Memories of SA," p. 2, Karl states only that "Before our father's marriage, he had been apprenticed to a harnessmaker in Cincinnati and later set himself up in this business in Camden" (to which town he moved from Morning Sun). Benjamin Dickey Anderson's death record gives his occupation as "Harness-maker"; Sutton, *TRTW,* pp. 493–94. "Historic Hopewell," leaflet obtained through the courtesy of Miss Eleanor I. Jones of Camden, Ohio. Irwin, or "I. N. [*sic*] Anderson" is listed as a dealer in "saddles and harness" at Morning Sun in *Williams Ohio State Directory for 1872–73* (Cincinnati, OH: Williams & Co., 1872?), p. 227. "Memories of SA," p. 2.
18. Margaret Austry's birth date and national origin are given on her certificate of death on file in the Division of Vital Statistics of the Ohio Department of Health at Columbus. One of her granddaughters told Sutton (*TRTW,* p. 477) that Margaret was born near Berlin and was brought to the United States when she "was perhaps three or four years old." Karl Anderson ("Memories of SA," p. 2) gives "Herdanstadt" [Hessen-Darmstadt] as her place of birth.
    Marriage certificate, Butler County, Record Book No. 3, p. 132. Margaret's last name is here spelled "Oystry." Karl Anderson twice characterized Smith as an Englishman and a teacher: in his letter of June 7, 1941, to the *Encyclopedia of American Biography,* where he states that his brother Ray agrees, and in "Memories of SA," p. 2. Emma (Anderson)'s birth date is given in her obituary in the Clyde (Ohio) *Enterprise,* May 14, 1895, p. 3. The divorce proceedings, source of the quotations in this paragraph, are recorded in *Code Record Butler County,* vol. 5, pp. 412–13, case no. 1362.
19. Evidence on the Louis Myers marriage is from several sources, some of them contradictory. The marriage certificate states that "Lewis Maer" (Louis Myers) was married to Margaret "Ostraey" (Austry) by a Reverend Edward W. Hood (possibly Edward W. Root, a Presbyterian pastor in Oxford). Louis Myers's gravestone in Oxford Township Cemetery gives his dates as "1828–1860." (See Hazel Stroup, compiler, *Butler County, Ohio, Cemetery Records,* vol. 6, Cincinnati, OH: [No pub.], 1964, p. 41; and letter from Mrs. Stroup

to WBR, Nov. 20, 1969.) Karl Anderson's account ("Memories of SA," p. 2) indicates that, contrary to Sherwood's recollection, it was Myers rather than Smith who met the unusual death. The Louis Myers who, according to Sutton "died of cholera at Oxford, Ohio, in September, 1861," appears to have been Louis Myers, Jr.

20. "Memories of SA," p. 2. Nellie Finch, the granddaughter of Margaret and Louis Myers, told Sutton (*TRTW*, p. 478) that Grandmother Myers was "'prudish, nasty-nice'": "As a Presbyterian church member she was shocked at the fact that her son-in-law, in whose home she lived the last thirty years of her life, did not attend church, and she took pains to mention his shortcoming to him frequently."

21. Church records furnished by Mrs. Dwight Sloane of the Records and History Committee of Oxford Methodist Church in a letter to WBR, Aug. 19, 1964; *Enterprise*, May 14, 1895, p. 3.

22. The Faris relationship, discovered by Sutton, is discussed in *TRTW*, pp. 482–83. "Memories of SA," p. 2. For the Morning Sun Academy, see *History of Preble County, Ohio, with Illustrations and Biographical Sketches* (Cleveland, OH: H. Z. Williams & Bros., 1881), p. 236.

23. Preble County Marriage Records.

24. Sutton, *TRTW*, pp. 494–95. Although no birth record exists for Karl, the place and date of his birth are confirmed by A/P Tapes, p. 1; hence the ascription of "Oxford, Ohio" as the birthplace in several biographical reference books is inaccurate. Various school records and newspaper references from the 1890s indicate that the first name was originally spelled "Carl." Karl presumably changed the spelling himself sometime after he reached maturity.

According to the *Minutes of Session & Church Register* of Hopewell Church, "Certificates of dismission were granted to I. M. Anderson and Emma J., his wife" on June 14, 1874. Unfortunately, the records of the Presbyterian Church in Camden, to which the Andersons presumably transferred membership, were destroyed by fire in 1929; hence an arrival date in Camden may only be surmised.

25. *History of Preble County, Ohio*, p. 306. Descriptive material on Camden in this paragraph is taken from this *History*, pp. 306–7; R. E. Lowry, *History of Preble County, Ohio: Her People, Industries and Institutions* (Indianapolis, IN: B. F. Bowen & Co., 1915), pp. 294–95; and B. F. Morgan, compiler, *Directory of Preble County, O. for 1875: Historical Sketches and Biographies of Eminent Pioneers: Advertisements, Home and Foreign* (Eaton, OH: B. F. Morgan, 1875), pp. 47, 49, 170–74.

26. Irwin's advertisement appears with four others from Camden on p. 42 of the Morgan *Directory of Preble County*. Three of the advertisements are larger than the other two; Irwin's is naturally one of these three. Statements by James Gift are from an interview conducted with him on June 20, 1938, by Mary Helen Dinsmoor, who included the interview material in her very useful "An Inquiry into the Life of Sherwood Anderson as Reflected in His Literary Works" (unpublished master's thesis, Ohio University, 1939), pp. 5–7. The first quoted statement by Morlatt comes from "The Story of Camden," Dayton

Daily News, Feb. 29, 1936, p. 3; the sentence concludes, "and [he] is not deserving of the knocks that Sherwood Anderson aims at 'daddys' in his story books." The second statement is from Dinsmoor, "An Inquiry," p. 7. The information came to Dinsmoor, not directly, but via Stephen Coombs, who grew up in Camden and began to collect information on Sherwood Anderson, including interviews with Gift and Morlatt, while in high school in the late 1920s.

27. The first three quotations are statements by Gift; the fourth, by Morlatt in "The Story of Camden." Although Irwin is not listed as a member of the band in Morgan's *Directory of Preble County* (p. 173), the preface to which is dated "July 28, 1875," both Gift and Morlatt affirmed that he did play in it, presumably subsequent to the time Morgan collected his information.

28. The birth record establishes date and place for the daughter. Her full name is given as "Estella Anderson," but she was always called Stella. The birth record gives the correct date for Sherwood's birth, but see Sutton, *TRTW,* p. 462, for a discussion of the erroneous entry of his name as "Lawrence Anderson." As for the unusual name, not a family one, Sutton notes on p. 465: "Mrs. Eleanor C. Anderson [Sherwood's fourth wife] has stated her husband told her he was named Sherwood after one of his mother's favorite teachers; conversation of April 8, 1962." Letter of Oct. 1, 1939, addressed to Sherwood Anderson by Karl Anderson, sworn to him before a notary public on Nov. 2. This letter was submitted to the Veterans Administration on a pension claim by Sherwood as legal evidence of his birth necessitated by the fact that his first name is erroneously entered on the Birth Record.

In July 1962, the house where Anderson was born was purchased by the Camden Progressive Club under the presidency of Mr. John Gray to be restored as a shrine. In Sept. 1963, the house was marked as the birthplace when a bronze plaque, donated by Mrs. Eleanor Copenhaver Anderson, was affixed to a rock placed in front of the building near the street.

29. The somewhat confused evidence on this matter is given in *TRTW,* p. 496–98, and Dinsmoor, "An Inquiry," p. 7. In addition one should note in Morgan's *Directory of Preble County,* p. 163, that a "B D Anderson" was then dealing in "Horses & Saddles" in "Fair Haven." Since Benjamin Dickey Anderson was a harnessmaker, it seems probable that this was Irwin's younger brother, an identification strengthened by the conflicting stories as to the town from which an Anderson left without paying a bill. Further, this identification may help explain Benjamin Dickey's removal by 1886 to California.

30. A. J. Baughman, *History of Richland County, Ohio, from 1808 to 1908* (Chicago: S. J. Clarke Publishing Co., 1908), vol. 1, p. 442. See also A. A. Graham, compiler, *History of Richland County, Ohio . . . Its Past and Present* (Mansfield, OH: A. A. Graham & Co., 1880), p. 634; and *Geo. W. Hawes' Ohio State Gazetteer, and Business Directory for 1860–61* (Indianapolis, IN: George W. Hawes, 1860), p. 54.

Young Irwin's birth is established by his birth record, recorded at Marion, seat of Marion County, in 1879, at which time the residence of the Anderson parents is given as Caledonia in Marion County. Information furnished WBR by Marion County Probate Court (letter postmarked Oct. 7, 1968) indicates that the new birth "would not have been recorded until the spring of [1879]" and then in Marion, rather than Richland, County. The older Irwin's Declaration for Pension under Act of May 11, 1912, states his places of residence in these years as "'77 to '79 Richland Co Ohio—'79 to '83—Marion Co. Ohio."

31. Information on C. S. Geddis is from an interview with him by Dinsmoor ("An Inquiry," p. 7) on Sept. 1, 1938, when Geddis was eighty-six. The residence and shop locations for "Irwin Anderson" are given in W. F. Stieff, *General Directory of Marion County* (Marion, OH: Christian & Vaughn, 1882), p. 51. Stieff lists Anderson's occupation specifically as "saddler," in distinction from the one other person in the craft, O. B. Smith, who is listed (p. 55) as "harness maker."

    In 1880 the population of Caledonia was 627. For information on the town see J. Wilbur Jacoby, ed., *History of Marion County, Ohio and Representative Citizens* (Chicago: Biographical Publishing Co., 1907), pp. 107–8, 110, 170, 258; and *The History of Marion County, Ohio Containing a History of the County; Its Townships, Towns, Churches, Schools, etc.* . . . (Chicago: Leggett, Conaway & Co., 1883), p. 706.

32. I have been unable to locate the Caledonia school records; but since the Andersons moved from Caledonia to Clyde, Ohio, in Mar., 1884, and Sherwood entered the second grade in Clyde the following October, he would have had his first year of schooling in Caledonia. Karl and Stella were to enter the sixth grade together in Clyde in Sept. 1884.

    In *Tar*, the visit to the harness shop is said to have occurred when the family was living in "quite a large town . . . a county seat." Either the family did live briefly in Marion or Mansfield, both county seats, or, as is more likely, Anderson in memory was confusing the town square of Caledonia with a county courthouse square. Description of the fire is from *The History of Marion County, Ohio, Containing a History of the County*, p. 706. Anderson was not quite seven years old at the time of the fire.

33. The first quotation is from an interview by Sutton with Mrs. Alice Irey (*TRTW*, p. 499); the second, from an interview by Dinsmoor with C. S. Geddis ("An Inquiry," p. 7). Letter to Eleanor Copenhaver Anderson from Mrs. Loren S. (Alice) Irey, Mar. 10, 1941. C. S. Geddis told Dinsmoor about Irwin's storytelling and playing in the band. According to Francis Russell (letters to WBR, Nov. 24, 1964, and Oct. 12, 1964), Harding joined the band in 1875 and played in it until the autumn of 1880; hence he and Irwin would have "overlapped" in Caledonia for at least a year. For Caledonia in Harding's time there and the band, see Joe Mitchell Chapman, *Life and Times of Warren G. Harding, Our After-War President* (Boston: Chapple Publishing Co., 1924), chapter 4; Ray Baker Harris, "Background and Youth of the Seventh Ohio President," *Ohio State Archaeological and Historical Quarterly* 52 (July-September, 1943), 260–75; Francis Russell, *The Shadow of Blooming Grove: Warren G. Harding in His Times* (New York: McGraw-Hill Book Co., 1968), chapter 4; Jack Warwick, "Growing Up with Harding," *Northwest Ohio Quarterly* 28 (Winter, 1955–56): 10–25.

34. See Sutton, *TRTW*, pp. 496–97, for an analysis of the chronological discrepancies in Nelson Evans's biographical sketch of Irwin Anderson and the evidence for Irwin's Mansfield residence. A description of Aultman & Taylor is in Graham, *History of Richland County*, pp. 499–510. Date and name of Ray given by Irwin Anderson in list of all his children on information form submitted to the Bureau of Pensions on Apr. 12, 1915. No county birth record has been located for this child.

35. Sutton, *TRTW*, pp. 499, 501; Dinsmoor, "An Inquiry," p. 7. On the basis of her interview with James Gift in Camden, Dinsmoor writes (p. 7): "there is no indication that [Irwin] was an excessive drinker."

36. This concluding section summarizes "Memories of SA," pp. 4, 6.

CHAPTER 2. CLYDE, OHIO

1. *Sherwood Anderson's Memoirs* (New York: Harcourt, Brace, 1942; Chapel Hill: University of North Carolina Press, 1969), p. 13. August Derleth, "Three Literary Men, a Memoir of Sinclair Lewis, Sherwood Anderson and Edgar Lee Masters," *Arts in Society* (Winter, 1959): 11–46, p. 29.

2. *Memoirs* (1942), p. 40.

3. For a detailed demonstration of Anderson's reliance on Clyde for the geography of Winesburg, see Evelyn Kintner, "Sherwood Anderson: Small Town Man: A Study of the Growth, Revolt, and Reconciliation of a Small Town Man" (master's thesis, Bowling Green State University, 1942), pp. 73–76. For my description of the town I have supplemented Kintner's work by my observations beginning with an extended visit in Sept. 1961, by interviews with a number of individuals who knew Sherwood Anderson in Clyde, and by various printed sources. Herman Hurd, Sherwood's "closest friend" in Clyde, and his son Thaddeus were especially well informed and helpful in several interviews with them during my initial visit.

4. *History of Sandusky County, Ohio: With Portraits and Biographies of Prominent Citizens and Pioneers* (Cleveland, OH: H. Z. Williams & Bro., 1882), p. 630.

5. "Memories of SA," p. 6. Interview, WBR with Mrs. Elizabeth Whaley, Sept. 9, 1961. Mrs. Whaley, who was several years younger than Sherwood, became a local historian. She reported to me what she was told by Mrs. Mary Whaley, her mother-in-law. The date of Earl's birth is from Irwin Anderson's Pension information statement of Apr. 12, 1915. No county birth record has been located.

6. *Directory of Clyde and Vicinity, January 1, 1887* . . . (Clyde, OH: A. D. Ames Publisher, 1887), p. 122. Quote, p. 28. In 1961 the building then occupied by the harness shop held the Citizen's Building and Loan Company. Terry's Opera House is now City Hall. "Memories of SA," p. 3. For further confirmation of Irwin's shift to painting of houses and signs and to paperhanging, see Sutton, *TRTW*, p. 513. In the *Memoirs* (1942), p. 26, Irwin is described as boasting of his skill in "graining" wood, at that time very much a decorating fad. He may have learned the technique, as Warren Harding did, from the

leader of the Caledonia band, who was a painter by trade and who by the process of "graining" could "convert honest white pine into imitation oak, cherry and mahogany." See Ray Baker Harris, "Background and Youth of the Seventh Ohio President," pp. 271–72.

7. F. Newlin Price, "Karl Anderson, American," *International Studio* 76 (Nov. 1922), 132–39, p. 134, 133. Judging by what facts can now be checked, this account is remarkably accurate. Although Sherwood Anderson embroidered on reality with such yarns as the Cabbage Story in *A Story Teller's Story* (pp. 50–54), the fact of the family's poverty has been confirmed by several Clyde people who knew them well.

8. Interview with Mrs. John Craun, Sept. 9, 1961. Mrs. Craun's father, Robert Jones, president of the Clyde Cutlery Company, was a good friend of Sherwood during the latter's subsequent business career in Elyria, but her mother considered him a boor and much preferred Karl for his "manners and polish."

9. Sutton, *TRTW*, p. 514. Interview, WBR with Herman and Thaddeus Hurd, Sept. 9, 1961.

10. Various Clyde people have confirmed the hatred of both sons for the father: interview, William Sutton with Jeanette Paden (*The Formative Years*, p. 46); interview, WBR with Mrs. Alfred Neuman, Dec. 22, 1961; interview, WBR with Karl Anderson, June 30, 1953. A manifestly Oedipal hatred on Karl's part is indicated by the manuscript of his unpublished semi-autobiographical novel, *Knots in the Weaver's Loom*, very kindly lent me by his son James B. Anderson.

    Enterprise, July 28, 1887, p. 2. The *Enterprise,* a firmly Republican weekly paper, had been founded in 1878 by Henry F. Paden, who died in 1889 after serving as Clyde's mayor. He was the father of Clifton Paden (later John Emerson), one of Sherwood's lifelong friends.

11. *Enterprise,* Mar. 17, 1887, p. 3. The issue for Mar. 31, 1887, reports (p. 3): "Major Anderson has not been able to perform a day's work since his fall into an unclosed ditch. He has suffered great pain, nearly all the skin from the elbow to the hand coming off." The reference to Irwin's painting in the issue for July 28, 1887, could conceivably have been on the occasion of his first work after the accident, in which case the family would have been without income from him for over four months.

12. See Kintner, "Sherwood Anderson," pp. 44–46, for the details of Sherwood's grade and high school records.

13. Karl James Anderson, "My Brother, Sherwood Anderson," *Saturday Review of Literature* 31 (Sept. 4, 1948), 6–7, 26–27, p. 6. Kintner, "Sherwood Anderson," pp. 46–47.

14. *History of Sandusky County,* pp. 622–23.

15. "Memories of SA," p. 7. Record of Birth, Sandusky County, vol. 3, p. 16. On his Pension information form of Apr. 12, 1915, Irwin erred in listing Fern's birth date as "Dec 11 1890."

    Enterprise, May 2, 1889, p. 3. Mrs. Anderson is not named in the newspaper account, but is referred to as "A neighbor lady who lives nearest the spring." Karl Anderson's account differs: "I recall a tragedy of a small child having fallen into the spring and of Sherwood's finding the drowned child. He ran to his mother, and she lifted the body out of the spring, directed him to notify the family that lived across the way. I remember a sort of enmity existed with that family because my mother had not found the child sooner, or it may be because the open spring existed on our place." ("Memories of SA," p. 3.) The newspaper account, being the contemporary one, is most likely to be correct.

16. Interviews, WBR with Herman Hurd, Sept. 7, 1961, and Mrs. James Stark, Sept. 9, 1961. Mrs. Stark was Herman Hurd's younger sister, Blanche.

17. "Memories of SA," p. 6. Anderson must have begun selling papers by early 1889, for Mayor Henry F. Paden died on Mar. 1 of that year and shortly afterwards the Paden family moved to Tiffin, Ohio. After a few years they moved to Chicago, where Anderson (see chapter 3) was to renew his friendship with his former competitor.

18. Interview, WBR with Herman Hurd, Sept. 8, 1961. "Memories of SA," pp. 6–7. The highly successful Clyde Kraut Company was established by Alonzo J. Wilder in 1890, a date that indicates that Sherwood must have been at least thirteen when he helped prepare sauerkraut. "Noted Author to Hear Nickname," *The Toledo Times*, Nov. 15, 1925, p. 14.

19. Interview, WBR with Herman Hurd, Sept. 7, 10, 1961. *Memoirs* (1942), p. 186, and *Tar*, p. 278. For confirmation that the unnamed "rich young man" was Frank ("Hal") Hadley Ginn, see SA to Karl Anderson, ca. June 1938 and W. Powell Jones to Fred Wieck, Aug. 23, 1951. Interview, WBR with Mr. and Mrs. W. Powell Jones, Sept. 11, 1961. Mrs. Jones was the daughter of Frank Ginn, who became a prominent lawyer in Cleveland and whose portrait Karl later painted.

20. *Enterprise*, Mar. 12, 1895, p. 4. The quotation is from Mark Twain, "What Paul Bourget Thinks of Us," *North American Review* 160 (Jan. 1895): 48–62, p. 51.

21. Interviews, WBR with Herman Hurd, Sept. 8, 10, 1961. John H. Sullivan in "Winesburg Revisited," *Antioch Review* 20 (Summer, 1960): 213–21, tells the Linwood Park story, calling the shoes a hat and making Sherwood's words a sly joke. When Mr. Hurd told me the story on Sept. 8 and repeated it on Sept. 10, he insisted on the detail of the shoes, and explicitly used the anecdote to illustrate Sherwood's "laziness" and "dreaminess."

22. Kintner, "Sherwood Anderson," p. 39. Kintner reports the testimony given her by both Herman Hurd and John Becker, a tailor in whose shop Sherwood often used to "hang out." Hurd repeated this observation to me in an interview, Sept. 7, 1961.

23. Neither of the Civil War books took a romantic view of the War, it may be noted. In his semifictional *Corporal Si Klegg*, published in 1887, Wilbur F. Hinman, who had been lieutenant-colonel in a regiment of Ohio volunteer infantry, deliberately aimed to present a truthful picture of soldiering. That Anderson may have known Hinman's book very well indeed is suggested both by the comments on it on p. 328 of *Tar* and p. 57 of the *Memoirs* (1942), p. 51 (1969) and by a comparison of the final paragraph of *Winesburg, Ohio* with

the first paragraph of chapter 4 in *Corporal Si Klegg,* which comments on the untired young volunteer's departure from a small Indiana town toward the war experiences that mature him through hard reality: "Si Klegg soon forgot the sad parting as the train swiftly bore him away. Visions of his new life took entire possession of his mind and heart, crowding out all other thoughts. The brightly-colored picture that his fancy painted was but the frontispiece to the volume whose dark pages were yet sealed to him."

24. Dinsmoor, "An Inquiry," p. 15; interview, WBR with Herman Hurd, Sept. 7, 1961. At this point in the interview Mr. Hurd explicitly stated that, on the other hand, Anderson never talked to him about being a rich and successful businessman.

25. Karl, or "Carl" as the name appears in the school records, "entered high school August 29, 1887, and withdrew about the middle of May, 1888." Quoted from letter to WBR, Apr. 30, 1969, from Miss Norma H. Miller, Clerk-Treasurer of the Board of Education of Clyde Exempted Village School District. Karl Anderson, "My Brother, Sherwood Anderson," p. 6; letter, Karl Anderson to W. Powell Jones, July 24, 1952, kindly lent me by Mr. Jones.

   Sutton's assertion of this point about boys can be supported by factual local evidence. According to the *History of Sandusky County* (1882), a cumulative total of seventy-five students had graduated from the Clyde High School from 1870 through 1881, of whom twenty-five were boys; and the *History* comments, "Few schools can show so large a proportion of male graduates" (p. 623). Likewise in the sketch of Clyde in Basil Meek, ed., *Twentieth Century History of Sandusky County, Ohio and Representative Citizens* (Chicago: Richmond-Arnold Publishing Co., 1909), it is stated that to date, "The graduates from the high school number, boys 94, girls 246, total 340." Herman Hurd was the one boy in his graduating class in 1896, all others having dropped out.

26. Kintner, "Sherwood Anderson," p. 40; Sutton, *TRTW,* p. 27. *Enterprise,* June 4, 1891, p. 3; June 11, p. 1; June 18, p. 2. Letter from Mrs. Bessie Neipp to Eleanor Copenhaver Anderson, May 1941. Mrs. Neipp was a member of the graduating class. For the Presbyterian Church building see *Enterprise,* Aug. 27, 1891, p. 3; Oct. 1, p. 3; Nov. 12, p. 2.

27. *Enterprise,* Aug. 25, 1892, p. 3; Jan. 5, 1893, p. 3; June 21, 1894, p. 3. Interview, WBR with Mrs. James Stark (Blanche Hurd), Sept. 9, 1961.

28. Presbyterian Church records cited by Kintner, "Sherwood Anderson," pp. 36, 39. *Enterprise,* Nov. 29, 1894, p. 3; Jan. 22, 1895, p. 1.

29. Presbyterian Church records cited by Sutton, *TRTW,* p. 30. "Noted Author to Hear Nickname," p. 14. *Enterprise,* Dec. 10, 1891, p. 3. The date of Fern's death is confirmed as Dec. 9, 1891, by the *Record of Deaths,* Sandusky County, vol. 3, p. 16, where the cause of death is also noted as "Congestion of Brain."

30. Attendance records furnished in letter to WBR from Miss Norma M. Hiller, Apr. 30, 1969. Only the total number of days present and absent are now available, not the specific dates.

31. Karl Anderson to W. Powell Jones, July 24, 1951. Lent by Mr. Jones. See also

A/P Tapes, p. 1. Price, "Karl Anderson," p. 133. Details confirmed by Herman Hurd in WBR interview, Sept. 7, 1961. In the living room of the Hurd home was in 1961 a charcoal portrait by Tichenor of Hurd's father, Thaddeus.

32. *Enterprise,* Oct. 22, 1891, p. 3. Details from Price, "Karl Anderson," p. 134, and from interview by WBR on Dec. 22, 1961, with Mrs. Alfred Newman, who knew Karl both in Clyde and in Chicago. The annual issues of the Art Institute's *Circular of Instruction of the School of Drawing, Painting, Modelling, Decorative Designing and Architecture . . . With a Catalogue of Students* list Karl (Spelled "Carl" but usually identified as Karl by his being from "Clyde, Ohio") in various life classes, usually both regular and Evening School, in the years 1892–93, 1893–94, 1894–95, and 1896–97. According to the Records Office of the Institute, he was also in the Evening School life class in 1895–96. The dates of Karl's residence in Chicago are important in helping to set the time when Sherwood left Clyde for that city.

33. *Enterprise,* Dec. 17, 1891, p. 1; Apr. 21, 1892, p. 3; Aug. 9, 1894, p. 3. The *Enterprise* invariably spells Karl's name as "Carl."

34. Karl Anderson, "My Brother, Sherwood Anderson," p. 6. See also Sherwood's letter to F. Newlin Price, reprinted in "Karl Anderson," p. 132: "I can well remember how proud we all were at the thought of this older brother of ours living an artist's life. In fact, so much did the life he had taken up influence ours that all, at one time or another, tried to be artists." Certainly both young Irwin and Earl did do some drawing. Price, "Karl Anderson," p. 132.

35. Interviews, WBR with Herman Hurd, Sept. 8, 7, 1961. For confirmation of Mr. Hurd's memory see items about the team in the *Enterprise,* May 10, 1894, p. 3; May 31, p. 1; June 7, p. 3; July 19, p. 3. These and other entries show that the local newspaper followed the fortunes of the team with great interest.

36. *Enterprise,* May 21, 1895, p. 1. Other details on the Greys confirmed in interview, WBR with Herman Hurd, Sept. 8, 1961.

37. Interview, WBR with Herman Hurd, Sept. 7, 1961. The expression "dream-girl" was Mr. Hurd's. The reminiscence, written in Feb. 1962, was passed on to me by Mrs. Clarence G. Fuller of Sandusky, Ohio, who was a niece of Bertha Baynes Whittaker and whose father, Burton H. Becker, was to employ Anderson in 1895 in his bicycle factory in Clyde. I am much indebted to Mr. and Mrs. Fuller for their hospitality during an interview on Sept. 10, 1961, and to Mrs. Fuller for making available to me in addition the written comments furnished by Helen Baynes and by a second niece, Mrs. David Lauster. The comments by Mrs. Whittaker's son Robert are from a letter to WBR, Nov. 3, 1964. Mrs. Whittaker's emphasis on her *walking* home with Sherwood may possibly be related to a date on which he took her out driving and had unfortunately hired a horse afflicted with the heaves.

38. Interview, WBR with Herman Hurd, Sept. 7, 1961.

39. Interview, WBR with Wharton Esherick, June 28, 1953.

40. Sherwood Anderson's Certificate of Discharge from the Ohio National Guard, dated Sept. 7, 1899. Photostatic copy in the Newberry Library.

41. *White's Business and Resident Directory of the Village of Clyde, Ohio. November 1st, 1895* (Homer, NY: A. J. White, Publisher [1895]), p. 74; *Direc-*

tory of Clyde and Vicinity, January 1, 1887, pp. 129, 131. For a brief biography of Captain Gillett, as for many other leading citizens of Clyde, see *Commemorative Biographical Record for the Counties of Sandusky and Ottawa, Ohio* . . . (Chicago: J. H. Beers & Co., 1896), p. 464. *Enterprise*, May 24, 1895, pp. 2, 3; June 7, p. 3; June 14, pp. 1, 3; June 14, 1894, p. 2; July 12, p. 3; Aug. 30, p. 1. Jan. 25, 1895, p. 3.

42. Interview, WBR with Herman Hurd, Sept. 8, 1961. Hurd believed that each son merely accepted his father's political position, but he insisted that he and Sherwood never argued on politics or on other matters. Interview, WBR with Herman Hurd, Sept. 10, 1961. Thaddeus Hurd, Hurd's son and a very knowledgeable local architect, specifically supported his father's assertion.

43. Information on the lodges from interview with Herman Hurd, Sept. 10, 1961, supported by the "lodge news" in the files of the *Enterprise*. Hurd, who was not a member of the Guard, joined the Masons at about the age of twenty-one on the invitation of B. F. Jackson, owner and editor of the *Enterprise*, who had married one of his sisters.

44. Karl Anderson, "My Brother, Sherwood Anderson," p. 6; "Memories of SA," p. 2; Sutton, *TRTW*, p. 515; "Noted Author to Hear Nickname," p. 14.

45. *Enterprise*, Jan. 16, 1890, p. 2; Jan. 11, 1894, p. 3. The records of the Eaton Post are missing, but the *Enterprise* carefully reported G. A. R. activities. *Enterprise*, Dec. 13, 1894, p. 2; Jan. 14, 1896, p. 3; May 13, 1897, p. 3; June 16, 1898, p. 3. Jan. 11, 1895, p. 2.

46. *Enterprise*, Apr. 30, 1895, pp. 1, 3. The long report on page 1 is signed "I. M. Anderson/J. B. Sprague/Sexton Duley," the order of the names indicating that Irwin was chairman of the committee. *Enterprise*, May 29, 1895, p. 3.

47. *Enterprise*, Mar. 15, 1895, p. 3.

48. *Enterprise*, May 7, 1895, p. 3; May 10, p. 2.

49. *Enterprise*, May 14, 1895, p. 3.

50. Death record of Emma Anderson, Record of Deaths (vol. 3, p. 41) Probate Court, Sandusky County, Ohio. Although this Record gives Mrs. Anderson's birth year erroneously as 1853, it corroborates the date of her death as May 10, 1895. In the *Memoirs* (1942, p. 75) Anderson writes that his mother died "in a few days" from pneumonia brought on by overwork and exposure as a washwoman during "a bitterly cold winter."

51. SA to Mary H. Dinsmoor, June 24, 1938. Dinsmoor had requested information in preparation of "An Inquiry," where the letter is reprinted, p. 64.

52. *Enterprise*, Apr. 14, 1887, p. 1; Apr. 21, p. 1; Mar. 13, 1890, p. 3.

53. *Enterprise*, Aug. 10, 1893, p. 3; Oct. 26, p. 3; Sept, 21, 1893, p. 3; Oct. 12, p. 3; Oct. 19, p. 3; Sept. 7, 1893, p. 3; Sept. [14], 1893, p. 3; Mar. 29, 1894, p. 3. "Clerk's Detailed Statement of the Receipts and Expenditures of the Village of Clyde, Ohio, For the Year Ending Mar. 18, 1895," *Enterprise*, Mar. 19, 1895, p. 1. That Sherwood, along with several other Clyde laborers, was paid by the village, not by the private contractor, supports his assertion in the *Memoirs* that he obtained the job from the village's Street Commissioner.

54. Interview, WBR with Herman Hurd, Sept. 8, 1961. The *Enterprise* for Aug. 2, 1895, p. 3, states that Sherwood went to Cleveland on July 31 "to see the

big races," that is, the harness or trotting and pacing races. *Memoirs* (1942), p. 83; interview, WBR with Herman Hurd, Sept. 7, 1961; SA to Mary H. Dinsmoor, June 26, 1939, reprinted in "An Inquiry," p. 72. Judging by entries in the *Enterprise* over several years, the trotting and pacing races usually were held from July through October.

55. *Commemorative Biographical Record,* pp. 704–5; *Enterprise,* 1894–96, throughout; interview, WBR with Herman Hurd, Sept. 8, 1961. Bert Ellison's younger brother was "mascot" for the Clyde Stars, the baseball team of which Sherwood was manager, and appears in the team snapshot. In connection with the Sandusky setting of "I'm a Fool" it is interesting to read in the *Enterprise* for Sept. 27, 1895 (p. 3), that "Solarion took third money in the free-for-all race at Sandusky last week." Herman Hurd recalled that Cedar Point, the resort near Sandusky where the narrator of "I'm a Fool" falls in love with Miss Lucy Wessen of Tiffin, Ohio, was a favorite of Clyde people. Occasionally during the summer the "whole town would shut down," take the "Big Four" train to Sandusky and then a boat across the bay to Cedar Point, spend the day, and come home. Sherwood often went along on these community jaunts.

56. Interviews, WBR with Herman Hurd, Sept. 8 and 10, 1961.

57. Interview, WBR with Herman Hurd, Sept. 7, 1961. *Enterprise,* Jan. 15, 1895, p. 3; Jan. 22, p. 1. The latter entry gives a detailed description of the factory and states: "The firm have sold over forty thousand bicycles for the season of 1895, and were compelled to decline an order for one thousand bicycles from a Chicago party." *Enterprise,* Feb. 1, 1895, p. 1; May 7, 1895, p. 3; Aug. 27, p. 3; Feb. 14, 1896, p. 3; Apr. 3, p. 3.

58. *Enterprise,* Oct. 29, 1895, pp. 1, 2. In his letter to Dinsmoor, June 24, 1938, Anderson states that his race track experience occurred *after* his employment in the bicycle factory; yet in another letter to Dinsmoor, June 26, 1939, he wrote, "My race track experience must have been when I was about fifteen or sixteen," which places the time as around 1891–93, *before* the Elmore factory was even transferred to Clyde. Whenever it was that he swiped for Tom Whitehead, he had gone to Cleveland to see the races in early Aug. 1895 and was working at the Elmore by early November of that year; the juxtaposition of racetrack life and factory life was real and was a decisive one for his scheme of symbolic values.

   White's Business and Resident Directory of the Village of Clyde, Ohio. November 1st, 1895 (Homer, NY: A. J. White, Publisher, [1895]), p. 9. The *Directory* was probably compiled in Oct. of 1895. Termini are set by (1) a reference in the text to the Taylor Greys, the baseball team organized in 1895, having "just finished a very successful season, winning 17 out of 21 games played"(p. 71) and (2) a notice in the *Enterprise,* Nov. 19, 1895, p. 3, that the *Directory* has just been issued.

   Interview, WBR with Mr. and Mrs. Clarence G. Fuller, Sept. 10, 1961. Both Mrs. Fuller and Herman Hurd separately pointed out that James Becker was the hard-driving one of the two brothers; hence Burton Becker's judgment of Anderson did not come from a demanding attitude. When I reported Mr. Becker's comment on Anderson's dreaminess on the job to Mr. Hurd, he thought it characteristic of Sherwood: "He was probably thinking how much he didn't like working there."

59. In this formulation I am indebted to Robert Blauner's acute analysis of alienation in the first two chapters of his *Alienation and Freedom: The Factory Worker and His Industry* (Chicago: University of Chicago Press, 1964). Cf. his summarized definition (p. 15): Alienation is a general syndrome made up of a number of different objective conditions and subjective feeling-states which emerge from certain relationships between workers and the sociotechnical settings of employment. Alienation exists when workers are unable to control their immediate work processes, to develop a sense of purpose and function which connects their jobs to the over-all organization of production, to belong to integrated industrial communities, and when they fail to become involved in the activity of work as a mode of personal self-expression. In modern industrial employment, control, purpose, social integration, and self-involvement are all problematic.

60. "A Testament," *Manuscripts* [New York], No. 1 (Feb. 1922), pp. 3–4.

61. *Enterprise,* Jan. 22, 1895, p. 1. Although Anderson invents an unvirtuous daughter for both Biffer Smith and Sponge Martin, the son that he assigns to each actually existed. "Peg" Rice, the son (cf. *Memoirs,* p. 88), did lose a leg while hopping rides on freight trains, but survived—as he does not in *Dark Laughter*—and even with a crutch caught freight trains more expertly than the average two-legged person. (Interview, WBR with Mr. and Mrs. Clarence G. Fuller, Sept. 10, 1961.) Both Mildred Becker Fuller and her husband, who also grew up in Clyde, knew Rice as children after Anderson had left town, and both specifically recalled his phenomenal ability to stripe either bicycles or the Elmore automobiles that the company soon began to manufacture instead.

62. *Enterprise,* June 2, 1896, p. 1; Sutton, *TRTW,* p. 42. Although there is no master list by name for this encampment, Sutton notes that all men in Anderson's company were accounted present and that hence Sherwood must have been there. *Enterprise,* June 30, 1896, p. 2; Sept. 22, p. 3.

63. SA to Dinsmoor, June 24, 1938.

64. Published in SA's newspaper, the *Smyth County News,* Oct. 25, 1928, p. 7.

65. Anderson's movements from about Nov. 1, 1895, when he was listed in the Clyde directory as an employee at the Elmore to Oct. 25, 1897, when he was definitely living in Chicago are far from clear. In *TRTW* (pp. 42, 53), Sutton gives the sketchy evidence suggesting that Anderson went from Clyde to Chicago at the end of summer of 1896, but he makes no attempt to fit in the substantiated period of Anderson's work in the factories of Erie and presumably other cities prior to his first going to Chicago. It is of course possible that this period occurred during the winter of 1895–96, but taken as a whole the evidence indicates to me the chronology I here propose. Interview, Sutton with Jeanette Paden, *TRTW,* p. 54.

66. Interview, WBR with Herman Hurd, Sept. 7, 1961.

67. Waldo Frank and others, eds., *America and Alfred Stieglitz: A Collective Portrait* (New York: The Literary Guild, 1934), p. 305. Sutton notes (*TRTW,*

p. 42) that for the National Guard encampment of late July, 1897, "the adjutant general's report . . . shows that one man from Company I did not attend camp." One assumes, though perhaps incorrectly, that the absentee was Anderson.

CHAPTER 3. YOUNG MAN FROM THE PROVINCES

1. *Memoirs* (1969) p. 165; (1942), p. 107.
2. The various residences of the Lay and Paden families and of Karl with them can be partly traced in the successive volumes of Reuben H. Donnelly, comp., *The Lakeside Annual Directory of the City of Chicago* (Chicago: The Chicago Directory Company, 1890–98); and the fact of the residences has been confirmed by Mrs. Alfred Newman (Bessie Lay), interviewed by WBR, Dec. 22, 1961, and by Miss Jeanette Paden, interviewed by Sutton (*TRTW*, p. 54). The Annual Directories list members of the Lay and Paden families for the first time in the 1893 volume. In 1894 and 1896, "[Anderson] Carl J. artist" is listed as living at the address of the Lays—no Carl J. appears in 1895—and in 1896 the Paden address is given for the first time as 708 Washington Boulevard. From 1897 on Karl's name is not listed—he left Chicago for New York in September of that year—but the Paden address remains the same until changed in the 1899 directory. Sherwood's name does not appear at all during these years, indicating that the directories were not without errors of omission. "[Anderson] Irwin clk [clerk]" is listed as living at the Paden address in 1898. This was certainly Sherwood's younger brother, who came to Chicago after Sherwood left for his Spanish-American War venture.
3. Karl Anderson, "My Brother, Sherwood Anderson," p. 6. John J. Flinn, *The Standard Guide to Chicago* (Chicago: The Standard Guide Co., [1893]), p. 539; *The Lakeside Annual Directory of the City of Chicago, 1897*, p. 2346; George W. Engelhardt, *Chicago: The Book of Its Board of Trade and Other Public Bodies* (Chicago: The Henry O. Shepard Co., 1900), p. 85; interview, WBR with Mr. Frank H. Collier, General Manager, Central Cold Storage Company, Chicago, Aug. 23, 1962. Quoted by Sutton from his interview with Jeanette Paden, *TRTW*, p. 56.
4. Interviews, WBR with Mrs. Alfred Newman (Bessie Lay), Dec. 22, 1961, and Mrs. W. K. Graham (Elizabeth Van Horne), Feb. 6, 1959. Little of the pleasantness of the Paden home life comes through in Anderson's subsequent portrait in *Windy McPherson's Son* (pp. 122–24) of the "ex-Caxton family named Pergwin" with whom Sam McPherson lives during "his first year in the city."
5. Interview, Sutton with Jeanette Paden, *TRTW*, p. 57.
6. Paden is so listed in *The Lakeside Annual Directory of the City of Chicago, 1897*, p. 1597, though his institution is not known. In the *Second Annual Register of the Lewis Institute* (Chicago, 1898), p. 70, "Anderson, Sherwood" is listed as taking "Arithmetic" and "Penmanship" in the 1897–98 session of the evening classes. In the unpaged volume of typed sheets of the Lewis Institute Registry for "Evening 1896–1922/Summer 1897–1917/A to L," "Anderson, Sherwood" is listed as taking only "Arithmetic" in 1897–98. See

also next note. Other details in this paragraph are from the *Second Annual Register* and the brochure *Lewis Institute, Chicago. Evening Classes and Lectures, Session of 1897–98.* These and related documents are in the Recorder's Office at the Illinois Institute of Technology, which subsequently absorbed the Lewis Institute.

In the *First Annual Register of the Lewis Institute* (Chicago, 1897), p. 62, "Jennie" (Jeanette) Paden is listed as a student in the special day class in cooking. Clifton Paden's name does not appear in any institute documents.

7. Lewis Institute Class Lists, "Evening Session 1897–1907": "Report of the Standing of Pupils in *Arithmetic* Section *Advanced* period *1st* [that is, 7:30 to 8:30 PM] during the *year* ending *Mch. 25 "98 J. C. South* Instructor" [italicized material is in the instructor's handwriting on the printed form]; *Second Annual Register of the Lewis Institute*, pp. 30, 53; *Memoirs* (1942), pp. 123–24, 247. South's "Final Estimate" ranking gives 91 to one Eugene Katz, 90 to Anderson, and 85 to the third best student.

Sherwood could have taken Advanced Penmanship at 8:30 PM on Mondays and Thursdays also; but the two different registers conflict as to his being in this course (see previous note), and the Institute's Class Lists contain no instructor's report for Penmanship. Anyone who has had to cope with Anderson's distinctive but difficult handwriting has a right to doubt that he took a course "calculated to secure ease, rapidity, legibility, and neatness in written work" (*Second Annual Register,* p. 53).

8. Price, "Karl Anderson," pp. 134, 137.

9. *Enterprise,* Mar. 3, 1898, p. 2. For Anderson's accounts of his Spanish-American War experience, see *A Story Teller's Story,* pp. 272–85, and the *Memoirs* (1942), pp. 120–35; (1969), pp. 166–98. Quotation in Karl Anderson, "My Brother, Sherwood Anderson," p. 6.

10. *The Lakeside Annual Directory of the City of Chicago,* 1898, p. 1072. Since Irwin is here listed as a clerk, it is unlikely that he took over Sherwood's job at the warehouse, as has sometimes been suggested. "Anderson, Irwin M." is also listed in the Lewis Institute Registry ("Evening 1896–1922") as taking accounting and arithmetic in both the ten-week terms into which the Evening Classes were divided in 1898–99. *Enterprise,* Apr. 28, 1898, p. 3. The newspaper account may refer either to a telegram from Anderson sent around the twenty-second or to his letter prior to Mar. 3. The details about Bertha Baynes were confirmed by Mrs. Clarence G. Fuller, a cousin of Bertha's, in a letter to WBR, Oct. 14, 1964. "The records of the Department of the Army show that Sherwood B. Anderson was enrolled Apr. 25, 1898, at Clyde, Ohio." (Letter to WBR from Elbert L. Huber, Chief, Navy and Military Service Branch, National Archives and Records Service, Washington, D.C., Sept. 30, 1964.) See *Enterprise,* Apr. 28, 1898, p. 2, for the account of the banquet and the departure of Company I from Clyde.

11. Mrs. Clarence G. Fuller's statement that "After Bertha married Sherwood came to their home to eat whenever he was in town" (letter to WBR, Oct. 14, 1964) is confirmed in a letter to Mrs. Fuller by Mrs. Whittaker herself dated Feb. 28, 1962.

12. *Enterprise,* Apr. 28, 1898, p. 2. The description of the departure from Toledo is based on the fervent account in Captain L. W. Howard, comp., *6th Ohio Volunteer Infantry War Album: Historical Events, Reminiscences and Views of the Spanish-American War, 1898-99* (Toledo, OH: Published by Captain L. W. Howard [n.d.]), unpaged section, "Who Would Not Be a Soldier?"

13. See *Enterprise,* May 5, 1898, p. 2, for quotations in this paragraph.

14. Feeling was also high against the quitters in Clyde when one of Company I's lieutenants returned to recruit replacements for them and new men to complete the company's complement of eighty-four men. See *Enterprise,* May 5, 1898, pp. 2, 3. In *TRTW,* p. 70, Sutton cites a home newspaper account of a similar mob action in Company H from Fremont, near Clyde.

15. Howard, *6th Ohio Volunteer Infantry War Album,* unpaged. The section of the album devoted to Company I summarizes the movements of the company from Apr. 25, 1898, to its return to Clyde on May 26, 1899. *Memoirs* (1942), p. 125; (1969), p. 172.

16. A letter from Harry Sergeant in the *Enterprise,* May 26, 1898, p. 2, confirms the conditions of Camp Thomas as described in such a history of the War as Walter Millis's *The Martial Spirit.* See also *Enterprise,* June 30, 1898, p. 2.

17. *Enterprise,* May 26, 1898, p. 2; June 2, 1898, p. 2; June 9, 1898, p. 2; June 16, 1898, p. 2. Harry D. Sergeant to Sutton, Nov. 14, 1942, quoted in Sutton, "Sherwood Anderson: The Spanish-American War Year," *Northwest Ohio Quarterly* 20 (Jan. 1948), 20-36, p. 33. Interview, Sutton with Dr. William A. Holtz, *TRTW,* p. 78.

18. *The Official Roster of Ohio Soldiers in the War with Spain 1898-1899* ([Columbus, OH]: Published by Authority of the General Assembly, 1916), p. 471.

19. The resolution was printed in full in the *Enterprise,* Oct. 13, 1898, p. 1. Interview, WBR with William L. White, formerly of Company I, Sept. 7, 1961. Mr. White was one of the Provost Guards (military police), who resented having to pay a fare in order to perform their duties in Knoxville. He recalls that the Provost Guards greased the tracks, thus preventing the little engine from making headway on them, until the train company capitulated and let the Guards ride free. Holtz quotation in Sutton, *TRTW,* p. 78, where the bracketed word reads "place." In Sutton, "The Spanish-American War Years," p. 33, the word reads "parlor," which seems more suited to the context.

20. See Howard, *6th Ohio Volunteer Infantry War Album,* "The Twin Regiments," a doggerel poem, and regimental movements.

21. Meek, *Twentieth-Century History of Sandusky County,* p. 280.

22. Letter from Lt. Jesse A. Douglas printed in the *Enterprise,* Jan. 19, 1899, p. 2, quoted in Sutton, *TRTW,* p. 77. Descriptive comments from Howard, *6th Ohio Volunteer Infantry War Album,* "First Impressions of Cuba." According to internal evidence this section of the book was written in 1899, when the impressions were fresh. Interview, WBR with Herman Hurd, Sept. 10, 1961.

23. Howard, "First Impressions of Cuba."

24. *Memoirs* (1942), pp. 127-28; (1969), pp. 184-86.

25. *Memoirs* (1969), pp. 186-87.

26. Howard, *6th Ohio Volunteer Infantry War Album,* "Happy Event at Camp Mackenzie." Letter to WBR from Elbert L. Huber, Chief, Navy and Military Service Branch, National Archives and Records Service, Sept. 30, 1964; *Enterprise,* June 1, 1899, p. 2.

27. *Enterprise,* June 1, 1899, p. 2; Feb. 23, 1899, p. 3; June 8, 1899, p. 2.

28. Letter to Sutton from Harry D. Sergeant, Nov. 14, 1942, quoted in "The Spanish-American War Year," p. 34. Sergeant's observations were corroborated by Herman Hurd, WBR interview, Sept. 10, 1961. Evans, *A History of Adams County, Ohio,* p. 678. Evans concludes his sketch, based on information supplied him by Irwin, with the statement that Irwin "has been very successful in his [dramatic] work." *Enterprise,* Nov. 24, 1898, p. 3. A summary of the play's plot in the *Enterprise* for Nov. 17, 1898, p. 3, establishes its highly melodramatic nature. *Enterprise,* Dec. 1, 1898, p. 3; Dec. 22, 1898, p. 3; Jan. 19, 1899, p. 3. This dramatic tour may be the factual basis for Sherwood's probably invented account in *A Story Teller's Story* (pp. 27–30, 73–76) of a traveling magic lantern show supposedly conducted by his father.

29. Irwin's post-Clyde years can be briefly documented. Statements in Nelson Evans's sketch of him in *A History of Adams County, Ohio* show that he was still at Clyde in June 1900, while various papers in his Civil War Pension File (No. WC 880 555) date his move to Connersville as not later than Mar. 13, 1901, when he married Minnie Stevens. His second wife had been born June 12, 1864, in Rush County, Indiana. On May 25, 1891, she married Frank C. Stevens in Connersville and on June 17, 1898, was granted a divorce from him, the court awarding her custody of their one child, Freddie. On Mar. 21, 1903, Minnie bore Irwin a son, Harold, the only child of their marriage. Irwin applied for an additional veteran's pension on May 18, 1912, under the provisions of the act of May 11 of that year, and on Jan. 12, 1914, he was admitted to the National Military Home in Dayton, Ohio. Here, at the National Home for Disabled Volunteer Soldiers, he died on May 23, 1919.

    Sutton records an interview with Irwin's stepson, Fred (Freddie) Stevens, in the early 1940s (*TRTW,* pp. 530–31). Irwin appears to have become somewhat, though not entirely, chastened in his later years. According to Fred Stevens, who recalled working very happily as a paperhanger with his stepfather, Irwin never drank heavily, was a good provider, talked much and entertainingly, and was active in the affairs of the local GAR post. While living at the National Military Home, he made regular trips to Connersville, and just before his death "he was training school children for Memorial Day exercises."

    "Memories of SA," p. 7. *Enterprise,* June 8, 1899, p. 3; Karl Anderson, "My Brother, Sherwood Anderson," p. 7.

    The "Anderson Irwin foreman" listed in the *Lakeside Annual Directory of the City of Chicago, 1899,* is almost certainly Sherwood's younger brother, and the "Anderson Irwin M asst supt" definitely is. Both the Lewis Institute Registry and Class Lists report Irwin as a student in 1898–99. In his two terms in J. C. South's arithmetic class, he had a final grade of 95; in his two terms of accounting, 88.

30. *Enterprise,* July 13, 1899, p. 3; interview, WBR with Herman Hurd, Sept. 7, 1961. In "City Plowman" Wallace is called "Jim," and the time is said to be just before Anderson left for Chicago for the first time. Interview, Sutton with Frank J. Wertel, quoted in *TRTW,* p. 88. The following account is taken from the beginning of Anderson's "Tim and General Grant," pp. 846–50, in Paul Rosenfeld, ed., *The Sherwood Anderson Reader* (Boston: Houghton Mifflin, 1947).

31. Ohio National Guard Form 84 in the Newberry Library. *Enterprise,* Sept. 14, 1899, p. 3.

32. For a picture and description of The Oaks see Jack Sullivan, "Sherwood Anderson's Year in Springfield Recalled," Springfield *Sun,* Jan. 3, 1961, pp. 1–2. The fullest account of his year is in William Baker, "Sherwood Anderson in Springfield," *American Literary Realism* 15 (Spring 1982): 47–61.

33. Letter to WBR from W. Emerson Reck, vice president, Wittenberg University, Jan. 7, 1965. In *TRTW* (p. 93), Sutton quotes the comment of Alice Mower, who taught Latin and English: "Even at that time he was plainly superior to most of the students of his age. He was in at least one of my classes and I remember him as a very fine student." Other quotations from Sullivan, "Sherwood Anderson's Year," pp. 1–2; letter to WBR from J. Fuller Trump, Dec. 24, 1964; Sutton, *TRTW,* p. 93; letter to WBR from Leon C. Dibble, Feb. 20, 1965; Baker, "Sherwood Anderson in Springfield," p. 52.

34. Harold H. Lentz, *A History of Wittenberg College (1845–1945)* (Columbus, OH: The Wittenberg Press, 1946), p. 181. *The Wittenberger,* Oct. 14, 1899, p. 3; Nov. 4, p. 2; Nov. 25, p. 8; Dec. 9, p. 6; Feb. 3, 1900, pp. 1, 6; Mar. 3, p. 2. On Mar. 30, 1900, Anderson was elected secretary of the Academic Athletic Association, but no one has been able to discover any other record of this organization or of his participation in it.

35. Letter to WBR from Mrs. Lorenz W. Carstensen (Margarete Hochdoerfer), Feb. 22, 1965. A number of the details on The Oaks are taken from this letter, from George H. Daugherty, "Anderson, Advertising Man," *Newberry Library Bulletin,* Second Series, No. 2 (Dec. 1948), 30–38, and from William Baker, "Sherwood Anderson in Springfield."

36. Lentz, *History of Wittenberg College,* p. 229. Hochdoerfer's one book-length publication was *Introductory Studies in German Literature,* published in 1904 in the Chautauqua Home Reading Series, but he was of sufficient distinction in the field of Germanic and Anglo-Saxon languages and literature to serve as vice president of the Modern Language Association of America.

Mrs. Carstensen to WBR, Feb. 22, 1965. Anderson's German teacher at the academy was Dr. Charles A. Wilson, not Dr. Hochdoerfer, who taught at the college; but the latter is almost certainly the one who, according to Karl ("My Brother, Sherwood Anderson," p. 7), "became interested in Sherwood" and helped "to prepare him to matriculate" in the academy.

SA to Mary Emmett, Jan. 4, 1939. Mrs. Carstensen to WBR, Feb. 22, 1965. Her comment continues: "After leaving the Oaks Miss White lived alone in an apartment near the city Library, entertained interesting people and had quite a correspondence with younger people. She was very proud of her friendship with Sherwood and kept all his letters. Unfortunately those letters were *destroyed* when her niece cleared out her apartment after her death."

37. Karl Anderson, "My Brother, Sherwood Anderson," p. 7.

38. Springfield *Republican-Times,* June 5, 1900, p. 5, quoted in Sutton, *TRTW,* p. 95. Mrs. Carstensen to WBR, Feb. 22, 1965.

39. Evans, *History of Adams County,* p. 678; Price, "Karl Anderson, American," p. 137. Entries in the volumes of the *Lakeside Annual Directory of the City of Chicago,* which apparently went to press on Aug. 1 each year, locate the family street addresses as follows: 1900 and 1901—1036 (now 2519) West Adams; 1902—4454 Oakenwald Avenue; 1903—245 (now 626) Oakwood Boulevard; 1904—235 (now 616) Oakwood Boulevard. (In 1909, the street numbering system in Chicago was changed; hence the two numbers for the West Adams and Oakwood addresses. Oakenwald numbers remained unchanged.)

   In her letter to WBR of Feb. 22, 1965, Mrs. Carstensen recalled Earl from Springfield days as "my play mate at croquet—a very quiet boy who clung to sister [Stella] and brother Ray."

40. "The Solicitor," *Agricultural Advertising* 11 (Aug. 1904), 21–24, p. 23. Cf. *Memoirs* (1942), pp. 137–38; (1969), p. 200.

41. Letter to Sutton from Marco Morrow, Oct. 11, 1941, quoted in Sutton, "Sherwood: The Advertising Years 1900–1906," *Northwest Ohio Quarterly* 22 (Summer 1950): 120–57, p. 120. In a letter to Eleanor Copenhaver Anderson dated Aug. 20, 1941, Morrow wrote: "I hired him to go to the Frank B. White Company as my assistant in the Copy Department," presumably the "literary" department Morrow was said to be in charge of in "Announcement," *Agricultural Advertising* 11 (Sept. 1904): 44.

42. Quoted from Morrow's letter to Sutton in "The Advertising Years," p. 120.

43. Interview, WBR with Mrs. Alfred Newman (Bessie Lay), Dec. 22, 1961, and Mrs. W. K. Graham (Elizabeth Van Horne), Feb. 6, 1959; letters from Mrs. Graham to SA, Mar. 18, 1931, and Oct. 25, 1939. In a letter of Feb. 24, 1948, to Stanley Pargellis, then librarian of the Newberry Library, Mrs. Graham likewise expressed her admiration for Stella Anderson's knowledge of literature and her devotion as "the home-maker for all those boys."

44. "The Farmer Wears Clothes," *Agricultural Advertising* 9 (Feb. 1902): 6; "Letter of an Advertising Solicitor to His Wife at Home," pp. 36–37; "A Soliloquy," p. 25; "Not Knocking," pp. 22–23; "Writing it Down," p. 46. Sutton, who first tentatively ascribed the "Letter" to Anderson, suggests the possibility that he may have contributed some of the unsigned articles in the magazine; but neither Sutton nor I have found convincing evidence for assigning any such articles to him.

45. All three of these "golden" categories are explicitly related to the brown and gold cover of the August issue, "conceived by Jerry of the Art Department," showing a farmer standing "with folded arms, amid his grain piles," and, across the bottom of the cover a row of half-husked golden corn ears. The cover is at least suggestive of Anderson's own future preoccupation with the symbolic values of corn.

46. See Earl Hilton, "Sherwood Anderson and 'Heroic Vitalism,'" *Northwest Ohio Quarterly* 29 (Spring 1957): 97–107, for a discussion of Carlyle's influence on the early Anderson.

47. The reorganization was announced in "Editor's Horizon," *Agricultural Advertising* 10 (Sept. 1903): 3–5, p. 3. The magazine and its staff were taken over by the new corporation, of which Long became president, Critchfield vice president. Already in March 1903, the White Company had expanded into new quarters in the Powers Building at 156 Wabash Street.

48. Letter to Sutton from Marco Morrow, Oct. 11, 1941, quoted in Sutton, "The Advertising Years," p. 123 (only summarized in *TRTW,* p. 104). In a letter to Eleanor Copenhaver Anderson, Aug. 20, 1941, Morrow wrote the same story in condensed form, concluding, "When he returned [from the trip], he told me he was going to write and from that time on he came in from trips with pages and pages and pages of ms." In an interview on Dec. 22, 1948, Morrow gave William L. Phillips a very similar account. See Phillips, "Sherwood Anderson's *Winesburg, Ohio,*" unpublished PhD diss., University of Chicago, 1949, p. 16.

49. "A Business Man's Reading," *The Reader* 2 (Oct. 1903): 503–4, p. 503; "The Man and the Book," *The Reader* 3 (Dec. 1903): 71–73, pp. 72, 73; "Why I Write," *The Writer* 49 (Dec. 1936): 363–64, p. 364.

50. "Letters from an Advertiser," *Agricultural Advertising* 10 (May 1903): 22–23, p. 23.

51. Freeman Kueckelhan, "Random Notes," *Agricultural Advertising* 11 (Oct. 1904): 57–58, p. 57.

52. Quotations from letters from Morrow to Sutton, Oct. 11, 1941 (quoted in "The Advertising Years," p. 149), and to George Daugherty, Sept. 21, 1947. In the version in the *Memoirs* (1969, pp. 211–13) Anderson writes that he saw Curtis at the Long-Critchfield office, talked with him (not Lorimer) in Philadelphia, "was offered a position as an editorial writer for the *Saturday Evening Post,*" and refused the position because the size of the Curtis Publishing Company "may have a little terrified me" and "perhaps already I had begun to be a little afraid of all bigness." Morrow, however, was in general more careful of facts than Sherwood, and the *Memoirs* version is suspect because of inconsistencies.

53. "Long-Critchfield Dinner," *Agricultural Advertising* 12 (May 1905): 421.

54. For many of the facts concerning Cornelia Platt Lane I am indebted to Sutton, *TRTW,* p. 133–35, to Mrs. Robert McNeill Lane, Cornelia's sister-in-law, interview, WBR, Sept. 6, 1961, and to Hilbert H. Campbell, "Cornelia's Grand Tour," *Winesburg Eagle* 15 (Winter 1990): 1–2. Information on her father from John M. Willets, ed., *Toledo and Lucas County, Ohio, 1623–1923,* 3 vols. (Toledo, OH: S. J. Clarke Publishing Company, 1923), vol. 1, p. 409, and from interview, WBR with Richard Faben, Sept. 6, 1961. Mr. Faben, who was born in 1899, lived next door to the Lane house from 1908 on and knew Robert Lane in his later years. Interview, WBR with Mrs. Robert McNeill Lane, Sept. 6, 1961. A number of details in the following paragraphs come from Mrs. Lane's very careful recollections.

55. Interview with Captain Raymond J. Toner, USN, June 15, 1961. Although Captain Toner knew Cornelia well only in the 1930s, he was speaking of long-standing characteristics.

56. Sutton, *TRTW*, p. 133. The research paper appeared in *The College Folio* (Jan. 1900): 105–9. Sutton quotes its concluding paragraph in *TRTW*, p. 134.

57. Summarized from Campbell, "Cornelia's Grand Tour."

58. Interview with Mrs. Alfred Newman (Bessie Lay), Dec. 22, 1961.

59. According to George A. Bottger, Anderson's business associate in 1906–7 (see chapter 4), Sherwood once told him that Cornelia's father had not approved of the marriage. Interview, WBR with Bottger, Sept. 12, 1961. The Mar. 6, 1904, note is the earliest of Anderson's letters in the Sherwood Anderson Collection in the Newberry Library. On his first trip to Europe Karl had met Helen Edgerton Buell of Marietta, Ohio, "who had made quite a success as a singer at Covent Garden" in London (A/P Tapes, p. 2). They were married on Sept. 1, 1904.

    The announcement in the *Blade*, which is printed on p. 6 as the first item in the Social column, refers inaccurately to "James" Anderson as the future groom and sets the time as "the middle" of May. The same error in Sherwood's name occurs in the *Blade* for May 3, 1904 (p. 8), but the date is accurately set as May 16 and the place as the bride's home. Social, *Toledo Daily Blade*, May 9, 1904, p. 6.

60. Quotations are from Mrs. Cornelia Anderson's remarks to Sutton in an interview, Oct. 10, 1946 (*TRTW*, 134–35, 104, 140). Some remarks are evidence of Sherwood's early interest in writing. Asked "if she knew when Anderson first considered himself a writer," she replied: "I had the feeling that he always did. When I first met him [1903], he had a lot of stories he'd written. Did you ever come across 'Girl in the Snow'? [Doubtless an early version of 'Death in the Woods.'] I imagine the *Agricultural Advertising* items were the first published. He had a scrapbook, it seems to me." (Bracketed material added by Sutton.) In a note on this passage, Sutton adds (p. 140): "In the same interview she also said, 'He just wrote all the time' and 'He was writing in a small way when I first knew him.'"

61. Social, *Toledo Daily Blade*, May 16, 1904, p. 6. This announcement is the lead item in the Social column, and the length of it is that reserved in the paper only for the more prominent marriages.

62. In 1904, both before and after the wedding, Anderson wrote a series of short essays and poetry that he kept in a notebook along with a journal of his honeymoon trip with Cornelia. This notebook was found among her effects after her death in 1967 by her daughter Marion (Mimi). She later turned it over to Hilbert H. Campbell, who edited and published it in "Honeymoon Journal and Other Writings, 1904," *Sherwood Anderson Review* 23 (Summer 1998). The notebook is now in the Anderson collection at the Newberry Library, Chicago.

63. Rosalie Court is now that part of Harper Avenue between 57th and 59th Streets just west of the Illinois Central tracks. Cornelia's summer school work is listed in her Teacher Record, Michigan City, Indiana, Public Schools. See

also Sutton, *TRTW,* p. 144, n. 79. *The Lakeside Annual Directory of the City of Chicago* for both 1905 and 1906 lists Anderson's business address after his name followed by "Riverside" as his home address. The *Directory* for 1906, the preface to which is dated July of that year, also gives a second entry, "[Anderson] Sherwood h[ome] 6126 Jackson Park av"; and even more confusingly this latter entry is given in the *Directory* for 1907, though by July of 1907 Sherwood and Cornelia had been in Cleveland nearly a year. There may have been a second Sherwood Anderson in Chicago at that time, though this seems unlikely. Possibly the second entry in 1906 indicates an early summer move to the Jackson Park Avenue address from Riverside, the *Directory* failing to correct its first entry. The 1907 listing would certainly seem a *Directory* error.

64. Letter to Sutton from Louis D. Wallace, Oct. 17, 1947, quoted in Sutton, "The Advertising Years," p. 153. Sutton, *TRTW,* p. 137.

65. For the letter recalling the incident see pp. 5–7 in William A. Sutton, ed., *Letters to Bab: Sherwood Anderson to Marietta D. Finley, 1916–33* (Urbana: University of Illinois Press, 1985).

CHAPTER 4. THE DREAM OF SUCCESS

1. "The Fussy Man and the Trimmer," *Agricultural Advertising* 11 (Dec. 1904): 79, 81–2, p. 82; "The Sales Master and the Selling Organization," *Agricultural Advertising* 12 (April 1905): 306–8, p. 307. One of Anderson's clients told Sutton that Sherwood "was disgusted with the commission-system of payment for advertising men" (*TRTW,* p. 138).

2. "'A Kalamazoo Direct to You': The Terse and Simple Story of a Half Million Dollar Business Built in Two Years," *Agricultural Advertising* 11 (Nov. 1904): 21–26, p. 21.

3. Most of the information on Anderson's association with the United Factories Company in 1906–7 comes from two interviews with Mr. Bottger. One of these was conducted by Sutton in the early 1940s and provided much of the material for chapter 7 of *TRTW,* from which I have drawn a number of details. The second interview I conducted on Sept. 12, 1961, covering much the same ground and obtaining additional information. The marked reliability of Bottger's recollections is indicated, among other ways, by the close agreement between the statements he made in two interviews twenty years apart.

   The head of Lord & Thomas was D. W. Taylor, who subsequently bought out the interest of Frank E. Long in the Long-Critchfield Corporation and made it Taylor-Critchfield. It was to this reorganized Chicago firm that Anderson returned in Feb. 1913 after his own failures as independent businessman.

   On Sept. 12, 1961, Bottger's comment on the deceptive engraving was: "You couldn't do that sort of thing nowadays." Such equivocations with the truth must be kept in mind as being accepted practices of the real business world in which Sherwood Anderson was functioning. Bottger could not recall whether Anderson was the man who persuaded United Factories to switch its account, but Sherwood's assignment to the account brought the two men into close acquaintance.

4. In my interview with him Bottger stated explicitly that it was Sherwood, not he, who suggested his transfer to United Factories.
5. Quotations from Sutton, *TRTW*, pp. 152–53.
6. Quoted in Sutton, *TRTW*, p. 152. Bottger told Sutton that: "The scheme failed for lack of a head. Each factory wanted to be boss." Actually United Factories continued in business until shortly after World War II (interview, WBR, Sept. 12, 1961).
7. Interview by Sutton of Mrs. Cornelia Anderson, Oct. 10, 1946 (*TRTW*, p. 157). Originally United Factories sold a roof paint called "Patch-a-Leak" or "New-Coat," later called "Unicoat." Anderson picked up a similar item— that is, "Roof-Fix"—from one of the several companies that made this sort of thing. At first Roof-Fix contained tar, but since tar dried out too readily, asphalt was substituted (WBR's interview with Bottger). Interview by Sutton of Baxter (*TRTW*, p. 157); interview by WBR of Bottger. Bottger recalled the church work for both Sutton and WBR. In her Oct. 10, 1946, interview with Sutton, Cornelia Anderson told him flatly, "We never went to church," though she later agreed that Sherwood may have gone this once. Description of SA by Mrs. Bottger at interview by WBR of Bottger.
8. Quoted from *TRTW*, p. 155. Sutton's summary in *TRTW*, p. 155, of statements made to him in an interview with the secretary, Mrs. William Puchta. Bottger emphasized this point about office routine in both the Sutton and the Rideout interviews.
9. Interview, WBR.
10. Bottger told Sutton that out of 3,200 incubators sold 600 were returned. Interview, WBR.
11. Quoted in *TRTW*, p. 154, from interview by Sutton of employee E. O. Schaad. In my lengthy interview with Bottger I questioned him carefully on this breakdown. Though he could give no details beyond those cited, he was absolutely certain about the fact of a breakdown in 1907 because it thereby became his responsibility to "pick up the pieces" of the incubator affair. When I described Anderson's breakdown in Elyria in 1912, Bottger insisted that he did *not* know about a later one, but *did* know about the one in Cleveland in 1907 because of the immediate consequences for himself and the United Factories Company. The incubator affair had been the crucial blow, Bottger emphasized to me, though Sherwood "didn't have business sense," especially in office organization. WBR: "Was business just too tough for him?" Bottger: "That's just right."

    Margaret Anderson, *My Thirty Years War': An Autobiography* (New York: Covici, Friede Publishers, 1930), p. 233.
12. Karl Anderson, "My Brother, Sherwood Anderson," p. 7. Karl gives the same account in "Memories of SA," pp. 8–9, but neither account includes any reference to the incubator episode. Bottger's statement in my interview with him struck me as circumstantially convincing.
13. Information on the development of Elyria is from *Picturesque Elyria: Her Enterprising Citizens and Her Industries* (Elyria, OH: Elyria Souvenir Co., 1903), from which most of the quotations are taken, and from G. Frederick

Wright, ed., *A Standard History of Lorain County, Ohio,* 2 vols. (Chicago and New York: The Lewis Publishing Co., 1916).

14. Wright, *Standard History,* vol. 1, p. 369.

15. Information on Dr. Philip D. Reefy comes from the following sources: Wright, *Standard History,* vol. 2, pp. 834–36; Anon., *Commemorative Biographical Record of the Counties of Huron and Lorain, Ohio* . . . (Chicago: J. H. Beers & Co., 1894), p. 784–87; *Picturesque Elyria,* p. 30; *Elyria Democrat,* Mar. 16, 1911, p. 8, and Feb. 15, 1912; interviews by WBR with Alma Galli (Mrs. Jack) Dillman and Richard Faxon, Sept. 13, 1961. Dr. Reefy died Oct. 7, 1913. For many years the Elyria Public Library was housed in his former home on Third Street.

16. *Elyria Evening Telegram,* Sept. 5, 1912, p. 1; Sept. 9, p. 1; Nov. 28, 1911, p. 1; Dec. 15, p. 1. *Elyria Republican,* Feb. 15, 1912, p. 5.

17. *Democrat,* May 28, 1908, p. 8. The first president of the club was Mrs. Walter E. Brooks, wife of the man who rented factory space to Anderson for his business and backed him financially. *Telegram,* Mar. 8, 1912, p. 1. Cornelia's membership is confirmed by the *Democrat,* Mar. 3, 1910, p. 8, "Personal and Social" column. *Democrat,* Jan. 31, 1907, p. 5. Other quotations in this paragraph from *Republican,* Feb. 15, 1912, p. 1, and *Telegram,* Nov. 26, 1912, pp. 1, 5. The prevalence of venereal disease suggests that, not surprisingly, actual sexual behavior of Elyrians was less strict than the public code professed.

18. *Democrat,* Mar. 23, 1911, p. 8. *Telegram,* Apr. 22, 1910, p. 6; Feb. 20, 1912, p. 4; Mar. 7, 1912, p. 4. Williams also combined his entrepreneurial and literary interests when in about Aug. 1911 he was one of the purchasers of what became the Central Book Store, run for years thereafter by his sister Claire and Annie J. Thomas. In addition to selling books the Central had a "Circulating" (rental) library containing many newly published volumes. See *Democrat,* Aug. 3, 1911, p. 5; *Telegram,* Feb. 7, 1912, "Special Bargain Section No. 1," p. 7. Wright, *Standard History,* vol. 2, p. 579. Sutton, *TRTW,* p. 182.

19. A reference in the *Telegram,* May 4, 1908, p. 5, places the Andersons in The Gray, while one in the *Republican,* Sept. 3, 1908, p. 8, places them on Seventh Street. Earl Anderson is located as living with Sherwood and Cornelia in *Moore's Standard Directory of Elyria, Ohio: 1908–1909.*

Anderson's tendency to mix fancy and reality in the *Memoirs* is well illustrated by his description of Delia (1942), pp. 163–64, 166–67, 170–72; (1969), pp. 254–55, 258, 262–63, 265–66. Mrs. Jack Dillman (born Alma Galli, daughter of Delia's brother-in-law) confirmed to me in an interview (Sept. 18, 1961) that her Uncle Angelo felt that Anderson indeed "looked down on him as a peasant" and that while the townspeople liked Delia, Angelo was never admitted to the "top group" of the city, as Anderson was. The Delias were already living on Seventh Street when the Andersons moved there, not vice versa as the *Memoirs* account implies, but Angelo did garden as a hobby. See also Alex Gildzen's interview with Mrs. Dillman reported in his "Sherwood Anderson, Elyria, and the Escape Hunch," *Serif* 5 (March, 1968): 3–10, and the accounts of Delia and Galli in Wright, *Standard History,* vol. 2, pp. 748–51.

20. The Topliff & Ely Manufacturing Company had made hardware for car-
    riages, but shortly before Anderson came to Elyria it had gone out of business,
    a victim, apparently, of the rising automobile industry. Sutton, *TRTW,*
    pp. 165–66, 157. Sutton notes that the Roof-Fix advertisement first appeared
    in the *Rural New-Yorker* for Sept. 14, 1907. I am indebted to Sutton's chap-
    ter 8, "Exit to Elsinore," for many details on Anderson's Elyria period. Let-
    ters to WBR from H. Kellogg Day (Dec. 31, 1964) and George M. Day (post-
    marked Jan. 8, 1965). The Day brothers were associated with their father in
    a hardware store, which, according to Kellogg Day, sold the tins and other
    "small items" to the Anderson Company.
21. Sutton, *TRTW,* p. 169–70; *Democrat,* Sept. 24, 1908, p. 5; *Telegram,* Aug.
    18, 1909, p. 1; *Democrat,* Aug. 19, 1909, p. 5; Apr. 22, 1909, p. 8; *Republi-
    can,* Jan. 20, 1910, p. 1. Although manufactured under the financial control
    of the Anderson Paint Company, the paints were marketed under the Wilcox-
    son brand name. Proof that Roof-Fix was now actually being manufactured
    at the Topliff & Ely Plant is provided by a report in the *Telegram* (June 10,
    1910, p. 1) of a small fire there caused by an overheated "kettle of the gums
    which are used in the Roof-Fix preparation."
22. Interview, WBR with Bottger, Sept. 12, 1961. Sutton, *TRTW,* pp. 169–70,
    201. "Memories of SA," p. 9. Sutton, *TRTW,* p. 165. Besides having been
    head of the defunct Topliff & Ely company—his first marriage had been to a
    Topliff daughter—Brooks was currently president of the expanding Elyria
    Telephone Company and had numerous other business interests. Like Ander-
    son he was a member of the Chamber of Commerce, the Elks, and the Coun-
    try Club. The close connection with Brooks shows how well Anderson had
    been accepted by the business leaders of Elyria.
23. My account of Commercial Democracy draws a number of details from Sut-
    ton, *TRTW,* pp. 170–72; other quotations from *Democrat,* Mar. 24, 1910,
    p. 8; *Telegram,* Mar. 21, 1911, p. 4.
24. "Memories of SA," p. 9. Cf. Cornelia Anderson's comment to Sutton on
    Commercial Democracy (*TRTW,* p. 201, n 43): "'Oh, yes, I believe we were
    socialists at one period. Perhaps he did have the idea of profit-sharing.'"
    George Bottger remembered Commercial Democracy as a political scheme,
    though Anderson never solicited him to join.
25. Sutton (*TRTW,* p. 172) quotes what he was told by Harry J. Crandall, an
    Elyria druggist who invested in another company Anderson was shortly to
    found. Crandall called *Commercial Democracy* "'an advertising pamphlet' to
    be sent to hardware dealers." Karl Anderson, "My Brother, Sherwood An-
    derson," p. 7.
26. Another indication of his business success was that in the fiscal year 1909–10
    the Anderson Manufacturing Company for the first time provided to the
    County Commissioners some of the materials and labor used for maintenance
    of bridges and highway railings. See *Democrat,* Oct. 27, 1910, Supplement:
    "The Annual Report of the Commissioners of Lorain County, O. For the Year
    Ending August 31, 1910." *Democrat,* Nov. 16, 1911, p. 5. My discussion of
    the company is based on this newspaper item; on Sutton, *TRTW,* p. 173; and

on the Articles of Incorporation, Charter Number 77798, Corporation Department, Office of the Secretary of State, Columbus, Ohio. Sutton refers to Anderson as a "director of the company" and notes that he "was apparently in complete charge"; in a news item on the Company on p. 1 of the *Telegram* for Aug. 17, 1912, Anderson is described as "president and general manager."

27. Sutton, *TRTW*, p. 173. Two investors Sutton interviewed told him that Brooks's support of Anderson was "very important" and that the "impression was that Anderson was a good advertising man and a good salesman."

28. *Telegram*, Jan. 4, 1903, p. 2; Oct. 30, 1911, p. 8. Dates confirmed by official birth records cited in Sutton, *TRTW*, p. 199, n 2. Although the Elyria Memorial Hospital opened on Oct. 30, 1908, Cornelia may have preferred having her second child in the same hospital where she had had her first.

29. *Democrat*, Apr. 9, 1908, p. 5; Aug. 20, 1908, p. 5; July 8, 1909, p. 8; Nov. 18, 1909, p. 8; Feb. 9, 1911, p. 8; Feb. 23, 1911, p. 4; June 1, 1911, p. 8. For "The Golf Ball" section of the *Memoirs*, see pp. 150–62 (1942); pp. 238–53 (1969). See also Ron Royhab, "Shades of Sherwood Anderson," *The Lorain, Ohio Journal*, Jan. 2, 1965, p. 5. The son of another Elyria businessman, when interviewed by Royhab, recalled caddying for Anderson on a golf course that, he insisted, his family and Anderson laid out together in the south part of the city.

30. *Telegram*, May 10, 1910, p. [5?]; *Democrat*, May 12, 1910, p. 8; May 26, 1910, p. 5.

31. *Democrat*, Sept. 30, 1909, p. 8. Sutton in *TRTW*, p. 162, points out the Helen Bowen Garfield connection. (The then Miss Bowen married John Garfield of Cleveland on Sept. 28, 1910.) Cornelia's social standing in Elyria is of considerable significance during the climactic year 1912. The status conferred by membership in the Fortnightly is indicated by the fact that the club's roster included the wives of a former mayor of Elyria, of a Congressman, of directors of two different banks, including the one where Sherwood did business, and of two descendents of the Ely who founded Elyria.

Evidence on the Fortnightly programs comes from various newspaper issues, chiefly of the *Democrat*. On June 9, 1910, Mrs. Anderson was elected corresponding secretary of the Club. Over a three-and-a-half-year membership she gave two readings, one of them at the meeting on the short story writers, and six papers, including "Stevenson and the Return of the Romance" (April 4, 1912) and "The Stage of Shakespeare" (Feb. 21, 1913). In view of Anderson's many references to "Elsinore" in the Amnesia Letter, it comes as rather a surprise that *Hamlet* was not among the six plays of Shakespeare studied by the club in 1912–13: *Henry the Fourth, As You Like It, Othello, King Lear, Antony and Cleopatra,* and *The Tempest.*

32. *Democrat*, Mar. 3, 1910, p. 8; June 29, 1911, p. 8.

33. *Democrat*, Jan. 26, 1911, p. 8; *Republican*, Jan. 26, 1911, p. 8.

34. Information on the Club from *Telegram*, Oct. 23, 1912, p. 2; Sutton, *TRTW*, p. 162; interviews, WBR with Richard Faxon, Nellie Lewis, and Mrs. Frank Wilford, Sept. 13, 1961; letter to WBR from Margaret E. Edwards, Mar. 2, 1965. The strong elements of progressivism and community service among

Elyria's "Establishment" is once again confirmed by the activities of Frank Wilford, who in 1911–12 was secretary and treasurer of the large Federation of Men's Clubs of Elyria and president of the Associated Charities; and by those of the very popular Comings, who in the rapidly expanding Elyria schools after 1900 instituted such innovations as manual training, domestic science, kindergarten, physical training, a vocational school, and special schools for ungraded children.

35. Interview with Nellie Lewis by Harvey Fisher reported in his "Sherwood Anderson," part 6, unpaged. This draft of an eight-part reporter's series on Anderson was written in 1961 for publication in the Elyria *Chronicle-Telegram* but was not used by this successor to the *Evening Telegram*. The draft was kindly lent to me for note-taking only, on Sept. 13, 1961, by Mr. and Mrs. Robert G. Peterson of Elyria. It was scrapped thereafter but not because Fisher's interview material was considered in any way dubious. Interviews, WBR with Mrs. Wilford and Miss Lewis, Sept. 13, 1961; with Mrs. John Craun, Sept. 10, 1961; with Mrs. Robert McNeill Lane, Cornelia's sister-in-law, Sept. 6, 1961; Captain Raymond J. Toner, USN, June 15, 1961. See also the letters to Sutton (quoted in *TRTW*, p. 184) from Florence Terry, a high school history teacher and close friend of the Andersons who in Oct. 1942 wrote: "'Cornelia's radical views . . . were along ultra modern lines on art and literature and social reforms. She seemed to think that new ideas in literature should be taught and studied even though real merit might be in question, time not having proved their worth.'"

36. Interview, Sutton with Cornelia Anderson, Oct. 10, 1946. See *TRTW*, p. 181.

37. Sutton, *Letters to Bab*, pp. 26–28. Anderson might have used "seven" as a nice-sounding, "magic" number, of course; but the possibility that for once he was remembering time accurately is strengthened by the fact that in the same letter he refers three times to "five years" as the length of his residence in Elyria, a fairly accurate statement of the actual five and a half years. "Memories of SA," p. 9. Karl's remark could mean that Sherwood had already begun a novel before being deflected from it by the need to meet competition; but at best it must have taken some time after Nov. 1909, for the scheme to achieve success and for other paint companies to have mounted a competitive reaction. If anything, Karl's testimony makes early 1910 rather than late 1909 the time at which Sherwood began writing. Letter, Purcell to Sutton, quoted in *TRTW*, p. 180.

38. Interview, Sutton with Cornelia Anderson, Oct. 10, 1946, quoted in *TRTW*, p. 181. Some years ago I ran across a striking instance of Anderson's power of eliciting the inner feelings of people met by chance. Dropping into the now defunct Peabody Bookshop in Baltimore, I got into conversation with its proprietor, the late Siegfried Weisberger. Learning of my interest in Anderson, Weisberger commented substantially as follows: "I remember he came in here once and introduced himself. He stood about as far from me as you are standing now, and when he asked me a question and looked at me with those dark brown searching eyes of his, I knew I just had to tell the truth."

39. Quotations in this paragraph are from Sutton, *TRTW*, pp. 180, 184, 203. For

newspaper references, see, for example, "Elyria Man Is Very Ill," *The Cleveland News*, Dec. 3, 1912, p. 1: "Sherwood Anderson, Elyria clubman, manufacturer and author . . ." For "Other friends," see *TRTW*, p. 180; interviews, WBR with Dorothy Jones, Sept. 12, 1961, and Mrs. Robert M. Lane, Sept. 6, 1961.

40. The argument favoring the prior *composition* of *Marching Men,* despite the priority in publication of *Windy McPherson's Son,* will be more fully presented in the discussion of *Marching Men* in a subsequent chapter, but order of composition is not the point here.

41. The information on Williams is drawn from Wright, *Standard History,* pp. 1033–34; *Memoirs* (1969), p. 301, 282–84; Sutton, *TRTW,* p. 178; interview, WBR with Mrs. James Thomas in Elyria Sept. 13, 1961. The material on the canoe trip is from Williams's own account in an article reprinted in Ron Royhab, "Shades of Sherwood Anderson," *The (Lorain, OH) Journal,* Jan. 2, 1965, p. 5. Since the year of the trip is mistakenly given as "1905"—Anderson did not settle in Elyria until 1907—the article would appear to have been written by Williams long enough after the fact for him to forget the correct date.

   In the *Memoirs* (1969), p. 301, Anderson writes that "my friend [Williams] was a great admirer of O. Henry." Williams did print three O. Henry stories in the *Telegram* in Jan. 1912 alone, and followed these with a serialization of Gene Stratton-Porter's popular *Freckles;* but in addition to his admiration for Twain and the prose styles of Howells and John Bunyan, he showed interest in literary creativity by printing on page 2 of the Feb. 20, 1912, issue of the *Telegram* a lengthy, unsigned article (possibly a "syndicated" one) summarizing the ideas of Havelock Ellis's *The World of Dream* (American edition, 1911). These ideas might well have interested Anderson, who was always fascinated by the imaginative life, for the summary pointed out that "dreams are merely the period of existence of another personality"; that for the great productive writer or artist dreams and reality "are no longer distinct" but "flow in the same channel"; that dreaming "resembles a cinematograph picture which is made up of many different pictures, but which are all related. They pass in quick succession without one word of explanation. Long before cinematograph pictures were invented children discovered how to make these pictures both when awake and on going to sleep. Most children love to close their eyes and to let a series of strange pictures pass on the curtain of the closed eyelids. They get their most interesting and unusual pictures in this way." The comments on the succession of pictures in the half-awake state is especially interesting when one recalls Anderson's frequent references to the procession of faces that would sometimes pass before his eyes, each face seeking to be expressed in one of Anderson's tales.

42. The information on Earl is drawn from *Memoirs* (1969), pp. 309–11; "Memories of SA," p. 9. See n. 19 for Earl's living at The Gray. *The Democrat* (Dec. 1, 1910, p. 8) lists Earl as one of the Elyria guests at the Anderson home for Thanksgiving dinner in 1910, a reference which suggests that he was not then living in the Seventh Street residence. A supplement to the issue of the *Demo-*

crat for Apr. 13, 1911, lists both Sherwood and Earl as contributors to the fund for a new YMCA building. I have located no subsequent references to Earl in any of the Elyria newspapers. His going to New Orleans may possibly be connected with Irwin's one reported visit to Elyria in late July 1911 (*Democrat,* July 27, 1911, p. 8).

Earl actually had had art training and experience. Interestingly, he is listed in the *Annual Directory . . . of Chicago* for 1904 as "artist" with the same business address as Sherwood's, which suggests that he too was then employed by Long-Critchfield, presumably in the Art Department. His home address is given as 235 Oakwood Boulevard, the number very likely being a misprint for 245 [now 626] Oakwood, where Sherwood is listed as living in 1903 and where the *Chicago Telephone Company Directory* places Stella in 1903 and 1904. The only other appearance of Earl's name in the *Annual Directory* for those years is in that for 1907: "[Anderson] Earl artist 5th fl 76 Sherman h[ome] studio bldg."

43. Interviews, WBR with Mrs. Frank Wilford, Sept. 13, 1961; Mrs. Robert McNeill Lane, Sept. 6, 1961; Captain Raymond J. Toner (friend of Mrs. John Sherwood Anderson), June 15, 1961. Statements to Sutton by Florence Terry, Cornelia Anderson, and Frances Shute are quoted from *TRTW,* pp. 181, 184. During my interview in Elyria on Sept. 12, 1961, with Dorothy Jones, daughter of Robert Jones, a good friend of Sherwood in Clyde, Miss Jones affirmed her own very strong impression, admittedly secondhand but gathered from several apparently informed people, that Cornelia did help her husband with his writing, "correcting his punctuation" and the like, an impression that tends to corroborate Florence Terry's flat statement about the specific nature of Cornelia's assistance.

44. *Democrat,* Oct. 27, 1910, Supplement; Oct. 5, 1911, p. 7; Sept. 26, 1912, Supplement. *Telegram,* May 15, 1912, p. 1; *Democrat,* May 16, 1912, p. 5. *Telegram,* Aug. 17, 1912, p. 1. Interview, WBR with Mrs. Frank Wilford, Sept. 13, 1961. According to Waldo Purcell (Sutton, "Formative Years," p. 191), "There was never very much actual cash paid in" from stock sales, beyond, that is, the initial investments, in which case Anderson presumably was operating on sales of goods and on bank loans. Interestingly, an obituary on Anderson in the Fremont (OH) *News Messenger* of Apr. 14, 1941, unpaged clipping, refers to Anderson's "growing certainty [in late 1912] that his bankers would foreclose on him."

A minor but unpleasant calamity occurred on Sunday, Oct. 20, 1912, when an angry former employee, a boy of nineteen recently paroled from the reformatory, broke into the paint factory and vandalized it, doing some slight damage. Anderson did not prosecute the boy, apparently feeling that returning him to parole authorities would be sufficient punishment. See *Telegram,* Oct. 21 and 22, 1912, p. 1.

45. An undated clipping from the *Cleveland Leader,* probably Dec. 3, 1912, gives this as Anderson's day and evening routine "in the last year or more" and states further, "He is the author of a quantity of magazine fiction."

Alma Galli Dillman spoke of her uncle's love of gardening (interview,

WBR, Sept. 13, 1961). Much of the Italian's garden episode may be fanciful of course, but it may be noted that in *Memoirs* (1969) Anderson places the episode in "the early spring of that year" (exact year unspecified) and says it occurred the day after he had gone to Cleveland with "three other young business men of the town." It may be mere coincidence that the one newspaper reference to a Cleveland trip by Anderson is that this "president of the American Merchants Company" attended "the Hardware Dealers' convention in Cleveland" on Feb. 29, 1912, a date fairly close to "early spring." See *Democrat,* Feb. 24, 1912, p. 8; *Telegram,* Mar. 1, 1912, p. 2.

Crandall quotation from Sutton, *TRTW,* p. 180.

46. Information for this paragraph is mostly from an undated clipping from the *Cleveland Leader,* probably Dec. 3, 1912 (see *TRTW,* pp. 181–82). The statement about Cornelia's persuading her husband to stop work late at night was made to William Phillips by George Daugherty, Anderson's friend at Long-Critchfield, who learned of this from Cornelia during one of his several visits to the Anderson home in Elyria. (Phillips, "Sherwood Anderson's *Winesburg, Ohio,*" pp. 18–19.) Mrs. Anderson told Sutton that "It was true that he was known to write all night" (*TRTW,* p. 181).

47. Interview, Sutton with Cornelia, Oct. 10, 1946 (*TRTW,* p. 184). Interview, WBR with Mrs. Robert McNeill Lane, Sept. 6, 1961.

48. Interviews, WBR with Mrs. Frank Wilford, Sept. 13, 1961, and with Mrs. Lane. Sutton, *TRTW,* p. 163.

49. *Democrat,* Nov. 7, 1912, p. 8.

50. SA to Finley, Jan. 12, 1917, pp. 44–45, in *Letters to Bab.* Interview, WBR with Alma Galli Dillman, Sept. 18, 1961.

51. Interview, WBR with Mrs. Frank Wilford, Sept. 13, 1961.

52. Interview, WBR with Mrs. Dillman, Sept. 18, 1961.

53. See *Democrat,* Nov. 28, 1912, p. 8. For many facts concerning Anderson's breakdown I am indebted to Sutton's account in *TRTW,* pp. 187–99, Sutton having first assembled the basic documents on the event. The quotation is his summary of information given him in an interview with Mrs. Frances Shute Howk.

54. See *TRTW,* p. 553. Although this quoted note, which is in the Newberry Library, is not in Anderson's hand and has not been confirmed as a copy of his original note, the contents accord with the situation. Anderson's admission to the Huron Road Hospital on Sunday, Dec. 1, 1912, is confirmed by hospital records (letter of Jan. 12, 1965, to WBR from Virginia B. Quinn, the Hospital's Medical Record Librarian). He was released from Huron Road on Saturday, Dec. 7.

55. Sutton, *TRTW,* p. 187. Quite typically Anderson was to write in the *Memoirs* (1942, p. 202) that the season was summer. The issues of the *Evening Telegram* for Nov. 27, 29, and 30 give the *noon* temperatures at Elyria as 39, 44, and 54 respectively with little change in temperature forecast for Sunday, Dec. 1.

56. "Elyrian Roves 4 Days in Daze," *Cleveland Leader,* Dec. 2, 1912, p. 1. This paragraph is based on the very circumstantial *Leader* account.

57. Kim Townsend, in his biography *Sherwood Anderson* (Boston: Houghton Mifflin, 1987), pp. 81–82, also identifies Anderson's condition as a "fugue state."

58. *Evening Telegram,* Dec. 2, 1912, p. 1; *Cleveland Press,* Dec. 2, 1912, p. 2; *Cleveland News,* Dec. 3, 1912, p. 1; *Democrat,* Dec. 5, 1912, p. 5. The definition for "dissociative reaction" and that for "fugue" are taken from Alfred M. Freedman and Harold I. Kaplan, eds., *Comprehensive Textbook of Psychiatry* (Baltimore, MD: Williams & Wilkins Co., 1967), pp. 380, 897. (I acknowledge gratefully the clinical information furnished me by Dr. Aristotle Alexander, then associate professor of Psychiatry in the Medical School of the University of Wisconsin.) Karl Anderson, "My Brother, Sherwood Anderson," p. 7.

59. *Telegram,* Nov. 27, 1912, p. 1. In the issue for the previous Apr. 30, the *Telegram* had also reported lengthily on its first page the account of Dr. William C. Freed, a thirty-seven-year-old physician, who, his mind "partially unbalanced" from "too ardent study of theosophy and kindred religious subjects," had twice disappeared from home and had been finally located "wandering about the fields" near Elyria after he had "spent forty-eight hours tramping country roads and fields in the rain without sleep and with but little food" except for an ear of corn he "had picked up along the road." Dr. Freed was certainly a man of ideas, possibly even an author of sorts, for the pockets of his wet overcoat bulged with water-soaked "Packets of typewritten documents . . . all of which were 'lessons in the study of the science of the soul, mind and body.'" After being returned to Cleveland, "he will be examined by specialists and if it is decided that he is of unsound mind will be taken to a sanitarium." Assuming, as seems likely, that Anderson had read of the Freed as well as the O'Connor case, one can only speculate as to its possible effect on his troubled mind, but the parallels with his own situation some seven months later are at least disconcerting.

60. Cf. Cornelia's comment to Sutton in the interview of Oct. 10, 1946: "He kept track of his whole adventure on a tablet." In a letter to Sutton she subsequently elaborated on this remark: "The notes that I said were kept during the amnesia trip were not a record of what Mr. Anderson actually did but of what he thought he did or impressions he got. They were patently a picture of his state of mind" (*TRTW,* p. 552).

    The passage relating to the story is worth quoting: "There is a place near Bedford [possibly the suburb southeast of Cleveland]. A child that cried looked at a man with a pipe in his mouth who growled like a yellow dog. I tried to drink some beer but it was bitter and the room was full of men who would have hit me but I ran." Three pages later appears the sentence: "Why did they hit me. There were so many negroes to look at" (*TRTW,* pp. 556, 557).

    The text of the Amnesia Letter is reproduced in *TRTW,* pp. 554–58.

61. The reference could be to either of two Mrs. Leonards in Elyria. (Anderson spells the name correctly on page 2.) One, Mrs. S. S. Leonard, was a member of the Round Table, where books were literally among the subjects discussed.

The other, Mrs. J. H. Leonard, was a prominent member of the Political Study Club, who at the meeting on Dec. 11, 1912, the day when Cornelia and a convalescent Sherwood left town for a visit to the Lanes in Toledo, read an "interesting paper prepared by Mrs. Sherwood Anderson" on Maria Montessori's "recent book," *The Montessori Method* (*Democrat*, Dec. 12, 1912, p. 8).

62. *Cleveland News*, Dec. 3, 1912, p. 1; *Cleveland Press*, Dec. 2, 1912, p. 2; *Telegram*, Dec. 3, 1912, p. 1.

63. Cornelia to Sutton in interview, Oct. 10, 1946, quoted in *TRTW*, p. 552.

64. See Sutton, *TRTW*, pp. 563–64, for the text of the interview article and for Mrs. Anderson's comment on it. See *Windy McPherson's Son*, p. 215, and *A Story Teller's Story*, p. 313.

65. Josephine Martin to Harvey Fisher, 1961, from notes by WBR on Fisher's draft for series on Anderson. *Democrat*, Dec. 12, 1912, p. 8; Dec. 26, 1912, p. 5; Aug. 21, 1913, p. 8; *Telegram*, Mar. 21, 1913, p. 21: Certificate of Dissolution of a Corporation for Profit, No. A228 243, furnished by Secretary of State of Ohio, Apr. 16, 1973. The certificate, dated Sept. 20, 1913, is signed only by Walter Brooks, vice president of the American Merchants Company, and Waldo Purcell, secretary.

66. *Democrat*, Feb. 6, 1913, p. 5; Feb. 13, p. 8; Apr. 17, p. 8; Apr. 24, p. 8. *Telegram*, Feb. 21, 1913, p. 2; Mar. 31, p. 3. Sutton, *TRTW*, p. 199.

CHAPTER 5. NEW MAN IN A NEW WORLD

1. The standard work is Milton W. Brown, *The Story of the Armory Show*, 2nd ed. (New York: Abbeville Press, 1988). Brown explains that the French modern section was sent from New York to Chicago "almost intact," but "the American, English, Irish, and German contingents" were reduced (p. 194). Attendance at the New York show had been slightly under ninety thousand. Floyd Dell, *Homecoming: An Autobiography* (New York: Farrar & Rinehart, 1933), p. 238; Harriet Monroe, "Cubist Art a Protest Against Narrow Conservatism," Chicago *Sunday Tribune*, Apr. 6, 1913, sec. 2, p. 5. This article was one of a series in which Miss Monroe explained and praised the new art to the *Tribune*'s wide audience, though she had her own reservations about Matisse as a "bore" and the Cubists as too "literary."

2. See Brown, *The Story of the Armory Show*, pp. 83, 243–44. Monroe, "Cubist Art," p. 5. (In the illustration an article "A" was inserted before "Glass" in Karl's title.)

3. In "Cubist Art" Miss Monroe singled out Karl and also Childe Hassam, who was represented by one painting at the International and had his own concurrent show of nineteen canvases, for extended praise, but concerning Hassam she warned of "the possibility that his best work is done." She noted as well that Karl's prizewinning painting, "The Idlers," at the 1910 Carnegie International had been purchased by the Art Institute.

4. Floyd Dell, "A New American Novelist," *The Masses* 9 (Nov. 1916): 17. For representative accounts of how Anderson became acquainted with the Dells,

see *Memoirs* (1942), pp. 234–40, and (1969), pp. 333–36; Karl Anderson, "My Brother, Sherwood Anderson," pp. 7, 26, and "Memories of SA," p. 8; Dell, "On Being Sherwood Anderson's Literary Father," *Newberry Library Bulletin* 5 (Dec. 1961): 315–21; Dale Kramer, *Chicago Renaissance: The Literary Life in the Midwest 1900–1930* (New York: Appleton-Century, 1966), pp. 232–36. Interestingly, many, though not all, of the details in the *Memoirs* can be corroborated by other evidence.

5. A standard account is Bernard Duffey, *The Chicago Renaissance in American Letters: A Critical History* (East Lansing: The Michigan State College Press, 1954). See also Kramer, *Chicago Renaissance*.

6. Maurice Browne, *Too Late to Lament: An Autobiography* (London: Victor Gollancz, 1955), p. 368, n. 18.

7. Material on the Dells is largely taken from Dell's *Homecoming*, Kramer's *Chicago Renaissance*, John E. Hart, *Floyd Dell* (New York: Twayne Publishers, 1971), and several articles by G. Thomas Tanselle based on his excellent "'Faun at the Barricades': The Life and Work of Floyd Dell" (PhD diss., Northwestern University, 1959).

8. Details about the art colony are from a variety of sources, including *Homecoming* (pp. 232–33), personal observation, and Daniel M. McMaster, ". . . And Here Was Bohemia," *Chicago Sunday Tribune Magazine of Books,* Mar. 14, 1954, pp. 6, 13. The area continued to be a bohemia until the structures housing it were torn down in the late 1950s as unrepairable. The portrait is now at the Newberry Library in Chicago. It further suggests the interrelationships among the Chicago Renaissance Groups that Nordfeldt had designed and painted scenery and sometimes acted for the Little Theatre.

9. See the 1942 (pp. 235–40) and 1969 (pp. 335–36) editions of the *Memoirs* for two versions of this episode. The versions differ in many details, the 1942 one being the more circumstantial, but they agree on an initial aborted attempt to meet and a second actual meeting.

10. Dell, "On Being Sherwood Anderson's Literary Father," p. 315.

11. Although Margaret Lane had left Elyria with Cornelia and the children on Apr. 21 en route to Little Point Sable, she and Superintendent Comings's daughter were to leave Boston on July 5 for a European trip, not to return "until the last of September" (Elyria *Democrat*, June 19, 1913, p. 5). After June, then, at least Margaret would not have been able to stay with the children while Cornelia might visit her husband.

12. Interview, William Phillips with Daugherty quoted in "Sherwood Anderson's *Winesburg, Ohio,*" pp. 26–27. See also Daugherty, "Anderson, Advertising Man," p. 34. Harry Hansen, *Midwest Portraits: A Book of Memories and Friendships* (New York: Harcourt, Brace and Company, 1923), p. 119. Dell's praise quoted from G. Thomas Tanselle, "The First Notice of Sherwood Anderson," *Notes and Queries* 207 (Aug. 1962): 307–9, p. 308. In the *Memoirs,* Anderson recorded his excitement at this notice, characteristically asserting that the notice, in early September, made him resolve to "meet this man," whom he had known at least since late in the previous spring.

13. Interview, WBR with Ernestine Evans, Dec. 11, 1960. Kramer in *Chicago*

Renaissance, p. 242, gives an account of the reading somewhat differing in details, though here as elsewhere in his book one misses the documentation he may have had but did not cite. For Lovett's recollection, see, for example, his article, "Sherwood Anderson," *New Republic* 89 (Nov. 15, 1936): 103–5. Dell, "A New American Novelist," p, 17.

14. The most detailed description is that of Vincent Starrett in his autobiography, *Born in a Bookshop: Chapters from the Chicago Renaissance* (Norman: University of Oklahoma Press, 1965), pp. 173–75. Starrett, who attended the meeting, was then like Margery Currey a reporter on the Chicago *Daily News*. Margaret Anderson, *My Thirty Years' War*, pp. 38–39, and "Our First Year," *Little Review* 1 (Feb. 1915): 1–6.

15. Phillips, "Sherwood Anderson's *Winesburg, Ohio*," pp. 28–29. Dell, *Homecoming*, p. 237.

16. Phillips, "Sherwood Anderson's *Winesburg, Ohio*," p. 29. Information to Phillips in interview with George Daugherty, Feb. 22, 1949. Hansen, *Midwest Portraits*, p. 166; letter from Mrs. Lorenz W. Carstensen (Marguerite Hochdoerfer) to WBR, Feb. 22, 1965. Mrs. Carstensen reported what she clearly remembered being told by Anderson's good friend from Wittenberg days, Trillena White, who "was very fond of the first wife [Cornelia] and used to tell of her heroism while Sherwood was threatened with T.B."

17. Hansen, *Midwest Portraits*, p. 119. Interview, Sutton with Cornelia, Oct. 10, 1946, reported in *TRTW*, p. 234; A/P Tapes, pp. 52–53.

18. Details of this visit are from Dell, "Anderson's Literary Father," pp. 318–20, and *Love in Greenwich Village* (New York: George H. Doran Co., 1926), pp. 29–30.

19. Sutton, *TRTW*, p. 234. Other details on the winter in the Ozarks are taken from Hansen, *Midwest Portraits*, pp. 166–68; Phillips, "Sherwood Anderson's *Winesburg, Ohio*," pp. 29–30; SA, "From Chicago," *Seven Arts* 2 (May 1917): 41–59, pp. 56–59; interview, WBR with John Anderson, June 19, 1953.

20. Cornelia told Sutton that "the company reneged" (*TRTW*, p. 234); Dell's version is given in Hansen, *Midwest Portraits*, p. 119. Correspondence that might settle the question has long since been discarded by the Henry Holt Company.

21. Waldo Frank, ?Mar. 1917. The following quotations in this paragraph are from Cornelia's letter to Sutton, Oct. 16, 1946, quoted in *TRTW*, p. 236.

22. Interview, WBR with John Anderson, June 19, 1953; A/P Tapes, pp. 52–53. Hansen, *Midwest Portraits*, p. 122. Cornelia's skepticism about his having thrown the manuscript of a novel away is recorded in Sutton, *TRTW*, p. 235. Typescripts of both novels, each with some missing pages, are in the Newberry Library. The former has been edited by Gerald C. Nemanic as "*Talbot Whittingham*: An Edition of the Text Together with a Descriptive and Critical Essay" (PhD diss., University of Arizona, 1969); the latter by William S. Pfeiffer as "An Edition of Sherwood Anderson's *Mary Cochran*" (PhD diss., Kent State University, 1975).

23. The particularity of the Jackson Park setting for parts of the novel is close to

that in the section of the *Memoirs* (1942, pp. 223–25) in which Anderson describes his wandering and writing in the Park in "early summer" of what is clearly 1913.

Writing of the Chicago period just before he met the Dells, Anderson comments in the *Memoirs* (1942, p. 220) that he "was under the spell of the earlier novels of H. G. Wells, and those of Thomas Hardy, Arnold Bennett and George Moore." That he had also read or knew of Wells's nonfictional *A Modern Utopia* is indicated by the narrator's remark in *Mary Cochran* that, "From a kind of class or sex consciousness [among such worker women as Mary] an indefinable unity, a sisterhood, an organization would spring up something akin to the 'Order of the Samurai,' conceived by the novelist Wells" (p. 187). Like Wells, Anderson is unsympathetic toward suffragist leaders, though not toward women's suffrage itself, and defines freedom for women in economic as well as sexual terms. In her marriage, however, Mary retains career independence while Ann Veronica prepares herself for motherhood. As early as his speech to the Teacher's Club of Elyria in Jan. 1911, Anderson had of course argued that a business career did not unfit women "for the home."

The date of composition of *Mary Cochran* is not yet fixed definitively, though the circumstantial evidence points strongly toward the Ozarks winter of 1913–14 as the period when he wrote most of the manuscript, though he may have begun it in the summer of 1913 as is suggested by his comment in a letter of Nov. 16, 1916, to Waldo Frank: "I met Floyd Dell . . . when I was at work on my third novel."

Critics who have dated both the *Talbot Whittingham* and *Mary Cochran* manuscripts as belonging to the Elyria period have relied on such remarks by Anderson in the *Memoirs* as that he had brought with him to Chicago early in 1913 the manuscripts of "four or five long novels" (1942, p. 217), and on Harry Hansen's assignment of these two unpublished novels to Anderson's "first period" of writing (*Midwest Portraits*, p. 117). Anderson, however, was unreliable about the dating of his various writings, and the *Memoirs* statement was made twenty years or more after the fact; the comments to Waldo Frank, coming only some three years later, in 1919, seem more reliable. Furthermore, Hansen is less precise than has been assumed. He accepts what SA told him, that the first period "began in Ohio," but he sets the ending of this period with the publication of *Marching Men;* hence all he really reports is that both *Talbot Whittingham* and *Mary Cochran* were written prior to (September) 1917. That Anderson's secretary in his Elyria firm, who typed his manuscripts, "could remember only *Windy McPherson's Son* and *Marching Men*" (Sutton, *TRTW*, p. 331), on the other hand, argues for a largely or entirely post-Elyria date of composition for the two unpublished novels.

24. "Some Contemporary Opinions of Rahel Varnhagen," *Little Review* 1 (March 1914): 28–29, p. 28. Cornelia's article is paired with Margery Currey's review of *Rahel Varnhagen*, pp. 25–27. Originally Margaret Anderson had asked the two women to collaborate on a single article (see Sutton, *TRTW*, p. 344). That they wrote separate pieces suggests that Cornelia was in Hooker at the time she wrote hers.

25. In "The New Note" Anderson refers to "last year's exhibit" (that is, the Armory Show), which would place the writing of the piece in 1914 but early enough for printing in a March issue. As the title suggests, "More About the 'New Note'" appears to be a sequel to the first article, perhaps, from the way it is printed, an afterthought expressed in a letter to Margaret Anderson. In this second piece Sherwood reminds a person addressed (unnamed but presumably Margaret) of a discussion of Coningsby Dawson's *The Garden without Walls,* a novel published in England and the United States in Sept. 1913. That Anderson was working on *Mary Cochran* at or near the time he was writing these two pieces is suggested by his using the term of the title in the novel itself. In his book Sylvester is trying to show that "one of the sweet new notes in the world was the modern middle aged efficient working woman."

William Phillips rightly questions Anderson's statement (in "On Being Published," *The Colophon,* part 1 [1930], unpaged) that he had received a letter from *Harper's* accepting the story while in the Huron Road Hospital in Cleveland in early Dec. 1912. Aside from the vague context of the statement, it would seem unlikely that *Harper's* would not print the story until a year and a half after such an acceptance date.

26. A/P Tapes, pp. 52–53, quoted from a letter by Karl to James Schevill. Cornelia told Sutton that Sherwood returned to Chicago in March (*TRTW,* pp. 234–35), a date confirmed by the divorce papers of 1916, which give "on or about the last of March, 1914" as the time when husband and wife ceased living together. Daugherty, "Anderson, Advertising Man," pp. 35–36.

27. [Donald M. Wright], "A Mid-Western Ad Man Remembers: Sherwood Anderson, Advertising Man," *Advertising and Selling* 28 (Dec. 17, 1936): 35, 68.

28. Most of the quotations in this paragraph are from Daugherty, "Anderson, Advertising Man," pp. 33–34, except for the long one, which is from Wright, "A Mid-Western Ad Man Remembers: Critchfield—Mother of (Agency) Presidents," *Advertising and Selling* 28 (Jan. 28, 1937): 34–35, 66–67, p. 66. Daugherty likewise told Phillips that "his friends at the agency remember" that "While he was ostensibly at work on advertising copy . . . he secretly scribbled on the lay-out sheets the beginnings of stories" ("Sherwood Anderson's *Winesburg, Ohio,*" p. 31). Letter to the friend, Burton Emmett, July 4, 1926. Anderson's disregard for "surface" facts is beautifully demonstrated by the two references to this episode in the *Memoirs* (1969). In the first (pp. 122–23) the assigned copy is for a laxative, in the second (pp. 432–33) for a commercial fertilizer. The "essence" of all three accounts—and of a fourth in the late, posthumously published *Writer's Book,* where the product is not named—is of course that he wrote "I'm a Fool" when he was supposed to be writing advertising.

29. See, for example, p. 187 of Ellen Key, *Rahel Varnhagen: A Portrait,* translated from the Swedish by Arthur G. Chater (New York: G. P. Putnam's Sons, 1913): "Rahel was a mystic in the sense that it was by intuition, by feeling, not by abstract reasoning that she gained insight into the depths of life, of death, and of the human soul, and when she was faced by the inscrutable or the unknowable, sought light in solitary contemplation or some other means that lay within herself."

30. The account in *Memoirs* (1942), pp. 212–13, is the fuller in detail and states that Anderson and Miss White were both visiting a house "in the suburbs," presumably of Chicago and at some time in 1913. The briefer version in *Memoirs* (1969), pp. 334–35, basically accords with the earlier one except that Miss White "had come to visit at my house," presumably in Elyria, where her only recorded visit was that of late Mar. 1910, though she may have made others. The imitative aspects of the story suggest that at least a first draft may have been written in Elyria. The July 1914 publication date, however, suggests that Anderson actually submitted it to *Harper's*, revised or unrevised, during the winter of 1913–14. In both versions he asserts that he received $75 for it.

31. Birth certificate furnished WBR by Richard D. Hitt, County Clerk, Jackson, Michigan, Oct. 1, 1974. Jay Mitchell had himself been born in Michigan, Mattie in Canada. For information on Tennessee's life up to 1914 I have drawn especially on (1) three printed accounts—Sutton, *TRTW*, pp. 242–55; Kramer, *Chicago Renaissance*, pp. 174–82; and Edgar Lee Masters, *Across Spoon River: An Autobiography* (New York: Farrar & Rinehart, 1936), Chapter 14, pp. 295–315, in which Tennessee appears under the name of "Deirdre"; (2) Tennessee's own "autobiography," a seventy-seven-page unfinished manuscript at the Newberry Library; and (3) interviews with Sue de Lorenzi, Aug. 15 and Sept. 14, 1960, and with Harriet Walker Welling, Feb. 21, 1970.

    Tennessee's birth certificate gives her first name as "Tenne" and lists no middle name or initial. Harriet Walker Welling, who came to know Tennessee well, has stated emphatically that both she and her sister knew Tennessee's middle name to be not Claflin but Content. As a child she may have been called "Tenne C." by her parents rather than simple "Tenne." In her autobiography Tennessee recalls having a "strange feeling" about her name: "In my embarrassment when I started to school, I called myself Tennie and later thinking it more substantial Tennis." In the Chicago *Annual Directory* for 1902 and 1903 and from 1906 to 1917 her name appears as Tennis Mitchell nine times and Tennis C. Mitchell five. With the next issue of the directory to be published that for 1923, her name begins to appear as Tennessee Mitchell. Sherwood always refers to her as Tennessee or "T." in his correspondence.

32. Tennessee gave this account of Amber's death to Mrs. Welling, and Dale Kramer ran across an account similar though differing in details (see *Chicago Renaissance*, p. 177). In her autobiography Tennessee writes merely that Amber fell ill one morning, became convinced that she would die, and did die the next morning while Tennessee was "out of the room for a few minutes." Like Sherwood, Tennessee appears to have varied her recollections for imaginative effect and to have little interest in exact dates. The Chicago *Annual Directory* lists her in 1902 (her first appearance in this annual) and in 1903 as "piano tuner" living at 5325 Washington Avenue (now Blackstone) on the South Side. She is not listed in the next two issues, but from 1906 on she appears as "music teacher" living at a succession of addresses on the Near North Side.

33. Interview, WBR with Mrs. Welling, Feb. 21, 1970. Mrs. Welling, then Harriet Walker, became a friend of Tennessee in 1910, the latter having been first

employed in that year to teach piano to Harriet's younger sister Carolyn, Harriet herself being eighteen at that time. Interview, WBR with Miss Sue de Lorenzi, Aug. 15, 1960. Mrs. Welling recalled that Tennessee had an arrangement with manufacturing friends back in Jackson whereby they sent her "the exquisite handmade French originals of lingerie (chemises petticoats & nightgowns) that had been used as models for their machine-made copies."

34. Mrs. Welling stated that when her mother employed Tennessee in 1910 to teach piano to her younger daughter, she knew that Tennessee had had an affair with Edgar Lee Masters; but since she was a very liberal person, she was less concerned over Tennessee's "lurid past" than was her husband, a judge (interview, WBR, Feb. 21, 1970).

35. Information on the Leathermans from interview with Mrs. Della Kruger, Sept. 5, 1961. Kruger, then Della Garland, lived with her grandmother next door to the Leathermans. Although only sixteen at the time, she came to know Cornelia well. She met Sherwood only once, when he was visiting his wife at the Leathermans' house, and could recall of him only that she thought him very handsome. Cornelia Anderson to Sutton in interview Oct. 10, 1946, quoted in *TRTW*, p. 236.

36. Interview, WBR with Margery Currey, July 1, 1953. Interview, WBR with Marion Lamphier, Sept. 14, 1960. Most of the information about the weekends at Union Pier comes from this interview and the interviews with Della Kruger and Margery Currey. Miss Lamphier, who grew up in Union Pier but then moved away, said she observed Anderson in the "Winchester House." Mrs. Kruger, who also grew up in Union Pier but remained there, could recall no Winchester House and instead gave circumstantial detail placing the Chicago group at Camp's Cottages, which stood on the "Bank of the Lake," that is, just about the beach.

37. Sutton, *TRTW*, p. 236. Her teacher record in the Public Schools of Michigan City, Indiana, where she taught English and Latin in the Isaac C. Elston High School from 1917 until her retirement in 1943, gives 1915-17 as the period of teaching in Union Pier.

38. Daugherty, "Anderson, Advertising Man," p. 36. Details about the Cass Street house are mainly from this account; from Phillips's interview with Daugherty recorded in "Sherwood Anderson's *Winesburg, Ohio*," pp. 35-36; and from SA's letter to Bab, Jan. 14, 1917. In a letter to Sutton, May 31, 1962, Bab wrote that Anderson was living at 735 Cass "as early as the fall of 1914" (*TRTW*, p. 306), while Max Wald, another lodger, told Phillips that when he moved in in Oct. 1914 Anderson was already living there (notes sent by Phillips to WBR, May 22, 1953). In his Jan. 1917 letter to Bab, written at 735 Cass, Anderson states that he began living there "two winters ago." The Chicago *Annual Directory*, normally published in August of each year, contains no Sherwood Anderson in 1914, but in 1915, 1916, and 1917 lists him, oddly, as bkpr (bookkeeper) living at 735 Cass Street.

39. Painting not located. A black and white reproduction of it appears on p. 2 of *Sherwood Anderson Writes of Himself*, an eight-page brochure prepared by the John Lane Company in 1918 to promote Anderson's first three books,

published by Lane. For Jack, see letters of Bronson Gobe to SA in the Newberry Library. Mary and the fat woman are described in Anderson's letter to Bab, Jan. 14, 1917.

40. Cf. *Memoirs* (1942), p. 243; (1969), p. 339, and *Mary Cochran* ms., pp. 71–73. The standard discussion of Anderson and Freudianism is Frederick J. Hoffman's *Freudianism and the Literary Mind* (Baton Rouge: Louisiana State University Press, 1957), pp. 229–50; but see also Phillips, "Sherwood Anderson's *Winesburg, Ohio*," pp. 60–71, and Trigant Burrow, *A Search for Man's Sanity: The Selected Letters of Trigant Burrow* (New York: Oxford University Press, 1958), pp. 39, 442–43, 558–62. Phillips points out that a long review by Alfred Kuttner of A. A. Brill's 1913 English translation of Freud's *Die Traumdeutung* (*The Interpretation of Dreams*) had appeared in Dell's *Friday Literary Review* section of the *Chicago Evening Post*, Aug. 29, 1913, p. 7. Anderson might have read the review and perhaps, though it is less likely, even looked at a copy of Brill's translation.

41. Ray Lewis White, "The Chicago Renaissance Discovers Gertrude Stein," *American Notes & Queries* 20 (March-April 1982): 111–13. *A Story Teller's Story*, pp. 359, 362. SA to Mary Chryst Anderson, Jan. 28?, 1934. SA, "Gertrude Stein," *American Spectator* 2 (April 1934): 3.

42. See pp. 8–18 of Gerald Nemanic's introduction to his edition of *Talbot Whittingham* for a discussion of the problem of dating the composition of the novel. Somewhat more external evidence exists in this case than in that of *Mary Cochran*, but his still slender evidence is flawed by the fact that some parts of it may refer, not to the full-length novel here discussed, but to other portions of the Whittingham material. Nemanic very tentatively suggests that of the five sections of "Books," book 2 and part of book 3 may have been written prior to 1913 and the remaining books between 1913 and 1916. (Book 1 is lost, as apparently are the opening page or pages of book 2.) Quite rightly, however, Nemanic points out that the crucial piece of evidence is Dell's comment quoted by Harry Hansen in *Midwest Portraits*, p. 123: "Sherwood Anderson used to send me as fast as written the chapters of a new novel upon which he was working called 'Talbot Whittingham.'" Although one cannot be certain that these chapters were from the full-length work Nemanic edited, the remark together with various pieces of internal evidence suggest to me a post-1913, probably a 1914–15 dating of the manuscript.

(In a letter to Sutton dated Feb. 5, 1964, Dell wrote that he saw, not successive chapters, but "only a sample of 15 pages on tablet paper" [*TRTW*, p. 334]; but Dell's memory in his later years was often inaccurate, and there is no reason to doubt his assertion to Hansen made much closer in time to the event.)

43. Letter from Sutton to Nemanic reporting Bab's recollection, quoted in *Talbot Whittingham*, p. 12, n. 21. The text of the report is given by Sutton in *TRTW*, pp. 584–88. Quotations in this paragraph are from the report except those in the parentheses, which are from the edited text, pp. 65–66.

44. An indication of how closely Anderson seems to be projecting through Talbot's action his own periods of emotional stress is the curious fact that in a

novel little given to naturalistic detail, the route of the hunted and hunter is traced by street name so exactly that an actual murder would have been committed in full view from Anderson's room at 735 Cass.

45. In her reader's report Bab found the manuscript "crude in many places, vague and blurred in others, faulty in construction at times" and not "Saleable to the majority" because of its unconventional moral values. Only after a third reading did she decide that with "careful remodeling" the manuscript's "great potentialities" as "a masterly depiction of the artist in modern times" could be realized.

46. Daugherty, "Anderson, Advertising Man," p. 37; letter from Bronson Gobe to SA, July 15, 1921. Of Anderson's "passing interest in Nietzsche" Daugherty further states: "The only thing in the Overman's philosophy that we ever heard him quote was the assertion to the effect: This is true—but the opposite is also true, which fitted in admirably with Anderson's well-known theory of the relation of truth and romance." Anderson may have been introduced to Nietzsche's thought by Daugherty himself if, as seems likely, the latter is the "Danaghy" Sherwood describes in a letter of Nov. 25, 1916, to Bab as an advertising copywriter who is "a devout student" of Nietzsche and often inveighs in public against Jesus and his appeal to pity (see Sutton, *TRTW,* pp. 589–91). Another or additional source might be *The Little Review.* The early issues contain many admiring references to Nietzsche, while from its first issue through that of Sept. 1915 the *Review* ran a series of fourteen articles on Nietzsche's ideas contributed by George Burman Foster of the University of Chicago.

47. Talbot's killing of Tom Bustard may be an echo of H. G. Wells's *Tono-Bungay* (1910), which it is likely (see n. 23) Anderson had read in the summer of 1913. Although the circumstances differ widely and George Ponderevo, the narrator of *Tono-Bungay,* feels guilt when he commits the murder, by the time he has come to write his "autobiographical" novel, he can refer to the act with a detachment surprisingly like Talbot's: "It is remarkable how little it troubles my conscience and how much it stirs my imagination, that particular memory of the life I took" (*Tono-Bungay* [New York: Scribner's, 1925], Atlantic Edition, vol. 12, p. 298).

48. See Phillips, "How Sherwood Anderson Wrote *Winesburg, Ohio,*" pp. 7–13, for the definitive discussion of the date of composition.

49. Ibid., pp. 16–17, for Wald's recollection.

50. SA to Floyd Dell, July 27, 1915.

51. SA to Theodore Dreiser, May 10, 1915; to Dell, July 27, 1915. J. J[efferson] Jones to SA, Jan. 17, 1916.

In "How Sherwood Anderson Wrote *Winesburg, Ohio,*" William Phillips astutely argued that *The Golden Circle,* and the other uncompleted fictions here discussed, preceded *Winesburg* and formed the pile of discarded sheets on the blank back sides of which Anderson wrote many of the *Winesburg* tales. Though the argument is generally persuasive, this original writing must be dated cautiously. At least one story, narrated in the first person by an advertising man named Sidney Melville, was certainly written well after the first

Winesburg tales were composed, since on p. 7 Melville says of a party that "now that prohibition has come, everyone got a little drunk." The Eighteenth Amendment did not come into effect until Jan. 19, 1919.

See chapter 2 for the real-life episode involving Emma Anderson.

52. The Scavenger [Ben Hecht], "The Dionysian Dreiser," *Little Review* 2 (Oct. 1915): 10–13, p. 13.

He may have taken the last name of the character from his Elyria friend Perry Williams, who was of Welsh extraction, a point he would emphasize about the protagonist of his remarkable later story, "An Ohio Pagan." The unusual first name, French in origin, he very likely got from Tennessee after her return from her summer at Lake Chateaugay, where she had met the early Freudian psychoanalyst Trigant Burrow and his wife at Camp Owlyout, and had spoken to him "frequently . . . of Sherwood" (Burrow, *A Search for Man's Sanity,* p. 558; Burrow later recalled that his and his wife's "meeting [Tennessee] was one of the outstanding experiences of the summer. We thought her charming, and greatly enjoyed knowing her" [p. 558]). In view of the considerable sexual content of the Trigant Williams and other manuscript efforts of this time, it is quite possible that Tennessee had picked up some further knowledge of Freudian theory from Burrow and was now passing it on to Sherwood. For Anderson's direct relation with Burrow see chapter 6.

53. The canceling of the title "Grotesques" *might* be the key to a more exact dating of the composition of this initial *Winesburg* story, for Anderson may have lined it out to avoid repeating the title of a one-act play by Cloyd Head, *Grotesques: A Decoration in Black and White,* which was first performed the evening of Nov. 16, 1915, at the Chicago Little Theatre and ran successfully for three weeks. It is not known whether Anderson saw the play or not, but he might well have been aware of the production at this time.

In Head's poetic drama the type characters are presented as puppetlike figures, or "grotesques," whose actions are controlled by the "designer" of the play, the character Capulchard. The latter, by introducing the play, has a slight functional resemblance to the old writer who "introduces" *Winesburg,* though Capulchard remains on stage as a kind of puppet-master throughout the drama. At one point in a specifically Nietzschean context he says of the characters under his control, "Grotesques are something that must be surpassed," a comment suggestive of Anderson's definition of the grotesque in *Talbot Whittingham.* In general, however, the play and the tales are quite unlike, and it is at most only conjectural whether *Grotesques* influenced Anderson in any way.

CHAPTER 6. THE DREAM OF FAILURE

1. For one of his accounts of the writing of "Hands" see *Memoirs* (1942, pp. 279–80; 1969, pp. 352–53).
2. SA to Frank, Nov. 14, 1916; to Bab, Oct. 23, 1916.
3. SA to Bab, Nov. 23, 1916. Phillips, "How Sherwood Anderson Wrote *Winesburg, Ohio,*" p. 15: "he had told his friends in the rooming house that he was

writing a trilogy about a woman named Tandy Hard; and Max Wald, the musician, had said that the name reminded him of nothing but hard candy."

In *Memoirs* (1942, p. 165; 1969, p. 257), Anderson refers to Bennett's "marvelous first books." He had read *Clayhanger* (published 1910), probably *Hilda Lessways* (1911), and possibly *These Twain* (1915 in U.S.), which make up the Clayhanger trilogy. Despite obvious differences, Anderson and Bennett had substantial points of comparison: both were provincials attracted to a great city and often wrote of provincial experience, both could reveal beauty beneath a drab or ugly surface reality, both had sharp insight into the minds of adolescents.

My source for information about Wright's venture is Shirley du Fresne McArthur, *Frank Lloyd Wright American System-Built Homes in Milwaukee* (Milwaukee: North Point Historical Society, 1985). Among other pieces of copy Anderson wrote the contents of a six-page folder on "ASBH" (pp. 15–18), from which my quotations are taken, and a "promotional letter directed to prospective dealers" (p. 19), also used as an advertisement, a somewhat condensed version of the folder. I am very grateful to Bruce Brooks Pfeiffer, director of the Frank Lloyd Wright Archives, who kindly sent me in a letter of Dec. 19, 1991, a photocopy of the letter/advertisement that states at the bottom in Wright's hand, "Written by Sherwood Anderson" with Wright's initials. In addition, Anderson prepared copy for a number of advertisements such as those of individual house models in the *Chicago Sunday Tribune* for Mar. 4, 1917, pt. 1, p. 7, and for June 3, 1917, pt. 1, p. 7. A number of these houses were built in Milwaukee and elsewhere until the entry of the United States into World War I brought a shortage of building materials and the end of the venture.

The quotation from SA's diary is from Nov. 14, 1940, p. 330 in Hilbert H. Campbell, ed., *The Sherwood Anderson Diaries, 1936–1941* (Athens: University of Georgia Press, 1987).

4. "'Queer'" is not included in the eleven stories presumably written first. See Phillips, "How Sherwood Anderson Wrote *Winesburg, Ohio,*" p. 11. SA to Mencken, Jan. 6, 1916. In his opening paragraph Anderson refers to "your letter of recent date," which had rejected "the Elmer Crowley story."

5. Dell, who still admired *Windy McPherson's Son,* would so characterize *Winesburg, Ohio* in his "Psychoanalysis and Recent Fiction," *Psyche and Eros* 1 (July 1920): 39–49, p. 44.

6. Dell wrote Sutton, Feb. 5, 1964, that, in Sutton's words, "the typescript he took with him to New York . . . was the reviser's typescript, because it did not seem to be a manuscript in need of revision." It is not likely, however, that Dell would attempt to place a revised version that both he and Anderson considered damagingly inferior to the one Sherwood had submitted to Holt. For the publishing history of *Windy McPherson's Son* see especially Dell, *Homecoming,* pp. 253–54; Hansen, *Midwest Portraits,* pp. 119–21; letters as noted. Jones to SA, Jan. 17, 1916.

7. Letter from the Grant Richards company to SA, Nov. 3, 1915. The letter thanks him for his payment, made in his Oct. 18 letter, for the typewritten

copy of *Windy McPherson's Son* and states that the manuscript, presumably the original from which the copy was made, would be sent to John Lane as Anderson had requested. SA to Dreiser, Jan. 10, 1916. Jones to SA, Jan. 17, 1916.

8. On Feb. 5, 1916, Mencken wrote Dreiser that he had sent the revised manuscript to Jones. Because of eye trouble he had not been able to read it after all, but he had asked Jones to send him galley (or perhaps page) proofs. Photocopy of Memorandum of Agreement, sent to WBR, Jan. 22, 1975, by Mr. John Ryder of the Bodley Head, founded by John Lane. The memorandum is apparently a copy sent to the English company for information, for it is not signed; however, it is authenticated by a handwritten notation on the first page: "Cancelled 1st Nov. 1922/£5 paid by B. W. Huebsch," Anderson's second publisher. The author's royalties were to increase to 12½ percent on copies sold from five thousand to ten thousand, and to 15 percent thereafter. In his letter of Jan. 17, 1916, Jones had informed Anderson of the Lane policy of requiring an author to offer his first three books for both English and American publication, but the memorandum stipulates the "next three," that is, the first four in all.

9. Dell, "On Being Sherwood Anderson's Literary Father," p. 320. Dreiser would subsequently assert on occasion that he himself was primarily responsible for John Lane's publication of Anderson's first two books. His recommendation must certainly have influenced Jefferson Jones's decision to accept *Windy McPherson's Son,* but the record shows Dell's efforts to have been even more essential.

10. In two of her art columns in the *Chicago Sunday Tribune* for 1913 (March 16, sec. 2, p. 8; Apr. 20, sec. 2, p. 9) Harriet Monroe had given the essentials of Blakelock's career, had urged her readers to visit the Moulton and Ricketts gallery's "loan exhibition of pictures by the three American masters," and had asserted that Blakelock's "large mystically beautiful 'Ghost Dance'" was "a superb picture, which art lovers should go miles to see."

For other details on Blakelock's life and work see especially Lloyd Goodrich, "Ralph Albert Blakelock," pp. 9–42 in *Ralph Albert Blakelock: Centenary Exhibition . . .* (New York: Whitney Museum of American Art, [1947]), and Florence N. Levy, ed., *American Art Annual,* vol. 13 (Washington, D.C.: The American Federation of Arts, 1916), pp. 325, 332. For SA's awareness of Blakelock and his work see Ray Lewis White, "Anderson, Blakelock, and 'Blackfoot's Masterpiece,'" *Winesburg Eagle* 15 (Winter 1990): 8–10. Evidence of the sensation caused by the sale of "The Brook by Moonlight" in Feb. 1916 is the fact that the picture, here titled simply "Moonlight," is reproduced as the frontispiece of the Levy volume in the annual series. The painting had been purchased for presentation to the Toledo Museum of Art, a circumstance that may have recalled for Sherwood associations with Cornelia.

A March date for the writing of "Blackfoot's Masterpiece" is suggested, not only by the schedule required for the acceptance of the story and its publication in the June issue of the *Forum* (probably distributed in late May), but by the narrator's statement that the "chattering thing up in the asylum . . . has nothing to do with the man who painted the canvas I saw sold to-day." As newspapers reported on Apr. 12, 1916, Blakelock had so far recovered his sanity that, accompanied by the Middletown asylum superintendent, he was able to come to New York to view and comment in accurate detail on the exhibition of his paintings at the Reinhardt Gallery. (On Sept. 5, 1916, he was released from the institution. He lived and painted under a guardianship except for a few months recommitment to Middletown, and died on Aug. 9, 1919, near Elizabethtown in the Adirondacks.)

11. Letter to WBR from Mrs. Florence Becker Lennon, Nov. 24, 1964.

12. Divorce documents, Cornelia L. Anderson, Plaintiff, vs. Sherwood Anderson, Defendant, in Docket L3025-8 filed in the Circuit Court for the County of Berrien [Michigan], In Chancery. The county seat of Berrien is St. Joseph. The Bill of Complaint avers that it had not been produced by any collusion between plaintiff and defendant, but the nonhostile tone of the proceedings suggests that this statement was included only to comply with the legal situation. Sutton apparently did not or could not question Cornelia Anderson as to the reason for the judge's denial of alimony, for in *TRTW* (p. 237) he merely states: "The tenor of the documents pertinent to the action is amicable (though accusative through legal necessity), and it seems likely that it was understood that no alimony was expected."

13. Most of the information on the summer at Upper Chateaugay Lake is from interviews, WBR with Sue de Lorenzi on Aug. 15 and Sept. 14, 1960. A few details are from Burrow, *A Search for Man's Sanity,* pp. 39–40, 328, 442–43, 558–62; Sutton, *TRTW,* pp. 255–57; and letter to WBR from Mrs. Florence Becker Lennon, Nov. 24, 1964.

   The camp was designed for women from the age of sixteen up, though Sue de Lorenzi, then in her twenties as were many others, recalled one season when the campers ran from a three-year-old to a woman in her early nineties.

14. Alys Bentley, *Child Life in Song and Speech: A Study in Development* (New York: The A. S. Barnes Company, 1910). See also Bentley's curious pamphlet, *The Dance of the Mind* (New York: The Shemin Printing Corporation, 1933).

15. Letter to WBR from Florence Becker Lennon, Nov. 24, 1964. In an interview in 1948, Marco Morrow informed William Phillips (see Sutton, *TRTW,* pp. 250–51) that Anderson had told him some years after his marriage to Tennessee that he had married her to protect her against a threatened newspaper exposure of Masters intended as an indirect attack on Clarence Darrow, Masters's former law partner. Morrow felt Anderson's story to be one of his "yarns," and there is no evidence to suppose otherwise; in fact, the evidence suggests that he was very much in love with Tennessee at this time as she was with him.

16. Details from a verified transcript from the Register of Marriages, Register No. 174, furnished by Archie McDonald, Town Clerk of Chateaugay, Aug. 19, 1960, and from letter to WBR from John F. Ryan, Town Clerk of Chateaugay, Feb. 8, 1975.

17. The Chicago Telephone Directory lists "Mitchell Miss Tennis" at 1244 Stone

in Oct. 1915 (p. 565) and "Anderson Tennis Mitchell" at 12 East Division in Oct. 1916 (p. 22). Since the Chicago *Annual Directory,* which was then published each August, lists "[Mitchell] Tennis" as residing at 1244 Stone Street in its 1916 issue (p. 1298), Tennessee would not have moved to Division Street until late spring of 1916 at the earliest. The 1917 issue of the *Annual Directory* places "[Mitchell] Tennis Miss [sic]" at 12 Division Street (p. 1247) and "[Anderson] Sherwood bkpr" at 735 Cass (p. 116). No *Annual Directory* was published from 1918 through 1922, but the yearly telephone directories list "Anderson Tennis Mitchell"—there is no "Anderson Sherwood" entry—at 12 East Division in the Oct. 1916 through June 1921 issues. In the Nov. 1922 issue, Tennessee and Sherwood are listed with the same phone number and address, 153 East Erie.

18. Publishing details by J. Jefferson Jones of John Lane, New York, as quoted in Hansen, *Midwest Portraits,* p. 121; *Chicago Daily Tribune,* Sept. 2, 1916, p. 7. No more advertisements for *Windy* appeared in the *Tribune* until Sept. 30 (p. 7), at which time it was listed with four other "New Autumn Books" from John Lane, including Mencken's *A Little Book in C Major,* a collection of 225 "original epigrams."

19. In *TRTW,* pp. 24, 363, Sutton shows that Sam's recollection of having once acted with Telfer in "an amateur performance" (*Windy McPherson's Son,* pp. 164–65) parallels the reports in the *Clyde Enterprise* in Feb. 1892 of the performance of the "Military Comedy Drama" *Allatoona,* in which Tichenor, his wife, who was a milliner in fact as in fiction, and the fifteen-year-old Sherwood took part. Telfer is not, of course, a literal portrait of Tichenor, who, among other differences from the fictional person, did practice his largely self-taught art in Clyde. Telfer's character and his "adoptive" relation to Same may have been colored by a recollection on Anderson's part of the loquacious and impractical Dr. Desprez and the quiet truth-telling boy he adopts in Robert Louis Stevenson's tale, "The Treasure of Franchard."

20. Without the evidence that now-lost manuscript versions might supply, it is impossible for the most part, of course, to say how much of these three Books, as well as of Book 1, represents the original Elyria draft and how much the author's additions and possible revisions from 1913 through early 1916, including the revision he certainly made late in 1915. Specific attitudes of Anderson's cannot, therefore, be assigned definitely to Elyria or post-Elyria periods.

21. Sam rises in Chicago at a slightly younger age and earlier period, the first half of the 1890s, than when Sherwood had been an unskilled worker in a cold-storage warehouse just across the Chicago River from the Market. In the 1890s South Water Street and its produce market extended west from its present location all the way along the edge of the Chicago River on the site of what is now Wacker Drive. In 1925 the Market's 265 produce commission houses were relocated south and west of the Loop off Racine Avenue between 14th and 15th Streets, but the well-known name of South Water Street Market was retained.

Anderson was definitely acquainted with some of Howells's fiction and

White's nonfiction. Whether he had read the novels listed is not known, but as a businessman reader he would almost certainly be aware of this type novel. Several reviewers would compare *Windy McPherson's Son* to Dreiser's *The Financier* (published Oct. 1912) and *The Titan* (published May 1914), but the dates of publication indicate that Dreiser's Frank Cowperwood could not have influenced the original conception of Sam McPherson. There is no evidence to disprove Anderson's insistence in letters to two of these reviewers, Waldo Frank (Nov. 6, 1916) and H. L. Mencken (Dec. 1, 1916), that he had already written *Windy* (that is, the original draft) before being introduced to Dreiser's work by Floyd Dell (that is, not before mid-1913). Whether Dreiser's novels may have influenced any subsequent revisions of Anderson's novel can be learned only from manuscript evidence, not now available.

In the *Memoirs* (1942, p. 289; 1969, p. 451) Anderson would also refer to the influence of H. G. Wells and others on his first two books. *Tono-Bungay,* it may be pointed out, describes the rise of an unscrupulous business man and rejects business attitudes, while the protagonist of *The History of Mr. Polly* revolts against his shopkeeper's existence and an unhappy marriage (cf. Book 2 of *Windy*), takes to the open road (cf. Book 3), and settles into a pastoral retreat (cf. Book 4).

22. For a striking example of popular romance language, see the third paragraph on p. 195 in the episode of the honeymoon camping trip on a wild Michigan river. The paragraph begins with a concreteness of perception and language that suggests something of what Hemingway may later have drawn from Anderson's style, but it ends in sentimental clichés. For the dissociative reaction see *Windy McPherson's Son*, pp. 215–19.

23. Connecting *Windy McPherson's Son* and *A Story Teller's Story* is not at all arbitrary. Each in a four-part structure describes a small-town boyhood and a feckless father and silent mother, an attempt to rise in business, a search for new values, and a mode of "return." Furthermore, several McPherson family events and persons described by Jane McPherson to Sam (see pp. 87–89 of *Windy McPherson's Son*) are closely parallel to those assigned in *Story* to the Anderson family.

24. In his discussion of the recently published *Windy* in "People Who Write" (*Chicago Daily News,* Oct. 4, 1916, p. 11) Anderson names Borrow and Fielding in the context of "what a novel should be," claiming expansively that "When I was a boy I continually read" them. Although he no longer read Stevenson as he had in the early 1900s, echoes of R. L. S. would recur in his writing.

Despite many differences there are striking resemblances between Book 3, which Anderson could have been writing or revising in the summer and early fall of 1913, and *The Friendly Road* by Ray Stannard Baker [David Grayson], the twelve episodes of which ran serially in *The American Magazine* from Nov. 1912 through Oct. 1913 and were collected into a highly popular book in Nov. 1913. Among the adventures that come to both Sam and "David" as they tramp the roads incognito are their meeting with and encouragement of a disheartened minister, involvement in a strike, and a sympathetic talk with a woman forced by economic circumstance into prostitution. Baker [Grayson] incidentally refers to two of Anderson's favorite books, *Huckleberry Finn* and George Borrow's *The Bible in Spain.*

25. *Windy McPherson's Son,* p. 128. For example, storms form part of the settings of episodes with Mike McCarthy and Mary Underwood that have a clear sexual content.

26. In *Homecoming* (pp. 253–54), Dell writes that, unknown to Anderson, he cut off half the final page of the *Windy* manuscript before he sent it to England and thus reduced the number of children Sam brings back to Sue from either five or seven to three. If Dell's recollection is accurate, then Anderson seems to have added much or all of Book 4 in his revision of late 1915. Not satisfied with the ending of the novel as published in 1916, he would later revise the last few pages for a reissue of *Windy* in 1922. In this last revision he would cut out Sam's moment of "revelation" and increase his hesitation about returning to a life with Sue.

27. SA to Frank, Nov. 6, 1916.

28. "People Who Write," *Chicago Daily News,* Oct. 4, 1916, p. 11.

29. "A New Novelist," *Chicago Evening Post,* Sept. 8, 1916, p. 11.

30. Gordon Seagrove, "Mr. Anderson's Novel Not Without Fault," *Chicago Daily Tribune,* Sept. 23, 1916, p. 7; Fanny Butcher, "Anderson's First Novel," *Chicago Sunday Tribune,* Sept. 24, 1916, sec. 7, p. 5; Jane Heap, "'Windy McPherson's Son,'" *Little Review* 3 (Nov. 1916): 6–7. Anderson's remark about Jane Heap was in a letter to Gertrude Stein, in spring 1923.

31. William Lyon Phelps, "Three Not of a Kind," *Dial* 61 (Sept. 21, 1916): 196–97; H. W. Boynton, "Some Outstanding Novels of the Year," *Nation* 103 (Nov. 30, 1916): 507–8, p. 508; Anon., "Windy McPherson," *New York Times Book Review,* Oct. 8, 1916, p. 423. Out of some sixteen reviews published from Sept. 1916 through Jan. 1917, seven were very favorable, four were favorable though with reservations, three were unfavorable though with some praise, and only two were completely unfavorable.

   Quotations from Jones are in Hansen, *Midwest Portraits,* p. 121. According to Jones, *Windy* "failed to sell in England" (*Midwest Portraits,* p. 121), not surprisingly considering that England was at war, the novel was about American experience, and its few English reviewers found the story sordid and, except for the Caxton section, unconvincing.

   SA to H. L. Mencken, Dec. 1, 1916. Mencken's review in is *Smart Set* 50 (Oct. 1916): 144. Although Mencken found major defects in the book, he felt that it contained "the gusto of a true artist" and held out "unmistakable promise." Jones reported to Hansen (*Midwest Portraits,* p. 121), however, that privately "'I sent a book to H. L. Mencken and he replied in a manner that proved he had no use for it.'"

32. Floyd Dell, "A New American Novelist," *Masses* 9 (Nov. 1916): 17.

33. *Memoirs of Waldo Frank,* ed. by Alan Trachtenberg (Amherst: University of Massachusetts Press, 1973), p. 84. The *Memoirs* contains the best account of Frank and of the magazine, *The Seven Arts* (pp. 83–95). For Frank's life and work see especially William Bittner, *The Novels of Waldo Frank* (Philadelphia:

University of Pennsylvania Press, 1958); Jerome W. Klocek, "Waldo Frank: The Ground of His Mind and Art" (unpublished PhD diss., Northwestern University, 1958); and Paul J. Carter, *Waldo Frank* (New York: Twayne Publishers, 1967). For *The Seven Arts* see also especially James Oppenheim, "The Story of the *Seven Arts*," *The American Mercury* 20 (June 1930): 156–64; chapter 2 of Van Wyck Brooks, *Days of the Phoenix: The Nineteen-Twenties I Remember* (New York: E. P. Dutton & Co., 1957); and the chapter "Roots and Skyscrapers," pp. 80–98, in Louis Untermeyer, *From Another World* (New York: Harcourt Brace and Co., 1939).

34. SA to Frank, Nov. 6 and 14 and Dec. 14 and 23, 1916; Frank to SA, Nov. 10, 15, 17, and Dec. 1, 1916. It should be noted that *The Masses* and *The Little Review* paid nothing to their contributors except the honor of being published. During its one year of life *The Seven Arts* printed of Anderson's work four of the Winesburg tales ("'Queer,'" "The Untold Lie," "Mother," and "The Thinker"), a group of essays and sketches in the May 1917 number, and a poem, "Mid-American Prayer," in the issue for June 1917.

35. SA to Frank, Jan. 2, 1917; to Bab, Nov. 27, 1916. That the passage is reminiscent of *Talbot Whittingham* does not mean that Anderson was merely inventing rage and horror.

36. In 1962 Marietta Finley, who had become Mrs. E. Vernon Hahn, presented to the Newberry Library some 275 letters written her by Anderson. This fine gift came about through the good offices of William Sutton, who edited them as *Letters to Bab: Sherwood Anderson to Marietta D. Finley 1916–33*. Information on reader's reports from two letters from Mrs. Hahn to Dale Kramer, Sept. 29, 1963, Oct. 22, 1963. In *TRTW*, Sutton dates the reader's reports as 1917 to 1919, but earlier he had written Gerald Nemanic (*"Talbot Whittingham:* An Annotated Edition," p. 12) that Mrs. Hahn "told me she thought she had written [the report on *TW*] about 1916." Since the only probable reference to the reports in the correspondence is a remark about *Mary Cochran* in a letter dated Oct. 25, 1916, it would seem likely that the reports had been written before the correspondence began. The reports for *Mary Cochran* and *Talbot Whittingham* are reprinted in *TRTW*, pp. 581–83 and 584–88.

37. In order the comments in this paragraph are from letters of Dec. 21, 1917; Jan. 12, 19, 26, 1917; and Oct. 24, 1916.

38. SA to Bab, Nov. 23 and Dec. 21, 1916, ca. Jan. 12, 1917. On Nov. 15, 1917, he wrote to Frank: "I have been rather open to the quick impressions that result in short stories this winter because I have not had a big job on. Now I have taken on such a job. Have begun a new book that I shall call 'Immaturity.'"

39. SA to Bab, Nov. 27, Dec. 3, Dec. 1, Nov. 26, and Dec. 21, 1916. The last two quotations are from letter of Nov. 26, 1916.

40. SA to Bab, Dec. 8, 1, 21, and 12, 1916, and ca. Jan. 4, 1917. The Jan. 15 letter is to Mrs. Florence H. Winterburn.

41. SA to Bab, Jan. 12, 14, 16, and 17, 1917.

42. "Hosanna" appears on p. 67. The list of place names reappears, somewhat changed, on p. 16 of *Mid-American Chants* in "Song of Industrial America."

43. SA to Bab, Jan. 22, 1917, Sept. 26, 1916.
44. The originals of SA's letters of Dec. 12, 1916, and Jan. 26, 1917, are in the Lilly Library of Indiana University. Sinclair's second letter was dated Dec. 22, 1916.

CHAPTER 7. THE NEW YORK ATTRACTION

1. The contract between Anderson and the John Lane Company for the publication of *Marching Men* has not been located, but the seven-month interval between mid-February and Sept. 14, publication date for this second novel, makes a Feb. conference and signing date reasonable, given the six-month interval for *Windy McPherson's Son*.
2. Frank to SA, Feb. 26, 1917; Brooks, "Letters to Van Wyck Brooks," *Story* 19 (Sept.-Oct. 1941): 42–62, p. 42; Oppenheim, "The Story of the *Seven Arts*," p. 161.
3. Letter to Bab, Feb. 26, 1917; Brooks, "Letters to Van Wyck Brooks," p. 42; Waldo Frank, "Sherwood Anderson: A Personal Note," *Newberry Library Bulletin,* 2nd Series, No. 2 (Dec. 1948): 39–43, p. 40; Paul Rosenfeld, "The Man of Good Will," *Story* 19 (Sept.-Oct. 1941): 5–10, pp. 5–6. The "female Falstaff" referred to in Rosenfeld's account was "Mama Geiger," keeper of a country tavern in Wisconsin, concerning whom Anderson often told a long earthy story and who may be the "huge red-faced woman" mentioned in *Windy McPherson's Son,* p. 132. Although there is no other evidence that Anderson had met Randolph Bourne earlier in this week, he very likely had done so. If Rosenfeld's memory of such a meeting is accurate, the political talk that interested Anderson would most likely have concerned Bourne's opposition to American entrance into the War in response to a recommendation for entrance by the editors of the *New Republic* now that unrestricted submarine warfare had begun on Feb. 1. Cf. the full-page advertisement signed by Bourne and three others published the week Anderson was in New York: "1917—American Rights—1798," *New Republic* 10 (Feb. 17, 1917): 82. *The Seven Arts* maintained an anti-war stand and would eventually suffer for its outspokenness.
4. Frank, "SA: A Personal Note," p. 41.
5. SA to Bab, Feb. 1917, Feb. 20, 1917; to Frank, Feb. 1917, May 1918. In Feb. 1917 Oppenheim (1882–1932) was six years younger than the forty-year-old Anderson. Although born in St. Paul, Minnesota, he had been brought up in New York, had attended Columbia University for two years, and had taught school for four years before becoming a novelist and then a poet. Brooks (1886–1963) reached his thirty-first birthday on Feb. 16, while Anderson was in New York. He had been born in Plainfield, New Jersey, had traveled in Europe with his family in 1898, had graduated Phi Beta Kappa from Harvard in 1907 after three years residence, had taught at Stanford University, and had lived in England off and on for some three years. Rosenfeld (1890–1946), fourteen years younger than Anderson, had been born into a cultivated, middle-class German-Jewish family in New York, had graduated from Yale in

1912, had traveled in Europe, and for several years had been a freelance writer specializing in the criticism of contemporary music.

6. SA to Frank, Jan. 10, 1917; Frank, "SA: A Personal Note," p. 157.

7. Anderson's poem "Chicago," which is printed as an introduction to this group of essays, is the first of the few songs that can be dated with some precision. Since Frank refers to "the poem" in a letter to Anderson of Feb. 26 as something already in Frank's hands, "Chicago" must have been written around Feb. 18–24. The two songs Anderson sent Frank of Mar. 5, "Assurance" and "The Planting," would be included in his third book, *Mid-American Chants.* In a letter to Frank, undated but probably from late Feb., he lists the titles of seventeen completed poems, not including these two. (The list is numbered up to eighteen, but one title is repeated.) Of these, sixteen titles are included in *Chants,* while the seventeenth, "Brief Barroom Songs," probably appears as "Song of the Drunken Business Man." Since there are forty-nine poems in *Chants,* Anderson had written approximately a third of the book in about two weeks and four-fifths of it in about a month and a half. "Mid-American Prayer," which was not printed as a pamphlet, appeared in the June 1917 issue of *The Seven Arts.* It was the second and last of the "songs" to be published in that magazine.

8. A number of the poems are slight in content, merely attempts to fix evanescent moods or recall memories, but a very large proportion of them are consciously "bardic." In his letter to Bab of Dec. 11, 1916, Anderson had portrayed himself in the role of artist as a "lover" embracing all the women in the world. Quotations are taken from *Mid-American Chants.* There is no evidence indicating that the "bardic" poems were more than slightly revised, if at all, from their original completed manuscript form.

Anderson's ascription of age and weariness to the *Seven Arts* men, his juniors, probably reflects his feeling that they were close, as he was not, to long-standing European cultural traditions. In poetry as in prose he was more interested in projecting emotional states than in presenting facts.

9. In his "The Story of the *Seven Arts*" Oppenheim would look back rather cynically on the "shockingly idealistic" belief he had shared with Frank and Rosenfeld in 1916 that "that lost soul among the nations, America, could be regenerated by art, and that the artist was always a Jean-Christophe with the power to do the job."

For a more detailed discussion of corn as symbol and other aspects of the songs see my essay, "Sherwood Anderson's 'Mid-American Chants,'" pp. 149–70, in Richard M. Ludwig. ed., *Aspects of American Poetry: Essays Presented to Howard Mumford Jones* (Columbus: Ohio State University Press, 1962). Corn, usually as cornfields, is referred to in twenty-six of the forty-nine poems in the *Chants,* and it is the central symbol in twelve of the twenty-six. No other symbolic motif so pervades the poems.

A late date for "Spring Song" is made likely by the fact that some of its phrases and images occur also in a letter to Waldo Frank of late Apr. or early May referring to Anderson's recent trip to Nebraska where he had seen the corn being planted.

10. SA to Brooks, May 23, 1918.
11. SA to Frank, May 7?, 1917.
12. In an undated reply to a letter from Frank dated May 3, 1917, he gives 12 East Division as his new address, but he may have stayed at 735 Cass Street as late as May 19. See Burton Rascoe, *Before I Forget* (Garden City, NY: Doubleday, Doran & Co., 1937), p. 344. SA to Bab, May 12, 1917, May 25, 1917.
13. Rascoe, *Before I Forget,* pp. 344–45, 433. Concerning Tennessee, Rascoe comments only that during the argument she "reclined in the big chair, smoking one cigarette after another, throwing in a gibe at Sherwood now and again but taking up not at all any thread of the argument and weaving it."
14. Quotations from letter to Bab, May 29, 1927.
15. Many details concerning Anderson's second summer at Upper Chateaugay Lake are from interviews by WBR with Sue de Lorenzi, Aug. 15, 1960, and Sept. 14, 1960.
16. SA to Bab, June 1917; to Frank, Sept. 5, 1917, June 1917.
17. Burrow, *A Search for Man's Sanity,* p. 559 (letter from Burrow to William L. Phillips, Mar. 4, 1949).
18. "Seeds" appeared in the July 1918 issue of *The Little Review* in a slightly longer text than that of the story collection *The Triumph of the Egg* (1921) and one more specifically identifying Burrow in the character of "a Doctor from Johns Hopkins," an identification subsequently confirmed by the psychoanalyst himself. Burrow's paper was read at the Fifteenth Annual Meeting of the American Psychoanalytic Association on May 12, 1925, and published in the *Psychoanalytic Review* 13 (April 1926): 173–86. Additional information on the Anderson-Burrow relationship from Burrow, *A Search for Man's Sanity,* pp. 39, 58, 269, 442, 558–61; undated letters from SA to Waldo Frank, ca. July 1917.
19. Letter to Trigant Burrow, Sept. 11, 1921. In a letter to Frank, Aug. 8, 1917, Anderson had written: "Burrow has been a sharp disappointment to me. Put to the test he proved to have no gift of companionship. The man wanted to reform, to remake me, his attitude was like Dell's."
20. Burrow, *A Search for Man's Sanity,* p. 442. In *TRTW* (p. 305) Sutton quotes a letter of Sept. 7, 1962, to himself from Marietta Finley, stating: "I discussed Freud with him, and he knew a lot of the answers. At least he hit the high places in Freud." See also Frederick J. Hoffman, *Freudianism and the Literary Mind,* pp. 229–50. Burrow was a key figure for Anderson's knowledge of Freud. Burrow, *A Search for Man's Sanity,* p. 559. In the letter to William L. Phillips, Mar. 4, 1949, here quoted from, Burrow corrects some statements made in his letter to Frederick J. Hoffman, Oct. 2, 1942 (pp. 442–43), but he does not qualify his admiration for Anderson's independent psychological insight.
21. Undated letters to Frank, July 1917. In a letter to Sutton dated May 31, 1962 (quoted in *TRTW,* p. 429), Marietta Finley commented that Anderson habitually left typed carbon copies of Winesburg stories with her when he visited her in Indianapolis: "These I kept and once, I recall, he was camping out in the Adirondacks at Chateaugay and there was a fire in his tent. He lost some of the Winesburg stories and asked me to send the copies I had."

Undated letters to Harriet Monroe, July–Sept. 1917; postcard to Harriet Monroe, July 9, 1917. Miss Monroe's side of the correspondence may be readily inferred from Anderson's side. The "Mid-American Songs" group was published in *Poetry* 10 (Sept. 1917): 281–91. Anderson substantially revised two of the six poems, "Song of the Drunken Business Man" and "Evening Song," before collecting all six in *Mid-American Chants,* and he also changed a line in "A Visit" which, as will be seen, had brought him some ridicule.

22. SA to Frank July–Aug. 1917, Aug. 27, 1917. Note that Phillips in "How SA Wrote WO" (p. 11), identifies the first two parts of "Godliness" as a separate and distinct unit, and that Anderson had his manuscript of the Winesburg tales, in some form, with him at the Tenthouse this summer.

23. SA to Frank, Aug. 31. 1917, Sept. 3, 1917. Paul J. Carter writes in *Waldo Frank* (p. 31) that "Frank was stricken by an illness that was incorrectly diagnosed as appendicitis and an unnecessary operation nearly killed him. He did not fully recover until Sept., 1918," but managed to continue active in his career.

24. SA to Frank, Sept. 5, 1917.

25. SA to Frank, Sept. 17, 1917, Sept. 1917, Oct. 1917, Nov. 1917.

26. SA to Frank, Sept. 1917. In a letter to Harriet Monroe written on or shortly after Aug. 22, 1917, Anderson thanked her for her letter, published on that date in the *Chicago Daily News,* protesting what he called "newspaper smartness in the News." Monroe's letter defended another poet than Anderson, however, and a search of the *News* has failed to locate the gibe at his poem "The Visit."

Hansen, *Midwest Portraits,* pp. 121–22. John Lane pushed the book in the Chicago newspapers. "Here is Sherwood Anderson's eagerly awaited second novel. A novel of men united, not for war, but for the world's work. It presents a timely new idea of the bringing about of better labor conditions through men marching shoulder to shoulder in time and union. The theme is absorbing and its treatment strong." (Advertisement in the *Chicago Daily News,* Sept. 26, 1917, p. 12.)

J. B. Kerfoot, "The Latest Books," *Life* 70 (Oct. 11, 1917), 601; Rascoe, "A Worth-While Chicago Novel," *Chicago Daily Tribune,* Sept. 22, 1917, p. 9; letter to Rascoe, Sept. 1917. The "old" *Life,* in some ways a forerunner of *The New Yorker,* is not to be confused with *Life* the picture magazine, which began publishing in 1936. In 1918 the John Lane Company would use a quotation from Kerfoot's review in its advertising brochure for Anderson's first three books, *Sherwood Anderson Writes of Himself.*

Anon., "Marching Men," *New York Times Book Review,* Oct. 28, 1917, p. 442; F[rancis] H[ackett], "To American Workingmen," *New Republic* 12 (Sept. 29, 1917): 249–50; H. L. Mencken, "Critics Wild and Tame," *Smart Set* 53 (Dec. 1917): 138–44, pp. 142–43; Ben Hecht, "Rewriting Homer," *Chicago Daily News,* Oct. 3, 1917, p. 13.

27. SA to Bab, Nov. 1917; interview, WBR with Eleanor Copenhaver Anderson, May 3, 1975. The assumption here that *Marching Men* preceded *Windy* in composition must necessarily be tentative, given the present, and perhaps the

future, state of the evidence. That *Windy* was published first has usually suggested it was written first, and there is some evidence appearing to support this suggestion. In his Sept. 1917 review of *Marching Men,* for example, Burton Rascoe reported Anderson as having told him, apparently around mid-1917, that "he had first written it five years ago," a statement that, if precise, would make the novel Anderson's second, the one he began writing furiously in the summer of 1912 just before his breakdown; yet Anderson's memory for dates was rarely precise. A similar problem of memory is involved in his statement to Waldo Frank that "I wrote *Marching Men* in the midst of the big readjustment in my own life," for the term "big readjustment" may well refer to the whole period of his growing interest in writing and not to the final year in Elyria. Again, in his comments quoted in "Literary Notes," signed "S. C. W." in an unidentified Boston newspaper just before the publication of *Windy McPherson's Son,* Anderson refers to this novel as his first, *Marching Men* his second, and *Mary Cochran* his third; yet the comment is such that he may well have been referring to the expected order of publication of these three volumes, rather than to the order of composition of the first two. (This newspaper clipping, which was pointed out to me by William S. Pfeiffer, is filed with the reviews of *Windy McPherson's Son* in the Sherwood Anderson Collection at the Newberry Library.)

On the other hand, one strong piece of external evidence favors placing *Marching Men* first in order of composition. When Anderson read the novel aloud to George Daugherty and Marco Morrow in Chicago in the spring of 1913, he read, Daugherty would recall, "the manuscript of what we understood to be his first novel" ("Anderson, Advertising Man," p. 34). True, Sherwood may have misrepresented the priority of *Marching Men* to his friends, but there is no need to assume that he did; and since Daugherty was accurate in many other details, the presumption must be that he was accurate in this one.

Other kinds of presumption likewise suggest that *Marching Men* was written first. It has already been pointed out (see p. 276) that to the extent that the book can be considered a "labor novel," the theme of worker solidarity appears to relate more closely to the period of Anderson's interest in Commercial Democracy, roughly around 1910, a time when he had expressed concern to Perry Williams with factory workers. (Although the detail hardly fixes the date of composition, it may be noted that David Ormsby, the wealthy manufacturer in *Marching Men,* had begun his rise as president of a "little plough company with its ownership scattered among the merchants and farmers of the vicinity" of a Wisconsin town, an economic arrangement suggestive of Commercial Democracy.) Likewise, quite aside from *Windy*'s being aesthetically superior to *Marching Men* and hence very likely representing an advance over an initial "apprentice" novel, the theme of the former seems of course much more consonant with Anderson's acute unhappiness with his business and personal life during his last year in Elyria.

28. That the "later fair copy" is the case may be implied by the fact that in this basic typescript is already included the episode concerning the barber who

deserted his wife and children in an Ohio town to devote himself to making violins—that is, devoting himself to art—in Chicago, an episode highly suggestive of Anderson's own post-Elyria situation.

29. SA to Rosenfeld, after Oct. 24, 1921.

30. Both McGregor and McPherson go to Chicago a few years before Anderson actually did and fairly quickly achieve success. Each pursues an ideal at approximately the time he was writing about them in Elyria. McGregor's Marching Man Movement, which is partly led by veterans of the Spanish-American War, apparently is conceived of as coming to a head at some time after 1907—see Ray Lewis White's note on the American politician Leslie Shaw, p. 154 of his edition of *Marching Men* (Cleveland, OH: Case Western Reserve Press, 1972)—and before Apr., 1912 (see the reference of p. 284 of the first edition to the sinking of the *Titanic* as being subsequent to the book's action).

31. Just as Anderson much changes the outward circumstances of his own vision of ordered power in describing McGregor's, so he changes, but also ascribes to McGregor, a secondary vision he reports in the *Memoirs* (1942, pp. 284–85; 1969, p. 186). Standing on a platform of the El in Chicago one late afternoon, he saw crowds of workers pouring out of buildings at closing time in a disorderly mass and suddenly perceived in them the potentiality for wordless unified movement that he had perceived in actuality on the training march. In *Marching Men* (pp. 235–37), McGregor likewise stands on a platform of the El but is filled with erotic emotion to see a regiment of uniformed "state troops" marching "with swinging measured tread" past a disorderly mass of striking teamsters.

32. The best statement of the critics' position is in Rex Burbank, *Sherwood Anderson* (New York: Twayne, 1964), chapter 2, "The Populist Temper," pp. 48–60. See also Irving Howe, *Sherwood Anderson* (New York: William Sloane Associates, 1951), pp. 83–88.

33. Quotations in the second sentence are from the Finley report reprinted in Sutton, *TRTW*, p. 369. That McGregor may have been creating beauty out of defeat is a concept Anderson apparently added to his ending only *after* he had given his manuscript to the typist for a fair copy. The last sentence of the text as published does not appear in the manuscript; instead, the manuscript ends with two sentences, themselves a corrected version of a previous single sentence. Ormsby thinks: "What if after all this McGregor and his woman knew both roads. What if they, after looking deliberately along the road toward *beauty and success* [author's italics] went without regret, along the road to failure."

34. Although McGregor's uneasiness about sex as a disruptive force appears in the "original" typescript, subsequent revisions give even more emphasis to this point. Anderson was consciously developing McGregor's rejection of sex as an important aspect of his personality.

Anderson introduced the theme of beauty coming from defeat at the end of his series of revisions of this scene, which occupies chapter 7 of Book 5, pp. 240–45 of the text. Page 240 through the paragraph ending at the top of

p. 244 are mostly in "original" typescript; the portion from the paragraph beginning at the bottom of p. 244 to the end of the chapter on p. 245 is in Anderson's own late typescript; all the paragraphs complete on p. 244 are in pencil handwriting. It is in this handwritten section that Edith asserts the nature of her beauty as opposed to Margaret's.

35. On the end of *The Seven Arts* see John Adam Moreau, *Randolph Bourne: Legend and Reality* (Washington, D.C.: Public Affairs Press, 1966), pp. 144–45, 162–64, in addition to the pieces by Brooks, Frank, Oppenheim, and Untermeyer cited in chapter 6, n. 47. SA to Frank, Oct. 1917, and Brooks Oct. 2, 1917. *Seven Arts* 2 (Oct. 1917) and (May 1917).

36. SA to Frank, Oct. 1917, ca. Nov. 1917; Frank to SA, ca. Nov. 1917.

37. SA to Frank, Nov. 1917.

38. "An Apology for Crudity," *Dial* 63 (Nov. 8, 1917): 437–38.

39. *Chicago Daily News*, Nov. 14, 1917, p. 13; Nov. 28, 1917, p. 13. SA to Frank, Nov. 1917, before Nov. 18, 1917, after? Nov. 18, 1917, late Dec. 1917; to Bab, Nov. 30, 1917.

40. SA to Frank, after Oct. 29, 1917; to Karl Anderson, ?Nov. 1917. Photocopy of Memorandum of Agreement between Sherwood Anderson and John Lane Company of New York, sent to WBR, Jan. 22, 1975, by Mr. John Ryder of the Bodley Head. The unsigned Memorandum is marked "copy" and was apparently sent to the English company for information. By the terms of the contract the royalty on each edition was set at 10 percent of copies sold up to two thousand (compared to five thousand copies for *Windy*) and 12½ percent on copies above two thousand to five thousand (compared to five thousand to ten thousand for *Windy*). A royalty of 15 percent was to be paid on copies of the American edition sold above five thousand; but this provision did not apply to the English edition, and "13," a baker's dozen, were to be "reckoned as 12" in the count of the English copies. As with the novel, six copies were to be furnished to the author free of charge.

41. "New Year Reception at the Cordon Club; Notes of Society," *Chicago Daily Tribune*, Jan. 2, 1918, p. 15. On Christmas Day of 1930 Anderson would write to a young painter friend, Charles Bockler: "I hate Christmas. The last two Christmasses before my mother died, she was ill at Christmas." Both Karl and he, he wrote, envied children in other families who received many gifts, which the brothers interpreted as signs of love not available to them. Tennessee's dislike of Christmas was believed by a friend to spring from some "childhood loneliness." "Chicago Culture," *Chicago Daily News*, Feb. 20, 1918, p. 7.

42. SA to Harriet Monroe, Mar. 21, 1918, Mar. 23, 1918. Anderson sent six poems to Miss Monroe on Mar. 23: "An Incident," "Plowing," "Oblivion," "Morning in Chicago," "Irene," and "Mother." In a letter received by her on Apr. 27, 1918, he added the "Spring Song," which, he wrote, "may help you to make up the group you are after." One of the two sets of sheets in the *Five Poems* folder in the Newberry Library bears notations by "H(arriet) M(onroe)" and "A(lice) C(orbin) H(enderson)" indicating their mixed response to the poems.

Of the seven pieces sent Harriet Monroe, five were subsequently printed as *Five Poems* (San Mateo, CA: The Quercus Press, 1939): "Morning in Chicago," "Oblivion," "In the Fields" (originally titled "Spring Song/For the Fields"), "Irene," and "Man in the Road" (originally titled "Plowing"). Heavy revisions of "In the Fields" and light revisions of the others, except for the untouched "Morning in Chicago," were made in more than one hand before publication, the emphasis in each case being on compression. The *Five Poems* is an unpaged brochure bound in heavy green paper covers and containing five pages of text, one poem to a page.

43. Frank to SA, ca. Feb. 1918; SA to Frank, ca. Mar. 18, Apr. 10, 1918; to Mencken, Mar. 12, 1918, Mar. 23, 1918, Apr. 5, 1918, Mar. 27, 1918.

44. SA to Brooks, early Apr. 1918 (or late Mar. 1918). Anderson's letters to Brooks over a number of years are reproduced in the "Homage to Sherwood Anderson" issue of *Story* 19 (Sept.-Oct. 1941): 42–62. Unfortunately Brooks's side of the correspondence on Twain has not been located. Brooks usually wrote letters in longhand without retaining copies, and despite his admiration for Brooks Anderson either threw away or lost most of the originals. "Letters to Van Wyck Brooks," *Story*, pp. 42–43. SA to Brooks, May 23, 1918.

45. Frank was still in New York when Anderson wrote him there on Apr. 10. Many details concerning the visit are drawn from the correspondence of Anderson with Frank and Brooks before and after Frank came to Chicago.

46. Rascoe began the fracas over Cabell with his "An Approach to James Branch Cabell," *Chicago Daily Tribune*, Saturday, Apr. 6, 1918, p. 12. The following Wednesday Hecht attacked Cabell in the book page of the *News,* and on the next Saturday, the thirteenth, Rascoe replied satirically in "News and Comment" (*Chicago Daily Tribune*, p. 11) that H. L. Mencken has just burlesqued himself under the pseudonym "Ben Hecht" in an attack on Cabell, whom Mencken admired highly.

According to Anderson's story of the affair in the *Memoirs* (1942, pp. 252–53; 1969, pp. 370–72), Hecht and Rascoe had agreed to stage a book page fight over Cabell, but that as the fight continued, Rascoe had begun to take it seriously and personally. In *Before I Forget* (pp. 358–59) Rascoe maintains that he had never met Hecht before the dinner to which Tennessee had invited him "to meet Waldo Frank, an earnest-minded New York intellectual." Both accounts, and that in a letter Rascoe wrote Cabell the day after the dinner, agree that Hecht and he had been invited as a practical joke, the letter implying that the scheme had been perpetrated by both Andersons. See Padraic Colum and Margaret Freeman Cabell, eds., *Between Friends: Letters of James Branch Cabell and Others* (New York: Harcourt, Brace & World, 1962), p. 45.

Sherwood may have felt that another kind of joke was on himself, for Hecht on Apr. 17 and Jones on the twenty-sixth, perhaps only the day before the dinner, had published humorous, mostly unfavorable reviews of *Mid-American Chants*.

47. Mencken's copy, now in the Enoch Pratt Free Library in Baltimore, contains

an inscription by Anderson referring to the book as "my illegitimate child," the same figure he used in a letter to Frank, Apr. 10, 1918. Tennessee's copy is in the possession of Professor James B. Meriwether of the University of South Carolina. SA to Frank, Apr. 10, 1918; Frank to SA, June 3?, 1918.

48. A typical review is that by "W. S. B." (presumably William Stanley Braithwaite), "The Lutanists of Midsummer," *Boston Transcript,* June 5, 1918, p. 6.

49. A(lice) C(ordin) H(enderson), "Mid-America Awake," *Poetry* 12 (June 1918): 155–58. In a letter to Frank ca. Jan. 4, 1919, Anderson explicitly stated this feeling in response to Henderson's second enthusiastic review, "The Soul of Man in Chicago," *New Republic* 17 (Jan. 4, 1919): 288–89, in which she perceptively commented, "For this poet the cornfields are a symbol of all that the machines have destroyed, of all that we must win back if we hope to be saved."

   SA to Bab, May 1918. See Untermeyer's largely adverse review, "A Novelist Turned Prophet," *Dial* 64 (May 23, 1918): 483–85. Ben Hecht, "On Sherwood Anderson," *Chicago Daily News,* Apr. 17, 1918, p. 9. In his review of the *Chants*—"Nascent Poetry," *Chicago Evening Post,* Apr. 26, 1918, p. 10—Llewellyn Jones reported: "I am told that [calling him a mystic] is the surest way to irritate beyond endurance my respected fellow-townsman, Mr. Anderson." On the evidence of the *Chants,* Jones went on to assert, Anderson was not a mystic but "an unterrified romanticist," one who could, furthermore, become a poet if he "took the trouble to learn the art." J. Smith, Letter to "Literary Editor The Daily News," *Chicago Daily News,* May 1, 1918, p. 12. Since a six-column headline about Hecht's review had inaccurately announced: "Sherwood Anderson's 'Mid-Western Chants,'" the title Smith gives implies a dig at the carelessness of the Literary Editor, Henry Blackman Sell, and hence seems further evidence that "J. Smith" was actually Anderson.

50. Hansen in *Midwest Portraits* (p. 122) apparently quotes Jones on the sales of the *Chants.* The John Lane Company advertised the book only once in the *Chicago Daily News.* On May 1, on the same page with the J. Smith letter, it was listed with five other Lane publications under the heading "Vital Spring Books" with the bland comment: "Mid-America has found a new poet who writes with seriousness of purpose and sincerity, verses that convey the rustle of the corn and the sweep of the wind across the prairies."

51. SA to Frank, Apr. 10, 1918, May 1918; to Laura Lou Copenhaver, Sept. 26. 1939; to Bab, [May] 1918. The letters to Frank and Mrs. Copenhaver confirm Sutton's conjecture (*TRTW,* p. 218) that Sherwood and Tennessee went to Harrodsburg. Before his friends, the Bohons, had arranged the automobile trip, Sherwood had planned to live for a week in one of the "many beautiful buildings of stone" in a village near Harrodsburg founded by Shakers.

   One of Anderson's relatively few references to orchestral music was made in connection with Dave Bohon as he recalled the man for Mrs. Copenhaver two decades later. Dave "was very dissipated," but "loved good music. He used to come to me in Chicago, go off on a debauch, drink and women, then come to me. We would go together to the Chicago orchestra to hear Bach."

Charles E. Modlin, "Sherwood Anderson's Kentucky Connections," *Winesburg Eagle* 21 (Winter 1996): 1–7, provides further information on the Bohon family and on the W. A. Steele family. In a letter to WBR, Feb. 7, 1996, Modlin writes of an interview he had with Hanly's daughter: "I know that SA said years after that Dave was the brains of the outfit, but [she] gave me the opposite impression—that Dave wasn't very businesslike and Hanly was the one who really ran the company. I realize a daughter might tend to be partial to her father, but, especially given Dave's funloving reputation, I tended to believe her."

52. SA to Frank, after June 5, 1918, on consultation with doctor.
53. SA to Frank, June 1918, on novel about Lincoln.
54. In *A Girl Like I* (New York: Viking Press, 1966) Anita Loos gives a lively account of John Emerson's early film career. John and Anita were married on June 15, 1919. SA to Frank June 1918; to Anita Loos July 19, 1918. *Memoirs* (1942), p. 304; (1969), p. 407. "The very thought of making the change . . . has rested me," he wrote Anita, gratefully, "and I feel as though I would be able to make a place for myself in some new field with real gusto."
55. SA to Brooks, June 1918.
56. For the June issue of *The Little Review*, "An American Number," the contributions had been "selected by their writers to represent them" ("I," p. 62). "The Man of Ideas" thus represented a choice by its author. A typescript of "Senility" now in the *Poetry* Collection at the Regenstein Library of the University of Chicago is dated "December 15, 1916."
57. "Here's Looking at You," *Chicago Daily News*, July 10, 1918, p. 12. The blunt-spoken Jane Heap was more flattering in her verbal impression of Sherwood in the "Glossary" of contributors, on p. 63 of the June issue of *The Little Review*: "*Anderson, Sherwood*: Like some portrait done with a palette knife. Dark hair falling over dark eyes. Mellowness and strength. Wide yellow trench-scarf; tweeds. A laugh dark and rich like earth just turned up by the plough. He is not Margaret Anderson's brother, we are sorry to say."

CHAPTER 8. ACHIEVEMENT

1. SA to Brooks, Aug. 3, 1918, after Aug. 5, 1918; to Waldo Frank, after Aug. 6, 1918; to Burton Rascoe, Aug. 1918; to Bab, Aug. 1918.
2. SA to Bab, Aug. 1918.
3. Interview, WBR with Anita Loos, Dec. 13, 1975.
4. SA to Frank, after Aug. 6, 1918.
5. SA to Rascoe, Aug. 1918; to Bab, Aug. 1918, Sept. 1918. Loos, *A Girl Like I*, p. 220.
6. Neither "The Dancer" nor "The Romanticist" has survived, at least under these titles.
7. SA to Rascoe, Aug. 1918, Sept. 1918. "Our Rebirth," *Chicago Daily Tribune*, Sept. 14, 1918, p. 10.
8. SA to Bab, Sept. 1918. Details or quotations in this and the following paragraph are from letters to her or to B. W. Huebsch, ca. Sept. 21, 1918.

9. A letter from SA received by Huebsch on Sept. 21 might be read as implying that the two men had not yet met, but since it invites Huebsch to an evening on the town with him and Tennessee, the stronger implication is that they had already become acquainted. SA to Huebsch, Dec. 12, 1918. Huebsch to William L. Phillips, June 22, 1949, quoted in "SA's *Winesburg, Ohio*," p. 159. Interview, WBR with Huebsch, Dec. 6, 1960.

10. Loos recalled that neither she nor John Emerson had ever had "a real press agent" and that John had hired "Swatty" on his own, not company, funds just to give him time to write. She also recalled that Anderson talked at the studio more than he wrote. The only publicity piece of his she could remember was "a kind of little story" that mentioned her and John but said nothing about them or the movies.

In a letter to Waldo Frank written early in Feb. 1919, after he had returned to Chicago, Anderson would comment: "You know after all I was a guy in New York. The moving picture world had an affectionate but patronizing regard for me." SA to Bab and Burton Rascoe, Oct. 1918.

11. Quotations in this paragraph are from a letter to Bab, Dec. 1918.

12. SA to Bab, Dec. 1918; to Huebsch, Dec. 2, 1918; to Frank, Dec. 1918.

13. Henry Blackman Sell, "This and That," *Chicago Daily News*, Dec. 18, 1918, p. 12. SA to Huebsch, Dec. 11. 1918. Copy of contract made available to WBR through the courtesy of Harold Ober Associates and The Viking Press, to which company Huebsch would join his own firm in 1925. The terms on *Marching Men* are not known, but those with Lane for *Mid-American Chants*, which as a book of poetry could not be expected to sell as well as fiction, were on paper very slightly more favorable than these with Huebsch. As with *Windy McPherson's Son* any payments for subsidiary rights to *Winesburg, Ohio*—serialization, drama or film adaptation, and the like—were to be divided equally between publisher and author. Perhaps because of Copeau's offers of assistance, Anderson specifically retained the rights for any translation of the book into French.

14. SA to Bab and Waldo Frank, Jan. 1919.

15. SA to Bab, Jan. 1919; Teacher Record of Cornelia Lane Anderson, Michigan City, Indiana, Public Schools. The record shows that Cornelia prepared herself for high school teaching with postgraduate summer training at the University of Iowa (1917), Michigan State Normal School at Ypsilanti (1918), and the University of Chicago (1919, 1921, 1925, 1926).

16. Howard Mumford Jones and Walter B. Rideout, *Letters of Sherwood Anderson* (Boston: Little, Brown, 1953), p. 43. The date of "? Late December, 1918" tentatively assigned this letter in *Letters of Sherwood Anderson* can now almost certainly be set as Jan. 8, 1919. SA may have been prompted to read the *Education* by Burton Rascoe, who had reviewed it in the *Chicago Daily Tribune* (Nov. 16, 1918, p. 8) under the heading, "An Autobiography to Rank with the Best We Have Had."

17. SA to Frank, ?May 1919.

18. The article is on p. 12 of the *Daily News*. Other firsthand accounts of the Dill Pickle Club are by Frank O. Beck, *Hobohemia* (Rindge, NH: Richard R.

Smith, 1956), pp. 78–83, and by Edna Fine Dexter, pp. 201–8 in Albert Parry, *Garrets and Pretenders: A History of Bohemianism in America* (rev. ed., New York: Dover Publications, 1960).

The fullest, though still sketchy, account of Jack Jones is in Elizabeth Gurley Flynn, *The Rebel Girl: An Autobiography: My First Life (1906–1926)* (New York: International Publishers, 1973), pp. 83–88, 103–6, 112–15, 152, 175, 332–33. Although Elizabeth Flynn left her husband in 1910, he did not obtain a divorce until 1920 just before his second marriage. Anderson writes of the tragic death of this second wife on their honeymoon in the *Memoirs* (1942), pp. 273–76; (1969), pp. 366–69. See chapter 10 of this book. Since Anderson considered Jones responsible for the death of his second wife, his subsequent attitude toward the Pickler was much less friendly; he found him basically vain and brutal, and contemptuously quoted him as once confiding of his ringmaster method, "'I give them the high-brow stuff until the crowd begins to grow thin and then I turn on the sex faucet.'" In *Hobohemia* Frank Beck recalls Jones less critically as a talented man devoted to truth and industrial justice.

19. Harry Hansen's account of Schlogl's in the first chapter of *Midwest Portraits* is the standard one. In *Before I Forget* (pp. 314, 365), Pascoe notes that the weekly meetings of the group occurred either at Schlogl's or at "a big table in the grill room at Marshall Field & Co."

20. Hansen, *Midwest Portraits*, pp. 6–7. Hansen of course is writing of the Anderson he best knew from 1920 to 1922. Rascoe's remarks are from his anonymously published "Sherwood Anderson," *The Bookman* 55 (April 1922): 157–62, reprinted in *Before I Forget*, pp. 427–34. The association of the two men was largely confined to the years in Chicago just before 1920.

21. SA the showman would eventually be the conviction of Pascal Covici who became acquainted with him when he used to drop in afternoons at the Covici-McGee bookshop. Curiously, Covici would remember him dressed, not as Rascoe and others have recalled, but "in a dark hunting shirt with a red scarf around his neck—every inch an artist from the Chicago South Side." Letter to WBR, Nov. 29, 1960; interview, WBR with Covici, Dec. 6, 1960.

22. SA to Brooks Mar. 31, 1919; to Burrow, ?Jan. 1919; to Heap ca. Mar. 1919. Considering this and subsequent letters to Heap, Anderson was being disingenuous toward either Heap or Burrow when he told the latter he was withdrawing the tale because *The Little Review* had "got too dreadfully inartistic and bad."

23. SA to Karl Anderson, Dec. 28, 1918.

24. SA to Frank, May 1919; to Bab, Feb. or Mar. 1919.

25. SA to Trigant Burrow, Feb. or Mar. 1919; to Jane Heap, Feb. or Mar. 1919, June 14, 1919. The letter to Burrow is dated "? October, 1919" in Jones and Rideout, *Letters of Sherwood Anderson*, p. 50, but must on later evidence be assigned to Feb. or Mar. of this year. The first definitely dated reference to *A New Testament* by title is in SA's letter to Brooks, Mar. 31, 1919. SA's undated letter to Heap announcing the change in title presumably antedates the letter to Brooks, while the use of the original title in the letter to Burrow places the latter even earlier.

26. The parts of the series were published as follows: 1 (Oct. 1919), 3–6; 2 (Nov. 1919), 19–21; 3 (Dec. 1919), 17–19; 4, 5 (Jan. 1920), 15–17; 6, 7, 8, 9 (March 1920), 12–16; 10 (April 1920), 58–60; 11, 12 (July-Aug. 1920), 58–61; "The Man in the Brown Coat" (Jan.-Mar. 1921), 18–21.

   Although SA would unsuccessfully submit "The Man in the Brown Coat" to the new magazine *The Freeman* in the summer of 1920, it is fairly certain that this unnumbered testament was originally sent to Jane Heap with the twelve numbered ones; the notice "(to be continued)" is printed after Testament 12 as at the end of each previous installment.

27. Although in one letter to Frank of early May 1919, SA refers to the "rugged, broken poetry of my New Testament," in another letter of May or earlier he describes his "new impulse" as a "new complexity of design in prose." All other references to the *Testament* in the correspondence of this period state or imply that the experiment is one in prose.

28. SA to Frank, ?May 1919. In a letter to Bab, dated by her only as 1919 but certainly written in late winter or spring, SA explains that, though he may or may not be a poet himself, his "new series of prose experiments" might help "to awaken the poetry in others." In addition to this apparent echo of the narrator's comment in "Hands" that "Perhaps our talking of them will arouse the poet who will tell the hidden wonder story," there are several other oblique references to parts of *Winesburg* in the first four testaments; furthermore, the dedication of that book to his mother, "Whose keen observations on the life about her first awoke in me the hunger to see beneath the surface of lives . . ." is in keeping with the dominant theme of this first part of the series. The "new impulse" for the testaments would seem to be as much an "extension" of the mood of the Winesburg stories as of the Chants.

29. SA to Brooks, Mar. 31, 1919.

30. *Memoirs* (1942), p. 294; cf. *Memoirs* (1969), p. 22. "The Reader Critic," *Chicago Daily Tribune*, July 12, 1919, p. 9. Anon, "*Winesburg, Ohio*," *Springfield Republican,* July 20, 1919, Magazine sec., p. 15A. Anon, *Sun,* June 1, 1919, p. 3. *New York Evening Post* attack quoted in John Nicholas Beffel, "Small Towns and Broken Lives," *Call Magazine,* Sept. 21, 1919, p. 10.

31. Broun, "*Winesburg, Ohio*," *New York Tribune,* May 31, 1919, p. 10. W. S. B., "Ohio Small Town Life," *Boston Transcript,* June 11, 1919, p. 6.

32. Boynton, "All Over the Lot," *Bookman* 49 (Aug. 1919): 729–30. Dell, "American Fiction," *Liberator* 2 (Sept. 1919): 46–47, p. 47. J. V. A. Weaver, "Sherwood Anderson," *Chicago Daily News,* June 11, 1919, p. 12. Jones, "The Unroofing of Winesburg," *Chicago Evening Post,* June 20, 1919, p. 9. Rascoe, "*Winesburg, Ohio*," *Chicago Tribune,* June 7, 1919, p. 13.

33. M. A. (Maxwell Anderson?), "A Country Town," *New Republic* 19 (June 25, 1919): 257, 260. Mencken, "Novels, Chiefly Bad," *Smart Set* 59 (Aug. 1919): 138–44, pp. 140, 142. Mencken, *Chicago American,* undated clipping in the Newberry Library.

34. SA to Mencken, July 7, 1919; to Rascoe, after June 7, 1919. Crane, "Sherwood Anderson," *The Pagan* 4 (Sept. 1919): 60–61.

35. SA to Brooks, June 24, 1919, Dec. 15, 1919.

36. SA to Huebsch, June 14, 1919; to Heap, ca. June 13, 1919. Sutton, *TRTW,* p. 450.

CHAPTER 9. IN THE TRAP

1. In view of the use of horse racing he shortly made in one of his best stories, it should be emphasized that SA had a genuine love for and considerable knowledge about both harness and thoroughbred racing. He and Tennessee had watched Willis Sharpe Kilmer's famous Exterminator unexpectedly win the 1918 Kentucky Derby after Kilmer had entered this gelding in place of his prize stallion Sun Briar. Having now seen Sir Barton win the 1919 Derby, SA would certainly have followed that thoroughbred's extraordinary and well-publicized performance over the next few weeks. On May 14, while SA was still in Owensboro, the Kentucky-born Sir Barton won the Preakness at Pimlico, Maryland, and on June 11 he won the Belmont Stakes at Belmont Park, Long Island. Sir Barton thus became the first thoroughbred in history to win all three top races, a feat for which in 1950 he would be posthumously named the first Triple Crown Winner. In addition Sir Barton had won the Withers at Belmont on May 24, no other Triple Crown horse also winning the Withers until Count Fleet did so in 1943. The point at the moment here is that the newspaper reports of Sir Barton's accomplishments would have helped keep SA actively aware of horse racing during this spring and summer of 1919.

   SA to W. A. Steele, Aug. 29, 1938. Letter to SA from Phyllis Hill Steele, Apr. 12, 1939. Modlin, "Kentucky Connection," pp. 3–5.
2. SA to Bab, before May 16, 1919.
3. Though Anderson's two published accounts of Copeau's visit differ in details—see *Memoirs* (1942), pp. 300–303; (1969), pp. 361–64—the fact of the theft is substantiated by SA's letters to Bab, May 1919, and Waldo, May 1919, May 27, 1919. For notices on Copeau's lectures see the *Chicago Tribune,* May 8, 1919, p. 21; May 18, 1919, sec. 7, pp. 5, 11; May 22, 1919, p. 19. In "The Theaters" (*Chicago Tribune,* May 25, 1919, sec. 8, p. 1), Percy Hammond quotes from Copeau's attack on "the decadence and the nullity of the modern theater."
4. SA to Frank, before May 19, 1919.
5. SA to Jane Heap, ca. June 14, 1919. As an instance of Anderson's "very bad English," the *Sun*'s reviewer cited the grammatical error in a sentence: "an intense silence seemed to lay over everything" (*Winesburg, Ohio,* p. 86, 1. 5). The correction of "lay" to "lie" in the second printing would eventually help William L. Phillips to distinguish between the first two printings of the book. See "The First Printing of Sherwood Anderson's *Winesburg, Ohio,*" *Papers of the Bibliographical Society of the University of Virginia* 4 (1951–52): 211–13.

   In "This and That" (*News,* July 30, 1919, p. 6), Harry Blackman Sell presumably reported one of Anderson's versions: "Before he picked the title . . . he scrutinized the map of Ohio for a town called 'Winesburg.' No such town was recorded, so he heaved a sigh of relief and named his book 'Winesburg, Ohio.'" It is barely possible that in shaping the name he was unconsciously affected by the title of Van Wyck Brooks's early book, *The Wine of the Puritans.*

6. SA to Bab, July 1919, Aug. 1919.
7. For the pongee suits see Howe, *Sherwood Anderson*, p. 113. For many details about the Ephraim vacation I am indebted to Mrs. Harriet Walker (Mrs. John Paul) Welling, interview, Feb. 21, 1970.
8. SA may have picked up his love of mushrooming from his friendship with Dr. Millspaugh (1854–1923), Curator of the Department of Botany from 1894 onward to Chicago's Field Museum of Natural History. In 1921 Millspaugh had published a revised and enlarged edition of Charles McIlwaine's *Toadstools, Mushrooms, Fungi, Edible and Poisonous; One Thousand American Fungi; How to Select and Cook the Edible; How to Distinguish and Avoid the Poisonous*. For years one of SA's prize possessions would be a copy of McIlwaine's original edition of 1900, commonly know as *One Thousand American Fungi*.
9. SA to Huebsch, ca. July 26, 1919. Huebsch to SA, Aug. 21, 1919. Replying to Huebsch on Aug. 23, 1919, SA stated that he "had been approached on the matter of writing such a book by another publisher," but references to "the Roxie stories" in subsequent correspondence with Frank suggest that Margaret had a special interest in them.
10. SA to Bab, Aug. 1919, ca. Sept. 8, 1919; *Memoirs* (1969), pp. 360–61.
11. SA to Frank, Aug. 1919, Sept. 1919. Frank to SA, Aug. 29, 1919, ca. Sept. 25, 1919.
12. See, for example, "Dope on the Ponies/Saratoga Results," *Chicago Sunday Tribune*, Aug. 10, 1919, sec. 2, p. 3. I have found no documentary evidence referring to the composition or sale of this story, "I Want to Know Why"; hence the one certainty is that it was written sometime prior to its publication in *The Smart Set* of Nov. 1919. The following paragraphs will show why I have assigned it an August date of composition, but it should be noted that if SA submitted the story to Mencken around the end of that month, the time-lapse before publication in the November issue is closely consistent with the documented time-lapse involved for "The White Streak" and the later story, "Unlighted Lamps." It would seem likely that SA sent "I Want to Know Why" to Mencken because of his praise for *Winesburg, Ohio* in the *Chicago American* (just prior to July 7) and in the August issue of *The Smart Set*. It is probably only a coincidence that in *The Smart Set* for Oct. 1919, Mencken's regular end-of-the-magazine book essay was devoted to Mark Twain. (See "Mark Twain," pp. 138–44.) Mencken praised Twain as "by long odds, the largest figure that ever reared itself out of the flat, damp prairie of American literature," and *Huckleberry Finn* as "the greatest work of the imagination that These States have yet seen."
    The "Mullford Handicap" is SA's invention, perhaps on the basis of the Waterford Handicap run at Saratoga on Aug. 23, 1919.
13. Banker Bohon may be a reference to George Bohon, "who had been employed at the [Harrodsburg] bank prior to his death in 1916," and who was the father of "Davis (Dave) T. Bohon (1878–1922) and his brother, Hanly (1885–1935)" for whose mail-order firm, D. T. Bohon Company, SA wrote advertising. (Modlin, "Kentucky Connections," pp. 2–3.) Modlin notes that two characters in SA's story are "*Dave* Williams and *Hanley* Turner." The latter character

was named "Pete Carroll" in *The Smart Set* printing of the story; when the story was collected in *The Triumph of the Egg*, he was renamed Hanley Turner.

If SA did go to Saratoga in Aug. 1917, he might have seen Sun Briar run. Sun Briar won four of the named races—the Albany Handicap on the ninth, the Saratoga Special on the eleventh, the Grand Union Hotel Stakes on the twenty-fifth, the Hopeful on the twenty-ninth. Exterminator won the Saratoga Cup on the last day of the 1919 Saratoga meetings—and went on to win it successively in 1920, 1921, and 1922.

14. Concerning Dave, SA to Laura Lu Copenhaver, Sept. 26, 1939. SA writes further that Dave's brother, Hanly Bohon, "was as vulgar and dissipated as Dave but more secretive about it."

15. SA to Bab, Sept. 1919; to Frank, Sept. and Nov. 1919; to Burrow, Sept. 15, 1919.

16. For a translation of the complete text of the appeal, see "Romain Rolland's Plea for Post-War Unity," *New York Times Current History* 11 (Oct. 1919): 148–50. In his *Quinze ans de combat (1919–1934)* (Paris: Les Editions Rieder, 1935), p. 3, Rolland lists "Sheervood Anderson (Etats-Unis)" as one of the fourteen American signers of the "Declaration."

Frank to SA, ca. Sept. 25, 1919, Oct. 1919. SA to Frank, ca. Sept. 27, 1919, Oct. 1919; to Burton Rascoe, Sept. 29, 1919, Oct. and Dec. 1919.

17. SA to Frank, just before Oct. 18, 1919.

18. SA to Frank, Oct. 22?, 1919. Waldo Frank, *Our America* (New York: Boni and Liveright, 1919), pp. 141–43, 146–47.

19. SA to Bab, ca. Nov. 1919. SA recognized the psychosomatic nature of some of his minor illnesses. As he wrote Frank, Nov. 5, 1919: "The body pays for what we do to the spirit."

20. For a discussion of the manuscript see William S. Pfeiffer, "*Mary Cochran:* Sherwood Anderson's Ten-Year Novel," *Studies in Bibliography* 31 (1978): 248–57. As will be seen, almost the only time when Anderson could have written "The Door of the Trap" was during Nov. 1919, perhaps around the eighteenth or nineteenth, when he told Frank by letter that "also I write the Mary Cochran stories." By Feb. 16, 1920, at the latest, he had sold this story to *The Dial*, which published it in May 1920. "Unlighted Lamps" would be published in *The Smart Set* for July 1921.

21. SA to Frank, Nov. and Dec. 1919.

22. SA to Frank, mid-Nov. 1919. Writing to Bab in December, he described a somewhat different focus: "I am sure the Testament will come to mean more than anything I have done, to many people. It seems to me to achieve a fine impersonality and to be more ascetic than anything else of mine. In a way that is the object."

23. Frank to SA, ca. Dec. 1, 1919. SA to Frank, ca. Oct. 18, 1919, late Nov. 1919.

24. The other two Testaments were an untitled one, sent before Nov. 27, 1919, printed in *A New Testament* as "Another Poet," pp. 114–15, and "Meditation," perhaps sent on Nov. 30, 1919, printed under the title "One Who Would Not Grow Old," pp. 91–92.

25. Frank to SA, early June 1919. SA to Frank, mid-Nov. 1919, prob. Nov. 30,

1919; *The Autobiography of Emanuel Carnevali,* comp. Kay Boyle (New York: Horizon Press, [1967]), p. 169. SA would describe Carnevali's passionate and violent nature in more detail in "Italian Poet in America," *Decision* 2 (Aug. 1941): 8–15, printed in an earlier form in *Memoirs* (1969), 396–404.

26. By the time SA printed this "perfect poem" in *A New Testament* (p. 50), however, he had dramatized it by titling it "The Minister of God" and by adding sharply physical details: "I was on my knees at prayer in a quiet dark place when lust for women came to me."

27. SA to Huebsch, Nov. 12, 1919. A year and a half later SA told Harry Hansen that *Sons and Lovers* was "one of the truly great books of our contemporary literature." (Hansen, "Gossip Over the Demi-Tasse," *Chicago Daily News,* Apr. 27, 1921, p. 12.) A tactful man, Huebsch probably never told SA of Lawrence's response to Huebsch on Dec. 3, 1919, giving his less enthusiastic reaction to a reading of *Winesburg:* "I have just received *Winesburg*—lay in bed and read it—gruesome it is—everybody dotty, *non compos* all the lot—good, I think, but somehow hard to take in: like a nightmare one can hardly recall distinctly. Thank you for sending it."(*The Collected Letters of D. H. Lawrence,* ed. Harry T. Moore, 2 vols. [London: Heinemann, 1962], vol. 1, pp. 599–600.)

The American edition of Maugham's novel had been published in late July, but SA would very likely have been prompted to read it by Mencken's admiring review in the November *Smart Set,* the issue which also carried "I Want to Know Why." Mencken asserted that most fictional portraits of "geniuses" had been unconvincing, but that "Maugham with his painting genius, his Kensington Gauguin, somehow achieves the impossible. . . . It is a novelistic feat of a high order" ("Novels for Indian Summer," p. 139).

28. W. Somerset Maugham, *The Moon and Sixpence* (New York: George H. Doran Co., 1919), p. 215. For SA's reactions cf. pp. 207–9, 224–25.

29. SA to Brooks, Dec. 15, 1919, late Dec. 1919.

30. SA to Rosenfeld, Dec. 15 or 16, 1915; to Frank, late Dec. 1919. The reorganization of *The Dial* was announced in the Nov. 29, 1919, issue of *The Dial,* the first under the new ownership. See "Casual Comment," p. 486.

"The Year's Achievement in Books: Important Landmarks of 1919 in Fiction, Poetry, History, Biography and Other Branches of Literature," *New York Times Book Review,* Dec. 7, 1919, sec. 8, pp. 724, 726–27, 730–36; p. 724. The other five books were Joseph Hergesheimer's *Java Head,* Harvey O'Higgins's *From the Life,* May Sinclair's *Mary Olivier: A Life,* Theodore Dreiser's *Twelve Men,* and Kathleen Norris's *Sisters.* The critic adds that *Twelve Men* and *Winesburg* "were greeted with perfervid praise by some reviewers, and just as enthusiastically condemned and ridiculed by others."

31. SA to Frank, Dec. 1919.

CHAPTER 10. EXPERIMENTS IN PROSE

1. SA to Sandburg, Jan. 4, 1920; to Frank, ca. Jan. 11, 1920; to Huebsch, ca. Feb. 25, 1920. Telegram to Sandburg, Jan. 3, 1920.

2. SA to Frank, ca. Jan. 11, 1920 (Jones and Rideout, *Letters of Sherwood Anderson,* no. 43, redated on new evidence), Feb. 1920; to Bab, Jan. 1920, "Feb. 1920" (but prob. Jan. 1920 also); to Hart Crane, Feb. 16, 1920.
3. SA to Bab, "Jan. 1920" (but prob. Feb. 1920), which states that he first went to Fairhope, "but could not stand it" and moved to Mobile; to Rosenfeld, Feb. 13, 1920. *Memoirs* (1942), pp. 267–68, and (1969), pp. 354–55, contains the only reference to finding the billfold.
4. SA to Hart Crane, Feb. 16, 1920. SA tells the ultimately tragic story of Ann (Anna) Mitchell in *Memoirs* (1942), pp. 269–76; (1969), pp. 356, 364–69. Certain details of this account can be documented by newspaper reports, but SA's letter to Hart Crane, Feb. 29, 1920, makes it almost certain that he first met Anna, not at Fairhope as stated in the *Memoirs,* but in Mobile.
5. SA to Frank, ca. Oct. 27, 1920; to Crane, Feb. 29, 1920; to Bab, ca. Mar. 1, 1920.
6. *Fairhope on Mobile Bay* (Fairhope, AL: Fairhope Courier, 1915); SA to Bab, ca. Mar. 1, 1920. *Memoirs* (1942), pp. 272–73; (1969), p. 365.
7. SA to Bab, ca. Mar. 1, 1920; to Huebsch, Mar. 7, 1920. *Fairhope on Mobile Bay,* pp. 6, 18–19. *Fairhope Courier,* Mar. 19, 1920, p. 1; Apr. 16, 1920, p. 2. SA to Crane, Jan. 29, 1920.
8. SA to Huebsch, ca. Feb. 25, 1920. Neither *The Freeman* nor *The Dial* offered to serialize *Poor White.*
9. SA to Karl Anderson, Apr. 1920; to Brooks, Mar, 7, 1920; to Huebsch, Mar. 7, 1920.
10. *A Story Teller's Story,* pp. 207–8. Cf. SA's Introduction, dated Nov. 10, 1925, to the Modern Library Edition of *Poor White,* p. vii. SA to Bab, Mar. 1920; to Karl Anderson, Apr. 1920. The manuscript was typed by Florence King, wife of Carl Zigrosser, who was then director of the Weyhe Gallery in New York.
11. Letters to the Blums, July 1920; to Bab, Mar. 1920. For his rejection of training see also his "Adventures in Form and Color," written for a subsequent exhibition of his paintings and published in *The Little Review* 7 (Jan.-March 1921): These watercolors were "done in the faith that an impulse needs but be strong enough to break through the lack of technical training. In fact technical training might well destroy the impulse."
12. The head is reproduced in Heywood Broun, "But It Is Art: The Plea of an Amateur Painter for an Appropriate Appreciation of the Aesthetic Urge," *Vanity Fair* 29 (Jan. 1928): 45, 106, p. 45. The "dark red sea" is mentioned by Rosenfeld in his letter to SA, July 11, 1920. John Hughes Thissen, "Sherwood Anderson and Painting," unpublished PhD diss., Northwestern University, 1974, p. 32. Thissen's is the standard discussion of the subject.
13. SA to Bab, May 1920, Apr. 1920; to Karl Anderson, Apr. 1920. Less expansively he wrote Burton Rascoe on May 15 that: "My painting is I am afraid like my poetry—a thing to puzzle the gods but it is the most fun of anything I have ever gone into. The two or three conventional painters who are here to look at it, shake their heads and then go home and take Epsom salts. That is no doubt the best way to take it."
14. Blanche C. Matthias, "Character Studies, Grotesques and Portraits: Woman Sculptor Holds Magic Key," *The Chicago Evening Post Magazine of the Art*

World, Nov. 24, 1925, pp. 1, 12. A copy of this article was very kindly sent me by its author.

15. *Fairhope on Mobile Bay,* pp. 28–29. *Fairhope Courier,* Apr. 9, 1920, p. 2. SA to Bab, Apr. 1920; to Crane, Apr. 24?, 1920; to Frank, Oct. 27?, 1920, Dec. 17?, 1920.

16. SA to Frank, May 7?, 1920; to the Blums, Dec. 24, 1920.

17. SA to the Blums, July 1?, 1920, Dec. 24, 1920. See also *Memoirs* (1942), pp. 316–21, (1969), pp. 480–85, for SA on the black stevedores.

18. Interview, WBR with Wharton Esherick, June 28, 1953.

19. SA to Bab, May 1920; to Frank, May 7?, 1920.

20. SA to Bab, Feb. 1920; to Brooks, May 15, 1920; to Karl Anderson, Apr. 1920; to Frank, May 7?, 1920. The echoes between the poem and the text of this letter to Frank strongly suggest that the letter may have been one of SA's characteristic "warm-up exercises" and that the writing of the poem followed on this morning in early May.

21. "Our Writers: Sherwood Anderson," Mar. 24, 1920, p. 22. The date of this "last meeting" cannot be determined, though it very likely was during SA's visit to New York in early Jan. 1920. Hind may have been echoing SA's own assessment in praising *Mid-American Chants:* "This is not his most popular book . . . but it may be his most significant, his most self-expressive book."

22. Hackett, "The Recent American Novel," and Mencken, "The Literary Capital of the United States," [London] *Nation* 27 (Apr. 17, 1920), 88, 90 and 90, 92, p. 90 and p. 92. Harry Hansen, in those days eager to praise Chicago's culture, reprinted Mencken's piece in the *Daily News,* May 5, 1920, p. 12, and in his book column for Aug. 4, 1920 (p. 12), noted that Huebsch was reprinting the Supplement as a pamphlet, which was issued under the title *On American Books.* Either Hansen or Huebsch could have sent SA word of the Supplement or a copy of it early in May.

23. Perhaps in April, SA wrote Gallimard "about the matter of bringing out Winesburg Ohio in France" (SA to Gallimard, Aug. 12, 1920), but received no reply for several months. Hansen's statement in his book column in the *News* for May 5, 1920 (p. 12), that *Winesburg* "is being translated into French" seems to have been based on some overconfident word to him from SA.

   SA to Brooks, May 15, 1920; to Bab, May 1920; to Frank, May 21?, 1920. Curiously, perhaps out of some habit of self-deprecation with Burton Rascoe, SA quoted Brooks's judgment to Rascoe in a letter of May 15, 1920, but added, "Just between us I think myself it's a little dull but there is some damned good writing in it."

24. SA to Brooks, May 15, 1920; to Bab, May 1920.

25. Harry Hansen, "These Wintry Evenings," *Chicago Daily News,* June 23, 1920, p. 12. SA's dislike for Christian Science as a "patent medicine religion" is expressed even more emphatically in his letter of May 15 to Rascoe protesting the *Tribune*'s summary firing of him as literary editor because of the complaints received when Rascoe in a review had made a casually slighting reference to Mary Baker Eddy's *Science and Health.*

26. SA to Bab, June 18?, 1920. Frank to SA, July 11, 1920. Rosenfeld to SA, July

14, 1920. Georgia O'Keeffe to WBR, Sept. 6, 1977. "Précisions sur la littérature américaine," *Mercure de France* 136 (Dec. 1, 1919): 535–40, p. 535: "Anderson a publié un roman, *Winesburg, Ohio,* qui est peut-être le meilleur de ceux parus dans n'importe quel pays depuis l'armistice."

27. Rosenfeld addresses SA as "Phallic Tchekoff" in a letter to him of July 4, 1920, and uses the same phrase in his article, "Sherwood Anderson" in *The Dial* 72 (Jan. 1922): 29–42, p. 35. The letter, however, refers to Brooks's account of the walk and conversation in his weekly column in *The Freeman* (see "A Reviewer's Note-Book" 1 [July 7, 1920], 407), in which Brooks circumspectly applies a bowdlerized version of the term ("our Dionysian Chekhov") to "Harwood" (pseudonym for Sherwood). In a letter to Rosenfeld, ca. Oct. 21, SA would write: "Brooks, I believe, once called me 'the phallic Chekhov.' I really do not believe I have a sex-obsession, as has so often been said" (Jones and Rideout, *Letters of Sherwood Anderson,* p. 78). His characterization of Brooks's "make-up" is in this same letter.

28. Frank to SA, July 11, 1920. SA to the Blums, ca. July 1, 1920; to Bab, Aug. 6, 1920. For a full discussion of SA's remarkable adaptation of the Twm O'r Nant material from *Wild Wales* see WBR, "A Borrowing from Borrow," pp. 162–74 in Hilbert H. Campbell and Charles E. Modlin, eds., *Sherwood Anderson: Centennial Studies* (Troy, NY: Whitston Publishing Co., 1976).

29. SA to Frank, July 22, 1920. Letter to WBR from David H. Stevens, Nov. 23, 1964.

30. *New Republic* 23 (July 21, 1920). SA to H. B. Hatfield, July 30, 1920.

31. SA to Brooks, Aug. 8?, 1920; to Frank, Aug. 1920, which makes clearer the causes of SA's anger.

32. Brooks to SA, Aug. 15, 1920. In SA's "Letters to Van Wyck Brooks" in *Story* (19 [Sept.-Oct., 1941]: 42–62, p. 57) Brooks appends to SA's angry question, whether Brooks thought him "not nice," the following note: "No, he was wrong here. I had no such thought." Anderson's claim to have been told that Brooks thought him "absorbed only in sex" appears to have been an invention based on the June 27 conversation in Westport.

33. This account is based on a letter to WBR from David H. Stevens, Nov. 23, 1964, and on newspaper reports. See "Dill Pickler's Chief and Bride Are Shipwrecked," "Bride Drowns; 'Dill Pickle' Chief Saved," and "Jones Tells How Waves Tore Dead Bride from Him," *Chicago Tribune,* Aug. 22, 1920, Pt. 1, p. 7, Sept. 12, 1920, pp. 1, 3, and Sept. 14, 1920, p. 1; "Artist Loses Bride in Storm on Lake," *New York Times,* Sept. 13, 1920, p. 1. Anna's body was subsequently recovered and identified by her husband on Sept. 24. Anderson's account in the *Memoirs* (1942), pp. 273–76, (1969), pp. 366–69, typically gives the essence of the event but is demonstrably inaccurate on details, partly because his memory fused matters from two summers, 1919 and 1920.

34. SA to Miss M. K. Propheter, possibly SA's secretary in his Chicago office, Aug. 11, 1920, concerning a company with which Steele was connected. SA to Bab, Aug. 29?, 1920, Sept. 1920.

35. SA to Frank, Sept. 1920. On Sept. 23, 1920, the *Chicago Tribune* ran its first front-page banner headline on the scandal: "Bare 'Fixed' World Series."

36. Much of the information about SA in Palos Park and village characters in this and following paragraphs is from interviews, WBR with Felix Russman, Aug. 26 and Aug. 29, 1958. SA to Bab, Oct. 14, 1920.
37. SA to Sandburg, mid-Oct. 1920; to Bab, Oct. 14, 1920.
38. Interview, WBR with Russman, Aug. 29, 1958.
39. *A Story Teller's Story,* pp. 359–60. Interview, WBR with Russman, Aug. 29, 1958.
40. Interview, WBR with Russman, Aug. 29, 1958. SA to Bab, Nov. 11?, 1920, Nov. 16, 1920; to Edward J. O'Brien, Oct. 21, 1920; to Rosenfeld, Nov. 11, 1920; to Huebsch, Dec. 10, 1920. James Schevill, *Sherwood Anderson: His Life and Work,* (Denver: University of Denver Press, 1951), p. 84. *Memoirs* (1942), p. 273; (1969), 367.
41. O'Brien to SA, Oct. 1, 1920. SA to O'Brien, Oct. 21, 1920; to Huebsch, Oct. 21, 1920.
42. SA to Bab, Oct. 26, 1920. In a letter to SA, Sept. 30, 1921, O'Brien requested permission to print "Brothers" in *The Best Short Stories of 1921.*
43. Reports on the Wanderer case appeared in many issues of the *Tribune* and the *Daily News* for about a month after the first account on June 22, 1920, and then almost daily from Oct. 4 through 31. The Oct. 18 issue of the *Daily News* had on its front page a six-inch story, "Wanderer Confession Read" and a news item, "Wanderer is becoming an obsession with some Chicago women," who bring lunches to the courtroom in order to watch continuously. Taken to Joliet State Prison, Wanderer was subsequently charged with the murder of the "ragged stranger," and on Mar. 19, 1921, a jury took only twelve minutes to decide that he should be hanged for the second murder.
44. Eleanor Copenhaver [Anderson], "Sherwood Anderson on *Poor White,*" pp. 61–66 in Campbell and Modlin, *Sherwood Anderson: Centennial Studies,* pp. 61–62. See also SA's "Introduction" (Nov. 10, 1925) to The Modern Library edition of *Poor White* (1926).
45. SA to the Blums, Nov. 12, 1920; to Rosenfeld, Nov. 11, 1920; to Bab, Nov. 16, 1920; to Rosalind Ivan, Jan. 2, 1921. Interviews, WBR with Russman, Nov. 26 and Nov. 29, 1958. SA's account of the visit in *Memoirs* (1942, pp. 313–14; 1969, pp. 427–29) is inaccurately dated as occurring after his summer in Europe in 1921.
46. SA to Frank, Nov. 1920; to Bab, after Oct. 14, 1920; to Rosenfeld, before Nov. 29, 1920. Rosenfeld to SA, Oct. 10, 1920, Nov. 29, 1920.
47. SA to Bab, Nov. 11?, 1920, Nov. 16, 1920, Nov. 24, 1920. Modlin, "Sherwood Anderson's Kentucky Connections," pp. 3–5.
48. Anon, "The Epic of Dulness," *Nation,* Nov. 10, 1920, p. 10. SA to Bab, ca. Nov. 11, 1920. Mencken, "Chiefly Americans," *Smart Set* 63 (Dec. 1920): 138–44, pp. 138–39. Jones, "Anderson / His Novel of Invading Industry," *Chicago Evening Post,* Nov. 19, 1920, p. 18. F[rancis] H[ackett], "*Poor White,*" *New Republic* 24 (Nov. 24, 1920): 330.
49. Modlin, ed., "The Owensboro School Bond Editorials," *Winesburg Eagle* 21 (Summer 1996): 6–8.
50. Hansen, "The Book of the Week," *Daily News,* Dec. 1, 1920, p. 12. Butcher,

"Tabloid Book Review," *Sunday Tribune,* Dec. 5, 1920, I, p. 9. Broun, "Books," *New York Tribune,* Dec. 13, 1920, p. 8. Genevieve Forbes, "Reporting, Not Criticizing," *Chicago Daily Tribune,* Nov. 27, 1920, p. 7. Rourke, "A New Middle West," *Literary Review* I (Dec. 4, 1920): 4. Lovett, "Mr Sherwood Anderson's America," *Dial* 70 (Jan. 1921): 77–79. Crane's letter seems not to have survived; his praise of SA and *Poor White* is taken from his letter of Nov. 23, 1920, to Gorham Munson, reprinted in Brom Weber, ed., *The Letters of Hart Crane, 1916–1932* (New York: Hermitage House, 1952), p. 47. SA replied on "Saturday," prob. Nov. 27, 1920, or Dec. 4, 1920. On Feb. 11, 1921, Crane commented to Munson that *Poor White* "certainly has made Anderson one of the most talked of artists there are" (*Letters of Sherwood Anderson,* p. 63).

51. SA to Mencken, Nov. 1920; to Lewis, Dec. 1, 1920, mid-Dec. 1920. Rosenfeld to SA, Dec. 15, 1920, the context of which indicates the nature of SA's suggested article. *Main Street,* almost immediately a best seller, sold more than one hundred thousand copies within its first four months.

52. On Dec. 22, 1920, a Knopf advertisement in the *Chicago Daily News* (p. 12) announced that *Moon-Calf* had gone into its fifth printing. This exchange of letters in Nov. 1920 has been reprinted in G. Thomas Tanselle, "Realist or Dreamer: Letters of Sherwood Anderson and Floyd Dell," *Modern Language Review* 58 (Oct. 1963): 532–37.

53. Rosenfeld to SA; Frank to SA.

54. SA to Bab, Dec. 1, 1920, Nov. 24, 1920, after Dec. 8, 1920 (misdated by Bab as "November 20th"), early Jan. 1931; to Huebsch, Dec. 10, 1920; to John Peale Bishop (at *Vanity Fair*), Dec. 13, 1920; to Rosenfeld, Jan. 14, 1921.

55. SA to Bab, Dec. 21, 1920, Dec. 25, 1920.

56. SA to Bab, Dec. 21, 1920, Dec. 25, 1920.

57. SA to Bab, after Dec. 25, 1920.

58. SA to Bab, Dec. 21, 1920.

CHAPTER 11. TO THE OLD WORLD, AND BACK

1. Rosenfeld to SA, Dec. 15, 1920. Except as indicated, quotations in these first three paragraphs are from SA's early January letters to Bab and his letter to Rosenfeld, Jan. 14, 1921. Hansen, "Gossip Over the Demi-Tasse," *Chicago Daily News,* Apr. 27, 1921, p. 12.

2. SA was presumably thinking of Alice Hindman in the *Winesburg* story, "Adventure."

3. Hansen, "The Way It Strikes Us," *Chicago Daily News,* Jan. 26, 1921, p. 12; Jewett, "A Riddle Is Posed for You to Read in Arts Club Show," *Chicago Sunday Tribune,* Jan. 23, 1921, p. 7. Jewett was sufficiently struck with the exhibit to write and include in her review a poem inspired by Anderson's pictures and entitled "Color Impulses." "The Gossip Shop," *The Bookman* 53 (Mar. 1921): 90–96, p. 93.

4. The telegram was received at Orland, a neighboring town to Palos Park, but since SA had no telephone, the telegram was mailed to him; hence the delay.

A second telegram from Rosenfeld on the twenty-fourth indicates that he had received a wire of acceptance.

5. *Vanity Fair* 15 (Jan. 1921): 55.
6. Actually Jean Catel did not "write up" SA until the issue of *Mercure de France* for Sept. 15, 1924, when he praised him briefly as knowledgeable about psychology and psychoanalysis and as "une des grandes figures du roman contemporain" (vol. 174, p. 828).
7. SA to the Blums, Jan. 7, 1921.
8. SA to Rosenfeld, Mar. 10, 1921; to Bab, before Mar. 10, 1921, ca. Mar. 17, 1921.
9. SA to Crane, Mar. 4, 1921, Apr. 2, 1921.
10. Rosenfeld to SA, Mar. 4, 1921; Thayer to SA, Mar. 14, 1921. SA to Bab, ca. Mar. 17, 1921.
11. Huebsch to SA, Mar. 30, 1921.
12. SA to Rosenfeld, Mar. 10, 1921; to Huebsch, Mar. 17, 1921; to Kreymborg, Apr. 19, 1921. Kreymborg to SA, Mar. 18, 1921, Mar. 30, 1921. SA to Mencken, Apr. 5, 1921, Apr. 11, 1921; to Rosenfeld, Apr. 19, 1921; to Bab, ca. Mar. 10, 1921. Cornelia Anderson to SA, ca. Mar. 30, 1921. Telegram, SA to Cornelia, Apr. 8, 1921.
13. Huebsch to SA, Mar. 20, 1921. Apparently either Grant Richards or SA had not followed up that English publisher's letter of Apr. 28, 1920, expressing a cautious interest in issuing SA's books.
14. This paragraph is based on the accounts in Carlos Baker, *Ernest Hemingway: A Life Story* (New York: Charles Scribner's Sons, 1969), pp. 78–79, and Charles A. Fenton, *The Apprenticeship of Ernest Hemingway: The Early Years* (New York: Farrar Straus & Young, 1954), pp. 98–110. The quotation about SA's "tales" is from a memoir by another tenant of the Smith apartment, William Horne, and was kindly furnished by Carlos Baker in a letter to WBR, Sept. 14, 1978.
15. Rosenfeld to SA, Apr. 16, 1921. SA to Rosenfeld, Apr. 19, 1921. O'Neil to SA, June 29, 1920. SA to O'Neil, Aug. 30, 1920. Peters to SA, Nov. 23, 1920. SA to Bab, ca. Jan. 31, 1921; to the Blums, Apr. 2, 1921.
16. SA to Bab, prob. Apr. 26, 1921, May 1, 1921; to Monroe, Apr. 28, 1921; to Cournos, Apr. 28, 1921. Baker, *Ernest Hemingway*, p. 79.
17. Mencken to Fanny Butcher, May 9, 1921, reprinted in Carl Bode, ed., *The New Mencken Letters* (New York: The Dial Press, 1977), pp. 142–43, p. 143. SA to Bab, May 6, 1921.
18. SA to Bab, Jan. 13, 1921, ca. May 6, 1921, May 12, 1921; to Frank, ca. May 21, 1921.
19. SA to Bab, May 12, 1921. Rosenfeld to SA, Apr. 16, 1921. "The Gossip Shop," *Bookman* 53 (July 1921): 471–80, p. 476.
20. Rosenfeld to SA, Mar. 4, 1921, prob. Apr. 20, 1921. "Adventures," *Little Review* 7 (Jan.-March 1921): 64. Hansen, *Midwest Portraits*, p. 165.
21. Huebsch to SA, May 14, 1921.
22. SA to Bab, ca. June 16, 1921. Interview, WBR with Ernestine Evans, Dec. 11, 1960.

23. SA to Huebsch, ca. June 21, 1921; to Frank, ca. June 20, 1921.
24. Lewis Galantière, "French Reminiscence," *Story* 19 (Sept.-Oct. 1941): 64–67, p. 64.
25. "The Gossip Shop," *Bookman* 54 (Oct. 1921): 183–92, p. 187.
26. Sylvia Beach, *Shakespeare and Company* (New York: Harcourt, Brace and Company, 1959), pp. 30–31. Shakespeare and Company, a bookshop specializing in modern British and American literature, had been established in the rue Dupuytren on Nov. 19, 1919, and later in that summer of 1921 was moved around the corner to its better known location at 8, rue de l'Odeon.
27. Interview, WBR with William Bird, June 23, 1962.
28. Evans interview, Dec. 11, 1960. SA to Huebsch, June 11, 1921; to Felix Russman, July 7, 1921. About Bazalgette, SA, "Death on a Winter Day," pp. 9–16, in *No Swank* (Philadelphia: The Centaur Press, 1934), pp. 9–10.
    Michael Fanning, *France and Sherwood Anderson: Paris Notebook, 1921* (Baton Rouge: Louisiana State University Press, 1976), p. 24. Fanning's transcription of SA's "Paris Notebook," including his misspellings, is printed on pp. 23–70. SA to Bab, ca. June 1, 1921.
29. SA to Bab, ca. June 1, 1921. "Paris Notebook," pp. 27–28. Noel Riley Fitch, *Sylvia Beach and the Lost Generation: A History of Literary Paris in the Twenties and Thirties* (New York: W. W. Norton, 1983), pp. 14, 84, 88. Although Joyce's visit suggests the extent to which Anderson's literary reputation had begun to spread abroad, Joyce was especially courteous; for he had learned only in early April that Huebsch, certain of prosecution on obscenity grounds, had reluctantly decided not to publish *Ulysses*, whereupon Beach had undertaken to publish it herself.
30. Beach to Stein, "June ? 1921," reprinted in Donald Gallup, ed., *The Flowers of Friendship: Letters Written to Gertrude Stein* (New York: Alfred A. Knopf, 1953), pp. 138–39. Beach, *Shakespeare and Company*, p. 31. Stein to SA, Fall 1921. "Paris Notebook," p. 51. The "individual" was Edmund R. Brown, whose Four Seas Press published Stein's *Geography and Plays* in 1922 with an introduction by SA. (Letter, Brown to George Gloss, Apr. 23, 1975.)
31. SA to Bab, ca. June 1, 1921, ca. June 10, 1921; to Felix and Helen Russman, after June 6, 1921. "Paris Notebook," pp. 29–30.
32. Evans interview, Dec. 11, 1960; "Paris Notebook," p. 30. With some inaccuracies SA describes "The Concord of the State," one of Rembrandt's very few allegorical paintings, and "Jacob Blessing the Children of Joseph," in the latter completely screening out the figures of Joseph and the two children and the aged Jacob's act of blessing the younger. The notebook entry was made between May 30 and June 2. In a letter to the Russmans, datable as after June 6, SA writes that he walks to the Louvre "almost every day," and reiterates his surprise at finding "fine and real" paintings by all "the masters."
33. SA to Bab, ca. May 29, 1921.
34. SA to Bab, June 10, 1921. For elements of this paragraph see "Paris Notebook," throughout. Dos Passos to SA, Jan. 7, 1922.
35. "Paris Notebook," pp. 32–33.
36. Galantière, "French Reminiscence," p. 65. This paragraph is based on Galan-

tière's account, pp. 66–67; "Paris Notebook," p. 40; SA to Russman, after June 6, 1921; to Bab, ca. June 10, 1921. Interview, WBR with Galantière, Mar. 15, 1973.

SA composed two Testaments in his notebook: "Paris Notebook," pp. 57–59, 61–62. A reference in the second to "a park in London," however, suggests that it was written after he had left France for England.

37. "Paris Notebook," p. 47. SA to Bab, June 24, 1921. *A Story Teller's Story*, p. 407. See also SA to Rosenfeld, Dec. 1921 (Jones and Rideout, *Letters of Sherwood Anderson*, p. 84).

38. For the information in this paragraph I am indebted to William Holtz, "Sherwood Anderson and Rose Wilder Lane: Source and Method in *Dark Laughter*," *Journal of Modern Literature* 12 (March 1985): 131–52. "Paris Notebook," p. 50.

39. SA to Bab, June 24, 1921; to Huebsch (cable), June 9, 1921, June 11, 1921, June 24, 1921. Huebsch to SA, May 26, 1921, June 10, 1921, June 23, 1921.

40. Gallimard to SA, Oct. 25, 1920; Galantière to SA, Feb. 3, 1921, Mar. 11, 1921. SA to Bab and to Huebsch, June 24, 1921. Galantière, "French Reminiscence," pp. 65–66. Galantière confirmed Madame Gay's "clairvoyance" in his interview, Mar. 15, 1973; she regarded SA, Galantière stated, as "an artist who understood people." "Paris Notebook," pp. 50–51.

41. SA to Mme. Gay, prob. June 29, 1921; to Bab, July 5–6, 1921. Mme. Gay to SA, Jan. 21, 1924.

42. SA to Bab, July 5–6, 1921; to Russman, July 7, 1921. Interviews, WBR with Evans, Dec. 11, 1960, and Galantière, Mar. 15, 1973. "Paris Notebook," p. 36.

43. "Paris Notebook," 51–56. SA to Huebsch, July 5, 1921, ca. July 28, 1921. Dating the composition of the separate pieces in the "writing-book" section of "Paris Notebook," which begins on p. 51, can be conjectural only. The last date given in "Paris Notebook" is "June 13" and is followed by only two Paris impressions of a paragraph each. The next three entries, beginning with the Stein portrait, follow immediately in the manuscript notebook with no distinctive break. Then come twenty-four blank notebook pages before the first of the two Testaments is entered, after which eight blank pages intervene before a prose piece, "A Forbidden Friendship," clearly "post-Cabourg" since it refers to "an American negro girl [Ruth Anna Fisher] met in London." The three entries described here could have been written in Paris after June 13, but about then SA had concentrated on quickly reading the remaining proof for *The Triumph of the Egg*, after which he continued the revision of *Windy* until at least June 24. Thereafter he seems to have had little time for writing while still in Paris.

44. "London's Water Falling in 100-Day Drought," *New York Times*, July 28, 1921, p. 15; SA to Bab, July 14, 1921, and Russman, July 15, 1921.

45. *Voices* 5 (Autumn 1921): 107–9. The pieces differ from the *Triumph of the Egg* versions in such formal matters as line-lengths, but there are only a few minor variations in wording. The untitled initial poem in *Triumph* is here called "The Teller of Tales," while the concluding "The Man with the Trumpet" is here called, oddly, "The Tired Man."

Interview, WBR with Cournos, Dec. 11, 1960. A bill dated July 19, 1921, from Burberry's in London indicates that by this date SA had also purchased a suit and extra pair of trousers for £16, 16s. See "Incoming Correspondence" file, Sherwood Anderson Collection, at the Newberry Library.

46. "Paris Notebook," p. 59. Fisher to SA, May 7, 1922, Apr. 5, 1925. SA to Huebsch, ca. July 20, 1921. Stearns, *The Street I Know* (New York: Lee Furman, 1935), pp. 204–5.

47. SA to Huebsch, ca. July 20, 1921. Huebsch to SA, Aug. 21, 1921. Cape published *Poor White* on Sept. 8, 1921. In an account, "Oxford," in his "What Say!" column of the *Smyth County News* for Oct. 11, 1928, p. 8, SA would state that a "London publisher" had paid his and Rosenfeld's expenses "for several weeks" at Oxford so that he could write an article on the English. Considering that his work was just beginning to be known in England, the *Review*'s payment of a fee seems much more likely than a publisher's (Cape's?) payment of two sets of expenses.

48. SA to Karl Anderson, July 24, 1921; to Bab, July 22, 1921; to Cournos, Aug. 1, 1921. SA, "Oxford."

49. SA to Huebsch, July 23, 1921. "'Hello, Yank,'" *Saturday Review* 132 (Aug. 6, 1921): 172–74.

50. SA, "Oxford." Bechhofer, "Impressions of Recent American Literature," *Times Literary Supplement,* May 26, 1921, p. 340; June 9, 1921, p. 372; June 16, 1921, pp. 387–88; June 23, 1921, pp. 403–4; June 30, 1921, pp. 419–20. Huebsch to SA, Aug. 2, 1921.

51. "Paris Notebook," pp. 59–61, 61–62.

52. "American on Ship Decry Vaccination," *New York Times,* Aug. 20, 1921, p. 2. SA to Burton Rascoe, prob. Aug. 26, 1921.

53. Manuscript evidence tends to support the argument that SA wrote the "Mother Winters" fragment on his homeward voyage. Whereas only three blank notebook pages intervene between "A Forbidden Friendship" and the Testament, forty-four intervene between the latter and "Mother Winters." Furthermore, no blank pages intervene between "Mother Winters" and the remaining three pieces, all likewise unfinished, in the notebook, an arrangement strongly implying that these four "suggestions for stories," as SA would term all his notebook fragments (SA to Frank, Nov. 18, 1921), were written very close together in time. The third of these last four pieces is "Embarkation," obviously written after the vaccination episode of Aug. 10.

The second of the four pieces is actually a summary of two scenes out of eight for a projected "Play: Making a Man," Anderson's earliest surviving attempt at drama. In the last of the four, "Adventures in Color," a reference to his Fairhope experience was apparently to lead as in "A Forbidden Friendship" to a story about relations between white men and black women.

54. SA to the Blums, prob. Aug. 23, 1921; to Rascoe, prob. Aug. 26, 1921.

CHAPTER 12. ARRIVAL AND DEPARTURE

1. SA to Rascoe, Aug. 26?, 1921; to the Blums, Oct. 15, 1921; to Rosenfeld, Aug. 26, 1921.

2. SA to Huebsch, Sept. 25, 1921; to Bab, Sept. 30, 1921. Frank to SA, Sept. 8, 1921. SA to Frank, ca. Sept. 20, 1921, ca. Oct. 26, 1921, Nov. 18, 1921.

3. SA to Burrow, Sept. 11, 1921, Oct. 12, 1921, Oct. 14, 1921. Burrow to SA, Oct. 9, 1921. In his Oct. 14 letter, SA mentions that his paintings had until recently "been showing at Washington," but there is no other evidence of such an exhibit after that at the Sunwise Turn in New York.

4. "We Nominate for the Hall of Fame," *Vanity Fair* 16 (July 1921): 48. "New York Notes," p. 12. O'Brien to SA, Sept. 30, 1921, from Oxford.

5. From "Announcement," *Dial* 70 (June 1921): 730–32, p. 730. SA's acceptance letter is dated Oct. 19, 1921. Seldes had presumably telegraphed the original notification on or just before that date. Rosenfeld to SA, Oct. 24, 1921.

6. SA to Rosenfeld, after Oct. 24, 1921.

7. SA to Huebsch, Oct. 14, 1921, Oct. 25, 1921; Huebsch to SA, Oct. 25, 1921, Nov. 9, 1921.

8. SA to Hart Crane, Oct. 31, 1921; to Karl Anderson, ca. Oct. 23, 1921; to Herbert Feis, Oct. 25, 1921; to the Blums, Nov. 1, 1921; to Bab, Nov. 6, 1921, Nov. 13?, 1921. Steele to SA, Oct. 25, 1921.

9. SA to Bab, ca. Nov. 14, 1921; to Frank, Nov. 18, 1921.

10. SA to Huebsch, Nov. 18, 1921, Nov. 21, 1921, Nov. 25, 1921, Nov. 28, 1921. Huebsch to SA, Nov. 23, 1921.

11. SA to Huebsch, Nov. 25, 1921. Reviews: "Accusation," *Nation* 113 (Nov. 23, 1921): 602; "Elemental Things," *New Republic* 28 (Nov. 23, 1921): 383–84; "The Distrust of Ideas," *Vanity Fair* 17 (Dec. 1921): 10–12, 118.

12. SA to Bishop, Nov. 21, 1921. The long quotation and those in the following paragraph come from several undated letters to Bab written in late November to mid-December.

13. Hansen, "Sherwood Anderson—and Others," *Chicago Daily News*, Nov. 30, 1921, p. 12; Hildegarde Hawthorne, "A Prize Winner's Ironical View of Life," *New York Times Book Review*, Dec. 4, 1921, pp. 10, 23, 29; *Nation* 113 (Dec. 7, 1921): 637.

14. Letters of introduction, dated Dec. 3, 1921. Baker, *Ernest Hemingway*, pp. 82–83; *Memoirs* (1942, p. 473).

15. SA to John Erskine and Franklin H. Giddings, Dec. 3, 1921; to Huebsch, ca. Dec. 3, 1921; to Bab, ca. Dec. 13, 1921.

16. SA to Huebsch, Nov. 25, 1921, Dec. 6, 1921; to Rosenfeld, ca. Dec. 13, 1921.

17. SA to Huebsch, Nov. 30, 1921.

18. SA to the Blums, ca. Dec. 13, 1921; to Frank, Nov. 18, 1921; to Bab, after Dec. 22, 1921. Dell was quoted in "The Gossip Shop," *Bookman* 55 (March 1922): 87–96, p. 91.

19. Gilman, *North American Review* 215 (March 1922): 412–16. SA to Karl Anderson, Feb. 1, 1922; to Bab, after Dec. 22, 1921; to Marguerite Gay, Jan. 19, 1922.

20. SA to Joseph Hergesheimer, Jan. 10, 1922; to Bab, ca. Jan. 12, 1922; to Rosenfeld, Jan. 12, 1922.

21. SA to Jerome Blum, Jan. 13, 1922, Feb. 2, 1922; to Hart Crane, Jan. 15?, 1922; to Marguerite Gay, Jan. 19, 1922.

22. Julius Friend, "The Double Dealer: Career of a 'Little' Magazine" in Leland H. Cox, Jr., "Julius Weis Friend's History of the *Double Dealer*," *Mississippi Quarterly* 31 (Fall 1978): 587–605, p. 598. Comments of Friend are from p. 1 of an unpublished "Article on Sherwood Anderson," which he sent to Irving Howe, Nov. 19, 1949, a copy of which Friend generously lent me in an interview, Dec. 9, 1959. Interview, WBR with Albert Goldstein, Dec. 8, 1959.

23. SA to Mencken, Jan. 25, 1922.

24. SA to Blum, Feb. 2, 1922; to Marguerite Gay, Jan. 19, 1922; to Karl Anderson, Feb. 1, 1922. Interview, WBR with James K. Feibleman, Dec. 10, 1959. "Orleans Is Warm While Cold Grips Most of Nation"; "Champion Oyster Husker of World is Mike Algero"; "Easy Victory for Joe Gans over Battiste," *Times-Picayune*, Jan. 29, 1922, sec. 1, 1; sec. 1, 1, 14; sec. 6, 11.

25. SA to Hart Crane, Jan. 15?, 1922; to Marguerite Gay, Jan. 19, 1922; to Rosenfeld, Jan. 18?, 1922; to Huebsch, Feb. 3, 1922.

26. SA to Bab, ca. Feb. 15, 1922; to Huebsch, ca. Feb. 15, 1922.

27. SA to Mencken, ca. Feb. 1, 1922; to Seldes, Apr. 24, 1922.

28. SA to Huebsch, Feb. 3, 1922, ca. Feb. 15, 1922; Huebsch to SA, Feb. 11, 1922.

29. Significant echoes of other Testaments occur in *Many Marriages*. For example, late in the previous November SA had written for Bab "a song" about the "lords of life," those vital, unconventional persons such as Webster wants himself and his daughter to be (see *Many Marriages*, pp. 194–97 and throughout). This song became the second part of "Testament of The Two Glad Men," the first part beginning with a close paraphrase of a sentence from Anderson's letter to Bab. The Testament was published in *The Double Dealer* for Apr. 1922.

30. Ralph Freedman, *The Lyrical Novel: Studies in Hermann Hesse, André Gide, and Virginia Woolf* (Princeton, NJ: Princeton University Press, 1963), pp. 1–2, 9.

31. Chase to SA, Jan. 11, 1922; SA to Chase, dated Feb. 16, 1922, but envelope postmarked Feb. 14, 1922.

32. SA to Lucile Blum, ca. Mar. 13, 1922.

33. Friend, "Article on SA," p. 4.

34. Interview, WBR with Mrs. Adaline Katz Samuel, Dec. 12–13, 1959. In his "Article on SA" Friend comments, p. 2: "If he had any affairs with women nobody ever heard about them. He did not evince the usual interest in pretty girls or make remarks about them as most men do as for instance while walking down the street. I have always thought that sex for Sherwood was mainly another symbol, the prime symbol of incorruptible life."

35. Interviews with Mrs. Samuel. Disastrously for her (and Anderson's biographers and readers) all this material was lost when Dr. and Mrs. Samuel's house in Bay St. Louis, Mississippi, was literally blown away by a hurricane in the summer of 1948.

36. Friend, "Article on SA," p. 1. SA to Karl Anderson, Feb. 1, 1922; to Huebsch, Feb. 6, 1922. Huebsch to SA, Feb. 11, 1922, Feb. 23, 1922. Gilman, "An American Masterwork," *North American Review* 215 (Mar. 1922): 412–16,

p. 416. C. E. Bechhofer, "Recent American Literature: 2," *Times Literary Supplement,* Jan. 19, 1922, p. 44.

37. *Survey* 47 (March 25, 1922): 997–1000.
38. "The Work of Gertrude Stein," *Little Review* 8 (Spring 1922): 29–32.
39. SA's article was published in the March issue of *The Double Dealer.*
40. SA to Bab, Mar. 1, 1922.
41. SA to Lucile Blum, ca. Mar. 13, 1922; to Huebsch, Mar. 13, 1922; to Seldes, Mar. 13, 1922; to Finley, Mar. 1922.
42. This paragraph is based on Hi (H. I.) Simons's "Notes on Sherwood Anderson—3-22-22," copy sent to Dale Kramer from original in possession of Bernardine Szold Fritz, Simons's former wife. See Kramer, *Chicago Renaissance,* p. 327.
43. Crane to SA, May 6, 1922. SA to Crane, May 9, 1922. Huebsch to SA, May 16, 1922, May 22, 1922. "Paris News Letter," *New York Tribune,* May 7, 1922, sec. 7, p. 6. SA to Huebsch, May 13?, 1922.
44. *Digest* 73 (April 1, 1922): 33; the quotations from West, "Notes on Novels," *New Statesman* 18 (Feb. 18, 1922): 564, 566.
45. SA to Lillian Marcus, Apr. 14, 1922. Rascoe, "A Bookman's Day Book," *New York Tribune,* Apr. 16, 1922, sec. 5, p. 7.
46. SA to Karl Anderson, ca. Apr. 15, 1922.
47. SA to Huebsch, May 15?, 1922, May 19, 1922.
48. Interview with Bernardine Szold (Simons) Fritz, June 22, 1976, by Lawrence J. Levin, who generously furnished me a tape transcription, Aug. 8, 1977.
49. SA to Ferdinand Schevill, Dec. 9?, 1923 (Jones and Rideout, *Letters of Sherwood Anderson,* p. 115). Tennessee Mitchell Anderson to Bernardine Szold Fritz, early 1926. Tennessee as dominating and jealous—"because he was a famous writer, she felt she should be a famous artist of some sort too"—was the analysis of Anderson's third wife, Elizabeth Prall Anderson, who drew on what Anderson and such mutual friends as Paul Rosenfeld told her but also on Tennessee's subsequent behavior during divorce proceedings. (Interview, WBR with Elizabeth Prall Anderson, Dec. 16, 1959.) SA to Bab, May 9?, 1922.
50. SA to Rosenfeld, July 8, 1922.
51. SA to Bab, June 14, 1922, July 6, 1922.
52. SA to Bab, June 14, 1922; to Rosenfeld, July 8, 1922. Rosenfeld to SA, June 24, 1922; Bernardine Szold Fritz to Dale Kramer, Oct. 6, 1963. Interviews, Lawrence J. Levin with Bernardine Szold Fritz, June 22, 1976; Dale Kramer with Helen Head Hunter and Y. K. Smith, 1963–64.

CHAPTER 13. A NEW LIFE

1. Hansen, "Eloquent Ancients," *Chicago Daily News,* July 5, 1922, p. 12. SA to Finley, July 6, 1922.
2. SA to Hart Crane, July 22, 1922; Huebsch to SA, July 7, 1922. The statement lists 383 copies sold of *Poor White* and 380 of *Winesburg, Ohio.* Less charges against his account, the royalties due him were $1,508.27. SA to Rosenfeld, July 11, 1922, Mar. 8, 1922; to Finley, July 7, 1922.

3. SA to Crane, July 8, 1922, July 20, 1922; to Rosenfeld, July 11, 1922. See "Alfred Stieglitz," *New Republic* 32 (Oct. 25, 1922): 215–17.
4. Munson to John Unterecker, quoted in Unterecker's *Voyager: A Life of Hart Crane* (New York: Farrar, Straus & Giroux, 1969), p. 250. My account is partly based on Unterecker's, which, however, disregards Crane's and Munson's share of blame in the episode.
5. SA to Rosenfeld, Aug. 7, 1922; to Crane, July 20, 1922, Aug. 17 or 24, 1922. Crane to Munson, Aug. 7, 1922.
6. SA to Karl Anderson, July 20, 1922.
7. "America's Literary Stars," *Literary Digest* 74 (July 22, 1922): 28–29, 44, 46–50.
8. SA to Rosenfeld, Aug. 7, 1922; to Harry Hansen, Nov. 29, 1922; to Finley, Aug. 1922; to Stieglitz, Sept. 6, 1922.
9. See n. 26.
10. This story was first published in *The Century Magazine* under the title "Broken." In *Horses and Men* it would appear, slightly revised, as part 2 of the two-part tale, "A Chicago Hamlet," a belated acknowledgment by Anderson, it would seem, of the Turgenev echo.
11. *Memoirs* (1969), pp. 77–78, 376–81. Daugherty as story teller was on SA's mind because his friend had "just written a novel" (SA to Finley, Aug. 1922).
12. Rascoe, "A Bookman's Day Book," *New York Sunday Tribune*, Aug. 20, 1922, sec. 5, p. 4. SA's reference to Cezanne was probably prompted by his having just read Clive Bell's *Since Cezanne* (1922), which he liked though feeling, characteristically, that Bell "does rather lay down too many laws." (SA to Karl Anderson, Aug. 21, 1922, late Aug. 1922.) A reference to Bell in "The Triumph of a Modern" helps date the composition of that story as mid-August.
13. SA to Karl Anderson and Stein, Aug. 21, 1922; Stein to SA, Sept. 1922.
14. SA to Finley, ca. Sept. 9, 1922.
15. Ibid.
16. SA to Karl Anderson, Sept. 16, 1922. Burdette I. Kinne's annotated copy of *The Triumph of the Egg*, autographed by SA as "A Christmas remembrance 1922," in WBR's possession.
17. Account of relationship of SA and Elizabeth Prall based on Elizabeth Anderson and Gerald R. Kelly, *Miss Elizabeth: A Memoir* (Boston: Little, Brown, 1969), pp. 47–55, and on interviews with her by WBR, Dec. 16, 1959, Dec. 17, 1959. Quotations are from *Miss Elizabeth*.
18. Entry on title page of Kinne's copy of *The Triumph of the Egg*. SA to Jerome and Lucile Blum, ca. Oct. 27, 1922 (misdated "?January, 1923" in Jones and Rideout, *Letters of Sherwood Anderson*, p. 90). In *Miss Elizabeth*, p. 54, Peg Lane is reported as "not at all upset about the news," but in a Dec. 17, 1959, interview by WBR, Elizabeth Prall Anderson stated that Peg was very much annoyed at her for deciding to marry SA, "that man," instead of Young.
19. Entry beneath SA's signature in Kinne's copy of *The Triumph of the Egg*, Kinne wrote: "Anderson shared my Apt. 12 St. Lukes Pl with me the fall + winter of 1922–1923. During this time he finished the writing and rewriting of *Many Marriages*, which was published early in 1923." Burton Rascoe, "A Book-

man's Day Book," *New York Tribune,* Oct. 1, 1922, sec. 5, p. 6. SA to Marguerite Gay, Sept. 13, 1922; to Gertrude Stein, Sept. 22, 1922; to Finley, ca. Sept. 9, 1922.

20. SA to Karl Anderson, late Aug. 1922; to Jerome and Lucile Blum, ca. Oct. 27, 1922. Contracts between SA and the American Play Company, Inc., represented by Otto Liveright, in the Berg Collection, New York Public Library. In addition, Liveright sold "Send for the Lawyer" (retitled "The Triumph of a Modern") to the *New Republic* on Oct. 26 for $60 ($54 to SA) and "Broken" to *The Century* on Nov. 24 for $400 ($360 to SA). Dates of contracts for the first four stories sold by Liveright help to confirm them as among the five SA wrote in August.

21. SA to Burdette Kinne, ca. Oct. 13, 1922; to Edmund Wilson, Oct. 13, 1922; to Lucile Blum, ca. Oct. 23, 1922; to Jerome and Lucile Blum, ca. Oct. 27, 1922; Bernardine Szold Fritz to Dale Kramer, Jan. 1964. Szold Fritz and Tennessee believed that Jerome Blum had much to do with SA's leaving Tennessee, but all other evidence suggests that Blum only strongly supported SA's action after the fact.

22. SA to Edmund Wilson, Oct. 23, 1922; to Stieglitz, Oct. 27, 1922; to Julius Friend, Oct. 26, 1922; to Jerome and Lucile Blum, Nov. 6, 1922.

23. SA to Bernardine Szold Fritz, ca. Nov. 17, 1922; to Jerome Blum, Nov. 13, 1922; to Jean Toomer, ca. Sept. 1922, Dec. 22, 1922, Dec. 1922. Huebsch to SA, Dec. 1, 1922. Toomer's "Nora" was included in his book *Cane* (1923) as "Calling Jesus."

24. SA to Harry Hansen, Nov. 29, 1922; to Finley, ca. Nov. 24, 1922, Dec. 1922. Stark Young to Gladys Coates Hamilton, Nov. 19, 1922, p. 176 in John Pilkington, ed., *Stark Young, A Life in the Arts: Letters, 1900–1962,* 2 vols. (Baton Rouge: Louisiana State University Press, 1975).

25. SA to Harry Hansen, Dec. 20–22, 1922; *Memoirs* (1942), pp. 344–45, (1969), pp. 434–35; *Miss Elizabeth,* pp. 51–52.

26. Martha Mulroy Curry, ed., *The "Writer's Book" by Sherwood Anderson: A Critical Edition* (Metuchen, NJ: Scarecrow Press, 1975), pp. 89–92, 225. Poems published in *A New Testament* as "Young Man Filled with the Feeling of Power," pp. 96–97, and, with the last two "stanzas" omitted, as "Man Lying on a Couch," p. 89.

27. *Bookman* 56 (Nov. 1922): 376–84, p. 376.

28. "Addressed to a Woman" and "The Word Maker," first printed in the Jan. 1920 *Little Review,* were reprinted in *A New Testament* as "A Persistent Lover" (pp. 50–54) and "Word Factories" (pp. 85–88). SA to Rosenfeld, Aug. 15, 1922. Wilson to Stanley Dell, Mar. 25, 1922; to John Peale Bishop, Sept. 22, 1922; to Maxwell Geismar, 1942, pp. 79, 97, 130 in Elena Wilson, ed., *Edmund Wilson, Letters on Literature and Politics 1912–1972* (New York: Farrar, Strauss & Giroux, 1977).

29. John Dos Passos, *The Best Times: An Informal Memoir* (New York: New American Library, 1966), p. 128. Fitzgerald to Perkins, [June 1, 1925], p. 111 in John Kuehl and Jackson R. Bryer, eds., *Dear Scott/Dear Max: The Fitzgerald-Perkins Correspondence* (New York: Scribner's, 1971).

30. SA's account in *Memoirs* (1942), pp. 333–35, (1969), pp. 451–53, is confirmed in *Miss Elizabeth*, pp. 49–50. SA to Mencken, ca. Nov. 1922; Dreiser to SA, Jan. 10, 1924.

31. Rascoe, *We Were Interrupted* (Garden City, NY: Doubleday, 1947), pp. 299–302. Other accounts drawn on are by Ernest Boyd, *Portraits: Real and Imaginary* (New York: Doran, 1924), pp. 221–22; Llewelyn Powys, *The Verdict of Bridlegoose* (London: Cape, 1927), pp. 89–90; Carl Van Vechten, "Theodore Dreiser as I Knew Him," *Yale University Library Gazette* 25 (Jan. 1951): 87–92, pp. 89–90. SA's account in *Memoirs* (1942), pp. 335–37; (1969), pp. 453–55, is largely contradicted by these.

32. Jean Toomer to SA, Dec. 18, 1922. SA to Toomer, Dec. 22, 1922; Toomer to SA, Dec. 29, 1922.

33. Of these Testaments the second, "The Lame One," was printed under that title in *A New Testament* (pp. 101–2), while the third, "A Young Man," was printed (pp. 98–100) under the title "A Dying Poet: To Emanual Carnevali." The first, titled simply "A Testament," SA's fanciful recollection of work in the Clyde bicycle factory (see discussion in chapter 2), was not reprinted. Entry on back end-paper of Kinne's copy of *The Triumph of the Egg* beneath pasted-in newspaper reproduction of this "portrait . . . made by Alfred Stieglitz at the time Anderson was sharing my Apt." Stieglitz had violently condemned a photograph he had seen of SA, perhaps the one reproduced in *The Literary Digest* for July 22. (SA to Stieglitz, Sept. 6, 1922.) SA to Stieglitz, May 18, 1923. The third photograph, reproduced in Paul Rosenfeld's *Port of New York,* opposite p. 175, shows SA without muffler and overcoat and wearing heavy tweed suit coat and vest.

34. SA to Karl Anderson, late Dec. 1922; to Finley, Jan. 2, 1923.

35. "The Bookman's Literary Club Service," *Bookman* 56 (Jan. 1923): 646–49. *New York Tribune*, Jan. 21, 1923, sec. 6, p. 27. Ochremenko to SA, Dec. 12, 1922; SA to Ochremenko, Jan. 1923.

36. Rascoe, "A Bookman's Day Book," *New York Tribune*, Jan. 14, 1923, sec. 6, p. 23. SA to Finley, Jan. 1923.

37. SA to Finley, Jan. 1923; to Karl Anderson, Jan. 1923.

38. Contract No. 121, American Play Company.

39. SA to Dreiser, ca. Feb. 8, 1923; to Rosenfeld, ca. Feb. 11, 1923.

40. SA to Karl Anderson, ca. Feb. 22, 1923.

CHAPTER 14. RENO

1. SA, "So This Is Reno," *Nevada Newsletter* 19 (April 5, 1924): 21, 23–25. SA to Karl Anderson, ca. Feb. 22, 1923.

2. SA to Finley, Feb. 22, 1923; to Rosenfeld, ca. Apr. 1, 1923. *Miss Elizabeth*, p. 56. In the following pages I have at several points relied on Elizabeth Prall Anderson's account of her life with SA, but on the basis of other evidence have corrected her occasional lapses of memory on details.

3. SA to Huebsch, Feb. 26, 1923, Mar. 6, 1923.

4. *New York Times:* Feb. 6, 1923, p. 23; Feb. 7, 1923, p. 19; Feb. 11, 1923, p. 8;

Feb. 25, 1923, sec. 1, pp. 1, 7, sec. 3, p. 10; Feb. 27, 1923, p. 18; Mar. 9, 1923, p. 17; Feb. 23, 1923, p. 2; Apr. 19, 1923, pp. 1, 4; May 3, 1923, pp. 1, 3. For a fuller account see Walker Gilmer, *Horace Liveright: Publisher of the Twenties* (New York: David Lewis, 1970), pp. 60–80.

5. SA to Huebsch, Mar. 13, 1923; Huebsch to SA, June 8, 1923, with royalty account dated May 1, 1923. On Mar. 25, the *New York Tribune* carried the Brentano's bookstores report that *Many Marriages* was third on the list of the six fiction books "having the best sale during the last week." It was described as: "The sad case of a middle-aged manufacturer of washing-machines who got tired of his wife and had to think up a good reason for running off with another woman" (sec. 6, p. 26).

6. *New York Times,* Feb. 25, 1923, sec. 3, p. 10; Mar. 15, 1923, p. 18 for quotation; Apr. 24, 1923, p. 20. Jones, "Sherwood Anderson's Biggest Achievement," *Chicago Evening Post Literary Review,* Mar. 2, 1923, n.p. Mencken, "Some New Books," *Smart Set* 71 (July 1923): 138–39.

7. SA to Rascoe, after Mar. 13, 1923. Henry W. Fisher to SA, Mar. 13, 1923. SA to Boyd, Mar. 1923; to Fitzgerald, Mar. 1923. Fitzgerald to SA, Apr. 1923.

8. SA to Huebsch, after Mar. 13, 1923; to Otto Liveright, Mar. 31, 1923; to Rosenfeld, Apr. 1923. "Censorship or Not," *Literary Digest* 77 (June 23, 1923): 27–29, 58–61, pp. 60–61.

9. SA to Stieglitz, Mar. 28, 1923; to Otto Liveright, Mar. 31, 1923; to Rosenfeld, Apr. 1923.

10. SA to Otto Liveright, Mar. 31, 1923; to Stark Young, ca. Apr. 4, 1923. Interview by WBR with William R. Dennes, May 29, 1959.

11. SA to Huebsch, Apr. 10, 1923; to Otto Liveright, Mar. 9, 1923, Apr. 25, 1923. In *Miss Elizabeth,* Elizabeth Prall Anderson implies that SA slept at night in his room at the Hotel Overland, but in an interview by WBR on May 26, 1959, with Margaret Bartlett Thornton and Dorothy Bartlett, who were daughters of the judge in SA's divorce case and who knew Sherwood and Elizabeth well, both women stated flatly that the couple lived together in Reno as, as it were, man and wife.

12. SA to Otto Liveright, Apr. 25, 1923, May 7, 1923, May 9, 1923, May 14, 1923; to Huebsch, ca. May 10, 1923, May 16, 1923.

13. *Memoirs* (1942), pp. 39–40; (1969), pp. 109–10. An analogous experience is described in *Tar,* pp. 104–6.

14. SA to Rosenfeld, Aug. 7, 1922; to Finley, Feb. 22, 1923.

15. SA to Finley, Jan. 1923.

16. *A Story Teller's Story,* pp. 134–35. SA to Huebsch, ca. May 10, 1923; to Rosenfeld, early Apr. 1923.

17. SA to Stark Young, late May 1923; to Karl Anderson, May 31, 1923; to Huebsch, ca. July 11, 1923; to Finley, July 6, 1923.

18. SA to Finley, July 6, 1923; to Van Wyck Brooks, July 23, 1923; to Karl Anderson, May 31, 1923; to Huebsch, ca. May 25, 1923; to Lucile Blum, July 1, 1923; to Stark Young, ca. July 25, 1923. *Miss Elizabeth,* p. 67, 69.

19. *Miss Elizabeth,* pp. 70–71, 75.

20. Undated letter from SA received May 31, 1923, by Louis N. Feipel, who

generously sent me a copy. SA to Stark Young, July 25, 1923; to Harry Hansen, May 27, 1923. Interview with Elizabeth Prall Anderson, Dec. 16, 1959.

21. SA to Huebsch, May 16, 1923; to Stark Young, late May 1923; Huebsch to SA, June 7–8, 1923, July 10, 1923.

22. Montgomery Gregory, "A Chronology of the Negro Theatre," in Alain Locke and Gregory Montgomery, eds., *Plays of Negro Life* (New York: Harper, 1927), pp. 419–20. Rascoe, "Day Book," *New York Tribune,* June 6, 1923, sec. 9, p. 26. Rosenfeld to SA, May 28, 1923; SA to Rosenfeld, July 8, 1923; to Otto Liveright, ca. June 3, 1923, ca. July 5, 1923.

23. SA to Huebsch and Otto Liveright, July 11, 1923; to Finley, July 6, 1923.

24. Huebsch to SA, July 10, 1923; Rosenfeld to SA, July 19, 1923; SA to Young, ca. July 25, 1923.

25. SA to Friend, after July 24, 1923.

26. SA to Brooks, before July 30, 1923.

27. SA to Huebsch, Aug. 4, 1923, ca. Oct. 1, 1923; to Ivan Dowell, late Aug. 1923; to Stieglitz, Sept. [3], 1923; to Stark Young, Aug. 1923. Huebsch to SA, Sept. 25, 1923. Thomas Smith to SA, Aug. 15, 1923. SA to Smith, late Aug. 1923. "Introduction," pp. v–x in Dreiser, *Free and Other Stories* (New York: Modern Library, 1924). SA to Roger Sergel, ca. Dec. 31, 1923. Burton Rascoe, "Day Book," *New York Tribune,* Nov. 11, 1923, sec. 9, p. 27.

28. SA to Karl Anderson, ca. Sept. 4, 1923; to Huebsch, Sept. 24, 1923; to Otto Liveright, Oct. 7, 1923; to Stieglitz, Sept. [3], 1923.

29. SA to Otto Liveright, Oct. 7, 1923, ca. July 19, 1923, ca. Sept. 24, 1923.

30. Rosenfeld to SA, Sept. 20, 1923; SA to Stieglitz, Oct. 18, 1923; to Otto Liveright, Oct. 7, 1923; to Ernest Ingersoll, Oct. 20, 1923; to Mrs. I. M. Dowell, after Sept. 17, 1923. "Berkeley Is Swept by a Great Fire; University Saved," *New York Times,* Sept. 18, 1923, pp. 1, 2. Case No. 19,875 in the Second Judicial District Court, Washoe County, Reno, Nevada.

31. Alyse Gregory, "Sherwood Anderson," *Dial* 75 (September 1923): 243–46. SA to Van Wyck Brooks, early Oct. 1923.

32. SA to Karl Anderson, ca. Sept. 4, 1923; Otto Liveright to SA, Sept. 18, 1923, Oct. 30, 1923; O'Brien to SA, Oct. 9, 1923; SA to Huebsch, ca. Nov. 5, 1923, ca. Oct. 24, 1923, Nov. 11, 1923.

33. SA to Lovett, early Mar. 1924.

34. Arvin, "Mr. Anderson's New Stories," *Freeman* 8 (Dec. 5, 1923): 307–8.

35. SA to O'Keeffe, Oct. 29, 1923; to Whitney Wells, ca. Dec. 1, 1923; to Otto Liveright, early Nov. 1923. Otto Liveright to SA, Nov. 27, 1923.

36. SA to Rosenfeld, Feb. 22?, 1924.

37. SA to Huebsch, Dec. 8, 1923; Canby to SA, Dec. 12, 1923.

38. SA to Wells, ca. Dec. 1, 1923; to Roger Sergel, Dec. 31?, 1923, ca. Dec. 31, 1923; to Ferdinand Schevill, Dec. 9?, 1923.

39. SA to Huebsch, ca. Nov. 13, 1923, ca. Dec. 3, 1923; to Otto Liveright, ca. Dec. 7, 1923.

40. SA to Rosenfeld, ca. Dec. 3, 1923, ca. Jan. 15, 1924; to Whitney Wells, ca. Nov. 13, 1923; to Georgia O'Keeffe, Oct. 29, 1923; to Stieglitz and O'Keeffe, Dec. 7, 1923.

41. SA to Stark Young, early Nov. 1923; to Otto Liveright, Nov. 21, 1923; to Ferdinand Schevill, Dec. 7, 1923, ca. Dec. 21, 1923.
42. SA to Whitney Wells, ca. Dec. 17, 1923, ca. Dec. 27, 1923; to Stark Young, mid-Dec. 1923; to Karl Anderson, ca. Jan. 3, 1924; to Stieglitz and O'Keeffe, Jan. 1, 1924.
43. SA to Otto Liveright, ca. Dec. 31, 1923; to Huebsch, Dec. 28, 1923; to Ferdinand Schevill, Jan. 3, 1924, ca. Jan. 3, 1924; to Stieglitz and O'Keeffe, Jan. 1, 1924.
44. SA to Huebsch, ca. Dec. 31, 1923; to Toomer, Jan. 3, 1924, Jan. 14, 1924.
45. SA to Rosenfeld, Jan. 15, 1924; to Alfred A. Knopf, ca. Jan. 16, 1924. Copy of Maurer broadside, very kindly presented to me by Erhard Weyhe.
46. *Miss Elizabeth*, pp. 68–69.
47. SA to Stieglitz and O'Keeffe, Jan. 1, 1924; to Rosenfeld, ca. Jan. 15, 1924; to Karl Anderson, ca. Dec. 3, 1923; to Huebsch, Jan. 13, 1924. "Biographer of Noted Author Here," *Reno Evening Gazette*, June 2, 1959, p. 8.
48. Bessie Beatty, *Who's Who in Nevada* (Los Angeles: Howe Printing Co., 1907), pp. 30–32; James G. Serugham, ed., *Nevada,* 3 vols. (Chicago and New York: American Historical Society, 1935), 1, p. 434; David W. Toll, *The Compleat Traveler* (Reno: University of Nevada Press, 1976), p. 82.
49. SA to Bartlett, ca. Jan. 13, 1924, copy very kindly sent me by Margaret Bartlett Thornton; SA to Stieglitz, Feb. 4, 1924; to Otto Liveright, ca. Feb. 7, 1924. Interview with Margaret Bartlett Thornton and Dorothy Bartlett, May 26, 1959.
50. SA to Rosenfeld, Jan. 15, 1924; to Ferdinand Schevill, Jan. 27, 1924; to Whitney Wells, ca. Feb. 28, 1924; to Huebsch, Jan. 29, 19; to Julius Friend, mid-Dec. 1923. Huebsch to SA, Jan. 28, 1924. The chapter of *Story* sold to *The Century* appeared in the Aug. 1924 issue as "When I Left Business for Literature," a title that helped establish the image of Anderson as the artist in rebellion against material affairs.
51. SA to Huebsch, ca. Feb. 14, 1924; to Rosenfeld, ca. Feb. 22, 1924; to Whitney Wells, ca. Mar. 19, 1924.
52. SA to Rosenfeld, before Mar. 19, 1924, Mar. 19, 1924; to Huebsch, ca. Mar. 19, 1924. Otto Liveright to SA, Mar. 19, 1924.
53. SA to Ferdinand Schevill, Apr. 4, 1924; Elizabeth Prall Anderson to Otto and Bernadine Liveright, Apr. 4, 1924. Schevill's notes for telegram to SA, Mar. 31, 1924. "Novelist Given Divorce Decree," *Reno Evening Gazette,* Apr. 4, 1924, p. 33. Decree of Divorce in Case No. 19,875, recorded Apr. 4, 1924, in Judgment Record Book 10, p. 440, Washoe County Clerk's Office.

CHAPTER 15. THE MOST CULTURAL TOWN IN AMERICA

1. *Miss Elizabeth*, pp. 72–74. Interview by WBR with Elizabeth Prall Anderson, Dec. 16, 1959. "Novelist Reweds 24 Hours After Obtaining Reno Divorce Decree," *San Francisco Chronicle*, Apr. 6, 1924, p. 1.
2. SA to Otto Liveright, May 19, 1924; to Stieglitz, ca. Apr. 10, 1924. Interview by WBR with Ralph Church, Apr. 24, 1959.

3. SA to Otto Liveright, May 19, 1924; to Huebsch, Apr. 19, 1924, ca. May 21, 1924; to Jerome and Lucile Blum, May 1924.

4. *Father Abraham: A Lincoln Fragment,* pp. 530–602 in Rosenfeld, *The Sherwood Anderson Reader,* p. 532. In my discussion of *Father Abraham* I have used this sole printed version for ease of reference.

5. SA to Sandburg, Aug. 1924; to Rosenfeld, ca. Aug. 10, 1924; to Stieglitz, ca. Aug. 3, 1924.

6. *Miss Elizabeth,* pp. 74–79. Interviews by WBR with Elizabeth Prall Anderson, Dec. 16, 1959, and William R. Dennes, May 29, 1959. SA to Ferdinand Schevill, ca. Apr. 19, 1924.

7. "Rebecca West to Speak This Week," *San Francisco Chronicle,* Apr. 20, 1924, sec. D, p. 5. Frederick O'Brien to SA and Elizabeth Prall Anderson, Apr. 24, 1924; SA to Stieglitz, Apr. 28, 1924, Apr. 4, 1924. The Cunningham portrait is reproduced as the frontispiece to James Schevill, *Sherwood Anderson.*

8. Interview by Suzanne B. Riess with Lehman, "Recollections and Reminiscences of Life in the Bay Area from 1920 Onward" (Regional Oral History Office, Bancroft Library, University of California, 1969), p. 82. This reference was kindly furnished me by J. R. K. Kantor, University Archivist.

9. Huebsch to SA, Apr. 7, 1924, Apr. 14, 1924, May 16, 1924, June 17, 1924, Apr. 25, 1924. In his letter of June 10, 1924, Huebsch also reports that Horace Liveright has just issued "another printing of 3000 copies" of the Modern Library *Winesburg, Ohio.* On July 22, Huebsch informed SA that Insel-Verlag had dropped their request for translation rights to *Horses and Men.*

10. Huebsch to SA, Apr. 7, 1924; Otto Liveright to SA, June 16, 1924. SA to Huebsch, ca. May 21, 1924; to Otto Liveright, ca. May 19, 1924.

11. SA to Huebsch, ca. June 5, 1924, June 26, 1924; to Ferdinand Schevill, early Mar. 1924. William Sutton has pointed out that "During the 1920s [Marietta Finley] contributed, over a number of years, $100 a month to Cornelia for support of the children." Sutton, *Letters to Bab,* p. xvi.

12. SA to Otto Liveright, ca. June 27, 1924; to Mencken, ca. June 16, 1924. Canby to SA, June 25, 1924.

13. SA to Huebsch, ca. June 26, 1924; to Otto Liveright, ca. June 27, 1924; to Mencken, June 27, 1924.

14. "Modernist Author Will Speak Friday," *The Summer Session Californian,* June 20, 1924, p. 1; "Sherwood Anderson," *The Summer Session Californian,* July 1, 1924, p. 4. Photocopies of these pieces were kindly furnished me by J. R. K. Kantor.

15. SA to Mencken, June 27, 1924; to Stieglitz, July 12, 1924.

16. Telegram, SA to Huebsch, June 28, 1924; Huebsch to SA, July 22, 1924; SA to Stieglitz, July 12, 1924.

17. Lillian Friend Marcus to SA, June 18, 1924; SA to Huebsch, ca. July 9, 1924.

18. SA to Whitney Wells, ca. July 15, 1924; to Mencken, ca. July 12, 1924; to Karl Anderson, early Aug. 1924; to Huebsch, July 24, 1924. A number of details concerning the New Orleans period, some corrected for accuracy, have been taken from *Miss Elizabeth.*

19. SA to Stieglitz, July 26, 1924; to Roger Sergel, early Aug. 1924; to Rosenfeld,

Aug. 10?, 1924; to Fletcher, ca. June 30, 1924; to Huebsch, ca. Aug. 10, 1924, ca. Aug. 16, 1924, ca. Sept. 15, 1924, ca. Sept. 16, 1924; to Karl Anderson, early Aug. 1924; to Otto Liveright, Aug. 17?, 1924; to Ferdinand Schevill, late Sept. 1924.

20. SA to Stieglitz, Sept. 4, 1924; to Calverton, Aug. 25, 1924.

21. Edward R. Gay, "Well Known Author Finds Field for Artists Here," *Times-Picayune*, Aug. 3, 1924, sec. 1-B, p. 2.

22. SA to Stieglitz, June 26, 1924, July 26, 1924, Aug. 3?, 1924. E. T. Booth to SA, July 22, 1924.

23. *Miss Elizabeth*, pp. 83–84.

24. James K. Feibleman, *Philosophers Lead Sheltered Lives: A First Volume of Memoirs* (London: George Allen & Unwin, 1952), p. 177.

25. SA to Stieglitz, Sept. 4, 1924, Sept. 23, 1924; to Ferdinand Schevill, late Aug. 1924; to Otto Liveright, Sept. 7, 1924; to Huebsch, Sept. 16, 1924, ca. Sept. 24, 1924.

26. SA to Clara Schevill, ca. Sept. 15, 1924; to Stieglitz, Sept. 23, 1924, Oct. 9, 1924; to Roger Sergel, ca. Sept. 4, 1924; to Huebsch, ca. Sept. 15, 1924. The lease from Roth & Rosenberg, [Real Estate] Agents, to SA was for twelve months commencing on the "first day of October 1924," but SA's correspondence confirms that he moved in on or close to Sept. 15. See also Cathy Harvey, "Dear Lyle/Sherwood Anderson," *Southern Studies* 18 (Fall 1979): 320–38, pp. 320–22.

27. SA to Huebsch, early Aug. 1924, ca. Sept. 15, 1924, Sept. 16, 1924, ca. Oct. 4, 1924. Huebsch to SA, Sept. 20, 1924, Aug. 25, 1924, Sept. 17, 1924.

28. *Miss Elizabeth*, pp. 107–8. Interview by WBR with Marc and Lucile Antony, Dec. 9, 1959. SA to Rosenfeld, Oct. 28, 1924. In her memoir Elizabeth names only Lucile as her partner, whereas the letterhead of Leonardi Studios gives only the names Elizabeth Anderson and Marc Antony.

29. Huebsch to SA, Oct. 20, 1924, Nov. 3, 1924, Nov. 17, 1924, Nov. 19, 1924, Nov. 24, 1924, Dec. 3, 1924. SA to Huebsch, ca. Nov. 5, 1924. Royalty statements, Oct. 31, 1924, and Apr. 20, 1925.

30. Huebsch to SA, Oct. 20, 1924. Morris, *New York Times Book Review*, Oct. 12, 1924, pp. 6, 22; Stallings, *New York World*, Oct. 14, 1924, p. 13, and Oct. 23, 1924, p. 11; McClure, *Times-Picayune Sunday Magazine*, Nov. 16, 1924, p. 6; Young, *New York Times*, sec. 8, p. 1; Lewis, *New York Herald Tribune Books*, Nov. 9, 1924, pp. 1, 2; Hemingway and Stein, *Ex Libris* 2 (March 1924): 176–77 and 177; Butcher, *Chicago Tribune*, Dec. 13, 1924, p. 9; Powys, *Dial* 78 (April 1925): 330–32; Walter Yust, *New York Evening Post Literary Review*, Nov. 1, 1924, p. 4; Van Doran, *Century* 109 (March 1925): 717–18, p. 717.

31. *New York Herald Tribune*, Dec. 12, 1924, p. 16. Sent a clipping of the story by a *Herald Tribune* reporter, Anderson replied that this praise for his book by one of "the more careful minds" in criticism "touched me deeply." (SA to David Karsner, ca. Dec. 15, 1924.)

32. SA to Finley, early Mar. 1925.

33. Because of editorial inconsistencies in Ray Lewis White's edition of *A Story*

Teller's Story: A Critical Text (Cleveland: The Press of Case Western Reserve University, 1968), I quote from the corrected third printing by Huebsch, Dec. 1924.

34. William Rose Benet, *Saturday Review of Literature* 1 (Oct. 18, 1924): 200.

CHAPTER 16. TURNING POINT

1. SA to Stieglitz, Oct. 9, 1924; Otto Liveright to SA, Oct. 22, 1924. The article was front-paged in *The Literary Review* for Oct. 25, 1924.
2. SA to Huebsch, ca. Oct. 11, 1924; to Otto Liveright, Oct. 25, 1924; to Rosenfeld, Oct. 28, 1924; Huebsch to SA, Oct. 15, 1924, Oct. 17, 1924, Oct. 20, 1924.
3. My description of the Anderson–Faulkner meeting draws on Joseph Blotner, *Faulkner: A Biography* (New York: Random House, 1974), 1, pp. 367–68; Ben Wasson, *Count No 'Count: Flashbacks to Faulkner* (Jackson: University Press of Mississippi, 1983), pp. 71–72; Hamilton Basso, "William Faulkner, Man and Writer," *Saturday Review* 45 (July 28, 1962): 11–14, p. 11.
4. Wasson to Carvel Collins, as reported in Collins's "Sherwood Anderson: Some Confusions Examined," paper delivered at the Sherwood Anderson Centenary, Michigan State University, Sept. 9, 1976. SA to Otto Liveright, prob. Nov. 8, 1924. Otto Liveright to SA, Nov. 12, 1924, states that "The Return," SA's second story has "just arrived" and that Liveright has received and read "A Meeting South," which indicates that the latter must have arrived at least by Nov. 11, a Tuesday. Copies of both stories were mailed to Huebsch on Nov. 10 and received on Nov. 12.
5. Otto Liveright to SA, Jan. 5, 1925, Mar. 4, 1925.
6. SA to Huebsch, Nov. 11, 1924, ca. Nov. 17, 1924, ca. Nov. 22, 1924, ca. Nov. 28, 1924; to Otto Liveright, Nov. 18, 1924, ca. Nov. 28, 1924, ca. Dec. 1, 1924; to Stieglitz, Dec. 1, 1924.
7. SA to Huebsch, ca. Nov. 11, 1924, ca. Nov. 18, 1924, ca. Nov. 22, 1924, ca. Nov. 28, 1924, ca. Dec. 1, 1924; to Otto Liveright, Nov. 28, 1924, ca. Dec. 1, 1924; to Stieglitz, Dec. 1, 1924.
8. Otto Liveright to SA, Oct. 27, 1924; SA to Otto Liveright, Nov. 3, 1924.
9. SA to Otto Liveright, ca. Nov. 18, 1924; to Horace Liveright, ca. Nov. 24, 1924; Otto Liveright to SA, Nov. 20, 1924; Horace Liveright to SA, Nov. 18, 1924, quoted from Gilmer, *Horace Liveright*, p. 109.
10. Sutton dates Bab's letter as "possibly Nov. 13–14, 1924" and notes that it is her "only existing letter" to SA before her marriage in 1928 to Dr. E. Vernon Hahn. (Sutton, *Letters to Bab*, pp. 197, 199, xiii.)
11. Rosenfeld to SA, Dec. 9, 1924.
12. SA to Karsner, ca. Dec. 15, 1924; to Huebsch, ca. Nov. 18, 1924; to Finley, Dec. 19, 1924; to Stieglitz, Dec. 12, 1924; to Young, Dec. 20, 1924. Leigh to SA, Nov. 11, 1924, Nov. 26, 1924, Dec. 25, 1924. Interview with Leigh by WBR, Dec. 5, 1960.
13. SA to Finley, Dec. 27, 1924; to Stieglitz, Dec. 12, 1924.
14. My account of SA's lectures in Cleveland, Hammond, and Topeka is partly

based on Sutton's notes to SA's letter of Jan. 8, 1925, *Letters to Bab,* pp. 205–6. SA to Edna Snow Lyons, Apr. 9, 1925; to Huebsch, Jan. 8, 1925; to Finley, Jan. 8, 1925.

15. Otto Liveright to SA, Jan. 5, 1925; Harris to SA, Jan. 5, 1925; SA to Harris, Jan. 14, 1925; Huebsch to SA, Jan. 3, 1925, Jan. 9, 1925; SA to Finley, Jan. 8, 1925; Hedwig Stieglitz Kuhn to SA, Nov. 7, 1924.
16. Clara Johnston to SA, Dec. 25, 1924. Clipping in Leigh, "Incoming Correspondence" File, No. 2, Sherwood Anderson Collection, at the Newberry Library.
17. SA to Finley, Jan. 8, 1925. [John Farrar], "The Gossip Shop," *Bookman* 61 (May 1925): 374–84, p. 384.
18. Although printed by Grabhorn, *The Modern Writer* was issued by Leon Gelber and Theodore M. Lilienthal's The Lantern Press of San Francisco in 1925. Fifty copies out of the printing were to be on vellum to be signed by SA and sold for $5 or $7.50 each instead of $2 for the regular copies. See Grabhorn to SA, Aug. 17, 1925; SA to Horace Liveright, Aug. 28, 1925; to Grabhorn, Aug. 28, 1925.
19. SA to Finley, Jan. [23], 1925; to the Sergels, ca. Jan. 25, 1925. Sutton, *Letters to Bab,* pp. 206–7, n. 3.
20. SA to Finley, Jan. 25, 1925, ca. Jan. 29, 1925; Nellie Nearing to SA, Jan. 31, 1925; Leigh to SA, Feb. 14, 1925. *Letters to Bab,* p. 207, n. 4.
21. Both Huebsch's invitations of Jan. 14, 1925, and the guest list give the place as The Lafayette Hotel, but a current commentary by Isabel Paterson, one of the guests, places the luncheon at the Brevoort. See Paterson, "Turns with a Bookworm," *New York Herald Tribune Books,* Feb. 8, 1925, 5, p. 13.
22. I am indebted to Ann Catherine McCullough for several documents concerning this luncheon used in her "A History of B. W. Huebsch, Publisher" (PhD diss., University of Wisconsin–Madison, 1979), pp. 304–8. Letter, Joseph Blumenthal (who made arrangements) to McCullough, Sept. 12, 1978. In his account in "Footnotes to a Publisher's Life" (*Colophon,* 2 n.s. [Summer 1937]: 406–26, pp. 416–17) Huebsch states that he invited "some eighty-five literary folk" for this "unprecedented gathering of important writers and critics." Farrar, "Pen-Enemies," *Time* 5 (Feb. 9, 1925): 15.
23. Maxwell Perkins to Charles Scribner, Feb. 24, 1925; H. L. Mencken to Sara Haardt, Jan. 30, 1925; Hendrik Willem Van Loon to Huebsch, July 18, 1925; SA to Huebsch, ca. Jan. 29, 1925; Huebsch to Hendrik Willem Van Loon, July 23, 1925; SA to Finley, Feb. 20, 1925.
24. SA to Gertrude Stein, early Mar. 1925; to Finley, Feb. 20, 1925. Baker, *Ernest Hemingway,* pp. 139, 147.
25. SA to Finley, Jan. 30, 1925, ca. Feb. 12, 1925, Feb. [25], 1925, Feb. 20, 1925. "Seven Alive," p. 3 in *Alfred Stieglitz Presents Seven Americans;* reprinted in Henry McBride, "Modern Art," *Dial* 78 (May 1925): 434–36, pp. 435–36.
26. SA to Finley, ca. Feb. 12, 1925, Feb. 11, 1925, Feb. 20, 1925; Otto Liveright to SA, Oct. 22, 1924; SA to Mary Blair, Feb. 15, 1926; SA to Ruth Anna Fisher, May 20, 1925; Raymond O'Neil to SA, Feb. 9, 1925. Adv. in *Guardian* 1 (Feb. 1925), facing inside back cover.

27. SA to Finley, Jan. 30, 1925, Feb. 20, 1925, Feb. [27], 1925; Leigh to SA, Feb. 18, 1925; SA to Leigh, Mar. 5, 1925; to John Emerson and Anita Loos, Mar. 5, 1925. *Miss Elizabeth,* p. 103.

28. SA to Huebsch, Mar. 5, 1925; Ochremenko to SA, Feb. 10, 1925; Otto Liveright to SA, Feb. 20, 1925, Mar. 4, 1925; SA to Otto Liveright, Mar. 6, 1925. "Betrayed" [the review], *Golden Book* 1 (May 1925): 743–44.

29. Blotner, *Faulkner,* 1, pp. 388–89, 397, 400–401; Carvel Collins, "Sherwood Anderson and William Faulkner: Some Confusions Examined," paper delivered at Michigan State University, Sept. 9, 1976; Carvel Collins, "Biographical Background for Faulkner's Helen," in William Faulkner, *Helen: A Courtship and Mississippi Poems* (New Orleans: Tulane University, Yoknapatawpha Press, 1981), pp. 16–17.

30. "Living in America," *Nation* 120 (June 10, 1925): 657–58; article sent to *Nation,* Mar. 9, 1925. SA to Ruth Kelso, Mar. 12, 1925; to George Sylvester Viereck, Mar. 21, 1925.

31. SA to Finley, Mar. 20, 1925, Apr. 11, 1925, Mar. 16, 1925; to Roger Sergel, ca. Mar. 20, 1925; to Robert Anderson, Sept. 9, 1925; to Otto Liveright, Mar. 20, 1925; to David Karsner, Mar. 13, 1925. Interview, WBR with Marc and Lucile Antony, Dec. 9, 1959.

32. SA to John Emerson and Anita Loos, Mar. 5, 1925; to Finley, Mar. 25, 1925, Mar. 16, 1925. First-person accounts of the cruise are in *Miss Elizabeth,* pp. 117–21, and William Spratling, *File on Spratling: An Autobiography* (Boston: Little, Brown, 1967), p. 29. See also Blotner, *Faulkner,* 1, pp. 417–18.

33. See "A Note on Sherwood Anderson," pp. 3–10, in James B. Meriwether, ed., *Essays Speeches & Public Letters by William Faulkner* (New York: Random House, 1965).

34. Spratling, *File on Spratling,* p. 22. SA to Faulkner, dated Spring 1925 by Meriwether. "Al Jackson," pp. 474–79 in Joseph Blotner, ed., *Uncollected Stories of William Faulkner* (New York: Random House, 1979). SA to Mencken, Mar. 1925.

35. Meriwether, *Essays Speeches,* pp. 7–8; Blotner, *Faulkner,* 1, p. 405; Jones and Rideout, *Letters of Sherwood Anderson,* pp. 139–41. *Memoirs* (1942), p. 18; (1969), pp. 35–36. SA to Finley, Mar. 20, 1925; to Otto Liveright, Mar. 25, 1925.

36. SA to Finley, early Apr. 1925; to Huebsch, Apr. 15, 1925, Apr. 1, 1925; SA's letter to Liveright appears to have been lost; to John Emerson, Apr. 5, 1925. Telegram, Emerson to SA, Apr. 5, 1925. Huebsch to SA, Apr. 6, 1925; statement, Huebsch to SA, Aug. 1, 1925; Emerson to SA, Apr. 13, 1925.

37. SA, "When the Writer Talks," *Literary Review,* Apr. 18, 1925, pp. 1–2, p. 1. SA to Julia Collier Harris, late Mar. 1925; to Otto Liveright, Apr. 5, 1925; to Finley, ca. Apr. 12, 1925.

38. SA to John Emerson, Apr. 5, 1925, Apr. 6, 1925. Baker, ed., *Hemingway: Selected Letters,* p. 157. *Miss Elizabeth,* pp. 96–97. Letter from Faulkner to his mother dated "[early Apr. 1925]," pp. 195–96 in James G. Watson, ed., *Thinking of Home: William Faulkner's Letters to His Mother and Father*

1918–1925 (New York: W. W. Norton, 1992). Despite repeated accounts by Faulkner and Elizabeth Anderson, as in WBR's interview with Elizabeth on Dec. 16, 1959, that Sherwood had agreed to recommend Faulkner's first novel to Liveright if he did not have to read the manuscript, both Andersons read chapters of the novel in progress and considered the completed work to be very good. See also Collins, "Faulkner and Anderson, Some Revisions," paper delivered at the Dec. 28, 1967, session of the American Literature Section at the Modern Language Association meeting in Chicago, abstracted in the Jan. 1968 report to the Section by its Secretary-Treasurer, Paul J. Carter, cited by Blotner, *Faulkner,* 1, p. 389.

39. SA to John Emerson, Apr. 5, 1925, Apr. 6, 1925; Horace Liveright to SA, Mar. 9, 1926. *Memoirs* (1942), p. 354; (1969), p. 491. *Miss Elizabeth,* p. 92.
40. SA to Otto Liveright, Apr. 11, 1925; Huebsch to SA, Feb. 11, 1925, Mar. 25, 1925, Apr. 6, 1925, Apr. 9, 1925. "Moonshine," with an afterword by William Holtz, has been published in *The Missouri Review* 12 (1989): 135–48.
41. SA to W. Orton Tewson, Apr. 17, 1925; to Anita Loos, Apr. 17, 1925.
42. Telegram, Otto Liveright to SA, Apr. 17, 1925. Otto Liveright to SA, Apr. 21, 1925, Apr. 29, 1925; SA to Mrs. Wharton Esherick, Apr. 15, 1925; to Anita Loos, Apr. 28, 1925.
43. "Modernist Beguiled By Old New Orleans: Anderson to Weave Charm of City Into His Stories," *Times-Picayune,* Apr. 19, 1925, pp. 1, 2, p. 1; "Artists to Replace 'Man of Action,' Anderson Says," *Times-Picayune,* Apr. 24, 1925, p. 24.
44. "Sherwood Anderson," reprinted pp. 132–39 in Carvel Collins, ed., *William Faulkner: New Orleans Sketches* (New York: Random House, 1958). Anderson's Al Jackson letter cannot be dated exactly but seems to have preceded the writing of the essay. There is no certain record of SA and Faulkner being on a boat together except for the *Josephine* cruise. In his 1953 "Sherwood Anderson: An Appreciation" Faulkner writes that Anderson told him the "dream," invented not dreamed, Faulkner knew, while they sat on a bench in Jackson Square, and then proceeds to invest it with symbolic meaning, as the essay does not.
45. Telegram, Otto Liveright to SA, Apr. 24, 1925. Otto Liveright to SA, Apr. 6, 1925, Apr. 21, 1925; SA to Ferdinand Schevill, May 6, 1925.
46. SA to Anita Loos, Apr. 28, 1925; to Ferdinand Schevill, May 6, 1925; to Horace Liveright, Apr. 18, 1925, May 6, 1925, June 1, 1925; to Finley, May 4, 1925.
47. Interview, WBR with Huebsch, Dec. 6, 1960; Huebsch to Swanberg, May 6, 1964. McCullough, "History of B. W. Huebsch," pp. 373–76.
48. SA to Horace Liveright, Apr. 18, 1925. SA's revisions are very capably discussed in Robert Lenhart Crist, "Sherwood Anderson's *Dark Laughter:* Sources, Composition, and Reputation," PhD diss., University of Chicago, 1966, pp. 89–121.
49. Horace Liveright to SA, May 1, 1925; SA to David Karsner, May 20, 1925; to Isidor Schneider, May 21, 1925; Marie-Celeste Maury Lyons to SA, May 18,

1925; SA to Finley, ?mid-May 1925, May 17, 1925, late May 1925; to Otto
Liveright, May 20, 1925.

50. SA to Finley, late May 1925; to Horace Liveright, June 1, 1925; to Stieglitz,
June 6, 1925.

51. Julia Harris to SA, ca. May 1, 1925, June 15, 1925; SA to Julia Harris, after
June 15, 1925. Harris's article appeared in *Journal of Social Forces* 3 (March
1925): 427–31.

52. SA to Stieglitz, July 10, 1925, June 20, 1925; to Julia Harris, ca. June 18,
1925; to Finley, ca. June 21, 1925.

53. SA to Finley, ca. June 21, 1925, ca. June 27, 1925; to Stieglitz, June 27, 1925.

54. Crist, "Sherwood Anderson's *Dark Laughter*," pp. 93–94. SA to Finley,
ca. June 27, 1925; to Horace Liveright, July 10, 1925; to Rosenfeld, July 10,
1925; to Julia Harris, July 10, 1925; Harris to SA, June 15, 1925.

CHAPTER 17. SPEAKING OF THE MODERN MOVEMENT

1. Robert F. Williams, "The Great Train Ride," *Winesburg Eagle* 1 (April 1976):
4–5. Caroline Greear, "Sherwood Anderson as a Mountain Family Knew
Him," *Winesburg Eagle* 14 (Summer 1989): 1–12.

2. Details about the stay in Troutdale in this and the following two paragraphs
are taken from the Greear account, *Miss Elizabeth,* pp. 133–35, and SA to
Finley, July 27, 1925, early Aug. 1925; to Julia Harris, before July 24, 1925,
July 24, 1925; to Gertrude Stein, Aug. 3, 1925; to Otto Liveright, Sept. 1,
1925; and *Memoirs* (1942), pp. 358–63; (1969), 485–90.

3. SA to Edwin Grabhorn, early Aug. 1925. "American Fiction," *Saturday
Review of Literature* 2 (Aug. 1, 1925): 1–3.

4. SA to Julia Harris, July 24, 1925; to John Emerson, Aug. 28, 1925; to Robert
Anderson, ca. Aug. 1, 1925, Sept. 9, 1925.

5. SA to Finley, Aug. 29, 1925, July 27, 1925, early Aug. 1925, Aug. 20, 1925.

6. SA to Barbara Miller, late Aug. 1925; to William Wright, Sept. 15, 1925, Sept.
30, 1925; to Finley, Aug. 20, 1925; to Julia Harris, late Aug. 1925. Interview,
WBR with William Wright, June 17, 1953.

7. SA to Huebsch, Aug. 17, 1925; Caroline Greear to SA, Aug. 25, 1925; John
Greear to SA, Aug. 29, 1925; SA to Caroline Greear, Sept, 30, 1925; R. L.
Greear (brother to John) to SA, Mar. 1, 1926, Mar. 17, 1926; Huebsch to SA,
July 8, 1925, Aug. 5, 1925.

8. Edwin Grabhorn to SA, Aug. 17, 1925; Horace Liveright to SA, June 24,
1925, Aug. 28, 1925 (telegram); SA to Grabhorn, Aug. 28, 1925; to Adam
Hull Shirk, Aug. 28, 1925; to Phil Stone, Aug. 17, 1925; to Horace Liveright,
Aug. 28, 1925; to John Emerson, Aug. 28, 1925.

9. SA to W. Colston Leigh, Aug. 28, 1925; to Julia Harris late Aug. 1925; to Finley, Sept. 1925; to Gertrude Lane, Nov. 26, 1925; to Otto Liveright, Sept. 9,
1925. "An Estimate and Appreciation of an Authentic American Portrait,"
Vanity Fair 25 (Nov. 1925): 57, 94, p. 94; reprinted in *Sherwood Anderson's
Notebook* as "After Seeing George Bellows' Mr. and Mrs. Wase."

10. SA to Horace Liveright, Sept. 30, 1925; to Roger Sergel, late Aug. 1925; to

Otto Liveright, Sept. 1, 1925, Sept. 15, 1925; Elizabeth Prall Anderson to Julia Harris, Sept. 27, 1925; SA to David Karsner, Sept. 20, 1925.

11. SA to Robert Anderson, Sept. 9, 1925; to William Wright, Sept. 23, 1925; to Julian and Julia Harris, Oct. 2, 1925; Elizabeth Prall Anderson to Julia Harris, Nov. 1, 1925. Interview, WBR with Mrs. Joel Harris Lawrence, Dec. 9, 1959.

12. SA to George Daugherty, Sept. 15, 1925; to Julia Harris, Sept. 15, 1925, Oct. 2, 1925. Stallings, "The First Reader: *Dark Laughter,*" *New York World,* Sept. 11, 1925, p. 15. "The Story Teller Goes South," *New York World,* Sept. 13, 1925, 3, p. 4. Calverton, *Evening Sun,* Sept. 12, 1925, p. 6. Anon., "Sherwood Anderson Contemplates Life on the Levee," *New York Times Book Review,* Sept. 20, 1925, p. 9.

13. Julia Harris to SA, Sept. 30, 1925; SA to Harris, Nov. 19, 1925. Sherman, *New York Herald Tribune Books,* Oct. 4, 1925, pp. 1, 2, 3.

14. Canby, "The Woman Talks," *Saturday Review of Literature* 2 (Oct. 10, 1925): 191. Lovett, "Dark Laughter," *New Republic* 44 (Oct. 21, 1925): 233–34. Mencken, "Fiction Good and Bad," *American Mercury* 6 (Nov. 1925): 374–81, pp. 379–80. K. S., "*Dark Laughter,*" *Boston Transcript,* Oct. 10, 1925, p. 4. Butcher, *Tribune,* Oct. 10, 1925, p. 14. Boni and Liveright royalty statement, Dec. 31, 1925.

15. SA to Otto Liveright, Sept. 7, 1924; to Daugherty, Sept. 15, 1925. This letter to Daugherty is Anderson's first direct statement that he possessed a copy of *Ulysses,* then banned from entry into the United States. According to Noel Riley Fitch in *Sylvia Beach and the Lost Generation* (pp. 138–39) the copy he had subscribed for in Paris in 1921, presumably from the first edition (Paris, Feb. 1922), was one of forty which had been smuggled into the United States from Canada by Barnet Braverman "before Christmas" of 1922 and soon distributed to subscribers. Curiously, the copy in Anderson's library is from the fourth "edition" (Paris, Jan. 1924). (See Charles E. Modlin and Hilbert H. Campbell, comps., "A Catalog of Sherwood Anderson's Library," pp. 83–144 in Campbell and Modlin, *Sherwood Anderson: Centennial Essays.*) Whatever happened to the first edition copy is not known, nor when and how he obtained the fourth edition copy. The letter to Daugherty and the text of *Dark Laughter* indicate that Anderson had read or read in *Ulysses* at the latest by July 1924.

SA to Arthur Palmer Hudson, quoted by Hudson in "The Singing South: Folk-Song in Recent Fiction Describing Southern Life," *Sewanee Review* 44 (July-Sept. 1936): 268–95, p. 284; to Rosenfeld, Aug. 19?, 1924.

16. In the *Memoirs* (1942), pp. 84–89; (1969), pp. 123–28, SA states that he used Rice as a model for Sponge and describes him. Interview, WBR with Mildred Becker Fuller, Sept. 10, 1961.

17. Holtz, "Sherwood Anderson and Rose Wilder Lane," pp. 143–45.

18. SA to Horace Liveright, Apr. 18, 1925.

19. SA to Helen Russman, late Sept. 1925.

20. SA to Finley, Oct. 6, 1925; to Sticglitz, Oct. 8, 1925; to Colston Leigh, Oct. 12, 1925; telegram to Julian Harris, Oct. 11, 1925; Leigh to SA, Sept. 29, 1925, Oct. 3, 1925. Sutton, *Letters to Bab,* pp. 231–34, n. 4.

21. Sutton, *Letters to Bab*, pp. 234–36, n. 2. Leigh to SA, Sept. 29, 1925; SA to Finley, Oct. 17, 1925.

22. Sutton, *Letters to Bab*, pp. 236–41, nn. 3 and 4. SA to Julian Harris, Oct. 23, 1925.

23. Greear, "Sherwood Anderson," pp. 23–25. SA to Karl Anderson, Oct. 28, 1925; to Lyle Saxon, Oct. 28, 1925; to Finley, Nov. 2, 1925; to Mrs. Leslie D. Hawkridge, Oct. 28, 1925. Leigh to SA, June 13, 1925.

24. SA to Karl Anderson, Oct. 28, 1925; to Mencken, Oct. 29, 1925, Dec. 19, 1925; to Bennett Cerf, Nov. 7, 1925, before Nov. 14, 1925; Leigh to SA, June 13, 1925, July 13, 1925, July 25, 1925; Cerf to SA, Nov. 14, 1925. Gilmer, *Horace Liveright*, pp. 90–91.

25. Leigh to SA, June 13, 1925, Nov. 4, 1925; SA to *New York Times*, Nov. 11, 1925, published as "Hamlet in Modern Dress," Nov. 15, 1925, sec. 8, p. 2.

26. "Sherwood Anderson Tells His Life Story," *Success* 10 (March 1926): 109–11, reprinted as Appendix B in Sutton, *Letters to Bab*, pp. 337–43.

27. SA to Stieglitz, Nov. 11, 1925; to Lyle Saxon, prob. Nov. 14, 1925. Leigh to SA, July 25, 1925, June 13, 1925. "Noted Author to Hear Nickname," *Toledo Times*, Nov. 15, 1925, p. 14. Richards, V. K., "Uplift the World? Not My Job, Says Sherwood Anderson," *Toledo Blade*, Nov. 19, 1925, p. 3.

28. SA to Leigh, Nov. 19, 1925; to Brooks, Nov. 14, 1925; to Harris, Nov. 19, 1925; to Stieglitz, Nov. 25, 1925; to Gertrude Lane, Nov. 26, 1925. Martha Kieffer to SA, Nov. 1925; Helen Peters to SA, Nov. 20, 1925; Otto Liveright to SA, Nov. 23, 1925. Brown, "It Seems to Me," *New York World*, Sept. 19, 1925, p. 15.

29. Leigh to SA, Aug. 29, 1925, Nov. 1925, June 26, 1925, Nov. 4, 1925, Nov. 27, 1925. SA to Leigh, Dec. 21, 1925; to Greear, Dec. 10, 1925; to Beach, Sept. 21, 1925, Oct. 13, 1925; to Stieglitz, Dec. 22, 1925. Beach, *The Outlook for American Prose* (Chicago: University of Chicago Press, 1926), pp. 247–80.

30. SA to Charles and Mabel Connick, Dec. 31, 1925; to Stieglitz, Dec. 31, 1925; to Leigh, Dec. 21, 1925. Leigh to SA, Mar. 10, 1926, notes probably unsent to SA, Dec. 1925; Mencken to SA, Dec. 22, 1925, Nov. 16, 1925; Otto Liveright to SA, Dec. 9, 1925, Dec. 28, 1925. I have adjusted minor discrepancies in Leigh's notes and his Mar. 10, 1926, letter to SA.

31. "Dreiser," *Saturday Review of Literature* 2 (Jan. 9, 1926): 475. SA to John Emerson, Dec. 31, 1925; to Finley, Dec. 24, 1925, Jan. 4, 1926.

32. Leigh to SA, Nov. 4, 1925, Nov. 24, 1925, Sept. 15, 1925, Jan. 7, 1926, Mar. 10, 1926; notes, Dec. 1925. "Visiting Author Discusses Beginnings of Literature," *Portland Oregonian*, Jan. 27, 1926, p. 7. "Tickets to Anderson Lecture Are Limited," "Anderson Says Americans Live in Factual Age," "Anderson Tells Colorful Story," *University of Washington Daily*, Jan. 27, 1926, p. 1; Jan. 29, 1926, pp. 1, 4; Jan. 28, 1926, p. 1. "Famed Author to Speak on 'America,'" "Author Likes Critics Even If They Hit Him," "Anderson Will Speak at U. W.," *Seattle Post-Intelligencer*, Jan. 24, 1926, sec. 2, p. D6; Jan. 28, 1926, sec. 2, p. 1; Jan. 27, 1926, p. H1. "Sherwood Anderson's Hobby Is His Vocation," *Seattle Times*, Jan. 28, 1926, sec. 1, p. 9. "Sherwood Anderson Talks to Students," *Seattle Star*, Jan. 29, 1926, p. 12.

33. SA to John Emerson, Dec. 31, 1925; to Finley, Jan. 27, 1926, ca. Jan. 18, 1926; to Frederick O'Brien, Feb. 15, 1926. Sutton, *Letters to Bab,* pp. 244–45, n. 2.

34. Leigh to SA, Mar. 15, 1926; SA to William Wright, Jan. 11, 1926; to Joseph Warren Beach, Feb. 5, 1926. Karsner, "Sherwood Anderson, Mid-West Mystic," *New York Herald Tribune Magazine,* May 16, 1926, sec. 8, pp. 8–9, 16. "Sherwood Anderson MS. Burned In Excitement Caused by Fire," *New York Times,* Jan. 26, 1926, p. 29.

35. Sutton, *Letters to Bab,* p. 246, n. 2.

36. Lardner to Zelda and F. Scott Fitzgerald, Feb. 23, 1926, printed pp. 215–16 in Clifford M. Caruthers, ed., *Letters from Ring* (Flint, MI: Walden Press, 1979); SA to Mencken, after Feb. 16, 1926. "Meeting Ring Lardner," *New Yorker* 9 (Nov. 25, 1933): 36, 38.

37. SA to Kate Scott, Feb. 15, 1926. *Miss Elizabeth,* pp. 100–101. Interview, WBR with Elizabeth Prall Anderson, Dec. 16, 1959, during which she insisted that Faulkner's rudeness to Schevill was the cause of the rupture.

38. SA, "They Come Bearing Gifts," *American Mercury* 21 (Oct. 1930): 129–37, p. 129. *Memoirs* (1942), p. 474; (1969), p. 462.

39. Spratling, *File on Spratling,* p. 28. Blotner, *Faulkner,* 1, pp. 491–92, 495, 497–98, 524–25. (See Blotner, 1, pp. 497–501, for a discussion of the SA–William Faulkner break.) Writing to the Antonys from Troutdale on May 28, 1926, SA asked them to give his love to "Bill" [Spratling], as he surely would not have done if he had known of any mistreatment of Bob by the two Bills prior to that time.

40. Blotner, *Faulkner,* 1, p. 501. The concatenation of two unpleasant incidents may also explain why Faulkner delayed presenting the copy of *Soldier's Pay* to the Andersons until three weeks after the novel was published rather than, as one would expect, presenting it immediately.

41. Blotner, *Faulkner,* 1, p. 496. Young to Harrison Smith, June 4, 1953, June 15, 1953, printed in Pilkington, *Stark Young,* 2, pp. 1255, 1256. Young wrote an article about SA in part commenting on the break "from Sherwood's side of it," but he withheld it from publication, and the manuscript has regrettably not been found.

42. Karl Anderson to SA, Feb. 17, 1926; SA to D. T. Flynn, Feb. 17, 1926; to Horace Liveright, Feb. 23, 1926. A/P Tapes, pp. 29, 40–50.

43. Karl Anderson to SA, Feb. 17, 1926; SA to Finley, after Feb. 17, 1926, ca. Feb. 23, 1926; to Karl Anderson, Feb. 22, 1926; to Horace Liveright, Feb. 23, 1926. A/P Tapes, pp. 29–30, 41, 42–43, 49–50.

44. A/P Tapes, pp. 29–30. SA to Finley, after Feb. 17, 1926, ca. Feb. 23, 1926; to Karl Anderson, Feb. 22, 1926; to Horace Liveright, Feb. 23, 1926; to Julian and Julia Harris, early Mar. 1926.

45. SA to Finley, early Mar. 1926, ?mid-Mar. 1926, late Mar. 1926; to Ferdinand Schevill, ca. Mar. 3, 1926; Wilson to SA, Apr. 10, 1926. "Reflections," *New Republic* 46 (April 28, 1926): 304–5.

46. "Dorothy Dix, Sherwood Anderson and Grace King Tell Everything About This Business of Writing," *Times-Picayune,* Mar. 14, 1926, pp. 1, 4.

47. SA to Finley, Mar. 29, 1926, before Apr. 25, 1926; to Karl Anderson, ca. Apr. 5, 1926; to Cornelia Anderson, Apr. 25, 1926; to Karl Anderson and Earl Anderson, Apr. 9, 1926; to Earl Anderson, ca. Apr. 9, 1926. Sutton, *Letters to Bab,* p. 255, n. 2.

48. SA to Karl Anderson and Earl Anderson, ca. Apr. 11, 1926; to Finley, before Apr. 25, 1926, ca. Apr. 6, 1926; to Karl Anderson, ca. Apr. 5, 1926; to Marguerite Gay, Apr. 20, 1926. Gay to SA, Feb. 2, 1926. *Les Cahiers du Mois* 18/19 (Paris: Editions Emile-Paul Freres, 1926). Michaud's lectures were published under the same title in Paris later in 1926. He concluded his two-chapter survey of the work of Anderson, "mystic" and "psychoanalyst," by stating that an indigenous American literature will owe "son emancipation et son originalite" to Anderson more than to any other writer.

49. SA to Karl Anderson, ca. Apr. 5, 1926; to Otto Liveright, Apr. 12, 1926; to Stieglitz, Apr. 19, 1926; to Frederick O'Brien, Apr. 20, 1926; to Finley, ca. Apr. 6, 1926, ca. Apr. 25, 1926.

50. SA to Otto Liveright, Apr. 25, 1926; Otto Liveright to SA, Apr. 16, 1926. "New Orleans" appeared in *Vanity Fair* 26 (Aug. 1926): 36, 97; "Hello, Big Boy" in *Vanity Fair* 26 (July 1926): 41-42, 88.

51. "Signers of Our Literary Declaration of Independence," *Vanity Fair* 26 (July 1926): 70.

52. SA to Otto Liveright, Apr. 12, 1926; to Finley, Apr. 25, 1926.

53. New Orleans, Louisiana Record Conveyance Office Book 409, Folio 305. SA to Cornelia Anderson, Apr. 25, 1926; to Finley, ca. Apr. 25, 1926.

CHAPTER 18. COLLAPSE

1. Caroline Greear to Julia Harris, May 6, 1926; SA to Helen Anderson, May 1926; to Finley, May 1926. Greear, "Sherwood Anderson," p. 10.

2. SA to Ferdinand and Clara Schevill, ca. June 23, 1926; to Marc Antony, May 28, 1926. *Miss Elizabeth,* 145; *Memoirs* (1942), pp. 364-67, (1969), pp. 493-96.

3. SA to Stieglitz, May 14, 1926; to Otto Liveright, May 26, 1926. Otto Liveright to SA, May 12, 1926, June 8, 1926, June 10, 1926. Donald Freeman to Otto Liveright, June 8, 1926, ca. June 14, 1926.

4. Burton Emmett to SA, May 2, 1926. SA to Burton Emmett, early May 1926, May 31, 1926. "Emmett, Burton," *National Cyclopaedia of American Biography* (New York: James T. White, 1941), 29, p. 432.

5. Elizabeth Graham to SA, May 17, 1926, June 12, 1926, June 21, 1926, June 24, 1926, ?July 1926, Aug. 2, 1926, Oct. 28, 1926. SA to Elizabeth Graham, dated May 21, 1926, Aug. 26, 1926. In my interview with Mrs. Graham, Feb. 6, 1959, she had nothing but pleasant early memories of SA.

6. SA to Otto Liveright, ca. May 14, 1926; to Stieglitz, May 14, 1926; to Finley, ca. May 9, 1926. Otto Liveright to SA, May 12, 1926, May 19, 1926.

7. SA to Otto Liveright, Apr. 12, 1926; to Finley, late May 1926.

8. Ray Lewis White, "'Death in the Woods': Anderson's Earliest Version," *Winesburg Eagle* 7 (Apr. 1982): 1-3; William V. Miller, ed., "The Death in the

Forest," appendix, pp. 231–36 in Ray Lewis White, ed., *Tar: A Midwest Childhood: A Critical Text* (Cleveland, OH: Press of Case Western Reserve University, 1969).

9. Otto Liveright to SA, June 8, 1926, June 23, 1926, July 9, 1926. Mencken to Otto Liveright, July 8, 1926.

10. SA to Gertrude Stein, Apr. 25, 1926, May 23, 1926. Yust, "Refreshingly Frank Confessional Notes by Sherwood Anderson," *New York Evening Post Literary Review,* May 22, 1926, p. 3; Hansen, "Anderson's Scrapbook," *The* [New York] *World,* May 9, 1926, M, p. 6; H. I. Brock, "Sherwood Anderson Reports on Life and Letters," *New York Times Book Review,* May 9, 1926, p. 2; "K. S.," "Sherwood Anderson," *Boston Evening Transcript,* May 29, 1926, p. 5. I have been unable to obtain from the paper's archives a copy of Julia Harris's review in the *Columbus Enquirer-Sun,* May 23, 1926, but in a mid-June letter SA thanks her for the "fine" review article.

11. Hemingway, *Ex Libris,* 176–77; Baker, *Hemingway,* pp. 159–60, 162–64; letter, Hemingway to Pound, Nov. 30, 1925; Szold quoted in Kramer, *Chicago Renaissance,* p. 338.

12. Horace Liveright to Hemingway, Dec. 30, 1925, quoted in Gilmer, *Horace Liveright,* pp. 123–25.

13. SA to Church, May 19, 1926; to Hemingway, May 19, 1926; Hemingway to SA, May 21, 1926.

14. SA to Finley, ca. June 23, 1926; to Hemingway, June 14, 1926. Benchley, "A Ghost Story (As Sherwood Anderson Would Write It If He Weren't Prevented)," *Life* 86 (Dec. 1925): 21, 64. Since Hemingway had mentioned Dos Passos but not Fitzgerald in his letter, SA's reference to the latter strongly suggests that he had already read "How to Waste Material."

15. SA to Finley, ca. June 23, 1926. In a sample review in *The Independent* for June 12, 1926 (p. 694), SA's "early admirer" Ernest Boyd commented acerbically that, "Watching the development of Sherwood Anderson, I have felt that his consecration as a national glory by eminent conservatives had coincided precisely with the revelation to his more critical readers of certain fundamental weaknesses in him."

16. SA to Otto Liveright, ca. mid-June 1926; to Stieglitz, June 23, 1926; to Finley, ca. June 23, 1926. Rosenfeld to SA, June 17, 1926, June 25, 1926.

17. SA to Finley, ca. July 1, 1926; to Stieglitz, July 12, 1926.

18. SA to Otto Liveright, ca. July 9, 1926, ca. July 11, 1926. "The South," *Vanity Fair* 27 (Sept. 1926): 49–50, 138; booklet reprint undated.

19. SA, "Look Out, Brown Man!," *Nation* 131 (Nov. 26, 1930): 579–80; letter to *The Crisis* (32 [May 1926], 36) in response to a query by assistant editor Jessie Fauset for the magazine's "The Negro in Art: How Shall He Be Portrayed: A Symposium" (pp. 35–36).

20. SA to Finley, ca. June 23, 1926, after July 19, 1926, ca. July 21, 1926; to Ferdinand and Clara Schevill, ca. June 23, 1926; to Donald Freeman, July 21, 1926; to Otto Liveright, ca. July 21, 1926.

21. SA to Finley, after July 19, 1926, mid-July 1926, ca. July 7, 1926.

22. SA to Finley, after July 19, 1926; to Robert Anderson, ?mid-Aug. 1926.

23. SA to Stieglitz, Aug. 5, 1926, Aug. 26, 1926; to Finley, mid-July 1926, ca. Aug. 3, 1926, Aug. 15, 1926, ca. Aug. 24, 1926; to Maurice Hanline, Aug. 26, 1926, Aug. 17, 1926. Otto Liveright to SA, July 23, 1926.

24. Otto Liveright to SA, Aug. 6, 1926; Robert Bridges to SA, July 2, 1926; Irwin Anderson to SA, July 15, 1926. SA to Elizabeth Graham, Aug. 26, 1926; to Earl Anderson, Aug. 19, 1926; to Robert Anderson, Aug. 24, 1926. "Another Wife" was published in the Dec. 1926 *Scribner's*, pp. 203–18.

25. SA to Karl Anderson, May 26, 1926; to Robert Anderson, Aug. 24, 1926; to Karl Anderson, late Nov. 1930. The portrait, "Three Anderson Brothers" is reproduced in Jones and Rideout, *Letters of Sherwood Anderson*, p. 152.

26. SA to Earl Anderson, ca. Aug. 18, 1926 (letter not sent, according to Charles E. Modlin, ed., *Sherwood Anderson: Selected Letters* [Knoxville: University of Tennessee Press, 1984], p. 82, n. 1), Aug. 24, 1926; to Roger Sergel, late Aug. 1926.

27. SA to Finley, early Sept. 1926, ca. Sept. 8, 1926.

28. SA to Burton Emmett, July 4, 1926, Sept. 6, 1926.

29. "Anderson Denies Dreiser Plagiarized His 'Tandy,'" *New York Herald Tribune*, Sept. 8, 1926, p. 20. SA to Finley, ca. Sept. 8, 1926; to Burton Emmett, Oct. 4, 1926.

30. SA to Karl Anderson, ca. Sept. 13, 1926; to Earl Anderson, Sept. 24, 1926; to Finley, ca. Sept. 8, 1926, ca. Sept. 25, 1926.

31. SA to Finley, late Sept. 1926.

32. Ibid.

33. SA to Karl Anderson, late Sept. 1926; to Finley, very late Sept. 1926; to Hemingway, July 17, 1926, Oct. 10, 1926; Lyle Saxon to SA and Elizabeth Prall Anderson, Sept. 12, 1926, Oct. 20, 1926; Hemingway to SA, July 1, 1926, ca. Sept. 7, 1926.

34. SA to Church, ca. Oct. 10, 1926; to Finley, late Oct. 1926.

35. SA to Finley, two letters, mid-Oct. 1926.

36. SA to Burton Emmett, early Nov. 1926; to Karl Anderson, late Sept. 1926; to Ferdinand and Clara Schevill, ca. Nov. 15, 1926; to Otto Liveright, mid-Sept. 1926; to William Wright, Nov. 23, 1926. *Memoirs* (1942), pp. 373–74; (1969), pp. 502–3.

37. *Memoirs* (1942), pp. 374–75; (1969), pp. 503–4. *Miss Elizabeth*, pp. 150–51.

38. *Memoirs* (1942), p. 372; (1969), p. 501–2.

39. SA to Ferdinand and Clara Schevill, ca. Nov. 15, 1926; to Burton Emmett, Nov. 15, 1926. Gorman, "Sherwood Anderson's Fancy of His Youth," *New York Times Book Review*, Nov. 21, 1926, pp. 2, 12; West, "Sherwood Anderson, Poet," *New York Herald Tribune Books*, Nov. 21, 1926, pp. 1, 8; Mencken, "Literary Confidences," *American Mercury* 10 (Mar. 1927), 382–83.

CHAPTER 19. THE DOOR OF THE TRAP

1. SA to William Wright, Nov. 23, 1926; to Karl Anderson, ca. Nov. 22, 1926; to Finley, ca. Nov. 26, 1926.

2. SA to Burton Emmett, ca. Dec. 8, 1926; to Marion ("Mimi") Anderson,

ca. June 5, 1927. *Miss Elizabeth,* pp. 154–55. Interviews, WBR with B. L. Dickinson, June 18, 1953; with Marion ("Mimi") Anderson Spear, Apr. 12, 1988; with Alma Schilf, Sept. 5, 1961.

3. SA to William Wright, ca. Dec. 2, 1926; to Swinnerton, ca. Dec. 10, 1926. *Miss Elizabeth,* p. 156.

4. SA to Swinnerton, ca. Dec. 10, 1926; ca. Dec. 13, 1926; to Burton Emmett, Jan. 19, 1927. *The Journal of Arnold Bennett* (New York: Viking Press, 1933), p. 918. *Memoirs* (1969), p. 438.

5. SA to Ralph Church, Dec. 22, 1927; to Gertrude Stein, Dec. 17, 1926. William L. Shirer, *Twentieth Century Journey: The Start, 1904–1930* (Boston: Little, Brown, 1976), p. 22.

6. SA to Karl Anderson, Mar. 15, 1927; to Stein, Dec. 1926; John Anderson to WBR, Dec. 12, 1988. Interviews, WBR with John Anderson, June 19, 1953; with Elizabeth Anderson, Dec. 16, 1959. Gertrude Stein, *The Autobiography of Alice B. Toklas* (New York: Literary Guild, 1933), p. 303.

7. SA to Finley, early Feb. 1927; to Otto Liveright, ca. mid-Jan. 1927. "Educating an Author," *Vanity Fair* 28 (May 1927): 47–48.

8. Interview, WBR with Maria Jolas, Feb. 21, 1964. SA, "[Homage] A Léon Bazalgette," *Europe* 20 (Aug. 15, 1929), 182–85, reprinted as "Death on a Winter Day," *No Swank* (Philadelphia: Centaur Press, 1934), pp. 9–12. Llona, "Sherwood Anderson," *Les Nouvelles Littéraires,* Jan. 1, 1927, p. 6. SA to EB, Jan. 19, 1927; to Sylvia Beach, ca. Dec. 29, 1926, Jan. 4, 1927; Marguerite Gay to SA, May 29, 1926; Gallimard to Sylvia Beach, Dec. 28, 1926, Jan. 3, 1927.

9. SA to Rosenfeld, early Dec. 1926. *Miss Elizabeth,* pp. 157–58. Shirer, *Twentieth Century Journey,* p. 251. Interview, WBR with Ralph W. Church, Apr. 24, 1959.

10. R. L. Samsell, "Paris Days with Ralph Church," pp. 145–56 in Matthew J. Bruccoli and C. E. Frazer Clark, Jr., eds., *Fitzgerald/Hemingway Annual 1972* (Washington, D.C.: Microcards Editions, 1973). Quotations concerning Hemingway are from Samsell's transcription of Church's manuscript, "Sherwood Comes to Town."

11. Samsell, "Paris Days with Ralph Church," pp. 152–53. SA to Mencken, mid-Feb. 1927.

12. Baker, *Ernest Hemingway: Selected Letters,* p. 241.

13. Elliot Paul, "Farthest North: A Study of James Joyce," *Bookman* 75 (May 1932): 156–63, p. 158. *Miss Elizabeth,* pp. 164–65.

14. Samsell, "Paris Days with Ralph Church," p. 149. Jolas and Paul, "Introduction," *transition,* No. 1 (Apr. 1927): 135–38; No. 27 (April-May 1938): 233.

15. SA to Sylvia Beach, Jan. 1927, ca. Mar. 7, 1927; to Adrienne Monnier, ca. Mar. 7, 1927, ?Apr. 1927; to Ralph Church, Sept. 28, 1927. Richard Ellmann, ed., *Letters of James Joyce,* vol. 3 (London: Faber & Faber, 1966), pp. 151–53. Fitch, *Sylvia Beach and the Lost Generation,* pp. 83, 98, 235–36. Marie Monnier, "Notes on Her Art by Marie Monnier," translation into English from a guide to an exhibit of her work, manuscript at Ripshin. Interview, WBR with William Wright, then owner of portrait, June 18, 1953.

16. SA to Monnier, ?Apr. 1927. Acton, *Memoirs of an Aesthete* (London: Methuen, 1948), pp. 175, 183. Huddleston, *Paris Salons, Cafés, Studios: Being Social, Artistic and Literary Memoirs* (Philadelphia: J. B. Lippincott, 1928), pp. 79–81.

17. Acton to WBR, Dec. 28, 1958. *Miss Elizabeth,* pp. 159–61. MacLeish to Ernest Hemingway, Feb. 14, 1927, in R. H. Winnick, ed., *Letters of Archibald MacLeish, 1907 to 1982* (Boston: Houghton Mifflin, 1983), p. 196. Stein, *Autobiography of Alice B. Toklas,* pp. 265–66, 303–4. SA, "Notebook," 1927. Toklas to Eleanor Anderson, Aug. or Sept. 1961, in Hilbert H. Campbell, "Three Unpublished Letters of Alice B. Toklas," *English Language Notes* 20 (March-June 1983), 47–51, p. 50.

18. Acton, *Memoirs of an Aesthete,* pp. 183–84. Stein, *Autobiography of Alice B. Toklas,* pp. 302–3. *Miss Elizabeth,* pp. 161–62.

19. SA to Karl Anderson, Mar. 14, 1927. *Miss Elizabeth,* pp. 162–63.

20. SA to Ralph Church, ca. Feb. 18?, 1927. SA, "Notebook [no. 3]. Paris, 1927."

21. SA to Mencken, ca. Feb. 18, 1927.

22. SA to Finley, ca. Feb. 23, 1927; to Karl Anderson, Mar. 14, 1927; to Church, ca. Feb. 17, 1927; John Anderson to WBR, Dec. 12, 1988. Interview, WBR with "Mimi" Spear, Apr. 12, 1988. Stein, *Autobiography of Alice B. Toklas,* p. 303.

23. *Miss Elizabeth,* p. 170. *Memoirs* (1942), p. 476, (1969), p. 465. Interview, WBR with Maria Jolas, Feb. 21, 1964.

24. SA to Ralph Church, ca. Feb. 18, 1927; to Georgia Church, ca. Mar. 6, 19; to Adrienne Monnier, Mar. 7, 1927; to Julia Harris, ca. Mar. 14, 1927; to Finley, Mar. 12, 1927; to Karl Anderson, Mar. 14, 1927; to Finley, ca. Mar. 18. Sutton, *Letters to Bab,* pp. 286–87.

25. A/P Tapes, p. 51. SA to Ettie Stettheimer, Mar. 17, 1927.

26. Sutton, *Letters to Bab,* p. 287, n. 2, n. 3. A/P Tapes, p. 43. SA to Finley, ca. Mar. 18, 1927, ca. Feb. 23, 1927, Mar. 12, 1927, ca. Mar. 29, 1927, Mar. 30, 1927; to Marion ("Mimi") Anderson, Mar. 30, 1927.

27. A. C. Senske, "Pithy Sayings in Anderson's Talk Take Attention," *Daily Cardinal,* Mar. 30, 1927, pp. 1, 8. SA to Finley, ca. Mar. 29, 1927, Mar. 30, 1927; to Mimi Anderson, Mar. 30, 1927.

28. SA to Finley, Mar. 30, 1927, ca. Apr. 8, 1927.

29. SA to Georgia Church, Apr. 8, 1927; to Stieglitz, Apr. 18?, 1927; to Karl Anderson, early Apr. 1927, late Apr. 1927; to Mimi Anderson, mid-Apr. 1927, early Apr. 1927, late Apr. 1927; to Ralph Church, May 19?, 1927.

30. SA to Georgia Church, Apr. 8, 1927; to Rosenfeld, Apr. 29, 1927. Interview, WBR with William Wright, June 17, 1953.

31. SA to Rosenfeld, Apr. 29, 1927; to Stark Young, late May 1927; to Burton Emmett, June 28, 1927; to Roger Sergel, ?Apr. 1927; to John Anderson, ?Apr. 1927.

32. SA to Mimi Anderson, early May 1927; to Karl Anderson, late Apr. 1927; to Finley, late May 1927; to Rosenfeld, May 19?, 1927; to Stark Young, late May 1927; to Ralph Church, ca. May 19, 1927, mid-Aug. 1927.

33. SA to David Karsner, May 23, 1927; to Mimi Anderson, early June 1927; to

Finley, late May 1927; to Karl Anderson, June 5, 1927. "Anderson at Wittenberg," *Winesburg Eagle* 15 (Summer 1990), 11.

34. SA to Karl Anderson, June 1927, after July 4, 1927; to "Davies," at O. K. Liveright's agency, late June 1927.

35. "New York" draft in "Notebook no. 2, 1927" in the Newberry Library, pp. 157–66. SA to Davies, late June 1927.

36. Interview, WBR with William Wright, June 17, 1953.

37. Hansen, "The First Reader," *New York World*, June 19, 1927, Sec. M, p. 8; "Sherwood Anderson's New Testament," *Boston Transcript*, June 22, 1927, p. 4.

38. SA to Karl Anderson, ca. July 5, 1927; to Lyle Saxon, early Aug. 1927.

39. SA to Ralph Church, mid-Aug. 1927; to Lyle Saxon, early Aug. 1927; to Karl Anderson, ca. July 5, 1927.

40. SA to Otto Liveright, July 1927. Aiken, "Sherwood Anderson, as Prose Poet, Plays Blind Man's Buff With Life's First Principles," *New York Evening Post Literary Review*, July 9, 1927, sec. 3, p. 8. Deutsch, *Herald Tribune Books*, July 24, 1927, p. 2. Morris, *New Republic* 51 (Aug. 3, 1927): 277–79.

41. SA to Karl Anderson, Aug. 25, 1927; to Finley, ca. Sept. 27, 1927; to Stieglitz, Aug. 18, 1927. Interview, WBR with Wright, June 18, 1955. *Miss Elizabeth*, pp. 174–76.

42. SA to Finley, ca. Sept. 27, 1927. *Miss Elizabeth*, pp. 177–79.

43. SA to Finley, Aug. 1927, ca. Sept. 27, 1927.

44. SA to Canby, late Sept. 1927; to Fagin, after Oct. 17, 1927. "America on a Cultural Jag," *Saturday Review of Literature* 4 (Dec. 3, 1927): 364–65; Johan Smertenko, "Anderson, the Writer," *Saturday Review of Literature* 4 (Feb. 25, 1928): 632.

45. SA to Finley, ca. Sept. 27, 1927, ca. Oct. 6, 1927, ca. Oct. 3, 1927; to Will Alexander, ca. Jan. 3, 1931; to Burton Emmett, ca. Oct. 22, 1927, ca. Oct. 4, 1927, Oct. 30, 1927 (agreement worded by Burton Emmett, signed by SA).

46. SA to Burton Emmett, Oct. 9, 1927, ca. Oct. 15, 1927, Oct. 16, 1927; to Ralph Church, Dec. 22, 1927.

47. SA to Burton Emmett, ca. Oct. 15, 1927, Oct. 16, 1927, Nov. 14, 1927, early May 1928; to Will Alexander, ca. Jan. 3, 1931. "Announcement," *Smyth County News*, Jan. 6, 1921, p. 1; "Raids the Whiskey Men," *Smyth County News*, July 9, 1925, p. 4; "The Scopes Trial, Tennessee and Darwinism," *Smyth County News*, Mar. 19, 1925, pp. 2–3; "Troutdale Chapter Red Cross Formed," *Smyth County News*, Sept. 9, 1926, p. 2; Announcement of Subscription Drive, *Smyth County News*, Aug. 18, 1927. Interview, WBR with Joe Stephenson, Sept. 6, 1955. "Gil: An Example for Others," *Smyth County News*, June 26, 1973, p. 15.

48. "Hotel Opens May The 27," *Smyth County News*, May 26, 1927, p. 1; "The Teachers Entertained," *Smyth County News*, Oct. 27, 1927, p. 1.

49. "In Gratitude," *Smyth County News*, Dec. 22, 1927, p. 1; "Up to Us," *Smyth County News*, Jan. 29, 1931, p. 1; "More News," *Smyth County News*, Nov. 3, 1927, p. 2; "To Our Readers!," *Smyth County News*, Jan. 26, 1928, p. 1.

50. SA to Lyle Saxon, Nov. 6, 1927; to Church, Dec. 22, 1927; to Will Alexander,

ca. Jan. 3, 1931; to Burton Emmett, Nov. 17, 1927, Oct. 21, 1927, Nov. 14, 1927, ca. Dec. 22, 1927.

51. SA to Burton Emmett, Nov. 2, 1927, Dec. 5, 1927; to Finley, ?early Nov. 1927. Interviews, WBR with Burt L. Dickinson, June 18, 1953, and Charles H. Funk, June 23, 1953. "Harry Gardiner . . ." *Smyth County News,* Apr. 14, 1927, p. 5.

52. SA to Burton Emmett, Nov. 6, 1927, Nov. 6, 1927, Dec. 5, 1927, Dec. 12, 1927.

53. "Sherwood Anderson Discovers America in a Small Town; Turning Editor He Learns the Value of Vital Statistics," *New York World,* Dec. 18, 1927, pp. M1, M15. "On Being a Country Editor," *Vanity Fair* 29 (Feb. 1928): 70, 92. "Nearer the Grass Roots," *Outlook* 148 (Jan. 4, 1928): 3–4, 27. SA to Burton Emmett, ca. Dec. 22, 1927.

54. SA to Church, Dec. 22, 1927, Aug. 15, 1928.

55. See Welford Dunaway Taylor, ed., *The Buck Fever Papers* (Charlottesville: University Press of Virginia, 1971) for a complete reprinting of Buck Fever's contributions.

56. Interview, WBR with Joe Stephenson, Sept. 6, 1955.

57. SA to Burton Emmett, Dec. 12, 1927, ca. Dec. 22, 1927; to Church, Dec. 22, 1927.

58. SA to Church, Dec. 22, 1927; to Burton Emmett, ca. Dec. 22, 1927, Dec. 12, 1927.

59. In *Letters to Bab,* p. 305, Sutton reads this handwritten word to be "seasons." Judging by both handwriting and context, I read it as here printed.

Selected Bibliography

PRIMARY SOURCES

Beyond Desire. New York: Liveright, 1932.
Dark Laughter. New York: Boni and Liveright, 1925.
Death in the Woods and Other Stories. New York: Liveright, 1933.
Hello Towns! New York: Liveright, 1929.
Home Town. New York: Alliance Book Corp., 1940.
Horses and Men. New York: B. W. Huebsch, 1923.
Kit Brandon. New York: Charles Scribner's Sons, 1936.
Many Marriages. New York: B. W. Huebsch, 1923.
Marching Men. New York: John Lane Company, 1917.
Mid-American Chants. New York: John Lane, 1918.
A New Testament. New York: Boni and Liveright, 1927.
No Swank. Philadelphia: Centaur Press, 1934.
Perhaps Women. New York: Liveright, 1931.
Plays: Winesburg and Others. New York: Charles Scribner's, 1937.
Poor White. New York: B. W. Huebsch, 1920.
Puzzled America. New York: Charles Scribner's Sons, 1935.
Sherwood Anderson's Notebook. New York: Boni and Liveright, 1926.
A Story Teller's Story. New York: B. W. Huebsch, 1924.
Tar: A Midwest Childhood. New York: Boni and Liveright, 1926.
The Triumph of the Egg. New York: B.W. Huebsch, 1921.
Windy McPherson's Son. New York: John Lane, 1916; rev. ed., New York, B.W. Huebsch, 1922.
Winesburg, Ohio. New York: B. W. Huebsch, 1919.

EDITED AND CRITICAL WORKS

Anderson, David. *Sherwood Anderson: An Introduction and Interpretation.* New York: Holt, 1967.
———, ed. *Critical Essays on Sherwood Anderson.* Boston: G. K. Hall, 1981.
Anderson, Elizabeth, and Gerald R. Kelly. *Miss Elizabeth: A Memoir.* Boston: Little, Brown,1969.

Bruyère, Claire. *Sherwood Anderson: L'impuissance créatrice.* Paris: Klincksieck, 1985.

Burbank, Rex. *Sherwood Anderson.* New York: Twayne, 1964.

Campbell, Hilbert H., ed. *The Sherwood Anderson Diaries, 1936–1941.* Athens: University of Georgia Press, 1987.

Campbell, Hilbert H., and Charles E. Modlin, eds. *Sherwood Anderson: Centennial Studies.* Troy, NY: Whitson Publishing Co., 1976.

Crowley, John W., ed. *New Essays on Winesburg, Ohio.* Cambridge: Cambridge University Press, 1990.

Curry, Sister Martha Mulroy, ed. *The "Writer's Book" by Sherwood Anderson.* Metuchen, NJ: Scarecrow Press, 1975.

Dunne, Robert. *A New Book of the Grotesque.* Kent, OH: Kent State University Press, 2005.

Fanning, Michael, *France and Sherwood Anderson: Paris Notebook, 1921.* Baton Rouge: Louisiana State University Press, 1976.

Howe, Irving. *Sherwood Anderson.* New York: William Sloane Associates, 1951.

Jones, Howard Mumford, and Walter B. Rideout, eds. *Letters of Sherwood Anderson.* Boston: Little, Brown, 1953.

Modlin, Charles E., ed. *The Egg and Other Stories.* New York: Penguin, 1998.

———, ed. *Sherwood Anderson: Selected Letters.* Knoxville: University of Tennessee Press, 1984.

———, ed. *Sherwood Anderson's Love Letters to Eleanor Copenhaver Anderson.* Athens: University of Georgia Press, 1989.

Modlin, Charles E., and Ray Lewis White, eds. *Winesburg, Ohio.* New York: Norton, 1996.

Ohashi, Kichinosuke, ed. *The Complete Works of Sherwood Anderson.* 20 vols. Kyoto: Rinsen Book Co., 1982.

Papinchak, Robert Allen. *Sherwood Anderson: A Study of the Short Fiction.* New York: Twayne, 1992.

Rideout, Walter B., ed. *Sherwood Anderson: A Collection of Critical Essays.* Englewood Cliffs, NJ: Prentice-Hall, 1974.

Rosenfeld, Paul, ed. *The Sherwood Anderson Reader.* Boston: Houghton Mifflin, 1947.

———, ed. *Sherwood Anderson's Memoirs.* New York: Harcourt, Brace, 1942.

Salzman, Jack, David D. Anderson, and Kichinosuke Ohashi, eds. *Sherwood Anderson: The Writer at His Craft.* Mamaroneck, NY: Appel, 1979.

Schevill, James. *Sherwood Anderson: His Life and Work.* Denver: University of Denver Press, 1951.

Sheehy, Eugene P., and Kenneth A. Lohf. *Sherwood Anderson: A Bibliography.* Los Gatos, Calif.: Talisman Press, 1960.

Small, Judy Jo. *A Reader's Guide to the Short Stories of Sherwood Anderson.* New York: G. K. Hall, 1994.

Sutton, William A. *The Road to Winesburg: A Mosaic of the Imaginative Life of Sherwood Anderson.* Metuchen, NJ: Scarecrow Press,1972.

———, ed. *Letters to Bab: Sherwood Anderson to Marietta D. Finley, 1916–1933.* Urbana: University of Illinois Press, 1985.

Taylor, Welford Dunaway, ed. *The Buck Fever Papers*. Charlottesville: University Press of Virginia, 1971.

Taylor, Welford Dunaway, and Charles E. Modlin, eds. *Southern Odyssey: Selected Writings by Sherwood Anderson*. Athens: University of Georgia Press, 1997.

Townsend, Kim. *Sherwood Anderson*. Boston: Houghton Mifflin, 1987.

White, Ray Lewis, ed. *Sherwood Anderson: Early Writings*. Kent, OH: Kent State University Press, 1989.

———. *Sherwood Anderson: A Reference Guide*. Boston: G. K. Hall, 1977.

———, ed. *Sherwood Anderson/Gertrude Stein*. Chapel Hill: University of North Carolina Press, 1972.

———, ed. *Sherwood Anderson's Memoirs: A Critical Edition*. Chapel Hill: University of North Carolina Press, 1969.

———, ed. *Sherwood Anderson's Secret Love Letters: For Eleanor, a Letter a Day*. Baton Rouge: Louisiana State University Press, 1991.

———, ed. *Sherwood Anderson's Winesburg, Ohio*. Athens: Ohio University Press, 1997.

Williams, Kenny J. *A Storyteller and a City*. DeKalb: Northern Illinois Press, 1988.

Index

Index

"A Business Man's Reading," 105–6
"Business Types" essay series, 99–107, 145
Butcher, Fanny, 234, 390, 547, 596
Butterworth, Clara (fictional character), 377, 381–86

Cabell, James Branch, 287–88, 400, 474
Caledonia, Ohio, 18–21
Calverton, V. F., 541, 595, 598, 599
Camden, Ohio, 16
Camp Owlyout, 219–22
Canby, Henry Seidel, 495, 516–17, 521–22, 569, 596, 683
Cane (Toomer), 490–91, 524–25
"The Can Factory," 114–15, 117
Cannan, Gilbert, 353
Cape, Jonathan, 406, 423, 577
Caples, B. H., 525
Carlyle, Thomas, 103; as influence, 97
Carnevali, Emmanuel, 347–48
Carr, Michael Carmichael, 171, 181
Cather, Willa, 400, 474
"Caught," 520, 535, 539
censorship, 173, 285, 316–17, 398, 451–52, 498–501, 575; magazines and reluctance to publish works, 614, 634; SA on, 501; SA's compliance with cuts, 285, 614
The Century (magazine), 528, 547, 560
Cerf, Bennett, 610
Chapman, Frederic, 213, 300
characterization, 288; dialogue and, 101–2, 108, 338, 599; empathic insight and, 27, 107–8; ethnicity and, 133; "Huck Finn" diction, 107–8, 230, 338, 340, 599, 625; imagination and development of, 661–62; of "Midwestern" man, 297; newspaper stories about invented characters, 693–95; plot defined by character, 662; in *Poor White*, 135, 138, 377–86; "real" *vs.* "puppet," 232–33, 556, 646; SA and discussion of characters during writing, 533, 546; Talbot Whittingham and development of, 200; town as protagonist, 377; in *Winesburg, Ohio*, 322–24; of women, 390. *See also specific characters*
Chase, Cleveland, 683
Chase, Lewis, 456
Chekhov, Anton, 365, 424
Chicago, 68–69, 93; Chicago Renaissance, 165–71, 599; Dill Pickle Club in, 305–6;

Jackson Park art colony, 169–71; as literary capital of U.S., 363; race riots in, 336; SA's return to, 163–64; as setting for works, 599; social milieu in, 169–71, 190, 284–85, 305–8, 527; as subject of works, 641; visits to, 565, 570; World's Columbian Exposition, 169
"Chicago," 259
"Chicago—A Feeling," 641
"Chicago Culture," 284–85, 307
"A Chicago Hamlet," 476, 503
Chicago Renaissance, 165–71, 599
chickens, 126–27
childhood and youth: animals as important during, 19, 21, 22; in Clyde, 25–26; education during, 18–19, 31; employment during, *xiii*, 31–32, 34; fiction linked to experiences of, *xii–xiii*, 100; poverty during, 27–29, 36; recollections of neighbors regarding personality of SA, 36, 612. *See also Tar*
children, 151; as audience for works, 336; as characters in works, 153, 210, 646–47 (*see also Tar*); Cornelia as custodian of, 191, 218–19; education of, 251, 355; education of SA's, 572, 616, 670–71; as obstacle or burden, 153; parenthood in *Windy McPherson's Son*, 153, 228–29, 230; procreation as function of women, 115, 117; as responsibility, 127, 153, 177; SA and Greear children, 589; SA as father, 152–53, 298–99, 304, 396, 401, 445, 496, 523, 572, 641–42; summer camp scheme, 337; support of, 218–19, 292; "teaching imagination" as parental role, 152; in works, 186, 506–7
Christ, 197–99, 245, 260, 284, 666
chronology, 207; alternatives to chronological structure in works, 268, 393–94; distortions in autobiographical writing, 57, 143; in *Poor White*, 379–80
Church, Ralph, 524, 636–37, 648, 661, 665, 667–68, 679, 693, 697
"City Plowman," 70, 87
Civil War, 25; Irwin Anderson's service, 4–10, 26, 52–53, 608; SA's interest in, 38, 51, 117–18, 664; as subject for works, 549–50, 582
Claflin, Tennessee, 187
Clarke, Mary, 409
Clean Books Bill, 498–99

Index

595; race in, 598; repeated motifs in, 604; revision of, 584–85, 587, 607; sales of, 597; SA's synopsis of, 584–85; sex in, 597, 602–3, 606; stream of consciousness, 597–98; structure of, 587, 601; style in, 597–98
The Dark Mother (Frank), 386–87, 398, 408–9, 436
Darrow, Clarence, 523
Daugherty, George, 90, 91–92, 172, 174, 182, 199, 305, 476, 504, 565, 585, 597
"Daughters," 33
Davidson, Donald, 609
daydreaming, 62, 65, 79, 123, 141, 151, 394
death: childhood experiences of, *xii–xiii*, 33, 41–43, 205; corn as symbol of rebirth and, 257–58, 395; "Elsinore" as metaphor for, 160; suicide in works, 229, 452, 455, 457, 460, 468; symbols of, 186, 507, 509; in works, 42–43, 57–58, 197–98, 205, 257–58, 426, 487, 507–9
"Death," 318
"Death in the Woods," *xii–xiii, xv,* 216, 425, 531–32, 631–33, 698–99; contexts of writing, 631–32; O. Henry Memorial Prize, 662; precursors for, 192–93, 396–97, 425–26, 632; publication of, 634, 641
"Declaration of Independence of the Mind" (Rolland), 342
Delia, Angelo, 133, 150–51
Dell, Floyd, 165, 168–70, 273, 391, 446; on Cornelia, 174; Freudian analysis and, 193; as mentor, 170–71, 214–15; publication efforts on SA's behalf, 172–73, 175, 177–78, 204–5, 212–13; on SA, 170, 173, 175, 214–15; on *Windy McPherson's Son,* 235
de Lorenzi, Sue, 219, 223, 261–63
De Mille, Cecil B., 642
Demuth, Charles, 569
depth *vs.* superficiality in works, 321–24
desertion: of Cornelia and children, 218; as grounds for divorce from Tennessee, 517; as theme, 154, 210; in works, 599
detail, surface *vs.* depth in works and, 321–24
Deutsch, Babette, 679–80
Dial Award, 437–40, 443–45, 468, 471
The Dial (magazine), 351, 354, 368, 387,

403, 463, 466–67, 471, 517, 519, 547, 560, 570
dialogue: character and, 101–2, 108; "Huck Finn" diction, 107–8, 230, 338, 340, 599, 625; monologue in works, 475
Dickinson, Burt L., 691
Dill Pickle Club, Chicago, 305–6, 354
"The Discouraged Man," 102, 107
"Discovery of a Father," 30–31
divorce: as escape, 458; in works, 154–55. *See also under* Lane, Cornelia; Mitchell, Tennessee; Prall, Elizabeth
Dix, Dorothy, 622
dogs, 21, 22, 162, 376–77, 632–33, 679
"The Door of the Trap," 344–46, 354, 405
Dos Passos, John, 416, 488–89, 494, 576, 635
Dostoyevsky, Fyodor, 296, 318, 402, 443, 464, 508; as influence, 505
The Double Dealer (magazine), 448–49, 462–63, 484, 539, 561
Dove, Arthur, 569
drama, 171, 302, 332, 608, 610–11, 642; dramatization of works, 407, 569
dreams, 389, 425–26, 698
"Dreiser," 215
Dreiser, Theodore, 173, 208, 213, 215, 400, 464, 479, 489–90, 516, 626, 686; plagiarism incident, 645–46; SA on works of, 614
"Drink," 199
Dudley, Bruce (fictional character), 597–601, 597–607
"The Dumb Man," 404
Dutch, translation of works into, 697

Eastman, Max, 212
economics, concentration of economic power as theme, 227
Edmonds, Ella G. and James, 535
"Educating an Author," 674
education: boyhood, 18–19, 31; of children, 251, 355, 388, 656–58, 660, 670; Cornelia and, 113, 153; of Emma Anderson (mother), 14–15; employment opportunities and, 87; experiments in children's, 251; Fairhope's School of Organic Education, 355; of Irwin Anderson (father), 10–12; Karl, 39–40, 44; at Lewis Institute, 75; of SA, 18–19, 73–74, 75, 88–92; SA's respect for, 113; sex

813

self-analysis in works, 206–7
self-destructive impulses, 49–50, 128, 154, 681
self-sacrifice as theme in works, 487
Sell, Henry Blackman, 307
Seltzer, Thomas, 498
"Senility," 293, 405
"A Sentimental Journey," 692
Sergel, Roger, *xvii*, 516, 566, 613, 644
Sergel, Ruth, 566, 613
Seven Arts (magazine), 235–38, 246, 247–49, 250–53, 254, 259, 268, 279–80
sex: brief relationships with women, 75, 95, 682; censorship of works with sexual content, 316–17; as compensatory in industrialized worlds, 67–68; corn as symbol of sexual force, 207, 208, 310–11; critics on timidity of treatment in works, 518; in *Dark Laughter,* 597, 602–3, 606; in *Father Abraham,* 532; "force of sex" as theme, 186, 215–16, 258, 278–79; forthrightness of SA in discussions of, 142; gender ambiguity in works, 504–7; gender roles in Troutdale, Virginia, 647; "gentlemanly" behavior, 81; homosexuality in works, 212, 382, 551–52; in *Horses and Men,* 366–67, 504–7; incompatibility between Cornelia and SA, 117, 151–52, 177, 180; in "I Want to Know Why," 338–39; lesbianism in works, 382; in "The Man Who Became a Woman," 504–7; in *Many Marriages,* 452–53, 456, 499–500, 542–43; in *Marching Men,* 278–79; in *Mary Cochran,* 178–79; in *Mid-American Chants,* 676; nature as symbol for, 207–8, 258, 310–11, 366–67; in *Ohio Pagan,* 366–67; in *Poor White,* 382; procreation as function of women, 115, 117; promiscuity or infidelity, 49, 154, 177, 361, 568; race relations and, 469, 639; repression in works, 310–11, 457, 508, 597; SA as "Phallic Chekhov," 365; SA on human relationships and, 586; SA's attitude toward, 193, 568, 586; SA's reputation as "sex obsessed," 365, 499–500, 608; SA's sexuality, 154, 398–99; in "Seeds," 266–67; sex as a symbol of something else, 340–41; sex education movement, 132; sexual initiation as theme, 178–79, 328, 338–39; sexual uncertainty as

theme, 338–39; social mores and, 171, 190–91, 316–17; symbolism and, 207–8, 215–16, 258, 310–11, 340–41, 366–67, 398, 456; in *Talbot Whittingham,* 203; in *Tar,* 633–34, 652–54; Tennessee M. and, 188–89; in *Windy McPherson's Son,* 154, 228; in *Winesburg, Ohio,* 316–17, 327–29, 368; youthful experiences in Clyde, 46–47, 69–70
Sherman, Stuart P., 547, 563, 567, 595, 612
Sherwood Anderson (Chase), 683
"Sherwood Anderson" (Faulkner), 580–81
Sherwood Anderson's Notebook (*Wind and Water,* working title), 612; contents of, 634; critical reception of, 634–35, 638; dedication to Marietta D. Finley and John Emerson, 614–15; epigram in, 634–35; publication of, 634
"Sherwood Anderson's Tale of the New Life" (Sherman), 596
Sherwood Anderson Writes of Himself, 323
Shirer, William, 658, 660
The Short Story's Mutations (Newman, ed.), 522
Shute, Frances, 125–26, 134, 144–45, 155, 273
"Sick of Words" (Morris), 680, 685
signed editions, 593
similes, 116
Simmons, Harry, 90, 92
Sinclair, Upton, 246, 248
"Singing Swamp Negro," 361
"Sister," 11, 192–93, 206–7
The Smart Set (magazine), 211–12, 234, 272, 293, 339–40, 406
Smith, Biffer (fictional character), 65
Smith, Henry Justin, 232, 307
Smith, J. (possible pseudonym for SA), 290
Smith, William (maternal grandfather), 13
Smith, Y. Kenley, 406–7
socialism, 131, 142, 246–47, 306, 342, 437; "Commercial Democracy" business scheme and, 135–36; SA and, 262; socially oriented aesthetics and, 168–69
social status, 133; advertising as white collar career, 92, 94; community membership and, 51–52; in Elyria, 139–42; marriage and, 113; National Guard service and, 51; relationship with Bertha Baynes and, 47–48

Index

"Unused," 366, 503, 518; precursors for, 200

The Unwelcome Man (Frank), 264

vacations, *xiv*, 204, 235, 259, 293, 334–36, 335, 370, 582, 586

Van Doren, Carl, 547

Van Gogh, Vincent, 673

Vanity Fair (magazine), 400, 437, 488, 542, 594, 612–13, 625–26, 629–30, 639–40, 642, 647, 656, 659, 663–64, 672; monthly series for, 639–40, 641, 648–49, 674, 679, 684, 692–93

Van Loon, Hendrik Willem, 567–68

Van Vechtan, Carl, 489–90

Van Volkenburg Browne, Maurice and Ellen, 168

Verrier, Charles Le, 412

"Vibrant Life," 215–16

Viereck, George Sylvester, 571–72

Viking Press, 583, 593

"A Visit," 268

"The Visit in the Morning," 361–62

Voices (magazine), 421–22

Wald, Max, 192, 204

walls, 450, 455, 486, 676

Wanderer, Carl, 375–76

war, 260–61, 282–83, 636; Civil War, 4–10, 25, 26, 38, 51–53, 117–18, 549–50, 582, 608; as context for art, 260–70; as context for writing, 256; as dehumanizing, 552; impact on publishing industry, 279–80; impact on reception of *Marching Men*, 271–72; military service, attitude towards, 282–83, 552; pacifism, 331; as subject in works, 254; as theme, 247–48; World War I, 247–48. *See also* Spanish-American War

"War," 216, 293, 405, 690

"The War and the Intellectuals" (Bourne), 279–80

Ward, Fred, 156

watercolors, 356–57

Watson, James S., 351

Weaver, John V. A., 307

Webster, Jane (fictional character), 452, 455, 459–60

Webster, John (fictional character), 452–55

Weeks, Jennie, 114

"We Enter In," 256–57, 261

wells, 450–51, 455–56, 486, 508

Wells, H. G., 172, 180

Wertel, Frank J., 87

West, Rebecca, 465, 563–64, 651

Westcott, Edith, 219–20

Western Union Cold Storage (Chicago), 73–74

"We Would Be Wise," 99

Whaley, Mrs. Mary, 26

Wharton, Edith, 400

"What Say!" (newspaper series), 689–90, 696

"When the Writer Talks," 579

White, Helen (fictional character), 47

White, Trillena, 91, 106, 139, 186, 226

Whitehead, Harry (fictional character), 60

Whitehead, Thomas "Tom" C., as character Harry Whitehead in works, 60

"The White Streak," 285, 293

Whitman, Walt, 74, 242–43, 245, 246, 255–56, 281–82, 312, 530; as stylistic influence, 598

Whittaker, Clarence, 76

Whittingham, Talbot (fictional character), 178, 194–206, 205, 208, 245, 624–25

Who and What: A Book of Clues for the Clever (Adams, ed.), 680–81

"Why There Must Be a Midwestern Literature," 392–93

Wickham, Anna, 665

Wilcoxson, L. L. "Daddy," 134, 137, 150

Wilcoxson Paint Company, 134

Wilford, Mrs., 148

Willard, George (fictional character), *xiii*, 325–29

Williams, Perry S., 131, 132, 136, 141, 146, 154

Wilson, Edgar (fictional character), 486–87

Wilson, Edmund, 475, 477, 478, 488, 519, 567, 621–22

Wilson, James Harrison, 6–9

Windy McPherson's Son, 34, 123, 145–46; abandonment of business and family linked to, 146, 162–63; autobiographical parallels in, 226–27; characters linked to Clyde citizens, 225–26; *Chicago Daily News* article about, 232–33; conclusion of, 231–32; contexts of writing, 150, 162–63; critical reception of, 172, 225,

as "secret" occupation, 146; self-analysis in process of, 206–7; self-identification as writer, 183, 214, 245–46, 283, 523, 659, 683; as self-revelation, 184; short forms and, 107; standardization of, 658; storytelling and, 38–39, 146–47, 184, 522; as subject of works, 254, 393, 520–21, 600; as theme in works, 144; as therapeutic, 43, 58, 145, 151, 156–61, 229, 240, 255, 272, 292, 369, 508–10, 597, 666; unpublished sketches in notebooks, 114–16; women writers as "mules," 611;

writers as protagonists in works, 194–204, 600. *See also specific works*
writing block, 586, 644, 658–59, 681, 682
"Writing it Down," 96

Xenia Female College, 10–12

Young, Kimball, 670
Young, Stark, 480, 482, 514, 572, 619
"The Younger Generation" (lecture), 607
"A Young Jew," 677
Yust, Walter, 634